American Reference Books Annual

1996 VOLUME 27

AMERICAN REFERENCE BOOKS ANNUAL

1996 VOLUME 27

Bohdan S. Wynar EDITOR IN CHIEF

Melissa R. Root ASSISTANT EDITOR

Comprehensive annual reviewing service for
reference books published in the United States and Canada

1996

LIBRARIES UNLIMITED
ENGLEWOOD, COLORADO

Copyright © 1996 Libraries Unlimited, Inc.
All Rights Reserved
Printed in the United States of America

No part of this publication may be reproduced, stored in a retrieval system, or transmitted, in any form or by any means, electronic, mechanical, photocopying, recording, or otherwise, without the prior written permission of the publisher.

LIBRARIES UNLIMITED, INC.
P.O. Box 6633
Englewood, CO 80155-6633
1-800-237-6124

Library of Congress Cataloging-in-Publication Data

American reference books annual, 1970-
  Englewood, Colo., Libraries Unlimited.

    v. 19x26 cm.

Indexes:
  1970-74. 1v.
  1975-79. 1v.
  1980-84. 1v.
  1985-89. 1v.
  1990-94. 1v.

    I. Reference books--Bibliography--Periodicals.
I. Wynar, Bohdan S. II. Root, Melissa R.
Z1035.1.A55   011'.02
ISBN 1-56308-431-7(1996 edition)
ISSN 0065-9959

Contents

Introduction xiii
Contributors xv
Journals Cited xxvii

Part I
GENERAL REFERENCE WORKS

1—General Reference Works

Acronyms and Abbreviations 3
Almanacs 4
Bibliography 5
   Bibliographic Guides 5
   National and Trade Bibliography 7
      International 7
      United States 8
      Other Countries 10
Biography 11
   International 11
   United States 15
   Australia 16
   Soviet Union 17
Catalogs and Collections 17
Dictionaries and Encyclopedias 18
Directories 23
Government Publications 25
Handbooks and Yearbooks 27
Indexes 29
Museums 31
Periodicals and Serials 31
Quotation Books 34

Part II
SOCIAL SCIENCES

2—Social Sciences in General

Social Sciences in General 41

3—Area Studies

General Works 45
United States 46
   General Works 46
   New York 46

Africa 47
   General Works 47
   Algeria 49
   Chad 50
   Eritrea 50
   Ethiopia 50
   Liberia 51
   Malawi 51
   Morocco 52
   São Tomé and Príncipe 52
   South Africa 53
   Swaziland 53
   Togo 53
   Uganda 54
   Zaire 54
Arctic Regions 55
Asia 55
   General Works 55
   Cyprus 56
   India 56
   Indonesia 57
   Iraq 58
Canada 58
Developing Countries 59
Europe 60
   General Works 60
   Eastern Europe 60
   Ireland 61
   Italy 61
   Poland 62
   Russia and the Successor States 62
   Scotland 63
   Spain 64
   Sweden 64
Latin America 65
   General Works 65
Middle East 67
   General Works 67
   Egypt 69
   Israel 69
   Lebanon 70
   Oman 70
Oceania 70
Pacific Area 71
West Indies 72

4—Economics and Business

General Works 73
   Bibliography 73
   Biography 74
   Chronology 74
   Dictionaries and Encyclopedias 75
   Directories 76
   Handbooks and Yearbooks 81
   Indexes 85
   Periodicals and Serials 86
Accounting 86
Business Services and Investment Guides . . . 87
   Bibliography 87
   Handbooks and Yearbooks 87
Consumer Education 88
Finance and Banking 90
Industry and Manufacturing 91
Insurance 92
International Business 93
   General Works 93
     Directories 93
     Handbooks and Yearbooks 94
   Asia 99
   Canada 102
   Europe 102
   Latin America 103
Labor 104
   Bibliography 104
   Dictionaries and Encyclopedias 104
   Directories 105
   Handbooks and Yearbooks 108
   Videographics 113
Management 114
Marketing and Trade 115
Office Practices 124

5—Education

General Works 127
   Bibliography 127
   Catalogs and Collections 127
   Dictionaries and Encyclopedias 128
   Directories 128
   Handbooks and Yearbooks 128
   Thesauri 129
Canada 129
Early Childhood Education 130
Elementary and Secondary Education . . . 131
   Bibliography 131
   Directories 131
   Handbooks and Yearbooks 132

Higher Education 134
   Bibliography 134
   Directories 134
   Handbooks and Yearbooks 143
International Exchange Programs and
   Opportunities 145
Learning Disabilities 147
Nonprint Materials and Resources 148
Reading 149
Vocational and Continuing Education . . 150

6—Ethnic Studies and Anthropology

Anthropology and Ethnology 153
Ethnic Studies 153
   General Works 153
   Africans 154
   Armenian Americans 155
   Asian Americans 155
   Blacks 157
   Gypsies 162
   Hispanic Americans 162
   Indians of North America 164
   Irish Americans 169
   Japanese Americans 169
   Jews 169

7—Genealogy

Heraldry 171
Genealogy 171
   Dictionaries and Encyclopedias 171
   Directories 172
   Handbooks and Yearbooks 172
   Indexes 174
Personal Names 175

8—Geography and Travel Guides

Geography 177
   General Works 177
     Atlases 177
       United States, 177; *International*,
       179; *Canada*, 182; *China*, 182
   Bibliography 183
   Biography 183
   Dictionaries and Encyclopedias 184
   Handbooks and Yearbooks 185
Travel Guides 186
   General Works 186
   Handbooks and Yearbooks 186
   International Travel 188
   United States 189

Europe 191
   General Works 191
   Ireland 192
   Latin America and the Caribbean 193

9—History

Archaeology 195
American History 195
   Archives 195
   Atlases 196
   Bibliography 197
   Biography 199
   Catalogs and Collections 201
   Chronology 201
   Dictionaries and Encyclopedias 203
   Handbooks and Yearbooks 207
African History 212
Asian History 214
   General Works 214
   Chinese 214
   India 215
   Japanese 215
   Korea 216
European History 216
   General Works 216
   British 217
   French 218
   German 219
   Italian 219
   Russian 220
   Yugoslav 220
Latin American and Caribbean
   History 221
Middle Eastern History 221
World History 222
   Atlases 222
   Bibliography 222
   Biography 223
   Catalogs and Collections 223
   Chronology 224
   Dictionaries and Encyclopedias 226
   Handbooks and Yearbooks 226

10—Law

General Works 229
   Bibliographies 229
   Biography 230
   Dictionaries and Encyclopedias 230
   Directories 233
   Handbooks and Yearbooks 237

Criminology 240
   Bibliography 240
   Dictionaries and Encyclopedias 240
   Directories 241
   Handbooks and Yearbooks 242
Human Rights 243
International Law 245
Sport Law 247
Victims of Abuse 247

11—Library and Information Science and Publishing and Bookselling

Library and Information Science 249
   General Works 249
      Bibliography 249
      Biography 250
      Handbooks 250
      Indexes 251
   Cataloging and Classification 252
   Comparative and International
      Librarianship 256
   Copyright 257
   Information Technology 257
   Interlibrary Loans 258
   Library Automation 259
   Periodicals 260
   Reference Services 261
   School Libraries 262
   Special Libraries and Collections 263
   Storytelling 267
Publishing and Bookselling 268
   General Works 268
      Bibliography 268
   Catalogs and Collections 269
   Dictionaries 269
   Directories 270
   Handbooks 271

12—Military Studies

General Works 273
   Atlases 273
   Bibliography 274
   Biography 275
   Dictionaries and Encyclopedias 276
   Directories 277
   Handbooks and Yearbooks 279
Air Force 281
Army 282
Navy 283
Weapons 284

13—Political Science

General Works 285
  Bibliography 285
  Biography 285
  Directories 286
  Handbooks and Yearbooks 287
Politics and Government 288
  United States 288
    Archives 288
    Bibliography 289
    Biography 290
    Dictionaries and Encyclopedias 291
    Directories 291
    Handbooks and Yearbooks 295
    Indexes 297
  Asian 299
  Canadian 299
  European 301
    General Works 301
    British 303
    Irish 304
    Spanish 304
  Latin American and Caribbean 305
  Middle Eastern 305
Ideologies 306
International Organizations 307
International Relations 309
Public Policy and Administration 311

14—Psychology and Parapsychology

Psychology 313
  Dictionaries and Encyclopedias 313
  Handbooks and Yearbooks 314
Parapsychology 315

15—Recreation and Sports

General Works 319
  Biography 319
  Chronology 321
  Directories 322
  Handbooks and Yearbooks 323
  Thesauri 323
Baseball 324
Basketball 326
Boating 326
Camping 327
Computer 328
Cricket 328
Cycling 329
Fencing 329
Fishing 329
Football 330
Golf 331
Hiking 332
Hockey 333
Mountaineering 334
Rugby 335
Soccer 335
Tennis 335

16—Sociology

General Works 337
  Bibliography 337
  Dictionaries and Encyclopedias 337
  Handbooks and Yearbooks 339
Aging 339
  Bibliography 339
  Biography 342
  Directories 342
  Handbooks and Yearbooks 343
Community Life 344
Disabled 345
Family, Marriage, and Divorce 348
Gay and Lesbian Studies 349
Men's Studies 350
Philanthropy 351
  Bibliography 351
  Directories 351
  Handbooks 356
  Indexes 357
Sex Studies 357
Social Welfare and Social Work 359
Substance Abuse 362
Youth and Child Development 363

17—Statistics, Demography, and Urban Studies

Demography 367
Statistics 371
Urban Studies 375

18—Women's Studies

Atlases 379
Bibliographies 379
Biography 381
Chronology 383
Dictionaries and Encyclopedias 383
Handbooks and Yearbooks 386

Part III
HUMANITIES

19—Humanities in General

General Works 391
   Bibliography 391
   Biography 393
   Dictionaries and Encyclopedias 393
   Directories 394
   Handbooks and Yearbooks 394

20—Communication and Mass Media

General Works 395
   Directories 395
   Handbooks and Yearbooks 395
Authorship 396
   General Works 396
   Bibliography 397
   Handbooks and Yearbooks 397
   Style Manuals 398
Newspapers and Magazines 399
   Bibliography 399
   Biography 400
   Directories 401
   Handbooks and Yearbooks 403
Radio, Television, Audio, and Video . . . 405
   Bibliography 405
   Dictionaries and Encyclopedias 405
   Directories 406
   Handbooks and Yearbooks 408
   Indexes 411

21—Decorative Arts

Collecting 413
   Antiques 413
   Books 414
   Coins and Paper Money 416
   Guns 417
   Toys 417
Crafts 418
Design 419
Fashion 420
Photography 420
Upholstery 421

22—Fine Arts

General Works 423
   Bibliography 423
   Biography 423
   Dictionaries and Encyclopedias 426
   Directories 428
   Handbooks and Yearbooks 428

Architecture 431
   Biography 431
   Dictionaries and Encyclopedias 432
   Handbooks and Yearbooks 432
   Indexes 434
Painting 435

23—Language and Linguistics

General Works 439
   Bibliography 439
   Dictionaries and Encyclopedias 440
English-Language Dictionaries 441
   Abridged 441
   Anagrams 446
   Etymology 446
   General Usage 447
   Grammar 450
   Idioms, Colloquialisms, and
      Special Usage 450
   Juvenile 452
   Obsolete Words 453
   Other English-Speaking Countries 453
   Terms and Phrases 454
   Thesauri 454
   Visual 456
Non-English-Language Dictionaries . . . 456
   Azerbaijani 456
   Bosnian 457
   Chickasaw 457
   French 458
   Fulani 459
   German 459
   Greek 460
   Haitian 460
   Hamito-Semitic 461
   Hebrew 461
   Hugarian 461
   Italian 462
   Japanese 462
   Kurdish 464
   Latin 464
   Lushootseed 465
   Norwegian 466
   Occult 466
   Russian 467
   Semitic 470
   Sign Language 470
   Somali 471
   Sotho 472
   Spanish 472
   Swedish 473
   Tatar 473
   Thai 474
   Uzbek 475

24—Literature

General Works 477
  Bibliography 477
  Biography 478
  Dictionaries and Encyclopedias 478
  Handbooks and Yearbooks 481
  Indexes 486
Children's and Young Adult Literature 487
  General Works 487
    Bibliography 487
    Biography 491
    Handbooks and Yearbooks 492
    Indexes 493
  Children's Literature 494
    Bibliography 494
Fiction 496
  General Works 496
  Crime and Mystery 498
  Historical Fiction 499
  Science Fiction, Fantasy, and Horror . . . 499
  Short Stories 501
National Literature 502
  American Literature 502
    General Works 502
      Bibliography, 502; *Biography*, 503; *Dictionaries*, 504; *Handbooks and Yearbooks*, 504
    Drama 505
    Fiction 505
    Individual Authors 507
      Robert Benchley, 507; *Rachel Crothers*, 507; *William Eastlake*, 508; *Allen Ginsberg*, 508; *Ernest Hemingway*, 509; *Herman Melville*, 509; *James A. Michener*, 510; *John Milton*, 510; *Eugene O'Neill*, 510; *John Steinbeck*, 511; *Mark Twain*, 512; *Jack Vance*, 512; *Kurt Vonnegut*, 512; *Tennessee Williams*, 513; *Virginia Woolf*, 513
    Poetry 514
  British Literature 514
    General Works 514
      Bibliography, 514; *Biography*, 515; *Dictionaries and Encyclopedias*, 516; *Handbooks and Yearbooks*, 518
    Fiction 519
    Individual Authors 521
      Joseph Addison and Richard Steele, 521; *George Herbert*, 521; *William Shakespeare*, 522
    Poetry 524
  African Literature 525
  Australian Literature 526
  Canadian Literature 526
  European Literature 527
  French Literature 527
  German Literature 528
  Indic Literature 529
  Irish Literature 529
  Latin American and Caribbean Literature 530
  Native American Literature 531
  Oceanian Literature 531
  Russian Literature 532
  Slavic Literature 532
Poetry 533

25—Music

General Works 535
  Bibliography 535
  Biography 535
  Dictionaries and Encyclopedias 536
  Discography 538
  Handbooks and Yearbooks 539
  Thesauri 540
Children's 540
Composers 541
Conductors 543
Instruments 543
  Cello 543
  Harp 544
  Harpsichord and Clavichord 544
  Organ 545
  Other 545
  Percussion 546
  Piano 546
  Recorder 547
  Voice 548
Musical Forms 549
  Choral 549
  Classical 549
  Operatic 550
  Popular 551
    General Works 551
    Country 558
    Jazz 558
    Rock 562
    Soul 565

26—Mythology, Folklore, and Popular Culture

Folklore 567
Mythology 569
Popular Culture 572

27—Performing Arts

General Works 577
  Biography 577
  Handbooks and Yearbooks 578
Film, Television, and Video 579
  Bibliography 579
  Biography 579
  Chronology 580
  Dictionaries and Encyclopedias 581
  Directories 586
  Filmography 589
  Handbooks and Yearbooks 593
  Indexes 599
Theater 599
  Dictionaries and Encyclopedias 599
  Directories 602
  Handbooks and Yearbooks 603

28—Philosophy and Religion

Philosophy 605
  Bibliography 605
  Biography 606
  Dictionaries and Encyclopedias 607
  Directories 608
  Handbooks 609
  Indexes 611
Religion 612
  General Works 612
    Atlases 612
    Bibliography 612
    Biography 614
    Dictionaries and Encyclopedias 614
    Handbooks and Yearbooks 615
    Periodicals and Serials 616
  Bible Studies 616
    Biography 616
    Dictionaries and Encyclopedias 617
    Handbooks and Yearbooks 620
    Indexes 621
  Christianity 621
    Atlases 621
    Bibliography 622
    Biography 623
    Dictionaries and Encyclopedias 624
    Directories 626
    Handbooks and Yearbooks 627
  Islam 628
  Judaism 628
  New Age 630
  Oriental 630

Part IV
SCIENCE AND TECHNOLOGY

29—Science and Technology in General

Bibliography 633
Biography 634
Dictionaries and Encyclopedias 637
Directories 642
Handbooks and Yearbooks 643

30—Agricultural Sciences

General Works 647
  Dictionaries and Encyclopedias 647
  Directories 648
  Handbooks and Yearbooks 648
Food Sciences and Technology 649
  Bibliography 649
  Dictionaries and Encyclopedias 649
  Directories 652
  Handbooks and Yearbooks 653
Forestry 656
Horticulture 656
  Handbooks and Yearbooks 656
Veterinary Science 660

31—Biological Sciences

General Works 663
Biology 664
Botany 665
  General Works 665
    Dictionaries and Encyclopedias 665
    Handbooks and Yearbooks 666
  Flowering Plants 667
  Fungi 671
  Grasses and Weeds 671
  Herbaceous Plants 672
  Herbs 673
  Molds 673
  Trees and Shrubs 674
  Vascular Plants 676
Natural History 676
Zoology 679
  General Works 679
  Bats 682
  Birds 683
  Domestic Animals 685
  Fishes 686
  Insects 688
  Mammals 689
  Marine Animals 691
  Reptiles and Amphibians 691

32—Engineering

General Works 695
Astronautical Engineering 696
Automation Engineering 697
Chemical Engineering 698
Electric Engineering and Electronics . . . 698
Environmental Engineering 699
Genetic Engineering 700
Materials Science 702
Mechanical Engineering 706
Petroleum Engineering 707
Plant Engineering 707
Tools 708

33—Health Sciences

General Works 709
  Dictionaries and Encyclopedias 709
  Directories 710
  Handbooks and Yearbooks 713
Medicine 714
  General Works 714
    Atlases 714
    Bibliography 715
    Dictionaries and Encyclopedias 715
    Directories 717
    Handbooks and Yearbooks 718
  Alternative Medicine 721
  Psychiatry 722
  Specific Diseases and Conditions 723
    AIDS 723
    Birth-Related Conditions 723
    Chemically-Related Conditions 724
    Childbirth 724
    Chronic Pain 724
    Depression 725
    Epidemics 725
    Oncology 726
    Poisoning 726
    Skin Conditions 727
    Sports Medicine 727
    Surgery 728
Nursing 728
Pharmacy and Pharmaceutical
  Sciences 729

34—High Technology

General Works 735
Artificial Intelligence 736
Computing 737
  General Works 737
  Dictionaries and Encyclopedias 737
  Directories 742

  Online 745
Telecommunications 747
  Directories 747
  Handbooks and Yearbooks 749

35—Physical Sciences and Mathematics

Physical Sciences 753
  General Works 753
  Chemistry 754
    Dictionaries and Encyclopedias 754
    Directories 754
    Handbooks and Yearbooks 755
  Earth and Planetary Sciences 756
    General Works 756
    Astronomy and Space Sciences 757
    Geology 758
    Meteorology 760
    Mineralogy 762
    Paleontology 763
    Volcanology 765
  Physics 765
Mathematics 767

36—Resource Sciences

General Works 769
  Dictionaries and Encyclopedias 769
  Directories 769
Energy Resources 770
  Acronyms 770
  Bibliography 770
  Directories 770
  Handbooks and Yearbooks 771
Environmental Science 775
  Acronyms 775
  Bibliographies 776
  Chronology 776
  Dictionaries and Encyclopedias 777
  Directories 780
  Handbooks and Yearbooks 781

37—Transportation

General Works 785
Air 785
Ground 787
Water 791

Author/Title Index 795

Subject Index 831

Introduction

PURPOSE AND SCOPE

American Reference Books Annual, a far-reaching reviewing service for reference books, is now in its 27th volume. The 1,898 books and CD-ROMs reviewed in this volume cover imprints from 1995 and some from 1994 that were received too late to be reviewed in the previous volume. In the 27 volumes of ARBA published since 1970, a total of 47,098 titles have been reviewed. Five cumulative indexes for ARBA cover the years 1970-1974, 1975-1979, 1980-1984, 1985-1989, and 1990-1994. These indexes facilitate the use of the annual volumes.

ARBA differs significantly from other reviewing media in its basic purpose, which is to provide comprehensive coverage of English-language reference books published in the United States and Canada during a single year. The categories of reference books reviewed in ARBA and the policy regarding them can be summarized as follows: (1) Dictionaries, encyclopedias, indexes, directories, bibliographies, guides, concordances, atlases, gazetteers, and other types of ready-reference tools are routinely reviewed in each volume of ARBA; coverage of this category of reference materials is nearly complete. (2) General encyclopedias that are updated annually, yearbooks, almanacs, indexing and abstracting services, and other annuals or serials are usually reviewed at intervals of three, four, or five years. The first review of such works generally provides an appropriate historical background. Subsequent reviews of these publications attempt to point out changes in scope, editorial policy, and similar matters. (3) New editions of reference books are ordinarily reviewed with appropriate comparisons to the older editions. (4) Traditionally, foreign reference titles have been reviewed only if they had an exclusive distributor in the United States. In 1987 coverage was expanded to include Canadian publications that do not have U.S. distributors. Prices for such titles are in Canadian dollars unless otherwise indicated. Substantial coverage of Canadian reference publications has been achieved and will continue until it is as complete for Canada as it is for the United States. Other foreign title coverage is restricted to English-language publications from Great Britain, as well as some from Australia and India. (5) Government publications are reviewed on a highly selected basis because other Libraries Unlimited works, *Government Reference Books* (published biennially) and *Government Reference Serials* (published irregularly) provide the library professional with comprehensive coverage of government reference publications. In ARBA 96 only Library of Congress publications and international publications, such as those of the United Nations, are covered. (6) Reprints are reviewed in ARBA on a selective basis as they often are produced in limited quantities. (7) Titles produced for the mass market in the areas of collectibles, travel guides, and genealogy receive selective coverage.

Certain categories of reference books are usually not reviewed in ARBA: those of fewer than 48 pages, those produced by vanity presses or by the author as publisher, and those generated by library staffs for internal use. Highly specialized reference works printed in a limited number of copies and that do not appeal to the general library audience ARBA serves may also be omitted.

Because there has been a significant increase and interest in electronic publishing, ARBA has begun reviewing this medium. More than 65 CD-ROMs receive comprehensive and lengthy evaluations in this edition. Future volumes will continue to include reviews of these state-of-the-art information storage devices in a variety of subject areas.

REVIEWING POLICY

To ensure well-written and erudite reviews, the ARBA staff maintains a roster of more than 300 scholars, practitioners, and library educators in all subject specialties at libraries and universities throughout the United States and Canada. Because ARBA is not a selective reviewing source, such as *Choice* or *Library Journal*, the reviews are generally longer and more critical, to detail the strengths and weaknesses of important reference works. Reviewers are asked to examine books and provide well-documented critical comments, both positive and negative. Coverage usually includes the usefulness of a given work; organization, execution, and pertinence of contents; prose style; format; availability of supplementary materials (e.g., indexes, appendixes); and similarity to other works and previous editions. Reviewers are encouraged to address the intended audience but not necessarily to give specific recommendations for purchase. An adequate description and evaluation of the reference book are sufficient. All reviews in ARBA are signed.

ARRANGEMENT

ARBA 96 consists of 37 chapters, an author/title index, and a subject index. It is divided into four alphabetically arranged parts: "General Reference Works," "Social Sciences," "Humanities," and "Science and Technology." "General Reference Works" is subdivided by form: bibliography, biography, catalogs and collections, dictionaries and encyclopedias, handbooks and yearbooks, indexes, and so on. Within the remaining three parts, chapters are organized by topic. Thus, under "Social Sciences" the reader will find chapters titled "Economics and Business," "Education," "History," "Law," and "Sociology."

Each chapter is subdivided to reflect the arrangement strategy of the entire volume. There is a section on general works followed by a topical breakdown. For example, in the chapter titled "Performing Arts," "General Works" is followed by "Dance" and "Film, Television, and Video." The latter is divided into sections by format, which include "Biography" and "Filmography." Subdivisions are based on the amount of material available on a given topic and vary from year to year.

ACKNOWLEDGMENTS

This 27th edition of ARBA has been assembled by four successive associate editors. The bulk of the work was done by Jeffrey E. Long; the current associate editor is Ed Volz.

In closing, we wish to express our gratitude to the many talented contributors without whose support this volume of ARBA could not have been compiled. We would also like to thank the members of our staff who were instrumental in the preparation: G. Kim Dority, Pamela J. Getchell, Kay Minnis, Stephen Haenel, Lori Kranz, Patricia B. Lutz, Judy Gay Matthews, Anna Grace Patterson, and Jo Anne Ricca.

Bohdan S. Wynar, Editor in Chief

Editorial Staff

Bohdan S. Wynar, Editor in Chief
Melissa R. Root, Assistant Editor

Contributors

Gordon J. Aamot, Head, Business Administration Library, Univ. of Washington Libraries, Seattle.

Debbie Abilock, Librarian/Information Specialist, The Nueva School, Hillsborough, Calif.

Stephen H. Aby, Education Bibliographer, Bierce Library, Univ. of Akron, Ohio.

Diana Accurso, Bibliographic Instruction Coordinator/Reference Librarian, Denison Univ. Libraries, Granville, Ohio.

January Adams, Asst. Director in Charge of Adult Services, Franklin Township Public Library, South Plainfield, N.J.

Laural L. Adams, Reference Librarian–Business, Univ. Library, New Mexico State Univ., Las Cruces.

Sandra Adell, Asst. Professor, Dept. of Afro-American Studies, Univ. of Wisconsin, Madison.

Walter C. Allen, Assoc. Professor Emeritus, Graduate School of Library and Information Science, Univ. of Illinois, Urbana.

Donald Altschiller, Reference Librarian, Boston University.

Mary Jo Aman, Education Librarian, Golda Meir Library, Univ. of Wisconsin, Milwaukee.

Elizabeth L. Anderson, Part-time Instructor, Lansing Community College, Mich.

Frank J. Anderson, Librarian Emeritus, Sandor Teszler Library, Wofford College, Spartanburg, S.C.

James D. Anderson, Assoc. Dean and Professor, School of Communication, Information, and Library Studies, Rutgers Univ., New Brunswick, N.J.

Robert T. Anderson, Professor, Religious Studies, Michigan State Univ., East Lansing.

Charles R. Andrews, Dean of Library Services, Hofstra Univ., Hempstead, N.Y.

Hermina G. B. Anghelescu, Fulbright Doctoral Student/Teaching Assistant, Graduate School of Library and Information Science, Univ. of Texas, Austin.

Susan B. Ardis, Head, McKinney Engineering Library, Univ. of Texas, Austin.

Henry T. Armistead, Adult Reference Librarian, Free Library of Philadelphia, Pa.

Roslyn Attinson, Professor Emerita, College of Staten Island, N.Y.

Lawrence W. S. Auld, Chairman, Dept. of Library and Information Studies, East Carolina Univ., Greenville, N.C.

Susan C. Awe, Arvada Branch Manager, Jefferson County Public Library, Colo.

Mary A. Axford, Reference Librarian, Georgia Institute of Technology, Atlanta.

Jan Bakker, Resource Center Director, North Central Regional Educational Laboratory, Oak Brook, Ill.

Jack Bales, Reference Librarian, Mary Washington College Library, Fredericksburg, Va.

JoAnn Balingit, Library Media Specialist, Bancroft Intermediate School, Wilmington, Del.

Gary D. Barber, Head of Reference, Daniel A. Reed Library, State Univ. of New York, Fredonia.

Helen M. Barber, Reference Librarian, New Mexico State Univ., Las Cruces.

Suzanne I. Barchers, Author/Consultant, Denver, Colo.

Donald A. Barclay, Reference Librarian, New Mexico State Univ., Las Cruces.

David Bardack, Professor, Dept. of Biological Sciences, Univ. of Illinois, Chicago.

Pam M. Baxter, formerly Psychological Sciences Librarian, Psychological Sciences Library, Purdue Univ., West Lafayette, Ind.

Craig W. Beard, Head of Reference Services, Mervyn H. Sterne Library, Univ. of Alabama, Birmingham.

Sandra E. Belanger, Reference Librarian, San Jose State Univ. Library, Calif.

Carol Willsey Bell, Head, Local History and Genealogy Dept., Warren-Trumbull County Public Library, Warren, Ohio.

George H. Bell, Assoc. Librarian, Daniel E. Noble Science and Engineering Library Arizona State Univ., Tempe.

Kenneth W. Berger, Team Leader, Reference/ILL Home Team, Perkins Library, Duke Univ., Durham, N.C.

Bernice Bergup, Humanities Reference Librarian, Davis Library, Univ. of North Carolina, Chapel Hill.

John B. Beston, Professor of English, Nazareth College of Rochester, N.Y.

Barbara M. Bibel, Reference Librarian, Science/Business/Sociology Dept., Main Library, Oakland Public Library, Calif.

Terry D. Bilhartz, Assoc. Professor of History, Sam Houston State Univ., Huntsville, Tex.

James E. Bird, Head, Science and Engineering Department, Raymond H. Folger Library, Univ. of Maine, Orono.

Ron Blazek, Professor, School of Library Science, Florida State Univ., Tallahassee.

Richard Bleiler, Reference Librarian, University of Connecticut, Storrs.

Daniel K. Blewett, Reference Librarian, Cudahy Library, Loyola Univ., Chicago.

Edna M. Boardman, Library Media Specialist, Minot High School, Magic City Campus, N.D.

George S. Bobinski, Dean and Professor, School of Information and Library Studies, State Univ. of New York, Buffalo.

Bobray Bordelon, Social Science Reference Center, Firestone Library, Princeton Univ. Libraries, N.J.

James K. Bracken, Head, Second Floor Main Library Information Services, Ohio State Univ., Columbus.

William Bright, Research Associate in Linguistics, Univ. of Colorado, Boulder.

Simon J. Bronner, Distinguished Professor of Folklore and American Studies, Capitol College, Pennsylvania State Univ., Middletown.

Barbara E. Brown, formerly Head, General Cataloguing Section, Library of Parliament, Ottawa.

Sue Brown, Reference Librarian, Louisiana State Univ., Shreveport.

Vik Brown, Assoc. Professor, Music Librarian, Southern Utah Univ. Library, Cedar City.

Judith M. Brugger, Catalog Management and Authorities Librarian, Cornell Univ., Ithaca, N.Y.

Patrick J. Brunet, Library Manager, Western Wisconsin Technical College, LaCrosse.

Betty Jo Buckingham, Consultant, Iowa Dept. of Education, Des Moines.

Joanna M. Burkhardt, Head Librarian, College of Continuing Education Library, Univ. of Rhode Island, Providence.

Lois J. Buttlar, Assoc. Professor, School of Library and Information Science, Kent State Univ., Ohio.

Hans E. Bynagle, Library Director and Professor of Philosophy, Whitworth College, Spokane, Wash.

Diane M. Calabrese, Research Associate for Planning and Eisenhower Grant Programs, Coordinating Board for Higher Education, Jefferson City, Mo.

John Lewis Campbell, Online Services Coordinator, Univ. of Georgia Libraries, Athens.

Joseph Cataio, Manager, Booklegger's Bookstore, Chicago.

Jo A. Cates, Former Head, Transportation Library, Northwestern Univ. Library, Chicago.

G. A. Cevasco, Assoc. Professor of English, St. John's Univ., Jamaica, N.Y.

Bert Chapman, Government Publications Coordinator, Purdue Univ., West Lafayette, Ind.

Boyd Childress, Reference Librarian, Ralph B. Draughon Library, Auburn Univ., Ala.
Stacey Ennis Chisholm, Staff, Libraries Unlimited, Inc.
Dene L. Clark, Reference Librarian, Auraria Library, Denver, Colo.
Paul F. Clark, Assoc. Professor, Pennsylvania State Univ., University Park.
Stella T. Clark, Professor, Foreign Languages, California State Univ., San Marcos.
Kathryn M. Cleland, Social Sciences Librarian, Swarthmore College, Pa.
Beth Clewis, Collection Specialist, Prince William Public Library, Va.
Barbara E. Clotfelter, Head, Business Department, Birmingham Public Library, Ala.
Harriette M. Cluxton, formerly Director of Medical Library Services, Illinois Masonic Medical Center, Chicago.
Gary R. Cocozzoli, Director of the Library, Lawrence Technological Univ., Southfield, Mich.
Donald E. Collins, Assoc. Professor, Dept. of Library and Information Studies, East Carolina Univ., Greenville, N.C.
Barbara Conroy, Career Connections, Santa Fe, N.Mex.
Kay O. Cornelius, formerly Teacher and Magnet School Lead Teacher, Huntsville City Schools, Ala.
Paul B. Cors, Catalog Librarian, Univ. of Wyoming, Laramie.
Angelo Costanzo, Professor of English, Shippensburg Univ., Pa.
Brian E. Coutts, Head, Dept. of Library Public Services, Helm-Cravens Library, Western Kentucky Univ., Bowling Green.
Bob Craigmile, Reference Librarian, Pitts Theology Library, Emory Univ., Atlanta, Ga.
Kathleen W. Craver, Head Librarian, National Cathedral School, Washington, D.C.
Milton H. Crouch, Asst. Director for Reader Services, Bailey/Howe Library, Univ. of Vermont, Burlington.
George M. Cumming Jr., Librarian III, Adult Services, Boston Public Library.
Gregory Curtis, Reference Librarian, Univ. of Maine, Presque Isle.
Mark Cyzyk, Reference Librarian, Albert S. Cook Library, Towson State Univ., Md.
William J. Dane, Supervising Librarian, Special Libraries, Newark Public Library, N.J.
C. B. (Bob) Darrell, Professor of English and Dept. Chair, Kentucky Wesleyan College, Owensboro.
Joseph W. Dauben, Professor of History and History of Science, City Univ. of New York.
Donald G. Davis Jr., Professor, Graduate School of Library and Information Science, Univ. of Texas, Austin.
Dominique-René de Lerma, Professor, Conservatory of Music, Lawrence Univ., Appleton, Wis.
Bonnie A. Dede, Head, Special Formats Cataloging, Univ. of Michigan Library, Ann Arbor.
Anthony J. Dedrick, Coordinator, Access Services, Auraria Library, Denver, Colo.
Barbara Delzell, Engineering Librarian, New Mexico State Univ., Las Cruces.
Margaret Denman-West, Professor Emeritus, Western Maryland College, Westminster.
Donald C. Dickinson, Professor, Graduate Library School, Univ. of Arizona, Tucson.
John B. Dillon, European Humanities Bibliographer, Memorial Library, Univ of Wisconsin, Madison.
Timothy A. Dixon, Manager of Content Acquisition and Evaluation, Edward Lowe Foundation, Cassopolis, Mich.
David Dodd, Cataloger and Archivist, Univ. of Colorado, Colorado Springs.
Sandra L. Doggett, Library Media Specialist, Linganore High School, Frederick, Md.
Margaret F. Dominy, Head, Mathematics-Physics-Astronomy Library, Univ. of Pennsylvania, Philadelphia.
G. Kim Dority, Staff, Libraries Unlimited, Inc.
John A. Drobnicki, Librarian, Queens Library, Jamaica, N.Y.

Joe P. Dunn, Charles A. Dana Professor of History and Politics, Converse College, Spartanburg, S.C.
Lee S. Dutton, Librarian, Hart Southeast Asia Collection, Founders Library, Northern Illinois Univ., De Kalb.
David Eggenberger, Freelance Writer and Editor, Vienna, Va.
Jennifer Comi Ellard, Young Adult Librarian, San Antonio Public Library, Tex.
Owen H. Ellard, Reference Librarian, San Antonio Public Library, Tex.
Marie Ellis, English and American Literature Bibliographer, Univ. of Georgia Libraries, Athens.
Jean Engler, Reference Librarian, Koelbel Public Library, Englewood, Colo.
Edward Erazo, Reference/Outreach Librarian, New Mexico State Univ., Las Cruces.
Jonathon Erlen, Curator, History of Medicine, Univ. of Pittsburgh, Pa.
G. Edward Evans, Univ. Librarian, Charles Von der Ahe Library, Loyola Marymount Univ., Los Angeles, Calif.
Elaine Ezell, Library Media Specialist, Bowling Green Jr. High School, Ohio.
Ian Fairclough, Head of Cataloging, Noel Memorial Library, Louisiana State Univ., Shreveport.
Kathleen Farago, Reference Librarian, Lakewood Public Library, Ohio.
Evan Ira Farber, College Librarian Emeritus, Earlham College, Richmond, Ind.
Adele M. Fasick, Dean and Professor, School of Library and Information Science, Univ. of Toronto.
Eleanor Ferrall, Librarian Emerita, Arizona State Univ., Tempe.
Ken Feser, London, Ont.
Judith J. Field, Senior Lecturer, Program for Library and Information Science, Wayne State Univ., Detroit, Mich.
Joan B. Fiscella, Bibliographer for Professional Studies, Library, Univ. of Illinois, Chicago.
Virginia S. Fischer, Reference/Documents Librarian, Univ. of Maine, Presque Isle.
Jerry D. Flack, Assoc. Professor of Education, Univ. of Colorado, Colorado Springs.
Patricia Fleming, Professor, Faculty of Library and Information Science, Univ. of Toronto.
Michael A. Foley, Honors Director, Marywood College, Scranton, Pa.
Joanna F. Fountain, Adjunct Faculty, Graduate School of Library and Information Science, Univ. of Texas, Austin.
A. David Franklin, Professor of Music, Winthrop Univ., Rock Hill, S.C.
David K. Frasier, Asst. Librarian, Reference Dept., Indiana Univ., Bloomington.
Suzanne G. Frayser, Social Science Research Consultant and Faculty, Univ. College, Univ. of Denver, Colo.
Susan J. Freiband, Assoc. Professor, Graduate School of Librarianship, Univ. of Puerto Rico, San Juan.
David O. Friedrichs, Professor, Univ. of Scranton, Pa.
Ronald H. Fritze, Assoc. Professor, Dept. of History, Lamar Univ., Beaumont, Tex.
Monica Fusich, Visual Arts Librarian, Willis Library, Univ. of North Texas, Denton.
Ahmad Gamaluddin, Professor, School of Library Science, Clarion State College, Pa.
Zev Garber, Professor and Chair, Jewish Studies, Los Angeles Valley College, Calif.
Joan Garner, Staff, Libraries Unlimited, Inc.
Gregg S. Geary, Music Librarian, Sinclair Library, Univ. of Hawaii, Honolulu.
Gerald L. Gill, Assoc. Professor/Business Reference Librarian, James Madison Univ., Harrisburg, Va.
Elizabeth A. Ginno, Coordinator of Library Computer Information Resources, Univ. Library, California State Univ., Hayward.
Barbara B. Goldstein, Media Specialist, Magothy River Middle School, Arnold, Md.
Allie Wise Goudy, Professor, Western Illinois Univ., Macomb.

M. Patrick Graham, Director, Pitts Theology Library, Emory Univ., Atlanta, Ga.
Marilynn Green, Sciences Reference Librarian, Information Service Dept., Univ. of Houston Libraries, Tex.
Rachael Green, Reference Librarian, Noel Memorial Library, Louisiana State Univ., Shreveport.
Leonard J. Greenspoon, Klutznick Chair in Jewish Civilization, Creighton Univ., Omaha, Nebr.
Richard W. Grefrath, Reference Librarian, Univ. of Nevada, Reno.
Arthur Gribben, Professor, Union Institute, Los Angeles, Calif.
Laurel Grotzinger, Professor, Univ. Libraries, Western Michigan Univ., Kalamazoo.
Leonard Grundt, Professor, A. Holly Patterson Library, Nassau Community College, Garden City, N.Y.
Kwabena Gyimah-Brempong, Professor of Economics, College of Business Administration, Univ. of South Florida, Tampa.
Stephen Haenel, Staff, Libraries Unlimited, Inc.
Susan B. Hagloch, Director, Tuscarawas County Public Library, New Philadelphia, Ohio.
Blaine H. Hall, English Language and Literature Librarian, Harold B. Lee Library, Brigham Young Univ., Provo, Utah.
Deborah Hammer, Head, History, Travel and Biography Division, Queens Borough Public Library, Jamaica, N.Y.
Joseph Hannibal, Curator of Invertebrate Paleontology, Cleveland Museum of Natural History, Ohio.
Constance Hardesty, Twenty-first Century Communications, Denver, Colo.
Roberto P. Haro, Director and Professor, San Francisco State Univ., Calif.
Chauncy D. Harris, Samuel N. Harper Distinguished Service Professor Emeritus of Geography, Univ. of Chicago.
Marvin K. Harris, Professor of Entomology, Texas A & M Univ., College Station.
Ann Hartness, Asst. Head Librarian, Benson Latin American Collection, Univ. of Texas, Austin.
Karen D. Harvey, Assoc. Dean for Academic Affairs, Univ. College, Univ. of Denver, Colo.
Joy Hastings, Manager, Technical Library, Hunt-Wesson, Inc., Fullerton, Calif.
Deborah S. Hatfield, Head Librarian, Lexmark Information Center, Univ. of Kentucky, Lexington.
Robert J. Havlik, Librarian Emeritus and Exhibit Coordinator, Univ. of Notre Dame, Ind.
Fred J. Hay, Librarian of the W. L. Eury Appalachian Collection and Assoc. Professor, Center for Appalachian Studies, Appalachian State Univ., Boone, N.C.
James S. Heller, Director of the Law Library and Assoc. Professor of Law, Marshall-Wythe Law Library, College of William and Mary, Williamsburg, Va.
Mary Hemmings, Technical Services Librarian, Law Library, Univ. of Calgary, Alta.
David Henige, African Studies Bibliographer, Memorial Library, Univ. of Wisconsin, Madison.
Carol D. Henry, Librarian, Lyons Township High School, LaGrange, Ill.
Mark Y. Herring, Dean of Libraries, Oklahoma Baptist Univ., Shawnee.
Susan Davis Herring, Reference Librarian, Univ. of Alabama Library, Huntsville.
Christopher J. Hoeppner, Reference Instruction Librarian, DePaul Univ., Chicago.
Richard E. Holl, Asst. Professor, History Dept., Lees College, Jackson, Ky.
Susan Tower Hollis, Independent Scholar, Reno, Nev.
Paul L. Holmer, Reference Librarian, Buley Library, Southern Connecticut State Univ., New Haven.
Curtis D. Holmes, Ph.D. Candidate in International Studies at the Univ. of Denver, Colo.
Teresa Holten, Media Generalist, Lyle Public School, Minn.
Shirley L. Hopkinson, Professor, Division of Library and Information Science, San Jose State Univ., Calif.
William E. Hug, Professor, University of Georgia, Athens.

C. D. Hurt, Director, Graduate Library School, Univ. of Arizona, Tucson.

Jonathan F. Husband, Program Chair of the Library/Reader Services Librarian, Henry Whittemore Library, Framingham State College, Mass.

Ludmila N. Ilyina, Professor, Natural Resources Institute, Univ. of Manitoba, Winnipeg.

David Isaacson, Asst. Head of Reference and Humanities Librarian, Waldo Library, Western Michigan Univ., Kalamazoo.

Barbara Ittner, Staff, Libraries Unlimited, Inc.

Peter B. Ives, Business Librarian, Parish Memorial Library, Univ. of New Mexico, Albuquerque.

Eugene B. Jackson, Professor Emeritus, Graduate School of Library and Information Science, Univ. of Texas, Austin.

Janice M. Jaguszewski, Mathematics Librarian, Univ. of Minnesota, Minneapolis.

Peggy Jobe, Government Publications Librarian for International Documents, Univ. of Colorado, Boulder.

D. Barton Johnson, Professor Emeritus of Russian, Univ. of California, Santa Barbara.

Richard D. Johnson, Director of Libraries, James M. Milne Library, State Univ. College, Oneonta, N.Y.

Marjorie H. Jones, Educational Media Specialist, Bryan Senior High School, Omaha, Neb.

Raymond E. Jones, Assoc. Professor of English, Univ. of Alberta, Edmonton.

Gary E. Joseph, Elementary/Middle School Library Supervisor, South-Western City Schools, Grove City, Ohio.

Suzanne Julian, Public Services Librarian, Southern Utah Univ. Library, Cedar City.

Jane Jurgens, Reference Librarian, St. Cloud State Univ., Minn.

Thomas A. Karel, Assoc. Director for Public Services, Shadek-Fackenthal Library, Franklin and Marshall College, Lancaster, Pa.

Edmund D. Keiser Jr., Professor of Biology, Univ. of Mississippi, University.

John Laurence Kelland, Reference Bibliographer for Life Sciences, Univ. of Rhode Island Library, Kingston.

Dean H. Keller, Assoc. Dean of Libraries, Kent State Univ., Ohio.

Barbara E. Kemp, Asst. Director, Dewey Graduate Library, State Univ. of New York, Albany.

Vicki J. Killion, Asst. Professor of Library Science and Pharmacy, Nursing and Health Sciences Librarian, Purdue Univ., West Lafayette, Ind.

Sung Ok Kim, Senior Asst. Librarian/Social Sciences Cataloging Librarian, Cornell Univ., Ithaca, N.Y.

Norman L. Kincaide, Citation Editor, Shepard's/McGraw-Hill, Inc., Colorado Springs, Colo.

Christine E. King, Reference Librarian, State Univ. of New York, Stony Brook.

Janet J. Kosky, Reader for Social Studies Dept., Ponderosa High School, Placerville, Calif.

Betsy J. Kraus, Librarian/Technical Editor, Environmental Evaluation Group, Albuquerque, N.Mex.

Linda A. Krikos, Head, Women's Studies Library, Ohio State Univ., Columbus.

Colby H. Kullman, Assoc. Professor and Editor, *Studies in American Drama*, Univ. of Mississippi, University.

Natalie Kupferberg, Health Sciences Library Coordinator, Ferris State Univ., Big Rapids, Mich.

Peter B. Kutner, Professor of Law, Univ. of Oklahoma, Norman.

Robert V. Labaree, Reference/Public Services Librarian, Von KleinSmid Library, Univ. of Southern California, Los Angeles.

Linda L. Lam-Easton, Assoc. Professor, Dept. of Religious Studies, California State Univ., North Ridge.

Renée J. LaPerrière, Reference Librarian/Music Coordinator, Newton Gresham Library, Sam Houston State Univ., Huntsville, Tex.

Mary Larsgaard, Asst. Head, Map and Imagery Laboratory Library, Univ. of California, Santa Barbara.

Brad R. Leach, Records Manager, Northern Colorado Water Conservancy District, Loveland.
Charles Leck, Professor of Biological Sciences, Rutgers Univ., New Brunswick, N.J.
Mary Lou LeCompte, Asst. Professor, Kinesiology and Health Education, Univ. of Texas, Austin.
Hwa-Wei Lee, Dean of Libraries, Ohio Univ., Athens.
Joann H. Lee, formerly Head of Reader Services, Lake Forest College, Ill.
R. S. Lehmann, Rocky Mountain BankCard System, Colorado National Bank, Denver.
Richard A. Leiter, Director and Assoc. Professor of Law, Regent Univ., Virginia Beach, Va.
John A. Lent, Drexel Hill, Pa.
Charlotte Lindgren, Professor Emerita of English, Emerson College, Boston.
Alan N. Livingston, Assoc. Production Editor, American Water Works Association, Denver, Colo.
Larry Lobel, Virtuoso Keyboard Services, Petaluma, Calif.
Koraljka Lockhart, Publications Editor, San Francisco Opera, Calif.
David V. Loertscher, formerly Staff, Libraries Unlimited, Inc.
Robert Logsdon, Assoc. Director/Public Services, Indiana State Library, Indianapolis.
Jeffrey E. Long, formerly Staff, Libraries Unlimited, Inc.
Jeffrey R. Luttrell, Leader, Humanities Cataloging Team, Princeton Univ. Library, N.J.
Patricia B. Lutz, Staff, Libraries Unlimited, Inc.
Marit S. MacArthur, Reference Librarian, Auraria Libraries, Univ. of Colorado, Denver.
Sara R. Mack, Professor Emerita, Dept. of Library Science, Kutztown Univ., Pa.
Theresa Maggio, Head of Public Services, Southwest Georgia Regional Library, Bainbridge.
Linda Main, Assoc. Professor, San Jose State Univ., Calif.
S. D. Markman, Professor Emeritus, Art Dept., Duke Univ, Durham, N.C.
Judy Gay Matthews, Staff, Libraries Unlimited, Inc.
Donald W. Maxwell, Reference Librarian, Stone Hills Library Network, Bloomington, Ind.
George Louis Mayer, formerly Senior Principal Librarian, New York Public Library and Part-Time Librarian, Adelphi, Manhattan Center and Brooklyn College, N.Y.
James R. McDonald, Professor of Geography, Eastern Michigan Univ., Ypsilanti.
Christopher Michael McDonough, Instructor, Dept. of Classics, Univ. of North Carolina, Chapel Hill.
Dana McDougald, Lead Media Specialist, Learning Resources Center, Cedar Shoals High School, Athens, Ga.
Robert B. McKee, Professor, Mechanical Engineering, Univ. of Nevada, Reno.
Susan V. McKimm, Business Reference Specialist, Cuyahoga County Library System, Maple Heights, Ohio.
T. McKimmie, Reference Librarian, New Mexico State Univ., Las Cruces.
Marian B. McLeod, Professor of Speech Communication and Theater, Trenton State College, N.J.
Maria O'Neil McMahon, Professor, School of Social Work, East Carolina Univ., Greenville, N.C.
Jean C. McManus, Asst. Reference Librarian, Tisch Library at Tufts Univ., Medford, Mass.
Margo B. Mead, Asst. Professor, Library, Univ. of Alabama, Huntsville.
Lillian R. Mesner, Technical Services Librarian, Agricultural Library, Univ. of Kentucky, Lexington.
Michael G. Messina, Assoc. Professor, Dept. of Forest Science, Texas A & M Univ., College Station.
G. Douglas Meyers, Chair, Dept. of English, Univ. of Texas, El Paso.
George A. Meyers, Chairman, National Labor Commission.
Jeffrey Meyers, Self-Employed Professional Writer, Kensington, Calif.
Bogdan Mieczkowski, Professor of Economics, Ithaca College, N.Y.

Seiko Mieczkowski, Hobart & William Smith Colleges, Geneva, N.Y.

Zbigniew Mieczkowski, Assoc. Professor, Dept. of Geography, Univ. of Manitoba, Winnipeg.

Bill Miller, Director of Libraries, Florida Atlantic Univ., Boca Raton.

Richard A. Miller, Professor of Economics, Wesleyan Univ., Middletown, Conn.

Carol L. Mitchell, Southeast Asian Bibliographic Services Librarian, General Library System, Univ. of Wisconsin, Madison.

James Moffet, Head, Reference Dept, Baldwin Public Library, Birmingham, Mich.

Janet Mongan, Research Officer, Cleveland State Univ. Library, Ohio.

Terry Ann Mood, Humanities Bibliographer, Univ. of Colorado, Denver.

K. Mulliner, Asst. to the Director of Libraries, Ohio Univ. Library, Athens.

Paul M. Murphy III, NREMT-Paramedic, Paramedic Division, EMS, Denver General Hospital, Colo.

James M. Murray, Director, East Bonner County Library, Sandpoint, Idaho.

Linda A. Naru, Planning and Development Officer, Center for Research Libraries, Chicago.

Danuta A. Nitecki, Assoc. Director for Public Services, Univ. of Maryland Libraries, College Park.

Eric R. Nitschke, Reference Librarian, Robert W. Woodruff Library, Emory Univ., Atlanta, Ga.

Christopher W. Nolan, Head, Reference Services, Maddux Library, Trinity Univ., San Antonio, Tex.

Carol L. Noll, Treasurer and Board Member, Tinton Falls Public Library, N.J.

O. Gene Norman, Head, Reference Dept., Indiana State Univ. Libraries, Terre Haute.

Marilyn Strong Noronha, Reference Librarian, Harleigh B. Trecker Library, Univ. of Connecticut, West Hartford.

Marshall E. Nunn, Professor, Dept. of History, Glendale Community College, Calif.

Barbara Jo O'Hara, Adult Services Librarian, Free Library of Philadelphia, Pa.

Herbert W. Ockerman, Professor, Ohio State Univ., Columbus.

Ray Olszewski, Computer Systems Specialist, The Nueva School, Hillsborough, Calif.

Berniece M. Owen, Coordinator, Library Technical Services, Portland Community College, Oreg.

John Howard Oxley, Halifax, N.S.

Mark Padnos, Humanities Reference Librarian, Mina Rees Library, Graduate School and Univ. Center, City Univ. of New York.

Robert Palmieri, Professor Emeritus, School of Music, Kent State Univ., Ohio.

Maureen Pastine, Director, Central Libraries, Southern Methodist Univ., Dallas, Tex.

Elizabeth Patterson, Head, Reference and Computer Reference Services, Robert W. Woodruff Library, Emory Univ., Atlanta, Ga.

Gari-Anne Patzwald, Freelance Editor and Indexer, Lexington, Ky.

Harry E. Pence, Professor of Chemistry, State Univ. of New York, Oneonta.

Karin Pendle, Professor of Musicology, Univ. of Cincinnati, Ohio.

Glenn Petersen, Professor of Anthropology and International Affairs, Graduate Center and Baruch College, City Univ. of New York.

Francis Poole, Assoc. Librarian, Univ. of Delaware Library, Newark.

Edwin D. Posey, Engineering Librarian, Purdue Univ. Libraries, West Lafayette, Ind.

Daphne Fallieros Potter, Database Specialist, American Mathematical Society, Providence, R.I.

Carl Pracht, Reference Librarian, Southeast Missouri State Univ., Cape Girardeau.

Ann E. Prentice, Dean, College of Library and Information Services, Univ. of Maryland, College Park.

Randall Rafferty, Reference Librarian, Mississippi State Univ. Library, Mississippi State.

Varadaraja V. Raman, Professor of Physics and Humanities, Rochester Institute of Technology, N.Y.

Kristin Ramsdell, Assoc. Librarian, California State Univ., Hayward.

Jack Ray, Asst. Director, Loyola/Notre Dame Library, Baltimore, Md.

Nancy P. Reed, Media Specialist, St. Mary Middle/High School, Paducah, Ky.

Lorna K. Rees-Potter, Asst. Professor, Graduate School of Library and Information Studies, McGill Univ., Montreal.

James Rettig, Asst. Univ. Librarian for Reference and Information Services, Swem Library, College of William and Mary, Williamsburg, Va.

Diane B. Rhodes, Life Sciences and Agriculture Librarian, Arizona State Univ., Tempe.

Jo Anne H. Ricca, Staff, Libraries Unlimited, Inc.

Constance Rinaldo, Head, Collection Services, Biomedical Libraries, Dartmouth College, Hanover, N.H.

Anne F. Roberts, Adjunct Professor, School of Education, State Univ. of New York, Albany.

John M. Robson, Institute Librarian, Rose-Hulman Institute of Technology, Terre Haute, Ind.

Ilene F. Rockman, Assoc. Dean of Library Services, California Polytechnic State Univ., San Luis Obispo.

Anne C. Roess, Librarian, Peoples Gas, Light & Coke Co., Chicago.

Deborah V. Rollins, Reference Librarian, Univ. of Maine, Orono.

John B. Romeiser, Professor of French and Dept. Head, Univ. of Tennessee, Knoxville.

Melissa R. Root, Staff, Libraries Unlimited, Inc.

Bertram H. Rothschild, Asst. Chief of Psychology, V.A. Medical Center, Denver, Colo.

Samuel Rothstein, Professor Emeritus, School of Librarianship, Univ. of British Columbia, Vancouver.

Michele Russo, Head of Public Services, Franklin D. Schurz Library, Indiana Univ., South Bend.

David E. Salamie, formerly Staff, Libraries Unlimited, Inc.

Edmund F. SantaVicca, Librarian, Information Commons, Estrella Mountain Community College Center, Litchfield Park, Ariz.

Frederick A. Schlipf, Executive Director, Urbana Free Library, and Adjunct Professor, Graduate School of Library and Information Science, Univ. of Illinois.

Diane Schmidt, Asst. Biology Librarian, Univ. of Illinois, Urbana.

Steven J. Schmidt, Assoc. Librarian, Indiana Univ.-Purdue Univ. at Indianapolis Libraries.

John P. Schmitt, Head of Reference, Univ. of Wyoming Libraries, Laramie.

Deborah K. Scott, Asst. Librarian, Employer's Reinsurance Corporation, Overland Park, Kans.

Ralph Lee Scott, Assoc. Professor, East Carolina Univ. Library, Greenville, N.C.

Robert A. Seal, University Librarian, Texas Christian Univ., Fort Worth.

Jonathan Seeley, Professor of Linguistics, Univ. of Arizona, Tuscon.

Margretta Reed Seashore, Professor of Genetics and Pediatrics, Yale Univ. School of Medicine, New Haven, Conn.

Ravindra Nath Sharma, Library Director, West Virginia State College, Institute.

Bruce A. Shuman, Adjunct Professor, Univ. of South Florida, Tampa.

Stephanie C. Sigala, Head Librarian, Richardson Memorial Library, St. Louis Art Museum, Mo.

Esther R. Sinofsky, Library Media Teacher, Alexander Hamilton High School, Los Angeles, Calif.

Robert Skinner, Technology Development Librarian, Central Univ. Libraries, Southern Methodist Univ., Dallas, Tex.

John David Smith, Alumni Distinguished Professor of History, North Carolina State Univ., Raleigh.

Nathan M. Smith, Director, School of Library and Information Sciences, Brigham Young Univ., Provo, Utah.

Mary Ellen Snodgrass, Freelance Writer, Charlotte, N.C.

Jerri Spoehel, Freelance Writer and Editor, Las Cruces, N.Mex.

Karen Y. Stabler, Head of Information Services, New Mexico State Univ. Library, Las Cruces.

Allen E. Staver, Assoc. Professor, Dept. of Geography, Northern Illinois Univ., De Kalb.

Kay M. Stebbins, Coordinator Librarian, Louisiana State Univ., Shreveport.

Norman D. Stevens, Director Emeritus, Univ. of Connecticut Libraries, Storrs.

John P. Stierman, Reference Librarian, Western Illinois Univ., Macomb.

John W. Storey, Professor of History, Lamar Univ., Beaumont, Tex.

William C. Struning, Professor, Seton Hall Univ., South Orange, N.J.

Bruce Stuart, Assoc. Professor of Health Administration, Pennsylvania State Univ., University Park.

Mila C. Su, Senior Asst. Librarian, Pennsylvania State Univ., Altoona.

Timothy E. Sullivan, Asst. Professor of Economics, Towson State Univ., Md.

Richard H. Swain, Reference Librarian, West Chester Univ., Pa.

James H. Sweetland, Assoc. Professor, School of Library and Information Science, Univ. of Wisconsin, Milwaukee.

Nigel Tappin, General Librarian, North York Public Library, Ont.

Deborah A. Taylor, Staff, Libraries Unlimited, Inc.

Glynys R. Thomas, Library Director, Ligature, Inc., Boston.

Katherine Margaret Thomas, formerly Biologist, Long Point Bird Observatory, Toronto.

Paul H. Thomas, Head, Catalog Dept., Hoover Institution Library, Stanford Univ., Calif.

Christine E. Thompson, Head, Catalog Dept. and Assoc. Professor, Univ. of Alabama Libraries, Tuscaloosa.

Mary Ann Thompson, Asst. Professor of Nursing, Saint Joseph College, West Hartford, Conn.

Angela Marie Thor, Information Consultant, Syracuse, N.Y.

Dianna Thor, Librarian, English as a Second Language Library, Univ. of Arizona, Tuscon.

Bruce H. Tiffney, Assoc. Professor of Geology and Biological Sciences, Univ. of California, Santa Barbara.

Carol L. Tilley, Library Media Specialist, Danville Community High School, Ill.

Andrew G. Torok, Assoc. Professor, Northern Illinois Univ., De Kalb.

Gregory M. Toth, Reference Librarian, State Univ. of New York, Brockport.

John U. Trefny, Head and Professor, Dept. of Physics, Colorado School of Mines, Golden.

Mary L. Trennery, Media Specialist, Millard Public Schools, Omaha, Nebr.

Carol Truett, Assoc. Professor, Appalachian State Univ., Boone, N.C.

Dean Tudor, Professor, School of Journalism, Ryerson Polytechnical Institute, Toronto.

Elias H. Tuma, Professor of Economics, Univ. of California, Davis.

Diane J. Turner, Science/Engineering Liaison, Auraria Library, Univ. of Colorado, Denver.

Robert L. Turner Jr., Librarian and Asst. Professor, Radford Univ., Va.

Michele Tyrrell, Media Specialist, Arundel Senior High School, Gambrills, Md.

Mary Lou Unterburger, Retired Branch Manager, Detroit Public Library, Mich.

Arthur R. Upgren, Professor of Astronomy and Director, Van Vleck Observatory, Wesleyan Univ., Middletown, Conn.

Joyce Kasman Valenza, Librarian, Wissahickon High School, Ambler, Pa.

Vandelia L. VanMeter, Assoc. Professor and Chair, Dept. of Library and Information Science, Spalding Univ., Louisville, Ky.

Dario J. Villa, Reference Librarian/Bibliographer, Ronald Williams Library, Northeastern Illinois Univ., Chicago.

Kathleen J. Voigt, Head, Reference Dept., Carlson Library, Univ. of Toledo, Ohio.

Ed Volz, Staff, Libraries Unlimited, Inc.

David V. Waller, Asst. Professor of Sociology, Dept of Sociology and Anthropology, Univ. of Texas, Arlington.

Wendy Waloff, Upper/Middle School Librarian, Friends Select School, Philadelphia, Pa.

Jeff Wanser, Coordinator, Reference and Government Documents, Hiram College Library, Ohio.

Richard S. Watts, Coordinator, Technical Processing Dept., San Bernardino County Library, Calif.

J. E. Weaver, Dept. of Economics, Drake Univ., Des Moines, Iowa.

Bruce H. Webb, Librarian/Asst Professor, Rena M. Carlson Library, Clarion Univ. of Pennsylvania.

Jean Weihs, Principal Consultant, Technical Services Group, Toronto.

Emily L. Werrell, Reference/Instructional Services Librarian, Northern Kentucky Univ., Highland Heights.

Nancy S. Weyant, Coordinator of Reference Services, Bloomsburg Univ., Pa.

Lucille Whalen, Dean of Graduate Programs, Immaculate Heart College Center, Los Angeles, Calif.

Carol Wheeler, Government Documents Reference Librarian, Univ. of Georgia Libraries, Athens.

David L. White, Professor, History Dept., Appalachian State Univ., Boone, N.C.

Marilyn Domas White, Assoc. Professor, College of Library and Information Services, Univ. of Maryland, College Park.

Robert L. Wick, Asst. Professor and Fine Arts Bibliographer, Auraria Library, Univ. of Colorado, Denver.

William H. Wiese, Science and Reference Librarian, Parks Library, Iowa State Univ., Ames.

Lorna A. Wiggins, Business Librarian, Social Sciences Dept., R. B. Draughon Library, Auburn Univ., Ala.

Lynn F. Williams, Professor, Division of Writing, Literature, and Publishing, Emerson College, Boston.

Wiley J. Williams, Professor Emeritus, School of Library Science, Kent State Univ., Ohio.

Frank L. Wilson, Professor and Head, Dept. of Political Science, Purdue Univ., West Lafayette, Ind.

Mark A. Wilson, Professor of Geology, College of Wooster, Ohio.

Patricia S. Wilson, Public Services Librarian, Agriculture Library, Univ. of Kentucky, Lexington.

William G. Wilson, Lecturer, Univ. of Maryland, College Park.

Glenn R. Wittig, Director of Library Services, Criswell College, Dallas, Tex.

Raymund F. Wood, Editor, *The Westerners*, Encino, Calif.

Bohdan S. Wynar, Staff, Libraries Unlimited, Inc.

Hope Yelich, Reference Librarian, Earl Gregg Swem Library, College of William and Mary, Williamsburg, Va.

A. Neil Yerkey, Assoc. Professor, School of Information and Library Studies, State Univ. of New York, Buffalo.

Henry E. York, Head, Collection Management, Cleveland State Univ., Ohio.

Arthur P. Young, Director, Northern Illinois Libraries, Northern Illinois Univ., De Kalb.

Louis G. Zelenka, Public Services Librarian, Satilla Regional Library, Douglas, Ga.

Magda Zelinska-Ferl, Professor/Faculty Advisor, Union Institute, Los Angeles, Calif.

Susan Zernial, Staff, Libraries Unlimited, Inc.

L. Zgusta, Professor of Linguistics and the Classics and Member of the Center for Advanced Study, Univ. of Illinois, Urbana.

Anita Zutis, Adjunct Librarian, Queensborough Community College, Bayside, N.Y.

Journals Cited

FORM OF CITATION	JOURNAL TITLE
BL	Booklist
BR	Book Report
Choice	Choice
C&RL	College & Research Libraries
JAL	Journal of Academic Librarianship
LJ	Library Journal
RBB	Reference Books Bulletin
RQ	RQ
SLJ	School Library Journal
SLMQ	School Library Media Quarterly
VOYA	Voice of Youth Advocates
WLB	Wilson Library Bulletin

Part I
GENERAL REFERENCE WORKS

1 General Reference Works

ACRONYMS AND ABBREVIATIONS

1. **The Barnhart Abbreviations Dictionary.** Robert K. Barnhart, ed. New York, John Wiley, 1995. 434p. $34.95. ISBN 0-471-57146-6.

Compiled by dictionary editors working from contemporary English-language resources such as books, newspapers, magazines, and technical and scientific publications, this work presents more than 60,000 entries in a user-friendly, two-way format. In its first section, the abbreviations and written symbols are listed alphabetically, with one or more definitions or subject labels, variant spellings, followed by a pronunciation guide, as appropriate. The second section is a mirror list of actual words and phrases, in alphabetical order, followed by their abbreviations. An introductory essay outlines the development of abbreviations and acronyms and identifies distinctions between the two forms, also discussing stylistic conventions for the preferred usage of abbreviations.

Similar in scope and coverage to the *Oxford Dictionary of Abbreviations* (see ARBA 93, entry 3), this work focuses on the most common English-language terms. Scientific, technical, and computing terms are well represented. Despite its title, however, a considerable number of the entries are acronyms, and distinctions made in the introductory essay between the two forms tend not to be observed in the actual selection of entries. The work is all the stronger for this lapse, and the volume will admirably serve as a handy reference guide for small- or medium-sized libraries and home use. Affordably priced and well designed as it is, those seeking a more comprehensive directory of abbreviations and acronyms are still advised to consult the more than 500,000 entries found in the classic, if pricey, *Acronyms, Initialisms & Abbreviations Dictionary* (see ARBA 93, entry 1).—**Elizabeth Patterson**

2. De Sola, Ralph, Dean Stahl, and Karen Kerchelich. **Abbreviations Dictionary.** 9th ed. Boca Raton, Fla., CRC Press, 1995. 1347p. $79.95. ISBN 0-8493-8944-5.

Since its appearance in 1958, this compact dictionary has provided a timely compilation of the many, and often confusing, abbreviations prevalent in modern society. This revised and expanded edition builds upon that tradition with more than 15,000 additional entries enhancing the comprehensive listing of abbreviations, acronyms, anonyms, appellations, contractions, eponyms, geographical equivalents, initialisms, nicknames, slang shortcuts, and toponyms.

Those familiar with the evolution of this dictionary will appreciate that the present title (sans cumbersome subtitle) does not do justice to the wide scope of its contents. In addition to the alphabetical listing of abbreviations, the final third of the work constitutes a ready-reference for useful information on a vast array of topics, including airlines of the world, inventions and inventors, international vehicle license letters, phobias, birthstones, national capitals, sobriquets, international conversions, signs and symbols, euphemisms, corrections facilities, superlatives, and much more. In these pages, one discovers that Bombay duck is a dried and salted lizard fish; that *fir* is Gaelic for a men's toilet; that Mildred E. Gillars was the real name of Axis Sally; and that arms making and trading is considered the world's second-oldest profession. Two additional lists are included in this recent edition: presidents and vice presidents of the United States, and national parks of North America.

The organizational scheme throughout, mainly alphabetical and numerical, is clear and well presented. The previous introduction is streamlined for this edition, resulting in a more concise user guide. This useful dictionary belongs in the reference collection of most, if not all, libraries.—**Owen H. Ellard**

3. **New Acronyms, Initialisms, & Abbreviations: A Guide to Acronyms, Initialisms, Abbreviations, Contractions.... Volume 2.** Jennifer Mossman and others, eds. Detroit, Gale, 1995. 247p. $250.00pa. ISBN 0-8103-5570-1. ISSN 0270-4404.

This is volume 2 of a 3-volume set: *Acronyms, Initialisms, & Abbreviations Dictionary* (AIAD) (see ARBA 93, entry 1), *New Acronyms . . .*, and *Reverse Acronyms . . .* (see ARBA 95, entry 2). In this supplement to the 19th edition of AIAD, the editors have increased their coverage of the most prolific sources of new abbreviations: architecture, aviation, computer science, engineering, mass media, and military affairs. They continue to provide acronyms, abbreviations, and initialisms from a long list of other fields. Editors have become aware of some entries through printed sources; the staff and submitters have encountered others in the media. Gale publishes 10 acronyms titles, including intereditions such as this. The fields of computers/telecommunications, business, periodicals, and international entries are treated in more detail in separate publications.

The book is divided into two parts. The first half lists the acronyms themselves; the second half lists entries by meaning. Most often the word given in the meaning section is the first word in the acronym. Material in the front of the volume explains the purpose and content, including a list of major sources.

New Acronyms is part of a standard work in libraries serving older teens, adults, and researchers. Libraries should acquire the specialized "cousins" if demand warrants. Gale updates this resource constantly, and that is especially important. It is also available on magnetic tape or diskette in a fielded format.—**Edna M. Boardman**

ALMANACS

4. **The Old Farmer's Almanac 1995.** Dublin, N.H., Yankee Publishing, 1995. 256p. illus. maps. $14.95pa. ISBN 0-89909-284-5. ISSN 0078-4516.

Published every year since 1792, *The Old Farmer's Almanac* is now in its 203d edition. As expected, the *Almanac* allots a great deal of space to weather and weather forecasting. The forecasts are broken down into 16 regions for ease of use. Other related features include information on daylight saving time, eclipses, holiday observances, astrological phases, sundials, tides, and windchill factors. There are feature articles on consumer tastes and trends for 1995; the practical pepper primer; the introduction of Jackie Robinson to major league baseball; chaos theory; cowboys; Ernie Pyle; and prize-winning recipes from U.S. food festivals. The volume is peppered with ads for everything from vacuum cleaners and weight loss regimens to woodworking patterns and videotapes. Every page brings a surprise, be it a recipe, a meteorological tidbit, or a medicinal recommendation. The hodgepodge format retains an antiquarian quality that gives the *Almanac* an appropriately nostalgic feel. There is no other volume like it. The almanac continues as a useful compendium of meteorological data, nostrums, and miscellanea that is nearly as old as the country—a veritable gold mine for social historians. Where else could one find a gestation and mating table, a manure guide, plants that attract butterflies, full moon names, and safe ice thickness? Recommended for libraries of all types, the work is especially recommended for public libraries with clientele who will inevitably want to verify the correctness of the fearless weather forecasts over the years.—**Arthur P. Young**

5. **The Universal Almanac 1995.** John W. Wright, ed. Kansas City, Mo., Andrews and McMeel, 1994. 760p. index. $19.95; $12.95pa. ISBN 0-8362-8033-4; 0-8362-8032-6pa. ISSN 1045-9820.

This attractive almanac continues to have much similar information as other almanacs, as indicated in a review of an earlier edition (see ARBA 92, entry 2). It contains calendars, chronologies, statistics, and historical documents. It also covers recent topics such as tabloid news on television, health care reform, and the civil war in the Balkans. The format of the *Universal Almanac* is one of the best of available almanacs. The print is clear with bold typeface used for emphasis and pleasant blue lines used for highlighting broad topics and tables. The index also has expanded from 20 to $24\frac{1}{2}$ pages, providing extended access to information.

Although the *Universal Almanac* does not replace the *World Almanac* (see entry 7), nor the *Information Please Almanac* (see ARBA 90, entry 2) it may be preferred due to its improved format, expanded articles, and the tendency to lie flat on a desk. The work under review provides more extensive coverage of AIDS worldwide and endangered species in the United States than the other two almanacs, and is the only almanac that summarizes recent sex research in the United States. The *World Almanac 1995* has flags of the world and birth dates and birthplaces of entertainment personalities not found in the *Universal Almanac*. Further, the *Information Please Almanac 1995* contains a crossword puzzle guide and pictures of national and world personalities, which the *Universal Almanac* lacks. Even so, every library can afford, and will benefit, from this appealing and informative work.—**O. Gene Norman**

6. **Whitaker's Almanack 1996.** 128th ed. London, J. Whitaker and Sons; distr., Detroit, Gale, 1995. 1279p. illus. maps. index. $80.00. ISBN 0-80521-254-5.

This remains, in its 128th edition, the standard single-volume reference book on all things British (see ARBA 95, entry 9, for a review of the previous edition). It explains everything from the mundane (bank holidays, population figures) to the exotic (copyright/patent/trademark laws), and the essential (currency exchange rates, forms of address). Tourists will find a list of London's sights, sports fans can locate performance records, and editors can learn what the abbreviation B CH [D] stands for (bachelor of dental surgery degree).

Lengthy chapters delineate the organization of both the Church of England and the British government, the Royal Family and the peerage. Annual summaries efficiently update the reader on developments in the arts, economics, the media, the sciences, and other fields. A general news update includes activities through August 1995; some are illustrated with color photographs. Maps and charts throughout the text add variety to the standard almanac format. A serviceable index aids access to the copious data contained in this resource. Libraries with all but the smallest reference collections should consider buying this annually.—**Ed Volz**

7. **The World Almanac and Book of Facts 1996.** Robert Famighetti and others, eds. Mahwah, N.J., World Almanac Books/Funk & Wagnalls, 1995. 975p. illus. maps. index. $24.95; $9.95pa. ISBN 0-88687-781-4; 0-88687-780-6pa. ISSN 0084-1382.

This compact volume continues to be one of the best values for purchase by any library or individual. Major features of the work include a review of the year (through October 1995); economic and business statistics and developments; data on computers, science, and technology; information on astronomy and the calendar; noted personalities of the year; profiles of U.S. states and cities; profiles of nations of the world; sports scores and other achievements; and vital statistics of the population.

Also included are notable U.S. Supreme Court decisions, 1995 Nobel prize-winners, a calendar of 1996 presidential primaries, notable quotations of the year, obituaries, disasters, flags and maps, a review of U.S. history, an overview of world history, profiles of historical figures, tables of weights and measures, lists of associations and societies, postal information and mailing rates, information on religions, Social Security and tax information, tables on crime and criminals, offbeat news stories, and miscellaneous facts. Added this year is a brief list of key sites on the Internet.

Color photographs of major events are divided into two sections. A table of contents, a quick-reference index, and a full index enhance the retrieval of information. Stalwart in any basic reference collection, the almanac is highly recommended.—**Edmund F. SantaVicca**

BIBLIOGRAPHY
Bibliographic Guides

8. **CD-ROM Finder: The World of CD-ROM Products for Information Seekers.** 1995 ed. Kathleen M. Hogan and James H. Shelton, eds. Medford, N.J., Learned Information, 1995. 764p. index. $69.50pa. ISBN 0-938734-86-5.

Ranking among the leading publications in the field, this resource is intended primarily for professionals, such as librarians, health care professionals, social scientists, attorneys, businesspeople, and scientists, as an aid to selecting the best possible product for their particular needs. However, this guide would also be helpful to the public and to students as a reference guide to CD-ROM products in public and academic libraries, respectively.

The burgeoning field of CD-ROM products is exemplified by an increase of nearly 1,000 additional CD-ROM publications since the last edition of this work (1994). While this work is important as a guide to the CD-ROM marketplace, the authors correctly point out that the rapidly developing field makes it dated almost immediately. Consequently, researchers are well advised to seek current information from, for example, more up-to-date sources, such as computer and CD-ROM periodicals.

The text is preceded by a brief introduction, a CD-ROM overview, and a "how-to-use" section. These are followed by the cornerstone of the work, entitled "Product Profiles," which consumes nearly all of the work. Each product is listed alphabetically. Products are described in detail; computer system requirements are listed for each item, and readers are provided what they need to know about acquiring the product, including the price. "Product Profiles" is followed by an applications index that lists each product under its major classification; a company/product index, which allows identification of a title with a specific organization; and a company index, which provides contact information on the publishers, distributors, and search software suppliers.—**James M. Murray**

9. Dority, G. Kim. **A Guide to Reference Books for Small and Medium-sized Libraries, 1984-1994.** Englewood, Colo., Libraries Unlimited, 1995. 372p. index. $49.00. ISBN 1-56308-103-2.

It has been 10 years since the previous edition of this work was published (see ARBA 85, entry 3). A few titles described in the 1st edition have been retained here, but most of the nearly 1,000 main citations and 400 secondary citations are for new works or new editions. Some older classics have been retained also. Generally excluded are government documents, children's materials, and works dealing with individual authors. The work has been arranged to correspond with the organization of *American Reference Books Annual*: a section on "General Reference Works," further divided into 13 subsections, followed by 34 subject sections. There are indexes to author/title and subject.

Each entry includes the title and edition of the work; the author, editor, or compiler; the publication data; the price; the ISBN and ISSN; the number of volumes for sets; and the frequency of publication for serials. Annotations are generally clearly written and informative, and alternative formats, such as CD-ROM and microform, are listed wherever possible. The work ably fulfills its aim of providing a helpful guide to those in smaller libraries who struggle to manage a viable reference collection on a tight budget.—**Dean H. Keller**

10. Krantz, Les. **CD-ROMs Rated: A Guide to the Best & Worst CD-ROMs & Multimedia Titles.** New York, McGraw-Hill, 1994. 304p. illus. index. $19.95pa. ISBN 0-07-912052-0.

The evaluations in this work are arranged according to 29 topics (e.g., atlases and travel, business and productivity, dictionaries and encyclopedias, erotica, games, performing arts, science, sports). Titles are rated on 7 factors—installation, breadth of content, depth of content, navigation, screen design, graphics, and multimedia aspects—with a resulting cumulative total between 1 and 100. In addition to a 100- to 250-word evaluative description, each entry notes publisher, price, and platform (DOS, Windows, or Macintosh); publication date is not included. The guide concludes with appendixes that cover the top-100 scoring titles, CD-ROM publishers, and reviewers' favorites, and includes a CD-ROM at the back of the book that demonstrates about 60 of the evaluated titles. Although the explosive growth in the CD-ROM publishing industry means that a work such as this is superseded by new titles almost immediately, *CD-ROMs Rated* provides librarians, teachers, and parents an excellent starting point from which to build a collection of worthwhile electronic titles. [R: WLB, Mar 95, p. 76]—**G. Kim Dority**

11. **Recommended Reference Books for Small and Medium-sized Libraries and Media Centers 1995.** Bohdan S. Wynar and Anna Grace Patterson, eds. Englewood, Colo., Libraries Unlimited, 1995. 280p. index. $45.00. ISBN 1-56308-352-3. ISSN 0277-5948.

Despite the doomsayers' prediction of the demise of the printed book, titles—including reference books—continue to multiply. Few library book budgets, however, are keeping up with spiraling costs and proliferating volumes, and beleaguered acquisition librarians at small or medium-sized libraries are particularly pulled in opposite directions by these two incompatible factors. This compilation of signed book reviews culled from the 1995 edition of *American Reference Books Annual* is designed to help these librarians select books for their reference collections. Published annually since 1981, types of works now reviewed in it include encyclopedias (one-volume and multivolume titles), dictionaries, indexes, bibliographies, guides, directories, almanacs, yearbooks, CD-ROMs, indexing and abstract services, and other works in all subject areas.

This 1995 volume lists 525 unabridged reviews chosen from the 1,796 entries in the 1995 ARBA. Entries are arranged under four major divisions—General Reference Works, Social Sciences, Humanities, and Science and Technology—which are further divided into topically organized sections. Complete bibliographical and ordering information is included with each citation, as well as, where appropriate, references to periodical reviews. The code(s) by each title indicate that a particular work is recommended for small college libraries, public libraries, or school media centers. Given ARBA's reputation as a reviewing service, this abridged version belongs in all libraries not having the parent work. One minor quibble: Perhaps introductions to future editions can detail the criteria used to select titles.—**Jack Bales**

12. **Reference Books Bulletin 1993-94: A Compilation of Evaluations September 1, 1993, Through August 1994.** By the American Library Association Reference Books Bulletin Editorial Board. Sandy Whiteley, ed. Lisa G. Orzepowski, comp. Chicago, Booklist/American Library Association, 1994. 181p. index. $26.00pa. ISBN 0-8389-7774-X. ISSN 8755-0962.

This familiar resource is a compilation of 564 reviews drawn from the "Reference Books Bulletin" section of the American Library Association's (ALA) monthly *Booklist*. Essentially a collection development tool, *Reference Books Bulletin 1993-94* groups its materials within broad subject areas (generalities, social sciences, language, science, and so forth); in addition to the specific book and CD-ROM reviews, there are six excellent omnibus articles that survey encyclopedias (the annual update), quotation books, reference sources on food and cooking, encyclopedia annuals and yearbooks, travel reference sources, and performing arts reference books. Although those who peruse the regular RBB section in *Booklist* may question whether they need to purchase this annual cumulation, its "all in one place" convenience and its reasonable price recommend it to those responsible for reference materials collection development.

—**G. Kim Dority**

National and Trade Bibliography

International

13. **Global Books in Print PLUS.** [CD-ROM]. New Providence, N.J., R. R. Bowker/Reed Reference Electronic Publishing, 1995. Minimum system requirements: IBM or MS-DOS compatible 286. CD-ROM drive with MS-DOS CD-ROM Extensions. MS-DOS or PC-DOS 3.1 (5.0 recommended). Hard disk space. 535K conventional memory. Monochrome or color monitor. $1,995.00/yr. ISBN 0-8352-3413-4.

The publishing aspect of the much-vaunted global marketplace is ably represented in this R. R. Bowker electronic reference. Intended for those "buying, selling, or selecting books" throughout the world, the CD-ROM includes information on 1.2 million U.S. books from *Books in Print* (BIP) (see entry 15); 500,000 U.K. books from *Whitaker's Bookbank* (see ARBA 94, entry 6); 220,000 titles from *International Books in Print* (Continental Europe, Africa, Asia, and Latin America [see ARBA 90, entry 10]); 57,000 titles from *Australian* and *New Zealand Books in Print* (see entries 22-23); and 32,000 Canadian titles produced in cooperation with *Canadian Telebook* or from *International Books in Print*. Only English-language books are listed.

In addition to providing full bibliographical citations, the disc displays integrated records that list all international editions and bindings (and prices) in a single citation. Pricing information encompasses price categories, such as retail, wholesale, short or long discount, and the like. The 16 access points include the standard items (author, title, ISBN) as well as such categories as audience, price, children's subject, and "special index," which supports searches for the presence of annotations, illustrations, and records by price source. As with several other of the resources in the electronic BIP series, the CD-ROM can be customized through vendor-supplied software to simplify electronic ordering with 22 distributors, wholesalers, and publishers.

Although this disc is probably most valuable to those in the bookselling and publishing industries, large public or academic libraries may also want to consider its purchase. However, purchasers should be aware that the disc's current installation procedure is challenging to say the least, and it will probably be necessary to rely on the computer support staff to get the program up and running initially.—**G. Kim Dority**

14. **Short-Title Catalogue of Books Printed in England, Scotland, Ireland, Wales, and British America and of English Books Printed in Other Countries 1641-1700. Volume 1: A1-E2926L.** 2d ed. Donald Wing, comp., and others, eds. New York, Modern Language Association of America, 1994. 954p. $400.00. LC 70-185211. ISBN 0-87352-661-9.

When the 2d edition of volume 1 of Wing's *Short-Title Catalogue* (Wing STC) appeared in 1972, it added numerous new entries and locations to those cited in the 1945 edition. However, Wing was roundly criticized for the bibliographical havoc he created by reassigning approximately 8 percent of the numbers from the 1st edition to totally different works. Other problems with the 2d edition of volume 1 involved the cancellation of entries without explanation or cross-references, inaccurate attributions, typographical errors, and inconsistent methodology. Wing died prior to the publication of volumes 2 and 3 of the 2d edition, and the editors of those volumes, which were published in 1982 and 1988 respectively, took the criticisms of the earlier volume to heart and strove to avoid repeating the errors of Wing's ways.

Now the Modern Language Association has released a revised and expanded version of volume 1, which not only adds a considerable amount of new material identified since 1972 but also establishes editorial consistency with volumes 2 and 3. Like its predecessor, this volume covers A-England, and it is bound to match the rest of the set. Thus, it fits neatly beside its two companion volumes. The editors have retained the numbering from the 1st edition of volume 1 and valid numbers from the 2d edition and have interpolated any additional numbers by adding a letter or letters to place them in correct numerical sequence. In addition, they have restored lost entries and provided cross-references for all canceled and moved entries. Moreover, they have corrected many errors of attribution and have expanded numerous titles to reflect the subject more accurately. Location reports now include libraries in Australia or New Zealand in addition to British, European, and North American institutions, and the number of locations provided has been increased to a maximum of 20.

The Wing STC continues to be an indispensable record of all extant books, broadsides, and pamphlets published in England, Ireland, Scotland, Wales, and British America, regardless of language, between 1641 and 1700 and of works printed elsewhere in English during the same period. Therefore, this is an essential purchase for all libraries holding the earlier version of volume 1.—**Marie Ellis**

United States

15. **Books in Print 1995-96.** New Providence, N.J., R. R. Bowker/Reed Reference Publishing, 1995. 9v. index. $475.00/set. ISBN 0-8352-3644-7. ISSN 0068-0214.

16. **Subject Guide to Books in Print 1995-96.** New Providence, N.J., R. R. Bowker/Reed Reference Publishing, 1995. 5v. index. $329.95/set. ISBN 0-8352-3655-2. ISSN 0000-0159.

R. R. Bowker's familiar *Books in Print* (BIP) publications are well known to librarians, primarily in their print iterations but more recently as CD-ROMs (see entry 17). When one attempts to quickly glean information from the nine volumes of *Books in Print 1995-96* or the five volumes of this year's *Subject Guide to Books in Print*, the utility of a CD-ROM version becomes immediately evident. Nevertheless, for those libraries still relying on the print publications, the multivolume BIP identifies nearly 1.6 million in-print titles published and distributed in the United States. More than 142,000 of these are titles new to this edition. Arguing for the health of the publishing industry, BIP's publishers' index lists more than 46,000 firms.

Entries provide the most complete bibliographical and ordering information available for each title, including number of pages, price, publisher, edition, binding, and ISBN. Occasionally, entries give brief annotations supplied by the publisher. Indexes include author, title, out-of-print and out-of-stock titles and authors, and wholesalers and distributors (both alphabetical and geographical). In addition, there are listings for publishers' and distributors' abbreviations and toll-free numbers, new publishers, and inactive and out-of-business publishers.

The *Subject Guide* respins a large portion of the information found in BIP (excluding fiction, literature, poetry, and drama by one author) under more than 74,000 Library of Congress subject headings. It remains an important companion set to BIP, providing subject access to the U.S.' annual publishing output that is available in no other print resource.—**G. Kim Dority**

17. **Books in Print with Book Reviews PLUS. October 1995.** [CD-ROM]. New Providence, N.J., R. R. Bowker/Reed Reference Electronic Publishing, 1995. Minimum system requirements: CD-ROM drive. $1,595.00/yr.

Of all the R. R. Bowker electronic *Books in Print* titles, this is perhaps the most valuable for librarians. As in its print counterpart (see entry 15), it identifies more than 1.5 million titles produced or distributed in the United States by some 46,000 publishers. Similarly, complete bibliographical citations accompany all entries. In addition, however, the CD-ROM provides roughly 225,000 full-text book reviews drawn from *Publishers Weekly*, *Library Journal*, *School Library Journal*, *Choice*, *ALA Booklist*, *Kirkus Reviews*, *The Bookstore Journal*, *Reference and Research Book News*, *SciTech Book News*, *University Press Book News*, *BIOSIS*, and *Voice of Youth Advocates*. Reviews date back to 1985, with about 30,000 added each year.

There are 18 different search capabilities: In addition to the standard access points (author, title, publisher), users can also search by Ingram title code, series title, audience, grade, language, and others. Search options include truncation and Boolean logic. For librarians who would like to order books while online, the CD-ROM can be customized through vendor-supplied software to promote electronic ordering with 22 distributors, wholesalers, and publishers. The program supports numerous search, display, and printing capabilities, all of which are well documented and easily implemented. Although it will probably be necessary to rely on the library's computer support staff to install *Books in Print with Book Reviews PLUS* initially due to its difficult installation procedure, it is well worth the inconvenience and time invested.—**G. Kim Dority**

18. **Books Out-of-Print PLUS. Summer 1995.** [CD-ROM]. New Providence, N.J., R. R. Bowker/Reed Reference Electronic Publishing, 1995. Minimum system requirements: IBM or full MS-DOS compatible 286. ISO 9660-compatible CD-ROM drive with MS-DOS Extensions-compatible device driver and MS-DOS CD-ROM Extensions. MS-DOS or PC-DOS 3.1 (5.0 recommended). Hard disk. 535K conventional memory. Monochrome or color display. $395.00/yr. ISBN 0-8352-2444-9.

Intended for booksellers and larger libraries that can afford it, this CD-ROM provides access to some 680,000 titles verified by the publisher to be out-of-print or out-of-stock indefinitely since 1982, plus another 75,000 additional titles listed in the *Books Out-of-Print* directories from 1979 through 1981. Titles reported only as out-of-stock (OS), as opposed to out-of-stock-indefinitely (OSI), are not included, as these titles often come back into print after a short time span. Although most American publishers participate in R. R. Bowker's out-of-print program, several notable presses (such as Basic Books, Cambridge University Press, and Scarecrow) do not; thus, users will need to verify whether the book they are searching for is from a participating publisher or not. Despite occasional errors of citation (such as mixing up names of authors), the information provided is for the most part reliable and contains more than 60,000 full-text book reviews from 12 key reviewing media.

Search categories (either singly or in combination) include by author, ISBN, keyword, LCCN, publisher, subject, children's subject, title, series title, audience, grades, illustrations, language, price, and publication year. The software offers four menus—search; browse; format; and action (help, save file, open bookmark, and so on)—that are easily understood and quickly mastered. The accompanying documentation is well organized and helpful; in fact, the manual is mostly generic to the entire *Books in Print* (BIP) electronic database products, so once a user has mastered one of the products, the rest are easily navigated.

The caveat with this R. R. Bowker BIP electronic product, as with all others in this series, is that only those with advanced technical computer skills should attempt to install the program. Due to the complex installation procedures involved, until the publisher comes out with a "plug-and-play" installation process, this resource can only be recommended to those organizations that have the technical support personnel on-site to support it.—**G. Kim Dority**

19. **Children's Books in Print 1995: An Author, Title, and Illustrator Index....** New Providence, N.J., R. R. Bowker/Reed Reference Publishing, 1995. 2v. index. $149.95. LC 70-101705. ISBN 0-8352-3593-9. ISSN 0069-3480.

20. **Subject Guide to Children's Books in Print 1995: A Subject Index to Books for Children and Young Adults.** By the R. R. Bowker Bibliographic Group, with the Publication Systems Department. New Providence, N.J., R. R. Bowker/Reed Reference Publishing, 1995. 1066p. $149.95. ISBN 0-8352-3596-3. ISSN 0000-0167.

This edition of *Children's Books in Print* (see ARBA 94, entry 9, for a previous review) has continued the two-volume format begun last year. Volume 1 includes awards, authors, and illustrators, and volume 2 covers titles and publishers. More than 94,000 titles appear, adding 10,000-plus titles from the previous year, some of which include publishers' annotations. This remains a useful tool for anyone working with children's books.

This edition of *Subject Guide to Children's Books in Print* (see ARBA 92, entry 17, for a previous review) includes more than 94,000 titles under 7,232 subject categories drawn from the 14th edition of *Sears List of Subject Headings* and the 15th edition of *Library of Congress Subject Headings*. The subject guide is a good source for beginning thematic searches, and coupled with *Children's Books in Print*, is an excellent tool for all those working with children's books.—**Susan Zernial**

21. **Children's Reference PLUS: Complete Bibliographic, Review, and Qualitative Information on Books....** [CD-ROM]. New Providence, N.J., R. R. Bowker/Reed Reference Electronic Publishing, 1994. Minimum system requirements: IBM or full MS-DOS compatible 286. ISO 9660 or compatible CD-ROM drive with MS-DOS Extensions. Hard disk space. 535K conventional memory. Monochrome or color display monitor. $595.00/yr. ISBN 0-8352-2839-8.

This CD-ROM source acts as both an acquisition and selection tool by bringing together a host of reviewing and verification sources. Titles from *Children's Books in Print*, *Subject Guide to Children's Books in Print* (see entries 19-20), and *El-Hi Textbooks and Serials in Print* (see ARBA 95, entry 350) are pooled with dozens of bibliographies and children's/young adult citations. These are gleaned from such tools as *Bowker's Complete Video Directory* (see entry 986) and *Ulrich's International Periodicals Directory* (see entry 88) to create a verification database. A reviewing database is compiled by gathering full-text reviews (again, children's/young adult titles only) from periodicals such as *Booklist*, *Library Journal*, and *Publishers Weekly*. The two databases can then be searched separately or jointly to simultaneously verify and evaluate a title being considered for purchase. This latest version of the database includes six new resources: "A to Zoo"; "Literature of Delight"; "Play, Learn, and Grow"; "Juniorplots 4"; "Middleplots 4"; and "PrimaryPlots 2." All citations and reviews are fully indexed; material can be downloaded into word processing programs (as long as copyright restrictions are heeded), and on-screen notes may be input into the margins.

This is a very convenient resource with only one short-term hassle. Loading the system is not painless, in part because the user's guide is not updated as each new disc is released. However, it is a clear time-saver and is recommended for any school and public libraries that can afford it.—**Ed Volz**

Other Countries

22. **Australian Books in Print 1995.** 33d ed. Port Melbourne, Australia, D. W. Thorpe/Reed Reference Publishing; distr., New Providence, N.J., R. R. Bowker/Reed Reference Publishing, 1995. 1332p. $115.00. ISBN 1-875589-58-9. ISSN 0067-172X.

In its 33d annual edition, this current *Australian Books in Print* (ABIP) continues its excellent coverage of Australian book publishing. "Australian" here includes books published in Australia, books by Australian authors published elsewhere, and books "with significant Australian content." Serials, media, and audiovisual materials are excluded. (For reviews of earlier editions, see ARBA 90, entry 23, and ARBA 79, entry 9.)

In addition to listings by author and title, other features include sections with directory listings of book trade and literary associations, series and imprints, Australian publishers and distributors, and overseas publishers and their Australian distributors. The print edition of ABIP supplies new books listed as of February 1995 in *Australian Bookseller & Publisher*. This edition is updated monthly on microfiche and on CD-ROM. For research library collections, ABIP is essential to worldwide bibliographical coverage.—**Bernice Bergup**

23. **New Zealand Books in Print 1995.** 23d ed. Wellington, New Zealand, D. W. Thorpe/Reed Reference Publishing; distr., New Providence, N.J., R. R. Bowker/Reed Reference Publishing, 1995. 435p. $70.00. ISSN 0157-7662.

This is the 23d annual edition of *New Zealand Books in Print*, the standard source for information in that area. A New Zealand book, for the purposes of this publication, means a book published in New Zealand, by a New Zealand writer living overseas, or a book about New Zealand. It also includes a number of English-speaking Pacific Islands. Books are listed alphabetically twice, in author and title sections. Names of publishers and distributors are given in full, as well as overseas publishers with New Zealand agents. There is a section listing antiquarian and secondhand booksellers.

This publication is an essential reference text for libraries and researchers. It is as up-to-date as possible: Published in February 1995, it lists books published through December 1994. (Monthly CD-ROMs are also available after that date.) This book contains important information concerning the New Zealand literary scene: lists of New Zealand literary awards in various categories (fiction, nonfiction, poetry, children's literature); past winners of New Zealand literary awards; sources of assistance for writers and academic fellowships available; and lists of literary journals. New Zealand, enviably, is one of the most literate of countries.—**John B. Beston**

BIOGRAPHY

International

24. **Biography Index: Indexing Coverage 7/84-7/95.** [CD-ROM]. Bronx, N.Y., H. W. Wilson and Norwood, Mass., SilverPlatter Information, 1995. Minimum system requirements: IBM or compatible. ISO 9660-compatible CD-ROM drive with cables, interface card, and MS-DOS CD-ROM Extensions 2.0. MS-DOS or PC-DOS 3.1. 640K RAM. 1.2MB hard disk space. Standard monitor. Floppy disk drive. Parallel printer port (optional). $1,260.00/yr. (single user).

H. W. Wilson's *Biography Index* (BI) has been a standard reference source for 50 years. Now drawing from more than 3,000 periodicals, plus some 1,900 current books containing biographical information, BI contains citations for people of all nationalities and fields, from antiquity to the present. Historically, the volumes have been issued annually. This has made it necessary for the user to check several volumes and copy the citations. If users wanted combinations of subjects, say O. J. Simpson and spousal abuse, or Simpson and Aleksandr Isayevich Solzhenitsyn, they had to look up the separate entries and cross-check them.

These chores have now been automated, thanks to the collaboration of H. W. Wilson and SilverPlatter Information, the CD-ROM manufacturers and developers of SPIRS (SilverPlatter Information Retrieval System). Once BI is digitized on a CD-ROM, the retrieval system performs the above tasks (and many others via Boolean operators) and either prints or downloads the results. Best of all, the CD-ROM covers an 11-year period (July 1984 to July 1995). As the data on the CD-ROM and in the long-familiar print editions (see ARBA 93, entry 33) are almost identical, there is no need to review it here. The package comes with the index CD-ROM, an easy-to-use installation CD-ROM, lucid SPIRS "User's Manual," "Quick References Guide" to the index, and SPIRS system in card format. Use requires only the most elementary computer sophistication. The disc is also available for Macintosh and Windows platforms and is highly recommended.—**D. Barton Johnson**

25. **Biography Today: Profiles of People of Interest to Young Readers. 1993 Annual Cumulation.** Laurie Lanzen Harris, ed. Detroit, Omnigraphics, 1994. 342p. illus. index. $42.00. ISBN 1-55888-345-2.

This second annual cumulation of *Biography Today* (see ARBA 94, entry 11) contains biographies of 42 individuals in entertainment, sports, politics, and other areas of current interest. Included are full biographies of the recently deceased Arthur Ashe, Dizzy Gillespie, and Rudolf Nureyev. The biographies are geared to children ages nine and up but are written in a style that will appeal to high school students and adults as well. Beginning in 1993, *Biography Today* was published as a magazine three times a year (January, April, and September) instead of four, but issues are still collected into the annual hardbound volume. The indexes in this latest volume are cumulative for the set. Because it is easy to read and it contains biographies of popular figures, *Biography Today* is a useful reference tool, even for libraries that have *Current Biography*.—**Kathleen Farago**

26. Fenwick, Gillian. **Women and the *Dictionary of National Biography*: A Guide to DNB Volumes 1885-1985 and *Missing Persons*.** Brookfield, Vt., Scolar Press/Ashgate Publishing, 1994. 181p. index. $74.95. ISBN 0-85967-914-4.

Fenwick has made a career studying the *Dictionary of National Biography* (DNB). She has written two books: *The Contributors' Index to the Dictionary of National Bibliography 1885-1901* (Oak Knoll Books, 1989) and *Leslie Stephen's Life in Letters* (see ARBA 94, entry 1261), as well as an article, "The Athenaeum and the Dictionary of National Biography" in *Victorian Periodicals Review* (vol. 23, pp. 180-88).

People in library school are taught that the DNB was a well-respected publication. Entry into the DNB was based on achievement, albeit accident of birth, rather than through paid self-promotion. Students learn that it was a product of scholarship, thorough research, and the ideals of the British Empire. Aside from the stringent standards it exercised, a person had to be a British subject as well as quite dead to be included.

Fenwick's introduction provides an excellent history of the DNB. Based on both secondary and primary sources, it probes the role of women in the creation of this ambitious publication. From the novelty of hiring a woman typist in 1888 to the decision to enter George Sand under her married name of Mary Ann Cross, Fenwick's essay on women as staff, contributors, and subjects is enlightening. This book goes well beyond being an index to women subjects listed in the DNB between 1885 and 1985 and the supplementary volume entitled *Missing Persons*. The introduction, as mentioned, provides a history of women associated with the DNB as well as an analysis of biography as a literary style.

The index itself is divided into four categories: an alphabetical listing of women as subjects; women contributors; male contributors (who wrote about women); and an occupations index. The headings in the occupations index tend to be more generalized and less colorful than the occupational descriptions listed in the alphabetical index. For example, Elizabeth Fenning (1792-1815) is described as "poisoner" in the alphabetical section. The occupational index holds no category for "poisoners," but rather lists the unfortunate Fenning under the sanitized and somewhat breathless category of "Law, lawyers, police, prisons, victims, criminals, imposters, witches and gamblers." Fenwick's guide to women and the DNB is an important and welcome addition to libraries already holding the DNB.—**Mary Hemmings**

27. **The Grolier Library of North American Biographies.** Danbury, Conn., Grolier, 1994. 10v. illus. index. $299.00/set. ISBN 0-7172-7246-X.

This 10-volume set provides basic information about approximately 2,000 famous North Americans, with emphasis on nineteenth- and twentieth-century figures. Each volume focuses on a theme: activists, athletes, entrepreneurs and inventors, explorers, performance artists, political and military leaders, scholars and educators, scientists, visual artists, and writers. The biographies, arranged alphabetically within each volume, range from one to four pages per entry. They include the person's birth and death date(s) if applicable, pertinent family background, and why the person is of historical significance. Some entries contain a small black-and-white photograph or illustration. Each volume has a glossary of appropriate words, sources, and further reading arranged by entry, and a volume-only index. The master index is in volume 10.

While females and minorities are well represented, North America translates into the United States with a Canadian flavoring. Is not Mexico still part of North America? Of course, this type of work is great for playing the "why" game. Why is Johnny Cash not listed in the performance artists volume alongside

Willie Nelson? What about Charlton Heston? Also, a typographical error appeared in the John Brown entry: 1932 was printed instead of 1832. People famous in more than one category (e.g., Benjamin Franklin) must be tracked down via the master index or by checking several tables of contents—a minor inconvenience.

The page layout, typeface size, and prose style will make this popular with students in grades 5-10, and those in English as a Second Language classes. It should be purchased by libraries that never have enough biographical information to go around.—**Esther R. Sinofsky**

28. Marzollo, Jean. **My First Book of Biographies: Great Men and Women Every Child Should Know.** New York, Scholastic, 1994. 78p. illus. $14.95. ISBN 0-590-45014-X.

My First Book of Biographies is a unique, international biographical book for girls and boys aged 6-10. Marzollo lists biographies of people from various fields of endeavor in one volume, along with vivid and entertaining illustrations in color. It should be included in all children's libraries.

Marzollo chose 45 people who can be role models for children who aspire to greatness of their own. These men and women are both historical and contemporary people, including political leaders, scientists, artists, and athletes such as George Washington, Marie Curie, Leonardo da Vinci, and Jesse Owens. Simple language to describe each person and full-page illustrations by Irene Trivas are good features for younger children. Yet, unlike *Twenty Names Series* (Marshall Cavendish, 1988), this book lacks a glossary and a bibliography for further reading for older children aged 9-10. Older children may need independent reading and a more detailed biographical book after they read these introductory stories. Trivas's pictures would also be more effective if accompanied by explanatory captions similar to those provided in the *Twenty Names* series. However, Marzollo's book is eye-catching and truly valuable for every child.
—**Sung Ok Kim**

29. **Merriam-Webster's Biographical Dictionary.** Springfield, Mass., Merriam-Webster, 1995. 1170p. $27.95. ISBN 0-87779-743-9.

This is a revised edition of *Webster's New Biographical Dictionary* published in 1988 (see ARBA 90, entry 34). Almost 40 pages have been added to the new edition. Important characteristics have been maintained from the earlier edition. These are no restrictions concerning the time, place, or country of origin of individuals selected for inclusion; clearly stated explanatory and pronunciation guides that provide easy understanding of the book's contents; and entries that remain succinct and informative. The original preface is included in the new edition so it remains unclear precisely what has been added or otherwise enhanced. Direct consultation with the publisher indicates that 287 new entries of deceased individuals have been added, all previous entries have been reviewed by the editorial staff, the size has been recomposed to make the volume easier to handle, and the book has been assigned a new copyright date. Given the low price, the comprehensive inclusion criteria, and the quality of presentation, this work remains a core research tool that must be considered an essential part of every library collection.—**Robert V. Labaree**

30. Morrow, Ed. **Born This Day: A Daily Celebration of Famous Beginnings.** New York, Citadel Press/Carol Publishing Group, 1995. 407p. index. $12.95pa. ISBN 0-8065-1648-8.

Books of days are fun for students, teachers, media specialists, and lay readers to turn to for finding out the famous as well as the infamous persons with whom their birthdays are shared. People born on April 6, for example, may be fascinated to learn that they celebrate their birthday with Merle Haggard, Billy Dee Williams, and Michelle Phillips. The majority of *Born This Day* is devoted to short vignettes about one famous person born on each of the 366 respective days of the calendar year (February 29 is included). All other prominent persons are listed only by name and the year of their birth. For example, January 1 features a short profile of Paul Revere and then lists the birth years of eight others, including Betsy Ross, J. Edgar Hoover, and Barry Goldwater.

School personnel need to be circumspect in their use of this resource. The author appears often to favor titillation more than good taste. How else to explain an account of John Barrymore's drunkenness and laziness as the profile of choice for February 14 birthdays while simply noting that Susan B. Anthony was born on the same day in 1820? The same question arises for the June 8 entries. Is Joan Rivers a more significant figure for young people to know than Frank Lloyd Wright or Barbara Bush? Of course, all such decisions are subjective. Nevertheless, the author seems to elect sensationalism over substance.

Even when the subject of the daily profile is justifiably famed, Morrow's source of information may be more appropriately geared to college youth than elementary or secondary school students. It may be interesting for some people to learn that pop singer Madonna scraped by early in her career by posing nude for artists at $7 per hour, but that is hardly the information teachers and parents have in mind when they send youth to the library. Although the book contains an index, only those persons fully profiled are listed. The reader will find Rivers in the index, but not Bush or Wright.

This limitation further weakens the value of the book as a reference tool. Morrow credits many sources he used, but he must have missed some vital ones. April 6 birthday celebrators will need to look elsewhere to learn that French revolutionary Maximilien de Robespierre and magician Harry Houdini celebrated their birthdays that day, as does Nobel prize-winning geneticist James Watson, who constructed the first model of DNA.—**Jerry D. Flack**

31. **The Oxford Children's Book of Famous People.** New York, Oxford University Press, 1994. 384p. illus. maps. $35.00. ISBN 0-19-910171-X.

Arranged alphabetically, this lavishly illustrated biographical dictionary contains sketches of 1,000 historical (e.g., Charlemagne) and popular (e.g., Madonna) individuals chosen by a team of consultants and authors. With an emphasis on politicians, writers, scientists, and actors, the result is a more representative selection of internationally known figures (e.g., Gabriel García Marquez, Imran Khan). Women represent approximately 20 percent of newer personalities, but significantly less from earlier eras.

Entries of varying lengths identify the role and achievements or failures for which the person is known, with appropriate *see also* references. Entries for well-known partnerships (e.g., [Meriwether] Lewis and [William] Clark) appear in a combined entry, a technique that fails when the appellation (e.g., [John] Lennon and [Paul] McCartney) is confusing and the expected cross-reference (Beatles) is missing. The thematic and chronological directories, with individuals listed by achievement and date of birth, are useful features but contain some errors.

Intended as an inspiring collection for family reference or browsing, this work is disappointing. The use of "children" in the title is misleading as the vocabulary employed is clearly beyond the scope of most elementary students, while middle school students require a level of detail or additional references that are absent here.—**Sandra E. Belanger**

32. Rolka, Gail Meyer. **100 Women Who Shaped World History.** San Francisco, Calif., Bluewood, 1994. 112p. illus. maps. index. $7.95pa. ISBN 0-912517-06-9.

33. Yenne, Bill. **100 Men Who Shaped World History.** San Francisco, Calif., Bluewood, 1994. 112p. illus. maps. index. $7.95pa. ISBN 0-912517-05-0.

These two slim companion volumes provide capsule views of 100 men and 100 women who made their mark in history. Each volume includes a table of contents with a timeline along the bottom showing the entry's place in history, an introduction, the individual entries arranged in chronological order, a trivia quiz based upon the entries, and an index. The one-page entries include at least one illustration (usually of the individual under discussion), a small map indicating the person's country, and a brief overview of the person's life with an emphasis on his or her contribution. The men's volume basically covers individuals who are readily found in general reference sources (e.g., Homer, William Shakespeare, Símon Bolívar, Thomas Edison, and Stephen Hawking). Similarly, the women's volume covers many predictable names (e.g., Harriet Beecher Stowe, Helen Keller, Golda Meir), but also highlights less well-known influences such as Marquise du Chatelet, Madame Lavoisier, and Mary Wortley Montagu. No bibliography or further reading list is furnished. These paperbacks would work best as circulating copies in the children's young adult section, or as supplemental texts in history or English as a Second Language classes.—**Esther R. Sinofsky**

34. **Who's Who 1995: An Annual Biographical Dictionary.** New York, St. Martin's Press, 1995. 2131p. $195.00. ISBN 0-312-12413-9.

This thick volume contains more than 29,000 separate biographical entries, arranged in alphabetical order according to last name. Each entry includes the person's current position, date of birth, family members, educational background, clubs, recreational activities, and an address. These individuals come from all disciplines (e.g., the arts, athletics, business, entertainment, politics, science) and from every continent. *Who's Who 1995* also provides an obituary of entrants who died from September 1993 to September 1994 and a complete roster of the British royal family.

An anonymous editorial board chose the individuals appearing in *Who's Who*, seeking to recognize men and women of achievement and influence. Many selections are outstanding, others only adequate. Unfortunately, traditional biases remain. The entrants hail disproportionately from Great Britain, and the vast majority are males. To cite one example, British singer Elton John is listed, while United States pop star Whitney Houston is not. Other omissions are even more glaring: Newt Gingrich, the U.S. Speaker of the House of Representatives, is nowhere to be found, nor is Vladimir Volfovich Zhirinovsky, the Russian ultranationalist. *Who's Who 1995* is a valuable work, rich in detail, but other biographical sources should be consulted in order to fill in gaps. This volume is recommended for college, university, and public libraries.—**Richard E. Holl**

United States

35. **The Cambridge Dictionary of American Biography.** John S. Bowman, ed. New York, Cambridge University Press, 1995. 903p. index. $44.95. ISBN 0-521-40258-1.

Librarians have long lamented that biographical dictionaries are often lacking. For instance, necrologies such as *Merriam-Webster's Biographical Dictionary* (see entry 29) bar the living, celebrity registers eschew the noncharismatic, and few works sufficiently accommodate the lives of important women and minorities.

Now joining the fray are editor Bowman and 94 subject consultants, who in an affordable volume have profiled 9,000 notable U.S. residents, past and present, many of whom are women or members of various ethnic groups. Of the total number of biographees, more than 200 were born before 1800, and more than 2,200 were alive at the time of publication. Unfortunately, despite the book's title, Canadians and Latin Americans are poorly represented. However, many of the covered subjects (e.g., Marlene Dietrich, Captain Kidd, and Sonja Henie) are not U.S. natives, but are people who have impacted U.S. culture. The breadth of this work is further widened by its 40-page names index, in which the main entries include individuals receiving mention within articles, as well as those accorded their own entries in the text.

Entries, which are unsigned, fall largely into the 75- to 250-word range, with articles on such figures as Jesse Jackson, Thomas Jefferson, and Elvis Presley, each exceeding 400 words. Besides year of birth and (when deceased) death, the entries scrupulously provide birthplace information, even giving birthplace name changes. Birth names, pen names, and nicknames are supplied, followed by highlights of the subject's life, including educational attainments, awards, publications, and his or her overall influence on the United States.

The publisher and editor deserve commendation for offering such a wide cross section of occupation holders. Here are criminals, judges and legal scholars, financiers, musicians, social activists, manufacturers and inventors, athletes and coaches, writers, and soldiers. Among the more obscure vocations covered are hat manufacturer, cartoon animator, army scout, and horse trainer. An occupational index affords access to the work's entries through more than 60 broad categories (e.g., theater, psychiatry, and journalism).

Significant omissions are few for a reference work of such ambitious compass. However, unaccountable absences include Jerry Brown, George Burns, John Dean III, Eliot Ness, John Wesley Hardin, Clarence Brigham, and Harry Combs. Also, it is noted that the entry for Robert Dworkin misspells "Worcester" as "Wooster." Despite such imperfections, this is the best one-volume biographical dictionary on the market today, and is strongly recommended for all libraries.—**Jeffrey E. Long**

36. **Dictionary of American Biography. Supplement 10: 1976-1980.** Kenneth T. Jackson, Karen E. Markoe, and Arnold Markoe, eds. New York, Scribner's/Simon & Schuster, 1995. 928p. index. $95.00. ISBN 0-684-19399-X.

Long the keystone of U.S. biographical scholarship, the *Dictionary of American Biography* (DAB) now offers its audience a 10th supplement, immortalizing 519 persons who impacted our nation's culture prior to their deaths during the period covered. Signed by more than 300 contributors, the profiles typically run 1,000-2,000 words. As in DAB's 9th supplement (see ARBA 95, entry 36), the editors' commitment to ethnic and occupational diversity is apparent. Perusing its pages, one finds articles on a football coach, a neuropsychologist, a clown, and a saloon keeper.

With a nod to our tabloid society, the editors have allotted space for personalities such as Bob Crane and Freddie Prinze. Users primarily familiar with the pre-supplement DAB may also be surprised to encounter sketches of Carlo Gambino, Sally Rand, and Jim Jones. A check against concurrent editions of *Current Biography* revealed some omissions (e.g., George R. Stewart, Mary Jo Shelly, Arnold Gingrich, and Ted Mack). It should be noted that the percentage of women in this book is 3 times that of the DAB 20 years ago.

In the cumulative name index to the supplements, pseudonym, nickname, and cross-reference entries prove their worth for such subjects as Edward Tanner ("Patrick Dennis") and "Willie" Sutton. Unfamiliar given names are usually parenthesized. This practice has occasionally been inexplicably abandoned, however, resulting in awkward index entries for such subjects as Allen Tate and Sebastian Cabot.

Despite such shortcomings, this is an essential acquisition for libraries owning previous volumes of the set. Besides its reliability and affordability for most institutions, librarians will continue to appreciate DAB's durable bindings that withstand chronic photocopying.—**Jeffrey E. Long**

37. **Who's Who in America 1996.** 50th ed. New Providence, N.J., Marquis Who's Who/Reed Reference Publishing, 1995. 3v. index. $459.95/set. ISBN 0-8379-0167-7.

This standard biographical reference source was reviewed in ARBA on many occasions. It was last reviewed in ARBA 94 (see entry 24). The 47th edition contained more than 80,000 biographies, using identical criteria as compared to previous volumes. The present edition substantially increases coverage, and now one discovers 92,000 entries, including prominent scholars, educators, industrialists, government officials, artists, and so forth.

All entries are updated every year, and deceased individuals are removed to the companion volume, *Who Was Who in America with World Notables* (see ARBA 94, entry 23). This source should be found in all major libraries.—**Bohdan S. Wynar**

38. **Who's Who of American Women 1995-1996.** 19th ed. New Providence, N.J., Marquis Who's Who/Reed Reference Publishing, 1995. 1229p. $239.00. ISBN 0-8379-0420-X.

Since 1958, 19 editions of this standard biographical source have been published. There are some 30,000 biographical sketches in this edition, more or less the same number as in the 17th edition reviewed in ARBA 93 (see entry 56). The criteria is similar to other works published by Marquis Who's Who, and this work should be found on shelves of most larger library institutions.—**Bohdan S. Wynar**

Australia

39. **Monash Biographical Dictionary of 20th Century Australia.** John Arnold and Deirdre Morris, eds. New Providence, N.J., Reed Reference Publishing, 1994. 568p. $50.00. ISBN 1-875589-19-8.

Compiled under the direction of the Australian Research Council and Monash University, this work provides brief biographies on more than "2200 Australians who have achieved prominence and/or made a contribution to their country this century" (foreword). It is another imprint in an unofficial series from Monash University, which has already produced *Who's Who of Australian Writers* (1991) and other reference works. Previous biographical works on Australians have included John Henniker Heaton's *Australian Dictionary of Dates and Men of the Time* (1879), Fred Johns's who's who series beginning with *Who's Who in Australia* (1906), and *Australian Dictionary of Biography* (1906-). While the *Australian Dictionary of Biography* has been updated through the years, this new twentieth-century dictionary is a welcome addition to the biographical information on Australians.

The criteria for inclusion in the *Monash Biographical Dictionary* do not require that each individual be of Australian birth or an Australian citizen, but that each has made a significant contribution to Australian society. In this respect, Australians who have simply gained a certain amount of fame for one reason or another are not necessarily included. Standard bibliographical form has been followed for each entry, which includes full name (including any nicknames or aliases), dates of birth and death, an indication of the occupation of the individual, and a brief biographical sketch. At the end of each entry, there is a reference code that corresponds to a chart of acronyms and abbreviations in the front of the volume referring to various organizations, associations, or honors common for Australians. In addition, there is a bibliography of works (67 items) used in the compilation of the volume. No other appendixes are provided.

This book will be an invaluable reference for biographical information on twentieth-century Australians, and it will act as a complement to the older Australian biographical dictionaries. It should be considered for personal collections and for all larger public and academic libraries worldwide.

—**Robert L. Wick**

Soviet Union

40. Morozov, Vladimir. **Who's Who in Russia and the CIS Republics.** New York, Henry Holt, 1995. 328p. index. $60.00. ISBN 0-8050-2691-6.

With the breakup of the Soviet Union and the ensuing establishment of the independent republics, many biographical sources are being published. Morozov's *Who's Who in Russia and the CIS Republics* is one example of such a compilation, but the reader will find a more comprehensive treatment of this topic in *Who's Who in Russia and the New States* (see ARBA 94, entry 136). The present volume provides brief biographical sketches of some 1,000 individuals, including political leaders, military commanders, scholars, artists, educators, sports stars, and prominent religious leaders. Morozov is a journalist and editor of *V.I.P. Magazine* who specializes in Russian foreign affairs. The treatment is sketchy, covering more than 25 academicians, 6 actors, 4 correspondents, 1 economist, and so forth. This work needs to be used with caution.—**Bohdan S. Wynar**

CATALOGS AND COLLECTIONS

41. Matz, David. **Ancient World Lists and Numbers: Numerical Phrases and Rosters in the Greco-Roman Civilizations.** Jefferson, N.C., McFarland, 1995. 254p. index. $44.50. ISBN 0-7864-0039-0.

Following the tradition of the *Book of Lists* tetralogy (see ARBA 78, entry 94, for a review of the 1st ed.), a number of reference works have appeared that enumerate sundry information: for example, John Boswell's *Five Rings, Six Crises, Seven Dwarfs, & 38 Ways to Win an Argument* (Viking Penguin, 1990) and *The Oxford Book of Ages* (see ARBA 86, entry 87). Matz has compiled an impressive array of rosters pertinent to historical, allegorical, and legendary topics ranging from prehistory through ca. A.D. 300.

Following a scholarly introduction that addresses such concerns as "A Brief History of Listmaking," "Inclusion Principles," and "Bibliographical Notes," Matz presents his lists, arranged in numerically ascending chapters ("The Threes," "The Fours," and so forth). Regrettably, he has no chapter for "The Ones" or "The Twos," in which either the eye of Homer's Cyclops or legendary twins Romulus and Remus could be cataloged. A chapter ("The Indefinites," perhaps) for the Hydra's tentacles and Polyphemus's shapes would be useful, also. Some entries could be merged to save space, as in the "Golden Apples" allusions found separately on pages 12 and 14. Matz's exhaustive index thankfully renders this but a petty annoyance, rather than an impediment to locating related topics.

Within the time frame from which he has drawn his selections, Matz has tended to overlook the obvious in favor of the obscure. For example, he omits the ancients' fundamental belief that the world was under the rule of three gods (Jupiter/Heaven, Neptune/Sea, and Pluto/Hades). Nor has he provided such biblical allusions as the Four Horsemen of the Apocalypse. This is not to say that Matz has not supplied much enigmatic information, such as the substantial listings he gives under "The Ten Plays of Menander," "The Twenty-Eight Kinds of Comic Masks," and "The One Hundred Forty-Seven Temples of Rome." This volume will also save librarians significant time searching for such elusive data as "The Seven Hills of Rome," "The Ten Events of the Ancient Olympics," and Marcus Terentius Varro's "Four Requirements for a Successful Dinner Party."

Somewhat troubling is Matz's habit of not always making clear whether a person, place, or event he refers to has a verified, fixed identity in history or has emerged from legend. For example, on page 27 he assures the reader that "The Amazons were a race of fierce female warriors," but adds that they battled "mythological characters" such as Hercules. A bibliography of nearly 200 classical citations follows the text. Despite the observed shortcomings of this work, it is clearly the culmination of sterling scholarship, and would fill an important need for anyone wishing to better understand the ancient allusions that permeate today's culture.—**Jeffrey E. Long**

42. Walsh, James E. **A Catalogue of the Fifteenth-Century Printed Books in the Harvard University Library. Volume III: Books Printed in Italy with the Exception of Rome and Venice.** Binghamton, N.Y., Medieval & Renaissance Texts & Studies, State University of New York, 1994. 397p. index. $50.00. ISBN 0-86698-174-8.

This is the third of a projected five-volume catalog of the fifteenth-century books in the Harvard University Library. The first volume was published in 1991 and described books in the Library that were printed in Germany, German-speaking Switzerland, and Austria-Hungary (see ARBA 92, entry 36), while volume 2 described books printed in Rome and Venice (see ARBA 94, entry 31). The present volume describes books printed in Italian cities other than Rome and Venice.

The 826 books described in this volume are arranged by city of publication, then by printer, and finally by date of publication. Entries include author, title, date, collation, notes about illustration and rubrication, citations to standard bibliographies, notes on provenance, and the location of the book in Harvard's libraries. There are indexes to author/title, editors and translators, printers and places, provenance, those books containing manuscripts, and identified bindings. Also provided are concordances for Ludwig Hain, Robert Proctor, the Gesamtkatalog, and Frederick R. Goff, and there are 16 plates representative of books described in the catalog. References are to works cited, which are additional to those in volumes 1 and 2.—**Dean H. Keller**

DICTIONARIES AND ENCYCLOPEDIAS

43. Bunting, Jane. **The Children's Visual Dictionary.** New York, Dorling Kindersley, 1995. 64p. illus. index. $14.95. ISBN 1-56458-881-5.

This attractive, visual dictionary for children ages 6 and up includes more than 700 high-quality color photographs and illustrations and more than 2,500 nouns, verbs, and adjectives to help enrich children's vocabularies. The individual pages, as well as the cover, are visually stimulating. Material is broken down by themes such as prehistoric life, school, and farm life. Many ideas are presented on each page. The sections on animals are exceptionally well done, with beautiful photographs. Most children will enjoy these sections. Each theme is introduced with a 50-word description of the theme. Adjectives, verbs, and nouns are placed in descriptive phrases to teach how these words work together. Some of the descriptive phrases are unusual, but overall, the selection of terms is very good. There is an obvious attempt to be multicultural in the illustrations and in the selection of terms. A simple index of terms is also listed. This book is a good purchase for libraries serving young children. If used correctly, it can be an effective device in building vocabulary.—**Carl Pracht**

44. **The Cambridge Encyclopedia.** 2d ed. David Crystal, ed. New York, Cambridge University Press, 1994. 1347p. illus. maps. $49.95. ISBN 0-521-44429-2.

Compared to its softcover offspring (see ARBA 95, entry 45), this one-volume reference is more comprehensive—if a bit more dated—in its subject coverage. It boasts nearly 8,000 additional entries: Its alphabetical listing accounts for more than 5,000 of these, with the other additions appearing in the 126-page ready-reference section. The editor states in his preface that this work contains approximately 1,500 more entries than its predecessor, and that about 30 percent of the entries carried forward into this edition have undergone revision. Crystal pledges subject currency through 1993 for all entries. An attractive 24-page, full-color world atlas follows the preface.

In this edition more space has been awarded to entries pertaining to popular culture, philosophy, mathematics, religion, and computer science, among other disciplines. The natural sciences remain well represented, with abundant entries on plant and animal species of the world. Impressive as well is the treatment given the performing arts, architecture, and music. Although entries average 125 words apiece, longer articles appear for countries, wars, major historical leaders, and broad subjects such as "Renaissance" and "ship."

With 6,000 biographical entries, *The Cambridge Encyclopedia* assembles persons from diverse backgrounds; for example, Raquel Welch, Simone Weil, John Coltrane, and Winnie Mandela. Some unfortunate absences include James Earl Jones, Cab Calloway, Nelson Rockefeller, and Donald Trump. Particularly troubling, however, is the absence of entries for notables who passed away before the book went to press; also, while death dates are provided for such personalities as Jacqueline Kennedy Onassis and Erich Honecker, none are given for such predeceased individuals as Helen Hayes, Peter Quennell, and Marian Anderson.

Although all of this edition's entries were examined for British bias by a specialist, a number of problems persist. Under such bicultural headwords as *sheriff* and *cabinet*, extended British definitions routinely tamp down American meanings into the lower third of the entry. Furthermore, *turnpike* is defined as "a gate across a road," and *salsa* is said only to be "a type of popular music of Cuban origin." Errors seem to be rare in this edition, although there are exceptions. Under *Denver*, the Forney Transportation Museum is misspelled as "Fornery Transport Museum." Also, embedded in the article on the Three Stooges is "(b. 1909)," after the name Joe de Rita; it is only after readers look at the end of the entry that they learn de Rita is actually deceased. Cross-references are profuse; there is no cross-reference, however, from "mythology" to a chart of "The 12 Major Gods of Olympus," nearly 200 pages removed.

Despite their drabness, *The Cambridge Encyclopedia*'s illustrations, charts, panels, and maps (now totaling 1,000) are clean, uncluttered, and usually informative. Regrettably, the compass rose seems to have become an endangered cartographic element, as it is absent from maps throughout this work. Overall, however, this is a remarkably accomplished piece of scholarship by diverse hands. For its asking price, no library should forgo its purchase.—**Jeffrey E. Long**

45. **The Concise Columbia Encyclopedia.** 3d ed. New York, Columbia University Press; distr., New York, Houghton Mifflin, 1994. 973p. illus. maps. $49.95. ISBN 0-395-62439-8.

Like its predecessors, this edition provides an up-to-date survey of persons, places, events, ideas, literature, and art. Although it is based on the two previous editions and on the 5th edition of the *Columbia Encyclopedia* (see ARBA 95, entry 49), the *Concise Columbia* does not simply duplicate. Some entries, such as *fuel injection* and *Getty Center*, appear only in the shorter encyclopedia.

While some entries appear unchanged, others have been revised. The entry for *folk art* adds the single word "idiosyncratic" to the definition found in the 2d edition. Still others, such as the separate entries for Chinese, African, and Japanese music, have been deleted. More prominent contemporary figures replace some biographees. Selected entries mirror social changes. The entries for *chlamydia* and *AIDS* have been expanded to more than twice their previous length. Articles are generally current. *Antarctica* mentions a 1991 protocol that was added to a 1959 treaty banning certain kinds of exploration, and the article on *marriage* notes the gay rights advocacy of marriage for gay couples.

Overall, the most significant changes reflect the collapse of communism in the Soviet Union and Eastern Europe. New articles cover the former constituents of the Soviet Union, replacing the long single article on the USSR. Entries, although generally brief, give clear definitions. Small capitals identify related entries and cross-references. Black-and-white photographs complement the line drawings, tables, and charts from the previous edition. The 16-page section of maps in the 2d edition has been replaced with individual country maps placed with their entries. Most libraries will want copies of this new edition. It carries on the tradition of selectivity, balance, and timeliness of earlier editions. [R: WLB, Feb 95, p. 64]—**Bernice Bergup**

46. **The Dorling Kindersley Visual Encyclopedia.** Anna Kruger and others, eds. New York, Dorling Kindersley, 1995. 456p. illus. maps. index. $44.95. ISBN 1-56458-985-4.

As with other Dorling Kindersley publications, this one-volume children's encyclopedia is lavishly illustrated with thousands of high-quality photographs and drawings. The graphics are not so useful as in some other visual reference books; where some books use graphics to convey information, the pictures in the *Visual Encyclopedia* are mostly just entertaining.

Ah, but what entertainment! The graphics truly are superb, and the work is visually stunning. This makes the book enjoyable to read, even if the approach does have a few drawbacks. There is simply no room for much text, and there are no long descriptions of subjects. Instead, paragraphs scattered among the illustrations give unconnected factoids. Each page or two-page spread covers a single subject; this is visually pleasing and appropriate for children's material, but it can lead to disproportionate space being assigned to subjects (e.g., Greenland gets as much coverage as China).

The encyclopedia is organized into 11 main subject areas (e.g., history, the human body) with a number of subheadings in each area. The general subject coverage is balanced: The arts, technology, science, geography, history, and social subjects all get reasonable treatment. The index is exhaustive, including everything down to the fine print on maps.

This book proves to be surprisingly good for ready-reference, full of most necessary facts and figures. It is also excellent for entertaining yet educational browsing. The book is less useful for research, even by children; there is no extensive coverage of most topics. If children like fun and aimless learning, they will like this book. If they are looking for in-depth subject coverage, enthusiasm will not be so high.

—Ken Feser

47. **Encyclopedia Americana, 1995.** [CD-ROM]. Danbury, Conn., Grolier Electronic Publishing, 1995. Minimum system requirements (Windows version): IBM or compatible 386/20MHz. MPC-rated 150KB/sec CD-ROM drive with MS-DOS CD-ROM Extensions 2.21. DOS 5.0. Windows 3.1. 4MB RAM. 4MB hard disk space. 520KB conventional memory. 16-color VGA or 256-color SVGA monitor. Windows-supported mouse or pointing device. Windows-supported printer with associated drivers. Minimum system requirements (Macintosh version): Macintosh LC II, 68020 CPU/16MHz. 150KB/sec CD-ROM drive. Macintosh 7.0. 2.5MB RAM. 4MB hard disk space. 12-inch, 16-color monitor (256 and higher recommended). Macintosh-compatible printer. $995.00 (2-8 users); $1,295.00 (9-20 users); $2,495.00 (21 or more users). ISBN 0-7172-7487-X.

Since 1829, *Encyclopedia Americana* (EA) has held a respected place among general-reference encyclopedias; today it is still ranked among the top five. However, similar to others in this genre, its print primacy is being challenged by substantially less expensive, glitzier multimedia encyclopedias such as *Microsoft Encarta* (see ARBA 95, entry 60) that attempt to replace in flash and dazzle what they lack in scholarship and depth. In *Encyclopedia Americana 1995* (EA95), Grolier has chosen to meet this market challenge halfway: Abjuring the graphics, videoclips, and audioclips favored by its competitors, EA95 has instead produced a text-only electronic version of its 30-volume print edition.

The CD-ROM reflects the strengths of its print parent. Its more than 50,000 articles, written at a level appropriate to secondary school students and adults, address a vast range of topics on both a national and international level. The editors intend the encyclopedia to serve "as a bridge between the worlds of the specialist and the general reader," and this goal is successfully achieved in clear, well-written articles that range in length from 600 to nearly 6,000 words. Although known for its coverage of United States and Canadian history, biography, and geography, EA is also increasingly treating international topics. Bibliographies accompany all major articles as well as many of the shorter entries. As would be expected, the 1995 edition continues EA's reputation for a high level of subject expertise.

Grolier has done an outstanding job in providing both easy-to-use, intelligent search options and easy-to-understand documentation, a rare feat in CD-ROMs these days. There are the usual toolbars, dialog boxes, and printing and copying capabilities; in addition, users can append notes to articles through an easily mastered process. Words and phrases are hot-linked to related entries. Especially helpful within long articles, users can ask to find a given term wherever it appears in an article, thus obviating a tedious screen-by-screen search for a specific item or topic. EA offers many access points, among the most powerful of which are the indexes, by article title, full-text, synopsis, bibliography, author, subject, geography, article form, date, and user notes (generated by the individual user).

Currency (or its lack) has always been a concern among librarians with EA, and it will be interesting to see what effect an electronic version of the encyclopedia will have on this issue. If Grolier elects to do a straight text dump of its print product into an electronic format, then the electronic product will be no more current than its print parent, as is the case here. For example, the entry on Colin Powell concludes with his retirement from the military on September 30, 1993. If, however, Grolier decides to create a database that can be updated on an ongoing basis, then perhaps an electronic product based on the currency of that database may help EA address this problem.—**G. Kim Dority**

48. **Encyclopedias, Atlases, & Dictionaries.** Marion Sader and Amy Lewis, eds. New Providence, N.J., R. R. Bowker/Reed Reference Publishing, 1995. 495p. illus. index. $85.00. ISBN 0-8352-3669-2.

Divided into six main parts, this evaluation guide to general encyclopedias, atlases, and dictionaries helps users select the most appropriate ones for their children, homes, offices, or libraries. Part 1 furnishes users with various acquisitions criteria: information about the scope, comprehensiveness, accessibility, and objectivity of a work; a comparative chart of each title referenced by a number of statistical categories such as price and number of volumes; and individual "What to Look for In" encyclopedias, dictionaries, and atlases chapters.

The main part of the text is composed of reviews, organized alphabetically, within classifications of similar titles. One chapter, for example, is devoted to children's encyclopedias, while another features secondary school through adulthood encyclopedias. Reviews are consistent in format and begin with a "Facts at a Glance" box that lists all pertinent ordering, price, and editorial information. Facsimiles of illustrations and diagrams from selected works are interspersed throughout various entries.

An outstanding aspect of this work is the excellent comparative data and evaluative criteria used to assess general reference works in electronic form. Acquisitions librarians and other potential purchasers will probably find this part of the book the most helpful. Reviews of electronic reference works contain information about hardware and installation, searching capabilities, downloading and printing, and documentation. Comparisons among other similar reference works are also supplied.

Although the editors and numerous librarian consultants have done an excellent organizational and display job with this work, there are several factors that weigh heavily against an unqualified recommendation for purchase. The first one relates to comprehensiveness. Designed to be a literary merger between *Reference Books for Young Readers* (see ARBA 89, entry 35) and *General Reference Works for Adults* (see ARBA 89, entry 32), this title describes and evaluates hard copy and electronic versions of general works. Lacking are evaluations for any specific reference works such as biographical, legal, medical, or scientific dictionaries.

A second factor that mitigates a mandatory purchase recommendation concerns timeliness. Both hard copy and electronic versions of these types of works are usually published on a yearly basis. Acquisitions librarians require the most recent reviews of the specific edition they are considering, not only to compare the work in question to similar ones, but also to compare previous editions for extensive changes or improvements. In the fast-moving publishing business, this work will become out-of-date and rather useless for potential acquisitions consultation.

The last factor influencing a purchase decision pertains to cost. Although this reference work is well organized and criteria-laden, its cost is substantial for its narrow focus and contemporary potential. Acquisitions librarians may just as easily rely upon *Booklist*'s annual evaluative and comparative review issues of encyclopedias, dictionaries, and atlases respectively. Reference librarians needing to stretch their acquisitions dollars can also offer these reviews to patrons needing to make similar purchase decisions. Therefore, purchase is recommended only if funding is sufficient and requests from adults wishing to purchase general reference works for personal use are numerous.—**Kathleen W. Craver**

49. **EXEGY: The Source for Current World Information.** [CD-ROM]. Santa Barbara, Calif., ABC-CLIO, 1994. Minimum system requirements: IBM or compatible 386SX/16MHz. CD-ROM drive with MS-DOS CD-ROM Extensions 2.2. DOS 3.3. Windows 3.1. 2MB RAM. 1.2MB hard disk space. 16-color 640x480 VGA monitor. Microsoft-compatible mouse. 6 issues/yr. $650.00/yr. (single user); $975.00/yr. (network of up to 10 users). ISSN 1076-8653.

As publishers look to new information packaging formats, CD-ROMs have provided increasing flexibility at decreasing prices. ABC-CLIO's entry into the market is *EXEGY*, which was developed from an earlier ABC-CLIO product, *KALIEIDOSCOPE*, which utilized 6-by-9-inch cards to report current events. *EXEGY* is an electronic encyclopedia that supplies a variety of information in an attractive, easy-to-use format, more appropriate for the school and public library but still a good choice for many academic libraries. The disc covers more than 2,000 news stories; 500 biographical sketches; political and organizational information; a broad range of statistical data; a basic documents collection; and maps, all representing the countries of the world as well as the 50 United States. The disc is updated every two months and coverage includes the most recent three years. The depth of coverage, biographies, and data makes *EXEGY* a reasonable encyclopedia/almanac resource.

Installation is simple, and system requirements are not demanding considering today's computer-based library environment. *EXEGY* does require Windows, but therein lies the ease-of-use factor of the disc. The initial screen provides several access points, including icons and buttons to four groups of information—countries, international, sports, and maps. Once an information screen appears, a category menu allows the user access to other fields of information—all within the Windows format. For example, if one clicks on countries, a country menu appears. A country can then be selected, which produces the category menu. These categories contain events, facts and figures, biographies, organizations, documents, and a map. Each screen allows access to the other screens in each of these categories. A button bar across the top of the screen provides access to a complete index and other function screens. The trail button provides the search history. The go-back button takes the user back a screen.

The help button leads to comprehensive instructions, including toll-free telephone numbers for technical and customer support. The help screens are quite instructional. Topic buttons on the bottom of the screen are used for printing, copying, and writing. *EXEGY* allows the user to copy information to the Windows clipboard, and then paste the text into a word processing system. The write button leads to Microsoft Write to create an original document, complete with text copied from *EXEGY*. This feature creates a system within a system for accessing information and writing term papers and reports.

Several additional features of *EXEGY* warrant mentioning. The search button allows the user to use basic Boolean logic. The facts and figures category lists an impressive array of factual country information. To list only a few, this category supplies land area and population density, time zones, average life expectancy, per capita income, religious demographics, natural resources, major industries, and transportation systems. The cutoff date for the initial disc (November-December 1994) is September 27, 1994. The documents section includes national constitutions and other significant international agreements. These are only a few of the strengths of *EXEGY*. In summary, *EXEGY* is an ideal selection for libraries that elect to provide access to an electronic encyclopedia—and networking is an even better reason to choose it.—**Boyd Childress**

50. **The Kingfisher Young World Encyclopedia.** New York, Larousse Kingfisher Chambers, 1995. illus. maps. index. $29.95. ISBN 1-85697-519-3.

An adult reviewer would crow over the spectacular coverage and layout of this full-color children's encyclopedia; a child, on the other hand, would just say "Wow" and demand one for a gift. A thorough study of earth science, the solar system, the sea, animals, plants, dinosaurs, the human body, machinery, physical science, and people and places, this 500-page volume anticipates questions before the reader asks them. Packed into well-paced, well-proportioned units are advisories ("Do not eat strange plants"), activities ("Make a cress head"), games ("Hatching Egg Game"), labeled drawings ("Helicopter"), charts ("Vertebrates"), word boxes ("Observation," "Experiment"), biography ("Helen Keller"), questions ("Find the Answers"), and stories and legends ("The Pumpkin Boat"). The art is crayon-bright without giving in to cartoonish overkill. The range of topics is superb—a boon for librarians, teachers, parents, and especially home schoolers.

The team who put this book together has managed problems of race, sex, religion, nationality, and taste by facing each issue and handling it with sensitivity and an appreciation of children's needs and interests. No entry appears gratuitous; each flows naturally in a rhythmic arrangement of ideas grouped under the heading, which appears at the top of each page. Boldface black captions focus the individual study, which fits nicely on two facing pages. Interactive questions and suggestions keep the reader involved. If the book could be improved, the editor should beef up the index and expand the literary element, which allies verse, stories, and lore. Also, their next task should be an adult encyclopedia that is this engaging and informative. [R: WLB, 1 & 15 June 95, p. 1826]—**Mary Ellen Snodgrass**

51. **The World Book Multimedia Encyclopedia: The Authoritative CD-ROM Encyclopedia.** [CD-ROM]. Elk Grove, Ill., World Book, 1995. Minimum system requirements (Windows version): Multimedia PC 386/SX. Multimedia CD-ROM drive (150 KB/second transfer rate) with MS-DOS CD-ROM Extensions 2.2. DOS 3.1. Windows 3.1. 4MB RAM. 5MB hard disk space. 640 X 480 256-color monitor and VGA card. Audio board with speakers or headphones. Minimum system requirements (Macintosh version): Macintosh LC or any color model. Multimedia CD-ROM drive (150 KB/second

transfer rate). System 6.0.7. 4MB RAM. 5MB hard disk space. Color monitor (14" or higher recommended). $119.00 (single user); $1,295.00 (network). [Also available for purchase with print version for $718.00 (single user); $1,598.00 (network).]

Although *World Book* is perhaps the quietest product on the student CD-ROM encyclopedia market, it is also the database most relied on for years. The publishers have always gone to great pains to make their product "curricularly relevant." Researchers tailor articles to the students most likely to read them. Articles begin on a basic level and get more detailed if it is deemed that higher-end users will be accessing them. *World Book*'s articles are, on the whole, longer than in other encyclopedias. Although it has the fewest articles (17,000) of the mass market products, it contains more or as many words as its competitors—*Grolier*, *Microsoft Encarta* (see ARBA 95, entry 60), and *Compton's* (see ARBA 95, entry 51).

The entire article runs on the right side of the split screen. The carefully prepared printable outline and graphic preview appear on the left. Fact boxes are detailed, appear as clear icons, and are printable. They are available for states, presidents, and countries. *World Book* wins the print flexibility award. Print options are by entire article, current selection, current page, selected text, or article outline. Print options even provide flexibility for tables; one can print the entire table or the current page. For graphics, clicking on "show it" enlarges the print preview and allows printing. The picture window may be hidden to allow full-column space for the article outline. Left and right arrows (previous/next controls) allow for easy flipping through illustrations and article hits.

The search interface is simple, but effective. Users choose to search either by topic or by word. A flexible proximity search feature will find words in the same sentence, word, paragraph, heading, or article. Although it is not mentioned on the screen, "Word Search" allows stringing of Boolean operators between words. The dictionary here is *World Book*'s own, accessible by clicking on any word of text. One may even click on text within the dictionary for further definitions. There are impressive bibliographies. *World Book* is the only product to include questions about the article.

The changes from last year's *Information Finder* (see ARBA 95, entry 67) include an increased number of illustrations, some video, animation, and sound. A feature new to this edition is "animation within animation." The segment about the heart includes buttons that lead users to other related animation, such as ones on the circulatory system, blood, respiration, and nutrition. *World Book*'s excellent, well-labeled diagrams, especially for science articles, continue to impress students and are popular printouts. Seventy-five percent of the images and all of the maps are printable. This year, a "copy" feature was added for graphics. Sound and video are not exportable. In preferences, graphics printing may be disabled and article length may be limited. Sound, video, and animation may be disabled. Videos and animation may be doubled in size.

World Book has strong curricular connections, a clear interface for younger users, and excellent maps and diagrams. The people at World Book are not marketing their product as entertainment. They are convinced that for students in need of a reliable research source, their product speaks for itself, albeit quietly. The CD-ROM is highly recommended for intermediate, middle, and high school students. (*Information Finder* is still available for DOS for those people who have not been able to upgrade their hardware.)—**Joyce Kasman Valenza**

DIRECTORIES

52. Crayton, Tabatha. **The African-American Address Book.** New York, Berkley, 1995. 288p. $14.00pa. ISBN 0-399-52148-8.

This is a brief compendium of names and addresses of individuals, organizations, and institutions presumed to have an African-American identity, although it is not clear what that means. Individuals can be identified, but how to identify organizations and institutions by race and ethnicity in a nonsegregated society? Is the identity a function of ownership of the organization, funding sources, majority of the clientele, or composition of the employees? Certainly the identity cannot be a function of the charter as segregation is prohibited by law.

The coverage is brief and supposedly covers most sectors of society: the media, entertainment, academia, the sciences, foundations, charities, sports, business, the professions, and more. Those included are supposed to be newsmakers and sources of influence in shaping society. Although no criteria for inclusion or exclusion are provided, it is possible to think of individuals who are prominent in state politics, major universities, and civil service who are not listed. On the other hand, there are addresses of people whose contributions to education and policymaking would require a microscopic search to observe. The longest list is of people in entertainment and sports, but do these people actually shape policy? Strangely, few names come from major universities, even though all major universities have African-American faculty members.

Evidently, the selection process is subjective and in that regard may be less useful than expected. Two major questions need to be answered: Have those included given their consent to have their addresses published, and is it necessary or even useful to have a separate address book for each racial and ethnic group in a country that aspires for integration and equality?—**Elias H. Tuma**

53. **The Gay & Lesbian Address Book.** By the Editors of *Out* Magazine. New York, Berkley, 1995. 309p. $13.00pa. ISBN 0-399-51933-5.

This handsome directory of individuals and organizations in the lesbian and gay community is marred by haphazard coverage and confusing arrangement. The editors give credit to a number of organizations for lists that have been incorporated into this directory, but apparently no independent effort was made to ensure some consistency in coverage. Take, for example, the section on "academics," which consists of individuals and organizations associated with colleges and universities in the United States. Several individuals associated with Rutgers University and two student organizations are listed, but the Office for Lesbian and Gay Concerns is omitted, while the Walt Whitman Center for the Culture and Politics of Democracy, which has little or nothing to do with lesbian and gay issues, is included. Why? Because Walt Whitman was gay?

However, directories are never complete, so incomplete and random coverage is easier to forgive than confusing arrangement. Entries are grouped in 20 categories, such as academics, AIDS/HIV, bookstores, business, fashion, libraries, publications, the religious, and writers. Writers can be listed in either "academics" or "writers," sometimes in both (e.g., George Chauncey). There is no overall alphabetical index, so users must check all possible categories.

Finding entries within categories can be a real challenge. Some are arranged alphabetically by name of person or organization, while others are arranged alphabetically by state and then city. The geographical arrangement makes sense for many categories, but the basis of this arrangement is hidden from the user—there are no headings or guide words to indicate this arrangement, so the actual display of entries appears to be chaotic. It would make sense to arrange the "academics" section geographically so that all the organizations and persons associated with a particular university or state would fall together, but this is not the case. Organizations from the same university are scattered all over. Entries are limited to names and addresses—no telephone or fax numbers or e-mail addresses are provided. Sometimes there is a line or two of commentary, such as the titles of books by a writer.

The venerable annual *Gayellow Pages* (Gayellow Pages) is a much more comprehensive source for addresses (and telephone numbers) for organizations. It has a consistent and clearly displayed geographical and topic arrangement, plus a comprehensive alphabetical index, and costs less ($11.95). However, it does not include many individuals other than service providers (e.g., lawyers, therapists). Libraries that want to provide addresses to prominent individuals in the lesbian and gay community may want *The Gay & Lesbian Address Book*, in the hopes that it might provide at least an address for the individual sought.
—**James D. Anderson**

54. Hammud, Zicky. **The Canadian Address Book: Who's Where and How to Reach Them.** Toronto, Macmillan Canada, 1994. 180p. index. $14.95pa. ISBN 0-7715-9030-X.

The Canadian Address Book celebrates the art of letter-writing. In his delightful introduction, Hammud outlines the purpose of his directory: to provide an easy-to-use guide and quick reference to famous Canadians. As Hammud notes, Canadians receive, on average, 350 pieces of mail per person annually. Because of the advent of e-mail, a thoughtful, well-crafted letter is more like a gift. Hammud also provides six rules of letter-writing etiquette to encourage users to present themselves well.

Listing the addresses of more than 2,000 individuals and organizations, this directory is indeed clear and simple. The entries are arranged in alphabetical order, and spacing, size, and typeface combine to make this an attractive reference book. The subject index collects the entries into broad categories that are easily understood and clearly referenced to the main body. Errors and omissions occur, however. Many prominent Quebec notables, such as Yvon Deschamps and Robert Charlebois, are excluded. Recent criminal "personalities," although listed in the main body of the book, are not indexed.

Much to his credit, Hammud's first effort is satisfying, concise, and a pleasure to handle. True to his philosophy, he welcomes letters from his readers and even provides his own address.

—Mary Hemmings

55. **International Research Centers Directory 1996-97: A World Guide to over 7,850 Government, University....** 8th ed. Anthony L. Gerring, ed. Detroit, Gale, 1995. 1674p. index. $430.00. ISBN 0-8103-8384-5. ISSN 0278-2731.

The 6th edition of *International Research Centers Directory* was reviewed in ARBA 93 (see entry 68) in a longer, critical review. The price of the 6th edition was $375; the 8th edition costs substantially more. Some 620 new entries have been added, so the total now is more than 8,000 entries. There is no change in subject coverage, and all entries are arranged alphabetically by country. It is divided into the same subject areas as in previous editions (e.g., agriculture, biology and life science, environment and conservation, health and medicine, physical and space sciences, and so on). The coverage is somewhat sketchy for Eastern Europe, where information is often not readily available. All larger educational institutions and research establishments should be interested in this directory. Gale publishes three additional directories of a similar nature: *Research Centers Directory* (see entry 340), *Research Services Directory*, and *Government Research Directory* (see ARBA 94, entry 740).—**Bohdan S. Wynar**

56. **The National Directory of Addresses and Telephone Numbers: The Business-to-Business Book That Covers the Entire USA.** 1995 ed. Detroit, Omnigraphics, 1994. 1698p. index. $95.00. ISBN 0-7808-0020-6. ISSN 0740-7203.

This new edition, containing more than 136,000 listings, covers the largest and most important businesses, organizations, government offices, and institutions in the United States and presents them both alphabetically and in a classified subject arrangement. Listings include organization name, address, and telephone and fax numbers, as well as toll-free numbers. This new edition also adds e-mail addresses when available. Furthermore, the 1995 edition introduces Internet coverage; access providers nationwide, publications and guides, mailing lists and Usenet sources, and organizations are listed. Freenets, community-based online bulletin board systems, are also included.

The classified section is now included in one A to Z ("Abrasive Products" through "Zoos and Botanical Gardens") arrangement. *See* and *See also* references are provided throughout the section to help users. The index to classified headings has been revised and is much more user friendly. Another handy feature is the fax and telephone numbers listed in the "Government—U.S. section" (i.e., senators, representatives, committees, regional offices, and information centers). However, the most useful new feature of the book is the "classification code," appearing in the alphabetical section. This feature enables users to identify the subject in the white pages that can be found in the yellow pages. Therefore, if one knows an Internet provider such as Colorado Supernet, looking in the alphabetical section supplies the classification code for the yellow pages, which lists similar organizations. Businesspeople, jobseekers, and market researchers will find this feature useful.—**Susan C. Awe**

GOVERNMENT PUBLICATIONS

57. **Bibliographic Guide to Government Publications—Foreign 1994.** New York, G. K. Hall/Simon & Schuster, 1995. 2v. $600.00/set. ISBN 0-7838-2179-4. ISSN 0360-280X.

58. **Bibliographic Guide to Government Publications—U.S. 1994.** New York, G. K. Hall/Simon & Schuster, 1995. 2v. $550.00/set. ISBN 0-7838-2182-4. ISSN 0360-2796.

Bibliographic Guide to Government Publications—Foreign 1994 and *Bibliographic Guide to Government Publications—U.S. 1994* are annual subject bibliographies of the materials cataloged by the Library of Congress (LC) and the New York Public Library (NYPL). The guides use a broad definition of "government publications" and contain materials about government publications. Access to the bibliographic guides is by main entry, added entries such as title, series title, and subject headings, arranged into one alphabetical sequence. The main entry provides the full bibliographical record including tracings, ISBNs or ISSNs, LCCNs, and an indicator and classmark for NYPL. Added entries contain abridged bibliographical information.

Both guides have been published annually since 1975. Works are listed in both guides based on date of cataloging, rather than on date of publication. The *Foreign* guide treats French materials published in 1795 and cataloged by NYPL in 1994. While most of the material included in the annual guides is more current than 1795, the inclusion criterion of cataloging date limits the usefulness of both guides in collection development. Both the Library of Congress (<telnet://locis.loc.gov>) and New York Public Library Research Library (<telnet://149.123.101.18 Login: library>) catalogs are Internet-accessible via TELNET. Access to their cataloging records is also available from bibliographical utilities such as OCLC Firstsearch *WorldCat* with author, subject, and title access.

The potential audience for both guides is research libraries that tend to have good network connections to the Internet. Widespread access to library catalogs from the Internet may have rendered annual publication of dictionary catalogs and supplements obsolete. Libraries that dislike "breaking a set" may wish to continue to receive the annual guides, but most users will prefer to search the individual libraries' catalogs to identify all materials on a topic, rather than just identifying material cataloged in a particular year.—**Peggy Jobe**

59. Lesko, Matthew. **The Federal Database Finder: A Directory of Free & Fee-Based Databases....** 4th ed. Detroit, Gale, 1995. 1253p. index. $125.00pa. ISBN 0-7876-0361-9. ISSN 0897-4810.

Anyone who needs further evidence that the federal government has become a ubiquitous presence in daily life need only take a look at Lesko's *Federal Database Finder*. Arranged by federal department or agency, the directory lists hundreds of databases on nearly every imaginable topic. There are, for example, the "Thunderstorm Beginning and Ending Times" and the ever-popular "Characteristics of Dental Hygiene Practice in Non-Traditional Settings." In general, however, there are many databases here that could be useful to patrons researching a wide variety of mainstream topics.

The directory leads off with a section that identifies public affairs offices and information resource management contacts for each agency, followed by a chapter of nearly 100 pages that surveys online sources, bulletin boards, and Internet access. After the preliminary material, the directory is organized by organization; for example, federal departments; independent agencies; the executive, judicial, and legislative branches; quasiofficial agencies; and boards, commissions, and committees. Entries include names; addresses; and telephone, fax, and data numbers. Descriptive annotations of 50 to 250 words identify the content of each database.

The previous edition of this work (see ARBA 92, entry 52) was criticized for inconsistencies in information provided, poor organization, and inadequate indexing. Although these issues have been addressed to some extent, there is still substantial room for improvement.—**G. Kim Dority**

60. Lesko, Matthew, with Mary Ann Martello. **1001 Free Goodies and Cheapies.** Kensington, Md., Information USA, 1994. 482p. illus. index. $19.95pa. ISBN 1-878346-25-3.

This 15th "help" book compiled by *The New York Times* syndicated columnist Lesko is basically a directory of telephone numbers and addresses for free and inexpensive information from the U.S. government. The guide provides sources for oral, print, and nonprint data for people of all ages. The subject range is broad, including such areas as birth, child care, business, hobbies, health, career, diet, education, investments, the home, pets, sex, and others. Each entry contains data on the usefulness of an item or items, as well as agency name, address, and telephone number for ordering purposes. A brief discussion of telephone etiquette when making requests is a useful feature, as is a state-by-state listing of federal and state information sources.

The book is well organized for ease of use. The table of contents groups items and information sources by broad subject, while a good index guides users to specific topics. The general public will find this to be a handy book for the home, and public libraries will find it a useful and inexpensive addition.—**Donald E. Collins**

HANDBOOKS AND YEARBOOKS

61. Ash, Russell. **The Top 10 of Everything.** New York, Dorling Kindersley, 1994. 288p. illus. index. $24.95; $14.95pa. ISBN 1-56458-721-5; 1-56458-703-7pa.

Issued annually in Great Britain and France for a number of years, this work now materializes in a first U.S. edition, edited with appropriate inclusiveness. Both highly informative and well formatted, *The Top 10* includes a wide variety of color photographs, illustrations, and other graphics that supplement text and category of information.

The work is arranged in 12 broad sections, each with subcategories and charts. Among the broad topics covered are the universe, science and medicine, nature, politics, crime, religion, war, population, art and architecture, media, culture, learning, music, theater and performing arts, business and industry, travel, tourism, sports and athletics, and toys and games—all under a variety of rubrics. Each topic has as many subcategories as Ash has deemed appropriate. In some instances, he places the American Top 10 next to the British Top 10 and sometimes includes a bit of annotation or historical information.

If one wants to know which are the 10 rarest birds in the world, what are the most common reasons for arrest in the United States, which countries have the most daily newspapers, who are the youngest recording artists to have a number one hit single in the United States, what are the most popular goods imported and exported by the United States, or what are the top occupations with fatal injuries at work, this volume will provide that information and more. Trivia buffs and reference librarians needing to provide such miscellany will find great value in this work. Even a personal library would benefit from the inclusiveness of topics.—**Edmund F. SantaVicca**

62. Johnsen, Ferris. **The Encyclopedia of Popular Misconceptions.** New York, Carol Publishing Group, 1994. 220p. $9.95pa. ISBN 0-8065-1556-2.

The Encyclopedia of Popular Misconceptions is more fun than Charles Panati's *The Browser's Book of Beginnings* (Houghton Mifflin, 1984) and John May's *Curious Facts* (Holt, Rinehart and Winston, 1980). But it is only nearly as much fun as David Feldman's *How Does Aspirin Find a Headache?* (HarperCollins, 1993). Of course, all three authors may rue the day they wrote such books with authors like Johnsen around waiting to catch a mistake or clarify a trifling point of historical accuracy.

Johnsen examines a host of wide-ranging subjects with an eye to correcting the outright errors or simple peccadilloes. Readers are regaled with various tidbits of trivia: Banana oil is not derived from bananas; the word *germ* is not a medical term but something that will grow into something larger; and rickshaws were invented by a U.S. Baptist minister and are only about 100 years old.

Most of the entries are 100 words long or less and usually involve an intellectual dispute of some kind. Is this the last word on each of these subjects? Hardly, for as everyone knows, if academics are laid end to end, one will never reach a conclusion!—**Mark Y. Herring**

63. **Pockets: Ancient Egypt.** By Scott Steedman. New York, Dorling Kindersley, 1995. 160p. illus. maps. index. (A DK Pocket). $5.95pa. ISBN 0-7894-0216-5.

64. **Pockets: Ancient Rome.** By Susan McKeever. New York, Dorling Kindersley, 1995. 160p. illus. maps. index. (A DK Pocket). $5.95pa. ISBN 1-56458-888-2.

65. **Pockets: Birds.** By Barbara Taylor. New York, Dorling Kindersley, 1995. 160p. illus. maps. index. (A DK Pocket). $5.95pa. ISBN 1-56458-661-8.

66. **Pockets: Buildings.** By Philip Wilkinson. New York, Dorling Kindersley, 1995. 160p. illus. maps. index. (A DK Pocket). $5.95pa. ISBN 1-56458-885-8.

67. **Pockets: Cats.** By David Alderton. New York, Dorling Kindersley, 1995. 160p. illus. index. (A DK Pocket). $5.95pa. ISBN 1-56458-886-6.

68. **Pockets: Dinosaurs.** By Neil Clark and William Lindsay. New York, Dorling Kindersley, 1995. 160p. illus. maps. index. (A DK Pocket). $5.95pa. ISBN 1-56458-662-6.

69. **Pockets: Earth Facts.** By Cally Hall and Scarlett O'Hara. New York, Dorling Kindersley, 1995. 160p. illus. maps. index. (A DK Pocket). $5.95pa. ISBN 1-56458-891-2.

70. **Pockets: Horses.** By David Alderton. New York, Dorling Kindersley, 1995. 160p. illus. maps. index. (A DK Pocket). $5.95pa. ISBN 1-56458-890-4.

71. **Pockets: Insects.** By Laurence Mound and Stephen Brooks. New York, Dorling Kindersley, 1995. illus. maps. index. (A DK Pocket) $5.95pa. ISBN 1-56458-887-4.

72. **Pockets: Inventions.** By Eryl Davies. New York, Dorling Kindersley, 1995. 160p. illus. maps. index. (A DK Pocket). $5.95pa. ISBN 1-56458-889-0.

73. **Pockets: Rocks & Minerals.** By Sue Fuller. New York, Dorling Kindersley, 1995. 160p. illus. index. (A DK Pocket). $5.95pa. ISBN 1-56458-663-4.

74. **Pockets: Space Facts.** By Carole Stott and Clint Twist. New York, Dorling Kindersley, 1995. 160p. illus. maps. index. (A DK Pocket). $5.95pa. ISBN 1-56458-892-0.

75. **Pockets: Trees.** By Theresa Greenaway. New York, Dorling Kindersley, 1995. 160p. illus. maps. index. (A DK Pocket). $5.95pa. ISBN 1-56458-884-X.

76. **Pockets: Weather Facts.** By Philip Eden and Clint Twist. New York, Dorling Kindersley, 1995. 159p. illus. maps. index. (A DK Pocket). $5.95pa. ISBN 0-7894-0218-1.

77. **Pockets: World Atlas.** By Esther Labi. New York, Dorling Kindersley, 1995. 160p. illus. maps. index. (A DK Pocket). $5.95pa. ISBN 0-7894-0215-7.

The Dorling Kindersley (DK) name—already a legend among librarians, teachers, children, and parents—maintains its product strength with a series of 15, 4-by-5-inch, full-color pocket books. The choices of subject matter, the pleasing layout, the bright maps and diagrams, the crisp photographs, and the labeled drawings and schematics are well worth the small price. Each book follows a pattern: color-coded sections, divisions of topics, sidebars, running heads, and annotations. The reference section at the end of the text uses the best of pedagogy by restating major principles, design, physical characteristics, and eras. The writers anticipate the kinds of questions children will ask (e.g., how to measure a tree, how to treat a sick or wounded cat, how to read a hieroglyph). A worthy example, *Rocks & Minerals* closes with valuable appendixes: minerals, elements, formulas, hardness, a geological timetable (unfolding from an ingenious spiral), advice on field studies and collections, resource material from the United States and Canada, a glossary, and an index. Another example, *Ancient Egypt*, lists museums, encouraging readers to seek more information about Egypt.

The best of the DK style is its respect for reader intelligence. Rather than following the dumb-down trend, this set uplifts, challenges, and entices the reader to turn another page, read another fact, and add to a growing base knowledge of the subject, as in the photographic study of how to ride a horse and practical, effective ways to feed birds. The entries are brief enough to cover central facts and to raise a few points that readers may not have encountered (for example, the zebra, horse, pony, and ass all belong to the Equidae family).

In contrast to DK quality and sensitivity to children and their needs, a few puzzling omissions pose serious questions about this series. Why are there no phonetic spellings of daunting terms: *El Niño*, *tsunami*, *Messier Catalogue*, *cotyledon*, *Chernobyl*, *praetorian guard*, *archosauromorphs*, *amulet*, and *ziggurat*? Likewise, the author of *Buildings* tiptoes all around North America's indigenous peoples, ignoring San Ildefonso, Mesa Verde, and the Taos pueblos, and the unique dwellings of the Inuit and Athabascan. More disturbing is the question of inclusion, a trend presently acknowledged by almost anybody who wants to sell books. Why does a prestigious house like DK limit its comments on women and black Africa in *Buildings*? The meager one-liner about Mumtāz Mahal and a frail caryatid are slim evidence of open-mindedness when weighed against the egregious neglect of Yoruba compounds, Nubian link houses, Malian compounds, town centers by Elizabeth Plater-Zyberk, or Julia Morgan's design for the Hearst mansion. Also, bindings are tight and inhibit a full spread to ease map reading, photocopying for report writing, or holding open during study and brief perusals.

In general, with a bit more effort, the authors might have noted Garret Augustus Morgan's traffic light and his gas mask, a major lifesaver during World War I; Benjamin Banneker's wooden clock; Elizabeth Scott's Shakespeare Memorial Theatre; Williamina Fleming's star classification system; Henrietta Leavitt's study of Cepheids; Rachel Carson's warnings on the dangers of pesticides; and the contributions of Nobel prize-winners Dorothy Hodgkin, Marie Curie, and her daughter, Irène Joliot-Curie. Young readers of both genders and all races deserve a full accounting of human knowledge and accomplishment. Also, the size and shape limit titles to individual use and discourage libraries from stocking so fragile and small a volume.—**Mary Ellen Snodgrass**

INDEXES

78. **ACCESS: The Supplementary Index to Periodicals.** John Gordon Burke and Ned Kehde, eds. Evanston, Ill., John Gordon Burke, 1995. 850p. $187.50/yr. ISSN 0095-5898.

ACCESS: The Supplementary Index to Periodicals is designed to provide information concerning the contents of magazines not included in the *Readers' Guide to Periodical Literature* (see ARBA 92, entry 60, and ARBA 88, entry 73). A secondary purpose of the volume is to provide indexing for national publications of general interest as they are first introduced. As a general principle (and a stated editorial policy), when a magazine is included in *Readers' Guide* it is dropped from *ACCESS*. Magazines included in *ACCESS* tend to be regional and city magazines and, to some extent, general and special-interest publications. Also, there is an emphasis on major professional journals in the area of library and information science.

The 1995 edition provides indexing for 108 magazines not included in the *Readers' Guide*. The arrangement of the work is by subject and author. The author index entries supply the name of the author, the title of the periodical article or work, the abbreviated name of the magazine, volume, pagination, and date. Additional information in each entry may include illustrations that are significant, the number of pages required to photocopy the item, and indications of entries that are fiction or poetry. The subject index provides access to nonfiction articles, including book, concert, and movie reviews; theater arts performances; and art criticism. A number of genre entries are listed to assist users, including "obituary," "review," "interview," and so on. Cross-references from one entry to another are provided when necessary. Beginning with this edition, *ACCESS* is also provided in electronic format on CD-ROM through SilverPlatter, and through The Library Corporation's online service NLIGHTN.

ACCESS provides a valuable supplement to the magazines supplied in the *Readers' Guide*. It is an easily used volume and covers a number of magazines generally not covered in other indexes. The work is recommended for school libraries that use the *Readers' Guide* as a primary index, as well as smaller public libraries. It may have limited value for large academic libraries where the collections encompass a large number of subject indexes and online indexing systems.—**Robert L. Wick**

79. **APT for Libraries 1995: Alternative Press Titles for the General Reader.** Charles Willett, ed. Gainesville, Fla., CRISES Press, 1995. 116p. index. $15.00pa/yr. ISBN 0-9640119-2-1.

The term *alternative press* refers to literature out of the mainstream, for one reason or another, which may deal with controversial subjects. This catalog is published by CRISES Press, a small, nonprofit corporation formed in 1991. These selections are recommended by CRISES for high school, college, and adult readers, and designed to challenge and expand library horizons through balancing mainstream publications that promote prevailing modes of thought and counter what the editors of this publication call "the corporate bias." The publishers hope that *APT* will take its place alongside more established publications that catalog alternative sources, such as *Alternative Press Index* (see ARBA 92, entry 53) and *Sipapu* (Noel Peattle, semiannual). While not an ordering tool, it does provide bibliographic data and annotations with addresses and prices for the publications it lists and recommends, which makes them easier to find and obtain.

Among form divisions listed are various kinds of American studies: African-, Arab-, Asian-, Jewish-, Latin-, and Native-American, along with materials dealing with disabilities, disease, health, ecology, science, technology, education, gay, lesbian, bisexual studies, political repression, covert action, resistance, revolution, rights, liberty, justice, and women's studies. A substantial bibliography contains separate sections for print sources, tapes, databases, videos, and periodicals.

Judging from the annotations, the general tone of the materials listed here is angry, and most authors represented have a grievance, feeling either disenfranchised, oppressed, or betrayed by "the system." The annotations range from descriptive to ranting, but accurately reflect content with a commendable economy of words. While the rhetoric may be impassioned, and the argumentation salted with invective, the material of alternative presses presents an effective counterpoise to the prevailing, politically correct universe of discourse found unchallenged on the shelves of many libraries. If democracy is anything other than a catchword, therefore, this booklet, and many of its recommended selections, belong side by side with the more conventional titles libraries order from their wholesalers.—**Bruce A. Shuman**

80. **CD-ROM Book Index: An International Guide to Full-text Books on CD-ROM.** Ann Niles, ed. Medford, N.J., Learned Information, 1995. 207p. $39.50pa. ISBN 0-938734-98-9.

This is a "no nonsense" index to printed books now on CD-ROM. The first section is called "CD-ROM Titles," and both the King James version of the Bible and the individual fables of Aesop make their first of several appearances throughout the volume. Each entry shows the software needed to access the CD-ROMs, and in too many cases the former are proprietary—thus complicating the life of the reference librarian/searcher.

Much space is devoted to publications of the Institute of Electrical and Electronics Engineers (IEEE), which searchers would naturally go to engineering tools to consult. The author index has four columns of names of Aesop titles and one of Jakob and Wilhelm Grimm. The title index has many references under "Acquired Immunodeficiency Syndrome" for conferences and symposia. There are also many related terms. The publisher index includes 120 names of both foreign and domestic firms.

Because this initial edition picks up a long backlog, there would not be a need for reference collections to anticipate waiting for a revised version. The book is recommended, if needed.—**Eugene B. Jackson**

81. **Essay and General Literature Index 1990-1994.** John Greenfieldt, ed. New York, H. W. Wilson, 1995. 2042p. $245.00. ISSN 0014-083X.

Nearing its centenary, *Essay and General Literature Index* (EGLI) in its 12th cumulation indexes some 19,000 writings collected in approximately 1,600 works (e.g., anthologies, studies, papers). Following the index are listings of indexed sources (with complete bibliographical information) and their publishers and distributors (with addresses and telephone and fax numbers).

Skewed as it has always been toward the humanities and social sciences, the work has but two citations under "Artificial Intelligence" and a handful under "Computers." Although there is no "High Technology" subject entry, a smattering of citations appear under "Chemistry," "Mathematics," and "Space Sciences." Consistent with Library of Congress subject headings, such quaint headings as "Boardinghouses," "Military Miniatures in Literature," and "Brigands and Robbers" appear. (Unfortunately, this last entry is cross-referenced from "Highwaymen," but not from the more accessible "Criminals.")

As a companion publication to H. W. Wilson's *Book Review Digest*, EGLI is spotty in its inclusion of citations to reviews and discussions of books, films, and other creative works. Citations appear under the title of the work, which is parenthetically followed by such identifiers as "motion picture" or "television program." Many personal name entries lack birth or death dates. Why include the birth year of Edward C. Halper, but not of Kate Simon?

Yet these are quibbles. In what other single-volume index can a researcher find 14 citations under "Authors and Patrons"; tables of contents reproduced from dozens of scholarly texts; and sources cited under such disparate headings as "Hamartia (The Greek Word)," "Preraphaelitism," and "National Socialism and Music?" As a means to buried articles and essays on a wide range of disciplines—as well as on the lives and works of scholars and other figures throughout world history—EGLI remains without peer.—**Jeffrey E. Long**

MUSEUMS

82. **A Bibliography of Museum Studies.** 11th ed. Simon J. Knell, comp. and ed. Brookfield, Vt., Scolar Press/Ashgate Publishing, 1994. 248p. index. $69.95. ISBN 1-85928-061-7.

This is a highly specialized unannotated bibliography of 4,254 journal articles and monographs examining all aspects of museum studies, museum collection management, and related disciplines. This edition is fully revised and reorganized from previous editions. Entries are arranged under broad subject headings such as "Material Culture," then further subdivided by more specific subheadings such as "Photography." There is an author index but no general subject index, and the book only contains citations to English-language materials. Although no doubt aimed to supplement previous editions, older references have been included if they are of historical importance or remain relevant. There is no cross-referencing, but entries have been placed under multiple subheadings when appropriate.

The lack of annotations significantly erodes the usefulness of this resource for those outside of the very specific discipline of museum studies. For many entries, it is difficult to ascertain an entry's scholarly worth based only on the title. The last section of the book contains a list of abstracts, bibliographies, directories, and periodicals related to the field of museum studies. This bibliography can only be recommended to those institutions with appropriate programs or information needs related to the topics and issues covered in this bibliography. However, for students and scholars in the field of museum studies and related disciplines, this is the most comprehensive, focused bibliographical resource available.—**Robert V. Labaree**

83. **The Volvo Guide to Halls of Fame: The Traveler's Handbook of North America's Most Inspiring and Entertaining Attractions.** By Paul Dickson and Robert Skole. Nancy Dickson, ed. Washington, D.C., Living Planet Press; distr., Chicago, Independent Publishers Group, 1995. 252p. illus. $12.95pa. ISBN 1-879326-26-4.

The publisher received a grant from the Volvo North America Corporation, hence the name. However, this title does not initiate a series of guidebooks to be sponsored by Volvo. With the exception of R. R. Bowker's *The Big Book of Halls of Fame in the United States and Canada* (see ARBA 78, entry 603), this is the most complete guide available, organizing 179 halls of fame into 2 primary sections: "Sports Halls of Fame" and "Non-Sports Halls of Fame."

Entries are well written; authors provide good coverage and engender interest. Included in each entry is information on admission fees, opening hours, addresses, telephone and fax numbers, directions, and helpful comments on public transportation. Most entries are attractively formatted and often provide additional background information under "The Inside Story," "In the Beginning," and "Hall of Famer" headings. Clip art illustrations add to the guide's attractiveness.

The nonsports section has additional entries for the offbeat and unusual ("Barbie Doll," "Route 66," "Exotic World," "Quackery," and so on). The final sections of the guide include "Coming Attractions" and a geographical directory. The authors and publisher have put together a nice traveling companion.
—**Milton H. Crouch**

PERIODICALS AND SERIALS

84. **CHOICE Reviews on SilverPlatter. September 1988-November 1994.** [CD-ROM]. Norwood, Mass., SilverPlatter, 1994. Minimum system requirements: IBM or compatible 386SX. ISO 9660 CD-ROM drive and controller with MS-DOS CD-ROM Extensions 2.1. MS-DOS or PC-DOS 3.1. Microsoft Windows 3.1. 4MB RAM. 8MB hard disk space. Monochrome VGA monitor (color recommended). Windows-compatible mouse. Windows-compatible printer (recommended). One high density floppy drive. $800/yr single; $1,200/yr network.

CHOICE Reviews on SilverPlatter, copublished by the Association of College and Research Libraries division of the American Library Association, contains more than 30,000 concise, evaluative reviews that were originally published in the journal *CHOICE: Current Reviews for Academic Libraries*. The purpose of the *CHOICE* reviewing service is to support and guide the development of library collections by providing information to librarians, faculty, students, scholars, and the public. The service informs these groups of significant current publications in terms of the relative place of the work in its subject field and in an undergraduate library collection. *CHOICE* is a monthly review service in the printed format, and the CD-ROM version is updated quarterly.

The subject fields in the humanities section range from "Art and Architecture" to "Religion"; in science and technology, from "Astronautics and Astronomy" to "Sports and Physical Education"; and in the social and behavioral sciences, from "Anthropology" to "Sociology." The contents of the individual entries include title, author, publisher, publication year, ISBN, physical description, the review itself, subject area, readership level, and reviewer's name and affiliation. The *CHOICE* citation, including issue number and year, is also provided.

Installation is straightforward. There is an online tutorial available by pressing the F1 function key. Users can define the search by using keywords. This product allows the user to do index searching. It also allows users to combine different topics together using Boolean operators. Users may combine alternate terms using the "OR" connector, or if the topic has more than one term that the user would like to combine, the two terms may be combined using the "AND" connector. A third option is the "NEAR" connector. After each search, the user has the option of clearing the thesaurus terms and restarting or else saving the search history.

To show on-screen records retrieved by the last search statement that was typed in, one can press the F4 function key. The search terms "architecture and landscap*" retrieved 165 hits (the asterisk [*] is the truncation symbol, replacing any number of characters with the same root word). The wild card truncation symbol that allows for variant spellings is the question mark (?). Search results can be printed by pressing the F6 function key or downloaded by pressing F11. Function keys are standard.

CHOICE has consistently promoted itself as a reviewing medium primarily for undergraduate library collections. *CHOICE Reviews on SilverPlatter* will be a valuable collection evaluation tool for subject selectors responsible for building those collections.—**Marilynn Green**

85. Katz, Bill, and Linda Sternberg Katz. **Magazines for Libraries: For the General Reader and School, Junior College, College, University, and Public Libraries.** 8th ed. New Providence, N.J., R. R. Bowker/Reed Reference Publishing, 1995. 1268p. index. $155.95. ISBN 0-8352-3570-X. ISSN 0000-0914.

It would be difficult to manage the serials collection of a library of any size without the benefit of *Magazines for Libraries*, now in its 8th edition. There were 6,600 entries culled from 70,000 choices in the 7th edition (see ARBA 93, entry 85); the 8th boasts 7,000 entries from the 147,000 titles considered. The preface states that about 80 percent of these carry over from the previous edition, but most have revised evaluative entries. The remaining 20 percent are included for the first time.

The entries are grouped into subject categories, which (in some cases) are further subdivided into more specific groupings. As a convenience, some titles appear in more than one category, and are cross-referenced for the browser (for example, *Whole Earth Review* is under the category "Alternatives" with a *see* reference to the entry within the "New Age" section). The title index and a newly enlarged subject index also simplify access.

Sections are organized in the following manner: related section headings of interest; a short introduction to the field or subject area describing what is or is not included; recommendations of basic periodicals that should be given first consideration, grouped by level; specialized abstracts and indexes in the field, and if there are none, which other indexes should be consulted; and the lists of journals with an evaluative abstract. Each entry includes an ISSN (new to this edition), frequency of publication, price, address, whether a sample copy is available on request, which online services and traditional services index it, and the level of interest or audience. Also, if a title's selection has been refereed by a panel of experts, it is noted, as is the circulation data, publisher address, the inclusion of book reviews, and so on.

With the never-ending increase of available periodical titles to consider, and the budgetary limitations that continue to plague libraries, this guide is more important than ever. However, the value of this work should not be treasured only by library staff. The enjoyable writing style and logical overall organization will satisfy all levels of library users who are seeking advice on which periodicals to read, research, or purchase.—**Gary R. Cocozzoli**

86. **Magazines for Kids and Teens: A Resource for Parents, Teachers, Librarians, and Kids!** Donald R. Stoll, ed. Newark, Del., International Reading Association and Glassboro, N.J., Educational Press Association of America, 1994. 101p. index. $10.00pa. ISBN 0-87207-397-1.

Formerly titled *Magazines for Children* (see ARBA 93, entry 87, and ARBA 85, entry 562), this updated and expanded edition is jointly published by the Educational Press Association, Rowan College of New Jersey, and the International Reading Association. The preface includes the criteria used in compiling this list and offers tips on selecting children's magazines. The preface also provides a motivational essay on the use of magazines by children. The magazines listed are for individuals from ages 2 to 17, with a good number of magazines listed at each of the various age/grade levels. The magazines must come out periodically during the year and contain editorial content, not just advertising or comics.

This book contains 249 entries, with each entry in alphabetical order by title, and supplies the following data: an approximately 50-word description of the magazine, editorial and ordering addresses, telephone numbers, editor's name, publisher information, information on the publication's audience, circulation, cost, information on obtaining a sample issue, and information on the types of work the magazine publishes. Indexes devoted to age/grade level and subject are furnished, as well as an index to magazines that publish readers' work in order to help readers find magazines devoted to a particular genre. This practical tool will inform librarians of appropriate magazines available for ordering, and is recommended for libraries serving children and teenagers.—**Carl Pracht**

87. **SPDCD 1995: The Standard Periodical Directory.** [CD-ROM]. New York, Oxbridge Communications, 1995. System requirements: IBM 386. MS-DOS 3.1 or higher. Windows 3.1 or higher. 4MB RAM. 6MB hard disk space. IBM VGA or EGA monitor. $695.00.

The Standard Periodical Directory has been a key resource for business libraries as well as large public and academic libraries since 1963. As with its print counterpart, this CD-ROM database includes 75,000 periodicals; however, in the electronic product, each periodical is accompanied by 125 different searchable fields of information (e.g., name of publishing company, frequency of issue, trim size). The entries themselves provide title, publisher, address, telephone and fax numbers, editor, a one-sentence description of editorial content, primary readership, frequency, trim size, subscription cost, circulation, advertising information, type of publication, and list rental costs. (Although one can search on ISSNs, they do not appear in the entry description.)

The disc has been configured using the Folio VIEWS search engine. Flexible and easily mastered, it supports both combined field searches as well as Boolean combinations; in addition, its use of a "shadow file" enables users to save custom queries, bookmarks, notes, and important searches. Further, templates for several different types of searchers—publishers, printers, advertisers, marketers, corporate/business librarians, public librarians, media relations people, and subscription/fulfillment people—are predesigned to reflect the types of information usually most valuable to these user groups. Is this CD-ROM worth its high price? Undoubtedly so for those who must frequently access this type of information. The electronic version of the directory is so versatile that it will save countless hours of flipping back and forth trying to pull together related groups of information.—**G. Kim Dority**

88. **Ulrich's International Periodicals Directory 1996: Including Irregular Serials & Annuals.** 34th ed. New Providence, N.J., R. R. Bowker/Reed Reference Publishing, 1995. 5v. index. $425.00/set. ISBN 0-8352-3676-5. ISSN 0000-0175.

The 33d edition of *Ulrich's International Periodicals Directory* was reviewed in *American Reference Books Annual 95* (see entry 87). The previous edition, also published in five volumes, contains 147,000 serials, with 11,500 appearing for the first time. The present edition is substantially enlarged, continuing information on some 165,000 serials with 112,000 serials added this year. The first 3 volumes cover, in classical arrangement, all the serials, while volume 4 is a cross-index to subjects, ISSN index, title index, title change index, and cessations. Volume 5 contains serials available on CD-ROM, producer listing/serials on CD-ROM, serials available online, an index to publications of international organizations, and controlled circulation serials.

There is also some change in publication schedules. The publication date of *Ulrich's* has moved from August to November, which is helpful with updating, and, for the first time, listings for the forthcoming serials are included. The coverage of document delivery services has been expanded to include ENDOCS, the EMBASE Document Delivery Service; Haworth Document Delivery Service; and the Petroleum Abstracts Document Delivery Service. All in all, this standard source for serials is the best publication available on the market and is a must purchase for all larger institutions.—**Bohdan S. Wynar**

QUOTATION BOOKS

89. **Cassell Dictionary of Cynical Quotations.** By Jonathon Green. London, Cassell; distr., New York, Sterling Publishing, 1994. 330p. index. $24.95. ISBN 0-304-34313-7.

Those who are familiar with Green's *Cynic's Lexicon* (see ARBA 86, entry 85) will immediately recognize the provenance of the *Cassell Dictionary of Cynical Quotations*. Minus the earlier work's introduction and thematic index and organized by topic rather than individual being quoted, this compendium mostly repackages *Cynic's Lexicon*. A random check of about $\frac{1}{10}$ of the work's roughly 3,000 entries indicates that approximately 4 percent are new to this edition. The entries themselves range from the witty to the wise to the abjectly mundane, but most of the really good lines are easily located in many of the other quotation books available in any public library. Given the abundance of excellent quotation books probably already on the shelf (including Jon Winokur's delightful *Portable Curmudgeon* [2d ed., New American Library, 1987]), there is little to recommend purchase of this repackaged work.

—**G. Kim Dority**

90. **Dictionary of Contemporary Quotations. [Volume 8].** 3d ed. John Gordon Burke and Ned Kehde, eds. Evanston, Ill., John Gordon Burke, 1994. 332p. $55.00. ISBN 0-934272-32-8.

Begun as a semiannual looseleaf periodical in 1976 (see ARBA 77, entry 90), the DCQ became a monograph in 1981 as volume 5. The current edition continues the same basic format as volumes 5-7 and has the same purpose—to record contemporary quotations with historical, sociological, and political significance, while using quotability as the major criterion for selection. New volumes have dropped some quotes—20 percent in volume 8—to make room for newer ones, and thus do not supersede previous volumes. The quotes, essentially 1- and 2-liners gleaned from about 175 source periodicals and newspapers, are provided for students of the humanities, social sciences, and popular culture. Entries are arranged in author and subject sections, with some quotations appearing under more than one subject. Subject searching is aided by *see* and *see also* references. Each quote includes the author's name, the quote, a source citation, an occasional descriptive annotation, and explanatory amplifications to establish the context of the quote when necessary. The example entry—*Polykoff, Shirley. If I've only one life, let me live it as a blonde! (advertising slogan) (New York 9:37 Aug. 23, 76)*—is typical. But how many students will have heard of Shirley Polykoff? Unfortunately, the failure to identify the persons being quoted diminishes the usefulness of the work, and this weakness will become even more serious as the volumes age and these names disappear from our recollections (if they were ever there). The editors would greatly enhance this work by adding parenthetical descriptions for all persons quoted similar to those in such rare entries as *Nieh, Jung-Chen (Chinese politburo member)*. Another weakness appeared in a check of five random entries, which disclosed two incorrect citations—a wrong issue month and a wrong page number. If pervasive, such errors could be a source of user frustration. However, the work is recommended for those needing sources of fairly recent quotes. [Note: Updates are available electronically by subscription from NLIGHTN (1-800-654-4486).]—**Blaine H. Hall**

91. **Gale's Quotations: Who Said What. Dos Version 1.0.** [CD-ROM]. Detroit, Gale, 1995. Minimum system requirements: IBM or compatible 286. ISO 9660-compatible CD-ROM drive with MS-DOS CD-ROM Extensions 2.1. MS-DOS or PC-DOS 3.3. 640 bytes RAM. 2.5MB hard disk space. VGA graphics card and monitor (color recommended). $400.00. ISBN 0-8103-9989-X.

This CD-ROM is a good example of the way electronic retrieval can simplify searching for information. The 117,000 quotations are searchable by 7 fields, with an easily mastered intuitive interface. An added feature is the background information given about the author/speaker, which contains birth and death dates, nationality, and citation of one or two of the author's major works. Pseudonyms are also cited if applicable.

When *Who Said What* (WSW) is compared to John Bartlett's *Familiar Quotations* (see ARBA 93, entry 89), it proves to be the electronic equal of that classic reference work. The disc makes searching easier, for once the keyword or phrase is entered, all references come up on one screen. A search for the phrase "bell the cat" shows two references in Bartlett: Aesop and William Langland. WSW, however, has three: Aesop, Archibald Douglas, and a Scottish proverb. "Only thing to fear is fear itself" has one reference in Bartlett—Franklin Delano Roosevelt—but two in WSW—Roosevelt and baseball pitcher Dan Quisenberry.

There are a few drawbacks to the program. One major problem is that phrases in foreign languages are entered both in the original language and in English, with only the citation to tie the two together and no cross-referencing. In the case of Virgil, with 104 entries, a non-Latin reader would have difficulty correlating the two by citation only. Also, the information about the author/speaker is not present for all the references; for example, Douglas, mentioned above, has none. The program installed easily into Windows but not into DOS. In addition, when the printer ran out of paper during printing, the entire program shut down.

This is, overall, an excellent program. For a small library that has Bartlett, the rather high price tag is a drawback. However, for networked sites it would be a most valuable tool, ranking along with other standard reference tools for online access.—**Nancy P. Reed**

92. **The Little Oxford Dictionary of Quotations.** Susan Ratcliffe, ed. New York, Oxford University Press, 1994. 481p. index. $15.00. ISBN 0-19-866207-6.

This book is good for browsing, principally because it is so small and can be carried around in a pocket. Unfortunately, as with similar books, it can also disappear from the collection. It is based on the 4th edition of the *Oxford Dictionary of Quotations* (see ARBA 93, entry 92). The preface notes that short quotations are preferred for this small compilation, along with short references. The full reference to the quotation is available in the larger book. "This book contains some one hundred quotations which have not previously appeared in any [Oxford] dictionary of quotations" (preface). Therefore, presumably the sources for these new quotations are given in full.

There are about 4,000 quotations given, sorted into more than 250 topics. Thus, this is the first thematic quotations dictionary available from Oxford University Press. The list of themes is given, as well as an index of authors. These categories include "Achievement," "Economics," "Old Age," "Idealism," and the like. However, ultimately, despite its usefulness to the individual purchaser, this is somewhat pricey for so small a book.—**Dean Tudor**

93. MacHale, Des. **Humorous Quotations.** Dublin, Mercier Press; distr., Chester Springs, Pa., Dufour, 1995. 221p. index. $15.95pa. ISBN 1-85635-076-2.

Of the making of quotation books there is no end. Certainly there are any number of dictionaries of humorous quotations including *Witty Words* (see ARBA 94, entry 70), *One-Line Quotations for Speakers, Writers, & Raconteurs* (see ARBA 82, entry 112), *The Book of Quotes* (see ARBA 81, entry 77), and A. K. Adams's classic, *The Home Book of Humorous Quotations* (see ARBA 70, v.2, p.63). Adams's dictionary, now very much outdated, nonetheless provides the most comprehensive coverage and the best arrangement, although it fails to provide access by author.

Humorous Quotations is designed more as a popular resource than as a library reference tool. It lists about 2,000 truly funny quotations arranged in 20 broad categories that include art, food, music, religion, sport, and the ever-popular miscellaneous assortment of odds and ends. The focus is on brief quotations, about 14 words each, that can be readily understood out of any larger context in which they may have originally appeared. The emphasis is on more contemporary quotations than those found in Adams's work. All of the usual people such as Woody Allen and Oscar Wilde are represented profusely. There is an author index but no keyword index. Primarily useful, as it was designed, for speakers or writers looking for brief bon mots, *Humorous Quotations* makes an excellent supplemental addition to the large collections of quotation dictionaries that many libraries maintain.—**Norman D. Stevens**

94. **NTC's Dictionary of Quotations.** By Robin Hyman. Lincolnwood, Ill., National Textbook, 1994. 515p. index. $19.95; $15.95pa. ISBN 0-8442-5753-2; 0-8442-5754-0pa.

A vast variety of quotations are furnished in this extensive dictionary. Criterion for selection was "what is likely to be familiar to the general reader whose mother tongue is English" (introduction). Some foreign quotations are included if they are deemed familiar to a general audience. In addition, 1,000-plus proverbs are provided.

The quotations are listed alphabetically by author. Sources, such as play, speech, hymn, poem, or general context, are given in italics in the right-hand margin at the end of the quotation. Anonymous works are listed under "Anonymous" (between Hans Christian Andersen and Arabian Nights), with subdivisions by type of quotation or language. Biblical citations are listed under "The Bible," broken down by books of the Bible in order. Proverbs are listed with a date when first written in a dictionary and the name of the dictionary, if known.

A comprehensive and thorough index (nearly 200 pages) by keyword eases access to the main text. For those difficult-to-remember quotations, the keywords in the index helpfully provide a path to the full saying. For example, looking under the term *hatred* leads one to such a quotation as "Heaven has no rage like love to hatred turned/Nor hell a fury like a woman scorned," written by William Congreve in *The Mourning Bride*. The index is keyed to page number and quotation number on that particular page.

This dictionary is both useful and entertaining. Its inexpensiveness and surprising thoroughness make it an important acquisition even for libraries with many quotation sourcebooks.—**Melissa R. Root**

95. Ruffin, C. Bernard. **Last Words: A Dictionary of Deathbed Quotations.** Jefferson, N.C., McFarland, 1995. 261p. index. $39.95. ISBN 0-7864-0043-9.

Last words of the rich and famous have always caught the attention of those left behind. In recent years, several reference works have appeared that fall under the narrow heading *thanatography* (writings about dead persons). Such volumes as Malcolm S. Forbes's *They Went That-a-Way—* (Simon & Schuster, 1988), Norman Donaldson's trilogy *How Did They Die?* (St. Martin's Press, 1989-1994), and a 100-page section of *Panati's Extraordinary Endings of Practically Everything & Everybody* by Charles Panati (HarperCollins, 1989) painstakingly recount the failure of health, inexorable decline, family vigil, and final words of people of renown.

Works such as Ruffin's pare away most of the degenerative preliminaries, jumping straight to the deadly wit, morbid bon mots, and other cryptic (and sometimes cryptlike) mutterings of the expiring scientist, king, singer, and so forth. Of course, despite the most rigorous research, one may never be assured of the veracity of the alleged final words of a wealthy or otherwise influential individual—especially when the death has been witnessed by few. As Ruffin notes in his introduction with the examples of Oscar Wilde, John Quincy Adams, and Sammy Davis Jr., the authenticity of reported last words may range from solid confirmation, to dubiety, to disputation, to entire discrediting.

In the more than 2,000 quotations in this dictionary, entry format is alphabetical by capitalized subject surname, followed by the person's years of birth and death and a brief identifying statement giving the person's occupation. Articles range from a few lines to several hundred words, as in the case of the lingering decline of Dwight L. Moody. Many cultures are represented in this collection, and all of recorded history is covered, including such recent deaths as Raymond Burr, John Candy, and Jacqueline Kennedy Onassis. (Unaccountable omissions are John Lennon, Anwar Sadat, Andy Warhol, Jean-Paul Marat, Nelson Rockefeller, and Gary Gilmore.)

Ruffin usually maintains a balanced perspective toward his subject, suppressing the possible urge to apply religious interpretations to such ambiguous dying remarks as Thomas Alva Edison's (window-side) observation, "It's very beautiful over there." (However, his assertion that Russian princess Anastasia survived the 1918 Bolshevik massacre, finally expiring in Virginia in 1984, will raise many eyebrows.) A useful subject index with single keyword and subject arrangement is provided. Quotation sources are gathered in a bibliography that follows the text. Integrating these source citations into their respective entries would have eliminated having to flip forward and backward to match a quote with its source.

Unfortunately, Ruffin supplies sources for the quotations only for those that he can attribute to a single source. Despite such minor quibbles, it is clear that, for now, Ruffin's treatment of this subject *is* the last word.—**Jeffrey E. Long**

96. **Talking Drums: An African-American Quote Collection.** Anita Doreen Diggs, comp. and ed. New York, St. Martin's Press, 1995. 177p. $14.95. ISBN 0-312-11745-0.

This collection of quotations highlights the statements of African-American writers and speakers and is divided into 76 subject categories. It includes a biographical list and a bibliography, although the absence of an index reduces the volume's effectiveness as a reference. The format closely resembles other, larger quotation collections such as *American Quotations*, edited by Gorton Carruth and Eugene Ehrlich (Wings Books, 1992). Comparing the biographical lists of the two works, one finds that only 6 of the 41 persons quoted under *A* and *B* in Diggs's collection, for instance, are found in the Carruth and Ehrlich volume, indicating that room exists for improving awareness of the memorable statements of African Americans.

Most of the subject categories found in Diggs's volume, however, are covered in the larger work. Some of the notable exceptions are categories for abortion, affirmative action, Harlem, Jews, drugs, and police found in *Talking Drums*. The biographical list in Diggs has more athletes and entertainers than in many quotation lists and overrepresents contemporary figures. Johnnie Cochran, made famous by the O. J. Simpson trial, is there, for example, as are entertainers Michael Jackson and Queen Latifah. Diggs even quotes herself in the section on affirmative action from her previous work *Success at Work* (Barricade Books, 1993). With its small format and scanty introduction, the book provides the overall impression that it is probably meant more as a gift book than as a reference.—**Simon J. Bronner**

Part II
SOCIAL SCIENCES

2 Social Sciences in General

SOCIAL SCIENCES IN GENERAL

97. **ASSIA PLUS. Summer 1995.** [CD-ROM]. New Providence, N.J., Bowker-Saur/Reed Reference Electronic Publishing, 1995. Minimum system requirements: IBM or compatible PC, XT, XT-286, AT, PS/2 Model 25, 30 286. IBM PS/2 Models 50, 60, 70, 80, or equivalent. CD-ROM drive with MS-DOS CD-ROM Extensions. 3MB hard disk space. 512K memory. Monochrome or color display. $1,895.00/yr. ISSN 0966-8764.

Whoever likes searching R. R. Bowker's *Books in Print* (BIP) on CD-ROM (see entry 17), will love *ASSIA*, for it is the identical search engine, complete in every detail right down to the same selections, command functions, displays, and search features. For those not familiar with the BIP search engine, suffice it to say that it takes some getting used to. It is not a difficult search engine, and for BIP, it does the job well. It can, in certain environments, require some computer expertise to make it function with other CD-ROMs (more so than others on the market), but this is not a significant drawback.

Installing *ASSIA* went without a hitch. The documentation did leave something to be desired, however. After opening the packet and pulling out the only disc in the box, the first instructions were: "During this process you will need to make backup copies of the Plus Series Install Diskettes." The instructions go on to inform about floppy disks and their sizes. Admittedly, this is a niggling detail that should go without notice, save for the fact that at nearly $2,000, it should not be too much to ask for documentation to match the enclosed contents. Beyond this detail, the documentation is explanatory enough, although it does contain much that most librarians will never use.

The search engine works off menus, function keys, and a couple of hot button commands. Searching functions, as mentioned before, in an identical manner to BIP. All search commands obtain: au=author, su=subject, ti=title, kt=key title, and so forth. Successful hits paint in a superimposed square box with truncated article and periodical titles. This gives rise to such perfectly unintelligible hits as "Mechanistic designs in me," so the user is forced to see the larger display. While certain searches will reveal comprehensible results, one must bear in mind that this electronic source indexes materials in the social sciences, not a field widely known for its ratiocination, title-wise. Printing also proved to be an interesting task, one that could generate reams of paper.

Installation options allow specification for various word processing systems that allow bibliographical manipulation. While certainly handy, one wonders if such an option would really be valuable in a public setting where many users must have access to the tool. The same is true of the Bookmark feature, where a user can open a small text screen, make a few notes, and retrieve them later. Is such a function useful in a setting where thousands will be using it?

What is obvious is that this search engine, when used with BIP, provides the acquisition librarian with various helpful features, but when cast for wider usership, proves of less striking value. Bowker would have done much better to spend the few extra dollars required to change the screens around in order to make them more valuable to citation searching rather than forcing the round peg of periodical citations into the square hole of a MARC record search engine. While *ASSIA* offers access to valuable materials in a somewhat easy-to-use format, the cost does not seem to justify itself. For the price, librarians should be able to offer patrons a ready tool of easy manipulation for research use. *ASSIA* offers patrons access to materials in a format better suited for an altogether different task.—**Mark Y. Herring**

98. **Building a New South: A Guide to Southern Social Justice Organizations.** Hayward Wilkirson and others, eds. Juneau, Alaska, Denali Press, 1994. 222p. index. $40.00pa. ISBN 0-938737-32-5.

Those living south of the Mason-Dixon line have had much history to live down. This would have remained the case following the desegregation of Southern schools had not busing also come to the North. Then we learned that prejudices were as frequent and as fierce there as in places where mint juleps were routinely served. Lamentably, the volume under review retains some of those stereotypes, as if the South still needed rebuilding. Why not simply, "Guide to Southern Social Justice Organizations"? "Building a New South" is unnecessary.

The volume provides names, addresses, telephone and fax numbers, issue focus, and a brief description of 513 social justice organizations in Alabama, Arkansas, Florida, Georgia, Kentucky, Louisiana, Mississippi, North Carolina, South Carolina, Tennessee, Texas, Virginia, and West Virginia. Arrangement is alphabetical, and a one-page summary to each section showcases a given state's social justice organizations.

The volume, however, is political widdershins: social justice as herein defined makes this the progressive "yellow pages" for Southern states. For example, Planned Parenthood is included, but alternative crisis centers are not. The volume completely ignores conservative groups who are also seeking social justice. Are readers to gather from this that only progressive (i.e., liberal) organizations care, or is it that only left-leaning organizations care the right way? Whichever way it is, if the volume is purchased, a counterweight is needed, such as *The National Review Politically Incorrect Reference Guide* (see ARBA 94, entry 726).—**Mark Y. Herring**

99. Hüttner, Harry J. M., and Pieter van den Eeden. **The Multilevel Design: A Guide with an Annotated Bibliography, 1980-1993.** Westport, Conn., Greenwood Press, 1995. 276p. index. (Bibliographies and Indexes in Sociology, no.23). $69.50. ISBN 0-313-27310-3.

This excellent annotated bibliography about literature on multilevel research covers the period 1980-1993. The authors define multilevel research as "empirical research into relationships of social phenomena differing in meaning and scope, where the higher level includes the lower level." The meaning of multilevel research is explicated in the preface through a discussion of four key terms: approach, theory, model, and procedure. Other topics covered in the preface are interpretation of an analytical group characteristic, multilevel design and research, and further developments of multilevel research.

The 589-item bibliography is arranged alphabetically within the following sections: theoretical issues and multilevel research; methodological issues in multilevel research; applications in educational research; applications in studies of voting behavior; applications in studies in deviant behavior and health care; applications in studies of organizations; applications in studies of spatial contexts; and miscellaneous. The bibliography deals with a complex sociological subject in a comprehensive manner. Author, title, and subject indexes enhance the volume. It is recommended for all academic libraries, especially graduate collections that specialize in education and sociopolitical analysis.—**Arthur P. Young**

100. Rosenfeld, Louis, Joseph Janes, and Martha Vander Kolk. **The Internet Compendium: Subject Guides to Humanities Resources.** New York, Neal-Schuman, 1995. 368p. index. $175.00/set; $75.00/v.pa. ISBN 1-55570-218-X.

This volume is one of a three-volume reference set on Internet access that covers the resources available in the humanities (see entries 101 and 1774 for reviews of the other volumes). The first two sections of the book consist of an introduction to the Internet and brief explanations of the various sources of information on the Internet and the ways to access them. The material is presented in a readable, easily understood manner that assumes the reader is a novice in online searching. Due to space constraints, however, the book does not pretend to be a complete manual for learning search techniques.

The third and largest section of the book contains the subject-oriented guides in the fields of literature, fine arts, religion, philosophy, library science, and education. Because each chapter in this section is compiled by a different person, each one an expert in that particular discipline, the format differs slightly from chapter to chapter. Generally, however, the sections cover listservs, Gopher collections, World Wide Web addresses, newsgroups, and FTP sites. The subject matter runs the gamut from architecture to Tibetan electronic resources. As fast as the Internet is growing, any listing of sites is obsolete before it leaves the presses; however, spot checks of several of the addresses listed in the various sections proved that the information is mainly accurate and accessible.

The book ends with a short list of favorite Internet sites and a complete subject index. Although the rather high cost makes it an optional purchase for a smaller library, it would be an invaluable resource for an organization that does a great deal of Internet searching, as the book gives many varied sources for information on a large number of subjects.—**Nancy P. Reed**

101. Rosenfeld, Louis, Joseph Janes, and Martha Vander Kolk. **The Internet Compendium: Subject Guides to Social Sciences, Business, and Law Resources.** New York, Neal-Schuman, 1995. 424p. index. $175.00/set; $75.00/v.pa. ISBN 1-55570-220-1.

One of a series of subject-specific Internet guides from this publisher, the work under review organizes its material by topic (e.g., employment opportunities and job resources, Latin American studies, U.S. federal government information, sources for women's studies). The work leads off with how-to information of interest to those unfamiliar with the intricacies of Internet searching: domain names; navigating with TELNET; using FTP; search tools such as Gopher, ARCHIE, and WAIS; and browsing the World Wide Web. Although too superficial to be of use to Internet novices, this introductory material might be helpful as a refresher for searchers with a bit of experience.

Eighteen chapters arranged by subject follow. Within these chapters, hundreds of entries describe listservs, Usenet newsgroups, forums, electronic journals, topical mailing lists, text archives, freenets, bulletin boards, FAQs, newsletters, real-time chats, databases, and library catalogs. In addition to notes on owner/editors, access, domain names and URLs, and other pertinent data, descriptive comments ranging from one sentence to several paragraphs accompany the majority of entries.

A list of 54 of the authors' favorite Internet sites and a reasonably detailed subject index conclude the compendium. As with all such print resources, the information in this guide will date rapidly; for the time being, however, for those who can afford the paperback's rather steep price, it will offer a good starting point from which to begin an Internet search in this topical area.—**G. Kim Dority**

102. **The Statesman's Year-Book: Statistical and Historical Annual of the States of the World for the Year 1995-1996.** 132d ed. Brian Hunter, ed. New York, St. Martin's Press, 1995. 1699p. maps. index. $95.00. ISBN 0-312-12749-9.

This one-volume work is a standard tool for basic questions on countries and many international institutions. It is organized into two sections. The first covers major international organizations giving basic historical, membership, and directory information. United Nations-affiliated organizations and approximately 25 others are included. These range from the World Council of Churches and the Organization of African Unity to the Arab League and the South Pacific Forum.

The second section covers the countries and territories of the world in alphabetical order. It provides textual and statistical information under standardized subject headings: history; territory and population; climate; constitution and government; defense; international relations; economy; energy and natural resources; justice, religion, education, and welfare; and diplomatic representatives (in the United States, Great Britain, and at the United Nations). These sections provide much basic information. A new feature this year is the addition of the UN Development Programme's "Human Development Index to the Capital," official name, population, and gross national product per capita in the masthead of each article. The other features include statistical tables on major grain and energy commodities indicating production by country, and indexes to places, organizations, and people.

Statesman's lacks much of the directory information in the two larger volumes of *The Europa World Year Book* (annual) (see ARBA 94, entry 82; ARBA 90, entry 91; and ARBA 86, entry 91), providing less data for international organizations and only key diplomatic addresses for countries. *Statesman's*, however, does have the advantage of compactness. The volume seems to be editorially finalized in March 1995, leaving it a mystery as to why some governments elected in late 1994 are listed not in the entry for that country but in an addenda. Inevitably, more dating occurs between final editing and actual publication. In sum, this standard reference tool is compact and comprehensive. It belongs in all but the smallest reference collections.—**Nigel Tappin**

103. **The Yearbook of Experts, Authorities & Spokespersons: "An Encyclopedia of Sources."** 12th ed. Washington, D.C., Broadcast Interview Source, 1994. 910p. illus. maps. index. $49.95pa. ISBN 0-93433-21-1. ISSN 1051-4058.

This work has a very narrow purpose. It "provide[s] bona fide interview sources to working members of the media." While "Great care . . . in the review and selection of sources for inclusion" is taken, no criteria for inclusion are offered. The experts, authorities, and spokespersons are self-selected, suggesting a bit of grandiosity in the title.

The topic index is alphabetically arranged, listing topics, the source, and the page on which a description of the source is located. Surprisingly, there are no cross-references. The listings contain advertisements by the participants commending themselves to potential media persons for interviews. They vary so much in size and style—some have photographs or logos—that it is evident that there is a charge for their inclusion. The geographical index is self-explanatory but is organized according to zip code. There is no explanation for this arrangement; the reader wonders why the entries were not arranged alphabetically by state. Then there are a telephone area code map, a list of participants, and survey forms for users to evaluate their contacts. Oddly, the table of contents is on the inside back cover.

Because of the extremely narrow scope of this work, it is hard to imagine that it will be of much interest to anyone except those in the media. Even then, because these are self-styled experts (although most are apparently bona fide), the interviewer would need to be on guard.—**Bertram H. Rothschild**

3 Area Studies

GENERAL WORKS

104. **Current World Leaders Almanac. Volume 38, Number 3, June 1995.** Santa Barbara, Calif., International Academy at Santa Barbara, 1995. 306p. $245.00pa./yr. (4-year colleges/universities, corporate libraries); $190.00pa./yr. (2-year colleges, public libraries, high schools, individuals). ISSN 0192-6802.

Current World Leaders has been published since 1957, and since 1981 has consisted of two parts, each alternately issued three times a year. There is the *Almanac* (issued in February, June, and October), *International Issues* (issued in April, August, and December, and formerly entitled *Biography & News/Speeches & Reports*), which contains original articles on a broad topic, along with a cumulative index. The major portion of the almanac, "National Governments" (191 of them), gives the name of the head of state/government, the ministers, and other important officials, with addresses and telephone numbers of the country's top leaders and the embassy in Washington, D.C. Also included are selected vital statistics regarding the economy, demographics, religion, and so on, and membership in international organizations. The "area" line compares the country to some portion of the United States.

In addition, there are directory sections for 35 major international organizations and "Colonies and Dependent Territories" (numbering 29), plus a list of acronyms and abbreviations. Information is mostly obtained from official sources; those items culled from the international news media are indicated with an asterisk. The International Academy at Santa Barbara (est. 1960; e-mail: iasb@igc.org; http://www.isab.org/intacad/) promotes interdisciplinary research in the social sciences and international relations and has recently been involved in environmental research.

The price for this work is steep, but one is paying for an updating service to keep the information current. Many libraries probably already own other standard annual sources, such as the (more expensive) *Europa World Year Book* (see ARBA 94, entry 82), *The CIA World Factbook* (see ARBA 95, entry 8), and *The World Almanac* (see ARBA 95, entry 6). This item is suitable for those libraries not owning or not able to afford the more expensive sources.—**Daniel K. Blewett**

105. **Worldmark Encyclopedia of the Nations.** 8th ed. Detroit, Gale, 1995. 5v. maps. index. $335.00/set. ISBN 0-8103-9878-8.

This encyclopedia offers detailed descriptions of the United Nations and the world's countries, protectorates, and territories through the five-volume arrangement employed in previous editions (see ARBA 85, entry 78). Revisions for this edition reflect current developments and analyze recent dissolutions (e.g., the Soviet Union, Yugoslavia), unifications (e.g., Germany, Yemen), and conflicts (e.g., Bosnia).

As with previous editions, the first volume relates UN structure, history, organization, and agencies. Because the focus is on structure rather than accomplishments, the factual—but largely uncritical—descriptions explain recent missions and financial problems more extensively than in previous editions. The appendixes offer glossaries, a general bibliography, and alphabetical indexes by country and agency name. Those seeking statistical comparisons between countries will be better served by *Europa World Year Book* (see ARBA 94, entry 82) and similar works.

The remaining volumes, divided by geographical area, consist of alphabetically arranged country profiles that vary in length from fewer than 10 pages (e.g., Fiji, Ukraine) to more than 20 pages (e.g., China, Japan). Each unsigned report contains the same 50 categories covering a variety of geographical, demographic, social, industrial, economic, and financial information, with up-to-date, useful bibliographies. The emphasis is on the political, economic, and social progress of each country.

Problems noted in previous editions such as map size and index location have been corrected; however, the absence of color is apparent and disappointing. Repeating identical country-name indexes in each volume has clearly improved access, but much information (e.g., historical events, places, famous personages) remains unindexed and undiscovered. The encyclopedia, successfully combining material from a number of sources and maintaining its excellent, factual descriptions, continues to be a useful, recommended addition to reference collections.—**Sandra E. Belanger**

UNITED STATES
General Works

106. **Worldmark Encyclopedia of the States.** 3d ed. Detroit, Gale, 1995. 758p. maps. $135.00. ISBN 0-8103-9877-X.

Continuing the format of the earlier editions published by Worldmark, this work covers each of the 50 states, the District of Columbia, and Puerto Rico. There are also chapters for the Caribbean and the Pacific dependencies of the United States, as well as one for the nation as a whole. While there is a historical section in each entry, the work's emphasis continues to be statistical, with a strong emphasis on fairly recent demographic, political, economic, and social data.

The arrangement is alphabetical by state, then the other locales, and ending with the United States as a whole. Each entry is divided into 50 sections, identical in arrangement and scope with the earlier editions (see ARBA 87, entry 90, and ARBA 82, entry 371). The length of each entry varies roughly with the size of the state's population. Each entry includes a black-and-white map of the state, reduced in detail from the previous edition (but adding interstate highways), and a few tables containing such data as recent presidential elections. Larger states also get more tables. Entries close with a short bibliography.

While nearly all the data are available in other sources, this remains a convenient source for ready-reference—for example, on variations in pronunciation of common words among the states. Obviously, much of the data provided is outdated rapidly. Unfortunately, the new publishers continue the practice of not citing their sources, although they do credit many individuals. This lack of attention to bibliographic detail is curious. For example, the Arizona entry includes reference to two of Gale's own products, *Gale State Rankings Reporter* (see ARBA 95, entry 895) and *Cities of the United States* (2d ed., Gale, 1993), and the Department of Education's *Digest of Education Statistics* (GPO, 1994), yet these do not appear in most of the other entries, nor in the general U.S. entry.

As a handy, if expensive, overview of a nation, this remains a useful but not essential tool, especially for the smaller library. For libraries that did not obtain the 2d edition, the 3d edition may be a consideration. For libraries with the 2d edition, the additional information is hardly worth the price.
—**James H. Sweetland**

New York

107. **The Encyclopedia of New York City.** Kenneth T. Jackson, ed. New York, New-York Historical Society and New Haven, Conn., Yale University Press, 1995. 1350p. illus. maps. index. $60.00. ISBN 0-300-05536-6.

More than a decade in the making, this product of 680 authors, historians, and specialists is unlike any other reference book on New York City. Among its 4,300 entries, users can read about both famous and not-so-famous individuals, institutions, neighborhoods, companies, objects, concepts, and ethnic groups. Most articles are brief, but several ("Architecture," "Housing") cover a few thousand words. Each entry contains bibliographical citations, and articles are arranged alphabetically by letter rather than word (e.g., "New Yorker" appears before "New York Ledger"), which will confuse some readers. There is a name index for those mentioned in passing, and nearly 700 black-and-white illustrations, portraits, photographs, maps, and tables. Since there is no overall subject index or schematic outline, which this book would have benefited from, the user must rely on the system of cross-references, which is in some cases too sparse—for example, there are no cross-references between the articles on "Child Welfare" and "Foundlings."

In any work of this scope, there will be controversy regarding both inclusions and exclusions. Because the editors wanted to include only those who left a permanent mark on the city's history or culture, several current pop icons (Madonna) and heroes (Mickey Mantle) are not included, while some obscure figures (Major Deegan, Captain Preserved Fish) and famous visitors (Charles Dickens and Abraham Lincoln) are. A few minor errors will always creep into a book of this size (1,350 pages) and magnitude: Bayswater is in southeastern Queens, not southwestern; the Queens Library book bus was not a bus to the library, but rather delivered books along routes in areas not served by a local branch library. Other errors will undoubtedly turn up, but this relatively inexpensive volume will prove a treasure trove of information about New York City from prehistory to the present for both serious students and general readers.—**John A. Drobnicki**

AFRICA
General Works

108. **Africa on File.** By Mapping Specialists, Ltd. New York, Facts on File, 1995. 2v. maps. index. $185.00/set looseleaf w/binder. ISBN 0-8160-3288-2.

Similar to many other volumes in this series (e.g., *Latin America on File* or *Asian History on File* [see entries 155 and 533]), this service incorporates an interdisciplinary approach, covering a broad range of subjects that include physical and human geography, economics, history, political science, and culture. The present volume highlights 52 African countries, emphasizing in more detail 6 major countries: Kenya, Tanzania, South Africa, Sudan, Nigeria, and Uganda.—**Bohdan S. Wynar**

109. Brockman, Norbert C. **An African Biographical Dictionary.** Santa Barbara, Calif., ABC-CLIO, 1994. 440p. illus. maps. index. $54.00. ISBN 0-87436-748-4.

This book provides biographical sketches of nearly 500 people who figure prominently in the history of sub-Saharan Africa. It includes non-Africans as well as Africans. The emphasis is on postcolonial contemporary history. North African states of the Mediterranean basin are not included; the island nations of the Indian Ocean are.

A listing of the entries under the following categories is given: politics, culture, economics, science and technology, religion, and geography and history. For example, under politics, there are traditional rulers, imperialists, anticolonial resistance leaders, postindependence heads of state or government, civil servants, political figures, and guerrilla leaders. Under culture, entries include sculptors and painters, novelists and writers, musicians, sports figures, and feminist activists and thinkers. Within economics, some subcategories are businesspeople and entrepreneurs, traders, and labor leaders. Science and technology is broken down into such subdivisions as physicists and mathematicians, wildlife and environmental advocates, engineers, medical and health care specialists, and paleontologists and archaeologists. The area of religion includes traditional religious leaders, Islamic leaders, African Christian leaders, Christian missionaries, and prophets and leaders of new religious movements. Finally, under geography and history, there are chroniclers and historians, and geographers and explorers.

An individual is sometimes listed under more than one heading. The headings indicate the spheres of activity of those included in this dictionary. Each entry starts with a short statement of the person's significance, followed by a chronological biographical sketch. Brief evaluations of their work are given for the cultural figures. Many of the entries refer the reader to one or more of 34 works listed in the book. Some entries list an autobiography and principal biographies where relevant. Several appendixes are given to aid the reader, and there is also an index.—**J. E. Weaver**

110. **Contemporary African Politics and Development: A Comprehensive Bibliography, 1981-1990.** Vijitha Mahadevan and others, eds. Boulder, Colo., Lynne Rienner, 1994. 1314p. index. (A Bibliography for the Study of African Politics). $160.00. ISBN 1-55587-334-0.

It would be unfair to characterize this compilation as anything but monumental—more than 16,000 entries covering just 10 years. There are undoubtedly some omissions, but they cannot be many. The volume continues the series edited by Richard Sklar covering and entitled A Bibliography for the Study of African Politics, but in considerably greater scope and detail.

All formats are represented: books, chapters, articles, reports, and government documents. The arrangement is the usual one. Entries are organized by country (Egypt is excluded) and subdivided within by topic; a detailed table of contents provides access to all parts of the work. Keywords are provided for all entries and annotations for entries published between 1986 and 1990. Cross-referencing is very limited. There are appendixes of 550 subject and topic headings, acronyms, changes in country names, and some 130 journals that were canvassed. The work closes with extensive author/editor and keyword indexes (the latter not always well differentiated within headings). The small section entitled "caveats" (p. xxi) is worth reading on its own terms.

Despite all these advantages, there are some problems. The editors decided to enter authors' names as they appeared on publications rather than consolidating them. As a result, for instance, D. B. Ndlela is indexed four times in slightly different ways, as well as once more under "Ndelela." The work shows again that getting keywords just right is notoriously difficult—the one for this reviewer's entry is wrong, as undoubtedly are others. Contextually, these are reasonably minor problems, although some could be troublesome, and most could have been corrected in the compiling stages. In its amplitude and generous accessibility, this work should be welcomed by Africanist political scientists and others as it stands. To what extent the burgeoning CD-ROM databases will replace such bibliographies remains to be seen; there is no indication that this work is online in any form, or that it could become so.—**David Henige**

111. **International Directory of African Studies Research. Repertoire International des Études Africaines.** 3d ed. Edited by International African Institute. Philip Baker, comp. New Providence, N.J., published for the International African Institute, Hans Zell/Reed Reference Publishing, 1994. 319p. index. $150.00. ISBN 1-873836-36-8.

The 1,800 entries in this edition exceed by more than 700 the number in the previous edition, which appeared in 1987, even though some 200 entries have been eliminated. As before, the information contained in this edition derives from replies to some 2,400 questionnaires. Inevitably in the circumstances, the coverage is both incomplete and inconsistent, as the questionnaires were apparently unedited, but still remarkably broad and useful.

The arrangement is alphabetical by, and within, country, and users should be aware that the choices for entries are frequently idiosyncratic (e.g., "African Studies Center" for Michigan State, "Center for African Studies" for Florida, but "University of California at Los Angeles" and "University of Wisconsin—Madison"). These peccadilloes aside, the work contains a large number of useful features: full mailing addresses, telephone numbers, and many fax numbers and e-mail addresses; research emphases; details on staff and activities; sizes of institutional libraries; and funding information.

Resources in Africa are surprisingly well represented—28 from Ghana, 120 from Nigeria, and 104 from South Africa, for instance, compared to 111 for the United Kingdom, 125 for France, and 116 for the United States. In all, more than 100 countries are represented.

The indexing is outstanding. There is a thematic index, one of international organizations, another (exceedingly useful) of serial publications, and one for personnel. Any work of this nature is vulnerable to obsolescence, but this work should be able to resist this fate better than most. The directory should be heavily used in libraries.—**David Henige**

112. Rake, Alan. **100 Great Africans.** Metuchen, N.J., Scarecrow, 1994. 431p. maps. index. $59.50. ISBN 0-8108-2929-0.

The subjects in this book are arranged into 11 topical chapters, with titles such as "Saints and Sinners," "Struggle Against Colonialism," and "Modern Rulers." There are nine maps for topics such as "Egypt and Kush," "The Golden Kings," and "Hannibal and Rome." The entries, averaging four pages each, are longer than those found in the older *Dictionary of Africa Historical Biography* (see ARBA 87, entry 96). The text in Rake's book flows a little better as well, but there are no source notes or bibliographies, a serious omission. Illustrations of these people would also have been nice, although that would have raised the book's price. Rake selected people whose significance was in Africa, regardless of their color or place of birth. He leaves out those whom he considered "essentially visitors doing a job on behalf of themselves or external powers" (p. viii), such as Henry Stanley and David Livingstone, General Charles Gordon, and Albert Schweitzer. The author is the managing editor of *New African* magazine, and also wrote *Who's Who in Africa: Leaders for the 1990s* (see ARBA 93, entry 760), which complements his newer title. Rake writes in the preface that "this book is essentially journalistic, not based on profound academic research." This biographical dictionary is suitable for the reference collections of all academic, high school, and public libraries. [R: WLB, Feb 95, p. 70]—**Daniel K. Blewett**

113. **Survey of Economic and Social Conditions in Africa, 1991-1992.** By Economic Commission for Africa. New York, United Nations, 1994. 1v. (various paging). $28.00pa. ISBN 92-1-125067-6. S/N 95-II-K.1.

This survey is one of a series published annually by the United Nations, prepared by the staff of the Socio-Economic Research and Planning Division of the United Nations Economic Commission for Africa. The quality of the data remains a concern, as numerous countries do not provide up-to-date and accurate information on their economic situation. After an overview of the world economy at the end of 1992 with emphasis on world trade, prices of internationally traded goods, and international finance, there is a chapter on the economy of developing Africa in 1992. The data are grouped in several different ways, with some discussion of policy issues for individual countries.

The next nine chapters are on the topics of fiscal, monetary, and price developments; external debt and resource flows; the external sector; agriculture, forestry, and fisheries; petroleum and natural gas; mining; the manufacturing industry; the construction industry; and transport, communication, and tourism. They contain specific information on production, policy, and prospects for the future. Selected social issues, such as health, education, and employment, are covered in the final chapter. The statistical annex has 34 tables with data by individual country on some of the topics covered in the text, including national accounts and the external sector. While years given vary from table to table, most are for the 1988 to 1992 time period.—**J. E. Weaver**

Algeria

114. Naylor, Phillip Chiviges, and Alf Andrew Heggoy. **Historical Dictionary of Algeria.** 2d ed. Metuchen, N.J., Scarecrow, 1994. 443p. maps. (African Historical Dictionaries, no.66). $55.00. ISBN 0-8108-2748-4.

This is another volume in the second round of historical dictionaries relating to Africa. As with other 2d editions in the series, it is superior to its predecessor, being in fact a combination of new and old. (See ARBA 82, entry 326, for a review of the previous edition.)

By the standards of the series, this is a large volume, and it possesses the usual accoutrements: a list of acronyms, a glossary, and tables of colonial and independence governments. There is also a 50-page bibliography that contains an appropriately large list of French-language materials, as well as a 40-page introduction providing some background. There is more on the precolonial period than in most of the African Historical Dictionaries, but this volume still remains largely biographical and contemporary in its focus. Chronologically, coverage extends back to pre-Roman times; geographically, there is relatively little on interior Algeria.

The entries seem accurate and internally well balanced, and it is a pity that the lack of an index—common to all volumes in this series—precludes convenient access to the materials in them. Although there is a good degree of cross-referencing (the entry for *Vandals* serves as an example), it remains that only luck or unnecessary persistence will bring users to much of the information in the work, and opportunities to discern patterns and commonalities are all but lost. Smaller print throughout would have permitted an index to be accommodated without additional pages.—**David Henige**

Chad

115. Joffe, George, and Valerie Day-Viaud, comps. **Chad.** Santa Barbara, Calif., Clio Press/ABC-CLIO, 1995. 188p. index. (World Bibliographical Series, v.177). $63.50. ISBN 1-85109-231-5.

Chad, situated in the center of the African continent, is one of the poorest nations in the world and has largely been ignored by the West. Formerly a French colony, what writings there are about it tend to be in French, including most of the somewhat uneven bibliographical coverage. Unfortunately, Chad's one claim to any notoriety is that it experienced a civil war between the Muslim north and non-Muslim south in the 1970s and 1980s, while simultaneously engaged in a border dispute with Libya. Most of what has been written about it since independence has tended to focus on these problems.

Preceded by a short introduction, this bibliography contains 650 entries (primarily books and journal articles) categorized by subject and accompanied by author, title, and subject indexes, and a map. Even though this bibliography, as with the others in this series, is designed for English speakers, the majority of entries are, of necessity, in French. Also, as with the other volumes in this series, it is not meant to be exhaustive. Each entry is accompanied by a short, useful annotation explaining its value.

There are a few anomalies, however. For example, it is the 1977 Scarecrow edition of the *Historical Dictionary of Chad* (edited by Samuel Decalo) that is listed, while only the 1988 edition is referred to in the annotation. Additionally, while the *Historical Dictionary* is found in the general history section, it also contains a significant bibliography, and so it would be useful to see some sort of reference to it in the bibliography section. These minor points aside, *Chad* is, overall, a useful work deserving a place in any serious Africana collection.—**Paul H. Thomas**

Eritrea

116. Fegley, Randall, comp. **Eritrea.** Santa Barbara, Calif., Clio Press/ABC-CLIO, 1995. 125p. index. (World Biographical Series, v.181). $56.00. ISBN 1-85109-245-5.

This excellent work is a recent addition to the World Bibliographical Series, which provides access to sources on the various countries and regions of the world. A volume on this newly independent state will likely prove particularly useful to researchers and students of the area.

The format of this series includes a useful introductory essay on the subject country by the compiler. In this case, Fegley provides readers with a thorough, fascinating, and readable 43-page overview of ethnic groups, languages, religions, history, and so forth, to help readers orient themselves to the ethnic and confessional complexities of Eritrea and its relationship with the Ethiopian and Italian colonizers.

The bibliography proper is divided into 31 subject sections covering a wide variety of social issues (e.g., women, refugee issues, human rights), economic and political matters; travel guides; explorer's accounts; coins and stamps; and much more. Citations include paragraph-length evaluative annotations. Most material is in English, although some Italian- and other European-language sources are listed. Inevitably, given its recent history, the work provides many items on Ethiopia. There are a general map of the country and a unified index of authors, titles, and subjects.

In sum, this is an excellent guide to finding sources of information on this Horn of Africa state. Its long introduction may make it of interest to larger public libraries as well as to strictly research institutions.—**Nigel Tappin**

Ethiopia

117. Munro-Hay, Stuart, and Richard Pankhurst, comps. **Ethiopia.** Santa Barbara, California, Clio Press/ABC-CLIO, 1995. 225p. index. (World Bibliographical Series, v.179). $69.00. ISBN 1-85109-111-4.

This is another welcome addition to an excellent series designed for English speakers, a series not intended to be comprehensive, but instead critically selective. The compilers are well-known scholars of Ethiopia, a fascinating land having a long history dating back to the pre-Christian era. This bibliography contains 610 entries, mostly books and journal articles and primarily in English, almost all of which have been insightfully annotated to be especially useful for users unfamiliar with Ethiopia (and that display the wide-ranging knowledge of the compilers).

The entries have been grouped into a number of topical chapters from flora, fauna, and urbanization to the arts, although history, travelers' accounts, language, linguistics, and literature are particularly well represented. Other currently important topics such as the Eritrean war for independence, famines, and international relief efforts are also included. Given that one of Munro-Hay's special areas of interest is numismatics, it is no surprise to see a chapter on this, too.

The bibliography is preceded by a short but useful introduction to Ethiopian history and a chronology and list of rulers. A serviceable index and an adequate map are appended. For smaller collections, especially in public and undergraduate libraries, this excellent bibliography is a must. Even for larger research collections serving scholars familiar with Ethiopian studies, which may already have many of the more comprehensive or specialized bibliographies on Ethiopia, this will still be a valuable addition given its wide-ranging scope and currency and its excellent, incisive annotations.—**Paul H. Thomas**

Liberia

118. Dunn, D. Elwood, comp. **Liberia.** Santa Barbara, Calif., Clio Press/ABC-CLIO, 1995. 207p. index. (World Bibliographical Series, v.157). $77.50. ISBN 1-85109-178-5.

Liberia has been much in the news during the past few years as it has undergone an almost fatal national trauma, so the appearance of the present work is at least timely. As typical of this series, the 656 items are divided into too large a number (28) of classifications, with some classifications having very few items. There is an author index; a subject index, which is oddly incomplete; and a title index, which is basically useless.

The most valuable component of the work is a listing by author of about 500 theses and dissertations more or less related to Liberia, so it is a pity that these entries are not included in any of the indexes. Both this listing and the main listing contain rather a large number of entries whose relevance to Liberia is unclear. An unfortunate and puzzling aspect of this work is the fact that so many of the entries seem unnecessarily outdated. Although the preface is dated 1994, two works published in 1989 (entry 635) are noted as "[f]orthcoming," while a bibliography of African art, published biannually, then annually since 1987, is listed (entry 653) only in its prototype published in 1985. Certainly there are a few entries from the 1990s, but the impression is that the labor of compilation effectively ceased far too many years before this work was published. One result is that the national trauma mentioned above is scarcely noticed at all.

In short, it needs to be said again that this volume, as so many others in this series, bears the hallmark of an attempt to compile to a formula—a formula that discourages innovation, comprehensive coverage, and currency at the same time that it rewards idiosyncrasy of choice forced onto a procrustean bed of format. Occasionally a volume rises above these constraints—unfortunately, this is not one of them.

—**David Henige**

Malawi

119. Decalo, Samuel, comp. **Malawi.** 2d ed. Santa Barbara, Calif., Clio Press/ABC-CLIO, 1995. 188p. index. (World Bibliographical Series, v.8). $62.00. ISBN 1-85109-238-2.

There are times when a comprehensive reference to works on different aspects of a particular country is needed. The World Bibliographical Series provides such readily available reference for many countries of the world. The 1st edition of volume 8 of the series, compiled by Decalo, was a comprehensive bibliography of works done on Malawi, in a user-friendly format. The 2d edition of the volume is even better. It is an updated and much-expanded version of the previous edition, with a comprehensive list of the latest written works on this country. From archaeology through economics, politics, and social issues to trade and commerce, the book is an unparalleled guide to works on all aspects of Malawi.

In addition to the list of dissertations and references cited, the book consists of 508 bibliographical entries. Each entry is accompanied by a short and insightful abstract and additional references. It is this feature that makes the book so useful to the researcher. The list of dissertations, as well as the reference works, are exhaustive. The author provides an excellent framework in which to appreciate this guide with a brilliant introductory chapter. This book is a must for anyone doing any serious research on Malawi. One wonders how researchers managed to work on this country in the past without this book.

—**Kwabena Gyimah-Brempong**

Morocco

120. Findlay, Anne M., and Allan M. Findlay, comps. **Morocco**. rev. ed. Santa Barbara, Calif., Clio Press/ABC-CLIO, 1995. 178p. index. (World Bibliographical Series, v.47). $61.00. ISBN 1-85109-216-1.

Morocco, part of the extensive World Bibliographical Series, is an annotated bibliography that supplements the 1984 edition (see ARBA 86, entry 113). The compilers state that the vast majority of citations are new and that the focus is on the last 10 years. The publication dates of the entries support those statements. The majority (approximately two-thirds) of the newer entries are from journals, followed in frequency by monographs and doctoral dissertations; these are supplemented by citations to key works from the earlier edition. The volume contains almost exclusively English-language entries, which of course excludes the vast amount of both Arabic- and French-language materials available.

Organizationally, the book is divided into a brief preface; an introduction; the core bibliography itself; a set of author, title, and subject indexes; and a map. The introduction is a broad description of Moroccan history, culture, and politics and, unlike the bibliography, is not restricted to the last 10 years. The core bibliography contains 622 entries arranged in 38 broad categories, some of which are further subdivided. The categories are logical and easy to use. Annotations range in length from very brief (1 sentence) to 120 or more words in length.

Despite the limited time frame covered and the English-language-only focus, this is a useful and easy-to-use reference work. The volume will be best suited for those libraries already owning either the earlier edition of this work or other materials similar in terms of comprehensiveness and time frames covered. It is recommended for academic and larger public libraries.—**Anthony J. Dedrick**

São Tomé and Príncipe

121. Shaw, Caroline S., comp. **São Tomé and Príncipe**. Santa Barbara, Calif., Clio Press/ABC-CLIO, 1994. 183p. index. (World Bibliographical Series, v.172). $54.00. ISBN 1-85109-181-5.

São Tomé and Príncipe is the smallest country in Africa, with an area of only 372 square miles and a population of about 120,000—in other words, it more resembles a city than a country. It owes its independent existence to the happenstance that it, alone of the former colonies in its region, ended up being ruled by Portugal rather than Great Britain, France, or Spain.

Under the circumstances, it would hardly seem to merit a bibliography similar in length to others in this series that address much more important nations. As this series goes, it is better than average, although inevitably suffering from some of the defects imposed by the publisher's template. Thus, there are 417 entries spread over the by-now standard 25 classifications, and there is the usual complement of space-wasting cross-references. On the other hand, a larger leaven than usual of the entries is devoted to non-English (i.e., Portuguese) citations, and a large proportion of these are substantial and useful, as is the work's introduction. On the whole, however, the citations lack a certain balance: fully 55 of them are on flora or fauna, compared to only 43 on historical matters and even fewer in other fields. The work concludes with a combined author/title/subject index.—**David Henige**

South Africa

122. Davis, Geoffrey V., comp. **South Africa.** rev. ed. Santa Barbara, Calif., Clio Press/ABC-CLIO, 1994. 463p. index. (World Bibliographical Series, v.7). $99.00. ISBN 1-85109-203-X.

This bibliography is not so much a revised edition as a supplement to the original 1979 publication. The 1st edition, edited by Reuben Musiker, suffered from a major handicap in that it was largely limited to works published in South Africa. Because of South African censorship laws in effect at the time, the result was that antiapartheid publications and materials published about black political life, especially from outside of South Africa, were not included. In this revised edition, Davis has set out to do two things. As one would expect, he has added many items published from 1978 to mid-1993 to update the listings with current materials. Yet, he has also supplemented the preceding work by restoring what he terms the classics. He attempts to include a generous selection of works published before 1978 on South Africa from outside the country and also to introduce works by South African exiles. Although this edition is able to provide only a sampling of the incredibly large number of materials published about South Africa, Davis has chosen to emphasize works on the African National Congress, the process of transition to majority rule, forced removals, censorship, prison literature, and the liberation struggle in general. In addition, what makes this volume of particular use is the author's insightful annotations on virtually every title listed. The 1,252 entries are well served by three indexes and a map. Any library with an interest in South Africa will want to add this bibliography to its collection.—**Paul H. Thomas**

Swaziland

123. Nyeko, Balam, comp. **Swaziland.** rev. ed. Santa Barbara, Calif., Clio Press/ABC-CLIO, 1994. 241p. index. (World Bibliographical Series, v.24). $64.50. ISBN 1-85109-226-9.

The new revised edition of *Swaziland* is greatly expanded from the 1st edition published in 1982. According to the author, only 40 percent of the entries in the 1st edition are repeated in the 2d. The book, now containing 705 entries, has 227 more entries, of which more than half have been published since 1983. Articles in journals make up about 400 of the entries. Other sources include books, chapters in books, reports, and government documents. An additional section on theses and dissertations has been greatly expanded.

In the 28 different subject categories, the largest are history (covering 26 pages), agriculture (23 pages), and law and constitution (20 pages). The smallest categories are tourism, literature, and art and music, with two pages each. The compiler, who selected works in English, has written informative annotations. As with the other publications in this series, there is only one map. Helpful would be a more detailed map of Swaziland, a regional map, and a map of Africa placing Swaziland in context with other African nations. This work is highly recommended for large public and academic libraries.—**Karen Y. Stabler**

Togo

124. Decalo, Samuel, comp. **Togo.** Santa Barbara, Calif., Clio Press/ABC-CLIO, 1995. 194p. index. (World Bibliographical Series, v.178). $57.00. ISBN 1-85109-160-2.

This series plods on remorselessly. The present volume is number 178, and now that subnational entities (e.g., Siberia, Texas, Wales) are being treated, the end is farther from sight than ever. Togo is one of Africa's smallest countries (approximately 22,000 square miles) and one of its most unlikely—the result of colonial legerdemain at the end of the nineteenth century.

Decalo, who has also compiled *Historical Dictionary of Togo* (see ARBA 89, entry 101), presents 565 main entries, and there are perhaps as many more citations within these (many of which are more significant than the entry within which they reside). As is all too typical of the volumes in the World Bibliographical Series, the entries are classified too finely; there are 28 of these, ranging from only 2 items to 50 (in history). No less typical is the fact that there are numerous misspellings of proper names, and too many items included that deal with Togo only in the most tangential way. There are author, subject, and title indexes. The last is by far the longest, and also the least likely to find use.

A volume such as this, dealing with so insignificant a country, naturally leads consumers to wonder what the point is of a series that treats the United States and Andorra (to cite extremes) in virtually the same way bibliographically. The inevitable result is that the compilers working on the smaller entities include numerous trivia in an effort to give their works specious substance (not always successfully; the Andorra volume is only 97 pages long [see ARBA 95, entry 148]), while the work on the major countries can only be woefully superficial. One rationalization would have been to combine, for instance, the island states of the Anglophone Caribbean into a single volume rather than lard each of the 11 volumes (so far) with multiple duplications from the others.—**David Henige**

Uganda

125. Pirouet, M. Louise. **Historical Dictionary of Uganda.** Metuchen, N.J., Scarecrow, 1995. 533p. (African Historical Dictionaries, no.64). $62.50. ISBN 0-8108-2920-7.

The *Historical Dictionary of Uganda*, part of the 66-volume African Historical Dictionaries series, is a 1st edition and typical of the series in terms of form and content. Preliminary sections include a brief note regarding the Bantu languages, a glossary of Bantu terms, abbreviations and acronyms, a 32-page chronology, several surprisingly crude maps, and a 20-page introduction. These are followed by the core of the work: a 250-page dictionary arranged alphabetically covering historical, cultural, and economic aspects of the country. These are supplemented with a substantial number of useful biographical sketches. Most entries are approximately one-half page in length with some topics treated more extensively. Cross-referencing is limited and there are no bibliographical citations within the entries themselves. The core dictionary is followed by a 158-page bibliography organized into 12 major areas. The bibliography, particularly in terms of journal articles, is quite dated; the vast majority of citations tend to be 20 to 30 years old or more, and in one section (the "Modern Sector," where one would expect some level of currency), only 2 of the 112 citations are more current than 1989. Despite these limitations, the work is a handy, comprehensive guide to the country and is recommended for most libraries.—**Anthony J. Dedrick**

Zaire

126. Williams, Dawn Bastian, Robert W. Lesh, and Andrea L. Stamm. **Zaire.** Santa Barbara, Calif., Clio Press/ABC-CLIO, 1995. 268p. index. (World Bibliographical Series, v.176). $77.00. ISBN 1-85109-218-8.

Similar to other works in the World Bibliographical Series, this bibliography provides a comprehensive overview of the literature related to Zaire. The work was prepared at the Melville J. Herskovitz Library of African Studies at Northwestern University and the vast majority of items cited are located within that premier collection. The titles selected for inclusion are primarily English-language, although a substantial number of the numerous French sources are also listed.

The core bibliography of 829 entries is preceded by a brief introduction, a chronology, and a name guide. The introduction provides an overview of general social, political, historical, and economic issues related to Zaire, while the chronology ranges from ca. 2000 B.C. to 1994. The name guide provides useful coverage of the numerous name changes that occurred between 1966 and 1971, when the Congo became the Republic of Zaire. The bibliography is divided into 38 categories ranging from "Explorers' Accounts," to "Languages and Dialects," to the more typical categories such as "Politics and the Arts."

The annotated entries are from 1 sentence to more than 250 words in length, and many contain bibliographies, providing the reader with additional avenues of research. The citations include a wide range of materials, such as monographs, journal articles, and reports from such organizations as Amnesty International. The bibliography is followed by author, title, and subject indexes, and a map. The work is an excellent introduction to the principal resources related to Zaire, despite the somewhat limiting English-language focus. The known location of most of the items cited is a major plus. This bibliography is recommended for academic and larger public libraries.—**Anthony J. Dedrick**

ARCTIC REGIONS

127. **Arctic & Antarctic Regions. September 1995.** [CD-ROM]. Baltimore, Md., National Information Services Corporation, 1995. Minimum system requirements: IBM or compatible 386. CD-ROM drive. 150K RAM (512K without extended memory). Color or monochrome monitor. $795.00/yr. ISSN 1043-7479.

Intended for librarians and scientists at major research centers, the *Arctic & Antarctic Regions* CD-ROM is a compendium of nine separate databases united by a common electronic search engine. The databases are Arctic Institute of North America (ASTIS, from the University of Calgary); Cold Regions Bibliography (from the Library of Congress's Science & Technology Division); Scott Polar Research Institute (SPRI, located in England); the Centre for Cold Ocean Resources Engineering (C-CORE, Memorial University of Newfoundland); Citation (World Data Center A for Glaciology, University of Colorado); USGS Antarctic Place Names; BOREAL and BOREAL Northern Titles (both from the Canadian Circumpolar Library); and INAC (from the Department of Indian and Northern Affairs, Canada). Together, these databases offer complete bibliographical records for some 680,000 items drawn from scientific journals, monographs, symposium and conference proceedings, government reports, books, theses and dissertations, and other salient documents. International in scope, coverage extends from the year 1800 through the present. Most entries include single-paragraph, well-written annotations or abstracts.

As with so many of the CD-ROM reference titles on the market, this one is supported by custom search-and-retrieval software, in this case a program called ROMWright. Although users will need to spend a substantial amount of time mastering its complexities, the program offers powerful, sophisticated search capabilities that will reward the determined individual. Also, this particular search engine is used on all of the National Information Services Corporation (NISC) electronic titles (e.g., *Fish & Fisheries Worldwide*, *Wildlife Worldwide*, *Species Information Library* [see entries 1605-1607]), so that science librarians who master it once will be able to easily navigate other NISC products.—**G. Kim Dority**

ASIA

General Works

128. **Economic and Social Survey of Asia and the Pacific 1995.** By Economic and Social Commission for Asia and the Pacific. New York, United Nations, 1995. 155p. $35.00pa. ISBN 92-1-119675-2. ISSN 0252-5704. S/N E.95.II.F.10.

The series is in its 48th year—the present volume covers data in 1994, with retrospective data back to 1990 in most cases. (There may be some confusion in that with 1995, the volume title year is the year of publication, rather than the preceding year; hence, there is no volume "1994.") The geographical coverage is for all of Asia and the Western Pacific. Many of the tables are regional in focus, with many detailing conditions in varying numbers of specific countries. Most of the information appears in narrative format, supplemented by 35 tables and 9 graphs (both with detailed source notes).

The major sections are "World Economic Developments and the ESCAP Region"; "Macroeconomic Performance and Policies"; "International Trade and Balance of Payments"; "Reform and Liberalization of the Financial Sector"; and "Social Security." Particularly useful are sidebars that elaborate on specialized topics such as "Japan's Pension System" and "Foreign Direct Investment Inflows: Prospects for the Least Developed Countries." Although there is no index, there are a few other supplementary sections: each country's fiscal year, the standard unit and abbreviation of its currency, and the exchange rate against the U.S. dollar in June 1994; abbreviations used; and a listing of special topics dealt with in each edition.

There is nothing flashy about this series. The information is straightforward in presentation and content. The extensive use of narrative content actually makes it more accessible to nonspecialist or casual users, although there is much of value for the serious researcher as well. Reasonably priced, the *Survey* is an appropriate acquisition for most academic and research collections.—**Kenneth W. Berger**

129. **Survey of Economic and Social Developments in the ESCWA Region 1993.** By Economic and Social Commission for Western Asia. New York, United Nations, 1994. 264p. $42.00pa. ISBN 92-1-128147-4. ISSN 0255-5123. S/N 94.II.L.11.

The annual *Survey of Economic and Social Developments* for 1993 will be of interest to specialists in the Middle East—the 12 Economic and Social Commission for Western Asia (ESCWA) members are the Arab countries west of Libya—as well as those with a more general interest in world trade. Since the *Survey*'s beginning in 1980, the emphasis has been on economic matters, and the range of topics includes energy, trade, finance, agriculture, water, manufacturing, transport, and environment, although in 1985 a social component was added with sections on demographics, literacy, health, and women. There is also an extensive analysis of regional cooperation for all subjects. A comprehensive series of tables are at the heart of each presentation, and these are augmented by a series of statistical annexes.

The current volume is primarily concerned with analyzing the relatively modest economic performance for 1993, a consequence of factors including lower oil prices, the sanctions against Iraq, internal conflicts in Egypt and Yemen, and the meager state of regional cooperation. In short, there are a combination of local and global elements in a world becoming ever more integrated (the year was to end with the General Agreement on Tariffs and Trade [GATT] accords).

The *Survey* provides a nice overview of a large subject suitable for both the novice and the advanced student, and is especially strong in placing events within the experience of the last two decades. Its lack of introductory material, however, makes its highly technical subject matter more intimidating than is desirable for a general audience. The work is recommended for libraries with an emphasis on international trade; it would also be a good addition to area studies collections.—**Paul L. Holmer**

Cyprus

130. Kitromilides, Paschalis M., and Marios L. Evriviades, comps. **Cyprus.** Santa Barbara, Calif., Clio Press/ABC-CLIO, 1995. 264p. index. (World Bibliographical Series, v.28). $76.00. ISBN 1-85109-213-7.

This bibliography of Cyprus, used in conjunction with the 1st edition of this work, is a useful first source for those wishing to learn more about many facets of Cyprus. There are more than 900 entries from a wide variety of sources, with most dating from after World War II. Although not an exhaustive bibliography, the section on archaeology is fairly extensive, but contains no references to articles from journal literature. Most of the material cited are from English-language sources, although there are a number of European-language citations in the "History" section.

As with other works in this series, the bibliography begins with short essays on the history of Cyprus historiography, the history of archaeology on Cyprus, British contributions during their occupation of the island, and the creation of Cyprus research organizations. The bibliography itself begins with a short section devoted to "The Country and Its People," which includes coffee-table books, then moves to sections that will be useful to businesspeople, travelers, academics, politicians, museum-goers, and many others. One of the last sections identifies Greek Cypriot, Turkish Cypriot, and English-language daily and weekly newspapers and other periodicals.

The entries are arranged by broad subject headings, with each entry providing normal bibliographical data and most providing a short description of the work with an indication of its usefulness and quality. Although works cited within sections are not arranged alphabetically, the volume is easy to use and concludes with indexes of authors, titles, and subjects, which make the bibliography accessible to scholars as well as the general public.—**David L. White**

India

131. Derbyshire, Ian D., comp. **India.** rev. ed. Santa Barbara, Calif., Clio Press/ABC-CLIO, 1995. 356p. index. (World Bibliographical Series, v.26). $90.00. ISBN 1-85109-200-5.

This revised edition on India has 1,039 annotated entries arranged under 34 subject headings, including history; religion; languages; minorities; politics and government; defense and military affairs; foreign relations; agriculture and food; science and technology; education; sports; Indians abroad; libraries; museums and archives; and bibliographies, abstracts, and indexes. All entries are arranged alphabetically with full bibliographical information, which includes author, title, place of publication, publisher, date of publication, and number of pages. It has separate author, subject, and title indexes for the benefit of researchers.

A special feature of this well-prepared bibliography is an excellent introduction to India by the compiler. It deals with India's place in the world, including its rich historical background, society, diverse cultures, religions, languages, and postindependence political and economic developments. A chronology of Indian history from 2500 B.C. to 1992 B.C.E. and a map of modern India have also been provided in the book. The work is a selective bibliography in which only English-language works, excluding articles, have been listed.

It is one of the best bibliographies; it supersedes the earlier volume compiled by Brijen K. Gupta and Datta S. Kharbas, published in 1984 (see ARBA 86, entry 121). The bibliography is highly recommended for researchers and scholars of India, and for academic and large public libraries interested in developing collections on India.—**Ravindra Nath Sharma**

132. **Reference Encyclopedia: India 2001.** New Delhi, Indmark Publishing and Columbia, Mo., South Asia Books, 1995. 1v. (various paging). illus. maps. $125.00. ISBN 0-945-921-42-X.

India is one of the oldest continuously inhabited regions of the world and has contributed to human development for more than 5,000 years. Yet, it is difficult to find a solid reference book published in India about this country. The editors of the proposed two-volume reference set are to be commended for publishing this first volume. The book has been divided into 26 sections and includes profiles of India and its people, religion, philosophy, freedom movement, currency, life styles, archaeology, architecture, art, education, science and technology, music, dance, festivals and fairs, and sports. Many articles are signed and provide references.

This is a well-prepared encyclopedia and covers all subjects from the prehistoric days to the present. It is an excellent overview of the history, civilization, and culture of India. Each section has separate page numbers and there are more than 900 pages in this volume. Many charts, maps, and photographs have been furnished in this valuable book to help readers understand India, Indians, and their history. It is one of the best reference books India has published. This book is highly recommended for the reference collections of all academic, public, and special libraries and for all scholars interested in India.—**Ravindra Nath Sharma**

Indonesia

133. **International Directory of Indonesianists.** 2d ed. Rita Smith Kipp, comp. and ed. Mt. Vernon, Ohio, Indonesian Studies Committee, Association for Asian Studies, Kenyon College, 1994. 249p. $20.00pa. (with disk).

Indonesian studies encompass a wide range of disciplines and interests. As chair of the Indonesian Studies Committee of the Association for Asian Studies, Kipp seeks to encourage the exchange of ideas and information among Indonesianists in academe, business, government, nongovernmental organizations, media, and elsewhere by updating the 1986 edition of the *International Directory of Indonesianists*. The result is a directory of almost 900 people from across the globe who have in-depth knowledge of Indonesia. The directory is arranged alphabetically in two sections. The larger of the sections consists of those individuals who provided complete information that includes degrees received, geographical areas of expertise, language proficiencies, professional experience related to Indonesia, and performances, exhibits, projects, and publications, as well as professional address, telephone number, and e-mail address. The second section of abbreviated entries contains information for known specialists who did not submit full profiles. Indexes to the specialists' country of residence as well as geographical and discipline specialization provide useful access points. An electronic form is available, but is not as easy to use as the paper because it is saved as an ASCII file. The directory is useful for those seeking Indonesian expertise or attempting to gain an understanding of this growing area of interest.—**Carol L. Mitchell**

134. Krausse, Gerald H., and Sylvia Engelen Krausse. **Indonesia.** Santa Barbara, Calif., Clio Press/ ABC-CLIO, 1994. 407p. index. (World Bibliographical Series, v.170). $94.50. ISBN 1-85109-127-0.

Indonesia is a vast island nation with a rich recorded history and culture. Although there are specialized bibliographies to this complex nation, *Indonesia* is a much-needed general bibliographical introduction to English-language scholarship. The inclusion of bibliographies in Indonesian serves as a source for indigenous scholarship. The 1,083 fully annotated entries cover all traditional disciplines from anthropology to urban studies, as well as topics of more general interest such as cooking and travel guides. Particularly welcome is the author's inclusion of women's studies as a category. There is a useful guide to English journals; unfortunately, some have already ceased. Although extremely useful, *Indonesia* falls short of expectations. While some of the best of Indonesian scholarship has been published by centers for Southeast Asian studies, many of these center publications are absent. The authors omit important literary translations. More problematic is the omission of several excellent recent publications (after 1991), including Robert Cribb's *Historical Dictionary of Indonesia* (see ARBA 94, entry 111). Despite its shortcomings, this is an important addition to the study of Indonesia.—**Carol L. Mitchell**

Iraq

135. Bleaney, C. H., comp. **Iraq.** 2d ed. Santa Barbara, Calif., Clio Press/ABC-CLIO, 1995. 237p. index. (World Bibliographical Series, v.42). $72.00. ISBN 1-85109-229-3.

Intended primarily for English-speaking nonspecialists, this selective, annotated bibliography contains 827 entries for books, book chapters, journal articles, and periodicals. Its 34 topics address Iraqi culture, social organization, and living conditions; history, literature, and language, both ancient and modern; economics, government, foreign relations, and national security; and other social science and science topics. Similar to others in the series, the book aims to express the country's "culture, its place in the world, and the qualities and backgrounds that make it unique" (series description). Although the items are primarily in English, some French-, German-, and other European-language materials are included to augment topics with a few English publications. Coverage is still uneven and most extensive for history, including the Persian Gulf War of 1991, and related topics, such as ethnic minorities. Most of the materials date from the 1980s to 1994, but some older items are listed. The annotations vary in content and style, but are primarily scope notes, with occasional references to related materials, authors' backgrounds, and purpose.

Arranged by broad subject, with some subtopics, the bibliography has an extensive combined author, title, and subject index, and cross-references to related items within the sections. Bleaney, joint editor of *Index Islamicus* (Mansell/Cassell, 1983-), produced at the Cambridge University Library, draws on the university's rich collection of Middle East resources to create a useful one-volume bibliography that includes a good synopsis of Iraqi history. In some cases, she has uncovered relevant chapters in obscure sources (e.g., a chapter on passive solar design in Iraqi courtyard houses in the proceedings of an international conference on renewable energy). Harriet Crawford, a noted authority on the ancient history and archaeology of Iraq, advised on materials in those areas.

The book updates A. J. Abdulrahman's *Iraq* (see ARBA 86, entry 152), which covers items published in the 1960s and 1970s. It is more comprehensive than the section on Iraq in Sanford R. Silverburg's *Middle East Bibliography* (see ARBA 93, entry 162). The *Bibliographic Guide to Middle Eastern Studies 1990* (see ARBA 93, entry 159) covers books and serials published in and about the Middle East, including non-English materials, but only from 1987 to 1990; it does not index periodical articles or book chapters as Bleaney does. For academic libraries, the book is a useful guide to more recent and readily available publications on Iraq.—**Marilyn Domas White**

CANADA

136. **Canadiana in United States Repositories: A Preliminary Guide.** William A. Gosling, comp. and ed. Halifax, Nova Scotia, Dalhousie University School of Library and Information Studies, 1994. 232p. index. (Occasional Papers Series, no.57). $26.95 spiralbound. ISBN 0-7703-9766-2.

In its chapter on libraries, the Royal Commission on National Development in the Arts, Letters, and Sciences reported in 1951 that "good collections of Canadiana are rare in Canada. The three best collections in the world are now in the United States, in the Library of Congress, in the New York Public Library and in the Library of Harvard University" (Ottawa: Queen's Printer, 1951, p. 103). Although this was an exaggeration even then, Canadian researchers remain eager for details about other collections while the development of Canadian Studies programs in U.S. universities has encouraged resource sharing.

Based on a survey of 350 libraries, this directory of 136 collections is a modest first step. Entries, alphabetical by library name, identify general and special Canadiana in all formats, subject strengths, published guides, and Canadian online databases. Directory information is standard with communications, hours, policies, online access, and Canadian Studies programs. Appendixes provide geographic listings as well as depository libraries for federal documents and maps. By definition, surveys are never complete, but notable omissions include the Boston Public Library and the Newberry Library.

The index is uneven in quality. It identifies single titles noted by respondents but none of their Canadian databases such as CAN/OLE, CBCA, and QL. Even more regrettable is a failure to provide access to the outstanding microfiche collection of the Canadian Institute for Historical Microreproductions that six of the libraries reported as *Pre-1900 Canadiana*, holding either the full set or important subjects such as history and literature. Other lapses (the National Agricultural Library is not indexed under agriculture) underline the need for searchers to read through the entries as well as the index.

—Patricia Fleming

137. Weihs, Jean. **Facts About Canada, Its Provinces and Territories.** Bronx, N.Y., H. W. Wilson, 1995. 246p. maps. $35.00. ISBN 0-8242-0864-1.

A valuable addition to the H. W. Wilson Facts About . . . series, this reference volume taps a wide range of federal and provincial information sources to focus on the individual provinces and territories that make up Canada. A brief introductory chapter on the country provides a basic background that incorporates statistical information from the 1991 census, used as the basis for data throughout the book. The author notes some difficulties encountered in using statistical formats supplied by the various official agencies between the provinces and territories.

Following the prefatory material highlighting information sources cited and an abbreviation listing, the provinces and territories are arranged alphabetically. Each chapter begins with a small map (inset) and description of the province or territory's geographical location within Canada. The first page details the historical and cultural facts unique to each—name derivations, confederation date, heraldry, and holidays. Following are subsections on geography and climate, parks and historic sites, demography, government, finances, economy, history, culture and education, and vehicle use. Three final sections vary considerably between the chapters: first/biggest/best, information sources, and selective bibliography.

While thousands of facts are presented, each area emerges as a definable entity within Canada. The inclusion of the bibliographies ensures opportunity for further reading and exploration. This unique reference volume fills well the need for provincial information about the nation of Canada.

—Virginia S. Fischer

DEVELOPING COUNTRIES

138. Shrum, Wesley, Carl L. Bankston III, and D. Stephen Voss. **Science, Technology, and Society in the Third World: An Annotated Bibliography.** Metuchen, N.J., Scarecrow, 1995. 399p. index. $47.50. ISBN 0-8108-2871-5.

This annotated bibliography is a guide to selected literature on science, technology, and social change in less developed countries of Asia, Africa, Latin America, and the Pacific (it does not cover Eastern European countries). It lists 978 interdisciplinary articles and books focused on science and technology, including all of the social sciences (sociology, psychology, economics, anthropology, political science, development studies, and so on). The bibliography has some important characteristics for readers and researchers. It lists current periodical articles and books published in the English language from 1975 to the fall of 1992. This interdisciplinary literature is available at any large university library or through the interlibrary system (dissertations, reports to funding agencies, departmental report series, and works that are not written in English are excluded).

The bibliography is grouped into three main parts so that readers can easily browse entries of interest. The first part includes general materials that may be used as a quick guide to the literature; the second part deals more with economics and innovation; and the third part deals with policy and political factors. The individual entries in each chapter are numbered and indexed by author and subject. This also enhances browsing entries. Although the Eastern European countries, which have been heavily focused on since the beginning of the post-Cold War period, are not included in this bibliography, it is a valuable reference book with current and readily available literature for English-speaking readers.—**Sung Ok Kim**

EUROPE
General Works

139. Urwin, Derek W. **Historical Dictionary of European Organizations.** Metuchen, N.J., Scarecrow, 1994. 389p. (International Organizations Series, no.4). $49.50. ISBN 0-8108-2838-3.

This dictionary does more than promised by its title. In addition to a comprehensive list of hundreds of postwar European organizations, it provides brief descriptions of key conferences, treaties, and policies related to European international organizations. Moreover, there are short biographical entries for leading statespeople involved in European politics. While most entries deal with West European organizations, the author also lists and describes the key East European Communist organizations. Further, there is a chronology of events in European politics since 1941. The author also provides an extensive bibliography of English-language secondary works on European diplomacy and politics. For convenience, the bibliography is arranged by topic (e.g., the German question, disarmament, Euratom).

This is a useful resource for journalists, students, scholars, and general readers who need accessible information on post-World War II Europe. While designed for general audiences, the dictionary, and especially its bibliography, will also be of use to specialists.—**Frank L. Wilson**

Eastern Europe

140. Burger, Robert H., and Helen F. Sullivan, with Lisa Radloff. **Eastern Europe: A Bibliographic Guide to English Language Publications, 1986-1993.** Englewood, Colo., Libraries Unlimited, 1995. 254p. index. $67.50. ISBN 1-56308-047-8.

As stated in the introduction, *Eastern Europe* "is a representative selection of titles as opposed to a comprehensive listing" (p. xi) of works that brings together more than 1,000 citations, primarily monographs, published about 8 Eastern European countries: Albania, Bulgaria, Czechoslovakia, the German Democratic Republic, Hungary, Poland, Romania, and Yugoslavia. The works selected for this bibliography are only in English, published mainly in the United States and Great Britain, from 1986 to 1993. Therefore, the volume abounds in references to the 1989 wave of social uprisings that led to the collapse of one of the gloomiest periods in world history—the communist dictatorship in the Eastern European part of the world.

The bibliography is aimed at students, teachers, and researchers in Eastern European studies. This is a valuable research tool for anyone interested in any of the European countries generically known as "beyond the Iron Curtain." It is also an extremely useful information resource for researchers in the Eastern European countries who are interested in analyzing the international perception of their countries during a period of dark censorship when they could not access the information included in this volume.

The entries are arranged by country and further subdivided by subject with headings specific to each country (e.g., "Reunification" for the German Democratic Republic, "Dissident Movements" for Poland and Yugoslavia, "Velvet Revolution" for Czechoslovakia). The citations, with full bibliographical information, are followed by a descriptive annotation, and whenever possible, by information on where the book was reviewed. The author and subject indexes provide quick access to the 1,008 entries of the volume. One can appreciate the effort to make specific headings to illustrate typically Eastern European concepts, such as "private plot agriculture," "central planning," "collective bargaining," and "collectivization of agriculture," which help both Eastern Europeans and English-speaking researchers familiar with the Eastern European phenomenon retrieve quickly the entries treating these subjects.

Eastern Europe reveals a multitude of sources and is one of the most comprehensive and up-to-date works that refer to this part of the world. Any library that supports a program of research in Slavic or Eastern European studies should have this book in its collection, and research libraries in the countries covered by this volume should have it as well.—**Hermina G. B. Anghelescu**

141. Gyeszly, Suzanne D. **Eastern Europe: A Resource Guide. A Selected Bibliography on Social Sciences and Humanities.** San Bernardino, Calif., Borgo Press, 1994. 242p. index. (Borgo Reference Guides, no.6). $33.00; $23.00pa. ISBN 0-8095-0702-1; 0-8095-1702-7pa.

Recognizing the increased interest and accessibility of materials concerning Eastern Europe, this research guide presents a core bibliography of work in the humanities and social sciences. It covers Czechoslovakia (now the Czech Republic and Slovakia), Hungary, and Poland, in addition to the Eastern European region as a whole. The emphasis is decidedly on current literature, with few entries dating before 1989. Pre-1989 entries are, for the most part, those published outside Eastern Europe and critical of political regimes. The decidedly revisionist tenor of this book leads to the suspicion that perhaps seminal works have failed altogether.

Foreign-language titles are translated into English for the benefit of researchers unfamiliar with the original languages. Books published in English and readily available in North America are useful starting points for novice scholars. The range of specialized titles within fields such as history is particularly encouraging for future editions of this research guide. Most of the entries have been verified by the author at the National Szechenyi Library of Hungary in Budapest, as well as the Library of Congress in Washington, D.C. Whereas this book is admittedly a research guide to core materials, rather than a mere fulsome bibliography, it remains a useful and promising contribution to scholarship.—**Mary Hemmings**

Ireland

142. Daly, K. S. **Ireland: An Encyclopedia for the Bewildered.** Berkeley, Calif., Ten Speed Press, 1995. 170p. illus. $7.95pa. ISBN 0-89815-749-8.

Ireland: An Encyclopedia for the Bewildered is a collection of items ostensibly about Ireland and things Irish. As such, the stated aim of the volume, according to the press release accompanying the encyclopedia, is to avoid the mistakes of other books and cartoons "littered with inaccuracies." Entries are listed alphabetically, beginning with *Abattoir* and ending with *Zozimus*. Of interest to readers will be items such as *Dáli Eireann* (Irish for "House of Parliament"), *GAA* ("Gaelic Athletic Association"), and *Gobshite* (an "idiot" or "fool"). The names and descriptions of some of Ireland's most notable literary and political figures are also provided.

Any dictionary or encyclopedia on a specific topic or subject is, by definition, a listing of terms, important words, and phrases pertaining to that topic—in this case, a clearly identifiable and delimited cultural and geographical entity known as Ireland. However, the volume is surely compiled with tongue in cheek and can only be read in this light. Otherwise, it is hard to imagine how a reader would be anything but bewildered by some of the entries in this "encyclopedia for the bewildered." Entries are frequently non sequitur in nature, and at least one entry might be considered insulting to the people of the town Navan, which is described in one line as "a backwards town in Co. Meath."—**Arthur Gribben**

Italy

143. Sponza, Lucio, and Diego Zancani, comps. **Italy.** Santa Barbara, Calif., Clio Press/ABC-CLIO, 1995. 412p. index. (World Bibliographical Series, v.30). $100.00. ISBN 0-903450-44-5.

This is a useful and comprehensive bibliography on literature dealing with Italy. It focuses on English-language publications, although there are some Italian titles in the section on bibliographies and in sections where there are few English-language listings. The volume includes not only books dealing exclusively with Italy but also collected volumes with chapters on Italy. It covers titles published through 1993. Each entry provides full bibliographical information and a helpful abstract of approximately 125 words. The abstracts summarize the book's contents and the author's general arguments.

The information is easily accessible. The main entries are arranged by general topic (history, politics, women, and the like). There are indexes by author's name, title, and subject matter. These indexes are thorough, including, for example, the names of authors of relevant chapters that are found in the abstracts. There is also a useful chronology of Italian history from prehistoric times to 1995. This volume is highly recommended for research libraries and general libraries with special interest in Italy.—**Frank L. Wilson**

Poland

144. Sanford, George, and Adriana Gozdecka-Sanford. **Historical Dictionary of Poland.** Metuchen, N.J., Scarecrow, 1994. 339p. (European Historical Dictionaries, no.3). $47.50. ISBN 0-8108-2818-9.

This is not a source for the serious scholar or student of Polish history, but for all others it is an excellent reference book that should be in any library collection providing some coverage of Poland. A 24-page introduction supplies an overview of the geography, history, and economy of Poland. This is followed by almost 400 alphabetical entries of important persons, places, events, and institutions. These entries range in size from two sentences on Biskupin, an important archaeological site, to seven pages on Roman Catholicism. The main entries are supplemented by a comprehensive chronology and a list of rulers and leaders of Poland. There is also a useful list of acronyms from the Communist and post-Communist eras, and an extensive bibliography that directs readers to added sources of information.

Polish history and politics are covered from the earliest time to the present, with an emphasis on the last 75 years. There is also coverage of the economy, society, culture, and religion. One can at times question the authors concerning some entries. For instance, there is none for Gniezno, an important site of the early Polish nation. The entries for Berman, Bierut, and Minc, the Stalinist Troika that ruled Poland until 1956, are much too brief. Yet as a whole, this is a concise and useful work and a valuable addition to the literature on Poland. The authors are both leading authorities who have published other books on Polish topics.—**George S. Bobinski**

Russia and the Successor States

145. **Longman Biographical Directory of Decision-Makers in Russia and the Successor States.** Martin McCauley, ed. Harlow, England, Longman; distr., Detroit, Gale, 1993. 726p. maps. index. $152.00. ISBN 0-582-20999-4.

Published in Great Britain and distributed by Gale, this biographical directory provides brief biographical sketches on decision-makers in Russia and the successor states, listing some 600-700 individuals. The information is recent as of 1992 (in some cases the first half of 1993), with an emphasis on Russia and, to some extent, Ukraine. Contrary to the statement in the preface, Belarus is not well worked (25 listings), and neither are some other countries: Armenia (2 listings), Estonia (3 listings), Lithuania (3 listings), and Kyrgyztan (6 listings). The introduction is dated July 1993, and 50 percent of the material is now somewhat obsolete. For example, there are only two entries for Chechnya (Husayn Akhmadov and Dzhokhar Dudaev) without any comment about Dudaev's role in the conflict with Russia (before the current war with Russia, Chechnya proclaimed its independence in 1991), and information on Ukraine's political leaders is also in many cases obsolete (for example: Boris Morozov, Vasyl Durdynets, and many others).

Nevertheless, the historical information provided for many individuals is interesting, describing important steps in their careers, political affiliations, imprisonment history (for former dissidents), educational background, and so on. This is an adequate dictionary and hopefully subsequent editions or supplements can be published in electronic form.—**Bohdan S. Wynar**

146. **The Military Encyclopedia of Russia and Eurasia. Volume 5: Adzhariia (Ship) - Aerial Blockade (Vozdushnaia Blokada), Concept of.** David R. Jones, ed. Gulf Breeze, Fla., Academic International Press, 1994. 242p. illus. maps. $37.00. ISBN 0-87569-028-9.

The main problem with Jones's work is that the editor had to choose between an encyclopedic format and a historical narrative. In the monumental task of collecting data from the former Soviet Union on military subjects, perhaps the editor has lost sight of what the purpose of an encyclopedia is. Some entries

(The Defense of the Adzhim-Ushkai Quarries, 1942 and Aerial Armament) are practically monographs in themselves. This does not lend the work to an encyclopedic presentation. In an endeavor to cover the vast amount of material coming out of the former Soviet Union, one cannot make out every defender of the quarries as a hero of the Soviet Union, nor describe every manner of aerial armament carried on every Soviet/Russian aircraft. The passionate description of the defense of the Adzhim-Ushkai Quarries is commendable, but deserves monographic presentation. A much shorter presentation would serve the encyclopedic purpose here, and without the historiographical debate.

The work needs serious editing and a narrower focus. The editor has tried to bring the work within the interest of both specialist and history buff. However, an encyclopedic presentation must be clear, concise, and factual, and direct the reader to other sources. Unfortunately, this volume tries to be factual and narrative, with a far too extensive bibliography in English and transliterated Russian. No doubt future volumes will be crammed with obscure and previously unresearched material; but again, the editor must choose between an encyclopedic presentation and a narrative one. With the editor unable to decide which presentation to follow, it is difficult for a reviewer to recommend this work to a readership. This work will satisfy neither Soviet/Russian specialist nor enthusiast.—**Norman L. Kincaide**

147. Poe, Marshall. **Foreign Descriptions of Muscovy: An Analytic Bibliography of Primary and Secondary Sources.** Columbus, Ohio, Slavica, 1995. 230p. index. $27.95. ISBN 0-89357-262-4.

Poe's analytical bibliography of Muscovy was compiled in order to provide a guide to the primary and secondary literature relating to foreign descriptions of Muscovy and more particularly, to correct errors and improve on *Kritisch-Literarische Ubersicht der Reisenden in Russland bis 1700*, which was published in 1846. The book is more than what it purports to be. The bibliography contains not only a chronological list of 638 foreign descriptions of Muscovy dating between 1450 and 1700, but large sections of other bibliographical material with works in many European languages as well.

There is a section of secondary studies on the conceptual, political, economic, and literary contexts of Western attempts to understand Muscovy. This section contains many works not specifically concerned with Muscovy but are focused on the general context of the period from 1450 to 1700. Another section lists monographs, compendiums, narratives, and political/scientific treatises dealing with Muscovy, including subsections such as "Muscovy in Cosmographies" and "Muscovy in Narrative Sources." Consequently, the bibliography ranges wider than just fifteenth- to eighteenth-century Muscovy.

The final section, which contains the foreign descriptions of Muscovy, provides useful information on the genre, other early editions, identified borrowings from other sources, location of original publication, modern translations, and secondary studies concerning the author and work cited. Useful appendixes cross-reference works from section 4 with *Kritisch-Literarische Ubersicht* and other works. Although each section is introduced with a short essay, this bibliography is for experts on the study of Muscovy in the fifteenth to eighteenth centuries, and therefore belongs in specialized libraries.—**David L. White**

Scotland

148. **Collins Encyclopaedia of Scotland.** John Keay and Julia Keay, eds. New York, HarperCollins, 1994. 1046p. illus. maps. index. $60.00. ISBN 0-00-255082-2.

A comprehensive national bibliography has eluded Scotland despite a tradition of scholarship that has been responsible for several outstanding reference works during its history, such as the *Encyclopaedia Britannica* and the *Dictionary of National Biography*. Edited by writers and broadcasters John and Julia Keay, the writing style is light and witty. Above all, it is an inviting encyclopedia, designed more for popular tastes than for serious research.

This encyclopedia arranges landmarks and institutions under individual cities, which proves troublesome for those not familiar with Scottish geography. For example, the entry for "Royal College of Physicians" cross-references the reader to "Edinburgh: Physicians Hall." However, its rival institution, located in the same city, merits a separate entry under "Royal College of Surgeons." This entry helpfully directs the reader to consider a related entry for "University of Edinburgh." There is no entry for the

University, nor is there a cross-reference to the correct entry. Searching under the city of Edinburgh also yields nothing. Persistence and chance finally uncovered a semicolumn under the heading "Edinburgh University."

Not without scholarly merit, the encyclopedia offers some well-written entries, such as the one for Scottish law. Populist balance, however, appears to demand an even longer and more detailed entry for "football." Although not as ambitious or as thorough as other national encyclopedias, this reference work makes up for those faults by its affordability and charming enthusiasm.—**Mary Hemmings**

Spain

149. Shields, Graham J., comp. **Spain.** 2d ed. Santa Barbara, Calif., Clio Press/ABC-CLIO, 1994. 448p. index. (World Bibliographical Series, v.60). $97.00. ISBN 1-85109-220-X.

This volume in the ever-increasing series is a revision of the 1985 edition (see ARBA 87, entry 133), necessitated by immense changes that have occurred in Spanish society, and the extensive new literature that describes them. The new edition follows the attractive and usable format of the other 172 titles in the series, and continues to fulfill its stated goal: "To provide English readers with an interpretation of the country's culture and the qualities that make it unique." This is achieved by means of 1,135 annotated bibliographical entries (increased from 982 in the previous edition) of published material concerning all aspects of Spanish life, arranged under 43 main subject headings.

The single index of the earlier book has been subdivided into author/title/subject indexes. An impressive feature of the index is its inclusion of subsidiary references in the annotations. The annotations are brief, well-written descriptions, and many include cross-references to related items in the volume, plus secondary references to items not included, apparently due to space limitations. Most entries refer to publications that have come out since the 1985 edition; the few duplications are apparently those that have not been improved upon or made obsolete by recent writings. This bibliographical resource is highly recommended.—**Larry Lobel**

Sweden

150. Scobbie, Irene. **Historical Dictionary of Sweden.** Metuchen, N.J., Scarecrow, 1995. 314p. (European Historical Dictionaries, no.7). $42.50. ISBN 0-8108-2922-3.

The *Historical Dictionary of Sweden* is the seventh publication in the series of European Historical Dictionaries published by Scarecrow. All of the dictionaries in this series follow a similar format and are intended for a general audience. Other titles to date include *Portugal, Turkey, Poland, Germany, Greece,* and *Cyprus* (see entries 144, 546). The dictionary contains a chronology of significant events in Sweden from 12,000 B.C. to April 1994, a historical overview of Sweden, a bibliography of selected works on Sweden published in English, and two appendixes listing Swedish rulers and prime ministers. The bulk of the dictionary is composed of more than 240 entries. The majority of these entries cover both general and specific topics such as emigration, music, neutrality policy, Uppsala, and visual arts. A smaller proportion of entries are biographical sketches of individuals who have made significant contributions to Sweden from the 1300s to the present day. The careers of these individuals are, with the notable exception of Gunnar Myrdal, not well known outside of Sweden. They include, for example, Ivar Kreuger, Christopher Polhem, Ingvar Carlsson, Eric XIV, and Tage Erlander. This historical dictionary as well as others in the series are recommended for most academic libraries. They are a quick reference tool to those who need some general information or an overview about a specific topic or personality.—**Jane Jurgens**

LATIN AMERICA
General Works

151. **Economic Panorama of Latin America 1995.** By Economic Commission for Latin America and the Caribbean. New York, United Nations, 1995. 83p. $12.00pa. ISBN 92-1-121201-4. ISSN 0259-241X. S/N E.95.II.G.15.

This volume reviews the economic conditions of nine Latin American countries: Argentina, Brazil, Chile, Colombia, Ecuador, Mexico, Peru, Uruguay, and Venezuela. The panorama is a description of three main elements for each country, namely the modest economic growth rates, the control over inflation, and the large and growing current account deficits.

This small statistical volume reports that modest growth rates make it difficult for these countries to generate enough jobs to lower unemployment and underemployment significantly. Each country has a series of statistical charts showing the quarterly evolution of the main economic indicators: gross domestic product crop farming production, industrial activity, unemployment rate, the trade balance, price indexes, index of real wages and industry, national treasury income and expenditure, inner interest rates, and the exchange rates. These specific economic guidelines allow the researcher to place individual companies and industries into the overall economic picture of the nine countries and Latin America strategically.

This is a handy guide for researchers wanting quick information in the 10 categories of each of these countries. This statistical guide, however, is a small supplement to *Cracking Latin America* (see ARBA 95, entry 288) and *Latin American Markets: A Guide to Company and Industry Information Sources* (see ARBA 95, entry 289).—**Gerald D. Moran**

152. Leonard, Thomas M. **A Guide to Central American Collections in the United States.** Westport, Conn., Greenwood Press, 1994. 186p. index. (Reference Guides to Archival and Manuscript Sources in World History, no.3). $65.00. ISBN 0-313-28689-2.

This guide to both large and small archival and manuscript collections in the United States on the six Central American nations—Costa Rica, El Salvador, Guatemala, Honduras, Nicaragua, and Panama—locates, identifies, and describes 768 collections in the possession of more than 200 institutions in 47 states and the District of Columbia. The work is arranged alphabetically by state, and then in apparently random order by holding institution. Information about each collection varies according to its nature, but may include identification of the individual for whom it is named, a general description, descriptions of record groups, particularly significant items, restrictions on use, and so forth. There is a name/subject index, but nonname subjects are very broad, such as "Guatemala, Historical Documents." This guide is recommended for academic and large public libraries with clientele interested in research resources for the countries of Central America.—**Ann Hartness**

153. **Social Panorama of Latin America.** 1994 ed. By Economic Commission for Latin America and the Caribbean. New York, United Nations, 1994. 206p. $25.00pa. S/N E.94.II.G.95.

This special reference source published by the Economic Commission for Latin America and the Caribbean is based on household surveys conducted in 13 Latin American countries. This edition emphasizes core issues concerning children and the family. Selective coverage is provided for Argentina, Bolivia, Brazil, Chile, Colombia, Costa Rica, Guatemala, Honduras, Mexico, Panama, Paraguay, Uruguay, and Venezuela.

Trends are analyzed for the period 1980-1992 in chapters on poverty, employment, income distribution, social expenditure, the family and children, education, and the social agenda. The last chapter looks at poverty; education; health; social security; and emerging issues such as rural conflicts, clashes of values, concerns about the environment, corruption, the military, and urban crime in terms of the region's social agenda. These 7 chapters are followed by 52 tables that provide background data for selected countries on the above topics.

Trends noted include a reduction in poverty indexes in Argentina, Bolivia, Chile, Mexico, Uruguay, and Venezuela; high employment rates for those who have 6 to 12 years of schooling, and an increase in unequal income distribution since 1980 in many countries. One interesting finding is that it is now necessary to have completed secondary school to have a good chance of earning an income above the poverty line. Used in conjunction with other Latin American statistical series, this special publication provides valuable information on a variety of social questions concerning Latin America for libraries with special interests in that area.—**Brian E. Coutts**

154. **Statistical Yearbook for Latin America and the Caribbean. Anuario Estadistico de America Latina y el Caribe.** 1994 ed. By Economic Commission for Latin America and the Caribbean. New York, United Nations, 1995. 782p. $70.00pa. ISBN 92-1-021034-4. ISSN 1014-0697. S/N E/S.95.II.G.1.

There are two standard compilations of Latin American statistics: the *Statistical Abstract of Latin America*, published annually by the University of California at Los Angeles' Latin American Center, and the bilingual *Statistical Yearbook for Latin America and the Caribbean*, published by the United Nations. Almost twice as long and issued in two volumes, the *Statistical Abstract* provides broader coverage of topics than does the *Yearbook*. However, its primary focus is on the traditional 20 "Latin" American countries. Since there are 33 members of the Economic Commission for Latin America and the Caribbean (ECLAC), the *Yearbook* provides some coverage for all of them. However, because of incomplete reporting from some Caribbean countries, most tables provide data for 25 countries. The 1994 *Yearbook*, published in February 1995, updates the main statistical series to December 1994.

Part 1 of the yearbook describes socioeconomic indicators such as growth rates, ratios of coefficients, and so forth, which give background information for the region. Part 2 provides historical series for selected topics to enable comparisons between countries. Balance of payments and national accounts are treated individually on a country-by-country basis. The ECLAC has analyzed such economic indicators as population, employment, poverty, nutrition, education, and housing since 1973. Among the more interesting tables are population projections for 33 countries for the period 1995-2025 and the annual consumer price indexes.

The *Yearbook* still lacks an index, making it time-consuming to find particular information quickly. The *Statistical Abstract* provides unique coverage for such topics as politics, religion and the military, illegal industry, and special subjects (e.g., U.S. foreign aid to Central America).

Large libraries and those with special interests in Latin America will want to acquire both statistical annuals. Libraries with limited reference budgets can answer many standard questions from the *Yearbook*. At $65, it costs $200 less than volume 31 of the *Statistical Abstract*.—**Brian E. Coutts**

155. Tomaselli-Moschovitis, Valerie. **Latin America on File.** New York, Facts on File, 1995. 1v. (various paging). maps. index. $155.00 looseleaf w/binder. ISBN 0-8160-3225-4.

Latin America on File, a Facts on File publication, is a compilation of black-and-white maps, graphs, and charts. The scope of the large looseleaf volume is on human and physical geography of Mexico, Central America, the Caribbean, and South America. The text is divided into 3 major parts. The 1st is composed of maps, graphs, and charts covering 24 major countries. Part 2 covers the minor countries and dependencies, which include French Guiana and the islands of the Caribbean, and the 3d part covers timely issues concerning those regions. Included for each country is a fact sheet that lists important data, such as climate, terrain, population figures, language(s) spoken, and type of government. As stated in the introductory notes, this volume should be used in conjunction with the other companion volumes.

On close evaluation, the information provided in this reference source is basic and therefore limited in scope. Furthermore, the data are readily available in other, more comprehensive sources. A further comment that needs to be made is that the information contained here is simply reformatted from other sources that are widely available in almost all academic libraries; many are now accessible on the Internet. This source is suitable for secondary education school libraries and large public libraries.—**Dario J. Villa**

MIDDLE EAST
General Works

156. **Arab Women in ESCWA Member States: Statistics, Indicators, and Trends.** By Economic and Social Commission for Western Asia. New York, United Nations, 1994. 301p. $42.00pa. ISBN 92-1-128148-2. S/N 95-II-L1.

157. **External Trade Bulletin of the ESCWA Region.** 7th ed. By Economic and Social Commission for Western Asia. New York, United Nations, 1994. 302p. $60.00pa. ISBN 92-1-128146-6. ISSN 0258-4948. S/N 94-II-l.10.

158. **National Accounts Studies of the ESCWA Region.** By Economic and Social Commission for Western Asia. New York, United Nations, 1994. 220p. (Bulletin no.14). $56.00pa. ISBN 92-1-128145-8. ISSN 1010-964X. S/N 94-II-L.9.

These are important and useful volumes of data on the countries represented by the Economic and Social Commission for Western Asia, membership in which seems somewhat arbitrary or politically oriented. For example, Egypt is included, although not in Asia; Israel is not, although it is located there. Other North African countries are not included, even though they have much affinity with the Western Asian Arab countries that are members of the Arab League. Nevertheless, these collections of data are useful as standardized measures of trade, national accounts, and, for the first time, conditions of women.

The economic data are presented in current and constant prices. The volumes on trade and national accounts are continuations of the series, and are, therefore, of great use to researchers. The volume on women was issued in preparation for the Conference on Women held in Beijing in September 1995. One hopes the promise to make it a continuing series will be possible to achieve. It is also hoped that some of the many gaps in the data will be filled in future editions. For instance, most data end in 1990, although even rough estimates for more recent years would be helpful. Another gap is on employment and unemployment: The data specify active and inactive percentages of the labor force by gender, but there are no data on unemployment nor on the distribution of the active labor force by occupation, except for those engaged in agriculture.

An interesting feature of the volume on women is the information on participation by women in public affairs, and the first time they had the right to vote and to run for election to public office. A more curious feature is the detailed entry on crime by gender (Table 25). This table can be highly misleading without explanation of the classification system. What does it mean that 52 percent of the crimes "against parental and maternal rights and family neglect" in Iraq in 1985 were committed by females and only 3.37 percent in Syria? Even so, the publication of this volume should be a tribute to women in the Arab world and a recognition of the place they occupy in Arab society and economy.—**Elias H. Tuma**

159. **Civilizations of the Ancient Near East.** Jack M. Sasson and others, eds. New York, Scribner's/Simon & Schuster, 1995. 4v. illus. maps. index. $449.00/set. ISBN 0-684-19279-9.

Joining its companion set, *Civilization of the Ancient Mediterranean: Greece and Rome* (see ARBA 89, entry 488), this handsome work lays out "the broad and varied scholarship on the ancient Near East, as carried out, internationally, at the close of the twentieth century" (p. xxxi). Neither an encyclopedia nor a specialized dictionary, *Civilizations* uses a thematic/topical structure in presenting multiple perspectives on this vast field and in incorporating new approaches and theories to the study of the past.

The beginning time period fluctuates, due in part to an ever-expanding knowledge about early peoples and their culture. For some articles, however, the time frame dates from around the third millennium B.C.E. when writing was invented and extends to the year 330 B.C.E. when Alexander the Great conquered the Persian Empire. Geographically, as beautifully mapped out on its end pages, the work surveys Egypt, Syro-Palestine, Mesopotamia and Anatolia, the Arabian Peninsula, Northeast Africa, and the Aegean and Anatolian cultures.

The 189 essays by a team of distinguished international scholars cover 11 subject areas that range from studies on the environment and population to social institutions. Introductory articles outline views of the ancient Near East in Western thought, and concluding essays present retrospective views. To accommodate these wide geographical areas and time spans, some essays treat a subject homogeneously and are non-place-specific. Other subjects are developed in a culture-by-culture sequence. Thus, while "The Agricultural Cycle, Farming, and Water Management in the Ancient Near East" is not limited to a particular physical area, the extensive section on social institutions has separate articles on private life in ancient Egypt and ancient Mesopotamia, as well as among the Hittites and in ancient Israel.

Essays conclude with lengthy critical bibliographies and cross-references to related articles. Interspersed throughout the text are graphs, line drawings, charts, and black-and-white photographs. Boxed inserts contain selections translated from ancient texts. A detailed, well-organized index in volume 4 forms an integral part of the work, allowing the user to pull together information on a subject treated in different articles.

While the depth and breadth of scholarship is immense, the language is straightforward and easily accessible not only to the specialist but also to the educated layperson as well. It is certain to pique the curiosity of the nonspecialist. *Civilizations* ranks as a major achievement. It deserves a place in research and academic libraries and in large public libraries serving a diverse population.—**Bernice Bergup**

160. **The Middle East and North Africa 1995.** 41st ed. London, Europa; distr., Detroit, Gale, 1994. 1022p. maps. $310.00. ISBN 0-946653-99-2. ISSN 0076-8502.

This is an outstanding reference work on the region and is commendably well organized and easy to use. The primary focus is on current social, economic, and political issues. The publication is organized into three sections: general survey, regional organizations, and country surveys.

The general survey has 14 topics ranging from broad subjects such as religions of the area to fairly specific topics. This section also contains a select bibliography.

The regional organizations section is small but usefully arranged. It includes major international organizations that are concerned with the region, such as the International Monetary Fund and UNESCO. Typical directory information such as addresses, telephone numbers, organization, and purpose is given.

The third section, country surveys, is the work's largest. Each of the 21 countries is described in terms of physical and social geography, history, and economics. A statistical survey and directory are included for each country. The data are primarily economic in nature, and the directories provide an overview of such topics as government structure, education, communications (press, television, and radio), and finance. This is an excellent and readable regional survey that is appropriate for both public and academic libraries.—**Anthony J. Dedrick**

161. **Who's Who in the Arab World 1995-1996.** 12th ed. Gabriel M. Bustros, ed. Beirut, Lebanon, Publitec Publications; distr., Detroit, Gale, 1994. 982p. index. $310.00. ISBN 2-903188-11-4. ISSN 0083-9752.

This hefty volume deserves a more descriptive title such as "Who's Who and What's What in the Arab World." In its three parts it covers biographies, profiles of countries, a brief historical survey, and essays and documents relating to specific topics, such as the Suez Canal, the Gulf Cooperation Council, and the Palestinian issue. There is a detailed index and a selected bibliography. The book is printed on good paper and looks elegant enough to (almost) justify its relatively high price. Having remained in publication since 1966, it no doubt serves a useful function. The work would, however, be much more useful as a "dictionary" of the Arab world if edited more carefully. Three kinds of problems should and can be removed: inadequate updating, imbalance in selection, and uncontrolled space and content of biographies. This reviewer's position and address are 12 years out of date. The profiles of Algeria, Iraq, and Palestine are other examples. The imbalance of coverage is shown by the 10-page index of individual biographies of Saudi Arabians, compared with less than 7 pages for Egyptians and $2\frac{1}{2}$ pages for Syrians. Prominent people such as Galal Amin, Heba Handoussa, Haseeb Sabbagh, and Antoine Zahlan are missing. The third problem relates to space and content of biographies. One biography fills four-and-a-half pages, most of which is useless detail. To admit that no editing or control of space for biographies was exercised is not an adequate explanation. More careful editing would minimize these defects, enhance the volume, and make it more useful.—**Elias H. Tuma**

Egypt

162. Goldschmidt, Arthur, Jr. **Historical Dictionary of Egypt.** Metuchen, N.J., Scarecrow, 1994. 369p. (African Historical Dictionaries, no.67). $42.50. ISBN 0-8108-2949-5.

This work extends the time period covered by an earlier series' volume on Egypt by Joan King (see ARBA 86, entry 149). Alphabetically arranged, clearly written entries cover individuals, places, events, organizations, and political, cultural, and religious issues from 1760-1994. The entries vary in length from a paragraph for such subjects as the 1992 earthquake, Omar Sharif, and the Arab League, to three pages for key leaders, including Gamal Abdel Nasser and Anwar al-Sadat.

Dictionary entries are complemented by an extensive introduction and a chronology outlining the political, social, and cultural development of Egypt beginning in 3100 B.C.E. The volume also includes a selective bibliography categorized by historical period and major subject categories. While this small volume cannot provide comprehensive coverage of a country whose history spans thousands of years, it is a strong basic reference source.—**Ahmad Gamaluddin**

Israel

163. Bleaney, C. H., comp. **Israel and the West Bank and Gaza Strip.** 2d ed. Santa Barbara, Calif., Clio Press/ABC-CLIO, 1994. 367p. index. (World Bibliographical Series, v.58). $86.50. ISBN 1-85109-176-9.

This new edition includes the changes that have taken place in Israel, the West Bank, and the Gaza Strip since the last edition appeared in 1985 (see ARBA 87, entry 148). English-language books (scholarly, semipopular, journalistic) are researched in an attempt to promote information on the history and culture of the area, and its modern economic, educational, political, religious, and social character. The strength of this annotated bibliography lies in the same area where its weaknesses become apparent: It does not aim to cover all aspects and expressions of life in the Holy Land. The text is merely expository and positive, but what makes this land between sea and desert unique is not clearly drawn or documented. For example, little is said on Eretz Israel as the cradle of Judaism and Christianity. Furthermore, for the informed reader, Bleaney treats disputed issues between Israelis and Palestinians gingerly, even superficially. Nonetheless, the volume is useful for a general audience. [R: Choice, Jan 95, p. 743]—**Zev Garber**

164. **New Encyclopedia of Zionism and Israel.** Geoffrey Wigoder, ed. New York, Herzl Press and Cranbury, N.J., Associated University Presses, 1994. 2v. illus. $185.00/set. ISBN 0-8386-3433-8.

Although this is titled the *New Encyclopedia of Zionism and Israel*, users will find it much the same as the premier volume of 1971 (see ARBA 72, entry 268), with most of the strengths and weaknesses of the original. As before, it is an invaluable guide to the leaders of modern Zionism. Here, one will find its major and minor players, enumerated and described, as well as information on the various kibbutzim, moshavim, towns, camps, organizations, political parties, factions, and other products of the movement. Interposed among these, the reader will also discover more general subject articles of varying length and quality. Many of these are on aspects of Israel and are among the least remarkable components, most being more extensively treated elsewhere, although a few, such as that on Israeli art, are models of their genre. Some are out-of-date, while others have been updated through the 1990s.

On the whole, the more current examples exhibit a more dispassionate view of contentious matters, although for really delicate questions, there is a tendency to resort to silence. There are only 11 lines on the *Shin Bet* (Secret Police), for instance, although the editors of a U.S. imprint are presumably beyond its jurisdiction. This is not the only charge that can be laid to the editors. Much of the weakness of this reference is the result of basic decisions of organization. There is no index, for instance, and the cross-references are inadequate. How is the novice to know that "immigration to Israel" and *aliya* are synonymous? Perhaps most serious, there are no bibliographies for individual entries, certainly one of the major purposes of a good encyclopedia. There is a general bibliography at the end, but this will be of little value to those with narrow questions. Librarians will need to carefully assess the needs of their users before purchasing this useful but limited source. [R: RBB, 15 Feb 95, p. 1111]—**Paul L. Holmer**

Lebanon

165. **Who's Who in Lebanon 1995-1996.** 13th ed. Gabriel M. Bustros, ed. Beirut, Lebanon, Publitec Publications; distr., Detroit, Gale, 1994. 496p. $155.00. ISBN 2-903188-12-2. ISSN 0083-9612.

This volume includes 270 pages of detailed biographical entries and about an equal number of broad survey pages covering history, geography, government, economy, education, international organizations, and cultural agencies. Individuals profiled appear to have widely varied professional backgrounds ranging from surgeons to former diplomats. Entries describe personal and professional background data and a current address and telephone number. The survey section is well organized and provides extensive background information on Lebanon, as well as useful directory listings for consulates, companies, libraries, museums, and the media. This book will be helpful to individuals with a need for a concise overview of Lebanon, or a need to make contact with agencies or well-known leaders in Lebanon.

—**Ahmad Gamaluddin**

Oman

166. Clements, Frank A., comp. **Oman.** rev. ed. Santa Barbara, Calif., Clio Press/ABC-CLIO, 1994. 346p. index. (World Bibliographical Series, v.29). $79.00. ISBN 1-85109-197-1.

As with other books in this series, the bibliography of Oman is a useful first source for material. The book is a revised and expanded edition, and should be used with the first. The more than 1,000 entries are from scholarly monographs and articles, government reports, and popular material, with most entries dating from the mid-1970s, although earlier works missed in the first edition have been picked up here. The bibliography contains only English-language material, although there are some references to works in other languages that include an English summary; there is also material from the non-Western world (e.g., India and Oman) produced in English.

The book begins with general information about Oman's past and present and contains an interesting and useful section identifying treaties concluded between the Sultanate and other powers throughout Oman's existence. Other useful sections identify general works on the Middle East that include material on Oman; a section on exploration and travel in Oman; one on Oman's flora and fauna containing numerous entries on the Arabian oryx; a historical section that, among numerous other entries, identifies works on the Imamate question, the Buraimi Oasis dispute, and the Dhofar War; several political, economic, and cultural categories; and a section on the mass media that lists journals, newspapers, and newsletters focusing on Oman.

Arrangement of the entries is by broad subject heading with titles in each subject listed alphabetically by author or title. Each entry is annotated with the best works in each category identified and some titles cross-referenced. The volume concludes with indexes of authors, titles, and subjects.—**David L. White**

OCEANIA

167. **The Far East and Australasia 1995.** 26th ed. London, Europa; distr., Detroit, Gale, 1994. 1142p. $360.00. ISBN 1-85743-000-X. ISSN 0071-3791.

There is no more accurate and up-to-date compendium of information about the Pacific Basin than this yearly survey. The book represents a vast, almost overwhelming undertaking, involving contributions from more than 50 experts on the geography, history, and economy of the area.

The survey covers essentially the Western Pacific Basin, but extends to include southern Asia and the Indian Ocean, ending with Pakistan. The Eastern Pacific countries are not included, although the editors do envision Chile as a growing force in the area. They see the coming century as the Pacific century—the area of chief economic power.

The book is arranged into three main parts. Part 1, a general survey section, contains a series of important essays on topics such as population growth in the area and global warming and its implications for the Pacific countries. Part 2, the main section, contains separate chapters on each country and a chapter on the Pacific Islands generally (including Hawaii). The format is the same for each country: detailed surveys of the country's geography, history, and economy, followed by a statistical survey, then a directory. The directory contains material on, for instance, the country's constitution, government, judicial system, religion, communications media, transport, tourism, and education. Finally, there is a bibliography that is admirably up-to-date. Part 3 contains regional information on organizations and research institutes. For those who need accurate and accessible information on this important area, the work is an indispensable sourcebook.—**John B. Beston**

168. Wuerch, William L., and Dirk Anthony Ballendorf. **Historical Dictionary of Guam and Micronesia.** Metuchen, N.J., Scarecrow, 1994. 172p. maps. (Oceanian Historical Dictionaries, no.3). $29.50. ISBN 0-8108-2858-8.

Wuerch and Ballendorf's *Historical Dictionary of Guam and Micronesia* is the third in a series of reference volumes, in dictionary form, that focus on Oceania. Within the vast Micronesian area of the western Pacific Ocean are some 2,106 typically small islands and atolls. Many of these are populated by peoples of predominantly Micronesian ethnicity. Guam, the most populous and the largest of the Micronesian islands, is an unincorporated territory of the United States.

The rather complex modern political evolution of the various Micronesian political entities is touched on by the authors in their introduction, in the historical chronology, and in certain entries in the body of the work. Entries in this compact volume are informative and offer insights on a variety of aspects of Micronesian life and culture. A 35-page selected bibliography of English-language references on the history, culture, and people of Micronesia concludes the volume. Among the small number of other substantial reference sources on Micronesia are two book-length bibliographies: *Micronesia, 1944-1974: A Bibliography of Anthropological and Related Source Materials* by Mac Marshall and James D. Nason (see ARBA 77, entry 744) and *Micronesia, 1975-1987: A Social Science Bibliography* by Nicholas J. Goetzfridt and Wuerch (see ARBA 90, entry 149). Wuerch and Ballendorf's dictionary is recommended for both general and specialized reference collections. [R: Choice, Feb 95, p. 920]—**Lee S. Dutton**

PACIFIC AREA

169. Gorman, G. E., and J. J. Mills, comps. **Fiji.** Santa Barbara, Calif., Clio Press/ABC-CLIO, 1994. 207p. index. (World Bibliographical Series, v.173). $59.50. ISBN 1-85109-078-9.

With this volume on Fiji, the World Bibliographical Series has issued its first survey of one of the smaller Pacific island nations. All the volumes in the series contain annotated entries on works dealing with a country's history, geography, economy, and politics, as well as its culture, social organization, and current living conditions. The compilers of this volume have surveyed and annotated some 700 works and journal articles, with primary emphasis on monograph literature of the last 25 years. They follow a standard subject arrangement (e.g., history, population, anthropology and ethnography, language, religion, health and welfare), with *see also* references in other related sections. They provide indexes at the end for authors, titles, and subjects.

The literature on Fiji is uneven in range of subject, and that aspect is necessarily reflected in the bibliography. As the compilers themselves point out, there are areas that have had ample or even excessive attention paid to them, and other areas that have not had enough. Anthropology and politics have had abundant coverage following the 1987 military coup and the subsequent flight of thousands of Fijo-Indians, whereas social and economic development has only begun to receive much scrutiny in the last 25 years or so. This volume is highly commendable for its up-to-dateness; Fiji is, after all, the first Pacific island nation to experience a military coup and to cut its links with its former colonial administrator.—**John B. Beston**

WEST INDIES

170. **Bahamas Handbook and Businessman's Annual 1995.** [35th ed.]. Paola Alvino and Suzanne Twiston-Davies, eds. Nassau, The Bahamas, Etienne Dupuch Jr.; distr., Bristol, Pa., Taylor & Francis, 1994. 548p. illus. maps. index. $30.00pa. ISBN 0-914755-59-5. ISSN 0067-2912.

For the individual who is seriously interested in matters of commerce, industry, history, and culture, this is an invaluable reference work. Even tourists who are anxious to learn more about the Bahamas than the special attractions of hotels and casinos would do well to consult it, for the handbook is a veritable treasure of serious information that is not found in histories or tourist guides—and it is well written, profusely illustrated, and crammed with official statistics, regulations, and abstracts of legislation. Whether one is interested in the "family islands," international investment, wildlife reservations, or the laws that govern tax havens, there is a comprehensive section of up-to-date information. However, the special value of the *Handbook* is the chapters on the culture of the Bahamas, which present the country as something more than a rendezvous for vacationers and offshore business registrants.

More than 150 pages of detailed information is provided on such subjects as costs of accommodation, accounting companies, art galleries and museums, the humane society, banking, birds, and broadcasting. A 30-page supplement covers Freeport, which is fast becoming a commercial and tourist center independent of Nassau and Providence Island. Compared to other Caribbean directories, this is a truly sophisticated one—a book that stresses tradition, continuity, and responsibility.—**Marian B. McLeod**

171. Crane, Janet, comp. **Martinique.** Santa Barbara, Calif., Clio Press/ABC-CLIO, 1995. 140p. index. (World Bibliographical Series, v.175). $55.00. ISBN 1-85109-151-3.

Crane has collected 380 citations into 21 broad subject chapters and prefaced them with an informative and perceptive introduction. The citation format conforms to that used throughout the series; citations are numbered, and list basic bibliographical data, translation of non-English titles, and annotations. This bibliography is more selective than many in this series. Important figures such as Lafcadio Hearn and Frantz Fanon are too briefly covered, and significant works such as Charles Wagley and Marvin Harris's important synthesis *Minorities in the New World* (Columbia University Press, 1964) are not listed.

This book was carefully produced and is amazingly free of error; the only ones identified concern Michel Laguerre, who is an anthropologist rather than a sociologist and whose name is rendered with different capitalizations (i.e., Laguerre or LaGuerre). Indexes for subject, title, and author, and a map of Martinique (which unfortunately does not include Morne-Vert, the peasant village that has been intensively studied by several North American anthropologists) are provided. Criticisms aside, this is an excellent selective bibliography of an island and community that have until now been poorly documented in the rapidly expanding reference literature on the Caribbean region.—**Fred J. Hay**

172. Moll, Verna Penn. **St. Kitts-Nevis.** Santa Barbara, Calif., Clio Press/ABC-CLIO, 1995. 185p. index. (World Bibliographical Series, v.174). $62.00. ISBN 1-85109-222-6.

This volume focuses on the island federation of St. Christopher (St. Kitts) and Nevis in the Caribbean. The introduction gives a six-page history of the islands, including geographical information on size, location, and topography. Following the uniform format of the series, theses and dissertations are listed first, followed by 565 annotated entries divided into 42 chapters by subject. A combined author and title index and an extensive subject index with cross-references conclude the volume. This is a useful compilation for libraries in that area and those researching the Caribbean.—**Elaine Ezell**

4 Economics and Business

GENERAL WORKS

Bibliography

173. **The Basic Business Library: Core Resources.** 3d ed. Bernard A. Schlessinger and Rashelle S. Karp, eds. Phoenix, Ariz., Oryx Press, 1995. 371p. index. $39.50. ISBN 0-89774-739-9.

As in previous editions, this most recent iteration of *The Basic Business Library* is intended to serve "as a checklist of essential business reference tools that smaller libraries can use to evaluate their business reference collections and services" and "as a core list and set of essays for smaller libraries beginning a business reference area" (preface). Within these parameters, the book evaluates and recommends 200 titles for a total budget outlay of $38,000.

The entries are organized alphabetically by title (rather than by subject); include abbreviated bibliographical information (e.g., price but no ISBN for monographs, no ISSNs, and inconsistent noting of frequency for periodicals); and note authority, scope, and reasons for recommendation. This "core resources" section is followed by an eclectic 60-page listing of articles from the literature of business reference and business libraries published between the years 1976 and 1994. Although a valuable compilation, this section's usefulness would be enhanced by organizing the articles by subject (an approach that would also improve the core resources bibliography).

The final section, comprising nine excellent essays on business reference sources and services, provides practical guidance in areas such as organization of materials, recommended investment sources, and core business periodicals. A thorough index concludes the work. Although this book could be greatly improved by organizing the core titles and articles by subject, it is nevertheless a valuable purchase for its intended audience.—**G. Kim Dority**

174. **Bibliographic Guide to Business and Economics 1994.** New York, G. K. Hall/Simon & Schuster, 1995. 3v. $625.00/set. ISBN 0-7838-2165-4. ISSN 0360-2702.

One of G. K. Hall's annual subject bibliographic guides, the *Bibliographic Guide to Business and Economics* follows the format found in the other titles (see entries 57-58, 398, and 489 for reviews of additional titles). Works in all languages and forms appear in a single alphabetical sequence, incorporating the main entry, added entries, titles, series titles, and subject headings. This guide includes titles cataloged during the past year by the Library of Congress in LC classification HA through HJ; it also lists publications cataloged by The Research Libraries of The New York Public Library if two or more of their subject headings correspond with two or more subject headings from the Library of Congress' MARC business and economics records.

The guide's durable buckram binding, along with its legible print on high-quality paper, guarantees ease of access and a long shelf life in spite of repeated usage. The guide would be highly useful in any library (academic, public, or special) that has major holdings in business or economics. Its usefulness would extend from reference to acquisitions to cataloging functions. The annual cost of buying this title will undoubtedly act as a barrier to its purchase by any but the largest or most heavily endowed libraries. However, any library that has the good fortune to acquire a substantial sum of money for business/economics library materials would be well advised to acquire this title for use as a buying guide.—**Dene L. Clark**

175. **Bibliography of Business/Competitive Intelligence and Benchmarking Literature.** By Washington Researchers. Washington, D.C., Washington Researchers, 1994. 246p. $275.00pa. ISBN 1-56365-049-5.

Bringing together two of corporate America's hottest topics—competitive intelligence and benchmarking—this 2-part bibliography identifies more than 2,000 items of interest to business researchers, corporate librarians, and others tracking this type of information. The book's first section is organized alphabetically by title, and comprises four chapters devoted to books; book chapters and periodical articles; audiotapes, videotapes, and transcripts; and miscellaneous materials such as conference findings, research papers, and government and private sector special reports. The second section is made up of 13 topical chapters that treat such areas as information-gathering tools and techniques, intelligence and technology, and ethical and legal issues. Publication dates range from the 1970s through 1994.

Although conceptually a good idea, this book will miss the mark for most librarians—as well as for most users—due to its lack of annotations and the lack of any bibliographical information save title and author for the monographs identified in the second section. In fact, the work often does not even provide the basic information one would glean from a rudimentary online search through one of the public library information utilities. There is, in fact, no added value here that would in any way justify the exorbitant price being charged for this paperback compilation of titles.—**G. Kim Dority**

Biography

176. **New Fortunes 1994: Biographical Profiles of 650 of America's Emerging Wealth Holders.** Catherine M. Ehr, ed. Detroit, Gale, 1994. 350p. index. $149.00pa. ISBN 1-56995-047-4. ISSN 1066-789X.

This book identifies 650 U.S. residents who have achieved a net worth of at least $2 million or have a significant record of nonprofit or philanthropic involvement. It focuses on those who accumulated their wealth in the last 20 years. Its purpose is to provide information on the "next tier" of U.S. wealth holders. The information on each person varies considerably, but the general headings of information are as follows: full name, birthplace/year, education, residences, current employment, contact address, wealth indicators, stock holdings, background, family, charitable activities, philanthropic affiliations, club affiliations, nonprofit affiliations, corporate affiliations, additional references, and further reading. The full entries are arranged alphabetically by last name. There are indexes to place of birth, state/country of residence, alma mater, corporate affiliation, nonprofit affiliations, philanthropic affiliations, club affiliations, and personal names. The book is aimed at prospect researchers, fund raisers, financial managers, investment bankers, and marketing professionals.—**J. E. Weaver**

Chronology

177. **Notable Corporate Chronologies.** Susan Boyles Martin, ed. Detroit, Gale, 1995. 2v. index. $375.00/set. ISBN 0-8103-9217-8. ISSN 1078-3865.

This is a useful and even delightful collection of timelines for 1,152 significant corporations that are currently operating in the United States or abroad. Each of these alphabetically arranged timelines describes 30 or more significant events in the history of an industrial, commercial, or financial firm. Significant events have been broadly defined to embody a variety of events in the history of the firm, including such things as its founding or any subsequent reorganization, the introductions of new products and product lines, mergers and acquisitions, stock offerings, major financial events, the tenure of its leading managers, and even notable scandals. Users will find these events both insightful and entertaining.

The events listed on each corporation's timeline are concise and informative. These entries not only provide the address and telephone number of each firm's corporate headquarters but also have short lists of further readings to facilitate additional research. This detailed reference work also includes four comprehensive and well-organized indexes (a master chronology, a geographical index, an alphabetical index, and an anniversary index) that not only make it easier to search and use the various corporate timelines but also encourage cross-referencing and thereby provide a more complete view of American and international business history. Among the more useful aspects of these indexes and chronologies is the determination of representative trends and patterns within the business world. These easy-to-use chronologies provide not only context but also an understanding of the growth and diversification of many of the world's leading corporations.—**Timothy E. Sullivan**

Dictionaries and Encyclopedias

178. Friedman, Jack P. **Dictionary of Business Terms.** 2d ed. Hauppauge, N.Y., Barron's Educational Series, 1994. 692p. (Barron's Business Guides). $11.95pa. ISBN 0-8120-1833-8.

Approximately 1,000 definitions of business terms have been added since the 1st edition (see ARBA 88, entry 163) appeared in 1987. The earlier work was praised for its clarity, conciseness, timeliness, and cross-references. All of these features are retained. This is a collaborative effort involving 16 subject specialists. While the work does cover many key terms, some newer subject-specific concepts such as Brady bonds, interest rate swaps, and keiretsu are not included. This work does not replace the more comprehensive subject-specific dictionaries. To ensure comprehensiveness, one should maintain a selection of dictionaries. A useful complement is Jerry M. Rosenberg's *Dictionary of Business and Management* (see ARBA 95, entry 187). Rosenberg includes approximately 7,500 terms as opposed to Friedman's 7,000 terms. Each contains terms that are not found in the other. This work is recommended as a ready-reference tool.—**Bobray Bordelon**

179. **The McGraw-Hill Encyclopedia of Economics.** 2d ed. Douglas Greenwald, ed. New York, McGraw-Hill, 1994. 1093p. index. $99.50. ISBN 0-07-024410-3.

Ever been frustrated by the need to look up an economic term or subject without having to master the technical aspects of economics, and finding no book that adequately explains the subject? The problem has been solved by the publication of *The McGraw-Hill Encyclopedia of Economics*. This expanded edition of the encyclopedia provides comprehensive coverage of various economic concepts in a format and language that are accessible to the noneconomist, and yet fully covers the subject to make it a reference of interest to the professional economist. Much has changed in the field of economics since the publication of the 1st edition in 1981, and the 2d edition reflects these changes. Some subjects have been dropped, more have been added, and coverage of all topics has been expanded. Topics covered include all the traditional subjects (ranging from acceleration principle to zero population growth) as well as new ones (such as supply-side economics), thus indicating that economics is, indeed, a living subject.

Most impressive about the book is that various contributors managed to cover the subjects they dealt with so well without recourse to technical jargon. From Kendrick's discussion of acceleration principle through Tobin's discussion of inflation to Knight's essay on zero population growth, all 307 essays in the *Encyclopedia* are easy to read, yet technically up-to-date. This reflects superb editorial work by Greenwald and McGraw-Hill. This book is by far the best this reviewer has seen in its class, and it should become the standard by which encyclopedias and dictionaries in economics, as well as in other subjects, will be measured. This book will be a superb addition to everyone's library, but to an economist, it is indispensable.—**Kwabena Gyimah-Brempong**

180. Terry, John V. **Dictionary for Business & Finance.** 3d ed. Fayetteville, Ark., University of Arkansas Press, 1995. 405p. $18.00pa. ISBN 1-55728-344-3.

The business world is undergoing dramatic changes in the 1990s, and one of the most striking changes is a blurring of the distinctions between financial and quasi-financial institutions. One net effect of this phenomenon is that most businesspeople now need to be familiar with terminology that was formerly outside their areas of competence. Today's practitioners need to be comfortable with terms in the fields of accounting, banking, economics, estate planning, finance, insurance, investments, management, real estate, securities, and statistics. They also need to understand Latin phrases that have been incorporated into the vocabulary of all these disciplines. An educated businessperson may not recognize business terms that are unknown, but the person will always have a business dictionary available.

Terry's *Dictionary for Business & Finance* is highly recommended as a suitable dictionary for the businessperson as well as the student. In the 3d edition Terry has added more than 200 terms, keeping the dictionary current with contemporary business usage. As an added feature for individuals who purchase this title for their home or office, the work includes appendixes for ratios, equations, formulas, and abbreviations. The dictionary is an important purchase for academic and public libraries, as well as special libraries that do any research in the area of business. In view of the encyclopedic nature of the definitions, the work should be a must-purchase in academic libraries that serve students in the field of business.

—**Dene L. Clark**

Directories

181. **The American Business Disc.** 1995 ed. [CD-ROM]. Omaha, Nebr., American Business Information, 1995. Minimum system requirements: IBM or compatible. CD-ROM drive with Microsoft CD-ROM Extensions 2.1. MS-DOS or PC-DOS 3.0. 4MB RAM. 6.2MB hard disk space. 480K conventional memory. $695.00.

The American Business Disc allows access to ten million businesses in the United States with information derived from the "yellow pages" and other sources. Each company's record includes its name; address; telephone number; number of employees and sales (both as ranges); and a notation of whether the business is a branch, subsidiary, or headquarters. A credit rating for each firm fills out the picture.

The user interface is straightforward and uncluttered. A search may be by company name, "yellow page" keyword, or SIC code. The geographical level is selected before the search and cannot be post-qualified. The user can make multiple state or county selections, but only one city or zip code may be chosen at one time. An "advanced searches" feature allows for qualification by headquarters/subsidiary designation, employee size, sales, public company status, and address.

The company records display is by brief listing of name and address alphabetically arranged by state and city. The full display provides the complete data. These records may be marked for printing or downloading. The brief records may be printed as a group while the full records may only be printed one at a time as they are viewed. The system allows six options for downloading, none of which are a plain ASCII text file. The WordPerfect download is formatted for the mail merge utility for labels and cannot be viewed as normal text without some knowledge of importing these mail files to text. Overall, this is a clean and easy-to-use system appropriate for both academic and public libraries.—**Gerald L. Gill**

182. **Directory of American Research and Technology 1995: Organizations Active in Product Development for Business.** 29th ed. New Providence, N.J., R. R. Bowker/Reed Reference Publishing, 1994. 818p. index. $329.95. ISBN 0-8352-3524-6. ISSN 0886-0076.

Many business directories provide basic information about companies. Finding a directory that describes research conducted by a given company or pinpoints which companies or organizations are engaged in research and development on a product or process, with commercial applications, is another matter. Fortunately, the *Directory of American Research and Technology* is available to answer just such questions. Dating back to the 1920s under an earlier publisher, the directory has been updated annually since 1984, an important point in an era when mergers and acquisitions are commonplace, and new technologies are emerging regularly. This one-volume work includes a principal section plus three indexes. The main section is an alphabetical list of parent organizations, followed by the central research and development center, if any, and then an alphabetical list of all divisions and facilities. The organization's professional staff and its fields of research are described briefly. The three indexes cover geographic, personnel, and classification. The latter index consists of broad subject headings subdivided into specific subheadings corresponding to the type of research performed by the more than 13,000 organizations that appear in the directory.

Research Services Directory (5th ed.; see ARBA 94, entry 165) is comparable, but revised only once every third year, and it lists only firms that provide research services to outside clients on a fee basis. *Research Centers Directory* (see entry 340), another comparable resource, is limited to university-related and independently operated nonprofit research facilities. The *Directory of American Research and Technology* is highly recommended for academic libraries with strong business or engineering programs, large public libraries, and special libraries that track research and development.—**Dene L. Clark**

183. **Directory of Companies Required to File Annual Reports with the Securities and Exchange Commission.** Washington, D.C., Securities and Exchange Commission; distr., U.S. Government Printing Office, 1994. 566p. $33.00pa. ISBN 0-16-045500-6.

The book under review lists the names, alphabetically and by SIC industry group, of all companies in the United States required to file annual reports with the Securities and Exchange Commission. As of September 30, 1994, more than 13,000 companies were required to report under the Securities Exchange Act of 1934. The companies involved are largely those with securities listed on national security exchanges or those whose securities are traded over the counter. Companies producing or marketing more than one class of product or service are placed in the SIC category that accounted for the greatest share of their gross revenue. A directory of SIC codes by industry is included to simplify searching by industry. Docket numbers and year of registration under the Securities Exchange Act are furnished in the alphabetical listing. The guide is an invaluable and authoritative reference for those who require the information supplied. Summaries and analyses are not provided.—**William C. Struning**

184. **The Fitzroy Dearborn Directory of Venture Capital Funds.** By A. David Silver. Chicago, Fitzroy Dearborn, 1994. 471p. index. $65.00. ISBN 1-884964-09-5.

Compiled by one of the leading authorities on entrepreneurship, this easy-to-read-and-understand resource is recommended for the reference collections of public and academic libraries. The work may also have great value in the collections of specialists in the field as well, as more than 400 active sources of venture capital funds are listed in the most current, available, and affordable resource.

The majority of the text consists of a venture capital directory or list broken down into five distinct types of funding sources: generic venture funds, medical/biotech/high technology venture funds, SSBIC/minority venture funds, socially useful venture funds, and strategic partners. More important, however, is the first part of the book, which is divided into five chapters that outline important information to have in hand prior to calling upon a venture capitalist. This information provides good insight and perspective into a field that can be both risky and stressful for those seeking funding for potentially successful business ventures.—**James M. Murray**

185. **Gale Encyclopedia of Business and Professional Associations: A Guide to More Than 8,000 Business....** Michael B. Huellmantel and others, eds. Detroit, Gale, 1995. 1184p. index. $75.00pa. ISBN 0-7876-0294-9. ISSN 1078-6775.

This directory is an 8,161-entry subset of the 23,000-entry *Encyclopedia of Associations* (EA) (see ARBA 94, entries 49-51), representing business, trade, labor, and professional groups of varying membership and budget size. More than 700 entries have been supplemented with information from *Trade Shows Worldwide* (see ARBA 94, entry 298). The work consists of a brief essay on its applications for a company's marketing department; a description of entry selection; an explanation of the entries' data elements and indexes; a list of terms used in the subject index; the association listings; and six indexes (subject, state/city, chief officer, acronym, budget size, and membership size—the latter two in ranked order).

Entries are arranged alphabetically and numbered. Although entries may have a maximum of 25 data elements, they commonly contain the entry number; the association name; an acronym; the address; telephone and fax numbers; the chief officer; the founding date; the number of members; the number of staff; the budget size; a description of purposes and activities; subgroups; former names and organizational changes; publications (both serial and other); and convention information—type, frequency, presence of exhibits, and future date/place.

In terms of coverage and type of information provided, this directory is similar to *National Trade and Professional Associations of the United States* (NTPA) (see ARBA 94, entry 54), published annually since 1966. The *Gale Encyclopedia* has 8 percent more entries than NTPA, but lacks 11 percent of NTPA's entries. NTPA has the same indexes, except one for membership size, but adds a list of association management companies.

A comparative analysis of 50 common entries revealed the following. *Gale* usually presents a much fuller picture of an association's purposes, activities, organization, and publications. NTPA more often gives dues, budget size (a range), and future convention sites. *Gale* more consistently traces former names and indicates the presence of exhibits at conventions. *Gale* has a superior entry layout and a more easily readable typeface size. Both directories should expand their subject headings list and more thoroughly index entries under all appropriate subject headings.

For public and academic business libraries, and corporate libraries and marketing departments that do not need the full national (and expensive) EA, *Gale* is a recommended—and modestly priced—purchase. For greater completeness of coverage and entry information, it should be owned in conjunction with the reasonably priced NTPA.—**John Lewis Campbell**

186. Glynn, Jeannette. **Who Knows Who [1996]: Networking Through Corporate Boards.** Berkeley, Calif., Who Knows Who Publishers; distr., Detroit, Gale, 1995. 871p. $150.00pa. ISBN 0-9638874-2-4.

Who Knows Who is similar to many other books (e.g., *Who Owns Corporate America* [see ARBA 94, entry 167] or *Who Knows About Industries and Markets* [see ARBA 93, entry 251]). It traces links among influential people working in nonprofit corporations. The material is arranged in six chapters: director-to-director links, an alphabetical list of organization-to-organization links, names of board members, a ranking of organizations by specifying the number of similar organizations, an alphabetical list of organizations, and a list of boards of directors for each of the covered organizations. The typeface is rather small, but still readable.—**Bohdan S. Wynar**

187. **Government Affairs Yellow Book: Who's Who in Government Affairs. Winter 1995: Volume 1, Number 1.** New York, Leadership Directories, 1995. 1024p. index. $180.00pa. ISSN 1078-9812.

The 11th title to be added to the Leadership Directory series, this book is a semiannual directory of government affairs experts who are employed by the leading business, government, and professional organizations to represent them before federal, state, and local governments. The directory covers 18,000 experts and gives their names, addresses, e-mail addresses, telephone and fax numbers, backgrounds, and the legislative issues in which they specialize. Corporations, financial institutions, trade associations, as well as subsidiaries, divisions, and joint ventures that run their own government affairs operations are profiled.

A large part of the directory includes listings of the Executive Office of the federal government, as well as key departments and agencies in the states and U.S. territories, major cities and counties, and authorities. The lobbying firms given in the other sections of the volume are also profiled separately. Indexes conclude the directory. They are excellent, and are broken down this way: legislative issues, industries, government subject areas, geography, personnel, and a master index. A user's guide is helpful for the first-time user of the directory. The work is a needed title in every reference collection of public and academic libraries.—**Kathleen J. Voigt**

188. **Guide to Private Fortunes: 1,000 New Descriptive Profiles of the Wealthiest....Volume 2.** Catherine M. Ehr, ed. Detroit, Taft Group/Gale, 1994. 644p. index. $235.00pa. ISBN 0-930807-82-0.

189. **Guide to Private Fortunes: 1,000 New Descriptive Profiles of the Wealthiest....Volume 3.** Catherine M. Ehr, ed. Detroit, Taft Group/Gale, 1995. 619p. index. $245.00pa. ISBN 1-569950-31-8.

Both of these volumes provide detailed biographical, historical, and corporate information on the wealthiest and most philanthropic people in the United States. *Guide to Private Fortunes* is not merely a list of the nation's wealthiest individuals, but rather a much more comprehensive portrait that includes such information as insider stock and real estate holdings, information on the individual's climb to affluence, and important charitable activities of individuals.

The biographical profiles (1,000 individuals in each volume), include the following information: name, birthplace/year, education, residence, current employment, wealth, stock holdings, background, family, charitable activities, philanthropic affiliations, club affiliations, and relevant articles and books about the listed individuals. There are eight separate indexes, which considerably enhance the usefulness of these volumes. They are arranged by place of birth; state or county of residence; alma mater; personal name; and philanthropic, nonprofit, corporate, and club affiliations.

These volumes will be of great value to institutional development officers, prospect managers, and those scholars and students who study the U.S. financial elite. The set is recommended for all types of libraries.—**Arthur P. Young**

190. **Hoover's Company & Industry Database on CD-ROM.** [CD-ROM]. Austin, Tex., Reference Press, 1995. Minimum system requirements: IBM or compatible. CD-ROM drive. DOS. Windows. $399.95 (single user); $499.95 (2-10 users); $599.95 (11 or more users) [with quarterly updates].

This is much more than a CD-ROM version of *Hoover's Handbook* (see ARBA 92, entry 145)—it provides information on 1,503 private and public companies, while the *Handbook* covers just more than 500. The CD-ROM also includes profiles of more than 35 industry groups in addition to the company profiles. It permits searching for company records by company name, company headquarters by state, by industry group, and also by words within profiles, providing hyperlinks from company profiles to industry profiles and competitor profiles. Corporate profiles consist of an overview (including a brief history of the operation and strategy of the company); a list of important executives ("who," which usually includes the name of the head of personnel or human resources services); directory information ("where"); a list of major products and services ("what"); a list of key competitors (including hypertext links); and financial information for five or more years ("how much").

The CD-ROM supplies both DOS and Windows software. The system requirements are reasonable and are spelled out clearly, and both versions of the software are easy to install and use. The database covers many fewer companies than the disc from Compact Disclosure, Standard & Poor's, or Moody's, and it does not provide the detailed information from Securities and Exchange Commission filings and annual reports required by investment firms or specialized business libraries. Nonetheless, it does furnish a depth of financial information suitable for most students and individual investors. It also covers the kind of historical and current business information most undergraduates are seeking, and it provides detailed information on both private and public corporations.

While this CD-ROM does not provide the depth of coverage of other databases of company information, the pricing of the more extensive databases is so much more expensive (approximately $3,500 for a single-user license for Compact Disclosure) that this database is in a class by itself. Because of its ease of use, reasonable price, timeliness, and coverage of public and private companies, this disc should be the first choice of most smaller public, college, and special libraries looking for a database of company and industry information.—**Richard H. Swain**

191. **Hoover's Handbook of American Business 1995.** Gary Hoover, Alta Campbell, and Patrick J. Spain, eds. Austin, Tex., Reference Press, 1994. 1275p. index. $39.95. ISBN 0-878753-65-7. ISSN 1055-7202.

Since the 1st edition of this handbook was published five years ago on a shoestring, Hoover's has expanded into a whole family of reasonably priced titles. This particular handbook contains somewhat fewer companies than the 1st edition, but there are several other handbooks plus online and CD-ROM sources to augment it. Thankfully, the binding on the later editions has drastically improved (the major flaw of the 1st edition), while the quality of the contents has remained high. The company profiles follow almost the same format as previously, giving an overview of the company's current market position, history and background, officers, address, key financial statistics, and competitors. Only the section listing where the company is ranked on various lists has been dropped. All profiles in the 1995 edition have been substantially revised, and include 1993 or 1994 financial data. The list section has been expanded, and now covers the complete Fortune 500 list, as well as the Standard & Poor's 500 and Midcap lists. Nonquantitative lists, taken from other sources, describe the best firms to work for and the most admired companies. There are numerous other lists, mainly rankings. The research involved in the company profiles and the wonderful compendium of lists make this book essential for even small libraries that provide some business information.—**Susan V. McKimm**

192. **Hoover's Masterlist of America's Top 2,500 Employers: A Digital Guide to the Largest & Fastest Growing U.S. Companies....** Austin, Tex., Reference Press, 1995. 415p. index. $19.95pa. (with disk). ISBN 1-878753-82-7.

Hoover is known for its series of business guides such as *Hoover's Guide to Private Companies* (see ARBA 95, entry 192) and *Hoover's Handbook of World Business* (see ARBA 92, entry 144). This paperback is aimed at jobseekers hip to the "information age"—it comes packaged in two editions. The standard text material is accompanied by 2, $3\frac{1}{2}$-inch diskettes (Windows based) containing the same data as the book, adding such features as data-exportation capability, the compiling of mailing lists, and the generation of cover letters.

So what is covered here? Twenty-five hundred employers listed by state and indexed by name, type of industry, and metropolitan area are included. It also has company profiles that list the usual addresses, telephone numbers, names of chief executive officers and human resources executives, the business type, the total number of employees, and the number of new hires in the past year. The reader can tell who is hiring and to what extent, which geographical areas are showing job growth, and in which industries that growth is occurring. In a more specific scenario, a nursing home administrator's wife is transferred to Albuquerque; he uses this book to discover that Horizon Healthcare and Sun Healthcare are headquartered there and added employees last year at a rate of more than 50 percent. He also sees that a medical services company in Albuquerque is growing at a rate of nearly 400 percent and composes some cover letters.

Almost as an aside, this resource also compiles 35 pages of lists that are regularly sought after, such as the top Hispanic-owned companies, most-admired companies, best companies for gays, and dozens more. Priced as it is, this extremely useful and compact directory is recommended to any libraries with jobseeking patrons.—**Ed Volz**

193. **National Directory of Nonprofit Organizations 1995.** Mollie B. Mudd, ed. Detroit, Taft Group/Gale, 1995. 3v. index. $450.00pa./set. ISBN 1-879784-86-6. ISSN 1048-8154.

Originally known as the *Taft Directory of Nonprofit Organizations*, this multivolume annual provides brief capsules of information on 185,000 organizations with annual revenues of $100,000 or more (volume 1, in 2 parts) and 75,000 organizations with annual revenues of $25,000 through $99,000 (volume 2). According to its editors, this work is intended for "marketers, sales staff, and nonprofit professionals who need information on the largest nonprofits in the U.S." (preface).

The set continues its previous organization: a main body of alphabetically arranged entries, followed by an activity index and a geographical index. The entries include name; address; telephone number; IRS 501(C) filing status; employer identification number (EIN); charitable deduction eligibility; the organization's annual income; and an activity-identifier code that indicates the organization's tax-exempt activity as assigned by the Internal Revenue Service (for example, health services or scientific research activities). The activity index organizes entries under 270 specific activities, while the geographical index provides access by zip code within state groupings.

Although the *Encyclopedia of Associations* (see ARBA 94, entries 49-51) furnishes much more depth of coverage (for example, the work under review offers no descriptive text, or any indication of when a nonprofit was established, number of employees, and so forth), large public and academic libraries may find the sheer volume of listings included here makes the set worth its purchase price.—**G. Kim Dority**

194. **National Directory of State Business Licensing and Regulation: A Descriptive Guide to State and Federal Licensing Requirements and Regulations for Specific Businesses.** David P. Bianco, ed. Detroit, Gale, 1995. 1139p. index. $89.50. ISBN 0-8103-9141-4. ISSN 1077-8063.

This useful new offering from Gale provides detailed federal and state licensing and regulatory information for more than 100 businesses. While some manufacturing industries are included, the directory's emphasis is clearly on the service industry, with more than three-fourths of the entries devoted to service-oriented businesses. The various businesses included in the volume range from accounting services to general contractors to tattoo parlors. The work is arranged alphabetically by industry, with four-digit level SIC (Standard Industrial Classification) codes included in each chapter heading, and a SIC thesaurus provided in the front matter for locating industries by SIC number. Also included is a geographical index that conveniently lists all covered industries for each state. Most industry chapters begin with an entry on federal licenses, and all give state-by-state listings of licensing and regulatory requirements. Each brief entry consists of a standard profile that may include directory information for the agency, licenses required to conduct business in the state, requirements that must be met to obtain a license or permit, activities authorized by the license, regulated activities and reporting requirements, and the statutory authority requiring the license.

The editor has done a commendable job of pulling together and conveniently packaging important information that has previously been scattered among state offices, trade publications, and compilations of state laws. All reference librarians serving patrons with an interest in small business will find this directory useful, and it will be a valuable addition to any business reference collection. [R: LJ, 1 Feb 95, pp. 68-70]—**Gordon J. Aamot**

195. Silver, A. David. **Quantum Companies: 100 Companies That Will Change the Face of Tomorrow's Business.** Princeton, N.J., Peterson's/Pacesetter Books, 1995. 342p. index. $21.95. ISBN 1-56079-373-2.

Quantum companies are, according to this book, energetic and enterprising organizations that create sustainable wealth. To arrive at a list of 100 such companies, financial, managerial, and environmental measures were examined. The result is a list of companies that the author believes are shaping the business world and will predict growth industries. Each profile consists of directory information, competitors, potential selling sites, and its problems and solutions that are being applied. A two-page narrative touches upon company highlights and innovative techniques employed. The book provides a roster for investors, jobseekers, and consumers. Ninety-six are United States businesses, three are Canadian, and one is British. Twenty are private firms. As with most works of this nature, it will quickly become dated. *Quantum Companies* does provide an interesting and easily readable look into some innovative companies, and is recommended as a source for information on emerging companies. [R: BL, 1 April 95, p. 1365]

—**Bobray Bordelon**

196. **Small Business Profiles: A Guide to Today's Top Opportunities for Entrepreneurs. Volume 2.** Jennifer Arnold Mast, ed. Detroit, Gale, 1995. 361p. index. $95.00. ISBN 0-8103-9325-5. ISSN 1076-8483.

This is the second volume of a set that was favorably reviewed in ARBA 95 (see entry 212). This adds 67 types of businesses to the 60 profiled in volume 1. The businesses in this second volume seem to be well selected, reflecting the types that entrepreneurs are actually starting. Examples include bars, business consultants, maid services, 900-number telephone services, and weight-loss clinics.

Most entries give a general description of the demands and nature of the business; data on costs and profits; financing options; suggestions for location, layout, setup, and inventory; and ideas for marketing and staffing. As with the previous volume, statistics are cited. Substantial numbers of outside resources are also mentioned. These are annotated, which is not the case with those in *Small Business Sourcebook* (5th ed.; see ARBA 93, entry 213).

Even though the individual signed chapters are written by different writers, some advice overlaps. For instance, although it is certainly sound advice, every chapter recommends that the entrepreneur contact the Small Business Administration. However, there is also much that is unique for each type of business, and this volume is highly recommended for all libraries that purchased volume 1 or that serve a significant number of entrepreneurs.—**Susan V. McKimm**

Handbooks and Yearbooks

197. **Business Rankings Annual, 1995: Lists of Companies, Products....** Compiled by Brooklyn Public Library Business Library Staff. Detroit, Gale, 1995. 787p. index. $170.00. ISBN 0-8103-8953-3. ISSN 1043-7908.

The librarians who produced this work have culled business rankings from some 1,400 periodicals and 18 newspapers to select "the lists that are most in demand by businesspeople, librarians, students, and the public . . ." (preface). Lists are grouped by alphabetically arranged subjects such as advertising agencies; Hispanic-American business enterprises; murder ("Occupations with the Highest Rate of Homicide"—number one is retailing!); outsourcing; toothpaste; and wine industry. Entries include title of ranking, ranking criteria, units of measurement, remarks (additional details as appropriate), number rankings, and source.

In addition to the listings, the annual provides a comprehensive index that enables the user to quickly identify in what rankings a specific company has been included, as well as a complete listing (title, publisher, contact information, frequency of publication, price, ISSN) of the more than 300 sources used to compile the ranking. Although *Business Rankings Annual* will be of value primarily to business researchers, it has a sufficient amount of strange and esoteric information (e.g., top-selling cocoa brands, best-selling ready-to-eat cereals, top soap operas) to be a favorite for browsing as well.—**G. Kim Dority**

198. **The Value of a Dollar, 1860-1989: Prices and Incomes in the United States.** Scott Derks, ed. Detroit, Gale, 1994. 559p. illus. $69.50. ISBN 0-8103-6841-2.

How much did a Buick cost in 1924? Did you know Cheerios were introduced in 1941 and Valium in 1963? A multitude of other prices and facts can be found in Gale's new reference book. From 1865 to 1989, *Value of a Dollar* attempts "to define the value of a dollar to the consumer at the point of purchase" (preface).

The work is divided chronologically. The first chapter covers the Civil War to 1899 and shows the groundwork being laid for a national consumer economy. As standard elements for five-year subchapters, each of the following four chapters includes a historical snapshot, consumer expenditures, investments, selected income, income standard jobs, food basket, selected prices, standard prices, and miscellany. The investment returns are compiled from Federal Reserve reports. Income was obtained from want ads of major newspapers. The food item prices came from four sections of the country. Standard prices are a selection of representative items tracked annually, allowing users to trace price fluctuations. A short appendix of sources concludes the volume.

Business historians, reporters, writers, and students will find this source, prepared for people curious about social history and economic trends in the United States, very helpful for historical research. Large public and academic libraries will want to purchase it.—**Susan C. Awe**

199. **Gale Business Resources.** [CD-ROM]. Detroit, Gale, 1995. 2 discs. Minimum system requirements: IBM or compatible PC 286 (386 recommended). ISO 9660-compatible CD-ROM drive with cables, interface card, and MS-DOS CD-ROM Extensions 2.1. MS-DOS or PC-DOS 3.3. 640K RAM (520K available). 5MB hard disk space. VGA monitor and graphics card (color recommended). Mouse (optional). Printer (optional). $7,995.00 (single user); $9,595.00 (2-8 users). ISBN 0-7876-0794-0.

This set of two CD-ROMs provides data on more than 216,000 companies in the United States, including brand information, company histories, complete text of 10-K reports for the top 1,000 firms, industry statistics, financial ratios, market share reports, rankings, and industry associations. The introductory screen menu offers four different ways to search for information. Entries that appear when searching by company include products and services, addresses, key officers, sales and revenue data, and a list of relevant Standard Industrial Classification (SIC) codes. Searching by product accesses 15,000-plus products and 185,000 brands. Searching by industry accesses data by SIC code, keyword, or type of industry. The final search option, extended search, introduces more detailed searching options under six categories: contact (any word in the company name, officer name, or parent company records); location; industry; scope (number of employees, year founded, revenue, stock exchange, or ticker symbol); profile (any word in the company profile, publications, special services, or seminars records); and product.

Although there are function keys and arrow keys that can be used to move from one option to the next, this is a Windows-based software system. Several factors make searching for information easy. An option menu is continuously displayed at the bottom of the screen with a "help" button always available to provide information about what the user is currently viewing, and a "main menu" button takes the user directly to the introductory screen menu. Only the available menu options at any given step within the database are highlighted, making it easy to see what information is available. This eliminates needless error messages. The software allows the user to jump from one option to the next throughout the database. The descriptions of SIC codes are taken from the *Encyclopedia of American Industry*, and industry rankings are collected from journal articles and trade magazines. There are also options to mark items and to save or print records. The displays, graphics, and menu screens are attractively laid out, easy to read, and consistently presented throughout the system.

Three problems are associated with determining the database's value over print sources, online systems, or other CD-ROM products. First, items chosen are not highlighted within the text of the entry. For example, this makes it difficult to locate exactly where in an entry there is reference to a specific brand name. Second, the need to switch to a second disc to view the 10-K reports means the system must be run on a multiple CD-ROM drive. Finally, while many are familiar with Windows-based computer use (scroll bars, point-and-click searching, and so forth), most commercial CD-ROM databases do not employ Windows-based searching; this forces users to make an adjustment in how they search the data, display information, and move through the system. In addition, extra space must be made available to allow for the use of a mouse and mouse pad.

Despite these misgivings, this database is easy to use, gives an enormous amount of business information in one place, and provides helpful supporting documentation. The system is highly recommended for those libraries that can afford it and have not yet invested in other systems. For those libraries that already have online systems and CD-ROMs that provide similar information, the *Gale Business Resources* database offers a comprehensive, easy-to-use alternative and an opportunity to consolidate information into one system.—**Robert V. Labaree**

200. **Global Trends: The World Almanac of Development and Peace.** Ingomar Hauchler and Paul M. Kennedy, eds. New York, Continuum Publishing, 1994. 416p. maps. index. $39.50; $19.95pa. ISBN 0-8264-0674-2; 0-8264-0785-4pa.

Originally published in German in 1993, this book contains 20 chapters addressing world order, society, peace, economy, ecology, and culture, designed to show global interdependence. The "World Peace" section, for example, includes chapters on military spending, arms transfers, and war. Written from an internationalist perspective, the book challenges the current development paradigm that emphasizes nationalist concerns. Hauchler, a Social Democrat member of the German Bundestag, and Kennedy, head of international security studies at Yale, are the editors and write at least the preface, but the authors of the individual chapters, referred to as "expert contributors" on the book's dust cover, are not identified in the text. A project of the International Development and Peace Foundation, which supports global reform based on the notion of the global community, the book was funded by the German government. The chapters are well documented with a wide range of international data drawn mainly from international organizations and German- and English-language sources. Several appendixes provide country statistics; a bibliography supplements chapter sources. The book has outstanding graphics, but the binding on the review copy was already tearing. The index has some strange entries: Entries are by acronym for most organizations, with no cross-references from the actual name. The book's point of view is obvious, but it would be a useful complement in larger collections, because of the integration of data from so many sources. World Watch's annual *State of the World* (Norton, 1984-) provides greater depth of analysis. [R: LJ, Mar 15, 95, p.60]—**Marilyn Domas White**

201. **Hoover's Handbook of World Business 1995-1996.** 3d ed. Patrick J. Spain and James R. Talbot, eds. Austin, Tex., Reference Press, 1995. 608p. index. $37.95. ISBN 1-878753-44-4. ISSN 1055-7199.

Reference Press aims to provide an affordable source of up-to-date and accurate information about the most important global companies, and this title fills the bill. This edition profiles 227 (42 more than the 2d edition) corporations headquartered outside the United States from the Bridgestone Corporation, Foster's Brewing Group Ltd., and Lloyd's of London to Volkswagen AC and the Union Bank of Switzerland. More than 100 European companies, 40-plus Japanese, and a dozen Canadian companies, in addition to companies in fast-growing countries such as Chile, Korea, Mexico, and Taiwan, are profiled.

Each entry, arranged alphabetically, contains operations, overviews, and histories; up to 10 years of key financial and employment data; lists of products and key competitors; foreign and U.S. executives; and U.S. and headquarters addresses, telephone, and fax numbers. To aid accessibility, these entries are indexed by industry, by headquarters location, and by people, companies, and brand names.

A four-page introductory section teaches users how to get the most out of the company profiles. The next section contains nearly 80 lists, including: "35 Wealthiest Non-U.S. Individuals and Families," "Europe's 20 Largest Banks," "Top 50 Emerging Market Companies," and "25 Largest Foreign Investors" in the United States, to name a few.

Hoover's Company and Industry Database on CD-ROM (see entry 190) makes this information plus business data from three other Hoover print publications available, and these profiles as well as more than 1,000 other company profiles may be viewed through 11 online services. If patrons are interested in global business, this abundant information for a terrific price is a must-acquisition.—**Susan C. Awe**

202. **How to Find Company Intelligence in State Documents.** 15th ed. Washington, D.C., Washington Researchers, 1994. 206p. index. $125.00pa. ISBN 1-56365-035-5. ISSN 1041-8024.

203. **How to Find Information About Divisions, Subsidiaries and Products.** 5th ed. Washington, D.C., Washington Researchers, 1994. 147p. index. $145.00pa. ISBN 1-56365-046-0. ISSN 0278-372X.

204. **How to Find Information About Foreign Firms.** 6th ed. Washington, D.C., Washington Researchers, 1994. 123p. index. $145.00pa. ISBN 1-56365-044-4. ISSN 0278-372X.

205. **How to Find Information About Private Companies.** 6th ed. Washington, D.C., Washington Researchers, 1994. 144p. index. $145.00pa. ISBN 1-56365-045-2. ISSN 0278-372X.

Washington Researchers is one of the oldest and best-known research firms in the country. These handbooks, based on the company's two decades of experience tracking down who, what, where, why, and how, are designed to help novice business researchers locate similar information on their own. All of the works lead off with an introductory overview of the special considerations and challenges of their topics (for example, information on subsidiaries is highly decentralized).

From there, each handbook organizes its material according to how one researches the topic at hand, including both the relevant information resources and guidance in how to most effectively use them. For example, when using federal resources to research private companies, the researcher is directed to first consider whether or not the "target" is a federal government supplier, is in a regulated industry, has employees, has a pension fund, makes consumer products, emits pollutants, is in an emerging industry, has patents or trademarks, or conforms to any of another slew of qualifying characteristics. Answers to these and other questions help shape the path of the research to be undertaken and the resources to be used. Supplementary materials include appendixes—"Publishers, Vendors, and Suppliers," "Using Your Telephone," and "State Offices of Economic Development"—in three of the books (not in *State Documents*), and all four contain a subject index.

Although there are a number of excellent guides to doing business research, few are as specifically targeted as these handbooks are. However, their exorbitantly high prices put them out of reach of all but the most affluent business libraries. Certainly there is no need to purchase the works, which had previously been issued on an irregular basis, biannually, as they are now being marketed.—**G. Kim Dority**

206. Randall, Richard C. **Randall's Practical Guide to ISO 9000: Implementation, Registration, and Beyond.** Reading, Mass., Addison-Wesley Publishing, 1995. 437p. index. $34.38. ISBN 0-201-63379-5.

Randall is the southeast regional director for National Quality Assurance, U.S.A., which is accredited by both the American National Standards Institute/Registrars Accreditation Board and the U.K. National Accreditation Council for Certification Bodies. In writing this excellent guide, he has used his expertise in discussing practical quality concepts and principles supplemented by examples from actual companies such as Varian Vacuum Products, General Electric Text Equipment Management Services, and Grayson Electronics.

This book is a pleasure to read because the author has clearly organized the subject, even using icons to designate specific items such as quality manual, procedure records, guidance, and so on. Beginning with the origins and history of ISO 9000, the reader is taken through implementation, definitions, and standards requirements for every part of the organization. Appendixes list organizations and publications related to ISO 9000. Because ISO 9000 does not define "how" to accomplish the desired result, Randall's book reflects his experience and that of certain companies by suggesting how a company can comply, always keeping in mind that individual companies are unique and should approach the problem in different ways. The book is not intended to take the place of a consultant and should be used as a reference guide for companies interested in achieving ISO 9000 certification. This volume will be a welcome addition to university, corporate, and large public libraries.—**Lorna A. Wiggins**

207. **StartSmart Small Business Advisor.** [CD-ROM]. Detroit, Gale, 1994. Minimum system requirements: IBM or compatible 286 (386 recommended). ISO 9660-compatible CD-ROM drive with cables, interface card, and MS-DOS CD-ROM Extensions 2.1. MS-DOS or PC-DOS 3.3. 640K RAM. 3MB hard disk space. VGA monitor and graphics card (color recommended). Mouse (optional). Printer (optional). $895.00. ISBN 0-8103-9846-X.

The setup routine allows the library to specify how many pages the patron can print (up to 999), whether or not they can download to disk, and whether and where they can save files. The software is menu-driven, which means searching is easy but time-consuming. The main menu offers six options: search by type of business, search for state resources, search for financing organizations, search by business topic, search for federal resources, and look at sample business plans. Under the first topic, there were about 855 choices. A comparison with the *Small Business Sourcebook* (SBS) (see ARBA 93, entry 213), however, shows that this large number of entries comes because the CD-ROM uses synonyms rather than cross-references as the book does. For instance, the same information appears under "Automobile auctioneer" and "Car engineer." Although a few types of businesses appear that are not in the 7th edition of the SBS (1993), most additional entries were merely synonyms.

Once one selects a business type, another menu allows one a choice of type of information, such as published sources, contacts, franchises, licensing, and so forth. Contacts include associations, trade shows, and consultants. The entries under "Education and Training" refer the patron to sources such as the *College Blue Book* (Macmillan), rather than directly to the actual schools or seminars. The licensing choice offers a further menu by state. In searching through the menus, occasional menu items were not selectable because there was no information. A trial printout of a list of approximately 80 articles on running a computer business did not appear to be sorted in any discernible fashion.

The state resources menu is arranged by state. Under Ohio, published sources include three titles, all by private publishers, and do not list such publications as the Ohio Secretary of State's booklet on how to incorporate. The Ohio Department of Development did appear under another heading. Again, SBS has a 300-page list of state resources. The financing organizations selection on the main menu similarly offers submenus, allowing the patron to select such topics as venture capital firms or small business investment corporations.

The section "Search by Business Topic" works similarly to "Search by Business Type." Again, there is no natural language searching and no cross-references, so one finds the same information under the headings "Collection, Bill," "Credit and Collection," and "Debt Collection." All main topics have the same subtopics, but not all headings are selectable or have information. The full-text articles that appear under some headings are definitely not available in SBS or other books published by Gale, even though SBS has extensive bibliographies on business topics.

A search for federal resources requires the selection of a specific agency. There is no alternative way to search, so it is necessary to guess what agencies may have programs. SBS lists 50 pages of federal resources. The sample business plans include 27 plans for a variety of businesses. Footnotes say that this portion of the CD-ROM is from Karin E. Koek's *Business Plans Handbook* (Gale, 1994). The majority of these plans are for businesses that have been operating a few years, not for start-up companies. There is also a template for a generic business plan.

In all, this is largely taken from Gale materials that have been published in book form, although abstracts and full-text materials have been added. It does not make use of advanced computer searching techniques, which would provide more access points to the data than are in the books. The disc would, however, be popular in a library serving entrepreneurs. Libraries who do not have the books, or who have large budgets and ample CD-ROM terminals, may therefore want this title.—**Susan V. McKimm**

Indexes

208. **World Index of Economic Forecasts: Including Industrial Tendency Surveys.** 4th ed. Robert Fildes, ed. Brookfield, Vt., Gower Publishing/Ashgate Publishing, 1995. 663p. $199.95. ISBN 0-566-07488-5.

This updated edition of the *World Index* (see ARBA 90, entry 195, for a review of the 3d ed.) indicates a new period of consolidation through mergers and closings of organizations engaged in international forecasting, while new entrants are also identified. A total of 217 organizations, covering all important countries, are included, some of them newly emerged or recently marketed, as those in Eastern Europe. The introductory essay on using macroeconomic forecasts is by the editor. It is followed by an international synoptical table.

The 2d section is on who is who in economic forecasting, and is divided into parts by organization, country, forecasting exchange rates, interest rates, commodity markets, labor, population, energy, company financial information, political risk, and shipping industry. Section 3, the main part of the book, provides detailed information on forecasters, including the types of macroeconomic measures used, production indexes, monetary indicators, labor market series, price indexes, foreign sector indicators, regional forecasts, and coverage of countries other than the country of origin.

The final section of this volume lists business cycles and tendency surveys by the forecasting organizations, providing their characteristics or components, and citing their publications. Contact information is given in sections 3 and 4. The *World Index* is a good reference guide to international forecasting. It provides information on expected future economic development and business activities for most countries of the world.—**Bogdan Mieczkowski**

Periodicals and Serials

209. **Directory of Business Periodical Special Issues: The Definitive Guide to Indexed Business, Science, and Technology Periodicals.** Trip Wyckoff, comp. and ed. Austin, Tex., Reference Press, 1995. 162p. index. $49.95pa. ISBN 1-878753-60-6.

As alluded to by the author of this invaluable reference source, an enormous amount of information is contained in the special issues of periodicals. This is particularly true with regard to specialized trade magazines. However, identifying these special issues is difficult given the very general coverage and underindexed content of most periodical indexes. This directory helps to bridge this information gap by listing the special issues of more than 1,300 periodical titles. The periodicals are arranged alphabetically with the editorial address and telephone number; the type of special issues published; and, if available, where the journal is indexed for each entry.

Although the subtitle indicates that the directory covers periodicals in the fields of business, science, and technology, a select number of journals outside of these disciplines are included (e.g., *History Teacher*). An unfortunate omission in an otherwise fine reference source is the lack of a key to the abbreviations of the periodical indexes—only a librarian or experienced researcher would know, for example, that "BPI" refers to the *Business Periodicals Index* or that "PAIS" refers to the *Public Affairs Information Service*. In addition, no reason is given as to why some indexing services were included while others were not. Despite this omission and a price of almost $50 for a 150-page paperback book, this directory remains an important guide to information contained in periodicals and is recommended for inclusion in any library collection.—**Robert V. Labaree**

ACCOUNTING

210. **A Dictionary of Accounting.** R. Hussey, ed. New York, Oxford University Press, 1995. 344p. $14.95pa. ISBN 0-19-280029-9.

There have been several dictionaries published on accounting. Although dated, one of the best is *Dictionary for Accountants* (Prentice-Hall, 1983), and more recently, *Encyclopedic Dictionary of Accounting and Finance* (see ARBA 90, entry 198). The volume under review is a British dictionary that reflects some of the recent changes in modern accounting practices.

This edition contains 4,000 entries, including common terms such as *cash* and *earnings*, as well as the lesser-known terms *daisy chain* and *Romalpa clause*. It furnishes definitions of the terminology used in financial accounting and reporting, financial management, management accounting, taxation, and treasury management. This dictionary's main focus is coverage of British accounting terms and concepts. However, it does provide broad coverage of United States terms where they differ from those in the United Kingdom. It also supplies explanations of the jargon used in both British and United States financial arenas. While giving many explanations of the various accounting terms, the reader would need to have a basic knowledge of accounting before attempting to use this resource. Most definitions include other accounting terms that, although also defined in the dictionary, would confuse the accounting novice.

While this dictionary cannot be recommended for the beginning accounting student, it could serve as a useful general reference source for advanced accounting students and individuals in the accounting and financial industries.—**Patricia B. Lutz**

BUSINESS SERVICES AND INVESTMENT GUIDES

Bibliography

211. Womack, Carol Z., and Alice C. Littlejohn. **The American Stock Exchange: A Guide to Information Resources.** Hamden, Conn., Garland, 1995. 225p. index. (Research and Information Guides in Business, Industry, and Economic Institutions, v.7; Garland Reference Library of Social Science, v.768). $35.00. ISBN 0-8153-0223-1.

Although mainly an annotated bibliography, this guide also includes a brief but informative history of the American Stock Exchange (AMEX) and a glossary. The bibliography itself has chapters covering various historical periods as well as trading, regulation, and economic aspects. Three indexes help access these chapters by title, name, and subject. In an unusual feature for a bibliography, appendix A goes through the annual reports from 1929 to 1993 (the cutoff date for this bibliography), and quotes highlights relating to trading, membership, and major developments. These highlights provide an abundance of AMEX statistics. Appendix B lists publications by and about the AMEX. Although described as "a sample," the list is quite extensive.

The annotations summarize the articles, containing enough facts and statistics to be useful in themselves. The last bibliographic entry is a 16-page list of every time *The Wall Street Journal* or *The New York Times* reported AMEX seat prices, giving the price in addition to the citation. The authors have excluded general information on the stock market from this work, which is part of a series of bibliographies that has already produced a guide to information sources on the New York Stock Exchange and on the U.S. Securities and Exchange Commission. In all, this is a thorough, well-organized, well-written, and potentially useful guide for anyone doing research on the AMEX.—**Susan V. McKimm**

Handbooks and Yearbooks

212. **The Dow Jones Guide to the World Stock Market.** 1995-1996 ed. By the Editors of Dow Jones & Company. Englewood Cliffs, N.J., Prentice Hall Career & Personal Development, 1995. 705p. maps. index. $34.95pa. ISBN 0-13-342296-8.

This 2d edition is a comprehensive guide that profiles 2,600 companies in 26 countries. The countries are listed alphabetically, and each entry includes a history of the stock exchange; trading hours and time differences from New York; gross domestic product with 3-year growth figures; main industries; consumer price indexes; monetary units and exchange rates; and the 10 largest capitalized companies, as well as a graph depicting the Dow Jones Equity Market Index Performance in local currency and U.S. dollars.

Each company profile provides the industry; goods produced or services provided; the 3-year history of sales, net income, book value, P/E ratio, P/B ratio, yield percentage, price as of September 30, 1994, and 52-week Hi-Lo; the address and telephone number of the company; and the names of the CEO and chair. There is a cross-index of all 2,600 companies alphabetically and by industry. This guide is a handy ready-reference tool for global investors as well as colleges or universities with international business studies.

—**Sue Brown**

213. **Flows and Stocks of Fixed Capital 1967-1992. Flux et Stocks de Capital Fixe.** Washington, D.C., OECD Publications, 1994. 51p. $24.00pa. ISBN 92-64-04120-6.

This title consists of tables of statistics for gross stocks, net stocks, gross fixed capital formation, and fixed capital consumption at current and constant prices for 13 of the 24 member countries of the Organization for Economic Cooperation and Development. Covering the period 1967 to 1992, the statistics are either provided by each country or gathered from other sources, which are cited in the introduction. Therefore, beginning dates and definitions may vary, although such variances are clearly stated in the notes.

Future editions are planned and will include statistics for additional member countries. The *Europa World Year Book* (see ARBA 94, entry 82) will provide fixed capital consumption and gross fixed capital formation totals, and *International Financial Statistics Yearbook* (see ARBA 92, entry 188) will also give gross fixed capital formation, but no other source is known to supply such in-depth statistical breakdowns. The work is recommended only for libraries needing such specialized information.—**Barbara E. Clotfelter**

214. **Standard & Poor's 500 Guide.** 1995 ed. By Standard & Poor's. New York, McGraw-Hill, 1995. 1021p. $19.95pa. ISBN 0-07-052099-2.

215. **Standard & Poor's MidCap 400 Guide.** 1995 ed. By Standard & Poor's. New York, McGraw-Hill, 1995. 817p. $19.95pa. ISBN 0-07-052100-X.

The extensive *Standard & Poor's Stock Reports* covers all companies listed on the New York and American Stock Exchanges and more than 1,000 other companies. These *Guides* extract from this extensive (and costly) source the reports for companies comprising the Standard & Poor's (S&P) 500 Index of large companies and the S&P MidCap 400 Index of medium-sized companies, respectively. Each company is featured in a two-page report that includes primarily factual information, accompanied by some brief evaluative comments and a rating (from A+ to D) from an S&P analyst. Ten years of balance sheets and income statement data are presented in summary tables, as are per share figures for earnings, cash flow, dividends, book value, price/earnings ratio, and stock price range. The stock's beta coefficient—a sometimes elusive statistic—is computed. Short narratives summarize the company's business and recent history of sales and dividend payments. Tables in an introductory section of each volume list rapid-growth stocks, stocks with A+ ratings, and stocks with consistently growing or rapidly growing dividends.

One consideration in selecting investment guides is currency. S&P analysts issue new reports weekly, with each company's report being updated every three months. The *Guides* are issued on an annual basis to include the latest reports available at press time. In summary, the *Guides* are a useful and low-priced tool providing basic data for assessing 900 of the more widely held stocks in the investment universe. While their coverage is much more limited, and issued less frequently, than that of other publications (both from S&P and from other publishers such as Moody's and Value Line), their cost is much lower as well. They merit a place in any investment collection where the *Standard & Poor's Stock Reports* are not included.—**Christopher J. Hoeppner**

CONSUMER EDUCATION

216. Bykerk, Loree, and Ardith Maney. **U.S. Consumer Interest Groups: Institutional Profiles.** Westport, Conn., Greenwood Press, 1995. 269p. index. $69.50. ISBN 0-313-26429-5.

This work provides in-depth profiles of 109 major nongovernmental organized interest groups, showing how they compete to protect consumer and business interests for products and services in all areas of life from baby foods to funerals. These organizations are arranged in alphabetical order. Each entry contains addresses and telephone numbers, followed by descriptions of organization and resources, policy concerns, and tactics. Examples of information included in these sections are basic goals, budget, publications, membership benefits, major issues concerning the group, and group activities used to influence public policy decisions.

Groups selected for inclusion were obtained from several standard reference sources such as *Encyclopedia of Associations* (see ARBA 94, entries 49-50, and ARBA 91, entries 37-38) and groups testifying before the House of Representatives. Information for the entries was obtained from publications supplied by the groups, which accounts for variance in detail, quality, and sophistication in the entries. In many cases, a further reading section is included, listing scholarly publications on the groups—these were also consulted for supplemental information.

Academic and public libraries will want to purchase the work. This reference is a treasure trove for interest group watchdogs, public policymakers, legislators, students, and private citizens.—**Susan C. Awe**

217. **Consolidated List of Products Whose Consumption and/or Sale Have Been Banned, Withdrawn, Severely Restricted, or Not Approved by Governments.** 5th ed. By the Department for Policy Coordination and Sustainable Development. New York, United Nations, 1994. 935p. index. $100.00pa. ISBN 92-1-130160-2. S/N E.94.IV.3.

This compilation has been developed by the United Nations to distribute information on products that have been banned, withdrawn, or severely restricted because they are harmful to health or to the environment. The consolidated listing of such regulatory decisions is intended to be used by the many small countries that lack the resources required to track the official actions of other nations. The list includes both regulatory and commercial information for about 700 pharmaceuticals, agricultural and industrial chemicals, and consumer products. Absence of a compound from the listings of a country does not, however, necessarily suggest that use of the compound is permitted in that country. For example, the substance may never have been officially submitted for approval or the results of a negative regulatory decision may not have been communicated to the appropriate UN agency.

The reference is well organized for easy reference. The products are indexed by common names, trade names, and Chemical Abstract Registry numbers. In many cases, the World Health Organization (WHO) has provided valuable summary comments. Most discussions of environmental regulations focus on only a few countries, and so researchers who wish a broader coverage may find this perspective to be beneficial.—**Harry E. Pence**

218. **Consumers Reference Disc 1985 - May 1995.** [CD-ROM]. Baltimore, Md., National Information Service Corporation, 1995. Minimum system requirements: IBM or compatible AT-class 286. CD-ROM drive. 512K RAM. 2MB hard disk space. Color or monochrome monitor. $695.00. ISSN 1053-1424.

This CD-ROM database is an amalgamation of *Consumers Index to Product Evaluations and Information Sources* (CI) (see ARBA 92, entry 174) and *Consumer Health & Nutrition Index* (CHNI) (see ARBA 93, entry 1614), which between them index more than 170 consumer-oriented journals (e.g., *Consumer Reports*, *PC Magazine*, *American Health*, and *FDA Consumer*). Produced by National Information Services Corporation (NISC), the disc is updated semiannually. The disc reviewed covers 1985-May 1995 and contains 235,000 records: 159,000 from CI and 76,000 from CHNI. Because CI and CHNI have overlapping journal coverage (currently 17 titles), there are articles with two records.

The base price is $695 for a stand-alone workstation (this is a 50 percent premium over the combined price of the print versions of CI and CHNI). The network price is the base price plus a scaled surcharge, ranging from 50 percent for 2-10 workstations to 250 percent for 36 or more. The ROMWright access software, developed by NISC, is DOS-based. Release of a Windows version is tentatively scheduled.

CI records typically have author, title, journal, major topic, keyword, and record fields. There are additional descriptive fields depending upon article type. Keywords correspond to primary section headings and subheadings used for the citation's placement in the print CI's hierarchical scheme. The major topic field, nowhere defined, ostensibly denotes the article type. However, in many records, it also contains the primary section heading from the keyword field. The field should be renamed and the section headings removed from it. Data errors in CI records were discovered. Many CD-ROM records without an author field have one in their corresponding CI print citations. There are many incorrect primary section headings in the CD-ROM records (e.g., some citations listed under the primary section "Sports, Recreation, & Hobbies" in the print CI were posted to "The Home" on the disc). CHNI records typically have author, title, journal, keyword, and record fields. Generally one to three keywords (from a controlled vocabulary) are assigned to each article. Duplicate CHNI records should be removed. There is a basic index of words and phrases from the title, keyword, abstract, and other descriptive fields; and separate indexes for author, major topic, keywords, journal, publication year, and subdatabase (CI or CHNI).

To accommodate users with differing experience, there are novice, advanced, and expert search modes. The novice search mode is highly structured and involves inserting terms into subject, author, and publication year boxes. The advanced mode is less structured and involves inserting terms into a list of fields. The expert mode is free-form and involves using field labels and creating and modifying sets. Boolean and proximity operators are functional in all modes, as is the Autodex, a scrolling list of index terms that pop up as one types search terms. Users can easily switch between modes and, in most cases, transport terms. The 200-page "User's Guide" is generic to NISC databases. Explanations are generally clear. Help screens are context-sensitive and heavily derived from the "User's Guide." On-screen instructions are clear and easy to locate.

This reviewer could identify no other similarly focused CD-ROMs; however, there are moderately priced CD-ROMs that include many of this database's journals as part of their coverage (e.g., the basic version of Ebsco's *Magazine Article Summaries*). The CI portion of the database is also available on OCLC's FirstSearch. Overall, CI and CHNI complement each other well. The data errors in many CI records are disturbing; however, when these are corrected, the disc will be serviceable, especially for medium- to large-sized public libraries owning many of the journals indexed.—**John Lewis Campbell**

219. **The Directory of Mail Order Catalogs, 1995.** 9th ed. Richard Gottlieb, ed. Lakeville, Conn., Grey House, 1995. 676p. index. $165.00pa. ISBN 0-939300-63-X.

This 9th annual edition of the *Directory* contains entries for 7,000 catalogs. This number has been steady for 3 years; however, the publishers find that approximately 800 companies are deleted each year with new enterprises taking their place.

The dramatic change has been in catalog revenues, up 33 percent in 1993 from 1987, and the forecast is for continued growth. Catalog revenues were estimated at $53.4 billion for 1993. Today, the industry employs 568,000 people, with a projected increase to 622,000 by 1997. In addition to catalog at-home shopping, home shopping networks are growing and large catalogers are beginning to merchandise products this way also. Various online services as well as the Internet are offering catalogs and e-mail ordering. CD-ROM catalogs are also becoming available.

Each entry in this directory provides company name; address; telephone, fax, and 800 numbers; product description; executive personnel; buyers; catalog circulation; printing information; credit cards accepted; catalog cost; mailing list information; company history; number of employees; and sales volume. The table of contents and the product and company indexes help users find the information desired.

The 1995 *Directory* is also available in a CD-ROM format and a computerized version that can be merged with most database software programs. It can also be purchased in mailing list form. Public libraries of all sizes will want to purchase, if possible. The directory will also be useful in business collections. (See ARBA 91, entry 193; ARBA 88, entry 236; and ARBA 86, entry 181, for reviews of previous editions.)—**Susan C. Awe**

FINANCE AND BANKING

220. Downes, John, and Jordan Elliot Goodman. **Dictionary of Finance and Investment Terms.** 4th ed. Hauppauge, N.Y., Barron's Educational Series, 1995. 682p. $11.95pa. ISBN 0-8120-9035-7.

This edition adds about 2,000 entries to the 3,000 in the 3d edition. Some examples of the additions are *named perils insurance*, *fully depreciated*, *Bo Derek stock*, *duration*, and *gross domestic product*. As a straight dictionary, this volume is wide-ranging, with clear definitions and, for some topics, a large amount of detail (e.g., U.S. tax acts of 1976, 1982, 1984, 1986, and 1993. The detail is superior to *A Dictionary of Finance* [see ARBA 94, entry 204]).

However, errors mar Barron's dictionary; for example, the entry on *antitrust laws* is incomplete (and misleading) and in spots just wrong; *gross domestic product* is identified as "formerly called *Gross National Product*," when in fact GNP and GDP, both still calculated and reported, are not the same. Also, *regression analysis* confuses regression and correlation.

This dictionary is particularly unhelpful (even when it is correct) when any quantitative entry is discussed (e.g., *discounted cash flow*, *net present value*, and *internal rate of return*). A superior source is *The McGraw-Hill Pocket Guide to Business Finance* (see ARBA 93, entry 241). While the volume under review is generally good, the next edition needs more than additional entries; it needs a thorough editing of all continued entries.—**Richard A. Miller**

INDUSTRY AND MANUFACTURING

221. **CDs, Super Glue, and Salsa: How Everyday Products Are Made.** Sharon Rose and Neil Schlager, eds. Detroit, U*X*L/Gale, 1995. 2v. illus. index. $34.95/set. ISBN 0-8103-9791-9.

CDs, Super Glue, and Salsa is a 2-volume work that provides clear explanations about the production and workings of 30 everyday products, with an emphasis on current technology. Averaging eight pages each, the essays provide background on the product, a section on design, and step-by-step descriptions of the manufacturing process, highlighted by line drawings. Boxed sections and margin notes provide related information, photographs add interest, and a brief bibliography tells where to learn more. A wide scope and nontechnical language make the essays entertaining and accessible. The most complex and sophisticated of processes are revealed in easily manageable terms, with each essay broken down into sections for ease of locating specific information. The inventor or development of the product is also covered.

Of course, many of the essays list David Macaulay's *The Way Things Work* (Houghton Mifflin, 1988) as a source for further research. This set makes an excellent companion to his classic work, and to Dorling Kindersley's *The Visual Dictionary of Everyday Things* (see ARBA 93, entry 1078). Yet, while they rely primarily on illustrations to convey information, and also focus on machines, *CDs, Super Glue, and Salsa* is language-based and tells the stories of a number of popular products that are both mechanical and nonmechanical. Commonly used at home or at school, the products are all more complex than they appear to be. Popular foods such as salsa, cheese, and chocolate are examined; clothing items on the order of blue jeans, running shoes, the zipper, and the bulletproof vest are explored. Collectors will enjoy a fascinating history of the postage stamp, while young technophiles will learn about the workings of CDs, optical fiber, bar code scanners, the combination lock, and the seismograph. These products have influenced contemporary industry, transportation, music, diet, entertainment, and lifestyle. The work is a smart, well-edited, and well-written reference set.—**JoAnn Balingit**

222. **The Chemical Industry in 1993. Annual Review: Production and Trade Statistics 1990-1992.** By Economic Commission for Europe. New York, United Nations, 1994. 237p. $42.00pa. ISBN 92-1-116604-7. ISSN 1020-0746. S/N E.94.II.E.26.

The chemical industry is an important gauge of most national economies; therefore, a review of international chemical production and trade such as this may be useful for investors and other analysts interested in the world economy or the economic health of specific nations. The report consists of two parts. Part 1 (73 pages) provides an overall assessment of the industry, a more specific summary focused on the developed nations, a briefer consideration of the less-developed countries, a listing of significant mergers or acquisitions, and a review of the major chemical product categories. Part 2 (157 pages) consists of statistical tables that cover the production, imports, and exports of 40 different countries in terms of major industry categories as well as many specific chemical products. Whether one needs to know how much sulfuric acid Albania produced or how much polyethylene Turkey imported, this is the place to look.

This publication offers a great deal of potentially valuable information, but the statistics only cover through 1992. Specialty chemical journals such as *Chemical and Engineering News* (American Chemical Society) present coverage that is more timely but is also less extensive, covering fewer specific countries and products. Those who are more in need of broad coverage than up-to-date data will find this publication to be a helpful resource.—**Harry E. Pence**

223. Lauber, Timothy J. **Furniture Associations in North America.** Hamburg, N.Y., AKTRIN Research Institute, 1994. 85p. index. $250.00 spiralbound. ISBN 0-921577-41-9.

The chief problem with *Furniture Associations in North America* (FANA) is its price, which will greatly limit the number of libraries able to purchase it. Also, it is a slender spiralbound paperback, which is sometimes a problem for public libraries. In checking the associations included against those listed in the *Encyclopedia of Associations* (see ARBA 94, entries 49-51) and in *National Trade and Professional Associations of the United States* (see ARBA 94, entry 54), there are only two U.S. associations in FANA that do not appear in both of the above titles. FANA, however, lists associations in Mexico and Canada, although there is only one completely Mexican association. The extremely thorough index points out which U.S. associations claim Mexican members.

The information given on the associations varies greatly but often exhibits insider knowledge in a way the other two directories do not. FANA also lists the membership fees for the various associations, which the other two do not provide. In many cases, the association's history, services, and other information (e.g., budget, a description of the membership) appear. FANA concludes that there are too many specialized associations and that what is needed is fewer, larger associations able to think and act internationally. The publishers are furniture industry consultants, and advertising for their other publications and services appears in the book. This title would be primarily useful to furniture companies who want to join and be active in trade associations.—**Susan V. McKimm**

224. **U.S. Industry Profiles: The Leading 100.** Diane M. Sawinski, ed. Detroit, Gale, 1995. 673p. maps. index. $95.00. ISBN 0-7876-0533-6. ISSN 1082-9798.

U.S. Industry Profiles (USIP) provides overviews of the present status and insights into the future of each of the 100 most important industries in the United States. The 1st edition of USIP takes the place of the now-defunct *United States Industrial Outlook*, published for 34 years by the U.S. Department of Commerce. More detailed coverage can be found in *Encyclopedia of American Industries*, also published by Gale (see ARBA 95, entry 236).

Each of the 100 profiles contains an overview; an outlook; significant features of the industry's organization and structure; work force characteristics; trends in research and technology; the position relative to the world market; a list of sources of additional data; suggestions for further reading; and, in some cases, other pertinent information such as environment and government. More than 400 charts, graphs, and maps draw attention to critical data. Industries are listed by SIC codes—an index of codes is included for searching by industry. A comprehensive alphabetical index permits access to companies, industries, organizations, and other key designations. No attempt is made to sum individual profiles to an aggregate for U.S. industry. However, this is a useful and accessible guide to U.S. industries.
—**William C. Struning**

225. **World Databases in Industry.** C. J. Armstrong, ed. New Providence, N.J., K. G. Saur/Reed Reference Publishing, 1995. 852p. index. (World Databases Series). $165.00. ISBN 1-85739-185-3.

Although an ambitious undertaking and unique in its approach, this source will not be needed by any library having access to a major database vendor, such as DIALOG. Those with such access will already have a catalog describing the databases available, an index listing the databases by subject, and a list of the journals available full-text with the databases in which they may be found. Unlike most guides, which profile online services and list their offerings, this directory takes the opposite approach and seeks to list and describe databases and indicate how they may be accessed. Many of the databases profiled consist of a single periodical title and its backfiles, instead of the usual online indexes.

The database descriptions vary in length and detail, but most records include type of database, years of coverage, language, geographical coverage, update frequency, name of the provider, description of the database, and keywords, and indicate the format options available, such as online, CD-ROM, tape, or real-time. A subject index, database name index, and addresses of the database providers are included.

World Databases in Industry is part of a series that is striving to become the authority on electronically published databases, but is for serious researchers only.—**Barbara E. Clotfelter**

INSURANCE

226. **Glossary of Insurance Terms: Over 2,500 Definitions of the Most Commonly Used Words in the Industry.** 5th ed. Thomas E. Green, ed. Santa Monica, Calif., Merritt Publishing, 1994. 276p. $14.95pa. ISBN 0-930868-68-4.

This is one of those books where the title nearly doubles as a table of contents. Terms are defined in entries that range from 6 to 100-plus words. Each entry is categorized by the type of insurance: the "livestock insurance" entry is labeled "PR" for property insurance, "hull policy" is categorized "OM" for ocean marine, and so forth. The types of insurance covered in the glossary are: annuities, automobile, aviation, crime, general, health, inland and ocean marine, legal, liability, life, pension and profit sharing, property, reinsurance, surety, and workers' compensation. Each chapter begins with a list of acronyms and abbreviations, which are explained either directly or through a *see* reference. Cross-referencing is used throughout the text to guide users to synonyms and antonyms. This 5th edition is a complete revision of the 4th.

Seemingly written for laypeople as well as insurance agents, the entries are understandable to the novice. Plain language is consistently used to explain concepts that are frequently abstruse for the average insurance consumer. The definitions are lengthier and more comprehensible than those found in the typical general-language dictionary. Libraries lacking such a glossary are advised to consider this inexpensive paperback resource.—**Ed Volz**

227. **Statistical Survey of Insurance and Reinsurance Operations in Developing Countries 1983-1990.** By the UNCTAD Secretariat. New York, United Nations, 1994. 468p. $50.00pa.

This volume continues the work of the United Nations Conference on Trade and Development (UNCTAD) in helping developing countries evaluate their market performance in insurance. The data use a uniform standard, the "UNCTAD Unified International System of Insurance Statistics," attempting to provide some compatibility across sources and countries. Additionally, the data were supplied to the secretariat of the UNCTAD via questionnaire for purposes of analysis.

All statistics are presented in table format, each clearly described and annotated. The three categories of analysis are the structure of the markets, the economic significance of the markets, and the insurance ratios in nonlife insurance. Combined, they provide a broad look at premium volume for various sectors of the industry and its relationship to that country's gross domestic product (GDP). For each analysis, the tables are organized alphabetically by country. The larger portion of the book is the annexes, each country's statistical submissions by category and year.

Statistical Survey contains valuable detail about the markets and provides a baseline to evaluate the insurance industry. However, the age of the data renders them virtually useless for product or market development research. The economic environment in these countries is so volatile that drastic changes have already occurred and more can be expected. In addition, the conclusion to section 1, note 19, acknowledges that "the analysis of investment returns which are essential for the profitability of insurance concerns in markets of developing countries" is missing from this statistical collection. Because similar resources, which also contain current economic information, are available from insurance industry vendors, the purchase of this book is recommended only for archival purposes and not as an addition to the reference shelf in a company focusing on the markets evaluation and product development necessary for twenty-first-century insurance practice.—**Deborah K. Scott**

INTERNATIONAL BUSINESS

General Works

Directories

228. **International Business & Trade Directories.** Richard Gottlieb, ed. Lakeville, Conn., Grey House Publishing, 1995. 636p. index. $125.00pa. ISBN 0-939300-64-8.

This directory of directories aims to fill a niche with its global approach. Arranged by broad industry categories (e.g., accounting, broadcasting, packaging, textiles), then divided by geographical regions (e.g., Africa, Eastern Europe, North America), each region may be broken down into specific countries. Entries vary in detail but may contain the publisher, publisher's address, telephone and fax numbers, frequency of publication, price, brief description of the contents, editorial staff, and pagination. A title index and publisher index are also included. An index of titles by country would have been useful.

While it may not have an equal with regard to global coverage, this title's errors involving standard business references lessens its effectiveness. On several pages the same content description is used for a number of different entries, resulting in titles such as *Moody's Handbook of Common Stocks* (see ARBA 93, entry 223) and the *United States Senate Telephone Directory* (U.S. Government Publishing Office) being described as a "who's who directory of services and supplies to the industry." In at least one instance, the price for a title published in the United States is given in British pounds, and, in another instance, both the current and previous title of the same source are listed as separate entries even though the title change occurred in 1990.

The *Encyclopedia of Business Information Sources* (see ARBA 93, entry 206, for a review of the 9th ed.) is a much-preferred source providing a wider range of topics. Its coverage is limited to the United States; however, a separate volume, the *Encyclopedia of Business Information Sources: Europe* (see ARBA 95, entry 277) is available. Due to its shortcomings, libraries needing this type of coverage may wish to wait for the 2d edition.—**Barbara E. Clotfelter**

229. **World's Major Companies Directory.** London, Euromonitor; distr., Detroit, Gale, 1994. 756p. index. $550.00. ISBN 0-86338-460-9.

This directory provides varying amounts of information on approximately 3,000 international companies from 95 countries. The geographical emphasis is heavily weighted toward North America, the European Union, Japan, and Australia. The entries are arranged in two categories—multinationals and nationals. The criteria for inclusion in the former category are annual turnover (sales) greater than $2 billion, and a substantial percentage of sales or corporate presence outside the home country. Entries in this category are in alphabetical order and often fairly detailed, but represent barely 20 percent of the total directory. The latter and largest category includes the biggest indigenous companies from each country—no subsidiaries of multinationals are listed—and, depending on the availability of information, may be quite brief. The arrangement is by region and country, and then alphabetically by company within the country. A typical company entry may cover company name and address, description of business, ownership, subsidiaries, key personnel, number of employees, main products and brands, and financial information. Financial information is presented in tabular form and, if the information is available, breaks out sales geographically by region. Supplemental notes highlight recent acquisitions, new products, market shares, and other items of interest. Useful lists of "top" companies, ranked by sales, precede the multinational section and selected country sections. Also furnished are a brief directory of published rankings listing special issues of journals and other international business directories that contain rankings, as well as an alphabetical company index for the volume.

The most significant contribution of this directory is the provision of company sales data broken out by region. There are also several shortcomings that should be noted. Most important is the fact that financial data for the majority of companies are only current through 1992, the lone exception being for those based in the United Kingdom, which have figures for 1993. Additional indexes (industry, for example) and a sturdier binding would also have enhanced its utility and value. On balance, however, upper-level and graduate business students should find the directory useful, and it is recommended for comprehensive international business collections.—**Gordon J. Aamot**

Handbooks and Yearbooks

230. Barbuto, Domenica M. **The International Financial Statistics Locator: A Research and Information Guide.** Hamden, Conn., Garland, 1994. 338p. (Research and Information Guides in Business, Industry, and Economic Institutions, v.11; Garland Reference Library of Social Science, v.924). $53.00. ISBN 0-8153-1483-3.

This guide is meant to help researchers locate financial and investment-related statistics as reported in 22 selected sources. These sources cover standard printed publications (*The Wall Street Journal*, *Barron's National Business and Finance Weekly*, and *The Federal Reserve Bulletin*) as well as sources in one or more other formats (online, magnetic tape, CD-ROM, and diskette) such as MARSTAT, DRICOM, and DRIFACS.

The work begins with a list of abbreviations for the sources and a short description of each source (including a notation of the formats in which the source is available). The major portion of the *Guide* is an alphabetical listing of countries and topics that refer one by abbreviation to the source providing the data in question. Under a country (e.g., Finland) the topics are divided by broad subject and then specialized heading. Under a particular topic, it generally refers one to the entry for a country or the entry for a broad range of information (e.g., commodities). Under *securities*, it gives a cross-reference to look under the names of individual countries.

An appendix, entitled "Directory of World Securities Markets," provides contacts for finding information not available from the 22 standard sources. The directory lists addresses, telephone, fax, and telex numbers. Internet addresses are not available.

The guide is a "second-order" reference work—that is, its function is to refer researchers to other sources. Among the most useful features of the guide is that it specifically indicates if some category of statistic (e.g., bank rates in Madagascar) is not available. This will clearly save the time a researcher would waste looking for a statistic that is not available in the standard sources. This is a useful resource for serious research in international finances and investment, and it would be a reasonable purchase for any library supporting such research.—**Richard H. Swain**

231. **Craighead's International Business, Travel, and Relocation Guide to 78 Counties 1996-97: The Most Comprehensive Reference Source....** 8th ed. Detroit, Gale, 1995. 3v. maps. $575.00/set. ISBN 0-7876-0840-8.

These 3 informative volumes cover 78 countries, 3 (Algeria, Sudan, and [the former] Yugoslavia) having been omitted from the preceding edition. The aim of this reference source is to provide working knowledge to those who plan to do business in foreign countries while living or temporarily residing in them. Academic and other temporary visitors will also find this source useful.

The country coverage (in the case of the Baltic countries, all three are lumped into one chapter) is standardized. A map of the country is followed by basic information and then by an orientation section on the people, geography, largest cities, shorthand history, climate (with some not completely correct comparisons), and diplomatic representation in and of the country. The next section is on developments and trends, with emphasis on the functioning of the economy and the country's politics; then comes a section on conducting business in the country, with such practical information as business customs, employment conditions and labor costs, hurdles for foreign investors, availability of on-site professionals, and various addresses.

A section on money and its use, banking conditions and addresses, and taxes follows. An important practical section is on communications, covering general telephone services, international calls, mail service, and English-language publications and broadcasting. Then comes information on living in the country; where to find housing; the cost of living, including automotive, recreation, and the like; the search for housing, its cost, leases, and information on schools for children; getting household help; utilities; food; driving conditions; religious services; social networking; and even information on importing pets. The section on health and safety provides data on insurance; emergency services; access to medical services (with addresses that seem to focus predominantly on the capital of the country), including dentists and pharmacies; and vaccination requirements. After providing all that information, *Craighead's* leads the traveler through the preparation for the trip (visas, work permits, customs and currency regulations); arrival hassles; lodging; dining and nightlife; and separately through the leisure activities, including shopping, sports, and tourist help. The country chapters close with bibliographies and lists of suggested reading.

The information is current to about mid-1993, and hence should be updated by the travelers themselves, especially with regard to countries with fast inflation or rapid institutional change, such as those in transition from communism to free markets. Many things have changed since 1993; for example, exchange rates, prices, and even currency systems. The changes—it is pleasant to report—have been generally for the better and for the greater comfort of travelers, but then *Craighead's* has omitted some countries (former Yugoslavia most of all). There are also the almost-inevitable spelling mistakes and minor factual errors. A page on "arrival survival language" is at times more amusing than useful and is found only for countries where English is not commonly known.

The general assessment of this source is that it is eminently useful to business and other travelers who, when embarking on their travel, may want to make photocopies of the relevant pages. *Craighead's* belongs in larger reference libraries, including those with multinational collections.—**Bogdan Mieczkowski**

232. **Economic Integration in Europe and North America.** M. Panic and Aleksandar M. Vacic, eds. New York, United Nations, 1995. 216p. (United Nations Economic Commission for Europe Economic Studies, no.5). $60.00pa. ISBN 92-1-100673-2. ISSN 1014-4994. S/N GV.E.93.0.24.

This is a series of academic papers on themes related to postwar attempts at integration in Europe, East and West. It has a chapter on the United States-Canadian trade treaty, with some concluding remarks on the North American Free Trade Agreement (NAFTA). Most of the papers were prepared in the early 1990s. They are intended to reflect the experience of the past half-century, to better understand options for the future.

Contributors come from academia and the staffs of intergovernmental organizations. Essays are grouped in three chapters: the main two on Western and Eastern European experiences and the final essay on North America. Papers on Western Europe deal with integration in the West (including those countries outside the European Community [EC]); the role of the European Free Trade Association (EFTA); and the effects of Western integration (with emphasis on the 1992 market completion program) on southern and Eastern European states. The Maastricht treaty and its programs for economic, monetary, and political union are not covered, nor is the accession of Sweden, Austria, and Finland to the European Union (formerly EC).

The papers on Eastern Europe cover the Council for Mutual Economic Assistance's (CMEA) integration efforts and its failure, prospects for future integration, and the impact of CMEA's collapse. Considering the rapid changes of past years, completion dates for papers on recent events would have been helpful. This is a useful volume of research papers that should be acquired by research collections. It is beyond the scope of most public libraries.—**Nigel Tappin**

233. Gottschalk, Jack A. **Directory of International Business.** Pasadena, Calif., Salem Press, 1994. 2v. illus. maps. index. $115.00/set. ISBN 0-89356-822-8.

This affordable two-volume set is a guide to international business practices, regulations, and laws, and is a library edition of the author's earlier trade publication *Global Trade and Investment Handbook* (Probus Publishing, 1993). The *Directory of International Business* is arranged alphabetically by country and provides information of interest to foreign investors and business students on 155 countries, from Albania to Zimbabwe. Each entry is 5-6 pages long and is arranged in 14 standard categories: political environment; foreign investment policy; formation and types of permitted business organizations; environmental protection; rights and obligations of foreign investors; labor; accounting requirements; currency controls; taxation; legal system; customs duties; protection of intellectual property; immigration and residence; and in-country sources of assistance for foreign investors. The length of each section varies from several paragraphs to a single sentence. Enhancements to the library edition include a black-and-white map showing the location of each country on its respective continent, with a depiction of its flag. Volume 2 also includes a list of the signatories to several of the most important international agreements.

While the original trade edition was intended as a convenient, desktop reference source for current trade and foreign direct investment information, the complexity and scope of the subject and the limitations of the format keep this work from being entirely successful as a serious business reference tool. The problems raised by squeezing 155 standardized country entries into a two-volume, monographic format are difficult to overcome. The summary of foreign investment policy in each entry is usually the longest of the 14 sections and is often quite good. In general, however, the other sections are too brief to provide much more than cursory information and none can be kept current, something vitally important to consumers of international business information. Also, there is no indication that the author's original 1993 work has been updated. The result is a work that is very broad in scope, but offers little depth of coverage. This work is suitable for general public and undergraduate library reference collections that need to include some basic coverage of international direct investment information, as well as those business collections not already owning the original trade publication from which the library edition is derived.—**Gordon J. Aamot**

234. **Handbook of International Trade and Development Statistics 1993. Manuel de Statistiques de Commerce International et du Développement.** By United Nations Conference on Trade and Development. New York, United Nations, 1994. 586p. $80.00pa. ISBN 92-1-012034-5. ISSN 0251-9461. S/N E/F.94.II.D.24.

This handbook arranges trade and development statistics generally reflective of development status by region. Under this scheme, four regional groupings are used: the developed market economies that have wide geographical distribution; Socialist economies of Asia; countries in Eastern Europe; and developing countries, which encompass countries in Africa, America, Asia, Europe, and Oceania that do not fit into the other groupings. These groupings are further subdivided by geographical distribution and political affiliations. This arrangement is designed to facilitate comparative analyses of the data, which have been presented as time series data wherever possible.

The handbook includes statistics on trade balances, the growth of world trade, patterns of trade, import/export patterns by major commodity, levels of external indebtedness, and social indicators. Other publications such as *Social Indicators of Development* (see ARBA 95, entry 870) and *World Tables* (see ARBA 95, entry 257) present data summaries primarily by country and may be easier to use in answering ready-reference questions about specific countries, but the analytical arrangement of *Handbook of International Trade and Development Statistics* makes it a good choice for libraries serving programs in international studies, marketing, or economics.—**Peggy Jobe**

235. Hargreaves, David, Monica Eden-Green, and Joan Devaney. **World Index of Resources and Population.** Brookfield, Vt., Dartmouth; distr., Brookfield, Vt., Ashgate Publishing, 1994. 417p. index. $149.95. ISBN 1-85521-503-9.

The purpose of this ambitious book is to quantify and project the interaction of 61 countries, 30 leading multinational companies, and 36 minerals (which make up more than 95 percent of the resources used) over a 30-year period.

The *World Index* is broken down into seven broad sections: world population trends, minerals, the energy industry, countries, companies, the automobile industry, and the environment. One drawback of the *Index* may be the brief attention (i.e., eight pages) given to automobile industry and the environment.

The easy-to-read text includes figures, charts, graphs, and summaries of activities for each of the sections and subsections discussed. The text is preceded by an informative introduction and how-to-use section, and it concludes with a glossary of terms and a brief but useful index.

The work, while somewhat pricey, is recommended for the reference collections of academic and public libraries. It would likely be used by any number of individuals, governments, and organizations interested in projecting the potential effects of future economic, population, social, and political trends.
—**James M. Murray**

236. **International Directory of Company Histories. Volume 9.** Paula Kepos, ed. Detroit, St. James Press, 1994. 730p. index. $145.00. ISBN 1-55862-324-8.

237. **International Directory of Company Histories. Volume 10.** Paula Kepos, ed. Detroit, St. James Press, 1995. 753p. index. $145.00. ISBN 1-55862-325-6.

238. **International Directory of Company Histories. Volume 11.** Paula Kepos, ed. Detroit, St. James Press, 1995. 753p. index. $145.00. ISBN 1-55862-326-4.

Since the initial volumes of this multivolume set first hit the shelves of reference collections across the country in 1988, librarians and library users have found the *International Directory of Company Histories* to be an important reference tool for all who want to learn more about the historical development of the world's largest and most influential companies. Volumes 9, 10, and 11 cover approximately 180 companies each, bringing the total number of entries in the set to more than 2,000. To be included, a company must have sales greater than $500 million or be a leader in its industry or geographical location. State-owned companies are discussed if they are important in their industry. Wholly owned subsidiaries may be listed if they meet the inclusion criteria.

Each company entry is between two and three pages in length and follows a standard format. It begins with a short section of basic directory information, including company name, address of headquarters, telephone and fax numbers, earliest incorporation date, number of employees, principal SIC (Standard Industrial Classification) codes, and stock exchanges where traded. Sales for the most recent year available are given in U.S. dollars and, if applicable, the country of origin. If the company has legal names in both English and the language of the country of origin, the English name is given, with the native name added in parentheses. The type of ownership—public, private, state, or parent—is also noted. In addition, a list of subsidiaries is provided. The majority of each article is composed of the narrative company history. The histories are compiled from publicly available sources and are uniformly well written and informative. Each article is signed by its author. A brief bibliography for further reading concludes each article. Volumes 9 through 11 all contain a cumulative company and personal name index for the entire set, so finding a particular company is quick and easy. A separate industry index, from "Accounting" to "Waste Services," is also supplied.

The latest volumes in the *International Directory of Company Histories* make an important contribution to the literature of business history, but some small criticisms need to be addressed. First, the sales data for each entry are described as being the most recent figures available, but no year is given. Second, although the title proclaims that these volumes are international in scope, it should be noted that this claim is fairly weak. A quick count of the foreign entries in volumes 9, 10, and 11 indicates that less than 10 percent of the companies are from countries other than the United States. Lastly, purchasers of these latest volumes should be aware that some articles are updates of earlier entries. Seventy-two (13 percent) of the 552 entries in volumes 9 through 11 fall into this category. While these updates are clearly marked as such, the fact remains that much of the revised article is derived from the original and that one may, in effect, be repurchasing information already contained in earlier volumes. On the other hand, it would be a disservice to readers to make them consult two different volumes to see the complete entry for a particular company, so this approach is preferable to the alternative. If the publisher continues to update previously covered companies, it might be useful to consider another format, perhaps CD-ROM. Despite these minor problems, the latest volumes of this important company directory are essential for both academic and public business reference collections.—**Gordon J. Aamot**

239. Miller, E. Willard, and Ruby M. Miller. **America's International Trade: A Reference Handbook.** Santa Barbara, Calif., ABC-CLIO, 1995. 325p. index. (Contemporary World Issues). $39.50. ISBN 0-87436-770-0.

This book is a reference handbook set at a fairly basic level. It begins by discussing how U.S. trade policy has evolved, and gives its current objectives. There are data presented that show the importance of international trade in general to the U.S. economy, as well as on some specific bilateral relationships of the United States. One chapter gives names and dates of major pieces of trade legislation along with a synopsis of the provisions. Another is a directory of world trade centers and organizations, giving an address, a description, a purpose, an activity, and publications when relevant. Approximately half the book is a bibliography, annotated for books, listings of journal articles, and government documents.

While the book can be a useful reference for many, it has shortcomings. The first is that even with a 1995 publication date, the material is dated. The omission of the most recent books and articles is not a serious problem, but the lack of mention of the World Trade Organization (WTO) is a major flaw. The organization came into being by treaty on January 1, 1995. It is now the most important international organization with regard to the establishment and enforcement of rules governing world trade. The WTO is the successor to, and qualitatively different from, the General Agreement on Tariffs and Trade (GATT), which is mentioned. The book is almost solely devoted to international trade, with investment, portfolio, or direct little mentioned. The omission can be justified, but given the interaction for companies and countries between direct foreign investment and international trade, it does limit the usefulness of the book.
—**J. E. Weaver**

240. Reddy, Marlita A., and Robert S. Lazich. **World Market Share Reporter 1995-96: A Compilation of Reported World Market Share Data....** Detroit, Gale, 1995. 602p. index. $295.00. ISBN 0-8103-9641-6. ISSN 1078-6783.

Business firms that seek a larger share of the market for a given product increasingly turn to foreign trade. The decision to sell one's product in the world market means that those companies that do so must conduct a tremendous amount of research—research about the importing country, as well as research about a specific importer. *World Market Share Reporter* (WMSR) is a welcome addition to the growing body of reference material addressing the needs of the American exporter. This new resource is a compilation of global market share data from periodicals literature. Each reference appears under a Standard Industrial Classification industry code. The appropriate International SIC (ISIC) and Harmonized

Code classifications also appear where applicable. In addition to the table of contents and an alphabetical table of topics, the nearly 1,650 entries may be accessed by company, product, brand, place, and source indexes. The majority of entries were extracted from newspapers and from general-purpose, trade, and technical periodicals. Rather than being exhaustive, the entries reflect the concerns of the business press, and those concerns generally mirror issues in the United States and abroad.

WMSR is modeled after the Gale business title *Market Share Reporter*, which covers North American market shares (Canada, United States, and Mexico). Reddy's and Lazich's work is a must-purchase for agencies that promote international trade or study the foreign economic scene. Likewise, academic libraries that support international marketing courses or international economic relations will wish to purchase this resource. Larger public libraries also have a ready clientele for such data.—**Dene L. Clark**

241. **USA Business: The Portable Encyclopedia for Doing Business with the United States.** By Karla C. Shippey and others. San Rafael, Calif., World Trade Press, 1995. 504p. illus. maps. index. (World Trade Press Country Business Guides). $24.95pa. ISBN 1-885073-01-1.

The intended audience for this particular title is companies or firms located abroad that wish to do business in the United States, whether as an investor, a manufacturer, or an exporter. This is the eighth book in the publisher's Country Business Guides series, and at least three more titles are planned. Currently, they are focusing on countries in Latin America and the Pacific Rim. While this title would be of little use in the United States, the other titles in the series would be useful for United States companies wanting to do business in such countries as Argentina or Korea.

While much of the information that has been included could be obtained from the U.S. Department of Commerce or the U.S. Chamber of Commerce operating in these countries, these are inexpensive books with much general information on such topics as taxation, business law, export policies, and business culture. The encyclopedias include addresses of government agencies and professional associations, maps of major cities, and information on trade fairs. They would serve as a good starting point for someone doing business in another country. People serious about doing business in another country would need to seek additional sources before entering into a business relationship. (See ARBA 95, entries 261-266, for reviews of other volumes in the series.)—**Judith J. Field**

Asia

242. **Consumer Asia 1995.** [2d ed.]. London, Euromonitor; distr., Detroit, Gale, 1995. 327p. $750.00pa. ISBN 0-86338-571-0.

Rich in statistics, this 2d edition on consumption in Asia is a treasure trove of comparative information and data on the development of individual countries over the period of 1989-93. Countries covered include East Asia (except for Japan), Southeast Asia, and South Asia, 12 countries in all. Overview sections deal respectively with: an overview of the region as a whole that contains a longer-period perspective, some forecasts, and a good discussion of data; marketing parameters for the individual countries of the region, as for instance the demographic statistics, retail sales, telecommunications, and tourism; and consumer markets for the 12 countries in individual products and product categories. Sections 2 and 3, as in the rest of this volume, only give statistics without discussing them, and they provide additional summary bar diagrams, graphically reinforcing the messages from the tables. The final 12 sections deal separately with the 12 countries of the region. They provide the background of demographics, labor markets, Gross Domestic Product (GDP), inflation, foreign trade, energy consumption, health, housing, advertising, expenditure patterns, and consumption of individual products and product categories, both durable and nondurable. The usefulness of the *Consumer Asia* volume is both personal—such as for information, research, tracing of trends—as well as institutional, for business and government to find information about the dynamically growing Asian markets, infrastructure needs, and possible health implications of the changes in consumption patterns. The importance of this volume cannot be underestimated, and it is therefore recommended for the widest possible use.—**Bogdan Mieczkowski**

243. **Indian Social and Economic Development 1993: An Index to the Literature.** Compiled by the Centre for Development of Instructional Technology (CENDIT). Thousand Oaks, Calif., Sage, 1994. 200p. index. $33.50. ISBN 0-8039-9167-3.

The Centre for Development of Instructional Technology (CENDIT), New Delhi, India, has prepared an index to the literature dealing with Indian social and economic development. An excellent index covering the period from 1989 to 1993, the focus of it is on the literature dealing with field experience, case studies, decision-making strategies, and resource-sharing tools for development. The book has six chapters under various subject headings such as ecology, human resources, women/children, income generation, empowerment, and debates.

There are a total of 514 entries selected for this index. They have been arranged alphabetically within chapters. Each entry provides complete bibliographic information, including author, title, place of publication, publisher, and page numbers. For journal entries, the information includes author, title, name of the journal, volume number, dates, and page numbers. A special feature of this index is a tailor-made abstract and subject heading for each entry. Books published by well-known publishers have been excluded, with a few exceptions. A few official documents, research reports, newsletters, seminar papers, monographs, and annual reports have also been supplied. In addition, a few entries dealing with other South Asian countries have been indexed.

This well-prepared book has author, title, subject, and geographical indexes. All entries in these indexes lead to entry numbers rather than page numbers. There is a list of abbreviations for all the states of India and other South Asian countries. The material furnished in this index has been identified with the state abbreviations for the benefit of all users. A list of periodicals cited in the book has also been included. The titles in this list lead to abstract numbers. This work is highly recommended for libraries interested in developing Indian collections, and for scholars and students interested in India.—**Ravindra Nath Sharma**

244. **Japan Directory of Professional Associations.** 3d ed. Tokyo, Intercontinental Marketing Corporation; distr., Bristol, Pa., Taylor & Francis, 1995. 400p. index. $300.00pa. ISBN 4-900178-09-8. ISSN 0287-9530.

The 3d edition of the *Japan Directory* lists about 8,700 organizations (encompassing associations, societies, and institutes), a 50 percent increase over the number of entries in the 2d edition. Arranged alphabetically, using names translated into English, entries include the Japanese name and, as available, the address, telephone and fax numbers, e-mail address, contact people, and subject categorization of activities. Many listings also have information about membership, activities, goals, regularly scheduled events, the existence of a library, and publications. As a significant improvement over previous editions, the directory has adopted a two-column format that is much easier to read.

There are two indexes, one for the Japanese names of the organizations, and the other for subject categories of activities. Supplementary sections cover finding information about Japan, the floppy disk version of the directory, the option of requesting special "start-up" research for business or industrial fields, the list of subject categories, some relevant magazines and journals, and a list of the directory's more commonly used abbreviations.

The extensive effort required (i.e., thousands of mailed questionnaires and follow-up telephone calls) to produce the directory has paid off in the creation of a directory that will meet the needs of the intended audience of businesspersons, researchers, students, and librarians needing brief information about a wide range of Japanese organizations. It is unfortunate that the high price of this paperback will limit its acquisition to business and academic libraries with adequate budgets and compelling needs for comprehensive coverage.—**Kenneth W. Berger**

245. **Major Companies of the Far East and Australasia 1995/96.** 12th ed. Jennifer L. Murphy, ed. London, Graham & Whiteside; distr., Detroit, Gale, 1995. 3v. index. $1,170.00/set. ISBN 1-86099-007-X(v.1); 1-86099-008-8(v.2); 1-86099-009-6(v.3). [Volumes also available separately.]

These volumes are 3 parts of a 12-volume set covering large companies worldwide. The set is updated annually; the individual volumes may be purchased separately. (Volume 1 was reviewed in ARBA 93 [see entry 281]). Company entries contain address; telephone/fax/telex listings; names of principal officers; types of business activities; banks used; date of establishment; number of employees; and essential financial data when available (about half the entries). The main text has company names arranged alphabetically under each country name (also alphabetical). Each of the volumes has three additional company name indexes: alphabetically regardless of country, alphabetically within each country, and country-by-country within a SIC code listing.

Although there is no summation of data for each country or business activity, this is still a valuable directory source for the business collections of large libraries. The information is presented in a more readable format than some other directories in this set. While small companies are not listed, these sources contain enough entries to satisfy all but the most curious and entrepreneurial.—**Ed Volz**

246. **The Ross Register of Siberian Industry 1995: A Directory of Resources....** Eugene L. Posadskov and Eugene D. Malinin, comps. Robert E. Ross, ed. New York, Norman Ross, 1995. 166p. maps. $119.00. ISBN 0-88354-125-4.

This premier edition of the directory has three main and two subsidiary parts. The first main part contains an extended narrative describing the resources of Siberia, including its history, weather, human resources, and management of the economically independent regions. Mineral and industrial resources are emphasized. A subsidiary part follows, listing product categories presumably found in the second main part, but not cross-referenced. The second main part lists major enterprises by product category, indicating the region of Siberia in which the enterprise is located, its address, telephone, and fax numbers. This part reveals a scarcity of service enterprises: This reviewer found here only banks and commodity exchanges. The third main part lists major enterprises by region, and has less than precise hand-drawn maps. The maps do not show the BAM railroad line as completed. The information about enterprises is more abundant in this part, providing also names of contacts, the number of employees, output by product, and exports. Finally, the subsidiary part lists territorial governments with addresses, contacts, telephone, and fax numbers. The *Register* can serve as a first step for business ventures, but it indicates also that careful individual exploration of business opportunities in Siberia is a prerequisite for a cautious businessperson. The directory is recommended for all multinational corporations.—**Bogdan Mieczkowski**

247. **The Russian Far East: An Economic Handbook.** Pavel A. Minakir and Gregory L. Freeze, eds. Armonk, N.Y., M. E. Sharpe, 1994. 495p. index. $150.00. ISBN 1-56324-456-X.

This unique reference book is the product of a joint publication venture by Russian and Japanese scholars, under the sponsorship of the Sasakawa Peace Foundation (Japan) and the Institute of Economic Research, within the Far Eastern Branch of the Russian Academy of Sciences. The work was stimulated by Japan's newfound interest in Siberia and the Russian Far East as a potential trading partner, as well as a place for new foreign investment. Therefore, the primary intended audience for the book is the international business community and those libraries that support research in the areas of international trade and finance.

The handbook contains much statistical data in addition to a considerable amount of text. The material is organized into three broad sections, covering natural resources and population, economic development, and economic reform and the system of economic regulation. Each section is subdivided into various chapters (14 in all) that deal with such topics as "the resource sector of the economy," "conversion of defense industries," and "international economic activity." A lengthy "Statistical Overview," consisting of 253 tables, is appended to the book, and numerous tables and figures are also found within the text of the chapters. Additionally appended is a classified list of Russian organizations active in foreign trade and investment; a list of basic laws, decrees, and normative acts that regulate international trade; and several maps of the Far East region. Although much of this material is highly specialized, the amount of statistical data and concise background information makes this work appropriate for most university library reference collections.—**Thomas A. Karel**

248. Williams, Dominic. **A Dictionary of Japanese Financial Terms.** Sandgate, England, Japan Library; distr., Atlantic Highlands, N.J., Humanities Press, 1995. 162p. $70.00; $19.95pa. ISBN 1-873410-11-5; 1-873410-12-3pa.

This unique dictionary is a product of the author's long experience with the translation of technical terms, and it is limited to terms used in financial communication. Japanese terms are provided only insofar as they pertain to finances, although some alternative uses are also indicated. The main, most extensive part of the dictionary has entries in Japanese, first in romanji and then in Japanese script (including katakana for Japanized English, kana, and Chinese characters), with alternative or related usage provided, and with clear and concise English translations. The second part is subsidiary, English-romanji, where the romanji equivalents of English terms can be checked more fully by going back to the first part. The final part contains 12 statistical tables for 1993, some with a historical 1991-93 perspective, covering up to 12 countries for international trade and its various components, including exchange rates and retail trade. The *Dictionary* is eminently practical, and is recommended to all firms or individual practitioners in financial transactions with Japan, or, when needed, to be used in conjunction with M. Matsuoka and B. Rose's *The DIR Guide to Japanese Economic Statistics* (Oxford University Press, 1994).—**Bogdan Mieczkowski**

Canada

249. Albala, Leila, and Elie Albala. **Catalogue of Canadian Catalogues.** 4th ed. Chambly, Quebec, Alpel Publishing, 1994. 168p. illus. index. $9.95pa. ISBN 0-921993-07-2.

The 1st edition was published in 1987 (see ARBA 88, entry 224), with 288 entries. Here, 900 Canadian mail-order (and mainly free) catalogs are described: names of companies, their addresses, telephone numbers, fax and toll-free numbers (if appropriate), and product lists, plus an indication of how long they've been in business, and a mission statement that should be taken at face value. The arrangement is by subject: There are about 100 categories, such as basketry, fabric, food, knitting, toys, organic gardening, pets, and winemaking. Most are for home crafts and family life. There are also pages of advertisements between the text and the index, but most are house ads from the publisher. This is a useful tool for Canadian libraries, and may even be useful for foreign libraries because most companies ship around the world (if not, the entry states "Canada only"). These are indeed the days of free trade.—**Dean Tudor**

250. **The Globe and Mail Report on Business: Canada Company Handbook 1994.** Toronto, Globe Information Services; distr., Austin, Tex., Reference Press, 1994. 1v. (various paging). $49.95pa. ISBN 0-921925-78-6. ISSN 0847-2831.

Now in its sixth year, this title contains material prepared for the "Report on Business" section of the *Globe and Mail* in Toronto, Canada. It is one of a series from the *Globe*. Since the *Globe* continuously gathers and analyzes financial information and news on thousands of Canadian companies, updated information is normally accessible through Info Globe on a daily basis. Of course, one must pay at a metered rate for this online delivery, but one's reward is last-minute details and computer-formatted material.

The arrangement is by major industry, such as oil and gas, automotive, chemical, transportation, banks and trusts, and utilities. For each of 417 public companies, there is current news, ratios and price performance charts, and quarterly financial information, with data current through 1993 or June 29, 1994. There is also an alphabetical directory of the top 1,000 public and private companies, crown corporations, and cooperatives, with addresses, stock symbols, descriptions of business, senior executives, assets, revenue, and net income. This work certainly has a good price for foreign libraries.—**Dean Tudor**

Europe

251. **Consumer Eastern Europe 1996.** London, Euromonitor; distr., Detroit, Gale, 1995. 581p. $750.00. ISBN 0-86338-570-2.

This massive volume contains many invaluable statistics plus a brief commentary on the economies of the Eastern European states and their economic prospects. The publisher has gathered an incredible amount of statistical data from national sources, no small task in view of the newly independent status of the Eastern European countries. Where necessary, the publisher has supplemented national data with figures from other sources. The statistical data range from birth rates, marriage rates, and population forecasts to ownership of television sets, washing machines, and refrigerators. Researchers looking for data on tourist accommodations in Bulgaria, per capita sales of soft drinks in the Slovak Republic, or per capita sales of household cleaning products in the Russian Federation will be rewarded. Likewise, they also will find data on new residential buildings constructed in Latvia, miles of East Germany's highway system (by state and class of highway), and newspaper and magazine circulation in Poland.

Consumer Eastern Europe includes nothing on Yugoslavia or its breakaway states. The spelling of "savoury" and "yoghurt" and the use of the British "petrol" will alert United States audiences that the title is published in London. Quibbling aside, the work unites in one volume data that, if available, is scattered throughout numerous sources, such as *Europa World Year Book* (see ARBA 94, entry 82) and various United Nations publications. It is highly recommended for corporate libraries serving firms with business interests in this region. Trade promotion organizations and economic think tanks that focus on Eastern Europe will need to acquire this title as well. Academic libraries supporting international marketing programs will also wish to purchase this title, budget permitting.—**Dene L. Clark**

252. **European Employment Law: A Country by Country Guide.** Trowers and Hamlins, eds. Burr Ridge, Ill., Irwin Professional Publishing, 1995. 353p. index. (Financial Times Series). $60.00. ISBN 0-7863-0152-X.

This is a guide to employment in Europe covering employment law both under the European Union and under 24 individual European countries in the European Community, European Free Trade Area, Eastern Europe, and Scandinavia. Each entry differs somewhat according to the legislation; however, the coverage generally includes types of employment agreements and contracts, collective agreements, termination, dispute settlement, and working conditions. Addresses and contacts throughout Europe who can offer further advice are given as well. The text is organized alphabetically by country, with a subject index at the back. Each section is written by an experienced business practitioner in the jurisdiction. The text is written in a general discursive manner without resorting to jargon or legalese. The text is aimed at the North American businessperson working in Europe, not legal experts. There are few references to actual legislation. Local legal advisers will be needed for detailed information.

The book will be a useful reference source for international business managers looking for information on employment issues. It would be helpful in any international business collection.

—**Lorna K. Rees-Potter**

253. **Major Companies of Europe 1994/5.** A. Wilson, S. Blackburn, and S. E. Hörnig, eds. London, Graham & Trotman; distr., Detroit, Gale, 1994. 4v. index. $450.00/set. ISBN 1-85966-099-1. ISSN 1356-2533.

This is the 14th annual edition of this work. There are 4 volumes containing information on Western Europe's 17,000 largest companies; the first covers those in Austria, Belgium, Denmark, Eire, Finland, and France; Germany, Greece, Italy, Liechtenstein, and Luxembourg are in the second; the third includes The Netherlands, Norway, Portugal, Spain, Sweden, and Switzerland; and the United Kingdom is the sole country in the fourth. While the information disclosed for each company varies, the following are given when available: name of company; address; telephone, fax, and telex numbers; name of chairman; president; board members; senior management; principal activities of the company; principal brand names and trademarks; parent company; principal subsidiaries and associates; bankers; auditors; principal shareholder; number of employees; and financial information for two years (such as sales turnover, profit [loss] before/after tax, dividends, earnings per share, share capital, and shareholder funds).

There are business activities indexes in English, French, German, and Italian that subdivide the 20 categories, such as consumer goods, mining and quarrying, and transport services. There is also a business activity index in each volume that lists companies by their various business activities within their main country of operation. In addition, there is an alphabetical index of all companies in each volume and an alphabetical index to companies within each country by their country of operation.—**J. E. Weaver**

Latin America

254. **Mexico Company Handbook: Data on Major Listed Companies.** 1995/96 ed. Mexico City, IMF Editora; distr., Austin, Tex., Reference Press, 1995. 117p. index. $34.95pa. ISBN 1-57311-000-0.

This guide provides succinct information on each of the 85 major companies listed on the Bolsa Mexica de Valores (BMV [the Mexican stock exchange]). Important data on the economy, the trade situation, and investment possibilities are provided for users. The book is especially designed to attract U.S. investment; therefore, it is published in English. Detailed information is given on the Mexican economy for 1994, with a five-year economic indicators chart.

The section on the Mexican securities market provides an overall view of the stock market; it also provides stock market data over a five-year period from 1990 to 1994 on trading volume, trading value in United States dollars, the highs and lows market capitalization, price earnings ratios, price book values, and public offerings. Another major section is on the securities market instrument, providing data taken from the book *Investing in Mexico* (Mexico City, Editorial Milenio SA de CV, 1989). The section on the Mexican stock exchange is quite interesting and gives the viewer a look at the BMV IPC Price & Quotations Index 1989-1995, and then a summary of the Mexican Securities Industry Association with a listing of the brokerage houses. Also included is an analysis of foreign investment in the Mexican stock market with a graph representing foreign investment in 1994.

Information is organized in alphabetical order for each company by the official Mexican corporation. Of the 75 companies, only 3 are listed as foreign-controlled corporations. The company information gives background, officers, number of shares, affiliations of markets and competition, main raw materials, and sources; it also gives a five-year historical background on sales per share data, balance sheets, income statement data, and ratios in dollars. A handy little guide that is a neat supplement, it works especially well for those who do not have *Moody's International Manual*, and is recommended for those who are developing commercial collections in Latin America, especially Mexico. In light of the North American Free Trade Agreement, this would be a good book to have.—**Gerald D. Moran**

LABOR
Bibliography

255. **Labor Arbitration: An Annotated Bibliography.** Charles J. Coleman and Theodora T. Haynes, eds. Ithaca, N.Y., ILR Press, 1994. 271p. index. (Cornell Industrial and Labor Relations Bibliography Series, no.17). $35.00. ISBN 0-87546-322-3.

Developed by practitioners, academics, and library professionals, this annotated bibliography is a comprehensive, well-crafted guide to literature in the field of labor arbitration. The bibliography lists entries from 154 books and monographs, and nearly 1,200 articles from professional and academic journals and the published proceedings of professional and academic meetings. Each entry includes a full citation and an efficient annotation. Books and articles are listed in separate sections, with each section broken down into subject areas such as arbitrator characteristics, advocacy, discipline and discharge, arbitration and the courts, interest arbitration, and arbitration in selected industries. A concise, well-organized section on the legal foundations of grievance arbitration is included. Subject and author indexes assist the reader in locating entries. *Labor Arbitration* is a very useful reference work that should be on the shelves of most professional and academic libraries, particularly those with substantial business and law collections.
—**Paul F. Clark**

Dictionaries and Encyclopedias

256. **Government Career Guides: Dictionary of Occupational Titles and Occupational Outlook Handbook.** [CD-ROM]. Detroit, Gale, 1994. Minimum system requirements: IBM or compatible 286 (386 recommended). ISO 9660-compatible CD-ROM drive with cables, interface card, and MS-DOS CD-ROM Extensions 2.1. MS-DOS or PC-DOS 3.3. 640K RAM. 1MB hard disk space. VGA monitor and graphics card (color recommended). Mouse (optional). Printer (optional). $199.00 (single user); $249.00 (2-8 users). ISBN 0-7876-0396-1.

Gale's *Government Career Guides* consists of a CD-ROM, a "Help Card," and a 70-page guide. The guide provides instructions for easy installation, an in-depth tutorial, and a very detailed explanation of the searches available under both the *Dictionary of Occupational Titles* (DOT) and the *Occupational Outlook Handbook* (OOH). The program will support either a keyboard or mouse operation, and it offers a truly intuitive approach. The "Help Card" will be sufficient aid for many users, while the tutorial in the guide is available for the novice. The tutorial is also useful for explaining the reports and occupational definitions in both the OOH and the DOT.

At each menu, the user selects items by highlighting them and pressing the enter key. On certain screens, letters and other menu items may be surrounded by a box to indicate that they are selected. Certain key combinations, shown in both the "Help Card" and the guide, have been assigned as shortcuts. From the main menu, the user selects either the OOH or DOT. The OOH table of contents offers three choices: job title, career category, and search by any word or phrase. When users narrow a search to a particular occupation, they are shown a screen with eight buttons along the right side of the screen. These eight operations correspond to the standard OOH contents for any job description. If users select the DOT button, they bring up the DOT table of contents, comparable to the OOH table of contents except it includes the option of locating a job title by DOT number. This CD-ROM is highly recommended for all libraries as well as employment counselors. Screens seem a little slow in changing, but the disc is exceptionally user friendly.—**Dene L. Clark**

257. **Roberts' Dictionary of Industrial Relations.** 4th ed. By Harold S. Roberts; revised by the Industrial Relations Center, University of Hawaii at Manoa. Washington, D.C., BNA Books, 1994. 874p. $85.00. ISBN 0-87179-777-1.

This latest edition of *Roberts' Dictionary of Industrial Relations* incorporates the changes in the U.S. workplace since the last revision done in October 1984. These include employer interest in union avoidance, participative management, innovations in work organization, and alterations in employee benefit plans. Some entries from the earlier edition have been expanded or changed to reflect current usage; others have been retitled to give the more popular term in use now. Of the more than 4,400 entries, almost 200 are new. Examples of the entries are cafeteria plan, job engineering, pork chopper, Section 301, and the Leather Workers International Union. Under labor secretaries, the 22 people who headed the U.S. Department of Labor are listed in order of their appointment, with their period of service. Some of the entries provide source references. Readers are also directed to other terms when appropriate. A listing of general source references is provided at the end of the book. This dictionary continues in its purpose to cover extensively terms used in industrial relations for those with a vested interest.—**J. E. Weaver**

258. Tracey, William R. **HR Words You Gotta Know! Essential Human Resources Terms, Laws, Acronyms, and Abbreviations for Everyone in Business.** New York, AMACOM, 1994. 166p. $17.95pa. ISBN 0-8144-7856-5.

This is a handy, current (although small) dictionary of terms that personnel in human resource departments will find useful. Approximately 1,100 terms have been excerpted from the author's larger work entitled *The Human Resources Glossary* (see ARBA 93, entry 302). The selection for this abridged work is based on terms that would be needed by human resource personnel in smaller companies or nonadministrative staff in larger firms. Terms and their standard abbreviations include many federal laws and regulations including the Americans with Disabilities Act, Equal Employment Opportunity Commission, and the Employee Retirement Income Security Act, and concepts such as on-the-job training, the mommy track, and unfair law practices. The definitions are brief and clearly written and provide the reader with basic information. A few definitions are almost too brief to provide much insight, such as the one on networking. The major strength of this book is the definitions that deal with laws and regulations that impact personnel policy, provide dates, and give straightforward explanations as to what these laws or regulations are supposed to accomplish. The book will be a useful addition to small business collections and to small companies. Those libraries that have the unabridged version will not need to acquire this book.
—**Judith J. Field**

Directories

259. Baker, Daniel B., Sean O'Brien Strub, and Bill Henning. **Cracking the Corporate Closet: The 200 Best (and Worst) Companies to Work for, Buy from, and Invest in If You're Gay or Lesbian....** New York, HarperBusiness/HarperCollins, 1995. 242p. index. $23.00. ISBN 0-88730-691-8.

This book is about how gay-friendly or gay-positive major firms are in the United States. The information on the subject came from surveys sent to more than 1,000 companies, supplemented by published stories and interviews with employees or former employees. The companies were in *Fortune* magazine's annual "Fortune 500" and "Fortune Service 500" in 1993. They are high-profile, privately owned companies; large U.S. companies that are divisions of foreign-owned companies; and smaller companies known to have especially good or bad records on the issues under concern. The three major categories addressed in the survey are: (1) whether the company includes sexual orientation in its antidiscrimination policy; (2) whether it offers domestic partnership benefits; and (3) whether it perceives the gay community as an important market and is sensitive about how to sell to that market.

Information from the survey is given by industry and for specific firms. Among the 18 industries covered are aerospace, defense, entertainment, and telecommunications. The response or lack of response is given for each firm contacted, with some discussion. Companies were sent earlier chapter drafts, and their comments or additional information provided were part of the final version of the book. The companies are rated with a listing of the best and worst from the authors' points of view.—**J. E. Weaver**

260. Gifford, Courtney D. **Directory of U.S. Labor Organizations.** 1994-95 ed. Washington, D.C., BNA Books, 1994. 124p. index. $45.00pa. ISBN 0-87179-850-6. ISSN 0734-6786.

The *Directory of U.S. Labor Organizations* is an up-to-date compilation of information pertaining to the trade union movement in the United States. It opens with a brief description of the history of the American Federation of Labor-Congress of Industrial Organizations (AFL-CIO), founded in 1955 by a merger of those two formerly competing union bodies.

Following the brief introduction, the directory presents a chart of the structure of the AFL-CIO, followed by the names of members of the AFL-CIO Executive Council. The Executive Council is the governing body between conventions that are held in odd years. Next is a complete listing of the AFL-CIO officers and the various departments, including department officers and addresses. Additionally, the addresses and directors of the 12 AFL-CIO regional offices are listed. All state and metropolitan Central Labor Councils are given, along with addresses and presiding officers. Each union affiliated with the AFL-CIO is listed, including addresses, officers and executive board members, and sizes of membership. There is also an alphabetical listing of all trade unionists whose names are found in the directory.

While major attention is given to the AFL-CIO, information pertaining to nonaffiliated unions is also available. Since the directory was compiled, one major change has begun. A merger between the two major unions in the garment industry, the Amalgamated Clothing and Textile Workers Union and the International Ladies' Garment Workers' Union, is at an advanced stage. The proposed name of the new organization is the Union of Needletrades, Industrial and Textile Employees, with a combined membership of 355,000.

The *Directory of U.S. Labor Organizations* is an invaluable source of readily available statistical information concerning the U.S. trade union movement.—**George A. Meyers**

261. **Graduate Group's New Internships for 1994-1995.** West Hartford, Conn., Graduate Group, [1994]. 173p. illus. maps. $27.50 spiralbound.

This volume, which the publisher has issued each year since 1993, contains reproductions of announcements, brochures, and forms regarding internship opportunities available at 46 public, private, and nonprofit organizations, ranging from the Smithsonian Institution to Apple Computer to the Lincoln Center for the Performing Arts. As the introduction points out, these materials are intended to update and supplement the publisher's other internship directories. These are similar in format to *New Internships* and include such titles as *Internships for Two-Year College Students* (1995), *Internships Leading to Careers* (1993), *Internships in State Government* (1995), *Internships and Job Opportunities in New York City and Washington, D.C.* (1994), and *Internships for Students Interested in Law, Medicine and Politics* (1994).

The publication of *New Internships* hardly seems necessary when so many of the titles it is intended to update are already issued annually. Moreover, as is the case with the other titles, the only access to the volume is the table of contents listing the organizations represented. No indexes by fields of interest or geographical area are provided. Nonetheless, those users who see an advantage to having the internship sponsors' forms and announcements may want to consider the other appropriate titles offered by this publisher, but they would not take the place of more comprehensive directories that offer indexes and a uniform format for entries—for example, *Peterson's Internships 1996* (Peterson's Guides, 1995) or the *National Directory of Internships* (9th ed.; see ARBA 95, entry 302).—**Gregory M. Toth**

262. Jankowski, Katherine. **The Job Seeker's Guide to Socially Responsible Companies.** Detroit, Visible Ink Press/Gale, 1995. 927p. index. $24.95pa. ISBN 0-8103-9987-3.

Definitions of "socially responsible" can differ greatly, a problem addressed at length in the introduction of this work. A wide variety of companies are included, "based on the selection criteria of 34 mutual funds that screen for social responsibility." These funds are listed, as are other resources for information on socially responsible firms. Even so, some selections seem controversial, such as Dow Chemical, which has been mired in the silicone breast implant controversy, and Exxon, still remembered for the Alaskan oil spill. Some might see the use of environmental and other programs by such companies as a public relations move, and may want to investigate the companies beyond what is in this directory. More obvious choices such as Ben & Jerry's also appear, of course. An index covers particular concerns, such as the environment.

Entries contain directory information; a description of the lines of business, including foreign and subsidiary operations; a mission or vision statement; a list of the funds holding the company's stock; a description of activities; employee benefits; and application procedures. What may have made this book truly outstanding would have been some commentary on criticism and lawsuits against the various companies. An appendix provides the Domini Social Index for 400 companies (1,000 are profiled in the directory), citing strengths and concerns. Dow Chemical and Exxon are not in this index. Ben & Jerry's is, with several strengths and no concerns. This title is recommended for libraries serving jobseekers, as it provides a starting point for those concerned about the values of their employer.—**Susan V. McKimm**

263. Lonier, Terri. **Working Solo Sourcebook: Essential Resources for Independent Entrepreneurs.** New Paltz, N.Y., Portico Press; distr., Emeryville, Calif., Publishers Group West, 1995. 315p. index. $24.95; $14.95pa. ISBN 1-883282-50-0; 1-883282-60-8pa.

Intended as a companion to Lonier's well-received *Working Solo: The Real Guide to Freedom & Financial Success with Your Own Business* (Portico Press, 1994), the *Working Solo Sourcebook* describes more than 1,200 information resources of interest to practicing and would-be entrepreneurs. These sources include books; magazines, pamphlets, and workbooks; audiotapes; videotapes; computer-based information; training programs; professional associations and networks; conferences; and suppliers and services. (Surprisingly, there are only a handful of Internet resources listed.)

The book's commonsense arrangement is alphabetical by topics familiar to all "independent entrepreneurs"; for example, advertising, barter, bookkeeping and accounting, choosing a business, employees, managing one's business, youthful entrepreneurs, and 30 other equally important subjects. All listings include complete bibliographical information plus a clear, informative, one- to three-sentence description; usage tips accompany many of the listings. Icons indicating type of resource—book, videotape, training program—set off each entry so that readers looking for, say, only training materials can easily identify just these resources. The sourcebook's index provides some subject access but primarily supplies names of resources. A minor problem, one that would appear to be an editorial oversight, is that approximately 125 entries beginning with "The" are indexed between *That's Guerrilla* and *Think and Grow Rich*. Written by an independent entrepreneur *for* independent entrepreneurs, this book provides a good starting point from which to explore further.—**G. Kim Dority**

264. Marsh, Arthur, Victoria Ryan, and John B. Smethurst. **Historical Directory of Trade Unions. Volume 4: Including Unions in Cotton, Wool and Worsted, Linen and Jute....** Brookfield, Vt., Scolar Press/Ashgate Publishing, 1994. 558p. index. $93.95. ISBN 0-85967-900-4.

This fourth of a projected five volumes is a compilation of historical information about British and Irish trade unions in the textile trades. The work is composed of a series of 13 industry sections with introductory essays covering the outlines of the history of the British Isles' union activities, the scholarly literature, and possible sources. Trades range from cotton, through lace and net to carpets and textile engineering. Introductions are followed by an alphabetical series of entries on the associations in the trade. There are *see* references from variant names to main entries. Entries vary from a sentence or two to a page for the better documented associations. There is an index of organization names covering all chapters.

Principal author Marsh is a retired fellow at St. Edmund Hall, Oxford, and is the author of the *Trade Union Handbook* (see ARBA 93, entry 305), a guide to contemporary British trade unions. The associate authors are a retired research officer at the St. Edmund Hall Industrial Relations Research Unit (Ryan), and a retired engineer and labor historian (Smethurst). They should be congratulated for their industry in retrieving so much organizational history from directories, government records, and surviving association documents. In this volume they have expanded coverage of Ireland.

This work is both an important piece of scholarship and an aid to future researchers in the field. Industrial relations research collections covering the British Isles should acquire a copy. The series of which it is a part would be a useful addition to general social history research collections. [R: Choice, Jan 95, pp. 754-56]—**Nigel Tappin**

Handbooks and Yearbooks

265. **The Adams Jobs Almanac 1995.** By the Editors of Adams Publishing. Holbrook, Mass., Adams Publishing, 1995. 915p. index. $15.00pa. ISBN 1-55850-422-2.

Intended as a comprehensive guide to career opportunities and search strategies, the directory combines industry forecasts and advice on résumés with the identification of companies, positions, and qualifications. Although such a combination is often in demand by students and other jobseekers, this work will not satisfy most patrons. The poor production quality (e.g., paper, binding) and failure to specify the research and data collection methods used are severe deficiencies. Although the industry descriptions are useful and the job search advice sound, the outlook for occupations sports two alphabetical listings without cross-references and a confusing arrangement in which teacher is listed under kindergarten. The largest section has 7,500 company entries arranged by industry. Entries offer basic information (e.g., name, telephone number), one-sentence descriptions, and broad position and background categories. For some companies, benefits (e.g., dental, day care); locations; and number of employees are also given. Unfortunately, most entries list a contact position rather than an individual. The state-by-state relocation guide is limited and contains inaccuracies. Several indexes to employers and state information complete the volume. A topical index would facilitate the use of certain sections (e.g., career outlooks). This work is not recommended.—**Sandra E. Belanger**

266. **American Salaries and Wages Survey: Statistical Data Derived from More Than 300 Government, Business, & News Sources.** 3d ed. Helen S. Fisher, ed. Detroit, Gale, 1995. 808p. $105.00pa. ISBN 0-7876-0059-8. ISSN 1055-7628.

Now in its 3d edition, this directory provides information on occupations and their corresponding salaries, obtained from hundreds of federal and state governmental agencies, trade associations, and journals. The wage data are collected for the period January 1990 through December 1995, covering some 35,000 salaries with more than 4,000 occupational classifications. Some subject descriptions are repeated many times (e.g., "clerk" or "guard") and this directory is certainly not easy to use. The reader is advised to refer to original sources when in doubt. Base salary figures that are provided in this directory are not always helpful because of supplemental compensations and other benefits. The Bureau of Labor Statistics (BLS) and other agencies should be consulted before any conclusions are reached in using this directory; it should be used with caution.—**Bohdan S. Wynar**

267. Barnhardt, Phillip. **Guide to National Professional Certification Programs.** Amherst, Mass., Human Resource Development Press, 1994. 650p. $99.95pa. ISBN 0-87425-965-7.

Certification, a growing requirement to assure career mobility, may be mandated or voluntary. This volume describes 531 voluntary certification programs in various occupations. Often, certifications are created, sanctioned, or affiliated with professional associations to define standards of performance via a third party. The authors describe this as "a quality enhancement mechanism" for occupations such as property manager, human resources executive, or plumbing inspector. The Gale *Professional and Occupational Licensing Directory* (see ARBA 94, entry 800) describes required state and federal licensing, registration, and certification. For the most part, certification attempts to apply a level of standard, objective measures to assure quality in performance. Thus, companies and organizations may use certifications in recruiting, training, and developing employees. These credentials are also used by employees to gain a new position or to qualify for new salary levels.

Twenty-two occupational categories contain the entries that describe each program, giving information on sponsor, examinations, costs, and the required qualifications. Requirements for achieving certification may include specified work experience or examination. An extensive 16-page introduction describes the value and use of certification, as well as the basis for establishing and qualifying such programs. Appendixes list official designations (i.e., CHRE for Certified Human Resources Executive, CPHQ for Certified Professional in Healthcare Quality) and sponsoring organizations for searching those aspects. Some expected credentials are not listed, and some programs did not respond to inquiries. No mental health, physician certification, or alternative medical practitioners are listed because of lack of agreement in acceptable certification criteria. This volume will become increasingly important to libraries, personnel and human resource professionals, and career guidance centers as trends toward certification and licensure intensify.—**Barbara Conroy**

268. Buckley, John F., and others. **State by State Guide to Human Resources Law, 1994.** New York, Panel, 1994. 1v. (various paging). $164.00pa. ISBN 1-56706-014-5.

269. Buckley, John F., and others. **State by State Guide to Human Resources Law, 1994: Midyear Supplement and Workers' Compensation Laws.** New York, Panel, 1994. 1v. (various paging). $69.00. ISBN 1-56706-073-0.

This is a comprehensive summary of the employment laws currently in effect in the 50 states and the District of Columbia. It provides the opportunity to quickly compare one state to another, particularly for organizations that have operations in more than one state. This edition introduces an introductory section entitled "Trends and Controversies in Human Resources Law," which provides the reader with some insight into current thinking on important issues or potential solutions being considered—this section is also included in the midyear supplement. The main volume describes information on fair employment practices; wages, hours, and holidays; employment at will; benefits; unemployment compensation; workplace privacy; health and safety; and a summary of federal legislation, guidelines, and policies on personnel law. Each section includes an introductory overview to the topic as a whole; within each part, tables are grouped in topical sections, each with a brief introductory comment.

In response to requests, the midyear supplement now covers new and revised tables that augment the topics in the main volume, and a compendium of workers' compensation statutes, which was prepared by the Chamber of Commerce. This set would be of use to libraries with strong legal collections, and also to human resource departments.—**Judith J. Field**

270. **Cuts in Defense Jobs in U.S. Counties, Metropolitan Areas, and States, 1992-2003.** 1994 ed. Washington, D.C., NPA Data Services, 1994. 141p. maps. $250.00 looseleaf w/binder (with disk). ISBN 0-936555-21-1.

With the end of the Cold War, the United States began reducing and restructuring its defense forces. At the conclusion of this defense conversion process in the year 2003, 2.6 million jobs will have been eliminated. This title compiles data from the Department of Defense, the Census Bureau, and the report from the Defense Base Closure and Realignment Commission in an effort to clarify and clearly present the data being released to the public in myriad reports and documents. The goal of this compilation is to alert community planners in defense-dependent areas to changes in defense employment in the coming years.

Tables cover defense employment at all levels: national, state, county, Metropolitan Statistical Areas (MSAs), and Consolidated Metropolitan Statistical Areas (CMSAs). Military, civilian, and private sector job statistics are included. Employment estimates are given for the years 1992, 1995, 1999, and 2003. Familiarity with census designations is presumed. An appendix includes lists of all MSAs and CMSAs, but an index of MSAs and CMSAs by state would be helpful. Also provided are the census state maps showing the counties.

This looseleaf notebook is accompanied by a disk that gives data for each year from 1992 to 2003 and provides further detail on active duty and civilian jobs. Libraries in defense-dependent areas may want this title for its clear presentation of a much-debated topic.—**Barbara E. Clotfelter**

271. **DISCovering Careers & Jobs. DOS Version 1.0.** [CD-ROM]. Detroit, Gale, 1994. Minimum system requirements: IBM or compatible 286. MS-DOS or PC-DOS 3.3. 640K of RAM (520K free). 2.5MB hard disk space. VGA card and monitor. $495.00; $700.00 network. ISBN 0-8103-5067-X.

DISCovering Careers and Jobs combines two well-known publications, *Occupational Outlook Handbook* (see ARBA 94, entry 281, and ARBA 91, entry 249) and *Dictionary of Occupational Titles* (4th ed.; see ARBA 93, entry 301), with sections on career information and potential employers. Career information includes job descriptions, bibliographies, and other data on 1,200 job titles in more than 250 careers. The potential employers division contains varying amounts of information on 40,000-plus U.S. firms.

The aspects of the program that access information from the *Handbook* and the *Dictionary* basically represent alternatives to the print versions within the same source. In some instances, however, they are more difficult to use than the originals. For example, in the *Dictionary*, browsing through the list of job titles is cumbersome because there is no way to jump ahead in the list. Searching by word or phrase is far more efficient.

The potential employers section is of dubious value. A search of the occupation "librarian" yielded a list consisting predominantly of hospitals and medical centers. When "librarian" was combined with New Jersey, the result was 11—certainly there are more library jobs than that. When these terms were further refined by adding a zip code, the result was zero—again a misleading result. Looking for all types of employers in the zip code area 07080 resulted in a list that excluded Home Depot, a major employer in the area. The advantages of this product as a whole include access to two popular publications on CD-ROM, and the ability to download or print out the information. Anyone who already has access to these publications, other directories listing employers in his or her state, and a copier would really not need this CD-ROM.—**January Adams**

272. Gonyea, James C. **The On-Line Job Search Companion: A Complete Guide to Hundreds of Career Planning and Job Hunting Resources Available via Your Computer.** New York, McGraw-Hill, 1995. 252p. illus. index. $14.95pa. ISBN 0-07-024068-X.

Gonyea's work combines traditional strategies for job hunting, such as ability assessment, career planning, networking, and company research, with newer online resources. A program disk for America Online is included with the book. Opening chapters instruct the reader how to use the book and provide an overview of career planning, education (notable for its case study of the Electronic University Network and list of other distance education resources), and job hunting using PC-based and online resources. An introduction to the Internet shows its value to a jobseeker and includes lists of Internet access providers. A chapter on commercial network providers suggests keywords for searching careers and job databases; another lists online bulletin boards with their modem telephone numbers.

Gonyea also provides information on how to make one's résumé available for online access and lists numerous resources available through telephone, fax, online, CD-ROM, or floppy disk access. This book provides helpful practical advice for the person just entering the workforce, or for one who is changing jobs mid-career. The recommended Online Career Center, reached through an Internet browser instead of the suggested Gopher access, is a sophisticated and easy-to-use resource. Developed by a nonprofit employer association, it lists classified advertisements and résumés, career assistance, a "cultural diversity" area, career fairs, and campus connections.

The book could be improved through more careful editing of text and organization of lists. For example, Internet providers are organized alphabetically instead of by location. The 160-item power tools annotated list is organized alphabetically and is located in a different chapter from the cross-reference index to it. The power tools list is unnumbered; once a user chooses a profile in the index, he or she must count the entries to reach the desired resource. A new edition of this book should address these changes and include more information on access to business information home pages.—**Joan B. Fiscella**

273. Griffith, Susan. **Work Your Way Around the World.** 7th ed. Oxford, England, Vacation Work; distr., Princeton, N.J., Peterson's Guides, 1995. 509p. illus. maps. $17.95pa. ISBN 1-85458-130-9.

For those who want to "work their way" through their travels or their stay in another country, this will be a useful resource. Written primarily for a British audience and with emphasis on Western Europe, this guide should nonetheless be of value for any English-speaker, regardless of destination. Indeed, it has apparently found a market in this country, as Peterson's has been distributing it here since the 5th edition in 1991.

While the first third of the book examines basic considerations such as preparations, red tape, transportation, taxes, and the major categories of work available, the remaining chapters proceed geographically, covering individual countries or regions and detailing regulations, accommodations, principal sources of employment, and the means of finding jobs in each one. The discussions are liberally illustrated with accounts of personal experiences from numerous contributors. A final chapter, entitled "In Extremis," describes last resort measures for coping with serious difficulties.

This is the sort of guide that users will want to study at some length and take along on their travels, for while its arrangement and detailed table of contents make it convenient to use, there are no indexes, and the wealth of specific information (publications, businesses, telephone numbers, agencies) is sprinkled throughout the largely expository text. It is this abundance of detail and concrete practical advice, as well as an exclusive focus on the concerns of the working traveler, that have no doubt earned earlier editions the loyal following represented by the many correspondents and contributors. The latest edition appears to be a continuation of that successful formula.—**Gregory M. Toth**

274. Jakubiak, Joyce, ed. **Specialty Occupational Outlook: Professions.** Detroit, Gale, 1995. 254p. index. $49.95. ISBN 0-8103-9644-0. ISSN 1077-3851.

This work (SOOP) expands on the coverage in *Occupational Outlook Handbook* (OOH) (see ARBA 94, entry 281) but does not overlap. Careers that were lumped under general headings in OOH have been pulled out and expanded so that they now have their own entries. For instance, convention managers, who were lumped under hotel managers and assistants in OOH, have been given a complete entry in SOOP. In most cases coverage of a career has been expanded from a brief mention to a complete article. In particular, the expanded career coverage includes a large number of scientific and technical occupations. The format of the entries in SOOP is modeled on OOH's tried-and-true model. It includes subheadings for nature of the work; working conditions; employment; training, other qualifications, and advancement; job outlook; earnings; related occupations; and sources of additional information. SOOP is intended as a supplement to OOH, and the index in SOOP refers the user to entries in both OOH and SOOP. Another volume is planned that will cover jobs not requiring college or advanced training. This title is reasonably priced, although not as inexpensive as OOH, and can be recommended for any library that makes extensive use of the type of information in OOH. This should include high school, public, and college libraries.—**Susan V. McKimm**

275. **JIST's Electronic Guide for Occupational Exploration.** [CD-ROM]. Indianapolis, Ind., JIST Works, 1995. Minimum system requirements: IBM or compatible 386DX. CD-ROM drive. Windows 3.0. 2MB RAM. 1.2MB hard disk space. SVGA monitor. Mouse. $295.00.

JIST's Electronic Guide for Occupational Exploration (EGOE) combines the resources of *Dictionary of Occupational Titles* (DOT) (4th ed.; see ARBA 93, entry 301), *The Complete Guide for Occupational Exploration* (GOE) (see ARBA 94, entry 387), and the *Worker Traits Data Book* (1994). It provides a 6-page report for more than 12,000 jobs. Each report includes: title; industry designation; summary of duties; interests; DOT number; training; aptitudes necessary; physical requirements; environment; temperaments; work fields; Materials Products, Subject Matter (MPSMS), Services; Standard Occupational Classification (SOC); Classification of Instructional Program (CIP); and Occupational Employment Statistics (OES).

The information following the profiles is presented largely in the form of numerical ratings. Aptitudes (rated from 1 through 5) are divided into 11 factors (e.g., verbal aptitude and motor coordination). A detailed manual, with appendixes describing the government classifications, is included. From the main menu, users may choose to search jobs by interests, using either GOE or DOT codes and their classification hierarchies. "Query," an advanced search mode, is also available. Users may print a complete report or select partial text. The manual recommends copying text to a word processor for greater print flexibility.

Although EGOE may be useful for counselors and employment professionals, it is far too frustrating for the average student searcher. The "Query" search mode confounded all testers. Less than a half page of each report is devoted to a narrative description of the occupations. Hypertext links are the same color as the regular text, making it difficult to determine where to click. Gale's *DISCovering Careers & Jobs* (see entry 271) provides substantially more detail for each occupation it profiles, as well as journal resources and company backgrounds. It is also far more user friendly. EGOE is recommended for optional purchase by employment professionals.—**Joyce Kasman Valenza**

276. Kuman, Arthur, Jr., and Richard D. Salmon. **Jobs for People over 50: 101 Companies That Hire Senior Workers.** Albany, N.Y., Brattle Communications, 1994. 112p. index. $9.95pa. ISBN 0-918938-06-6.

Self-proclaimed as the "only book of its kind today," this slim volume lists 101 companies with reputations for hiring older workers. Entries are divided broadly by industry, such as "Computers & Electronics" and "Financial Services." Each entry contains the company's address and telephone number, notes on the company's philosophies on older workers, and the types of jobs available to them. There is advice on writing résumés and cover letters, dealing with age discrimination, interviewing, and competing with younger workers. The book abounds with hints, such as how to emphasize one's experience, how not to reveal prejudices, and refraining from talking about grandchildren during an interview. While the advice will seem basic or obvious to many, the book will provide older persons inexperienced in jobseeking with added confidence, realistic expectations, and solid starting points. It is recommended for public libraries and career counselors.—**Laural L. Adams**

277. **OSHA Field Inspection Reference Manual.** By the U.S. Department of Labor, Occupational Safety and Health Administration. Rockville, Md., Government Institutes, 1995. 1v. (various paging). index. $59.00pa. ISBN 0-86587-426-3.

This is a commercially published government document from a publisher who has been publishing in the area of environmental concerns for more than 20 years. This is not the first government publication they have reprinted in their attempt to make environmental rules and regulations more widely available. Depository libraries and other libraries and firms that acquire material directly from the Occupational Safety and Health Administration (OSHA) may already own this publication. Others may want to acquire the publication, which reflects regulations in effect as of September 26, 1994; each page of the manual has this date stamped at the top. The *OSHA Field Inspection Reference Manual*, while published for compliance officers in their field offices to assist them in their inspection duties, would also be useful to others who must meet these compliance standards. An index has been included so the user can quickly identify the section that needs to be consulted.—**Judith J. Field**

278. **Overseas Summer Jobs 1995.** 26th ed. David Woodworth, ed. Oxford, England, Vacation Work; distr., Princeton, N.J., Peterson's Guides, 1995. 256p. $14.95pa. ISBN 1-85458-123-6. ISSN 0070-60.

279. **Summer Jobs Britain 1995.** 26th ed. David Woodworth with Hannah Start, eds. Oxford, England, Vacation Work; distr., Princeton, N.J., Peterson's Guides, 1995. 255p. maps. $15.95pa. ISBN 1-85458-126-0. ISSN 0143-3490.

Retaining the format used successfully in previous editions (see ARBA 92, entry 218), current summer overseas employment opportunities are identified. Compiled from information supplied by employers and agencies, the country and British regional entries are arranged alphabetically. Beginning with an overview of the employment climate and procedures and regulations for foreign workers (e.g., visas, permits), entries offer a combination of basic data (e.g., address); opportunity descriptions (e.g., agriculture, camping); and position qualifications (e.g., duties, rates of pay). While the unemployment rate in some locales influences the job market, an excellent case is made for seasonal work and for volunteer organizations that are willing to accept unskilled workers. With availability ranging from none (e.g., India) to numerous (e.g., Germany), most of the jobs will appeal to college students for whom experience rather than remuneration is a primary goal. Separate sections consider au pair, winter work, and—for Great Britain—vacation traineeships and on-the-job experiences.

Although applicable only to the current summer season, the globalization of markets and the competition for employment ensure a continuing place for these two works in collections serving young adults.
—**Sandra E. Belanger**

280. **Peterson's Job Opportunities in Business 1995.** Princeton, N.J., Peterson's Guides, 1994. 402p. index. $18.95pa. ISBN 1-56079-386-6. ISSN 1070-6615.

Aside from slight changes in section titles, the information in the first portion of this edition is essentially the same as in the 1994 edition—how to succeed in business in the 1990s, how to check out potential employers, and how to be a stand-out job candidate. A chapter on finding jobs in small, rapid-growth companies is new, however, as is an accompanying list of 50 such firms.

As in the previous edition, the largest portion of *Peterson's Job Opportunities in Business 1995* is devoted to a listing of approximately 2,000 of the United States' major employers. Corporate and government organizations profiled in this guide are selected based on the number of people they employ. The entries include name and address of the organization, date founded, annual sales, number of employees, fields of expertise needed, and a contact person's name and telephone number. Some companies augment their entries with a short description. Longer descriptions are included in a separate section.

The volume is completed by three indexes. The first classifies companies according to the primary industries in which they operate. The second, a geographical index, lists profiled companies in alphabetical order by state. The third, an index by hiring needs, presents companies by areas of expertise sought.

Together, these features provide a useful companion volume to the *Occupational Outlook Handbook* (see ARBA 94, entry 281). This Peterson's guide has a place in any career library; however, because it is likely to be heavily used, the paper binding may become problematic.—**Rachael Green**

281. Postic, Lionel J. **Wrongful Termination: A State-by-State Survey.** Washington, D.C., BNA Books, 1994. 822p. $125.00. ISBN 0-87179-843-3.

Postic begins this work with an introduction to the doctrine that an employee is presumed to be hired at-will, and he then reviews four recognized exceptions: public policy, oral assurances, handbooks, and implied covenant of good faith and fair dealing. He outlines problems dealing with the exceptions and with other subjects related to the exceptions. The introduction concludes with a table briefly summarizing each state's position about the exceptions and employment-related torts.

The body of the book is organized into chapters, arranged alphabetically by state, and each follows the same outline: introduction, public policy, employment contract, implied covenant, burdens of proof, attendant torts, and statutes. A finding list by topic is useful for quick access to the appropriate information for every state. Two appendixes conclude the work; the first is a model employment-termination act that, if adopted by all states, would ensure uniform law in the United States; the second is an alternative model. The material covered in each chapter provides a broad overview of the legal position of each state, with extensive citations to relevant state laws. The material is current through August 1993, and the author foresees annual updates. Postic does not give in-depth analysis, nor does he cover issues such as privacy, drug testing, public employment, associations, or employers' defenses.

This book will be very useful to people needing basic legal information about the topic of wrongful termination with reference to legal precedent for each state. Postic's clear focus and his careful statement of what is covered and what is omitted from the book will make this useful for libraries collecting materials about legal aspects of human resource management.—**Joan B. Fiscella**

Videographics

282. **Field Guide to Current Training Videos.** Laura Winig with William Ellet, eds. Boston, Harvard Business School Press, 1995. 248p. $49.95pa. ISBN 0-87584-566-5.

This is a guide to 100 training videos that were reviewed from 1993-94 in the industry's newsletter, *Training Video Review*. The editor of this publication serves as the publisher of the newsletter, and she asked practicing trainers, consultants, and line managers to write the reviews, enhancing their value. The primary focus of the videos that were selected is management and supervisory skills in such areas as innovation, leadership, sexual harassment, team building, and diversity. Each review summarizes and evaluates the content of the video being reviewed, describes the intended audience, and tells how it should be used. Ratings of one to four stars are given to each video in such categories as entertainment value, production quality, and portrayal of women and minorities. The user will find an explanation of the evaluation system in the introduction. A few classic videos that have been recently reissued have also been included. Less intimidating, comprehensive, and costly than other publications currently being published, the guide at hand focuses on current management concerns. The editor has also included a brief article on the evolution of training films, which would be of interest to staffs that are considering acquiring films for staff training programs. Human resource departments and smaller business collections will find this a useful tool.—**Judith J. Field**

MANAGEMENT

283. Kemper, Robert E., and Daniele Renee Kemper. **Negotiation Literature: A Bibliographic Essay, Citations, and Sources.** Metuchen, N.J., Scarecrow, 1994. 479p. index. $55.00. ISBN 0-8108-2776-X.

The authors' stated intent for this work is to identify and cite materials pertaining to the processes of global organizational negotiations. *Negotiation* is defined as the process of bargaining to achieve a goal, and other terms such as bargaining, conflict resolution, conflict management, and dispute resolution are used interchangeably with the term.

This volume consists of 4,855 citations, listed alphabetically by first author's name, with a subject and cocontributor index. A review of these citations is offered in a 30-page bibliographical essay preceding the bibliography. The essay highlights the key items by formats (e.g., bibliographies, book collections, journals, and dissertations); other relevant resources (e.g., associations and publishers); and two contextual areas: (1) theoretical approaches to negotiation (including learning process, decision-making process, psychological, sociological, prescriptive, descriptive, game theory, communication, and collective bargaining); and (2) special areas of negotiation literature (including third-party negotiation, collective action, social power, negotiatory conduct, dispute resolution, and pedagogy).

Items are identified through the process of citation indexing, with starting points in course syllabuses and recommendations from surveyed faculty teaching relevant courses or doing research in negotiation. Criteria for inclusion in the bibliography are aimed to establish a list of items that are: (1) primarily concerned with organizational behavior, (2) highly regarded recent volumes, and (3) representative of a variety of disciplinary and methodological focuses.

Prepared by a professor of management and a student of social work, this extensive bibliography's creation relies on others citing a work, but reflects very little explicit evaluation of individual entries. Although the help of librarians is acknowledged, no mention is made that the authoritative *ISI Social Science Citation Index* was used in the process of creating this bibliography. It is recommended as a beginning point of reference for students of the topic, including researchers studying negotiations, practicing members and managers of organizations who negotiate daily, and students of negotiations who seek an area for imaginative study and research.—**Danuta A. Nitecki**

284. **The McGraw-Hill Encyclopedia of Quality Terms & Concepts.** By James W. Cortada and John A. Woods. New York, McGraw-Hill, 1995. 392p. index. $34.95. ISBN 0-07-024099-X.

Prepared by experts in the field, this encyclopedia offers concise definitions of more than 600 quality-related terms and concepts. Designed as a professional-level reference for those interested in applying quality management principles to their organizations, key terms (e.g., benchmarking, reengineering), approaches (e.g., TQM), methods (e.g., Taguchi), and measurement tools (e.g., standard deviation) used in the quality field are discussed, with appropriate figures and illustrations.

Organized alphabetically, with three appendixes and a topical index, the definitions, varying in length and detail, are followed by a short list of references to other McGraw-Hill publications. The addition of quotations in the margin from referenced works is an interesting touch. Most of the basically well-crafted definitions begin with the same word (this), an indication of insufficient editing. The appendixes offer a comprehensive annotated bibliography, organized by category, and lists of quality management journals and worldwide organizations.

The brief index is inconsistent in its inclusion of acronyms and fails to offer page numbers for textual cross-references, thereby inhibiting rather than promoting ease of use. Despite these minor flaws, this timely reference, although unexciting, will prove a useful addition, particularly to academic and corporate libraries.—**Sandra E. Belanger**

285. Newman, Barry M., Virginia S. Peabody, and Joan M. Vigliotta. **Quick Reference to ERISA Compliance.** New York, Panel Publishers, 1995. 481p. index. $125.00pa. ISBN 1-56706-147-8.

ERISA—the Employee Retirement Income Security Act of 1974—is a piece of legislation that requires advance study and interpretation before an employee benefit professional may implement its provisions with confidence. The detail and complexity of the law make it mandatory that those persons who are responsible for complying with its provisions purchase a practitioner's manual such as the book under review. Any person, business, or library that seeks out a "how-to" guide on ERISA is concerned, first of all, with its authoritativeness. Do the authors know what they are writing about? The next consideration is the organization of the "how-to" manual. Is it arranged so that knowledgeable people can locate quickly the material they need? The *Quick Reference to ERISA Compliance* scores well on each of these points.

The three authors, all associated with the Alexander Consulting Group (a global human resource management consulting firm), possess a rich background in employee benefits. They obviously devoted considerable thought to the layout of the manual. ERISA covers pension plans as well as welfare plans. The law makes provision for many exemptions, but it also requires the filing of many reports to numerous entities, using special forms. By means of a compliance calendar, tables, and flowcharts, the authors are successful in implementing an orderly process that employee benefit professionals may adopt.

The work is highly recommended for all persons who administer employee benefit plans. It will also be useful in large public libraries and academic libraries that support major human resource management programs.—**Dene L. Clark**

MARKETING AND TRADE

286. **American Export Register 1995.** New York, Thomas Publishing, 1995. 2v. $120.00/set. ISBN 0-937200-89-1. ISSN 0272-1163.

Published annually, this directory provides an international marketplace for U.S. products and services. The 2 volumes contain more than 4,200 product and service headings, listing related companies in alphabetical order along with a mailing address, telephone and fax numbers, and sometimes a brief product or service description. A company profile segment in the second volume expands on this information and gives sales contacts for more than 45,000 companies which are arranged alphabetically. It is indexed in nine languages as well as English and includes such helpful features as a chart of time zones around the world and a measurement conversion table. Other special sections cover informational, financial, and transportation services associated with the export business.

Among the competition for this resource is the *U.S. Export Directory* published by Reed Reference Publishing, which catalogs some 25,000 companies for about twice the price. Another consideration is the *United States Importers & Exporters Directory* (see ARBA 90, entry 286), which covers both aspects of international trade, but currently sells for about $600.—**Jean Engler**

287. **Annual Bulletin of Statistics of World Trade in Steel 1993.** By Economic Commission for Europe. New York, United Nations, 1994. 155p. $28.00pa. ISBN 92-1-016302-8. ISSN 0501-3062. S/N E/F/R.94.II.E.37.

This work consists of only three tables plus notes and cross-reference tables. The titles and notes are in French, English, and Russian, but the tables are English only. The cross-references contain coding and translations, so that someone fluent in only French or Russian could decipher the tables. The languages of the two countries that export the most steel, Japan and Germany, are not used. The three tables consist of two summary tables and a major table (which is most of the book) listing exports by product (wire rods, plates, and so on), by region and country of origin, and giving countries of destination. The first of the summaries gives steel exports of major countries in 1980, 1985, 1990, 1992, and 1993. Not all countries are included, and not all have data for all years.

The other presents trade of steel products among Economic Commission for Europe (ECE) nations. Although the data are probably not as readily obtainable, production figures also would have been useful. The lengthy table composing most of the book covers all countries for which 1993 data were available, excluding such major exporters as Korea and Belgium-Luxembourg. The publishers did well to get the data published so quickly, but for some countries, 1992 figures could have been included with a footnote. Despite some gaps in the data, which are probably inevitable in a project of this scope, this book is recommended for any library with a subject interest, and the price is reasonable, given its specialized nature.—**Susan V. McKimm**

288. **The Arthur Andersen North American Business Sourcebook: The Most Comprehensive, Authoritative Reference Guide....** Chicago, Triumph Books, 1994. 621p. maps. index. $150.00; $175.00 w/Spanish suppl. ISBN 1-880141-51-5.

The Arthur Andersen North American Business Sourcebook provides information on the North American trading area, which covers 360 million consumers with a $6.5 trillion marketplace all within the North American Free Trade Agreement (NAFTA). This one-volume executive guide is an encyclopedia to all aspects of the North American trading block, with current trends to economic integration that entrepreneurs and corporate strategists can use to get a comprehensive overview of NAFTA and trade within the North American partnership and other world areas.

The work reviews 10 industry sectors affected by NAFTA: agribusiness, automotive goods, electronics, energy, financial services, pharmaceuticals, services, telecommunications, textiles and apparel, and transport by land. Most of the text examines the impact for corporations doing business in and from Mexico, the United States, and Canada. The *Sourcebook* overview is not as comprehensive in the treatment of NAFTA as the *Encyclopedia of North American Free Trade Agreement* . . . (see entry 305).

The guide includes important information regarding other global trading sectors, as well as the details of an integrated North American economy and information to help businesses identify profitable opportunities; executive guidance to locate funding and joint venture partners; understand complex rules and regulations; and monitor strong new competitors. Extensive appendixes cover other world areas and their interactions with the North American trade block, issues of foreign investments, exporting programs, and an extensive summary of the NAFTA text. The bibliography is helpful for finding informational gateways to international trade in North America. The detailed index makes it a CEO trading bible and an outstanding library reference tool. A Spanish supplement is available to assist Spanish-speaking businesspeople in taking full advantage of the information in the *Sourcebook*. This one-volume guide for North American trade is an excellent and highly recommended resource.—**Gerald D. Moran**

289. **Directory of Import Regimes. Part I: Monitoring Import Regimes.** By United Nations Conference on Trade and Development. New York, United Nations, 1994. 145p. $10.00pa. ISBN 92-1-112349-6. S/N E.94.II.D.6.

290. **Directory of Import Regimes. Part II: Descriptions of Import Regimes. Section A: OECD.** By United Nations Conference on Trade and Development. New York, United Nations, 1994. 137p. $15.00pa. ISBN 92-1-112341-0. S/N E.94.II.D.6.

Countries, for various reasons, establish import regimes to control trade. These trade control measures (TCMs) take numerous forms, among them tariffs/duties, surcharges, quotas, preferences, price controls, import licenses, antidumping actions, and product standards. As a follow-up to its *Handbook of Trade Control Measures of Developing Countries 1987* (United Nations, 1987), the United Nations Conference on Trade and Development (UNCTAD) has undertaken the issuance of a multivolume directory describing the TCMs of both developed and developing countries.

Thus far, the UNCTAD secretariat, with the cooperation of various intergovernmental organizations and the countries themselves, has prepared individual chapters on the European Union (EU) and 67 countries that have adopted the Harmonized Commodity Description and Coding System to classify their imports. Following the pattern of the first published volume of country chapters (part 2) reviewed here, subsequent volumes will focus on a single trade group.

Part 1 discusses UNCTAD's methods for monitoring changes in countries' TCMs, down to the tariff-line level; the construction of a sophisticated database that chronicles these changes; and how the information in that database has been disseminated and used to investigate the effects of trade barriers. A substantial supplement provides 2 pages of statistical charts for each of 50 (primarily developing) countries, showing the relationship between indicators of their import regimes for major product categories and the value of imports in those same product categories, for the period 1982-1992.

Part 2 covers the TCMs of Organization for Economic Cooperation and Development (OECD) members, with a chapter on the EU and separate chapters on each of the 13 other OECD members not part of the EU (as of 1994). Chapters range in length from 4 pages (Turkey) to 24 (the EU), and average 10 pages. A chapter typically identifies each of that country's TCMs, with widely varying detail about how and to what categories of products it is applied. TCMs are arranged in a standard pattern, according to an elaborate numerical coding scheme explained in part 1. The use of this system simplifies cross-comparisons between countries. There is extensive citation of source documents and referral to governmental agencies (with their addresses) for further information.

This directory's content and technical vocabulary would appeal more to an audience of trade policymakers and scholars. However, exporters who use the annual *Exporters' Encyclopedia* (Dun & Bradstreet) and the looseleaf *International Trade Reporter: Export Shipping Manual* (Bureau of National Affairs) may discover here information that supplements those two sources' coverage of trade regulations. Because rapid change seems to be the norm for TCMs, one hopes that new editions of this directory will be published on a regular basis to keep it reasonably current. This directory is highly recommended for libraries with collections on international trade.—**John Lewis Campbell**

291. **The Directory of Importers in Latin America.** 1994 ed. New York, Americas Research Group; distr., Bristol, Pa., Taylor & Francis, 1994. 260p. maps. $195.00pa. ISBN 0-9642542-0-4.

This directory identifies Latin American companies likely to import products that can be supplied by U.S. companies. According to the introduction, it is designed "to help you do business profitably in Latin America. . . . By compiling the names of the most important importers in Latin America, we hope to give you a tool that will make your sales and marketing efforts more successful." It covers the 11 countries considered to "provide the best opportunities for exporters, both currently and in the foreseeable future": Argentina, Bolivia, Brazil, Chile, Colombia, Costa Rica, Mexico, Paraguay, Peru, Uruguay, and Venezuela.

The work is divided into four major sections: an alphabetical listing of all companies included in the directory, an alphabetical product listing, a numerical product code listing, and an alphabetical listing of companies under countries. The latter section serves as a directory of companies in each country, providing the following information about each one—address, telephone, and fax number; chief executive officer; nature of the business (distributorship, end user); legal characteristics (locally owned, foreign owned); annual import volume; and products imported.

Also provided is general information about the geography of each country with an outline map on which principal cities are located, and short summaries about the macroeconomic environment, trade, recent developments, and so forth. These summaries are outdated, since they are based on 1991-1993 economic data; they should not be depended upon for current economic information as the economic environment in many countries is undergoing rapid change. This directory of Latin American export markets will be useful in libraries serving a business clientele, as well as in those libraries with users interested in Latin America in general.—**Ann Hartness**

292. Douglas, Livingston G. **The Bond Markets: A Desktop Reference to World Debt Market Performance and Analysis.** 1995 ed. Chicago, Probus Publishing; distr., Burr Ridge, Ill., Irwin Professional Publishing, 1995. 269p. $35.00pa. ISBN 1-55738-553-X.

A sequel to the author's *Fixed Income Almanac* (Irwin, 1993), this book reviews the performance of world bond markets for 1994 via statistical tables and charts. For a few key series (e.g., inflation, bond market returns), the data cover a broader time period to provide historical perspective. Although the audience is not stated, the book is more useful for investors interested in the U.S. bond market because data are more comprehensive for U.S. bonds. Arranged in eight sections, the book briefly capsules bond market behavior in 1994 and factors affecting it. The reference provides a chronology of key events, then covers economic statistics, inflation, U.S. federal budget, and monetary policy; the remaining segments review U.S. government securities, mortgage-backed and asset-backed securities, corporate and municipal bonds, international bonds, and derivative securities. Each of the 21 chapters is prefaced with a 2- to 6-paragraph summary of the data presented in tables and charts. The tables or charts are documented briefly with the organizational source, which includes securities firms and government agencies, but more complete documentation should have been provided.

Experienced in fixed income portfolio management at several firms, the author has written several books on finance. The book's primary usefulness is as a convenient means of getting access to data series useful for investors interested in the bond market; many of them, however, are readily available in a more timely fashion in government sources or investment services, and the data's usefulness is hampered by the fact that they are provided for one year only, although they do show month-to-month fluctuations over the year. The book is probably more useful in specialized business collections or to individuals interested in a historical perspective on 1994 bond market activity.—**Marilyn Domas White**

293. **External Trade Monthly Statistics.** Brussels, Office for Official Publications of the European Communities; distr., Lanham, Md., UNIPUB, 1994. 111p. $30.00pa. ISSN 1017-6004.

An overview of trends in world trade is found in this statistical periodical published by the Statistical Office of the European Community (EUROSTAT). It provides import and export data on products traded, the value of products traded, and geographical patterns of trade of member states. The publication gives data of the European Union with its main trading partners, as well as developing countries. EUROSTAT compiles tables from detailed data provided by member states on magnetic tape. These trade statistics also are available online through EUROSTAT data banks. Symbols and data sources used in this issue are located on an introductory page (p. ix).

Statistics found in the issue examined (no. 5, 1994) were classified by EUROSTAT as short-term trends in external trade. Libraries that require a longer overview of trends in external trade and world trade since 1958 are referred to the *External Trade Statistical Yearbook* (Series A), which is also issued by the publisher.—**O. Gene Norman**

294. **Foreign Trade Statistics for Africa. Statistiques Africaines du Commerce Exterieur.** New York, United Nations, 1994. 181p. (Direction of Trade, Series A, no.36). $35.00pa. ISBN 92-1-025044-3. S/N E/F.95.II.K.4.

This handbook from the United Nations Economic and Social Commission for Africa provides detailed statistical information on the trade of African countries on an annual basis from 1984 through 1992, both within the continent and with the rest of the world. There are no tables for imports or exports for Gambia, Chad, Western Sahara, and South Africa.

The prefatory material is quite brief and consists of a page of definitions (duplicated in French and English), a table of contents, a schematic map of African states, and a table grouping the states by region of Africa. The numbers for the countries on the map are somewhat mysterious, with no units or explanation given. Other numbers in the regions table are also unexplained.

The substantial part of the book starts with a summary table, "Total Trade," listing imports and exports by country (including Chad and the Gambia this time) in millions of U.S. dollars for the years indicated above. Regional totals are also given. The country tables are arranged by region, with an alphabetical ordering within regions. Imports are on the left page and exports on the right, with the countries and regions of origin or destination along the sides and the years across the top. Curiously, text on the export side is always in French. (Country names are duplicated.) Some figures in the tables are in millions of U.S. dollars; most are in thousands.

In sum, this is a useful source providing detailed trade figures for African states and regions. It should be acquired by business or economics collections with the relevant client interests and budget.
—**Nigel Tappin**

295. **Foreign Trade Statistics of Asia and the Pacific 1988-1992. Statistiques du Commerce Exterieur de l'Asie et du Pacifique.** By Economic and Social Commission for Asia and the Pacific. New York, United Nations, 1995. 627p. $45.00pa. ISBN 92-1-119683-3. ISSN 1011-4858. S/N E/F.95.II.F.18.

Foreign Trade Statistics of Asia and the Pacific, as the title states, is devoted entirely to the presentation of import and export data for 22 countries of Asia and the Pacific for the years 1988-1992. The book was published by the Economic and Social Commission for Asia and the Pacific (ESCAP) of the United Nations, using data provided by the UN Statistical Division. All data are presented in thousands of U.S. dollars to provide a common basis. Countries that supply trade statistics to the UN have been included.

Data are presented in four formats, or tables. The first classifies each country's imports and exports by trading partner (i.e., source and destination country). The second provides, for each of the 22 countries, a listing of exports and imports by broad categories of commodities (standard industrial trade classification [SITC] sections). The majority of the book is occupied by a third table, a more detailed classification of commodities (SITC groups) for each country. The first three tables show each commodity section/group classified by world total, as well as by both developed and developing ESCAP country. The final table places each country's trade into broad economic SITC categories.

Other than tabular classification, the book contains no analysis or summary and, thus, will be appreciated only by those seriously interested in trade patterns of Far East nations. However, it serves as the most reliable and comprehensive source available, at relatively modest cost, for such data. The rapid expansion of the economies of the countries included in the volume, as well as their promise for the future, makes this a valuable data source for those interested in development or in expanding trade with those countries.—**William C. Struning**

296. Ganly, John. **Data Sources for Business and Market Analysis.** 4th ed. Metuchen, N.J., Scarecrow, 1994. 458p. index. $55.00. ISBN 0-8108-2758-1.

Revised from the 3d edition published in 1983 (see ARBA 84, entry 779), the 4th edition identifies print and online data sources for U.S. and international business. The publications of the U.S. Bureau of the Census and other federal government agencies are covered in detail. Regional and local sources such as professional and trade associations, business firms, periodicals, abstracts, and indexes are then covered. Basic foreign and international sources are dealt with in a separate chapter, a section of which is devoted to listing the statistical abstracts of individual countries. The entries are linked by commentary and explanatory text that is very helpful.

The titles included are well chosen and often accompanied by a brief description. They include monographs, periodicals, and online sources. The entries for monographs provide place, publisher, date, and paging. Many U.S. entries include the complete address, telephone number, and fax number for the issuing body. However, the entries for periodicals do not include the date of the first issue or a history of the publication (for example, change of title, change of issuing body). An exception is *Gale Directory of Publications . . .*, published as *Ayer Directory . . .* for more than a century (1869-1982).

The index at the end provides an approach by subject, title, and issuing body, including subdivisions. The entry for a government department is by keyword. In many cases, an entry is indexed under title or under publisher, but not under both. In effect, this provides an excellent source for current information, including online data sources, and will be useful for a wide group of researchers, especially for marketing and statistics. [R: RBB, 1 Feb 95, pp. 1024-25]—**Barbara E. Brown**

297. Hinkelman, Edward G., and others. **Exporting to the USA: The Single Source Reference Encyclopedia for Exporting to the United States.** 1995-96 ed. San Rafael, Calif., World Trade Press, 1995. 756p. illus. index. $87.00. ISBN 1-885073-02-X. ISSN 1081-9746.

This volume is useful for those seeking to export to the United States. It is divided into seven sections: information lists; legal issues; banking; U.S. customs entry and clearance; packing, shipping, and insurance; commodity index; and a general index. The first 5 sections contain the requirements for exporters from the different countries, followed by 500 pages discussing commodities by subject. Each chapter provides information on key factors, general considerations, customs classification, sample import duties, entry and documentation, prohibitions and restrictions, marking and labeling requirements, shipping considerations, publications available, relevant government agencies, sources of additional information, and principal exporting countries. This book is a valuable source of information concerning the rules and regulations relating to exporting to the United States, along with information by product. It is highly recommended as a basic reference tool for those in the foreign trade business.—**Barbara E. Brown**

298. Hinkelman, Edward G., and others. **Importers Manual USA: The Single Source Reference Encyclopedia for Importing to the United States.** 1995-96 ed. San Rafael, Calif., World Trade Press, 1994. 844p. illus. index. $87.00. ISBN 1-885073-00-3. ISSN 1065-5158.

This volume is useful for importers in the United States. Similar to *Exporting to the USA* (see entry 297), it is divided into seven sections on such categories as international law, international banking, U.S. customs entry and clearance, packing, shipping, and insurance. A commodity index and a general index are also provided. The first 5 sections contain the requirements for importing into the United States, followed by 600 pages discussing commodities by subject. Each chapter provides information on key factors, general considerations, customs classification, sample import duties, entry and documentation, prohibitions and restrictions, quotas, marking and labeling requirements, shipping considerations, publications available, relevant government agencies, laws and regulations, and principal exporting countries. In effect, this book is a valuable source of information concerning the rules and regulations relating to importing, possible exporters, and useful information by product. It is highly recommended as a basic reference tool for those in the foreign trade business.—**Barbara E. Brown**

299. **International Advertising & Marketing Information Sources.** Gretchen Reed, ed. Washington, D.C., Special Libraries Association, 1995. 97p. $36.25pa. ISBN 0-87111-447-X.

This slender source encompasses some otherwise hard-to-find information in a usable and handy package. Arranged by global areas such as Asia/Pacific or Europe, and then by country, this volume is a directory of foreign contacts who can provide information of interest to marketers and advertisers. Each listed country may cover agency/client directories, media expenditure sources, periodicals in the field, sources of print advertisements and commercials, and advertising associations. Coverage depends on the country, with some having only one or two categories, while others such as France have them all. For publications, the publisher, address, telephone number, and frequency of publication are provided. Fax numbers are given when available.

Forty-two countries are included in this book. It definitely fills a gap in business reference collections, although some of the information is available in the U.S. International Trade Administration's *Overseas Business Reports*. This directory is a solid source of leads on foreign marketing and advertising. One hopes that there will be future regular editions, and that more countries will be covered in them. The work is recommended for any library with a need for information on international business.—**Gerald L. Gill**

300. **International Trade Fairs & Conferences Directory 1995: An Authoritative Guide....** 10th ed. Toronto, Co-Mar Management Services, 1994. 522p. index. $104.95pa. ISSN 0844-2762.

This well-produced tool provides access to events worldwide by industry classification, country and city, and date and conference name. The main listing (397 double-columned pages) is arranged alphabetically, first by industry and then by show name. Examples of the more than 100 categories are animals and livestock, fashion and accessories, gemology, new ideas and technology, subcontracting, and women. There is an index to the page on which each classification starts, just before the main section that is duplicated at the end of the listings (curiously, only the latter is included in the contents). The listing itself covers frequency; subject matter; date and location; market area (e.g., regional, national, local, international); trade and public attendance where applicable; number of exhibitors and countries from which exhibitors come; total space available; cost information (e.g., per square meter or foot, per booth, upon demand); and the full name and address of the organizer including telephone and fax numbers. The publisher indicates that the information is usually supplied by the organizer or other reliable sources.

The geographical and date indexes provide conference name and a reference to the main listing. For some reason, the U.K. listings are under four separate "countries"; namely, England, Scotland, Wales, and Northern Ireland. Additional features are clear prefatory material, a directory of trade fair representatives in North America (in sections for Canada, the United States, and Mexico), and a one-page article by Barry Siskind on the pros and cons of exhibiting. In sum, this is a professional directory giving access to international shows and conferences, although perhaps with a North American emphasis. The guide is a must for larger business collections and smaller resource centers where customer interest warrants.—**Nigel Tappin**

301. **Latin American Advertising, Marketing, and Media Sourcebook.** London, Euromonitor; distr., Detroit, Gale, 1995. 182p. maps. index. $470.00. ISBN 0-86338-544-3.

This is a highly specialized and expensive reference source that provides background information and detailed statistics on the news and broadcast media in Latin America, with a focus on advertising and marketing aspects. The advertising data are broken down by country, and further subdivided by the number of television and radio stations and sets, by television viewing habits, by the amount spent on advertising, and by households with VCRs. Most of the statistical data date from 1990-1993, with occasional 1994 figures in some of the tables, so this can be a useful resource for tracking cultural trends within the selected countries. Although the title indicates coverage of Latin America, the only non-South American country included is Mexico.

In addition to the statistical material, there is a substantial directory section that lists and profiles the leading advertising agencies (arranged by country); leading advertisers; major newspaper and magazine publishers; other media operators; business associations; and market research companies. Only libraries that support programs or research in international marketing or advertising will need to purchase this sourcebook.—**Thomas A. Karel**

302. **The Leo Burnett Worldwide Advertising and Media Fact Book.** Chicago, Triumph Books, 1994. 498p. maps. $250.00. ISBN 1-880-141-57-4.

This compendium covers major media in more than 50 countries, including the United States, citing trends, statistics, and the top companies. Important regulations, such as prohibitions on advertising alcoholic beverages, are summarized. Media research firms, similar to A. C. Nielsen or Arbitron in the United States, are described where relevant. The average cost of advertising in different media is examined. Other items of interest, such as economic and demographic data and holidays, are briefly tabulated.

The book would definitely be useful in trying to figure out which media to use to reach a target audience. As an example of the specific kinds of information imparted, one learns that 57 percent of Filipino households have television, but in metropolitan Manila the figure is 91 percent. However, the Philippines has 1,200-plus movie theaters at which commercials may be shown. Media covered include television, radio, cable, satellite television, videocassettes, cinema, newspapers, magazines, outdoor/transit, direct marketing, and (briefly) nontraditional.

Attention is paid to children's as well as adult advertising. The languages used in advertisements are rated by percent, so one learns that 70 percent of Swiss television commercials are in German. Many more tidbits of information are included in this wonderfully complete but concise book. Perhaps the only major piece of information omitted is addresses, which can often be found in *The Europa World Year Book* (see ARBA 94, entry 82; ARBA 90, entry 91; and ARBA 86, entry 91). This work is recommended for any library with patrons who have an interest in international business or advertising.—**Susan V. McKimm**

303. **Market Trends for Selected Chemical Products 1985-1990 and Prospects to 1995.** By Economic Commission for Europe. New York, United Nations, 1994. 96p. $28.00pa. ISBN 92-1-116603-9. S/N E.94.II.E.25.

The present study is the sixth five-year survey of market trends and prospects for chemical products in the Economic Commission for Europe (ECE) region. This survey provides a review of developments in the chemical industry during the period 1985 to 1990. Sources of data include material by national and international institutions, technical magazines, and materials submitted by governments in response to requests by the ECE. Unlike previous surveys, the current edition does not contain cumulated statistics of key chemicals or product groups dating back to 1965; thus earlier surveys will remain relevant. The textual part of the volume concentrates on a few major products or product groups, and as in previous editions, projections for selected groups of hydrocarbon and olefins have been described. While of limited applicability outside the chemical industry, this volume provides substantial information often found in significantly more expensive industry newsletters.—**Andrew G. Torok**

304. Rosenberg, Jerry M. **Dictionary of Marketing and Advertising.** New York, John Wiley, 1995. 371p. $17.95pa. ISBN 0-471-02502-X.

People in the business world, as well as students and laypeople, have the need to consult a dictionary of business terms from time to time. Rosenberg, a renowned business lexicographer, has assembled one in the areas of advertising, merchandising, packaging, sales, and consumer behavior. Rosenberg's work defines more than 5,500 words, terms, and phrases in their current professional context. Synonyms are referenced to one definition; acronyms are typically referenced to the full phrase. With thousands of entries included, many of Rosenberg's definitions are brief, but all are clear and concise. Users who need a more in-depth definition may consult *The Marketing Glossary* by Mark N. Clemente (AMACOM, 1992), a dictionary that gives more encyclopedic detail but covers only a quarter as many terms as the *Dictionary of Marketing & Advertising*.

Few fields in contemporary society operate in such a state of flux as marketing and advertising. On the assumption that new words first enter our written vocabulary in periodicals, the reviewer selected 137 marketing and advertising terms from one current issue each of six journal titles: *Journal of Marketing* (American Marketing Association), *Journal of International Marketing* (Michigan State University Press), *Journal of Marketing Research* (American Marketing Association), *Journal of Consumer Research* (University of Chicago Press), *Industrial Marketing Management* (Elsevier Science), and *Advertising Age's Business Marketing* (Crain Communications). Ninety-one percent of these terms or phrases appear in the dictionary. In view of the dictionary's comprehensiveness as well as clarity, the title is highly recommended for all academic libraries with business programs, all special libraries in business, and midsize and larger public libraries.—**Dene L. Clark**

305. Rosenberg, Jerry M. **Encyclopedia of the North American Free Trade Agreement, the New American Community, and Latin-American Trade.** Westport, Conn., Greenwood Press, 1995. 562p. index. $79.50. ISBN 0-313-29069-5.

This reference volume has clear, concise definitions and explanations of concepts, specific issues, rationalizations, ideologies, controversies, and recommended actions in the 5-volume, 2,000-page treaty called the North American Free Trade Agreement (NAFTA) between Canada, Mexico, and the United States. Also, explanations are provided in regard to the new creation called New American Community (NAC). The NAC will create a trade and economic zone for 700 million people in North and South America. This is the major resource for industry, government, and academics and business decisionmakers on NAFTA and the NAC.

The dilemma is that a library would almost have to have the original document in hand in order to use the (usually very short) definitions and explanations. However, the encyclopedia does provide information on specific issues, rationales, ideologies, controversies, and actions needed to increase understanding in the pursuit of cooperation and productivity among the free trading countries of North and South America. Also, the library should use this encyclopedia in conjunction with the NAC in response to the European-Asiatic trading partnership challenges.

Since there is so much controversy and misunderstanding about NAFTA, this encyclopedia would provide quick-reference action in regard to the interpretation of the document itself. There are long quotations and sections cited in the text of some definitions. The author is an expert on the North American trading situation and international business. The encyclopedia is recommended for all academic international business and historical economics collections, plus special libraries dealing in international trade.—**Gerald D. Moran**

306. **Trade Data Elements Directory: UNTDED 1993. Volume I: Standard Data Elements.** New York, United Nations, 1994. 272p. $95.00pa. ISBN 92-1-116585-7. S/N E.94.II.E.4.

Issued annually, volume 1 of this directory contains International Standard ISO 7372, which was prepared by the United Nations Economic Commission for Europe. The purpose of providing these standard data elements is to make easier the interchange of data in international trade. An index of data element names referring to Tag Numbers (section 3) follows the introductory part (section 1) and the maintenance of trade data element part (section 2). A numerical listing of data element tags continues the alphabetical listing. Section 4 constitutes the main part of the book, which presents and identifies the standard data elements. These elements include: the layout; dates and periods of time; parties, addresses, places, and countries; and amounts by weight or other measures, charges, and percentages of amounts used for value. Four appendixes cover change request forms, a numerical listing of data element tags, recommendations and standards, and how to change an EDIFACT-coded message to a paper document.

Volumes 2 and 3, which contain the USER Code List and the Compendium of Trade Facilitation Recommendations, were not seen by this reviewer. This is an expensive, but important, addition for libraries frequently needing information on international trade or international standards.—**O. Gene Norman**

307. **United Nations Commission on International Trade Law Yearbook, Volume 24: 1993.** New York, United Nations, 1994. 440p. $60.00pa. ISBN 92-1-133478-0. ISSN 0251-4265. S/N E.94.V.16.

This yearbook is a detailed review of the United Nations Commission on International Trade Law for the year 1993. It is divided into three main parts: the report of the commission on its annual session, studies and reports on specific subjects, and annexes. It is laboriously documented and referenced, and the annexes, particularly the summaries of meetings, provide rare insight into the workings of such international organizations.

A broad range of people and academic departments would find this book interesting, from international law to business schools to businesspeople involved in international marketing and trade. Yet the work of such organizations, especially in the efforts to provide a "model law" or a set of standards for international trade, are often irrelevant to day-to-day practical concerns. It may, therefore, be of limited use.

The meticulous documentation of most UN publications make for poor readability for a general audience, and this work would most likely be encountered only for a specific reference, a piece of information, or as part of detailed research. As such, even libraries with appropriate departments or patrons that do not already receive UN publications will want to carefully review its utility, with special consideration to this volume's relation to the whole series. Those holding UN documents or already having other volumes in this series will want to make sure this is part of their collections, especially as trade law and international economics seem to be of current major international concern.—**Curtis D. Holmes**

308. Welch, Jeanie M., comp. **The Spice Trade: A Bibliographic Guide to Sources of Historical and Economic Information.** Westport, Conn., Greenwood Press, 1994. 188p. index. (Bibliographies and Indexes in World History, no.37). $65.00. ISBN 0-313-29117-9.

This work is a thorough annotated bibliography on a significant historical topic. The result is a fascinating professional research aid. The book focuses on the history of the spice trade from ancient times through the present. The compiler (head of reference at the University of North Carolina at Charlotte) points out that this commerce was a major force behind European exploration and colonization, as well as an influence on the empires of the Mediterranean world and Asia. The subject is thus central to world history.

A brief introduction to the trade provides a definition and description of the main spices (black pepper, cinnamon, cloves, ginger, nutmeg and mace, and vanilla). There is also a clear methodological and definitional note. Citations are primarily in English and mostly those likely to be available through research facilities in the United States. Popular and scholarly monographs, periodical articles, pamphlets, and manuscripts are included. Annotations (a mix of description and evaluation) range from a sentence to a paragraph; these represent an impressive commitment to thoroughness on the part of the compiler. The citations are arranged in five chapters by period covered (general, ancient, Dark and Middle Ages, exploration and colonialism, 1945 to date) and then by type of work. Access is provided through a subject and geographical index.

This guide should be purchased by all major research libraries, along with more specialized collections in economic and social history.—**Nigel Tappin**

309. **The World Directory of Exhibitions and Trade Fairs 1995.** London, Euromonitor; distr., Detroit, Gale, 1995. 396p. index. $390.00pa. ISBN 0-86338-453-6.

An important means of promoting a firm's products or services, searching for suitable suppliers, or keeping abreast of competitive offerings is through exhibitions and trade fairs, *The World Directory of Exhibitions and Trade Fairs* enables a firm to determine what are the most appropriate events for its purposes. Information on more than 4,000 exhibitions and trade fairs in 90-plus countries is included, such as country and place where an event is held; organizer; when held (month, year); frequency; number of exhibitors; number of visitors; and sectors (product/service) covered. Organizers are listed by country with addresses, telephone and fax numbers, and specific exhibitions and trade fairs managed. Searching for particular exhibitions or trade fairs is eased by a country index and a sector index. A specific organizer can be located by means of an index of organizers. This is a new and useful addition to Euromonitor's series of business directories.—**William C. Struning**

OFFICE PRACTICES

310. Branchaw, Bernadine P., and Joel P. Bowman. **Delmar Reference Manual: Essentials for the Electronic Office.** Albany, N.Y., Delmar, 1994. 456p. index. $17.95 spiralbound. ISBN 0-8273-6473-3.

Individuals who prepare and process the written word—from secretaries to educators, students to editors—will find the *Delmar Reference Manual* a useful and unique reference tool. Its contents focus on rules for common tasks used in preparing and managing documents (forms of address, grammar usage, and the like), with special coverage on the principles of communication (telephone techniques, electronic correspondence). In addition to features usually found in a reference manual, *Delmar* includes special sections that make it a unique resource: a glossary of terms for the electronic office, a guide to dictionary entries, a perpetual calendar, a word processing guide, and a section on desktop publishing. There is also a detailed but easy-to-use index. The preface states that supplements are available: *Worksheets* for the *Delmar Reference Manual* (student exercises) and *Instructor's Guide* for the *Delmar Reference Manual* (teaching techniques).

Both in physical format and in presentation of rules, the manual is arranged primarily in alphabetical order and formatted in a general-to-specific organization: The table of contents identifies the general area of interest, while each chapter page has a detailed list of contents. Two-color presentation and design elements aid the user in quickly picking out important information, which is presented in clear, concise prose. This manual is highly recommended for those who want quick answers to a wide variety of up-to-date office procedure questions as well as information found in a traditional reference manual.—**Stacey Ennis Chisholm**

311. **Forms of Address: A Guide for Business and Social Use.** Andrea Holberg, ed. Houston, Tex., Rice University Press, 1994. 216p. index. $27.50; $12.95pa. ISBN 0-89263-333-6; 0-89263-334-4pa.

The purpose of this useful guide is to explore the practical issues of protocol in the modern, increasingly international city. The book is a departure from guides on business etiquette and protocol in several ways. It has a narrow focus, encompassing only the proper forms of address for titled officials in all levels of U.S. government, foreign government, royalty, religion, U.S. military, and others. The book is formatted for easy use; all entries follow a basic graphic, citing the style and format considered most appropriate for business correspondence, personal correspondence, place cards, introductions, and conversation. Unusual items are clarified by footnotes. A product of years of research and experience gained by the Houston International Protocol Alliance, the book addresses issues nonexistent until recently—such as married couples with different last names and female elected officials—and questions unique to local government that are not addressed in books targeting a mostly federal audience.

The book is not intended to be exhaustive but to be used as a reference tool for helping readers make educated decisions when confronting individual situations. A limited bibliography is included. This guide will prove a considerable help to government personnel, business executives, and social and community leaders, as well as anyone interested in proper forms of address.—**Stacey Ennis Chisholm**

312. **The Professional Secretary's Handbook.** New York, Houghton Mifflin, 1995. 578p. index. $18.95. ISBN 0-395-69621-6.

This reference pulls together into a single format copious details and information on dealing with modern office life. The format is similar to the previous edition, reviewed in ARBA 94 (see entry 301). Fifteen chapters provide information on such topics as human relations, word processing, telecommunications, conventional and electronic mail, international and domestic travel, and accounting and data processing. The informative text is interspersed with various helpful tables. For example, a table in chapter 5 ("Correspondence") lists common abbreviations found in place-names (e.g., canyon [cyn], harbor [hrbr]). A table in chapter 8 ("Telecommunications") supplies dialing codes and time differences for countries of the world, an important aspect in today's global marketplace. In chapter 2 ("Professional Career and Development"), an interesting table entitled "Body Language and the Messages It Conveys" provides insight into various behaviors coworkers may adopt (although it is both questionable and annoying to state that a woman who crosses her legs is being flirtatious).

Although it is convenient to have all this information at one's fingertips, some of the problems addressed in the review of the previous edition have remained unresolved. The index is still rather limited, although the table of contents is detailed and helpful. The chapter on business English is complicated and continues to assume extensive prior knowledge of English grammar; the chapter on business style still follows, rather than precedes, the business English chapter. The real updating in this edition from the previous one is the inclusion of details on the electronic office and the changing secretarial functions that this entails. Also, brief information on ergonomics is provided.

Beginning secretaries and libraries seeking to answer general reference questions pertaining to the office may be better served by *Merriam-Webster's Secretarial Handbook* (see ARBA 95, entry 328), which is more user friendly and accessible and contains a grammar section that is easier to understand. The work under review seems geared more toward the experienced secretary. However, the information contained herein would also be helpful to others besides secretaries; those who purchase this work may well want to acquire a copy for their boss as well.—**Melissa R. Root**

5 Education

GENERAL WORKS

Bibliography

313. Stitt, Beverly A. **Gender Equity in Education: An Annotated Bibliography.** Carbondale, Ill., Southern Illinois University Press, 1994. 168p. index. $24.95. ISBN 0-8093-1937-3.

The purpose of this annotated bibliography is to provide professional sex equity staff, administrators, teachers, and counselors with a reliable, easy-to-use guide for selecting specific resources, materials, and readings to further their attempts to overcome gender role stereotyping and sex bias in schools. Recent studies show that either consciously or unconsciously, teachers fail to practice gender equity in the classroom. They call on boys more often than girls and encourage boys to pursue careers from which girls are excluded. This bibliography is an annotated list of hundreds of currently available books, articles, videos, classroom activities, and curriculum and workshop guides to help provide the tools needed for educators to become more gender-conscious and to develop a gender-fair educational system.

Begun in 1985 and continuing through early 1993, it includes some material developed in the 1970s and 1980s that remain useful. The book is divided into 23 subject categories. Each entry's annotation provides a short description of the content and the age group to which the resource applies. Ordering information is provided (if available), but no cost information because of price adjustments over time. Also included is additional information for available videotapes, filmstrips, and slide presentations. Each entry appears once in the bibliography, under the most pertinent category. Entry codes are listed in the index under other relevant categories, so that readers may look up specific categories of interest to them in the index and locate the entry codes indicating the bibliographical categories in which the resources are described.—**Janet Mongan**

Catalogs and Collections

314. **The ETS Test Collection Catalog. Volume 2: Vocational Tests and Measurement Devices.** 2d ed. Compiled by Test Collection, Educational Testing Service. Phoenix, Ariz., Oryx Press, 1995. 200p. index. $52.50pa. ISBN 0-89774-743-7.

Taken from the Test Collection Data Base, available on the Internet through the Catholic University of America's Gopher, this volume of the Test Collection focuses on those tests that provide information on a broad range of vocational measures, including attitude measures, career planning aids, and vocational aptitudes. Tests cover all age groups and all grade levels. Unless they are part of a collection of tests or a kit, no tests published prior to 1980 are included.

Each entry lists the test title, the author, descriptors, availability source, and an abstract. Additional information such as copyright date, number of items, and time it takes to complete the test are included when available. Subject, author, and title indexes provide access to entries. The *Catalog* is well organized and provides a wide variety of tests to determine aptitudes and ways of measuring success. It is a useful tool for educators, managers, and others involved in evaluating success and potential for success in a wide variety of work and work environments.—**Ann E. Prentice**

Dictionaries and Encyclopedias

315. Ward, Robert E. **An Encyclopedia of Irish Schools, 1500-1800.** Lewiston, N.Y., Edwin Mellen Press, 1995. 251p. (Mellen Studies in Education, v.25). $89.95. ISBN 0-7734-9050-7.

This compilation is the result of a felt need by a U.S. professor of British literature to know what schools and schoolmasters stimulated the great Irish authors. Utilizing primary sources as well as secondary accounts by nineteenth- and twentieth-century scholars, he has brought together authentic information on various types of schools and on outside influences on Irish education. There are chapters on types of schools, such as charter work, academy, bardic, grammar, foundation, independent, and proprietary schools.

Other chapters are devoted to schools of denominations dissenting from the Church of Ireland: Presbyterian, Huguenot, Quaker, and Catholic—including the underground hedgeschools. Still others present topics such as laws against educating Catholics, educational endowments such as that of the Erasmus Smith schools, European influences on Irish education, treatment of education in the Irish newspapers, and methods and teaching materials. A chronology of events relating to education; a map showing the provinces and dioceses of the Church of Ireland, 1152-1833; and a bibliography of sources used in the preparation of the encyclopedia supplement the entries.

This will be a useful research aid for specialists in Anglo-Irish literature, for students and scholars such as Ward who wish to have a more thorough understanding of the Irish, for students of the history of education or of comparative education, and for students of political and social conditions in Ireland during this time period.—**Shirley L. Hopkinson**

Directories

316. **American Association of Colleges for Teacher Education (AACTE) Directory of Members 1995.** Washington, D.C., American Association of Colleges for Teacher Education, 1995. 143p. maps. index. $50.00pa. ISSN 0516-9313.

This publication could serve as the American Association of Colleges for Teacher Education's handbook. It does indeed contain a directory section geographically listing the approximately 720 member institutions of AACTE with their addresses and telephone numbers, and the names and titles of association representatives at each school. However, it also has sections listing the Association's officers and directors, its committees and their members, its council of state representatives, and the members of its advisory boards. The text of the Association's *Articles of Incorporation, Bylaws, and Resolutions of the Membership* are included as well. Yet another section, in tabular form, indicates the teacher education and related programs offered at each member institution and the numbers of students completing them in the 1992-93 academic year. Finally, indexes of institutions and representatives' names provide access to the directory section.

However, because not all institutions involved in teacher education are AACTE members—some 1,150 schools grant bachelor's degrees in education in the United States, for example—this work cannot serve as a comprehensive source of information about this field. It will be of value primarily to individuals and organizations connected with or interested in the AACTE.—**Gregory M. Toth**

Handbooks and Yearbooks

317. Hubbs, Don. **Home Education Resource Guide: A Comprehensive Guide for the Parent-Educator....** 3d ed. Cheryl Gorder and Erika Gravlin, comps. Tempe, Ariz., Blue Bird, 1994. 144p. illus. $11.95pa. ISBN 0-933025-25-4.

Home schooling, the process by which families educate their children at home rather than sending them to public or private schools, is growing in popularity. This self-published guidebook to home education resources contains a variety of information, such as suppliers of home schooling books and other curricular materials; lists of correspondence courses; Christian-oriented teaching resources; and lists of support groups, magazines, how-to books, and speakers supportive of the home education concept.

Brief essays ("Children Educated at Home Don't Become Social Misfits" and "What in the World Is a Social Studies/Science Project?") precede the core of the book—17 chapters devoted to such topics as legal information, educational toys and games, help for the handicapped, home businesses, and suppliers of materials. The work concludes with a series of full-page advertisements for teaching materials, accompanied by an order form.

One can question the advice given in the legal information chapter, which suggests that people contact a local support group rather than a state education code or a licensed attorney for the most up-to-date information. In addition, the lack of a unified, centralized index makes it difficult to pinpoint specific information. For example, the Home School Legal Defense Association (which sponsors seminars, conferences, and a speakers bureau, according to the *Encyclopedia of Associations*), is listed only under the chapter "Legal Information About Home Education," and not "Speakers and Seminars." The source is targeted to a specialized audience of families who wish to teach their children at home, and is recommended for specialized collections.—**Ilene F. Rockman**

Thesauri

318. **Thesaurus of ERIC Descriptors.** 13th ed. James E. Houston, ed. Phoenix, Ariz., Oryx Press, 1995. 704p. $69.50. ISBN 0-89774-788-7. ISSN 1051-2993.

The Educational Resources Information Center's (ERIC) national information system has provided access to education-related literature since 1966. Its database is now the world's largest source of information on education. It currently contains abstracts of more than 850,000 books, documents, and periodical articles. ERIC's controlled vocabulary is recorded in this printed thesaurus. The latest edition contains 10,363 vocabulary terms, of which 5,759 are main-entry descriptors and 4,604 are nonindexable USE references or dead terms. Approximately 200 new descriptors and 199 new USE references have been added.

The terms are organized in four sections. The alphabetical display contains the complete records of all of the thesaurus terms in alphabetical order. The rotated descriptor display is a permuted alphabetical index of all words that form thesaurus terms, whether they are descriptors or USE references. The two-way hierarchical term display groups terms into families or generic trees related by the taxonomic concept of class membership. The descriptor group display arranges 41 groups in 9 broad subject categories and serves as a table of contents to the thesaurus.

There are also lists of descriptors new to this edition and of transferred, invalid, or dead descriptors. An introduction describes the ERIC system and its indexing methods and procedures. This publication is an essential tool for those searching the ERIC database in the print indexes (*Resources in Education* [RIE] and *Current Index to Journals in Education* [CIJE]), the online database, or ERIC on CD-ROM.

—**Shirley L. Hopkinson**

CANADA

319. **The Directory of Canadian Schools.** 6th ed. Cheryl Cooper, ed. Don Mills, Ont., Southam Magazine and Information Group, 1995. 674p. index. $98.00pa. ISBN 0-919217-82-6.

Because education is a provincial responsibility in Canada, entries in the directory are arranged geographically by city within the 10 provinces, the Northwest Territories, and the Yukon Territory. Elementary and secondary schools and school boards take up most of the work. The minimum entry for each school provides address; telephone and fax numbers; language of instruction (English, French, or both); religion (nondenominational, Catholic, or Protestant); admission (coed, male, or female); grade range; and school board affiliation. Additional information in most entries records names of the principal, librarian, and guidance counselor; enrollment figures; and programs such as gifted, special needs, English as a Second Language, French immersion, before and after school, and daycare.

Other chapters offer access in the same format to schools or military bases, private schools, special needs schools, and native schools. There is a small section of adult education institutions and Bible colleges as well as a brief listing of universities, colleges, and Quebec colleges (CEGEPs). Entries for the postsecondary institutions are minimal, with no information about enrollment, programs, or facilities; in the case of this reviewer's institution, the large and complex University of Toronto, entries are muddled, one college has been omitted, and a residence is identified as a university while its distinguished parent is called a community college.

Directories of provincial ministries and educational associations precede the school listings, and an index completes the work. Printed in four-column format on green paper, it provides access by name to all the schools, school boards, and associations entered in the directory. With the exception of the postsecondary institutions, this directory works: appropriate information in accessible format. The addition of e-mail addresses might be considered for the next edition.—**Patricia Fleming**

320. Paul, Kevin. **The Complete Guide to Canadian Universities: How to Select a University and Succeed When You Get There.** 3d ed. Bellingham, Wash., Self-Counsel Press, 1994. 260p. maps. index. $14.95pa. ISBN 0-88908-524-2.

Now in its 3d edition, this comprehensive profile of Canadian universities is intended primarily for people seriously considering attending a university in Canada. The focus of the work is on undergraduate programs. The material is well presented. The first 77 pages provide useful insight into such matters as how to use the text, whether a university is the right choice, how to choose a university, admissions and finance issues, and study and success skills. The remainder of the book consists of brief but informative descriptions of accredited universities, military colleges, and francophone universities. The universities are profiled individually according to the provinces where they are located.

Many of the descriptions include maps of the universities. Each of the profiles includes the following: history, campus and city, important contacts, enrollment figures, tuition fees, residences, degrees offered, orientation, and facilities and services. The body of the work is followed by three appendixes that include useful self-help exercises; addresses of important associations and councils, provincial ministries, and departments; and student organizations. This work is recommended especially for school and public libraries, especially those in Canada, or those in states bordering Canada.—**James M. Murray**

EARLY CHILDHOOD EDUCATION

321. Denenberg, Dennis, and Lorraine Roscoe. **Hooray for Heroes! Books and Activities Kids Want to Share with Their Parents and Teachers.** Metuchen, N.J., Scarecrow, 1994. 243p. index. $27.50. ISBN 0-8108-2846-4.

Activities related to biographies are offered in this title for preschool and primary school children and for intermediate grades and young people. After the activities, biographies—frequently more than one title per person—are listed in alphabetical order by biographee, with author, title, publisher, date, and pages. Series titles are also included. A few collective biographies conclude the book, which also offers an appendix of notable children's trade books in the field of social studies and indexes for series titles, descriptor, and hero.

There are some clever activities that could be useful if tied with appropriate curriculum and reading projects, as well as extensive lists of biographies written for children and young people about "heroes." The idea of heroes is extended to include athletes, inventors, politicians, military leaders, entertainers, saints, singers, and the like. However, the biographees selected are predominantly white and male. For example, in the preschool and primary sections more than 70 white male biographees were identified, more than 30 white female biographees, more than 30 nonwhite male biographees, and more than 25 nonwhite female biographees. When titles, rather than biographees, are considered, the comparison is at least 200 titles for white males, more than 80 for nonwhite males, less than 60 for white females and more than 25 for nonwhite females. One presumes that this count reflects the published materials, although the compilers could have striven harder to achieve a balance. Indeed, the activities sampled—again the Preschool/Primary section—reflect the same bias. Less than 25 percent of the activities that named specific persons mentioned females, and only four were noted to refer to both sexes.

—**Betty Jo Buckingham**

ELEMENTARY AND SECONDARY EDUCATION

Bibliography

322. **Educators Grade Guide to Free Teaching Aids 1995.** 41st ed. Thomas John Haider and Kathleen S. Nehmer, eds. Randolph, Wis., Educators Progress Service, 1995. 1v. (various paging). index. $44.95 looseleaf. ISBN 0-87708-275-8.

323. **Elementary Teachers Guide to Free Curriculum Materials 1995.** 52d ed. Thomas John Haider, ed. Randolph, Wis., Educators Progress Service, 1995. 371p. index. $25.95pa. ISBN 0-87708-278-2.

The *Educators Grade Guide to Free Teaching Aids 1995* and the *Elementary Teachers Guide to Free Curriculum Materials 1995* are nearly indistinguishable. Both provide an abundance of identical information about free materials for teachers. Either resource also should be of interest to home schoolers, librarians, and professors of elementary education. The organization is user friendly, including directions for obtaining the materials, advice regarding writing the sponsors of the resources, and suggestions for evaluation of the received materials.

The heart of each resource includes more than 2,000 titles from a wide variety of topics ranging from "Accident Prevention and Safety" to "Teacher Reference and Professional Growth Materials." The annotations provide just enough information for judicious selection and are cross-referenced to a source index for ordering. Recognizing that many materials encompass a variety of topics, a subject index provides additional support when searching for materials on specific subjects. This also assists when some sections are not truly subject-oriented, such as "Visual and Audiovisual Aids."

The primary difference between the two resources is the addition of four "Illustrative Units" and a supplement to the *Educators Grade Guide*. The units, such as "Why Astronauts Envy Bears" for intermediate grades or "Pollution Prevention Is Everyone's Job" for middle school, demonstrate how teachers can weave supplementary resources into a unit. Although interesting, the units are dispensable. This resource also includes a supplement with an additional 177 items. Potential purchasers should consider whether the sample units and supplement justify the higher price. The *Elementary Teachers Guide* is undoubtedly a bargain.—**Suzanne I. Barchers**

Directories

324. **The Encyclopedia of Education Information for Elementary and Secondary School Professionals, 1994/95.** Leslie Mackenzie, ed. Lakeville, Conn., Grey House Publishing, 1994. 563p. index. $125.00pa. ISBN 0-939300-59-1.

This directory is a valuable resource for K-12 educators, as it provides easy and efficient access to a considerable amount of information especially relevant to elementary and secondary school teachers and administrators. There are nearly 5,400 numbered entries, some annotated with 1-2 sentences, others not, that are organized into the book's 10 major sections: associations, organizations, and government agencies; conferences and trade shows; databases, directories, and centers; employment resources; grants and fund-raising; the school library; books for professional development; publications (magazines and newsletters); publishers; and suppliers. Each section is organized clearly and logically—for example, the section on employment resources includes a large subsection on teaching abroad that lists schools worldwide and groups them by location. The section on grants is organized by state, and magazines and newsletters are grouped by subject matter. Each entry includes an address and telephone number, and sometimes a fax number and the name of a contact person. Three indexes—by entry, by publisher, and by subject—facilitate information retrieval. This is a well-organized directory; the only major flaw is the omission of e-mail addresses as part of the vital statistics for each entry. The work is recommended for all collections that serve elementary and secondary school professionals.—**G. Douglas Meyers**

Handbooks and Yearbooks

325. **The Blackwell Handbook of Education.** By Michael Farrell, Trevor Kerry, and Carolle Kerry. Cambridge, Mass., Blackwell, 1995. 333p. $59.50. ISBN 0-631-19279-4.

Purchase of this esoteric title is necessary only if a collection requires material concerning aspects of education in England and Wales. While well organized and filled with recent data and significant educational research, its use will probably be limited to academics and administrators seeking definitions for comparative studies and publications.

Using an appropriate A to Z format, the authors—each of whom has instructional experience at either British universities or the Department of Education—present information within several broad areas. Entries are included if they pertain to one of the following subfields of education: concepts and recent issues, educational institutions or organizations, educator duties and responsibilities, rules and regulations, learning differences, curriculum matters, and pedagogies or resources. The remaining three sections furnish lists of acronyms and abbreviations, educational organizations, and education-related legislation, respectively. A classified list of all cited entries concludes the text.

The approximately 370 entries are not uniform in length or content and sometimes suffer from redundancy. "Montessori, Maria (1870-1952)," for example, is described in one entry as a "pioneering educator" and reference is made to Montessori Schools within this entry. The subsequent entry is "Montessori Schools," which also refers to Maria Montessori and credits her teaching approaches and methods. The need for two entries for these items seems unnecessary. In some cases, a one-sentence definition for "Nursery Classes," for example, could easily be subsumed into either the "Nursery Education" or "Nursery School" entry.

Coverage of the field of education, however, is still broad. Users will be struck by the inclusion of many educational terms and issues such as hyperactivity, multicultural education, and readiness that are familiar to those used in the United States. Education professors and administrators needing information on specific British government-sponsored reports and legislation from 1861 to the present will find the chronological list in section 4 especially helpful.—**Kathleen W. Craver**

326. **Guide to Summer Camps and Summer Schools 1995/96.** 27th ed. Boston, Porter Sargent, 1995. 560p. illus. index. $35.00; $25.00pa. ISBN 0-87558-133-1; 0-87558-134-Xpa. ISSN 0072-8705.

In its 27th edition, the *Guide to Summer Camps* is published every 2 years in the interest of helping parents, their children, teachers, doctors, counselors, and other interested people in the choice of a camp or school for the summer months. It has a most unusual—partly geographic—arrangement for a reference book. Within the descriptive main body of the text, summer camps and schools are pigeonholed by emphasis: academic programs, unusual programs, summer study and travel abroad, programs for special needs, and that age-old favorite, the recreational camp. It is here that camp listings are presented geographically. This arrangement seems to reflect the greater density of population in the eastern half of the country, and the naturally larger number of summer camps in that area. Descriptive entries are listed from east to west in the United States; this is followed by Canadian camps and schools. Thus, in certain descriptive sections, entries move from Maine or Massachusetts through to Hawaii. This is a selective listing, in that the editors obtained information from camp directors by questionnaire, and later follow-up, if necessary. Camp accreditation may be included in the description, but it is not stressed, as it is in the American Camping Association's *Guide to Accredited Camps* (see entry 811).

The features of a camp or school are one means of access. For example, religious education, diving, weight loss, military training, preschools, English as a Second Language, and wilderness are some of the types. Librarians will also appreciate the complete master index that is provided. The information presented is well organized and everything is well written. Layout is neat and compact; readability is high. Still, one wishes for more detail in the text. Perhaps that is the purpose of the so-called announcements illustrated section, in which summer programs have paid for the space. This fine book has previously been reviewed in ARBA 84 and 80 (see entries 555 and 621, respectively), as well as in ARBA 72 (see entry 619).—**Randall Rafferty**

327. **The Handbook of Private Schools 1995: An Annual Descriptive Survey of Independent Education.** 76th ed. Boston, Porter Sargent, 1995. 1396p. illus. maps. index. $85.00. ISBN 0-87558-135-8. ISSN 0072-9884.

In its main section, "Leading Private Schools," the *Handbook of Private Schools* provides parents, counselors, and others with comparative information on 1,652 private schools in the United States. Information supplied is based on questionnaires returned by the schools, which then receive a free listing. Schools are arranged geographically by state, then alphabetically by city within each state. (A "Features Classified" index provides access by type of school, e.g., military, single-sex, schools for students with learning disabilities.) Common statistical information provided for the schools in the main section is: address, telephone, and fax numbers; name and qualifications of the administrator and director of admissions; grade range, academic orientation (college preparatory, general academic, vocational, and so on), and curriculum (availability of advanced courses; foreign language, fine arts, and computer courses; tutoring, remedial classes, and English as a Second Language); number of new admissions yearly as well as admissions tests used; enrollment and faculty (number of boys and girls enrolled at each level of schooling; number of male and female full- and part-time faculty as well as number holding doctoral, master's, and bachelor's degrees); graduate record (number in previous year's graduating class plus number entering college or preparatory school); tuition costs and scholarship information; summer session information; information on the school's physical facilities; and date of establishment, religious or other affiliation, and association membership (including accrediting agency). In addition, the main section presents paragraph descriptions for each school, intended to be a historical summary as well as an overview of recent innovations. Descriptions vary in length from a five-line paragraph to well over a page. This somewhat unbalanced coverage may be a result of schools supplying differing amounts of information on their questionnaires.

Two hundred and fifty of the schools have purchased space in the *Handbook*'s "Private Schools Illustrated" section. Through photographs and narrative, schools stress features they consider significant about their purposes and programs. A "Concise Listing of Schools" section contains single-paragraph descriptions of more than 900 schools—similar to those in the main section—for which insufficient information was available or those in which enrollment is limited to a local area or with specialized objectives and programs.

Libraries limited to the selection of one private school directory should consider this one. It describes more schools than Bunting and Lyon's *Private Independent Schools* (1995 edition), and has a more balanced coverage, although the Bunting and Lyon includes schools that the *Handbook* does not. Librarians should also make patrons aware that many private schools simply are not included in either reference work. The only rationale for the *Handbook*'s scope is that it includes schools that the editors judged to be of interest to a national audience.—**Jan Bakker**

328. Roberts, Patricia L. **Alphabet: A Handbook of ABC Books and Book Extensions for the Elementary Classroom.** 2d ed. Metuchen, N.J., Scarecrow, 1994. 264p. index. (School Library Media Series, no.3). $32.50. ISBN 0-8108-2823-5.

The expressed purpose of this reference source on alphabet books is to provide information from which librarians and teachers can select ABC titles that are varied in both topic and art style. The book is divided into three sections. Part 1 divides titles into a collection that has words and illustrations related to 9 selected themes. The grade level of each title is listed along with suggested activities that can be used. Part 2 focuses on the art of presenting the letters of the alphabet. Once again, grade level and activities for each title in this section are given. Part 3 is an annotated bibliography of all 262 books included in the work. A short summary of each book is provided. Entries represent titles that are currently in publication, including titles from mass market areas. There is a short bibliography of related readings, as well as a combined author/title index.

This work will be useful to preschool and elementary teachers as well as librarians. Narrow as the scope of this work may be, it is the only single source available for alphabet books. This book deserves a place in most large libraries and professional education collections. [R: Choice, Feb 95, p. 919]

—**Gary E. Joseph**

329. **Teacher Education Policy in the States: A 50-State Survey of Legislative & Administrative Actions, December, 1994.** Washington D.C., State Issues Clearinghouse/American Association of Colleges for Teacher Education, 1994. 108p. $25.00pa. ISBN 0-89333-128-7.

This edition of the 50-state survey updates earlier editions, with an emphasis on K-12 educational reform that was first reported in the spring 1994 edition of this survey. The introduction summarizes the data gathered and gives an overview of educational practices throughout the United States. The list of acronyms is especially helpful. The categories found in the survey include teacher entrance and exit requirements, regular licensure, emergency or shortage-driven credentials, and licensure with alternative preparation. Also provided are the categories of standards boards, minority teacher recruitment, teacher education review and study, and response to violence.

This survey defines all the categories as they apply to this work. Each state differs in the amount of information given in each area. Some of the categories are listed as "no state programs were reported in this area." Each state is responsible for what is included in the survey, and so the amount of information for each state ranges from one-and-one-half pages to three pages. The use of standardized categories enables users to consult one reference tool in order to compare regulations in all the states. This is a useful survey of teacher education policies, especially for student teachers who are job hunting.—**Mary Jo Aman**

HIGHER EDUCATION
Bibliography

330. Buchanan, Anne L., and Jean-Pierre V. M. Herubel, comps. **Doctor of Philosophy Degree: A Selective, Annotated Bibliography.** Westport, Conn., Greenwood Press, 1995. 125p. index. (Bibliographies and Indexes in Education, no.15). $59.95. ISBN 0-313-29539-5.

This volume is composed of 484 annotated bibliographical entries concerning the Ph.D in the United States, its history and evolution, as well as its nature in the sciences, social sciences, and humanities. As the title denotes, this is a *selective* bibliography in perhaps the best sense of that term. Here are almost 500 informative, well-written, annotated entries purportedly covering the best of what has been written on the topic. It is unclear, however, what criteria were used for including citations in this volume; a clear annunciation of the methods and criteria used in compiling this bibliography would have made it a much better work.

Another thing that would have made the bibliography much more useful is if, for each of the four chapters, entries were listed primarily by date and secondarily by author. (As it stands now, each chapter lists items alphabetically by author.) It is surprising that the compilers did not choose to do this, as they emphasize the fact in their introductory essay that the literature and research on the Ph.D is protean in nature; one would expect to find bibliographical listings in chronological order, so that one could trace the transformation of the research into this diverse entity more easily.

The bibliography should prove useful not only to those researching higher education in the United States but also for those currently enrolled in a Ph.D program or contemplating study at the doctoral level. It is recommended for libraries maintaining graduate collections in higher education research.—**Mark Cyzyk**

Directories

331. **Barron's Best Buys in College Education.** 3d ed. By Lucia Solórzano. Hauppauge, N.Y., Barron's Educational Series, 1994. 706p. index. $14.95pa. ISBN 0-8120-1857-5.

Profiling 299 schools, ranging from large state universities to small liberal arts colleges, this directory claims to identify best buys based on tuition rates, selectivity, or academic emphasis. Herein lies the problem with this type of selective and subjective work. In order to include a range of schools from all 50 states, and private as well as public institutions, many schools that may offer equal or even better value have been excluded. The schools profiled were selected initially from questionnaires obtained for the 1994 edition of Barrons's *Profiles of American Colleges*, the publisher's comprehensive guide to four-year schools. Questionnaires were then sent, through deans of students, to students at the schools identified for possible inclusion. Readers are not told how many students were contacted or how they were selected, although the introduction states their opinions weighed heavily in the final selection decision.

Arranged alphabetically by state, the descriptions of individual schools are detailed and useful. They describe the student body, academics, facilities, campus life, financial assistance, graduation rates, and types of jobs obtained by graduates. Five "quick lists" at the beginning of the book help prospective students target their choices. These include size of undergraduate population, cost of tuition, predominantly single-sex schools, and colleges with Phi Beta Kappa chapters. Students and parents will need to look at more comprehensive works to identify all the appropriate schools for their budgets and interests. However, if any of the colleges profiled here are on the lists they compile, the descriptive reviews in this work will provide them with some sense of what the individual schools are like.—**Christine E. King**

332. **Business Week Guide to the Best Business Schools.** 4th ed. John A. Byrne with the editors of *Business Week*, eds. New York, McGraw-Hill, 1995. 351p. index. $14.95pa. ISBN 0-07-009422-5.

This highly selective guide to master of business administration (MBA) degree programs has nearly doubled in size since it first appeared in 1990 (see ARBA 91, entry 139). As in previous editions, this one focuses on the strengths and weaknesses of the 20 best schools of business in the United States as rated by recent graduates and corporate recruiters polled by *Business Week*. The results of the 1994 survey are presented in graphs, tables, and anecdotal descriptions of nearly 60 outstanding MBA programs.

The top 20 schools (listed in rank order) are each discussed in 8-page articles filled with facts about admissions criteria, the student body, faculty, curricula, teaching methods, the campus atmosphere, costs, placement services, job offers, starting salaries, and alumni, as well as pithy comments by 1994 graduates. Entries for the 20 runners-up (listed alphabetically) are each only 4 pages long; they cover in less detail the same topics as the articles about the 20 elite schools. In addition, 6 top business schools outside the United States are profiled in 2-page essays, and 15 other programs in this country that offer "MBAs for bargain hunters" are described in 1-page entries.

This current, reliable, and interesting information source includes introductory chapters that discuss the value of an MBA degree and how to gain admission to an outstanding program. All libraries serving potential business school students will find it useful. [R: BL, 15 May 95, p. 1620]—**Leonard Grundt**

333. Cassidy, Daniel J. **Dan Cassidy's Worldwide College Scholarship Directory.** 4th ed. Franklin Lakes, N.J., Career Press, 1995. 249p. index. $19.99pa. ISBN 1-56414-208-6.

This directory is an abridged version of the National/International Scholarship Research Services database, claimed to be the largest private sector financial aid research service in the world. Begun in the late 1970s with information on national programs, the database today contains information on thousands of aid programs from 75 countries. This printed directory cites 1,256 scholarship programs, giving brief information about the amount of financial aid, deadlines, fields of study supported, and special eligibility for recipients, in addition to an address where to write for full information and application forms. These are arranged alphabetically by broad fields of study. Further information about college and financial aid subjects may be found in the more than 100 "helpful publications" cited in an annotated listing. A list of 170 organizations is also included, with encouragement for students to write to those in their fields of interest to get career information.

Three indexes simplify the use of this guide. The quick-find index consists of reference numbers to the award listings, arranged by common requirements used for eligibility qualifications for most private sector awards. Among the categories in this index are country of intended study, country (as well as city and county) of residence, current grade point average, ethnic background, family ancestries, and religious affiliation. The field of study index is arranged like a college catalog with groupings by broad field (e.g., "School of Business"), subdivided by specific areas (e.g., "Accounting"), and by specific subjects (e.g., "Banking"). An alphabetical index lists all awards, books, and career organizations cited in the directory.

The book's preface furnishes advice to the student starting to look for financial aid, including a sample letter to request application information and a plan to organize mailings into separate boxes for government funding, school endowments, and private sector sources of aid. Encouragement is repeated for students to seek information and submit applications to effectively compete for billions of available dollars. For its reasonable price, this directory is a useful guide for any student seeking financial aid, but particularly to those in high school planning for college.—**Danuta A. Nitecki**

334. Cassidy, Daniel J. **Dan Cassidy's Worldwide Graduate Scholarship Directory.** 4th ed. Franklin Lakes, N.J., Career Press, 1995. 295p. index. $26.99pa. ISBN 1-56414-209-4.

This is another in a series of books compiled by Cassidy and his staff at the National Scholarship Research Service in Santa Rosa, California. Although identified as the 4th edition, it is the first edition to offer international coverage. The style and format are identical to previous editions (see ARBA 94, entry 331, and ARBA 89, entry 283). There are helpful sections, such as practical advice on requesting and returning applications, a list of organizations offering career information, and a bibliography. The body of the directory consists of 1,536 brief entries (fewer than the previous edition), organized alphabetically within broad subject areas. Each entry includes the address and telephone number of the organization, the amount of the award, the application deadline, and eligibility requirements.

For this edition, the author has included scholarships and awards for foreign citizens who want to study in the United States and for U.S. citizens who want to study abroad. However, this directory offers relatively few of these and should not be considered a substitute for *International Scholarship Directory* (3d ed.; see ARBA 94, entry 332). Despite repeating the page of instructions on using the guide three times, the author offers no explanation of the criteria used for inclusion in the directory or when the entries were last updated. This, and more minor criticisms aside (the number of entries in sections of the "Quick Find Index" are too numerous to be useful; the adhesive binding will not withstand heavy use), this directory is recommended for academic collections. Books on this subject are always popular, and no scholarship directory is comprehensive.—**Hope Yelich**

335. **Chronicle Two-Year College Databook: For 1995-96 School Year.** rev. ed. Moravia, N.Y., Chronicle Guidance, 1995. 366p. index. $22.46pa. ISBN 1-55631-241-5.

This is an excellent, easy-to-use guide to 733, 2-year majors offered at both 2-year and 4-year institutions. The introductory sections include useful advice on how to select a college, with a number of considerations briefly discussed. As in past editions (see ARBA 93, entry 369, and ARBA 90, entry 334), there are two main sections. The first section lists the majors, with the institutions arranged by state, that offer certificates or diplomas, associate degrees, and transfer programs. The "Two-Year College Charts" composes the second section. Information for 2,408 colleges and universities is presented here in tabular form and provides an address, telephone and fax numbers, the calendar, the location, enrollment figures, admissions requirements, the application deadline, costs, and financial aid information.

Although more detailed information can be found in other sources such as *Peterson's Guide to Two-Year Colleges* (see ARBA 94, entry 343), the basic data presented are enough to allow a student to compare schools and to decide whether or not to write to an institution for complete information. As noted in past reviews, no one source gives a comprehensive list of majors and institutions offering them. Libraries will need several such directories. The *Databook* is a worthy addition to this section of any reference collection.—**Michele Russo**

336. **Directory of Graduate Student Employee Bargaining Agents and Organizations.** Rachel Lanzerotti, Melissa Hayes, and Jon Curtiss, eds. New York, National Center for the Study of Collective Bargaining in Higher Education and the Professions, School of Public Affairs, Baruch College—City University of New York, 1995. 95p. $40.00. ISBN 0-911259-32-5.

This is a handy guide in the area of union development among higher education employees in the United States, providing information on recognized collective bargaining agents for graduate students for the Coalition of Graduate Employee Unions. Information is provided on each locale: unit size, membership, the kind of union organization, and contract highlights of unions that are in existence in 10 of the 50 states. It also covers unions that are operating in private institutions as well as public sector institutions. Four private institutions are covered—Cornell, Notre Dame, Syracuse, and Yale. The directory also contains entries with information contributed by organizations that have not been recognized as collective bargaining agents. These include union-affiliated organizations that have attempted or are in the process of pursuing recognition of graduate student governments that are advocates for graduate student employees and have expressed interest. There is a third section of the directory that lists names and addresses of graduate employee organizations in Canada. Specific information concerning name, address, telephone number, e-mail address, names of individuals, and a short history of the bargaining unit itself is provided. This is an important addition to the directory and guide literature of higher education in the United States.—**Gerald D. Moran**

337. **Education for the Earth: The College Guide for Careers in the Environment.** 2d ed. Princeton, N.J., Peterson's Guides, 1995. 319p. illus. index. $14.95pa. ISBN 1-56079-407-0. ISSN 1077-1883.

This is a college guide to environmental education programs in the United States and Canada covering 211 institutions. Both undergraduate and graduate programs are listed in the five broad career areas of environmental engineering, environmental health, environmental science, environmental studies, and natural resource management. There are informative essays on specific career paths for each of these career areas, and a chapter devoted to internships.

The colleges are arranged alphabetically by name. A geographic index at the end of the volume enables one to locate the colleges by state or country. A second index is arranged by subject area of specialization, with listings of colleges offering fields of study in that area. Using this source, the career seeker can identify well-established programs in various colleges, compare the programs, and choose the college with the desired course of study.

An interesting feature of this book are the profiles of working environmentalists complete with picture, educational background, what kind of work they do, and what they like about their career. They also give advice to persons just entering the field. The table of contents provides easy access to the information. The volume quickly pinpoints pertinent information for the future environmentalist. A "How to Use" section in the beginning of the volume assists the reader in understanding the purpose and organization of the book, and provides suggestions as to where additional information may be found. This work will be of value in career and college guide sections in libraries. In keeping with the environmental theme, the book is published on recycled paper. [R: C&RL, Mar 95, p. 194]—**Marilyn Strong Noronha**

338. **Guide to American Studies Resources, 1994.** John F. Stephens, ed. Baltimore, Md., Johns Hopkins University Press, 1994. 285p. $25.00pa. ISBN 0-8018-4935-7.

This directory, published as a supplement to the *American Quarterly*, official journal of the American Studies Association (ASA), provides a broad overview of membership and services related to American Studies programs. Profiles of college programs from the University of Alabama to Youngstown State University form the first 100 pages of the guide. Each entry briefly describes the program, and lists the degrees offered by the institution, tuition, deadlines for application to the program, and faculty serving the program.

The second half of the directory presents an alphabetical listing of the complete institutional and individual membership in the ASA. Additionally, this guide lists fellowships and grants, a calendar of meetings and conferences, ASA awards and prizes, and useful addresses such as publishers and libraries, all of which are of interest to persons studying or working in the field of American studies.—**Jerry D. Flack**

339. **New Research Centers 1996. The Supplement to the 20th Edition of Research Centers Directory: A Guide to Over 13,400 University-Related and Other Nonprofit Research Organizations....** Anthony L. Gerring, ed. Detroit, Gale, 1995. 1v. index. $330.00pa. ISBN 0-8103-9097-3. ISSN 0028-6591.

340. **Research Centers Directory 1996: A Guide to More Than 13,400 University-Related and Other Nonprofit Research Organizations....** 20th ed. Anthony L. Gerring, ed. Detroit, Gale, 1995. 2v. index. $485.00/set. ISBN 0-8103-9094-9. ISSN 0800-1518.

This annual guide to North American Research Centers and independent nonprofit research organizations was reviewed in ARBA several times. For the latest review, see ARBA 94 (entry 345). It covers some 13,000 organizations in 2 volumes. Institutions are in subject arrangement, covering life sciences, physical sciences and engineering, private and public policy and affairs, social and cultural studies, and multidisciplinary and research coordinating centers. Subject, geographical, name, and master indexes conclude these volumes. The supplement covers several hundred additional institutions.
—**Bohdan S. Wynar**

341. **Peterson's Colleges with Programs for Students with Learning Disabilities.** 4th ed. Charles T. Mangrum II and Stephen S. Strichart, eds. Princeton, N.J., Peterson's Guides, 1994. 674p. index. $31.95pa. (with disk). ISBN 1-56079-400-3.

Awareness of and attention to the needs of the disabled were greatly facilitated by the 1990 ADA (Americans with Disabilities Act). Thousands of first-year college students report having a learning disability, and they and their parents are interested in identifying a college that will provide them the optimum educational setting in terms of programs and services, special assistance, diagnostic and prescriptive planning, advising, counseling, remediation, tutoring, and specially designed courses. The latter could address developmental reading, language remediation, study skills, writing research papers, note-taking techniques, personal psychology, and college survival, among others. This specialized directory in the Peterson's Guides series describes more than 800 programs in the United States, its territories, and Canada. This edition is accompanied by a computer disk for searching the guide.

The introductory material provides useful answers to questions such as: What are learning disabilities? What are the characteristics of college students with learning disabilities? How are students with learning disabilities admitted to college? What types of assistance do colleges provide for students with learning disabilities? "A Checklist for Comparing LD Programs and Services" helps users match special needs with schools. "A Quick Reference Chart of Colleges" is arranged by state for geographical identification.

College profiles are arranged alphabetically in two major listings: comprehensive programs designed specifically for LD students, and schools that offer special services that are beneficial to LD students. Entries typically range from one-half to two pages in length and begin with a chart summarizing information related to: the year the program began, special fees, diagnostic testing, subject area tutoring, basic skills remediation, special courses, taped textbooks, alternate exam arrangements, note taking, LD support group, staff, and students. The profile gives additional details about the LD program as well as general information about the college.

An alphabetical index to academic institutions concludes the volume. Prospective students, parents, high school media specialists, guidance counselors, librarians, and other educators will find this guide useful and informative. It will be an important addition to collections in high school, academic, and public libraries.—**Lois J. Buttlar**

342. **Peterson's Contract Services for Higher Education.** Princeton, N.J., Peterson's Guides, 1995. 447p. index. $89.95pa. ISBN 1-56079-442-9. ISSN 1080-2541.

This 1st edition lists contract and outsourcing providers for higher education services, in 15 categories such as athletics; computer facilities and systems; public relations; and financial, library, and personnel services. Organized by major category, each service provider entry contains (as available) company name, address, annual sales, number of employees, year founded, type of services, area served, names of clients, and contact person with telephone and fax numbers. The initial information was gathered through surveys of business officers of higher education institutions followed by questionnaires to the service providers.

Directory introductory material includes use instructions, information about the development of the directory, and an essay on making decisions for contract management. These materials allude to the question of determining appropriate services for outsourcing and the importance of assessing the value of various alternatives for providing the services in question. Indexes provide access by services, suppliers and contact names, locations by state, and advertisers. The directory also includes a list of university and college business officers with their telephone numbers.

There are areas for improvement for subsequent editions of the directory. Minor inaccuracies in the suggestions for using the directory need correction. More importantly, the terminology used for the services listing for each provider and the service categories is very general. Concrete examples of the kinds of projects or services for which providers have been responsible would be more useful. Finally, if the section on library services is indicative of other services, many more service providers in each of the subcategories are available. Although the directory is potentially a valuable resource for higher education institutions, it will not replace other formal and informal information resources.—**Joan B. Fiscella**

343. **Peterson's Guide to Colleges in the Midwest 1995.** 11th ed. Princeton, N.J., Peterson's Guides, 1994. 339p. index. $13.95pa. ISBN 1-56079-360-0. ISSN 0742-4949.

344. **Peterson's Guide to Colleges in the South 1995.** 10th ed. Princeton, N.J., Peterson's Guides, 1994. 282p. illus. index. $13.95pa. ISBN 1-56079-361-9. ISSN 1069-0085.

345. **Peterson's Guide to Colleges in the West 1995.** 9th ed. Princeton, N.J., Peterson's Guides, 1994. 189p. illus. index. $13.95pa. ISBN 1-56079-362-7. ISSN 0888-8159.

346. **Peterson's Guide to Middle Atlantic Colleges 1995.** 11th ed. Princeton, N.J., Peterson's Guides, 1994. 215p. illus. index. $13.95pa. ISBN 1-56079-363-5. ISSN 0742-4957.

347. **Peterson's Guide to New England Colleges 1995.** 11th ed. Princeton, N.J., Peterson's Guides, 1994. 134p. illus. index. $13.95pa. ISBN 1-56079-359-7. ISSN 0742-4973.

348. **Peterson's Guide to New York Colleges 1995.** 11th ed. Princeton, N.J., Peterson's Guides, 1994. 129p. illus. index. $13.95pa. ISBN 1-56079-358-9. ISSN 0742-4965.

The majority of each volume under review provides information on the two-year and four-year colleges (including those that are part of universities), both general and technical, in that region. The information is given in categories similar to those contained in the single-volume Peterson guides (see ARBA 94, entries 342-343)—academic information, student body statistics, expenses, financial aid, first year admission, transfer admission, entrance difficulty—although with fewer details. In addition to those standard categories, a number of the institutions have had their admissions officers provide statements about the social life, the academics, campus visits, and the interviewing process at their respective institutions.

Each guide begins with useful general information on transferring and on financial aid, with fairly specific information on the financial aid provisions for each of the states covered in that volume. Four indexes conclude each guide: majors and degrees offered; athletic programs and scholarships available; ROTC programs; and finally, an alphabetical index of all the institutions covered in that guide (except for the New York volume). These guides will be useful for high school and public libraries in the respective regions, but they are probably not necessary where the more general Peterson guides (or other major national guides) are available.—**Evan Ira Farber**

349. **Peterson's Guide to Graduate and Professional Programs: An Overview 1995.** 29th ed. Princeton, N.J., Peterson's Guides, 1995. 1198p. illus. index. (Peterson's Annual Guides to Graduate Study, bk 1). $24.95pa./v.; $145.30pa./set. ISBN 1-56079-380-5.

350. **Peterson's Guide to Graduate Programs in Business, Education, Health, and Law 1995.** 29th ed. Princeton, N.J., Peterson's Guides, 1995. 1614p. illus. index. (Peterson's Annual Guides to Graduate Study, bk 6). $24.95pa./v.; $145.30pa./set. ISBN 1-56079-385-6. ISSN 0894-9387.

351. **Peterson's Guide to Graduate Programs in Engineering and Applied Sciences 1995.** 29th ed. Princeton, N.J., Peterson's Guides, 1995. 1409p. illus. index. (Peterson's Annual Guides to Graduate Study, bk 5). $34.95pa./v.; $145.30pa./set. ISBN 1-56079-384-8. ISSN 0894-9387.

352. **Peterson's Guide to Graduate Programs in the Biological and Agricultural Sciences 1995.** 29th ed. Princeton, N.J., Peterson's Guides, 1995. 2635p. illus. index. (Peterson's Annual Guides to Graduate Study, bk 3). $41.95pa./v.; $145.30pa./set. ISBN 1-56079-382-1. ISSN 0894-9360.

353. **Peterson's Guide to Graduate Programs in the Humanities, Arts, and Social Sciences 1995.** 29th ed. Princeton, N.J., Peterson's Guides, 1995. 1466p. illus. index. (Peterson's Annual Guides to Graduate Study, bk 2). $34.95pa./v.; $145.30pa./set. ISBN 1-56079-381-3. ISSN 0894-9352.

354. **Peterson's Guide to Graduate Programs in the Physical Sciences and Mathematics 1995.** 29th ed. Princeton, N.J., Peterson's Guides, 1995. 778p. illus. index. (Peterson's Annual Guides to Graduate Study, bk 4). $31.95pa./v.; $145.30pa./set. ISBN 1-56079-383-X. ISSN 0894-9387.

This set, published annually since 1966 with various titles and number of volumes, is a standard source for comprehensive information on postbaccalaureate education offered by accredited institutions in the United States and its territories, and by those Canadian, Mexican, European, and African institutions accredited by United States' accrediting bodies. The information, collected by the publisher directly from deans, department heads, and other administrators at some 1,500 institutions offering graduate and professional programs, is subject to editorial revision. Each volume begins with a graduate adviser section consisting of two essays and other information. The first essay is on applying to the schools (the application process: forms, transcripts, letters of recommendation, and so forth; special remarks addressed to older, returning students and part-time and international students). The second essay, on financial aid, offers tips on applying for aid; types of aid available; aid for minority students, women, and disabled students; and international education and study abroad information. This section concludes with data on major standardized admissions tests and a directory of institutional and specialized accrediting agencies.

Graduate and Professional Programs provides information on the institutions as a whole, including: (1) a directory of programs by fields (publisher's statement: 322; reviewer's count: 318) and the institutions that award degrees in these fields; (2) a directory of institutions and their offerings—the same information as in the first directory, but listed alphabetically by institutional name and subdivided by fields; (3) a combined degree programs directory arranged alphabetically by field and thereunder by institution(s); (4) profiles of institutions offering graduate and professional work, providing general institutional information (public/private; coed/unisex; expenses; enrollment; number of faculty members; library, computer, and special research facilities; general application contact) and similar information for individual graduate units within the institution; (5) 2-page essays of selected institutions, furnishing statements on degree programs, research facilities, financial aid, costs, application forms, tests, fees, contact person/office, and faculty; (6) 2 appendixes (reproduced in all other volumes)—a list of institutional changes (closures, mergers, name changes) and abbreviations of degrees, tests, organizations; and (7) 2 indexes, the first giving page references to the profiles and the 2-page essays in this book, and the second providing references to the directories and subject areas in the other books under review.

Using the same format, the remaining in the Graduate Studies series are guides to programs in specific subject areas: the humanities, arts, and social sciences; biological and agricultural sciences; physical sciences and mathematics; engineering and applied sciences; and business, education, health, and law, respectively. Each volume includes, in sequence, a directory of institutions with their respective areas, a directory of programs, announcements, and descriptions in the subareas of the given book title. For instance, *Physical Sciences and Mathematics* is divided into eight sections (subareas): physical sciences, astronomy and astrophysics, chemistry, earth and planetary sciences, marine sciences/oceanography, mathematical sciences, meteorology and atmospheric sciences, and physics. Physics is further subdivided into six fields: acoustics, applied physics, mathematical physics, optical sciences, physics, and plasma physics. Two of the three indexes in each book (the index of full descriptions and announcements and the index of directories and subject areas) relate to a given book; a third index (also in *Graduate and Professional Programs*) is to directories and subject areas in all books in the series. Its comprehensiveness, annual updating, and ease of use make the Peterson's Annual Guides to Graduate Study series a most valuable resource for academic and public libraries.—**Wiley J. Williams**

355. **Peterson's Guide to MBA Programs: A Comprehensive Directory of Graduate Business Education....** Princeton, N.J., Peterson's Guides, 1995. 1000p. illus. index. $19.95pa. ISBN 1-56079-366-X. ISSN 1080-2533.

This guide to master of business administration (MBA) programs is a new addition to the Peterson's Guides series. It covers 700-plus MBA and equivalent programs in the United States and Canada, as well as selected courses elsewhere in the world. The work is based on a survey and responses to it sent to the schools involved in late 1994 and early 1995. The main section contains information on entrance requirements, including grade point average and GMAT levels, facilities, program components and types of work required, student backgrounds by subject and geographic origin, placement, finance, and more.

This section is arranged geographically by state and school, with Canadian entries separately listed by province and institution. Schools in other countries follow by country and program. There are also a comparative chart on the programs and a section of two-page profiles for those schools providing them.

Other features are essays on seven aspects of the MBA choice from finance to trends; and indexes by category of program (including equivalents to MBA programs), by school name, and by areas of concentration offered. There are also extensive sections on how to use the volume and how the information was obtained. In sum, this seems to be a good, inexpensive one-volume directory of business schools from a reputable series that should be considered for addition to business or education guide collections.

—Nigel Tappin

356. **Peterson's Guide to Nursing Programs: Baccalaureate and Graduate Nursing Education in the U.S. and Canada.** Princeton, N.J., Peterson's Guides, 1994. 675p. illus. index. $21.95pa. ISBN 1-56079-355-4. ISSN 1073-7820.

In cooperation with the American Association of Colleges of Nursing, Peterson's Guides has added nursing to its series. Criteria for inclusion in the guide are appropriate accreditation of the parent institution and accreditation of the nursing program by the National League of Nursing (NLN) or the Canadian Association of University Schools of Nursing. Responses from questionnaires sent to over 600 nursing programs are included. The introduction provides a background for using the guide and includes helpful essays on career planning, advice to the practicing nurse who is returning to school, suggestions to the international student, and information on financial aid including contact information for public and private funds. A quick-reference chart is followed by profiles, arranged geographically by state or province, that provide a variety of data about the institution and the nursing program along with contact name and address. A section of two-page descriptions submitted by the school or department personalizes some of the programs. There is an index to specialties for master's degree programs, another by program type, and a third by name of the institution.

This volume will replace *Guide to Programs in Nursing in Four-Year Colleges and Universities* (see ARBA 88, entry 1683). Although some of the information is available from other sources, such as NLN publications, this is the most comprehensive, one-stop guide to education in a profession that is adapting its educational expectations for rapidly changing and more challenging career opportunities. The intended audience and the modest price make it practical for all libraries.—**Margo B. Mead**

357. **The Princeton Review Student Access Guide: The Big Book of Colleges.** 1996 ed. By Edward T. Custard. New York, Princeton Review/Random House, 1995. 1237p. illus. index. $25.00pa. ISBN 3-679-76152-7. ISSN 1081-2415.

In comparison to *The Princeton Review Student Access Guide to the Best 309 Colleges* (see entry 358), this volume offers information on some 1,200 institutions covering almost identical information: economics, facilities, student and faculty information, extracurricular activities, admissions, and financial aid policies. There is a fairly detailed section, "How to Use This Book"; a separate section, "What's the Admissions Wizard?"; an alphabetical listing of colleges and universities; and an alphabetical index. It should be noted that the Princeton Review is not affiliated with Princeton University or the Educational Testing Service.—**Bohdan S. Wynar**

358. **The Princeton Review Student Access Guide to the Best 309 Colleges.** 1996 ed. By Tom Meltzer and others. New York, Princeton Review/Random House, 1995. 707p. index. $18.00pa. ISBN 0-679-76146-2. ISSN 1067-215X.

Updated annually, this edition offers a fairly detailed description of some environmental factors on 309 well-known colleges in the United States. Edited by the staff of *The Princeton Review* and published by Random House, this directory offers information based upon ongoing surveys of students attending these institutions, covering such aspects as "students speak out," admission requirements, financial aid, student body demographics, average SAT scores, and so on. There are a helpful index of independent counselors arranged by state, an index of learning disability programs, and a general index of schools. All in all, this is a helpful directory that will be used with guides published by Barron's Educational Series or Peterson's Guides.—**Bohdan S. Wynar**

359. Roes, Nicholas A. **America's Lowest Cost Colleges.** 9th ed. Barryville, N.Y., NAR, 1995. 184p. index. $9.95pa. ISBN 0-89780-041-9.

With college costs rising rapidly, a new edition of this comprehensive directory of more than 2,000 colleges and universities with low tuition is welcome. Low tuition is defined as no more than $3,500 (for tuition and other mandatory fees) for a full academic year. Readers must realize that this is for in-state tuition and that out-of-state tuition is considerably higher. This directory includes community colleges, junior colleges, and four-year colleges, as well as universities with graduate schools. All schools listed must offer an academic program. Only seminary schools, trade schools, and technical schools that also have academic programs are listed. All educational institutions covered are accredited by one of the six major regional accreditation associations. Entries are arranged by state. Basic information includes name, address, and telephone number of institution; tuition (both in-state and out-of-state); and degrees offered.

The need for a comprehensive, inexpensive guide such as this one is great. Unfortunately, there are numerous errors. For example, two institutions in Utah have changed their names: Southern Utah State College changed its name to Southern Utah University in 1991, and Utah Valley Community College changed its name to Utah Valley State College in 1993. Neither has been updated in this directory. Degree offerings from these two institutions are also incorrect: SUU has offered a master of accountancy for years and UVSC offers numerous baccalaureate degrees. UVSC has also been left out of the index of four-year schools. These are not recent changes and there is no excuse for such inaccurate research. This source may be a good beginning point in the search for an inexpensive college or university, but the information must be checked for accuracy.—**Vik Brown**

360. **Summer on Campus: College Experiences for High School Students.** [2d ed.]. New York, College Board, 1995. 321p. $15.00pa. ISBN 0-87447-526-0.

Even though identified as a 2d edition, there are improvements that need to be made to this guide to summer programs at colleges and universities. While some 400 programs are listed, these are by no means the only ones available for new and continuing students. The advantage of this compilation is that it provides the advisor or counselor with a handy guide, and a variety of indexes, to some of the programs available in a particular state. A helpful addition might be to identify large standard metropolitan areas such as Boston, Chicago, Denver, Los Angeles, New York, and Washington, D.C., where a student might have several options for summer study or education. The addition of an e-mail address for the contact person or office for programs in this guide would expedite access to pertinent information. Increasingly, students are using e-mail to secure information from target colleges and universities and avoid delays in reaching people by telephone, or sending letters via fax.

Some of the information contained in this guide is obsolete even at the date of printing. As an example, fees at many of the included programs tend to change annually. Users should be prepared to engage in telephone, fax, or e-mail follow-up with a prospective program to verify actual costs. Overall, this guide provides useful information to assist students in selecting a summer program of interest at a college or university campus. Public libraries, high school counseling offices, and some academic libraries may be interested in purchasing this new edition. Perhaps in the near future additional information on other summer programs will be incorporated and made available on CD-ROM.—**Roberto P. Haro**

361. **World List of Universities and Other Institutions of Higher Education.** 20th ed. Ann C. M. Taylor, ed. New York, Stockton Press, 1995. 875p. index. $160.00. ISBN 1-56159-109-2.

This publication of the International Association of Universities (IAU) provides concise information on more than 11,000 institutions in 178 countries. It includes university level institutions, as so defined by each country, other institutions offering three- or four-year degree programs, and national organizations and agencies concerned with higher education. Military academies and independent theological schools are not listed. Entries are arranged by country and then usually grouped in the three categories mentioned above, although other categories are used to subdivide entries for countries that have many institutions or use different designations for them. These variations and the lack of an index by institution name can create difficulties for users attempting to look up a particular school, even when its location is known.

The section entitled "Index" is in fact a table of contents, which does at least indicate any special categories under which institutions are grouped for each country. The entries themselves are generally brief, including the name, address, telephone number, and founding date of each institution, along with two or three top administrators and any affiliated faculties, schools, centers, or other subunits (or simply the major disciplines or areas of study offered).

As the editor notes in an introductory section, more extensive information about the universities—roughly half the schools covered here—can be found in the IAU's *International Handbook of Universities* (13th ed., Stockton Press, 1993). The *World of Learning* (45th ed., Gale, 1995) likewise includes fewer institutions and provides more detailed entries. As an alternative to these titles, the *World List* offers greater comprehensiveness, a more convenient size, and a lower price.—**Gregory M. Toth**

Handbooks and Yearbooks

362. **American Community Colleges: A Guide.** 10th ed. Robert H. Atwell and David Pierce, eds. Phoenix, Ariz., Oryx Press, 1995. 909p. index. $135.00. ISBN 0-89774-874-3. ISSN 1079-7599.

Ten years have passed since the last edition of this important reference work was published under the title *American Community, Technical, and Junior Colleges*. During that time, community colleges have continued to grow in importance, enrolling 60 percent of first-year students in U.S. higher education. The need for an accurate, up-to-date, and comprehensive guide to these colleges is thus self-evident. This volume has been prepared by the American Council on Education and the American Association of Community Colleges; its editors are presidents of these associations. It describes 1,812 accredited public and private 2-year colleges in the United States, plus those in American Samoa, Guam, and Puerto Rico.

The guide's main section contains detailed and complete entries for each college. The entries include data on general background, academic information, and financial information. A subject index follows, arranged alphabetically by headings based on major curriculum areas and programs. The last part of the book is an institution index. The book's information is indeed definitive and authoritative. It is sturdily bound and printed on high-quality paper. On the negative side are its expensive price and the fact that its information will date rather quickly. Perhaps its main value is as a permanent reference source on U.S. community colleges rather than as a current guide to them (unless it is revised more frequently or becomes available on electronic databases).

Peterson's Guide to Two-Year Colleges (see ARBA 94, entry 343) is an alternative acquisitions choice in this area. Revised annually, it is priced reasonably. *Peterson's* covers much the same information as *American Community Colleges* and is also available in online and CD-ROM databases. As a bonus, Peterson's Electronic Application Service allows students "to complete applications on disks and send them electronically to college admission offices" (p. iv).—**Marshall E. Nunn**

363. Bear, John, and Mariah Bear. **College Degrees by Mail 1996: 100 Accredited Schools That Offer Bachelor's....** rev. ed. Berkeley, Calif., Ten Speed Press, 1995. 216p. illus. index. $12.95pa. ISBN 0-89815-760-9.

John Bear is *the* respected and established authority on nontraditional education. His daughter Mariah joins him as the coauthor of this revised and expanded edition of *College Degrees by Mail* (a somewhat misleading title—a more accurate and appropriate one would be *College Degrees by Nontraditional or Distance Learning Methods*). The book is valuable as it shows the many different ways learning can occur outside the classroom through correspondence courses; courses offered via cable television or videotape; independent study; courses available over home computers, often via the emerging Internet; and extension courses.

In the first section of the book, the authors draw upon their wide experience and knowledge to offer wise words and counsel on degrees, accreditation, and different ways of earning credit. These include foreign academic experience and the interesting idea of the Regents Credit Bank Service. The core of the book is its one-page descriptions of each of "One Hundred Accredited Schools Offering Degrees Entirely or Almost Entirely by Home Study." This section lists schools in Canada, Israel, England, South Africa, and Wales. The descriptions are concise and informative.

Eleven appendixes follow, including ones on diploma mills and unaccredited colleges; "Advice for People in Prison" (and other institutions)—it is actually possible to earn a Ph.D. from the University of South Africa from prison!; a glossary; and two indexes. Humorous illustrations enliven the text. The Bears' book is an indispensable guide through the terra incognita of distance learning and nontraditional education. (See ARBA 94, entry 351, and ARBA 92, entry 300, for reviews of earlier editions of this work.)
—**Marshall E. Nunn**

364. **Chronicle Financial Aid Guide: For 1995-96 School Year.** rev. ed. Moravia, N.Y., Chronicle Guidance, 1995. 320p. index. $22.47pa. ISBN 1-55631-242-3.

This guide is an excellent source of financial aid prospects for undergraduate students. More than 900 scholarships, loans, and grants from the private sector, states, and federal government are listed. The sources of financial aid are arranged alphabetically by the name of the award or sponsoring agency. Each entry provides a concise profile about eligibility requirements and restrictions, number and dollar amounts of awards, selection criteria, application procedures, and deadlines.

Thorough indexing by subject, target audience, and sponsoring agencies, along with a lengthy table of contents by broad subject, makes specific information easy to locate. An introduction provides general information about seeking financial aid and specific information on how to use this book, with examples of how to write letters to the sponsoring agencies. A bibliography of other resources about financial aid is included near the end of the volume. There are many sources of aid here for students with disabilities. This guide covers all the essential information necessary to aid the beginning college student in locating financial assistance, and will be of value in every school, academic, and public library.—**Marilyn Strong Noronha**

365. Hamel, April Vahle, with Mary Morris Heiberger and Julia Miller Vick. **The Graduate School Funding Handbook.** Philadelphia, University of Pennsylvania Press, 1994. 162p. index. $36.95; $13.95pa. ISBN 0-8122-3232-1; 0-8122-1447-1pa.

This guide is primarily concerned with external financial aid for graduate study; that is, funding available from sources outside students' own institutions. The first chapter surveys types of graduate degrees, describes the various forms of institutional financial aid typically available within universities, and offers advice on selecting and applying to graduate schools. The remainder of the work focuses on external funding, devoting a chapter each to: individual fellowships, research and study abroad, research grants, dissertation fellowships, and postdoctoral fellowships. Each chapter provides general information on the funding type in question, including advice on applying for it, and then specific information and comments on selected programs of that type.

Although provided with an index and a detailed table of contents, this work is less a reference source than a treatise on financial aid for graduate study. Considered as such, it should be of value to students (and those advising them) who are seeking such aid. However, because its listing of funding programs and sources is very selective, the handbook must be used in conjunction with more comprehensive directories and guides, a fact the authors acknowledge both explicitly and in the lists of references for further reading provided in most of the chapters.—**Gregory M. Toth**

366. **National Profile of Community Colleges 1995-1996: Trends & Statistics.** Kent A. Phillippe, ed. Washington, D.C., American Association of Community Colleges, 1995. 82p. $65.00pa. ISBN 0-87117-278-X.

This compilation of statistics and accompanying text provides a broad overview of community colleges in the United States, both public and private. The compilers define *community college* as an institution separately accredited, or in the process of becoming accredited, by one of the six regional accrediting bodies, and offering, as their highest degree, the associate degree. Also included are the unique systems or campuses of accredited baccalaureate or higher-degree-granting institutions that offer the associate degree.

Data collected from a large number of statistical sources, both print and electronic, are presented in graphs, pie charts, tables, and maps, each citing the source of the data shown. Each section has an introductory text and brief statements interpreting or analyzing the statistical findings. The reader is able to draw a profile of student enrollments and characteristics, costs and financial aid, institutional revenues and expenditures, faculty and staff characteristics and salaries, and the impact of community colleges on the workforce, by pursuing the graphic materials and the analyses.

An introductory chapter gives a short history of the development of the U.S. community college and a comparison of community colleges and public four-year institutions. A concluding chapter examines the possible future of the colleges. A bibliography lists references and electronic data sources. Students, instructors, researchers, and writers in the field of higher education; sociologists; and community college administrators and boards will find this compilation to be an excellent source of statistical information. It should also be of interest to higher-education specialists in other countries.—**Shirley L. Hopkinson**

367. **Peterson's Summer Study Abroad: A Guide to Summer Academic and Language Programs.** Princeton, N.J, Peterson's Guides, 1995. 570p. illus. $18.95pa. ISBN 1-56079-444-5.

This book outlines more than 800 summer international study programs offered in 80 countries. The introduction discusses the proper use of the book—matching the student with the best summer program for his or her needs. Most of these programs are schools that offer academic credit, but a few language schools are included. The book contains program descriptions, and each profile discusses comparative data such as subjects taught, dates, admission requirements, costs, living arrangements, and so on. These program descriptions are mostly listed by country and then by city. Advertisements are found, but are carefully done and do not take away from the presentation of the programs. Black-and-white photographs found throughout the book are attractive and inviting. Indexes on fields of study, program sponsors, and host institutions are included.

This book is a good purchase for libraries wanting to provide accessible information on summer study abroad programs. Peterson's also publishes a guide on semester and academic year programs (see ARBA 95, entry 382), but the information in the two guides is sufficiently different to warrant the purchase of both.—**Carl Pracht**

INTERNATIONAL EXCHANGE PROGRAMS AND OPPORTUNITIES

368. **Academic Year Abroad 1995/96.** Sara J. Steen, ed. New York, Institute of International Education, 1995. 612p. index. $42.95pa. ISBN 0-87206-211-2.

369. **Vacation Study Abroad 1995/96.** Sara J. Steen, ed. New York, Institute of International Education, 1995. 388p. index. $36.95pa. ISBN 0-87206-212-0. ISSN 1046-2104.

These study abroad books are produced by the Institute of International Exchange (IIE), the largest U.S. higher education exchange agency. More than 2,200 programs are outlined in *Academic Year Abroad* and 1,600 programs in *Vacation Study Abroad*. These programs are designed mainly for U.S. students at the undergraduate and graduate levels. Paid advertisements are also included. In each volume, the preface furnishes an extensive explanation on how to use the information provided. An interesting essay entitled "Planning for Study Abroad" gives advice on selecting a program, visas, medical insurance, transportation, and many other helpful topics.

Programs are broken down first by continents and next by country. They are then listed alphabetically. Listings include site, dates, subjects taught, eligibility, credit, information on instruction, costs, housing, deadlines, other information, and contact persons. The indexes are the greatest strength of these two books. They list sponsoring institutions; consortia; fields of study; special options (e.g., internships, student teaching, independent study, and the like); and cost ranges.

While the books under review are in direct competition with *Peterson's Study Abroad* (see ARBA 95, entry 382) and *Peterson's Summer Study Abroad* (see entry 367), there is surprisingly less overlap than one would expect. The IIE books include more programs than the Peterson's guides, but the latter guides provide slightly better program descriptions. These two IIE books are worthy purchases for libraries wanting to provide patrons with current study abroad information.—**Carl Pracht**

370. Altbach, Philip G., and Eng Thye Jason Tan. **Programs and Centers in Comparative and International Education: A Global Inventory.** rev. ed. Buffalo, N.Y., State University of New York, Graduate School of Education Publications, 1995. 145p. (Special Studies in Comparative Education, no.34). $15.00pa. ISBN 0-937033-57-X.

This book lists university-based programs and centers in comparative and international education worldwide. The information on the 79 programs, centers, and institutes outlined was gathered through questionnaires sent to members of various professional organizations. This revised edition includes a significant number of additional listings over the preliminary edition, although the authors state that this inventory is not complete. A brief introduction discusses the method used in compiling the data for the book. Following the introduction is an essay on current trends and issues in comparative education. Programs and centers are listed geographically. Each listing has such information as the full name and location of the institution; the names, ranks, and specializations of academic staff; key courses and textbooks; and a full address, telephone number, and e-mail address for each program or center. A name index is included for academic staff. Appendixes containing the titles of textbooks and other publications conclude the book. Information is provided on university-based programs and centers in comparative education, as well as brief information on faculty members. Libraries wanting to offer accessible information on this topic will find the book helpful.—**Carl Pracht**

371. Hawks, John. **Youth Exchanges: The Complete Guide to the Homestay Experience Abroad.** New York, Facts on File, 1994. 234p. index. $22.95. ISBN 0-8160-2922-9.

Homestay is the name given to exchange programs in which students live with a host family in another country, often attending school, and learning about another culture in great detail. This guide, written by a former exchange student who now edits travel publications, describes such programs. The first part of the work discusses youth exchange in general terms and answers questions about choosing a program, preparing for it, learning about destinations, typical experiences of exchange students, concerns of parents, and hosting in the United States. The second half is a directory of 50 exchange programs. Each entry includes the destinations, the number of students who participate in the program each year, descriptions of the different options offered, the length of the stay, ages served, approximate fees, and the selection process. Most of the programs are aimed at teenagers, but some allow young adults to participate. Many of the programs also furnish options for international students to visit the United States.

Seven appendixes provide such additional information as exchange programs arranged by country, addresses and telephone numbers of passport agencies, foreign embassies in the United States, and organizations involved in youth exchange. A bibliography of additional sources and an index complete the book. This work would be useful to students, parents, and guidance counselors. Because most of the exchange programs are aimed at high school students, it would be an appropriate purchase for public and high school libraries, but not so necessary for most academic libraries.—**Christine E. King**

372. **The ISS Directory of Overseas Schools: The Comprehensive Guide to K-12 American and International Schools Worldwide.** 1994-95 ed. Princeton, N.J., International Schools Services; distr., Peterson's Guides, 1994. 531p. maps. index. $34.95pa. ISBN 0-913663-11-5.

International Schools Services is a not-for-profit educational organization providing a wide variety of support services to American and international schools. The *Directory of Overseas Schools* is just one of their many services and publications. Focusing on grades K-12, the directory is arranged alphabetically, first by country, then by city or town, and finally by school name. For ease of use, the volume is indexed by school, city, and country names. The very thorough entries include such information as mailing and street addresses and other contacts (this year including e-mail addresses when available), names of chief school officers and heads of libraries and computer centers, number of teaching staff, ratio of faculty to students, student and staff nationalities, information on enrollment, boarding, tuition and fees, accreditation, and languages of instruction. Bringing the 1994-95 edition up-to-date is the inclusion of entries from schools in the former Soviet Bloc regions, Eastern Europe, and Vietnam; the work is recommended for libraries that have not updated this volume in recent years.—**Diana Accurso**

373. **Japan: Exploring Your Options. A Guide to Work, Study & Research in Japan.** Washington, D.C., Gateway Japan, 1995. 437p. index. $20.00pa. ISBN 0-89068-131-7.

Produced by Gateway Japan, a nonprofit project of the National Planning Association, and based on responses to questionnaires sent to the profiled programs, *Japan: Exploring Your Options* provides comprehensive and detailed information for anyone considering a substantive, extended stay in that country. The major portion of the guide is the profiles of 117 programs, arranged under four broad categories: "Cultural Programs & Homestays," "Directed Study & Degree Programs," "Fellowships, Scholarships & Research Opportunities," and "English Teaching." The categories describe introductory information about each type of activity. For each entry, as appropriate, there are addresses and telephone numbers; contact people and other personnel; statements about the program's purpose, main activities, and future plans; costs and financial assistance; logistics (e.g., travel and living arrangements); application information and applicant requirements; and credentials. Supplementary materials include a bibliography of more than 30 related guides (most published after 1990); a name and address list of several dozen other relevant organizations, arranged by the same categories; and an alphabetical index of profiled programs. Although some information (such as financial data) will undoubtedly become dated quickly, there is much continuing value in this resource. It will prove an invaluable, focused supplement to the more general standards such as *Study Abroad* (see ARBA 90, entry 348) and *Work, Study, Travel Abroad: The Whole World Handbook* (12th ed., St. Martin's Press, 1994). Furthermore, the reasonable price makes it an affordable purchase for many public and academic libraries.—**Kenneth W. Berger**

LEARNING DISABILITIES

374. **The Complete Learning Disabilities Directory, 1995/96.** Leslie Mackenzie and Amy Lignor, eds. Lakeville, Conn., Grey House Publishing, 1995. 649p. index. $125.00pa. ISBN 0-939300-67-2.

The Complete Learning Disabilities Directory is an interesting compendium that has the potential to end the frustration involved in locating accurate information and referrals for individuals in need of learning disability services. While this 3d edition appears to be under the sponsorship of the National Center for Learning Disabilities, it in fact only contains a general introduction from the current chair, Anne Ford. The National Center has extensive disclaimers on the verso of the title page to any information contained in the work.

The publisher has included an extensive copyright notice on the verso of the title page, including the following statement that strikes this reviewer as sort of odd: "Grey House has added value to the underlying factual material through one or more of the following efforts: unique and original selection, expression, arrangement, coordination and classification." Similarly odd is the accompanying statement that any "Errors brought to the attention of the publisher and verified to the satisfaction of the publisher will be corrected in future editions." These types of statements coupled with the $125 price would ordinarily raise a warning flag in this reviewer's mind. The layout of the book and the typesetting is best described as routine. While the publisher/editor Mackenzie claims to have added value by arrangement and expression of the material, the book is in fact a computer typeset group of lists without any artistic embellishment. The book is a folio-sized paperback.

The directory covers universities, learning centers, organizations, government agencies, vocational training programs, and special schools that have programs aiding the learning disabled. Also treated are newsletters, workshops, assistive devices, and other teaching materials of interest to the learning disabled person. The editors have provided name, subject, and publisher indexes to the entries in the volume. The work appears to be compiled from responses to a questionnaire, a copy of which is appended at the back of the book. According to the publisher's blurb, the earlier editions were well reviewed as the most comprehensive of their kind.

While the volume is no doubt useful to those needing information on the subject, the presentation of the material is rather mundane. The entries are sometimes repetitive and routine. For example, many colleges have the canned notation: "Offers a variety of services to students with disabilities including notetakers, extended testing time, counseling services and special accommodations." Casual readers may think that this entry was specially constructed for the college they were considering, when in fact it is not. Most libraries with special populations will have need of this directory. A more attractive format would add much to this work.—**Ralph Lee Scott**

NONPRINT MATERIALS AND RESOURCES

375. **Educators Guide to Free Films, Filmstrips, and Slides 1995.** 55th ed. John C. Diffor and Elaine N. Diffor, eds. Randolph, Wis., Educators Progress Service, 1995. 351p. index. $32.95pa. ISBN 0-87708-276-6.

376. **Educators Guide to Free Videotapes 1995.** 42d ed. James L. Berger, ed. Randolph, Wis., Educators Progress Service, 1995. 545p. index. $27.95pa. ISBN 0-87708-277-4.

In this rapidly changing world, schools or libraries cannot provide their own resources for keeping abreast of all types of material from all sources. To solve this problem, educators and distributors of films and videos compiled indispensable tools for librarians or directors of audio/visual materials in these guides.

The 42d edition of *Educators Guide to Free Videotapes* and the 55th edition of *Educators Guide to Free Films, Filmstrips, and Slides* list carefully selected current and authoritative films and videotapes. The *Videotapes* volume lists 514 new titles and provides 2,621 titles in total. Most additions among 514 new titles are made in engineering (103) and science (205), which support educational policy to enhance science education for grade-school students. This edition of the *Films, Filmstrips, and Slides* volume combines, for the first time, all films, filmstrips, slides, audiotapes, and audiodiscs in one physical volume. It lists 1,290 films, 93 filmstrips, 198 sets of slides, 13 audiotapes, 119 audiodiscs, and 10 compact discs, including 118 new titles since the previous edition.

These guides provide an informative summary, the date of release, the size, sound versus silent, the format, the running time, and distributor information with branch offices. The user-friendly guides have fingertip references identified by five different colors, which are extremely helpful for finding a desired title using the title index (blue paper) or the subject index (yellow paper). The guides also provide a sample letter suggesting how to request items effectively from the distributors.

Providing a format index (e.g., Beta, U-matic, VHS) for a listing of each videotape found in the text is also an excellent feature of this edition of the guide to videotapes. If the guide to films provided a format index such as the videotapes guide, it would be much more useful and convenient. However, these guides are a must to update annually for any school, library, or business.—**Sung Ok Kim**

377. Mood, Terry Ann. **Distance Education: An Annotated Bibliography.** Englewood, Colo., Libraries Unlimited, 1995. 191p. index. $27.50pa. ISBN 1-56308-160-1.

Distance education means that instruction and learning take place in different locations. Mood provides more than an annotated bibliography to this increasingly common form of education. She not only summarizes the literature of distance education, but also introduces readers to the philosophical and pedagogical issues associated with this field.

Mood has produced a well-organized, well-written, and informative book that offers ample information in an easily accessible format for readers. She clusters the 297 sources into 7 chapters that follow a logical sequence of content, beginning with the history and philosophy of distance education, and then moving into core areas of application—administrative planning and management of a distance education program; the teacher's role, responsibilities, and problems; and the student's special position and need for resources in this context. Final chapters focus on nonacademic and international applications of distance education (e.g., in industry, for the physically disabled, and in cross-cultural contexts).

Mood introduces each chapter with an overview of its content, highlighting major themes in the literature. A clear, succinct, and thorough description of the content of each source accompanies the alphabetically arranged entries. The table of contents as well as the subject, author, and topical indexes provide additional ways of accessing material. The two appendixes give information about journals and online sources that concentrate on distance education. Anyone interested in distance education—from the casual reader to the professional involved in implementing programs of this sort—will benefit from this excellent overview of the field.—**Suzanne G. Frayser**

378. **The Visual Resources Directory: Art Slide and Photograph Collections in the United States and Canada.** Carla Conrad Freeman and Barbara Stevenson, eds. Englewood, Colo., Libraries Unlimited, 1995. 174p. index. $45.00pa. ISBN 1-56308-196-2.

For the purpose of this directory, a visual resource collection is defined as any organization or unit having as its primary function the collection of photographic images for such uses as research, teaching, or historical documentation. The directory lists 528 collections in the United States and Canada. Of these, 253 are in departments of art or art history, 104 in art museums or galleries, 98 in general libraries, 36 in architecture libraries or departments, 19 in historical archives, 8 in research centers, 7 in media or instructional resource centers, and 3 in humanities departments of academic institutions.

Entries in the directory are grouped by country, then by state or province. Each gives a name; an address; the name and title of the person in charge; the date of establishment; staffing; hours; services; size; annual circulation; information on programs supported by the collection, including subject concentrations, special collections, and classification systems; and the extent of automated cataloging, subject retrieval access, and electronic imaging projects. A history of visual resource collections in the United States is included in the preface, while that of Canadian collections appears in an appendix. Another appendix lists names and addresses of professional organizations in the field and gives information on visual resource journals.

The directory is thoroughly indexed by institutional name, by names of persons mentioned in the entries, by subject, and by type or category of collection or type of parent organization. This is the most comprehensive directory of its kind. It will be a useful tool for visual resource personnel and for administrators considering establishing a collection or wishing to compare theirs with similar centers, vendors, teachers, students, and art historians.—**Shirley L. Hopkinson**

READING

379. Lundin, Anne H., and Carol W. Cubberley. **Teaching Children's Literature: A Resource Guide, with a Directory of Courses.** Jefferson, N.C., McFarland, 1995. 355p. index. $42.50. ISBN 0-89950-990-8.

The McFarland bibliographical reference series has always been somewhat uneven in quality and usually requires judicious decision making on the part of an acquisitions librarian. Many times the cited materials are dated, the annotations are wooden, and the subject matter rather esoteric. Such is not the case, however, with this outstanding resource for teaching and researching children's literature.

The introduction provides an interesting and provocative overview of the evolution of children's literature from the "stepchild discipline" into an acceptable area of study for scholars and educators. Part 1 contains well-written, insightful annotations concerning children's literature reference works, journals, textbooks, and articles. Part 2 furnishes a potential teacher of children's literature with 8 representative syllabuses, including sample assignments and term projects. Part 3 provides a directory of children's literature courses offered at various 4-year colleges in each state. The directory concludes with appropriate author/title and subject indexes.

The authors, both professors of children's literature, clearly demonstrate expert knowledge of their subject. Their guide is comprehensive in scope, and different pedagogical teaching philosophies are well represented. Acquisitions librarians seeking to broaden their children's literature history and teaching sections will find many valuable sources cited. Scholars and teachers of children's literature will find it a first-stop source before embarking upon any further study. Purchase of this title is recommended where there are researchers, students, teachers, and aficionados of children's literature. It is a gem.

—**Kathleen W. Craver**

380. Pearlman, Mickey. **What to Read: The Essential Guide for Reading Group Members and Other Book Lovers.** New York, HarperPerennial/HarperCollins, 1994. 228p. index. $9.00pa. ISBN 0-06-095061-7.

Reading groups will enjoy using *What to Read*, a collection of 33 annotated book lists, as a resource when looking for themes or titles. Bibliophiles will delight in browsing through it, recalling favorite books already read and looking for new titles to explore. Lists are organized by topic, sometimes predictably (e.g., "Native American Literature," "Go West," "Mothers and Daughters"). Other lists are surprising: "Fairy Tales for Grown-ups," "New York Stories," and "la, la, la It's Magic." The author and title indexes add to the usefulness of the book.

Pleasing to see is the occasional worthy young adult novel interspersed with adult fiction. However, displeasing to see is the Newbery Award repeatedly spelled as Newberry. "In the Hammock," with diverse recommendations such as *Sisters and Lovers* by Connie Briscoe, *The Way to Cook* by Julia Child, and *Having Our Say* by Sarah and A. Elizabeth Delany, is a favorite list. More "Dream Lists" (reading lists supplied by writers themselves) would have been appreciated. All in all, *What to Read* provides book lovers with pleasurable reading itself.—**Suzanne I. Barchers**

VOCATIONAL AND CONTINUING EDUCATION

381. **Chronicle Vocational School Manual: For 1995-96 School Year.** rev. ed. Moravia, N.Y., Chronicle Guidance, 1995. 295p. $22.48pa. ISBN 1-55631-239-3.

Users of earlier editions (see ARBA 93, entry 406) of this well-established source will find the distinctive "chart" format used once again as the vehicle for presenting basic information on more than 3,600 institutions that offer occupational education at the postsecondary level in the United States, Guam, and Puerto Rico. These schools are all accredited by 1 or more of the 18 bodies listed in the introductory pages. Together they offer 921 programs of study. The tabular chart section, which occupies just over half the volume, is arranged by state and lists each school's name; address; telephone number; founding date; and abbreviated information on admission requirements, tuition and fees, enrollment, government aid and training programs, other financial aid, and the availability of counseling services and housing. An extensive and detailed index by program of study points the user to schools of interest.

Because the information offered here is basic and brief, this volume serves best as a starting point in searching for vocational training programs. Indeed, the introduction urges users to contact and, if possible, visit schools they are interested in for further information. The *Chronicle Vocational School Manual* will be useful in this capacity for students, guidance counselors, career counselors, and in school and public libraries. *Peterson's Vocational and Technical Schools* (see ARBA 95, entry 389) lists more schools and offers lengthier entries, but its two large volumes are a much more expensive purchase.

—**Gregory M. Toth**

382. **Encyclopedia of Careers and Vocational Guidance.** [CD-ROM]. Chicago, J. G. Ferguson, 1994. Minimum system requirements (Windows version): IBM or compatible 386. CD-ROM drive with MS-DOS CD-ROM Extensions 2.0. DOS 5.0. Windows 3.1. 4MB RAM. VGA monitor with 1MB video memory. Minimum system requirements (Macintosh version): System 7. CD-ROM drive. 4MB RAM. Color monitor. Mouse. $199.95. ISBN 0-89434-153-7.

The *Encyclopedia of Careers and Vocational Guidance* on CD-ROM provides a database of current information for more than 2,000 jobs in 544 occupational interests. Students can select careers using any one or a combination of search fields:

- *Job Titles*. This is an alphabetical index of jobs from accountants to zookeepers. Students have direct access to job titles by specific occupations. They can either scroll down one by one or jump to an individual career.

- *Industry Profile*. Seventy-three industries are listed from accounting to wood, with general information, outlook for employment, related industries, and related careers.

- *School Subjects.* From agriculture to sociology, the jobseeker can obtain information about which class subjects relate to which job titles.

- *Occupational Categories.* Included are 12 job categories from agriculture to structural work.

- *Interests.* From airplanes to writing, students can scan a list of 18 interests that lead to a list of related jobs.

- *Level of Education.* From "some high school" to "graduate school," students can access jobs according to the amount of education required.

- *Earnings.* By looking at five earning categories, users can see at a glance how jobs rate according to earnings.

The program also allows the student to perform customized searching in which specific terms are put into the database (e.g., earnings, education, interests), and then a list of occupations is given according to the student's preference.

The directions for the installation of the CD-ROM program are easy to follow. There is a technical support 800-number available for any problems that might arise during either the installation or execution of the program. This program will be useful for students who are looking for careers in their favorite school subjects or even for class assignments. Non-college-bound students can access jobs that require little or no training beyond high school; it is also helpful for people who are re-entering the job market. The CD-ROM will be a welcome addition to assist high school and college students with career choices.
—**Barbara B. Goldstein**

383. **Free and Inexpensive Career Materials: A Resource Directory.** Cheryl S. Hecht, ed. Garrett Park, Md., Garrett Park Press, 1995. 1v. (unpaged). $19.95pa. ISBN 1-880774-09-7.

This directory is a new source of career information available from associations, governmental agencies, and academic departments that provide their publications free, on a "for cost" basis, or for $5 or less. The directory lists more than 800 organizations that offer career material on 320-plus occupations. The principal sections of this work are an alphabetical index of occupations followed by entry numbers that lead the user to the appropriate organizations, and an alphabetical list of organizations and governmental agencies, each of which has a sequential entry number. The directory provides the full name of the organization, its address, telephone number, title of career item, and price, if any.

The directory duplicates the *Educators Guide to Free Guidance Materials* (30th ed.; see ARBA 93, entry 400), but only in small part because the latter source emphasizes media materials. *Free and Inexpensive Career Materials* is easy to use; the typeface is very readable. The one feature that needs closer attention in successive editions is the alphabetical index of occupations. For example, the index refers the user to two organizations under the heading "interior design," yet the directory also lists a third organization—the American Society of Interior Designers—in the organization listing. In spite of such quibbling, the directory serves such a highly useful purpose that it is a must-purchase for most public, school, and academic libraries, as well as all career counseling centers.—**Dene L. Clark**

384. **Gale's Career Guidance System.** expanded ed. [CD-ROM]. Detroit, Gale, 1995. Minimum system requirements: IBM or compatible 286 (faster recommended). MS-DOS or PC-DOS 3.3. 640K RAM. 6MB hard disk space (16 recommended for optimal speed). VGA monitor and color card. $4,995.00 (single user); $6,262.00 (network).

The present CD-ROM has just about everything that librarians would normally expect to find. Installation of this system is remarkably easy. All is menu-driven and just about all "techie" jargon is missing. For example, the installation menus are short and descriptive: "Install on drive?" Rather than asking one to figure it out, a descriptive screen explains that most such installations are made on drive C:/ and that selection is automatically made. The directory choice is also made, requiring a change if the default is rejected. Screens to allow printing, whether exporting will be an option wanted and on what drive, and so forth, come next. Finally, a lengthy screen asking purchasers to install *Dictionary of Occupational Titles* (DOT) and *Occupational Outlook Handbook* (OOH) files (with size implications) is offered. Once these screens have been completed, a final screen appears with all the choices made and with a chance to change any of them. Instructions for loading onto a network are also provided and are equally easy to follow.

Once installation is completed, the searching begins. Mouse operations are a must, although Gale instructions argue that keyboard operations are supported. This is largely true, but users trying to execute this program without a mouse will most likely be frustrated. The main menu to this system offers four options: "Career Opportunities," "Potential Employers," "Career Information," and "Government Career Guides." The first one allows users to perform an online self-analysis. Once completed, one must enter command searches for the best match. All of this is menu-driven and easy to use.

The "Career Information" menu offers the following options: job descriptions, current trends and advice, projected growth, wages, job qualifications, licensing and rules, helpful publications, helpful organizations, and potential employers. Each option supplies easy-to-read information can be either downloaded or printed. Here disappointment abounds, as much of the information viewed on several searches revealed data nearly 10 years old. One item referenced a 1991 library publication; another, a 1988 government publication. These would have been fine if other data or resources much more recent were not available.

The "Potential Employers" screen simply lists just about every employer in a given region. Granted, this information can be searched by zip or area code, state, industry, or company name, but the only information provided is the address. If one wished to blanket a state or area code with résumés in a given job area, this might be a good idea. However, if one wished to find viable, open jobs, the better option would be standard job listing sources. In the DOT source, users are able to search by job name, career category, DOT number, or any word or phrase. All of the sections have on-screen help that is actually helpful. The handbook accompanying the boxed set is also well written and easy to follow. Some of the screen captures are hard to read by virtue of being too dark, but most are legible. Appendixes and a full index round out this printed guide.

On the whole, this is a most useful CD-ROM, and one that would get constant use. Having the frequently used DOT and OOH publications online would certainly be valuable, but the drawback with the source is the same for nearly all of Gale's tools: the cost. How many small- and medium-sized libraries have $5,000 for one source? Publishers of reference material must be repaid for their considerable costs, but trying to garner that much money seems untoward.—**Mark Y. Herring**

385. Wright, Philip C., Josée G. Guidry, and Judy Blair. **Opportunities for Vocational Study: A Directory of Learning Programs Sponsored by North American Non-Profit Associations.** Toronto and Cheektowaga, N.Y., University of Toronto Press, 1994. 412p. index. $35.00pa. ISBN 0-8020-7776-5.

This work is noteworthy for its focus on the training, educational, and certification programs offered by more than 270 nonprofit trade, professional, and industry associations in Canada and the United States. Some technical associations are also included, but most medical and health-related programs are not. The entries constituting the body of the work are arranged by organization or association name and contain contact information and a general description of each organization, the educational programs it offers, how these are delivered and evaluated, qualifications required of participants, and any recertification requirements. An index provides access to the entries by profession, craft, or trade.

The authors have identified a class of alternative education opportunities not directly or fully covered by the various guides currently available on internships, apprenticeships, occupational training programs, nontraditional colleges, and the like. Thus, their work will be of considerable value to high school graduates not pursuing traditional postsecondary education; workers seeking specialized training or skills even if they have attended college; persons changing careers or returning to the job market; vocational and career counselors; and personnel and human resources managers.—**Gregory M. Toth**

6 Ethnic Studies and Anthropology

ANTHROPOLOGY AND ETHNOLOGY

386. Schobinger, Juan. **The First Americans.** Grand Rapids, Mich., William B. Eerdmans, 1994. 193p. illus. maps. $39.99. ISBN 0-8028-3766-2.

This book, translated from the Spanish, gives basic information to general readers about the prehistory of humans in the Americas. The information presented is similar to other books of the same title (for example, by Geoffrey Bushnell Hext [McGraw-Hill, 1968]). Part 1 gives a good geographical and climatic discussion of the areas where the first human remains in the New World have been found. Hunters and gatherers are then introduced via their tools, artwork, and campsites. The Neolithic and the first evidence for agriculture at widespread points in the Americas follow in part 2. From part 3 to part 4, the book focuses on specific cultures: Teotihuacán, Olmec, Maya, Chavín, Nazca, Moche, Tiahuanaco, and Inca. Segments of each culture, such as art, religion, and politics, are presented in basic terms. The briefest of sketches is devoted to the Inca culture.

There are several faults that make this work less than perfect. For example, there is no glossary. When presenting general readers with abbreviations such as *B.C.E.* or words that are (presumably) unfamiliar, such as *petroglyph*, a glossary is essential. The book contains a section entitled "History of Scientific Research." It gives a sketchy description of scientific research, but provides the reader little information or explanation about techniques used in archaeology to discover, salvage, or interpret data. There is no explanation of carbon dating, for example.

Picture captions are unclear in many cases, and the maps of the glaciations are difficult to read and interpret. The book has no summary to pull the information presented into a meaningful whole. It simply stops after a brief introduction to the Incas. The work has a large number of beautiful illustrations and many full-page color photographs, but there is no bibliography. This book may be a reasonable addition to the circulating collection of a public library, but the information provided is not particularly useful for reference purposes.—**Joanna M. Burkhardt**

ETHNIC STUDIES
General Works

387. **Gale Encyclopedia of Multicultural America.** Judy Galens, Anna Sheets, and Robyn V. Young, eds. Detroit, Gale, 1995. 2v. illus. index. $125.00/set. ISBN 0-8103-9163-5.

Public libraries will find this resource useful in meeting the student demand for multicultural information. According to the 1990 census, there are 215 ethnic groups in the United States. In Gale's 2-volume set, the editors have collected more than 100 essays on the groups most commonly researched in high schools and colleges, along with those ranking high in population. At the same time, essays reflect a broad scope and recent immigration patterns. Selections include both foreign and native cultures, as well as ethnoreligious cultures such as the Amish.

Entries are alphabetical, ranging in length from 5,000 to 20,000 words. The entries provide information about the country of origin, immigration circumstances, culture and religion, language, cuisine, economic and political dynamics, special issues, and significant contributions. In addition, they list relevant periodicals, radio and television stations, museums, organizations and associations, and other bibliographical resources. This is great for students, but also for immigrants who are seeking contact with their ethnic communities in the United States.

The work contains an introduction describing the history of multiculturalism in the United States, a subject index, and an extensive bibliography that does not duplicate resources listed in the entries. More than 150 black-and-white photographs complement the well-organized text. This is another reliable product from Gale.—**Jean Engler**

388. Kennett, Frances, with Caroline MacDonald-Haig. **Ethnic Dress.** New York, Facts on File, 1995. 192p. illus. maps. index. $40.00. ISBN 0-8160-3136-3.

Ethnic dress is an expression of a people's traditions, customs, and history. This guide, intended for a wide audience including both professionals and amateurs, covers contemporary costume from around the globe. It is profusely illustrated, with about 500 color photographs and regional maps.

Arrangement is by 10 geographical areas, which are then further subdivided. Factors influencing the development of costume and its etiquette are discussed, such as social history, environment, and religious beliefs. The main section is followed by a glossary of clothing terms and by an index that enables access by country, specific group, or type of costume.

The volume is billed as being comprehensive, which may be true about its scope. Coverage, however, is uneven. While Native American crafts are well displayed, other ethnic groups are underrepresented. The three Baltic countries, for example, are dismissed with three sentences and two illustrations. Perhaps future editions could expand their coverage to include such groups and countries.—**Anita Zutis**

389. Levinson, David. **Ethnic Relations: A Cross-Cultural Encyclopedia.** Santa Barbara, Calif., ABC-CLIO, 1994. 293p. illus. index. (Encyclopedias of the Human Experience). $49.50. ISBN 0-87436-735-2.

This volume is part of the Encyclopedias of the Human Experience series and covers a very broad topic from an international standpoint. It does fill a need for a comprehensive work on the topic, although other regionally specific works are available that provide much more depth and, in particular, ethnic relations in the United States—for example, the *Harvard Encyclopedia of American Ethnic Groups* (see ARBA 82, entry 438). Likewise, many of the general concepts are also covered in much greater depth in other works. If there is a fault with the work, it is that it attempts to cover a very large topic in a single volume containing only 89 entries.

The entries average 2 to 3 pages in length with citations for 3 to 10 supplemental readings attached. These entries are divided into 2 types: general concepts and profiles of 38 specific conflicts. The collection of specific conflicts is an excellent resource that provides an international perspective along with giving specific examples to supplement the concepts discussed in the more theoretical sections. The volume is indexed and includes a description of 17 international organizations whose missions are related to ethnic relations, and a 16-page bibliography. Both of the latter sections are brief and of marginal value. The strength of the work lies in its global perspective and coverage and the summaries of specific conflicts selected. Recommended for both public and academic libraries, it should particularly be acquired as part of the entire series. As a single volume, its academic value would be primarily for the undergraduate student or public patron.—**Anthony J. Dedrick**

Africans

390. Haskins, Jim, and Joann Biondi. **From Afar to Zulu: A Dictionary of African Cultures.** New York, Walker, 1995. 212p. illus. maps. index. $18.95. ISBN 0-8027-8290-6.

Haskins, author/compiler of a great many juvenile books, and journalist Biondi have used Haskins's regular formula: Identify a topic for which there is both a market and a body of easily accessible information (especially from scholarly reference books) and then repackage it in a more pleasing and easy-to-use format. Thirty-two of the better-known and more populous African ethnic groups are included, excluding North Africa and white African groups, and those from the islands off the east coast of the continent. Each chapter begins with a map, a population figure, a list of modern countries in which the group lives, the language spoken, and foods eaten. The text gives a thumbnail history and account of customs, beliefs, and lifeways. Most chapters have black-and-white photographs (avoiding any that might have an unacceptable degree of nakedness) and many present illustrations of the group's art for photocopying. Also included is a brief chapter on historic cultures, a list of African ethnic groups and their locations, a glossary, a selected bibliography, and an index.

This work is a nicely produced and accurate reference book with only a few problems: the consistent confusion of culture and society, the inconsistent use of Ivory Coast and Côte d'Ivoire, a poor understanding of the complexities of African religions, confusion of the terms matriarchy/patriarchy with the appropriate terms matrilineality/patrilineality, and the omission of variants of an ethnic group's name from index (e.g., Mandingo for Malinke).—**Fred J. Hay**

Armenian Americans

391. **Armenian American Almanac: An Encyclopedic Guide....** 3d ed. Hamo B. Vassilian, ed. Glendale, Calif., Armenian Reference Books, 1995. 496p. illus. $45.00pa. ISBN 0-931539-09-9.

As the subtitle of this reference work implies, it is a comprehensive encyclopedic guide to all kinds of information sources related to Armenians in the United States and Canada. The work is arranged in seven parts that are further subdivided. Part 1, for example, has nine sections: organizations, churches, newspapers and periodicals, schools, Armenian studies programs, libraries and special/private collections, bookstores, video and book publishers, and nonprint media; it has an organizational index, as well. Information in part 1 is similar to that in the *Encyclopedia of Associations* (see ARBA 94, entries 49-51) and includes the name and address of the organization, sponsoring (or owning) organization, person in charge, library holdings, bibliographic aids, availability (open to the public), description of the collection, and contact person.

Part 2 is devoted to financial aid to Armenians in terms of scholarships, loans, grants, and fellowships. Part 3 is a directory to Armenian professionals in two lists. The first is alphabetical by profession (e.g., accountants, attorneys, dentists); the second is a straight alphabetical listing. Part 4 lists marketplaces that sell Armenian food; part 5 is a list of 1,100 popular Armenian names. (It would be useful for non-Armenians if the gender associated with the names were identified.) Part 6 is a very important part of the guide: a 587-entry bibliography of English-language materials about Armenian Americans. Part 7 is a telephone directory containing names and addresses of over 63,000 Armenian Americans.

The number of pages increased by almost 25 percent from the 2d to the 3d edition; however, a larger font has been used. This makes the work very readable, but it is hard to determine whether actual content is larger or smaller, as the entries are no longer numbered. A count of entries for organizations reveals that there are actually fewer listed in this edition, which may be explained by the aging or assimilation of the ethnic group. This is an outstanding resource on Armenian Americans for ethnic studies scholars and a must for scholarly academic libraries and those public libraries in areas heavily populated by Armenians.—**Lois J. Buttlar**

Asian Americans

392. **The Asian American Almanac: A Reference Work on Asians in the United States.** Susan Gall and Irene Natividad, eds. Detroit, Gale, 1995. 834p. illus. index. $95.00. ISBN 0-8103-9193-7.

The premier edition of *The Asian American Almanac* is quite simply the single most important volume ever published on the subject. Two facts increase its significance: It is the most substantial reference work in this area in many years, and it concerns the fastest-growing ethnic group in the United States. It is also quite comprehensive and authoritative.

Natividad, the most prominent Filipino-American and Asian-American woman on the national political scene, is the managing editor. She is especially active in the areas of women's rights and political empowerment. As Natividad states in the preface, "Our goal was to describe the Asian American experience in general, while preserving the distinct aspects of each group's journey from their native land to the U.S." (p. xv). They have succeeded admirably. The contributors are outstanding and come from all walks of Asian-American life: journalism, law, business, community activism, writing, librarianship, military service, and academia.

Chapter 1 describes the Asian Pacific Americans in general and includes a helpful map of Asia. The next 14 chapters give information on specific Asian-American groups, from Cambodian Americans to Vietnamese Americans. In each chapter is information on country of origin; immigration patterns; culture; assimilation and acculturation; political, economic, and health issues; community organizations and associations; and a listing of notable personages. Many of these chapters have bibliographies. The use of illustrations and statistics enriches the text throughout. Much of the data is based on the 1990 U.S. census, although some of it is more recent.

Chapters 16-41 are a valuable source of information on all important aspects of Asian-American life: chronology; laws and key documents; immigration; civil rights; military service; family and women; languages; education; labor; organizations; sports, including martial arts; biographies (with photographs) of prominent Asian and Pacific Islanders (including one of Judge Lance Ito of O. J. Simpson trial fame); historic landmarks of Asian America; speeches; a bibliography; and a detailed and useful index. This volume joins other Gale publications on this subject, such as *Notable Asian Americans* (see entry 396), *Who's Who Among Asian Americans* (see ARBA 95, entry 402), *Asian American Information Directory* (see ARBA 93, entry 421), and *Statistical Record of Asian Americans* (see ARBA 94, entry 401). Together, they form a distinguished body of literature on this ethnic group.—**Marshall E. Nunn**

393. **Asian American Biography.** Helen Zia and Susan B. Gall, eds. Detroit, U*X*L/Gale, 1995. 2v. illus. index. $55.00/set. ISBN 0-8103-9687-4.

More than 130 profiles of living and deceased individuals are included in this 2-volume set for people ages 10 and above. Although it is unclear how these prominent men and women of Asian and Pacific Island descent were selected, many names are well known. Included are television (e.g., Margaret Cho) and sports (e.g., Greg Louganis) figures, along with those from academia (e.g., Ron Takaki); the arts (e.g., Maya Lin); business (e.g., Phyllis Jean Takisaki Campbell); government (e.g., Norman Mineta); medicine (e.g., Lillian Gonzalez-Pardo); the military (e.g., William Shao Chang Chen); music (e.g., Zubin Mehta); science (e.g., Yuan T. Lee); and technology (e.g., An Wang). Some omissions were noted. Profiles span two to three pages and most include a black-and-white photograph of the subject. Each sketch concludes with a brief unannotated bibliography of sources, and the entire work is rounded out by a field of endeavor index.

This set is complementary to U*X*L's three other publications—*Asian American Almanac* (see entry 392, *Asian American Chronology* (1995), and *Asian American Voices* (1995). This biographical set will be welcomed by academic education and curriculum collections, by literacy centers helping new immigrants to learn English, and by both school and public libraries serving young readers. It is an inspiring tool, especially for young Asian Americans looking for role models.—**Ilene F. Rockman**

394. **The Asian American Encyclopedia.** Franklin Ng, ed. New York, Marshall Cavendish, 1995. 6v. illus. maps. index. $449.95/set. ISBN 1-85435-677-1.

This timely and helpful encyclopedia of Asian-American culture is an important addition to any reference library. The material has never been so comprehensively assembled. The 6 volumes serve as a history of this growing American culture as well as a reference to the 2,000 entries of biographical sketches, historical articles, immigration, community studies, and demographics on the 6 largest Asian-American groups. These six largest groups—Chinese Americans, Filipino Americans, Japanese Americans, Asian Indian Americans, Korean Americans, and Vietnamese Americans—are covered in great detail. The charts, tables, graphs, maps, and chronologies as well as exhaustive indexes complement the text. Lists of organizations, museums, research centers, libraries, university programs, newspapers, newsletters, magazines, and journals are helpful. Asian Americans are multicultural, and great care has been taken to be comprehensive on the various ethnic populations. These volumes are invaluable to the understanding of the history and cultural contributions of Asian Americans.—**Linda L. Lam-Easton**

395. Bionat, Marvin P., ed. **Who's Who in the Asian-American Community 1994-95.** Boston, PacRim Publishing, 1994. 171p. index. $19.00pa. ISBN 0-9642151-0-1.

This book is the 1st edition of what is intended to be a serial publication. It has the standard arrangement of biographical directories. A somewhat unusual feature of the criteria for inclusion allows self-nomination. This practice may raise a few eyebrows. The brief introduction traces the outlines of Asian-American history and immigration with its sociological implications in a rather cursory manner. The main section of the biographees' listings is 131 pages long. This seems rather short for such a fast-growing and dynamic segment of the U.S. population. A random check of entries for well-known Asian Americans such as I. M. Pei, Daniel Inouye, and George Takei finds them present and accounted for. But where are the entries for March Kong Fong Eu and Harry H. L. Kitano?

Next comes "Asian-American Organizations" (including social service groups that cater primarily to Asians), arranged alphabetically by state. Why does Hawaii have only one listing? A three-page unannotated bibliography follows. The last part of the book is an occupational index. Is there a need for this directory? Not really. Two Gale serials are far superior, albeit much more expensive. They are *Who's Who Among Asian Americans* (see ARBA 95, entry 402) and *Notable Asian Americans* (see entry 396).

—Marshall E. Nunn

396. **Notable Asian Americans.** Helen Zia and Susan B. Gall, eds. Detroit, Gale, 1995. 468p. illus. index. $65.00. ISBN 0-8103-9623-8.

Notable Asian Americans profiles 250 Asian Americans whose significant contributions in more than 130 fields have had an impact on U.S. and world culture. The biographical entries are written in an informal style by contributors who have often gathered their material firsthand in personal interviews with their subjects. The essays are relaxed, inspirational, and conversational; they are divided into sections by subtitles, and are edited to provide a succinct introduction to each life in terms of youthful influences, education, formative experiences, and major accomplishments.

Although *Notable Asian Americans* is suitable for readers and researchers of all ages, one intention of this volume's editors is to inspire young Asian American people. The editors note the absence, up until recently, of resources available to teach the Asian-American community about the extent of its own creativity, contributions, and multiethnic vitality. This volume goes a long way toward filling the gap. As George Takei of *Star Trek* fame points out in the foreword, looking at these different lives can be a means to understanding U.S. pluralism.

The scope and range of the book are eye-opening: from Asian Indian to those of Vietnamese descent, 15 ethnic groups are represented. Weight lifters, physicists, photographers, law enforcement officers, engineers, conductors, illustrators, poets, farmers, members of Congress, costume designers, comedians, architects, activists, and astronauts are presented in sketches that highlight personal drive and integrity. The occupation and ethnicity indexes complement the comprehensive subject index. A few notables have been overlooked, but omissions are hard to avoid in an undertaking of this size. Also, the sketches should have provided bibliographies of the noted person's works, where applicable. The oversights will no doubt be addressed in the next volume of *Notable Asian Americans*, for which lists are already being compiled.

—JoAnn Balingit

Blacks

397. **African American Breakthroughs: 500 Years of Black Firsts.** Jay P. Pederson and Jessie Carney Smith, eds. Detroit, U*X*L/Gale, 1995. 280p. illus. index. $29.00. ISBN 0-8103-9496-0.

Hundreds of milestones involving African Americans are described in this new entry from U*X*L. The book, appropriate for ages 10 and up, is arranged by subject categories, including business and labor, civil rights and protest, education, fine and applied arts, literature, media, the military, performing arts, politics, religion, science, and sports. Readers and browsers will find the typical well-known historical facts of black history as well as little-known information about people such as Mary Fields, or "Stagecoach Mary," the first black woman and only the second woman ever to serve as a U.S. mail coach driver; Joseph L. Searles III, the first black member of the New York Stock Exchange; Lucy Stanton, the first black woman to graduate from college; and Bessie Coleman, the first black woman to earn a pilot's license.

First events cover the first law passed that protected slaves fleeing brutal treatment by their masters; the first recorded antislavery petition presented to Congress (it was rejected); the production of the first American-made film with an all-black cast; and the organization of the first black labor union on record.

Introduced by a "Calendar of Firsts" and an illustrated "Timeline of Important African American Events," the attractive format of the book makes for easy reading, with boldfaced headings before each category and at the top of each page. Numerous photographs of people and events provide added interest. Appendixes list a bibliography of sources and a comprehensive index.

Related references are *Black Firsts* (see ARBA 95, entry 412), which follows a similar format but provides more extensive coverage (2,000 years of black history as opposed to 500 years), and *Milestones in Twentieth Century African-American History* (Visible Ink Press, 1993), arranged chronologically into 9 significant historical eras of this century, each introduced by an essay ranging in length from 1 to 13 pages.
—**Dana McDougald**

398. **Bibliographic Guide to Black Studies 1994.** New York, G. K. Hall/Simon & Schuster, 1995. 395p. $180.00. ISBN 0-7838-2164-6. ISSN 0360-2710.

This subject bibliography lists African-American items cataloged during 1994 by the New York Public Library's Schomburg Center for Research in Black Culture. Since 1926, when the NYPL acquired black bibliophile Arthur A. Schomburg's magnificent library of African Americana, this collection has been one of the leading international repositories for the study of the African Diaspora.

The Schomburg Center's holdings include manuscripts and books by authors of African descent regardless of subject or language. The collection prides itself on its breadth and has rich holdings in such diverse areas as art, biography, folklore, geography, history, literature, languages, music, religion, and sports. *Bibliographic Guide to Black Studies* serves as an annual supplement to the *Dictionary Catalog of the Schomburg Collection of Negro Literature and History* (1962; *First Supplement*, 1967; *Second Supplement*, 1972).

As with other annual subject bibliographies published by G. K. Hall, the compilation includes complete Library of Congress cataloging information for each title, along with an ISBN and identification of holdings at the NYPL. Access is provided by entry, added entries, titles, series titles, and subject headings. All are integrated in alphabetical sequence. Full bibliographical information appears in the main entry. Shortened citations appear for secondary entries.

Well produced and carefully edited, the *Bibliographic Guide* nonetheless fails to provide a means to identify nonbook materials. Also, because the Schomburg's catalogers were inconsistent in their assignment of subject headings, some works receive more thorough coverage than others. Despite these quibbles, *Bibliographic Guide to Black Studies* is an excellent and valuable bibliographical tool. Up-to-date access to the Schomburg's holdings offers scholars one of the best windows to the wealth and breadth of the African-American experience.—**John David Smith**

399. **Black Studies on Disc.** [CD-ROM]. New York, G. K. Hall/Simon & Schuster, 1995. Minimum system requirements: IBM or compatible. CD-ROM drive with MS-DOS CD-ROM Extensions 2.0. 512K RAM. $995.00. ISBN 0-8161-1653-9.

Black Studies on Disc combines the cumulative catalog of the New York Public Library's Schomburg Center for Research in Black Culture with the years 1989-1993 of the annual *Index to Black Periodicals* (see ARBA 94, entry 403, and ARBA 91, entry 390). G. K. Hall plans to update this product annually and standing order customers will receive the updates for $495. The site license permits an unlimited number of simultaneous users within one building at no additional charge.

The Schomburg Center is an important repository for African documentation and is the most significant discrete collection of materials relating to the African Diaspora in the Western Hemisphere, and especially North America. The Schomburg's catalog (more than 108,000 citations), combined with five years of the *Index to Black Periodicals* (for a total of approximately 130,000 citations), makes this product an unsurpassed bibliographical source for African-American studies. This disc replaces three print/microform products from the same publisher: *Index to Black Periodicals*, *Dictionary Catalog of the Schomburg Collection of Negro Literature and History* (1962-1976), and the Schomburg's annual acquisitions list, *Bibliographic Guide to Black Studies* (see entry 398).

G. K. Hall's CD Searcher software has been improved. Although not the most powerful or easy-to-use CD-ROM search software, G. K. Hall has demonstrated their commitment to continue improving their product. The software permits customization of the interface and simultaneous use of different customized interfaces.

The disc can be searched by material type, standard bibliographical field (including standard, LC, and OCLC numbers), or free-text. Material types include archives and manuscripts (the majority of which are microform sets and theses); audio; books; film and video; articles; photographs; scores serial titles; and 705 citations in an "undetermined" category (an assortment of formats, including videos, rare books, microforms, and artifacts). Indexes can be browsed or term searched with Boolean operators. The search interface permits use of internal and end-of-word truncation, search set combination, and nesting with parentheses. Search sets can be easily sorted, saved, printed, or downloaded. This disc provides good context-specific help screens but lacks cross-references or a command that will search for similar subjects.

This product is the most comprehensive database of its kind, but could be made better by the addition of the back files of the *Index to Black Periodicals* and by the inclusion of indexing for historically important serials such as *Phylon, Journal of Negro History*, and others. Another nice addition would be the Schomburg's *Kaiser Index to Black Periodicals, 1948-1986* (see ARBA 93, entry 425). The most significant problem with this disc is the need for comprehensive name authority work. For instance, there are three citations under three different versions of Harriet Ottenheimer's name. They follow one another in the author index if one uses the "browse" command. There are 13 versions of W. E. B. Du Bois, and they are not all found together browsing the author index. Correcting this problem will make this excellent resource a much friendlier one.—**Fred J. Hay**

400. **Contemporary Black Biography: Profiles from the International Black Community. Volume 8.** L. Mpho Mabunda, ed. Detroit, Gale, 1995. 314p. illus. index. $45.00. ISBN 0-8103-5739-9.

Volume 8 of what is now a standard Gale reference product shares the same format and presentation strategy of the preceding volumes of this title, as well as with most of Gale's other biographical/critical collections. The 73 new entries average 3 pages in length, and are usually accompanied by 1 or more black-and-white photographs of the subject (why there are no pictures for Corinne Mitchell or Kristin Clark Taylor is not explained). Biographies contain a bibliography and a highlighted "At a Glance" box that briefly reports the subject's life, dates, education, major accomplishments, awards, and address. All entries, except the long-overdue biography of the controversial Leonard Jeffries, are signed. Four cumulative indexes are included: one for nationality, occupation, subject, and name.

The quality of research and writing is up to Gale's usual high standard, although Gale continues to have trouble reporting on African-American music. For instance, bluesman Son House richly deserves inclusion in Volume 8, but certainly not before the more accomplished and influential musicians/composers of his era such as Charlie Patton, Blind Lemon Jefferson, or Tampa Red are covered. The sketch of House fails to cite several of the more important works about him or the standard biographical reference work for the blues, Sheldon Harris's *Blues Who's Who* (Arlington House, 1979). Also lacking is mention of the various compilations of House's classic Paramount recordings now available. There are similar problems with the W. C. Handy biography, including the listing of sheet music rather than discs in the selected discography.—**Fred J. Hay**

401. **Contemporary Black Biography: Profiles from the International Black Community. Volume 9.** L. Mpho Mabunda, ed. Detroit, Gale, 1995. 319p. illus. index. $45.00. ISBN 0-8103-5740-2. ISSN 1058-1316.

The 9th volume of Mabunda's *Contemporary Black Biography* is an eclectic reference work chronicling the lives of 71 internationally acclaimed blacks. These men and women of African heritage, according to the editor, "have changed today's world and are shaping tomorrow's" (p. ix).

The alphabetically arranged biographies include men and women of distinction, as well as lesser-known individuals "likely to be ignored by other biographical reference series" (p. xi). Some are from the fields of architecture, art, business, dance, education, fashion, film, industry, journalism, and law. Others work in the worlds of literature, medicine, music, politics and government, publishing, religion, science and technology, social issues, sports, television, and theater.

In a curious editorial decision, Mabunda chose to profile not only contemporary blacks, but also "selected individuals from earlier in this century whose influence continues to impact on contemporary life" (p. ix). Thus, in a work that provides sketches of contemporary businessman Wally Amos (b. 1937), historian David Levering Lewis (b. 1936), and talk show hostess Rolonda Watts (b. 1959), one also finds articles on such pioneer blacks as former Haitian king Henri Christophe (1767-1820), civil rights activist Archibald H. Grimké (1849-1930), cowboy Nat Love (1854-1921), politician P. B. S. Pinchback (1837-1921), bibliophile Arthur A. Schomburg (1874-1938), activist Mary Church Terrell (1863-1954), and abolitionist Harriet Tubman (1820[?]-1913). Not only have these latter figures attracted considerable historical and biographical treatment, but they fit poorly into a reference work that highlights modern figures. In addition, although the articles are signed, the editor fails to identify the contributors and to establish their credentials for the respective assignments.

On a happier note, Mabunda's work is attractively designed and well illustrated. Each article supplies sources for additional information, and the volume contains cumulative nationality, occupation, subject, and name indexes for the nine-volume set. Despite its weak conceptualization, these strengths render *Contemporary Black Biography* an attractive acquisition for public, school, and junior college collections.
—**John David Smith**

402. Glover, Denise M. **Voices of the Spirit: Sources for Interpreting the African-American Experience.** Chicago, American Library Association, 1995. 211p. index. $25.00pa. ISBN 0-8389-0639-7.

Glover's *Voices of the Spirit* provides a basic introduction to resources on the African-American experience for high school and undergraduate teachers, students, and the general public. Glover's goal is to "breathe three-dimensional life into the faceless, nameless victims we passively read about or encounter in our daily routines" (p. viii) and integrate them into a multicultural framework.

In six chapters, the work annotates a highly selective corpus of African-American resources, including general reference books, collective biography and genealogy, historiographical works, general historical surveys, documentary histories, and historical works by chronological period. In addition, Glover discusses historical photographic books, traveling exhibits, and videotapes. She makes a special effort to examine resources by and about African-American women. Author/title and subject indexes, and a list of the 14 sources consulted, complete the volume. Unfortunately, Glover's book falls terribly short in terms of coverage, analysis, and accuracy.

First, her decision to annotate only 179 titles severely limits the usefulness of *Voices of the Spirit*. While few collections should have to start from scratch, librarians nonetheless should be introduced to the classic works. For example, Glover mentions only in passing Monroe N. Work's dated but invaluable *Bibliography of the Negro in Africa and America* (Wilson, 1928, repr., Octagon, 1965). Also, she inexplicably omits the superb *Black Biography, 1790-1950* (3 vols., Chadwyck-Healy, 1991), edited by Henry Louis Gates Jr. There are numerous other omissions.

Second, Glover's annotations are generally mere pedestrian summaries of the books. Her occasional criticisms focus on format, not content or research design, and whether an author includes African-American women in her/his coverage. Historians will find her comments both uncritical and uninformed. For example, when discussing the underground railroad, Glover is unfamiliar with the standard scholarly treatment, Larry Gara's *The Liberty Line* (University of Kentucky Press, 1961). More serious is her misunderstanding of how scholars employ the term *historiography*, confusing it with the term *history*. It is doubtful that such thin and confused analysis will assist collection managers.

Third, Glover's book is riddled with errors. For example, she repeatedly refers to Louisiana State University Press as "Louisiana University Press." She refers to publisher Harry N. Abrams as "Barry N. Abrams" and author Alrutheus A. Taylor as "Alritheus Taylor." Finally, Glover incorrectly includes historian C. Vann Woodward among "a group of liberal Jewish historians who wrote on African-American history" (p. 57). Woodward was raised by devout Methodists. In short, this is an incomplete and terribly flawed book. One expects more from the American Library Association.—**John David Smith**

403. **Historical Statistics of Black America.** Jessie Carney Smith and Carrell Peterson Horton, comps. and eds. Detroit, Gale, 1995. 2v. index. $125.00/set. ISBN 0-8103-8542-2.

In 1990 Gale published *Statistical Record of Black America* (see ARBA 92, entry 348), a valuable reference work that provided a wealth of statistical data on the status of African Americans from 1975 to the present. *Historical Statistics of Black America*, a companion work totaling 2,244 pages, provides significantly broader chronological coverage of the African-American experience—from the eighteenth century to 1975. While *Statistical Record*, which focused keenly on the contemporary period of African-American history, and *Historical Statistics* contain many of the same categories, the two compilations differ both in chronological and thematic coverage. *Historical Statistics*, for example, includes a lengthy chapter on agriculture, reflecting the key role that African Americans historically have played in crop production, especially in the South. While Smith and Horton have gleaned most of their 2,320 tables and text reports from U.S. government publications, they also have drawn upon important and often neglected pioneer African-American sources, including *The Negro Year Book* (1912, 1914, 1918, 1919, 1925, 1937-1938) and *The Negro Handbook* (1942, 1944, 1947, 1949).

Historical Statistics of Black America is divided into 19 topical chapters from agriculture to vital statistics. Data appear in several formats: tables, charts, and short narratives. Each chapter contains thematic sections that are arranged alphabetically, then chronologically. "Slavery and the Slave Trade," for example, contains 10 sections: families, growth and size, population, private families, protests, slave labor, slave prices, slave trade, slaves escaped, and taxable persons. This chapter includes 56 tables spanning the period 1619-1950. Perhaps not surprisingly, population and vital statistics are the most complete chapters, including 18 sections and 336 tables, and 6 sections and 232 tables, respectively. In addition to a list of reference sources, the editors provide two indexes: a subject index with more than 1,600 terms, and an index by year with more than 1,590 references arranged by year and major topic.

Unfortunately, this indexing scheme falls seriously short of providing thorough access to the extraordinary mass of quantitative data amassed by Smith and Horton. For example, while an entry appears in the subject index under "Churches in Ohio," the index contains no entry for Ohio. Also, *Historical Statistics* provides no cross-references. As a result, someone studying miscegenation, for instance, would find some page references in the subject index under "Mulattos" [sic] but might not know that one would in fact find more complete listings under "Population—mulatto" and "Population—mulattoes." In short, the editors apparently were overwhelmed by the sheer volume of the data they compiled. This problem is exacerbated by their failure to provide any significant interpretive analysis of the methodological pitfalls that await researchers who use such raw data. The two-paragraph "Interpreting the Data" (volumes 1 and 2, page lxxxii) is woefully inadequate.

Despite these problems, *Historical Statistics* provides a convenient assemblage of quantifiable data on more than 350 years of African-American life. While they will not necessarily satisfy all patrons, the volumes nonetheless will be a welcome addition to all reference collections. [R: RBB, 15 Feb 95, p. 1110; WLB, Mar 95, p. 80]—**John David Smith**

404. **Statistical Record of Black America.** 3d ed. Jessie Carney Smith and Robert L. Johns, eds. Detroit, Gale, 1995. 1145p. index. $99.00. ISBN 0-8103-8419-1.

The 3d edition of Gale's *Statistical Record of Black America* builds upon the strengths and weaknesses of the 1st edition (see ARBA 92, entry 348). Determined to cull valuable data pertaining to blacks from the flood of statistics published mainly by the U.S. government, editors Smith and Johns have compiled thousands of bits of information gleaned from 39 obscure government and nongovernmental sources.

The data are arranged in 1,155 tables in 17 topical chapters: the arts; attitudes, values, and behavior; business and economics; crime, law enforcement, and legal justice; education; the family; health and medical care; housing; income, spending, and wealth; labor and employment; military affairs; politics and elections; population; the professions; social and human services; sports and leisure; and vital statistics. An easy-to-use index provides subject access by page and table number. To their credit, the editors have made every effort not to duplicate data from the two earlier editions or from the companion two-volume *Historical Statistics of Black America* (see entry 403). They unearth an abundance of recent statistics that document many of the main currents of contemporary black life.

Despite its strengths, *Statistical Record of Black America* succeeds only partially, and the volume will have a limited clientele. Because tables are not reproduced in their entirety, advanced researchers will gain only partial glimpses of statistics available in the original sources. Moreover, users at all levels must depend on the editors' idiosyncratic selection of topics for inclusion. For example, the section "Higher Education" in the chapter on education contains 36 tables that provide considerable detail on black enrollments in colleges and universities in the late 1980s and early 1990s. The section "Higher Education Faculty" presents six tables that enumerate faculty characteristics by race, gender, and rank. The volume contains only two tables, however, that document the number of black faculty at predominantly white institutions. While their database may not yield more information on this topic, in the end Smith and Johns unfortunately offer students limited information with which to begin their research.

Statistical Record of Black America ultimately falls short because of the sheer enormity of its research design. Nevertheless, the volume is a noble effort at social science compilation on the contemporary black experience. While of marginal value to major research collections, it will fill an important void in high schools, junior colleges, and other institutions that lack comprehensive document holdings.—**John David Smith**

Gypsies

405. Tong, Diane. **Gypsies: A Multidisciplinary Annotated Bibliography.** Hamden, Conn., Garland, 1995. 399p. illus. index. $60.00. ISBN 0-8240-7541-2.

This selection of recent writings by and about Gypsies includes articles, books, theses, and dissertations, with some government reports and similar materials as well. The 1,075-plus citations cover nonfiction from 1960 to 1992, and include even older fiction titles. While the emphasis is on English, Romanes, and southern, eastern, and central European language material, there are citations to other languages. Entries are alphabetical by author under 22 broad topics, with numerous cross-references. Access is provided by subject, title, and personal name (not author) indexes. An interesting humanizing touch is the six photographs of Greek Gypsies by the compiler.

Much more selective than Dennis Binns's *Gypsy Bibliography* (Manchester, England, the author, 1982, 1986, 1990, and supplements) that covers almost solely English-language material, the present title's primary contribution to the field is in its annotations, which taken as a whole, provide a very useful review of the literature. Eschewing objectivity, Tong clearly has a point of view and sticks to it. Because there are many stereotypes and even outright errors in much of the material, such evaluations are both useful and necessary. Unfortunately, Tong is unclear as to the sources of her material, or the criteria for selection. For example, while her citations to fiction are detailed to the point of including references in specific paragraphs in some stories, they are nearly silent on major characterizations in speculative fiction.

The only truly significant problem with this work, however, is the poor indexing. The name index does not distinguish between authors and references in the annotations. The subject index is so sparse as to be nearly useless. For instance, while many cited items refer to fortune-telling, there is no such subject index entry. Again, while many of the citations deal with a specific cultural or language group or even one family, there are no index entries for groups at all. With continuing interest in multicultural studies, most academic and many public libraries could benefit from this book. It is truly unfortunate that so little concern appears to have been devoted to the indexing.—**James H. Sweetland**

Hispanic Americans

406. **Dictionary of Twentieth Century Culture: Hispanic Culture of South America.** Peter Standish and others, eds. Detroit, Gale, 1995. 340p. illus. index. $60.00. ISBN 0-8103-8483-3.

From architecture to theater, researchers can locate brief overview information from the Spanish-speaking countries of South America. The editors define culture as people of like backgrounds communicating through shared knowledge. Unfortunately, religion (as a reflection of culture) is not covered. Instead, art, music, literature, drama, film, radio, television, and dance are viewed as cultural phenomena. Hence, Yiddish theater, for example, is missing.

Organization is alphabetical by term or individual. Entries range from one paragraph to several pages (longer essays are devoted to such luminaries as Gabriel García Marquez and Pablo Neruda). Each entry is descriptive and evaluative, signed with the initials of the author, and may provide a photograph or references to further readings, depending upon the significance of the subject. Special features include a map and a timeline of political and cultural events (with no mention of the restrictive United States immigration policies that led many individuals to immigrate to South America from the 1920s to the 1950s). Rounding out the work is a general name and word index keyed to page, not entry, numbers.

Geared to secondary school, public, and academic libraries, this source provides help for answering quick overview and ready-reference questions. A companion volume, *Dictionary of Twentieth Century Culture: Hispanic Culture of Mexico, Central America, and the Caribbean*, is scheduled to follow. (See entry 545 for a review of another companion volume.)—**Ilene F. Rockman**

407. **Hispanic American Biography.** Rob Nagel and Sharon Rose, eds. Detroit, U*X*L/Gale, 1995. 2v. illus. index. $55.00/set. ISBN 0-8103-9828-1.

This 238-page set profiles 93 well-known Hispanic-American figures. Although the emphasis is on contemporary figures, some historic personalities are included. The majority of the biographies come from the fields of literature, television and film, music, and sports. The entries are arranged alphabetically in each volume, with a complete listing in the table of contents. Each entry furnishes the place and date of birth (and death, when appropriate), a quote, a two- to three-page description of the life and contributions of the figure, a black-and-white photograph, and a short bibliography.

There is a brief "Reader's Guide" in each volume identifying the scope of the work, and describing three important related reference sources: *Hispanic American Almanac* (U*X*L/Gale, 1995), *Chronology of Hispanic-American History* (see entry 550), and *Hispanic American Voices* (U*X*L/Gale, 1995). Each volume also includes a useful "Field of Endeavor Index" listing the entries by subject fields.

The work is oriented toward the middle and high school level. However, it would also be appropriate for a popular public library audience. The presentation is attractive, the profiles easy to read and interesting. They are presented in two columns, and subdivided into sections, using various styles and sizes of typeface to facilitate easy reading. The book is a convenient source of up-to-date information on Hispanics in the United States who have made and are still making significant contributions to life today.
—**Susan J. Freiband**

408. Novas, Himilce. **The Hispanic 100: A Ranking of the Latino Men and Women....** New York, Citadel Press/Carol Publishing Group, 1995. 495p. illus. index. $24.95. ISBN 0-8065-1651-8.

Novas points out in her introduction "that by the year 2000 Latinos will be the largest single minority group in the United States and account for one out of every three U.S. citizens" (page xi). She goes on to mention that even though Hispanics represent such a large group, there still is very little known about them by mainstream America. This biographical dictionary presents 100 leading Hispanic Americans from every walk of life who have made outstanding contributions to such varied fields as entertainment, science, education, government, and labor relations. The individuals are listed in order of influence to U.S. thought and culture.

At first glance, it is difficult to determine the basic criteria for selection of the individuals included, as they come from such varied backgrounds and have made such varied contributions. Cesar Chavez is listed first, and Elizabeth Pena (the wonderful actress who appeared in such films as *Down and Out in Beverly Hills* and *The Milagro Beanfield War*) is listed last. Three criteria were used in compiling the 100 individuals listed: the heroes and heroines had to be trailblazers, legends in their own time or later, and recognized on a far-reaching or international level. For the most part, this kind of ranking is a popularity rating, but that aside, Novas's work provides valuable biographies of 100 outstanding Hispanic Americans.

Each entry contains the name, birth and death dates, a black-and-white photograph, and a biography covering the main events in the individuals life, along with important publications, plays, political positions, and other major events. The entries are written clearly and in an entertaining manner without being cute. An index is provided for both the individuals featured (because they are in order of importance, not alphabetical order) and all other names listed in the entries. The index makes the work more valuable as a reference source. *The Hispanic 100* is highly recommended for individual purchase and for academic and public libraries of all sizes. It is especially recommended for smaller public and academic collections where major biographical sources are not available.—**Robert L. Wick**

409. **Who's Who Among Hispanic Americans 1994-95.** 3d ed. Amy L. Unterburger and Jane L. Delgado, eds. Detroit, Gale, 1994. 990p. index. $100.00. ISBN 0-8103-8550-3. ISSN 1052-7354.

Who's Who Among Hispanic Americans 1994-95 is an important revision that provides biographical information on prominent Hispanics (Latinos) in the United States. There are, however, some serious omissions and outdated data in this new edition that require attention. Juan Mestas, the deputy director of the National Endowment for the Humanities, is not listed. Raymund Paredes, the highest-ranking Latino scholar/administrator at the University of California at Los Angeles, is also not listed. Neither is Hector Garza, the director of the Office of Minorities in Higher Education at the American Council on Education in Washington, D.C. Moreover, the address and position given for Eugene Cota-Robles are incorrect. As this is the 3d edition of the work, such omissions and incorrect information require better attention from the editors.

This who's who would be strengthened by including e-mail addresses and fax numbers for those listed. Electronic access to artists, business and political figures, and others is expedited by e-mail contact; long-distance telephone calls are expensive. A word of caution regarding the foreword by Ricardo R. Fernandez: Several Mexican-American leaders were disappointed that Fernandez did not mention that people of Mexican origin constitute about 75 percent of the Hispanic population in the United States. The omission of such factual information about the Hispanic population does not provide a complete picture about this rapidly increasing group in our society. The work is recommended for purchase by all libraries.
—**Roberto P. Haro**

Indians of North America

410. Aaseng, Nathan. **Athletes.** New York, Facts on File, 1995. 118p. illus. index. (American Indian Lives). $17.95. ISBN 0-8160-3019-7.

As part of a new multivolume series, American Indian Lives, for young adult readers, *Athletes* makes an exciting and extraordinary contribution to the understanding of the careers and accomplishments of American Indian athletes and of how racism, prejudice, and discrimination have affected the lives of all American Indian people. All of the men and women athletes were influenced in varying degrees by their culture and all experienced the ugliness of discrimination. Photographs and a selected bibliography add to the readability and value of the book.

The book begins with a meaningful introduction to the impact of culture in the lives of American Indian people and how American Indian traditions and values have positively and negatively affected the ability of American Indian athletes to succeed in the non-Indian sports world. The writing is frank and honest throughout, presenting American Indian lives with empathy and respect. The reader is caught up in the joys and triumphs as well as the setbacks and tragedies of the men and women athletes. Young readers will experience the thrill of running along with Billy Mills as he ran to win the Olympic gold medal, and the pain of Jim Thorpe when his medal was taken from him. They will feel the tragic loss of a young and promising Sioux athlete and role model, Suanne Big Crow.

These captivating stories of the athletes lead the reader to a greater understanding of traditional and contemporary American Indian cultures, as well as encourage the examination of the enduring discrimination that American Indian people experience. This book should be in all school libraries; it will fascinate those readers who are dedicated to sports, as well as those who are interested in American Indians. Teachers will find it invaluable.—**Karen D. Harvey**

411. Durham, Michael S. **Guide to Ancient Native American Sites.** Old Saybrook, Conn., Globe Pequot Press, 1994. 260p. illus. maps. index. $15.95pa. ISBN 1-56440-492-7.

At some point the market for travel guides to North American archaeological sites will be saturated. Durham, who writes very well, describes 144 sites located in 29 states (an interesting note is that the cover incorrectly states 150 sites in 30 states). Each entry provides the usual information about location, hours, fees, and so forth; following the basic information is a relatively brief description of the site with some historical background information. The maps and illustrations are adequate and typical of other travel guides. This guide is similar to a half-dozen other guides that have appeared in the past few years, no better or worse. If a library already has two or three guides such as *Indian America* (see ARBA 91, entry

395), *Native America* (see ARBA 93, entry 431), or *North American Indian Landmarks* (see ARBA 94, entry 416), this could be a pass. If there is a need for an inexpensive guide, this would be a reasonable, if unexceptional, choice.—**G. Edward Evans**

412. Klein, Barry T. **Reference Encyclopedia of the American Indian.** 7th ed. West Nyack, N.Y., Todd, 1995. 883p. index. $125.00; $75.00pa. ISBN 0-915344-45-9; 0-915344-46-7pa.

The difference between the 6th and 7th editions is length. Most of the more than 200 additional pages in the 7th edition are the result of more information in section 1, the U.S. directory section (100-plus additional pages), and 50 more pages in the biography section. There are 3 new divisions in section 1: "Indian Education Programs in Public Schools," "Tribally Owned Casinos and Bingo Halls," and "Native American Events." A number of the biographical entries are updated; for example, the entry for Jamake Highwater in the 6th edition provided an address and telephone number—in this edition, the statement is "address unknown." Other entries remain unchanged; for example, Charlotte Heath's entry still lists her as a faculty member at the University of California, Los Angeles, rather than indicating her position with the National Museum of the American Indian (a post she has held for several years). For some individuals whose 6th edition listing was merely name and address, there are full entries (e.g., Norbert S. Hill Jr.). Maintaining good biographical information is difficult; therefore, it is not surprising that there are inconsistencies and inaccurate information. The coverage of activists has improved somewhat over previous editions. This remains one of the best single sources of current directory information on native peoples of North America. (See ARBA 94, entry 419, for a review of the 6th ed.)—**G. Edward Evans**

413. Legay, Gilbert. **Atlas of Indians of North America.** Hauppauge, N.Y., Barron's Educational Series, 1995. 95p. illus. maps. index. $16.95. ISBN 0-8120-6515-8.

By presenting Native American life in the context of the 10 environmental areas most commonly described by scientists and used in classroom instructional materials, the *Atlas of Indians of North America* helps young readers understand the fundamental connection between culture and the physical and natural environment. The diversity of traditional American Indian clothing, foods, shelters, tools and technologies, arts, family and tribal organizations, and religious ceremonies come to be understood as creative and sensible adaptations to the world that surrounded America's indigenous peoples.

One of the book's great strengths is the colorful and accurate illustrations that demonstrate this remarkable diversity, ingenuity, and creativity. The maps are bright and clear and include such valuable information as physical features of North America, linguistic families, and general locations of historical American Indian nations. Because of the abundance of illustrations, this is a valuable reference for the classroom as well as a book that students will enjoy just browsing through. Much of the text is presented by bullets in shaded boxes, one for each of the major tribes, making specific information easy to locate and quick to scan.

Of necessity, the information is general and brief, making the book a captivating introduction to the diversity of American Indian people or a quick reference. While the belief that American Indians are a part of the historical past tends to be reinforced by the title of the book, nonetheless, the text alludes to the viability and contemporary presence of American Indians by providing recent population data. Contemporary American Indians would resent the reference to their "historical" names when, in fact, most tribes are ridding themselves of names given to them by others and returning to the names given to them in their own creation stories. These transgressions could be easily avoided by having American Indians review texts written by non-Indian authors.—**Karen D. Harvey**

414. Miller, Jay, Colin G. Calloway, and Richard A. Sattler, comps. **Writings in Indian History, 1985-1990.** Norman, Okla., University of Oklahoma Press, 1995. 216p. index. $27.95. ISBN 0-8061-2759-7.

Anyone doubting the level of scholarly interest in Native American history needs only to look at this compilation to have all doubts removed. The compilers identified 2,951 items on American Indian history published from 1985 through 1990. Francis Prucha's works—*A Bibliographical Guide to the History of Indian-White Relations in the United States* (see ARBA 78, entry 345) and *Indian-White Relations in the United States* (University of Nebraska Press, 1982)—provided bibliographical coverage of similar materials published up to 1980. There is a gap that remains unfilled: the period 1981-1984.

There are broad similarities in the structure of all the bibliographies; an introductory section covering guides, bibliographies, and manuscript finding aids, followed by a topical arrangement of journal articles and books. In this volume, there are 12 topical chapters—precontact (subdivided by traditional culture areas); Indian-white relations in terms of governmental and military affairs; economic life, trade, and traders; missions and missionaries; legal relations (including treaties); ethnohistory (again by culture area); Métis; biographies; social life and relationships; environment (an unusual mix of physical and spiritual material); Indian history and historians; and finally, Native American literatures. Entries only provide basic bibliographical information; there are no annotations.

Given the broad topical approach, the detailed combination author-and-subject index is a helpful means of access to the material. An example of the level of detail is a surprising "postcard" entry that lists two items. This is a useful addition to general Native American reference collections or collections on U.S. history.—**G. Edward Evans**

415. **Native North American Chronology.** Duane Champagne and Michael A. Paré, eds. Detroit, U*X*L/Gale, 1995. 185p. illus. maps. index. $29.00. ISBN 0-8103-9818-4.

This work is a shortened, revised, and simplified version of Champagne's previous *Chronology of Native North American History* (see ARBA 95, entry 433) intended for middle and high school audiences. Providing several hundred short entries on the people, places, and events of native North America, it spans the prehistoric and historic periods, with particular concentration on the twentieth century. Entries are well written, sometimes better written than those in the above-mentioned work, but with less detail and with simplified terminology (such as changing "Franciscan" to "Catholic"). Many entries from the larger volume are omitted, such as biographical notes and less prominent events, but the result is a smooth-flowing chronology that captures the essence of the larger work.

Other sections rounding out the volume include a series of short tribal chronologies, and a good, although not comprehensive, subject index. Numerous black-and-white photographs, illustrations, and maps aid the text and add dimension to the book. The only serious omission is a bibliography. Finally, the editors do a good job of covering historical events in Canada and the Spanish Southwest, as well as the Anglo-American United States. In summary, this work is recommended for middle, high school, and public libraries. Postsecondary libraries and the adult sections of public libraries will need the more thorough *Chronology* instead.—**Jeff Wanser**

416. **Notable Native Americans.** Sharon Malinowski, ed. Detroit, Gale, 1995. 492p. illus. index. $65.00. ISBN 0-8103-9638-6.

This easily readable biographical dictionary contains more than 265 men and women (70 percent contemporary, 30 percent historical) from all disciplines (activists to writers). Sketches are signed, vary in length from 1-3 pages, and often contain photographs or illustrations along with an appended bibliography.

An advisory board suggested names, and those selected are considered noteworthy by the Native American community. These names are not collectively available in any other reference source.

Prefatory materials include a provocative essay by George H. J. Abrams entitled "Race, Culture, and Law: The Quest of American Indian Identity"; a list of entries by surname, tribal group or nation, occupation or tribal role; and sketches of the contributors. A 13-page subject index rounds out the work.

Not all tribal groups are represented (there are no entries for Algonquian or Chumashan, for example), but the sketches are better written and more extensive than those in the *Reference Encyclopedia of the American Indian* (see entry 412), *Who Was Who in Native American History* (see ARBA 91, entry 402), and in the companion volume, *The Native North American Almanac* (see ARBA 95, entries 439 and 443). It is a useful tool for all libraries.—**Ilene F. Rockman**

417. **Ready Reference: American Indians.** Harvey Markowitz, ed. Pasadena, Calif., Salem Press, 1995. 3v. illus. maps. index. $270.00/set. ISBN 0-89356-757-4.

More than 160 U.S. scholars contributed 1 or more entries for this impressive 3-volume set. Entries vary in length from a few hundred words for some biographies to several pages (for example, the entry for the Arctic culture area). They are arranged in dictionary order and cover individuals, tribes, organizations, historical events, cultural traditions, and contemporary issues. While there is some coverage of

Mesoamerica (major groups such as Maya, Aztec, and Toltec), the focus is on areas north of Mexico. Canadian material is represented, but spotty. (For example, there are no entries for Canadians such as Mary Sillett, Nelson Small Legs, Butch Smitheram, or Ralph Steinhauser.)

Each entry begins with some basic information; biographies provide birth and death dates, and who the person was or is—politician, writer, tribal leader, and so forth. Next comes tribal affiliation information and a sentence or two about why the person is important. What then follows is a narrative about the individual's life and major accomplishments. The narrative varies in length from two pages to two paragraphs. Extensive use of cross-references leads the user to related topics, and often entries provide one or two citations to more detailed material. Tribal entries supply 1990 census data and historic and contemporary information. Archaeological sites (Chaco Canyon), complexes (Mogollon), and material (Folsom point) furnish concise information and place the site or complex into the broader context of Native American history.

The more general articles, usually labeled pantribal, are of mixed content and value. For example, the article on food preparation and cooking attempts an overview of techniques across a continent in less than one full page. Needless to say, much is missing from such attempts. There are approximately 75 such "general" entries. It is unclear why some are single entries and some are more specific. Other general entries, such as "Buffalo," provide good facts but do not attempt to explore the implications. In the case of the buffalo entry, a paragraph discusses the slaughter of the herds in particular between 1870 and 1880, without commenting on why this took place. The concluding sentence of the entry will probably raise more questions than it answers: "Once the herds were destroyed, the Plains Indians were reduced to extreme poverty and had little alternative to the reservation system" (p. 126). Interestingly enough, there is no cross-reference to the entry on "Reservation System of the United States." Entries for religious ceremonies cover the most widely known, such as Shalako, Shaking Tent, and Peyote Religion.

Much of the appendix directory material is better covered in other sources such as Barry T. Klein's *Reference Encyclopedia of the American Indian* (see entry 412). The four-and-one-half pages of glossary are too short, as is the mediagraphy (seven pages). The bibliography provides sound selective references. The index is helpful and makes up for the occasional lack of cross-references.

If a library already has the *Native North American Almanac* (see ARBA 95, entry 439) and *Native America in the Twentieth Century* (see ARBA 95, entry 434) and is not serving a large community interest in Native American issues, it may be difficult to justify acquiring this set. If it does not have these titles and is seeking a solid single source of information, this would be a good choice.—**G. Edward Evans**

418. Sherrow, Victoria. **Political Leaders and Peacemakers.** New York, Facts on File, 1994. 146p. illus. index. (American Indian Lives). $17.95. ISBN 0-8160-2943-1.

Reflecting the increasing interest in American Indian people, *Political Leaders and Peacemakers*, as part of the multivolume series American Indian Lives, presents bibliographies of 12 American Indian leaders of the past and present. From Deganawidah and Hiawatha, creators of the unique Iroquois League, to Wilma Mankiller, Principal Chief of the Cherokee Nation, these stories honor those who have led American Indian people during difficult and turbulent times. Some of those who are honored by inclusion in this book are better known than others; however, the book is not limited to famous chiefs about whom much has been written and who have traditionally formed the non-Indian conception of American Indian leadership. The photographs are valuable, as is the selected annotated bibliography.

Considerable debate is centered on the issue of whether or not non-Indians should write about American Indian peoples and cultures. The author has endeavored to research the subjects well and has listed American Indian resources. This research, quite naturally, is easier when the people are still alive, and these chapters are more interesting and more readable. Small errors in the text could have been avoided by having an American Indian edit the text. For example, a tribal powwow is not a religious ceremony as stated in the introduction. Unfortunately, these admittedly small factual errors raise doubts in the informed reader's mind and misinform the young reader—a much more serious consequence.

The chapters that involve much historical information could become confusing and even boring if the reader did not have some knowledge of this period of history or the benefit of a teacher's guidance. The book would also have been strengthened by the addition of at least one political leader who did not accept the inevitability of history and who did not earn the general appreciation of the non-Indian public.
—**Karen D. Harvey**

419. Sonneborn, Liz. **Performers.** New York, Facts on File, 1995. 112p. illus. index. (American Indian Lives). $17.95. ISBN 0-8160-3045-6.

Performers is part of a multivolume series, American Indian Lives, written for young readers. In presenting the stories of Native American dancers, actors, and singers, the book fills a void in the literature by combining the engrossing stories of American Indian people in the performing arts with an enlightening picture of their audiences and the society in which they performed. The traditional role of performer was to ensure the continuity of the culture; the contemporary role has been as a representative of American Indian cultures to non-Indian cultures. Both roles have great responsibility.

Each biography is carefully crafted to engage the young reader in the power and excitement of each story, and the photographs and selected annotated bibliography contribute to the readability and usefulness of the book. Young readers are likely to be drawn to the life stories of those contemporary performers that they know, such as Graham Greene or John Trudell, but they will be attracted also to the stories of those who are not as well known but whose powerful stories of ambition, training, and persistence are compelling. Through the biographies, the reader will develop a greater understanding of how American Indian performers have confronted both positive and negative stereotyping in their roles and prejudice in the entertainment industry, and how they have helped to shape the perceptions of American Indians through their work. They bring their Indian traditions and values to their work, enriching everyone. The book expands understanding of American Indians in a manner that has been ignored in the past and makes a valuable contribution to the field.—**Karen D. Harvey**

420. **Statistical Record of Native North Americans.** 2d ed. Marlita A. Reddy, ed. Detroit, Gale, 1995. 1272p. index. $105.00. ISBN 0-8103-6421-2. ISSN 1082-7811.

The 1st edition of this book was published in 1993 and reviewed in ARBA 94 (see entry 422). This new edition has expanded coverage of American Indian areas from the 1990 census, including Alaska Native Statistical Areas (ANVSAs), reservations and trust lands, Tribal Designated Statistical Areas (TDSAs), and Tribal Jurisdiction Statistical Areas (TJSAs). As was the case with the 1st edition, data were obtained through a library search and contacts with federal agencies, national organizations, and associations. There are 12 chapters on broad topics such as "History" or "The Family," and within these chapters, data are organized by topics. All in all, this is the most comprehensive single reference source on this subject.—**Bohdan S. Wynar**

421. White, Phillip M. **American Indian Studies: A Bibliographic Guide.** Englewood, Colo., Libraries Unlimited, 1995. 163p. illus. index. $29.00. ISBN 1-56308-243-8.

Focusing on reference material for American Indian Studies (AIS), this guide has reasonably comprehensive coverage for publications issued between 1970 and 1993. (The 1993 date is probably to about mid-year, as *The Sioux and Other Native American Cultures of the Dakotas* [see ARBA 95, entry 428] is missing.) Perhaps two-thirds of 385 entries cover titles that are exclusively Native American studies in scope. The balance of the entries are for more general reference works that contain material that is relevant to AIS. It is the latter category that is the weakness of this guide. Given the broad nature of Native American studies, almost any general reference work may contain useful material. Therefore, where to stop the listing of general reference titles is a difficult decision. The author's decision appears to have been to include tools undergraduate students and younger would use. However, some electronic databases are included that may not be widely accessible in public and smaller academic libraries (e.g., LEXIS/NEXIS and DIALOG).

The material is arranged by typical reference tool types (encyclopedias, bibliographies, indexes, and so forth). Entries have basically descriptive annotations, although there are occasional evaluative comments. The majority of entries for bibliographies do not have annotations. While the coverage is far above average for this type of guide, it is not comprehensive. For example, although there are several guides to archives included, there is no entry for *A Guide to the Archives of Hampton Institute* (see ARBA 87, entry 341). This is an example of the difficulty in where to cut off more general reference works. In the case of Hampton Institute, the work should be included, as the Institute played a major role in U.S. Indian education from 1878 to 1923 and has substantial AIS material. Overall, this is an excellent, modestly priced guide that will be useful to college, public, and school libraries.—**G. Edward Evans**

Irish Americans

422. Barnes, John A. **Irish-American Landmarks: A Traveler's Guide.** Detroit, Gale, 1995. 590p. illus. maps. index. $34.95. ISBN 0-8103-9603-3.

This is an idiosyncratic work, designed to serve as a vade mecum rather than to grace a reference shelf. It provides thumbnail introductions to historical sites that are in some way identified with Irish Americans. Most of its 300 entries treat Irish-American-related aspects of buildings, churches, museums, and memorials. There are, however, sites of broader historical significance, such as the Alamo, the Gettysburg battleground, and Baltimore's B&O Railroad Museum.

The volume is organized by region, state, and city, and although it includes sites located in 46 states and 2 Canadian provinces, coverage is heavily slanted: More than one-third of its pages are devoted to the Northeast. This plan does indeed make it handy for travelers, but the reliance on geographical and alphabetical order communicates to the reader no sense of pattern or process in the Irish-American experience in the United States; it would seem to lack any comprehensive intellectual vision.

Irish and Irish-American participation in both the Revolutionary and Civil Wars is given extensive treatment, as are the birthplaces and homes of U.S. presidents. Sites devoted to such entertainment luminaries as Jackie Gleason and John Wayne also abound. Reliance on movie photograph stills for many of the illustrations does not instill a great deal of confidence in the book's historical accuracy. *Irish-American Landmarks* is well written and well designed. Collections specializing in ethnic coverage, along with those insatiable friends of all things Hibernian, may find this worth acquiring.—**Glenn Petersen**

Japanese Americans

423. **Academic Focus Japan: Programs and Resources in North America.** Gretchen Shinoda, ed. Washington, D.C., Gateway Japan, 1994. 647p. $45.00pa. ISBN 0-89068-125-2.

This directory gives information on 410 academic programs and related resources in North America that focus on Japanese studies or the Japanese language. Of these, 104 are degree programs at universities and colleges. Other resources include publishers, periodicals, databases, repositories, funding programs, cultural activities, and the like. The program profiles are arranged alphabetically by name, and each follows a standard format. Information is given on the purpose, subject matter covered, audience, programs and activities, tuition and financial aid, personnel, financial support of the program, and contact people.

Supplementary reference lists categorize the organizations and programs into three groups for ease of access: study and overseas experiences; supported research and training and other sources of funding for research; and related organizations and resources such as libraries, museums, government agencies, databases, and software. There is also a list of opportunities for teaching English in Japan, with names of placement services. In addition, programs and institutions are listed by state and in a separate alphabetical reference list.

The compilers have asked each institution to review and verify the information on their programs or resources, but issue a caveat regarding costs and other specifics that are subject to change. Spot checking indicates that the information is accurate and complete. This directory will be of use to students interested in a course of study on Japan or its language; to those wishing to study overseas; to counselors; to teachers of Japanese culture, history, or language; and to those wishing to teach in Japan.—**Shirley L. Hopkinson**

Jews

424. Castelló, Elena Romero, and Uriel Macías Kapón. **The Jews and Europe: 2,000 Years of History.** New York, Henry Holt, 1994. 239p. illus. index. $50.00. ISBN 0-8050-3526-5.

This outstanding book has more than 350 full-color illustrations, many of them full-page, illustrating an authoritative text that covers nearly all aspects of Jewish life and survival in the mostly inimical lands of Europe, both Christian and Islamic. The text is interspaced in symmetrical paragraphs between the illustrations so as to maximize the interrelationships between text and pictures. This brings the reader's attention even more forcefully to Jewish art, architecture, painting, dance, folk art, literature, cinema, music, costume, religious practices, holidays, jewelry, and many other aspects of Jewish achievement and survival during two millennia.

The writers are well known in their fields, the principal author being a researcher for the Consejo Superior de Investigaciones Cientificas in Madrid, and under her name of Romero has published books on Sephardic ballads and on the development of Hebraic law. The present work, copyrighted and printed in Italy (and there is also an Italian text), is presented to the U.S. public with U.S. spelling and usage. There is a glossary of Jewish terms and phrases, with their literal meanings and sometimes lengthy explanations, such as those for *Bar Mitzvah*, *Haggadah*, *Ashkenazi*, *shofar*, *Sukkot*, *yeshiva*, and *Yom Kippur*. There are also a good bibliography and an index of names going back at least to Alexander the Great. This splendid volume should be in every public library, whether or not it has a large Jewish population in its area, and is recommended especially for libraries serving students for the ministry, both Christian and Jewish.—**Raymund F. Wood**

425. **The "Jewish Question" in German-Speaking Countries, 1848-1914: A Bibliography.** Rena R. Auerbach, ed. Hamden, Conn., Garland, 1994. 385p. index. (Garland Reference Library of the Humanities, v.1571). $62.00. ISBN 0-8153-0812-4.

At first glance, the subject of the "Jewish question" in German-speaking countries may appear to be a rather narrow field to cover, but this professionally prepared bibliography containing 3,734 entries shows otherwise. It offers extensive coverage of issues raised by the participation of Jews in German-speaking countries—Germany, Austria-Hungary, and Switzerland—prior to World War I. The use of this material suggests significant research into the background of European anti-Semitism, the prologue to events of the Holocaust, and the ethnic politics and social relations of European history.

The book continues the *Bibliographie zur Geschichte der Judenfrage*, by Volkmar Eichstadt, published in 1938 (Hamburg, Germany, Hanseatische Verlagsanstalt) and reprinted in 1969 (West Mead, England, Gregg International). Eichstadt covered the period 1750-1848 and treated tolerance, improvement of civil rights, equality, emancipation, selected material on missionary work, Judaism in literature, and the internal Jewish debate about religious reform of Judaism. Auerbach adds subjects of the army, demography and statistics, economics and finance, ideologies, law and justice, racism, and the "solution of the Jewish Question." She conveniently arranges her bibliography according to subject and numbers each entry, whereas Eichstadt listed entries mostly chronologically. An appendix to Auerbach's bibliography lists newspapers and periodicals by categories (general, anti-Semitic, confessional, Jewish, and missionary). Indexes to authors and subjects follow the appendix. Auerbach offers a brief preface to explain the format of the bibliography, followed by an all-too-brief introduction to the significance of the "Jewish Question" by Otto Kulka of Hebrew University.

The most impressive aspect of the bibliography is its international coverage. Most entries come from German sources, but a substantial number are in English, French, Hebrew, and several other European languages. The German titles are not translated into English, but Hebrew titles (rendered in Hebrew letters) are given English translations, although the Hebrew transliterations are not offered. Entries include complete publication information, length of the work, and its location. The bibliography is especially useful for getting a handle on the immense pamphlet literature of the period. The bibliography will be of use to collections of Jewish studies and European history and sociology.—**Simon J. Bronner**

7 Genealogy

HERALDRY

426. **Debrett's Peerage and Baronetage [1995].** Charles Kidd and David Williamson, eds. New York, St. Martin's Press, 1995. 980p. illus. $250.00. ISBN 0-312-12557-7.

Revised every five years, *Debrett's* is a comprehensive record of titled nobility in the United Kingdom. This new edition contains 2,500 heraldic entries, listing descendants and siblings, collateral branches living, and (when appropriate) predecessors. Most entries contain a description and a small black-and-white illustration of the coat of arms. Royal crowns, coronets, and various decorations are also illustrated in miniature.

Main sections cover the royal family, the peerage, and the baronetage. In addition, the volume provides tables of precedence, forms of addressing persons of title, a guide to the wearing of Orders, and other relevant information. Special articles included in this edition are: "Baronies by Writ and the Barony of Grey of Codnor, Its History and the Investigations Involved in Having It Called Out of Abeyance" by Thomas Woodcock and Somerset Herald; "The Debrett Family: Ancestors and Descendants of John Debrett" by Frances-Jane French; and "A Rare Honour: British Marquessates Through Six Centuries" by Robert Horley. This valuable resource, founded in 1769, is important for those researching the British aristocracy.—**Jean Engler**

GENEALOGY

Dictionaries and Encyclopedias

427. **A Dictionary of English Surnames.** 3d ed. By P. H. Reaney; revised by R. M. Wilson. New York, Oxford University Press, 1995. 508p. $15.95pa. ISBN 0-19-863146-4.

This represents the 3d edition of Reaney's classic *A Dictionary of British Surnames* (see ARBA 79, entry 500, and ARBA 77, entry 489, for reviews of the earlier editions) under a slightly different title and with a slight shift in orientation toward names of specifically English rather than Celtic origin. The 2d and 3d editions were prepared by Wilson. He took over for Reaney, who died in 1967.

Wilson adds 4,000 names to those found in the 2d edition, and points users to other works that are useful for finding information on Irish, Welsh, and Scottish names. Purchasers should be aware that the purpose of the dictionary is to explain the meaning of names, not to treat their genealogy and family history. A bonus feature of the book is the introductory essays on naming practices in each of the regions of the British Isles, which only adds to the value of the dictionary. It is highly recommended for any library with an interest in names and genealogy.—**Donald E. Collins**

Directories

428. Bentley, Elizabeth Petty. **The Genealogist's Address Book.** 3d ed. Baltimore, Md., Genealogical Publishing, 1995. 653p. index. $34.95pa. ISBN 0-8063-1455-9.

Given the importance of identifying and locating repositories, agencies, and various other institutions and organizations for family and local history information, this is an essential book for library reference collections. This edition adds several hundred new entries and updates approximately 80 percent of the entries from the previous volume.

The work is, as the title states, primarily an address book of agencies, archives, libraries, publishers and publications, historical societies, and other repositories and resources of genealogical and local history information or interest. The scope is broad enough to cover sources of even marginal relevance to the topic. Entries include names, addresses, telephone numbers, contact persons, business hours, publications, and frequently parenthetical notes concerning the resources of the repository or agency. The book is logically divided into sections according to national, then state, then ethnic and religious interests. The final section provides similar information regarding various types of publishing and publishers, computer interests, adoption registries, surname registries, and more.

There are only two points of criticism. Because users would normally expect to find state vital statistics agencies listed under the appropriate state, it is difficult to understand why these offices are found within the national addresses section. In addition, access would be greatly improved if the organization name entries, which now make up the entire general index, were liberally supplemented with keywords taken from within the main entries in the text, as well as from the book's table of contents, headings, and subheadings. At present, a search for Georgia vital statistics will be unsuccessful through a search of either the general index or the Georgia entries in the state addresses section. An improved index will turn an already very good reference source into an excellent one.—**Donald E. Collins**

Handbooks and Yearbooks

429. **African American Genealogical Sourcebook.** Paula K. Byers, ed. Detroit, Gale, 1995. 244p. index. $69.00. ISBN 0-8103-9226-7.

This is the second of a series of four books designed to aid persons in minority and ethnic groups in tracing their family histories. The present volume treats the peculiarities of genealogical research and the difficulties faced by African Americans in researching their ancestry.

The first half of the volume consists of three essays. African-American researchers are first introduced to historical and background information preparatory to research. This is followed by a discussion of general methods and materials useful to family researchers of all races; it concludes with an explanation of research materials that are specific to African Americans. The three authors possess impressive credentials in black genealogy, and the essays, particularly the third, are well written. Illustrative examples of research materials that are common to books of this nature are few in number in this volume and are confined to materials of significance exclusively to African Americans. Given the authors' premise that certain materials are useful to all races, perhaps the use of illustrations should be broadened.

Fully half of the book consists of a directory of genealogical sources. The basic organization is by type of repository and material: libraries and archives, private and public organizations, print sources, and other media. Each of these is further subdivided geographically: national and regional, state, and foreign. Researchers will find the book generally easy to use through its logical organization and indexes.

Although the book is generally well constructed, there are criticisms. Repositories and organizations are frequently described in overall terms that give little attention to genealogical or African-American collections. For example, the genealogy department at the North Carolina State Library goes virtually unmentioned in describing the library as a whole. Attention to this oversight would make this an even better book.

The book is an education to Americans of all races in the problems faced by African-American family researchers, and is a good and useful introduction to black genealogy. It is recommended for public and college libraries and for African Americans with an interest in genealogy.—**Donald E. Collins**

430. **Asian American Genealogical Sourcebook.** Paula K. Byers, ed. Detroit, Gale, 1995. 280p. maps. index. (Genealogy Sourcebook Series). $69.00. ISBN 0-8103-9228-3.

A unique and valuable source, this is the third volume in the Genealogical Sourcebook Series. "This series is designed to be a first-stop guide to researching the genealogy of any person with an Asian, African, Hispanic, or Native American heritage," (p. xiii) (see entries 429, 432, and 433 for reviews of other volumes in the series).

This work is organized into three main parts as delineated in the user's guide. Part 1, "Conducting Genealogical Research," consists of three chapters of essays written by experts in the field of Asian-American genealogy. These essays combine historical data and practical genealogical advice, and they indicate what must be done in a successful search for data. This information is detailed and explicit. For example, the section on the Republic of the Philippines is 83 pages long and is packed with much specific information on genealogical records in each province and important municipality.

Please note that the chapter "Records Specific to Asian America" covers research and sources for only three major groups: Chinese, Japanese, and Korean. This part also contains a chapter that lists, with descriptive notes, libraries, archives, and repositories both within and outside the United States that hold relevant genealogical materials. Each of the three chapters in this part concludes with a bibliography. Part 2, "Directory of Genealogical Information," consists of four chapters that provide information on libraries and archives, private and public organizations, print resources, and media. Part 3, "Indexes," has author, title and organization, and subject indexes. The quality of this work is high. Gale plans to publish the volumes in the Genealogical Sourcebook Series on an ongoing basis. They have certainly produced an outstanding volume in this particular title.—**Marshall E. Nunn**

431. Bremer, Ronald A. **Compendium of Historical Sources: The How and Where of American Genealogy.** rev. ed. Salt Lake City, Utah, Progenitor Genealogical Society, 1994. 914p. index. $100.00pa.

Rather than dealing with history, as the title suggests, this is in fact a compendium of miscellaneous articles, forms, lists, and suggested methodologies of concern to genealogists. The 30 chapters cover a wide range of genealogical interests, including principles of genealogical research, correspondence, notable genealogical libraries and archives, and various categories of records and record sources. Access to the book's 900-plus pages is barely adequate at best through a 1-page table of contents and a 2-page index.

This reviewer found the book to be a disappointment. Typographical errors, misspellings, incorrect grammar, wrong and obsolete titles, references to out-of-date sources, and unidentified/unexplained illustrations are evident throughout the volume. An examination of the volume gives the impression that it is a haphazard collection of documents, tidbits, and personal views gathered over many years of genealogical work. Experienced genealogists will question some of the author's suggested methods, and trained librarians will find much wrong with his discussion of libraries. The suggestion on page 35, for example, that jam, cheese, or candy be sent to communist countries in order to prompt replies to correspondence is not only out-of-date since the fall of communism, but is too amusing to be taken seriously. The placement throughout the book of advertisements for the author as a genealogical speaker also causes readers to question the author's purpose. The book is overpriced and, regardless of cost, cannot be recommended to either individuals or libraries. [R: LJ, Jan 95, p. 82]—**Donald E. Collins**

432. **Hispanic American Genealogical Sourcebook.** Paula K. Byers, ed. Detroit, Gale, 1995. 224p. index. $69.00. ISBN 0-8103-9227-5.

This volume, one of a proposed series to be originated by the publishers, has been created to focus on the many ethnic groups in America and to direct the researcher to remote sources and repositories (see entries 429, 430, and 433 for reviews of other titles in the series). It has accomplished its goal.

In addition to giving useful background material about conducting genealogical research, the editor concentrates on the applications to Hispanic Americans and records specific to this group. Included are notarial records, heraldry, inquisition records, and records of religious orders and of the secular church. Libraries and archives in the United States are outlined with their holdings, including some special collections pertinent to Hispanics. Among these are the Chicano Research Collection at Arizona State University and the Benson Latin American Collection at the University of Texas, Austin. Useful is a list of archives outside the United States that gives a brief description of their holdings. Historical data help to orient the searcher, and in-depth discussions about folklore, family traditions, and many more topics open the doors to numerous avenues to follow.

An extensive bibliography of printed sources, both in English and in Spanish, leads the researcher to an abundance of material. A glossary of terms relative to the topic would have been a useful addition for the uninitiated. The sourcebook is highly recommended for genealogical and reference collections, particularly in areas with a large Hispanic population.—**Carol Willsey Bell**

433. **Native American Genealogical Sourcebook.** Paula K. Byers, ed. Detroit, Gale, 1995. 219p. maps. index. (Genealogy Sourcebook Series). $69.00. ISBN 0-8103-9229-1.

As part of the Genealogy Sourcebook Series (see entries 429, 430, and 432 for reviews of other volumes in the series), this volume provides useful chapters on information specific to Native Americans as well as on general genealogical resources. The first 110 pages address Native American issues in 5 essay chapters. Mary Lynn Sharpe provides a general overview of United States Native American history (note: This work does not cover Canada, is weak on Alaska, and has nothing for Hawaiians) and addresses potential problems the research may encounter when attempting to interpret Native American data. Her chapter concludes with a selective but useful bibliography. George Nixon has contributed three chapters. The first is a chronology of major Native American events, similar to such lists in other reference works on Native Americans. His second contribution is a 35-page guide to basic genealogical research methods and how to apply them to Native American research. A particularly good section in this chapter is the "case history," which illustrates some of the complexity and methods for resolving questions when conducting Native American genealogical research. Jimmy B. Parker's essay on records for Native Americans is a solid review of the general resources for records. The last essay is the last of Nixon's and covers records specific to the "Five Civilized Tribes" (Cherokee, Choctow, Chickasaw, Creek, and Seminole Nations).

Part 2 presents general genealogical information. The first section is a directory of libraries and archives with large genealogical collections. Entries are arranged by state and provide brief descriptions of each organization, location, and telephone number(s) as well as highlighting some of its special collections. The second section is a list of organizations of national and state significance in the field of genealogical or Native American studies. The final section is a short (three-page) list of other media; this is of limited value. An author, a title and organization, and a subject index round out the volume. This is a source to seriously consider for libraries with a service community that have a strong interest in Native American issues.—**G. Edward Evans**

Indexes

434. **Index to the Roll of Honor.** Martha Reamy and William Reamy, comps. Baltimore, Md., Genealogical Publishing, 1995. 1164p. $75.00. ISBN 0-8063-1483-4.

The title of this work refers to those who died in the service of the Union during the Civil War. Originally published by the Government Printing Office between 1865 and 1871 and reprinted in 1974 by Genealogical Publishing, the 10-volume set (see ARBA 95, entry 547) provides a valuable service in identifying and locating the graves of soldiers. It also indicates in many cases where and when they fell. The present volume serves as a much-needed cumulative index to the original work.

Martha and William Reamy give organization to the helter-skelter approach taken by the earlier compilers. The "Index to Burial Sites" pulls together the numerous and widely scattered individual cemetery indexes, arranging them alphabetically by states, with volume and page numbers. The primary index lists the deceased alphabetically, providing volume and page number to their location in the original work. An informative essay by Mark Hughes relates the history of the original project and the difficulties faced in attempting to retrieve and identify the dead. He points out the problems of determining the exact number of dead—deciphering almost unreadable script, incompetence in gathering the original data by careless or inept officers, and the multiple listing of some names. Although the compilers' intent was to list all Union deaths, they do not. Cemeteries have been missed, soldiers who died in the Western states and territories have been purposely omitted, and men who died after going home and many whose bodies were retrieved by their families are not recorded. Nevertheless, this massive undertaking was well worth the effort.

All libraries that possess the original or the reprint of the *Roll of Honor* will want to add this volume. Additionally, any library with an interest in genealogy or the Civil War should consider purchasing at least the index, if not the entire set, of this valuable work.—**Donald E. Collins**

PERSONAL NAMES

435. **Collins Scottish Clan & Family Encyclopedia.** By George Way and Romilly Squire. New York, HarperCollins, 1994. 512p. illus. maps. index. $40.00. ISBN 0-00-470547-5.

There has long been a need for a reference source to explain the often confusing world of clans, tartans, heraldry, and family names in Scotland. This work seeks to fill that need in a colorful and understandable manner. In-depth discussions cover clanship and the law of the clan, as well as the tartan that denotes family allegiance and pride. Heraldic terms are well explained and illustrated. Arranged alphabetically by family name, each segment for primary families includes arms, crest, and motto, with a colored representation of the tartan. Family names belonging to the member clans of the Standing Council and the armigerous clans and families are treated separately. Several appendixes review chronology, lists of monarchs, and heraldic terms.

The index is difficult for the casual user, as names appear in ordinary, boldface, and italic print, requiring the reader to check the instructions each time. Some errors appear; the name OLIVER is not found on page 449 as stated. Nevertheless, this lovely work is highly recommended for both individuals and libraries.—**Carol Willsey Bell**

436. Faulkner, Benjamin. **What to Name Your African-American Baby.** New York, St. Martin's Press, 1994. 178p. index. $7.95pa. ISBN 0-312-11348-X.

Typical of the genre of baby-name books, this volume makes no claims to scholarship. The first of six chapters illustrates current trends in making new names (e.g., adding a new beginning to a traditional name—changing Ellen to Triellen, or combining parts of both parents' names—Dawn and John to baby Dawnjohn). African-American heroes include political, educational, and arts leaders; businesspeople; and athletes. The book contains an extremely select list of jazz and soul artists, but no rappers, gospel performers, and only one name from the blues. The blues has been one of the most influential of American musical forms, and certainly one of the more African of American musical idioms. The omission of such names as Muddy Waters and Joe Willie Wilkins reveals Faulkner's superficial understanding of African-American cultural history.

African names include ones from the past (especially royalty), divinities (often without any ethnic identifier), ancient cities and kingdoms, topographical features, and the names of modern African states and cities. Lists of traditional names are given for four African languages—Yoruba, Hausa, Zulu, and Swahili. If, as the author states, these groups were chosen because they are ancestral for many African Americans, ones more appropriate than Zulu and Swahili could have been chosen. A list of English-language words (e.g., ability, poet, fox), not necessarily the same ones for each language, are translated into each of the four African languages used. The work has a pronouncing guide for the African languages, a brief bibliography, and a name index.—**Fred J. Hay**

437. Robb, H. Amanda, and Andrew Chesler. **Encyclopedia of American Family Names.** New York, HarperCollins, 1995. 710p. $45.00. ISBN 0-06-270075-8.

This collection of more than 10,000 surnames was inspired by newspaper columns entitled "Is Your Name . . . ?," published by the grandfather of one of the authors. Because most of the surnames published were of Western European origin, the authors expanded on the original work by studying the *Report of Distribution of Surnames in the Social Security Number File*, and added only those surnames showing a frequency of more than 5,000.

Arranged in alphabetical order, each entry includes the family name, the "root" name, and variations; the ranking (in the Social Security Administration's frequency table); the number of persons with this name found in the Social Security database in 1980; the national and etymological origin of the surname; prominent Americans of this family name; and genealogies published on the family name, as found in the Library of Congress card catalog. This work is far more comprehensive than others on the subject, and should certainly be included in reference and genealogical collections.—**Carol Willsey Bell**

8 Geography and Travel Guides

GEOGRAPHY

General Works

Atlases

United States

438. **Connecticut, Maine, Massachusetts, [and] Rhode Island: Atlas of Historical County Boundaries.** John H. Long, comp. and ed. Gordon DenBoer, comp. New York, Simon & Schuster Academic Reference Division, 1994. 412p. maps. $50.00. ISBN 0-13-051947-2.

439. **New Hampshire [and] Vermont: Atlas of Historical County Boundaries.** John H. Long, ed., and Gordon DenBoer with George E. Goodridge Jr., comps. New York, Simon & Schuster Academic Reference Division, 1993. 216p. maps. $40.00. ISBN 0-13-151954-5.

Two of a projected forty-volume series covering the contiguous states and Hawaii, these atlases trace the evolution of each county within the specified states from the 1630s to 1990. The boundary changes are shown via text and maps. Long, associated with the Newberry Library's Center for Family and Community History, was formerly assistant editor of the *Atlas of Early American History: The Revolutionary Era, 1760-1790* (see ARBA 77, entry 375) and editor of *Historical Atlas and Chronology of County Boundaries, 1788-1980* (G. K. Hall, 1984), an earlier version of the atlases covering only the 14 eastern and central states in the *Atlas of Early American History*. The project has been funded by the National Endowment for the Humanities.

The books are arranged by state, then alphabetically by county. For each county, there is a chronology, accompanied by sets of maps to show each boundary change. Included in the chronologies are not only boundary changes, but also "county name changes, unsuccessful authorizations for new counties, redefinitions and clarifications of existing lines" (*New Hampshire [and] Vermont*, p. xi). The rationale for the changes or events leading to them is not documented, only the actual decisions. The county chronologies are consolidated into a state chronology, which is documented to show primary sources of information for each change. These, plus other sources that may provide insights into rationales and background events, are listed in a bibliography. Some of these are discussed in detail in the introduction. Each introduction is a mix of information pertinent to the series as a whole and unique, state-specific information. The introduction is a model for introductions, documenting the purpose, audience, scope, and other editorial decisions, and putting the atlases in the context of similar reference works.

The atlases are based on original research in legal documents. The historical boundaries are marked on special versions of the U.S. Geological Survey (USGS) state base maps for each state. Drawn at the scale of 1:500,000 (8 miles per inch), they show current coastlines, rivers, lakes, names of water features, place-names, longitude and latitude lines, land survey lines, and county and state boundary lines, but eliminate other characteristics for legibility. Counties too large to fit on one page are covered by USGS maps drawn at the 1:2,500,000 scale (40 miles per inch). All maps have been reduced for publication.

These two volumes are admirable historical atlases—thorough, carefully researched, well documented, and well designed to convey information effectively. Their subject matter is useful to historical, geographical, and demographic researchers. Two earlier books—*Historical U.S. County Outline Map Collection, 1840-1980* (University of Maryland, Baltimore County, Department of Geography, 1984) and *Map Guide to the U.S. Federal Censuses, 1790-1920* (see ARBA 88, entry 861)—provide similar materials, but are less comprehensive, covering fewer boundary changes with small-scale maps. A useful feature for the atlases would have been a name index to geographical features. With the current arrangement, a researcher wanting to know what counties a particular city had been in throughout its history would have to use another source to find a county location, then follow the changes affecting that county and possibly other counties. Several tables effectively summarize data (e.g., county creations for each state). The volumes are highly recommended for larger academic libraries and other collections serving historical researchers.—**Marilyn Domas White**

440. Goins, Charles Robert, and John Michael Caldwell. **Historical Atlas of Louisiana.** Norman, Okla., University of Oklahoma Press, 1994. 99p. maps. index. $65.00; $29.95pa. ISBN 0-8061-2589-6; 0-8061-2682-5pa.

This volume contains a broad range of information that is well presented for readers of all ages and is suitable for multiple levels of scholarship. The maps and text are worthy for serious research or for leisurely browsing in the pursuit of interesting knowledge. A concise seven-page overview of the Bayou State provides a capsule of the geologic and human cultural history of Louisiana. Much of the material that follows is in the form of nearly 100 maps and accompanying text that detail the physical setting and natural resources of Louisiana and the settlement of the area from aboriginal to modern times, and subsequent chapters that devote special attention to economic growth as seen in transportation, agriculture, and commerce and industry. A final chapter pertains to the cultural growth of the state as measured by museums, historic sites, libraries, archives, fairs, festivals, and other events.

Anyone fascinated with the proliferation of Cajun cultural material within U.S. life over the past 2 decades will benefit greatly from a study of map 97, along with the subsequent 1 page of information, showing the selected folk regions of Louisiana. An explanation of the evolution of North (Hill Country) versus South (Cajun Country) cultures within the state is found here. Interestingly, the authors do not hesitate to add tiny bits of information and references that add depth to the atlas and prevent it from becoming dry reading. Just one example suffices to illustrate this: The authors indicate that the past glory of railroads is memorialized in the ballad of the once-great Illinois Central train, "The City of New Orleans." This atlas brings demographics and additional facts up-to-date through the 1990 federal census. Because of this factual content, the clearly presented maps, plus the readable style, this volume should be in the holdings of all libraries in the state.—**Louis G. Zelenka**

441. **Hammond Road Atlas America.** Maplewood, N.J., Hammond, 1994. 96p. maps. $5.95pa. ISBN 0-8437-2704-7.

Road atlases are one of the most popular reference sources for the home. The small, 24-by-31-centimeter size of this atlas makes it easy to handle and store. The regional arrangement, beginning with the Northeast states and progressing southward, then westward, makes the table of contents especially helpful to those readers seeking an alphabetical arrangement. Maps of the Canadian provinces are also arranged from east to west and are followed by a map of Mexico and 21 maps of National Parks and recreation and vacation areas. The 17 special vicinity maps dispersed throughout are often 2-page spreads providing easy-to-read detailed maps of larger cities. A typical two-page regional/state map also includes a travel guide listing historical sites and other attractions of interest, a topographical map of the area, and an alphabetical index of city and town names. Travelers of small rural roads may not find the atlas adequate as small communities and less-traveled roadways are not included.

Other helpful information includes mileage distance tables of 105 United States and 20 Canadian cities, as well as communication codes on the front and back inside covers, addresses and telephone numbers for additional travel information, a page location key for state maps, a time zone and interstate highway map, and a guide to using the atlas. The wide use of color makes it attractive, appealing, and easy to use.—**Elaine Ezell**

442. **Hammond Road Atlas and Vacation Guide.** Maplewood, N.J., Hammond, 1994. 48p. maps. $2.75pa. ISBN 0-8437-2702-0.

If this work is intended as a competitor to the annual *Rand McNally Road Atlas* (see ARBA 93, entry 468), then Hammond has more work to do. The only ways in which the Hammond atlas might possibly be judged to be a better buy are that it is half of Rand McNally's size ($8\frac{1}{2}$-by-11 inches as compared to 11-by-17 inches)—and thus easier to handle (perhaps it was designed for use in compact cars)—and that its price is under half that of the Rand McNally. This atlas has a mileage chart, 17 metro-area maps, and as the heart of the atlas, a series of maps of areas (e.g., New England), generally of areas about 200 by 400 miles or smaller. For each area, scenic points are noted, and there are excellent brief summaries of what to see while on vacation. There are a gazetteer, a location map, and color photographs with each major map. It seems to this admittedly map-bound person that one would need more detailed maps for driving in metropolitan areas, such as greater Los Angeles; the highways given are not sufficient for getting one where one needs to go in these areas. The major maps of the northern United States also include bordering areas of Canadian provinces. Appropriate for persons who find the Rand McNally atlas to be too awkward to handle in a car, this atlas is also useful for those who need less information than the Rand McNally atlas provides.—**Mary Larsgaard**

International

443. **Around the World: An Atlas of Maps and Pictures.** Skokie, Ill., Rand McNally, 1994. 79p. illus. maps. index. $14.95. ISBN 0-528-83691-9.

As a slogan at the bottom of the title page—"Rand McNally for Kids"—indicates, this is an atlas intended for use by children. No indication is given as to what specific age group would find this volume of most use, but one would estimate grades 2-4. Instead of photographs, this atlas has color drawings of such items as "Harvesting Wheat," or of children of different countries, along with reproductions of national flags. This Western-focused atlas begins with North America and South America, and proceeds to Europe, Asia, Oceania, Africa, and the Poles. The Americas and Europe are represented on 57 percent of the map pages, although they cover only approximately 21 percent of the Earth's land surface. Relief is depicted in antiquated fashion, with inverted, clustered v's. For each continent or country, various statistics (e.g., area, population) are given, as is a location map (the globe, with area discussed in red). The atlas concludes with a one-page picture index and a three-page place-name index. More suited to home use than school use, it is nonetheless an attractively presented volume.—**Mary Larsgaard**

444. **Atlas of World Development.** Tim Unwin, ed. New York, John Wiley, 1995. 346p. maps. index. $79.95. ISBN 0-471-94991-4.

This interesting and well-crafted atlas—the product of several primarily British geographers and cartographers—was produced on behalf of the Developing Areas Research Group (DARG) of the Institute of British Geographers. The topical scope encompasses the geopolitics and geography of social and economic change of the developing world. The work as a whole is divided into the following six subject areas: "Definitions of Development and Historical Context"; "The Environment of Development"; "Population, Class and Education"; "Production and Exchange"; "States, Wars and Elections"; and "Images, Religion and Language." These subject areas, or chapters, are further subdivided into individual articles and maps on such varied topics as the geography of the death penalty, and plate tectonics and world development.

Outstanding black-and-white graphics make this volume lively and interesting. The fact that the maps are not in color in no way detracts from their visual appeal, and all maps and graphics effectively convey a maximum amount of information with a simplicity that is refreshing. There are a few maps/graphics that are truly unusual and, in fact, force one to look through the eyes of the developing world (for example, the "Sino-Centric 'Turnabout' Cartogram of World Population," a purposely disorienting world map on which individual countries are projected not by land area, but rather by total population, and on which the traditional north/south convention of cartographic layout is inverted). Recommended for academic libraries maintaining collections in geography and cartography, this atlas will also serve such geopolitically relevant disciplines as economics and political science.—**Mark Cyzyk**

445. Brawer, Moshe. **Atlas of Russia and the Independent Republics.** New York, Macmillan/Simon & Schuster, 1994. 144p. maps. index. $75.00. ISBN 0-13-051996-0.

This is the first atlas to examine geographical features of the former Soviet Union and the changes introduced since the collapse of the Soviet Union in 1991. It covers Russia, Ukraine, Belarus, Moldova, Georgia, Armenia, Azerbaijan, Kazakhstan, Turkmenistan, Uzbekistan, Tajikistan, and Kyrgyzstan. The coverage is region-by-region and describes national resources, climate, ethnic divisions, population density, economy, religious composition, industry, trade, agriculture, and similar topics, including brief descriptions of capitals. Maps are well integrated with the text, and there is an adequate index.

Unfortunately, there are also some deficiencies. A list of sources consulted contains a number of rather obsolete books, and occasionally provided information is not complete. For example, in an entry for Kubjovyc, the name is misspelled Kubiojovyc, and the author apparently used only the first volume of *Encyclopedia of Ukraine* (see ARBA 94, entry 138). This particular work was published in 5 volumes with Volume 5, which was issued in 1993, reflecting many changes in Ukraine. Using again Ukraine as an example, only very few major cities, primarily limited to the first map, indicate Ukrainian spelling of their names (and none of the rivers). The rest are in Russian. All in all, it is a well-executed atlas for popular consultation that has to be used with some caution.—**Bohdan S. Wynar**

446. **Cosmopolitan World Atlas.** Skokie, Ill., Rand McNally, 1994. 304p. maps. index. $70.00. ISBN 0-528-83674-9.

A recent earlier edition of the *Cosmopolitan World Atlas*, under the title *The New Cosmopolitan World Atlas*, was favorably reviewed in ARBA 95 (see entry 486). The basic maps of this new edition are the same, although there have been numerous small revisions of boundaries, names, and information. The main change is the inclusion of an extended new essay, "The Real World," by Professor Marvin W. Mikesell. This beautifully illustrated and clearly written, thoughtful essay covers the Earth as viewed from space and its terrain, climate, settlement, population, resources and industry, economic activity, environmental change, transportation, communication, and peoples and countries. This essay forms a cohesive introduction to the physical Earth and humankind's activities thereon, with illuminating detail on such topics of current interest as the complexity of distribution of ethnic groups in southeast Europe. This medium-sized atlas with maps, extended tables, and a detailed place-name index that places emphasis on country units and, in the United States, maps of states with county divisions, has a long history. The *Cosmopolitan World Atlas* continues to be an up-to-date, useful reference source. [R: WLB, Mar 95, p. 83]
—**Chauncy D. Harris**

447. **The Eyewitness Atlas of the World.** New York, Dorling Kindersley; distr., Boston, Houghton Mifflin, 1994. 160p. illus. maps. index. $24.95. ISBN 1-56458-297-3.

This is a fine basic, introductory atlas for home or school. It is organized by continents or large regions and further breaks down into countries or groups of countries on two-page spreads. Relief is well indicated by shading. Economic symbols show locations of crops, industry, tourism, and the like. Maps are surrounded by iconic illustrative matter—small photographs with brief text, highlighting cultural, economic, or historical points of note.

The introductory chapters succinctly demonstrate the great thematic characteristics of our planet. Earth's geology, landscape, climate and vegetation, population, boundaries, and astronomical position are displayed on two-page spreads. Each is a balance of small but distinctive illustrations and photographs of notable features with short commentary.

There is a helpful index map on the frontispiece as well as a gazetteer, a glossary, and a display of national flags. The book is moderately oversized at 14-by-10.5 inches. Color and printing is crisp, and the binding is sewn. The cover may be a weak feature: It appears to be made of paper that looks as if it could tear easily. In addition, there is no preface, introduction, or foreword to explain the contents or rationale. One typographical error was found: The elevation of Mt. Whitney (p. 20) is given as "1,4492 ft." For the price, however, it is an adequate learning tool. [R: BR, Jan/Feb 95, p. 59]—**Peter B. Ives**

448. **Hammond Students Atlas of the World.** Maplewood, N.J., Hammond, 1995. 52p. maps. index. ISBN 0-8437-7926-8.

A surprisingly slender compendium for so much data, this well-organized, up-to-date atlas presents a comprehensive overview of land masses, beginning with Europe and moving east around the globe to Africa and including both the north and south poles. The computer-generated maps appear in low-key colors, with each country depicted in a neutral tone and waterways in blue. The work features no colored indications of mountains. Island clusters, such as the Solomons and Northern Marianas, are clear. Paper content and size readily suit the fingers and eyes for easy management and perusal during searches of difficult terrain.

A pleasing work, this atlas attempts to keep the student in mind. Endpapers list facts and figures on seas, canals, continents, islands, the solar system, mountains, rivers, and lakes. The editors preface the text with a two-page explanation of use, including an alphabetized list of abbreviations, scales, and an unusual system of arrows that indicate how one map connects with another. From a section explaining four types of global projection, the editors move to an unappealing, artistically scrambled table of contents and symbol chart. The text opens with four pages of full-color world flags, a two-page world map, and individual land mass entries, including an inset to demonstrate position and a page detailing topography, demography, land use, and mineral resources. The atlas concludes with a limited index and three appendixes naming territories, major cities, and time zones. Overall, Hammond could increase the usability and appeal of its atlas with more extensive indexing and a bit more artistry in layout.

—**Mary Ellen Snodgrass**

449. **The New International Atlas.** 25th ed. Skokie, Ill., Rand McNally, 1994. 1v. (various paging). maps. index. $150.00. ISBN 0-528-83693-5.

This 25th edition continues Rand McNally's goal of bringing to a worldwide audience the most up-to-date, comprehensive, authoritative, and beautiful atlas possible. With international use in mind, the maps use the metric system of measurement, and local geographic names are in the local language (English is used for geographic features that cross borders) and are used as an alternate for major cities. The entire introductory section is presented in five languages—English, French, German, Portuguese, and Spanish. Country names appear in English and the local language.

Another significant feature of the *Atlas* is the classification of the maps into five series, using a limited number of map scales. Each series has a distinctive style and content. The first portrays the continents as they might appear from 4,000 miles in space; then, the major world regions maps are shown in a political style and content. The third covers nearly all inhabited areas with physical and cultural detail emphasized. The fourth portrays key regions in each continent selected for their importance, high population density, or complex development. Finally, the world's major metropolitan areas are mapped, emphasizing the complex patterns characteristic of large urban areas.

The art form called "shaded relief" is used to symbolize the Earth's terrain. The variations in shading give the maps a three-dimensional appearance, and add to their ability to provide important information as well as contribute to the unique quality of the atlas. A comprehensive glossary of geographic terms, the "World Information Table," and the index, which provides map location references, enhance the usefulness of this valuable reference source. For libraries or individuals seeking to purchase only one quality world atlas, *The New International Atlas* will be a good choice. [R: WLB, Mar 95, p. 83]

—**Susan C. Awe**

450. **PC Globe Maps'n'Facts: The Comprehensive World Atlas for the Entire Family.** [CD-ROM]. Novato, Calif., Broderbund Software, 1994. Minimum system requirements: MPC-compatible 386SX (486 recommended). Double-speed CD-ROM drive. Windows 3.1. 4MB RAM. 6MB hard disk space. Microsoft or compatible mouse. $49.95.

Maps'n'Facts, produced by Broderbund Software, is a geography reference tool for all ages that offers all the features of printed atlases and almanacs. With the click of a button, one can switch from maps to facts, see flags, or hear the country's national anthem (even though it sounds like a funeral dirge).

Data can be compared for countries, regions, or groups. Zooming in on any part of the world is a feature of this program. The user can print out maps and even create custom-made ones. Names can be searched for in the feature index; bookmarks can save one's place. *Maps'n'Facts* can remember where one is and what one is looking for to easily switch back and forth and see different views of the same subject. There are six map views available on the CD-ROM: political, physical, statistical, group, time zones, and custom. There are five ways to look at information: country profiles, city profiles, statistical charts, world rankings, and flags and anthems.

Maps and data are included for approximately 227 countries, including the newly emerging states of Eastern Europe, in addition to information on groups of countries and individual cities. Current events reflected in this program include the dissolution of the Soviet Union, the split of Czechoslovakia into the Czech Republic and Slovakia; the independence of Eritrea from Ethiopia; and the departure of Slovenia, Croatia, Macedonia, and Bosnia and Herzegovina from the Yugoslav Federation. The disc maintains entries in its database for both former countries and their successor states. These former countries include West Germany, East Germany, Czechoslovakia, Yugoslavia, and the USSR.

This program provides in-depth information that is user friendly. Compared to *The Software Toolworks World Atlas*, there is more written information. *World Atlas* does include video clips and photographs, which are not a part of the *Maps'n'Facts* program. However, for a reference tool in information gathering, the disc under review will be an important part of a CD-ROM collection of reference materials in any media center.—**Barbara B. Goldstein**

Canada

451. **Reader's Digest Atlas of Canada.** Montreal, Reader's Digest Association (Canada), 1995. 176p. maps. index. $50.00. ISBN 0-88850-248-6.

As the prosperous North American country that refrains from attempting to impose its agenda on the rest of the world, Canada is an immensely popular nation. Its images of vast spaces, impressive resources, functional cities, and strong individualism combined with social concern represent a most attractive package. Not surprisingly, a number of quality Canadian atlases have recently appeared.

This is a particularly well-produced volume that seems much in keeping with the overall quality that has characterized other Reader's Digest publications. Roughly the first half of the work is devoted to a "Portrait of the Nation" and "Facts About Canada," in which virtually every aspect of the history, geography, economy, and culture of the nation is presented, usually with the aid of photographs, tables, thematic maps, and often-imaginative graphics. The second half consists of a more conventional atlas in which the country is shown in a series of 27 maps of varying scale, followed by a section of city maps. Topography is approximated by shading, while the cultural information is quite detailed. Colors are sharply printed (although some are a bit garish), while indexes to places and physical features complete the volume. The atlas is "politically correct" in that French and English are used jointly on all maps (although the text is only in English). This is a quality atlas at a moderate price. The publishers no doubt breathed a sigh of relief on October 30, 1995, when Québec voted narrowly to remain part of Canada!
—**James R. McDonald**

China

452. Hsieh, Chiao-min, and Jean Kan Hsieh. **China: A Provincial Atlas.** New York, Macmillan/Simon & Schuster, 1995. 303p. maps. index. $125.00. ISBN 0-02-897184-1.

This hefty volume offers less than expected. Nearly half of its 303 pages are taken up with a locator index, which offers only 29 names per page with an indication of type of entity (e.g., city, county, or river); administrative category (usually a province); page of the map on which it is found; and grid. Despite the focus on provinces in the title, the first 49 pages provide national thematic maps and information on subjects such as agriculture and transportation for all of China, although mention is made of regional considerations.

The thematic general maps are striking, and for the most part, informative; however, the map and information for each province or administrative unit comprise only three or four pages. Within such limited space, descriptions necessarily run to the general. Important cities within a province receive only a sentence or two each, although plates of the largest cities are inset in provincial maps.

The provincial maps use the Hachuring cartographical method—for the first time in a U.S. publication (according to the publisher)—to provide a three-dimensional view of the topography. Unfortunately, a good number of the maps seem blurred, with many black-lettered place-names barely discernible against dark backgrounds. Moreover, the cartographical method, which is described as "most effective for small-scale maps," greatly reduces the comparative use of the plates. Only with familiarity of the topography can the user discern that Tibet (the Xizang Autonomous Region) is far higher and more rugged than a province such as Fujian. Exhibiting political correctness acceptable to both the mainland and Taiwan governments, Tibet and Taiwan are treated like other provinces. Despite these many shortcomings, this work must be recommended as illuminating the regional and provincial bases of the nation, which are often obscured in national atlases.—**K. Mulliner**

Bibliography

453. **World Databases in Geography and Geology.** C. J. Armstrong, ed. New Providence, N.J., Bowker-Saur/Reed Reference Publishing, 1995. 1255p. index. (World Databases Series). $195.00. ISBN 1-85739-111-X.

An inevitable escalation in the information revolution the world is experiencing is the "database of databases." The amount of information has grown so rapidly that people now need guides to the guides to the information. This massive book is two distinct database directories (Geography and Geology) with a single comprehensive set of indexes.

The organization of all this data is remarkable. The two directories are divided into primary subjects (cartography, regional studies, demography, mineralogy, mining, and so on), and then within each subject, the major databases are listed in what is called a "family tree" structure of "parent" databases and "spin-offs." Each listing includes the usual library data, thorough descriptions, and often brief reviews and references to fuller reviews. The directories are thus more than just tables of data and addresses—they provide initial evaluations for librarians and researchers. Each item has a unique reference number in a decimal system, making it easy to move from the indexes to the listing details. The index even contains miniature icons of the database media (online, CD-ROM, disk, tape, videotex, fax, and so forth).

The editor was liberal in the definition of what databases to list in the directories. Many other sources often neglect, for example, to include items such as the *Zoological Record* in a geology database, assuming only biologists would be interested. This editor knew that paleontologists use this source often, along with other biological databases. Geographers have an even greater variety of databases to search, from land-use surveys to disease demographics.

The only significant criticism of the book is its combination of the geography directory with the geology directory. They seem an obvious pair to all but geographers and geologists. There are some important overlaps between the two disciplines (maps and aerial photographs, for instance), but most of the material in one directory will be of no use to those using the other. "Immunization Demographic Data" is unlikely to be used by geologists, and geographers probably have little need for paleontology databases.—**Mark A. Wilson**

Biography

454. Saari, Peggy, and Daniel B. Baker. **Explorers & Discoverers: From Alexander the Great to Sally Ride.** Detroit, U*X*L/Gale, 1995. 4v. illus. maps. index. $76.00/set. ISBN 0-8103-9787-8.

This series breaks former molds of the stodgy reference book by offering young researchers a cornucopia of information in an attractive, vigorous worldview of exploration and discovery. A simple but exacting preface explains the authors' working method—a study of lives and times, including women and non-European adventurers whom former histories have passed over. A single sentence expresses to the user a researcher's most valuable tool—an inquiring attitude toward who, when, and how alongside why and what consequences resulted. Following the introduction and picture credits are rather spare maps devoid of the minutiae that often mar or obscure cartography in adult reference works.

Similar in style and scope to U*X*L's *Performing Artists* series (see entry 1363), this attractive work summarizes lives and expeditions along with black-and-white photographs, line drawings, portraits, and sidebars. For example, the entry on Abu Abdallah Ibn Battutah cites a significant issue of the Middle Ages—the influence of bubonic plague on travelers, city officials, and whole nations devastated by the disease. Each volume concludes with a timeline by global regions, explorers by country of origin, and an index of minor and major figures, with the most important appearing in boldface. Along with the *de rigueur* Marco Polo, Jacques Cousteau, and Captain Cook, U*X*L juxtaposes the flight of Beryl Markham, Will Steger's study of the North Pole, and Herodotus, who became the father of history. For no obvious reason, certain prominent travelers receive no mention, notably Margaret Mead, Heinrich Schliemann, and Louis S. B. and Mary Leakey. Detailed views of Christopher Columbus's landfalls in the Caribbean and the shape and record of *Sputnik I* fill in many gaps for a generation still learning that exploration has always been a global project.—**Mary Ellen Snodgrass**

Dictionaries and Encyclopedias

455. Biger, Gideon, with the International Boundaries Research Unit. **The Encyclopedia of International Boundaries.** New York, Facts on File, 1995. 543p. illus. maps. index. $125.00. ISBN 0-8160-3233-5.

National boundaries are as much integral parts of the world as economic policies and political leaders. This new reference encyclopedia combines the history, politics, economics, and military aspects of international borders. Arranged in an alphabetical format listing two nations with boundaries in dispute (e.g., Canada-United States), the individual entries focus on geography, history, and the present border situation. The information is accurate and presented in a straightforward, well-written style. Included are contemporary border disputes between nations (e.g., Iraq-Kuwait). Excluded are boundary conflicts within nations, such as provinces or states, and maritime disputes.

Other features include cross-references, a brief glossary and bibliography, a list of maps, and several useful indexes. Worth mentioning are indexes by treaty, boundary lakes, rivers, and mountain ranges. This reviewer would have preferred a greater use of maps, which are most useful accompanying the text, and fewer photographs, which add virtually nothing to the volume. In addition to 16 pages of black-and-white photographs, useless pictures such as the Greek-Macedonian border are scattered throughout. Overall, however, the authors are to be applauded for an innovative, timely, useful, and handsome reference work.—**Boyd Childress**

456. **World Geographical Encyclopedia.** English Language ed. Sybil P. Parker, ed. New York, McGraw-Hill, 1995. 5v. illus. maps. index. $500.00/set. ISBN 0-07-911496-2.

This major encyclopedia was originally published in Italy as *Enciclopedia Geografica Universale* in 1994, with an Italian board of editors and a list of international scholars as contributors. It has been felicitously translated into English. The first volume, covering Africa, is arranged with an introduction and an overview of the continent as a whole, including natural environment, geological structure and relief, climate, hydrography, flora and fauna, population, economic summary, and history and culture. Then the various parts of the continent are considered, region by region, with information about the countries within the region. Each country entry visually locates the country within an outline map of the continent and has a depiction of the national flag in color, followed by "Geopolitical Summary" of pertinent facts. Next, more extensive physical, political, economic, and cultural geographical information is provided.

A major feature of this encyclopedia is the 750 color photographs that embellish the text and help the reader envision the areas discussed. The format used in the African volume is followed in the other volumes which cover the Americas, Asia, Europe, and Oceania, in that order. At the back of each volume there is a section of colored maps with explanatory text entitled "Great Routes and Voyages of Discovery." Volume 5 has a 45-page section on general geography, with colored maps and diagrams; a section of world statistics; a lexicon; a works cited list that is international in scope and ranges from the sixteenth century into the late 1980s; and a 32-page, 5-columns-per-page index of names. There is no subject index or cross-references, which might impede access to information. The encyclopedia considers the recent major political changes in the world and is as up-to-date as possible.—**Frank J. Anderson**

Handbooks and Yearbooks

457. **Geography on File.** 1995 ed. New York, Facts on File, 1995. 1v. (various paging). illus. maps. index. $155.00 looseleaf w/binder. ISBN 0-8160-3172-X.

The 1995 edition of *Geography on File* updates the 1992 edition (see ARBA 92, entry 401). It includes a chapter specifically on the Commonwealth of Independent States (the former Soviet Union) and other new maps and charts that reflect worldwide demographic shifts. There are more than 250 maps, charts, and graphs divided into two principal sections—the first contains graphics suitable to support the study of basic geographical topics such as climate, topography, people, economy, and resources; the second covers the major geographical regions.

These copyright-free maps, charts, and graphs feature concise captions and crisp, easy-to-read print. Individual regional maps cover political boundaries, major geographical features, major cities, climate, railroads, population distribution, languages, agricultural and industrial areas, products manufactured, natural resources, and similar topics intended to support units of study. The sturdy paper, looseleaf binding, informative table of contents, and indexing make this a suitable work for all school, public, and academic libraries. Updates, with a new cumulative index, are available annually.—**Vandelia L. VanMeter**

458. **Masterworks of Man & Nature.** 2d ed. New York, Facts on File, 1994. 400p. illus. index. $35.00. ISBN 0-8160-3177-0.

This armchair tour of 400 natural and cultural sites throughout the world that are worthy of preservation is a visual delight. Frederico Mayor, director general of UNESCO, sums up the mission of this book—to "increase awareness of the urgent need to save the 1,001 natural and cultural beauties of our planet which we hold in trust for future generations" (p. 7). The work is a joint venture of the World Heritage Committee of UNESCO and the World Conservation Union. It visualizes the most beautiful sites in our world, including natural as well as human-made. These wonders have been a source of inspiration throughout the generations. The authors discuss the fragility of these places and the efforts being made to preserve them for our children's children. Vice President Al Gore states that environmental threats are just as dangerous as a nuclear threat.

The sites are arranged alphabetically by their country name within their region. Each site has a glossy, sumptuous color photograph, a description of the location including latitude and longitude, a brief detailing of the site, and a description of the site's larger significance as a masterwork. It also includes essays by scholars and world leaders encouraging conservation and preservation of these historic sites. Well-known locations such as the Great Wall of China and the Taj Mahal are described, as well as lesser-known places such as the Old City of Dubrovnik in Croatia. Country names are up-to-date, as in Uzbekistan and Benin. Maps of the sites with political boundaries would have been useful for students. A glossary, an index, and a table of contents make it accessible to report writers. The eye-appealing format encourages the reader to jump around from country to country.—**Sandra L. Doggett**

459. **Middle East and North Africa on File.** New York, Facts on File, 1995. 1v. (various paging). maps. index. $155.00 looseleaf w/binder. ISBN 0-8160-3106-1.

This looseleaf publication covers all the nations and territories of North Africa and the Middle East, including the Western Sahara, Cyprus, and the Israeli-occupied territories of the Gaza Strip, Golan Heights, and the West Bank as separate entities. In addition, it contains a section of maps dealing with contemporary regional issues such as boundary disputes, the Kurds, the Palestinians, Islam, suffrage, water use, oil exports, and so forth. Each of the national entries contains maps; basic facts (e.g., capital, total area, climate, head of state); a brief chronology of important events; statistical charts and maps for demographics and economics; and a cultural synopsis and overview of everyday life. Also appended is a brief, two-page bibliography of reference sources for the Middle East and North Africa, and an index.

This work is obviously intended for a student audience, probably high school and middle school as well as teachers of those age groups, and is designed for use along with the publisher's *Maps on File* (annual updates) and *Geography on File* (see entry 457). It comes with its own "reproduction certificate" that authorizes photocopying of any of its materials by and for nonprofit and educational organizations, or for private use. In middle or high school libraries, it should serve as a ready-reference, an easy place to start a student paper, or to provide handout materials for teachers, and should come in quite handy with its more than 300 maps and diagrams. Larger libraries, with any sort of collection of Middle East materials, may find this convenient but redundant.—**Paul H. Thomas**

TRAVEL GUIDES
General Works
Handbooks and Yearbooks

460. **Adventure Holidays 1995.** 18th ed. Victoria Pybus and Caroline Ingram, eds. Oxford, England, Vacation Work; distr., Princeton, N.J., Peterson's Guides, 1995. 223p. illus. maps. index. $12.95pa. ISBN 1-85458-128-7. ISSN 0143-389X.

This vacation planner is published by a British company, Vacation Work, and distributed by Peterson's Guides in the United States. The guide advertises "adventure and special interest holidays for independent holidaymakers" (p. 5). That is, the compilation is meant to offer adventurous travelers unusual and active vacation tours, as antidotes to traditional packaged tours and beach vacation routines.

The information is assembled for a British audience; thus, most of the holidays described, and the companies who sell them, are located in the British Isles. There are other, although fewer, listings for each type of adventure covered in Africa, Asia, Europe, the Americas, and Australasia. Prices for almost all the tours are quoted in British currency (pounds). A few U.S.-based businesses that sell adventure tours in the United States are included.

American vacationers and travelers may not consider all of these activities wildly adventurous—although Murder and Mystery Weekends, or Montana's Cattle Moovers [sic] are unusual ways to spend summer vacation. Many Americans may wonder what is so adventurous about canoeing, motorcycling, or bird watching. However, the book does offer listings of many uncommon pleasures: parascending, snowboarding, survival courses, historical re-creation, camel caravanning, Arctic exploration, and botanical safaris. Some listings are for women only, for kids only, or even for those who cannot bear to leave work: "Specialist Activities" lists management training courses.

Outside of the British Isles, coverage is spotty. For example, the surfing holidays are limited to England, Scotland, Ireland, Wales, and Europe. What, no Australia, Costa Rica, California, or Hawaii? *Adventure Holidays 1995* is ideal for planning outdoor adventures in, or from, Great Britain.
—**JoAnn Balingit**

461. Hawks, John K. **Career Opportunities in Travel and Tourism.** New York, Facts on File, 1995. 212p. index. $27.95. ISBN 0-8160-3036-7.

Those seeking information on professions often need to go beyond the *Occupational Outlook Handbook* (see ARBA 94, entry 281, and ARBA 91, entry 249) for more detailed descriptions about work life. This specialty volume offers in-depth information about positions in any phase of the travel industry, such as travel agent, hotelier, tourism director, casino croupier, or airport manager. The header of each job profile notes general duties; salary ranges; employment prospects (from poor to excellent); and education, training, experience, personality traits, or special skills that are expected of an applicant. Next follows expanded details (usually two to three pages) of general job duties and of the segments listed above. The "Tips for Entry" give positive ideas to assist those who want to plan their career, and there is even a suggested career ladder showing a typical pattern others may have used to prepare for the job being highlighted.

The index is helpful, but has a few oddities. For example, the job title "purser" has no entry; it is under "chief purser," with no cross-reference. On the other hand, the entry under "salary range" provides a handy list of jobs grouped by general salary expectations. The five appendixes list college programs in travel and tourism (certificates, diplomas, or associate degrees) arranged by state; trade associations and unions, major national travel employers (travel agencies, car rental firms, cruise lines, theme parks, hotel chains); travel recruiting and placement firms; and a classified bibliography of books and travel-interest periodical titles. The specific content of travel entries is similar to those in *Career Information Center* (Macmillan, 1992), although entries are not as in-depth as those in the *Encyclopedia of Careers and Vocational Guidance* (see entry 382 for a review of the CD-ROM edition), the work as a whole is handier and much better organized. It is suitable for public, school, and community college libraries.

—Gary R. Cocozzoli

462. Shirk, Martha, and Nancy Klepper. **Super Family Vacations.** 3d ed. New York, HarperCollins, 1995. 440p. index. $15.00pa. ISBN 0-06-273330-3.

Like clockwork, families plan vacations each year, and just as regular are the publications of travel books—outlining trips, sights, and expenses. Predictably, *Super Family Vacations* is no exception. Rather expensive for a paperback, the book is divided into seven general categories—resorts, guest ranches, ski areas, historical sites, cruises, adventure trips, and natural settings. Following introductory remarks and an outline for planning family vacations, each of the categories is divided into a variety of destinations designed to provide a broad range of activities and attractions, arranged geographically. Each entry includes general information, a guide to accommodations and dining, an outline of activities, children's attractions, nearby sites of interest, and price range indicators. Locations are in North America and the Caribbean, and two indexes provide ample, although not extensive, access points.

A typical entry is the five pages devoted to Colonial Williamsburg. The history of the town and community and Rockefeller involvement in restoration precedes brief information on accommodations and dining, followed by a list of activities, separate activities for children, and nearby sites such as Jamestown, Yorktown, and Busch Gardens. Typically, several telephone contacts are provided for additional information. The lack of more exact price information is a cause for concern. For example, no mention of the range of ticket prices to the restored village is given, which should be a concern for all travelers. This, and other bits and pieces of information, are available in sources in most libraries. Although an interesting mix of ways and means of travel and tourism, this is one on which most librarians can pass.—**Boyd Childress**

463. **Yearbook of Tourism Statistics. Annuaire des Statistiques du Tourisme. Anuario de Estadisticas del Turismo.** 46th ed. Madrid, World Tourism Organization; distr., Lanham, Md., UNIPUB, 1994. 2v. $125.00pa/set. ISBN 92-844-0078. ISSN 1001-8977.

This trilingual two-volume publication of the World Tourism Organization (WTO) is the best source of international tourism statistics in the world. Volume 1 is topical and regional; volume 2 contains country statistics. The former provides data on tourist arrivals and receipts starting from world level, then on continental level, and then according to various groupings of countries, such as World Bank classification, level of economic development, and Organization for Economic Cooperation and Development members. Interesting are tables on world top destinations, earners, and spenders. Data for receipts per tourist are also provided. The rest of the volume is devoted to regional summaries (Africa, Americas, East Asia/Pacific, Europe, Middle East, and South Asia).

Volume 2 presents tourist statistics according to countries in alphabetical order of their English names. The tables contain six groupings: arrivals of tourists (leisure and business tourists spending at least one night in a foreign country); arrivals of visitors (tourists and excursionists or day-visitors); arrivals in hotels and similar establishments; arrivals in all accommodation establishments; nights in hotels and similar establishments; and nights in all accommodation establishments. Technical notes are appended to the first volume and contain a number of imperfections that cannot be discussed here in detail (e.g., Zambia and Zimbabwe in eastern Africa, Israel and Turkey in Europe). The World Bank classification of economies is in need of updating. In addition, the inadequacies of world tourism statistics, resulting from differences of definitions and data collection methodology, are insufficiently explained, although a reference to a relevant 1985 publication is made. The market for the yearbook is wide: Virtually everyone who deals with international tourism should be interested.—**Zbigniew Mieczkowski**

International Travel

464. Herbote, Burkhard. **World Tourism Directory '95/96. Part 1: Europe.** 3d ed. New Providence, N.J., K. G. Saur/Reed Reference Publishing, 1995. 579p. $325.00/set; $140.00/v. ISBN 3-598-11181-9/set; 3-598-11202-5/v.

465. Herbote, Burkhard, and Marian Goldberg. **World Tourism Directory '95/96. Part 2: The Americas.** 3d ed. New Providence, N.J., K. G. Saur/Reed Reference Publishing, 1995. 660p. $325.00/set; $140.00/v. ISBN 3-598-11181-9/set; 3-598-11203-3/v.

466. Herbote, Burkhard. **World Tourism Directory '95/96. Part 3: Africa, Middle East, Asia, and Oceania.** 3d ed. New Providence, N.J., K. G. Saur/Reed Reference Publishing, 1995. 706p. $325.00/set; $140.00/v. ISBN 3-598-11181-9/set; 3-598-11204-1/v.

It would be difficult, if not impossible, to locate a more comprehensive resource to travel in the world than this multivolume resource directory. The directory lists 63,000 addresses of tourist contacts for 330 countries. In the process of reading the directory, one learns that tourism is the world's largest industry and continues to experience an economic growth rate surpassing any other sector of the global economy. This expansive resource consists of three volumes, covering Europe; the Americas; and Africa, the Middle East, Asia, and Oceania, respectively. Each volume lists countries alphabetically. The country entries contain information about government tourism agencies; tourism schools; tourism associations; air, rail, bus, land, and ferry transportation information; noteworthy recreational activity contacts such as national parks and sports and conservation associations; travel publications and travel bookstores; immigration and customs authorities; Chambers of Commerce, especially in the U.S. entries; regional and local tourism information offices; embassies and consulates; and miscellaneous information that may include trade, investment, and development contacts. Individual listings include name, address, telephone, and fax and telex numbers.

Virtually no area of the world is omitted. For example, in part 2 (*The Americas*), the reader discovers an amazing breadth of contacts for travel in Antarctica. The International Antarctic Centre is in Christchurch, New Zealand, and additional travel information contacts may be made in Argentina and through Falkland Islands Tourism. Travel operators may be located in Florida, Washington, New York, Argentina, Germany, Great Britain, and the Netherlands. A host of governmental and private agencies provide research data, magazines, maps, and additional information about Antarctica. In part 3 (*Africa, Middle East, Asia, and Oceania*), a traveler wishing to learn more about Zambia can send a fax to the Ministry of Tourism in Lusaka, telephone more than 20 tour operators, or make reservations through Zambia Airlines at 25 different sites. Contacts for hunting, fishing, and canoeing information in Zambia are provided, as are consulate addresses and information relative to the Zambian Ornithological Society. The information found in the *World Tourism Directory '95/96* is thorough, well arranged, and easily located. [R: RQ, Summer 95, p. 470}—**Jerry D. Flack**

467. **International Dictionary of Historic Places. Volume 1: Americas.** Trudy Ring, Robert M. Salkin, and Sharon La Boda, eds. Chicago, Fitzroy Dearborn, 1995. 804p. illus. index. $125.00/v. ISBN 1-884964-00-1.

468. **International Dictionary of Historic Places. Volume 2: Northern Europe.** Trudy Ring, Robert M. Salkin, and Sharon La Boda, eds. Chicago, Fitzroy Dearborn, 1995. 860p. illus. index. $125.00/v. ISBN 1-884964-01-X.

469. **International Dictionary of Historic Places. Volume 3: Southern Europe.** Trudy Ring, Robert M. Salkin, and Sharon La Boda, eds. Chicago, Fitzroy Dearborn, 1995. 818p. illus. index. $125.00/v. ISBN 1-884964-02-8.

Here are the first three volumes of a projected five-volume set. (Volume 4 will cover the Middle East and Africa; volume 5 will cover Asia and Oceania.) When completed, the set will provide information on nearly 1,000 sites of historical interest that have been preserved or restored and are accessible to the public.

Each article contains a three- to five-page essay relating the historical events that occurred on or near the site, their significance, and information about what the site offers to contemporary visitors. Each article is accompanied by one or two black-and-white photographs, and a headnote with locational data, a brief description of the site, and addresses and telephone numbers of site headquarters or other information sources. Suggestions for further reading are given in short critical notes.

Within each regional volume, entries are arranged alphabetically by name of site location (sometimes under the name of the city where the site is located; e.g., there are six entries each for New York, Rome, and London). A detailed keyword index in each volume helps to locate information. Information has been compiled from such publicly available sources as material supplied by the site offices. Authors, who may be responsible for one or more essays, are likely to be freelance writers or journalists (few academics are represented). A sampling of essays on sites familiar to this reviewer indicates that they are predominantly given over to historical narrative: Relatively little space is devoted to describing the sites as they are today. The essays are accurate, readable, and accessible to an adult or high school audience.

Arrangement is not entirely consistent: The essay on Lexington-Concord is filed under Boston, while Harvard Square, a subway ride from Boston, is filed under Cambridge. No articles are listed for Lisbon, but the index reveals two separate essays about sites within easy reach of Lisbon. The essays basically stand alone, and there is no linkage between sites. The only help provided for planning a travel itinerary are the maps on the inside covers of each volume.

General encyclopedias and historical dictionaries cover much of the same ground, but not in such depth. Approximately 70 percent (131 of 187 sites) in volume 1 are in the United States, including, but not restricted to, many listed in the *National Register of Historic Places* (2d ed., Preservation Press, 1994). Public and academic libraries can purchase individual volumes as needed. They will be useful for student papers or inquiries about historical places or events.—**Jonathan F. Husband**

United States

470. **Exploring Our National Parks and Monuments.** 9th ed. By Devereux Butcher; revised by Russell D. Butcher. Washington, D.C., National Parks and Conservation Association and Boulder, Colo., Roberts Rinehart, 1995. 477p. illus. index. $16.95pa. ISBN 1-57098-025-X.

Russell Butcher, taking over for his father Devereux, has completely redone this edition of *Exploring Our National Parks and Monuments*, the first revision since 1985. Many new areas are included, reflecting the system's growth. Older articles have been rewritten, but all still concentrate on the geological and natural history aspects of the areas. Some of the black-and-white photographs are new, and a helpful feature puts travel directions and brief facilities information in a gray highlighted box.

The table of contents has been redone to reflect the increasing size and diversity of the system, dividing the areas covered into national parks, monuments (both natural and archaeological), historical parks, preserves, seashores and lakeshores, rivers and riverways, recreational areas, and trails. New sections have been added on the presence of Native Americans, sites for future parks and monuments, and the history of the National Parks and Conservation Association. The essay on threats to the natural environment has been totally revised and expanded to discuss new or aggravated problems such as geothermal drilling in Yellowstone, the *Exxon Valdez* oil spill that impacted Katmai and Kenai Fjords, and noise pollution from snowmobiles at both Acadia and Voyageurs Parks.

This is not the book for someone who needs to know hotel accommodations, the number of campsites available, or the names and routes of specific trails. Butcher speaks to the traveler who wants to know why certain areas of the United States were deemed important enough to protect—what they can teach him or her about the natural landscape and its history—and why, of course, these special places must remain as pristine as they are. Once the need to visit these spectacular places has been created, other, more specialized guidebooks can be consulted. Butcher's book is a wonderful place to begin any exploration of the natural United States.—**Deborah Hammer**

471. **Fodor's Great American Vacations for Travelers with Disabilities.** New York, Fodor's Travel Publications, 1994. 600p. maps. $18.00pa. ISBN 0-679-02591-X.

Permanent and artificial barriers can limit travel opportunities for individuals with disabilities. As U.S. federal and state governments continue to provide employment opportunities and job protection for the disabled, consumer institutions have paralleled these developments by adapting facilities for the vision, hearing, and movement impaired. Fodor's, long the established leader in travel books, has produced a convenient one-volume vacation guide for persons with disabilities.

The book documents 39 vacation destinations, either cities or areas/regions (e.g., the Maine Coast, the Lincoln Trail, North Carolina's Outer Banks). Each site receives thorough attention (Savannah, Georgia, for example, is accorded 11 pages), and coverage includes accommodations, restaurants, and attractions—all focusing on facilities for the disabled. For each location, a brief description is followed by travel information and advice on what time of the year to go; how to get there; and various attractions and activities, ranging from parks and museums to shopping, sports, and entertainment. A list of lodging and dining facilities completes most entries. When relevant, symbols for mobility, hearing, and vision accessibility are indicated, as is other pertinent information for travelers with disabilities. Telephone Device for the Deaf (TDD) (now known as TDY) numbers are provided when available. This guide, containing precise travel information, is highly recommended for reference collections in public and academic libraries as well as for travel agents and tour-booking agencies. [R: BL, 15 Mar 95, p. 1347]—**Boyd Childress**

472. Gordon, William A. **Shot on This Site: A Traveler's Guide....** New York, Citadel Press/Carol Publishing Group, 1995. 274p. illus. index. $14.95pa. ISBN 0-8065-1647-X.

If people cannot visit their favorite stars, at least they can visit the buildings, sites, and locations where the stars filmed favorite movies or television series (e.g., Yuma's Algonbones Sand Dunes [*Return of the Jedi* and *Stargate*], Blair House Inn [*Murder, She Wrote*], Oregon's Timberline Lodge [*The Shining*], Boston's Bull & Finch Pub [*Cheers*], and numerous places in New York City, San Francisco, Seattle, and Utah). Sites in 48 of the 50 states are covered—there appears to be no referenced places in Idaho and North Dakota.

This volume reveals where approximately 900 movies and 90 television series were filmed. Gordon notes that this is not an all-inclusive or definitive guide—as no one book could realistically cover the tens of thousands of films released in the United States alone—so he has concentrated on box office favorites released over the past 15 years and a few pre-1980 classics. Chosen sites had to be accessible or at least visible, if not open to the public. The guide is arranged geographically and is up-to-date, as many 1995 releases are included. The three indexes, by film, name, and television program, are helpful. This volume is a fun, informative travel guide for tourists, travelers, and film buffs.—**Joy Hastings**

473. Ocko, Stephanie. **Adventure Vacations: A 50 State Guide....** New York, Citadel Press/Carol Publishing Group, 1995. 286p. illus. index. $14.95pa. ISBN 0-8065-1632-1.

This 50-state guide to adventure will appeal to anyone looking for outdoor excitement, escape, or discovery in the United States. Covering a wide diversity of activities, such as airship adventures, bird watching, cooking, house building, mountaineering, and windsurfing, this source will provide ideas on getting away from the rat race and doing something truly exciting, educational, risky, or just plain fun. The author admits this is not a complete list of all that is available in the world of adventure, but she tries to provide something for everyone.

Entries are arranged alphabetically and provide background on the particular adventure and who to contact. Some entries furnish insight into activities that have an element of risk, while others give brief but interesting historical background on unique places one can visit. The appendix gives insurance and safety tips, telephone numbers for state tourism offices, and how to obtain maps to plan adventures. The alphabetical index provides access to the fun and adventure just waiting to be found by the explorer in everyone. This informative guide would be a worthwhile addition to any public library.—**Diane J. Turner**

474. Wiggers, Raymond. **The Plant Explorer's Guide to New England.** Missoula, Mont., Mountain Press Publishing, 1994. 601p. illus. maps. index. $18.00pa. ISBN 0-87842-306-0.

Wiggers is a former New England resident, trained in geology, botany, and horticulture. In this paperback book he has illustrated and written narratives for 54 walking and driving tours throughout New England, from Maine to Connecticut. Each chapter features a map, the estimated tour driving distance, and a starting point. Tour highlights open each chapter; unexceptionally reproduced black-and-white photographs break up the text every couple of pages. A combined annotated bibliography and recommended readings list includes a wide range of texts in such fields as geology and botany. A thorough index, with entries for illustrations and italicized captions, completes the book.

The author knows his material and cogently shares information. This reviewer enjoyed the ongoing references to Henry David Thoreau and Ralph Waldo Emerson, as well as other New England literati. Other readers could find such diversions irrelevant. The theme of the book is scarcely more plant information than travel guide; buyers should be aware that there is as much scenic description here as scientific discourse. This guide is recommended for only the deepest botanical and travel collections.—**Ed Volz**

475. Wolverton, Ruthe, and Walt Wolverton. **The National Seashores: The Complete Guide to America's Scenic Coastal Parks.** rev. ed. Niwot, Colo., Roberts Rinehart, 1994. 287p. illus. maps. index. $13.95pa. ISBN 1-879373-86-6.

Much is heard about our National Parks, but little is heard about our National Seashores, which stretch along the East Coast from Massachusetts to Florida, around to the Gulf Coast, with one on the West Coast. *The National Seashores*, revised from its 1988 printing, will supply information on these national treasures, explaining the unique features of these unspoiled areas.

General information includes how the National Seashores were started and a full description of what a beach is. Each National Seashore has an entry that provides a history of the area, directions to the site, and what to expect upon arrival. The "Where to Stay" section gives broad information about motels and camping facilities, mainly of the "contact the Chamber of Commerce" type. Specifics are provided for park-run facilities, and a directory of further contacts is listed. The beaches, trails, wildlife, and historic points are all dealt with, as well as a brief look at regulations concerning what activities are allowed in the park. A checklist compares all the parks and their activities, making it easy to find which ones allow specific activities. There is a reading list for those who wish to learn more about a particular area. The index provides basic access, but lacks cross-references, and occasionally suffers from poor term selection.—**Angela Marie Thor**

Europe

General Works

476. **Amsterdam.** By Robin Pascoe and Christopher Catling. New York, Dorling Kindersley, 1995. 312p. illus. maps. index. (Eyewitness Travel Guides). $22.95. ISBN 0-7894-0186-X.

477. **Provence & the Côte D'Azur.** By Roger Williams. New York, Dorling Kindersley, 1995. 264p. illus. maps. index. (Eyewitness Travel Guides). $22.95. ISBN 1-56458-860-2.

478. **Venice & the Veneto.** By Susie Boulton and Christopher Catling. New York, Dorling Kindersley, 1995. 312p. illus. maps. index. (Eyewitness Travel Guides). $22.95. ISBN 1-56458-861-0.

479. **Vienna.** By Stephen Brook. New York, Dorling Kindersley, 1994. 288p. illus. maps. index. (Eyewitness Travel Guides). $22.95. ISBN 1-56458-647-2.

There are thousands of traveling guides on the market. Most librarians are used to such standard names as the French *Guides Bleues*, the Baedeker series, Nagel's travel guides, Fodor's travel guides, more inexpensive Frommer or Mobil guides, and many others. Dorling Kindersley started distributing travel guides in the United States two or three years ago; most of them were not reviewed in ARBA and are not very well known. Editorial work is conducted in Great Britain, and the guides are printed and bound in Italy. Illustrations are executed in Italy and Singapore. All aspects of the text and the illustrations are well done.

The structure of the text is similar in all volumes. For example, the description of Venice starts with a brief historical introduction, including statistics and well-executed illustrations and maps. Introductory remarks take some 50 pages, and this is followed by a detailed description of Venice area by area (e.g., "A View from the Grand Canal," "San Marco," "San Polo and Santa Croce," "Castello," "Dorsoduro,"

"Cannaregio," and "The Lagoon Islands"). Similar treatment is found for Veneto, with concluding chapters entitled "Travelers' Needs" (hotels, restaurants, shops, entertainment, and the like). Also included are a section called "Survival Guide" (practical travel information), a general index, and a small but helpful phrase book. It is well executed, and the text is very readable. The illustrations, all in color, are superb.

While in Venice last summer, this reviewer used this guide successfully, especially covering the territory region by region. One feature of those guides is, in this reviewer's opinion, very good: One can walk street by street in a city and have no problems in finding a desired item. Information is reliable and up-to-date. Everyone has his or her preferences, and this reviewer would give an "A" to Eyewitness Travel Guides and only a "B+" to Baedeker or Fodor's. The guides under review are recommended for all public and some university libraries.—**Bohdan S. Wynar**

480. **Great Britain.** By Michael Leapman. New York, Dorling Kindersley, 1995. 672p. illus. maps. index. (Eyewitness Travel Guides) $29.95. ISBN 0-7894-0187-8.

481. **Ireland.** By Lisa Gerard-Sharp and Tim Perry. New York, Dorling Kindersley, 1995. 384p. illus. maps. index. (Eyewitness Travel Guides). $24.95. ISBN 0-7894-0188-6.

The volume on Great Britain covers in some detail information on London (more than 140 pages of general information on England plus London) and covers in separate chapters Southeast England, the West Country, the Midlands, and Scotland. Chapters on travelers' needs (hotels, restaurants, shops, and so forth) and a "Survival Guide" with useful, general travel information conclude this volume. Information on Ireland is similarly structured. Both volumes are very useful companions to many visitors of this beautiful part of Europe. (See entries 476-499 for reviews of other volumes in this series.)

—**Bohdan S. Wynar**

Ireland

482. Sullivan, Frank, and Fran Sullivan. **The Irish Bed & Breakfast Book: Country and Tourist Homes, Farms, Guesthouses, Inns.** Gretna, La., Pelican Publishing, 1994. 182p. illus. maps. index. $12.95pa. ISBN 1-56554-034-4.

The Irish Bed & Breakfast Book is a list of some 100 inns, farmhouses, guesthouses, and tourist homes in Ireland. Arranged by county, it provides both basic information and a more subjective assessment of each establishment. The former includes name, address, and telephone number of the bed-and-breakfast; its size; the number of bedrooms; bathroom facilities available (e.g., private or shared, shower or tub only); daily rates; whether or not smoking is allowed; and whether there is access for the handicapped. Since these are small family-run establishments, the Sullivans include information on the family itself: how many children the proprietors have and whether there are pets.

Most guidebooks give such information. The Sullivans also give more impressionistic information: what attractions are near enough to visit; a description of the house and grounds; and special features of the house, such as the availability of musical instruments for the guests' use or of a library of tourist information. Descriptions of the breakfasts are particularly appealing and helpful when deciding where to stay. Does one want a typical Irish breakfast, with homemade scones and black-and-white pudding, or a more continental one, with cereal, cheese, yogurt, and fruit? Or how about "a trolley of apricots, grapefruit, and mandarin oranges, fresh fluffy scones, and home-baked currant bread"?

Small and light in weight, this is a book to take with you when you travel. With it, you can plan your trip a day or two at a time, ringing ahead to reserve a room at the perfect guesthouse. Libraries with extensive travel collections will want to add this, but be prepared to have it checked out all the time.

—**Terry Ann Mood**

Latin America and the Caribbean

483. **Frommer's Comprehensive Travel Guide: Caribbean '95.** By Darwin Porter and Danforth Prince. New York, Prentice Hall General Reference/Simon & Schuster, 1994. 708p. maps. index. $18.00pa. ISBN 0-671-88480-8. ISSN 1044-2375.

Frommer's Comprehensive Travel Guides are well known to tourists, and most public libraries will acquire them from time to time. They were reviewed in ARBA several times, and there is no need to repeat the same comments again. Most volumes are reviewed on an annual basis; they contain black-and-white maps but no illustrations. The present volume covers 12 groups of islands. If one wants to know more about Puerto Rico or Jamaica, this author would recommend the use of more specialized guides. It should be noted that bulk purchases of Frommer's Comprehensive Travel Guides carry special discounts, depending on the quantity, and can be purchased with special imprints or logos. Many corporations use them for promotional purposes.—**Bohdan S. Wynar**

9 History

ARCHAEOLOGY

484. Bybee, Howard C., and Conrad L'Heureux. **Bibliography of Syrian Archaeological Sites to 1980.** Lewiston, N.Y., Edwin Mellen Press, 1995. 236p. index. $89.95. ISBN 0-7734-9040-X.

Boasting the world's two oldest cities of continuous habitation—Aleppo, known to the ancients as Halab, and Damascus, cited often in the Bible—Syria is an archaeological treasure trove. It affords an opportunity to survey human development from prehistoric times to the present. Also adding to Syria's appeal is the richness of its history. Situated astride important commercial routes between Egypt and Mesopotamia, Syria was drawn unavoidably into the political and military struggles of greater powers. The ancient Assyrians, Babylonians, Egyptians, Hittites, Mitannians, and Canaanites, and later the Greeks and Romans, all traversed the region. In light of its past, it is easy to appreciate that there are currently more than 50 ongoing excavation sites in Syria, and Syrian authorities are supportive of such scholarly efforts.

This bibliography will be of value primarily to scholars. It contains 2,000-plus entries, mostly in French, with a sensible arrangement. Part 1, comprising about two-thirds of the study, is an alphabetical listing of archaeological sites, and subsumed under each is an alphabetical inventory of the literature on that site. Part 2 tabulates scholarly works of a broader, general nature that touch on Syrian archaeology, while part 3 gives the sources from which the bibliography was compiled. Works printed since 1980 were omitted on the assumption that this material is readily available via computer. This shortcoming not withstanding, the volume would be a worthy addition to the reference collections of university and college libraries.
—John W. Storey

AMERICAN HISTORY
Archives

485. **Twentieth-Century America: A Primary Source Collection from The Associated Press.** By The Associated Press. Danbury, Conn., Grolier, 1995. 10v. illus. index. $349.00. ISBN 0-7172-7494-2.

This impressive 10-volume set relates the major and many lesser events of the past 95 years as written by Associated Press (AP) correspondents and presented to subscribing newspapers and radio and television stations. Told in a "you-are-there" style, it brings to life U.S. history in a manner and detail that is missing from standard encyclopedias and histories. The first thing noticed in reading this work is a feeling of immediacy, the sense of reading history as it occurs. The second is the presentation of details of the events in history that are omitted from books and journal articles.

The set is well constructed. Political and social history, sports, legal and criminal happenings, and other areas of historical interest are related in chronological order and tied together by introductory comments and notes that place the stories in perspective. Each volume begins with a timeline illustrated with well-chosen photographs. Volumes, as well as individual chapters, are introduced by detailed tables of contents. Significant events are told in series of articles that follow stories as they developed. Hundreds of photographs throughout the set make this a quality resource for pictures of the people and events of the period. Excellent access is provided through tables of contents and individual volume indexes, and there is a comprehensive index for the set. This work is highly recommended as a resource for teachers, students, librarians, and any individual who enjoys twentieth-century history.—**Donald E. Collins**

Atlases

486. **The Atlas of the Civil War.** James M. McPherson, ed. New York, Macmillan/Simon & Schuster, 1994. 223p. illus. maps. index. $40.00. ISBN 0-02-579050-1.

This superb atlas was prepared by Pulitzer prize-winning author McPherson with the assistance of nine other historians. Their combination of narrative accounts, contemporary statements by participants in the war, more than 200 black-and-white and color illustrations, and 200 full-color maps especially prepared for this volume provides users with a colorful, comprehensive, and authoritative overview of the campaigns and battles of the Civil War.

The volume is organized for ease of use. Each battle or campaign is described in a two-page spread that includes a narrative description, a timeline, contemporary quotes, and one or more maps that show troop positions, movements, and other pertinent data. These are easily located through several devices. Theater of operations maps identify battles in broad geographic areas, with page numbers in parentheses leading to more substantial treatment in the body of the book. The table of contents provides a chronological overview, and the two indexes give alphabetical access. The body of the book itself is arranged chronologically. The volume is divided into five sections, one for each year of the war. Each section is preceded by a narrative account of the year written by editor McPherson.

Despite the excellence of this work, there are criticisms, such as several typographical and factual errors. For example, the Battle of Manassas map on page 33 mistakenly spells the alternate name as Ball Run; the locator map on page 12 includes wrong page numbers; and one reference to First Manassas on page 13 actually leads users to the Battle of Second Manassas. Southern readers may also disagree with the apparent Northern view of the war in the yearly surveys. These surveys additionally contain a number of questionable statements. The claim that no Southerner became president for a century after the war obviously overlooks Woodrow Wilson; and McPherson's doubts in regard to whether African Americans would fight for the Confederacy overlooks a growing body of literature on the subject. An occasional lack of balance is also demonstrated in the treatment of the prisons and prisoner of war issues.

The book is priced within the range of most individuals and all libraries, and is highly recommended for any person or library with an interest in the Civil War.—**Donald E. Collins**

487. Homberger, Eric, with Alice Hudson. **The Historical Atlas of New York City: A Visual Celebration of Nearly 400 Years of New York City's History.** New York, Henry Holt, 1994. 192p. illus. maps. index. $45.00. ISBN 0-8050-2649-5.

Homberger, reader in American studies at the University of East Anglia, has produced an attractive and much-needed visual record of the United States' premier urban center. Combining new maps produced for the book with historical maps, photographs, and illustrations, he examines the history of New York City from its geological beginnings to the present. Eight chapters divide the city's chronology, covering the Dutch and English colonial periods and various phases of growth, rebuilding, and consolidation through the nineteenth and twentieth centuries. Homberger approaches the task from several directions, alternately focusing on places, such as Central Park and Harlem; events, including the British occupation during the American Revolution and the Civil War draft riots; and topics, such as tenements and skyscrapers. Most discussions are placed within two-page layouts, combining text, maps, and other graphics, that are generally well organized and pleasing to the eye. Unfortunately, a few maps overlap pages, and portions are lost in the gutters.

Coverage is fairly even in terms of time periods, but this is not so geographically. For the majority of the book, New York City is Manhattan, and the other boroughs are given only small sections for summarizing their preconsolidation histories. Also, few maps or discussions treat the city as a whole, making the full picture of the city's growth harder to perceive. Other, minor problems include place-names in the text that do not appear on the maps, and occasional typos and other errors. The text is well written, if concise, and the volume is rounded out with a timeline, biographical sketches, and a good bibliography.

Aside from the above complaints, this is an excellent atlas and a good introduction to the history of the city. Recommended for most academic and public libraries. [R: WLB, Mar 95, p. 80]—**Jeff Wanser**

488. Wexler, Alan. **Atlas of Westward Expansion.** New York, Facts on File, 1995. 240p. illus. maps. index. $40.00. ISBN 0-8160-2660-2.

This work is governed by its title in its coverage and arrangement. Therefore, it arranges the entire process of our expansion into the West into eight significant groupings, disregarding other important topics such as the War for Independence and the Civil War, but concentrating on events that shaped the West rather than the nation. Specifically, the book contains these chapters: "Colonial America Looks to the West," "The U.S. Extends Its Empire," "Crisis on the Frontier," "An Expanding Nation," "A Transcontinental Republic," "Wealth of the West," "Reshaping the West," and "Frontier's End."

Each of these chapters, with its respective period of one or two decades indicated, consists of a combination of text and maps. Chapter 1, for example, has 24 pages with 19 maps, some full-page, others half- or quarter-page. Also included in the chapters are contemporary drawings, engravings, or photographs; in addition, there are occasional drawings, by Molly Brown, of contemporary artifacts, such as a handmade ax, a shovel, an original Bowie knife, a water pump with hand-operated lever, and the like.

The text is written in a lively but objective style. It is not intended to glorify, nor to explain away faults, but simply to recount events that happened. For example, with regard to the 1836 Texan account of the defense and capture of the Alamo, no comment is made about Mexican General Martin Perfecto de Cos's seeming violation of his parole. Similarly, in the Battle of the Little Bighorn, the text is straightforward, making no comment about General George Armstrong Custer's character or military ability.

Interspersed throughout the work are several sidebars (not necessarily related to nearby text), such as those on the Cherokee alphabet, the Colt pistol, or women of the West. Appendixes include a profile and a chronology of U.S. territorial expansion from 1750 onward, an extensive bibliography, and an index of names and topics. This excellent work on the expansion into the West is a must-buy for high school, college, and public libraries.—**Raymund F. Wood**

Bibliography

489. **Bibliographic Guide to North American History 1994.** New York, G. K. Hall/Simon & Schuster, 1995. 741p. $335.00. ISBN 0-7838-2194-8. ISSN 0147-6491.

The latest volume of G. K. Hall's Bibliographic Guide series continues the lavish format and organization that have characterized previous volumes. Twenty-one fields are now covered by these guides. This volume lists publications dealing with North American history cataloged between September 1, 1993, and August 31, 1994, by the New York Public Library and the Library of Congress.

Previous reviews have complained about the price of these volumes (ever rising and approaching the prohibitive) and the prodigious amount of shelf space that they consume. Those structural problems remain. Viewed in splendid isolation, these volumes are masterpieces of bibliography, but when the levels of potential usage and the other competing and readily available venues for bibliographic research are considered, many libraries will probably reach the conclusion that these bibliographic guides are impressive but unnecessary luxuries.—**Ronald H. Fritze**

490. Dougan, Michael B., Tom W. Dillard, and Timothy G. Nutt, comps. **Arkansas History: An Annotated Bibliography.** Westport, Conn., Greenwood Press, 1995. 365p. index. (Bibliographies of the States of the United States, no.5). $75.00. ISBN 0-313-28226-9.

This is the fifth volume to appear in the Greenwood Press Bibliographies of the States of the United States series. The preceding volumes are on Kansas (see ARBA 93, entry 513), South Dakota (1993), Illinois, and North Carolina (see entries 492-493). State history bibliographies are extremely valuable resources, and this is an excellent one for a state that has not received a great deal of attention in Southern or national history surveys. In the preface the compilers note that *The Journal of Southern History* recorded more entries on Ohio than Arkansas and that significant works on the South ignored Arkansas.

Professor of history Dougan (Arkansas State University) and librarians/archivists Dillard (University of Central Arkansas) and Nutt (Central Arkansas Library System) provide 2,970 citations to printed sources, many with brief annotations. The listings are arranged topically under "Environment and Climatology," "Prehistory," "Indigenous Peoples," "Exploration and Colonial Period," "Territorial Period," two chapters on the "Statehood Period," and such specialized topics as minorities, business and transportation, social life, local and county history, and many others. The volume also includes a chronology, subject and author indexes, and information on major archives and historical sites in the state.

Comprehensive, well-arranged, and enlightening, this compilation will help to alleviate the problem of Arkansas' relative neglect in historical accounts. It is a first-class work that should be in all major research libraries and in all school and public libraries in the South and in states surrounding "the Bear State."
—Joe P. Dunn

491. Giglio, James N., comp. **John F. Kennedy: A Bibliography.** Westport, Conn., Greenwood Press, 1995. 425p. index. (Bibliographies of the Presidents of the United States, no.34). $75.00. ISBN 0-313-28192-0.

While a great deal of popular and revisionist literature has been written concerning John F. Kennedy in the past 30 years, there are surprisingly few current, comprehensive, and authoritative reference sources, especially bibliographies. This title admirably fills that void. Number 34 in the Bibliographies of the Presidents of the United States series, this well-researched tool is strong in its coverage of both primary and secondary sources, regardless of format. The organization is primarily by chronological aspects of Kennedy's life (childhood, congressional years, and so on), with chapters on archival sources such as manuscripts and oral histories, concluding with sections on historiographical and iconographical materials. Most of the 4,349 entries have one- or two-sentence annotations concisely describing the item's focus or content. Indexes to authors and subjects further expedite access to the wealth of research material in this book.

With the constantly evolving evaluation of Kennedy the president and the complex, driven human being, current and exhaustive research sources are essential for those who would attempt to understand him. This title will undoubtedly remain the standard, or at least the customary starting point, until such time as something in the future appears to update it. Research libraries or large public institutions with presidential collections will find that this work is invaluable as an addition to their Kennedy materials.
—James Moffet

492. **Illinois History: An Annotated Bibliography.** Ellen M. Whitney, comp. Janice A. Petterchak and Sandra M. Stark, eds. Westport, Conn., Greenwood Press, 1995. 603p. index. (Bibliographies of the States of the United States, no.4). $85.00. ISBN 0-313-28235-8.

The Illinois State Historical Library and the Illinois State Historical Society cosponsored this work, and their monographic and serial publications form the core of the volume. The book is composed of 4,620 numbered references to books, articles, and primary research materials. The entries are broadly divided by chronological period, with other sections on subjects such as biographies, reference sources, and historic sites. The entries are arranged by author within each section. Some of the bibliographic citations have a line or two of annotation when the title does not clearly reflect an item's content, or if the item is important. There is a helpful 18-page chronology on the state's history, followed by an outline map of the state, with its counties and county seats. The book has an author and subject index; one wishes that a title index had been compiled as well.

Greenwood Press had previously published *A Guide to the History of Illinois* by John Hoffman, which was composed of bibliographic essays and fewer citations (see ARBA 92, entry 471). This new title is now the first bibliographic tool to use for research on Illinois. A review of the first volume in this series, for Kansas, can be found in ARBA 93 (entry 513). The publisher is willing to take personal phone orders at 1-800-225-5800. The item under review is recommended for academic and public libraries. (See entries 490, 493, and 494 for reviews of other titles in the series.)—**Daniel K. Blewett**

493. Jones, H. G., comp. **North Carolina History: An Annotated Bibliography.** Westport, Conn., Greenwood Press, 1995. 796p. index. (Bibliographies of the States of the United States, no.3). $95.00. ISBN 0-313-28255-2.

A mammoth collection of materials covering every aspect of North Carolina, this bibliography encompasses history, society, arts, and natural history in more than 11,000 entries. Described as a source for primary materials, the bibliography includes books, pamphlets, theses and dissertations, and articles from more than 300 periodicals and serials. It generally excludes creative writing except for that which has become historical. Genealogical sources are included, but genealogies are not.

For Jones, dealing with such a large and disparate collection presented no little challenge. Materials are grouped broadly into chronological periods, then categorized within each period under religion, government, ethnic and racial groups, economic and social history, science, and literature. Because some items have been entered under more than one section, each with a distinct entry number, the number of entries represents fewer discrete items.

According to the compiler, annotations "consist chiefly of the classification of entries into chronology and subject" (p. xiii). Occasionally an entry's focus or contents may be noted in a descriptive phrase. Users will rely heavily on the subject index, along with the work's organization, to fully utilize the bibliography.

Jones brings to the work his extensive knowledge of North Caroliniana. He is presently a research historian at the University of North Carolina at Chapel Hill, having served also as curator of the University's North Carolina Collection, as the state archivist of North Carolina, and as director of the State Department of Archives and History. Academic and research libraries with large historical collections will want to acquire this important contribution to North Carolina history.—**Bernice Bergup**

494. Tate, Michael L., comp. **Nebraska History: An Annotated Bibliography.** Westport, Conn., Greenwood Press, 1995. 549p. index. (Bibliographies of States of the United States, no.6). $79.95. ISBN 0-313-28249-8.

Tate's *Nebraska History* is the 6th volume in a series of book-length bibliographies designed to "systematically review the components of local, state, and regional history within the chronological framework of the states' histories" (p. ix). This work includes a listing of more than 5,000 monographs, journal articles, theses, and dissertations about Nebraska history that have been published prior to 1994. These citations are arranged in 16 convenient divisions, the largest of which include: "Native Americans in Historical Times"; "Frontier Period"; "Land, Agriculture, and Livestock, 19th and 20th Centuries"; "Economic Life, 19th and 20th Centuries"; "Government, 19th and 20th Centuries"; and "Cultural Life." With few exceptions, notably the works cited in the "Community and County Histories" section, the entries are annotated. The volume also includes a 9-page chronology of significant events in Nebraska history, and comprehensive, 70-page indexes to authors and subjects.

As the first systematic bibliographical reference guide on Nebraska, this work will be a valuable tool for students interested in doing historical research on this state. Although some scholars will be disappointed with the brevity of the annotations, this volume deserves to be included on the acquisition list of all major research libraries.—**Terry D. Bilhartz**

Biography

495. **Biographical Dictionary of the Union: Northern Leaders of the Civil War.** John T. Hubbell and James W. Geary, eds. Westport, Conn., Greenwood Press, 1995. 683p. index. $99.50. ISBN 0-313-20920-0.

Researching individual leaders of the U.S. Civil War has never been easy due to the large variety of possible sources. This biographical dictionary goes a long way toward solving this problem. *Biographical Dictionary of the Union* provides information on more than 800 individuals who are considered leaders in the Union army, as well as civilians. The editors point out that "The main criterion used in determining the final choice of biographical entries centered on those men and women who influenced the course of public policy, opinion, and events. The list is comprehensive for political leaders (presidents, congressmen, senators, governors, cabinet officers, Supreme Court justices) and selective for others (e.g., foreign service officials, editors, photographers, abolitionists)" (introduction).

Military leaders were selected based on their contribution to the Union cause and, for the most part, include division commanders and other officers who became prominent. The entries have been written by numerous Civil War historians, scholars, and enthusiasts. Each entry contains the individual's name, employment (e.g., officer, senator, congressman), birth and death dates, education, positions held, and a brief biography based on the person's activities during and after the Civil War. In most cases, the source of the information is also included. Most references are to standard works such as the *Dictionary of American Biography* or *Generals in Blue* by Ezra Warner. In a few instances, the references are to primary sources that may be out-of-print. There are entries to some individuals "whose obscurity is breathtaking" (introduction), but the documentation available is always provided.

Even though it is a reference work, this book is a delight to peruse. The entries are uneven and vary in their approach due to the use of dozens of authors, but this adds to the work's charm. The entries are loaded with fascinating information and serve to point out how the nation was consumed by the war. Appendixes furnish an extensive bibliography, an index, and a list of contributors. This book is especially recommended for all larger academic and public libraries with special Civil War collections. It will also be a valuable resource for historians and Civil War enthusiasts.—**Robert L. Wick**

496. Cook, James F. **The Governors of Georgia, 1754-1995.** rev. ed. Macon, Ga., Mercer University Press, 1995. 341p. illus. index. $25.00. ISBN 0-86554-480-8.

Cook, professor of history at Floyd College in Rome, Georgia, offers an interesting and useful resource in this revised and expanded edition of a work originally published in 1979. He provides in-depth sketches on each of the 76 men who have served as the chief executive of the state, from the first Royal Governor John Reynolds in 1754 to the incumbent Zell Miller. The individuals are an eclectic lot, from obscure figures to national leaders, including a president of the United States. Sixteen governors also served as U.S. senators, seventeen served in the U.S. House of Representatives, several held cabinet positions, and Alexander Stephens was vice president of the Confederacy. The composite biographies provide a history of a state that was founded as a haven for the destitute and remained abjectly poor throughout much of its history until its emergence in the last two or three decades as the center and capital of the upscale Sunbelt South.

The chronologically arranged sketches focus on the major achievements of each governor's administration, but also include references to the individual's family, background, personal traits, and subsequent political or professional career. All the entries are well researched, judicious, and compactly written. Most of the entries supply a picture of the governor. The selected bibliography is outstanding, as it lists all the significant books, dissertations and theses, and articles on the governors and other major works on Georgia history. It would be wonderful if a book such as this existed on every state. In the meantime, this valuable volume should be in all libraries with significant collections on Southern history; in every academic, school, and public library in Georgia; and in larger collections in surrounding states.—**Joe P. Dunn**

497. **Encyclopedia of Frontier Biography on CD-ROM.** [CD-ROM]. Lincoln, Nebr., University of Nebraska Press, 1995. Minimum system requirements: IBM or compatible. Double-speed CD-ROM drive (recommended). VGA monitor (color recommended). $150.00.

A catalog of significant persons and personalities of the U.S. West, this menu-driven CD-ROM contains some 5,700 biographical entries that can be accessed by both alphabetical and chronological listings. Clearly the principal advantage of creating a CD-ROM from what was initially published as a three-volume set of books (by Dan L. Thrapp [1991-1994]) is that its digital format encourages searches of any and all of these entries for similar themes, words, or phrases, or to cross-reference persons and events.

The individuals included in this reference work were chosen for the significance of their actions and lives on the U.S. frontier. The people selected include a wide variety of men, women, and Native Americans who were settlers, explorers, outlaws and desperadoes, writers, scientists, and military figures. Entries are linked together and identified by name (and aliases if any), fields of significance, dates of birth and death (if known), summaries of their careers, and various facts and places of interest. Entries also typically provide useful biographical notes to guide further research.

The entries in this encyclopedia are concise and informative and reflect Thrapp's background not only as a historian but also as a journalist. He has achieved his objective of creating a permanent record of a fascinating era of U.S. history and legend. The lives and times of the famous and the infamous, the recognizable and the obscure, reveal much about who people are and how they became what they are. Students and researchers alike will benefit from either casually browsing or thoroughly studying this practical reference work.—**Timothy E. Sullivan**

Catalogs and Collections

498. **Landmark Documents in American History.** [CD-ROM]. New York, Facts on File, 1995. Minimum system requirements: IBM or compatible PC 386. CD-ROM drive. MS-DOS 5.0. Windows 3.1. 8MB RAM. 3MB hard disk space. 640KB main memory. VGA 16 color or SVGA 256 color monitor with 512KB video memory. Windows-compatible mouse. Printer. $295.00. ISBN 0-8160-3247-5.

The demand for primary source materials to support the history curriculum has grown dramatically in recent years. Facts on File answers the call with this comprehensive collection of nearly 1,300 of the most-requested full-text documents. The disc spans 500 years of U.S. history, from the privileges granted Christopher Columbus through the Republican's 1994 "Contract with America" and the 1995 "Glass Ceiling Commission Report."

Among the documents are major Supreme Court decisions (150); letters, party platforms, inaugural addresses, and speeches of all the presidents (200); debates and treaties (100); photographs (250); and legislation (400). All but the longest documents are full-text. Documents are introduced with commentary describing their significance and historical context. Relevant biographies are accessible from the document screen. Users may search by subject, period, year, historical figure, or title of document. A flexible advanced search mode allows for combinations of keyword, field, and date searching. Resulting lists supply the date and the document type. The "further readings" function provides users with a bibliography to inspire further research. Hypertext links allow easy navigation among related documents. The Windows version includes 20 QuickTime movies, including Martin Luther King Jr.'s "I Have a Dream" speech and an excerpt from the Richard M. Nixon-John F. Kennedy debates.

One minor concern is that users cannot select text and print portions of documents without first saving to a file. An online list of the videos available in the Windows version would have been helpful as well. *Landmark Documents* makes accessible an abundance of critical curricular materials. Its approach is more comprehensive than the Primary Source's *American Journey* CD-ROM series and its scope is broader than Oryx Press's *Famous American Speeches* (1995). *Landmark Documents* will be of permanent value to most high schools, colleges, and larger public library branches.—**Joyce Kasman Valenza**

Chronology

499. **America in the 20th Century.** Paul Humphrey and others, eds. New York, Marshall Cavendish, 1995. 11v. illus. maps. index. $399.95/set. ISBN 1-85435-736-0.

This fine set offers additional proof that social history has moved far beyond "pots and pans"—that is, a rather conventional political and economic framework enlivened by a few interesting tidbits about the way people lived. Each of these 10 volumes covers a decade, and within each decade several common themes are explored, ranging from health and medicine, the media, literature and the arts, and education to technological change, family life, sports, and the environment and natural resources. Every volume highlights the struggles of women, indigenous peoples, and racial minorities. Overall, the study presents an excellent picture of the dramatic changes in life in the United States, from a predominantly rural landscape in 1900 to an urban metropolis by 1994.

Each volume has approximately 150 pages and contains about 100 photographs, political cartoons, and advertisements of the time; at least a score of brief biographies of prominent figures from varied walks of life; a list of important dates; suggested readings; and an index. Enhancing the set's usefulness is an 11th volume that is an exhaustive index of events, places, social issues, women, scientists, minorities, laws, treaties, the arts, and popular culture. Intended primarily for a general audience, this study will be of little value to scholars, for its treatment of many subjects is superficial. An example is religion, which is completely ignored until volume 6. In this reviewer's copy, moreover, the text in volume 9 is upside down. Such criticism aside, this reference will be very appealing to lay readers, and public and high school libraries should have a set.—**John W. Storey**

500. **Chronicle of America.** John W. Kirshon and Ralph Berens, eds. New York, Dorling Kindersley, 1995. 1008p. illus. maps. index. $59.95. ISBN 0-7894-0124-X.

Imagine *USA Today*, with its eye-catching color photographs, reporting U.S. history and trivia: "Jackson is President after tough race," or "Grain overcooked; now it's corn flakes." This colorful newspaper approach to U.S. history is best described as a cross between a chronology and a historical dictionary. Similar to a chronology, it presents year-by-year the events of U.S. life; similar to a historical dictionary, it gives brief descriptions of these events. Yet does *Chronicle of America* satisfy a library's need for both? Compared to a standard chronology, such as *The Encyclopedia of American Facts and Dates* (see ARBA 94, entry 504), *Chronicle* has about half as many dates or entries. Compared to a thorough historical dictionary or one-volume encyclopedia, such as *The Reader's Companion to American History* (see ARBA 92, entry 468), *Chronicle*, with numerous photographs and entries, does not have the space to go into as much detail or list additional sources of information.

The primary reason to use *Chronicle of America* is for visual stimulation. It contains a treasure trove of photographs, illustrations, and paintings, which will help students of U.S. history locate unusual pictures, such as a photograph of King Camp Gillette's safety razor (1901) or "Scarface" Al Capone in "his favorite pose" (1931). Beyond the visual facets, this work includes facts or events that do not always appear in chronologies or historical dictionaries, such as the introduction of paper cups: "You just drink up and toss cup away" (1908). A general index provides access. As with an enjoyable coffee-table book, this book is much fun to browse and will be especially useful for those who need a visual history of the United States.—**John P. Stierman**

501. **The Columbia Chronicles of American Life, 1910-1992.** By Lois Gordon and Alan Gordon. New York, Columbia University Press, 1995. 837p. illus. index. $39.95. ISBN 0-231-08100-6.

The Columbia Chronicles of American Life brings to the casual and to the serious student of U.S. history a comprehensive mosaic of the U.S. scene from 1910-1992. Included in this well-organized, 800-page, single volume are news items; facts and figures for such diverse topics as unemployment, quotes, economic profiles, best-sellers, films; and the most popular songs, musicals, and films that encapsulate American culture. More than 500 well-chosen photographs, many from the Library of Congress, the National Archives, and the Smithsonian Institution, add visual impact to the text. Of special interest is the "Quotes" section; for example, in 1917, at the height of the Great War, "We [Germany] make Mexico a proposal of alliance . . . to recover the lost territory in Texas, New Mexico, and Arizona" (the intercepted Zimmerman note preceding the United States' declaration of war).

This volume is also a chronicle of the men and women who stood apart from the ordinary, and participated in exploration, the political, the literary, and the popular culture of music and film, forever leaving their mark on the U.S. scene. One proofing error found that Damon Runyan was listed as having died in 1946 and again in 1947. This well-thought-out chronology is an educational tool that both enlightens the mind and is fun reading. At the reasonable price, this volume is highly recommended for all academic and public libraries.—**Dario J. Villa**

502. Flanagan, Mike. **The Old West: Day by Day.** New York, Facts on File, 1995. 498p. illus. index. $60.00. ISBN 0-8160-2689-0.

From a socioeconomic point of view, this work essentially narrates the day-by-day events that took place during—to quote from the introduction—"a quarter century, from the end of the Civil War until 1890, (which) was all it took either to relocate or to eliminate the native population of a continent." From a reference point of view, the work is a treasure trove of daily events, culled largely from the newspapers of the plains states, dealing with historic persons, places, or activities of the period. It does actually cover a somewhat longer period, beginning with summary entries for the years from 50,000 B.C. to 1848; an epilogue covers 1891 to 1993. All these entries are narrated in the present tense. There are also many sidebars and boxes covering related events or biographies; these are narrated in the past tense.

The most valuable portions of the book for reference librarians are the 3 excellent indexes: a name index (12 pages), a place index (7 pages), and a subject index (11 pages)—all of them 4 columns to the page and in small print. All important topics are subdivided. The entry for Cheyenne Indians, for example, has 16 subdivisions. Considering the thousands upon thousands of entries for names and dates and places, the very few errors that were turned up during the review may well be disregarded. Even so, Vardis Fisher's novel is *Mountain Man*, not *Mountain Men*; Pinnacles is in California, not Utah; and "Francis Fuller," noted in the name index, is in reality Frances (Fuller) Victor, and she is correctly identified on page 224 of the text. The work is recommended for all libraries that have a clientele of Western history enthusiasts.—**Raymund F. Wood**

503. Meltzer, Ellen, and Marc Aronson. **Day by Day: The Eighties.** New York, Facts on File, 1995. 2v. illus. index. $195.00/set. ISBN 0-8160-1592-9.

This work is the fifth in a series of decade-by-decade chronologies beginning with the 1940s. The extensive information contained in this resource is gleaned from the Facts on File Yearbooks, which in turn derive their information from public events as reported in the news media.

The atlas-sized, 1,659-paged compilation is divided into 2 volumes covering 1980-85 and 1986-89. It is intended as a quick-reference guide to specific events having an impact on humankind in order to give the reader or researcher an idea of the sense and feel of what the years and decade were like. In this respect, the material has additional value to public and academic libraries as a beginning point for any in-depth research projects concerning significant events in the 1980s.

Day-by-day entries along the left-hand page are matched with 10 broad categories along the top of both pages. The five categories on the left-hand page cover international events, while the first four categories on the right-hand page cover U.S. developments. The 10th category covers worldwide cultural events.

The first volume begins with a brief, one-page preface. It is followed by a 10-page introduction that provides a snapshot of the decade. The second volume concludes with useful name and subject indexes, which are arranged alphabetically and chronologically. Each index entry includes the year, month, day, and column location in the reference guide.—**James M. Murray**

Dictionaries and Encyclopedias

504. **The American Civil War: A Multicultural Encyclopedia.** By the Civil War Society. Danbury, Conn., Grolier, 1994. 7v. illus. maps. index. $179.00/set. ISBN 0-7172-7348-2.

Produced in seven thin volumes, with copious black-and-white illustrations, this is a young adult title, although not so labeled. After a brief introduction, there are approximately 300 alphabetical entries for major persons and battles, as well as most ethnic and national groups involved in the war. Biographical entries tend to cover a person's life from birth to death, rather than being limited only to the war years. There are cross-references within the articles and an index. While the set concludes with a short bibliography (of adult-level sources) none of the individual articles provide any citations.

Other than the attraction of the rather thin multicultural articles, this work has significant flaws, the result of poor writing and worse editing. For example, the reader learns that all Civil War Cavalry were called dragoons, the Merrimack was a Union ironclad ship seized by the Confederates, and Philip Sheridan was a "Calvary" leader. Cross-references are erratic: For example, there is no reference in the Benjamin Butler article to the "Contrabands" entry, nor references under "Zouaves" to the articles on "French-Americans" or "Vivandieres." Illustrations are curious: A full-page reproduction of a song sheet about Sheridan's ride appears with no textual reference to the ride; a photograph of Charles Francis Adams Jr. illustrates the entry for his father. Possibly to avoid offense, William Tecumseh Sherman's well-known comment that "war is hell" is replaced by the lesser-known "war is cruelty." Religion apparently is not part of multiculturalism: Although Quakers and Mormons get entries, Roman Catholics do not, and Dunkers get short shrift under the Dunker Church reference. Less explicable is the absence of references to age groups; although the "Drummer Boy of Shiloh" and a photograph of a powder monkey appear, neither drummer boys nor powder monkeys rate an entry—curious omissions in a work aimed at youth.

A well-designed reference book emphasizing the role of ethnic groups and their members in the Civil War would be of great value. The idea is good; the execution in this title is not. [R: RBB, 1 Feb 95, p. 1021]—**James H. Sweetland**

505. **The American West: A Multicultural Encyclopedia.** Danbury, Conn., Grolier, 1995. 10v. illus. maps. index. $279.00/set. ISBN 0-7172-7421-7.

This rather overpriced set of 10 volumes of Western history and biography is aimed at young readers from grades 6 through 10 or 11. The print is clear and large, and well paragraphed; the illustrations are numerous (about one every third page); and *see* references are frequent, and in all capital letters. The introductory matter, consisting of a map of the United States about 1875; a brief explanation of the set, as well as the end matter; a glossary of Western words used in the specific volume; some four pages of suggested further reading for the topics of that volume; and a good index to the entire set are repeated in each volume.

The final volume has a comprehensive glossary that condenses all previous glossaries into a single list. There is also a comprehensive bibliography, but it does not bring all previous bibliographies into a single list. Rather, it is a listing of more general works (and perhaps also some "afterthought" titles; for example, the first book to be listed is *Peyote Religion Among the Navajos*. This title is not listed in volume 7, where there is an article on Navajos). There are also examples of misplaced books: Don Berry's . . . *History of the Rocky Mountain Fur Company* is listed in volume 7, but the pertinent article appears in volume 8. Most volumes also have an additional set of maps, placed just before the index. The number varies from none in 2 of the volumes to up to 12 in volume 4. No explanation for the variation is given, and it may simply be a question of how many pages were left over after the last article in each volume.

As with other multiauthored sets (six writers in this case), there are discrepancies. General Philip Kearny appears sometimes with an extra *e* in his name. Some articles place the meeting of the transcontinental rails at Promontory Summit, others at Promontory Point. There are some questionable statements: Harry Love (not named in the text), who led the posse that captured Joaquín Murieta, was not a "visiting Texas Ranger." He had been living in California for about three years by 1853. Also, the Nieto family were not granted "200,000 acres" in 1844. A better figure would be 150,000 acres; and the date must have been prior to 1834, because in that year the land was regranted, causing confusion as to the total acreage, some land being counted twice.

A rather amusing error is in the article on the Franciscans, wherein the Mission of San Xavier del Bac in Arizona, an abandoned Jesuit foundation (although the text erroneously calls it Franciscan), was being restored by Francisco Garcés, "a Spanish priest known as the White Dove of the Desert." Garcés might have been honored to be so termed, but unfortunately it was the mission building itself that acquired that name, by reason of its magnificent white architecture.

A large majority of the biographees in the work will also be found in the *Encyclopedia Americana* (see entry 47 for a review of the CD-ROM edition), as well as in others aimed at youth readership. Under the letter C of the work being reviewed, 70 percent of the biographees are also listed in *Americana*. On the other hand, a 12-year-old girl, wanting to read about Annie Oakley, may be put off by the small print and more adult language of a major encyclopedia, but would enjoy the fine article in volume 7 of this work. As an inducement to school librarians to purchase the set, it comes equipped with card pockets ready to be glued in, and date due slips ready for use. For middle school libraries with inadequate access to other Western sources, and for the families wherein the pupils of these schools reside, the work is recommended.—**Raymund F. Wood**

506. Boatner, Mark M., III. **Encyclopedia of the American Revolution.** 3d ed. Mechanicsburg, Pa., Stackpole Books, 1994. 1290p. maps. index. $32.95. ISBN 0-8117-0578-1.

Upon close examination, this 3d edition of Boatner's *Encyclopedia* turns out to be an exact reprint of the 1974 bicentennial edition (see ARBA 75, entry 365). The 1974 volume, in turn, is the same as the original 1966 edition, except for a half-page addendum to the bibliography. This one-volume source covers the period from 1763 to 1783, and contains alphabetically arranged entries on people, events, battles, and issues. There are many black-and-white maps but no portraits, and for all intents and purposes, the bibliography has not been updated since the original—thus, several citations are incomplete (e.g., L. H. Gipson's *British Empire Before the American Revolution* turned out to be 15 volumes, not 9). Essentially, this is a comprehensive source based on scholarship until 1966, therefore ignoring nearly 30 years of valuable historical writings on the American Revolution.

Those libraries that already own either the 1st or 2d edition can safely pass up this one, unless they need an additional copy for circulation. Libraries looking for a more up-to-date (and much more expensive) source should consider the two-volume *The American Revolution, 1775-1783: An Encyclopedia*, edited by Richard L. Blanco (see ARBA 94, entry 503), which concentrates on military aspects, or *The Blackwell Encyclopedia of the American Revolution*, edited by Jack P. Greene and J. R. Pole (see ARBA 92, entry 470), which contains long, topical essays.—**John A. Drobnicki**

507. **James Madison and the American Nation 1751-1836: An Encyclopedia.** Robert A. Rutland, ed. New York, Macmillan/Simon & Schuster Academic Reference Division, 1994. 509p. illus. maps. index. $95.00. ISBN 0-13-508425-3.

Rutland and a distinguished group of scholars have produced what should prove to be the definitive reference source on both James Madison and the Early National Period. The 400 signed articles, each with a bibliography, are arranged alphabetically and range in length from a few paragraphs to several pages. Included are biographical sketches of Madison's famous and not-so-famous contemporaries, as well as articles on places ("Mississippi Territory"), events ("Federal Convention"), and things ("Jay's Treaty"). As one would expect, the entry on Madison himself is quite lengthy, and is subdivided into seven articles covering his entire life and career. There are many portraits, illustrations, and facsimiles, and a handy chronology compares events in Madison's life with events in both the United States and the world. Cross-references, an index, and a synoptic outline make the copious information in this volume easily accessible. The work is highly recommended.—**John A. Drobnicki**

508. **Larousse Dictionary of North American History.** Min Lee, ed. New York, Larousse Kingfisher Chambers, 1994. 308p. $8.95pa. ISBN 0-7523-0005-9.

Based on the *Larousse Dictionary of World History* (see ARBA 95, entry 582), this is an alphabetically arranged dictionary that focuses on the political, diplomatic, and military history of the United States, Canada, and Mexico. Most of the roughly 1,000 entries range from 5 to 10 lines in length, although some number as few as 3 (e.g., Crispus Attucks), and others cover about $1\frac{1}{2}$ pages of more than 60 lines (e.g., Immigration Legislation, Civil Rights Movement). Although no index is included, many of the entries have cross-references. In terms of scope and currency, Christopher Columbus is mentioned, as are Bill Clinton, Bob Dole, and the Iran-Contra Affair.

Admittedly, space limitations preclude any work of this type from being comprehensive, but the brevity of most of the entries will send most students and librarians to either an average encyclopedia or a work that concentrates on a specific North American country, such as the *Dictionary of American History* (see ARBA 77, entry 384), *The Reader's Companion to American History* (see ARBA 92, entry 468), or the *Dictionary of Canadian Military History* (see ARBA 94, entry 517).

Although mistakes are to be expected in any reference work (e.g., Horatio Alger was born in 1832, not 1834, and he did not, as his entry states, help prepare James A. Garfield's presidential campaign literature), readers will be distracted by the many grammatical and punctuation errors. Students needing a quick reference may find this book useful, but most libraries will find it of limited value.—**Jack Bales**

509. **Profiles in American History: Significant Events and the People Who Shaped Them.** By Joyce Moss, and George Wilson. Detroit, U*X*L/Gale, 1994. 8v. illus. maps. index. $29.95/v.; $225.00/set. ISBN 0-8103-9208-9(v.1); 0-8103-9209-7(v.2); 0-8103-9210-0(v.3); 0-8103-9211-9(v.4); 0-8103-9212-7(v.5); 0-8103-9213-5(v.6); 0-8103-9214-3(v.7); 0-8103-9215-1(v.8); 0-8103-9207-0/set.

The roughly 165 profiles that make up this excellent resource are arranged in volumes that encompass broad United States historical eras: exploration to revolution, the Constitutional Convention to the War of 1812, the Indian removal to the abolition movement, westward expansion to the Civil War, Reconstruction to the Spanish American War, the Chinese exclusion to the women's rights movement, the Great Depression to the Cuban missile crisis, and the civil rights movement to the present. Within each chronological span, profiles are grouped according to noteworthy historical eras or events. For example, one section devoted to the Harlem Renaissance profiles Marcus Garvey, James Weldon Johnson, and Zora Neale Hurston, while a section on the Vietnam War features Lyndon B. Johnson, J. William Fulbright, Daniel Ellsberg, and Richard M. Nixon. The engagingly written biographies run from 10 to 20 pages; each includes personal background; events participated in; an "aftermath" paragraph that discusses the long-term impact of the individual's actions on society; a 2- to 5-item bibliography; and a single-page, black-and-white portrait. The text is further supplemented by reproductions of well-known art works, maps, illustrations, chronologies, comparative tables, and sidebars of highlighted information.

The goal of *Profiles in American History* is to present for its secondary school audience "the roles played by significant individuals, including many women and minorities, in historical events," with a guiding principle of achieving "balance not only in gender and ethnic background but in viewpoint" (preface). This goal is admirably met; for example, the profile of Christopher Columbus goes out of its way to position Columbus's "discovery" of North America within the context of its effects on the Native Americans who were already in residence. The work is similarly competent in its profiles of less controversial (in today's world) but equally important individuals, such as Supreme Court Chief Justice John Marshall or First Lady Eleanor Roosevelt. Although readers will always question selection in works such as these (how could Ralph Waldo Emerson not be included in the Transcendental Movement profiles?), this well-done, reasonably priced set will be a solid addition to secondary school and public libraries. [R: VOYA, Feb 95, p. 372]—**G. Kim Dority**

510. Slatta, Richard W. **The Cowboy Encyclopedia.** Santa Barbara, Calif., ABC-CLIO, 1994. 474p. illus. index. $54.00. ISBN 0-87436-738-7.

Those previously acquainted with Slatta's *Cowboys of the Americas* (Yale University Press, 1994) will find familiar material here, but now in dictionary format. Some 1,300 entries focus on the equestrian cattle cultures of the Americas, with the majority given to the English-speaking areas, and the rest spread among the Latin nations, most especially Mexico, Venezuela, and Argentina. Many are brief definitions, but others are of essay length—that for the *gauchos*, for example, covers some 10 pages. Extensive treatments are also found in the appendixes on films, periodicals, and museums; these are among the strongest parts of the volume.

Taken as a whole, this is a treasure trove of information, much of which is not easily available elsewhere. It is also a source that will be read as well as merely consulted, and the librarians who place it on their reference shelves will need to be prepared to do battle with the patrons who will want to take it home. Its readability cannot disguise a central flaw, however: It is never made clear why such diverse cultures profit by being discussed together. Aside from cows and horses, their commonalities derive from a shared Iberian ancestry, or so the reader infers. Yet this tradition is ignored, as are the two other "ancestral" cattle cultures brought to the new world: the Celtic and the African.

This want of a unifying historical perspective is glaring in the absence of any other principle that can give meaning to the whole. It is true that Slatta is attentive to the multitude of racial and social indignities visited on most cowboys, but a moral sensibility is not a principle of analysis and such ethical sensitivity only serves to heighten the great question: why such groups of underpaid and oppressed rural laborers should have become established in the national myths of places as diverse as the United States and Argentina. For this answer, the reader must seek elsewhere.—**Paul L. Holmer**

511. **Utah History Encyclopedia.** Allan Kent Powell, ed. Salt Lake City, Utah, University of Utah Press, 1994. 674p. illus. maps. index. $50.00. ISBN 0-87480-425-6.

Covering Utah's history from early geologic times to the present, this long-needed reference work includes 500 entries in 7 major categories—people, events, organizations, institutions, places, themes, and subjects—written by 270 historians and writers. The subject entries cover such topics as the geology of the state; plant life; archaeology; immigration and settlement; ethnic groups; the fur trade; elections; higher education; dinosaurs; political and social issues; religions (not only the Mormons); polygamy; industry; politics; economics; transportation; the arts; folklore; the towns and counties; and many other subjects from Maurice Abravanel (the legendary director of the Utah Symphony) to Zion's Cooperative Mercantile Institution (known today as ZCMI, the United States' first department store, founded in 1868).

These are not dry, data-filled chronicles, but often lively, personalized interpretive essays that provide an informative, basic introduction to the state. Its pages explore the forces—natural, social, political, religious, and economic—that have given Utah its unique heritage. The work features 250 black-and-white historical photographs from the Utah State Historical Society archives, an extensive index, and bibliographic references for further reading at the end of many articles, primarily to works likely found in public libraries. As a lifelong Utah resident with pioneer roots, and a Utah history buff, this reviewer found the articles not only accurate and readable, but informative and enlightening. The encyclopedia is highly recommended for all libraries needing an authoritative, readable, one-volume reference work on a state with a unique past and a bright future.—**Blaine H. Hall**

Handbooks and Yearbooks

512. **America: History and Life on Disc. Volumes 19-31, 32:1-2 1982-1995.** [CD-ROM]. Santa Barbara, Calif., ABC-CLIO, 1995. Minimum system requirements: IBM or compatible PC/XT/AT. ISO 9660-compatible CD-ROM drive with controller and interface cable. MS-DOS or PC-DOS 3.0. 720KB hard disk space. 512KB memory (384K free). Floppy disk drive. $4,250.00 (single user); $5,500.00 (network). ISSN 1076-5484.

America: History and Life on Disc is identical in scope and content to the printed version, *America: History and Life*, the standard index to the history and culture of the United States and Canada from prehistoric times to the present. Articles are abstracted from more than 2,100 journals. Abstracts from core journals contain 75 to 100 words. Book reviews are cited from 140 journals. Dissertation information is obtained from *Dissertation Abstracts International*.

The electronic version makes the abstracts and bibliographical citations back to 1982 quickly available from a computer. Three cumulative updates are issued each year. The latest, for fall 1995, contains two useful enhancements: The list of journals indexed is now provided in a text file on the CD-ROM, and the entries from searches are listed in reverse chronological order. There are two basic choices in searching the CD-ROM: the general search, which appears as the opening screen, and the specific fields search, intended for more detailed searching. The general search offers an impressive number of access points: subject (free-text), descriptors, author/editor, title, date, journal name, time period (centuries or decades), document type, and language. The specific fields option offers many additional fields such as review; author; abstracter; publication date; and documentation (the existence of bibliographies, illustrations, maps, and the like). The manual that accompanies the disc explains all these options, offers sample search strategies, and provides instructions on sorting search results and printing.

This work features menu bars on the screen, pull-down submenus, and context-sensitive help at any time in a search. It is not difficult to use, but it certainly is not transparent. Without the publisher's "Quick Reference Card," a novice may have difficulty in spite of the on-screen prompts. The number of search options may be perplexing. Nonetheless, this CD-ROM is a most efficient way for searching the periodical literature on U.S. history.—**Henry E. York**

513. **American Decades 1930-1939.** Victor Bondi, ed. Detroit, Gale, 1995. 612p. illus. index. $75.00. ISBN 0-8103-5725-9.

The editors of this title in Gale's American Decades series do an admirable job of chronicling the major events of the Depression era. Editors' names are listed at the beginning of each section. As in other books in this series, events are arranged into a dozen or so topical chapters: art, business, education, fashion, government and politics, law and justice, lifestyles and social trends, media, medicine and health care, religion, science and technology, and sports. The chapters average 42 pages, but range between 30 and 65 pages in length (religion and art, respectively). The Great Depression's distinguishing features are highlighted in an introduction that touches on such 1930s phenomena as joblessness, bank closures, the New Deal, and the gap between the rich and the poor. Events outside the United States are also listed here.

Chapter formats are repeated as follows: chronology of events; overview of the topic's historical importance; two- to three-page summaries of topics in the news (usually with brief bibliographies); one- or two-page biographies of headline makers; a few sentences on people in the news; awards granted, such as the Oscars, Nobel and Pulitzer prizes, and the like; deaths; and a list of publications for further reading. Black-and-white photographs appear on almost every page, and sidebars highlight particular events or people, often using contemporary sources. A general reference bibliography and a detailed index complete the volume.

Whether placed in reference or circulating collections, this handy summary of the 1930s will prove invaluable to high school and undergraduate students looking for term paper ideas and "best books" recommendations. (See entries 514-516 for reviews of other volumes in the series.)—**Gary D. Barber**

514. **American Decades 1940-1949.** Victor Bondi, ed. Detroit, Gale, 1995. 641p. illus. index. $75.00. ISBN 0-8103-5726-7.

This is the fourth volume in the American Decades series to be published. (Previously published volumes are reviewed in this edition of ARBA [entries 513, 515, and 516] and in ARBA 95, entry 544.) All volumes, treating 1 twentieth-century decade from 13 different perspectives, have a similar format. First comes a chronological listing of world events, followed by 13 chapters in alphabetical order, covering such aspects as the arts, business and the economy, education, law and justice, lifestyle and social trends, medicine and health, religion, science and technology, and sports. The chapters are similarly organized: a chronology of events; an essay overview of the chapter's subject area; discussions of particular aspects of the subject area; brief biographies of "Headline Makers"; biographies, 400 to 1,000 words in length, of eminent "People in the News"; deaths of notables during the decade, and finally, a list of the decade's important publications in the particular subject area. (The "General References" section toward the end of the volume contains a selective listing of more recently published items on each of the 13 subject areas.) Many black-and-white illustrations are scattered throughout the volume, as well as frequent sidebars on more entertaining, although not necessary, information. The volume concludes with a list of contributors, an index to the photographs, and a detailed general index.

As with the other volumes, this one can be recommended to a wide audience. The information is accurate and nicely encapsulates the decade; the editor's style makes for good reading; the treatment of issues, including controversial ones (e.g., the bombing of Hiroshima and Nagasaki), is clear and balanced; the bibliographies, although brief, are well chosen; and it is all put together in an attractive, sturdy volume. While the American Decades series is particularly appropriate for high school and public libraries, it should also prove useful in libraries serving undergraduates.—**Evan Ira Farber**

515. **American Decades 1960-1969.** Richard Layman and James W. Hipp, eds. Detroit, Gale, 1994. 595p. illus. index. $75.00. ISBN 0-8103-8883-9.

The *American Decades* series, of which this is the first to be published, treats in each volume "a single twentieth-century decade from thirteen separate perspectives, broadly covering American life" (introduction). The volume begins with a chronological listing of world events, providing context for American events. The chapters then follow in alphabetical order. All chapters are similarly organized: a chronology of events; an essay overview of the subject area; discussions of particular aspects of that area; brief biographies of headline makers; biographies—400-1,000 words in length—of eminent people in the news; deaths of notables; and finally, a list of the decade's important publications in respective subject areas. (The listing of general references toward the end of the volume contains more up-to-date items on each of the 13 subject areas.) Black-and-white illustrations are scattered throughout the volume, as well as frequent sidebars on interesting, although not necessarily important, information. A list of contributors, an index to the photographs, and a general index conclude the volume.

For a number of reasons, the work can be recommended to a wide audience: The information provided is accurate and encapsulates the period; the editors' style is readable; the treatment of issues, including controversial ones, is clear and balanced; the bibliographies, although brief, are carefully chosen; and it is put together in an attractive, sturdy package. While *American Decades 1960-1969* is especially appropriate for high school and public libraries, it will also prove useful in libraries serving undergraduates.
—**Evan Ira Farber**

516. **American Decades 1970-1979.** Victor Bondi, ed. Detroit, Gale, 1995. 623p. illus. index. $75.00. ISBN 0-8103-8882-0.

The third volume in a series covering the twentieth century by decades is suitable for high school students and adults seeking an overview of the significant people, events, and issues of the 1970s. As in the previously published volume on the 1960s (see entry 515), this one chronicles the 1970s from 13 perspectives (world events, mostly but not exclusively non-U.S. occurrences; the arts; business and the economy; education; fashion; government and politics; law and justice; lifestyles and social trends; media; medicine and health; religion; science and technology; and sports). Each perspective except the first includes a chronology and overview, short essays on the decade's events, sidebars of interesting information (e.g., 20 top-grossing movies of the 1970s in the arts chapter, malpractice insurance premiums in 1975 in medicine and health); brief biographies of key people; brief notices of significant accomplishments by prominent persons; awards (if applicable); deaths; and publications. The volume concludes with a general bibliography, an index of photographs, and a comprehensive index of subjects (e.g., persons, books, periodicals, plays, movies, television shows, songs, universities, corporations, government agencies, laws, court cases).

Readers are reminded that *American Decades* is complementary to both the Time-Life series, *This Fabulous Century* (1969-70), "century" being defined in this profusely illustrated, limited text set as 1870-1969, and the Facts on File's Day by Day series (see entry 503), covering each decade since 1940. Most of the material in the latter set is based on the *Facts on File Yearbooks*, rearranged into 10 columns across 2 pages. Entries on left-hand pages cover world affairs, Europe, Africa and the Middle East, the Americas (except the United States), Asia and the Pacific; the five columns on the right-hand pages deal with U.S. developments. While each series contains information not in the others, readers will surely appreciate a current re-review, which *American Decades* offers. Recommended for academic, public, and high school libraries.—**Wiley J. Williams**

517. Eicher, David J. **Civil War Battlefields: A Touring Guide.** Dallas, Tex., Taylor Publishing, 1995. 228p. illus. maps. index. $19.95; $14.95pa. ISBN 0-87833-886-1; 0-87833-881-0pa.

Five years of on-site battlefield exploration, mapping, and photography went into this attractive, easy-to-use handbook. Here is an on-the-ground history of the Civil War in 40 detail and area maps, 130 photographs, and locations and descriptions of more than 1,350 specific features still to be seen. Writer and editor Eicher covers 12 major battlefield areas comprising 22 campaigns and some 40 separate battles. Alphabetically, the battles run from Antietam to the Wilderness, and chronologically from Bull Run to Appomattox Court House.

The author provides a short but useful narrative of each battle, tying the background and combat action to the sightseeing features on the field. His history is well written and probably more accurate than the usual travel book. The analytical index is excellent. As prize-winning historian James M. McPherson says in the foreword, "A whole new exciting world awaits" the visitor who tours with this book in hand. But not so "exciting" are the many cemeteries with their numerous graves of unknowns, Union and Confederate.—**David Eggenberger**

518. Gregory, Ross. **Modern America 1914 to 1945.** New York, Facts on File, 1995. 455p. illus. maps. index. (Almanacs of American Life). $70.00. ISBN 0-8160-2532-0.

This reference source chronicles developments in U.S. history during the three-decade period encompassing both World Wars and the Depression. Author Gregory uses a topical approach, opening individual chapters with a contextual introduction augmented by statistics from government documents and other sources. Subjects addressed reflect the diversity of the U. S.' historical and cultural evolution. These include economics; religion; military forces; weather; state profiles; biographies of individuals such as Louis Brandeis, Calvin Coolidge, Amelia Earhart, Jesse Owens, and Frank Lloyd Wright; education; science; entertainment; and crime and punishment.

Illustrated with contemporary photographs accompanying the exhaustive array of statistics, this is a worthy addition to any library's twentieth-century U.S. history collection. Its use of diverse U.S. government statistical publications such as *Historical Statistics of the United States* (1989) and *Handbook of Labor Statistics* (1989) is especially commendable. One hopes the use of such primary source materials will prompt users to become better acquainted with these publications as tools for historical research.—**Bert Chapman**

519. Hyland, Pat. **Presidential Libraries and Museums: An Illustrated Guide.** Washington, D.C., Congressional Quarterly, 1995. 175p. illus. index. $39.95; $29.95pa. ISBN 0-87187-960-3; 0-87187-961-1pa.

Presidential libraries have a dual character—they serve as research centers and tourist attractions. The present work is a useful, well-written, and readable guide for visitors who wish to visit these centers as historical sites rather than to use them as research institutions. It describes the 10 presidential libraries administered by the U.S. Archives, as well as the privately operated Rutherford B. Hayes Library.

The organization is logical and easy to follow. One chapter is devoted to each president, and these are arranged in chronological order by presidency. A typical chapter provides historical information about the library itself and takes the reader on a walk-through of the building or buildings and grounds. Numerous illustrations accompany the entertainingly and informatively written text.

The volume concludes with two appendixes: general descriptions of materials to be found in each library and lists of books about each of the presidents included. This is a useful book that should be considered for purchase by public and academic libraries.—**Donald E. Collins**

520. **Reference Guide to United States Military History: 1945 to the Present.** Charles Reginald Shrader, ed. New York, Facts on File, 1995. 328p. illus. maps. index. (Reference Guide to United States Military History, v.5). $50.00. ISBN 0-8160-1840-5.

Last in the series, this volume is organized exactly like the previous volumes. Part 1 deals with the organization of armed forces and their history, part 2 with biographies, and part 3 covers battles and events. Six sections cover the historical chronology of the Cold War, the Korean War, two sections on Vietnam, the era of flexible response, and the Persian Gulf War. This well-designed work discusses the progress of U.S. military commitment around the world from the end of World War II to the breakup of the Soviet Union. The major players in this era are identified; in this respect, the biographical entries bring the various personalities alive. This era carried a strange dichotomy of preparedness for total nuclear war and the commitment of U.S. forces to small regional conflicts. The commitment by U.S. presidents to meet the threat of communism anywhere in the world with military forces chained an inflexible policy to a so-called flexible response militarily. With the fall of the Soviet Union and the breakup of the Warsaw Pact, U.S. military commitments around the world changed dramatically and produced some confusion as to when, where, how, and for what purpose the forces should be used. This work points out the challenges ahead for a well-equipped and trained U.S. armed force. Most challenging have been the commitment of forces to "peacekeeping" operations in Somalia, Bosnia, and Haiti.

Only a few deficiencies detract from the overall quality of this book. More could have been said about the rearming of Germany under NATO and a mention of at least one German officer who was instrumental in that undertaking. Overall the entries are clear, concise, and insightful. This volume is highly recommended for college, university, and government reference collections.—**Norman L. Kincaide**

521. **Scholastic Encyclopedia of the Presidents and Their Times.** By David Rubel. New York, Scholastic, 1994. 216p. illus. index. $16.95. ISBN 0-590-49366-3.

Each year of U.S. history is allotted one page in this introduction to its presidents, from George Washington through Bill Clinton. On the first page covering a given presidency, basic information is provided. A running narrative that extends throughout the presidency explains the overall issues of the times, and provides context for significant political, social, and economic events that are highlighted through the use of boxes, maps, and sidebars. The small, but clearly reproduced, photographs and cartoons and judicious use of touches of red, with shades of gray providing the background for special topics, result in an attractive format. The extensive index indicates all entries on a topic, and signals those pages that provide the most detailed explanations; words within the text that are carefully explained elsewhere are highlighted in red. A table of information on presidential elections is appended. This overview, with its unique structure, is recommended for its own sake and because the topics chosen to be emphasized will appeal to the intended audience and encourage further research. It is suited for students grades four through eight.—**Vandelia L. VanMeter**

522. Sifakis, Stewart. **Compendium of the Confederate Armies: Kentucky, Maryland, Missouri, The Confederate Units and the Indian Units.** New York, Facts on File, 1995. 234p. index. $27.50. ISBN 0-8160-2294-1.

523. Sifakis, Stewart. **Compendium of the Confederate Armies: Louisiana.** New York, Facts on File, 1995. 144p. index. $24.95. ISBN 0-8160-2291-7.

524. Sifakis, Stewart. **Compendium of the Confederate Armies: Mississippi.** New York, Facts on File, 1995. 154p. index. $24.95. ISBN 0-8160-2292-5.

525. Sifakis, Stewart. **Compendium of the Confederate Armies: South Carolina and Georgia.** New York, Facts on File, 1995. 311p. index. $29.95. ISBN 0-8160-2290-9.

526. Sifakis, Stewart. **Compendium of the Confederate Armies: Texas.** New York, Facts on File, 1995. 147p. index. $24.95. ISBN 0-8160-2293-3.

Like the first five *Compendium* volumes (see ARBA 93, entries 711-715), these books are the Confederate companion to Frederick H. Dyer's *A Compendium of the War of the Rebellion* (Dyer Publishing, 1908). Border states having Confederate units and Indian Confederate units compose one volume, as do South Carolina and Georgia; the other three treat the states of Louisiana, Mississippi, and Texas, respectively. Artillery, cavalry, and infantry units are dealt with separately. For each, units having a numerical designation are listed first, followed by those using the name of their commander, home region, or other name. Units are then listed alphabetically by size (i.e., battalions, batteries, companies, and regiments). Any nicknames or mistaken designations are noted, as well as the details of the time and place the unit was organized, the number and nature of its constituents, and time and place of its disbandment or mustering out. Commanding and field-grade officers are listed alphabetically. Also included is a list of all the engagements in which the unit participated. The entry concludes with suggested further reading, if any. Each volume also contains a bibliography and an alphabetical index of battles and names.

Librarians report heavy use of the first five volumes in the series. Scholars and others interested in tracing the participation of individuals and units in various battles will no doubt welcome the publication of the latest books in the series.—**Kay O. Cornelius**

527. **U.S. Presidents: A History of the Presidents of the United States of America.** [CD-ROM]. Minneapolis, Minn., Quanta Press, 1994. Minimum system requirements (DOS version): IBM or compatible. CD-ROM drive with MS-DOS CD-ROM Extensions. 640K RAM. Minimum system requirements (Macintosh version): Macintosh Plus. CD-ROM drive with Foreign File Access. 1MB RAM. $49.95.

This CD-ROM is easy to install and use but comes with very little documentation and offers surprisingly limited information about U.S. presidents considering the large amounts of data that can be stored in CD-ROM format. No more than two or three pages of written text are provided for each of the presidents, from George Washington to George Bush. Color portraits of reasonably good quality are also provided, but it would have been helpful to know the source or location of the portraits and photographs used. The single source used throughout for virtually all of the presidential biographical information provided here is *The Presidents*, edited by Robert Ferris in 1977 for the U.S. National Park Service as part of a survey—not of presidents, but of national historical sites. (Information for presidents Reagan and Bush was provided by their respective press offices.)

The one useful feature of the CD-ROM format is the ease with which cross-referenced searches for specific information may be conducted. For example, it is possible to determine very quickly which presidents went to college or served in the Navy (or who both went to college and served in the Navy). Brief information is given about each of the first ladies, along with pertinent statistics concerning each presidency. For students, however, the information provided here is of such limited scope that even a good encyclopedia article would in most cases provide more in-depth material, along with bibliographies for further reading—which are not included in this CD-ROM "history." Indeed, users should be warned that the writing is full of misspellings and is often grammatically incorrect and inappropriately opinionated; in the article on Reagan, for example, one finds "Inn 1980," "with who . . .," and the unqualified assertion that "his sound fiscal policy and wise managerial skills won great accolade from the people of California." Strange locutions abound: Washington is said to have been "irritated by the dilution of his rank," and Lincoln's parents are said to have been "progenitors of a daughter named Sarah." Inattentive proofreading has also left incomplete sentences, overlooked missing words, and failed to correct faulty punctuation and formatting. Clearly readers, especially students, need to proceed at their own risk with this product.—**Joseph W. Dauben**

528. **The Young Reader's Companion to American History.** John A. Garraty, ed. New York, Houghton Mifflin, 1994. 964p. illus. maps. index. $39.95pa. ISBN 0-395-66920-0.

Packed into these 964 pages is a work of extraordinary scope, lavishly illustrated with photographs, maps, cartoons, tables, and color plates. Inspired by *The Reader's Companion to American History* (see ARBA 92, entry 468), *The Young Reader's Companion to American History* is organized in dictionary format, with articles ranging from 250 words to 4 or 5 pages. These articles serve to identify a topic and offer a jumping-off point for further research. Entries conclude with a discussion of the importance or influence of the subject. The material is aimed at students ages 11 and up, but would certainly have appeal to high school students and adults as well. Included are biographical sketches and essays concerning American culture: rock music, all major sports, religious groups, and child labor. (The editor admits that decisions about inclusion of biographies were challenging and that some omissions were dictated by audience interest. John Smith is treated; John Rolfe is not.) The full-color sections on advertising, architecture, fashion, and painting are particularly usable and appealing. Introductions to controversial issues such as abortion, affirmative action, gun control, and censorship are detailed. Most articles are signed. The impressive list of contributors includes Dee Brown, who writes on Sitting Bull, and Julian Bond on the Civil Rights Movement. Some noted authors for young people covered are Milton Meltzer, Russell Freedman, Paula Fox, Jim Haskins, Brent Ashabranner, Elizabeth George Speare, and Joan Blos.

There are numerous cross-references and a thorough index. The appendix contains the Declaration of Independence and the U.S. Constitution, a table of information on the states, and population statistics. *The Young Reader's Companion to American History* invites browsing. Although much of this information is available in other sources, this is a quality, convenient, one-stop-shopping approach that deserves a spot on the reference shelf of every school library and many homes. [R: BR, Mar/Apr 95, p. 55; SLJ, Feb 95, p. 129]—**Joyce Kasman Valenza**

AFRICAN HISTORY

529. **African History on File.** By the Diagram Group. New York, Facts on File, 1994. 1v. (various paging). $155.00 looseleaf w/binder. ISBN 0-8160-2910-5.

Despite its title, this work is basically schematic, presenting a series of more or less standardized maps that illustrate the major political trends in African history. Each map is accompanied by a brief text and a timeline that does no more than repeat information in the text. In turn, the latter—perhaps necessarily—reflects the unproblematic approach to the African past that characterized the 1960s and early 1970s, a state of affairs that is reinforced by the bibliography, far too much of which is devoted to books published during this time rather than more recently.

In many cases, the maps are illuminating and orienting, but frequently their scale is too small to permit needed detail. Also, all too often they are in error. For instance, on page 3.21, the map and the text both suggest that Spain was entirely under Islamic rule in 711, the year of the first invasion. In fact, all of Spain was never under Muslim control. As well, comments such as "the formation of the Macedonian Empire in 332 [BC]" (p. 3.05) are both wrong and oddly stated, as are frequent variations of "between 1497 and 1498" (p. 4.05). In a work more contextually situated, this propensity to give drawn-out processes a specific date would be a peccadillo, but here the practice is certain to puzzle and mislead the uninitiated readers for whom the work is largely intended.

History viewed so largely through cartographic lenses is bound to oversimplify, for instance, in picturing states as more extensive, common, and coherent than they were—a case exemplified by the discussion and description of the medieval states of the western Sudan. If not swallowed whole, however, there can be a place for a work such as this at the first stages of introducing users to the African past. It can be useful as a point of departure, but should be used with other, more nuanced, African historical atlases, of which several have been published in the past decade or so. In particular, its bibliography should be ignored in favor of any number of better alternatives.—**David Henige**

530. Cook, Chris, comp. **The Making of Modern Africa: A Guide to Archives.** New York, Facts on File, 1995. 218p. index. $35.00. ISBN 0-8160-2071-X.

The title of this work implies, and its preface asserts, that it is concerned with all of Africa, but the vast majority of entries relate to British Africa. There are more than 1,000 entries, arranged alphabetically by individual, and covering personalities from 1878 to ca.1980. Rationale for inclusion is missing and, while many major figures are represented, even more are not, to be replaced by some very minor figures indeed. Each entry consists of a skeletal curriculum vitae and details as to scope and location of personal archival holdings. Both European and African archives are included. Nearly 300 entries, or almost 10 percent of the total, refer to the copious collections at Rhodes House Library in Oxford, for which a substantial, if now dated, guide has been published. German, South African, and Zimbabwean archives are also well represented, although not nearly on such a scale. There are archive and subject indexes (almost too small to read) and a token bibliography of a mere 11 items.

The value of this inchoate work would have been measurably increased had it also furnished a list of the addresses of, and other relevant information concerning, the archives represented in it; however, there is none, nor is there the slightest indication as to how interested parties may secure such information. This is an extraordinary lapse—one that could have been remedied in fewer than 10 pages or simply by having streamlined the presentation of certain information. Its absence renders the work of little practical value, especially in light of the fact that more complete details about almost everything in it are available in other sources. Happily, it is not as pricey as many other recent Africanist reference works, but for a few dollars more it could have been made much more useful.—**David Henige**

531. Fage, J. D. **A Guide to Original Sources for Precolonial Western Africa Published in European Languages....** rev. ed. Madison, Wis., University of Wisconsin, African Studies Program, 1994. 200p. index. $30.00pa. ISBN 0-942615-24-7.

This guide is a revision of the 1987 edition, and the 833 citations contain 65 new entries along with 75 other entries containing substantial revisions. In the introduction, Fage provides a relatively brief but comprehensive overview of the other major reference works dealing with this topic, including those by Ternaux-Complans, Hess and Coger, Cox, Paulitschke, and Mauny. The strengths, weaknesses, and coverage of these works are compared to his publication. Virtually all entries focus on the time period from 1500 to 1865 and represent a variety of sources in European languages. Wherever possible, the author has identified available English-language translations for the reader. Works published in other, non-European languages, most notably the many Arabic sources, are listed only if there was a European language translation known to the author.

The entries are chronologically grouped into 15 categories and can be further accessed via several thorough indexes, including title ("headword"), author, and other individuals significant to a given work such as editors, compilers, and translators. The organization, sequence, and bibliographical notations related to the citations are carefully explained within the "Notes on Entries" section.

While the annotations accompanying most of the entries tend to be brief, the author supplements them with many cross-references, translation availability notes, and historical background information. Fage's guide is a comprehensive, meticulously documented tool for the African scholar. This work will be appropriate for the larger academic library already possessing significant African resources.—**Anthony J. Dedrick**

532. Nuñez, Benjamin. **Dictionary of Portuguese-African Civilization. Volume I: From Discovery to Independence.** New Providence, N.J., Hans Zell/Reed Reference Publishing, 1995. 532p. $110.00/v. ISBN 1-873836-10-4.

For many years, the Portuguese language in the United States was taught as a dialect of Spanish. While the language and culture of Portugal began to be appreciated in their own right after World War II, many universities still combine their Portuguese and Spanish departments. What this indicates, of course, is that Portuguese has not been one of the primary languages for study in the United States.

That has steadily changed as Brazil has democratized, become more important as a U.S. trading partner, and is figuring larger in world and regional politics. A remaining weak link in English-Portuguese-language and -culture study is the realization of the importance of Portuguese as a spoken language in many former African colonies, and the cultural relationship between Brazil and many Portuguese-speaking African countries.

The *Dictionary of Portuguese-African Civilization* is a remarkable step in giving English-speaking students access to the vast language, literature, culture, and politics of these countries. It includes background data for the primary Portuguese-speaking African countries—Angola, Cape Verde, Guinea-Bissau, Mozambique, and São Tomé and Príncipe—as well as a table of abbreviations and acronyms, and an indispensable bibliography. The entries—words, terms, and phrases—are arranged alphabetically.

The dictionary is an essential acquisition for libraries that serve Portuguese language departments, as well as African studies, international studies, and political science departments. Because of the paucity of information in English in this subject area, it is also valuable for any major research library. While narrow in its field, it is a valuable and easy-to-use reference. Others outside these categories should still review the book for special circumstances and patron requirements.—**Curtis D. Holmes**

ASIAN HISTORY
General Works

533. **Asian History on File.** By the Diagram Group. New York, Facts on File, 1995. 1v. (various paging). illus. maps. index. $155.00 looseleaf w/binder. ISBN 0-8160-2975-X.

A companion volume to the publisher's *African History on File* (see entry 529) and *Time Lines on File* (1988), this volume consists primarily of black-on-white line maps of Asia: from South Asia (Pakistan in the west) through Japan and Korea. It is divided into five major sections: prehistory, South Asia, China, Japan and Korea, and Southeast Asia, each composed of maps, timelines, and chronologies—all complemented by a graphic table of contents and concluding with a bibliography and index. Authorization to reproduce the contents for "non-profit, educational, or private use" is explicit, simplifying use in classrooms or papers.

Maps are wonderful aids, but do have limitations. They may offer illusory clarity or reflect ignorance or political purpose. This volume evidences both the strengths and weaknesses. Historic borders that likely were never static nor clearly defined are represented by a single line covering decades or centuries. Exemplifying the importance of perspective, a South Asian map shows the Chola Empire conquering Sumatra (p. 2.21), while a Southeast Asia one (p. 5.07) shows Srivijaya dominant there in the same period. Sometimes a thousand words are needed (but not provided here) to qualify what is too obvious in a picture.

Less bothersome but worth noting is that the volume is not free from occasional inaccuracies and inconsistencies (such as the use of "Burma" on a map and "Myanmar" in its legend [p. 5.02]). The chronologies and timelines will be useful reference aids, and the maps, with their breadth and depth, will serve courses and research touching on Asia, but should have been available also on CD-ROM (removing the need to photocopy or scan and reducing the cost).—**K. Mulliner**

534. Schmidt, Karl J. **An Atlas and Survey of South Asian History.** Armonk, N.Y., M. E. Sharpe, 1995. 168p. maps. index. (Sources and Studies in World History). $45.00; $17.95pa. ISBN 1-56324-333-4; 1-56324-334-2pa.

The 96 maps that make up this simple historical atlas of South Asian history will delight the visual learner. The power of mapping the changes in the subcontinent's history is shown clearly by the perceivable shifts in the topographical world. Dangers accrue to this process. Particularly in the early stages, the shadowy history in South Asia is presented as clear and complete. Scholars' disagreements and dissents are forged into maps of certainty. However, taken as a whole, this is a very useful volume. Read alone it gives a rudimentary overview of South Asian history. An even more valuable use would be in conjunction with a course or text that complicates the subject sufficiently. Four thousand years of history are presented from the economic, social, cultural, political, and geographical perspectives. Specific maps concerning Nepal, Bhutan, Sri Lanka, Pakistan, Bangladesh, and India are included. For the college student, the general reader, and the merely curious, this atlas will serve its purpose. Carefully used, it will enhance a scholar's or specialist's work.—**Linda L. Lam-Easton**

Chinese

535. Zurndorfer, Harriet T. **China Bibliography: A Research Guide to Reference Works About China Past and Present.** New York, E. J. Brill, 1995. 380p. index. (Handbook of Oriental Studies). $99.50. ISBN 90-04-10278-7.

This extensive and scholarly research guide to major reference works for the study of modern and historic China is well crafted. It is by a sinologist who has been teaching at the Sinologisch Instituut at Leiden University since 1978 and has spent more than 10 years painstakingly gathering useful information about important reference works covering a wide range of subjects, published in China or elsewhere in the world, during the past 300 years.

The 1-volume guide has 11 chapters beginning with an extensive introduction and followed by "Bibliographies," "Journals and Newspapers," "Biography in China: Past and Present," "China's Geography: Historical and Modern Sources," "Dictionaries," "Encyclopedias, Yearbooks, and Statistical References,"

"*Ts'ung-shu* and Miscellaneous Collectanea," "Indexes and Concordances," "The Chinese Calendar," and "Translations." Each chapter also begins with a useful introduction. The most important feature of this guide is the inclusion of Chinese characters for all Chinese names and titles cited. The whole work provides a systematic way for its readers to approach the overwhelming number of publications related to China in Chinese and other languages.

With wider scope and currency, this guide supplements, updates, and extends (but does not necessarily duplicate) major earlier publications such as *The History of Imperial China* by Endymion Wilkinson (see ARBA 74, entry 331); *Updating Wilkinson: An Annotated Bibliography of Reference Works on Imperial China Published Since 1973* by James H. Cole (n.p., 1991); *Modern China, 1840-1972* (see ARBA 74, entry 252); *An Annotated Bibliography of Selected Reference Works* (3d ed.; see ARBA 72, entry 249); *Modern China: A Bibliographical Guide to Chinese Works 1898-1937* by John Fairbank and K. C. Liu (Harvard University Press, 1950; repr., 1961); *Contemporary China* by Peter Berton and Eugene Wu (Hoover Institution on War, Revolution and Peace, 1967); and *Early Chinese Texts* by Michael Loewe (Institute of East Asian Studies, University of California, 1993). In view of the growing interest in the study of China and the need for an up-to-date research guide, this volume is highly recommended for all libraries with a major reference collection.—**Hwa-Wei Lee**

India

536. Carter, April. **Mahatma Gandhi: A Selected Bibliography.** Westport, Conn., Greenwood Press, 1995. 169p. index. (Bibliographies of World Leaders, no.2). $59.95. ISBN 0-313-28296-X.

This descriptive bibliography of works written by and about Gandhi, the second in the Bibliographies of World Leaders series, is a valuable addition to Gandhi studies. Considered a saint by many Indians and an inspiration to many others in the West, there is abundant literature on Gandhi. A subject-phrase search on him in the Research Library Group's RLIN database produced 2,458 titles. Jagdish Saran Sharma's comprehensive work, *Mahatma Gandhi: A Descriptive Bibliography* (2d ed., Delhi, S. Chand & Co., 1968) lists more than 4,500 works on Gandhi.

This selective bibliography, however, concentrates only on English-language works and contains only 489 books and articles. It sets Gandhi in his historical and political context, covering his life, political campaigns, philosophy, and the strategy of nonviolence. There are 49 entries for Gandhi's own writing; 72 for general biographies; 204 on political campaigns; 85 on Gandhi's social, political, and ethical thought; 51 on Gandhi's place in history; and 30 on the Gandhian movement since 1948.

This bibliography also includes works on colleagues and contemporaries relevant to understanding Gandhi's life and thought, a summary biography, a chronology of his life, a glossary of Indian terms, author and subject indexes, and Gandhi's picture as a frontispiece. This is a useful reference book for English-speaking students.—**Sung Ok Kim**

Japanese

537. Dower, John W., with Timothy S. George. **Japanese History and Culture from Ancient to Modern Times: Seven Basic Bibliographies.** 2d ed. Princeton, N.J., Markus Wiener Publishing, 1995. 459p. index. $59.95; $34.95pa. ISBN 1-55876-097-0; 1-55876-098-9pa.

When the 1st edition of Dower's *Seven Basic Bibliographies* appeared in 1986 (see ARBA 87, entry 112), it filled a significant bibliographical gap in English-language Japanese studies. Even though it was primarily the reading lists used in the author's classes, lacking annotations and a subject index, with typeface too small for easy reading, it was still the best work of its type in print. Since then, other bibliographical works in Japanese studies have appeared, including Frank Joseph Shulman's well-indexed and -annotated *Japan* (see ARBA 91, entry 103), as well as computer databases. Japanese studies students and scholars have greater expectations from bibliographical resources.

This 2d edition adds many books, dissertations, articles, government documents, and other publications that have appeared since 1986. The volume is more than twice the size of the original, but the typeface has nearly doubled as well. The last two sections, "Bibliographies & Research Guides" and "Journals &

Other Serial Publications," show the most substantive increase in entries. The table of contents, virtually unchanged, still forms the basic subject access to the materials: There is still no topical index. The present work also lacks annotations.

Taken as a whole, the Dower and George bibliographical resource is still a useful reading and research list for undergraduate and possibly graduate students, as well as nonacademic clientele. Furthermore, the reasonable price encourages its wide acquisition by both public and academic libraries. It is hoped that the next revision and updating will provide its audience with more complete and accessible information.—**Kenneth W. Berger**

Korea

538. **The Korean War: An Encyclopedia.** Stanley Sandler, ed. Hamden, Conn., Garland, 1995. 416p. illus. maps. index. (Military History of the United States, v.4; Garland Reference Library of the Humanities, v.872). $75.00. ISBN 0-8240-4445-2.

There are many reference books covering the Korean War, including the *Historical Dictionary of the Korean War* (see ARBA 92, entry 648). There is an older work that provides access to many works on this subject: *The Korean War: An Annotated Bibliography* (see ARBA 87, entry 493). This encyclopedia on the Korean War offers articles of varying lengths on several topics connected with the war; for example, ground, naval, and air operations; the POW issue; armistice negotiations; large military units; civilian and military leaders; and so on. Longer articles are signed and include bibliographies on a given topic. A chronology, a bibliography of pertinent works, and an index conclude this handy volume on one of the most important topics in U.S. military history.—**Bohdan S. Wynar**

EUROPEAN HISTORY
General Works

539. Vincent, Mary, and R. A. Stradling. **Cultural Atlas of Spain and Portugal.** New York, Facts on File, 1994. 240p. illus. maps. index. $45.00. ISBN 0-8160-3014-6.

Facts on File's Cultural Atlas series has won applause from previous reviewers for its unique combination of cultural history with historical and contemporary maps. Previous volumes have described Japan (see ARBA 89, entry 108), Russia and the Soviet Union (1990), and France (see ARBA 93, entry 143). The present volume focuses on the Iberian countries of Spain and Portugal, described here as being on the peripheral, edge, or fringe of Europe. This geographical isolation is explored in part 1, "Physical Background." According to the authors, it accounts for the persistent localism so apparent in the peninsula.

Part 2 explores the history of the peninsula in 5 chapters from the earliest Iberians, whose origin is a matter of dispute, through the establishment of democracies in the late twentieth century in both Spain and Portugal. Some 40 maps drawn to scale, ranging in size from $\frac{1}{2}$ to $\frac{3}{4}$ of a page, accompany the text and describe historical and contemporary events that include Iberian, Visigothic, Greek, Roman, and Moorish occupations; the Reconquest; Imperial Spain and Portugal; the Wars of Independence; and the civil wars of the last two centuries. Part 3 describes the geographical regions of the peninsula, including the South, the Mediterranean, the Center, the Ebro Valley, the Atlantic Coast, and the Atlantic Islands.

The text and maps are complemented by 240 beautiful color photographs that highlight many important historical and cultural events. These encompass features on art, palaces, buildings, artists, posters, food, and even Expo '92 in Seville. A chronology, dynastic chart, glossary, short bibliography, and gazetteer complete the volume.

Vincent, a lecturer in modern history at the University of Sheffield, and Stradling, a reader in history at the University of Wales, know the region well, having published widely on Iberian topics. This atlas will make an excellent addition to the reference shelves of academic, public, and school libraries, and it will also prove a useful guide to anyone contemplating a trip to the peninsula.—**Brian E. Coutts**

British

540. Englefield, Dermot, Janet Seaton, and Isobel White. **Facts About the British Prime Ministers: A Compilation of Biographical and Historical Information.** New York, H. W. Wilson, 1995. 439p. illus. index. $55.00. ISBN 0-8242-0863-3.

This is a new addition to H. W. Wilson's Facts About . . . series, and it closely resembles *Facts About the Presidents* (6th ed.; see ARBA 94, entry 499) in format and scope. However, while there are numerous reference books on U.S. presidents, there are few on British prime ministers, making this an important new work. All 50 prime ministers, from Sir Robert Walpole in 1721 to the present John Major, are profiled. The first and main section of the book consists of chronological entries, each about seven pages in small typeface. Following a brief overview of the individual's career is a section on family members, Parliamentary elections and experience, governments formed, and a list of important dates in the person's life. The sketches end with background information on the PMs, including appearance; education; hobbies; memorable quotes; locations of portraits, statues, and personal papers; and a short bibliography.

In the second part of the book, information on the prime ministers is rearranged into 80 tables that compare personal and professional characteristics. Here is a playground for trivia fans. Where else can one find out easily that "since 1730, a Prime Minister has been born on average every 5 years and 69 days" (p. 371)? Other features of the book are an introduction to the role of the prime minister in the twentieth century, a discussion of the official residences, a glossary, and a subject index.

The authors are all affiliated with the Library of the House of Commons, and they share a librarian's love of detail. They have done an excellent job presenting their facts in an attractive, logically organized format, but with enough anecdotes to make the work entertaining. *Facts About the British Prime Ministers* is recommended for high school, public, and academic libraries that field questions on recent British history.—**Hope Yelich**

541. Larousse Dictionary of British History. Min Lee, ed. New York, Larousse Kingfisher Chambers, 1994. 330p. $8.95pa. ISBN 0-7523-0004-0.

Adapted from the *Larousse Dictionary of World History* (see ARBA 95, entry 582), this work covers the history of the British Isles (including Ireland) from earliest times until the 1990s. The arrangement is alphabetical, with names or phrases highlighted in the text that are referred to further entries. People, events, important legislation, and major periods and concepts in British history are included. Only political, diplomatic and military, and, to a lesser extent, religious history are covered. There is no reference to cultural figures or the arts, except for the inclusion of a few writers, such as Thomas Paine or Mary Wollstonecraft, noted for their political views and writings. The entries vary in length from a few lines to several pages for major events such as the American Revolution or World War I. They provide concise accounts of the significance of the individuals and events included in the context of their period of British history.

The coverage of the dictionary is necessarily highly selective, and weighted toward modern personalities, events, and government legislation. This has led to some insignificant twentieth-century political figures being included at the expense of such major historical figures as Saint Patrick. However, this is a useful, current, and reasonably priced ready-reference source, probably more appropriate for a personal than a library collection, since many more substantial sources of British biography and history exist.—**Christine E. King**

542. Rosenthal, Joel T. **Late Medieval England (1377-1485): A Bibliography of Historical Scholarship 1975-1989.** Kalamazoo, Mich., Medieval Institute Publications, Western Michigan University, 1994. 371p. index. $36.00. ISBN 1-879288-16-8.

Authoring a bibliography is like the toiling of Sisyphus. Even before it is published, the bibliography is rendered out of date and incomplete by the appearance of new scholarship. Scholars and students of late medieval England (1377-1485) will still be most grateful to Rosenthal for his labors in compiling this new bibliography of 1,910 items of historical scholarship published during the years 1975-1989. Individual entries provide full bibliographical information and are usually briefly annotated. The bibliography is organized into 11 chapters (e.g., political history, social and economic history, and fine arts and crafts). Particularly useful is the second chapter: "Bibliographies, Catalogues, Guides, Handbooks,

Historiography, and Reference Studies." A simple index of authors, editors, or compilers concludes the volume. Rosenthal's work serves as a useful and needed supplement to DeLloyd J. Guth's *Late-Medieval England, 1377-1485* (see ARBA 77, entry 409) and Edgar B. Graves's *A Bibliography of English History to 1485* (see ARBA 77, entry 408). One only hopes that Rosenthal or someone else is already busily compiling the next supplement for 1990-2004.—**Ronald H. Fritze**

543. **Twentieth-Century Britain: An Encyclopedia.** F. M. Leventhal, ed. Hamden, Conn., Garland, 1995. 902p. illus. index. (Garland Reference Library of the Humanities, v.1378). $95.00. ISBN 0-8240-7205-7.

This work is a topical dictionary covering twentieth-century British historical development. It opens with a contents listing by topic, a preface, and a chronological listing of important events for every year from 1900 to 1994. The encyclopedia consists of descriptive and analytical entries ranging from 500 to 3,000 words. Written by United States and British scholars, these alphabetically arranged entries chronicle individuals, events, social conditions, and legislation affecting British life during this century.

Subjects covered in this encyclopedia include political thought, historical preservation, publishing and publishers, imperial preference, Open University, the Falklands War, the Official Secrets Act, genetics, coal mining, detective fiction, Ralph Vaughan Williams, the Conservative Party, Methodism, cricket, the National Health Service, and marriage. Each entry also features a selective bibliography.

One weakness of this effort is the absence of an essay on the evolving role of the monarchy in light of historical controversy over King Edward VIII and ongoing royal marital scandals. Nevertheless, this work is sufficiently comprehensive in scope and serves as a useful introduction to contemporary British history that will be a welcome addition to academic library reference collections.—**Bert Chapman**

544. Wilson, Eunice. **Dangerous Sky: A Resource Guide to the Battle of Britain.** Westport, Conn., Greenwood Press, 1995. 128p. illus. maps. index. (Bibliographies of Battles and Leaders, no.14). $65.00. ISBN 0-313-28216-1.

This book is a welcome addition to the voluminous literature about World War II, especially as it developed in the European theater in 1940. *Dangerous Sky* seeks to compile the main sources of information published through 1989 about the activities of the Royal Air Force (RAF) during the Battle of Britain. While the aerial combat, pitting crack Luftwaffe pilots against outnumbered but valiant RAF squadrons, was by no means a pivotal battle, its symbolic value was of considerable weight for the embattled British. After occupying most of the European continent by June 1940 and driving the British army into the sea at Dunkirk, Adolf Hitler's next objective was to control Great Britain. Neither the Battle of Britain, nor the ensuing blitzkrieg bombing of civilian populations, nor four long years of war would give him that victory. One interesting aspect of the Battle of Britain is that the RAF pilots were an international group, consisting of the British, North Americans, Australians, Czechs, and Poles, among others. U.S. pilots volunteered to join the RAF and fight in a war that was as yet undeclared for the United States, thereby risking their citizenship.

Dangerous Sky is an essential starting point for further research on the Battle of Britain. It organizes materials that range from official documents through memoirs and biographies to secondary histories under major categories. Within each category, materials are listed in alphabetical order, and there are short descriptive comments. The bibliography of works related to the Battle of Britain and the onset of World War II is particularly rich. This research guide is highly recommended for military buffs, researchers, and students.—**John B. Romeiser**

French

545. **Dictionary of Twentieth Century Culture: French Culture 1900-1975.** Catharine Savage Brosman and others, eds. Detroit, Gale, 1995. 449p. illus. index. $60.00. ISBN 0-8103-8482-5.

This work is the second volume in an ambitious series designed to summarize worldwide cultural trends in regional settings (the first volume dealt with American culture after World War II, and 18 other volumes are in preparation). The layout of each book consists of a foreword and editorial plan, a topical index, and a timeline of contributions and events covering the period of the work. The time span covered seems in many ways an odd temporal framework for such a book dealing with France, but decisions obviously had to be made. A more comprehensive general index concludes the volume. The roughly 550 major entries cover most aspects of the French scene during the selected time frame; they range from a few lines to more than two pages in length. Photographs are widely used for illustration, although many of these are poorly reproduced. Amazingly, there is not a single map, although many of the entries would clearly profit from cartographic expression.

The basic problem with such a work is to define *culture* and to draw appropriate boundaries of inclusion. This book is generally strong in art, architecture, literature, cinema, and media (although failure to mention *Le Canard Enchaîné*, in many ways the most influential of post-World War II French newspapers, seems inexplicable), but the editors ignore science, although many famous scientists have strongly influenced French culture. They also seem unable to resist edging into politics, although the sketchy coverage here largely slights many figures who have played a prominent role in the interlinked recent political/cultural history of France. Nonetheless, this is an impressive volume, and should find a place on the bookshelf of anyone interested in twentieth-century France.—**James R. McDonald**

German

546. Thompson, Wayne C., Susan L. Thompson, and Juliet S. Thompson. **Historical Dictionary of Germany.** Metuchen, N.J., Scarecrow, 1994. 637p. illus. maps. $62.50. ISBN 0-8108-2869-3.

This is a very useful dictionary covering the history of Germany from Roman times to the Maastricht treaty of 1993. It includes a chronology of events; a dictionary of persons, political parties, events, and terms; and a selected but impressive bibliography of works dealing with the country's history, politics, economy, and culture.

While the dictionary's subject is the whole of German history, its emphasis and strength are its coverage of topics from the mid-twentieth century to the present. This emphasis is seen in the chronology, which uses 24 pages for events from A.D. 9 to 1945 and devotes 60 pages to the events from 1946 to 1993. When one gets into the dictionary proper, one is greeted by copious information on political parties, programs, incidents, persons, and cultural topics. Biographical entries are for the most part devoted to politicians and military leaders, but many artists, musicians, authors, and philosophers are also included. To suggest the scope of the dictionary with a few sample entries risks misrepresenting the breadth of its coverage, but a few random selections follow: *German Empire, Grand Coalition, Weimar Republic, Socialist Initiative, Family, Education, Helmut Schmidt, Revolution of 1848*, and *Change (Wende)*. All subject entries are in English and there is no index or *see* references from the German form to the English, so it is necessary to know the English form. On the other hand, the German version is usually given in the text of an entry. Numerous *see* references connect English entries and *see also* references lead the researcher from one related article to another. Abbreviations for political parties are liberally used, and there is a helpful and necessary glossary of abbreviations and acronyms at the beginning of the work. The abbreviations are those used in German but the definitions include both the English and the German forms. For example, SED is defined as "Socialist Unity Party (Sozialistische Einheitspartei Deutschlands)."

The dictionary will be invaluable to students of history and political science and its 80-page bibliography of English-language book sources will provide a fine beginning for further research. It is recommended for all academic libraries and those public libraries supporting research in German history and politics.—**Eric R. Nitschke**

Italian

547. Adkins, Lesley, and Roy A. Adkins. **Handbook to Life in Ancient Rome.** New York, Facts on File, 1994. 404p. illus. maps. index. $40.00. ISBN 0-8160-2755-2.

Although a significant number of handbooks, guides, and encyclopedias already exist on ancient Rome, the *Handbook* succeeds in making an original contribution to this much-studied civilization. Designed as a ready-reference tool for both beginning and more advanced students, the handbook has incorporated much of the recent scholarship in the field of ancient Roman studies as well as preserving older but still valuable material. The organization falls under nine broad headings: "Republic and Empire";

"Military Affairs"; "Geography of the Roman World"; "Towns and Countryside"; "Travel and Trade"; "Written Evidence"; "Religion, Economy and Industry"; and "Everyday Life." Each heading is divided into subtopics. The user who is used to a straight alphabetical listing of subjects may be confused, even discouraged, by the arrangement. Use of the detailed index is a must in finding information; the index should be used in locating individual topics under each heading.

Useful features of the *Handbook* include a "Gazetteer of Place Names," which lists both the original Roman name and modern equivalents; a list of "Authors and Their Works" that contains a brief biographical sketch of each author, together with a detailed list of writings; and the "Numbering and Stations of Legion," a convenient section on the various units in the Roman army and their role in history. It is a welcome addition to any library's reference collection and will complement other current reference sources on Roman history such as *Encyclopedia of the Roman Empire* (see ARBA 95, entry 579), *Civilization of the Ancient Mediterranean World* (see ARBA 89, entry 488), and *Chronicle of the Roman Emperors* (Thames & Hudson, 1995). Many of the entries that are furnished in the bibliography are current sources published in the 1980s and 1990s. The work is illustrated with black-and-white photographs and line drawings, and is recommended for all libraries.—**Jane Jurgens**

Russian

548. Frame, Murray, comp. **The Russian Revolution, 1905-1921: A Bibliographic Guide to Works in English.** Westport, Conn., Greenwood Press, 1995. 308p. index. (Bibliographies and Indexes in World History, no.40). $79.50. ISBN 0-313-29559-X.

With the dissolution of the Soviet Union and the opening of archives to broader and more diverse research in Russia and the new countries formed from the breakup of the Soviet Union, a bibliography of works in English on the Russian Revolution is a welcome source for research in the field of Russian history. The work includes published material from 1905 to 1994, the main criterion for inclusion being that the work concern the period of the Russian Revolution from 1905 to 1921. There are 24 thematic sections, which include political structures; revolutionary movements; civil war; the military; personalities; and diaries, memoirs, travel, and eyewitness accounts.

The significance of this volume is that it comes out at a time when old attitudes about the Russian Revolution may be changing, particularly in the countries of the former Soviet Union. One hopes that this volume can help to bridge material produced before the fall of the Soviet Union to material that will place the Russian Revolution in a clearer perspective, minus the Socialist/Communist ideological persuasion. But perhaps a whole generation will have to pass before the Russian people and the nationalities of the various countries of the former Soviet Union can gain a more dispassionate view of one of the most important events of the twentieth century. This work brings to light the progress that is being made, and that needs to continue, in understanding the Russian Revolution, not only by the Russian people, but by the English-speaking and -reading countries of the world. This work is therefore highly recommended for college, university, and government reference collections.—**Norman L. Kincaide**

Yugoslav

549. Stallaerts, Robert, and Jeannine Laurens. **Historical Dictionary of the Republic of Croatia.** Metuchen, N.J., Scarecrow, 1995. 341p. (European Historical Dictionaries, no.9). $45.00. ISBN 0-8108-2999-1.

Beginning with a chronology and overview of Croatian history and economic geography, which demonstrate that the Croatian nation is much older than the present country, the authors provide articles on more than 550 people, places, institutions, events, and political parties in Croatia past and present. The majority of articles are brief (few exceed one page), and there are many *see* references. Students and researchers will be disappointed that the biographical entries give years of birth and death but rarely months or days, and few personal details. The entry on the Ustasa discusses the deaths of 700,000 Serbs, but does not mention the persecution of Jews. The articles on Croatia's relations with other countries are superficial and only cover from 1990 on (i.e., the time since Croatia's rebirth). Astonishingly, there is no major article on the historical relationship between Croatia and either Serbia or Bosnia.

The approximately 100-page bibliography has more than 800 items, covering a wide variety of scholarly and popular articles, books, and government reports, primarily in English, but also in Croatian and French. Entries give full bibliographical information and are arranged under broad subject headings and subtopics, with no accession numbers and no index. Although Francine Friedman's *Yugoslavia: A Comprehensive English-Language Bibliography* (see ARBA 94, entry 139) contains many more items for the former Yugoslavia in general, the dual role of this historical dictionary makes it a unique source at the present time for information on Croatia.—**John A. Drobnicki**

LATIN AMERICAN AND CARIBBEAN HISTORY

550. Kanellos, Nicolas, with Cristelia Perez. **Chronology of Hispanic-American History: From Pre-Columbian Times to the Present.** Detroit, Gale, 1995. 427p. illus. maps. index. $49.95. ISBN 0-8103-9200-3.

Chronology of Hispanic-American History is divided into 11 chapters dealing with key historical figures, places, and events placed in chronological context. Included also are regional histories, a "historical timeline," citations or excerpts from pertinent historical documents, a glossary, a category or subject index, and a general index. The book covers a plethora of subjects, among which are agriculture, anthropology, art and architecture, civil rights, economics, education, film and theater, labor, literature, music, politics and law, religion, science, medicine, sports, and women's issues. The object of the book is to provide a concise, one-volume form of basic information of significance regarding people, places, and events in the history of Hispanic America from pre-Columbian times through the twentieth century.—**S. D. Markman**

551. Whigham, Thomas, and Jerry W. Cooney. **A Guide to Collections on Paraguay in the United States.** Westport, Conn., Greenwood Press, 1995. 114p. index. (Reference Guides to Archival and Manuscript Sources in World History, no.4). $59.95. ISBN 0-313-29203-5.

This guide is a specialized resource to collections and scattered archival and manuscript materials on Paraguay located in libraries and research centers in the United States. Arranged geographically by state, the work provides the complete name and address of each institution together with a list of its collections. Brief descriptions of the contents of a particular collection as it pertains to Paraguay are also provided. The guide includes collections of personal and family papers and conference and society papers, as well as state and federal documents. Relevant materials on Paraguay are highlighted within general collections, such as U.S. Department of Commerce General Records and the Pam American Health Organizations. The guide contains both a collection and a subject index and is recommended for research libraries with strong collections in Latin America.—**Jane Jurgens**

MIDDLE EASTERN HISTORY

552. Edelheit, Hershel, and Abraham J. Edelheit. **Israel and the Jewish World, 1948-1993: A Chronology.** Westport, Conn., Greenwood Press, 1995. 413p. index. (Bibliographies and Indexes in World History, no.39). $69.50. ISBN 0-313-29275-2.

This reference work in Jewish and Israeli studies should be purchased by larger public and research libraries, and smaller or more specialized collections where client interest and funds warrant. The work is of obvious use in Middle East studies collections, although it is inevitably written from a pro-Israeli viewpoint. The 14-page introduction summarizes the end of the Holocaust and the main currents in the Jewish Diaspora and international relations that led to the Zionist movement and the establishment of Israel.

There are nine chapters focused on the main experiences of the Israeli state. The chronology appears complete to a nonexpert. There are individual indexes to names, places, and subjects. The usefulness of this separation is questionable; it creates extra work and some confusion. For example, Abu Nidal is in the subject (and not the name) index, apparently because the references are to the acts of his terrorist group. (The terrorist "Carlos" is for some reason in neither index, although one would think his associations with Middle East terrorism would make him relevant to Israel.) Original language terms (transliterated) for Israeli and European organizations may diminish the user friendliness for the nonspecialist, although the substantial glossary alleviates this problem. In summary, this is a professionally produced reference work on a high-profile topic.—**Nigel Tappin**

WORLD HISTORY
Atlases

553. Howarth, Sarah. **The Children's Atlas of the 20th Century: Chart the Century....** Brookfield, Conn., Millbrook Press, 1995. 95p. illus. maps. index. $19.40; $12.95pa. ISBN 1-56294-563-7; 1-56294-885-7pa.

This overview of the twentieth century covers the time period in a 5-part study composed of summaries, sidebars, 200 photographs, glove insets, and color-coded maps of most world areas. A clever timeline device appears on the right outer edge of 30 pages. The two-page index refers users to significant concepts, movements, leaders, events, and places. The initial appeal of sharply defined territorial boundaries, transportation lines, and readable legends suggests that students, teachers, parents, and librarians will profit from owning and using this atlas. However, in this case, looks are deceiving.

As is true of many repackaged books from European publishing houses, this atlas belies its seemingly generous, inclusive coverage. The cover is a warning that a focus on mostly white males and war deprives the reader of a fuller knowledge of the world. The author violates basic rules governing diction, pronoun reference, passive voice, verb-subject agreement, and rhetorical variety. Quality black-and-white and color graphics appear alongside fuzzy photographs and smeared sepia prints. Cutlines in several places identify a male in the picture but ignore the female or other significant males. In most examples, the single reference leaves the reader with no clue as to which person is the focal figure. Many photographs featuring women depict them in passive, subservient roles or as victims, and Native Americans are conspicuously absent from pictures and text. Commentary lacks specificity; no charts or tables orient the reader with census figures or proofs of generalizations. A stronger editorial hand may have saved this work from the ignominy of inept writing and weak presentation.—**Mary Ellen Snodgrass**

Bibliography

554. **The American Historical Association's Guide to Historical Literature.** 3d ed. Mary Beth Norton and Pamela Gerardi, eds. New York, Oxford University Press, 1995. 2v. index. $150.00/set. ISBN 0-19-505727-9.

This set of annotated bibliographies covers all regions and periods of history. Through it the American Historical Association seeks to provide a guide to the historical literature for the scholar and serious student. It supersedes the 1931 and 1961 editions. The volumes are divided into 48 sections with 26,926 citations, extensive subdivisions, and cross-references. Most sections are geographical, emphasizing Europe, Asia, and North America. Subjects for nongeographical sections are: the theoretical and practical aspects of history; prehistory; world history; international relations; science, technology, and medicine; and natives of the Americas. Each chapter is edited by a specialist.

Each section has an introduction discussing major themes in the historiography of its topic. Annotations for the section are written by the editors and a team of academics and graduate students. Some annotations are evaluative, others purely descriptive. Responsibility for each annotation is indicated by contributor initials. Full bibliographic information is provided. Both monographs and journal articles are covered. Most works are in English, but foreign-language material is present. Most of the contributors have American academic affiliations. The detailed subject index will greatly aid those interested in topics transcending section headings. There is an index to the authors cited. Added features include a list of journals publishing materials on historical subjects.

The listings appear balanced and extensive, but not exhaustive of the literature. For example, while the introduction to the Soviet section mentions legal history, the author index contains no mention of Peter Solomon of the University of Toronto who has published extensively in this area. These sorts of omissions do not detract from the impressive whole, but need to be noted: For the specialist there can be no substitute for thorough literature searches! In sum, all research libraries must buy this work. It would be of value to nonresearch public libraries where funds permit.—**Nigel Tappin**

555. Latham, A. J. H., comp. **Africa, Asia, and South America Since 1800: A Bibliographical Guide.** Manchester, England, Manchester University Press; distr., New York, St. Martin's Press, 1995. 259p. index. $90.00. ISBN 0-7190-1877-3.

In the style of Latham's occasional annotations, this book is a brave compilation of colonial and native, capitalist and labor spokespersons on economics and politics. Perhaps a quarter of the entries have comments. But the titles, and sometimes authors' reputations, tell the good news that there is information available to help people be good citizens of the world and vote wisely on leaders, if they will read. Most of the publications were published between 1970 and 1990, and would need to be constantly updated.

The subject of the guide is the last two centuries in Africa, Asia, and South America. The rationalizations of the powerful and the cries of the masses are considered and debated. Even humanists are included, when they elucidate the necessity of caution as people exercise the inevitable need for livelihood and security and the social responsibility of entrepreneurship and political intervention. That expert writers have gathered facts and hypothesized theories, that there are bibliographies of these writings, is reason to celebrate.—**Elizabeth L. Anderson**

Biography

556. Hamilton, Neil A. **Founders of Modern Nations: A Biographical Dictionary.** Santa Barbara, Calif., ABC-CLIO, 1995. 505p. illus. maps. index. $60.00. ISBN 0-87436-750-6.

This is an intriguing title. According to the preface, *Founders of Modern Nations* is divided into two parts: biographical entries and national entries. There is an explanation of criteria that, unfortunately, can only add to the confusion. Who is a "modern" founder in Russia? According to the entry locator, there are the following political figures: Catherine II (the Great), Mikhail Gorbachev, Ivan III (the Great), Peter I (the Great), and Boris Yeltsin. For the United States, John Adams, Samuel Adams, Benjamin Franklin, Alexander Hamilton, Thomas Jefferson, James Madison, Thomas Paine, and George Washington are listed. Indeed, as the preface indicates, "exhaustive coverage of the United States would, in itself, require a dictionary of formidable size." Yes, there are several scholarly dictionaries for the United States, but why include Gorbachev and Yeltsin and omit Franklin Roosevelt? The second part, "Country Profiles," is simply not sufficient for any user, including the elementary school student. Hamilton is an associate professor of history at Spring Hill College in Mobile, Alabama. It is difficult to recommend this book to even the uninitiated.—**Bohdan S. Wynar**

Catalogs and Collections

557. **Imperial War Museum Film Catalogue. Volume I: The First World War Archive.** Roger Smither, ed. Westport, Conn., Greenwood Press, 1994. 592p. index. (Bibliographies and Indexes in Military Studies, no.7). $115.00. ISBN 0-313-29379-1.

The Imperial War Museum was founded in 1917 to record a war that was perceived as unique and, it was hoped, the war to end all wars. The Museum assembled vast collections from aircraft and artillery to art. One component was film, and the First World War film collection is one of the first film archives in the world. This collection is an invaluable resource for scholars, researchers, and educational program makers. This is the first volume in the museum's plan to publish catalogs of all their collections.

The catalog covers all 1,217 items in the World War I collection, including documentaries and newsreels, instructional and propaganda materials, and animation. It treats the battlefields and the home front, and traces the evolution of combat camera work and the filming of the war. Virtually all are silent films. Each entry gives a Museum index reference number, the country of origin, the date of release or production, the title, the length of the film and other technical description, a summary of contents, other notes about the film, and the identity of the cataloger and date of entry. Many of the entries supply an evaluation of the film. The volume has an excellent index, and a superb introductory essay on World War I film and the evolution of the archives by Stephen Badsey of the Royal Military Academy, Sandhurst. Although this is a mammoth effort and an extremely valuable source for employing the film archive, it is an esoteric source of interest only to a small number of highly specialized researchers. Very few libraries need this volume.—**Joe P. Dunn**

Chronology

558. **Chronicle of the 20th Century.** Clifton Daniel and others, eds. New York, Dorling Kindersley, 1995. 1486p. illus. maps. index. $69.95. ISBN 0-7894-0332-3.

A less-than-stellar first impression is made by a book featuring multiple typographical errors in a portentous foreword. Luckily, the body of this oversized chronology is unpretentious and compulsively readable. Dividing the century into monthly chunks, each month's entry contains the following: a day-by-day calendar for that month; three to six brief newspaper stories written in pseudo-wire service style; a news headline for most days of the month; and photographs. The illustrations are the book's strength. There are thousands of portraits, action shots, print advertisements, movie posters, propaganda banners, and fine art reproductions. Nearly a half of each page is devoted to engrossing images. A flaw in the "newspaper stories" is that they are not wire service stories but are formatted as such, giving the reader the impression that they are reprints of newspaper stories of the day. It is a small point but one worth making—news copy written in hindsight is more knowing than wire service copy of the moment.

Arrows throughout the text lead the reader forward in the book to follow up on story developments and resolutions. The July 12, 1966, entry on mass murderer Richard Speck (the Chicago nurses were slain that week) contains an arrow pointing the reader to August 1, 1966, the date of his "not guilty" plea, then to April 15, 1967, for his conviction, and to June 5, 1967, for his death sentence. It is a handy device for tracking stories; however, the book's index picks up the 1967 entries, but not those for 1966. With one or two pages assigned to each month, the coverage of events is at times skimpy (unavoidable) and shallow (questionable). The December 1971 page states "conceptual art becomes fad in U.S." Think of this oversized book as a historical chronology as presented by *USA Today*. With all of its photographs, it is really fun to browse, but in-depth factual work would mandate the use of a second source. Reluctant writers of history papers would likely reach for this resource first.—**Ed Volz**

559. **Chronology of the Ancient World: 10,000 B.C. to A.D. 799.** By H. E. L. Mellersh. New York, Simon & Schuster, 1994. 500p. index. (Chronology of World History). $70.00. ISBN 0-13-326422-X.

560. **Chronology of the Expanding World: 1492 to 1762.** By Neville Williams. New York, Simon & Schuster, 1994. 700p. index. (Chronology of World History). $75.00. ISBN 0-13-326406-8.

561. **Chronology of the Medieval World: 800 to 1491.** By R. L. Storey. New York, Simon & Schuster, 1994. 705p. index. (Chronology of World History). $75.00. ISBN 0-13-326465-3.

562. **Chronology of the Modern World: 1763 to 1992.** 2d ed. By Neville Williams and Philip Waller. New York, Simon & Schuster, 1994. 1136p. index. (Chronology of World History). $90.00. ISBN 0-13-326695-8. [The above 4 titles may be purchased as a set: $310.00. ISBN 0-13-326430-0].

This series of volumes provides month-to-month descriptions of important political and military events on the left-hand pages, while the right-hand pages describe developments in economy, science, religion, literature, scholarship, and the like, and important births and deaths for the year under consideration. The first volume emphasizes Greco-Roman and early Medieval European history. The second contains material on the Islamic world and China and Japan, as well as Medieval Europe. Volumes 3 and 4 treat most of the world; however, the approach to the events listed remains Eurocentric.

There is an obvious abundance of material in the combined 3,000-plus pages, but several flaws mar the volumes' usefulness. The volumes emphasize European and, in the modern era, English details. For instance, most entries under "scholarship" and "sports" in the *Modern World* list British accomplishments.

While there is some treatment of the non-Western world in all the volumes, there are a number of mistakes and misstatements. For instance, Siddhārtha Gautama is referred to as a Bengal prince (*Ancient World*, p. 91), the caliph Abū Bakr is credited with making the Koran (*Ancient World*, p. 433), and Robert Clive is stated to have taken Plassey (*Expanding World*, p. 536). No entry could be found in the index for the Taj Mahal, and its builder, Shāh Jāhan, is listed under Jāhan, Shāh. Technical terms are not explained, and official explanations are given in place of more accurate history, as in "only Israel accepted a British-French ultimatum to withdraw from Sinai" in 1956 (*Modern World*, p. 652). Readers are cautioned, therefore, to use these volumes with care.—**David L. White**

563. Hutchison, Kevin Don. **Operation Desert Shield/Desert Storm: Chronology and Fact Book.** Westport, Conn., Greenwood Press, 1995. 269p. illus. index. $69.50. ISBN 0-313-29606-5.

The war may have been brief, but a whole cottage industry of quick histories and reference works, including encyclopedias, almanacs, chronologies, and fact books, has quickly emerged. This volume by an information specialist and military historian—whose earlier book *World War II in the North Pacific* (see ARBA 95, entry 684) is the best source on that topic—is the most comprehensive work yet on the Desert Shield/Desert Storm operation. The heart of the volume is a day-by-day chronology of the conflict that addresses movements, events, units, missions, equipment, and personnel for the United States and the entire Allied coalition.

Appendixes include a glossary; lists of coalition personnel killed and taken prisoner; the various ground, naval, and air forces in the conflict for both the coalition and Iraq; and 50 pages of biographies of key coalition personnel. The volume also furnishes maps, charts, full-page official photographs of the primary U.S. command and of some of the key weaponry, an excellent bibliography, and an index. If one wants to know any factual information about the Persian Gulf War of 1991, this is the reference work to consult. It is valuable for all libraries that maintain these types of reference sources on U.S. wars.—**Joe P. Dunn**

564. Mellersh, H. E. L., and others. **The Chronology of World History.** compact ed. Santa Barbara, Calif., ABC-CLIO, 1995. 516p. index. $44.55. ISBN 0-87436-866-9.

Historical chronologies have become standard library reference tools since their introduction in the 1960s. This resource is a condensation of other chronologies reviewed elsewhere in this ARBA volume: *Chronology of the Ancient World*, *Chronology of the Expanding World*, and *Chronology of the Modern World* (see entries 559-562). The book's title describes its organization—a straight run from 10,000 B.C.E. to 1994 C.E. More events are listed for later years than early years, with the space devoted to an individual year steadily increasing as the text and time progress. The same amount of space is used for the period 1200-1000 B.C.E. as for the year 1951—one page.

Events are sometimes highlighted, or sometimes not, with headers for music, art, politics, and other broad categories. Such random application is a minor annoyance that is easily ignored. A typical twentieth-century year will have these elements listed: general sociopolitical news; memorable events in the sciences, arts, and sports; musical hits; popular films released; top television shows; and notable books of that year. All such lists are selective. An 85-page index to people, places, and things helps guide the reader through the text.

Given that this is a condensation of other chronologies, the selection of material for inclusion is necessarily selective and somewhat arbitrary. Tracking 12,000 years of history in 430 pages is a challenge. With so little space available for a given year, the reader is tempted to question what is included (e.g., the obscure "industrial" musical group Einsturtzende Neubauten for the year 1984; the equally obscure 1970 film *Kes*—one could nitpick for hours). It is more reasonable to question factual errors, and these are evident as well. Allen Ginsberg's name is listed as "Ginsburg"; Led Zeppelin's second album is listed as a 1970 release, not 1969. Fittingly, this is recommended as a secondary source. Libraries are recommended to buy it if they cannot afford a more comprehensive chronology and to double-check the facts in another source when possible.—**Ed Volz**

Dictionaries and Encyclopedias

565. Bunson, Matthew E. **Encyclopedia of the Middle Ages.** New York, Facts on File, 1995. 498p. illus. maps. index. $45.00. ISBN 0-8160-2456-1.

If, as the song says, you "don't know much about the Middle Ages," this book will end that condition. The approximate chronological scope of the volume covers the years 400-1500. Geographically, it focuses on Europe and the Islamic lands of North Africa and the Middle East. Consisting of 2,000 alphabetically arranged entries on all aspects of the Middle Ages, including people (e.g., Al-Hakim); places (e.g., Kiev); groups (e.g., flagellants); ideas (e.g., Arianism); laws (e.g., Golden Bull); and institutions (e.g., Witan), this volume contains a surprisingly large amount of information.

Individual entries are well written and range in length from a few words to several thousand. Numerous chronologies, genealogies, and maps are provided to complement and supplement the text. *See* and *see also* entries, along with a general index, aid the reader in locating specific topics. Three appendixes of the rulers and dynasties of medieval Europe and Islam, followed by a brief glossary of medieval terms, provide additional information.

Needless to say, a single volume dealing with such a large subject cannot cover everything, but a few entries (e.g., Ethiopia, Mali, Mansa Musa) on the medieval Sudan of Africa are needed. The text contains a few errors and omissions. The Ilkhanids, a Mongol dynasty in Persia, deserve a separate entry, while some material is missing from appendix 3 on page 475. These problems, however, are minor and do not detract from the overall excellence of this book. Its inexpensive price, handy size, and high quality make it a must-purchase for any library, even if its collection already contains the massive classic *The Dictionary of the Middle Ages* (12 vols.; see ARBA 90, entry 533; ARBA 89, entries 484-486; ARBA 88, entries 549-550; ARBA 87, entries 429 and 531; ARBA 86, entry 510; ARBA 85, entries 485-486; and ARBA 84, entries 335-336).—**Ronald H. Fritze**

566. **Larousse Dictionary of Twentieth Century History.** Min Lee, ed. New York, Larousse Kingfisher Chambers, 1994. 767p. $12.95pa. ISBN 0-7523-0003-2.

This work is a concise overview of twentieth-century history, based on the more comprehensive *Dictionary of World History* (formerly the *Chambers Dictionary of World History*, issued by Larousse, 1994), but updated in this concise version when necessary. Unfortunately, no bibliography or references are listed, so readers wishing any additional information will have to seek further help elsewhere. Ready-reference is provided, however, for the influential figures of this century, with an emphasis on diplomatic, military, and political history; little is included of cultural or social significance. Nineteenth-century figures whose influence was felt into the twentieth century are discussed. Coverage of African, Asian, and Latin American personalities is noteworthy, as is the attention paid to recent political developments in Eastern Europe. Anyone needing nothing more than brief information on topics related to current events in this century will find this a helpful reference of first resort, but not for detailed material on any of the topics covered. No maps or illustrations are provided. Cross-references alert users to related topics, but an index would have been equally useful in further enhancing the value of this work.

—**Joseph W. Dauben**

Handbooks and Yearbooks

567. **Eyewitness History of the World.** [CD-ROM]. New York, Dorling Kindersley, 1995. Minimum system requirements: IBM or compatible 386DX/33MHz. CD-ROM drive. Windows 3.1. 4MB RAM. SVGA 256-color monitor. Mouse. Sound card. Loudspeakers or headphones. (Also available in Macintosh version). $79.95. ISBN 0-7894-0042-1 (Windows); 0-7894-0096-0 (Macintosh).

This multimedia reference guide to world history may provide some educational entertainment for children in secondary schools, but its treatment is selective and far too cursory to be of any substantial use, even to high school students. The emphasis here, in at least a few noteworthy instances, is "eyewitness" (as the title indicates). This product's most engaging feature is the use of actual videoclips, often from newsreel footage, of such historic moments as the explosion of the Hindenberg zeppelin at

Lakehurst, New Jersey in 1937, and the actual landing and first words by Neil Armstrong and Edwin Aldrin on the moon in July 1969. Major historical figures are also shown, including Vladimir Lenin during the Bolshevik Revolution; quotations from Mao Tse-tung; Martin Luther King Jr.'s "I Have a Dream" speech; and footage of protesters in Tiananmen Square, Beijing, in June 1989.

Likewise, audio/video explanations are especially useful in making clear, for example, exactly what a Chinese musical instrument such as the *Q'in* is, how it is played, and what it sounds like. These are graphically illustrated in sight and sound. Yet in either case, both voice-over narration and video presentations are less than a minute apiece, and the latter are limited to a small 3-by-5-inch rectangle (some are smaller), the quality of which is grainy in appearance. Similarly, written copy never exceeds a page or two of the most basic information. Graphics and photographs used to illustrate the text, similar to the videos, are of a low resolution.

Apart from the presentation, the range of subjects covered is ambitious, from ancient civilizations and such specialized topics as Greek philosophers and Roman Emperors to the Six Day War (1967) and the Persian Gulf War (1990-91). However, as an example of how limited coverage is, of the Greek philosophers, only the Sophists, Socrates, Plato, and Aristotle are covered, and under "Roman Emperors," only Octavian, Caligula, Nero, Trajan, and Hadrian are to be found, with no more than a few short paragraphs devoted to each.

Options allow viewers to search through such broad categories as "Everyday Life," "Culture," "Documents," "Innovations," and "Who's Who." "Key dates" are easily accessible, and some, but not much, cross-referencing is provided. There is a "Quiz Master" game that will test basic knowledge and is designed to allow a number of participants to compete with each other in answering three broad categories of questions. The package is easy to install, and the audio quality is good, but the narration is usually too fast for students to catch easily. The computer action itself is a bit slow, and moving from one screen to another often takes an unnecessarily long time. For users with questions, minimal help is available on the computer as the software is being used; otherwise, telephone and fax numbers for direct contact with the manufacturer in both New York and London are also provided. Clearly, a considerable amount of technical expertise went into the making of this product. It is only release 1.0, and possibly future versions will build on the strengths of this edition, but they will have to provide substantially more historical information if this CD-ROM is ever to be more than simply a novelty.—**Joseph W. Dauben**

568. **History of Humanity. Volume 1: Prehistory and the Beginnings of Civilization.** S. J. De Laet and others, eds. Paris, United Nations Educational, Scientific, and Cultural Organization and New York, Routledge, 1994. 716p. illus. maps. index. $175.00. ISBN 0-415-09305-8.

Focusing the study of history on a world or global perspective is all the rage among certain circles of the historical profession. The United Nations Educational, Scientific, and Cultural Organization (UNESCO) has labored to foster and to publish historical works of this nature. Its first effort was the *History of the Scientific and Cultural Development of Mankind* in six volumes (1963-1975) followed by various regional histories such as *The General History of Africa* (1980-). The present volume, along with its forthcoming six companion volumes, will supersede the earlier *History of Mankind* (see ARBA 72, entry 291). Unlike its predecessor, the volumes of the *History of Humanity* are collaborative works with many authors writing individual chapters.

The first volume, *Prehistory and the Beginnings of Civilization*, contains 59 chapters written by 49 experts from all over the world. Chronologically, the volume starts with the era of *Homo habilis* and *Homo erectus* and ends about 5,000 years before the present. The chapters are divided into four sections covering *Homo habilis* and *Homo erectus, Homo sapiens neanderthalensis, Homo sapiens sapiens*, and the beginning of food production and the rise of the first states. Within each of the sections, some chapters provide an overview of the period while others concentrate on specific geographical areas. Such an arrangement allows the reader to locate information on various topics or geographical areas. The text contains a generous number of maps and black-and-white drawings with an additional 140 black-and-white photographic plates gathered at the end of the volume. Individual chapters include extensive bibliographies, while a detailed index concludes the volume.

As an up-to-date summary of current scholarship, the volume is valuable, although many prehistorians of the Americas will find chapter 29, "The Origins of Humanity in America," to be unsatisfactory. Its conclusions are also in conflict with the material in chapter 30, "Prehistory of North America." The level of the writing in this volume is fairly technical, due to the nature of the subject, and general readers will find it to be difficult. Furthermore, this volume is obviously intended for a more academic rather than a general audience, and as such it should find a welcome place on the bookshelves of academic libraries.

—**Ronald H. Fritze**

10 Law

GENERAL WORKS

Bibliographies

569. Doyle, Francis R. **Searching the Law: The States. A Selective Bibliography of State Practice Materials....** 2d ed. Irvington-on-Hudson, N.Y., Transnational Publishers, 1994. 737p. $125.00. ISBN 0-941320-88-X.

Francis Doyle offers a simple and useful guide to state laws. In fact, there is little that needs to be said here. The guide offers no preface or introduction to the state-by-state bibliographic entries. Clearly the purpose was to provide a coherent research guide for ferreting out the state laws in which one might have an interest. The table of contents lists a preface, which is preceded by an acknowledgments page. No such preface exists in this reviewer's copy. Still, that does not detract from the value of this research guide. States are listed alphabetically. Within each state, bibliographical entries are listed by subject headings (there are 75 such categories) and include accounting, arbitration, bankruptcy, civil procedure, computer law, constitutional law, consumer law, contracts, criminal law and procedure, digests, education law, environmental law, evidence, family law, juvenile law, labor law, local government, probate law, property, taxation, torts, and trial practice. (Obviously, one will not find every subject heading in every state listing.) Within each subject heading, the entries are listed alphabetically by title or author. The final section of the book contains a useful list of addresses for many of the publishers cited in the entries. For those who need to know where to go for information on a specific state issue, this work would be a useful place to begin that research.—**Michael A. Foley**

570. **Index to Law School Theses and Dissertations.** By Sanford R. Silverburg. Buffalo, N.Y., William S. Hein, 1995. 512p. index. $85.00 looseleaf w/binder. ISBN 0-89941-903-8.

Silverburg has compiled a comprehensive listing of nearly 4,600 theses or dissertations from approximately 30 U.S. law schools. Nearly all the papers listed were submitted to complete the requirements for a master of laws (LL.M) degree; a small number were submitted for various other advanced degrees. The author index serves as the master list for the bibliography. It includes the name of the author, the title of the thesis or dissertation, the degree issued to the student/author, and the degree-granting institution. Silverburg adds a separate, very detailed subject index, and finally, a listing by degree-granting institution.

In his introduction, Silverburg notes other more limited compilations, such as the *Greenwood Annual Abstract of Legal Dissertations and Theses, 1985-1987* by Kenneth Brown (Greenwood Press, 1988). He also recognizes two electronic listings of legal theses and dissertations, one at the Washington and Lee Law School, the other at the University of Maryland Law School. (The Maryland list, which also includes dissertations from Canadian universities, is updated to 1993. Washington and Lee no longer maintains its list.) *Index to Law School Theses and Dissertations* is a welcome addition to legal bibliography. Easily supplemented in a looseleaf binder, Silverburg plans to update the index annually. Researchers should expect to find the Silverburg index on the reference shelves of all libraries with substantial legal collections.—**James S. Heller**

Biography

571. Secrest, William B. **Lawmen & Desperadoes: A Compendium of Noted, Early California Peace Officers, Badmen, and Outlaws, 1850-1900.** Spokane, Wash., Arthur H. Clark, 1994. 343p. illus. index. $37.50. ISBN 0-87082-209-9.

Supplementing the 1992 *Encyclopedia of Western Lawmen and Outlaws* by Jay R. Nash (see ARBA 93, entry 609), which largely ignores California badmen and their legal nemeses, this volume presents extensive biographical/historical articles on approximately 50 lawmen and badmen prominent in California during the half-century shown in the title. Although the book is well researched and well written, there seems to be an overall defect in the editing, resulting in a simple lack of cross-referencing. For example, in the sketch of the notorious George Contant (also known as Sontag), there is no indication that more information may be found in other articles—some under Charles Aull (a warden at Folsom), and more under John Sontag (George's older brother) and Christopher Evans (John's father-in-law). In a book catering to a nationwide readership, not just to California aficionados, this lack of cross-referencing is a distinct weakness in the composition of the book.

More careful editing also would have avoided some unanswered questions: The article on Contant refers to "his small book," entitled *A Pardoned Lifer*. But the author is given later as Opie L. Warner. Was he an editor? A ghost writer? No explanation is given. There is a report of the Los Angeles Rangers capturing a gang of horse thieves near La Puente, Los Angeles County, and bringing them before a local justice, who said they must deliver their prisoners to a justice in Shasta County (about 500 miles away). With no explanation, one wonders—is it a misprint? Or did the Rangers embark on a 1,000-mile journey?

The collection of biographies is well illustrated and well written, despite the author's tendency to lapse occasionally into twentieth-century slang. One reads that one desperado already had a rap before entering California; and also that Sara Hill insisted in court that she did not shack up with Senator Sharon, but was his truly wedded wife. Libraries wanting to give their readers a broader view of law and outlawry in the Far West should order this book.—**Raymund F. Wood**

572. **The Supreme Court Justices: A Biographical Dictionary.** Melvin I. Urofsky, ed. Hamden, Conn., Garland, 1994. 570p. illus. index. (Garland Reference Library of the Humanities, v.1851). $75.00. ISBN 0-8153-1176-1.

The Supreme Court Justices is a biographical dictionary of 107 men and women Supreme Court justices, from the first Chief Justice John Jay to Ruth Bader Ginsburg. The analytical and interpretive essays vary in length from 1 to 12 pages. Each essay has a picture of the justice, and a biographical sketch concentrating on legal career and significant cases. The essay is completed with a bibliography that notes important publications by the justice, information on the location of personal papers and documents, and further biographical publications. The essays are written in easy-to-understand, nonlegal language by an array of noted American legal scholars. The volume is completed by a topical index and an index of cases.

This is an excellent addition to any law library collection. Because of its readable style, the book is most suitable for any collection that needs to provide a historical overview of the development of American justice—especially any public library collection. [R: WLB, Jan 95, pp. 84-86] —**Lorna K. Rees-Potter**

Dictionaries and Encyclopedias

573. **Crimes and Punishment: The *Illustrated* Crime Encyclopedia.** Westport, Conn., H. S. Stuttman; distr., North Bellmore, N.Y., Marshall Cavendish, 1994. 28v. illus. index. $279.95/set. ISBN 1-85435-793-X.

This set merges the texts of three works first issued in Great Britain: *Murder Casebook*, *Science Against Crime*, and *Crime and Punishment*. A mélange of tabloid-toned articles and often-lurid illustrations, the work describes heinous crimes and their perpetrators that occurred in the United States and Great Britain this century. Sensational unlawful acts from other times and locales are sporadically represented, as evidenced by the inclusion of such miscreants as Italy's Lucrezia Borgia, New Zealand's John Merrett, and Scotland's Madeleine Smith.

The best feature of this compilation is the "Murder Casebook" section that appears in each volume. Most of these focus on one criminal, such as Jeffrey Dahmer, Peter Sutcliffe, or Charles Starkweather. Others, however, are emblazoned with such provocative catch-all titles as "The Man-Haters" and "Cults of Evil." (The latter piece devotes pages to the Jonestown tragedy of 1978, while saying nothing of the 1993 siege in Waco.)

Most distracting are *Crimes and Punishment*'s hyperactive treatments of its subjects and its carrying forward into this United States edition such British spellings as "cheque," "behaviour," and "tyre." Also unsatisfying are the impediments to information access engendered by undocumented materials, the awkward general format, and an uneven index. Arranged alphabetically under such inconsistent and opaque headings as "Women Who Kill," "Wood, Ida," and "YWCA Murder," this encyclopedia's hundreds of articles appear without signatures or bibliographies. Further, no names or credentials of contributors are acknowledged or listed.

Ready access to information is hindered by the absence from the volumes' spines of any alphabetical, page number, or subject tags. Thus, the user is forced to rely either on the set's table of contents (found only in volume 1) or on the work's integrated index (only in volume 28). Most of the index entries are criminals' names, with a lesser number of such subject entries as "Bullets," "Photography," and "Truckee Lake." (Despite the presence of this last entry, geographical entries are sparse.)

A cursory inspection revealed several other indexing flaws. Under "Zodiac Killer," no citation for page 679 appears. No entry appears for pirate Anne Bonney, although her exploits are detailed in an 8-page essay in volume 3. Finally, there are no boldfaced page citations under the Hindenburg entry, even though a sizable reproduction of the famous photograph of that German airship's conflagration appears on page 1406.

The index, as with the chapter headings, is marred by its unpredictable selections of terminology. Also, while one is gratified to find listings for such individuals as Gary Gilmore, John Hinckley Jr., and Willie "the Actor" Sutton, one is nonplused by the absences of Richard Hickock (of *In Cold Blood* notoriety), Lynette "Squeaky" Fromme, and "Baby Face" Nelson. Neither Robert Stroud nor the "Green River Killer" (of the U.S. Northwest) are present in the index. Given these deficiencies, librarians should opt for such alternatives as Jay Robert Nash's works, most notably *Encyclopedia of World Crime* (see ARBA 92, entry 552); *Encyclopedia of American Crime* (see ARBA 83, entry 520); or Michael Kurland's *A Gallery of Rogues* (Prentice Hall General Reference, 1994).—**Jeffrey E. Long**

574. Dahl, Henry Saint. **Dahl's Law Dictionary: French to English/English to French. Dictionnaire Juridique Dahl.** Paris, Editions Dalloz and Buffalo, N.Y., William S. Hein, 1995. 851p. $68.00. ISBN 0-89941-919-4.

This dictionary is not to be confused with another bilingual *Dahl's Law Dictionary*, subtitled *Dictionario Juridico* (see ARBA 94, entry 552), which is by the same author but covers Spanish and English rather than French and English. The author is a United States citizen educated in Argentina who practices law and teaches at the Texas Wesleyan School of Law and as a visiting professor at the Conservatoire National des Arts and Metiers (Paris). He has been assisted by native French speakers.

This work, as with Dahl's Spanish dictionary, offers two kinds of definitions. Synonym-based definitions offer short translations of terms likely to be used in legal matters. Authoritative definitions explain the French or United States legal systems (i.e., English definitions of French words explain French law) and quote directly from both treatises and authoritative sources, such as the French Penal Code. Tables list all the sources quoted.

Such substantive definitions are unusual in dictionaries and are helpful in understanding a foreign legal system, but cannot, of course, take the place of consulting an expert in the law concerned. Because this is a new dictionary, it is more up-to-date on slang and other new terminology than other bilingual dictionaries, including translations of terms such as "shark repellents." This work would be useful to large law libraries or libraries serving those dealing with French-speaking countries. Although the law explained is that of France, the French legal system has strongly influenced those of its former colonies.
—**Marit S. MacArthur**

575. DeBeer, Shane R. **Dictionary of Business & Legal Terms: Russian-English/English-Russian.** New York, Hippocrene Books, 1995. 814p. $50.00. ISBN 0-7818-0-163-X.

This bilingual legal and business dictionary contains some 20,000 entries with a pronunciation guide for each; grammatical indications of gender, adjectives, and the like; and many subentries that illustrate proper usage of the terms in speech and correspondence. It is a popular dictionary, but the explanations are not always accurate. One example will illustrate this: *predlagat' - platezhei* does not mean "to propose a payment plan" but simply "to propose payments." Nevertheless, because of the many changes in Eastern Europe, this dictionary will be of assistance to travelers and some businesspeople.—**Bohdan S. Wynar**

576. **A Dictionary of Law.** 3d ed. New York, Oxford University Press, 1994. 433p. $13.95pa. ISBN 0-19-280000-0.

Fortunately, law has a better public relations agent provocateur and thus fares better in the public eye than lawyers. This new edition of an old favorite provides users with a paperback version of the same old, same old. Three thousand "clear and concise" entries have been provided. Asterisks (*) have been helpfully placed by those entries with new material added to them.

The whole point of this volume is to demystify legal matters by descrying legal terminology. Changes in legal concepts have been updated throughout. This tome cannot compare with *Black's Law Dictionary* (6th ed.; see ARBA 92, entry 529) and is not as complete as Bryan A. Garner's *A Dictionary of Modern Legal Usage* (see entry 577), but it is a handy reference tool. Although written for the uninformed, here is something for everyone.

Of course, the bashing of the legal profession will continue. The preface opens with a line meant to instill great faith: The volume was put together by a distinguished team of academic and practicing lawyers (the oxymoron notwithstanding). It cannot be helped that such tools must always look a bit like the fox in the hen house.—**Mark Y. Herring**

577. Garner, Bryan A.. **A Dictionary of Modern Legal Usage.** 2d ed. New York, Oxford University Press, 1995. 953p. $65.00. ISBN 0-19-507769-5.

The 2d edition of *A Dictionary of Modern Legal Usage* expands considerably on the 1st edition (see ARBA 88, entry 564) by including more terms and by providing illustrative quotations—and citations to them—from court decisions, books, articles, and other sources. Much more than a legal dictionary—of which there are literally dozens to choose from—Garner defines thousands of law-related words and phrases, but also counsels his readers on matters of style; grammar and usage; legal lexicology and special conventions; word formation, inflection, spelling, and pronunciation; and punctuation and typography.

In what other legal dictionary can one find an exposition on the use of the dash, of which Garner describes two types? First is the em dash—represented by two hyphens to "enclose a parenthetical remark or to mark the ending and the resumption of a statement by an interlocutor"—that Garner calls the second-most underused mark of punctuation in legal writing. The second is the single-hyphen en dash, which usually substitutes for the word *to*.

The 1st edition was called "the best legal dictionary now available in the English language" and "a work of learning, taste, care, and wit." The 2d edition is that and more. There exists no reason to doubt Charles Alan Wright's statement that Garner "has established himself as the world's leading authority on the language of the law." *A Dictionary of Modern Legal Usage* is a treasure to have and a delight to read. Much different from the other legal dictionaries on the market, it should appear on the shelves of every law library.—**James S. Heller**

578. Hill, Gerald N., and Kathleen Thompson Hill. **Real Life Dictionary of the Law: Taking the Mystery Out of Legal Language.** Los Angeles, Calif., General Publishing Group, 1995. 479p. $19.95. ISBN 1-881649-74-1.

This volume may be the only thing to replace the O. J. Simpson/Susan Smith trials: a guide to understanding them! Only in the United States could coverage of trials—forums of one of the most arcane professional languages in the world—become the most watched television. Now, at long last, a volume to help people wade their way around Judge Lance Ito's "voir dire" and Johnnie Cochran's "Sidebar!" demands. This is a book that makes the doublespeak of law a single-tined tongue.

More than 3,000 definitions are included here, enough terms to get the Menendez brothers a new trial, or sufficient legal sayings to provide Lorena Bobbit with an old saw. What makes this volume so appealing is that it demystifies legalese for those who have not had the fortune it takes to secure the degree. With decisions like *Adarand* and *Rosenberger v. University of Virginia*, this tome is sure to find uses in and out of the academy.

Not only are the entries accurate, but they are also written in a provocative style meant to entertain. Interlaced among the definitions are quotes illustrative of the inscrutable law or its tendency to evoke universal contempt of its advocates. The appendixes on the Constitution, the U.S. court system, major Supreme Court decisions, state bar associations, legal trivia, and more will provide scholars and laity alike with ready answers to niggling law questions. This volume is a must for all libraries.—**Mark Y. Herring**

579. Hopkins, Bruce R. **Nonprofit Law Dictionary.** New York, John Wiley, 1994. 361p. $49.95. ISBN 0-471-01632-2.

As anyone ever involved in running a nonprofit organization can attest, the legal requirements for achieving and maintaining nonprofit status can be both complex and intimidating. This volume is intended to provide definitions of nearly 2,000 legal and tax terms applying to this field in terminology that are both technically correct for the lawyer and comprehensible to those without legal training. In particular, the author sets himself the challenge of making the puzzling terms and concepts used by the Internal Revenue Service intelligible.

Hopkins, a lawyer specializing in tax-exempt organizations, has published five other titles on the subject, all in Wiley's Nonprofit Law, Finance, and Management series. This volume provides cross-references to discussions of topics in all other volumes in the series. Definitions range in length from a sentence to almost a page and are uncommonly clear for a law dictionary. Words in a definition that have their own definitions elsewhere in the volume are boldfaced. Definitions often provide summaries of the law as well as explanations of the meaning of a term.

The content of this work is different from that in *Facts on File Dictionary of Nonprofit Organization Management* (see ARBA 88, entry 297), with its emphasis on management rather than law. Because so many people are involved in nonprofit professional or community organizations, this volume should be of use in a wide variety of public and academic, as well as law, libraries.—**Marit S. MacArthur**

580. Redden, Kenneth R., and Gerry W. Beyer. **Modern Dictionary for the Legal Profession. 1994 Supplement.** Buffalo, N.Y., William S. Hein, 1994. 69p. $19.95pa. ISBN 0-89941-829-5.

Emphasis is on the word *modern* in the title of this dictionary. In 1993 Redden and Beyer produced a useful compendium of up-to-date terms and jargon common to lawyers and their clients. This is the first supplement, and once again the authors include an interesting and eclectic mix of definitions. For example, the "International Herald Tribune World Stock Index; Trib Index" precedes "Internet," which is followed by "Interpersonal Therapy" and "Inverse Floater." The value of this dictionary is that Redden and Beyer select many current phrases that are not easy to find in other sources. There are over 600 new terms in this supplement. Annual editions are planned.—**Berniece M. Owen**

Directories

581. **Barron's Guide to Law Schools.** 11th ed. Hauppauge, N.Y., Barron's Educational Series, 1994. 410p. index. $14.95pa. ISBN 0-8120-1754-4. ISSN 1062-2489.

Barron's 11th edition of the *Guide to Law Schools* maintains the quality of previous editions. Since 1967, Barron's has published guidebooks to law schools at periodic intervals. Information and statistics in the 11th edition have been updated to 1993 accuracy. Concern for accuracy is apparent. An example is the statement on the verso of the title page right under the copyright date, noting the necessity of checking for this year's costs and statistics. The publisher also desired to provide the reader with a complete picture, beginning with points to consider if thinking about attending law school through a sample LSAT exam, on to the admissions process, and profiles of ABA-approved law schools. An index concludes the work.

Throughout the guidebook, facts are presented in a consistent, clear, and attractive manner. Wherever appropriate, charts, tables, or graphs are used. Each is precisely labeled and highly readable. Copious material on each ABA-approved law school is condensed in identical layouts. Readers will find very little omitted from any law school profile. One addition would be to mention any increases or decreases in the number of admissions over the last five years. Many law schools are reducing their enrollment in response to the occupation's current surplus. One chapter entitled "The Job Outlook" addresses this issue of oversupply. It candidly relates the job statistics for the class of 1992. The three other chapters in that section cover the requirements of prelaw education, the practical aspects of law school, and the realities of legal practice in an honest yet witty manner.

Undergraduate institutions need several copies of this work for their reference rooms and career centers. High schools will also find the information useful for students thinking of a future in the legal world. Any individual contemplating law school should purchase a personal copy to aid in making this major decision.—**Marjorie H. Jones**

582. **The Insider's Guide to Law Firms.** 2d ed. Sheila V. Malkani and Michael F. Walsh, eds. Boulder, Colo., Mobius Press, 1994. 734p. $79.95; $48.95pa. ISBN 0-9637970-3-4 (hardcover and paperback).

The Insider's Guide to Law Firms consists primarily of 3-page profiles of more than 200 large law firms in a dozen large cities: Atlanta, Baltimore, Boston, Chicago, Dallas, Houston, Los Angeles, New York City, Philadelphia, Pittsburgh, San Francisco, and Washington, D.C. The editors constructed the firm profiles primarily from information received from law students who had clerked with the firms, and to a lesser extent from associates at the firms.

The editors' concede that the firm profiles provide an anecdotal snapshot of the firms, rather than a scientific study. Still, the *Guide* serves as an invaluable aid to law students interested in working in large firms. The profiles provide a revealing portrait of the atmosphere of each firm: work environment; professional development for entering associates; management; practice areas; pro bono policy; social interaction between associate and associate, and associate and partner; ethnic and gender diversity; and facilities. The 2d edition adds a short chapter on the hiring process, as well as some rudimentary interviewing strategies that will probably benefit only students in law schools without professionally staffed placement offices or an adequate law placement library.

The statistical summaries for each firm—which for the most part contain information current to 1994—include the number of firm partners and associates, women and minority lawyers, and attorneys in each of the firm's practice areas. The editors also furnish salary information for both summer clerks and associates; the number of hours a year a young associate might expect to work (which appear low) and bill; and the percentage of entering associates who eventually make partner. Law students understand it has been a "buyer's market" for the last few years, and most students who yearn for a job with a big name firm would delight in receiving an offer from any of the firms profiled. However, students wishing to target—or avoid—firms with a certain atmosphere would definitely benefit by looking through the *Guide* first, and those who receive multiple offers will find the profiles enlightening.

The *Guide* offers unique information that should be available in every law school placement office. The editors acknowledge that much of the information represents the views of a small number of people. They even suggest that those who read something in this guide that does not appeal to them should get additional opinions. Even so, the profiles are fun to read, and provide some inside information about the firms read about in *Legal Times*, *National Law Journal*, or *American Lawyer*. The work under review is a steal for the paperback edition, but libraries should be advised to put it on a chain, or it may disappear quickly.—**James S. Heller**

583. **Martindale-Hubbell Dispute Resolution Directory: The Single-Source Reference Guide to Dispute Resolution.** New Providence, N.J., Martindale-Hubbell/Reed Reference Publishing, 1994. 1v. (various paging). $85.00. ISBN 1-56160-109-8.

As court dockets have become increasingly congested and the costs of litigation have soared, extrajudicial dispute resolution has become increasingly common. New forms of dispute resolution, such as early neutral evaluation and minitrials, have taken their place alongside more familiar arbitration and mediation procedures. With this inaugural volume, law directory publisher Martindale-Hubbell provides not only a directory of practitioners but also a cogent introduction to the entire field of dispute resolution. Following an explanation of each type and subtype of dispute resolution, there are profiles of several practice areas (e.g., business, family, environment, maritime) that outline how dispute resolution techniques typically operate within each one.

The directory itself lists practitioners alphabetically by state and city. Entries range from a single line in normal type for nonsubscribers to extended listings in boldface type for subscribers (i.e., as with the telephone yellow pages, the more a firm pays, the more prominent is its listing). Information on a firm may be as little as street address (but no zip code or telephone number) or as great as services offered, practice areas, and detailed profiles of individual partners (even including lists of their articles/publications). There are indexes of personal names, practice areas, and service roles. Additional features are statutes/acts, rules and codes, model programs, and forms pertaining to dispute resolution, as well as profiles of national organizations such as the American Arbitration Association. In spite of the unevenness of directory coverage, this will be a valuable resource for public, academic, and law libraries.—**Jack Ray**

584. **Martindale-Hubbell Law Directory on CD-ROM.** [CD-ROM]. New Providence, N. J., Martindale-Hubbell/Reed Reference Electronic Publishing, 1995. Minimum system requirements: IBM PC, XT, AT, PS/2 Model 25, 30 or compatible 286. ISO 9660-compatible CD-ROM drive with 680MB capacity and MS-DOS CD-ROM Extensions. MS-DOS or PC-DOS 3.1 (5.0 recommended). Hard disk. 640K memory. 535K free base memory. Monochrome or color monitor. $995.00.

CD-ROMs are sold to reference librarians with promises of vastly improved retrieval capability, of instant data recovery, and of myriad searchable fields. The eight-volumes-to-one-disc transformation of the *Martindale-Hubbell Law Directory* is more welcome than most such dramatic reductions in space. Since the 1860s, this has been an essential directory for law firms and attorneys throughout North America and beyond. All the usual directory elements are offered: name, educational background, job title, firm size, representative clients, and fields of law. However, with keyword searching, one can look up specific lawyers without first knowing the city and state where their practice is located. Records for firms and lawyers are also available in both abbreviated and complete formats. While a full entry for a law firm will give biographies of all firm members, the brief record has just members' names.

Moving around the record fields is a simple activity; creating files and downloading them is similarly easy. Help screens appear with a keystroke; Boolean operators may be used—all the standard CD-ROM tools are in place. A WATS line is available for technical support. Libraries that can afford this resource as a CD-ROM will enjoy the benefits and conveniences of that medium. The disc is recommended for any library experiencing a demand for legal directory information.—**Michael A. Foley**

585. **The Princeton Review Student Access Guide to the Best Law Schools.** 1996 ed. By Ian Van Tuyl. New York, Princeton Review/Random House, 1995. 463p. illus. maps. index. $20.00pa. ISBN 0-679-76148-9. ISSN 1067-2168.

Enclosed in Van Tuyl's guide are the evaluative ravings of 22,500 law school students on the nation's schools of law. Thus, Yale's is the toughest to get into, requiring both a high grade point average and a high Law School Admission Test (LSAT) score, and is also the number one "demand" school. Northern Kentucky University ranks at the bottom of the 170 schools in student/faculty ratio, while Boston College has the best teaching faculty. If one is looking for a high female law school faculty, Brigham Young is the worst. If private practice is what one yearns for, University of Detroit, Mercy will be the school of choice.

This is only the beginning of what users will find in this helpful text. Each profile contains information about the curriculum, quality of teaching, quality of student life, facilities, salary expectations, and whether or not the school is ideologically conservative or liberal. Sprinkled throughout are comments from students that run the gamut of "We are one of the BEST law schools in the country," to "With lockers, gossip, it's a bit too much like high school." The overall effect is to give one the milieu of the school of one's choosing.

Also added to this guide are state locators of the school, statistics on cost, enrollment, student/faculty ratios, and diversity statistics. Also included is a comparison of a given school ranking with national rankings relative to employment in private practice, government, judiciary, business, research, and politics. Coleridge once wrote that the Devil saw a lawyer killing a viper on a dunghill near a stable and smiled, for it put him in mind of Cain killing Abel. As long as that sort of thing is going around, it may be that such books as these, providing profiles of the best places to learn that sort of execution, will be essential.—**Mark Y. Herring**

586. **REA's Authoritative Guide to Law Schools.** rev. ed. Piscataway, N.J., Research & Education Association, 1994. 416p. illus. $18.95pa. ISBN 0-87891-920-1.

REA's Authoritative Guide to Law Schools adds to the ever-growing list of publications designed for those who plan to attend law school and have a choice as to which school they will attend. What this reviewer finds most surprising is that the Research and Education Association (REA) apparently has not recognized the recent drop in the number of law school applicants and the number of competing (and superior) publications.

Similar to other law school guides, *REA* includes a brief chapter on applying to law school that answers such questions as "Why do I want to go to law school?," "What good is law school if being a lawyer is so unrewarding?" (REA answered an earlier question with many negative opinions about a career in law), and "What undergraduate classes will help me prepare for law school?" The authors also spend a few pages describing the law school application process, the LSAT, and financing a legal education.

Much of the guide includes profiles of the 177 or so American Bar Association (ABA)-accredited law schools, 27 non-ABA-accredited schools (most of which are in California), and 15 Canadian law schools. As in similar guides, each short profile offers a snapshot about the law school, the admissions process, costs and financial aid, minority programs, student organizations, the faculty, the curriculum, the library, law school publications, and the application procedures. These profiles offer basically the same information found in other guides, such as the number of applicants, how many the school accepted, and the number who enrolled; the mean grade point average (GPA) and LSAT score of the entering class; and the percentage of men, women, and minorities. However, the REA guide seems to have less current information than its competition.

So what is the competition? The current champion must be *The Official Guide to U.S. Law Schools* (Bantam Doubleday Dell, annual). Not only does the *Official Guide* have more information about a career in law, applying to and choosing a law school, and finding a job, but also their data are much more current. For example, the 1996 edition contains application data for the 1994-1995 academic year, more up-to-date than the REA publication. *Barron's Guide to Law Schools* (see entry 581) also proves superior to *REA*, with more extensive discussion on factors in choosing a law school and the application process, as well as the requisite profiles. Another, more selective guide is *The Princeton Review Student Access Guide to the Best Law Schools* (see entry 585), which profiles the top 170 ABA-accredited schools. In sum, the REA guide was not needed and does not compare to the *Official Guide* or to *Barron's*.—**James S. Heller**

587. **World Databases in Patents.** C. J. Armstrong, ed. New Providence, N.J., Bowker-Saur/Reed Reference Publishing, 1995. 324p. index. (World Databases Series). $165.00. ISBN 1-857-39106-3.

This is the fourth work in a series of guides aiming to provide a comprehensive listing of world database resources by subject (see entries 225, 453, and 1788 for additional reviews in the series). This volume covers not only patents but all aspects of intellectual property including trademarks, trade names, standards, and copyright. The arrangement is alphabetical by database name as provided by the producer. Under each is a general description, keywords, start year, update period, and the like, followed by separate subentries for each available version of the database in various formats (online, CD-ROM, tape, diskette, and so forth) and through various vendors (e.g., DIALOG, NEXIS).

Information provided varies from entry to entry; for instance, pricing is sometimes supplied and sometimes not. A few Internet sources are listed. The introduction stresses that databases merely including patents are not furnished unless they are "deemed to make a significant contribution to patent searching" (introduction). The omission of Chemical Abstracts, a highly significant source, seems puzzling, especially when seemingly more peripheral databases such as BNA Books and PTS Newsletter are included. Also puzzling is the omission of any mention that the Derwent World Patents Index is available on DIALOG or STN.

Following the main guide is a list of publishers' addresses and subject and database name indexes. The database name index should allow one to look up all versions of a database, but there are problems. In the text, DIALOG databases are referred to only by number rather than name, and these numbers are not in the index. The titles of print versions of databases are given in the text, but not in the database index. Because of its inconsistencies, omissions, and high price, this book is recommended only for libraries specializing in patents, which need as much information as possible on individual foreign databases.
—**Marit S. MacArthur**

Handbooks and Yearbooks

588. Bentley, Elizabeth Petty. **County Courthouse Book.** 2d ed. Baltimore, Md., Genealogical Publishing, 1995. 397p. $34.95pa. ISBN 0-8063-1485-0.

The format of this update remains the same as that of the 1990 edition (see ARBA 91, entry 584). As before, the information was gathered through a questionnaire sent to more than 4,700 counties, cities, and towns; while the response rate has increased from 55 percent to nearly 65 percent, there are still a significant number of jurisdictions for which the data are fairly sketchy and unverified. For those that did respond, the questionnaire elicited information on four major groups: land, naturalization, probate, and vital records. In many cases, fees for searching and photocopying are indicated. As was true of the 1990 edition, the usefulness of this directory will depend greatly on the researcher's area of interest.—**Jack Ray**

589. Carr, Fred K. **Patents Handbook: A Guide for Inventors....** Jefferson, N.C., McFarland, 1995. 221p. index. $38.00. ISBN 0-7864-0026-9.

Carr, chair of a small electronics firm, attributes his firm's competitiveness to patents. He has written this practical, informative book from a businessperson's perspective. This is an excellent first source for those with patent-related questions. Carr's intended audience includes researchers; prior art researchers (i.e., those who search previous patent documents); and investors.

The 17 chapters cover a general introduction to patents; the invention; conditions for patentability; the application; claims; examination of the application; applicant's response; petition and appeal; allowance, issue, and correction; interference; patents as information tools; major patent offices; the U.S. patent classification system; the international patent classification system; searching patent documents; requirements of a reference; and patent rights. The appendix shows a sample patent. The index only refers to a topic's main reference; for example, *Official Gazette* is listed as being on page 123, although it is mentioned in other discussions.

Carr relied on 35 U.S. Code and 37 Codes of Federal Regulations for this work, and recommended Irving Kayton's treatise, *Patent Preparation and Patent Practice*. With the exception of a handful of court cases, no other sources or further reading titles are indicated. A few may quibble about some of Carr's definitions (e.g., copyright). Although not set up as a reference book, this source will prove handy for answering basic questions. Business libraries should consider a copy for the circulating collection.
—**Esther R. Sinofsky**

590. Fishman, Stephen. **The Copyright Handbook: How to Protect and Use Written Works.** 2d ed. Berkeley, Calif., Nolo Press, 1995. 1v. (various paging). illus. index. $24.95pa. ISBN 0-87337-241-7.

Continuing its fine tradition of providing easy-to-read and authoritative guides to law for the nonlawyer, Nolo Press presents the 2d edition of this excellent copyright handbook. Author Fishman is an attorney with experience in the government and in private practice. He has written reference books for other lawyers as well as two books on software copyright for Nolo Press.

This guide is for "the entire universe of people who deal with the written word." The first four chapters make up an overview of copyright law, including basic information on how authors can make sure they protect their work under the law. The following 11 chapters discuss copyright law in detail. Fishman defines exactly what copyright does or does not cover and how long it lasts. He discusses what constitutes infringement, and in this edition, he adds a chapter on electronic publishing. He notes that new copyright legislation will be under consideration in 1995.

Of particular interest to authors is the fact that the handbook ends with a section of forms required for registering copyrights. There are samples of filled-in forms and blank, tear-out forms ready to use. For librarians and teachers, there is a clear and simple explanation of fair use. There is a chapter on international copyright protection and, finally, a chapter on other resources, including addresses of legal aid groups. This handbook will enhance the basic reference collection of most libraries.—**Berniece M. Owen**

591. Goode, Steven, and Olin Guy Wellborn III. **Courtroom Handbook on Federal Evidence.** 1995 ed. St. Paul, Minn., West Publishing, 1995. 495p. index. $31.00pa. ISBN 0-314-06129-0. ISSN 1080-9457.

Goode and Wellborn designed this handbook for attorneys to carry with them into the courtroom. The first half of the manual includes the text of the Federal Rules of Evidence, selected constitutional and statutory provisions, and other court rules that affect admissibility of evidence or relate to the evidentiary rules. The second half consists of the authors' commentary on each rule of evidence. Goode and Wellborn make reference to and cite significant court decisions interpreting the rules, and also include cross-references to related statutes and rules, and even some treatises.

The authors list 89 common objections an attorney is likely to make to introduction of certain types of evidence, as well as possible responses by the attorney attempting to introduce the evidence. They also provide a fairly thorough subject index, and tables that refer to the statutes, rules, and cases cited throughout the text.

The handbook is not designed to compete with law school hornbooks such as *McCormick on Evidence* (4th ed., West Publishing, 1991) or even Anderson Publishing's *Weissenberger's Federal Evidence* (1992), an excellent and inexpensive paperback that offers a more scholarly application and interpretation of the rules. However, the handbook offers more than pocket-sized guides such as *Federal Rules of Evidence with Objections* (NITA, 1994) or Myron H. Bright and Ronald L. Carlson's *Objections at Trial* (Butterworth, 1993). Attorneys will find *Courtroom Handbook on Federal Evidence* a handy, straightforward manual that will help them more readily negotiate the evidentiary rules.—**James S. Heller**

592. Hempelman, Kathleen A. **Teen Legal Rights: A Guide for the '90s.** Westport, Conn., Greenwood Press, 1994. 236p. illus. index. $39.95. ISBN 0-313-28760-0.

A check of young adult library shelves for books about the legal rights of teenagers will almost certainly turn up a majority dated in the 1980s. The legal presence of young people in the courts has expanded, so it is time for an authoritative update. Using a question-and-answer format, Hempelman, an attorney in private practice in Phoenix, Arizona, speaks to the teens themselves and to the adults around them. Her answers are clear and in language accessible to most students who have the maturity to be interested in the questions.

Categories are teen friendly. They include the rights of teens as drivers and as children at home. Hempelman sorts out their rights as independent persons who may marry, have children, work, and determine their own dress. Chapters deal with age, sexuality, money, alcohol, abuse, religion, a teen's rights if parents divorce, and a teen's rights in the school setting. Sections totaling 31 pages treat rights if a young person is accused of or convicted of a crime or appears in court. There is an odd omission in the section on religious groups in schools: Hempelman does not mention that such groups must be student led.

Appended materials include "How to Find the Law," a glossary, a summary of abortion laws, and lists of child protection agencies and national organizations that assist young people in legal matters. Bibliographies are also provided (although the final bibliography lists books too old to cover current decisions; bibliographies at the ends of chapters have several newer titles). An index completes the work.
—**Edna M. Boardman**

593. Houdek, Frank G., comp. **AALL Reference Book: A Compendium of Facts, Figures, and Historical Information About the American Association of Law Libraries.** Buffalo, N.Y., William S. Hein, 1994. 1v. (various paging). $55.00 looseleaf w/binder. ISBN 0-89941-893-7.

Houdek clearly states the purpose of this work in the title, *AALL Reference Book: A Compendium of Facts, Figures, and Historical Information About the American Association of Law Libraries*. Houdek organized the facts, figures, and historical information concisely and chronologically. Dates are given for everything from the founding of the association in 1906 to the years individuals served on committees. History, officers, committees, chapters, meetings, programs, publications, and awards are covered in a factual manner with quotations and notes appropriately inserted for interest and explanation. When necessary, further related details on items are marked, and the notes conclude the section.

Concern for clarity and precision can also be seen in the materials layout. Pages are arranged in columns with people identified by title, position, and institution of employment, as applicable. Tab dividers separate chapters, and the looseleaf binding simplifies the addition of pages. Houdek does not mention any sequels to this work, but the binding would allow for periodic updates. In the dedication,

Houdek mentions previous efforts to preserve the AALL's history, but does not refer to an earlier compendium. Several books are listed under the history section of the selected bibliography, which is most complete for all of the chapters. Emphasis is on recognizing the leadership and activities of the American Association of Law Libraries. An index would assist the reader in locating specific information and people. Although the work is attractive and well organized, its appeal is limited to the targeted audience. Mostly members of the association and law librarians would use this reference book. [R: LJ, 1 Feb 95, p. 105]—**Marjorie H. Jones**

594. Ryan, Patrick J. **Organized Crime: A Reference Handbook.** Santa Barbara, Calif., ABC-CLIO, 1995. 297p. index. (Contemporary World Issues). $39.50. ISBN 0-87436-746-8.

Ryan, an associate professor of criminal justice at Long Island University, is uniquely qualified to discuss the world impact of organized crime. Prior to becoming an academic, he logged 21 years as a New York City police officer (retiring as a detective sergeant) and at one time served as the executive director of the International Association for the Study of Organized Crime. In this well-crafted ready-reference handbook, he notes that organized crime is now a multiethnic and multinational phenomenon that generates worldwide profits of hundreds of billions of dollars a year.

Brief chapters on the nature, extent, and activities of organized crime are deftly written and segue into succinct and informative discussions of international crime groups and the historical efforts of the U.S. government to control organized crime in this country. Biographical sketches on members of organized crime (John "the Dapper Don" Gotti and the like) are offered, as are thumbnail entries on those who fight the problem ("Interdictors") and those who study it ("Researchers and Students"). A chronology traces organized crime from the emergence of immigrant gangs in the United States in 1850 through the efforts of the Russian government in 1995 to control the mob.

Especially useful is a bibliographical essay that cites selected books, government documents, journals, and nonprint resources (CD-ROMs, videos, and so forth) essential to the study of this global problem. A strong entry in ABC-CLIO's Contemporary World Issues series, this reference guide is recommended for all academic, college, and special libraries supporting criminal justice programs.

—**David K. Frasier**

595. **State Legislative Summary, 1994: Children, Youth, and Family Issues.** Denver, Colo., National Conference of State Legislatures, 1994. 144p. $20.00pa. ISBN 1-55516-649-0.

Since 1982, the National Conference of State Legislatures' Children and Families Program has compiled summaries of recent state legislation affecting children and families. Each year, state legislative staff provide the Children and Families Program with the latest legislation. Program staff summarize the legislation (in anywhere from one to five sentences), which is then reviewed (and presumably edited) by state legislative staff.

The legislative summaries are arranged into 11 main subject areas: "Child Abuse and Neglect," "Child Care/Early Childhood Education," "Child Health," "Child Mental Health," "Child Welfare," "Family Law," "General Children, Youth, and Families," "Juvenile Justice," "Public Assistance," "Substance Abuse and Control," and "Youth at Risk." These broad topics are then subdivided into narrower categories, where the summaries are presented alphabetically by state. Each summary is preceded by a citation to the state session law where the complete text of the legislation may be found. An appendix includes citations, but not abstracts, to recent child support legislation.

The *State Legislative Summary, 1994* will prove useful to legislators and others who research these policy areas. It is recommended particularly for law and governmental libraries, and other libraries with comprehensive youth and family law collections.—**James S. Heller**

CRIMINOLOGY

Bibliography

596. Friedmann, Robert R., comp. **Criminal Justice in Israel: An Annotated Bibliography of English Language Publications, 1948-1993.** Westport, Conn., Greenwood Press, 1995. 211p. index. (Research and Bibliographical Guides in Criminal Justice, no.4). $75.00. ISBN 0-313-29439-9.

This is an interesting bibliography of criminal justice in a country that is less than a half-century old but in which the system of justice and due process appears mature and well grounded in the daily life of the people—although the problems associated with the Arab-Israeli conflict may belie this assertion. The collection at hand includes publications in English, and is annotated and classified into 21 categories, such as addiction to drugs and alcohol, crime and society, juvenile delinquency, political deviance and violence, rape, and social stress. There is an extensive index, and every entry has keywords. Given the detailed classification and the small number of entries (824), the index seems redundant and just adds to the cost. Although the bibliography should be useful, it raises critical questions: Why a special bibliography for Israel? Should there be such a reference book for each country in the world? Why are only the English publications listed? Should the scholar not consult references in other languages, or should there be a separate reference book for each language? Friedmann could have avoided these queries by writing an introduction explaining why criminal justice in Israel offers special experiences that deserve particular attention. Israel has developed a highly modern and progressive system of justice, dedicated to due process, rehabilitation, and humaneness. Its treatment of addicts and juveniles suggests rehabilitation. Its virtual abolition of the death penalty, the Mosaic Laws notwithstanding, testifies to its humaneness, and the fact that the high court sometimes overrules even military courts testifies to its dedication to due process—even though enforcement of such overruling may be lacking. Yet, personal status is left to the religious authorities.—**Elias H. Tuma**

Dictionaries and Encyclopedias

597. Anderson, Sean, and Stephen Sloan. **Historical Dictionary of Terrorism.** Metuchen, N.J., Scarecrow, 1995. 452p. (Historical Dictionaries of Religions, Philosophies, and Movements, no.4). $57.50. ISBN 0-8108-2914-2.

No more timely a tool may be available to us than the dictionary in hand. Anderson and Sloan, from the helpful and explanatory first chapter, to the terms and definitions, to the most helpful bibliography closing out the volume, have covered the gamut of terrorism around the world. The authors use as a jumping-off place a selected topology to define a matrix of terrorism into nine types of groups: state repressive, state revolutionary, and state limited; revolutionary repressive, revolutionary, and revolutionary limited; and entrepreneurial repressive, entrepreneurial revolutionary, and entrepreneurial limited. However, this is only the beginning of the story. Other examples and definitions abound. For those seeking the identification of groups, places, dates, and events regarding or surrounding the issue of terrorists and terrorism, this volume will become a chief source.

If any objections can be made, it must be to the paucity of materials on domestic terrorism. Indeed, the title should insert the word "international." While recently, the press sees militia groups at every corner, Anderson and Sloan all but ignore them. This should be remedied in the next edition.
—**Mark Y. Herring**

598. Ballinger, Erich. **Detective Dictionary: A Handbook for Aspiring Sleuths.** rev. ed. Minneapolis, Minn., Lerner, 1994. 144p. illus. index. $14.21. ISBN 0-8225-0721-8.

First published in Germany in 1987, the *Detective Dictionary* calls itself a reference book. As such, entries are arranged in alphabetical order with guide words at the top of each page. "Detective related words" are also indexed. The similarity to standard reference books ends here. Unfortunately, this work does not seem to know what it wants to be. In form, the book does resemble a dictionary. In tone, it ranges from silly to serious, from reference to ridiculous. The arrangement of the material is also puzzling.

Ballinger intersperses serious content with games and puzzles, with the solutions presented at the end of the book. (Admonitions concerning the difficulty of the puzzles are more off-putting than encouraging.) Black-and-white illustrations, photographs, and sketches add little.

The dictionary appears to have been written for a middle school audience. Few middle schoolers, at least in the United States, will understand or appreciate the humor, the references to famous celebrities (Evita P.?), or be interested in biographical information about Ellery Queen, Dorothy Sayers, or Georges Simenon. Furthermore, the information presented will not inspire them to go read mysteries by these authors, even if those detective novels would be comprehensible or interesting to them. Also, the humor is heavy handed. In trying to make the serious subject of crime enjoyable, Ballinger is often condescending instead. Besides, everyone, especially middle schoolers, loves to read about blood and gore—the subject does not need to be made funny to be interesting. Readers of the Fear Street series and fans of Lois Duncan and Joan Lowry Nixon will not be amused. This is a marginal purchase at best.—**Michele Tyrrell**

599. **The Encyclopedia of Police Science.** 2d ed. William G. Bailey, ed. Hamden, Conn., Garland, 1995. 865p. index. (Garland Reference Library of the Humanities, v.1729). $95.00. ISBN 0-8153-1331-4.

Perhaps no other reference tool comes at so opportune a time. In the 6 years between 1985 and 1991, for example, homicides committed by males between the ages of 15 and 19 increased 154 percent. Between 1982 and 1991, the juvenile arrest rate rose 93 percent, while aggravated assault and forcible rape increased 72 percent and 24 percent, respectively. Clearly, society is on a violent rampage.

When the 1st edition of this work appeared 6 years ago, more than 140 entries had been penned by the best police scholars in the world. With this 2d edition, more than 4 dozen entries have been added (including a new entry on Rodney King and 9 references) and scores of others have been updated or substantially revised. This edition concentrates more energy on drug-abuse suppression, new crimes, international developments, and federal pressures in the form of mandates. In light of recent developments, articles on terrorism in the United States will seem more important than ever before.

Contained in the text are elaborate explorations of topics with ample cross-references and an excellent index. Important law cases, widely publicized events, and international developments help to make this an outstanding reference source. Some curiosities do exist, however. There is no entry or index reference to Waco, the Branch Davidians, David Koresh, or Randy Weaver. Apart from these oversights—and they are significant ones—the volume is a must-buy for any library with an interest in the field.
—**Mark Y. Herring**

Directories

600. Bosoni, Anthony J. **Post-Release Assistance Programs for Prisoners: A National Directory.** 2d ed. Jefferson, N.C., McFarland, 1995. 181p. index. $34.50pa. ISBN 0-7864-0025-0.

This 2d edition of a national directory is certainly timely, insofar as the size of the U.S. prison population has increased dramatically in recent years, and a large proportion of these prisoners will eventually be released into larger society. In the current political environment, much more attention has been directed toward facilitating the incarceration of those convicted of serious crimes than reintegrating rehabilitated human beings into the social mainstream. The present volume provides a listing—first by state, and then broken down into cities—of more than a thousand agencies that assist parolees. Some brief descriptive material on two major agencies, the Salvation Army Adult Rehabilitation Centers and the Delancy Street Foundation, is given up-front, but many other public and private agencies are listed within. The information is then provided in a very user-friendly format, with the address and telephone number of the organization, eligibility requirements for assistance (e.g., "anyone in need" or "non-violent, sober, drug free people in need"), fees (if any), and services provided (e.g., emergency food and clothing, shelter, substance abuse counseling, and so on).

Obviously, this volume should prove a useful addition to any public library that ex-offenders may patronize, and any agencies that work directly with inmates and parolees. The author is himself a prison inmate who has found an especially constructive way to do time.—**David O. Friedrichs**

601. **Terrorist Group Profiles.** [CD-ROM]. Minneapolis, Minn., Quanta Press, 1994. Minimum system requirements: IBM or compatible 386. ISO 9660 CD-ROM drive with MS-DOS CD-ROM Extensions. MS-DOS 2.X. 640K RAM (1MB for SVGA). $49.95.

CD-ROM is an enticing medium of information storage. Instead of huge bound sets that take up space and gather dust, there is compact, speedy retrieval of needed facts. When a great user interface with attractive graphics is added, the combination is hard to resist. In this disc, such is not the case. When a document that is 7 years old (and in its printed incarnation only 131 pages long) is coupled with minimal graphic interest (grainy black-and-white photographs) and combined with a pedestrian but usable interface, the result is an expensive but dull CD-ROM. Seven years is a long time in the world of current affairs. The original print version, published in 1988 by the Joint Task Force on Terrorism with a foreword by Vice President George Bush, cost $8 from the Government Printing Office (GPO), and although it is no longer in print, it is readily available at the nearest GPO Depository Library. Unless a collection emphasizes terrorism and *Terrorist Group Profiles* was missed when it was first published, libraries are urged to buy something else.—**George M. Cumming Jr.**

Handbooks and Yearbooks

602. **City Crime Rankings: Crime in Metropolitan America.** Kathleen O'Leary Morgan, Scott Morgan, and Neal Quitno, eds. Lawrence, Kans., Morgan Quitno, 1995. 284p. index. $19.95pa. ISBN 1-56692-307-7.

This volume is a companion to the same publisher's earlier *Crime State Rankings* (see ARBA 95, entry 624). It is current through 1993 with statistics made available by the FBI. The purpose of this reference work is immediately evident: It is intended to provide data allowing for a comparison of major crime rates in 274 metropolitan areas and 100 of the largest U.S. cities (or at least those for which data were available).

Following an exceptionally brief preface providing a rationale for the publication, and a few words about the basis for the city-by-city rankings, the balance of this volume is composed principally of tables. The first table combines data on reported major index crimes to arrive at a ranking of alphabetically listed metropolitan areas from the most to the least safe. Most of the first half of the volume is devoted to ranked data (on absolute numbers and rates) for metropolitan areas on crime generally, and on such specific index crimes as murder, rape, robbery, aggravated assault, burglary, larceny, and motor vehicle theft. Tables are provided to reveal percentage changes in the one-year period between 1992 and 1993, and for the longer period between 1989 and 1993.

The second half of the volume is principally taken up with the same type of tables for the 100 largest cities. Some data on metropolitan and city populations during the period in question are included in appendixes; abbreviated descriptions of metropolitan areas, a county index, and some summary data are also supplied.

The 90 tables found in this volume are certainly easy to understand, but as with the *Crime State Rankings* volume, very little discussion is included on the question of what such rankings do and do not mean. Accordingly, unsophisticated readers who consult such a work may draw questionable conclusions about this sort of data. With that caveat in mind, *City Crime Rankings* will be useful to individuals (students, journalists, politicians, and the like) who seek current comparative crime data. [R: Choice, July/Aug 95, p. 1704]—**David O. Friedrichs**

603. Kinnear, Karen L. **Violent Children: A Reference Handbook.** Santa Barbara, Calif., ABC-CLIO, 1995. 251p. index. (Contemporary World Issues). $39.50. ISBN 0-87436-786-7.

The Contemporary World Issues series to which this volume belongs focuses on timely and often contentious issues of current concern. There is considerable alarm in response to widely publicized data suggesting dramatic increases in juvenile involvement in violent crimes during the most recent period. Following the format of the other volumes in this series, the present work provides a well-organized capsule review of some aspects of the problem of violent children.

The first chapter focuses especially on causes of juvenile violence, and some treatment or prevention strategies. A second chapter summarizes significant developments in the societal response (almost entirely restricted to the twentieth century). The third chapter is composed of brief biographical sketches of individuals, from pediatrician T. Berry Brazelton to sociologist Murray Straus, who are considered to have made some significant contributions to the public's response to the violence of children. The fourth chapter, covering facts and statistics, provides recent data, in addition to excerpts from relevant appellate court decisions and other documents. A fifth chapter supplies an annotated listing of organizations concerned in some way with youthful violence (e.g., understanding it or addressing it directly). Two final chapters are composed of highly selective listings of print and nonprint resources. An index completes this volume.

The books in this series, including the present title, are most appropriate for secondary school and public libraries. Due to the exceptionally selective (and inevitably superficial, in places) coverage of a large research literature, this book is less appropriate for college and university libraries. Any student of violent children, however, can identify some useful tidbits of information in this user-friendly volume.—**David O. Friedrichs**

604. Peterson, Marilyn B. **Applications in Criminal Analysis: A Sourcebook.** Westport, Conn., Greenwood Press, 1994. 312p. index. $79.50. ISBN 0-313-28577-2.

Television portrayals of crime and punishment are often reduced to memorable one-liners—"Book 'em, Dano," or, "Just the facts, ma'am,"—but one knows there is more to it than that. The volume under review here describes just how complicated and difficult the process is. No other social issue has received as much attention, nor is on the mind of the public more often, than the issue of crime. Criminal analysis, a broad term that describes the analytical work that occurs in criminal justice, involves so much that, after examining this book, one is left more in awe of how many criminals *are* caught, rather than the many that get away. Criminal analysis involves analyses of three sorts: crime, intelligence, and strategic. But what do those things involve? This volume attempts to answer that complex question.

The first chapter provides a most informative, helpful, and descriptive overview. The remaining nine chapters cover various techniques in criminal analysis, first in terms of what is available to prosecuting officers (databases, forecasting, matrices profiles), and second in terms of how crime is executed by its perpetrators (violent crime, organized crime, narcotics, white-collar and street crimes). Both current leaders and future trends are also examined. While it is a reference tool with an extremely narrow field of interest, making it suitable for only the largest of libraries with criminal law curricula, the volume is well written and expertly researched.—**Mark Y. Herring**

HUMAN RIGHTS

605. Bennett, James R. **Political Prisoners and Trials: A Worldwide Annotated Bibliography, 1900 Through 1993.** Jefferson, N.C., McFarland, 1995. 363p. index. $68.50. ISBN 0-7864-0023-4.

Anyone conducting research on political trials and political prisoners in the world between 1900 and 1993 will find this reference work essential. It begins with a wonderful 25-page introduction that offers a brief history, citing the important work the United Nations and Amnesty International have done to bring to the attention of the world travesties of justice throughout the world. Indeed, the author notes that these two human endeavors constitute "two of the noblest enterprises in the history of humankind" (p. 1). The introduction also contains some working definitions of political prisoners. In addition, there is a very good section on torture.

Within the introduction, the researcher will find smaller sections on trials, prisons, secrecy and censorship, the death penalty, genocide, women, children, disappearances, trade unionists, conscientious objectors, writers and journalists, institutional reporting, the media, the United States, and research methods, among other topics. The introduction ends with a bibliographic list of works cited within it. The bibliographic entries begin with a list of general works, a listing of some 24 pages. Thereafter, the entries occur alphabetically, beginning with Afghanistan and ending with Zimbabwe. The work concludes with an excellent 47-page index; it is highly recommended.—**Michael A. Foley**

606. Chandler, Ralph C., Richard A. Enslen, and Peter G. Renstrom. **The Constitutional Law Dictionary. Volume 1: Individual Rights, Supplement 3.** Santa Barbara, Calif., ABC-CLIO, 1995. 189p. index. $50.00. ISBN 0-87436-758-1.

This publication is the third compilation since the original volume was published in 1985. It covers U.S. Supreme Court decisions concerning individual rights from 1990 to 1994. A companion work, volume 2, on governmental powers, was published in 1987, and it appears that this volume has not as yet been supplemented, because the law in this area has not experienced any significant changes.

The specialized nature of this work and its companion volumes indicates that it is best used by researchers at academic, political science, and law libraries as an introductory summary of, or guide to, Supreme Court activity. While this volume is useful, it is most valuable when included in library collections as a part of an entire set, as the contents are constructed around the earlier supplements and main volume.

Beginning with notes on how to use the book, acknowledgments, and an alphabetical list of new case entries, the text is divided into five chapters covering the first, fourth, fifth, sixth, and eighth amendments. The book concludes with an updated chapter on equal protection and privacy. Cross-references in dictionary references are found at the end of a number of paragraphs in the work. The text is followed by updated appendixes that list all the justices of the Supreme Court and an outline of the composition of the Supreme Court since 1900. The volume concludes with a useful alphabetical index of terms and cases.—**James M. Murray**

607. **Civil Rights Decisions of the United States Supreme Court: The 19th Century.** Maureen Harrison and Steve Gilbert, eds. San Diego, Calif., Excellent Books, 1994. 239p. (Civil Rights Decisions Series). $16.95pa. ISBN 1-880780-04-6.

608. **Civil Rights Decisions of the United States Supreme Court: The 20th Century.** Maureen Harrison and Steve Gilbert, eds. San Diego, Calif., Excellent Books, 1994. 273p. index. $16.95pa. ISBN 1-880780-05-4.

These two small volumes present the official texts of the Supreme Court decisions in what the editors consider the most important civil rights cases of the nineteenth and twentieth centuries. The first volume, covering the nineteenth century, is devoted to decisions relating to Native Americans, African Americans, and Chinese Americans, while the second volume, covering the twentieth century, includes decisions relating to Japanese Americans and African Americans. Some of the more prominent cases included are *Dred Scott v. Sandford*; *Brown v. Board of Education of Topeka, Kansas*; and *University of California v. Bakke*.

The opinions are those written by the justice chosen to speak for the majority. Although the decisions are almost entirely taken from the official documents, certain words and phrases that might not be easily understood by the average reader have been translated into understandable language and placed in brackets following the original text, as for example, prima facie is followed by [in the face of it]. Lengthy alphanumeric legal citations and wordy disputes over abstract points of procedure have been omitted to make for easier reading. In each case, however, reference is made to the volume and page of the unedited text in the *United States Reports*.

Additional material supplied in each volume is a brief history of each case, a list of the members of the Court deciding the case, a bibliography of works relating to each case, an index, and a copy of the U.S. Constitution. All of these add to the usefulness of the volumes. Although these decisions are available in standard reference sources, these volumes are much easier to use, particularly for students, and are well worth the modest cost. They are recommended for academic and public libraries.—**Lucille Whalen**

609. **Human Rights on CD-ROM.** 2d ed. [CD-ROM]. New York, United Nations, 1995. Minimum system requirements: XT PC. CD-ROM drive. DOS 3.2. 1MB hard disk space. 430K conventional memory. $190.00. ISBN 92-1-100691-0. S/N GV.95.0.2.

This new CD-ROM from the United Nations Library in Geneva, Switzerland will ease research relating to human rights throughout the world. There are more than 14,000 entries, encompassing the complete texts of 95 international instruments, including such documents as the "Universal Declaration of Human Rights," the "Declaration on the Granting of Independence to Colonial Countries and Peoples," and the "Declaration on Race and Racial Prejudice," among others. In addition, each of the texts and any bibliographical entry can be printed. In less than five minutes, this reviewer had copies of the "Principles of Medical Ethics Relevant to the Role of Health Personnel, Particularly Physicians, in the Protection of Prisoners and Detainees Against Torture and Other Cruel, Inhuman or Degrading Treatment or Punishment" and the "Code of Conduct for Law Enforcement Officials."

One can conduct a search for documents through 12 different query points, including "Title," "Subject(s)," "Personal Author," "UN Issuing Body," "Session," "UN Document Series Symbol," "Publication Date," or "Full Texts of Instruments." The more one can narrow the field of search, the better. For example, a "human rights" search will net 3,500-plus entries, whereas a "human rights of prisoners" brings up 74. There are many roads one can travel, however, and it is recommended that all possible reference points be searched.

The printed document that comes with the CD-ROM provides useful information about the package and its contents. This should be read before doing any search. There is also an online thesaurus to search topics in English, French, and Spanish. However, the disc was not as easy to use as the document suggests. Yet, for anyone doing UN research on human rights, this is a CD-ROM to access.—**Michael A. Foley**

INTERNATIONAL LAW

610. Boczek, Boleslaw Adam. **Historical Dictionary of International Tribunals.** Metuchen, N.J., Scarecrow, 1994. 361p. (International Organizations Series, no.5). $45.00. ISBN 0-8108-2903-7.

This book is a much-needed resource for researchers and reference librarians who find themselves increasingly drawn into research on international law. Anyone with any amount of research experience in international law certainly knows how complex and potentially confusing the field can be. Due to the fact that international law is a field governed only by mutual agreement and respect among nations, and obviously not enforceable or regulated by any specific governmental body, the field is chronically underpublished and underreported. In addition, as there is no central administrative body for international regulation or adjudication, there are few publishers that have taken on the responsibility for disseminating information on a global basis. Even though this source does not provide actual text of sources, it does provide a central location where one can turn in order to obtain insight and information about where to find materials.

There are many useful features in this book. One is a chronology of the activities of international tribunals. This chapter helps one gain a historical perspective on the sources of, and the development of, the international courts and tribunals. Other useful features are six annexes that list, in chronological order, opinions and other important actions of the international tribunals. Summaries of all the disputes listed are included in the dictionary portion of the book. The summaries are succinct and clear, and provide references to reported versions of each action of the relevant tribunal.

The book's main feature is a dictionary that defines terms in addition to providing biographies and describing events and institutions regarding the field of international law. Essentially, the work is more like an encyclopedia than a dictionary, although it is packed into a little more than 350 pages. An excellent bibliography, list of abbreviations and acronyms, and glossary are also included, adding to the usefulness of the book as a selection tool as well as a reference book.

All in all, the book is recommended to libraries with any size collection of resources in the field of international law, or with patrons who might have occasion to engage in such research. If nothing more, this work will provide researchers with enough information to help them get pointed in the appropriate direction to obtain copies of needed materials, and perhaps, even give them basic information to solve an otherwise difficult research problem. [R: Choice, Mar 95, p. 1074]—**Richard A. Leiter**

611. Maddex, Robert L. **Constitutions of the World.** Washington, D.C., Congressional Quarterly, 1995. 338p. index. $69.95. ISBN 0-87187-992-1.

This compendium provides descriptive information on the constitutional arrangements of 80 countries. It gives more constitutional information than *Statesman's Yearbook* (see entry 102) or *Europa World Year Book* (see ARBA 94, entry 82). Entries are arranged alphabetically by country from Algeria through Zimbabwe. Most major countries seem to be covered. Exceptions include states for which the political situation is particularly unsettled (as in Afghanistan or the former Yugoslavia). Entries are from three to five pages long. Each begins with a brief characterization of the country, its economic base, form of government, dates of constitutions, and location, followed by a summary of the constitutional history. In a useful (politically correct) touch, the compilers have included local traditions of government to emphasize the non-Western elements in constitutional development. The section on the present constitution is the longest. This furnishes information on basic rights; the distribution of powers; the executive, legislative, and judiciary—plus amendment procedures.

There is a "Constitution at a Glance" table, giving the type of government, unitary or federal state, most recent constitution or revision, sort of parliament, whether there is judicial review, and whether there is an ombudsman. There are also a sources section by country, an index, and a brief (four-page) glossary. On balance, this would make a useful but not essential addition to larger reference collections where budgets permit. Other sources of similar information in the collection should be accessed before acquisition.
—**Nigel Tappin**

612. **Multilateral Treaties Deposited with the Secretary-General: Status as at 31 December 1994.** New York, United Nations, 1995. 1024p. index. $75.00pa. ISBN 92-1-133484-5. ISSN 0082-8319. S/N E.95.V.5.

The 1994 volume is the latest in this standard serial that has been published, with title changes, annually by the United Nations since 1967. The main section contains information on multilateral treaties, the original of which is deposited with the secretary-general of the UN. This section is arranged by chapters related to various topics such as health, the status of women, and navigation. A smaller section, arranged chronologically without the subject breakdown, deals with multilateral treaties formerly deposited with the secretary-general of the League of Nations.

For each treaty covered, this volume provides full title, its entry into force and registration, and a list of nations that have signed and ratified the treaty. There is also information on where the text of the treaties may be found, either in the *Treaty Series* or other UN documentation. This is a straightforward publication that will be extremely useful for anyone requiring a listing of multilateral treaties or information on them, especially on the current status of their acceptance by the international community.
—**Henry E. York**

613. **Tuttle Dictionary of Legal Terms: English-Japanese, Japanese-English.** rev. ed. By Richard S. Keirstead. Rutland, Vt., Charles E. Tuttle, 1995. 561p. $18.95pa. ISBN 0-8048-2039-2.

This new edition of the *Tuttle Dictionary of Legal Terms* has the same features as the 1st edition (see ARBA 95, entry 605). It has more than 6,000 entries; in addition to the legal terms, the dictionary introduces conventional words. In the appendixes, compilers introduce the constitutions of both the United States and Japan, useful information with regard to both countries' legal education systems; the Japanese number system; and the addresses of the organizations that are connected with law and litigations. The lexicographers of both editions introduce and translate into Japanese such familiar English words as *high school* [kootoo gakkoo], *OK* [noroshii], *the United States of America* [Amerika Gasshuukoku], and the like.

On the other hand, the same compilers introduce a number of unfamiliar English words or terms without translating them into Japanese, instead simply supplying them in the forms of Japanese pronunciation (e.g., *impact loan* [inpakuto roon], *offshore company* [ofushoo kanpani], *slot machine* [surotto mashin], and *green card* [gureen kaado]. The lack of definitions in Japanese words or terms translated from English may cause frustration to the user. Thus, the *Tuttle Dictionary* is for legal professionals with some knowledge of the language.—**Seiko Mieczkowski**

614. **Yearbook of the International Law Commission 1992: Summary Records of the Meetings of the Forty-Fourth Session....** New York, United Nations, 1994. 2v. $55.00pa.(v.1); $38.00pa.(v.2). ISBN 92-1-133461-6. ISSN 0082-8289. S/N E.94.V.3(v.1); E.94.V.4(v.2).

The 34 members of the International Law Commission are charged by the United Nation's General Assembly to promote the progressive development of international law and its codification. Created in 1947, the ILC prepares draft conventions on subjects either not yet regulated by international law, or those for which the law is not well developed. Its codification efforts are intended to systematize international law where there already exists extensive state practice, precedent, and doctrine. The ILC's draft articles have formed the basis of numerous international conventions, including the Geneva Conventions on the Law of the Sea. The 1992 *Yearbook of the International Law Commission* focuses on the Commission's activities during its 44th session.

The yearbook provides a thorough record of the Commission's activity. Volume 1 covers summary records of the meetings of the session. Volume 2 (part 1) supplies reports of special rapporteurs, and the texts of other documents considered during the session. Volume 2 (part 2) contains the Commission's report to the General Assembly, including draft articles approved by the Commission during the year. In addition to listing the 34 members of the Commission and its officers, volume 1 includes the Commission's agenda and a listing of multilateral conventions cited during the session. The detailed meetings of the session discuss debate over establishment of an international criminal court and state responsibility for internationally wrongful acts. The report provides a paragraph-by-paragraph listing of proposed, amended, and adopted articles.

Volume 2 furnishes a summary of the debate over the Draft Code of Crimes against the Peace and Security of Mankind, and an account of the working group's deliberations on international criminal jurisdiction. The report also lists draft articles on State Responsibility for International Crimes, a summary of the debate on those articles, and a synopsis of the debate over International Liability for Injurious Consequences Arising Out of Acts Not Prohibited by International Law, and other decisions and conclusions of the Commission. The *Yearbook* provides essential source material for those who research public international law, and should be found in all serious international law collections.—**James S. Heller**

SPORT LAW

615. Wong, Glenn M., and T. Jesse Wilde. **The Sport Lawyer's Guide to Legal Periodicals: An Annotated Bibliography. 1995 Supplement.** Buffalo, N.Y., William S. Hein, 1995. 189p. $20.00pa. ISBN 0-89941-989-5.

As the earlier *American Reference Books Annual* review indicates, the original edition of *The Sport Lawyer's Guide to Legal Periodicals* is a tremendous resource for those interested in the burgeoning field of sports law (see ARBA 95, entry 599). The fact that there is so much material, and such intense interest, in the subject fully justifies this first annual supplement only a year after the publication of the original edition. There is, in fact, a clear need for the regular supplements that one hopes the authors will produce. This is evident from the fact that the supplement contains 200 articles published in 1993 and 1994, against the total of just more than 900 articles listed in the original edition that covered through the end of 1992.

As they should be, the format, content, and indexes are exactly the same as the premier edition. Law libraries, because of their commitment to historical precedent, will need the original edition and this, and future, supplements. Academic libraries, where students may be looking for related information when writing term papers on sports issues, may be able to get by with purchasing this supplement, and future supplements, that are more reasonably priced than the previous edition.—**Norman D. Stevens**

VICTIMS OF ABUSE

616. **Child Abuse & Neglect: 1965 - July 1995.** [CD-ROM]. Baltimore, Md., National Information Services Corporation, 1995. Minimum system requirements: IBM or compatible 386. CD-ROM drive. 150K RAM (512K without extended memory). Color or monochrome monitor. Free (contact publisher for more information).

Anyone working in the area of child abuse and neglect will benefit from this CD-ROM. The publisher claims that this disc "offers the world's largest collection of bibliographic databases on the maltreatment of children," and the product supports this claim. It offers a tremendous amount of research information that can be retrieved in a variety of ways. There are citations and abstracts to books, journal articles, conference papers, and descriptions of service programs and prevention and treatment strategies, among other sources.

The CD-ROM contains the following databases: child abuse and neglect documents (the major subjects on child maltreatment here, for example, are physical abuse, sexual abuse, emotional and psychological abuse, and child neglect); public awareness materials for adults and children; national organizations; audiovisuals; state statutes; program directories; and a child abuse and neglect thesaurus. The child abuse and neglect documents database, for example, includes among others the following key topics: definition and etiology of child abuse and neglect, social and economic factors, identification, treatment and prevention strategies, legal issues, federally funded research projects, and abuse and developmental disabilities.

The disc could not be easier to use, and if there are problems, an accompanying user's guide will answer questions. On entering the main search screen, three options are presented: a basic search, an author search, and a broad topic search. For an index of entries, the user simply hits F2. Under "abrogation," 39 entries were found; under "democracy," 3. To print, the user hits command F5. Once a topic has been selected, F3 displays the records for that search. The abstracts appear to be uniformly excellent. This disc is highly recommended.—**Michael A. Foley**

617. Hall, Rob. **Rape in America: A Reference Handbook.** Santa Barbara, Calif., ABC-CLIO, 1995. 202p. index. (Contemporary World Issues). $39.50. ISBN 0-87436-730-1.

Rape in America, arranged in seven chapters, is a compendium of information on sexual assault. Three chapters are composed of sections of from one to several pages on such topics as pornography, law enforcement, corrections, types of rapes, and statistics. One chapter is a chronology of miscellaneous events involving sexual assault, beginning with the biblical story of Joseph and Potiphar's wife, and ending with a 1994 Oklahoma court case. A chapter of biographical sketches features brief descriptions of 23 contemporary "'movers and shakers' [sic] in the field of sexual assault." A chapter of references describes 30 books and 15 audiovisual programs, almost all of which are aimed at popular audiences.

The most useful chapter is a directory of organizations, which describes national, state, and local organizations involved in various aspects of sexual assault advocacy and service. The index is useful for locating subjects in the text, but provides inadequate access to figures. Some chapters include reference lists of popular and scholarly books and articles along with an annoying number of personal interviews.

This work is of limited reference value but may serve as an introduction to its subject for the layperson or undergraduate student. It should be for circulating collections in larger public and undergraduate libraries.—**Gari-Anne Patzwald**

618. Kinnear, Karen L. **Childhood Sexual Abuse: A Reference Handbook.** Santa Barbara, Calif., ABC-CLIO, 1995. 333p. index. (Contemporary World Issues). $39.50. ISBN 0-87436-691-7.

Kinnear presents a reference handbook that builds a foundation of facts and understandings concerning child sexual abuse, then points to sources for further information. Paragraph-long annotations accompany a 26-page bibliography of video and audiocassettes, and there are addresses of suppliers. A few of the videocassettes are suitable for use with children. Books and other print resources, also with detailed annotations, cover 43 pages. The author made a solid effort to list the most up-to-date sources available but does not lead the reader to CD-ROMs or Internet listings.

The 36-page directory of organizations lists activities, emphases, and publications, and gives telephone and fax numbers. The book further fulfills its usefulness as a reference by including 23 pages of court decisions and excerpts from federal laws. Kinnear has assembled biographical sketches of recognized authorities, a chronology, key studies and their results, and guidelines and position statements from professional organizations and religious and policymaking groups.

There is suggested introductory reading for a wide variety of audiences who may need to be sensitized to indicators: clinicians and therapists, parents of children who have been molested, survivors' groups, doctors, social workers, and law enforcement personnel. The book will serve instructors looking for training materials and writers who wish to locate studies or contact authorities. It is accessible to older high school students and general readers in public libraries. The series title, Contemporary World Issues, is a misnomer as the book delineates the child sexual abuse problem only as it exists in the United States.
—**Edna M. Boardman**

11 Library and Information Science and Publishing and Bookselling

LIBRARY AND INFORMATION SCIENCE

General Works

Bibliography

619. **Information Science Abstracts. Volume 29, No. 12 December 1994: Abstracts 94—7751 to 94—8500.** New York, Plenum, 1994. 1447p. $535.00 (12 issues). ISSN 0020-0239.

Founded by the American Society of Information Science, the Division of Chemical Information of the American Chemical Society, and the Special Libraries Association, *Information Science Abstracts* covers the worldwide literature and data on information, its science, management, and technology. Its initial title was *Documentation Abstracts* (see ARBA 91, entry 603, and ARBA 87, entry 592, for reviews of earlier volumes).

Each monthly issue contains some 750-800 bibliographic citations with abstracts selected from journals, books, conference proceedings, reports, and patents. Approximately 50 core journals, and report and conference series are comprehensively abstracted; a considerable number of other journals and reports are abstracted selectively. In general, the abstracts are selected from materials available either through purchase, by photocopy, or interlibrary loan from institutions or libraries.

Citations list the number of references and note the language of the original; the abstracts themselves are in English. Entries are organized into seven major categories, including, among others, sections on information systems and applications, and on libraries and information services. Monthly issues are indexed by subject under broad headings; for example, an article entitled "Automatic parallelization framework for multicomputers" is indexed under the heading "parallel architecture." The cumulative index in issue 12 provides entry numbers only, making it somewhat cumbersome to use. Fortunately, an online version of *Information Science Abstracts* from 1966 to the present is available for searching through DIALOG Information Services as File 202. Information science collections and large research libraries should consider acquiring this work.—**Bernice Bergup**

620. Karp, Rashelle S. **The Academic Library of the 90s: An Annotated Bibliography.** Westport, Conn., Greenwood Press, 1994. 337p. index. (Bibliographies and Indexes in Library and Information Science, no.9). $69.50. ISBN 0-313-29301-5.

Given the availability of electronic databases dedicated to library and information science, one might justifiably question the need for this annotated bibliography. Yet its organizational format, succinct valuative summaries, and comprehensiveness easily support the need for purchase by academic libraries and library science departments. Its purpose is to provide the user with abstracts of library literature articles that were published between 1990 and 1993, and when studied, to furnish librarians with current trends, major research findings, and forecasts of the future of academic libraries. Unlike the neutral abstracts found in online database articles, these abstracts supply users with detailed précis rather than traditional subject descriptions and article outlines.

For accessibility, the articles are divided into six chapters: "Academic Librarians," "Administrators and Administrative Concerns," "Access Services," "Collection Management," "Technical Services," and "The Future and Role of Academic Libraries and Librarians." Several indexes (author, article, book/journal title, and subject) facilitate browsing and locating information among a total of 1,662 articles. A perusal of the journals cited reveals thorough selection criteria. Librarians and researchers will find this bibliography a timesaving and valuable tool to consult for information about their profession and its myriad activities.—**Kathleen W. Craver**

Biography

621. **Quién es Quién: A Who's Who of Spanish-Speaking Librarians in the United States 1994.** 4th ed. Arnulfo D. Trejo, Marta Stiefel Ayala, and Reynaldo Ayala, eds. Tucson, Ariz., Hispanic Books Distributors, 1994. 103p. index. $24.95. ISBN 0-938243-02-0.

Because of the dwindling number of Spanish-speaking librarians in the United States, the editors of *Quién es Quién* began including paraprofessionals in the library community in the 4th edition of this directory. Criteria for inclusion of paraprofessionals rest not only on their fluency in Spanish but also on a minimum of five years employment in the field and recommendations from professional colleagues.

The 259 people profiled returned questionnaires, which supplied the information used in this book. A typical entry consists of brief personal information with ratings of fluency in Spanish and any other languages, education, employment history, and a work or home address. Additional information may refer to areas of expertise, affiliations, accomplishments, reference sources, or honors. Thus, the amount of data varies significantly from person to person, with accuracy dependent on the responding individual. Five indexes—alphabetical, geographical, country of origin, ethnic/cultural background, and professional/paraprofessional categories—complete the work. In recognizing talented individuals in the field, this directory is also useful as a selective recruitment tool for libraries or businesses requiring fluency in Spanish.

—**Jo Anne H. Ricca**

Handbooks

622. **Annual Review of Information Science and Technology. Volume 29: 1994.** Martha E. Williams, ed. Medford, N.J., published for the American Society for Information Science, Learned Information, 1994. 455p. index. $95.00. ISBN 0-938734-91-1. ISSN 0066-4200.

As noted in its preface, "ARIST is an annual publication that reviews numerous topics within the broad field of information science and technology. The contents vary from year to year; no single topic is treated on an annual basis.... ARIST chapters are scholarly reviews of specific topics as substantiated by the published literature." The topics covered in this volume are arranged within four broad categories—planning information systems and services, basic techniques and technologies, applications, and the profession—and include such articles as "Information Retrieval Techniques," "Digital Image Representation and Access," "Managing Information Systems in State and Local Government," and "LIS Professionals as Knowledge Engineers." The articles, all of which are written at a scholarly level, range from 15 pages (including an 8-page bibliography) to 33 pages (with a 12-page bibliography) and conclude with a brief summary of key points.

As with previous editions, this volume will be of great value to those interested in advanced information studies. Given its price, however, most public libraries will want to seriously consider whether this information is sufficiently important to them to merit purchase.—**G. Kim Dority**

623. **The Bowker Annual Library and Book Trade Almanac, 1995.** 40th ed. Catherine Barr, ed. New Providence, N.J., R. R. Bowker/Reed Reference Publishing, 1995. 828p. index. $159.95. ISBN 0-8352-3613-7. ISSN 0068-0540.

This annual, reviewed in ARBA many times (39th ed.; see ARBA 95, entry 644), is one of the most essential ready-reference sources used by both librarians and publishers. Coverage and structure is the same as in previous volumes, including, for example, such sections as "Reports from the Field"; "Legislation, Funding, and Grants"; "Library/Information Science Education, Placement, and Salaries"; "Research and Statistics"; "Reference Information"; and "Directory of Organizations." This 40th edition contains 4 special reports on library networking and the impact of new technologies, as well as an informative account of the Library of Congress's digitization program under the Federal Agency and Federal Library Reports. A number of well-known librarians have contributed to this volume (e.g., R. Kathleen Molz, Ken Haycock, Mary Jo Lynch). All in all, this annual is indispensable for all libraries that can afford the rather high price tag.—**Bohdan S. Wynar**

624. Eberhart, George M., comp. **The Whole Library Handbook 2: Current Data, Professional Advice, and Curiosa About Libraries and Library Services.** Chicago, American Library Association, 1995. 521p. illus. index. $30.00pa. ISBN 0-8389-0646-X.

The Whole Library Handbook is basically an almanac for libraries and librarianship. In concise articles, the compiler has produced an informative, easy-to-read, and enjoyable compendium of library-related information for use by both the professional and the layperson. His use of visuals adds interest, and often a chuckle, to the text. The entries are arranged into 10 categories and subdivided into topics. The use of boldface type calls attention to important aspects within the articles, making this an easy-to-use ready-reference.

The title identifies this publication as a 2d edition (see ARBA 92, entry 570, for a review of the previous edition); however, it is more than an update and revision of the original publication. Although the purpose, scope, and format remain the same, and the revisions are primarily updates of statistical data, approximately two-thirds of the topics are new material. New subtopics cover issues of current interest, including the Internet, recycling and the library, the deacidification process, bookmobile services, and library promotions by type of library. (Be sure to check the especially delightful chapter entitled "Librariana.") This edition is not intended to replace the 1st edition, but rather to complement it. It is highly recommended to all who are looking for concise information related to the library profession, or to those who just enjoy browsing.—**Margaret Denman-West**

Indexes

625. **LISA PLUS.** [CD-ROM]. New Providence, N.J., Bowker-Saur/Reed Reference Publishing, 1995. Minimum system requirements: IBM or compatible 286. CD-ROM drive with MS-DOS CD-ROM Extensions. 3MB hard disk space. 512K conventional memory. Monochrome or color monitor. $1,575.00. ISSN 0966-8799.

The database consists of *Library & Information Science Abstracts* (1969-) and *Current Research in Library and Information Science* (1981-). Coverage and content correspond to the print publications. In addition to standard access points (author, title, subject, keyword, publisher, date, and so on), other search limiters include language, country of research, and author affiliation.

The reviewed disc (spring 1995) was tested on a Dell Pentium/90 with 16 MB RAM and a quad-speed modem. In this configuration, the system worked quickly. However, a drawback of the A&I Plus software used with Bowker-Saur products is that it is demanding on system memory (so that the system would not load while network drivers were running). It was also difficult to load on another computer (Gateway 2000 486/66), as it did not want to recognize that system's Microsoft Extensions; no other CD-ROMs have caused similar problems on that system.

The accompanying manual was the 1st edition (1992), inadequate for the present product. For example, the installation instructions were for floppy disks, which are no longer used; there were no instructions on how to install from the CD-ROM. The instructions for navigating through the database were satisfactory. While clearly appropriate for libraries serving library and information science programs, at the price, most other libraries would have to consider whether their use would justify the alternative forms of access: print subscription and online searching through DIALOG.—**Kenneth W. Berger**

Cataloging and Classification

626. Brown, Lorene Byron. **Subject Headings for African American Materials.** Englewood, Colo., Libraries Unlimited, 1995. 118p. $31.00pa. ISBN 1-56308-252-7.

This work is a compilation of some 5,000 terms that can be used to access information and materials related to the African-American experience. Gleaned partly from a list generated for the author's 1974 dissertation, the terms are structured in the style of the Library of Congress Subject Headings (LCSH) and arranged in a similar thesaurus-like presentation. Terms from the LCSH itself are used in the list but are not distinguished from those derived from the author's "A Thesaurus of African-American History Terms." Therefore, a cataloger using them in an automated catalog would need to enter them either in MARC field 653 (Index term—Uncontrolled) or in 69x (Local Subject Access fields).

There are relatively few name headings; however, a helpful list of subdivisions is provided under the heading *King, Martin Luther, Jr., 1929-1968*, which serves as a pattern heading for personal name headings. The introduction, while designed to benefit high school and college students, focuses primarily on grammatical forms of headings, and makes no reference to uses of the terms beyond library catalogs in other library indexes. The book is well designed and easy to use with its softcover, $8\frac{1}{2}$-by-11-inch format.—**Joanna F. Fountain**

627. Chan, Lois Mai. **Library of Congress Subject Headings: Principles and Application.** 3d ed. Englewood, Colo., Libraries Unlimited, 1995. 541p. index. $46.00; $35.00pa. ISBN 1-56308-195-4; 1-56308-191-1pa.

The Library of Congress (LC) system of subject headings, originally designed for use in the card catalog of a single library, is increasingly used internationally in electronic library catalogs and bibliographical utilities, and also in electronic indexes for other types of materials such as periodical articles. This is so at least in part because LC cataloging has been so readily available, now even through the Internet. It seems likely that LC headings will continue to be widely used, as an economically practical alternative has yet to appear.

Since publication of the 1st edition in 1978 (see ARBA 79, entry 278), Chan's book has provided the best available explanation of the history, structure, and use of LC subject headings. This 3d edition brings her work up-to-date with new and timely examples; expanded coverage of electronic developments, including USMARC coding; and discussion of the efforts made to update and improve the list, such as the 1991 Airlie House conference on subject subdivisions. The bibliography is also updated, with new entries added and old ones dropped.

Part 1 gives a history of the system, analyzes its principles, and explains subject authority control; part 2 deals with the application of subject headings as they are currently assigned to USMARC records; and part 3 discusses the future prospects of the system as an online retrieval tool. Although part 2 explains current practice rather than what ought to be, Chan is aware of valid criticisms of the system, and parts 1 and 3 offer lucid commentary on historical reasons for problems with the system, progress being made to overcome them, and what further changes may be made. Because an increasingly electronic environment means LC subject headings will be encountered even by users of libraries using other subject heading lists, this volume would be helpful in all libraries.—**Marit S. MacArthur**

628. **Class FC: A Classification for Canadian History.** 2d ed. Ottawa, National Library of Canada, 1994. 129p. index. $15.95; $20.75 (U.S.). ISBN 0-660-15428-5.

This is a revision and expansion of the 1976 edition. The classification system is currently in use by the National Library of Canada's Canadiana bibliography and library collection. The FC schedule is officially endorsed by the Library of Congress as an alternate to its F1000 class, and LC states that no other schedules will be developed to conflict with FC. American libraries can use FC instead of F1000, but it is not necessary. Certainly the FC schedules are useful and inexpensive enough for all Canadian Studies programs, and even if not all programs use it, its outline and shape of Canadian history is relevant as a guide.

Additions and changes from the previous edition are slight, and more expansionary than anything else. Historical time periods for the nation have been brought up-to-date, and there are newly established time periods for the provinces. There are also more examples for the biographies and special subjects (Cuttering is based on the NLC's shelflist). And—most important—names have been established by *AACR2* (1988).

The National Library says that this schedule is also on computer for ease of updating. Thus, it should also be made available *now* on disc so that all can use it. Electronically, it will be easier to search with little need for an index, more examples will be possible, hypertext links can be established, and libraries can update as changes occur. Do not hesitate to purchase this work.—**Dean Tudor**

629. **ERIC Identifier Authority List (IAL) 1995.** James E. Houston, Carolyn R. Weller, and Carol A. Patt, eds. Phoenix, Ariz., Oryx Press, 1995. 591p. $59.50. ISBN 0-89774-890-5. ISSN 1062-0508.

Robert Fugmann, a leading theoretician of indexing, draws a sharp distinction between the appropriate treatment of "general concepts" and "individual concepts," the latter of which, represented by "identifiers" in the Educational Resources Information Center (ERIC) system, refer to particular persons, institutions, publications, programs, events, and similar unique phenomena (quoted from *Subject Analysis and Indexing* [Frankfurt, Indeks Verlag, 1993, p. 134]). While the effective management of general concepts requires careful placement in a relational semantic structure for effective management, individual concepts need only be standardized and listed with equivalent terms. This is exactly the approach used for many years by the ERIC system, in which general concepts are placed in its structured thesaurus, and individual concepts are compiled here in its Identifier Authority List. This is the 2d published edition of the identifier list.

Here are more than 50,000 terms arranged alphabetically, with interfiled cross-references from unused equivalent terms. Most entries consist of no more than the term itself, its postings (i.e., number of times used) in the two ERIC databases, and a category number. Some entries include equivalent (used for) terms, and a few provide scope notes, which often refer to related terms. The traditional structure of broader, narrower, and related terms is not provided.

These terms are also listed in 20 conceptual categories, such as conference meetings, curriculum areas, equipment, places, groups, events, languages, organizations, persons, projects, and publications. Some categories, such as "health-related," "methods/theories," and "science & technology," list terms Fugmann would not call "individual concepts." These often are candidate terms for the *Thesaurus of ERIC Descriptors* (see entry 318). Recent examples of terms that have "graduated" from this list to the thesaurus are "aesthetics," "bus drivers," and "decision support systems."

The terms are listed to encourage uniformity in indexing and improved performance in searching. No one is helped when the name of a drug company such as Hoffman La Roche Company is spelled or formulated in six different ways. Indexers can use this list to provide helpful control for the terms listed, and they can use its guidelines to formulate similar terms as well.—**James D. Anderson**

630. **LC Period Subdivisions Under Names of Places.** 5th ed. Compiled by Office for Subject Cataloging Policy. Washington, D.C., Cataloging Distribution Service, Library of Congress, 1994. 123p. $16.00pa.

An aid to catalogers of historical materials and area studies collections, this compilation reflects place-names and related historical periods entered in the online subject authority database of the Library of Congress through January 1994. Place-name headings are arranged alphabetically, and repeated with each free-floating topical subdivision that may be used under the place-name. Topical subdivisions are in turn further subdivided by applicable authorized time periods; for example, **BRAZIL—HISTORY—1964-1985**, or **MARYLAND—SOCIAL LIFE AND CUSTOMS—TO 1775**. Beginning and closing dates of periods authorized for use under the free-floating subdivisions **—FOREIGN RELATIONS** and **—HISTORY** are those generally recognized by historians for the specified period.

The primary value of this publication is as a work-saver in assigning authorized time-period subdivisions to cataloging records and referring to the large tomes of *Library of Congress Subject Headings* (LCSH) and the *Subject Cataloging Manual: Subject Headings*. Nevertheless, the book's preface reminds the user that this is not a comprehensive or definitive statement of date subdivisions found in LCSH, and established as they are needed for works being cataloged at the Library of Congress. This listing replaces the 4th edition, published in 1990, before a large number of place-names and period subdivisions were modified due to changes in governments—especially in Eastern Europe. *LC Period Subdivisions* may serve as an aid to searching in library catalogs for information in works related to particular times and places in history. The format is an easy-to-handle 28-centimeter paperback with a clearly legible typewritten appearance.—**Joanna F. Fountain**

631. McCroskey, Marilyn. **Cataloging Nonbook Materials with AACR2R and MARC: A Guide for the School Library Media Specialist.** Chicago, American Association of School Librarians/American Library Association, 1994. 77p. $20.00pa. ISBN 0-8389-7736-7.

The author, audiovisual cataloger and head of the catalog department of the Meyer Library of the Southwest Missouri State University Library System, teaches cataloging and was formerly a school librarian for five years before joining the staff at SMSU. This book was originally prepared for a workshop presented at the 1992 American Association of School Librarians (AASL) Conference. It is geared primarily for use by the many people staffing school libraries who are not librarians, and who may not have any background in cataloging. Indeed, the author does not assume her audience has had experience in computerized catalogs as opposed to card catalogs. Thus, her examples are shown in both Machine Readable Cataloging (MARC) format (for those who use or are already familiar with computerized cataloging) and in card format.

The author bases her guidelines on *Anglo-American Cataloging Rules*, 2d edition (*AACR2*), and its 1993 amendments. Format integration is mentioned as being in the pipeline, although given the date of publication, there are no examples of how it affects nonbook cataloging. General guidelines for cataloging and creating MARC records for audiovisual items are discussed in the first chapter of this book, followed by separate sections on the various formats, such as videos, filmstrips and slides, nonprojected graphics, three-dimensional materials, sound recordings, and computer files and software. McCroskey does a good job of presenting her information to the lowest common denominator. For example, she explains what copy cataloging is, what MARC is, and she admonishes her readers to never accept someone else's cataloging without double checking all the information—an interesting thought in this era of "push-button" cataloging.

Overall, McCroskey's book does well at providing some basic knowledge for library technicians who are faced with the prospect of creating records for nonbook materials in small libraries. Given the complexities of cataloging in general, and of cataloging nonbook materials in particular, it probably would not be appropriate for use by itself in larger (especially research) libraries; but overall, it provides basic guidance to paraprofessionals working on their own without the supervision of a librarian.

—**Paul H. Thomas**

632. **Subject Headings for Children 1994: A List of Subject Headings Used by the Library of Congress with Dewey Numbers Added.** Lois Winkel, ed. Albany, N.Y., OCLC Forest Press, 1994. 2v. $70.00pa./set. ISBN 0-910608-46-6.

Subject Headings for Children is a two-volume reference book for catalogers, children, parents, teachers, and children's librarians. The first volume is an alphabetical list of subject headings used by the Library of Congress with Dewey numbers added. The headings in this list are current only through August 1993. The second volume, a keyword index, provides access to entries with subject headings by listing all significant words in main headings and the first word in each subdivision. Numbers and personal names are excluded. Both volume 1 and volume 2 provide instructions on how to use the book. Specific explanations are given for codes and abbreviations, fiction, biographies, Dewey numbers in brackets, more than one Dewey number, poetry and drama, filing order, and scope and exclusion.

The source and authority for classification numbers is the 20th edition of the *Dewey Decimal Classification* (Forest Press, 1989). Subject headings used fewer than five times and entered into the OCLC Online Union Catalog before 1983 are excluded, as are obsolete headings and those not likely to be used with children's materials. Both *Sears List of Subject Headings* (15th ed.; see ARBA 95, entry 652) and Dewey have served media specialists and librarians well all these years. Why reinvent the wheel?

—**Barbara B. Goldstein**

633. **SUPER LCCS CD.** [CD-ROM]. Detroit, Gale, 1995. System requirements: IBM or compatible 386. ISO 9660-compatible CD-ROM drive with cables, interface card, and MS-DOS CD-ROM Extensions 2.0 (double speed). MS-DOS or PC-DOS 3.1. Windows 3.1 or 3.0 with Multimedia Extensions. 8.5MB hard disk space for full installation. 4-8MB memory. CGA, EGA, or VGA monitor (VGA color recommended). Mouse. Parallel or serial printer port (optional). $3,200.00/qtr. (1 user); $3,850.00/qtr. (2-8 users). ISBN 0-7876-0006-7.

This new CD-ROM version of Library of Congress (LC) classification enables a cataloger to find up-to-date LC classification numbers without leaving a workstation. Installation is straightforward. One can set up the program to run off either the hard disk or the CD-ROM; the latter will be slower but will take up less disk space. The 139-page manual is well written and explains basic Windows concepts for those with little experience. Each section explains a task and how to perform it, concluding with a tutorial. Most functions can be performed using either the mouse or keyboard equivalents; users can customize the "look" and "feel" of various windows and functions to specific tastes.

When viewing the text of SUPER LCCS, one sees two windows simultaneously, one containing an expandable table of contents, the other the text. When scrolling through one window, the position in the other changes, so that the table of contents can be used to navigate around the text. Cross-references provide hyperlinks between sections. The text exactly reproduces that in the official LC schedules, with the occasional addition of Gale notes. The software supports searching by class number, word, or phrase, using complex Boolean and proximity searches; there are 12 predefined search forms that can restrict the search to specific categories or schedules. Multiple "hits" can be viewed sequentially, or users can have many windows open and visible at one time for comparison. If a displayed class number requires the use of a table, a hyperlink will enable one to quickly display it; unfortunately, users must still do their own arithmetic.

Text can be copied from one place to another for searching or exporting to a cataloging application. Journal and search history features allow retracing of movements through the text or previous searches. A future release will allow users to add their own hyperlinks, notes, and bookmarks, either private or available to anyone. Rather confusingly, these features are already documented in the manual, showing features that do not appear on the screen; there are also other minor differences between the manual and the program.

It will be interesting to compare *SUPER LCCS* with the Library of Congress's own product, due out in January 1996. *Classification Plus* will contain both LC subject headings and the LC classification, although at first the classification will be limited to the *E-F, H, L, R, T,* and *Z* schedules. The LC product will sell for a considerably lower price than *SUPER LCCS*. However, *SUPER LCCS* offers sophisticated capabilities that will make it attractive to those comfortable with technology. The manual is generally informative, but this is a complicated product and it will take time to learn, especially for those unfamiliar with Windows. Those contemplating its purchase must weigh its high price and the learning curve for staff against its potential convenience and ability to boost productivity.—**Marit S. MacArthur**

634. **USMARC Format for Bibliographic Data: Including Guidelines for Content Designation.** 1994 ed. By the Network Development and MARC Standards Office. Washington, D.C., Library of Congress Cataloging Distribution Service, 1994. 2v. $60.00 looseleaf w/binder. ISBN 0-8444-0809-3.

This edition of the USMARC bibliographic format incorporates the 1988 edition, the four published updates, and the approved format changes made to February 1994. It is the first edition to reflect format integration in which data elements are valid for all types of materials. Previous to this there were seven published formats—for books, archival materials, computer files, maps, music, serials, and visual materials. (Archival materials are called mixed materials in this edition.)

The changes dictated by format integration are not totally reflected in the 1994 edition. The 010-886 fields have been amended, but format integration has not been applied to the leader, field 006 (linkages) and field 007 (physical description fixed field). However, proposed changes for the latter are listed at the end of the appropriate field descriptions. Previously published separately, the national-level record and minimum-level record requirements are now found in the appendixes of this edition. The omission of deleted content designations is another change from the 1988 edition.

This work is an essential purchase for any library that does original cataloging and wishes to conform to Library of Congress practice. Those libraries that derive Library of Congress cataloging copy may also find it contributes to an understanding of Library of Congress MARC records.—**Jean Weihs**

Comparative and International Librarianship

635. **Academic Libraries in the United Kingdom and the Republic of Ireland 1994.** 3d ed. Ann Harrold, ed. London, Library Association; distr., Lanham, Md., UNIPUB, 1994. 148p. index. $50.00pa. ISBN 1-85604-114-X.

First published in 1987 as *Libraries in Colleges of Further and Higher Education in the UK*, this updated and expanded edition includes almost 700 universities, polytechnic equivalent institutions, colleges of further and higher education, and specialized colleges (sixth form colleges are excluded). This directory complements the annual publication *Libraries in the United Kingdom and the Republic of Ireland* (see ARBA 91, entry 627; ARBA 86, entry 584; and ARBA 85, entry 546), also edited by Harrold. Arrangement is alphabetical by name of institution or location (in the case of institutions beginning with the word "University"). Basic information for each institution is given: telephone, fax, and e-mail numbers; address; controlling authority; chief librarian or manager; hours; collection size; special collections (with areas of concentration); links with other departments and institutions; reporting relationships; and in some cases, history of the institution.

Comprehensive indexes assist the user: an institutions index; a subject index; a special collections index (by name of institution); and a geographical index (England, Irish Republic, Northern Ireland, Scotland, and Wales). This is a useful publication for academic and public libraries interested in international librarianship, interlibrary loan, and cooperative collection development, and for researchers in general. For future editions, the subject index might be expanded to include the specific subject areas of concentration of the special collections.—**Bonnie A. Dede**

636. Leeves, Juliet, and others, comps. **Library Systems in Europe: A Directory & Guide.** Washington, D.C., TFPL, 1994. 401p. index. $69.00pa. ISBN 1-870889-47-9.

Library Systems in Europe was written to assist libraries in the European Union (EU) select an appropriate integrated library system. The guide looks at issues such as language (What official EU languages does the system support? Does the system support a language in all modules of the system and in the documentation?), and at the import/export capabilities of the system (Will the system import and export UKMARC, USMARC, DanMark, IBERMARC, or other European record exchange formats?), and the availability of a multilingual search function. The guide provides an overview of the issues, with charts by library system listing available modules, charts documenting installed customer base by country and type of library, and another chart of library systems by language. Using information reported by the vendors, the guide then summarizes information about technical requirements, price, and functioning of the modules within each system. Modules discussed include cataloging, authority control, public and staff access to the catalog, circulation control, acquisitions, serials control, management information, and future developments of each system.

The guide furnishes a thorough but concise introduction to each of the systems that met the criteria for inclusion as a "European" system. It does much of the necessary groundwork needed to change or upgrade systems. While oriented primarily toward the European market, the guide has some useful features for libraries in countries outside of Europe but speaking European languages. The work could be improved with the addition of TELNET-accessible addresses for representative libraries using each system to enable prospective purchasers/evaluators to search and compare the public access modules of the various systems.—**Peggy Jobe**

637. **Libraries in the United Kingdom and Republic of Ireland 1995.** Ann Harrold, ed. London, Library Association Publishing; distr., Lanham, Md., UNIPUB, 1994. 245p. index. $19.25pa. ISBN 1-85604-091-7.

This 21st edition has listings for more than 1,700 libraries in the United Kingdom, the Republic of Ireland, the Channel Islands, and the Isle of Man, arranged in groups for public, academic, and selected government, national, and special libraries. A typical listing includes the name of the contact person, an address, telephone and fax numbers, and an e-mail address. The directory, first published before 1960, has appeared annually since 1988. The directory is also available in the form of mailing labels.

—Lawrence W. S. Auld

Copyright

638. Schultz, Jon S., and Steven Windsor. **International Intellectual Property Protection for Computer Software: A Research Guide and Annotated Bibliography.** Littleton, Colo., Fred B. Rothman, 1994. 1v. (various paging). index. (AALL Publications Series, no.46). $52.50 looseleaf w/binder. ISBN 0-8377-9294-0.

Computer software has proven notoriously resistant to intellectual property rights protection, especially on the international front. In an attempt to help remedy this situation, Schultz and Windsor provide a solid starting point from which researchers, businesspeople, and software developers can explore the issues. The selective bibliography is organized into three main parts: a brief overview of the international copyright's legal and technical background; the bibliography section, comprising descriptions of English-language books as well as general and country-specific periodical articles published between the early 1980s and the 1990s; and an appendix that reproduces the texts of the four major international treaties related to software protection.

The bibliography first treats general/multinational sources, then items grouped by country. (Readers will especially appreciate the fact that the authors lead off each country's articles section with a list of relevant treaties, copyright laws, and patent laws.) Annotations range from a single sentence to a paragraph in length and are primarily descriptive, although they are occasionally evaluative. An author index concludes the book; there is no subject index, although entries are cross-referenced as appropriate. The American Association of Law Libraries is to be commended for their sponsorship of *International Intellectual Property Protection for Computer Software*, for it will help many individuals and companies figure out how and where to start researching this thorny issue.—**G. Kim Dority**

Information Technology

639. **Who's Who in the European Information World 95/96.** 2d ed. Jorund B. Nordin, comp. and ed. Washington, D.C., TFPL, 1995. 899p. index. $230.00. ISBN 1-870889-51-7.

This directory provides information on personnel working in the information industry and in special libraries in Europe. The eastern countries of the former Soviet Union are not included. The information industry is widely defined to include online and CD-ROM database producers; automated library systems vendors; faculty teaching in library or information science fields; information brokers; consultants; and relevant personnel in public, national, or academic libraries. As such, the directory provides a useful source of contacts.

At the beginning of the directory there is a listing of international and Pan-European professional associations. Each country also has its national professional associations listed. The main part of the directory is a listing by country of information professionals. Within each country, names are listed alphabetically. A full entry provides the name and address of the organization for which the person currently works, the person's position in the organization, and how long he or she has held the position. Telephone and fax numbers, e-mail addresses, total years of work experience, previous positions, main areas of professional activity, languages spoken, personal interests and hobbies, and memberships in professional associations are listed. Not all entries are full, due to the fact that entries are self-submitted. The entries are clear and easy to read.

The directory contains three indexes: an organizations index that lists each organization alphabetically with its employees; an activities index following a modified UK Standard Industrial Classification (SIC92) system (organizations and their employees decided themselves to which category they belong, and there is much cross-listing); and a surnames index that does not refer back to a page number, but lists the country under which the individual is entered.—**Linda Main**

640. **Who's Who in the UK Information World 95/96.** 5th ed. Jorund B. Nordin, comp. and ed. Washington, D.C., TFPL, 1995. 600p. index. $155.00pa. ISBN 1-870889-50-9.

Task Force Pro Libra (TFPL), a British company offering employment services and training programs in the United Kingdom, publishes two directories of information professionals, one for the United Kingdom (reviewed here) and one for Europe (see entry 639). Criteria for inclusion include three years' working experience in a special library or information department, and status as a senior public librarian, a senior academic librarian, the manager of a special library or information department, an information broker, or an active board member of a professional body in the information sector. Not all British librarians or information professionals qualify, but the majority could be included, and the publication solicits qualified entrants with a notice at the bottom of each page and an entry form in the back of the directory. It appears that there are many more entries for special libraries than academic or public libraries.

The work has a brief introduction including criteria for entry, a description of the format of entries, and a description of the indexes. The body of the work includes 468 pages of entries in alphabetical order. Entries contain name, current position, contact address and numbers, relevant qualifications and memberships, library or information science training institution attended, years of professional experience (total and in current position), names of the two most recent positions held, foreign languages spoken, and brief descriptions of current responsibilities and interests. There are three indexes: employing organization, employing organization main area of activity, and library and information science institution attended. The indexes improve the utility of the publication, and similar indexes may profitably be included in U.S. directories of librarians and information professionals.

The work is paperbound and includes advertisements for other TFPL publications and programs and for Whitaker Bibliographic Services. While a specialized publication aimed at a British audience, this work should prove useful for academic, public, and special librarians looking for contacts in the United Kingdom. It would thus be an excellent addition to the libraries of schools of information and librarianship. Also, the organization activity index makes it a useful resource for researchers in the information business.—**Richard H. Swain**

Interlibrary Loans

641. Morris, Leslie R. **Interlibrary Loan Policies Directory.** 5th ed. New York, Neal-Schuman, 1995. 828p. index. $119.95pa. ISBN 1-55570-198-1.

Contrary to trends in rising interlibrary loan (ILL) activity and the rallying cry of access-over-ownership, the 5th edition of the *Interlibrary Loan Policies Directory* contains fewer entries (1,425) than the previous edition (1,550) (see ARBA 93, entry 657). The author attributes this decrease in entries to a number of California libraries cutting ILL service in response to budget constraints. In fact, this directory covers a small part of the ILL world, describing the policies of approximately 4 percent of the total number of U.S. libraries counted by R. R. Bowker for the *American Library Directory* (32,441 U.S. libraries counted in the 1995-96 ALD).

The libraries discussed in this work are academic, public, and special libraries, mostly in the United States; also included are entries for 23 Canadian libraries. As in the previous edition, the arrangement of entries is by state, then alphabetically by name of institution. Each entry consists of several data elements, from the directory information (address, telephone, and fax numbers) to specific policies on various formats of materials, terms of loan, costs, and so forth. There are some new data elements in this edition: Ariel address, listed under "Acceptable Methods of Transmission," which does not answer the question of whether the library will supply via Ariel; e-mail address; and a yes/no indication of whether an institution also has a separate document delivery service (no information is given for the few "yes" answers).

The directory has indexes, actually lists of libraries or institutions by name with state, telephone and fax numbers, e-mail addresses, and Ariel addresses; there are lists by specific types of materials or material formats for libraries that will lend them. This directory is not comprehensive, not without errors, and not as updatable as the OCLC Name Address Directory; it is not an essential tool for an ILL office. This is not a general reference work and is recommended for library staff new to the ILL business or for those for whom this is the only available source of ILL information.—**Linda A. Naru**

Library Automation

642. **Directory of Canadian Library & Information Science Consultants.** Helen Rogers, ed. Ottawa, Canadian Library Association, 1994. 240p. index. $29.95pa. ISBN 0-88802-262-X.

Included here in alphabetical order by surname are the profiles/biographies of 175 Canadian librarians and information science professionals (current through 1994). Information provided was taken from a questionnaire completed by each individual. Each profile presents the following information: areas of expertise, address, career history, education, awards received, facility with computers, languages other than English, international experience, conference participation, association memberships, publications, previous clients, availability of services, willingness to travel, and fee charged for service. Geographical, language, and subject indexes supplement the work, followed by an eight-page directory of businesses and agencies offering library and information science services.

Although the primary audiences for this work are likely to be Canadian and other Commonwealth institutions, it will be of use on an international level as well, signaling as it does so much experience and expertise to be shared in the consulting and problem-solving arena. The directory is recommended for libraries collecting in the area of library and information science, consulting, architecture, and facilities management.—**Edmund F. SantaVicca**

643. **Directory of Library Automation Software, Systems, and Services.** 1994 ed. Pamela R. Cibbarelli, comp. and ed. Medford, N. J., Learned Information, 1994. 374p. index. $79.00pa. ISBN 0-938734-82-2.

Librarians contemplating any aspect of library automation, be it retrospective conversion, new online software, additional electronic modules, or CD-ROM and online database acquisitions should consider the 1994 edition of this directory a core reference work. The first part provides an alphabetized, formatted entry listing of all software systems marketed and commercially available in North America and designed primarily for libraries and information management systems. One-page entries, under the name of the specific software package, furnish the following data: company name, ordering information, hardware and system requirements, programming language, components and applications, updating modes and features such as Boolean and full-text capabilities, MARC formats, type of library most suited for, installations, bar code formats, published reviews and articles, and price and suppliers comments.

A second directory contains a listing, in similar format, of retrospective conversion services and products. This listing is followed by a section that includes database hosts. These are companies such as Auto-Graphics, Inc. and EBSCO, which supply online database management and bibliographical utilities to libraries. Another section includes a list of CD-ROM and portable database distributors. Among those cited are Brodart Automation, which markets a CD-ROM-based public access catalog, and Gale, which sells a full-text, literary criticism database entitled DISCovering Authors. A final section called "Brief Info" alphabetically lists library automation software for which it was not possible to provide complete information.

The directory concludes with a selected bibliography of additional library automation reading, a list of library automation periodicals and recent books, a chronology of library automation conferences and meetings scheduled through December 1995, and an index. Coverage in this directory is comprehensive. This reviewer, who has investigated many library automation systems for possible purchase, could not find a significant system that was omitted. Librarians will find this directory an essential resource not only for locating and comparing systems, but also as an excellent criteria-based source from which to base a final financial decision.—**Kathleen W. Craver**

644. Kurth, Martin, and Thomas A. Peters. **Browsing in Information Systems: An Extensive Annotated Bibliography of the Literature.** Ann Arbor, Mich., Pierian Press, 1995. 275p. index. (Library Hi Tech Bibliography, v.10). $45.00pa. ISBN 0-87650-341-5.

This work deals with a topic of great interest to both library users and library professionals. As stated in the authors' introduction, "Virtually all the information environments described in this bibliography enable users to browse intertextually and intratextually; that is, they allow users to browse among texts and within texts, regardless of whether those texts contain verbal or pictorial information."

This volume includes articles published in periodicals or as monographs or chapters, papers presented at conferences and symposia and published in the proceedings of these events, and unpublished master's theses and doctoral dissertations. The authors also include articles from the Internet. The annotations vary from one paragraph to eight or nine long paragraphs. The more than 700 entries annotate works published in the last 15 years. They cover only English-language materials that have a variety of countries as their place of publication, such as Italy, Canada, Japan, Great Britain, Australia, and Switzerland. The inclusion of non-English materials would have been useful and would have provided a wider perspective on the subject.

The material is structured into 10 chapters that focus on general browsing behavior, browsing the library shelves, browsing the rooms, browsing in retail environments, online browsing in general, browsing in programming environments, browsing on Online Public Access Catalogs, hypertext and hypermedia browsing, surfing the Internet, and browsing among images and sounds. Each chapter is preceded by a succinct introduction, written by the compiler of the chapter, that briefly highlights the major issues included and points out the most prominent entries.

The 70 entries of the 1st chapter offer a general background on the nature of information; browsing and serendipity in searching for information; and information-seeking behavior of different categories of browsers, such as scholars, students, and physicians in a variety of environments, both physical and virtual. The multidimensional information retrieval system within the framework of hypertext and hypermedia environments is extensively explored. The authors analyze the most recent developments in the area of browsing computer networks and electronic databases that enable end-users to navigate through pictorial and auditory representations by using fast and sophisticated search engines.

With three fine indexes—by author, title, and subject—*Browsing in Information Systems* represents an excellent tool for library professionals, information scientists, and automation specialists. It provides a wide overview of the best recent literature devoted to the process of finding information resources.
—**Hermina G. B. Anghelescu**

Periodicals

645. *The Emergency Librarian* **Index. Volumes 1-20: 1973-1993.** By Ken Haycock. Seattle, Wash., Rockland Press, 1994. 332p. $20.00 spiralbound. ISBN 0-920175-12-0.

Begun in 1973 as a "Canadian librarians' underground newsletter," an alternative to publications of the professional associations, *The Emergency Librarian* originally focused on women in librarianship. By 1979, the focus had shifted to library services for children and young adults in school and public libraries. In addition to its feature articles, it has included useful reviews of professional books and numerous "best" lists of the notable and recommended books in various categories, which still have retrospective usefulness. This work supersedes an earlier index by Lynne Lighthall, bringing the indexing through volume 20, 1993.

The index consists of three alphabetized main sections, each entry providing a complete citation: an author index, including the subject descriptors, in all capital letters, assigned to each article; a title index, with article titles italicized; and a subject index. Three additional alphabetized lists complete the work: the titles reviewed in the "Professional Reading" section of the journal but not titles of works reviewed in other columns of the journal, article authors, and the subject headings. For those libraries needing an index to their back issues of this journal, this work fills the bill.—**Blaine H. Hall**

Reference Services

646. The Burwell Directory of Information Brokers 1994. Helen P. Burwell and Carolyn N. Hill, eds. Houston, Tex., Burwell Enterprises, 1994. 649p. illus. index. $79.50pa. ISBN 0-938519-10-1.

The 11th edition of this basic directory continues to grow, now listing 1,527 individuals and organizations worldwide. Included are information brokers, document delivery firms, freelance librarians and information specialists, information packagers, and public and academic libraries—all of whom provide services for a fee. The basic listing is in two parts, first for the United States by state or territory, and second for other nations, alphabetically by country. Each entry furnishes standard directory information, followed by subject expertise, services offered, hours, and fees. A short paragraph concludes each entry with background information on the organization.

Two appendixes give acronyms of professional associations and directory information on them. Indexes, by city, company name, names of contacts, foreign country experience, foreign database expertise, foreign language expertise, subjects covered, and services offered, conclude the volume. The indexes of foreign country, foreign database, and foreign language expertise are new with this edition. Entries in the directory are arranged by serial numbers, used in the indexes. The typeface, although small, is clear, with the name of the state or country as a running head on each page. Serial numbers are prominently featured adjacent to each entry; thus, the volume is easy to scan. As the book is paperbound, the cover will merit reinforcement if subjected to heavy use. This directory can prove useful in a variety of ways in all large public and academic libraries, as well as specialized information centers. The directory is also available on computer disk (DOS 3.31 or higher). (For reviews of earlier editions, see ARBA 93, entry 654; ARBA 90, entry 583; and ARBA 86, entry 568 [under the title *Directory of Fee-Based Information Services*]).—**Richard D. Johnson**

647. Reference and Information Services: An Introduction. 2d ed. Richard E. Bopp and Linda C. Smith, eds. Englewood, Colo., Libraries Unlimited, 1995. 626p. index. $47.50; $35.00pa. ISBN 1-56308-130-X; 1-56308-129-6pa.

For students in library schools and their instructors, the publication of the 2d edition of *Reference and Information Services* by Bopp and Smith, both of the University of Illinois, comes as a welcome introduction to reference services and materials. The purpose of the volume is the same as the 1st edition (see ARBA 92, entry 604). To achieve this goal, the first 11 chapters treat such generalized topics as "The Reference Interview," "Reference Staff Training and Development," and "A Philosophy of Service." This portion of the book is followed by a series of 10 chapters dealing with specific types of reference sources such as encyclopedias, dictionaries, bibliographies, and indexes and abstracts. The well-written, up-to-date text, thoroughly revised from the 1st edition, is augmented with a generous scattering of boxed sample reference questions, representations of entries from standard reference sources, and, at the end of each chapter, an annotated bibliography of additional readings.

As with the 1st edition of this book, comparison with William Katz's *Introduction to Reference Work* (6th ed., McGraw-Hill, 1991) is inevitable. In this case, the Bopp and Smith text has the obvious advantage of currency. A chapter on "Trends in Electronic Reference Services—Opportunities and Challenges" includes a lengthy section on the Internet, hypertext, hypermedia, and related topics. These discussions are backed by footnotes to readings published as recently as 1993 and 1994. The Katz text, however, still earns first place in any contest for style. While the Bopp and Smith compilation conveys the issues of reference service and evaluates the standard works in an accurate, straightforward manner, Katz enlivens the same topics with a dash of humor and a sense of excitement. With all that said, *Reference and Information Services* is recommended as the current text of choice for beginning graduate reference students.—**Donald C. Dickinson**

648. The Reference Assessment Manual. Compiled and edited by the Reference and Adult Services Division of the American Library Association. Ann Arbor, Mich., Pierian Press, 1995. 372p. index. $35.00pa.; $45.00pa. (with disk). ISBN 0-87650-344-X.

A decade's work of a committee of the Reference and Adult Services Division of the American Library Association, this publication summarizes the insights of librarians such as Marjorie E. Murfin on the assessment of reference services. The book's information is organized into three major parts. The first third of the manual consists of 15 chapters addressing components of the reference process, such as question classification, users, collection use, communication, training, costs, and outcomes. Although not identically organized, each chapter covers common elements, including the scope, importance of research, state of the field, research needs, and instruments of the particular component of reference assessment addressed.

The second third of the book consists of an annotated bibliography of more than 300 citations relating to reference assessment. Entries, many of them recent, include mostly publications in library journals but also dissertations, Educational Resources Information Center (ERIC), and other specialized reports. The third section of the manual contains annotated summaries of 91 instruments. Each entry includes the author and name of the instrument, a brief statement of its purpose, a description of and experience with its use, an account of its use, a review, noted validity and reliability factors, bibliographical references, and a comment on its availability. Many of the summaries indicate availability of the instrument on an accompanying disk (the disk was unavailable for review).

Although the manual is well organized, location of an appropriate instrument requires knowledge of its author or title (for entry by indexes); otherwise, one must read one of the appropriate chapters covering the topics where specific tools are cited. Also, one is cautious of the claim that "most of the instruments . . . can be easily adapted for assessment of reference service in an electronic environment," as many of the instrument descriptions note that no data are available on the tool's reliability or validity. Still, this is a rich source of information for the student, practitioner, or beginning researcher to identify instruments and cases in which reference services and related factors have been evaluated. It is recommended for inclusion in most collections serving reference providers or students of any type of library.—**Danuta A. Nitecki**

School Libraries

649. **Children's Media Market Place.** 4th ed. Barbara Stein and Lucia Hansen, eds. New York, Neal-Schuman, 1995. 284p. $49.95pa. ISBN 1-55570-190-6.

Information sources related to children's media and services are the focus of this comprehensive directory, now in its 4th edition. This reference tool is arranged in two parts: "Directory of Children's Media Sources" and "Names and Numbers Index to Children's Sources." The directory section provides names, addresses, and other ready-reference information related to publishers; computer software and audiovisual producers and distributors; wholesalers; children's booksellers; antiquarian booksellers; book clubs; agents; periodicals for children (as well as parents and professionals associated with them); review journals; museums; associations (state library and media associations, state school media offices); grant sources that fund children's programs (including objectives and eligibility requirements); awards (state and national literary awards); events; conferences; and selection tools covering materials and services for children.

The most active publishing houses and companies selling children's books, computer and A/V software and equipment, both large and small, are described, accompanied by indexes to individual sections. New sections in the revised and expanded edition include an annotated list of cooperative networks, listservs, and user groups that deal with K-12 education, as well as lists of organizations that provide children's and youth programs representing different cultures, in addition to multicultural bibliographies, teaching aids, and other resources of interest to teachers and students.

The index section supplies each organization's name, address, and telephone and fax numbers, followed by a code number that designates the section in the directory containing the entry describing that particular organization. The code number then immediately identifies for the user the nature of the organization (e.g., whether it is a producer/distributor, publisher, children's bookseller, museum, conference, and so forth). This work is an invaluable, all-in-one-volume source to aid school media specialists, teachers, librarians selecting materials and providing services for children, and other educators and professionals whose work is with or about children.—**Lois J. Buttlar**

650. **Middle and Junior High School Library Catalog.** 7th ed. Anne Price and Juliette Yaakov, eds. New York, H. W. Wilson, 1995. 988p. index. $175.00. ISBN 0-8242-0880-3.

Formerly titled the *Junior High School Library Catalog*, this standard core reference tool has been renamed *Middle and Junior High School Library Catalog* to reflect the increasing presence of middle schools as an educational division and the expansion of its coverage. Issued every 5 years with annual supplements scheduled for 1996, 1997, 1998, and 1999, this new edition contains 4,224 titles and 4,490 analytical entries. These numbers represent a significant increase over the 3,219 titles and 3,600 analytical entries of the previous edition (see ARBA 91, entry 650).

The 6th edition correctly concerned itself with adolescent stresses, contemporary social problems, health-related issues, and the treatment of ethnic groups. This edition wisely focuses on cultural diversity, technology, personal values, and contemporary social and political concerns. For example, the nonfiction section lists works about AIDS, homelessness, poverty, virtual reality, and DNA fingerprints.

An examination of selected subject headings noted in both editions revealed many new titles in this edition that bear a 1994 copyright date. While several advisory committee members and consultants worked on both editions, many new names are cited for this edition. The addition of new contributors is evident in the diversity of titles listed, especially in multicultural areas.

The organization of the catalog is virtually the same as the previous edition's. It consists of three parts. Part 1, the classified catalog, lists books in Dewey Decimal order under specific subject classifications. Part 2, an author, title, subject, and analytical index, provides quick access and entry points to the classified catalog featured in part 1. Part 3 furnishes a directory of publishers and distributors.

School librarians should be cautioned, however, about the contents of this work. While it is definitely a voluminous catalog, it does not include textbooks, periodicals (except for professional review media), adult fiction, "plot-your-own-story" books, nor nonprint materials. It does, however, for the first time, list CD-ROM versions of a print equivalent such as generalized and specialized encyclopedias. For school librarians, this catalog should be considered a mandatory purchase. Media specialists will find it an invaluable tool for acquisitions, reading guidance, confirmation of information, and collection development.—**Kathleen W. Craver**

651. **School Library Media Annual 1995: Volume Thirteen.** Betty J. Morris, Judith L. McQuiston, and Cecile L. Saretsky, eds. Englewood, Colo., Libraries Unlimited, 1995. 320p. illus. index. $45.00. ISBN 1-56308-388-4. ISSN 0739-7712.

An emphasis on technological change, the role of automation, and the Internet marks the 13th volume of a reference that focuses on school library media centers. The authors perceive the need for schools to look ahead, to access the new information environment in which almost anything ever produced, print and nonprint, is available to school-aged researchers.

The book is divided into 3 parts, each of which is made up of short items by 53 writers interested in and involved with school library media. Only three are working school library media specialists. David Calliston, in "Restructuring Pre-Service Education," decries the slowness with which school library media specialists are perceived as leaders. In this volume, actual scenarios help one envision how the media-resource specialist might fit into a world of change. Part 1 projects the future of school library media programs, part 2 reviews research in progress or completed, and part 3 provides information about organizations and sources.

Even schools that do not normally subscribe should consider adding this edition. Its vision will be valuable for school library media specialists, students in training for that position, and administrators and governing boards who wish to know in what direction to move as they plan for growth and development of their school library media centers.—**Edna M. Boardman**

Special Libraries and Collections

652. **A Checklist of Painters c1200-1994: Represented in the Witt Library Courtauld Institute of Art, London.** 2d ed. London, Mansell/Cassell and Chicago, Fitzroy Dearborn, 1995. 557p. $95.00. ISBN 1-884864-37-0.

With nearly 2 million photographs and reproductions, the Witt Library is one of the world's largest visual archives of art historical works. Although few Americans have the opportunity to visit the collection in London, publication of the list of painters included in the Witt Library has proved an invaluable authority tool for slide curators and art librarians worldwide. The 1st edition has been a common source for name and date authorities since 1978 (see ARBA 79, entry 905), when the collection was composed of works of some 40,000 European artists. Now expanded to 66,000 artists working in the Western tradition of European-style painting, the Witt checklist is most useful for relatively contemporary minor European artists who do not appear in older, standard sources. In addition, this edition is an affordable and handy alternative to the *Union List of Artists Names* now produced by the Getty Art History Information Project on diskette (1994; distributed by G. K. Hall).—**Stephanie C. Sigala**

653. Craig, Barbara L., and Peter D. James. **A Guide to the Fonds d'Archives and Collections in the Holdings of the York University Archives.** Toronto, ECW Press, 1995. 636p. index. $70.00. ISBN 1-55022-229-5.

This book describes the holdings of the York University Archives. The history of each *fonds d'archives* is explained in-depth, and the reader is guided to related *fonds*. Besides descriptions, the guide has an explanatory introduction, appendixes that note archival procedures, and an index with name and subject references.

The Archives contain material from a number of different sources. Perhaps half of the *fonds* are records from York University; the other half are from a variety of sources. Much of the private material comes from Toronto or Ontario, which are York's home city and province. There is some interesting material, such as the papers of bill bissett (a Canadian poet) and a collection of folklore tapes from Ontario and Newfoundland.

This guide was well prepared. The descriptions and indexing are meticulous, and the archival procedures used in creating the guide are well explained. However, the value of the book is questionable compared to the electronic database on which it is based. The electronic version of this guide contains extra information, such as restrictions on the use of particular materials. The database is also more current; the book only covers material cataloged as of 1993.

The very existence of this book is an achievement for the York University Archives; it represents much work spent documenting and promoting the collection. However, the electronic version of the book is a more powerful tool. The Archives expects to make the electronic guide available on the Internet through the university library Online Public Access Catalog (OPAC) by early 1996. When it is available, the electronic version will be the preferred tool for most scholars and researchers.—**Ken Feser**

654. Fowler, David J. **Guide to the Sol Feinstone Collection of the David Library of the American Revolution.** Washington Crossing, Pa., David Library of the American Revolution, 1994. 515p. index. $60.00. ISBN 0-9643693-0-3.

A longtime devotee of the founding years of U.S. history, businessman and philanthropist Feinstone (1888-1980) spent 50 years collecting more than 2,400 manuscripts, records, diaries, and other primary source material pertaining to the Revolutionary era (1750-1800). These documents, as well as printed materials, reference books, journals, and some 10,000 reels of microfilm, compose the David Library of the American Revolution, which he established on his farm in Washington Crossing, Pennsylvania, in 1959.

Today, the privately endowed foundation is a leading research center of the Revolutionary era, and this guide to its primary resources will be welcomed by its users and other scholars. Each of the nearly 2,500 entries includes an item number, which corresponds to the organization of the microfilm edition of the collection; a subject heading; the location identification (where the item was written); a date; the recipient's name; the number of pages or volumes; and an abstract, which succinctly summarizes the content of the item.

Not only is the *Guide*'s introduction clear, concise, and well written, but its index is a model of detail and thoroughness, enabling one to find easily, for example, documents concerning Benedict Arnold's treason or the battle at Yorktown. An appendix lists chronologically arranged item numbers. This guide is for special and university library collections.—**Jack Bales**

655. **International Directory of Serials Specialists.** Jean I. Whiffin, ed. Binghamton, N.Y., Haworth Press, 1995. 156p. index. $24.95. ISBN 1-56024-943-9.

This work is the first international directory in the field of serials librarianship. Persons included are those whose record of contribution to the profession is recognized regionally, nationally, and internationally. The principal section lists serials experts alphabetically, first by country and then by surname. It covers 144 individuals in 46 countries. Full address, telephone, and fax information is provided. Many listings also give telex numbers. Entries contain areas of serials expertise, career highlights, conferences organized, papers presented, publications, and research in progress. Indexes by personal name and areas of expertise follow the listings of individuals. This guide also includes directory information for administrators in more than 60 regional, national, and international centers that comprise the network for assigning International Standard Serial Numbers. While of limited appeal to those outside the library or book trade, *International Directory of Serials Specialists* will be helpful to librarians, publishers, serials agents, and library associations.—**Rachael Green**

656. Janes, Robert W., with Katherine R. Tromble. **Scholars' Guide to Washington, D.C., for Peace and International Security Studies.** Washington, D.C., Woodrow Wilson Center Press and Baltimore, Md., Johns Hopkins University Press, 1995. 407p. index. $65.00; $24.95pa. ISBN 0-8018-5218-8; 0-8018-5219-6pa.

This is another splendid addition to the Scholars' Guide series from the Woodrow Wilson International Center for Scholars (see ARBA 95, entries 164 and 938, for other recent titles in the series). The format of this volume conforms to the series standard: a listing of collections and organizations found in the greater Washington, D.C., area, arranged into broad categories. In addition to libraries of all types (public, academic, governmental, special), other collections that are identified are located in museums, archives, film or map repositories, and within databases. The organizations profiled in this book, which focuses on peace and international security issues, include research centers, academic programs, governmental agencies, international organizations based in Washington, D.C., and cultural exchange groups.

For each of the more than 750 collections or institutions, a helpful profile is supplied. Names of key contact persons are given, as are the hours of availability, services provided to the public, any limitations to use of materials, a brief description of the organization (or collections), and any associated publications. There are several indexes, with each item keyed to a section and number in the main portion of the book. In addition to a detailed subject index, there are indexes of personal papers, organizations, and libraries according to their subject strengths. One of the appendixes also identifies the libraries with the best collections in this field. The guide will be an indispensable resource for anyone doing research in the area of peace and international security, and is highly recommended for all academic libraries, regardless of location.
—**Thomas A. Karel**

657. **The Mexican-American War of 1846-1848: A Bibliography of the Holdings of the Libraries, The University of Texas at Arlington.** By Jenkins Garrett. Katherine R. Goodwin, ed. College Station, Tex., published for the University of Texas at Arlington by Texas A&M University Press, 1995. 693p. illus. index. (Special Collections Publication, no.2). $75.00. ISBN 0-89096-587-0.

This bibliography provides access to the vast collection of materials on the Mexican-American War (1846-1848) at the libraries of the University of Texas at Arlington. Looked at another way, it is an archive of the period. Indeed, the holdings were prepared (and edited) by an archivist, Goodwin, of the University of Texas. The materials were collected by Fort Worth attorney Jenkins Garrett, representing more than 40 years of dedicated work.

The holdings are divided into chapters and consist of all manner of archival materials—histories, fiction, speeches, cartographical materials, manuscripts, sheet music, and newspapers. In all, there are approximately 2,500 items, each fully described. The book contains 37 illustrations, an extensive index, and more than 60 pages of appendixes, which provide an alternate method of referencing data. As befitting a volume of 700 pages, the book is well made with jacket, boards, and head bands and foot bands.—**David Eggenberger**

658. Moore, Jean M., comp. **Mapping the Territory: A Guide to the Archival Holdings, Special Collections, University of Calgary Library.** Marlys Chevrefils and Apollonia Steele, eds. Calgary, Alberta, University of Calgary Press, 1994. 150p. illus. index. $19.95pa. ISBN 1-895176-53-0.

This work is a guide to archival collections at the University of Calgary. The library maintains primarily Canadian archival collections in history, publishing, the petroleum industry, and architecture, with particular strengths in Canadian literature and music. The main body of the text, following international standards, is composed of descriptive entries for the archival collection, giving creator name, title, dates of creation, extent, biographical/historical notes, scope, and content of the unit, as well as specialized information unique to the entry. There follows a subject index using Library of Congress subject headings and an index of names in the Archival Collection. The publication is composed from an Inmagic database searchable through the University of Calgary Library. It is hoped that more archives will publish guides to their holdings.—**Lorna K. Rees-Potter**

659. Phillips, Faye. **Local History Collections in Libraries.** Englewood, Colo., Libraries Unlimited, 1995. 164p. index. $32.00. ISBN 1-56308-141-5.

This new guide to administering local history collections is more comprehensive than two earlier volumes: Enid T. Thompson's *Local History Collections* (American Association for State and Local History, 1978) and James H. Conrad's *Developing Local History Programs in Community Libraries* (American Library Association, 1989). It also includes discussions of new technological advances for access to and preservation of collections. The author goes beyond public libraries and considers local history collections in academic libraries as well. She features a description of the Research Libraries Group Conspectus for collection evaluation and provides samples of forms for academic libraries.

Phillips organizes her material well. She proceeds systematically from collection building, through organization and preservation, to use, public relations, and outreach. She gives relatively full descriptions of operations so that a nonlibrarian can immediately use this volume to begin organizing a local history collection. Numerous sample forms are furnished.

Appendixes give examples of a collection development policy statement, a collection strategy, a collection inventory, and an appraisal checklist. Unfortunately, there are no photographs (a handsome feature in Thompson). A lengthy bibliography, unhappily not organized by subject, and an index complete the volume. The work is recommended for all libraries, both public and academic, and for circulating and reference collections.—**Richard D. Johnson**

660. Sapp, Gregg. **Building a Popular Science Library Collection for High School to Adult Learners: Issues and Recommended Resources.** Westport, Conn., Greenwood Press, 1995. 329p. index. $45.00. ISBN 0-313-28936-0.

While being surrounded with new scientific and technical gadgets in daily life, most people passively accept them or in extreme cases reject them without consideration of their effect on life and culture. The need for what is called "science literacy," or the science knowledge one needs to understand public issues, has been growing over the years. To compound the issues, there has been a spate of published popular science books, both good and bad, dealing with science and technology issues that may or may not be of importance in our lives.

Librarians and science teachers feel a particular responsibility to help out in this situation. This book is an attempt to present sound advice to ease the problem. It is divided into two parts, the first being a series of essays by the author defining scientific literacy and then discussing the history, understanding, and evaluation of popular science information resources.

The second part consists of short evaluations of more than 2,500 print and nonprint works in 9 of the most-read subject fields of popular science literature that can be recommended or collected to teach science literacy. The author's role as writer of the annual *Library Journal* column "Best Sci-Tech Books for General Readers" adds much credibility to his selections. There are also author, title, and subject indexes to the recommended books.—**Robert J. Havlik**

661. **Special Collections in Children's Literature: An International Directory.** 3d ed. By Association for Library Service to Children. Dolores Blythe Jones with National Planning for Special Collections Committee, comps. and eds. Chicago, American Library Association, 1995. 235p. illus. index. $40.00pa. ISBN 0-8389-3454-4.

Since its first release in 1969, this work has evolved to become the definitive directory of special collections relating to children's literature. It is intended to help bibliophiles, researchers, and librarians identify and locate institutions with holdings of materials pertinent to the study of children's and young adult literature.

The 3d edition includes 300 U.S. institutions (that is an addition of 82 since the 2d edition [see ARBA 83, entry 131]) listed by collection and subject and representing children's literature holdings listed in any format—print, illustration, or audiovisual. The directory is arranged alphabetically by state, city, and institution. Each collection within an institution is described as specifically as possible. All entries include full addresses, fax and telephone numbers, contact names, and e-mail and Internet addresses. New to this edition is a directory of international collections, describing the holdings of 119 institutions in 40 countries. Private collections are not included. This definitive directory is a must-have for scholars, collectors, or anyone researching or interested in the history of children's literature.

—**Jennifer Comi Ellard**

662. **University of London Library Catalogue of the Goldsmiths' Library of Economic Literature. Volume V: Additions to the Printed Books, Periodicals, and Manuscripts to 1850.** Angela Whilelegge and Ruth Vyse, comps. London, for the University of London Library, Athlone Press; distr., Atlantic Highlands, N.J., Humanities Press, 1995. 101p. index. $120.00. ISBN 0-485-15020-4.

This volume includes 600 entries that are unique new additions to the Goldsmiths' Library of Economic Literature at the University of London since the last supplement to their catalog was published in 1982. This is the second supplement to the original catalog, which was published in two volumes in 1971 and 1975 respectively. In 1984, following the publication of the first supplement, a general comprehensive index to the set was produced. This catalog is designed for the researcher who is concerned with contemporary sources in economic literature, and the arrangement is therefore by year of publication, including entries for printed books, periodicals, manuscripts, and autographs.

The earliest title listed in this supplement is dated 1549. The entries are numbered in such a manner as to relate these publications with those in the first two volumes. This is important because entries from 1601, in addition to being arranged chronologically, are also subdivided by 14 subject divisions such as corn laws, social conditions, and the colonies. Users of this set will find that the entries in this volume are more descriptive than in the previous ones. There is a general index to this volume, followed by a few amendments and corrections to the previous four volumes. Libraries already owning the first four volumes will want to acquire this one for their collection.—**Judith J. Field**

Storytelling

663. Freeman, Judy. **More Books Kids Will Sit Still For: A Read-Aloud Guide.** New Providence, N.J., R. R. Bowker/Reed Reference Publishing, 1995. 869p. illus. index. $45.00; $29.95pa. ISBN 0-8352-3520-3; 0-8352-3731-1pa.

Marketed as a companion volume to *Books Kids Will Sit Still For* (see ARBA 92, entry 62), this annotated compilation is an excellent stand-alone acquisition either in the hardcover or more-affordable paperback version. It contains more than 1,400 new titles about picture books, poetry, folklore, fiction, and nonfiction for children in preschool through sixth grade. The essential author, title, illustrator, and subject indexes even cite reference entry numbers to the previous volume. Thus librarians, teachers, and parents owning both works can easily combine current and retrospective lists of titles, literature extension activities, and stories that children will love and enjoy.

Beginning with a charming foreword by prolific author Daniel Pinkwater about the myriad possibilities to be discovered in a single book, the author describes 50 ways to recognize a good read-aloud. These recognition standards serve as criteria for the 1,400 annotations grouped within 12 chapters. These chapters range from fiction for preschool students to fiction for students in grades 5-6. Separate chapters are devoted to collections of folk and fairy tales, myths, and legends; poetry, nonsense, and language-oriented nonfiction; and nonfiction and biography. A preceding chapter provides future booktalkers and storytellers with memorable tips and examples of reading with expression and integrating literature into various teaching curricula. A second chapter focuses solely on the importance of a school library/media center program.

What distinguishes this volume and its previous companion work from other similar compilations are the refreshing, enticing annotations. Their originality and citations to additional related works leave no doubt that Freeman has read and probably used each title in a read-aloud, workshop, or booktalk session. Her "50 Ways to Recognize a Read-Aloud" constitutes an almost guaranteed basis for acquisitions that are certain to be borrowed by users of any age.

Librarians, teachers, and parents who work with children should consider this a mandatory purchase. It succeeds in furnishing not only a list of new materials, but even more important, the methods and programs to bring literature to life.—**Kathleen W. Craver**

PUBLISHING AND BOOKSELLING

General Works

Bibliography

664. Rosenblum, Joseph. **A Bibliographic History of the Book: An Annotated Guide to the Literature.** Metuchen, N.J., Scarecrow and Pasadena, Calif., Salem Press, 1995. 425p. index. (Magill Bibliographies). $55.00. ISBN 0-8108-3009-4.

Having previously edited *American Book-Collectors and Bibliographers: First Series* (see ARBA 95, entry 971), bibliophile Rosenblum has selected, annotated, and compiled some 1,400 titles for this wide-ranging bibliography. With an emphasis on twentieth-century items from the West, his list is preceded by a well-researched introduction (16 pages), which provides a solid historical overview to the subject for the uninitiated. This discursive essay traces the courses of literacy and book publishing through time, pointing out how they were promoted by such forces as religion, the railroad, and the cylinder press. No selection criteria are given regarding Rosenblum's choice of entries; however, they appear to display balance in the topics represented.

Subtended into 19 chapters, the work's 4 parts have the headings "Resources," "Technical Aspects," "History," and "Miscellaneous Subjects." Part 1 canvasses general reference works on book history and those focusing on bibliography as a discipline. Part 2 contains annotations on titles that address such pursuits as papermaking, illustration, typography, and binding technologies. Part 3 provides a chronological roster—from antiquity to today—of works devoted to illuminated manuscripts, Renaissance printing, the United States' present reading culture, and so forth. Part 4 offers a mix of entries on such subjects as the history of private presses, book collecting techniques, and booksellers' memoirs. These are followed by author and subject indexes. Rosenblum's annotations, averaging about 150 words, carry the ring of authority. With their crisp style, they are saturated with the author's insights, comparisons to works' previous editions, and occasional references to other scholars' appraisals of the works in question.

If the publisher ever considers issuing a 2d edition of this title, the annotated citations should be assigned entry numbers, to improve accessibility from the indexes. Pagination information included within the respective citations, illustrations, a publisher index, and a glossary (of such terms as *scriptorial* and *marbling*) would also be helpful. Although this book will not enjoy a wide audience among library patrons, it is valuable for its assembling, under one cover, perspectives and citations on a subject that is underrepresented today in most libraries' reference and professional collections. Rosenblum's work should be considered for purchase by any library with staff or patrons who retain a sense of reverence for the preelectronic printed word.—**Jeffrey E. Long**

665. Speck, Bruce W. **Managing the Publishing Process: An Annotated Bibliography.** Westport, Conn., Greenwood Press, 1995. 350p. index. (Bibliographies and Indexes in Mass Media and Communications, no.9). $69.50. ISBN 0-313-27956-X.

Encompassing works published between 1960 and the early 1990s, *Managing the Publishing Process* annotates approximately 1,200 topically arranged articles, book chapters, proceedings, and other materials related to the myriad steps involved in taking a project from conceptualization to printed book. Focus is on the practical aspects of the publishing process; thus, there is substantial material on computers, copyright, marketing and sales, electronic production, paper, printing, scheduling, and other day-to-day concerns, as well as thorough coverage of such areas as acquisitions, author relations, and editing.

The bibliography leads off with a chapter on comprehensive sources (17 monographs, with contents described in great detail), followed by topical chapters subsumed under the broad categories of "products," "personnel," and "other topics." The single-paragraph annotations are clearly written and informative, and taken together present a clear-headed overview of what publishing actually involves. Subject and author indexes conclude the work. Academic and large public libraries will find this title a valuable addition to their mass media and communications collections.—**G. Kim Dority**

Catalogs and Collections

666. **Type Foundries of America and Their Catalogs.** rev. ed. Maurice Annenberg, comp.; revised by Stephen O. Saxe. New Castle, Del., Oak Knoll Books, 1994. 286p. illus. index. $49.95. ISBN 1-884718-06-X.

The 1st edition of this, the definitive bibliography of U.S. type specimen books, was published in an edition of 500 copies in 1975. It quickly went out of print and is difficult to find, and costly on the antiquarian book market. Now printing historian Saxe and Oak Knoll Books have reprinted the work with some significant additions and an index by Elizabeth K. Lieberman.

Annenberg began his work with an account of the United States' earliest type founders, such as David Mitchelson, Abel Buell, Christopher Sower, Benjamin Franklin, and Adam Mappa, and then moved to an alphabetical consideration of 67 firms that produced foundry types. A history of each firm is provided, followed by a list of specimen books issued by the firm. Each entry in the list contains the year of issue, the size of the page in inches, the number of pages or leaves, the locations of copies, and notes. Many entries are illustrated. Saxe has added 73 previously unknown type specimens to Annenberg's list, and he has discovered one additional type foundry, Abraham Riggs of New York City.

The additional listings and an account of Riggs are provided in appendixes 2 and 3, while appendix 1 lists type specimen collections. Appendixes 4, 5, and 6 describe type specimen holdings in the New York Public Library, the Smithsonian Institution, and in the personal collection of Saxe. Appendix 7 records errata, omissions, and duplications, and a select bibliography of 20 items makes up appendix 8. Saxe has provided a brief biography of Annenberg, and Annenberg's original, informative introduction has been retained in this very welcome updated and amended edition.—**Dean H. Keller**

Dictionaries

667. Eckersley, Richard, and others. **Glossary of Typesetting Terms.** Chicago, University of Chicago Press, 1994. 169p. $20.00. ISBN 0-226-18371-8.

In the burgeoning field of typesetting, how is one to stay current with terminology? The venerable University of Chicago Press has provided a possible solution in this easy-to-use glossary for typesetters, editors, proofreaders, and designers. More than 900 entries provide up-to-date meanings for terms such as *ASCII, kerning,* and *widow,* and definitions of new phrases such as *global search and replace* and *page description language* used in digital technology. While acknowledging word and phrase differences between this glossary and the terminology in *The Chicago Manual of Style* (14th ed., University of Chicago Press, 1993), no apologies are made for the rigorous selection of terms to include or exclude. Cross-references are provided where appropriate and overview paragraphs for terms that require more explanation are used frequently to highlight concepts or provide historical information. Eight appendixes offer guidance to type styles, parts of a book and letter, marking manuscripts, proofreaders' marks, and special characters. There are no references to specific products, equipment, or photocomposition systems.

Typographic terms can take on the flavor of the localized areas in which they are used and understood, and a book such as this helps to clarify and unify terms in a particular industry. The impact of desktop publishing and related developments in typography makes this glossary imperative as a way to bring a useful technical vocabulary to anyone who works in publishing or printing. There is nothing to fault in this ambitious and satisfying project, and it is recommended for the target audience.

—**Judy Gay Matthews**

Directories

668. **Alternative Publishers of Books in North America.** 2d ed. By the American Library Association Social Responsibilities Round Table Alternatives in Print Task Force. Byron Anderson, comp. Gainesville, Fla., CRISES Press, 1995. 80p. $12.00pa. ISBN 0-9640119-1-3.

This directory provides detailed information about 119 United States and Canadian small presses that have been in business for at least 5 years and that publish thought-provoking novels and works of nonfiction. Each entry supplies the usual directory information; a detailed statement of the aims and goals of the press; and detailed information about its output, such as average number of books published per year.

The 2d edition differs from the 1st (published in January 1994) by virtue of its greater comprehensiveness (44 more small presses are included) and by its inclusion of more Canadian publishers as well as the presses of various associations. Although many of these same presses are included in the annual *Literary Market Place* (see ARBA 95, entry 672), LMP does not provide as much detailed information as APOB and is 13 times more expensive. Future editions of this useful directory should include an appendix listing the best-selling titles of these presses.—**Joseph Cataio**

669. **Cabell's Directory of Publishing Opportunities in Accounting, Economics and Finance.** 6th ed. David W. E. Cabell and Deborah L. English, eds. Beaumont, Tex., Cabell Publishing, 1994. 2v. index. $59.95pa./set. ISBN 0-911753-07-9.

Contrary to what is printed on the title page, this is the 1st edition of this directory, not the 6th. It resulted from *Cabell's Directory of Publishing Opportunities in Business, Administration and Economics* (see ARBA 82, entry 810 and ARBA 80, entry 41) being split into two publications, this one and *Cabell's Directory of Publishing Opportunities in Management and Marketing* (see entry 670).

Cabell's Directory of Publishing Opportunities in Accounting, Economics and Finance lists alphabetically by title more than 300 journals dealing with accounting, economics, finance and investments, insurance, and real estate. Each entry provides the information necessary for manuscript submission, such as an address, desired manuscript topics, type and length of review process, acceptance rate, readership data, frequency of issue, circulation data, and publication guidelines, which may include a very detailed style guide. An index that classifies journals according to manuscript topics completes the work.

As with its predecessors, this up-to-date, reliable, and useful directory will help authors in the fields covered identify which journals are most likely to accept their manuscripts for publication. Highly recommended for academic and business libraries.—**Leonard Grundt**

670. **Cabell's Directory of Publishing Opportunities in Management and Marketing.** 6th ed. David W. E. Cabell and Deborah L. English, eds. Beaumont, Tex., Cabell Publishing, 1994. 2v. index. $59.95pa./set. ISBN 0-911753-08-7.

The names of more than 400 journals are provided as a table of contents in volume 1, followed by descriptions in the two volumes. Each entry includes the editor's name, address, and telephone and fax numbers; publication guidelines, such as manuscript length, style manuals to be used, number of copies required, and acceptable electronic format; description of the review process; number of articles accepted for publication; and topics appropriate for the publication. Each journal is also described by its readership, frequency of publication, copies produced per issue, and subscription price. An index allows users to identify publishing opportunities based on broad topic areas, types of reviews (e.g., blind, external, optional), numbers of external reviewers, and acceptance rates. Quite valuable are the suggestions on how journal attributes should be applied to formulating manuscripts and to choosing journals most likely to publish one's submissions. The major change in this edition is the division of the former directory into two volumes: this volume for marketing and management, and another for accounting, economics, and finance. As with Cabell's other directories, the bindings are poor and the font and layout lack polish. The price is high, but the directory is extremely useful for scholars publishing in these areas.

—**Laural L. Adams**

671. Kiefer, Marie. **Directory of Printers.** 1994-1995 ed. Fairfield, Iowa, Ad-Lib; distr., Chicago, Login Publishers Consortium, 1994. 389p. index. $14.95pa. ISBN 0-912411-43-0. ISSN 0895-139X.

Last reviewed in ARBA 92 (see entry 638), this directory lists more than 700 printers of books, catalogs, magazines, and other bound publications. Each entry provides company name; contact person; address; telephone, toll-free, and fax numbers; optimum printruns; standard book sizes; and binding capabilities. No e-mail addresses were noted. Information was gathered by survey; secondary sources were used for nonrespondents. Each company also indicated whether they could do color separations, maintain mailing lists, handle fulfillment, and provide typesetting and layout services. Extensive indexes lead to printers of books and specialty items (e.g., calendars, comics, computer documentation, cookbooks, maps). Binding capabilities, equipment and services, and printers by state are also listed. Familiarizing oneself with the abbreviations used to indicate services and equipment is essential, as many listings run to more than 25 items in one category alone. There has been a 66 percent price increase since the 1991 edition.

Special items are how to select a printer, how to request a quotation, tips for saving money, standard contract terminology, how to use this book, and a glossary. Easy to use, with information accessible in a variety of ways, this directory complements *Literary Market Place* (see ARBA 95, entry 672), and should see extensive use. Publishers, advertisers, and professional and trade organizations will welcome this practical updated guide.—**Judy Gay Matthews**

672. **Publishing Market Reference PLUS 1994-1995.** 2d ed. [CD-ROM]. New Providence, N.J., R. R. Bowker/Reed Reference Electronic Publishing, 1995. Minimum system requirements: IBM or compatible 286. CD-ROM drive. MS-DOS or PC-DOS version 3.1. 535K conventional memory. Monochrome or color display. Compatible MS-DOS Extensions device driver. $795.00. ISBN 0-8352-2840-1.

Formerly known as *Library Reference PLUS*, this CD-ROM encompasses six book trade directories: *American Book Trade Directory*; *American Library Directory*; *World Guide to Libraries*; *Literary Market Place*; *International Literary Market Place*; and *Publishers, Distributors, & Wholesalers of the United States*. In addition, the work provides the full text of *The Bowker Annual Library and Book Trade Almanac* for the current year as well as the preceding four years, and the U.S. government-supplied database of almost 103,000 schools and school agencies that have been assigned Standard Address Numbers (SANs).

The key value of *Publishing Market Reference PLUS*, aside from bringing together such an abundance of industry resources, is its database format and accompanying multiple access points. Users can perform a title-specific or global search on any (or a combination of) the following categories: institution/company name, personal name, other names, position, classification/section/database, subject, description, titles published, ISBN prefix, SAN, date established, city/state/zip code, country code, area code, keyword, automation, conferences/meetings, membership, expenditures, income, salaries, holdings, store area (in square feet), audiovisual holdings, and total population served. In addition, there are numerous report and print options.

The detailed user manual that accompanies the disc provides excellent documentation and information once the user has the program up and running, but doing so can be a nightmare. As with others in the R. R. Bowker/Reed Reference Electronic Publishing series, this CD-ROM would be impossible for the average librarian to install. It requires extensive knowledge of technical aspects of computers, which most people still have not mastered. Therefore, until R. R. Bowker comes out with a "plug-and-play" installation process, this resource can only be recommended to those organizations that have the technical support personnel on site to support it.—**G. Kim Dority**

Handbooks

673. **Consumer Research Study on Book Purchasing, 1993.** By the NPD Group, Inc., and Carol J. Meyer. New York, Book Industry Study Group, 1994. 1v. (various paging). $175.00pa. ISBN 0-940016-47-8.

This informative but expensive market research report provides detailed information about which U.S. residents purchased what kinds of books from what sources in 1993. It also provides some comparative data for the years 1991 and 1992. The data are based on the monthly purchasing diaries of some 16,000 U.S. households, a sample that the researchers believe is representative of the total U.S.

white population, but which they admit is not representative of the African-American or Hispanic populations. The data are presented primarily in chart form and focus on adult books, although there is a small section discussing the juvenile book market.

Those who read *Publishers Weekly* (Cahners Publishing) regularly will find no surprising new revelations and little that is new in this report. Those seeking detailed information about the kinds of books that people in the United States buy will be greatly disappointed that this report uses only nine broad subject categories, such as popular fiction and general nonfiction, in its analysis. Thus, it cannot answer such a question as how the sale of mystery novels compared to the sale of science fiction novels in 1993. Those seeking detailed subject information will be better served by the various special subject issues of *Publishers Weekly* and by magazines covering specific genres, as *Locus* (Locus Publications) does for the science fiction and fantasy genres.—**Joseph Cataio**

674. Kim, David U., and Craig A. Wilson. **Policies of Publishers: A Handbook for Order Librarians.** 1995 ed. Metuchen, N.J., Scarecrow, 1995. 296p. $35.00. ISBN 0-8108-3017-5.

The aim of this handbook is to provide in a single source the information librarians need in order to place direct orders with publishers. The information was gathered through questionnaires sent to publishers and also from several standard reference sources and recent publisher's catalogs. Alphabetically arranged by publisher, each entry contains name, address, order address, telephone and fax numbers, e-mail address, divisions, imprints or subsidiaries, prepayment, discount, return invoice, back order, and special order plan policies. If publishers have electronic ordering systems or online catalog access, this information is also provided.

This resource will be an important aid in helping librarians make purchasing decisions—purchasing library materials from the most prompt and economical vendors. Although acquisitions librarians will find this book a dream come true, it is limited to book publishers, and media materials and periodicals for libraries are in high demand and a growing part of most collections. With so small a target group and these other limitations, this title has a slim chance for widespread success.—**Susan C. Awe**

12 Military Studies

GENERAL WORKS

Atlases

675. Gilbert, Martin. **Atlas of World War I.** 2d ed. New York, Oxford University Press, 1994. 164p. maps. index. $19.95; $12.95pa. ISBN 0-19-521075-1; 0-19-521077-8pa.

This 2d edition of an acknowledged classic atlas provides ready-reference to much information relating to World War I operations. Five new maps have been added, using the same presentation style as the author's *Atlas of the Arab-Israeli Conflict* (see ARBA 76, entry 358). It complements *The Historical Atlas of World War I* (see ARBA 95, entry 681) by giving much more detailed economic and political coverage than the latter title. Land events are grouped by year with separate sections for the air and sea war, global affairs, and the war's aftermath. Bibliographical endnotes guide one to additional readings.

The focus in this volume is the monochrome maps, most with detailed captions. The battle maps give only a general overview; forces in each battle and their movements are not annotated, and topographical detail is minimal. Instead, the real strength here is the "big picture": clear representations of complex topics such as food riots in Germany or British court-martial executions. Some maps give ready access to esoteric information, such as the layout of U.K. antiaircraft barrage dispositions in 1917 with the codename of each emplacement.

The book maintains a high standard of accuracy, resulting from regular updating since its initial publication in 1970. The array of information provided is competently indexed, making this a valuable supplement to World War I studies. Clearly printed on good-quality paper in a durable lay-flat binding, this title will be useful for any collection supporting twentieth-century history. [R: RBB, 1 Jan 95, p. 836]
—**John Howard Oxley**

676. Smurthwaite, David. **The Pacific War Atlas 1941-1945.** New York, Facts on File, 1995. 141p. illus. maps. index. $24.95; $15.95pa. ISBN 0-8160-3285-8; 0-8160-3286-6pa.

With a text-to-image ratio of 3:1, this book is closer to an illustrated history than an atlas per se, narrating the Pacific War through a focus on the major campaigns, which are depicted in 65 maps together with an assortment of monochrome photographs. Unfortunately, this entire production suffers from rather slipshod editing. While the narrative text is crisply written to make several interesting points, a bevy of major and minor slips were noted. For example, the USS *Arizona* did not blow up at Pearl Harbor "under a hail of bombs" as described on page 26, but from a single bomb hit; similarly, describing the postattack condition of all 8 battleships present as "sunk" or "severely damaged" overstates the effects on 3 of these ships, which were only lightly damaged. Map and illustration captions are plagued with misspellings and outright errors: On page 14, General Georgy Zhukov is on the right of the picture, not the left, as the caption says; on page 110, Admiral Raymond Spruance is cropped out of the photograph in which he supposedly appears; and on page 122, the map's north direction indicator in fact points south.

Errors aside, the quality of the contents is insufficient. While the small 10-by-7-inch format simply does not allow many details in even the largest map, most of the maps show no land topographical features whatsoever; some lack a scale; the colors used for Japanese and British forces are so similar in some cases that they cannot be told apart; and in those maps depicting naval actions, the lack of time indicators renders the track charts nearly useless. In the perfect-bound paperback edition, two-page maps lose important detail in the gutter. Many of the photographs are literally the size of postage stamps, and the two-page index is completely inadequate for a serious scholarly tool. Given the fact that a number of alternatives exist for this title, the fact that it is clearly printed on good-quality paper does not redress its considerable shortcomings as a ready-reference source on the Pacific Theater of World War II.—**John Howard Oxley**

677. **The West Point Atlas of American Wars. Volume I: 1689-1900.** Compiled by the Department of Military Art and Engineering, the United States Military Academy. Vincent J. Esposito, ed. New York, Henry Holt, 1995. 1v. (unpaged). maps. $75.00. ISBN 0-0850-3391-2.

This is a reissue of the first volume of a classic military atlas (initially published in 1959) encapsulating the expertise of the U.S. Army's foremost officer training institution to create an atlas concentrating on land warfare events. Apart from an updated reading list (which is no longer annotated), no changes have been made in the maps or text, both of which have stood the test of time. Coverage is chronological by war, campaign, and battle on a corps/division basis (with brigades or regiments singled out only occasionally). The text integrates military issues with the battle narrative, giving critical evaluations of command decisions and unit performance; its close linkage with the maps enables a reader to follow the flow of action as it unfolds chronologically.

The maps are excellent examples of military cartography, limning the opposing sides in blue and red on a pale olive relief (slightly more prominent in the new edition and therefore easier to grasp). Crucial aspects of topography receive unobtrusive emphasis to give clear, concise descriptions of complex strategic and operational decisions. Compared to the original edition (which had blue text on thick cream paper), the reissue is slightly more utilitarian, being clearly printed in black ink on good-quality white paper but with a binding that is neither as elegant nor as sturdy as the original. Any library serving U.S. military history interests will find this an effective background reference tool, despite the lack of an index.
—**John Howard Oxley**

Bibliography

678. Blewett, Daniel K. **American Military History: A Guide to Reference and Information Sources.** Englewood, Colo., Libraries Unlimited, 1995. 295p. index. $52.00. ISBN 1-56308-035-4.

A good guide to the reference literature of a subject will be logically organized; it will be annotated so that important characteristics of cited titles are evident; it will, should it cover a large subject, bear evidence of judicious selection so that the most important and most useful sources are included; finally, it will be well indexed so that, in conjunction with its organization, users will find what they need. In respect to these criteria, Blewett's guide is a very good one indeed.

This work lists printed and electronic reference materials focusing on or useful for the study of U.S. military history. Atlases, directories, bibliographies, indexes, dictionaries, guides to archives and special collections, journals, statistical sources, and chronologies are some of the types of materials cited. The guide begins with a long chapter on materials covering U.S. military history in general; this is followed by chapters on individual conflicts, disarmament, terrorism, and other topics, and is concluded by chapters on libraries, archives, organizations, and journals specializing in military history. There is an author/title index and a subject index.

Libraries owning Robin Higham's superb *Guide to the Sources of United States Military History* (see ARBA 76, entry 1675) and its supplements (see ARBA 94, entry 680; ARBA 87, entry 652; and ARBA 82, entry 1652) will certainly want to purchase this work. The two guides complement each other splendidly: Higham is critical for identifying primary and secondary information sources on U.S. military history, while Blewett provides a terrific survey of the reference sources covering the field. Blewett's guide should be in every public and academic library that has readers interested in U.S. military history.
—**Eric R. Nitschke**

679. Morriss, Roger, comp. **Guide to British Naval Papers in North America.** New York, Mansell/Cassell, 1994. 418p. index. $120.00. ISBN 0-7201-2162-0.

This fine work is certain to find a place in all reference collections supporting research involving the Royal Navy. Its scope, however, is very precisely defined and is not as broad as the title might suggest to some. It describes and locates "original documents, official and unofficial, generated by British naval personnel or government officials and exported artificially to North America" (p. xvii). An artificial export refers to a document purchased by manuscript collectors from British sources and deposited in North American collections. The survey excludes collections of microforms or other copies; materials relating to the British navy but not originated by British naval or government personnel; archives of private companies referring to the navy; and official correspondence of Canadian and United States governmental units. Nevertheless, almost 1,200 collections are described, of which more than half are composed of personal papers and diaries. Thirty-four Canadian and eighty-three United States libraries, archives, museums, and societies are represented.

The arrangement of the guide is by document type: government records, ship's records, and personal papers. Within each category, collections are listed alphabetically by source and are accompanied by an appropriately detailed description of size and content, with references to descriptions supplied by other printed guides. The indexes tie the work together and include: a chronological index; a general index of proper names, places, and subjects; and an index by library. The library index, in addition to listing the collections in each institution, provides addresses, telephone numbers, hours of operation, and titles of printed guides or catalogs referring to the collections. All in all, this is a most professional and handsome work that scholars will be most grateful to have.—**Eric R. Nitschke**

Biography

680. Dever, John P., and Maria C. Dever. **Women and the Military: Over 100 Notable Contributors, Historic to Contemporary.** Jefferson, N.C., McFarland, 1995. 163p. index. $24.95. ISBN 0-89950-976-2.

The nonspecialist authors explain that their purpose in compiling the 21 biographies and 83 briefer capsules is to demonstrate the important role that women have played in military affairs in diverse cultures from antiquity to present. Although most of the entries treat women from the United States, a few cover historical figures from Europe, Asia, and Africa. The time frame is from the ancient Israel prophet Deborah through Paula Coughlin of the Tailhook sexual harassment case.

Although the longer biographies have some value as a quick reference, the short profiles, many of which do little more than identify the individual, are of minimal value, and the book is not a significant contribution. More appropriate for high school and public libraries than for more scholarly collections, the volume has some utility, but libraries can let it pass without serious consequence to their reference holdings.
—**Joe P. Dunn**

681. **Who's Who in World War II.** John Keegan, ed. New York, Oxford University Press, 1995. 182p. $14.95pa. ISBN 0-19-521080-8.

Keegan, defense editor of London's *Daily Telegraph* and author of many books, is one of the world's most renowned military historians. This concise, paperback volume is a useful addition to the vast number of reference works on World War II. Keegan offers brief, compactly detailed sketches on more than 300 of the most important characters in this global conflict, including the military and political leaders of all the powers involved and other notable participants. Keegan's authoritative stature and his evenhanded balance of all participant countries in the war enhance the book's status. The format is alphabetical and provides dates of birth and death and a chronological sketch of the individual's life. The entries are cross-referenced. The book's major weakness is that it does not include bibliographical references.

Although more comprehensive and more detailed specialized sources exist on World War II, the virtue of this volume is that it is particularly valuable for the introductory student. The inexpensive price of this paperback makes it worthwhile for all libraries to acquire as a quick reference, but it is especially appropriate for secondary school, college, and public libraries.—**Joe P. Dunn**

Dictionaries and Encyclopedias

682. **Brassey's Encyclopedia of Military History and Biography.** Franklin D. Margiotta, ed. McLean, Va., Brassey's, 1994. 1197p. illus. maps. index. $44.95. ISBN 0-02-881096-1.

The important wars of the world and the military leaders who fought them are presented in this large volume. It consists of alphabetically arranged articles drawn from the 1993 six-volume *International Military and Defense Encyclopedia* (see ARBA 94, entry 688). As such, it illustrates the expertise gained from two impressive editorial boards that served the parent publication enhanced by a short foreword by John Keegan. Margiotta is a retired U.S. Air Force combat pilot and current author/editor of four books. Some 80 knowledgeable contributors authored the 200 articles selected for this volume.

The text begins with a four-page account of Afghanistan's invasion by the Soviet Union and ends with a four-page biography of Georgy Zhukov. There are 35 entries on wars, conquests, and so on, from classical times to the Gulf War. Of course, in the sorry history of man's combativeness, this number covers only the major engagements. There are no entries on individual battles. Some 100 biographies are well written, but interesting for their selections as well as omissions. Highlights include a 14-page discussion of terrorism, 30 pages on aircraft and air power, and such thoughtful pieces as "Armed Forces and Society," "Principles of War," "War," and "Science of War."

Although copyrighted in 1994, bibliographic citations later than 1988 are scarce, missing, for example, Keegan's own *The Second World War* (Penguin, 1990). Illustrations are few and trite and there are not nearly enough graphics for such articles as "American Civil War," "Punic Wars," and "Roman Empire." However, the 76-page index is excellent and all things considered, the book is worth the price, especially if the 6-volume parent publication is not available.—**David Eggenberger**

683. Møller, Bjørn. **Dictionary of Alternative Defense.** Boulder, Colo., Lynne Rienner, 1995. 553p. $79.95. ISBN 1-55587-386-3.

This dictionary examines the concepts, individuals, and events influencing nontraditional military defense strategies. The author sees the principal goals of alternative defense as including disarmament; war prevention; defensive strength; damage limitation; and détente, entente, and democracy in international political relationships.

An introduction provides a historical and contextual overview of alternative defense theories and perspectives. The majority of this work is a dictionary defining terminology relevant to alternative defense strategies. Examples of featured entries include "Alternative Defense Commission," "bridge building," "crisis stability," "Mohandas Gandhi," "indirect approach," "minimum deterrence," "preventive diplomacy," "Anatoli Rapoport," "totally destructive conventional war hypothesis," and other relevant terms. The dictionary concludes with an exhaustive multilingual bibliography.

This reference book is well arranged, featuring succinct writing, extensive bibliographic references, and entry cross-references. While the overall intellectual merit and public policy value of alternative defense are highly problematic, this work will introduce readers to currents of thought influencing many national security policy debates as well as scholarly analysis in this field.—**Bert Chapman**

684. **The New Grolier Encyclopedia of World War II.** Danbury, Conn., Grolier, 1995. 8v. illus. maps. index. $249.00/set. ISBN 0-7172-7508-6.

This eight-volume set is a beginner's introduction to World War II. The writing is clear and straightforward (at about middle school level) with the text and graphics set in large typeface. There is at least one illustration, and more often two or more, on every page. Many of the illustrations are run in two- and four-color. Sidebars are employed to provide biographical information, war stories, and special effects such as wartime posters from both Allied and Axis nations. The page layouts are attractive, and the overall design is pleasing.

Volume 1, "The Home Front," sets the tone for the other seven volumes. It consists of 137 well-illustrated pages and, as in all the volumes, carries in 7 pages the complete index for the encyclopedia. Germany is represented here as well as the United States, Great Britain, and France. National leaders receive a chapter-length biography, but the headings are a bit grating—Adolf Hitler is the "Evil Genius," Winston Churchill the "Bulldog Leader," Benito Mussolini the "Comic Dictator," and Joseph Stalin the "Man of Steel." Better are the sidebars on lesser-known but key people—Jean Moulin and Leni Riefenstahl, for example.

Volume 2, "War in the Mediterranean," begins in North Africa and ends with victory in Italy. Graphics summarize battles, the strength of contending forces, and casualties. Sidebars report on military commanders. Similar presentations are used in the other combat volumes. Volume 3, "War in the Pacific," runs from Pearl Harbor through the conquest of the Marianas in 1944. Volume 4, "The Air and Sea War," opens with the battle of Britain, covers the blitz, the Flying Fortress raids on Europe, and ends with the battle of the Atlantic and the ultimate victory over the German U-boats.

Volume 5, "The Eastern Front," presents the Nazi invasion of the Soviet Union, the crucial battles of Moscow, Stalingrad, and Kursk, the Soviet counterattack, and the failure of the 1944 Warsaw uprising. Volume 6, "The March on Berlin," traces the progress of Allied troops from D-Day in Normandy to the crossing of the Rhine, and concludes with the Soviet capture of Berlin. Volume 7, "Victory in Japan," closes the ring on Japan from India to Okinawa, including both conventional and atomic bombing of the Japanese homeland. Volume 8, "Behind the Fighting," covers a broad array of subjects—advances in technology, intelligence, propaganda, entertainment, and the Holocaust.

For its intended audience, this is an excellent reference work. It is authentic, comprehensive, and a pleasure to research in or just to browse through. (For an adult history of World War II, see Gerhart Weinberg's *A World at Arms* [Cambridge University Press, 1995].)—**David Eggenberger**

685. **The United States in the First World War: An Encyclopedia.** Anne Cipriano Venzon, ed. Hamden, Conn., Garland, 1995. 830p. maps. index. (Military History of the United States, v.3; Garland Reference Library of the Humanities, v.1205). $95.00. ISBN 0-8240-7055-0.

The Garland series of encyclopedias on the Military History of the United States proves to be an outstanding contribution. This is the third volume to appear. The first two are entitled *The American Revolution 1775-1783* (see ARBA 94, entry 503) and *The War of 1898 and U.S. Interventions 1898-1934* (see ARBA 95, entry 685). Volumes on the Korean Conflict, the Vietnam War, and the Colonial Wars of North America, among others, are scheduled to be forthcoming.

More than 200 authors contributed to the alphabetically organized volume, which covers the period of preparation prior to U.S. entry into the conflict through Armistice Day. It treats leaders, major campaigns and battles, and the histories of military units, as well as foreign leaders, foreign relations, and other aspects that place the United States in an international context. Domestic topics include entries on the political, industrial, and moral support of the war and organizational and individual opposition to it, as well as the role of women and minorities in the war. A good index supports the volume. However, the brief bibliographies at the end of the major entries are often disappointing. Usually limited to two or three sources, they sometimes do not list the latest and best works on the subject.

All research libraries and most smaller collections will want this volume and the others in the series to augment more general military reference works such as *The Harper Encyclopedia of Military Biography* (see ARBA 93, entry 698), *The Harper Encyclopedia of Military History* (4th ed.; see ARBA 94, entry 687), and *The Military History of the United States* (see ARBA 93, entry 700).—**Joe P. Dunn**

Directories

686. **Carroll's Military Facilities Directory: September 1995/February 1996.** Ronald Weston, ed. Washington, D.C., Carroll Publishing, 1995. 118p. index. $75.00pa./yr.

This directory lists 550 military installations and centers, including guard and reserve bases. The directory is composed of three parts: military facilities, a listing of naval ships and aircraft units, and two appendixes (units and activities) and a military facilities index.—**Bohdan S. Wynar**

687. **Directory of U.S. Military Bases Worldwide.** William R. Evinger, ed. Phoenix, Ariz., Oryx Press, 1995. 412p. index. $125.00. ISBN 0-89774-822-0.

This ready-reference volume provides details on U.S. military establishments worldwide, so the "base" concept includes support as well as combat facilities administered by the Department of Defense. Base profiles form the heart of the work, and are listed in U.S. and overseas sections, broken out alphabetically by location within each state or country. While the information herein is relevant for 1993, two appendixes cover base closures for this and subsequent years to maintain currency.

Each major base has entries for its address, organizational components, history, visitor attractions, key contacts, and services. This information is laid out clearly in an easily accessed format. Apart from the rare typographical error, the entries are exact and accord with other reference sources. Many interesting information snippets flesh out the basic facts; among them, that the first U.S. Air Force Reserve all-female mission was performed at Castle AFB; that the Marine Barracks in Washington, D.C., is the oldest Marine Corps base; that the first warship built in North America was built on the site of Portsmouth Naval Shipyard, Maine; and that the chapel organ at West Point is the largest in the world.

Worth particular mention are the excellent detailed indexes: alphabetical by base, branch of service, state/country and branch of service, and numerical/alphabetical by unit (so the 1183 Ordnance Detachment [MLRS Maintenance] at Camp Grayling is as easy to find as the U.S. Army Headquarters at Fort Myer, Virginia). In summary, the directory is a clearly printed subject guide in a sturdy attractive binding, with the only reservation being the degree to which some of the information contained is likely to become stale in a short period of time.—**John Howard Oxley**

688. Johnson, Richard S. **How to Locate Anyone Who Is or Has Been in the Military: Armed Forces Locator Directory.** rev. ed. Burlington, N.C., MIE Publishing, 1995. 271p. index. $19.00pa. ISBN 1-877639-16-8.

In two prior ARBA reviews (see ARBA 91, entry 679, and ARBA 90, entry 654), this concise locator has received scant comment, but deserves more. The first 2 editions were much less extensive (50 and 83 pages respectively) but the 1995 revision covers more than 270 pages. Divided into 12 chapters, Johnson includes seemingly endless ways to identify and locate vital statistics and other records for any military personnel—past or present. Just some of the chapters focus on obtaining records of unit and ship rosters, veterans, and Reserve and National Guard members. A useful introductory chapter details the assignment of social security and military service numbers and their use in locating personnel. As a result of the nearly unending listings, addresses and telephone numbers (and zip codes where applicable) are listed for all domestic and foreign U.S. military bases, as well as contact points for Navy ships. Also included are lists for state veterans' offices, state reserve and national guard headquarters, military reunion organizations, and various other military and veteran associations.

Among other useful bits of information are military insignia, sample personal information forms, and several lists of abbreviations. If one ever wants to find an old Army buddy, boyfriend from the past, or long-lost friend—then this is an ideal how-to reference book. The price has more than doubled since the book's original 1989 edition, but so has the number of pages. This handy volume is an ideal choice for all types of libraries as well as genealogical organizations, law offices, and credit agencies, to mention only a few potential consumers.—**Boyd Childress**

689. Lang, George, Raymond L. Collins, and Gerard F. White, comps. **Medal of Honor Recipients 1863-1994.** New York, Facts on File, 1995. 2v. index. $99.00/set. ISBN 0-8160-3259-9.

Not until the U.S. Civil War was there a military-wide medal that could be earned by deserving soldiers and sailors. President Abraham Lincoln signed a bill creating the Medal of Honor for the Army in 1862. The Medal of Honor became an instant success, with more than 1,500 being awarded during that conflict. One hopes this two-volume set will be just as successful, for it is a welcome addition to any military history reference collection, be it public, college, university, government, or private.

Recipients of the Medal of Honor are organized alphabetically in two volumes, the first of which covers the Civil War to the Second Nicaraguan Campaign. The second volume covers World War II to Somalia. Each entry identifies the vital statistics of each recipient and the relevant data pertaining to the action for which the award was given. The award citations make for interesting, inspiring, and at times moving reading. There is little to fault in these volumes, except that the editors may want to add color plates of the medal as it evolved and halftones of recipients or ceremonies to break up the text.

—**Norman L. Kincaide**

690. Schlachter, Gail Ann, and R. David Weber. **Financial Aid for Veterans, Military Personnel, and Their Dependents 1994-1996.** San Carlos, Calif., Reference Service Press, 1994. 310p. index. $38.50. ISBN 0-918276-23-3.

As in the 1st (1988) and 2d (1990) editions of this biennial directory—enthusiastically reviewed in ARBA 89 (see entry 297) and ARBA 92 (see entry 651)—the 4th edition brings together descriptive information on a wide variety of financial aid programs (959 entries, an increase of about 100 over the 3d edition) open to veterans, military personnel, and their dependents from state and federal government agencies, professional organizations, foundations, educational associations, and military/veterans organizations. These programs are open to applicants at all levels (from high school through postdoctoral) for education, research, travel, training, career development, or emergency situations. The main body of this volume consists of entries grouped in six categories—scholarships, fellowships, loans, grants-in-aid, awards, internships—each divided into the three population groups named in the title. Within these subdivisions, entries are arranged alphabetically by program title. Entries typically include address, telephone and fax numbers, availability, purpose, eligibility, financial data, number awarded, and deadline information. More than half of the programs listed provide aid for postsecondary education. The second section of the book identifies the state agencies to contact for information on benefits. The agencies are grouped by type of support provided (financial aids, student loan programs, and state veteran agencies); states are listed alphabetically within each category. The 3d section is an annotated bibliography of 60 key recently published general financial aid directories. In the fourth and final section are five indexes: program title, sponsoring organization, geographic (state or country), subject, and calendar (listing entry numbers for programs with established filing dates).

This comprehensive, current directory to financial aid for military-related persons will be extremely useful in public, academic, and some high school libraries, and libraries serving the armed forces and their dependents. For noneducational or nonmonetary federal benefits for military personnel, veterans, and their dependents (pensions, disability compensation, correcting military records, Department of Veterans Affairs medical centers and clinics), *Veterans Benefits* by Keith D. Snyder, Richard E. O'Dell, and Craig Kubey (see ARBA 95, entry 696) may prove useful.—**Wiley J. Williams**

Handbooks and Yearbooks

691. **Civil War.** [CD-ROM]. Minneapolis, Minn., Quanta Press, 1994. (USA War Series). Minimum system requirements (DOS version): IBM or compatible XT. CD-ROM drive with MS-DOS CD-ROM Extensions. 640K RAM. Minimum system requirements (Macintosh version): Macintosh Plus. CD-ROM drive with Foreign File Access. 1MB RAM. $69.95.

692. **Korea.** [CD-ROM]. Minneapolis, Minn., Quanta Press, [1994]. (USA War Series). Minimum system requirements (DOS version): IBM or compatible XT. CD-ROM drive with MS-DOS CD-ROM Extensions. DOS 2.x. 640K RAM. Minimum system requirements (Macintosh version): Macintosh Plus. CD-ROM drive with Foreign File Access. 1MB RAM. $69.95.

693. **Normandy: The Invasions of France.** [CD-ROM]. Minneapolis, Minn., Quanta Press, 1994. (USA War Series). Minimum system requirements: IBM or compatible. CD-ROM drive with MS-DOS CD-ROM Extensions. Windows. $69.95.

694. **Vietnam.** [CD-ROM]. Minneapolis, Minn., Quanta Press, 1994. (USA War Series). Minimum system requirements (DOS version): IBM or compatible XT. CD-ROM drive with MS-DOS CD-ROM Extensions. 1MB RAM. VGA monitor. Minimum system requirements (Macintosh version): Macintosh Plus. CD-ROM drive with Foreign File Access. $69.95.

Ken Burns's popular television series *The Civil War*, the events surrounding the 50th anniversary of D-Day, the continued attraction of the Vietnam Veterans Memorial, and similar events have helped inspire public interest in U.S. military history. Those events and that interest have led to the publication of a wide range of related printed and electronic materials. Quanta Press has produced these four CD-ROM products, and a fifth and sixth on Desert Storm and World War II, to provide a wide variety of textual and visual information about those military conflicts derived from public and private information. At first glance, the products appear to be similar but, in fact, there are substantial differences in both the nature and quality of the information and the means of access. Libraries interested in building their military history collections should, therefore, evaluate these CD-ROM products as individual items.

The best of these products, but one for which there is likely to be limited demand, is that on Normandy. It was produced by two professional military historians with connections to the U.S. Army Military History Institute at Carlisle Barracks in Pennsylvania. Much of the material, similar to the material in the other CD-ROMs in this series, is derived from government documents that are in the public domain, especially, in this case, the American Forces in Action series. The contents are accessible through five main points of entry that are initially displayed visually: media clips, photographs, references, monographs, and interviews. In some of those categories the amount of information is limited. There are, for example, a small number of War Department newsreels produced for soldiers, sailors, and air personnel; five audioclips; 650 high-resolution images; a few maps; and a handful of interviews with participants collected shortly after the invasion by trained military historians. The main and most useful feature is the text itself, which provides a brief history of the invasion, a chronology, a list of codewords, statistics on the levels of firepower of both sides, a list of Distinguished Service Cross recipients, a glossary of military terms (but not slang), a translation of Adolf Hitler's defense directive, and a recounting of the lessons to be learned. The software makes all of the contents easily accessible.

Equally accessible is the information in the CD-ROM on Vietnam. With that product the user is presented initially with a screen that offers access to either all of its contents or to one of 14 categories, including Agent Orange (48 entries), background (412 entries), chronology (41 entries), glossary (1,638 entries), missions (58 entries), and statistics (32 entries). The user has the option of either scrolling through the records in each category or of conducting a search using a word or words, with AND as a default Boolean operator in multiword searches to access particular parts of a category or the entire file. An assortment of bitmapped black-and-white photographs of key figures accompanies the biography category, while a number of high-resolution color images accompany the glossary category. A useful feature is that either the images can be retrieved from the associated textual file or the image file can be scrolled and the textual file retrieved from the image.

This product, like the remaining two, appears to have been produced by an amateur historian. The result is that the contents and quality of it, and the others, are uneven. There may be some useful information here, but most of it duplicates what is readily available elsewhere, and much of it is derived from public documents. The Civil War CD-ROM, for example, relies heavily on a U.S. history text published by the Immigration and Naturalization Service and a secondary school text, *The Civil War*, by James I. Robertson. At first glance, it appears to be a comprehensive product that covers such things as the forces leading up to the war, a listing of battles in chronological order, and biographies of major civil and military leaders. Its 714 cards (screens) contain, however, only 109 entries for Abraham Lincoln, and, it turns out, more than 550 of those cards are devoted to photographs. That makes it a rich visual resource, but the images are grainy and there is no good way to reproduce them. The key feature of this product, and the others in the series, is that searches of the entire file can be carried out by a single word, a phrase, or the use of standard Boolean operators. In some ways, therefore, it may be somewhat easier to find the information about a specific event or person here than it is in the original printed source. Records or reports can be printed out or written to an ASCII text file.

The CD-ROM on Korea contains 429 cards with 2,055 unique words and 1,071 visual images. Much of the content was derived from a government publication, *U.S. Army in the Korean War*. Perhaps the only unique feature is a series of several interviews, produced specifically for this CD-ROM, with individuals who served in combat roles during the war; these are on an audio track. The format and points of access for this product are identical to those for the Civil War CD-ROM.

Ultimately, none of these products seems to have any special value as library reference sources, largely because while they may provide multiple points of access, they depend heavily on other sources and provide little unique material. Except for the Normandy item, they have not been assembled by professional historians and, therefore, lack credibility as authoritative sources. They are, at best, interesting supplementary materials that are most likely to be useful at the secondary school level and then, perhaps, primarily in connection with a classroom study of the particular war. The only file in the entire series that may have wider appeal and value is that of the entire list of the 58,136 names of those on the wall at the Vietnam Veterans Memorial. That is because the file, like the rest of the contents of these products, can be searched in a variety of ways to provide a level of access (e.g., individuals from a particular locality) that may not be available in other listings.—**Norman D. Stevens**

695. Gazit, Shlomo, and Zeev Eytan. **The Middle East Military Balance 1993-1994.** Jerusalem, published for the Jaffee Center for Strategic Studies, Jerusalem Post and Boulder, Colo., Westview Press, 1994. 575p. maps. $98.50. ISBN 965-459-012-3.

This annual publication of the staff of the Jaffee Center for Strategic Studies of Tel Aviv University has two parts. Part 1 consists of 9 essays by leading Israeli defense specialists on various strategic topics, including the peace process in 1993-1994, the armed dimensions of the intifada, Israel's quantitative security edge in Arab eyes, progress toward Middle East arms control, and proliferation of nonconventional weapons. The essays are good and the tables provide sound information. The Israeli perspective is evident.

Part 2 looks at the military forces and infrastructure of Israel, Iran, and 18 Arab countries. The outline provides basic information on the country, security alliances and assistance, infrastructure, size and composition of the military, and weapons systems. These features are augmented by 19 tables of data and figures. Other attributes include a glossary of terms, a chronology of events of 1993-1994, a list of abbreviations, several fine maps, and the biographical data on the contributors to part 1.

Although this is a useful source, the book is quite expensive for a perennial volume that is dated at the time of publication and has a short shelf life. It is recommended only for very large libraries with extensive national security collections.—**Joe P. Dunn**

696. Vogel, Frederick G. **World War I Songs: A History and Dictionary of Popular American Patriotic Tunes....** Jefferson, N.C., McFarland, 1995. 530p. illus. index. $85.00. ISBN 0-89950-952-5.

More than 35,000 copywrited songs—marches, patriotic anthems, and ballads—were stimulated by World War I. Only World War II produced more music. The overwhelming majority of these pieces were never published, and many that were remained obscure. Vogel, coauthor of an earlier study of music of the movies and movie musicals, approaches the subject of this book in four parts. Part 1 is a series of essays on various genres of music such as the "Outbreak of Hostilities" before U.S. entry into the war, "Beating the Victory Drum," or "Homeward Bound." Part 2 lists all World War I songs published in the United States, complete with title, lyricist, composer, and year of publication. Part 3 gives the complete lyrics to 300-plus selected songs of the era. A massive index lists song titles, composers, lyricists, publishers, textual subjects, and key words of the songs. The volume also contains a two-page bibliography.

The essays are an interesting research source, and the volume is the place to locate desired information about any song of the era. However, this is a rather esoteric reference tool. Only very large research libraries will have need of this book.—**Joe P. Dunn**

AIR FORCE

697. Francillon, René J. **The Naval Institute Guide to World Military Aviation 1995.** Annapolis, Md., Naval Institute Press, 1995. 745p. illus. $125.00. ISBN 1-55750-252-8.

Compiled by one of the major experts in aviation writing, this guide provides data on more than 350 fixed/rotary-winged aircraft with more than 1,000 photographs and 115 line drawings. All current in-service military aircraft are described (whether in production or not) in detail with precision. An air order-of-battle composes the first third of the book, and aircraft descriptions the remainder: Each has a general introductory essay and an acronym glossary.

Such order-of-battle tabulation for the world's air forces is a major research and analysis tool, unmatched in the open literature. It outlines not only air forces, but also separate naval, army, coast/border guard, and armed police formations. Some national organizations are still not public, but ex-Warsaw Pact states such as the former Soviet Union are now described in much more detail. Where known, the order-of-battle cites squadron and aircraft type nicknames.

The squadron/basing information is supplemented by the concept of an "aircraft census" for each nation, an especially good idea relating aircraft type to operational tasks, while enabling readers to judge data precision. The census also makes an approximation of squadron sizes possible (e.g., the Albanian

People's Army Air Force groups 174 aircraft in 14 squadrons; the Netherlands Army Light Aviation group has 90 aircraft in 5 squadrons). The number of aircraft types each nation uses can also be derived: Compare Italy's relatively homogenous air force with 881 aircraft in 31 types to Colombia's hodgepodge air force with 265 aircraft in 50 types.

The aircraft descriptive section details the aircraft type; the manufacturer; the program history; variants in detail (some major types may have upwards of two dozen significant variants); current military operators; and basic data. Aircraft statistics are cited in both English and metric measures, including wing loading for fixed-wing aircraft and rotor loading for helicopters. The monochrome photographs are clear and large, but several are rather dark, and some consume too much space: The opportunity to provide detailed captions has been almost totally foregone. The diagrams have been drawn from a mix of manufacturer and secondary sources, resulting in a nonstandard appearance.

While a massive amount of information is provided with care and accuracy, more than a dozen problems were noted. The most serious omission is the failure to provide an index by aircraft type designator (a user wanting to know about the *A-6* must know either that the aircraft is manufactured by Grumman or that its popular name is *Intruder*), but the fact that Russian acronyms are used throughout the book without a glossary is also a major lapse. The fact that the prospective *EH-101* is in the book, while the far more important *Lockheed F-22 "Lightning II"* is not, is perplexing. Most errors are minor misspellings, but persistent inaccuracy in converting Mach numbers and metric speeds to English measures are not trivial.

In comparison with *Jane's All the World's Aircraft* (see ARBA 93, entry 178), the *Naval Institute Guide* has both plusses and minuses. Both have the same number of editorial pages. The former covers aero engines and civilian airplanes; the latter does not, although its orders-of-battle are unique. *Jane's* has slightly more detailed coverage of major types, is more thoroughly indexed, covers projected aircraft uniformly, and is particularly better in its coverage of Chinese aircraft. The *Guide* has more extensive treatment of types no longer in production; both appear to have equally reliable data.

Overall, this is a comprehensive ready-reference source to its topic, sturdily bound and crisply printed on good-quality paper. Despite rather inadequate indexing, this may be the only source on its topic that many smaller libraries need, and any institution serving military history interests will find it valuable.

—**John Howard Oxley**

ARMY

698. **The Army Times Book of Great Land Battles: From the Civil War to the Gulf War.** By J. D. Morelock. Walter J. Boyne, ed. New York, Berkley Books, 1994. 331p. illus. maps. index. $28.95. ISBN 0-425-14371-6.

This work looks at 14 land battles selected by the author for their importance either to the military arts or to modern history. Each battle is analyzed in terms of its historical and political setting, leadership, weaponry, and tactics. A concise but clear account of the battle as it unfolded is presented, along with a discussion of the consequences of the loss or victory to the combatants and to later history. Some battles included are Gettysburg, Sedan, Port Arthur, Tannenberg, Stalingrad, the Korean War, Sinai and the Golan Heights, and the Gulf War. The accompanying maps are quite good. There is an index but no bibliography or source notes. Because of this, and because it is likely to be a work readers will wish to read all the way through rather than consult, libraries may wish to add it to their circulating collection rather than their reference collection. In spite of being a little strong on hyperbole and cliché, this book will be of interest to teenage and older readers. It would be a suitable purchase for school, public, and academic libraries.

—**Eric R. Nitschke**

699. **On the Trail of the Buffalo Soldier: Biographies of African Americans in the U.S. Army, 1866-1917.** Frank N. Schubert, comp. and ed. Wilmington, Del., Scholarly Resources, 1995. 519p. $125.00. ISBN 0-8420-2482-4.

The title under consideration is a fine addition to the ranks of African-American military history reference books. It is composed of thousands of entries on black soldiers for the period from the end of the Civil War to the beginning of American involvement in World War I. In these 50 years, black regiments served primarily in the West (with some service in Cuba and the Philippines), where they earned their nickname while fighting the Native Americans. Most of the alphabetically arranged entries contain only the basic information, such as birthplace, rank and unit, and a sketch of their service history, while others have much more information, with excerpts from official reports, their circumstances prior to emancipation, and relatives' names included. Virtually every entry contains a source note, and there are some cross-references. The bibliography contains citations to books, articles, newspapers, government documents, unpublished manuscripts, archival collections, military records, and Veterans Administration pension files. The appendixes list the number of black men enlisted in the army, dates of service of sergeants major of the black cavalry regiments, soldiers killed in action, recipients of the Medal of Honor, and dates and locations of the various regimental headquarters. Schubert is the Chief of the Operations History Division, Joint History Office, U.S. Joint Chiefs of Staff. One can use Robert Greene's *Black Defenders of America, 1775-1973* (Johnson, 1974) and *Black Soldiers-Black Sailors-Black Ink* by Thomas Truxton Moebs (Moebs Publishing, 1994) to complement the work. This well-constructed book is well worth its price, as it presents so much information in one volume. It is recommended for military history, genealogical, African-American, and general reference collections of all academic and public libraries. [R: RBB, 15 Feb 95, pp. 1111-12]—**Daniel K. Blewett**

NAVY

700. Garzke, William H., Jr., and Robert O. Dulin Jr. **Battleships: United States Battleships, 1935-1992.** rev. ed. Annapolis, Md., Naval Institute Press, 1995. 386p. illus. index. $75.00. ISBN 1-55750-174-2.

The 1st edition of this work (see ARBA 77, entry 1649) set a standard for the scholarly, technical, yet accessible, illustrated ship history. Covering physical characteristics such as propulsion, armament, communications, and radar as well as design, development, and operational history, this revision, like the original, is concerned with battleship classes built since 1935: the fast battleships. Well illustrated with line drawings and photographs, the current edition, sadly, does not have the excellent pull-out plans that are but reproduced at a smaller scale.

The 1995 edition contains much new material concerning the *North Carolina* and *South Dakota* classes, but it is the chapters concerning the *Iowa*-class battleships, the never-built *Montana*-class BBs, and the *Alaska*-class battlecruisers that have been extensively rewritten and substantially added to. Additional information has been found, especially for the sections dealing with armaments, radar, hull, and performance characteristics. A completely new chapter details the role of the *Iowa*s in Lebanon and Desert Shield/Storm, and the modifications made to them for their return to service. A new appendix discusses the role of President Franklin D. Roosevelt in battleship design and construction, and there is an extended treatment of the turret explosion aboard *Iowa* in 1989. All in all, the revised edition has added 110 pages of new material.

Norman Friedman's fine *U.S. Battleships: An Illustrated Design History* (Naval Institute Press, 1985) is worthy of mention here, but it complements rather than competes with the Garzke and Dulin work. Their excellent new edition should be in all libraries serving readers interested in modern warship history.
—**Eric R. Nitschke**

701. **The Naval Institute Historical Atlas of the U.S. Navy.** By Craig L. Symonds. Annapolis, Md., Naval Institute Press, 1995. 241p. illus. maps. index. $39.95. ISBN 1-55750-797-X.

This atlas is a compilation of 94 maps covering more than 200 years of U.S. Navy actions and activities from the American Revolution to the Persian Gulf War. It is arranged in 10 sections: "American Revolution, 1775-1883"; "The Age of Sail, 1783-1812"; "The War of 1812, 1812-1815"; "Pirates, Explorers, and War with Mexico, 1815-1860"; "The Civil War, 1861-1865"; "Retrenchment and Renaissance, 1865-1900"; "A Global Navy and a World War, 1901-1939"; "World War II, 1939-1945"; "The Cold War Navy, 1946-1980"; "The Pax Americana, 1980-1994." Additionally, there is an epilogue on the U.S. Navy in the twenty-first century.

Each section is preceded by a thoughtful essay about the historical period with relevant illustrations. Then, particular important events are described on a verso page, with the facing page carrying the map showing deployment of ships, their tracks, and, in some cases, shore activity. The atlas has an index. The author is a professor of history at the U.S. Naval Academy. William J. Clipson, the cartographer, has illustrated more than 500 books. An atlas of this nature has not previously been available; students and scholars of the U.S. Navy's history will welcome this volume. The reasonable price puts the book within reach of individuals.—**Frank J. Anderson**

WEAPONS

702. Citino, Robert M. **Armored Forces: History and Sourcebook.** Westport, Conn., Greenwood Press, 1994. 308p. illus. index. (Histories and Sourcebooks on Combat Forces). $75.00. ISBN 0-313-28500-4.

Citino has written an excellent narrative on the development of armored forces and the historical debate over their employment and who was primarily responsible for formulating armored warfare doctrine in the twentieth century. He details the development of the tank during the Great War and identifies the primary personalities in the debate over the development and employment of armored forces during the interwar years. J. F. C. Fuller, Basil Liddell Hart, Charles de Gaulle, and Heinz Guderian were all studying the employment of armored forces during this period and had varying success in their attempts to influence the development of armored forces in their countries. Citino's graceful narrative goes on to describe the armored campaigns of World War II: France 1940, North Africa 1940-1943, Russia 1941-1944, and Western Europe 1944-1945. Modern tank warfare is described as those campaigns following World War II. Korea was a kind of sideshow to the much-predicted and -anticipated Anglo-Soviet conflict prepared for in central Europe. The Arab-Israeli wars provided a glimpse of what that larger conflict might have been like, as did the Iran-Iraq war. Finally, the Gulf War gave us a clear idea of how that major conflict between Anglo-Soviet forces might have turned out. Citino's main point is that tanks are just part of a combined force, part of that combined arms concept that was developing during the middle and late nineteenth century. Citino also provides a biographical section that includes the major personalities in the armored warfare debate as well as the most prominent commanders. This volume is highly recommended for college, university, and military library reference collections as well as for military historians.—**Norman L. Kincaide**

703. Dastrup, Boyd L. **The Field Artillery: History and Sourcebook.** Westport, Conn., Greenwood Press, 1994. 220p. index. $65.00. ISBN 0-313-27264-6.

The field artillery, as opposed to coastal or antiaircraft artillery, is used on the battlefield to project explosives against enemy troops and fortifications. The title reviewed here is a fine bibliography of materials relating to this subject and its history, technology, tactics, and organization. The book begins with a history of field artillery, from its origins in the fourteenth century to the recent Persian Gulf War. Extensive footnotes in this section introduce a wide range of sources, some of which deal with general military history and the history of warfare, others with artillery in general, and still others with particular guns. Most sources are books. Journal articles are cited from history, military studies, and armed forces journals rather than general interest or buffs' magazines.

The second part of the work contains bibliographic essays paralleling the chronological and thematic arrangement of the first part. In these essays, Dastrup succinctly summarizes the uses and values of the various works cited in the histories. The result is a skillful blending and arranging that guides the researcher through the subject from the general to the particular, all the while providing the basis for knowledgeable selection of titles helpful for researching a particular interest. Biographies of notables in the technical and military development of artillery, along with a chronology and several appendixes of technical information on selected field pieces of the fifteenth to twentieth centuries, conclude the book.

All in all, this is a very good work on a specialized topic. Libraries whose users are interested in military history in general or the field artillery in particular will find this a useful purchase.

—**Eric R. Nitschke**

13 Political Science

GENERAL WORKS

Bibliography

704. Eccleshall, Robert, and Michael Kenny, comps. **Western Political Thought: A Bibliographical Guide to Post-War Research.** Manchester, England, Manchester University Press; distr., New York, St. Martin's Press, 1995. 342p. index. (History and Related Disciplines Select Bibliographies). $79.95. ISBN 0-7190-3569-4.

This book provides a good, although not comprehensive, resource of the literature since 1945 concerning the history of political thought in the Western tradition. The entries are briefly annotated in eight chronological categories and subdivided variously by subject, place (e.g., Greece), and person. The authors note the work's many restrictions, including its geographical scope (limited to Great Britain, Europe, and North America), the exclusion of primary writings (assumed to be better known to students and researchers), and the exclusion of most post-World War II political philosophy and the topic of political ideologies, among others. Nevertheless, the book is a valuable and timely tool for sorting through the exploding literature in this area. The work that has been done for this volume will be appreciated by researchers, teachers, students, and librarians assisting them. Cross-references and an index add significantly to the book's versatility.—**Curtis D. Holmes**

Biography

705. Axelrod, Alan, and Charles Phillips. **Dictators and Tyrants: Absolute Rulers and Would-Be Rulers in World History.** New York, Facts on File, 1995. 340p. illus. index. $45.00. ISBN 0-8160-2866-4.

For those who have ever drawn a blank on where to begin researching a Hapsburg prince or a Middle Eastern tyrant, this unique single-volume reference book would be a good place to start. The comprehensive text profiles nearly 600 tyrants and would-be tyrants from world history. People chosen for inclusion by the editors are those who ruled unlawfully according to the standards of the society in which they originally came to power. Beginning as far back as King David of Israel and Genghis Khan, the coverage extends to the modern day with dictators such as Adolf Hitler, Muammar Muhammad al-Qadhafi, and Manuel Antonio Noriega.

Arranged alphabetically by name, each entry is 3 to 15 paragraphs long and begins with an explanation of how the rulers overstepped their power, a description of their rise to power, and their final demise. The writing is easy to read, particularly for the junior high and high school student. Most entries end with suggestions for further reading and many have black-and-white photographs, often of sculptures or paintings. The book concludes with a useful index that not only lists the biographical entries, but also includes subjects such as biblical figures, English monarchs, massacres, political purges, and poison. This is a well-made reference book with an unorthodox slant on world history.—**Carol D. Henry**

706. **Great Leaders, Great Tyrants? Contemporary Views of World Leaders Who Made History.** Arnold Blumberg, ed. Westport, Conn., Greenwood Press, 1995. 354p. index. $49.95. ISBN 0-313-28751-1.

The distinction between leadership and tyranny has produced debates among historians and political scientists concerning numerous contemporary and historical figures. This compilation, edited by Towson State University history professor Arnold Blumberg, is an attempt to synthesize such debate over the political assets and tyrannical liabilities personified by numerous historical leaders.

Blumberg presents succinct portraits of 52 historical rulers. Personalities examined include Fidel Castro, King Charles I of England, Mikhail Gorbachev, Ho Chi Minh, Mao Tse-tung, Maximilien Robespierre, and the Roman emperor Vespasian. Entries begin with contextual introductions and proceed with concise biographical portraits. The principal features of each entry include assessments of why the individual should be regarded as a great leader or great tyrant. Portraits conclude with a bibliography of selected readings.

This work can serve as a useful introduction to the lives and policies of numerous historically prominent rulers. Some will object to the exclusion of figures such as Kim Il Sung and Ayatollah Ruhollah Khomeini, as well as other historically significant leaders. Nevertheless, *Great Leaders, Great Tyrants?* should initiate study and analysis, and lead to consultation of more substantive works describing and analyzing the lives and policies of these individuals.—**Bert Chapman**

Directories

707. **The International Directory of Government 1995.** 2d ed. London, Europa; distr., Detroit, Gale, 1995. 830p. $345.00. ISBN 1-85743-004-2. ISSN 0956-0998.

More than 190 nations are included in this directory, many of them new to the world since the 1st edition in 1990 (see ARBA 91, entry 719). Each country chapter begins with two boxes listing the head of state and the legislature, followed by directory information for government ministries, departments, agencies, and other organizations, covering subject areas such as agriculture, art and culture, business, tourism, the news media, defense, judiciary, nationalized industries, and so on. There are more than 15,000 entries. International organizations are not included. A list of abbreviations and international telephone codes are at the beginning; no index is provided. The data contained within these pages can also be found in the *Europa World Year Book* (see ARBA 94, entry 82, and ARBA 90, entry 91), and the *Year Book* is the more useful title as it contains a multitude of statistical and textual information not found in the *International Directory of Government*. One wonders why Europa went to the trouble of publishing this title. While a good source, libraries that already own the *Year Book* can safely pass on this expensive item.
—**Daniel K. Blewett**

708. **Profiles of Worldwide Government Leaders 1995.** Todd Leeuwenburgh and others, eds. Bethesda, Md., Worldwide Government Directories; distr., Detroit, Gale, 1995. 855p. index. $297.00. ISBN 0-96929283-9. ISSN 1080-7063.

This biographical directory is a companion volume to *Worldwide Government Directory*, the 11th edition of which appeared in 1995 (see entry 709). What distinguishes *Profiles* is its detailed information on key officials in 195 countries. Arranged by country, the directory lists major officials, detailing for each entrant birth date, education, family status, political party, private and political career, and agency contact. However, addresses and telephone numbers are not provided for these contacts, so users must consult other directories.

Data for some entries are scant, while others are more complete. "Private career" may simply be "lawyer." In some cases, as for Rfaiddin Şahin, minister of Agriculture and Village Affairs in Turkey, "private career" consists of "Languages: Turkish, French, English." Names of political parties are in English, with abbreviations for the name in the original language. For example, in Turkey, the True Path Party is identified as DYP—but the official name is not given. This may have resulted because the biographies were collected in a variety of languages, including Arabic and Chinese.

Information in the directory was compiled from multiple sources and claims to be current as of January 1995. The introduction notes that among the sources used were ministers themselves, government ministries worldwide, foreign diplomatic agencies in Washington, D.C., and New York, U.S. government files, world news and media services, and correspondents for Worldwide Government Directories on five continents.

Profiles will provide cursory biographies of a country's officials with sketchy information on party affiliation and political career. Within these limitations, journalists, government foreign officers, and political analysts will find it useful for quick identifications.—**Bernice Bergup**

709. **Worldwide Government Directory with International Organizations 1995.** Ken Gause and others, eds. Bethesda, Md., Worldwide Government Directories; distr., Detroit, Gale, 1995. 1477p. $347.00. ISBN 1-886994-00-5. ISSN 0894-1521.

The 11th edition of this standard directory is again divided into 2 main sections. The first and principal section outlines, country by country, the structure and personnel of the governments of 195 nations. Each entry provides information on the head of state, the head of government, executive agencies, the major legislative and judicial entities, senior defense organs, the central bank, and foreign embassies located in the country. For all of these agencies, there is a listing of senior officials with addresses and telephone and fax numbers. The strength of this directory is the inclusion of personnel at the deputy minister/assistant secretary level. The first section ends with brief information on languages, ethnic and religious composition, currency, political parties, and the international and regional organizations of which each nation is a member.

The second section profiles more than 100 worldwide and regional organizations. Each entry identifies the chief officers and provides addresses and telephone and fax numbers. All information in this edition is current as of January 1995. This directory invites comparison with the *Europa World Year Book* (see ARBA 94, entry 82; ARBA 90, entry 91; and ARBA 86, entry 91). While the Europa publication has less directory information, listing only the chief officer for each major governmental agency, it has much statistical, economic, and historical information not covered in the *Worldwide Government Directory*. The international organizations sections of the two publications exemplify their different approaches. The *Europa World Year Book* has much more information on their activities and functions, but identifies far fewer officials. For those who are interested principally in the directory function of identifying personnel, the Central Intelligence Agency's monthly *Chiefs of State and Cabinet Members of Foreign Governments* may be a better alternative to the annual *Worldwide Government Directory*.—**Henry E. York**

Handbooks and Yearbooks

710. **Countries of the World and Their Leaders Yearbook 1995: Supplement.** Brian Rajewski, ed. Detroit, Gale, 1995. 498p. maps. index. $85.00pa. ISBN 0-8103-6843-9. ISSN 0196-2809.

Intended as a one-stop reference source for students, teachers, and travelers, this new edition is formatted the same as the previous edition, reviewed in ARBA 91 (see entry 723). The first section contains background notes on a selected number of countries. There are also sections on foreign travel, travel warnings and consular information sheets, and international treaty organizations. As in previous editions, the information is reprinted from publications from the Department of State, the Customs Service, the Passport Office, the National Climactic Center, and so forth. Obviously, some information is fairly current and some is not. The volume is attractively bound and well laid out, but the price tag is substantial for information obtainable in any depository library.—**Bohdan S. Wynar**

711. **The Facts on File World Political Almanac.** 3d ed. Chris Cook, comp. New York, Facts on File, 1995. 536p. index. $45.00. ISBN 0-8160-2838-9.

Political changes occur at a dizzying pace throughout the world, especially since World War II. Without an orderly account of the past, it becomes difficult to recall specific happenings or to identify trends. Cook (head of Modern Archives Unit at the London School of Economics) provides access to political events in the years between 1945 and 1994 via the 3d edition of *Facts on File World Political Almanac*. The author uses chronological listings as a basis for reviewing categories such as international organizations, heads of governments, legislative bodies, diplomatic agreements, political parties, elections, internal and external conflicts, and arms control agreements. A sufficient, but minimum, amount of text conserves space, thus permitting inclusion of a comprehensive assortment of essential information. Even data on population and urbanization can be found, as well as a dictionary of terms, events and actions, and a biographical dictionary. A table of contents and a detailed index ease the task of searching. The almanac is excellent as a general review of recent political history or as a point of departure for deeper investigations. The compiler has sifted through many sources to place important political facts within the convenience of a single volume.—**William C. Struning**

712. **Federal Systems of the World: A Handbook of Federal, Confederal, and Autonomy Arrangements.** [2d ed.]. Daniel J. Elazar and the staff of the Jerusalem Center for Public Affairs, comps. and eds. Harlow, England, Longman Group and New York, Stockton Press, 1994. 364p. $175.00. ISBN 1-56159-086-X.

This is a miniencyclopedia of federal and confederal arrangements in the modern world. Its chapters cover constitutional and political overviews of approximately 60 federal or quasi-federal systems, 9 confederal associations between states, and 4 recently dissolved federal states.

A detailed introduction includes a theoretical overview, definitions of related terms, and general information on federal arrangements. This section also contains the editors' argument that federalism is the wave of the future in a world of multiethnic states. The body of the work is divided into three parts (federal arrangements, confederal arrangements, and dissolved federations), further subdivided into chapters on individual systems. The chapters sampled seem detailed and accurate, outlining constitutional arrangements, the national and provincial/state/regional governments, and the main features of the party system.

The editors drew on standard reference works present in most larger libraries as well as input from the International Association of Centers for Federal Studies. Entries for countries vary greatly from more than 10 pages for states such as Canada, India, the United Kingdom, the United States, or the Russian Federation, to a few pages for smaller states such as Monaco or Vanuatu. Confederal arrangements outlined include the European Union, the Caribbean Community, and the Commonwealth of Independent States. There are four tabular appendixes, but no subject index. In sum, this work belongs in research collections in comparative politics or international relations. Where funds permit, it would also be useful for larger public libraries.—**Nigel Tappin**

713. **Handbook of the Nations: A Brief Guide to the Economy....** 14th ed. Compiled by U.S. Central Intelligence Agency. Detroit, Gale, 1995. 512p. maps. $120.00. ISBN 0-8103-8586-4. ISSN 0194-3790.

This edition is a reprint of *The World Factbook* (see ARBA 95, entry 8, for a review of the CD-ROM edition) published annually by the Central Intelligence Agency (CIA). The CIA is using data provided by various departments of the agency, as well as the Defense Intelligence Agency, the U.S. Bureau of the Census, the Defense Nuclear Agency, the U.S. Coast Guard, the U.S. Department of State, and other government agencies. The previous print edition, entitled *The World Factbook 1991-92* and published by Brassey's, was reviewed in ARBA 93 (see entry 105). It should be noted that the price was $28. Gale increased the price substantially to $120. The new edition contains 100-plus more pages, but this hardly justifies such a significant increase in price. The volume contains government information that is free to all.—**Bohdan S. Wynar**

POLITICS AND GOVERNMENT

United States

Archives

714. **The Sourcebook of State Public Records: The Definitive Guide to Searching for Public Record Information at the State Level.** 2d ed. Tempe, Ariz., BRB, 1995. 339p. (The Public Record Research Library). $33.00pa. ISBN 1-879792-22-2.

The 2d edition of the *Sourcebook* has more than 40 pages of enhancements. It now includes profiles of state agencies that keep sales tax records and has added 900-plus occupational licensing entries in an easier-to-use topical format (the 1st edition required users to browse an entire list of boards and departments—see ARBA 95, entry 730). The book contains about 5,000 state-level locations for more than 20 different types of information: criminal records; corporation records; trademarks and tradenames; workers' compensation records; driver records; and birth, death, marriage, and divorce records, among others.

Listed among the 12 occupational licensing groups are those for architecture, business, construction, education, the environment, finance, health, social services, and transportation. Each entry furnishes addresses, telephone and fax numbers, business hours, how far back records are available, fees, turnaround times, and restrictions. The editors also offer advice on what to look for and how to obtain specific records. This paperbound directory has a sturdy binding, wide inner margins, and is reasonably priced. Most academic and public libraries will want this convenient source in their reference collections.—**Gary D. Barber**

Bibliography

715. Goehlert, Robert U., and Fenton S. Martin. **The United States Congress: An Annotated Bibliography 1980-1993.** Washington, D.C., Congressional Quarterly, 1995. 640p. index. $185.00. ISBN 0-87187-810-0.

This excellent bibliography continues the work begun in *The United States Congress; a Bibliography* (Free Press, 1982). It offers annotated references to books, articles, dissertations, and essays that discuss Congress's history, development, power, and relations with other branches of the federal government. The collection is aimed at the student/researcher and cites materials that should be available at medium or large public libraries as well as academic ones. The 14 major categories cover congressional investigations, foreign affairs, committee structure and work, legislative case studies, pressures on Congress, and Congress and the electorate. Subheadings include congressional immunity, human rights, committee reform, the veto power, and campaign finances. Subject and author indexes are useful for locating the clearly written annotations. Particularly unique is the introduction, which is actually a detailed guide to the major sources available for congressional research, from almanacs to biographical dictionaries to journals, newspapers and CD-ROM products, as well as sources for information on committees, elections, and statutory law. Goehlert and Martin have created a superior research guide that belongs in larger public and all academic libraries.—**Deborah Hammer**

716. Lowenthal, Mark M. **The U.S. Intelligence Community: An Annotated Bibliography.** Hamden, Conn., Garland, 1994. 206p. index. (Organizations and Interest Groups, v.11; Garland Reference Library of the Humanities, v.1765). $25.00. ISBN 0-8153-1423-X.

This annotated bibliography is part of Garland's Organizations and Interest Groups series. The author, a noted scholar and former intelligence official, provides a useful roadmap to a diffuse and extensive body of literature. The bibliography focuses on books and journal articles published between 1946 and 1993 that address specific roles the intelligence community has played in national policymaking.

The 225 entries are grouped into 5 chapters: "Intelligence Theory and Practice," "History and Organization," "Intelligence Oversight," "Compilations of Documents," and "Bibliographies." While studies on analysis predominate, the operations side is not neglected. Also included are post-Cold War writings that tend to focus on economic rather than military intelligence gathering.

More than half of the volume consists of reproductions of important U.S. government documents such as the National Security Act (1947), the Foreign Intelligence Surveillance Act (1978), the Central Intelligence Agency Information Act (1984), and various resolutions and executive orders. Separate author and subject indexes are also provided. All academic libraries will want to acquire this reasonably priced guide to intelligence literature.—**Gary D. Barber**

717. Reams, Bernard D., Jr., comp. **Federal Legislative Histories: An Annotated Bibliography and Index to Officially Published Sources.** Westport, Conn., Greenwood Press, 1994. 595p. index. (Bibliographies and Indexes in Law and Political Science, no.21). $99.50. ISBN 0-313-23092-7.

This bibliography identifies and describes 255 legislative histories covering legislation from 1796 (4th Congress, 1st session) to 1990 (101st Congress, 2d session) that have appeared in committee prints, hearings, or Congressional Research Service publications. Publication dates range from 1862 through 1990. Arranged chronologically by public law number, the publication has indexes by author, popular name of the law, congressional session, public law and bill numbers, and a table providing reference from Statutes at Large citations. Each entry includes a bibliographic citation, relevant locational information (e.g., Superintendent of Documents classification and CIS microfiche number, but not Library of Congress classification), reference to bills mentioned in history, and an annotation. The annotations are clear, complete descriptions of the contents and arrangement of the history. A brief introductory chapter discusses the use of legislative history in interpreting statutes.

The author of several legislative histories and other legal books, Reams is both a law professor and director of the law library at Washington University School of Law. The completeness of the entries and thoroughness of the annotations make this a valuable resource for identifying legislative histories that are readily available. The American Association of Law Libraries' *Sources of Compiled Legislative Histories* (Rothman, 1988) covers a wider range of sources but not as much time.—**Marilyn Domas White**

Biography

718. Hendrickson, Kenneth E., Jr. **The Chief Executives of Texas: From Stephen F. Austin to John B. Connally Jr.** College Station, Tex., Texas A&M University Press, 1995. 246p. illus. index. (Centennial Series of the Association of Former Students, Texas A&M University, no.55). $29.50. ISBN 0-89096-641-9.

Outside the Lone Star State, this reference tool will be of only marginal value. Inside the "whole other country" of Texas, this tome will be viewed with skepticism, dismay, and outright regret. No little part of the skepticism exhibited by Texans will reside in the one small but significant fact that the author was educated at none other than the University of Oklahoma, longtime longhorn rival, and therefore the bane of all "true" Texans.

Hendrickson has attempted to combine scholarship with diatribe and has come up with this volume. Trying to avoid commonplace hagiography in the treatment of former governors of Texas, the author careens to the other side of the road, smashing spades into spades, and wrecking jackanapes into jackanapes. The sore contention of this volume is that Texas has not been blessed with good leadership; on the contrary, it has been cursed with knaves and only by the grace of God has not fallen into mediocrity, although its leadership has weltered in it.

Forty-four heads of state appear in this volume posthumously. Of the six living governors, only the scantiest mention is made of five. The text reads hotter than a Texas pepper in the Rio Grande. For example, of the sainted Coke Stevenson, Hendrickson writes, "Throughout his political career, Stevenson . . . exhibited no liberal tendencies . . . and few that could be even described as constructive. [H]e was reactionary, penurious, and in some cases downright cruel." Ouch! Do not look for this to get the Texas Popular Book of the Year award.—**Mark Y. Herring**

719. Quinn-Musgrove, Sandra L., and Sanford Kanter. **America's Royalty: All the Presidents' Children.** rev. ed. Westport, Conn., Greenwood Press, 1995. 286p. illus. index. $59.95. ISBN 0-313-29535-2.

Little research has been conducted about the lives of presidential children. In fact, in the current age of television, the media seems to treat them more as ornaments or curiosities of an incoming administration than as contributors to a president's life experience and mental well-being. This book represents a step forward in the knowledge about the offspring of the United States' presidents and helps to illustrate the fact that with the exception of James Buchanan (the only president to never marry), the election of a new president represents not only an individual ascending to office but also a family beginning a new life.

The book begins by briefly describing the lives of six presidents who never had children, followed by a description in chronological order of the children of the presidents. This revised edition includes biographical sketches of George Bush's six children and Bill Clinton's one child, as well as changes to the text "reflecting the maturing technical or mechanical skills of this edition's author" (preface). When known, the date of birth, birthplace, date of death, age at death, cause of death, educational background, profession or occupation, name of spouse, and number of children for each child is given. The data are followed by an essay providing a detailed description of the child's life, accomplishments, and failures. A list of further readings concludes each presidential entry, although there is no list after the chapter devoted to childless presidents. The book concludes with an appendix listing shared characteristics among the presidential children, a bibliography, and an index.

This book is well written and informative, and is unique in that it describes in-depth the lives of the president's children. It is recommended for all libraries.—**Robert V. Labaree**

Dictionaries and Encyclopedias

720. **The Encyclopedia of the United States Congress.** Donald C. Bacon, Roger H. Davidson, and Morton Keller, eds. New York, Simon & Schuster Academic Reference Division, 1995. 4v. illus. maps. $355.00/set. ISBN 0-13-276361-3.

The publishers consider this set the most definitive and comprehensive reference on the U.S. Congress. Other recent titles that might dispute this claim are mostly Congressional Quarterly publications such as *Congress and the Nation* (see ARBA 95, entry 731) and *Congress A to Z: CQ's Ready Reference Encyclopedia* (see ARBA 94, entry 728). These excellent titles, however, focus on the activity and functioning of the body and feature many lists and statistical compilations. The focus of the *Encyclopedia of the United States Congress* is quite different: the historical development of the body from 1789 to 1995.

The 4-volume set comprises 1,056 alphabetically arranged articles written by 550 authorities, mainly U.S. professors but also government officials, researchers, and congressional staff. The Congressional Research Service is well represented. The articles vary in length and style. For example, under "History of Congress" there are 8, 10-page historical essays tracing the development of the institution; some articles are only a paragraph or two with brief, factual summaries of historical events. There are 247 biographies of former senators and representatives. All articles have bibliographies. There are a comprehensive index and a glossary of terms in the last volume. In addition, there are more than 900 illustrations, tables, charts, and graphs. At a time of intense interest in Congress, this encyclopedia provides comprehensive coverage of this institution that is suitable for general audiences and for the needs of specialists.—**Henry E. York**

Directories

721. **Carroll's County Directory: November 1995/April 1996.** Tracey A. Ryan, ed. Washington, D.C., Carroll Publishing, 1995. 559p. index. $150.00pa./yr. ISSN 0742-1702.

Carroll's County Directory, one of many volumes published by Carroll Publishing, has several sections, each devoted to a different profile. The introductory section contains abbreviations, national associations, state associations of counties, and associations of county officials affiliated with National Association of Counties. The directory covers some 3,100 counties in the United States. Counties are listed alphabetically by state, and their population is based on 1994 Bureau of the Census information. Counties with a population over 50,000 include names and office telephone numbers of all council members; counties with a population under 50,000 list only the chief elected official and chief administrative official.—**Bohdan S. Wynar**

722. **Carroll's Federal Advisory Directory 1995.** Tracey A. Ryan and Laura Crow, eds. Washington, D.C., Carroll Publishing, 1995. 662p. index. $137.00pa./yr. ISSN 1074-2727.

There are approximately 19,000 people serving on more than 950 federal advisory committees. Only 122 committees have been terminated to date. This directory, with a committee index and a membership term length index, provides basic information on all committee members in such sections as "Executive Office of the President," "Cabinet Departments," and "Administrative Agencies."—**Bohdan S. Wynar**

723. **Carroll's Federal Directory: Executive, Legislative, Judicial. November/December 1995.** Albert Ruffin, ed. Washington, D.C., Carroll Publishing, 1995. 640p. index. $197.00pa./yr. ISSN 1080-4919.

This directory consists of several parts—an alphabetical list of executives; an organizational listing; Congressional listings (Senate leadership and members' offices, committees, and the same coverage for the House of Representatives); judicial listings; and a keyword index.—**Bohdan S. Wynar**

724. **Carroll's Federal Regional Directory: September 1995/February 1996.** Tracey A. Ryan, ed. Washington, D.C., Carroll Publishing, 1995. 512p. index. $150.00pa./yr. ISSN 1082-3182.

One of several directories published by Carroll Publishing, this volume consists of several sections. The alphabetical listing of executives provides names of individuals with their telephone numbers. This is followed by cabinet departments, administrative agencies, Congress, and judiciary. A keyword index and a geographical index conclude this volume. Also of some help will be the detailed table of contents. For example, under Department of Agriculture, the reader will find a listing of 17 agencies starting with Agricultural Marketing Service and ending with Rural Utilities Service. The usefulness of this volume will defend the frequency of updating.—**Bohdan S. Wynar**

725. **Carroll's Municipal Directory: October 1995/March 1996.** Tracey A. Ryan, ed. Washington, D.C., Carroll Publishing, 1995. 590p. index. $150.00pa./yr. ISSN 1083-933X.

Carroll's Municipal Directory consists of a listing of executives, an organizational listing of municipalities, municipalities with a population under 15,000, and a geographical index.

—**Bohdan S. Wynar**

726. **Carroll's State Directory: Executive, Legislative, Judicial. November 1995/February 1996.** Tracey A. Ryan, ed. Washington, D.C., Carroll Publishing, 1995. 758p. index. $140.00pa./yr. ISSN 1082-1929.

Similar in detail to other volumes published by Carroll Publishing, this directory has an alphabetical list of executives, followed by an organizational list, a legislative list, supreme courts, and a keyword index.—**Bohdan S. Wynar**

727. **County Executive Directory: May/October 1994.** Tracey A. Ryan, ed. Washington, D.C., Carroll Publishing, 1994. 399p. $127.00pa. ISSN 0742-1702.

728. **Municipal Executive Directory: April/September 1994.** Tracey A. Ryan, ed. Washington, D.C., Carroll Publishing, 1994. 552p. index. $130.00pa. ISSN 0742-1710.

729. **State Executive Directory: March/June 1994.** Tracey A. Ryan, ed. Washington, D.C., Carroll Publishing, 1994. 637p. index. $127.00pa. ISSN 0276-7163.

These three directories are part of a series of directories published by Carroll Publishing, which also includes *Federal Executive Directory* (see ARBA 95, entry 725, and ARBA 89, entry 644) and *Federal Regional Executive Directory* (see ARBA 95, entry 726, and ARBA 89, entry 645). Together, the five volumes offer one of the most comprehensive current listings of governmental personnel available.

The *State Executive Directory* is published three times a year and contains listings for executives in departments, agencies, and the legislature. The volume under review lists more than 36,000 names along with corresponding telephone numbers for each executive. There is also legislative reference information listing legislators, their telephone numbers, and dates for state legislative sessions.

The *Municipal Executive Directory* is published twice a year. The issue under review contains more than 33,000 names, divided by size of municipality. The listings for municipalities under 15,000 in population include only the name, address, and telephone number for the top elected official. The listings for places of more than 15,000 itemize major officials (frequently even the librarian) and can be quite lengthy. For example, Los Angeles has a full two-column page of listings.

The *County Executive Directory* is also published twice a year and is divided by size, with divisions at the 25,000 and 50,000 population marks. As in the large municipalities, the listings for counties larger than 50,000 can be quite extensive and may cover county offices such as surveyor, sanitation supervisor, constable, and dog officer. Each directory uses consistent color-codes to divide the major sections, providing for easy, quick usage. All five titles are available both in paper binding and as a floppy disk. The set is recommended for large public and academic libraries.—**Christine E. Thompson**

730. **The Directory of Professional and Occupational Regulation in the United States and Canada.** Lise Smith-Peters, ed. Lexington, Ky., CLEAR/Council of State Governments, 1994. 327p. $30.00pa. ISBN 0-87292-985-X.

This work provides readers with a single-source list of regulatory and licensing bodies in the United States, its territories, and the Canadian provinces. It is divided into two sections. Section 1 lists the names of the governing bodies, their addresses, and telephone and fax numbers under 185 broad professional or occupational headings. These are listed by individual state, territory, or province. Section 2 provides a table that clarifies the type of regulation (license, certification, or registration) required.

This publication combines and updates two previous works of the Council on Licensure, Enforcement and Regulation (CLEAR); *The Directory of State Licensing Officials* (1989) and *Occupational and Professional Regulation in the States* (1990) and has been expanded to include data from the U.S. territories and the Canadian provinces. This work is to be updated every two years.

While the book is helpful in providing contact information for the respective state, territory, or province, it is much less informative than Professional and Occupational Licensing Directory, published by Gale (see ARBA 94, entry 800), which provides not only contact and regulation clarification but also specific job titles, requirements, examination guidelines, exemption and reciprocity information, fees, and more. Thus, the only advantage the title under review has is its coverage of information from the territories and provinces. Because of this, libraries may want both publications; otherwise, their best purchase would be the Gale volume.—**Robert Logsdon**

731. **Federal Regulatory Directory.** 7th ed. Jon Preimesberger, ed. Washington, D.C., Congressional Quarterly, 1994. 1017p. illus. index. $139.95. ISBN 0-87187-811-9. ISSN 0195-749X.

The 7th edition of this directory (see ARBA 92, entry 687, for a review of the previous edition) provides updated information on the regulatory system of the United States. Following the same format as previous editions, the main body is divided into three separate sections. The largest section covers the 13 major regulatory agencies (e.g., Environmental Protection Agency, Food and Drug Administration). The following information is provided for each agency: an in-depth description of its powers and responsibilities; a detailed history; the future outlook for regulatory action; a brief biography and a photograph of commissioners or board members; organizational information, including names, telephone numbers, and organizational charts; public information sources within the agency; congressional committees with legislative responsibilities related to the agency; major legislation with regulatory provisions administered by the agency; and a bibliography of reference works and periodicals.

The other 2 sections cover 16 regulatory agencies (e.g., Federal Election Commission, Nuclear Regulatory Commission) and more than 80 agencies with regulatory powers within executive branch departments (e.g., Patent and Trademark Office, Immigration and Naturalization Service, National Highway Traffic Safety Administration). The information provided for each agency in these two sections is briefer in narrative and organizational detail, yet includes the essentials of the agency's authority, organization, and contacts.

Other features of the directory include a section on how to use the *Federal Register* and *Code of Federal Regulations*, the texts of five pieces of legislation and four executive orders relating to the regulatory process, a name index, and a detailed subject/agency index. Cornelius M. Kerwin's updated introduction provides a thorough background of the regulatory process and traces regulatory changes through successive presidential administrations. This outstanding directory will be useful to anyone dealing with the federal regulatory bureaucracy from a personal, business, or academic perspective.
—**Carol Wheeler**

732. **The Government Directory of Addresses and Telephone Numbers 1995: A Comprehensive Guide to Federal, State, County, and Local Government Offices in the United States.** 3d ed. Detroit, Omnigraphics, 1994. 1376p. index. $150.00. ISBN 0-7808-0017-6. ISSN 1062-1466.

All major federal, state, county, and municipal government offices are listed in this convenient, one-volume directory. More than 100,000 listings provide complete names, addresses, and telephone numbers for each office. The entries are divided into sections for the four levels of government included. Each section begins with a quick reference listing for frequently called numbers. The federal section contains the Executive Office of the President, cabinet departments, and the full range of administrative agencies. Congressional lists include the offices of all members of both houses. The outcome of the 1994 elections makes some of the information outdated. An extensive section covers the regional federal offices. It has useful maps delineating the federal regions for many agencies and programs. The state listings provide similar coverage for each of the states, the District of Columbia, Puerto Rico, and U.S. territories. The municipal and county sections provide telephone numbers and addresses for cities with populations over 15,000 and for counties over 25,000. A very useful feature is the keyword indexes after the federal and state sections, providing access for those not familiar with the organizational intricacies of the government.

This directory is a good buy for those who need more information than is available in standard directories, such as *The United States Government Manual* (see ARBA 84, entry 456), *The Book of the States* (see ARBA 94, entry 721; ARBA 91, entry 743; ARBA 88, entry 727; and ARBA 85, entry 655), and *The Municipal Yearbook* (see ARBA 83, entry 482), but do not need or wish to pay more for the four editions of the "Yellow Book" series (for federal, congressional, state, and municipal levels) published by Leadership Directories. These offer comparable coverage but are updated quarterly and include the names of current officeholders in addition to addresses and telephone numbers.—**Henry E. York**

733. Nelson, Garrison, with Mary T. Mitchell and Clark H. Bensen. **Committees in the U.S. Congress 1947-1992. Volume 2: Committee Histories and Member Assignments.** Washington, D.C., Congressional Quarterly, 1994. 1048p. $230.00. ISBN 0-87187-611-6.

This reference book is the second of a two-volume set on the U.S. Congress. Volume 1, published in 1993, was entitled *Committee Jurisdictions and Member Rosters* (see ARBA 94, entry 741). While the first volume dealt with formal jurisdictions of the committees, Volume 2 deals with the individual member's congressional career on committees. This book is divided into two major sections. Part 1 is organized by member and includes a biographical sketch of each member of Congress. Biographical sketches list name, party and state, dates of birth and death, dates of service, and reason for the ending of each period of service. The second section furnishes a committee assignment list that shows committee membership throughout Congressional representatives' careers, including rank held. This work covers more than 28,000 member assignments for the 23 Congresses from 1947 through the end of 1992.

Part 2 of this work provides a brief history of the more than 150 standing, select, special, and joint committees that have existed since 1947. Each history discusses the formation of the committee, the reasons for its existence, names of its prominent chairs, and the reasons for the committee's termination. The work is a most comprehensive source of information on committees of the U.S. Congress and should prove a useful resource for both public and college libraries.—**Gary E. Joseph**

734. **Washington Information Directory 1995-1996.** Christopher M. Karlsten and Paul McClure, eds. Washington, D.C., Congressional Quarterly, 1995. 1143p. maps. index. $99.95. ISBN 0-87187-847-X. ISSN 0887-8064.

Maintaining current information about contact personnel in Washington, D.C. is crucial for many businesses and public policy organizations. Possessing such current information is also crucial for countless library reference departments. *Washington Information Directory* has proven an essential reference source on Washington, D.C. for all sizes of libraries.

This newest edition (see ARBA 93, entry 743, for a review of an earlier edition) provides users with the names, addresses, telephone and fax numbers, and in some cases, e-mail and Gopher server addresses for the diverse variety of government and nongovernment individuals and organizations that make and influence federal public policy. Organization of this work is broken down by subject into 18 sections that cover areas such as economics and business, advocacy and public service, national security, transportation, and Congress and politics.

Entries for organizations feature the names of principal contact personnel, statements of organizational purpose, and print and electronic contact information. Examples of listed individuals and organizations include Oklahoma Representative J. C. Watts, the Latvian Embassy, the National Wildlife Federation, the Health Care Financing Administration, and mayors of major U.S. cities.

Directories such as this cannot keep track of all information changes. For instance, an entry for the Commerce Department's International Trade Administration lists the *U.S. Industrial Outlook* as one of its publications, even though that title has ceased publication. Another area of enhancement would be listing World Wide Web server addresses for federal agencies, as that has become the primary means for government agencies to disseminate their information on the Internet. These caveats aside, this directory remains an essential source for libraries wishing to possess relatively current information about influential individuals and organizations in the Washington, D.C. area.—**Bert Chapman**

Handbooks and Yearbooks

735. **America Votes 21: A Handbook of Contemporary American Election Statistics.** Richard M. Scammon and Alice V. McGillivray, comps. and eds. Washington, D.C., Congressional Quarterly, 1995. 498p. maps. $142.00. ISBN 0-87187-842-9.

This product of Congressional Quarterly's Elections Research Center continues to be a standard source for information on U.S. election results, particularly at the presidential, congressional, and gubernatorial levels. Even the *Statistical Abstract of the United States* (see entry 920) draws on *America Votes* for some of its tables. The newest volume of this biennial series includes detailed results of the 1993 and 1994 votes cast county-by-county in every state for governors, senators, and congressional representatives, with registration figures, vote totals, percentages, and pluralities. This handbook is highly recommended.—**Bohdan S. Wynar**

736. Bosnich, Victor W., comp. **Congressional Voting Guide: A Ten Year Compilation.** 5th ed. Dallas, Tex., CVG Press, 1994. 621p. index. $39.95. ISBN 0-9618958-5-3.

This volume provides reports on U.S. congressional voting by House member or Senator from 1984-1993 for everyone sitting in the 1993 Congress. Data are provided on approximately 150 of the most important roll call votes in each chamber over this 10-year period, with a larger share of the votes from the most recent years. In addition, a presidential support score is calculated for each member on all 1992 and 1993 votes. Each of the votes in the sample is identified by number and title with a brief description of its content. The results (by party) of the roll call vote are also provided, along with the president's position. Also included is a brief biographical note on each member. The guide is politically neutral; the selected votes reflect no partisan bias and offer a fair cross section of the most important roll call votes.

This is a convenient resource for general citizens, students, and scholars interested in the U.S. Congress. While this volume already appears dated because of the extraordinary turnover in the House and Senate in 1994, its impartial presentation and coverage of 10 years, and its fair price, make it particularly valuable.—**Frank L. Wilson**

737. **Congressional Quarterly's Desk Reference on American Government.** By Bruce Wetterau. Washington, D.C., Congressional Quarterly, 1995. 349p. index. $49.95. ISBN 0-87187-956-5.

This well-crafted reference book is designed to present information about the U.S. government in a manner easily understood by the ordinary citizen. Wetterau has done an outstanding job of developing a book that succeeds in achieving this goal. The material is presented in a lively question-answer format that makes for fascinating browsing. After reading an entry, one is compelled to read more. In addition, many of the answers direct the reader to other questions on related subjects, encouraging further research. All answers are annotated with the source of the information, which is listed in the bibliography. The listing of reference materials contains many standard works on U.S. history, such as *Dictionary of American History* (see ARBA 77, entry 384), as well as the latest works available on U.S. government.

For the individual who needs a quick reference for a specific fact, this book is invaluable. The 62-page index is complete and extremely detailed. There are numerous charts in the text that give information not easily found elsewhere. For example, there are 16 Supreme Court Justices who have retired for reasons other than health. The book lists them and the reasons for their retirement. All in all, this is an excellent reference work that would be an asset to even the smallest library. The work is both entertaining reading and a compilation of invaluable information on U.S. government.—**Nancy P. Reed**

738. **Congressional Quarterly's Politics in America 1996: The 104th Congress.** Philip D. Duncan and Christine C. Lawrence with CQ's Political Staff. Washington, D.C., Congressional Quarterly, 1995. 1541p. illus. $89.95; $54.95pa. ISBN 0-87187-843-7; 0-87187-844-5pa. ISSN 1064-6809.

This latest edition of Congressional Quarterly's biennial political compendium will serve as a useful guide to the members of the revolutionary 104th Congress. Although there are many new faces and newly renamed committees, the CQ approach is virtually identical to that of previous editions (see ARBA 94, entry 749, and ARBA 90, entry 691, for recent reviews). Information on the senator or representative is divided into two sections—"In Washington" and "At Home," with a brief demographic and political profile of the congressional district. For newly elected members of Congress, profiles are simply titled "The Path to Washington," in which much election strategy is discussed. Basic election data, key votes, voting analysis, and interest group ratings are provided. For each state, there is a brief political sketch of the Governor and Lieutenant Governor, plus basic state data, a map showing congressional districts, and information on redistricting. The appendixes include a listing of Senate and House committees with members, a seniority list for each house, campaign finance information for every 1994 congressional race (new in this edition), a pronunciation guide for difficult names, a list of "close calls" in the election, and a list of proposed military base closings linked to the affected representatives (also new).

A new bonus feature of this edition is the inclusion of a CD-ROM that duplicates the information in the book and provides expanded district profiles. The CD-ROM uses Adobe Acrobat software and supports Macintosh, Windows, and DOS systems. It is easy to use (if one's computer has the required version of Acrobat Manager installed), but the searching limitations are disappointing. Perhaps future CD-ROM versions will utilize the technology more effectively. With or without the CD-ROM, this publication remains an essential purchase for most reference collections and is rivaled only by the Almanac of American Politics series (see ARBA 94, entry 746).—**Thomas A. Karel**

739. **The Congressional Yearbook 1993: 103rd Congress, 1st Session.** Washington, D.C., Congressional Quarterly, 1994. 352p. illus. index. $29.95; $21.95pa. ISBN 1-56802-011-2; 1-56802-009-0pa. ISSN 1079-8129.

The intended audience for this reference source is anyone interested in the makeup, operation, and legislative actions of Congress. This book is the first in an annual series that will cover issues for one session of Congress, in this case the 1st session of the 103rd Congress. The information covered in this yearbook is divided into five major areas. The introduction gives an overview of information on freshman members, women, and the Black Caucus. The second and largest part of the book deals with 12 subject areas that received legislative consideration, ranging from agriculture to transportation. Information on presidential cabinet nominations is provided, when appropriate, with each subject area listed. The third section, entitled "Inside Congress," deals with congressional issues such as ethics and campaign finance, as well as recommendations for the operation and reform of Congress. The appendix includes a glossary of congressional terms as well as Senate and House membership information. The subject index is comprehensive, with cross-references given.

This is an excellent and inexpensive single source for information on sessions of Congress, and will be useful for patrons in all high school, college, and public libraries.—**Gary E. Joseph**

740. **Lobbying, PACs, and Campaign Finance: 50 State Handbook.** 1994-95 ed. By the State Capital Law Firm Group. Eagan, Minn., West Publishing, 1994. 1061p. index. $63.50pa. ISBN 0-314-04216-4.

This 1st-edition handbook, expected to be updated annually, is intended to provide general information for those interested in state legal requirements affecting lobbying, PACs (Political Action Committees), and campaign finance. This volume is a recent example of the work of the State Capital Law Firm Group, a nonprofit corporation founded in 1989 of 50 independent law firms located in or near their respective state capitals. Their goal is to provide information on state laws on particular subjects and their interpretation and implementation by state judicial and executive agencies. The Group thus recognizes the continuing shift in lawmaking and regulation from the federal government to the states. To this end, this volume summarizes in a uniform state-by-state manner more than 40 selected topics on lobbying and campaign finance laws and ethical considerations. Each state presentation first identifies a state's code number (6 for California, 24 for Michigan, 52 for Wyoming), then the code number for a specific topic. Each state presentation then includes an overview followed by three categories—"Lobbyists and Lobbying," "Other Considerations When Dealing with Public Officials and Public Employees," and

"Campaign Finance"—each subdivided. For example, "Lobbyists and Lobbying" covers four sections on definitions; six on registration, record keeping, and reporting requirements; five on prohibited practices and penalties; and two miscellaneous sections (where to go for help—agency name, address, and telephone number; and forms used by a state). "Campaign Finance," the third category, is divided into such subcategories as contributors (with sections on who may give, how much, when, reporting the contributions, and prohibited practices) and PACs (their organization and formation, registration, and reporting). Each category furnishes a "where to go for help" section.

The handbook concludes with a reference table and a subject index. The table connects the section/chapter or other number of a state primary legal source to its location in the handbook. Many index entries list subentries. *Lobbying, PACs, and Campaign Finance* will be useful to lobbyists (who are lawyers, political consultants, consumer activists, trade association representatives, or government affairs specialists) and other civic-minded individuals interested in understanding lobbying and campaign regulation in the states and improving this process. The handbook thus should be a worthwhile purchase by law and other special libraries, and large academic and public libraries.—**Wiley J. Williams**

741. **Survey of Social Science: Government and Politics Series.** Frank N. Magill, ed. Pasadena, Calif., Salem Press, 1995. 5v. index. $375.00/set. ISBN 0-89356-745-0.

Magill's ready-reference format is familiar to most librarians. The *Government and Politics Series* is the fourth in the Survey of Social Science set, following sets on economics (see ARBA 92, entry 127), psychology (see ARBA 95, entry 782), and sociology (see entry 836). Averaging 6 pages in length, the set's 342 articles have a standard structure. Each article provides a brief definition followed by an overview (a general introduction to the topic); applications (discussions of case studies that demonstrate how the topics work in actual practice); and the context that places the subject within its broadest historical, geographical, and philosophical framework. An annotated bibliography concludes the article. All articles are signed by specialists, usually faculty members of North American universities. All in all, this set will assist most specialists in getting familiar with basic information on subjects covered in this well-edited, recommended set.—**Bohdan S. Wynar**

742. Wright, Russell O. **Presidential Elections in the United States: A Statistical History, 1860-1992.** Jefferson, N.C., McFarland, 1995. 187p. maps. $29.95. ISBN 0-89950-770-0.

This small volume presents the results of presidential elections since 1860. Between 1860 and 1948, only national figures on percentage of votes and electoral count are provided. For the elections from 1952-1992, Wright provides more information at the national, regional, and state levels. However, even for these elections, some important data are omitted, such as the turnout rates.

This appears to be less a reference volume than a collection of data designed to develop a model that will allow the prediction of future elections based on results in a few Eastern Seaboard states and a broader trend toward Republican presidential success. The work is based on regional and state analyses and trends. The predictive model suggests that the election outcome may be a Republican victory if Georgia, New Jersey, and Connecticut vote Republican. The long-term Republican trend is supported by past results and anticipated population growth.

While Wright's arguments are interesting, those looking for election data rather than his interpretation would be better advised to consult *America Votes 21* (see entry 735), the latest edition of a series published by Congressional Quarterly.—**Frank L. Wilson**

Indexes

743. **American Foreign Policy Index 1995: A Guide to Foreign Policy and Foreign Relations Publications of the U.S. Government. Volume 3, Number 2.** Bethesda, Md., Congressional Information Service, 1995. 229p. index. $995.00/yr.

AFPI, as the *American Foreign Policy Index* is generally called, is the Congressional Information Service's (CIS) attempt to cover major unclassified foreign policy publications, all printed or duplicated materials issued by the U.S. government. These publications analyze or record U.S. foreign policy, foreign relations, and relevant conditions in foreign countries. CIS minimizes overlap with their *American Statistics Index* (see ARBA 90, entry 837) and *CIS Index to Publications of the U.S. Congress* by eliminating from AFPI titles basically statistical in nature and those dealing with the deliberative process of Congress. Statistical and congressional publications with substantial analysis or policy discussion are included.

AFPI is published quarterly with a cumulated clothbound annual volume. Each issue contains two parts. The *Abstracts* volume contains the bibliographic entries with abstracts for each publication covered. The *Index* volume contains five indexes: by subjects and names, by titles, by agency report numbers, by congressional bill numbers, and by Superintendent of Documents numbers. The subjects and names section is by far the largest, with many cross-references to aid research.

A useful option by CIS is the provision, at a substantial price, of the full text of all publications included in AFPI in a companion microfiche collection. This is especially valuable for the nondepository materials. There is also a "Documents on Demand" service that sells individual microfiche or paper copies of the indexed documents. There is an extensive user guide that provides easy-to-read instruction on how to use the indexes. CIS has provided the most efficient, if not the cheapest, way to identify and locate documents related to U.S. foreign policy.—**Henry E. York**

744. **The Cumulated Indexes to the Public Papers of the Presidents of the United States: George Bush, 1989-1993.** Lanham, Md., Bernan Press, 1995. 264p. $65.00. ISBN 0-89059-028-1.

745. **The Cumulated Indexes to the Public Papers of the Presidents of the United States: Ronald Reagan, 1981-1989.** Lanham, Md., Bernan Press, 1995. 307p. $75.00. ISBN 0-89059-027-3.

The Public Papers of the Presidents series has been published by the Office of the Federal Register since 1957 in response to a recommendation from the National Historical Publications Commission to systematically collect, organize, and publish materials of U.S. presidents. The series contains a chronological compilation of papers, speeches, and writings of each president beginning with Harry S Truman. The information contained in the Public Papers series represents an important resource for scholars of U.S. history and politics. Unfortunately, a cumulative index is not published after a particular president's term in office has ended. The Cumulated Indexes series alleviates this problem by providing a comprehensive, cumulative index to accompany each set of the Public Papers series.

The Reagan administration volume is divided into two parts. The first part indexes the Public Papers series by name, and the second part indexes materials by subject. The volume covering the Bush administration includes these parts plus an additional index to materials listed under specific document categories. The categories generally refer to broad administrative topics, such as appointments, nominations, and bill vetoes. It provides access to topics otherwise buried within the subject and name indexes. The document categories index was not included in the Reagan volume because there was no corresponding indexing system contained in the Public Papers series. References to documents are identified by volume year in bold typeface, followed by a page number in each volume.

Given the importance of this resource to scholars and the fact that the Office of the Federal Register does not publish a cumulative index to accompany the Public Papers series, these and previously published cumulative indexes represent an essential supplement to a vital resources of information that documents the policies, actions, and decisionmaking framework of each U.S. presidential administration since Truman.
—**Robert V. Labaree**

746. **Reports Required by Congress, 1995. Volume 2, Number 1: Covering Executive Communications Listed in the Congressional Record January-March 1995.** Bethesda, Md., Congressional Information Service, 1995. 95p. index. $595.00pa.

Few people outside of government can appreciate the complexity of communication that takes place in the U.S. political arena. One of the least known areas of political communication is the submission to Congress of what is collectively known as Executive Communications (EC). Most of these reports must be submitted under the provisions of public laws and vary in length from 2 to 50 pages. ECs provide Congress with essential information about, among other things, the activities of agencies, commissions, programs, and federal projects as well as actions brought about under laws affecting specific agencies. For example, many agencies are required by law to submit reports with regard to actions taken under the

Freedom of Information Act. Obtaining these reports can be difficult because they are rarely published by the Government Printing Office, they are difficult to access through the Congressional Record, and the congressional committee that received them is frequently unable to distribute copies of the reports.

By compiling this index, Congressional Information Service (CIS) has opened a window into a little-known arena of political communication and administrative law. The index is published three times a year with an annual cumulative edition. Each volume contains a list of reports by accession number, a comprehensive subject index, an index under House and Senate by Executive Communication Number, and an index by statutory authority. The publication is accompanied by a microfiche collection that contains reproductions of the reports. Each entry includes the title of the report, the date it was issued, the frequency of publication, the statutory authority requiring its publication, the EC number assigned to it in the Congressional Record, the committee to which the report is assigned, and a list of descriptors assigned by CIS describing the subject of the report. The index excludes reports that are the result of legislative actions taken by the District of Columbia's city council and draft legislation proposals submitted in Congress.

Typical of other CIS titles, this publication has an easy-to-use presentation, a comprehensive index, and an informative introduction. Any institution with a large clientele interested in government, political science, administrative law, public administration, or policy studies should seriously consider adding this to their collection, because it covers a unique area of political communication and accesses information otherwise difficult to obtain independently.—**Robert V. Labaree**

Asian

747. Leifer, Michael. **Dictionary of the Modern Politics of South-East Asia.** New York, Routledge, 1995. 271p. index. $59.95. ISBN 0-415-04219-4.

The *Dictionary of the Modern Politics of South-East Asia* is a welcome addition to both political science and area studies reference books. Leifer, Southeast Asian specialist and professor of international relations at the London School of Economics and Political Science, has written an excellent guide to the politics of Southeast Asia since 1945. Leifer begins with brief essays covering each of the 10 states that comprise the region. These are followed by more than 350 alphabetically arranged entries that provide information on important people, events, political parties, and issues. From Lee Kuan Yew of Singapore to General Suchinda Krapayoon of Thailand and Corazon Aquino of the Philippines, the political names encountered in the news can be confusing. The inclusion of nearly 150 biographical entries makes the *Dictionary* a valuable guide to the political personalities of the region. Most entries are about a half-page and include cross-references. Additional access is provided by a geographical index. Leifer's suggestions for further reading provide those interested with a list of some of the best research done on the region, but it is not meant to replace the Southeast Asian volumes in the more comprehensive World Bibliographical Series of ABC-CLIO. Leifer's work supplements Scarecrow's Historical Dictionary series, providing concise information on a rapidly changing region, and updates Lawrence Ziring and C. I. Eugene Kim's *Asian Political Dictionary* (see ARBA 86, entry 662). This excellent dictionary for specialist and nonspecialist alike would have benefited from chronologies listing the events included in the text.
—**Carol L. Mitchell**

Canadian

748. **A Bibliography of Works on Canadian Foreign Relations 1986-1990.** Compiled by the Staff of the John Holmes Library. Toronto, Canadian Institute of International Affairs, 1994. 1v. (various paging). index. $45.00. ISBN 0-919084-59-1.

Fifth in a series of bibliographies published by the Canadian Institute of International Affairs, this volume contains publications issued between 1986 and 1990, although materials covered concern the period 1945-1990. Coverage may not be exhaustive although all inclusions have been examined. As with previous volumes (see ARBA 88, entry 746), the scope is broad, including both Canadian and foreign materials from the perspectives of foreign relations, defense, economic relations, foreign aid, international law, and environmental concerns. An asterisk denotes that the item is available in the other official language.

Prefaced by user guidelines, a journals listing, and a complete list of all subject headings used, the volume is divided into two primary indexes. The subject index is arranged alphabetically by subject term and cross-listed under as many terms as appropriate. Full records appear under each heading, subarranged by author/editor, with records without authors appearing first. The author/editor index that completes the bibliography also contains a full record entry. For students and researchers in all Canadian disciplines, as well as those interested in foreign affairs and international relations, this compilation is a valuable addition to the bibliography series.—**Virginia S. Fischer**

749. **Canadian Representatives Abroad.** Ottawa, Minister of Supply and Services Canada, Department of Foreign Affairs and International Trade; distr., Canada Communication Group, 1995. 1v. (various paging). $20.95pa. (U.S.). ISBN 0-660-59797-7.

750. **Diplomatic, Consular, and Other Representatives in Canada.** Ottawa, Minister of Supply and Services Canada, Department of Foreign Affairs and International Trade; distr., Canada Communication Group, 1995. 1v. (various paging). $20.95pa. (U.S.). ISBN 0-660-59798-5.

These two publications of the Canadian Department of Foreign Affairs and International Trade share a similar format and purpose in providing reference aids for government services in Canada. Text is in English and French. Current as of December 1994, each seems to be updated on at least an annual basis. As with many government publications, the emphasis is utilitarian rather than designed for popular publication, and the cover and design are reflective of this purpose.

Canadian Representatives Abroad deals with, as the title states, Canadian representation abroad and is prefaced by a brief table of contents and a list of cities with such representation. The next section alphabetically details the countries with local street or mailing address, telephone number, and a list of representatives and their positions. A similar short list of international organizations and their representatives follows. A middle section highlighted by yellow pages gives a complete alphabetical cross-listing by name and location.

Diplomatic, Consular, and Other Representatives is tricolored, with a colored section for diplomatic, consular, and international representatives in Canada. Although there is no table of contents or an index, the sections are easily distinguished. Each listing is alphabetical by country or organization as appropriate and details pertinent addresses and positions. Included in the third section is a list of national holidays as well as those celebrated federally in Canada. For users who need access to these types of federal references to Canada, both volumes are available through booksellers in that country or by mail from the Canada Communications Group.—**Virginia S. Fischer**

751. Mahler, Gregory, comp. **Contemporary Canadian Politics, 1988-1994: An Annotated Bibliography.** Westport, Conn., Greenwood Press, 1995. 204p. index. (Bibliographies and Indexes in Law and Political Science, no.23). $69.50. ISBN 0-313-28924-7.

This is a bibliography of books and articles on Canadian politics published between 1988 and 1994. It follows publication of a volume covering the years 1970 to 1987. It is limited to writings primarily concerned with government and politics, as distinct from combinations of economics and politics, sociology and politics, political histories, and biographies.

There are more than 1,500 entries, a substantial minority of which are annotated. The entries are divided into general works on Canadian politics; the Canadian constitution and legal system; federalism, finance, and public policy; regionalism and local politics; English Canada and its political culture; French Canada and Québec; public opinion and citizen participation; political parties, ideology, and elections; the executive; Parliament and the provincial legislatures; the administrative process; and foreign policy. There is also an extensive subject (but no author) index to the entries. An unusual but welcome additional feature is a compendium of Canadian studies associations and Canadian studies centers and programs throughout the world. There is also a listing of periodicals that regularly publish a substantial amount of material relating to Canadian politics.

That a bibliography covering only seven years contains such a large volume of entries demonstrates the increased activity of recent years in the field of Canadian studies. Although some of the articles and many of the books in the bibliography are intended for a wide readership, the bibliography itself primarily serves students and scholars of Canadian or comparative politics. It does so quite well and merits acquisition by academic libraries.—**Peter B. Kutner**

752. McMenemy, John. **The Language of Canadian Politics: A Guide to Important Terms and Concepts.** Waterloo, Ont., Wilfrid Laurier University Press, 1995. 322p. $29.95pa; $35.00 (U.S.). ISBN 0-88920-230-3.

A revision of the author's original 1980 work, this reference book reflects the profound changes that have occurred in the Canadian political system since that time (for example, the 1982 repatriation of the Constitution). Designed initially to meet general as well as academic needs, the revision will serve the same basic purpose in providing a concise yet comprehensive summary of terminology and basic concepts fundamental to an understanding of Canadian government and politics.

Arranged in a straightforward, alphabetical, dictionary-style format, each entry provides a succinct although complete explanatory definition averaging a paragraph in length but, in some instances, a page or more. Examples are provided to elucidate concepts and brief historical background is included for clarification. Highlighted *see* references refer the user to related or alternative entries. An alphabetical contents listing prefaces the work, so pertinent terminology can be located quickly. For political science or government students and researchers as well as those interested in any aspect of Canadian studies, this reference compilation will be an invaluable resource.—**Virginia S. Fischer**

European

General Works

753. **Guide to the Community Initiatives 1994-99.** Brussels, Office for Official Publications of the European Communities; distr., Lanham, Md., UNIPUB, 1994. 104p. maps. $10.00pa. ISBN 92-826-8437-7.

The European Union's (EU) (formerly the European Communities) Commission adopted guidelines for the allocation of the Union's regional development funds for the period 1994-1999. These funds are designed to reduce regional economic differences within the EU. The funds represent one of the EU's major financial undertakings.

This guide provides a summary of these initiatives. It is designed for potential beneficiaries of the Commission's initiatives. The guide includes an explanation of the general priorities and objectives for the initiatives. It also provides a summary of the background to each of them and their goals. It gives the full text of the Commission's guidelines for the 13 programs and provides telephone and fax numbers for the directorates responsible for each of the initiatives.

This document will be useful only to a small handful of specialists in the EU's regional policies. In most cases, it will be needed only in depository libraries that receive full collections of EU publications.
—**Frank L. Wilson**

754. **Interinstitutional Directory: European Union.** Brussels, Office for Official Publications of the European Communities; distr., Lanham, Md., UNIPUB, 1994. 332p. maps. index. $25.00pa. ISBN 92-826-9029-6.

This directory provides telephone numbers for European Union (EU) personnel, members of the European Parliament, and member countries' permanent representatives. The listings are given by institution. A name index and a comprehensive table of contents by organization provide access to the appropriate individual or office. Brief summaries of the institutions and their responsibilities precede each institution's listings. The directory covers information through fall 1994 and includes the names and telephone numbers of the newly elected European Parliament.

This is a hard copy of the EU's online interinstitutional directory IDEA, which offers even more up-to-date information. (Unfortunately, the section that explains access to the online service, along with the first 30 pages of the directory, were omitted from the review copy.) Given this high-tech approach, it is unfortunate that the directory does not include e-mail addresses. Still, this is a useful guide for research libraries and libraries serving those involved in international business.—**Frank L. Wilson**

755. **Official Journal of the European Communities. Volume 38: Legislation.** English ed. Brussels, Office for Official Publications of the European Communities; distr., Lanham, Md., UNIPUB, 1995. 935p. $25.00pa.

This is volume L 142 of the "L" series of the European Communities (EC) *Official Journal*. The series publishes all EC legislation. It still uses the "European Communities" terminology despite the Maastricht Treaty's alteration of the name to European Union (EU). According to *The European Communities Encyclopedia and Directory 1992* (see ARBA 92, entry 71), the other two series contain draft legislation; information and notices (the "C" series); and notices for staff vacancies, tenders, and the like (the "S" series).

As a reference source, the individual issue is not of great interest unless one happens to have a clientele interested in the specific legislation it promulgates—a Commission regulation amending and repealing various other regulations relating to the Common Customs Tariff of the EU. Even then, commercial update services are likely to be more user friendly for many purposes. This work contains no prefatory materials; nothing appears but the text of the legislation itself, apart from sales information on the back cover. The series will be of interest to larger research libraries in law or government documents where client interest balanced against costs justify an original legislative series from this important supranational legislation.—**Nigel Tappin**

756. **Political Leaders of Contemporary Western Europe: A Biographical Dictionary.** David Wilsford, ed. Westport, Conn., Greenwood Press, 1995. 514p. index. $115.00. ISBN 0-313-28623-X.

This volume contains 71 biographical essays on politicians in postwar Europe. Subjects come from 14 of the 15 European Union countries and Norway. Contributors are academics with affiliations in the United States and Europe. The articles are arranged alphabetically from Konrad Adenauer through Harold Wilson with the leaders also listed by country. Darkly influential figures, such as Jean-Marie Le Pen, are included. Papers average just under seven pages. One anomaly is the short (three-page) entry for the colorful Bavarian Franz-Josef Strauss. Brief bibliographies are appended. Many entries sampled seem detailed and make fascinating reading. François Mitterrand's biography, for example, accurately matches this reviewer's memories of his career as reflected in the "Le Monde" section of the *Manchester Guardian Weekly* from 1977 to the present. There is also an introductory essay on influential theories of leadership by the editor. The leaders are also listed by country.

The selection of subjects is a difficult and thankless task. Thus, Winston Churchill was excluded as a politician whose main impact was prior to 1945, while Neil Kinnock was included among the few British politicians, presumably because he started the reform of the Labour Party in order to restore it as a credible party of government. Why was John XXIII discussed, but not John Paul II? On the whole, however, the selection is a good one.

There is an index, but it does not seem to be complete—odd in this age of computer-assisted indexing. For example, the entry for Helmut Kohl lists his profile, with references to those on Hans-Dietrich Genscher, Ruud Lubbers, and Helmut Schmidt, but not those on Mitterand or Strauss. This work should be purchased by research libraries with the relevant client interests and other large libraries if budgets permit.—**Nigel Tappin**

757. **Political Parties of Eastern Europe, Russia, and the Successor States.** 2d ed. Bogdan Szajkowski, ed. Harlow, England, Longman Group and New York, Stockton Press, 1994. 735p. index. $195.00. ISBN 1-56159-079-7.

The 2d edition of this British imprint is somewhat enlarged, including dates on 1,435 parties and movements covering, in alphabetical order, all countries in Eastern and Southern Europe plus countries of the former Soviet Union located in Asia. In examining the coverage of Ukraine written by Andrew Wilson of Sidney Sussex College, University of Cambridge, one finds the account to be concise and well written. It opens with a brief historical note about development of political parties in Ukraine, followed by a statistical table on party representation in the 1990 and 1994 parliaments. There is a directory of various parties and movements including minorities (e.g., the Christian Democratic Alliance of Romanians in Ukraine [CDARU]). All in all, it is a useful compilation for the uninitiated.—**Bohdan S. Wynar**

British

758. Butler, David, and Gareth Butler. **British Political Facts 1900-1994.** 7th ed. New York, St. Martin's Press, 1994. 541p. index. $49.95. ISBN 0-312-12147-4.

Historians, political scientists, and other people interested in twentieth-century Great Britain will enthusiastically greet the appearance of the 7th edition of this valuable reference work. Updated to 1994, its true scope of coverage extends well beyond narrow political concerns. Aside from lists of government ministries, parties, elections, and the civil service, it also supplies detailed information about social conditions, the economy, the royal family, the media, and religion. One particularly interesting chapter deals with political allusions by providing lists of famous political place-names, quotations, scandals, civil disturbances, and assassinations.

Those familiar with earlier editions (see ARBA 87, entry 692) will find the basic organization to be the same, although the chapters on the economy and the public sector have been expanded. A brief bibliography lists other reference works on twentieth-century Great Britain, while a modest general index supplements the volume's detailed table of contents. Readers seeking more current information will still need to consult the annual *Whitaker's Almanack* (see entry 6).—**Ronald H. Fritze**

759. Lawrance, Alan, and Peter Dodd. **Anthony Eden, 1897-1977: A Bibliography.** Westport, Conn., Greenwood Press, 1995. 190p. index. (Bibliographies of British Statesmen, no.20). $75.00. ISBN 0-313-28286-2.

Anthony Eden is perhaps best known as the British prime minister during the Suez Crisis of 1956, although his public career began in 1931 with the British foreign secretariat. This new bibliography provides a narrative overview and a handy chronology of Eden's life and career. The bibliographical section covers manuscript and archival collections of Eden's papers and official British government publications relevant to his career, as well as Eden's own published writings (with selected reviews of Eden's books included).

The majority of the bibliography is composed of books and articles written about Eden. A chapter is devoted solely to Eden biographies; each entry provides a brief annotation. The remaining chapters divide Eden's public career into phases, with nearly 40 pages of references on the Suez Crisis. There are nearly 800 entries in the book, with author and subject indexes appended and keyed to the numbered entries.

This bibliography will be most appropriate for college and university libraries that support graduate programs in British history and politics or in international relations. The selection and presentation of the material meets the normally high quality expected in a Greenwood Press book.—**Thomas A. Karel**

760. Mieder, Wolfgang, and George B. Bryan, comps. **The Proverbial Winston S. Churchill: An Index to Proverbs in the Works of Sir Winston Churchill.** Westport, Conn., Greenwood Press, 1995. 434p. (Bibliographies and Indexes in World History, no.38). $79.50. ISBN 0-313-29433-X.

This book is an obvious labor of love by two Churchill devotees and will be best appreciated by those readers with similar interests. Churchill, the former British prime minister, was both an eloquent public speaker and a prolific writer who made great use of proverbs in his speeches and writings. Mieder and Bryan (both of the University of Vermont) contributed a 93-page essay on Churchill and the proverb, which is filled with many examples taken from Churchill's writings. They provide an itemized listing of the editions of Churchill's writings used in this book—965 specific pieces are identified and numbered consecutively.

The heart of this book is a keyword index to the proverbs used by Churchill. This arrangement allows the user to locate the proverbs by using a specific subject approach. Each proverb is linked to two citations: The first refers to the piece of Churchill's writing that alludes to the proverb (with a page number and date); the second refers to a standard reference source where the complete proverb can be located. The reference sources include the Bible, six major collections of proverbs (such as *The Oxford Dictionary of English Proverbs* [3d ed.; see ARBA 72, entry 1330] and *A Dictionary of American Proverbs* [see ARBA 93, entry 1299]), and a dozen additional dictionaries and quotation books. Appended to the index are several frequency and distribution tables, which only a fanatic Churchillian would consult. Although this is a specialized reference work, it may be appropriate for upper-level rhetoric collections as well as for libraries with a strong interest in Churchill.—**Thomas A. Karel**

Irish

761. Flackes, W. D., and Sydney Elliott. **Northern Ireland: A Political Directory 1968-1993.** rev. ed. Belfast, Blackstaff Press; distr., Chester Springs, Pa., Dufour, 1994. 513p. index. $29.00pa. ISBN 0-85640-527-2.

Northern Ireland: A Political Directory is 513 pages of detailed and sometimes intriguing documentation on the 25 years since the beginning of the area's present troubles. This 4th edition reference work—first published in 1980 (see ARBA 82, entry 525)—is a credit to its authors. Presented here is a chronology of events since 1968; an alphabetical dictionary of people, parties, organizations, and key places; an account of election results; full descriptions of the government and the security systems; and a comprehensive index section. The chronology section covering 1968-93 offers a helpful preliminary sketch of the years from 1921 to 1967, giving key events that helped shape both modern Northern Ireland and the Irish State. Beginning with Terence O'Neill's television interview on March 25, 1968, his fifth anniversary as prime minister of Northern Ireland, the reader gets an in-depth chronology of hundreds of political and sectarian events up to December 31, 1993.

In the dictionary section, we learn the back- and foreground of individuals such as Gerry Adams, Ian Paisley, John Hume, and many more. Even a quick glance at the amount of space allotted to certain names clearly indicates the importance of these players in this 25-year drama. Events, organizations, and key places are described, offering a much-needed guide to interested outsiders. Anyone confused about political parties and affiliations can find information at a glance. The deeds of all sides are objectively presented in a scholarly and reportorial way, the result of scholar Elliott and journalist Flackes's collaboration. The section on election results offers statistics and general commentary on local, district, Westminster, and European Parliamentary races for these years. The systems of government and security systems sections, respectively, offer an overview of the origins of Northern Ireland and the Republic as states, and a clear picture of the prisons, police, military and paramilitary, special powers, courts, internment, intelligence agencies, and security statistics. This book is a must for anyone seeking a source of factual information on Northern Ireland objectively presented and precise in its definition of political positions and personages.—**Arthur Gribben**

Spanish

762. **The Treaties of the War of the Spanish Succession: An Historical and Critical Dictionary.** Linda Frey and Marsha Frey, eds. Westport, Conn., Greenwood Press, 1995. 576p. index. $125.00. ISBN 0-313-27884-9.

The War of the Spanish Succession, instigated by the death of Spain's last Habsburg King Carlos II, convulsed Europe and portions of North America between the years 1702 and 1714. This compilation profiles important individuals and events influencing this protracted conflict. An introduction opens with an overview of the issues and results of this war. The principal contents feature a dictionary of pertinent individuals and events involved in this particular conflict. Entries are included for subjects such as Queen Anne of Great Britain, the Battle of Blenheim, Canada, King Charles XII of Sweden, the five Iroquois nations, Montréal, Rio de Janeiro, the Treaty of Ryswick, Jonathan Swift, and Utrecht. These are written by the editors and other scholars, feature cross-references to other entries, and provide a select bibliography. A more detailed bibliography is furnished at the end of the volume.

This effort will serve as a helpful introduction for those wishing to study this important conflict, which had international impact. Each entry is well written, and the multilingual bibliographical entries are helpful, as are the Spanish Succession chart and the chronological timeline of this conflict at the end of the volume. The exorbitant price, unfortunately, will deter many libraries from purchasing this valuable source.—**Bert Chapman**

Latin American and Caribbean

763. Camp, Roderic Ai. **Mexican Political Biographies, 1935-1993.** 3d ed. Austin, Tex., University of Texas Press, 1995. 985p. $75.00; $24.95pa. ISBN 0-292-71174-3; 0-292-71181-6pa.

This 3d edition provides nearly 2,000 brief biographical sketches of Mexican political figures prominent since 1935. The 1st edition, printed in 1976, contained approximately 900 entries, and the 2d (1982) edition provided 1,350 entries. Significant updates have been made to many of the original entries. The author used more than 200 sources to identify and update this information. The criteria for inclusion combined using Frank Brandenberg's top six levels of political prestige outlined in *Making of Modern Mexico* (1964) and cross-referencing of data from at least two sources.

This book is a continuation of the author's 1991 book entitled *Mexican Political Biographies 1884-1934*. Both books, organized in the same manner, contain such information as birth date; birthplace; education; elective and party positions; appointive governmental and private positions; interest group activities; parents, spouses, and friends; military experience; and additional sources of information. Ten helpful appendixes provide a chronological list of Supreme Court justices; senators; federal deputies; directors of federal departments, agencies, and banks; major ambassadorial posts; governors; rectors of the national universities; national executive committees of the Partido Nacional Revolucionario (PNR), the Partido de la Revolución Mexicana (PRM), and the Partido Revolucionario Institucional (PRI); presidents of major parties; and secretaries-general of large labor organizations. This excellent, up-to-date, ready-reference book includes reliable biographical information that is extremely difficult to locate, and is highly recommended for large public and academic libraries.—**Karen Y. Stabler**

Middle Eastern

764. **The Middle East.** 8th ed. Daniel C. Diller, ed. Washington, D.C., Congressional Quarterly, 1994. 432p. illus. maps. index. $42.95; $29.95pa. ISBN 1-56802-038-4; 0-87187-999-9pa.

The title under review can be categorized as an encyclopedia, due to the wide variety of information and numerous section headings found within it. The text is explanatory, and not just an arrangement of miscellaneous facts. While not containing as much directory or statistical data as Europa's *The Middle East and North Africa* (see entry 160), this edition does provide more up-to-date information than the U.S. Army's *Country Study* series. There are chapters on the Arab-Israeli conflict, the Gulf War, Mideast oil, U.S. policies for the area, and a history of Islam. Biographical sketches of important political figures are in the appendixes, along with reprints of 13 relevant documents, such as "Israeli-Palestinian Declaration of Principles." An individual country profile includes a line map, a picture of the country's leader, a few key facts, a brief history of the country, a section on the economy and national security, and a final portion that looks ahead to the future of the country. For most nations in that volatile region, the outlook is cloudy and uncertain. With 19 maps, a 6-page bibliography, 7 statistical tables (6 of them on oil), photographs, and an index, the hardbound edition also comes with a full chronology of events for 1900-1994 (the paperback edition has only an abbreviated version). What is lacking is a list of acronyms and abbreviations. Diller previously edited *Russia and the Independent States* (1992) for Congressional Quarterly. This is an easy-to-read book that is recommended for high school, public, and academic libraries. (The 7th edition was reviewed in ARBA 92, entry 724.)—**Daniel K. Blewett**

765. **Political Parties of the Middle East and North Africa.** Frank Tachau, ed. Westport, Conn., Greenwood Press, 1994. 711p. index. (Greenwood Historical Encyclopedia of the World's Political Parties). $125.00. ISBN 0-313-26649-2.

The presence of politics is widespread, as the present volume makes painfully apparent. Its design is to present as exhaustive a compendium of information regarding the evolution, impact, formation, and interactions of said political parties as possible. The volume is a trove of information both current and historical.

Middle East is defined as countries lying between Morocco to the west and Iran to the east, north of the Sahara Desert, and south and east of the Mediterranean Sea, including Turkey. The volume does not contain descriptions of political parties in Afghanistan, Pakistan, countries in the Horn of Africa, or central or west Africa.

The arrangement is alphabetical. Each entry begins with a brief history that covers more than just the political, but also the geographical and social. Tables regarding certain votes, party makeups, election results, and so forth round out the entries. Each historical description ends with a bibliography. This is immediately followed by an alphabetical listing of the country's political parties (with internal cross-referencing), accompanied by narrative descriptions where appropriate. Appendix 1 consists of a chronology of political events for all countries, while appendix 2 provides readers with a genealogy of each listed party. An ample index makes searching easy.

Each entry is signed, and the entries average about 30 pages each. The tone of the volume is erudite, but even novices will benefit much from its use. While the volume is decidedly reference in nature, libraries may wish to purchase two as use of the volume will require considerable reflection. Of course with the price of the volume, many libraries will have to forego what is surely one of the best reference tools in its class.—**Mark Y. Herring**

IDEOLOGIES

766. Button, John. **The Radicalism Handbook: Radical Activists, Groups, and Movements of the Twentieth Century.** Santa Barbara, Calif., ABC-CLIO, 1995. 460p. index. $49.50. ISBN 0-87436-838-3.

This text opens with a lengthy and insightful essay on "Radicalism in the Twentieth Century," followed by a chapter of brief biographies on 38 pre-1900 intellectual extremists. The next section comprises the majority of the work—page-length profiles of 380-plus sociopolitical twentieth-century figures. A briefer chapter follows, describing radical groups and movements. The text concludes with an extraneous appendix simply entitled "Other Notable American Radicals," and other appendixes categorizing the book's personal subjects by country and activity (e.g., Tibet, suffragists).

While many of the people and topics covered are predictable—Emma Goldman, environmentalists, the Yippies—the book's value is in its inclusion of lesser-known figures and groups. Dozens of such obscure organizations as the antinuclear Livermore Action Group and the self-help Sarvodaya Movement are given generous, cogent descriptions. All entries are followed by bibliographic references for further information. There is a single index for all of the book's sections.

This volume updates *The Cassell Handbook of Radicalism*. The author is a longtime environmental activist. The book's political range is limited to what is generally considered to be the liberal/left-wing spectrum. Elements of the conservative/right-wing spectrum (e.g., survivalists, paramilitary groups, Aryan nation members, fervent antiabortionists) are not included in this text. Representation of the full political spectrum would have made this an invaluable resource. As it is, this text is still appropriate for academic and large public libraries, especially those lacking liberal/leftist journal collections, where information about such people and groups may otherwise be found.—**Ed Volz**

767. **Radicalism in Minnesota 1900-1960: A Survey of Selected Sources.** By the 20th-Century Radicalism in Minnesota Project. Carl Ross, Project Director. St. Paul, Minn., Minnesota Historical Society Press, 1994. 109p. illus. index. $17.95pa. ISBN 0-87351-307-X.

Minnesota has a rich tradition of left-wing labor, farm, and farm-labor movements that have influenced American radical thought and action over the past 125 years. The Minnesota Project of the Minnesota Historical Society has compiled a description of nearly a thousand sources on twentieth-century radicalism in Minnesota. A broad range of radical causes is covered, from communism to labor unions to ethnic groups. The bibliography also covers literature and materials from opponents to radical causes.

The types of materials covered include pamphlets, newspapers, periodicals, oral histories, manuscript collections, sound and visual materials, articles and books, and unpublished papers. Entries provide summaries of the nature of the item or collection, background on the group or individual involved, and the archive location. A comprehensive index allows researchers to find references to a group, individual, or publication that is described in the main listings. This is a specialized bibliography but one that is important because of the key role Minnesotans have played in American radicalism.—**Frank L. Wilson**

INTERNATIONAL ORGANIZATIONS

768. **Directory of Community Legislation in Force and Other Acts of the Community Institutions.** Brussels, Office for Official Publications of the European Communities; distr., Lanham, Md., UNIPUB, 1994. 2v. index. $135.00pa./set. ISBN 92-77-82774-2.

The European Union (EU) has developed a vast body of laws and regulations. This directory is designed to assist lawyers and others to locate agreements and conventions; legislation in the form of regulations, decisions, and recommendations; and important nonbinding acts in force as of December 1994. Each entry provides brief information on the content, nature, and date of the legislation. They give citations that allow the user to find the legislative action in the appropriate *Official Journal of the European Communities* (distr. by UNIPUB) and on the CELEX, the EU's computerized online source for all its legal order. Because the descriptions of the individual pieces of legislation are brief and sometimes cryptic, the directory is useful only as a guide to locating legislation that is already known by the user. The directory includes a master list arranged by subject matter and supplementary indexes based on chronological order and alphabetical listing of the act's title. This directory will be of use to libraries serving the needs of international lawyers and businesspeople.—**Frank L. Wilson**

769. **Directory of United Nations Information Sources.** 5th ed. Compiled by the Advisory Committee for the Co-ordination of Information Systems. New York, United Nations, 1994. 574p. index. $45.00pa. ISBN 92-1-100681-3. ISSN 1014-8035. S/N GV.E.94.0.14.

The 5th edition of this directory updates earlier editions with variant titles, including *Directory of United Nations Databases and Information Services* (4th ed., United Nations, 1990) and *Directory of United Nations Databases and Information Systems* (see ARBA 86, entry 706). It also incorporates information previously published in *Directory of Applications Software of the United Nations System* (see ARBA 92, entry 736). The new edition covers information services, databases, and software provided by 36 organizations of the UN system. Each color-coded section is arranged in broad subject categories. Subject, organization, and name indexes are also provided.

Entries in the yellow "Information Services" section provide name, organization, contact person, description, holdings, subject scope, and services available to specific categories of users. Because the names of some services are generic-sounding or unfamiliar to someone outside the organization, the indexes are essential. Although the indexes include geographic locations for some services, a geographic index or other means of access to services by location would be useful. The number of entries in this section has increased from 325 in the 4th edition to 450 in this edition, and includes more UNESCO offices/libraries and UN information centers in various countries.

Entries in the blue "Databases" section furnish database name, organization, contact person, description, subject scope, availability/distribution media, and printed products. Listings of online hosts and CD-ROMs refer to entries for specific databases. Separate listings provide addresses for online hosts and CD-ROM producers. The number of databases covered has increased from 547 to 605 in this new edition. Entries in the green "Software" section cover software name, organization, contact person, description, user support, system requirements, and cost. The number of software packages covered has increased from 81 in the previously separate directory to 137 in this newly combined one.

This directory has improved in several ways since previous editions: format, typography, information provided in entries, inclusion of information services in more countries, and addition of the section on software. The principal weakness is a lack of geographic access by separate index or other means. Because ACCIS was discontinued in 1993, the future of this directory is in doubt.—**Carol Wheeler**

770. **A Guide to Information at the United Nations.** New York, Department of Public Information/United Nations, 1995. 119p. index. $9.95pa. ISBN 92-1-100542-6. S/N E.95.I.4.

This basic guide is designed to assist the media, researchers, nongovernmental organizations, and others in finding information on a particular aspect of the work of the United Nations. It provides brief descriptions of the work and structure of the UN's agencies, departments, and programs. The main body is divided into three parts. The first includes 12 entries covering the UN Secretariat and other offices (e.g., the Department of Peace-keeping Operations, the Department of Public Information). The second part contains 25 entries covering UN programs and other bodies (e.g., the 5 regional commissions, the UN Environment Programme, the International Court of Justice). The third part lists 16 entries covering specialized agencies and other organizations (e.g., UNESCO, the World Trade Organization).

All entries provide administrator's name and country, general mandate, programs, information products, and contact information. Entries in the second and third parts also generally furnish a list of major publications (title, frequency, languages, price [if applicable]) and a pie chart showing estimated percentages of expenditures in major areas. Completing the work is an annex consisting of a list of acronyms, a chart of the UN System, and an index. The index provides a selective list of primary subject areas in which various bodies are involved, and provides the acronym and page number for the body's entry. The subject terms in the index are not always specifically mentioned in the entry.

This guide does not cover all the working bodies of the UN. Researchers, diplomats, and others needing detailed information on the current membership, mandate, and structure of all the organizations within the UN System will still need to consult the New Zealand Ministry of Foreign Affairs and Trade's annual *United Nations Handbook*. Nevertheless, anyone needing subject access and basic information will find this attractively formatted new guide useful.—**Carol Wheeler**

771. **Index to Proceedings of the Economic and Social Council. Organizational Session—1992. Substantive Session—1992.** New York, United Nations, 1995. 155p. (Dag Hammarskjold Library Bibliographical Series, no.E.69). $25.00pa. ISBN 92-1-100553-1. ISSN 0082-8084. S/N E.95.I.13.

This annual bibliographical guide indexes the proceedings and documentation of the United Nations Economic and Social Council (see ARBA 92, entry 739, for review of an earlier edition). Its format is identical to previous editions and also mirrors indexes produced for the General Assembly, the Security Council, and the Trusteeship Council. The only difference between this and previous editions is this one reflects changes in the Economic and Social Council's pattern of meetings (locations, dates, and structure) instituted in 1992.

The index is arranged in three sections. The first covers sessional information, including members, terms of office, officers, and rules of procedure. For each session, the second section provides a checklist of meetings; agenda; a subject index; and three indexes to speeches (by corporate names/countries, speakers, and subjects). The third section lists resolutions adopted, documents issued, and reports forwarded to the Council by the sessional committees assigned to work on specific topics.

This index is important for Model UN students and all others who need to use documentation from the Economic and Social Council. By providing UN document symbols, it allows researchers to find the documents they need in paper UN documents collections or in the Readex microfiche collection *United Nations Documents and Publications*. Chadwyck-Healey's new *UNBIS Plus on CD-ROM* (1994) provides electronic access to the UN database from which this printed index is produced. It remains to be seen whether the search capabilities of the CD-ROM product can replicate all the features of the printed index and in a more timely fashion.—**Carol Wheeler**

772. **Revenue Statistics of OECD Member Countries 1965-1993. Statistiques des Recettes Publiques des Pays Membres de L'OCDE.** Washington, D.C., OECD Publications, 1994. 255p. $50.00pa. ISBN 92-64-04176-1.

This annual statistical publication provides data on the tax levels and structures of the 24 (as of 1993) member countries of the Organization for Economic Cooperation and Development (OECD). Most data are taken from statistical publications of the individual national governments. Data are generally shown in national currencies and cover selected years between the years 1965 and 1992 or 1975 and 1992. Data are not provided for all countries for all years. Diskettes containing the data in this publication are available separately.

As in previous editions, the data are presented in eight parts, with effective access provided by a detailed table of contents. The first part contains a series of charts comparing the tax levels and structures of the different countries. The second part provides a detailed explanation of the OECD tax classification system and its relationship to the United Nations' System of National Accounts, the European Communities' European System of Integrated Economic Accounts, and the International Monetary Fund's (IMF) system. The next three parts contain detailed tax revenue data for different years. The sixth part attributes 1992 tax revenues to the subsectors (supranational; federal or central; provincial, regional, or state; local; and social security funds) of the general government. The seventh part presents data from the IMF's *Government Finance Statistics Yearbook* on nontax revenue, capital revenue, and grants. The final part is an overview of tax revenues, nontax revenues, and grants.

This is an important and well-formatted source for revenue data. Anyone needing data on a country not belonging to the OECD will need to consult the UN's *National Account Statistics* (see ARBA 95, entry 254) or the IMF's *Government Finance Statistics Yearbook*. Both of these sources cover more countries but present generally less detailed revenue data in a different format.—**Carol Wheeler**

773. Williams, Phil, comp. **North Atlantic Treaty Organization.** New Brunswick, N.J., Transaction Publishers, 1994. 283p. index. (International Organizations Series, v.8). $69.95. ISBN 1-56000-154-2.

This selective bibliography provides annotations for 899 English-language books, journal articles, research reports, and the like about the North Atlantic Treaty Organization (NATO). In addition, there is an unannotated listing of 100 doctoral dissertations written between 1958 and 1991. A separate listing of 13 congressional documents supplements the small number of government documents included in the main annotated bibliography. A list of acronyms, a chronology, and separate author, title, and subject indexes complete the volume.

The main body of this work is the annotated bibliography. It is divided into 19 subject categories, with further subdivisions in some by date, geography, or type of strategy. The well-written annotations provide useful information on content and perspective. In a few instances, Williams includes works with negative annotations because those works represent a perspective that contributed to debate at the time written.

There are a few shortcomings in the work. A few acronyms appearing in annotations are not provided in the list of acronyms. The computer's ordering of titles beginning with "NATO" and "NATO's" is a problem in the title index. There are a few errors in titles, authors, publishers, and places of publication, including the baffling movement of all Yale University Press publications from Connecticut to New Jersey. It would also have been useful to supply a section for bibliographies about NATO. Neither Garland's 1985 unannotated but comprehensive bibliography *NATO: A Bibliography and Resource Guide* (see ARBA 86, entry 711) nor Senate Print 101-37, *NATO at 40*, prepared in 1989 by the Congressional Research Service, are listed.

In spite of those few shortcomings, this is an excellent work. The layout and typography are effective and easy to read, and the indexing provides good access. However, most important of all, the selection of works included and the well-written annotations make this a useful reference work for anyone doing research on NATO.—**Carol Wheeler**

INTERNATIONAL RELATIONS

774. **Index to Documents of the National Security Council.** Bethesda, Md., University Publications of America, 1994. 721p. $450.00. ISBN 0-89093-994-2.

This book indexes two valuable series of documents on microfilm from the same publisher: *Documents of the National Security Council* (1947-1977, through the 4th supplement) and *Minutes of Meetings of the National Security Council* (original and 1st supplement). This series makes available for research collections all United States National Security Council (NSC) documents that have become public through the Freedom of Information Act. Further volumes of the index are projected to cover later issues of the microfilm series.

The prefatory material provides brief descriptions of the various sorts of NSC materials available in the series, along with an explanation of the codes used to reference locations by series or supplement, reel, and frame. They also contain a list of abbreviations used for security classifications of the documents, from "Confidential" through "Top Secret/Sensitive," and a source note. The main body of the index is divided into 13 sections by category of document, from NSC policy papers through presidential review memoranda, and from presidential directives to NSC directives. Each of these sections has a brief introduction to that specific category of papers.

The entries themselves contain title and authorship information, NSC classification numbers, length and date of publication and declassification, a long paragraph-length descriptive annotation, related documents, and references or subject headings. These last items are used in the subject index. Thus, there are not only subject access and solid annotations to aid the scholarly researcher, but also *see* references to related documents. In sum, this is an important access tool for this major research series. Research collections that own the microfilm should strongly consider purchasing it.—**Nigel Tappin**

775. Lapin, Lee. **The Whole Spy Catalog.** San Mateo, Calif., Intelligence Incorporated; distr., Chicago, Independent Publishers Group, 1995. 426p. illus. index. $44.95pa. ISBN 1-880231-10-7.

This entertaining and intriguing compilation purports to be the result of a mysterious desert encounter between Central Intelligence Agency agents and librarians en route to an online searching conference. The result of this encounter was an exchange of information-finding perspectives by each of these professional groups. The range of material in this compilation is impressive. Topics covered include information on locating and investigating individuals, genealogy and adoption searches, books on intelligence and intelligence services, data on researching through DIALOG and the Internet, private detectives, video surveillance, telephone tapping, security specialists, and nocturnal surveillance. Entries within individual chapters feature bibliographic annotations for books, organizational addresses, photographs, illustrations, prices for individual items, and technical descriptions of paraphernalia described. Most material related to normal library information gathering is quite useful.

Unfortunately, this work has problems. There is no way of independently verifying that the CIA or other intelligence officers actually contributed material to this compilation, or of determining the validity of such material in relation to actual intelligence practice and operations. Placing real or purported information about bugging individuals, illicit telephone tapping, and computer hacking in a publicly accessible book for the ready consumption of unstable individuals is a major ethical problem the author and publisher should soberly consider. Publication of such information can and does have negative consequences on legitimate governmental operations, law enforcement officials, and individuals with the misfortune of being targeted by illegal surveillance operations.—**Bert Chapman**

776. Tarragó, Rafael E. **Early U.S.-Hispanic Relations 1776-1860: An Annotated Bibliography.** Metuchen, N.J., Scarecrow, 1994. 171p. index. $25.00. ISBN 0-8108-2882-0.

Tarragó has written a useful annotated bibliography of important works on relations between the fledgling United States and its Central and South American sister states. The period covered, 1776 to 1860, is significant because of a growing U.S. concern with restricting the influence of European powers in the Western Hemisphere (i.e., the Monroe Doctrine).

While Tarragó's work is a slight volume with fewer than 800 citations, it fills an important niche in the relationships between the United States and its southern neighbors. The organizational structure of the book tends to be a compromise between a chronology and a subject interpretation. Some cross-referencing would be desirable to allow overlaps that should bring together important themes and perspectives. This would assist users as they utilize the subject index, or identify an important item that is related to another citation in the bibliography. There are a few typographical errors in the book. One in particular on the second page of the table of contents is quite glaring.

This type of printed bibliography may still be justified because of its newness and first-time compilation of important sources. However, included information should find its way into standard online catalogs and bibliographic databases. The work is recommended for large academic libraries and specialized collections on United States-Latin American relations and history.—**Roberto P. Haro**

PUBLIC POLICY AND ADMINISTRATION

777. **APELL Annotated Bibliography.** New York, United Nations Environment Programme Industry and Environment/United Nations, 1994. 117p. index. (Technical Report no.21). $25.00pa. ISBN 92-807-1411-2. S/N E.94.III.D.10.

This bibliography is one of a series of reports distributed by the United Nations Environment Programme Industry and Environment (UNEP IE) Centre. It serves as a supplement to an earlier publication entitled *Awareness and Environment for Emergencies at Local Level (APELL): A Process for Responding to Technological Accidents* (United Nations Environment Programme, 1988), and provides readers with a listing of works pertaining to emergency planning for hazardous incidents. Titles listed in the bibliography were published in English, Spanish, or French between the years 1980 and 1992. Included are ". . . books, articles, pamphlets, monographs, guidelines, seminar and conference proceedings, and case studies . . ." (p. ix).

The publication is divided into eight sections beginning with "Basic Documents" and concluding with "Other Bibliographies." Entries are arranged alphabetically by title within each of the sections. Listings are first by English titles, then French, and finally Spanish works. Citations and annotations are in the language of the publication. Altogether, there are 209 citations; this is broken down into 173 English, 34 Spanish, and 2 French works. The works in English represent publications from Australia, Canada, the United Kingdom, and the United States.

Access to the bibliography is through a table of contents and several indexes for author, corporate author, and title. There are also an acronyms index and a listing of publishers with their addresses. The bibliography has well-written annotations and an easy-to-use arrangement. Although it is for a specialized topic, it should be a useful reference work for libraries with extensive collections in the areas of the environment, hazardous materials, and emergency planning.—**Robert Logsdon**

778. **The Librarian's Guide to Public Records.** special ed. Tempe, Ariz., BRB, 1995. 299p. (The Public Record Research Library). $39.00pa. ISBN 1-879792-23-0.

This is a directory of public records housed in county courts and recorder's offices, state agencies, and federal courts. Section 1 contains county records; section 2, state records; and section 3, federal records. Information on felonies, misdemeanors, landlord/tenant actions, and civil judgments, among other records types, can be accessed at the county level. Driving records, vital records, and pertinent data on the Uniform Commercial Code can be found in state repositories. The federal records section lists locations where public record documents are held, including U.S. District Courts, U.S. Bankruptcy Courts, U.S. Courts of Appeals, and Federal Records Centers. A chart alerts the reader to state regulations governing access to public records; another chart cross-references states to their corresponding Circuit, Appeals Court, and Federal Record Center.

There are extensive listings. More than 11,500 locations are mentioned; no state or county is left out. Each location is accompanied by addresses, telephone numbers, office hours, and types of records available. The information provided is valuable, but limited; those who seek a full description of records at each site, and detailed instructions on how to use them, should consult other Public Record Research Library publications. Nor are the listings absolutely complete. While the Federal Records Center at Suitland, Maryland is noted, the Washington, D.C. address of the National Archives is not. A quick-reference only, the *Librarian's Guide to Public Records* will be useful for businesspeople, insurance investigators, and lawyers. Scholars will receive somewhat less benefit. The work is recommended for public libraries.
—**Richard E. Holl**

14 Psychology and Parapsychology

PSYCHOLOGY

Dictionaries and Encyclopedias

779. Lewis, James R. **The Dream Encyclopedia.** Detroit, Gale, 1995. 416p. illus. index. $49.95. ISBN 0-7876-0155-1.

This work presents brief articles on some 250 topics, from adaptive therapy and astral projections to Zulu and Zuni myths. Each entry contains a brief listing of sources for further reading and, where applicable, relevant cross-references to other citations within this work are highlighted in boldface. In addition to the main encyclopedia, a short introductory overview of dream and sleep research and a subject index are included. Also provided is a list of "dream resources," with the names and addresses of many of the organizations now focusing on the study of dreams and sleep research. In addition, a lengthy, if cursory, introduction to some 700 dream symbols or "occurrences" is furnished. The work is heavily illustrated with black-and-white photographs and drawings, as well as "dream symbol" pictographs that refer from specific encyclopedia entries to the more detailed review of the imagery cited in the dream symbols section.

The focus of this work is clearly popular and suited to the casual reader, with an emphasis placed on nontraditional religious and therapeutic interpretations. Taken in that light, this work offers some interesting alternative approaches to the study and interpretation of dreams. However, students and researchers seeking more substantive studies into the etiology, neurology, and pathology of dreams and sleep states will be better served by such works as the *Encyclopedia of Sleep and Dreaming* (see ARBA 94, entry 808).—**Elizabeth Patterson**

780. Noll, Richard, and Carol Turkington. **The Encyclopedia of Memory and Memory Disorders.** New York, Facts on File, 1994. 265p. index. $45.00. ISBN 0-8160-2610-6.

Containing more than 700 entries, *The Encyclopedia of Memory and Memory Disorders* presents the basic vocabulary of memory and memory research with extensive discussions. The entries cover major theories; clinical terms for neurological, biological, and genetic research; drugs and mnemonic therapies; and profiles of researchers and famous patients. The book demystifies complex information about human memory by explaining concepts in language accessible to the general reader. The combined efforts of a scientist and medical writer improve clarity for the layperson attempting to understand intricate scientific research.

This volume covers ideas proposed by Plato through current research investigations. Some entries have short, specific bibliographies. More of this direct referencing would be helpful, especially when the material presented is potentially controversial (such as alternative therapies). The general bibliography is extensive.

Disappointingly, there is no mention of recovered memory or false memory syndrome, both topics in the news now. The topic of recovered memory is implied in the section on child abuse, memory, but not cross-referenced. Otherwise, the entries are extensively cross-referenced. Entries might benefit from being more concise or organized differently, as some broad concepts have been treated in rather expansive essays (e.g., "neurons and memory"). An alternate format to the two-column, dictionary-like page would improve readability for many entries. The appendixes are useful and the index is good.

Overall, this book accomplishes the stated objectives, and is easy to use and browse. It would be a useful tool for patients and their families, as well as medical professionals needing an introduction to topics in memory research. [R: RBB, 15 Feb 95, p. 1109]—**Constance Rinaldo**

781. Thomson, Sandra A. **Cloud Nine: A Dreamer's Dictionary.** New York, Avon Books, 1994. 576p. $6.99pa. ISBN 0-380-77384-8.

This work makes many claims but breaks virtually no new ground in the field of dream research and analysis. It is divided into two parts. The first purports to be a "practical guide to understanding your dreams" and is composed of 6 topical chapters and 25 "dreamercises" to aid the reader in remembering, interpreting, and directing dreams. The author presents an extremely condensed reworking of selected popular and scholarly studies in a chatty New Age format. Each chapter includes brief annotated references to works cited in passing. Part 2 contains more than 2,200 brief interpretations of dream symbols and themes, as well as a short index to sources used. Cross-references to related terms are provided.

Although this work claims to be the most complete and comprehensive dream dictionary available, in many respects it is no more than a reworking of earlier titles such as R. E. Guiley's *Encyclopedia of Dreams* (Crossroad Publishing, 1993) or G. S. Miller's *Dictionary of Dreams* (Prentice Hall, 1986). While some readers may find the informal and cozy tone and the promise to realize one's personal potential through dream interpretation quite appealing, students and scholars will find little new offered by this latest addition to the vast literature of dream analysis.—**Elizabeth Patterson**

782. **Wiley's English-Spanish, Spanish-English Dictionary of Psychology and Psychiatry. Diccionario de Psicología y Psiquiatría Inglés-Español, Español-Inglés Wiley.** By Steven M. Kaplan. New York, John Wiley, 1995. 594p. $45.00. ISBN 0-471-01460-5.

This dictionary of equivalent terms in English and Spanish includes more than 60,000 entries, about 30,000 English-to-Spanish and another 30,000 Spanish-to-English translations. The work covers general and technical terms in a wide range of areas in both psychology and psychiatry, such as abnormal psychology; applied psychology; cognition and language; developmental psychology and psychiatry; marriage and family; psychometrics; sexuality, attraction, and intimacy; and therapy. The author is a renowned lexicographer who has written several English-Spanish guides for John Wiley.

This reference work is both current and comprehensive, making it an indispensable tool for instructors, students, therapists, patients, and translators. The dictionary does not include cross-references (e.g., the terms *obsessive compulsive disorder* and *obsessive compulsive neurosis* are listed separately) so users have to know exactly what they need. However, terms do appear in phrasal entries (i.e., those starting with the same first word), which makes finding related terms easy enough. The two-column format is easy to both read and use. This handsome work is highly recommended for both public and academic libraries.
—**Edward Erazo**

Handbooks and Yearbooks

783. Parker, Julia, and Derek Parker. **Parkers' Complete Book of Dreams.** New York, Dorling Kindersley, 1995. 208p. illus. index. $24.95. ISBN 1-56458-855-6.

The Parkers have intended this book to be used as a guide for those interested in interpreting their own dreams. As background to the subject, they include sections on the mechanics of sleep, the history of dreams, and how best to remember your dreams. The majority of the book, however, consists of dream themes. The length of the entries varies from one sentence to approximately 75 words, and they usually include cross-references to other sections of the work. In addition, several types of dreams (e.g., rock star, wedding) and their analyses are covered. The themes can be accessed in two ways: through a thesaurus that lists dream images and their related topics, and through a short index.

This is an attractive, oversized book with text that has been liberally supplemented with colorful illustrations. One can easily imagine it residing on a coffee table where it will entice people to browse through it, perhaps checking on a recent dream. Its usefulness as a reference work, however, is more limited. Despite the authors' claim that it is a definitive guide, the book falls short of this goal. This becomes evident when it is compared to Tom Chetwynd's *How to Interpret Your Own Dreams* (Random

House, 1988). For example, when the subject "water" is examined, one can see that the Parker book lists half the number of entries found in the Chetwynd work. The Parker book also would have been strengthened by a bibliography, multiple interpretations for each subject, and more information on the sources of the interpretations. Overall, the authors provide information that is most useful to the casual reader.
—**January Adams**

PARAPSYCHOLOGY

784. Cavendish, Richard. **The World of Ghosts and the Supernatural.** New York, Facts on File, 1994. 160p. illus. maps. index. $22.95. ISBN 0-8160-3209-2.

Cavendish has been writing on occult topics for many years. Organized geographically, this book gives an overview of the beliefs of regions of the world concerning the supernatural. Topics include witchcraft (treated in more than one geographic region, but never including an explanation of modern witchcraft, or Wicca), ghosts, werewolves, vampires, psychic surgery, alien encounters, sexuality and the sacred, and Cargo Cults.

The book makes no pretense of being scholarly. It is a coffee-table book filled with photographs. There are no footnotes or bibliography; one feels grateful for the page of photograph credits and the two-page index. It is frustrating to read a tale and have no supporting documentation as to where the author obtained the information. The introduction is vague and gives little idea as to the overall purpose of the book and nothing on the sources (and thus validity) of the information. At the same time, because there are many similar books, one has seen the same stories over and over. Therefore, in effect one has the worst of both worlds—no way of verifying the truthfulness of the accounts, but little new information. In sum, the book has an interesting format and is well written but unscholarly. Buy it for personal enjoyment but not as a reference work.—**Mary A. Axford**

785. George, Leonard. **Alternative Realities: The Paranormal, the Mystic and the Transcendent in Human Experience.** New York, Facts on File, 1995. 360p. index. $35.00. ISBN 0-8160-2828-1.

This book purports to be the first one-volume reference to cover a wide variety of unusual experiences. The entries, 450 in number, discuss the paranormal, mystic, and transcendent in human experience. George is a psychologist and compiled the selections according to his parameters of the subject. While fascinating, it is clearly an idiosyncratic collection.

His introduction, "Beckoning the Darkness," states that this is a book about shadows and light. The directory of entries gives a clue to his vision of the subject. Under interpretation, he mostly catalogs the field of psychology and includes mental and organic disorders. Under varieties of unusual experience, he mostly catalogs memory, phobias, sleep-related experiences, and sensory anomalies. Under deliberate inducement of experience, his largest section is on drugs. While this has so far shown to be a very Western and psychology-influenced selection, his real weakness lies in his "Specific Tradition" section. His understanding of religious experience from Christianity, Islam, and Judaism to Taoism, Hinduism, and Buddhism is very elementary and obviously based on secondary sources. Consult with caution.
—**Linda L. Lam-Easton**

786. Guiley, Rosemary Ellen. **Atlas of the Mysterious in North America.** New York, Facts on File, 1995. 178p. illus. maps. index. $35.00. ISBN 0-8160-2876-1.

Guiley is the author of numerous works relating to the occult, including the excellent *Encyclopedia of Witches and Witchcraft* (see ARBA 90, entry 755). The current work is well described by the title. The atlas is organized by types of mysterious places: power points and sacred places, earthworks and mounds, stoneworks, haunted places, ghost lights, phantom and mystery ships, water monsters, and mysterious creatures. Each section has introductory text that defines the phenomenon and proposes possible explanations for it. The following section lists places where the phenomena occur, organized by country (United States and Canada), then state or province; a map at the beginning of each section includes a reference number for each site. A short description of the site gives the name, the reference number, and a brief description. The text is supplemented by numerous black-and-white illustrations. The book is fun to browse. Selecting the section on water monsters, for example, allows one to read the mythological meanings of such creatures, followed by a discussion of the history of scientific studies of sea serpents and their kin. The maps with their associated site descriptions will be useful to those planning a vacation trip.

While there are no footnotes, there is a nicely organized bibliography and suggested reading list. Some of the works listed are scholarly books on folklore and history, as well as some of the more well-known popularizers of the occult. The index is comprehensive. *Atlas of the Mysterious in North America* is recommended for collections on folklore or the occult.—**Mary A. Axford**

787. Hollander, P. Scott. **Tarot for Beginners: An Easy Guide to Understanding & Interpreting the Tarot.** St. Paul, Minn., Llewellyn, 1995. 359p. illus. $12.95pa. ISBN 1-56718-363-8.

This work describes and interprets the symbolism of each of the 78 cards in a Tarot deck and shows the reader how to lay out the cards and interpret them in relation to each other. It explains that the cards may be used for fortune telling or meditation to provide spiritual self-development. It also includes a short history of tarot and two sample readings of the cards. The work is an attempt to teach beginners how to read the cards for themselves or others. A detailed description of each card with illustrations gives the meaning of the card and how to read it in conjunction with other cards.

The chapters are arranged logically, and the text is clearly written so that no prior knowledge is necessary to use this book. No bibliography or footnotes tell the reader where to find further information. *Encyclopedia of Tarot* by Stuart R. Kaplan (3 vols.; U.S. Games Systems, 1978-1990) provides more in-depth history and examples. This book is definitely for believers, as no criticism of the method is even alluded to.—**Sandra L. Doggett**

788. Matthews, Caitlín, and John Matthews. **Encyclopaedia of Celtic Wisdom: The Celtic Shaman's Sourcebook.** Rockport, Mass., Element Books, 1994. 456p. illus. index. $39.95. ISBN 1-85230-561-4.

This encyclopedia is unique in its field for its careful presentation of translations of original materials. The subtitle's reference to Celtic "shamans," however, confuses the issue. This detail may mislead researchers and cause them to overlook an interesting work. This anthology combines the translations of many respected scholars and researchers, representing a wide range of Celtic eras. All were originally transcribed in the Christian era, and this may affect their contents and references. The texts are for the most part presented without commentaries and annotations. While this makes the volume readable, for the scholar the lack of background and annotation causes the need for further research. The book is divided into three parts. Part 1 is the contribution of "memory" (of the earth, trees, animals, and ancestors) to the "shamanistic" tradition. Part 2 deals with spiritual specialists, and part 3 contains materials on healing, divination, and prophecy. This book is compiled by practitioners of the shamanic tradition and the "spirits" are the prime acknowledged helpers. If this suits the reader, all is well, but for the scholar, this may pose an insurmountable problem.—**Linda L. Lam-Easton**

789. Ritchie, David. **UFO: The Definitive Guide to Unidentified Flying Objects and Related Phenomena.** New York, Facts on File, 1994. 264p. illus. maps. index. $40.00. ISBN 0-8160-2894-X.

David Ritchie's *UFO: The Definitive Guide to Unidentified Flying Objects and Related Phenomena* fills a real need in the reference collection for the paranormal. Items are easily found in the dictionary format, and the exhaustively thorough index provides ample material for cross-reference. A short bibliography follows the text for those looking for further information. The breadth of data covered here is impressive: For example, one can read about not only the "Little Blue Man" incident in England in 1967, but also the encounter of St. Anthony and a mysterious satyr in the fourth century. Terms such as *kundalini* (a mysterious bodily energy experienced in many close encounters) are explained as well. The text throughout is readable and informative. The illustrations, however, are a disappointment: More eyewitness drawings of the sightings would be preferable to the author's own cartoons. Also desirable is a better use of maps, as it would be interesting to get a geographical sense of UFO activity worldwide. Despite these criticisms, Ritchie's UFO dictionary still provides a down-to-earth guide to the odd happenings above. [R: Choice, Jan 95, p. 758; LJ, Jan 95, pp. 90-92]—**Christopher Michael McDonough**

790. Schwartz, Jacob. **Asteroid Name Encyclopedia.** St. Paul, Minn., Llewellyn, 1995. 372p. index. $19.95pa. ISBN 1-56718-609-2.

This reference work is based on the author's premise that one's future can be determined through the careful observation and charting of asteroids that carry the same names as people, places, or things that are significant in one's life. This theory is described in the introduction, in which the author uses such examples as the history of Russia and the O. J. Simpson case to support his ideas. Entries are arranged alphabetically by name, and each includes the number assigned by the IAU (International Astronomical Union), date(s) of discovery, the intended meaning of the name, variations of the name, and famous people or places with the name.

This encyclopedia also contains exhaustive cross-references to numerical and zodiacal order of the asteroids, as well as an index that cross-references to asteroid numbers (as opposed to page numbers). As the index corresponds only to the small section arranged numerically, it seems somewhat unnecessary. The index is also visually difficult to read, arranged with four vertical columns per page.

This encyclopedia is designed to be read by a very specific audience: those who are familiar with astrological terminology and are willing to devote much time to drawing the recommended personal charts that can be used to plot significant asteroids in the readers' lives. As a casual tool, it is likely to have the appeal of a novelty item, rather than being a core reference work.—**Teresa Holten**

791. Shaw, Eva. **Divining the Future: Prognostication from Astrology to Zoomancy.** New York, Facts on File, 1995. 293p. illus. index. $35.00. ISBN 0-8160-2937-7.

This encyclopedia of fortune-telling practices from historical times to the present provides a fascinating account of the best known to the obscure. Humankind has attempted to predict the future through the ages by a multitude of ingenious divination practices. This work thoroughly details more than 150 of them, illustrating an incredible diversity (e.g., those involving smoke, water, stones, and animals, to name a few). Entries on psychics, mystics, prophets, numerologists, spiritual teachers, and astrologers are also included, from Pythagoras and Nostradamus to Jeane Dixon and Uri Geller. Each entry has a brief definition followed by an explanation of several paragraphs and a bibliography for further reading. Pen drawings enhance the text. Cross-referencing and a 13-page index make locating entries quick and easy.

The author's entries both entertain and educate the reader. Explanations of well-known divination practices such as palm and teacup reading, Tarot cards, the I Ching, and numerology are among the most detailed entries, but the entries of some obscure practices make this work unusual. This book makes not only a fine reference guide, but enjoyable general reading on the subject as well. It is recommended for public, academic, and high school libraries.—**Edward Erazo**

15 Recreation and Sports

GENERAL WORKS

Biography

792. **African-American Sports Greats: A Biographical Dictionary.** David L. Porter, ed. Westport, Conn., Greenwood Press, 1995. 429p. illus. index. $59.95. ISBN 0-313-28987-5.

Despite the plethora of recent books on African-American and black sports figures, this is the first all-sport collection of biographies that is exclusively devoted to the greatest African-American athletes. In the recent past, there have been histories of black athletic development and biographies of U.S. sports greats and Olympic sports heroes, all of which have included African Americans among the biographees. However, none has covered all sports and all places and times in the United States.

The editor has had some experience in this field. Here he has marshaled the contributions of many people who come from a variety of backgrounds. The entries, two to three pages in length, are written to a standard that is perhaps a testimonial to his previous work: the six-volume *Biographical Dictionary of American Sports* (see entry 793). The 166 men and women profiled in the work under review represent figures from the early days (boxer Jack Johnson) to the present day (football player Emmitt Smith), as well as some administrators and coaches.

Porter's approach is fresh and satisfying. He insists on presenting a picture of the whole person. If there are difficulties in an athlete's private life, the editor does not shirk from dealing with them, although always in an unemotional and factual way. The sensational murder case involving football and sports personality O. J. Simpson is included (the book is current through mid-1995), but the event is placed in the context of his life. The same can be said for boxing great Mike Tyson, in that his legal troubles and turbulent life are examined. Entries are about 800 to 1,000 words in length; use quotations liberally from knowledgeable people; and cover the subject's family, education, personal struggles, career achievements and records, and awards and honors. Each entry concludes with a bibliography of books and articles on the biographee.

This biographical dictionary is a fine contribution to the literature. Any U.S. sports fan would enjoy it, and it is well suited for school, public, and some academic libraries. It is sturdily bound in an attractive cover and printed on permanent paper. Photographs and appendixes are provided.—**Randall Rafferty**

793. **Biographical Dictionary of American Sports: 1992-1995 Supplement for Baseball, Football, Basketball, and Other Sports.** David L. Porter, ed. Westport, Conn., Greenwood Press, 1995. 811p. index. $89.50. ISBN 0-313-28431-8.

This is the second supplement to the four-volume set that appeared in 1987-89 (see ARBA 90, entries 757 and 769; ARBA 89, entry 735; and ARBA 88, entry 798); a first supplement came out in 1992 (see ARBA 93, entry 817) and a separate cumulative index in 1993. The format remains unchanged: signed articles of 200-600 words arranged by sport, each with several bibliographical references. The subjects include not only players, but also managers, coaches, league administrators, broadcasters, and others who have achieved prominence in American sports. Of the 616 entries in this volume, the majority (383) are from baseball and football; the next greatest is basketball, with 58 entries. While some of the subjects have gained fame only since the late 1980s, most of them were active at an earlier time, suggesting that they probably do not rank as highly in importance as the subjects of the earlier volumes.

While there are numerous contributors, the entries are stylistically similar and the quality of the writing is uniformly good. There is an alphabetical index of all subjects, as well as listings of entries by subject's place of birth, women athletes by sport, major U.S. sports halls of fame, and sites of Olympic games. A cumulative index of subject names would have been a desirable feature. Libraries owning the earlier volumes will obviously wish to add this supplement; others should seriously consider purchasing the entire set.—**Jack Ray**

794. **Great Athletes. Supplement 21-23: The Twentieth Century.** Pasadena, Calif., Salem Press, 1994. 3v. illus. index. $75.00/set. ISBN 0-89356-819-8.

This set updates and broadens the coverage of the original 20-volume edition by examining the lives and careers of 106 athletes, many of whom have risen to prominence since the 1st edition's publication in 1992 (see ARBA 93, entry 816, for previous review). The final volume lists recent major accomplishments by and recent deaths of athletes profiled in the first edition.

As previously, each article is uniform in its format, averaging about four pages long, and includes a photograph of the athlete, ready-reference data, early life, the road to excellence, the emerging champion, continuing the story, and a summary. Each entry is supplemented by tabular materials that contain information such as career statistics, honors and awards, records set, and other individual milestones.

The supplement volumes continue the volume- and page-numbering of the original edition. New in the final volume is a year-by-year chart of highlights in world sports during the century. The indexes and timeline have been updated, and each references all 23 volumes. These works have a clear, readable format for middle school students, and also are conducive to browsing by adults.—**Kathleen J. Voigt**

795. Jacobs, Timothy. **100 Athletes Who Shaped Sports History.** San Francisco, Calif., Bluewood, 1994. 112p. illus. index. $7.95pa. ISBN 0-912517-13-1.

Sports have played an important part in history and to this end, *100 Athletes Who Shaped Sports History* encompasses 100 athletes whose birth dates range from 558 B.C. through 1966.

Arranged in chronological order, male and female athletes of various multicultural backgrounds are presented in one-page descriptions. Each page includes an athlete's name in bold capital letters, the dates of birth and (if applicable) death, the sport in which he or she excelled, and a locator map to show birthplace. The biographical sketches address each athlete's personal and unique talent. There is also a line drawing of each athlete. Cross-references to other athletes in the book are included. These are in boldface print for easier reference.

This book has a timeline cross-referenced to each athlete and an extensive index arranged by name, sport, and organization to assist the reader. For extra fun, the author includes a trivia quiz. The answers to the questions are given as clues (i.e., see #_____).

With just enough writing for explanation, this compact and concise book will be a valuable addition to a middle school collection, both as a reference source as well as a part of the regular nonfiction collection.—**Barbara B. Goldstein**

796. Steele, Sandy. **The Official Celebrity Registry 1994-1995: Intimate Information on the World's Most Popular Sports Stars.** Los Angeles, Calif., General Publishing Group, 1994. 415p. illus. $9.99pa. ISBN 1-881-649-09-1. ISSN 1071-5789.

One of a series of Official Celebrity Registries by the same publisher, this work bears the official imprimatur of no organization other than the publisher. The author is described as an "insider" who was assisted by a sportswriter. Although the cover states that each edition provides the latest up-to-date information, this volume was out-of-date before it went to press: before Jennifer Capriati and O. J. Simpson went to jail, before Nancy Kerrigan won her controversial silver Olympic medal, and while Jimmy Johnson still coached the Dallas Cowboys.

Brief sketches and black-and-white photographs of 200 of the world's most popular sports stars fill the pages. Of these stars, 20 are female, and more than 90 percent were born in the United States. Most are still active, and fewer than 10 percent are coaches or administrators. Among the notable omissions are Mary Lou Retton, Dorothy Hamill, Bonnie Blair, and Dan Jansen. There is no index or appendix, and many of the photographs are of poor quality; several are more than 10 years old. Coverage is uneven. Michael Jordan and Earvin "Magic" Johnson are listed as members of the 1992 Olympic "Dream Team"; Larry Bird is not. The author mentions the several marriages of such people as Bruce Jenner and Chris Evert, but not of others such as O. J. Simpson or Joe Montana. Many sketches mention neither spouse, offspring, nor parents. Most of the information has been published elsewhere and very little of it is "intimate." Many other works, including the annual encyclopedias published for most major sports, provide more accurate data. Therefore, the work is not recommended.—**Mary Lou LeCompte**

797. Sugar, Bert Randolph. **The 100 Greatest Athletes of All Time: A Sports Editor's Personal Ranking.** New York, Citadel Press/Carol Publishing Group, 1995. 446p. illus. index. $24.95. ISBN 0-8065-1614-3.

Greatness, as defined by Sugar, "is a combination of things, an equation that includes dominance, perceived greatness, consistent performance, accomplishments that transcend time, and overall excellence" (p. xiii). With this definition, and a dose of "Sugar," comes this ranking of the 100 greatest athletes of all time. Conducting his research at "watering holes," gathering nominees from new acquaintances, reading and rereading yellowed newspapers and clips of bygone eras, Sugar has ranked the 100 greatest athletes according to their contribution to sports history.

Each ranking is accompanied by a photograph and an insightful biography of the athlete. The biographies range from two to six pages each and are succinctly written with a summary of the biographee's childhood, college achievements, amateur and professional accomplishments, and statistics. Although there is a profusion of information in each biography, Sugar also manages to capture the essence of the personal side of the athlete.

The rankings encompass athletes from around the world, and from all eras of the twentieth century. They have been pulled from predominately U.S. sports, such as baseball, boxing, football, golf, and tennis. To the casual observer, the list includes anyone and everyone worthy to be among the greatest 100, but in the addendum entitled "101," Sugar lists another 250 athletes who could have easily made the cut.

Sugar has covered the sports scene for more than three decades, both in print and on television. He wrote this book to be the source of endless arguments among sports fans. He does not seek to convince the reader, as there is no such thing as objective truth, but merely to stimulate. This book belongs in the library of every sports fan, and it can be considered a benchmark for those sports figures who are deemed to be "great."—**Deborah A. Taylor**

Chronology

798. **Sports in North America: A Documentary History. Volume 4: Sports in War, Revival, and Expansion 1860-1880.** George B. Kirsch, ed. Gulf Breeze, Fla., Academic International Press, 1995. 416p. index. $75.00/vol. ISBN 0-87569-135-8.

The development of sports in North America between the years 1860 and 1880 is documented in one source with this publication—the fourth in the Sports in North America: A Documentary History series (see ARBA 94, entry 826, for a review of the third volume). This era is indicative of the fury of athletics that swept through North American colleges, the domination of amateur athletics and clubs, and the early development of professionalism and commercialism in individual and team sports.

In the introduction and in chapter 1, "Cultural Issues," Kirsch overviews the process of modernization that influenced the development of sports and characterized a new style of athletics throughout the United States and Canada. He details the era that experienced the United States Civil War, the influence of British sportsmen and traditions, industrialization, urbanization, and changes in transportation and communication trends. Kirsch also addresses the social and cultural issues of ethnicity, social class, gender, and religious issues. Remaining chapters reprint more than 150 annotated documents that chronicle the diversity of North American sporting activities.

Each chapter begins with an introduction to the sport that examines the issues of the era and how they affected the sport's evolution. Important primary source documents have been reprinted as they originally appeared and include rules and regulations, constitutions, bylaws for clubs and associations, personal accounts, and newspaper editorials. Emphasis is placed on the major sports of the period—aquatics, baseball, boxing, cricket, equestrianism, football, gymnastics, lacrosse, and track and field. Also covered are bicycling, blood (animal) sports, croquet, field sports, pub sports, racquet sports, and winter sports.

A selected bibliography of primary and secondary sources and indexes by names, subjects, institutions, and geographical and place-names completes the work. This is the first comprehensive collection of important primary source documents to chronicle the development of sports in the United States and Canada, and it will prove invaluable to sports historians.—**Deborah A. Taylor**

Directories

799. **Athletic Scholarships: A Complete Guide.** Cleveland, Ohio, Conway Greene Publishing, 1994. 561p. index. $20.95pa. ISBN 1-884669-05-0.

For many high school athletes—both male and female—the only thing more competitive than sports is the competition for athletic scholarships. Literally hundreds of colleges award athletic grants to enable young men and women to continue their education and play sports. Far exceeding *The Winning Edge* (2d ed.; see ARBA 95, entry 799), *Athletic Scholarships* is a comprehensive guide to scholarships at more than 1,000 institutions, from National Collegiate Athletic Association (NCAA) Division 1-A level programs to National Association of Intercollegiate Athletes (NAIA) schools. NJCAA (junior colleges) are also listed.

A typical institutional entry includes the address; telephone and fax numbers; organizational association (NCAA, NAIA, NJCAA); athletic conference affiliation; and name of the athletics director. Information concerning to whom student inquiries should be made, the individuals making scholarship decisions, the financial value of an athletic award, and graduation rates are indicated where applicable and available. Finally, the number of scholarships for each sport (men's and women's) is listed, along with average grade point averages, Standardized Achievement Test, and American College Test scores by sport. Gathered from the institutions, conferences, and other sources of public information, these figures and rates are generally reliable and accurate.

Entries are arranged alphabetically by the school name and are easy to read. Indexes are by institution, by sport (for men's and women's), and by state/city. Coverage is not just for the major sports, but includes sports such as wrestling, hockey, fencing, dance, and crew—in all, nearly 60 sports. Recommended for all types of libraries, *Athletic Scholarships* is a must for high school, prep school, and junior/community college collections. [R: RBB, 1 Feb 95, pp. 1021-22]—**Boyd Childress**

800. **Playground Industry Reference Directory 1995.** North Vancouver, B.C., International Trade Publishing, 1995. 230p. maps. $29.95 spiralbound; $49.95 spiralbound (U.S.).

This publication is for specialists in the playground industry, to whom it will be an invaluable resource. In the slim, spiralbound volume, there is copious information for those who deal in playground equipment. To those whose activities revolve around trampolines, slides, bicycle racks and lockers, gazebos, park benches, rotomolding, playground surfacing—or those who need them—this book will provide ample information.

The beginning of the book features more than 60 yellow pages interspersed with advertisements, all arranged in the manner of a telephone book and covering entries for the United States and Canada. The white pages list manufacturer profiles arranged in alphabetical sequence. Next, the same manufacturers are listed, with their profiles, in geographical order, from Alabama to the Yukon Territory. The entries for dealers and agents in the industry follow, arranged in a similar order. The back of the book has several useful sections: state and province postal abbreviations, metric/U.S./imperial conversion tables, international long distance telephone country and city dialing codes, North American telephone area codes in numerical order, and a map of North America with the area and time zone map.—**Koraljka Lockhart**

Handbooks and Yearbooks

801. Berlow, Lawrence H. **Sports Ethics: A Reference Handbook.** Santa Barbara, Calif., ABC-CLIO, 1995. 204p. index. (Contemporary World Issues). $39.50. ISBN 0-87436-769-7.

Sports run deep in our lives—as deep as the baseball fans who lament the 1994 players' strike to the workers preparing for the 1996 Olympic Games in Atlanta. The ethical aspects of sports, which have a significant impact on many Americans, are becoming as integral to sports as individual participants, leagues and teams, and major events such as the Kentucky Derby and the Masters Golf Tournament. No doubt CBS television golf analyst Ben Wright's comments on the women's professional tour reflect a preoccupation with ethics in sport and lend support to the need for such a book as *Sports Ethics*. A part of ABC-CLIO's series on Contemporary World Issues, the book includes a narrative description of ethical issues in sport, a brief chronology, a handful of biographical sketches, a loose collection of relevant documents, an annotated list of sports organizations, and 50 pages of resources—print and nonprint. An index, albeit far too brief for a reference book, concludes the volume. In summary, the book provides an overview of ethics in various sports.

The argument here concerns not so much what the book includes as what it does not. For example, boxing, which many do not consider a sport but others do, is hardly mentioned, nor are gambling and sports odds making, certainly worthy of consideration in any discussion of ethics in sports. Also absent in the biographical section are boxing promoter Don King and former University of Nevada, Las Vegas basketball coach Jerry Tarkanian, whose long battle with the National Collegiate Athletic Association (NCAA) is also excluded. There is no mention of the gambling suspensions of professional football players Paul Hornung and Alex Arras (1963), the tragic suicide of baseball pitcher Donnie Moore, or the National Association for Stock Car Auto Racing's controversy over the regulation of engines in auto racing, all of which again center on ethical arguments. In the feature movies listed, *The Natural* is included while 1994's highly acclaimed *Hoop Dreams* is not. Among the books missing are *Under the Tarnished Dome: How Notre Dame Betrayed Its Ideals for Football Glory* (Simon & Schuster, 1993) and John Feinstein's fine books on college basketball. All things considered, *Sports Ethics* is a disappointment and a missed opportunity to explore a vital issue in sports today.—**Boyd Childress**

Thesauri

802. **Sport Thesaurus: The Thesaurus of Terminology Used in the SPORT Database.** 1994 ed. Richard W. Stark and others, eds. Gloucester, Ont., Sport Information Resource Centre, 1994. 297p. index. $115.00 spiralbound; $95.00 (U.S.). ISBN 0-921817-23-1.

This thesaurus lists approximately 7,500 keywords used in the SPORT Database (known as SPORT Discus in its CD-ROM version). As in the more familiar *Thesaurus of ERIC Descriptors* (see entry 318), keywords are accompanied by broader, narrower, and related terms. Cross-references are provided from terms not used to approved keywords, and scope notes are supplied to explain keywords that may be ambiguous. Quite a few nonsport keywords are included because of their connection with sports topics (e.g., anatomical and medical terms). Many specific sports events (e.g., the National Invitational Tournament) are listed as keywords, as are individual years, decades, and centuries. There are separate listings of geographical headings (Aberdeen to Zurich) and proper names of teams, clubs, leagues, and associations. The thesaurus concludes with several classified and alphabetical lists of numerical codes that can be combined for subject searching. British rather than American spelling has been used (e.g., colour, fibreglass), but this affects only a small minority of entries. Clearly, this admirable thesaurus will be necessary for libraries that have the SPORT Database.—**Jack Ray**

BASEBALL

803. **The Baseball Encyclopedia Update, 1995: Complete Career Records for All Players Who Played in the 1994 Season.** New York, Macmillan/Simon & Schuster, 1995. 169p. $12.00pa. ISBN 0-02-860089-4.

This update is presented in virtually the same format as the main encyclopedia, which was last reviewed in ARBA 94 (see entry 830). A section on the teams and their players features capsule statistics for each team's principal players, arranged by position. Following are complete final standings of the teams for this regrettably truncated season. The player and pitcher registers are separate alphabetical lists of every person who appeared in a game in the 1994 season, along with complete major league statistical records. A final section lists 1994 managers and their managerial records in the major leagues.

Although this supplement is not expensive, it must be said that the initial section on teams and their players is the only feature that can definitely recommend it (and this will be repeated in the next edition of the encyclopedia). Team standings can be found in any almanac or encyclopedia annual, while the *Sporting News Baseball Register* (Horton Publishing) is much preferred for information on current players (and costs about the same). *Baseball Register* lists not only all 1994 players, but also many who did not play that year but are playing in 1995. There are many more details provided on each player's career, and all minor league records are included. Moreover, pitchers are integrated into a single alphabetical register of players. Likewise, the roster of managers includes their major and minor league managing statistics, as well as their major and minor league playing records.—**Jack Ray**

804. Faber, Charles F. **Baseball Ratings: The All-Time Best Players at Each Position.** 2d ed. Jefferson, N.C., McFarland, 1995. 269p. $27.50. ISBN 0-7864-0030-7.

The Holy Grail of baseball fans and researchers is surely the definitive determination of the best players of all time. Faber's effort toward this end must rank as one of the more complex and sophisticated attempts. He has devised separate point systems for rating hitters, fielders, pitchers, relief pitchers, and players (an amalgam of the hitting and fielding rankings). For each category, he assigns points for criteria that he deems to be of paramount significance and makes adjustments for each year to factor in the performance of the league as a whole. To this basic scenario he adds a number of other wrinkles and exceptions that he believes will allow for more valid comparisons. From these calculations Faber generates lists of greatest players in 70 different categories (e.g., leading hitters by club, best hitting teammates, best double-play combinations, best seasons by a starting rotation, most underrated players). He has lists by year, by team, by decade, by position, even by year and place of birth. His most startling conclusion: The greatest player (in terms of Faber points) was not Babe Ruth or Ty Cobb, but the lesser-known Napoleon Lajoie, who last played in 1916 (although the Babe, Cobb, and Honus Wagner are not far behind). Another rank heresy (Faber's term): Richie Ashburn was a better fielding centerfielder than Willie Mays. Even those who disagree with Faber's system cannot fail to be impressed with his thoughtfulness and devotion to the game. However, it must be questioned whether this book, based as it is on selective and subjective data, belongs on the reference shelf. Inclusion in the general collection is probably a better choice.—**Jack Ray**

805. **Official Athletic College Guide: Baseball.** 1995 ed. Charlie Kadupski, comp. and ed. Chicago, Triumph Books, 1994. 733p. maps. $24.95pa. ISBN 1-57243-070-2.

This is a guide for high school students who hope to play baseball in college. Useful not only for the state-by-state directory of community college, four-year college, and university baseball programs that forms most of the book, it is also useful for the introductory information on factors to consider in selecting an institution, making campus visits, communicating with targeted schools, National Collegiate Athletic Association recruiting rules, and eligibility requirements. Helpful features include sample questions to ask the baseball coach, a college planning checklist that lists activities that should be accomplished (e.g., researching sources of financial aid) on a quarterly basis from the high school sophomore year on, and a sample résumé. The editors stress that students pay careful attention to the academic program a school offers, as most college players will never have professional careers.

The directory information is quite variable, no doubt reflecting the fact that a large part of it was gathered from questionnaires. Moreover, the amount of detail provided does not correlate with the size or scope of the program. However, each entry does include an academic profile (standard college guide data) and an athletic profile. The latter may cover information on baseball scholarships, practice and playing facilities, number of games played in the spring and fall, achievements of recent players, backgrounds of coaches, and positions needed for the next recruiting class. In spite of the unevenness of coverage, this source will be a useful complement to general college guides available in school and public libraries.—**Jack Ray**

806. Walker, Donald E., and B. Lee Cooper, comps. **Baseball and American Culture: A Thematic Bibliography of Over 4,500 Works.** Jefferson, N.C., McFarland, 1995. 257p. index. $39.95. ISBN 0-7864-0049-8.

Baseball as an aspect of American culture has become a legitimate area of academic study in the last 25 years. This bibliography, compiled by two college history professors, purports to document this linkage, but unfortunately is considerably flawed in its execution. One might have hoped that this work would concentrate on sources that somehow intend to explore the baseball/culture nexus; while there are a number of these references, the majority of entries are articles in popular magazines, biographies, team histories, and anthologies that are in no way distinctive for their treatment of baseball as a cultural phenomenon.

The book is divided into 25 subcategories; a few of these (e.g., "Women in Baseball") are useful, but the majority are unfocused or ambiguous (e.g., "The Anti-Democratic Nature of Baseball," "Geography and Baseball," "External Influences on Baseball"), and sometimes overlap each other. Many items are listed more than once, which not only suggests the book's lack of focus but also considerably reduces the number of sources announced in its subtitle.

A section called "Communication Systems in Baseball" is mainly concerned with sportswriters and sportscasters; "Health Hazards in Baseball" runs the gamut from players with handicaps to the off-field shooting of umpire Steve Palermo. A listing of individual players in the section on biographical studies of ballplayers includes many nonplayers—most notably Fidel Castro, Billy Crystal, Richard Nixon, and Roseanne (formerly) Arnold—and misspells the names of Dan Quisenberry, Dusty Rhodes, and Edd Roush. This bibliography would have been more useful if it had expanded its publication date scope (which is 1985 to mid-1993) and included only sources that truly do address the cultural implications of baseball.—**Jack Ray**

807. Wright, Russell O. **The Best of Teams, the Worst of Teams: A Major League Baseball Statistical Reference, 1903-1994.** Jefferson, N.C., McFarland, 1995. 189p. index. $29.95. ISBN 0-7864-0011-0.

Wright has mined the vast resources of *The Baseball Encyclopedia* (9th ed.; see ARBA 94, entry 830) and *Total Baseball* (2d ed.; see ARBA 92, entry 786) to assemble this cornucopia of highs and lows. The book is divided into five parts: "Winning and Losing," "Offensive Highs and Lows," "Defensive Highs and Lows," "Best Teams in Franchise History," and "Team Summaries." The first three sections are divided by league and often by time periods (e.g., before and after the designated hitter) that Wright deems to be significant.

One can see at a glance the best and worst years each franchise has ever had in a wide variety of categories (e.g., won/lost percentage, average runs scored, team batting average, average home runs per game, earned run average, double plays). Additionally, for many of these categories average figures over time are presented. In the fourth section, each franchise is separately profiled for best and worst years; the last section reorganizes all the data presented in the first three parts and summarizes it for each team.

All this would have been labor enough, but Wright adds a considerable amount of narrative description to accompany each table of data. One might quibble with Wright's decision to lump all manifestations of a franchise together; this means, for example, that many of the low marks attributed to the Orioles were in fact achieved by their pre-1954 evil twins, the St. Louis Browns. Nevertheless, this distillation of the best and worst of major league baseball (the title's Dickensian pun is apt) will be of enormous interest to fans and researchers.—**Jack Ray**

808. Young, Ken. **Cy Young Award Winners.** New York, Walker, 1994. 152p. illus. index. $14.95. ISBN 0-8027-8300-7.

The Cy Young Award for the major leagues' best pitcher originated in 1956; beginning in 1967 one winner was selected from each league. This book is a collection of profiles of 10 prominent winners: Whitey Ford, Sandy Koufax, Denny McLain, Tom Seaver, Bob Gibson, Jim Palmer, Steve Carlton, Fernando Valenzuela, Dwight Gooden, and Roger Clemens. Except for an appendix listing all winners and their records for the year they won, there is little or no information on other Cy Young pitchers. There is very little background on the award itself: how it began, who makes the selections, criteria for winning, or controversy about selecting relief pitchers. The profiles themselves are serviceable, if somewhat bland, and seem aimed at a teenage audience. A couple of factual errors leaped out: Palmer's Aberdeen minor league team was in South Dakota, not Maryland; Seattle's Gorman Thomas is twice referred to as Gordon Thomas. This is a reasonable choice for the YA sports shelf, but not appropriate for a reference collection.—**Jack Ray**

BASKETBALL

809. Douchant, Michael. **Encyclopedia of College Basketball.** Detroit, Visible Ink Press/Gale, 1995. 615p. illus. maps. index. $42.95; $19.95pa. ISBN 0-8103-9640-8; 0-8103-9483-9pa.

As Dick Vitale says in his introduction, this jam-packed encyclopedia of the minutia of college basketball is "Awesome, baby! With a capital A!" But do not be put off by his typically obnoxious and overstated comments. The few other reference books on college basketball that exist, such as *NCAA Basketball's Finest* (see ARBA 93, entry 827) or *Final Four Records, 1939-1991* (see ARBA 94, entry 839) pale in comparison because they are far more limited in scope. This splendid compendium covers every last detail of this increasingly popular collegiate sport, even including records since 1985 in the Final Four based on the teams' sneaker contracts. Perhaps because it is published by a standard reference book publisher rather than a sports association or organization, this is a sensible, well-organized, complete, and comprehensive guide to college basketball that can serve as a model for other sports reference books. Eighteen separate chapters begin with six that provide an excellent narrative and statistical summary of the game broken down by era, also including brief year-by-year sketches. The remaining chapters cover the National Invitation Tournament (NIT), a register of outstanding players and another of eminent coaches, profiles of college players who later achieved fame in other settings, women's basketball, small colleges, the Olympics, a conference directory, a school directory, NCAA awards, NCAA records, and a miscellanea of fascinating statistical odds and ends. The information is easy to find as arranged, but there is also an excellent index. One minor quibble is that the fair assortment of black-and-white photographs of individuals might have been somewhat larger.

This is a reference book that is also fun to read. It should be of special interest to the many academic libraries in institutions with strong basketball programs.—**Norman D. Stevens**

BOATING

810. **McKnew & Parker's Buyer's Guide to Sportfishing Boats.** 1995 ed. By Ed McKnew and Mark Parker. Blue Ridge Summit, Pa., International Marine/McGraw-Hill, 1994. 246p. illus. index. $19.95pa. ISBN 0-07-045171-0.

This descriptive guide to 300 current and out-of-production post-1975 power fishing boats in the 25- to 82-foot range is especially recommended for public libraries in affluent communities with boating areas. Many people who never buy such boats still attend boat shows, so other public libraries may want to at least consider adding it to their collections. Listed alphabetically by name, each entry provides a set of brief standard specifications (e.g., length, beam, draft, weight) accompanied by an advertising-style annotation, a black-and-white photograph, and one or more line drawings. The guide also provides some basic questions to ask when buying a boat, a directory of U.S. yacht brokers and dealers, another of U.S. marine surveyors, and a new and used boat price guide showing high and low retail prices. At the price (especially when the boats it lists start at about $20,000), this guide is a bargain.—**Norman D. Stevens**

CAMPING

811. **Guide to Accredited Camps, 1995/96.** 39th ed. By the American Camping Association. Martinsville, Ind., American Camping Association; distr., Chicago, Independent Publishers Group, 1995. 296p. illus. $12.95pa. ISBN 0-87603-144-0. ISSN 1046-5774.

The American Camping Association (ACA) began publishing its directory of accredited camps in 1957. Its purpose then, as now, is to guide parents in selecting an ACA-accredited summer camp for their children. Features added since then, as intimated below, expand its usefulness for today. In its purpose and arrangement, the new version seems hardly to differ from that of a decade ago (see ARBA 86, entry 764). Of course, there are a few more entries now, for summer camping and retreats are apparently a growth industry. Some camps have dropped off the list, having lost their accreditation. The 2,000 main entries have been updated from last year's data by camp directors/owners as they renewed their membership in the American Camping Association.

There are some advertisements in the front matter, but it is the introductory pages of essays and advice columns that will aid in answering parents' questions, and in helping the prospective camper prepare as well. Among the subjects engaged here is the not inconsiderable cost of camp. It may surprise some readers to learn that aid in the form of "camperships" is available from public and private sources (named here only in a general way).

Main entry coverage includes the date of founding of the camp, the director, the operator, the type (e.g., boy, girl, coed, adult), the ages, the capacity, the facilities, and the seasonality. For an activities index, the publisher has retained the matrix in which the camps are listed on one axis, and all possible activities on the other. Where a "hit" occurs, a symbol appears—*G* (part of general program) or *N* (new program), for example. Camps for special groups are listed separately: families, disadvantaged, international, overweight, as well as programs for campers with special needs, such as the physically or mentally challenged.

A recent addition to the guide is a listing of ACA approved "sites." These sites may be reserved for seminars, retreats, meetings of schools, family reunions, or company picnics. Most states are represented among the 400-odd sites. At its price, the *Guide* compares favorably with *Peterson's Summer Opportunities for Kids and Teenagers*, in which ACA accreditation is noted. It is a nice complement, but only that, to the *Masters Guide to Sports Camps* (see ARBA 88, entry 790). Of course, those others include non-ACA-accredited camps as well.—**Randall Rafferty**

812. Maniguet, Xavier. **Survival: How to Prevail in Hostile Environments.** New York, Facts on File, 1994. 454p. illus. maps. index. $40.00. ISBN 0-8160-2518-5.

Survival, an excellent source of information, is as easy to read as it is informative. The title accurately describes Maniguet's work; the book instructs how to live through situations in inhospitable places with few resources—as opposed to getting out as quickly as possible. Indeed, most survival experts agree that staying put is the best bet for being rescued. The book also explains how to prepare before going into sparsely populated or dangerous areas. Examples include the detailed list of equipment that must be aboard a lifeboat, and the instructions on how to catch, kill, and eat turtles.

The book is presented in three parts: major threats (e.g., cold, heat, thirst); hostile environments (e.g., deserts, jungle, mountains); and science and survival (e.g., weather, orientation, medicine). Also included are an appendix concerning technical equipment, a glossary, a selected bibliography, a suggested further reading section, and an index.

This is not a coffee-table book but it is easy and enjoyable to read. If a library can get only one book on survival, this is the one to choose. Recommended for adult and young adult collections concerning travel, outdoor recreation, extreme sports, and expeditions.—**Alan N. Livingston**

COMPUTER

813. Maloni, Kelly, Derek Baker, and Nathaniel Wice. **Net Games: Your Guide to the Games People Play on the Electronic Highway.** New York, Michael Wolff, and New York, Random House Electronic Publishing, 1994. 272p. illus. index. $19.00pa. ISBN 0-679-75592-6.

What is playing in cyberspace? What kinds of entertainment are available via the Internet? These questions are increasingly asked by home computer users. The answer to both queries is "Plenty!" A staggering array of contests, games, activities, and learning experiences is available to users of commercial online systems or anyone with a computer, telephone, and modem. For example, there are *Doom*, *Dungeons and Dragons*, *Star Wars*, *Mortal Kombat*, *X-wing*, and various trivia contests. Challenging games are downloadable—some free and some as shareware. There are already thousands of such games available and more (or updated versions) coming all the time. This easy-to-use handbook lists, describes, and comments on thousands of games played on the Information Superhighway. There are games for all tastes and at all user levels, from beginner to expert, using all operating systems or offered by commercial online services.

There are thousands of shoot-'em-up, beat-'em-senseless games available, with full color, realistic sound effects, and satisfying blood and gore. This book lists them, reviews them, provides hints on effective strategies, and provides information on how to get connected and what they are likely to cost. There is plenty of downloadable software, too, if you would prefer to own them rather than just visit. The writing is crisp and colloquial, and the book will open a new world of learning to those not familiar with the Internet. Entries are organized within chapters (e.g., shoot-'em-up; role-playing and adventure; strategy and classics; sex, hubs, and MUDs). Each entry is listed under the name of the game, with information on how to get at it, and a lively, incisive review.

Sounds good? It is, but a few warnings are in order. Many popular games are built around themes of death and destruction, and most of them involve competition, with winners and losers. These exciting, attractive options often carry additional charges beyond monthly fees incurred for basic service. Electronic games can become seriously addictive and may lead to spending unconscionable amounts of time alone and inside. Finally, as Internet services change or expand almost daily, new editions of this book are bound to come along at frequent intervals; libraries are well advised to consider standing orders. Enthusiastically recommended!—**Bruce A. Shuman**

CRICKET

814. Rundell, Michael. **The Dictionary of Cricket.** 2d ed. New York, Oxford University Press, 1995. 214p. $19.95. ISBN 0-19-866198-3.

Rundell's fascinating dictionary appears to be the standard for this international sport. As more immigrants enter the United States, there will be greater demand for reference material on cricket. For instance, a Sri Lankan amateur cricket league exists in metropolitan Washington, D.C. Cricket is an old game, played mostly in countries formerly part of, or influenced by, the British Empire. As of 1992, when Zimbabwe was admitted to the International Cricket Council, there were 9 "Test" (qv)-playing countries and 20 associate members, including the United States.

Even if one is not particularly interested in sports, cricket can arouse interest on grounds of lexicography (Rundell is a professional lexicographer); social comment (e.g., *Anyone But England: Cricket and the National Malaise*, by Mike Marqusee); or popular culture (e.g., Tom Melville's *Cricket for Americans* [Bowling Green University Press, 1993]). There are more than 12,000 citations in *Padwick I* and *II*, bibliographies published by the Library Association in 1977 and 1991.

For many U.S. citizens, cricket terminology is obscure. For instance, there is a 600-term glossary in the 117-page paperback by Robert Eastaway, *Cricket Explained* (1992). Also, the 1992 edition of "The Laws of Cricket" (42 of them) fills more than 50 pages. Rundell has approximately 1,100 entries (e.g., *crease*, *tonk*, *limited-overs*, *county championship*, *lbw*, and *V*) arranged alphabetically. The definitions are long, based upon historical principles and quoting from many books, newspapers, and periodicals.

The technical and legal aspects of the game are well explained. Approximately 20 line drawings depict such things as playing stances and signals of the umpire. In short, this fine dictionary is highly recommended for comprehensive collections on either sport or British culture.—**William G. Wilson**

CYCLING

815. **Mountain Bikers Almanac, 1996.** Peter W. Grant, Mark Langton, and Brian Hemsworth, eds. Stateline, Nev., Grant Wolf, 1995. 247p. illus. maps. $19.95pa. ISBN 0-9647601-0-X.

More than 200 pages of mountain biking information—cool! Part editorial, part equipment catalog, part advertisement, part directory, this book/magazine has something for all mountain bikers. The work contains information about the history of mountain biking; descriptions of selected riding havens; a 1996 calendar (24 wasted pages); an equipment gallery; notable mountain biking records; a 1996 "who's who"; equipment/company/club/association and e-mail directories; a glossary; tour and festival listings; and miscellaneous tips, such as courtesy rules.

The book is lavishly illustrated with quality photographs and easy-to-read maps. Design and production are outstanding, although a bit confusing at times as each section has its own style, and because of the lack of running heads. The almanac is recommended for high school, public, and college libraries, although it should be considered for the circulating rather than the reference collection.—**Alan N. Livingston**

FENCING

816. Evangelista, Nick. **The Encyclopedia of the Sword.** Westport, Conn., Greenwood Press, 1995. 690p. illus. index. $79.50. ISBN 0-313-27896-2.

Although there are numerous books on various aspects of swords and swordplay, and short entries in many standard encyclopedias, *The Encyclopedia of the Sword* is the first comprehensive treatment of the weapon that has played a key role in human history. Evangelista has assembled a massive amount of information about virtually every artistic, cultural, historical, literary, popular, and symbolic aspect of the sword at all times and in all countries. This will truly serve as the definitive text on the subject for many years to come.

The encyclopedia's hundreds of short entries appear, at first glance, to concentrate primarily on classical European fencing. There is, indeed, exhaustive treatment of key contemporary and historical fencers and highly specialized terms for that important element of sword history. In addition, however, there is excellent coverage of other aspects of the subject, such as swords and swordplay in Japan and other non-European countries, legendary swords, the treatment and use of swords in literature and the movies, and many other arcane aspects of the subject. Nearly 250 different kinds of swords, for example, are identified and described.

Appendixes that list types of swords, fencing masters, noted swashbuckler films, actors who fenced in movies, film fencing masters, and historical and modern fencing organizations add to the value of this comprehensive encyclopedia. Libraries of all kinds should consider this as a valuable addition to their social history collections and not simply as another weapons book with limited value.—**Norman D. Stevens**

FISHING

817. Roberts, George V., Jr. **A Fly-Fisher's Guide to Saltwater Naturals and Their Imitation.** Camden, Maine, Ragged Mountain Press/McGraw-Hill, 1994. 163p. illus. index. $34.95. ISBN 0-07-053166-8.

A unique resource, it combines a basic introduction to saltwater gamefish food sources with one of the most comprehensive guides to the associated fly patterns available. The book consists of three parts: predation and imitation, saltwater forage species, and directory of fly patterns. The principal sections are supplemented by color plates of 89 fly patterns and 41 forage types, a bibliography, and a comprehensive index. Part 1 is a concise overview of predation habits and discusses topics such as prey recognition, forage habits, and pattern selection. Part 2 covers the life histories of most of the major forage species in the Western Hemisphere commonly imitated by fly patterns, consisting of fish, crustaceans, squids, and worms. Part 3 is the directory of fly patterns that includes tying instructions, fishing techniques, and a brief history of the patterns.

Saltwater fly-fishing is a rapidly growing sport, and Roberts's book fills a major void in the contemporary literature. This definitive work will likely become a classic on the topic of saltwater fly imitations and is highly recommended for any public library located in a coastal area, and for medium to larger public libraries located inland.—**Anthony J. Dedrick**

FOOTBALL

818. Gutman, Bill. **The Kids' World Almanac of Football.** Mahwah, N.J., World Almanac Books/Funk & Wagnalls, 1994. 275p. illus. index. $7.95pa. ISBN 0-88687-764-4.

Balancing brief biographies, historical narrative, and statistical data, the author gives young readers a grasp of football's greatest players and achievements. The professional sport's corporate history is outlined, as well as that of the game's different leagues and specific teams. Individual record holders and assorted past players are briefly profiled in text and black-and-white photographs. Professional football championship games are given capsule summaries; Super Bowls are reviewed in entries a few sentences in length. College football records are presented, major historical figures profiled, and bowl games and Heisman trophy winners listed in charts. Gutman notes odd events in both the professional and college games: lopsided scores, the 1968 pro game telecast interrupted by the start of the movie *Heidi*, and other memorable and trivial occurrences. Canadian football is given a one-chapter explication, as are general football terminology and strategy (for older readers). The book's general index appears complete enough to guide one to a needed information.

As a breezily written browser for young adult fans, this source cannot fairly be compared to the sport's standard sources: *Canadian Football League Facts, Figures, and Records* (see ARBA 95, entry 819); *Sports Encyclopedia: Pro Football. The Modern Era, 1960-1993* (see ARBA 95, entry 820); and others published nearly every season. This could, however, be an effective resource for ready-reference work in smaller children's libraries. Although sportswriting cliché abound, and the arrangement favors browsing over research, there is sufficient information here to support both roles.—**Ed Volz**

819. **NCAA Football: The Official 1995 College Football Records Book.** Shawnee Mission, Kans., National Collegiate Athletic Association; distr., Chicago, Login Publishers Consortium, 1995. 532p. illus. $16.95pa. ISBN 1-57243-032-X. ISSN 0735-5475.

Literally hundreds of teams and thousands of players compete for records—wins and losses, touchdowns, passes, receptions, and interceptions. *NCAA Football* captures those exploits on all levels—1A, 1-AA, and Divisions 2 and 3. In more than 500 pages, the volume includes all sorts of team and individual performances and records, coaching records, game and stadium attendance records, conference records, and postseason bowl game scores.

Initially, the book is divided into divisional records, followed by various categories—bowl games, coaching records, and so on—and 1994 statistical leaders and 1995 team schedules with 1994 results. Compiled and published by the National Collegiate Athletic Association (NCAA), the data and records appear impeccable. Virtually hours spent reading and examining the records and scores resulted in locating no errors.

It was rewarding to see academic all-Americans included in an NCAA-sponsored volume. Omissions were few. For example, teams generally maintain more defensive statistics than those included here—fumbles caused, sacks, and individual tackles, to name a few. Postseason bowl games are detailed, but preseason games (Kickoff Classic, Pigskin Classic) are excluded. These minor criticisms detract only slightly from a comprehensive record book, which is easily recommended as a replacement for volumes on college football records.—**Boyd Childress**

GOLF

820. Johnson, Salvatore. **The Official U.S. Open Almanac.** Dallas, Tex., Taylor Publishing, 1994. 320p. illus. $18.95pa. ISBN 0-87833-884-5.

1995 marks the centennial of the national championship of American golf, the U.S. Open. Sports fans around the world have heard of the U.S. Open and know that it is one of the premier golfing tournaments in the United States. Both professional and amateur golfers compete for the prestigious title and large purse. The U.S. Open is a major annual sporting event and yet, as Johnson notes, there is no source of complete information on it. Johnson wrote this almanac to fill that void and commemorate the centennial. This work combines facts, statistics, and trivia about the U.S. Open into an interesting and entertaining historical review of the championship. Golf enthusiasts will enjoy reading the detailed accounts of each tournament and the biographical sketches of every winner. Each entry presents the statistics in table format, with an anecdotal review of the tournament or winner's life followed by related trivia and facts.

Johnson writes in a witty, yet concise, journalistic manner. Unfortunately, he does not reveal his credentials or association with the U.S. Open. Another omission is that of an index. With the copious amount of information packed into these 320 pages, a reader would find an index beneficial for locating information about specific golfers and championships. Information about each year's championship is arranged chronologically, while the biographies and host golf course facts are alphabetical. A few black-and-white photographs illustrate the biographies and host courses; this breaks the condensed text and tables of statistics. Championship records and odd facts are listed at the end of the work, prior to the selected bibliography. The facts and trivia contained in this almanac will spice many rounds of golf for years to come.—**Marjorie H. Jones**

821. Lane, James M. **The Complete Golfer's Almanac 1995: A Compendium of Useful Golfing Facts and Information.** New York, Berkley, 1995. 395p. index. $13.95pa. ISBN 0-399-52151-8.

It now seems that the game that has outpaced all others in the past few years is golf. Golf is presently enjoying an immense surge in popularity. There is talk of a new cable television channel devoted entirely to golf. Ratings are on the increase for the professional men's and women's golf events on network television.

Golfing equipment has also played a role in the boom. The advent of metal woods and oversized heads has made the ball a little easier to control for the general player. So the time would seem to be right for another fact book on golf. Already in the mix are *The Hamlyn Encyclopedia of Golf* by Ian Morrison (see ARBA 87, entry 769) and the *Information Please Sports Almanac* (see ARBA 94, entry 818), an annual that offers a summary of golfers and golfing considerably briefer than that of this almanac.

As with most sporting reference books, this has that readability that makes it a joy to open up. It includes brief biographies of leading players past and present and playing results from the careers of many active men and women. For some spectators and readers, the aging, over-50 players that make up the Senior PGA Tour are more interesting than the Normans, Prices, Pavins, and Faldos. These results have also been supplied. There are sections on the events of 1994 and some prescient (as it turns out) predictions for the 1995 majors. Although the book was published well before any of the events were held, *The Complete Golfer's Almanac* correctly named the eventual winners of The U.S. Open (Corey Pavin) and the British Open (John Daly).

Further sections of the book are arranged as follows: people, which was mentioned above; history, in which most of the tournament results and rankings for both men and women, amateur and pro, college and junior, are enumerated; places, in which golf is summarized for countries, states of the United States, top courses in the world (sorry, no pictures), and schools, which gives just enough information to get started. A glossary, a list of world associations, equipment sales data (something not seen everywhere), and an index are in the last pages.

The *Almanac* will be hungrily devoured by the legion of players and television fans of this wildly flourishing game, one that is at once fascinating and frustrating; it will be useful in large public libraries. What the almanac does not have: the rules of the game, which are available from the United States Golf

Association or the Royal and Ancient Club at St. Andrews. However, rules would have added another 30 or 40 pages to the book as the editors have made lavish use of typeface sizes and white space. The pleasing effect is that of readability.—**Randall Rafferty**

822. **PGA Tour, 1995: Official Media Guide of the PGA Tour.** Chicago, Triumph Books, 1995. 407p. illus. index. $12.95pa. ISBN 1-880141-79-5.

The *PGA Tour* is a book to delight any golfing fan. A complete reference for the professional golf world, it contains information about every facet of the tour. The most prominent professional golfers, 154 in number, are profiled in detail; each page-long biography, which includes a picture, gives personal as well as career data, with a brief summary of their 1994 seasons. Following these pages are shorter entries about other professional golfers. Also included in this portion of the book are some of the more famous international players, not mentioned in the first group because they do not play the PGA tour full-time.

The rest of this book contains every fact about professional golf that any aficionado could possibly desire. Every possible record seems to be included, except negative ones. For example, one can learn who is the best putter, but not the worst. Each sanctioned tournament is covered, giving the final results for each event in 1994, as well as a listing of all winners since the tournament's beginning. A brief chronology of the tour rounds out this interesting volume.

Spot checks found no apparent errors in the book's information, although the lack of an index does make using it more difficult. For a golfing fan, the book is a marvelous vade mecum, invaluable for keeping informed about this very popular spectator sport that draws thousands of fans every week all over the world.—**Nancy P. Reed**

823. **Senior PGA Tour, 1995: Official Media Guide of the Senior PGA Tour.** Chicago, Triumph Books, 1995. 251p. illus. index. $12.95pa. ISBN 1-880141-80-9.

With the increased popularity of golf, the Professional Golf Association has expanded its activities. The Senior PGA Tour is one highly successful expansion. Since the tour's beginning in 1980, each year has shown an increase in tournaments and prize money. The *Senior PGA Tour, 1995* chronicles the development of the tour, and provides players' statistics and tournament facts. A table of contents and an index guide the reader through the vast information. The stated purpose of this guide is to provide writers, broadcasters, and fans with the knowledge and records that will enable them to follow the tour each week throughout 1995. At times, fine print is necessary to present all of the information; yet, the detail contained in 251 pages is impressive.

No author or editor is cited. The verso on the front cover notes that the work was produced by PGA Tour Creative Services. Further explanation of that entity would be beneficial. Credit and responsibility of the work do increase that work's validity. If numerous people contributed sections or chapters, authors could have signed their parts. Someone wrote a fine, 2-page history of the Senior PGA Tour, but did not clearly note that a PGA member qualifies for senior status at age 50.

Biographies of the top 31 players on the 1994 Senior Tour Money List are most complete. The photographs are black-and-white, yet very clear, so that players can be easily identified. Even the weather was described in the summaries of each 1994 Senior event. Facts, figures, and records of the Senior Tour are well arranged and easy to read. Practicality and usefulness of information are consistently demonstrated: The list of PGA schedules for 1995 is just one example. A more convenient and complete work on the 1995 Senior PGA Tour would be hard to find; this is probably the best source available.—**Marjorie H. Jones**

HIKING

824. Cook, Charles. **The Essential Guide to Wilderness Camping and Backpacking in the United States.** New York, Michael Kesend Publishing; distr., New York, Talman, 1994. 324p. illus. maps. index. $24.95pa. ISBN 0-935576-46-0.

This handy reference for anyone wanting to camp in America's backcountry is divided into two parts: essentials of wilderness camping and backpacking and a complete guide to U.S. parks and other natural areas open to wilderness camping, along with the best trails for backpacking. The work includes an index.

The first part of the book is for people with limited backcountry experience. It covers topics such as camping fundamentals, equipment, food, clothing, planning and preparation for a trip, camp setup, and safety.

Part 2 is the real treasure. It is divided by state, each having a list of places where backpacking and wilderness camping are permitted, with applicable regulations and sources of other information. In addition, descriptions of "major backpacking trails," defined as "scenic trails . . . at least 40 to 50 miles long and open to backpacking," are provided, including trail regulations. The "Activities" list possible outdoor activities for the region in question, such as kayaking or rock climbing.

This book is a good starting point for backpacking in unfamiliar places. However, additional detailed maps and trail descriptions will be required for most places listed. This book is a companion to Cook's *The Essential Guide to Hiking in the United States* (see ARBA 93, entry 835). Recommended for developing outdoor activity collections.—**Alan N. Livingston**

825. Rajtar, Steve. **Hiking Trails, Eastern United States: Address, Phone Number, and Distances for 5000 Trails....** Jefferson, N.C., McFarland, 1995. 343p. index. $39.95pa. ISBN 0-7864-0142-7.

While there are many hiking guides for the eastern United States, the unique approach of this guide makes it a reference tool that academic and public libraries with any interest in outdoor recreational activities will find invaluable. In an extremely compact format this guidebook provides brief listings for nearly 500 trails or hiking areas in the United States east of the Mississippi River. It needs to be used with other guidebooks, maps, and similar resources because the information it provides is so sketchy. Each entry usually consists of the name of the trail; the name, address, and telephone number of the organization responsible for maintaining it; the length; whether or not there are awards associated with hiking that particular trail; and citations to 1 or more of about 250 trail guides.

The basic entries, which are numbered consecutively, are arranged alphabetically by state—a geographical arrangement that located states contiguously would be preferable as trails are necessarily confined by state borders—and, within each state, alphabetically by the name of the trail. There is an index by city at the end of each state entry. A final entry provides a separate listing of interstate trails. The references to other guidebooks consist of simple abbreviations that refer to a detailed list of the sources used at the end of the text. This innovative approach to providing access to information about a popular recreational activity deserves attention and should prove to be a most useful reference tool.

—**Norman D. Stevens**

HOCKEY

826. Fischler, Stan. **Bad Boys: Legends of Hockey's Toughest, Meanest, Most-Feared Players!** Toronto, Warwick Publishing; distr., Willowdale, Ont., Firefly Books, 1994. 238p. illus. $15.95pa. (U.S.). ISBN 1-895629-42-X.

Fischler has written more than 60 books on hockey. In view of this remarkable number, one may safely conclude that there is a substantial audience for specialized publications on hockey and that Fischler has the experience, knowledge, and skill to command that audience. Indeed, by now his reputation is such that his name alone is enough to characterize and, in effect, guarantee his wares.

Bad Boys is standard Fischler. The subject this time around is the rough-and-tough players who act as "enforcers" or "policemen" for their teams. Fischler provides profiles of 26 current National Hockey League players famed for their ability at violence, as brought out by the questions and answers of an interview. A page of biographical information and commentary precedes each interview, and a concluding chapter (by Eric Servetah) rates the best fighters by their standing with respect to such indispensable skills-of-the-trade as "knockout punch," "tying up," and "intimidation."

There is no index, but because each chapter deals with just one person, the book permits fairly easy consultation. However, it is unlikely that any but the largest or most specialized libraries will want *Bad Boys* for its reference value. The appeal here is to readers who find pleasure in learning more about hockey violence and its star practitioners. Apparently there are many such readers; Fischler serves them well.

—**Samuel Rothstein**

827. Fischler, Stan. **Goalies: Legends from the NHL's Toughest Job.** Toronto, Warwick Publishing; distr., Willowdale, Ont., Firefly Books, 1995. 196p. illus. $14.95pa. (U.S.). ISBN 1-895629-40-3.

There is no end of excellent hockey reference books, but this is not one of them. In fact, it is doubtful whether this will be used as a reference book despite the fact that it contains short biographical sketches of 24 prominent professional hockey goalies. The text is divided into three sections. The 1st section deals with 12 former goalies of note. After this come six short tales of memorable incidents involving goalies (e.g., the goalie who scored a goal). Finally, there are sketches of 12 contemporary National Hockey League goalies. The main problem is that all of the pieces are sketches rather than true biographies. They provide the bare minimum of biographical information—no birth or death dates, and none of the detailed statistical information that many fans look for. The net result is a book that is fun to read but that has little lasting reference value. Public libraries in areas where there is great interest in professional hockey are the most likely buyers of this text, and they, for the most part, are apt to put it in their circulating collections.—**Norman D. Stevens**

828. *The Sporting News* **Complete Hockey Book.** 1995-96 ed. Craig Carter, George Puro, and Kyle Veltrop, eds. St. Louis, Mo., Sporting News Publishing, 1995. 784p. $18.95pa. ISBN 0-89204-529-9.

Previously published as two volumes, this resource incorporates both the *Guide* and *Register*. The table of contents divides the resources into five sections: National Hockey League (NHL) year in review, minor leagues, history, college, and the register. The coverage on the NHL teams is excellent. Team information includes statistical data on the players, a schedule, the club directory, draft selections, and the training club roster. The section on NHL history provides records in the various leagues, past winners of the Stanley Cup, All-Star Games, awards, hall-of-famers, milestones, and information on the history of the teams (including defunct teams and teams that have moved).

The Minor League section covers the American, International, East Coast, Central, and Colonial Hockey Leagues. General information on each league is provided, as well as team information, individual statistics, awards, and league playoff records. The leagues and team information of the Major Junior's are also listed. The college section covers primarily National Collegiate Athletic Association (NCAA) Division 1 teams and a brief listing for some of the Canadian University Leagues. The entry on college independents is very limited (two teams). There are many teams and leagues that fall into this category, but there is no definition in this source of what *The Sporting News* classifies as independents.

The other piece of hockey information that is missing that would truly make this a complete guide of hockey in North America is information on the collegiate women's teams in the United States and Canada. The register of players provides the player's history and important transitions and career notes, but no pictures. Lastly, there is a section with information on NHL coaches. At the time of this review, no other hockey guides of equivalent coverage were in print. The price for this two-in-one volume is reasonable for any hockey fan or hockey collection.—**Mila C. Su**

MOUNTAINEERING

829. Child, Greg, comp. **Climbing: The Complete Reference.** New York, Facts on File, 1995. 264p. illus. index. $39.95. ISBN 0-8160-2692-0.

Although *Climbing* is more a string of extended definitions than a practical guidebook, it offers a survey of the tools, techniques, people, and places involved in all aspects of mountaineering. While its information is plentiful and accurate, it gives little feeling of the techniques, challenges, and pleasures of climbing itself. Many states have entries under their own names, including suggested local guidebooks. However, there is no listing for New York State although the Shawangunk Mountains, one of the best areas in the state for rock climbing, have a separate listing. Surely New York State merits a mention of its own, if only in the index. The sparse illustrations and photographs add little to the text. A better choice for libraries would be *The Handbook of Climbing* (Viking Penguin, 1991), despite its British orientation. The work under review is recommended only for large outdoor collections.—**Natalie Kupferberg**

RUGBY

830. **Rugby Catalogue of Information Sources. Répertoire de Sources d'Information sur le Rugby.** International Rugby Information Centre, ed. Gloucester, Ont., International Rugby Football Board and Sports Information Resource Centre, 1994. 228p. index. $39.95pa. ISBN 0-921817-27-4.

Professional and amateur rugby players will find invaluable this bibliography of more than 5,300 citations on all aspects of the sport. Arranged in broad subject categories, it covers children and adolescents, coaching, diseases, drugs and doping, injuries and accidents, nutrition, officiating, physiology, psychology, and training and conditioning. Within each category the entries are arranged alphabetically by title, and complete standard bibliographic information is provided for each entry. Each entry is also assigned a research level rating to assist users in determining if the material is appropriate to their need. Abstracts are generally provided for advanced materials, as well as for some intermediate or technical materials.

The book has a brief English and French topical index, but lacks an author index, which makes it virtually impossible to locate items on an author basis. A listing of information resource centers in various countries is intended to assist users in locating copies of the material listed. That is an important need, since much of the material listed is not readily available even in larger academic libraries. Judging by the seven U.S. centers listed, however, that listing is not likely to be of any real help.

In the end, this bibliography can be recommended only as a secondary source for larger academic libraries with a strong sport, leisure, and exercise science or sports medicine program, and for public libraries serving an active rugby community.—**Norman D. Stevens**

SOCCER

831. Howard, Dale E. **Soccer Stars.** Chicago, Childrens Press, 1994. 48p. illus. index. $13.45. ISBN 0-516-08047-4.

Soccer Stars is a juvenile title giving biographies of the 10 best soccer players the world has ever seen, including Sir Stanley Matthews, Lev Yashin, Pelé, Franz Beckenbauer, George Best, and Diego Maradona. The author states that many others could have been included as well. Each three-page biography contains the soccer player's birth and death dates, country, position, numerous photographs, and a narrative. A glossary of world soccer terms and an index are included. This is an easy, large-print reader that should be very popular with juvenile soccer enthusiasts, as there are few soccer biographies that they are able to read. *Soccer Stars* is a must for public library juvenile sports collections.—**Kathleen J. Voigt**

TENNIS

832. **WTA Tour: Official 1995 WTA Tour Media Guide.** Compiled by the WTA Tour Communications Staff. Chicago, Triumph Books, 1995. 414p. illus. $19.95pa. ISBN 1-57243-025-7.

Ever wonder how tennis commentators display a remarkable grasp of history, trivia, and minutia to capture and hold the attention of the television viewing audience? The answer is a media guide. Initially, *WTA Tour* presents a historical overview of the Women's Tennis Association since its inception, including its history, its function, its staffing, a tournament schedule for the upcoming year, award winners, and philanthropic work. The next section, the most important and valuable, offers player biographies of registered amateurs, professionals, and noteworthy retired professionals. Requisite birthplace and vital statistics sections lead off each alphabetically ordered biography, followed by career highlights and personal information. The third section lists winners of tournaments for the past 10 years, rankings and how they are figured, prize monies, and the complete draw for the past year's grand slam events. Contact information for each country's tennis federation, a listing of Hall of Fame inductees, and credits round out the volume.

Despite the lack of an index, this compact book is easy to read, browse, and search. Judicious typography, photographs, and charts add to the entries. The presentation of facts and the all-inclusive treatment of women's professional tennis are the strong points in this media guide. Controversial on-court events are recounted (e.g., the attack on Monica Seles), while off-court, headline-grabbing behavior has no mention. Any library maintaining tennis, up-to-date sports, recreation, or sports history reference collections would be well served by this reasonably priced volume.—**Timothy A. Dixon**

16 Sociology

GENERAL WORKS

Bibliography

833. Nordquist, Joan, comp. **Theodor Adorno (II): A Bibliography.** Santa Cruz, Calif., Reference and Research Services, 1994. 72p. index. (Social Theory: A Bibliographic Series, no.35). $15.00pa. ISBN 0-937855-69-3.

Number 35 in the series Social Theory: A Bibliographic Series, *Theodor Adorno (II)* is a supplement to the 1988 bibliography of the same title (see ARBA 89, entry 748). Section 1 contains all the books and essays by Adorno reprinted since 1988 with a listing of book reviews and essays that pertain to each title. Essays, interviews, and articles by Adorno are listed in section 2 with citations to their sources. Section 3 lists books, dissertations, and theses in English about the works of Adorno and biographies of him. Section 4 contains the critical literature in English about Adorno in books and journal articles. Additional features in this publication are a two-page introduction to Adorno and keyword-in-title indexes to the entries.

In the days of on-demand online computer searches, the value of printed indexes like the ones in this series is sometimes questioned. (This particular book has a folded and stapled binding.) Various databases will certainly satisfy many with easy access to a number of citations. These searchers will not be interested in finding a printed bibliography. However, for those who need greater coverage of the literature, this series offers extensive coverage of English-language sources. It covers the literature found in edited books as well as the periodical literature. The publishers state that particular effort has been made to include citations from the alternative, left, feminist, and small presses. Also, this bibliography lays out the principal works and the critical literature in a very clear and easy-to-use manner. Although the citations lack annotations and non-English-language works are omitted, the work will be appreciated by anyone doing in-depth research.—**Henry E. York**

Dictionaries and Encyclopedias

834. **The Concise Oxford Dictionary of Sociology.** Gordon Marshall, ed. New York, Oxford University Press, 1994. 571p. $29.95; $13.95pa. ISBN 0-19-211670-3; 0-19-285237-Xpa.

This dictionary, written by a team of 30 sociologists who at the time of its conception were all affiliated with the University of Essex, has about 2,500 unsigned entries, including hundreds of *see* references. Entries, which range in length from five lines to two pages, provide definitions of terms and biographical sketches. British spelling (e.g., "behaviour," "ethnocentricism") is used throughout. Not only are sociological concepts and sociologists included, but also related terms and major names in anthropology, economics, philosophy, political science, and psychology. However, because the contributors could not agree on what leading contemporary authorities to include, there are no entries for living sociologists such as Jürgen Habermas, Claude Lévi-Strauss, Seymour Martin Lipset, and Robert K. Merton.

Within entries, asterisks are used frequently to denote *see also* references. Bibliographical citations provide only authors, titles, and dates. There is no separate bibliography with complete publication data, such as can be found in another recent work, *The HarperCollins Dictionary of Sociology* (see ARBA 93, entry 848). Also, there are far fewer illustrations than in *The Encyclopedic Dictionary of Sociology* (4th ed.; see ARBA 93, entry 849), a more physically attractive book.

Despite its faults, students of sociology will find this Oxford University Press publication useful. However, it is not an essential purchase for libraries possessing the two dictionaries mentioned above.

—**Leonard Grundt**

835. Levinson, David. **Aggression and Conflict: A Cross-Cultural Encyclopedia.** Santa Barbara, Calif., ABC-CLIO, 1994. 234p. illus. index. (Encyclopedias of the Human Experience). $49.50. ISBN 0-87436-728-X.

While aggression and conflict are centuries-old behaviors, people have found numerous ways to resolve conflicts peacefully. Both points are covered in this cross-cultural survey of expressions of, and reactions to, harmful behavior. The encyclopedia is meant for high school and college students, and others interested in human behavior. Ninety subject entries (e.g., peacemaking, rape, war) focus primarily on non-Western cultures and on customs still practiced in some cultures. Black-and-white photographs enhance the descriptions.

Each entry defines the behavior or custom, describes its variant forms and distribution, and gives examples. Sources used for each entry, and those providing additional information, are cited at the end. Cross-references serve to link entries. A cumulative bibliography collates sources, and a subject index provides quick access.

This volume, as well as others in Encyclopedias of the Human Experience, is based on ethnographic research and cross-cultural surveys. Such works serve to promote global understanding and the concept that there are nonviolent ways to manage and resolve conflicts.—**Anita Zutis**

836. **Survey of Social Science: Sociology Series.** Frank N. Magill, ed. Pasadena, Calif., Salem Press, 1994. 5v. index. $375.00/set. ISBN 0-89356-739-6.

This affordable encyclopedia of sociology is a five-volume reference work that will make a useful addition to many library reference collections. Most potential users will be favorably impressed by the breadth of material (338 articles) covered in the *Sociology Series* and the consistent organization of substantive material in each selection. The articles cover a number of specific topics, many of traditional concern to specialists in the discipline, along with others of more topical or popular interest. Various reference aids are provided to make this volume easy to access. Each selection contains keywords stating the area of study to which each article's topic belongs, a list of key terms with practical or working definitions, an annotated bibliography directing the reader to accessible sources, and a list of cross-references of related articles. Moreover, the articles are arranged alphabetically by article title, and each volume begins with a list of its contents and ends with a list of the entire series contents grouped by category.

The series concludes with a glossary of all key terms and definitions in the series and a cross-referenced index of topics, concepts, and personages. As for each article, a standard text format is consistently applied: One section introduces and explains the topic, a second section illustrates applications of the concept in sociological studies, and a third section relates the concept to the field of sociology as a whole and to relevant historical or cultural concerns. This straightforward presentation of each subject is fresh, accessible, and welcome.

On the whole the *Sociology Series* is an impressive collection of articles written by reputable scholars in the discipline. As such, the prospective user should feel confident that the quality of the articles is superb and authoritative. The series is designed to provide nonspecialists with views of areas "increasingly important to the layperson." The articles cover a wide range of intellectual concerns in the discipline, but the intent of the series is not to represent the entire discipline to a general audience. This limitation is especially notable in several emergent research areas, such as the sociology of emotions, the social studies of science, and new social theory. However, given the intent and length of the project, such a limitation should not prevent most public libraries and undergraduate college libraries from acquiring the *Sociology Series* for their reference collections.—**David V. Waller**

Handbooks and Yearbooks

837. Johnson, Richard S. **Find Anyone FAST: By Phone, FAX, Mail, and Computer.** Burlington, N.C., MIE Publishing, 1995. 175p. index. $19.00pa. ISBN 1-877639-20-6.

This handbook by the author of *How to Locate Anyone Who Is or Has Been in the Military* (see entry 688) expands upon information given in that book, so that someone searching for a missing person without a military connection may find it useful. Johnson describes how to organize and conduct a search, how to determine if the person being sought is deceased, where to find important identifying information, and what assistance is available from federal, state, and local governments as well as businesses and other private sources. The book includes search techniques employing mail, telephone, facsimile transmission, and computers.

Brief descriptions of missing person cases solved by the author are provided, as are sample copies of forms, lists of agencies and telephone numbers, and a glossary. Unfortunately, the book is poorly edited, so that there are frequent grammatical inconsistencies and the same information is unnecessarily repeated in several places. Furthermore, the index is woefully inadequate, bibliographical references are incomplete, and—worst of all—the author advertises his publications and personal research service ad nauseam. Ted Gunderson's *How to Locate Anyone Anywhere Without Leaving Home* (see ARBA 90, entry 778) is a much better reference source for those needing to find missing people.—**Leonard Grundt**

AGING

Bibliography

838. Folts, W. Edward, and others. **Aging Well: A Selected, Annotated Bibliography.** Westport, Conn., Greenwood Press, 1995. 156p. index. (Bibliographies and Indexes in Gerontology, no.31). $55.00. ISBN 0-313-28771-6.

The well-qualified authors of this skillfully annotated bibliography admit that they are not always in complete agreement as to what "aging well" really means. At any rate, they have used this concept as the criterion for selecting entries from literature and research about normal aging—the positive aspects of growing old successfully as opposed to the more usual negative viewpoint of a period of problems, deteriorating health, and loss.

Consecutively numbered, 500 entries are arranged alphabetically by author under 9 general topics: physical aging, psychological aging, social aging, family issues, living arrangements, work and economics, education and leisure, politics, and religion. These categories are explained in the introduction. Specific subjects for needed future research on aging well are also suggested.

The appendix lists articles grouped under the title "Instruments for the Measurement of Aging Well." There are subject and author indexes. Researchers and specialists from many disciplines dealing with aging and the elderly should find this volume from the series on gerontology of significant interest.
—**Harriette M. Cluxton**

839. Hayslip, Bert, Jr., Heather L. Servaty, and Amie S. Ward, comps. **Psychology of Aging: An Annotated Bibliography.** Westport, Conn., Greenwood Press, 1995. 134p. index. (Bibliographies and Indexes in Gerontology, no.28). $59.95. ISBN 0-313-29376-7.

This is one of the volumes in the Greenwood Press series Bibliographies and Indexes in Gerontology. In the series, Greenwood Press presents what is known about gerontology, and this particular volume contains an annotated bibliography on the psychology of aging, with the subject classified into 14 topics, each topic constituting a chapter in the book. The topics include theory, research methods, psychophysiology, sensory-perceptual processes, learning and memory, intelligence, creativity, personality, interpersonal relations, work and retirement, and death and dying. Bibliographic entries, acquired from scientific articles, books, or book chapters, are from the past 10 to 15 years; some older materials, considered by the authors to be classics, are also listed. Textbooks are excluded.

The bibliography is not intended to be exhaustive, but it does reference 546 items. Some items, because they cover more than one topic, are repeated in various chapters. Sources are arranged alphabetically within each chapter, and the book contains a helpful author and subject index. The work, although not intended to be a substitute for a thorough literature search, serves as a useful guide to recent literature. This annotated bibliography will be of most help and interest to graduate students and beginning researchers, but it can also be helpful to mental health workers, psychologists, and teachers.—**Nathan M. Smith**

840. Koenig, Harold G., comp. **Research on Religion and Aging: An Annotated Bibliography.** Westport, Conn., Greenwood Press, 1995. 172p. index. (Bibliographies and Indexes in Gerontology, no.27). $55.00. ISBN 0-313-29427-5.

The past two decades have witnessed an explosion in geriatric-related literature. Currently there are more than 40 professional journals and dozens of monographs published annually on some aspect of gerontology. This bibliography is part of the definitive gerontology reference series Bibliographies and Indexes in Gerontology. Koenig, this volume's compiler, is the director of the Duke University Program on Religion, Aging, and Health, thus making him eminently qualified for this project.

Intended for a diverse audience, ranging from ministers and policymakers to psychiatrists and other mental health professionals, this volume covers 291 journal and monographic entries published between 1980 and 1995. These items were selected after an examination of the leading medical and sociological literature, as well as searches run on MEDLINE, PsychLIT, and Sciofile databases. Each citation is thoroughly annotated, covering five aspects of the publication: objective, sample and method, results, conclusions, and the compiler's quality rating. Regrettably, almost all entries are drawn from the clinical health care literature, while the scholarly religious publications are mostly ignored, as was the Health, Medicine, and Bioethics Database created by the American Theological Library Association. Despite the oversight, this reference bibliography will provide an excellent starting point for most researchers investigating the relationship between religion and aging in the Western world.—**Jonathon Erlen**

841. Koff, Theodore H., and Kristine M. Bursac, comps. **Long Term Care: An Annotated Bibliography.** Westport, Conn., Greenwood Press, 1995. 128p. index. (Bibliographies and Indexes in Gerontology, no.25). $59.95. ISBN 0-313-28583-7.

This book is one in a series of bibliographies on gerontology. Aimed at researchers, clinicians, and public policymakers in medical and social work fields, the work is not for the lay public. The compilers define *long term care* as any services provided for the chronically ill or impaired, thus including both institutional and home-delivered services.

The 249 entries are divided into 12 chapters, based on broad topics. Subjects covered include the history of long-term care, institutionalized care, community services, services to special population groups, and public policy issues. Most entries represent journal articles, books, or government reports. Many are chapter- or book-length reviews of various aspects of the field. Each entry is accompanied by full bibliographical information and a one-paragraph abstract. There are complete subject and author indexes. Although the existence of online databases makes such bibliographical publications less essential, there is still something to be said for letting experts in the field list and summarize the work that forms an outline of the basic knowledge of a particular field.—**Carol L. Noll**

842. Rife, John C., comp. **Employment of the Elderly: An Annotated Bibliography.** Westport, Conn., Greenwood Press, 1995. 133p. index. (Bibliographies and Indexes in Gerontology, no.23). $59.95. ISBN 0-313-29191-8.

Designed for researchers, practitioners, and policymakers, this annotated bibliography is intended as a current reference guide to employment- and unemployment-related issues as they pertain to the elderly. With inclusions (e.g., books, periodicals), exclusions (e.g., newspapers), and categories (e.g., 50-plus, 1980-94) clearly defined in the preface, selected works are arranged in nine topical chapters (e.g., age discrimination, self-help). The best, most comprehensive chapters are those on training and the implications of an aging workforce for the economy. The two indexes—author and subject—are inadequate, with spotty keyword indexing and a lack of important cross-references.

Meant as a survey of the significant research from the last 20 years, this work suffers from design, editing, and content flaws. While many of the annotations are both descriptive and analytical, too many begin with the word "this." Chapter 3, which lists selected archives, databases, and periodicals, fails to mention several important databases (e.g., Sociofile, ABI/Inform) and indexes (e.g., Work Related Abstracts). The chapter on special populations should be a highlighted feature, given the multicultural nature of our populations; instead, in focusing entirely on African Americans, it ignores the numerous Hispanic, Native American, and Asian-American elderly residing in the country. The author has created an introductory rather than authoritative work for this important topic.—**Sandra E. Belanger**

843. Schwiebert, Valerie L., and Jane E. Myers, comps. **Counseling Older Persons: An Annotated Bibliography.** Westport, Conn., Greenwood Press, 1995. 119p. index. (Bibliographies and Indexes in Gerontology, no.26). $49.95. ISBN 0-313-29277-9.

Counseling Older Persons is in the series Bibliographies and Indexes in Gerontology by Greenwood Press. The bibliographies provide answers to what is know about specific fields in gerontology through literature reviews. The book is divided into nine chapters and subchapters including normative experience of aging; older persons with impairments; needs and services for older persons; population and special situations; theories on counseling the elderly; ethics in counseling; practicums and internships; the gerontological counselor; and pharmacology and aging. The preface acknowledges the demographic changes in the population over age 65. The annotations are up-to-date and cover a wide range of professional research publications, books, and reports. The book could be improved by making the annotations more substantial. Access to the book is accomplished through an author and subject index. *Counseling Older Persons* is more limited in its appeal not only because the annotations are shorter, but also because it is not as comprehensive as *Topics in Gerontology* by the same publisher (see ARBA 95, entry 832). This book is more specialized and would appeal to those who want to specialize in gerontological counseling or research. This would be a nice addition for the larger academic and public libraries that have gerontological programs and collections.—**Theresa Maggio**

844. Walker, Bonnie L., comp. **Injury Prevention for the Elderly: A Research Guide.** Westport, Conn., Greenwood Press, 1995. 311p. index. (Bibliographies and Indexes in Gerontology, no.30) $75.00. ISBN 0-313-29670-7.

Injury is one of the top 10 causes of death, and is responsible for excessive morbidity and health care expenditures among the elderly. Therefore, this book is a welcome addition to the ongoing series of gerontological bibliographies and indexes published by Greenwood Press. As with previous works in the series, this book provides annotated reviews of the literature on the topic, citing more than 600 books or articles from professional journals or the popular press.

The book begins with an overview of injury theory and epidemiology; it then proceeds to individual chapters on various causes of injury in the elderly (e.g., burns, falls, abuse, alcohol, suicide, hypo/hyperthermia). An added value is the inclusion of chapters on topics not usually addressed in the gerontological injury literature: choking, drowning, food poisoning, and malnutrition. Within the topical chapters, the epidemiology of the injury as well as prevention is discussed. A broad range of literature, dating up to and including 1994, is reviewed. Two cross-indexes, by author and by subject, simplify the use of the reference. This comprehensive collection would be helpful for professionals in gerontology, as well as undergraduate and graduate students in many academic fields.—**Mary Ann Thompson**

845. Yahnke, Robert E., and Richard M. Eastman. **Literature and Gerontology: A Research Guide.** Westport, Conn., Greenwood Press, 1995. 231p. index. (Bibliographies and Indexes in Gerontology, no.29). $69.50. ISBN 0-313-29349-X.

This book continues a series of annotated bibliographies on various topics in gerontology. The purpose of this new addition, as stated in the introduction, is to highlight "the ways in which literary works illuminate the problems and potentials of older persons." The reference is divided into two main sections. The first presents a series of 44 short bibliographic essays, bringing together the literature that speaks to a particular subject, such as ageism, older couples, or aging-in-place.

The second major section contains the citations, subdivided into novels, plays, poems, and stories. Although not every piece of literature that relates to aging could be included, the listing is comprehensive, covering more than 350 works dating from the time of William Shakespeare to the present. A section citing other anthologies on literature and aging is supplied. The book is organized, easy to use, and contains a number of indexes. This work would be invaluable for the gerontologist wanting to integrate literary works into a course or for the English professor wanting to integrate gerontological concepts.
—Mary Ann Thompson

Biography

846. Achenbaum, W. Andrew, and Daniel M. Albert. **Profiles in Gerontology: A Biographical Dictionary.** Westport, Conn., Greenwood Press, 1995. $85.00. 396p. index. $85.00. ISBN 0-313-29274-4.

Profiles in Gerontology provides biographical information on more than 300 researchers, practitioners, and teachers in the field of aging. While most of the individuals represented are North Americans, there are a number from Great Britain and Europe. The work begins with an introduction by the authors that provides a brief history of the study of gerontology and some predictions for the field. Each individual's entry contains place of birth, education, prominent positions held, and a brief biography, including prominent publications and places of employment. Honors, awards, or memberships in scholarly organizations may be included.

The authors obtained the information for the volume through the use of profile questionnaires sent out during fall 1994. Several prominent gerontologists preferred not to participate, and they were not included. The entries are even and provide comparable information from one gerontologist to the next.

The book is extremely useful as a biographical source, and the name and subject indexes allow for more general reference on the subject. The name index indicates the main entry for each individual along with page references in other entries. It is possible to look up colleges and universities in the subject index to find the faculty in the area of gerontology at a particular university and to trace their research efforts.

While the work is an important reference tool in the area, a complete bibliography of all works referred to in the entries and a list of individuals by specialty would have been useful. However, *Profiles in Gerontology* is still a useful source. The only other sources for information on individuals in the field that come to mind are *American Men and Women of Science: The Medical Sciences* (see ARBA 76, entry 1542) and *Dictionary of American Medical Biography* (see ARBA 85, entry 1535). Andrew W. Achenbaum's *Crossing Frontiers* (Cambridge University Press, 1995) identifies individuals who are important to the field. The work under review is strongly recommended for all medical libraries and for larger university and public library collections.—**Robert L. Wick**

Directories

847. **The Directory of Retirement Facilities, 1995.** Baltimore, Md., HCIA, 1994. 1377p. index. $249.00pa. ISBN 1-880678-96-9. ISSN 1053-6825.

This annual publication of HCIA serves as a guide and basis for general comparison of retirement facilities currently in operation in the United States. Most of the facilities listed are intended to serve the elderly, but some also provide housing for low-income families and the handicapped. The four types of facilities listed here are: *Assisted Living*, combining shelter along with help as required for daily activities such as laundry; *Congregate Care*, private living quarters with centralized dining services and access to social and recreational activities and transportation; *Independent Living*, homes, apartments, condominiums, or mobile homes where the residents retain an independent lifestyle; and *Continuing Care*, providing a broad range of care from skilled nursing to housekeeping for the balance of a person's life.

Arrangement is state-by-state and then alphabetical by town or city, listing the facilities located there. The information for the retirement facilities varies. Some entries indicate, in addition to the address, telephone number, and contact person, kinds of activities, monthly services (housekeeping, central dining, kinds of nursing care), date opened, whether state licensed, private for profit, and private nonprofit. A few entries include the costs, but most do not. A facility index at the end of the volume lists each facility alphabetically by name and indicates in which city or state it is located. This substantial volume lists information in one source that would be difficult to locate elsewhere. It is a good starting point for senior citizens in selecting a retirement home and will be of great value in public libraries.—**Marilyn Strong Noronha**

848. **KR Information OnDisc Grants Database. July, 1995.** [CD-ROM]. Phoenix, Ariz., Oryx Press, 1995. Minimum system requirements: IBM PC/XT/AT or PS/2 or compatible 286. CD-ROM drive with MS-DOS CD-ROM Extensions 2.1. PC-DOS or MS-DOS 3.1. 512K RAM. 1MB hard disk space. Color or monochrome monitor. Printer (optional). $850.00/yr.

Easy-to-follow, precise directions with helpful examples make installation of this product quick and simple. Security features are useful and easy to lock in; users can be forced to save to a disk in either drive A:\ or B:\, not the hard disk. As with other KR Information OnDisc products, users can choose either the "Easy Menu Search" or "DIALOG Command Search" to look up information. Customer and technical support is also readily available from KR's able customer service representatives, while questions on file content are answered by Oryx Press.

This directory database provides standard grantseekers information with myriad access points and covers all academic disciplines, as well as performance and programmatic grants in the arts, humanities, and social and physical sciences. Subject terms are taken from the more than 200-term *GRANTS Subject Authority Guide* (see ARBA 93, entry 637). Many choices of formats for records are available, as well as sorting and formatting options. Records all seem current and accurate.

As usual, DIALOGLINK allows users to conduct their search online if that option is made available by the library. Updated every other month, the Grants Database will be well used in any academic library.
—**Susan C. Awe**

849. **National Guide to Funding in Aging.** 4th ed. C. Edward Murphy, comp. and ed. New York, Nassau County Department of Senior Citizen Affairs and Foundation Center, 1994. 454p. index. $80.00pa. ISBN 0-87954-559-3.

Any group or organization seeking to develop research projects or programs for older adults would do well to investigate this new edition of funding resources. Information is given on more than 1,000 governmental, private, and voluntary organizations that do, or could potentially, provide project financing. The publication is well organized and easy to use. It is divided into four main sections: federal government, state governments, private foundations, and voluntary organizations. The state government and foundation sections are organized alphabetically by state; the federal section is organized by program type (e.g., housing, health, veterans); and the voluntary groups are arranged by type of organization (e.g., universities). The federal government and foundation chapters are the most valuable in regard to potential funding. Each of these two sections has a brief introduction that gives basic, but important, information on how to apply for grants from the respective resources. This is followed by individual resource entries that include such information as what is funded, the amounts of money available, how to apply, who to contact, and what types of programs have been funded in the past. A comprehensive index cross-references all the sources by name. This invaluable guide for geriatic program planners and researchers is highly recommended for general as well as college and university libraries.—**Mary Ann Thompson**

Handbooks and Yearbooks

850. **The Encyclopedia of Aging: A Comprehensive Resource in Gerontology and Geriatrics.** 2d ed. George L. Maddox and others, eds. New York, Springer Publishing, 1995. 1216p. illus. index. $159.00. ISBN 0-8261-4841-7.

This publication belies the negative stereotype that often accompanies a book known as an "encyclopedia." Rather, this reference is an outstanding and valuable contribution to the literature on aging. The editors note that extensive revisions have occurred since the 1st edition in 1986 (see ARBA 88, entry 819); more than 80 percent of the book is updated or new. The list of contributors, representing a range of disciplines, reads like a "who's who" in gerontology.

The 545 alphabetized entries are concise but substantive and are written at a level that is appropriate for many types of readers. Entries include appropriate references for further research. The references are compiled in a 190-page section at the conclusion of the book, an asset that, in itself, is worth the price of the book. Subject and author cross-indexes simplify use. This book is a must for academic, health care, and public libraries and is highly recommended.—**Mary Ann Thompson**

851. **International Handbook on Services for the Elderly.** Jordan I. Kosberg, ed. Westport, Conn., Greenwood Press, 1994. 501p. index. $99.50. ISBN 0-313-28338-9.

The 32 countries covered in this handbook were selected to represent regions of the world, levels of development, and the diversity among societies' attitudes toward and care of the aged. Although Europe is heavily represented with 13 countries, the 32 span the globe and include Canada and the United States; Argentina and Barbados; France, the Netherlands, and Sweden; Israel, India, China, and Thailand; Ghana and Sudan; and Australia and New Zealand. Editor Kosberg, a specialist in gerontology with academic experience on both sides of the U.S.-Canadian border, developed a uniform structure for each national chapter that, despite the diversity of his international cast of contributors, has been observed assiduously throughout.

The essays' structure opens with an introduction that explains the national definition of old age, characterizes societal attitudes toward the elderly, and provides an overview of government's role in providing services. Other sections cover income maintenance and employment, health care services, housing resources, supportive services, leisure-time resources, advocacy and protection organizations, and future projections regarding the effectiveness of the national service program for the elderly. "Supportive services" includes information and referral services, nutrition programs, home care programs, and mental health services.

Each essay concludes with a bibliography of cited sources. Topical entries in the index are followed by numerous geographic subdivisions, just as geographic entries are followed by topical subdivisions. The index, combined with the regular structure of the chapters, facilitates international comparisons of how countries address an issue. As the worldwide population ages, these issues will demand more attention from policy makers. The handbook will be a very useful tool for both students of these issues and policy makers who must deal with them.—**James Rettig**

COMMUNITY LIFE

852. **Communities Directory: A Guide to Cooperative Living.** 1995 ed. Rutledge, Mo., Fellowship for Intentional Community, 1995. 440p. illus. maps. index. $20.00pa./individual; $30.00pa./institution. ISBN 0-9602714-3-0.

Intentional communities—from cohousing groups to religious communities—are on the rise. This book documents their growth with listings for more than 600 intentional communities in the United States and abroad. Entries are arranged alphabetically by community name within two broad categories—North American and International. Most annotations include a mailing address, a telephone number, and a brief description that outlines the basic goals and policies of the group. Detailed charts list other features, such as size, how often members eat together, what type of diet is followed, number of children in the community, and chosen spiritual path. An index by state and province follows the North American community listings, and maps indicate the location of groups within larger regions.

In addition to the directory, the book offers 31 articles on various aspects of community living. These are intended to guide readers in such endeavors as finding a community to join, identifying cults, financing, and taking social action. Appendixes provide a calendar of events, information on the International Community World Wide Web Page, and other available resources and services. With its home-grown layout, newsprint pages, and snapshot photographs, the book is reminiscent of *The Whole Earth Catalog* (see ARBA 70, v.1, p. 161) of the 1960s and 1970s. Perhaps the directory would be more user friendly if arranged by geographical location; however, the index certainly makes up for this inconvenience. Anyone interested in finding out more about intentional communities should refer to this book.—**Barbara Ittner**

DISABLED

853. **Accent on Living Buyer's Guide: Your Number One Source of Information on Products for the Disabled.** 1994-95 ed. Betty Garee, ed. Dorothy Foran, comp. Bloomington, Ill., Cheever Publishing, 1994. 144p. illus. index. $12.00pa. ISBN 0-915708-35-3.

The rapid growth of rehabilitation science and other parallel health care fields has led to the creation of a large number of devices and equipment designed to help physically disabled individuals. This brief volume is an easy-to-use shopping guide for some of this difficult-to-locate technology.

The items included in this guide are divided into 32 broad categories of specialized apparatus, ranging from devices to assist with automobile travel to gardening, eating, and writing. Each category lists companies that sell/provide the specific equipment that falls within this section's purview. Coverage is national, but limited. The basic "yellow pages" provides more complete listings for each community. Some categories list a few books and videotapes dealing with this segment's field. Perhaps the work's most useful feature is a list of addresses and telephone numbers for all firms with products listed in the text.

There are a number of troubling aspects of this quasi-reference work. The compilers fail to explain, or even mention, what, if any, criteria are used for selecting items for their book. Only firms that paid for advertising space have illustrations and descriptions of their apparatus. All other listings are mere one-line mentions that a firm produces specialized equipment. It is important not to confuse this book with *Consumer Reports* (Consumers Union of United States) and similar high-quality publications. This volume is an unusual cross between a traditional reference tool and a paid advertising brochure, thus making it of questionable worth to all libraries and their patrons. [R: BL, 15 Mar 95, p. 1345]—**Jonathon Erlen**

854. Backstrom, Gayle. **The Resource Guide for the Disabled.** Dallas, Tex., Taylor Publishing, 1994. 172p. index. $10.95pa. ISBN 0-87833-845-4.

Backstrom lists approximately 500 associations, agencies, and service organizations that provide referrals or services to handicapped or chronically ill individuals and their families. Each entry in the alphabetical listing contains names, addresses, and telephone numbers; type (e.g., nonprofit, government, research facility); its audience and range of services offered; and a brief description of the organization's focus or current emphasis. Most serve a national audience and offer services and referrals directly to individuals from a national office or from regional or local units. Others refer clients to service points or agencies. A few serve only local or regional needs, but are included as models or address needs outside a defined area on a resource-available basis. The index by disability, illness, or chronic condition is designed to identify agencies serving a specific clientele.

The *Resource Guide* joins several similar, current directories; therefore, there is considerable overlap with existing publications. *The Complete Directory for People with Disabilities* (see ARBA 93, entry 862) and *Resource Directory for the Disabled* (see ARBA 93, entry 864) have a similar scope, but also include information on media, mobility devices and coping aids, and other products. The *Directory of National Information Sources on Disabilities* (U.S. Department of Education, National Institute on Disability and Rehabilitation Research, 1991) describes fewer national programs but in greater detail. Despite overlap with these publications (and with comprehensive works such as *Encyclopedia of Associations*), the reasonable cost makes this volume useful for libraries where such information is frequently requested, and for specifics on little-known organizations.—**Pam M. Baxter**

855. Buchanan, Robert J., and Kenneth Lewis. **The Complete Directory of Nursing Facilities for Younger Adults with Chronic Physical Disabilities, 1994.** Lakeville, Conn., Grey House Publishing, 1994. 333p. index. $85.00pa. ISBN 0-939300-57-5.

Finding nursing facilities for young adults who are physically but not mentally disabled is difficult. Their needs are not necessarily well suited to facilities catering to children or the elderly. This directory describes more than 270 facilities around the United States that primarily serve young adults or provide special care units for that population.

Entries are arranged alphabetically by state and then by institution name. For each facility there are four major categories of information: facility related data, admissions criteria, staff and services, and resident information. Facility-related data include information on number of beds, ownership, payment options, levels of care, patient mobility requirements, and room options (e.g., semiprivate, accepts couples). Admissions criteria include such items as age requirements, restrictions, required medical conditions, and most frequent locations for discharge (e.g., home, assisted living facility, health care facility). Staff and services describe the number and variety of professional staff; the kinds of nursing, medical, dietary, and therapy services offered; and recreation, educational, and social programs. Resident information provides a variety of age-related data on the facility's residents, as well as a breakdown of the most frequent physical disabilities treated. Additional access is provided by an entry name index and a disability index.

This is a valuable directory from a publisher experienced in providing directories to other kinds of health care services. The only caveat has to do with the method of gathering data. As with many other sources similar to this, data on the facilities were gathered from surveys filled out by the facility administrators. There is no independent verification of the details, nor are there distinctions made between facilities in the quality of care provided. As a starting place, however, this source is recommended for public and medical libraries.—**Stephen H. Aby**

856. Cremona, Candida H. **ACCESS Travel U.S.A.: A Directory for People with Disabilities.** Fort Lauderdale, Fla., Creative Hospitality Concepts, 1994. 170p. illus. index. $19.95pa. ISBN 0-9642279-0-8.

Especially since the passage of the Americans with Disabilities Act in 1990, libraries welcome patrons with disabilities. In addition to providing access to the entire collection, libraries house materials of particular interest to people with disabilities. Resources that expedite travel and recreation, such as this reference guide, are essential.

Using this guide, readers will know what to expect from any of 15 cruise lines, 27 ski areas, and hundreds of hotels throughout the United States. For cruise lines and hotels, charts present 40 pieces of information including dimensions of cabins/rooms, bathrooms, and fixtures. Vital information on public areas (e.g., elevators, dining rooms) is included, and nonaccessible areas are indicated. Hotel listings describe services designed to assist travelers with hearing impairments. A comprehensive section on ski areas indicates special instruction available to travelers with a variety of requirements, while the transportation section provides limited information about airlines, bus lines, vehicle rental agencies, and train services. The valuable "Information Resources" component lists organizations that provide services—including travel-related services—to people with disabilities.

A few weaknesses were noted. The hotel section, while presenting in-depth information for most hotels listed, is inadequate in breadth of coverage. For some states, including Iowa, Connecticut, Oklahoma, and Alabama, only one hotel is listed; coverage of some of the larger cities is also limited. Another weakness relates to format; the book is attractive, but some charts may be unreadable to people with visual impairments. A printing error on page 78 of the review copy makes it impossible to comprehend data there.

Despite these concerns, *ACCESS Travel U.S.A.*, with its depth of coverage and low cost, is a good addition to libraries that already have a basic work such as Lewis and Sygalls's *A World of Options for the 90's* (see ARBA 92, entry 315). [R: BL, 15 Mar, p. 1347]—**Jan Bakker**

857. Lang, Harry G., and Bonnie Meath-Lang. **Deaf Persons in the Arts and Sciences: A Biographical Dictionary.** Westport, Conn., Greenwood Press, 1995. 424p. illus. index. $69.50. ISBN 0-313-29170-5.

This fascinating biographical work has about 150 articles on deaf leaders in the arts and sciences throughout modern history in the Western world. The articles average more than two pages in length and have two to five bibliographical references. There are 34 illustrations of the biographees. An appendix of brief entries covers an additional 120 persons in the 4 main fields represented: art, entertainment, science, and writing. An 11-page index simplifies the use of this book.

Besides being a useful reference tool for any comprehensive biographical collection, this book will be even more relevant in all libraries that serve young deaf readers by presenting readable information about persons who can serve as role models. Both persons deaf from birth and those adventitiously deafened by accident or disease are included. Persons covered who will entice young readers include Heather Whitestone, the 1995 Miss America; Marlee Matlin, the U.S. actress; Irving King Jordon, the first deaf president of Gallaudet University; and Andrew Foster, the founder of the Christian Mission for Deaf Africans and of more than 20 schools for deaf people in Africa.

For a general adult reader, this book is most interesting because it reveals information about people known for their accomplishments but not their deafness, such as Ruth Benedict, the anthropologist; Annie Jump Cannon, the astronomer; Harriet Martineau, the British writer; and George Catlin, the painter.

Lang and Meath-Lang are both professors at the National Technical Institute for the Deaf in Rochester, New York. Lang has nine entries in the library catalog of Gallaudet University, including his 1994 *Silence of the Spheres*, which also should be widely purchased. He has written more than 35 articles and essays on science education and deaf studies. There is no comparable biographical dictionary available. Only a few of the biographees herein are included in the *Gallaudet Encyclopedia of Deaf People and Deafness* (see ARBA 88, entry 824). In short, this book is highly recommended.—**William G. Wilson**

858. Schlachter, Gail Ann, and R. David Weber. **Financial Aid for the Disabled and Their Families 1994-1996.** San Carlos, Calif., Reference Service Press, 1994. 321p. index. $38.50. ISBN 0-918276-22-5.

One of the ongoing problems with the provision of aid or social services to individuals is informing them of what exists. For the disabled and their families, there is a substantial amount of public and private financial aid available. The aid can be used for further education, training, research, emergency situations, career development, and more. This guide pulls together that diverse list of sources of aid and provides key information on the application process. It updates program details for 75 percent of the original entries and adds 100 new programs, totaling more than 1,000 funding sources, state agencies, and relevant reference works.

The guide is organized into three sections. The first, and major, section lists aid sources by the type of disability, including a general category and one for family members. These categories are further subdivided by type of aid, covering scholarships, fellowships, loans, grants-in-aid, awards, and internships. Aid programs are then listed alphabetically by title. The information on each program includes not only an address and a telephone number, but also the purpose, eligibility requirements, financial data, duration of the aid, special features, number awarded, and application deadline. The second section of the book lists state agencies that provide financial aid and related services. It has categories for state financial aids, student loan programs, and vocational rehabilitation services. The state services are then listed alphabetically by state. The third section is an annotated bibliography of general reference sources identifying scholarships, fellowships, grants, internships, and related types of aid. These sources do not exclusively focus on the disabled. The supplemental indexes for program title and sponsoring organization also indicate by code letters the target disability and type of aid. There are also subject, geographic, and calendar (application deadline) indexes.

This work is clearly written, well organized, and thoroughly indexed. The review of the 1st edition in ARBA 89 (see entry 762) stated that if it were updated regularly, it would be a "major reference tool." Given that it is biennially issued, it should easily earn a spot in any reference collection.—**Stephen H. Aby**

859. **A Woman's Guide to Coping with Disability.** Lexington, Mass., Resources for Rehabilitation, 1994. 224p. index. $39.95pa. ISBN 0-929718-15-1.

This publication deals with the needs of women who have chronic and disabling conditions. Information is provided about the nature of the disease, treatment, and an overview of the condition regarding the special concerns of women in relation to sexual functioning, pregnancy and childbearing, and the psychological effects. The introductory chapters discuss how disabilities generally affect women, how to deal with the health care system, coping with daily activities and working, housing applications, recreation and travel, and laws that relate to women with disabilities. The disabilities covered are arthritis, diabetes, epilepsy, lupus, multiple sclerosis, osteoporosis, and spinal cord injury. For each, there is a discussion about the nature of the illness, the treatment, and impact on lifestyles. There is also information on professional service providers who treat the condition and where they might be located.

Each chapter has bibliographies of articles and books about the condition, as well as lists of organizations where one can find support and additional information. For each organization there is complete directory information with telephone and fax numbers. Each chapter also includes a list of publications and videos dealing with rehabilitation, exercise, physically managing the illness, treatment, and self-care. Full directory information is provided to make these materials easily available. A lengthy table of contents makes all information easy to locate.

Not every disabling disease is covered here, but the three introductory chapters do provide information useful for any kind of disability. The strengths of the work are that it is aimed at the particular concerns of women and that it provides a large quantity of resources. It will be of great value in libraries, for support groups, for health organizations with information centers, and for individuals coping with disabilities.

—Marilyn Strong Noronha

FAMILY, MARRIAGE, AND DIVORCE

860. **The Adoption Directory: The Most Comprehensive Guide to Family-Building Options....** 2d ed. Ellen Paul, ed. Detroit, Gale, 1995. 571p. index. $65.00. ISBN 0-8103-7495-1. ISSN 0077-4472.

This directory is for prospective adoptive or foster parents, adoption professionals, pregnancy counselors, and birth parents considering adoption, attorneys, physicians, and support groups. It lists both public and private adoption agencies, adoption exchanges, foreign agencies, foster parenting information, and support groups. The work is divided into six sections; the first lists the state and province statutes and adoption agencies in the United States and Canada. Arranged alphabetically by state, the Canadian entries follow the United States entries. In each entry, the individual state's policy regarding adoption is followed by a listing of the public, then private, agencies within that state. The second section describes foster care agencies and gives, information on financial assistance, requirements, and the types of children placed. Section 3 lists independent adoption services. These people provide professional intermediary services, such as locating adoptable children and performing home studies.

Section 4 lists information on support groups for adoptive families, prospective adoptive parents, foster parents, special needs children, and so forth. Section 5 lists adoption exchanges that provide exposure to waiting children by compiling lists. Most cover wide geographical areas, and so are listed alphabetically, not geographically as in the other sections. Section 6 lists countries that will place children with U.S. families. The countries included are Bolivia, Chile, Colombia, Paraguay, the Philippines, and Ukraine. There is a glossary and a bibliography of new titles on adoption. There are two appendixes, one on where to write for vital records, the other on immigration and naturalization services information. This was completely redone from the 1st edition, with questionnaires sent out to nearly 7,000 agencies. Those libraries owning the 1st edition should replace it with this.—**Robert L. Turner Jr.**

861. **Association for Population/Family Planning Libraries and Information Centers—International (APLIC-I) Union List of Serials.** Michael F. Zimmerman, comp. and ed. New York, Association for Population/Family Planning International, 1995. 403p. (APLIC Special Publication, no.7). $35.00. ISBN 0-933438-22-2.

This publication lists more than 3,500 serial titles held by members of the Association for Population/ Family Planning Libraries and Information Centers - International. The holdings of 24 institutions, 23 in the United States and 1 in Canada, are included. For each participating library, a three-letter symbol, a complete address, and (usually) the name of a contact person and a brief description of interlibrary loan policies are provided. Because the institutions were asked to report all of their holdings, many titles not directly related to population and family planning, such as *Consumer Reports*, *Journal of Agricultural Economics*, and the *UN Chronicle*, are listed. Complete bibliographical data are supplied, wherever possible, for each title on the list. The information is current as of November 1994.

Since the material is somewhat out-of-date, the coverage is limited to only two dozen libraries, and the subject matter is quite specialized, few libraries will need to acquire this publication. Those requiring current holdings information should consult one of the more comprehensive online databases, such as OCLC's Union Catalog.—**Leonard Grundt**

862. Broude, Gwen J. **Marriage, Family, and Relationships: A Cross-Cultural Encyclopedia.** Santa Barbara, Calif., ABC-CLIO, 1994. 372p. illus. index. (Encyclopedias of the Human Experience). $49.50. ISBN 0-87436-736-0.

As part of ABC-CLIO's new series this volume is a questionable addition. Cross-cultural essays cover subjects including courtship, divorce, kinship, and reproductive strategies. The book also addresses more controversial societal issues such as prostitution, premarital pregnancy, homosexuality, and incest.

Listed alphabetically by topic, each entry ranges in length from 1,500 to 2,000 words. Appropriate black-and-white photographs enhance the text and highlight a particular culture's customs regarding an aspect of marriage, family life, or associations. The essays conclude with a short list of readings about the topic. A bibliography and a thorough subject index complete the volume.

It is important to note that the subjects addressed in short survey essays (e.g., rape, sexual behavior, and family) have been and are the focus of voluminous writing by social scientists. With this brief entry format, it is difficult to do more than mention a culture's treatment of newlyweds, for example, or the remarriage of widows. In the latter instance, the author does an admirable job of describing the widow-remarrying practices of at least 23 cultures in approximately $2\frac{1}{2}$ pages. Weaving succinct references to each culture's customs is a challenge given this entry length. Perhaps in doing so, however, it was difficult to separate past and present cultural practices. This failure to distinguish between superannuated and contemporary customs gives the user the impression that many behaviors are still indigenous to a specific culture when indeed they are not. Citing articles from 1884, 1928, 1939, and 1951 as evidence of contemporary customs does nothing but perpetuate primitive cultural stereotypes.

Users of this volume will need to rely upon their own skepticism and perhaps even travel experiences to discern that the author is describing past practices rather than present ones with regard to most cultures. Public and academic libraries needing marital and familial multicultural materials should consider *Encyclopedia of World Cultures* (see ARBA 95, entries 397-398; ARBA 94, entries 395-396; ARBA 93, entry 413; and ARBA 92, entries 334-335) or *The Illustrated Encyclopedia of Mankind* (see ARBA 91, entry 75) instead of this historically dated encyclopedia. [R: LJ, 1 Feb 95, p. 66]—**Kathleen W. Craver**

863. **Encyclopedia of Marriage and the Family.** David Levinson, ed. New York, Macmillan/Simon & Schuster, 1995. 2v. index. $175.00/set. ISBN 0-02-897235-X.

Levinson, as editor of the outstanding *Encyclopedia of World Cultures* (Macmillan, 1991-), is well qualified to produce this two-volume set containing information about marriage, familial issues, health-related problems, sexual beliefs and behaviors, parenting, reproduction, and sociocultural influences on the family. The set consists of 169 articles contributed by a majority of college and university professors with appropriate subject expertise. Access is alphabetical by topic, with each entry ranging in length from 6 to 10 pages and concluding with a bibliography. Where necessary, relevant charts and tables provide statistics from primary sources in support of generalizations and conclusions. A cumulative index is included in volume 2.

The language of each article is clear, concise, and understandable. High school students should be able to grasp most of the issues and concepts for research assignments, as well as parents or adults searching for information about, for example, family rituals, child abuse, love, remarriage, and self-help groups. A broad, interdisciplinary approach has been successfully elicited by the editor and executed superbly by each contributor. In the section concerning extramarital sex, this proclivity is examined from biological, psychological, and religious perspectives.

Compared to *Marriage, Family, and Relationships* (see entry 862), this two-volume set is a better acquisition. Although both works address similar issues involving family, marriage, and relationships, Levinson's work is more in-depth and current. Articles about gangs, incest, family violence, and cohabitation, for example, reflect the latest analyses and implications for society as a whole. The articles provide an excellent overview of broad topics and furnish the user with valuable, up-to-date sources for additional information. This set is a worthwhile reference and is relevant to all school, public, and academic libraries' social science collections.—**Kathleen W. Craver**

GAY AND LESBIAN STUDIES

864. **Cassell's Queer Companion: A Dictionary of Lesbian and Gay Life and Culture.** William Stewart, ed. New York, Mansell/Cassell, 1995. 278p. illus. $18.95pa. ISBN 0-304-34301-3.

This is a dictionary of 2,500 terms that relate to the politics, history, film, theater, popular culture, style, and slang of the gay and lesbian community (primarily in the United States and the United Kingdom). Entry headwords are clear boldface type on two-column pages, and white space and font size and variety make the book easy to use. Definitions are clearly written and range from a brief phrase to several columns; terms are often cross-referenced to others. Much positive information is presented about the diversity of the gay and lesbian community. This dictionary will be a valuable addition to any public or academic library, and should be considered a must for collections specializing in lexicography.

—**G. Douglas Meyers**

865. Russell, Paul. **The Gay 100: A Ranking of the Most Influential Gay Men and Lesbians, Past and Present.** New York, Carol Publishing Group, 1995. 386p. illus. index. $24.95. ISBN 0-8065-1591-0.

Those in search of a definitive "who's who" of gay men and lesbians will find this book vexing in its subjectivity, but taken as one man's idiosyncratic collection of 100 gay men and lesbians who have made the most influential contributions to American/European gay/lesbian identity, it provides a good deal of interesting information. It begins with an introduction outlining the project and touching on key questions about the meaning of such terms as *influential*, *gay*, *lesbian*, and *gay/lesbian identity*. It ends with a selected bibliography of 57 sources and an index.

Most of the book consists of the author's essays about his subjects. These are arranged by ranking, starting with #1 in importance (Socrates) to #100 (Michelangelo Signorile). Activists, artists, authors, military leaders, politicians, and thinkers spanning 2,400 years are discussed for their important contributions to history in general, and to gay/lesbian identity in particular. Of the 100 entries, 60 are about men, sketching such figures as Magnus Hirschfeld (#4), Alexander the Great (#14), Jean Genet (#45), Francis Bacon (#81), and Ian McKellen (#97). Thirty-eight entries are about women, from Sappho (#2) to Susan B. Anthony (#12), Adrienne Rich (#47), Mary Renault (#80), and Ethel Smyth (#94). Two entries are shared by men and women—the Patrons of the Stonewall Inn (#5) and Harold Nicolson/Vita Sackville-West (#64). This is a well-researched and highly readable book; while not a rigorous scholarly work, *The Gay 100* deserves a place in any library that takes seriously the ideal of diversity.—**G. Douglas Meyers**

MEN'S STUDIES

866. August, Eugene R. **The New Men's Studies: A Selected and Annotated Interdisciplinary Bibliography.** 2d ed. Englewood, Colo., Libraries Unlimited, 1994. 440p. index. $45.00. ISBN 1-56308-084-2.

In contrast to the assumption that traditional scholarship is synonymous with men's studies, August, alumni chair in the Humanities at the University of Dayton, argues that past studies rarely touched upon the lives of men as men. Gender-conscious scholarship focusing on the lives of ordinary men and their private spheres of male existence differentiates the new men's studies from traditional ones. These new men's studies make up August's selected and annotated interdisciplinary bibliography of 1,049 sources.

As in *Men's Studies* (1985), August chooses to include more scholarly than nonacademic books, although many of the sources are appropriate for the general reader. Limited to books in English or in English translation, entries span all major disciplines, represent a range of philosophical and political views, and embrace most significant books in the field. August comments on the burgeoning literature and interest in the field. He has added more than 500 new sources to this 2d edition. The 27 alphabetically arranged chapters divide the sources, also alphabetical, into major content areas. Division by broader content areas might have simplified access, as chapter headings can be clustered by discipline (e.g., anthropology, sociology, psychology, health); politics (e.g., feminism, men's rights); type of account (e.g., bibliography, men's studies); life cycle issues (e.g., single men, males in families); and so forth. Plentiful cross-references in addition to author, title, and subject indexes enhance the ease of finding sources.

The author provides a succinct overview of the field in his introduction, as well as useful definitions of terms (e.g., misandry, patriarchy, feminism, masculinities). His full, clear descriptions of the content of sources go beyond annotations. August has made a significant contribution to organizing the literature on men's studies. His bibliography should be a basic source for the general reader, and also for anyone interested in examining and developing gender-balanced scholarship.—**Suzanne G. Frayser**

PHILANTHROPY

Bibliography

867. Brackney, William H. **Christian Voluntarism in Britain and North America: A Bibliography and Critical Assessment.** Westport, Conn., Greenwood Press, 1995. 306p. index. (Bibliographies and Indexes in Religious Studies, no.35). $85.00. ISBN 0-313-28421-0.

The author has three primary objectives: (1) to trace the historical evolution of Christian voluntarism; (2) to assess the important literature on voluntarism in Great Britain and North America; and (3) to provide a selected listing of voluntary associations in Great Britain, North America, and other continents. Most of the information located here deals with the United Kingdom, Canada, and the United States. The author, a professor of historical theology at McMaster University, provides scholars with a tool that may be pronounced definitive for the period covered (events prior to 1900). Bibliographic citations to both primary and secondary sources are complete; the brief annotations serve as a model of their kind, and users will appreciate having the superior scholarship identified. The initial chapters provide excellent explanations for the origin and the purpose of Christian voluntarism in Great Britain and North America. Laypersons should find these introductory chapters well worth the time it takes to read them (approximately two hours).

The publisher has been unstinting in an effort to produce a quality product: binding, format, typeface, and paper quality are excellent. Brackney's subject bibliography is highly recommended, a required purchase by university libraries and divinity schools, large and small.—**Milton H. Crouch**

Directories

868. **Alternatives to the Peace Corps: A Directory of Third World & U.S. Volunteer Opportunities.** 6th ed. Annette Olson, ed. Oakland, Calif., Food First Books, 1994. 88p. $6.95pa. ISBN 0-935028-62-5.

Based on the premise that hunger is a political problem of food production, distribution, and consumption, this guide, published by the Institute for Food and Policy Development (Food First), introduces the personal and political aspects of voluntarism in both developing countries and the United States. Practical advice—including the need to question the motives for volunteering, how to evaluate a voluntary service organization, and the application of lessons learned abroad to domestic activities—dominates the introductory material.

Volunteer service organizations are classified under the divisions of international, U.S., and alternative travel and study overseas. Information on each organization covers title; address; telephone, fax, and telex numbers; and profiles of its affiliations, purpose, activities, and requirements. Further divisions of the guide note other voluntary organizations, guides to U.S. and international opportunities, and publications on travel and tourism programs. The final division addresses job or career opportunities in development. The index is to the names of listed organizations.

While far less comprehensive than *Volunteerism: The Directory of Organizations, Training, Programs and Publications* (see ARBA 92, entry 829) and *International Directory of Voluntary Work* (see ARBA 94, entry 894), this guide's value lies in its low cost and frank appraisal of methods and motives operating under the rubric of community development through voluntarism.—**Eleanor Ferrall**

869. **Directory of International Corporate Giving in America and Abroad 1995.** Katherine E. Jankowski, ed. Detroit, Taft Group/Gale, 1995. 825p. index. $180.00pa. ISBN 1-56995-035-0. ISSN 1046-4263.

This work is one of a number of authoritative publications from the Taft Group (see ARBA 95, entry 643, and ARBA 91, entry 864, for other examples). It provides information on charitable giving in the United States by foreign-owned companies and on the International giving of U.S. multinational corporations. There are 460 profiles of corporate giving programs; this new edition includes 159 new profiles—135 foreign-owned and 24 U.S. multinationals. Biographical information has been added for corporate and contributions officers. Section 1 includes profiles of the contributions programs of 460 companies that are at least 10 percent foreign-owned. Section 2 profiles the international giving programs of 184 U.S. multinationals. Each section has its own indexes, and there is also a short master index.

The prefatory materials are particularly helpful and clear. The preface contains a statement of what is new to this edition, an explanation of the method of compilation, and an explanation of the indexes. There are excellent explanations of the content of a profile for sections 1 and 2. There are a list of abbreviations, a revised list of nonprofit recipient categories, a list of recipient organization types, and a glossary.

The directory is a model of organization and utility. It is extremely well thought out, with an excellent explanation of layout, content, and function. Each section provides information on the contacts within the organization, a list of typical recipients, a summary of giving, a list of recent grants, and application information. The indexes are exemplary, and the inclusion of the "other things you should know" section in each entry allows the editors freedom to present useful materials that could not otherwise be included. This is an essential work for any institution seeking grant funding.—**Richard H. Swain**

870. **Directory of New and Emerging Foundations.** 3d ed. Margaret Mary Feczko and Linda Tobiasen, eds. New York, Foundation Center, 1994. 437p. index. $95.00pa. ISBN 0-87954-553-4.

In the digital age, specialized spin-offs from standard reference works such as *The Foundation Directory* (see ARBA 94, entry 890, and ARBA 91, entry 866) have become common practice among reference works publishers. The first challenge is to recognize that much of the information may be already contained in a previously acquired work from the same publisher. The second challenge is to decide whether this usually esoteric information is essential to one's user population. In the case of an extremely active academic development office, research institution, and other fund-raising activities, the answer may be yes.

The *Directory of New and Emerging Foundations* (DNEF) follows the same format as *The Foundation Directory*. It supplies donor, foundation type, financial background, limitations, trustee information, and application information on approximately 2,950 U.S. grantmaking foundations established from 1989-1992. Four classes of foundations are included: independent, company-sponsored, operating, and community. Tables furnish aggregate fiscal data for all listed foundations by type, region, and state, and assets over $2 million, respectively. A detailed user's guide sheet, glossary, and an additional list of Foundation Center publications constitute the beginning contents. Standard donor, geographic, types of support, subject, and foundation title indexes conclude the listing of entries.

Ease of access is not a problem with DNEF. The problem concerns entry overlap. Listing, for example, the Annenberg, John W. Kluge, and Anheuser-Busch Foundations as new and emerging is stretching even the "poetic license" line. Granted, the above foundations have slightly altered their entry descriptions since incorporation. Each, however, was clearly established prior to 1989. All of these foundations are also listed in the 1992, 1993, and 1994 editions of *The Foundation Directory*.

Libraries needing fund-raising information are strongly advised to purchase the latest edition of *The Foundation Directory* and the supplement, if necessary, before acquiring this somewhat duplicative volume. Libraries already owning *The Foundation Directory* may wish to consider other Foundation Center publications that may specifically match one's institutional profile, such as *AIDS Funding* (see ARBA 93, entry 1653), *Guide to Funding for International and Foreign Programs* (see ARBA 93, entry 880), or *National Guide to Funding in Religion* (see ARBA 93, entry 1411), before acquiring this volume.—**Kathleen W. Craver**

871. **The Foundation Directory Supplement.** 1995 ed. Margaret Mary Feczko and Elizabeth H. Rich, eds. New York, Foundation Center, 1995. 626p. index. $115.00pa. ISBN 0-87954-613-1. ISSN 0071-8092.

The Foundation Directory Supplement contains updated entries for 2,462 of the 22,565 major foundations listed in *The Foundation Directory* and *The Foundation Directory Part 2*, published six months earlier than this supplement. When users identify a potential source of foundation support in these two volumes, they should check the supplement to see if these revised entries reflect changes in foundation names and addresses, personnel, funding program interests, limitations of grants, or procedures for applying for support, as well as information related to foundations that have permanently terminated operations, temporarily discontinued funding activities, or merged with other organizations. Information in each entry that has changed is highlighted in bold typeface.

The supplement is arranged geographically; entries, numbered consecutively throughout the directory, are listed alphabetically by foundation name within each state category. A useful section precedes the main body of the work with instructions on how to use the supplement and background information on the role and definition of a foundation. A glossary of some of the terminology commonly used in the field of grantsmanship, a section that describes major publications and services of the Foundation Center, and a state-arranged list of cooperative libraries that house Foundation Center collections are also included.

Grantseekers may consult any of six indexes to access information about funding for research and other projects: the index to donors, officers, and trustees; the geographical index (state and city where foundation is headquartered); the international giving index (entry numbers to foundations with interest in projects beyond the United States); the types of support index (including definitions of terms for major support categories; for example, curriculum development, debt reduction, emergency funds); the subject index; and the foundation name index.—**Lois J. Buttlar**

872. **Foundation Grants to Individuals.** 9th ed. L. Victoria Hall and others, eds. New York, Foundation Center, 1995. 630p. index. $65.00pa. ISBN 0-87954-604-2.

Individuals seeking financial aid often cringe when faced with the research necessary to discover sources for help, but *Foundation Grants to Individuals* makes the search almost simple. As a listing of private U.S. foundations that give financial assistance to individuals, this volume is both a guide for grantseekers and a reference tool for those interested in foundation giving. It includes 2,658 entries, 579 of them new to this edition.

The descriptive listings are of grants for educational support (scholarships, graduate fellowships, postgraduate research grants, student loans, internships, residencies, and research grants); for general welfare; and for cultural support. Also listed are many foundations with restrictions (such as those given only for Buddhist studies, or assistance to disabled Connecticut seamen). Amounts given can vary from as low as $64 to highs of more than $20,000.

Additional help offers income tax considerations, information for international applicants, and an excellent bibliography. Entries are logical and well indexed. All information is easily located. Omissions of some foundations may be a concern. One such oversight is the Educational Foundation of the American Association of University Women, although two of its branches are mentioned. A warning issued repeatedly says, "If you do not qualify, do not apply." However, the text explains very well how to qualify, so the reader can easily follow the instructions.—**Jerri Spoehel**

873. **The Foundation 1000 1995/1996: In-Depth Profiles of the 1000 Largest U.S. Foundations.** Francine Jones, Katie Reiser, and Georgetta Toth, eds. New York, Foundation Center, 1995. 2945p. index. $265.00pa. ISBN 0-87954-645-X.

The Foundation 1000 provides grantseekers with the facts that they need to identify and contact appropriate funding sources among the United States' 1,000 largest foundations, which account for approximately 65 percent of all foundation grant dollars awarded in a given year. The information supplied for each foundation cites a number of useful details. In addition to complete addresses and names of contact people, one finds brief information on purpose, limitations, support area, financial data, officers and number of staff, background, and policies and application guidelines, plus detailed and well-presented data on grants analysis, including subject, recipient type, type of support, and geographical. There are many specialized directories (e.g., *National Guide to Foundation Funding in Health* [see ARBA 90, entry 1622] or *Money for Visual Artists* [see ARBA 92, entry 991]), but this directory, not limited to a particular subject area, will be of substantial assistance to most larger institutions.—**Bohdan S. Wynar**

874. **Guide to Federal Funding for Volunteer Programs and Community Service.** 3d ed. Alvin C. Lin, ed. Arlington, Va., Government Information Services, 1995. 1v. (various paging). index. $114.95 looseleaf w/binder. ISBN 0-933544-84-7.

What does this looseleaf service do? Patrons looking to identify volunteer services funded through taxpayer conscription will find these services here: AmeriCorps, Vista, National Senior Corps, Department of Education programs, and C-Sap (Center for Substance Abuse, not a tongue-in-cheek dig at those funding it). Each entry has information regarding eligibility, restrictions, funding potential, and key grants made the previous year. Matching it up with funding opportunities (e.g., libraries, Native Americans, antipoverty) could help tailor grant requests to specific areas. Other programs (more than $2 billion in grants) dealing with fungibility between student aid and services rendered are also here. The looseleaf format allows for updating the service.

An overview of the work of the government in this area, along with subject and program indexes, makes it readily accessible to patrons. However, other sources abound for locating these programs; hence, the selection is superfluous.—**Mark Y. Herring**

875. **Guide to Funding for International and Foreign Programs.** 2d ed. Margaret Mary Feczko, Ruth Kovacs, and Carlotta Mills, eds. New York, Foundation Center, 1994. 316p. index. $85.00pa. ISBN 0-87954-546-1.

Thousands of foundations and corporations in the United States make more than $10 billion available to those seeking grants. However, without a guide, a grantseeker would face a tedious search to locate a potential donor for a specific situation. The Foundation Center was created to ease that problem by serving as a unified source of information on available grants from foundations and corporations. *Guide to Funding for International and Foreign Programs* provides a starting point for those seeking funding for foreign or international programs. The roughly 5,700 grants listed were drawn largely from other publications, broader in scope, of the Foundation Center. The *Guide* contains suggestions for grantseeking in general, explanations and directions for use of the guide, a glossary, and a bibliography. Especially useful are several indexes: by names of key personnel, by state in which the grantmaker is located, by state within subject, by state within type of support, and by program—as well as a detailed subject index. Each entry contains considerable information, including address, financial data, names of donors, areas of giving, staff, directions for applying, and examples of recent grants. The *Guide* represents an authoritative, current, and comprehensive (although not quite all-inclusive) point of departure.—**William C. Struning**

876. **Guide to Greater Washington D.C. Grantmakers 1994-1995.** Washington, D.C., Washington Regional Association of Grantmakers and New York, Foundation Center, 1994. 149p. index. $45.00pa. ISBN 0-87954-552-6.

Building on an earlier work, *The Directory of Foundations of the Greater Washington Area* (1984), the Foundation Center—in collaboration with the Washington Regional Association of Grantmakers—has produced a directory of 789 grantmakers. Fewer than 115 of the grantmakers are included in the *Foundation Directory*. This publication is similar in style to other Foundation Center publications and achieves their excellent publication standard.

Summarized information in four interesting tables begins the work: Table 1 covers aggregate data by grantmaker type; table 2, the 50 largest grantmakers by assets; table 3 lists the 50 largest grantmakers by total giving; and table 4, grantmakers by asset categories. This volume has an alphabetical arrangement with a sequence number for each foundation. This number is used in the four indexes: to donors, officers, trustees; by types of support; by subject (i.e., giving interests of grantmakers); and to grantmaker name.

For each foundation, up to 33 basic elements are listed. Besides the expected name, address, telephone number, and contact person, the amounts and types of grants are given as well as fields of interest. The coverage includes foundations, direct corporate giving programs, public charities having either a primary or an application address in the greater Washington, D.C., area, and current members of the Washington Regional Association of Grantmakers. This publication has a limited scope, but because it covers Washington, D.C., five Maryland counties, and seven Virginia counties, public and academic libraries in all these areas should have copies.—**Lorna A. Wiggins**

877. Kovacs, Ruth, and Ben McLaughlin, eds. **Who Gets Grants/Who Gives Grants: Nonprofit Organizations and the Foundation Grants They Received.** 2d ed. New York, Foundation Center, 1994. 1469p. index. $95.00pa. ISBN 0-87954-542-9.

This work's primary emphasis is on nonprofit organizations that receive foundation funding. It provides direct access to grant recipient information in 19 subject areas by geographic regions. The more than 18,000 nonprofit organizations covered in this volume receive more than 50 percent of all foundation grant dollars. The grant sample includes only grants of $10,000 or more awarded to nonprofit organizations in 1991-1992. Only those nonprofit organizations that received a total of $25,000 or more in grant dollars in the year reported are included.

This edition is organized in four sections. First, it lists nonprofit organizations alphabetically, each with a reference number for access to listings in other sections. Second, within each of the 19 major subject fields, nonprofit organizations are listed alphabetically by their state or foreign country. Each organization's grants are listed alphabetically by the name of the foundation awarding the grant. Third, for each foundation in this volume, all the organizations that have received grants ($10,000 or more) from the foundation are listed. This section is arranged alphabetically by foundation state, then foundation name. Fourth, each foundation is listed alphabetically, with name and address and any geographical, program, and type of support limitations on the foundation's giving program.

Who Gets Grants/Who Gives Grants is a useful source for developing an initial list of potential funding sources. It complements the *Foundation Directory* (see ARBA 94, entry 866).—**Roslyn Attinson**

878. **National Guide to Funding for the Environment and Animal Welfare.** 2d ed. Margaret Mary Feczko, Ruth Kovacs, and Carlotta Mills, eds. New York, Foundation Center, 1994. 411p. index. $85.00pa. ISBN 0-87954-551-8.

As one of the Foundation Center's many publications, this particular work is intended to help those involved in the areas of the environment and animal welfare target those foundations most likely to award them grants. The work includes more than 1,200 entries for grantmaking foundations and 89 direct corporate giving programs that have shown interest in these areas. The editors are quick to point out that the guide is not comprehensive and that grantseekers should investigate all avenues—especially local possibilities. To help in this search, the editors have included a bibliography, a glossary, sections on the services of the Foundation Center, and information on how to use the guide and to apply for grants.

The guide is arranged alphabetically by state. Foundations are then listed alphabetically within each state. The entries may be accessed through six indexes, assuring ease of use. The listings themselves are composed of 33 informational items, including: assets, grants paid, types of support, publications, and application information. A random check of these entries showed the information to be current and accurate. This work fulfills its stated goal and is a pleasure to use.—**January Adams**

879. Schlachter, Gail Ann. **Directory of Financial Aids for Women 1995-1997.** San Carlos, Calif., Reference Service Press, 1995. 496p. index. $45.00. ISBN 0-918276-27-6. ISSN 0732-5215.

This is a directory of scholarships, fellowships, loans, grants, awards, and internships designed primarily or exclusively for women, state sources of educational benefits, and reference sources on financial aid. Funding opportunities at any level (high school through postdoctoral and professional) designed primarily or exclusively for women for study, research, travel, training, career development, or innovative effort are covered. All areas of the sciences, social sciences, and humanities are discussed in the awards listed. The directory is divided into four separate sections: a descriptive list of financial aid programs designed primarily or exclusively for women, a list of state sources of educational benefits, an annotated bibliography of directories listing general financial aid programs, and a set of six indexes.

The 1995-1997 edition completely revises and updates the earlier biennial edition and identifies more than 1,500 scholarships, fellowships, grants, loans, awards, and internships set aside for women and women's organizations. More than 70 percent of the entries have been substantially updated, and 300 new programs have been added. Each entry provides detailed information on program title; sponsoring organization address and telephone number (including toll-free, fax, and e-mail numbers); purpose; eligibility; remuneration; duration; special features; limitations; number of awards; and deadline dates. The information is indexed by program title, more than 500 sponsoring organizations, geographical coverage, subject, and deadline date. The volume lists the addresses and telephone numbers of state sources of educational benefits and describes the 60 key directories that any individual can use to locate additional sources of financial assistance.—**Janet Mongan**

880. Schlachter, Gail Ann, and R. David Weber. **Directory of Financial Aids for Minorities 1995-1997.** San Carlos, Calif., Reference Service Press, 1995. 663p. index. $47.50. ISBN 0-918276-28-4. ISSN 0738-4122.

For years, Reference Service Press has produced reference serials targeted to specific populations, from veterans to the disabled. The authors of the 6th edition of this particular work (one of whom is also the publisher) tell us that the work reflects 350 new additions and updated information for 70 percent of the entries. More than 2,000 scholarships, fellowships, loans, grants, awards, and internships are listed for both individuals and organizations.

It appears that the information was gathered from questionnaires distributed through 1994. Unfortunately, there is no indication of how the sources were selected, the criteria for inclusion, and if inclusion constitutes any form of endorsement. A quick perusal, for example, shows no entry for the California-based [J. Paul] Getty grant program, "Undergraduate Multicultural Summer Internships." Plans call for the next edition to be issued in early 1997, but again it is unclear if the data will be compiled from standard sources, mail surveys, solicitations, or other means.

By far the largest portion of the work contains the sort of financial aid program described, subdivided by ethnic group (Asian, black, Hispanic, or Native American). Entries provide 11 elements, including the purpose, the eligibility requirements, the duration, the limitations, and financial aid directories. Rounding out the work are indexes by program title, sponsoring organization, residency, tenability, subject, and calendar.

Although the work notes that portions of the information are available electronically through commercial services (such as America Online and e-world), there is no indication if CD-ROM or computer programs are also available (similar to *Scholarship 101* from Pinnacle Peak Solutions, which allows for easy access to the data for Macintosh, DOS, or Windows platforms). This source can be useful for those seeking to defray educational (study) or professional development (travel or research) costs.—**Ilene F. Rockman**

Handbooks

881. **Food Aid in Figures. Volume 11: 1993. L'Aide Alimentaire en Chiffres. La Ayuda Alimentaria en Cifras.** Rome, Food and Agriculture Organization of the United Nations; distr., Lanham, Md., UNIPUB, 1994. 138p. $40.00pa. ISBN 92-5-003530-6.

This 138-page handbook presents statistical data on sources of food aid and recipient countries for shipments of food aid. Both English and Italian languages are used to present the data. It is a valuable guide to transactions reported to the Consultative Subcommittee on Surplus Disposal, food aid through the World Food Programme and other organizations, and food aid budget allocations.

The information was pulled from a comprehensive database of food-aid flows for better planning. The information was supplied by donor countries, complemented by data from the Food and Agriculture Organization's (FAO) AGROSTAT computerized system. The data in the extensive tables cover the periods from 1970-1971 for cereals (wheat, rice, and coarse grains), and from 1977 for noncereals (skimmed milk powder, other dairy products, vegetable oil, and butteroil).

Donors include such countries as Australia, Belgium, Canada, Denmark, France, Germany, Ireland, Italy, Japan, Luxembourg, New Zealand, Portugal, Spain, the United Kingdom, and the United States. The largest donors are from the European Community, the United States, and Canada. Recipient countries are primarily the least developed countries, such as Afghanistan, Burundi, Chad, Madagascar, Malawi, Rwanda, Sudan, and Yemen.—**Maureen Pastine**

882. **Guide to Federal Funding for Governments & Nonprofits, 1995.** Native American ed. Heather C. Bodell, Alvin C. Lin, and Natascha M. L. Ovando, eds. Arlington, Va., Government Information Services, 1995. 2v. index. $379.00/set looseleaf w/binder. ISBN 0-933544-83-9. ISSN 1055-596X.

A two-volume set in looseleaf format for convenient updating, this source provides information on several hundred current programs that offer grants and financial or other assistance to Native American organizations, tribal groups, local governments, and individuals. Subscribers receive new program descriptions as well as the Federal Grant Deadline Calendars to update application deadlines. The work organizes programs into 14 categories, with tabs in the looseleaf, such as community development, job training and employment, health, and housing, with a separate section for new programs. Each program entry is two to four pages in length and follows a standard format that describes the flow of funds from the federal government to the recipient, eligibility requirements, uses of the funds, selection criteria, how to apply, and other information.

Summarizing each program in capsule form is a "Program Profile," which includes a "funding opportunity index rating," a measure of program competitiveness. Title, subject, and keyword indexes make location of appropriate programs a bit easier, but are not as user friendly as they could be. The keyword index leads from everyday language to government-speak (i.e., "Prisons—*see* Corrections") and then to the subject index for page numbers. An additional index cross-references programs listed with those in the *Catalog of Federal Domestic Assistance*. Overall, this guide will be a useful, if expensive, source of federal funding information. It is recommended for libraries that serve Native American populations.—**Jeff Wanser**

Indexes

883. **The Foundation Grants Index 1996: A Cumulative Listing of Foundation Grants Reported in 1994.** 24th ed. Compiled by the Foundation Center. Linda G. Tobiasen and Denise McLeod, eds. New York, Foundation Center, 1995. 2266p. $150.00pa. ISBN 0-87954-648-4.

The 24th edition of *The Foundation Grants Index* provides access to the funding interest of major foundations by subject area, geographical focus, types of support, and types of organizations that receive grants. The 18th edition of this work was reviewed in ARBA 90 (see entry 823), and this new edition remains basically the same. As a companion volume to *The Foundation Grants* (see ARBA 91, entry 867), this index is useful in developing an initial list of potential funding sources based on a foundation's giving program, its application procedures, and other relevant information. A general introduction furnishes information about how to use this index and describes trends in 1994 giving. The index is highly recommended to all interested parties.—**Bohdan S. Wynar**

884. **Philanthropic Studies Index: A Reference to Literature on Voluntarism, Nonprofit Organizations, Fund Raising and Charitable Giving. 1995 Cumulative Index.** Janet S. Huettner, ed. Bloomington, Ind., Indiana University Center on Philanthropy/Indiana University Press, 1995. 316p. $75.00/yr.

This index breaks new ground as the first single-source provider of access to articles and book chapters in the emerging discipline of philanthropy. PSI is published three times each year in paperback, in addition to this clothbound annual cumulative index. Rather than list specific journals that are indexed, the editions of PSI reflect online searches done regularly in 8 databases that monitor about 5,000 journals in disciplines such as economics, business, social work, psychology, and the humanities. In addition, the editors examine scholarly journals, books, and news publications in the fields of law, hospital management, and philanthropic studies.

For entries selected, information noted includes a main subject heading, with an added second- or third-level subject heading if appropriate. Entries provide the name(s) of the author(s), title, an indication of illustrative material, name of publication, volume, issue number, and publication date. No information appears available on the source or control of the subject headings used. A six-month lag time may occur between publication date and indexing date, but the editor plans for more timely coverage when additional electronic sources become available (for example, the cumulative index will be available via the Internet). While such an index may appear too narrowly focused, its small cost may well be considered a productive investment for organizations and institutions facing reduced funding, and the subsequent need for information on the status and trends within philanthropic activities.—**Eleanor Ferrall**

SEX STUDIES

885. **The Complete Dictionary of Sexology.** new expanded ed. Robert T. Francoeur and others, eds. New York, Continuum Publishing, 1995. 790p. illus. $29.95pa. ISBN 0-8264-0672-6.

This "new expanded edition" of the 1991 *The Complete Dictionary of Sexology* (Greenwood Press) offers 130 additional entries in a 21-page addendum at the end of the 766-page original text, which contained more than 6,000 entries. Otherwise, the dictionary remains the same as its precursor. No new preface or introduction informs the reader of how or why the editors chose the new entries. Their goal and basis for selection probably remained the same—to provide "a common basis for communication by bringing together terms and definitions from all the disciplines" (p. ix).

The merits of this edition are the same as those of the 1st: incorporating and clarifying sexual terms from a variety of contexts; ease of use by professionals from a variety of disciplines; extensive cross-references, appendixes, and citations from the professional literature; contribution to the development of a consistent vocabulary within the field and across disciplines; and definitions composed by contributors well trained in the field of sexuality. Integration of the new entries would have facilitated the reader's ease of use. However, the paperback version, at its inexpensive price, makes this valuable resource affordable to a wider audience.—**Suzanne G. Frayser**

886. **Fetishes, Florentine Girdles, and Other Explorations into the Sexual Imagination.** Harriett Gilbert, ed. New York, HarperPerennial/HarperCollins, 1994. 290p. illus. $15.00pa. ISBN 0-06-273313-3.

Described as a feminist companion to various theories about sexuality, this book also discusses the artists who have grappled with the subject. This description is accurate but requires qualification. Gilbert, a writer and broadcaster, intends that the guide should serve to illuminate the structures that contain, explain, and express female sexuality. Interspersed with an eclectic selection of 35 black-and-white illustrations (e.g., Japanese comics, a Robert Mapplethorpe photograph, a painting by Frida Kahlo), the 350 miniessays by an international team of 95 feminist authorities are an idiosyncratic collection. The essays cluster around a number of themes related to creative endeavors in various geographical regions, historical periods, cultures, and perspectives: (1) the lives of poets, writers, novelists, playwrights, painters, photographers, social scientists, feminists, political activists; (2) novels, works of art, classics in philosophy and religion; and (3) aspects of sexuality and gender.

In this unusual resource, contributors provide well-written critiques of their subjects, bibliographical citations, and numerous cross-references. Many of the topics are "common sense" selections that are easy to find (e.g., Sigmund Freud, Alfred Kinsey, patriarchy, orgasm, androgyny). However, alphabetically arranged entries and the lack of an index or table of contents make it difficult to locate unusual topics such as "The Clit Statement" or the "Hetaira." Arrangement according to themes (e.g., biographical sketches, psychological concepts) would have facilitated access to the materials. Nevertheless, the essays are interesting, informative, and often humorous. The contributors succeed in probing and sparking the sexual imagination. Unfortunately, there is no easily discovered definition of what a "Florentine Girdle" is! Perhaps that is left to the imagination.—**Suzanne G. Frayser**

887. Frayser, Suzanne G., and Thomas J. Whitby. **Studies in Human Sexuality: A Selected Guide.** 2d ed. Englewood, Colo., Libraries Unlimited, 1995. 737p. index. $85.00. ISBN 1-56308-131-8.

This new expanded edition expresses the same purpose as the 1st edition, which is to "provide scholars, professionals, students, and laypersons with a bibliographic guide, to the best books comprehensive in scope, in human sexuality" (p. xi). Thus, the material included has both titles published prior to 1980 as well as those published in the 1990s. The number of books abstracted has grown from 627 in the 1st edition to 1,091 in this one. Highlighted are more of the pressing issues of the day such as abortion, AIDS, child sexual abuse, incest, rape, sexual harassment, homosexuality, pornography, and prostitution. The focus is on monographs and not periodical literature. Books were selected from varied viewpoints to provide balance. Reading levels of the books listed are indicated at the head of each entry. These range from professional, intelligent layperson, and popular, to young adult and children. This is a useful feature for collection development or for use with particular groups.

The volume is arranged in three parts. Part 1 covers books on general works such as reference, research, and statistical surveys. Part 2, the largest section, is a topical guide arranged by broad subject areas, which are subdivided into more narrow topics. Part 3 is a listing of bibliographies. The volume covers every aspect of sexuality and all the included titles have lengthy, informative abstracts. A table of contents in the front is arranged the way the book is organized. The separate author, title, and subject indexes, found at the end of the volume, are necessary to assist the researcher in locating specific topics because of the large volume of material here. This well-researched edition will be necessary for most research libraries, and will be of great value for counselors and therapists.—**Marilyn Strong Noronha**

888. Hartel, Lynda Jones, and Helena M. VonVille. **Sexual Harassment: A Selected, Annotated Bibliography.** Westport, Conn., Greenwood Press, 1995. 158p. index. (Bibliographies and Indexes in Women's Studies, no.23). $59.95. ISBN 0-313-29055-5.

This work serves as a sequel to *Sexual Harassment: A Guide to Resources* (see ARBA 86, entry 813), which covered the literature from 1974-1984. Hartel and VonVille have searched a number of sources to create a reference that ranges from January 1984 through late 1994. From an initial search result of more than 1,000 items, the authors selected and annotated some 535 print items that include articles, books, and dissertations. Omitted from the scope were editorials and letters, generic works on harassment, materials unavailable in the United States, newspaper articles, popular press publications, works where sexual harassment was not the primary focus, anecdotal reports, and articles specific to the Bob Packwood or Tailhook controversies.

Annotated entries are arranged in four major sections: history, theories, and consequences of sexual harassment; sexual harassment in various workplace settings; sexual harassment in academic, social, and living environments; and legal aspects of sexual harassment. These are further subdivided into 18 chapters. The body of the text is supplemented by a brief chronology of significant sexual harassment legislation and publications, followed by author and subject indexes. The bibliography is recommended as a necessary addition for public, academic, special, business, and organizational reference collections.

—**Edmund F. SantaVicca**

889. Thomsett, Michael C., and Jean Freestone Thomsett. **Sex and Love Quotations: A Worldwide Dictionary....** Jefferson, N.C., McFarland, 1995. 226p. index. $35.00. ISBN 0-7864-0048-X.

Despite the advent of a wide variety of electronic reference sources, there is still room for another high-quality topical quotation book. The 2,406 entries in *Sex and Love Quotations* make it a comprehensive guide to virtually every aspect of the physical and emotional elements of human relationships as viewed by writers from all times and all places. Some of the entries may be found in standard general-purpose dictionaries of quotations, but there are a substantial number of entries that will not be found there, or readily located anywhere else.

The topical arrangement is an interesting one, especially valuable for those who may be looking for a quotation to use in a paper or speech. Each of 11 major headings—on everything from love, to being single, to physical love, to multiple sex partners—is broken down into 4 to 12 categories (ranging from romance to rape) under which the quotations are randomly arranged for ease and enjoyment. A lengthy index of keywords-in-context makes it easy to locate a particular quotation (each individually numbered) by virtually any uncommon word. Only the author, title of the work, and date are given, as is true in most quotation dictionaries, so actually tracking down the exact location, and more complete context, of a quotation may still be difficult. All in all, this is a valuable addition to the realm of quotation dictionaries.

—**Norman D. Stevens**

SOCIAL WELFARE AND SOCIAL WORK

890. Barker, Robert L. **The Social Work Dictionary.** 3d ed. Washington, D.C., NASW Press, 1995. 447p. $34.95pa. ISBN 0-87101-253-7.

The field of social work is much broader in its areas of concern than the non-social worker may suspect, covering such subjects as family therapy, counseling and group work, cognitive and moral development, educational equity, social theory, criminal justice, health care, and more. This breadth of responsibility necessitates being familiar with terminology from many subjects and disciplines. Theories, theorists, key concepts, organizations, court cases, and various pieces of legislation may need to be understood for one to practice most effectively. All of these kinds of terms are covered in this dictionary, which is intended for both social workers and related human service professionals.

This 3d edition of the dictionary is approximately twice as large as the 1st (see ARBA 88, entry 851). As in the earlier edition, definitions range in length from a sentence to a long paragraph; italicized words in definitions are defined elsewhere in the dictionary. Cross-references direct the user from unused words, phrases, or acronyms to the preferred terms. Supplementary information includes a chronology of milestones in the history of social work, the National Association of Social Workers (NASW) Code of Ethics, and lists of state regulatory boards and NASW chapter offices.

This source has been regularly updated and expanded, which should ensure that the terminology is current. The definitions themselves are well written and cover such a broad range of topics that most libraries, whether they have social work collections or not, should find this source a valuable complement to sociology and social science dictionaries.—**Stephen H. Aby**

891. **The Big Book of Minority Opportunities: The Directory of Special Programs for Minority Group Members.** 6th ed. Willis L. Johnson, ed. Garrett Park, Md., Garrett Park Press, 1995. 449p. index. $39.00pa. ISBN 0-912048-89-1. ISSN 0093-9501.

This impressive compendium of opportunities for minorities should be of great use to students, advisors, employers, and program directors. The volume is divided into 19 sections. Sections A-M classify opportunities by field, such as agriculture, health, law, and social science. Sections N-Q present programs by universities and colleges, associations, states, and federal government. Sections R and S classify opportunities by the targeted minority group, African American, Hispanic, and so on. The volume includes a glossary of terms, an index, and a useful list of other sources of information. Interestingly enough, opportunities for women are not displayed separately, as would be expected under affirmative action principles. The announced opportunities cover financial, occupational, and advisory services.

Each entry (there are 4,312 in all) provides basic information and application deadlines if known. In its 6th edition, this volume is up-to-date in terms of the politics of affirmative action, as indicated by the shift from the concept of affirmative action to diversity in order to comply with new laws. The reader finds guidelines on how to use the information and a warning that simply reading the book does not guarantee benefits; one has to go after the opportunities to realize the benefits.

The book would be even more helpful than it is were it classified and published in separate volumes, each specific to the level of education of the potential beneficiaries. One volume would serve high school students aiming at a college education. Another would help college students exploring graduate and professional education. A third would be for job placement and training opportunities. Such specialization would lower the cost and make its contents more accessible not only at the reference libraries, but also on the desks of student and career advisors everywhere.—**Elias H. Tuma**

892. **Carroll's Federal Assistance Directory: Fall 1995.** Jill Conley, ed. Washington, D.C., Carroll Publishing, 1995. 775p. index. $137.00pa./yr. ISSN 1083-8813.

Carroll's Federal Assistance Directory lists 1,390 programs, and each program outline provides the following information: title of the program, purpose, type of assistance, applicant eligibility, uses and limits of program benefits and restrictions, criteria for selecting proposals, procedure for applying, deadline (if any), finances, and contact name and telephone number. The table of contents is helpful in finding needed information.—**Bohdan S. Wynar**

893. **The Encyclopedia of Social Work.** 19th ed. Richard L. Edwards and others, eds. Washington, D.C., NASW Press, 1995. 3v. index. $150.00; $120.00pa. ISBN 0-87101-255-3; 0-87101-256-1pa.

The 19th edition of *The Encyclopedia of Social Work* is a three-volume, expanded collection of articles (290), including bibliographies (142), on subjects relating to professional social work. Topics are easily located by a table of contents in each volume, with subject cross-references, comprehensive indexes, and reader's guide boxes following articles with related topical entries. Clearly, much effort has been made to present each topic objectively and thoroughly.

Readers need to keep in mind, however, that the content of each article is dependent on the knowledge, experience, and judgment of the author or authors assigned to write on the topic, and may not be reflective of the entire profession. For example, the article on direct practice with children gives little attention to the use of play; yet, social workers around the world frequently use this medium for communication, assessment, and treatment of children. In the article on abortion, it appears that the author is a strong proponent for the inclusion of funding for abortion in any national health policy. In the article on generalist practice, little recognition is given to the central characteristics commonly acknowledged as basic to generalist practice, namely, a multilevel approach, a systems perspective, and a problem-solving process. This encyclopedia offers a broad overview of the multiple dimensions of social work today, and is highly recommended for social work educators, practitioners, and professional social work libraries.—**Maria O'Neil McMahon**

894. Ginsberg, Leon. **Social Work Almanac.** 2d ed. Washington, D.C., NASW Press, 1995. 390p. maps. index. $34.95pa. ISBN 0-87101-248-0.

Social workers, like other professionals, have a recurring need for statistical data on issues affecting their practice. Data on health care, crime, educational attainment, poverty levels, homelessness, and mental illness, among other topics, are important for policy decisions, reports, and intervention. However, given the amount and diversity of statistical data sources, a handy compilation would be an invaluable timesaver. The *Social Work Almanac* meets this need by drawing data from government and private sources to present a statistical portrait of some of the country's most important social issues.

The data, which are as recent as 1993, are organized into nine chapters dealing with population and demography, children, crime, education, health, mental illness and disabilities, older adults, social welfare, and the social work profession. Within these chapters, there are subsections addressing more specific topics. For example, the chapter on older adults covers population trends, living arrangements, poverty, public expenditures, abuse, and criminal victimization. The data are arranged well in charts, graphs, and tables; source documents are cited. One of the nicest features of this book is its discussion of the various tables and figures. These brief discussions are often fairly educational, providing a context for the value of the data. There is a supplementary list of references, as well as a subject index that includes institutions and program names.

This source is not just for social workers. It covers major social issues of interest to those in the social sciences and is, for a statistics book, reasonably user friendly. Regular updates, as was the case between the 1st (see ARBA 94, entry 911) and 2d editions, will ensure its utility. Both public and academic libraries will find it a valuable tool for answering a range of questions dealing with social statistics.
—**Stephen H. Aby**

895. Loescher, Gil, and Ann Dull Loescher. **The Global Refugee Crisis: A Reference Handbook.** Santa Barbara, Calif., ABC-CLIO, 1994. 261p. index. (Contemporary World Issues). $39.95. ISBN 0-87436-753-0.

The authors of this compact handbook, a professor of international relations at the University of Notre Dame and a teacher/author, have attempted to create a multipurpose reference source intended for the general public and students at all levels. The result is a somewhat superficial work that tries to do too many things. The book consists of seven sections, beginning with an overview that defines the topic and outlines the nature, extent, and causes of the refugee problem in the post-World War II era. The focus is on the United Nations High Commissioner for Refugees and the activities of that office, with less attention paid to other international organizations. The other sections vary considerably in scope and depth of presentation. A brief chronology covers the twentieth century from World War I. A weak biographical section includes sketches of prominent refugees and activists for refugees, but provides information on only 27 individuals. The longest and most comprehensive section consists of statistics on refugees, and reprints or summaries of legal documents from the UN and other international bodies. A directory of organizations and government agencies involved in refugee issues is provided, with short summaries of their activities. The last two sections consist of selective bibliographies of books, periodicals, and audiovisual and electronic sources for further research. They cover mostly recent resources, current through 1993, and materials for children as well as adults. A glossary, a list of acronyms, and an index round out the volume.

The information presented appears accurate overall, although occasional value judgments appear in the text that seem inappropriate for a reference work. In summary, this one-stop-shopping approach to reference works on particular topics seems problematic, as it mixes together information that will become obsolete at various times, and shortchanges some aspects of the topic under consideration. Still, this volume will be useful as an introduction to the refugee crisis, and is recommended as such for public, school, and college libraries.—**Jeff Wanser**

SUBSTANCE ABUSE

896. **National Guide to Funding in Substance Abuse.** James E. Baumgartner and others, eds. Washington, D.C., Foundation Center, 1995. 238p. index. $95.00pa. ISBN 0-87954-602-6.

This volume is intended as a starting point for grantseekers looking for foundation and corporate contributions for various programs in the area of substance abuse. The volume contains 530 entries for grantmaking foundations and 75 entries for direct corporate giving programs with substantial interest in substance abuse. A total of 695 grants in substance abuse are listed for 209 foundations. An introduction, a how-to-use section, and a glossary of terms explain how the volume is organized. Information includes the criteria by which foundations were selected for inclusion and how to select the best foundation for one's needs. There is also a bibliography on substance abuse funding and a lengthy listing of other publications of the Foundation Center.

The main body of the book consists of a directory with a state-by-state listing of the foundations containing the essential information for each foundation listed, including address, telephone number, fields of interest, and types of support. At the end of the volume are six lengthy indexes, four of which would be of particular use to the grantseeker. These are the geographical index, listing foundations by state and city indicating whether the grants are national, regional, or international; the types of support index indicating the areas in which grants are given, such as fellowships, program development, and the like; an index of foundation and corporate giving programs by broad subject, such as alcoholism; and an index to grants by subject that is narrowly defined, such as birth defects and child development.

With its lengthy introduction regarding use and many indexes, persons seeking funding in this field should be able to locate the information they need with ease. The guide will be of great value to individuals and institutions who are involved in education or research in the field. Most university libraries should acquire this.—**Marilyn Strong Noronha**

897. Osgood, Nancy J., Helen E. Wood, and Iris A. Parham, comps. **Alcoholism and Aging: An Annotated Bibliography and Review.** Westport, Conn., Greenwood Press, 1995. 250p. index. (Bibliographies and Indexes in Gerontology, no.24). $65.00. ISBN 0-313-28398-2.

Experts in the fields of gerontology, clinical psychology, and geriatric medicine have compiled this analytical bibliography providing lists and abstracts of research dealing with alcoholism and aging over the past 30 years. The 301 annotated references and 100 unannotated references indicate the research done to date on prevalence, causes, effects, diagnosis, prevention, and treatment of alcoholism in the aging. The annotated section lists sources by types of work: bibliographies, overview articles, books and book chapters, empirical studies, and miscellaneous works.

A large overview section in the beginning of the work provides a summary of the many facets of the problem, citing the research that has been done. Problems with existing data are discussed and areas in which more research is needed are presented. Cross-references and author and subject indexes make this guide very accessible to the user. The work is comprehensive but not exhaustive, as not all works by an author could be included. A representative sampling from major authors is presented. The bibliography is a good starting point for the researcher to get a general survey of this multifaceted problem and to become aware of major studies already done on the topic. It will be of value for health professionals, social workers, sociologists, and those in public health. The work should be in libraries that serve these populations.—**Marilyn Strong Noronha**

898. Single, Eric, and Diane McKenzie. **Canadian Profile: Alcohol, Tobacco, & Other Drugs 1995. Profil Canadien: L'Alcool, le Tabac, et les Autres Drogues.** Toronto, Canadian Centre on Substance Abuse and Addiction Research Foundation, 1994. 414p. index. $34.95 spiralbound. ISBN 1-896323-02-2.

This is a handbook of statistics on drug use in Canada. It is the result of collaboration between the staffs at two leading drug abuse think tanks. The information is drawn from Statistics Canada and other government sources. Previous editions were published in 1992 and 1994. The work is an important source of drug use information for book collections with client interests in Canada.

There are 12 chapters in the work on various categories of licit and illicit drugs and on social and economic aspects of drug use. The latter include such topical issues as aboriginal peoples, street youth, public opinion, steroid use, spending on drugs, crime, and AIDS. Chapters include introductory lists of figures and tables (with no page references), textual material and highlights, and tables and graphs. There is an idiosyncratic table of contents with abstracts but no page numbers. However, many chapters have tabs for easy location. A subject index to the tables gives table numbers. Other features include a note on information gaps and research implications.

The book is in parallel columns of English and French. There are a few puzzling aspects to the English, for example, where the French (and context) seems to indicate that hospital visits or possibly admissions is meant, the English is rendered "hospital separations." Either this is a term unknown to this reviewer or a strange editorial mistake. This is an important source on substance abuse in Canada and should be added to Canadian studies and relevant specialist collections.—**Nigel Tappin**

YOUTH AND CHILD DEVELOPMENT

899. Carpenter, Kathryn Hammell. **Sourcebook on Parenting and Child Care.** Phoenix, Ariz., Oryx Press, 1995. 269p. index. $35.00pa. ISBN 0-89774-780-1.

This comprehensive, practical, well-designed guidebook provides solid, timely information for those concerned about infants, children, and adolescents. More than 900 entries are descriptively annotated and reflect the "best" current popular and professional books and journals published in the United States, primarily from 1990-1993 (with a few 1994 and classic titles included). The one-paragraph annotations address the purpose, audience, and special features of the works.

The book is organized into 26 chapters covering such topics as the adoptive family, the humorous side of parenting, growth and development issues, parental responsibilities, and children in crisis. Resources in each chapter are preceded by a brief introduction, and recommended titles are starred. Entries provide full bibliographic information, including the price. A useful directory of organizational and social service agencies concludes each chapter. Appendixes of parenting videotapes, statistical data, and indexes (author, title, subject) round out the work. Since the author has experience as a book reviewer, health sciences bibliographer, and acquisitions librarian, the work is well conceived and easy to use. The nominal price will make it a popular purchase for academic, public, school, and special libraries.—**Ilene F. Rockman**

900. Deaton, Wendy, and others. **The Child Sexual Abuse Custody Dispute Annotated Bibliography.** Thousand Oaks, Calif., Sage, 1995. 117p. $27.50. ISBN 0-8039-5861-7.

The 137 items covered in this bibliography include much more than just items that deal with sexual abuse in custody disputes. Most of the items would be classified under sexual abuse, child abuse, divorce, and so forth, without specifically dealing with custody. A quick search on PsyLit, using sexual or child abuse and child custody or joint custody, found 67 articles that seemed relevant to this bibliography. Many were not included here. When the search was broadened, looking at child abuse and sexual abuse, many more were found. When the annotations in this bibliography were compared with those in PsyLit, it was found that only some were more detailed here, while others were shorter: surprising, since more detail, not less, was expected in this specialized bibliography. There were some errors in this bibliography such as wrong article titles and page numbers.

In this time when electronic databases are becoming more and more available, it is questionable whether patrons will use bibliographies such as this one, when they can get more current information, select those things that are held by the institution where they are searching, and download the information to use in their word processors. This book is for comprehensive collections without electronic access.—**Robert L. Turner Jr.**

901. DeFrancis, Beth. **The Parents' Resource Almanac: Where to Write, Who to Call....** Holbrook, Mass., Adams Publishing, 1994. 779p. index. $39.95; $15.00pa. ISBN 1-55850-396-X; 1-55850-394-3pa.

Beginning with a well-deserved cover blurb from *Parent's Choice* magazine, this accurately priced guide to parenting and child care should be a mandatory purchase for all types of libraries. The author, a freelance writer and mother of two small children, has succeeded admirably in compiling a list of annotated sources with useful tips concerning such subjects as adoption, clothing, disabilities, nutrition, and nonprescription drugs.

Twenty-seven chapters and nine appendixes are devoted to topics including parenting techniques, grandparenting, family travel, health matters, education, children's literature, and child development. Under each subject are listings of books, periodicals, associations, computer software, cassettes, videotapes, and businesses that provide relevant information or services. Addresses and telephone and fax numbers are also supplied where appropriate. Subsequent appendixes furnish lists of juvenile products, U.S. government publications, youth orchestras, national parks and forests, and mail order catalogs, respectively. A thorough index concludes the text.

Despite the publication of *The Parent's Desk Reference* (see ARBA 92, entry 842), *The Childwise Catalog* (3d ed.; see ARBA 94, entry 921) and *Sourcebook on Parenting and Childcare* (see entry 899), this title makes an indispensable contribution to the genre. None of the previously cited titles is as comprehensive as this easy-to-use almanac—a truly all-in-one guide to whatever parents and interested educators need to know.—**Kathleen W. Craver**

902. Erickson, Judith B. **Directory of American Youth Organizations 1994-1995: A Guide to 500 Clubs....** 5th ed. Minneapolis, Minn., Free Spirit, 1994. 189p. index. $18.95pa. ISBN 0-915793-63-6. ISSN 1044-4440.

This directory is a valuable resource for parents, children, youth, and professionals seeking information about nationally organized youth organizations. More than 500 social groups are identified according to name, address, contact person, telephone number, and brief organizational description. The listings are well indexed and categorized according to similarity in purpose or focus. The book contains information regarding youth organization changes in name or status. Content following the directory listings includes a presentation on such topics as recognition of the important role played by volunteers in youth organizations, a brief history and comparison of organizations, and a consideration of trends and future directions in American youth organizations. The book concludes with a listing of resources for administrators and workers in youth organizations, and a brief description of selected relevant readings. The book provides its readers with the opportunity to become more aware of the vast number of social, recreational, educational, and civic outlets available for children and youth in North America today. The directory is highly recommended for libraries and agencies serving children and teens.—**Maria O'Neil McMahon**

903. Feinberg, Sandra, Barbara Jordan, and Michele Lauer-Bader. **Parenting: An Annotated Bibliography 1965-1987.** Metuchen, N.J., Scarecrow, 1995. 806p. index. $97.50. ISBN 0-8108-2664-X.

This bibliography is a guide to books published between 1965 and 1987 concerning each stage of parenting from pregnancy and childbirth through adult children and care of aging parents. Comprehensive rather than selective, the 2,947 entries are annotated and cover a range of topics, including Benjamin Spock's child-rearing methods, Jane Fonda's pregnancy workout, families as a public policy issue, financial planning, helping children with school work, coaching soccer effectively, special-needs children, and where to turn for help with adoption. Books on fathering and the experience of fatherhood are also included. Entries are alphabetical by author and numbered, with cross-references to title and subject indexes. The subject index is similar to that in *Psychological Abstracts*, so scholars will find it familiar.

This is a quick reference to general topics that will prove useful to parents, child psychologists, family counselors, social workers, and others working with children and their families. It may not suffice for graduate students, who will also need the Educational Resources Information Center (ERIC) and *Psychological Abstracts* and any of the numerous subject-specific bibliographies on children and parenting. Comprehensive collections on child development and those serving practitioners in family counseling will want to own this title, although the price may prove too steep for some academic and public libraries.
—**Glynys R. Thomas**

904. Stoppard, Miriam. **Complete Baby and Child Care.** New York, Dorling Kindersley, 1995. 351p. illus. index. $29.95. ISBN 1-56458-850-5.

Complete Baby and Child Care is aptly titled; it is indeed a remarkably complete compendium of information on child care from birth through early childhood. Written in a clear, nonpatronizing tone, Stoppard begins with the period just after birth, discussing such things as weight and size; feeding;

bonding; and possible medical conditions such as jaundice, premature delivery, Down's syndrome, and so on. Her urge to be reassuring in completeness means that there is a section on types of birthmarks as well as one about the different sounds a baby is liable to make (e.g., snuffling, sneezing, burping, hiccups).

Proceeding chronologically through the baby's life, Stoppard covers child development; emotional and physical needs at each age; medical situations likely to be encountered (stuttering, Attention Deficit Hyperactivity Disorder, to name two of many); and such topics as eating and sleeping patterns, toilet training, types of preschools, family dynamics, and much more.

This hefty book is attractive and inviting, with wide margins and clear color photographs in addition to occasional charts and diagrams. The diagram showing how to fold a cloth diaper is a perfectly obvious choice for such a book, but one that is not likely to be found elsewhere. There are also specific case histories, with photographs, of babies and parents at different stages of development, which describe particular stories and include the parents' feelings and points of view. There is an index, a list of useful addresses, and a first aid section. All in all, this is a valuable book for the target audience.—**Wendy Waloff**

17 Statistics, Demography, and Urban Studies

DEMOGRAPHY

905. **Gale Country & World Rankings Reporter: 3,000 Country & World Area Rankings on a Variety of Topics....** Charity A. Dorgan, ed. Detroit, Gale, 1995. 1091p. index. $129.00. ISBN 0-8103-9876-1. ISSN 1079-929X.

For almost all countries in the world, comparative data are given in this compendium on a multitude of subjects. The tabular material alone takes more than 50 pages to list, and consists of more than 3,000 tables, grouped into 5 broad categories called "thematic profiles." They are, in order, a social profile and a physical profile, followed by one on transportation and public utilities. The concluding profiles cover political and economic information. A surprising variety of vital statistics, economic indicators, and technical, cultural, and educational parameters is included among the data.

An introduction gives a detailed account of the lists and tables presented, along with the methods of compilation. The balance of the volume is devoted to the tabular material and its sources, and a general index; consequently, this is a reference book, and only likely to be used as such in an office or library. There is less here for the general student or businessperson, but trivia buffs and the curious may find a number of topics of interest to them. The work is a useful source for demographics, trade, and other yardsticks by which societies are measured around the world.—**Arthur R. Upgren**

906. Gerhan, David R., comp. **Bibliography of American Demographic History: The Literature from 1984 to 1994.** Westport, Conn., Greenwood Press, 1995. 339p. index. (Bibliographies and Indexes in American History, no.30). $79.50. ISBN 0-313-26677-8.

One in the important Bibliographies and Indexes in American History series, this volume surveys contributions to the literature on the demography of the United States that appeared during the referenced decade. As such, it is a logical companion to the earlier *Retrospective Bibliography of American Demographic History* (see ARBA 90, entry 835). Coverage is comprehensive, and the definition of *demography* is broad enough to include many considerations of cultural and social interactions as well.

The 8,902 entries are arranged in 6 chapters, covering theory, method, and general background; marriage and fertility; health and death; migration, pluralism, and local patterns; family and demographic history; population; and economics, politics, and society. Within each chapter, references are arranged both chronologically (before 1800, 1800-1920, and post-1920) and in appropriate topical subdivisions. Prefacing each subdivision is a brief overview, highlighting the more significant contributions. The books and journals referenced are primarily American; but increasing international scholarship on American historical questions is reflected in entries from many (especially European) countries. There is a list of journal abbreviations, and detailed author, place-name, and topical indexes.

Sociology, political science, geography, and economics (apart from history) are among the professional disciplines amply represented in the collection. For anyone concerned with virtually any aspect of America's population, this will be an indispensable volume.—**James R. McDonald**

907. **Migration Statistics 1994.** Brussels, Office for Official Publications of the European Communities; distr., Lanham, Md., UNIPUB, 1994. 109p. $14.00pa. ISBN 92-826-9228-0.

Since the mid-1980s, strong immigration pressures on the part of both political and economic refugees have led to migration policy becoming the subject of heated debate in many Western European nations. This detailed collection of migration statistics dating from 1991-1992 provides a useful database for the comparative analysis of migration trends by country, nationality, and certain socioeconomic characteristics.

Part of the voluminous Eurostat series published by the Statistical Office of the European Communities (now the European Union [EU]), the book presents 53 tables offering information for each country on the number of residents from every other country included in the survey and the numbers and origins/destinations of international immigrants and emigrants. Data are broken down by sex, age, citizenship, and nations of previous and next residence. The 19 Western European countries surveyed include the 12 members of the EU (which grew to 15 in 1995) and 7 additional members of what was known as the European Economic Area. Immigration and emigration tables use selected nations from other parts of the world. Except for a few summary graphs and a brief introduction, the tables are presented without discussion.

Because the data have largely been provided by the statistical offices of the countries surveyed, there is considerable variety of both definitions and coverage. France, for example, is notoriously parsimonious, providing no data on migration by previous/next residence or emigration, and little on immigration. Despite these problems, it is useful to have reasonably comparable migration information from several countries collected in a single volume.—**James R. McDonald**

908. Mitchell, Susan. **The Official Guide to the Generations: Who They Are. How They Live. What They Think.** Ithaca, N.Y., New Strategist, 1995. 414p. index. $69.95. ISBN 0-9628092-8-4.

In an era in which competition for U.S. consumer markets has become increasingly severe, specific niches—economic, geographic, sociological—have emerged as serious marketing targets. Not surprisingly, publishers are attempting to capitalize on this trend by producing reference works that identify highly focused subgroups in the overall national cultural fabric. This, for example, is the fourth "official guide" (although "official" by whose criteria is never specified) offered by the publisher (see *The Official Guide to the American Marketplace*, entry 911) that proposes to provide a helpfully categorized population profile.

The premise of the volume is that, in the 1990s, the consumptive United States may usefully be divided into four generations: (1) "World War I," those born before 1933; (2) "Swing," 1934-45; (3) "Baby-boom," 1946-64; and (4) "Generation X," 1965-76. Oddly, no consideration is given to the post-1976 generation, which, for many commodities, is the most consumptive of all. Employing data largely derived from the 1990 U.S. census, with additional inputs from the Bureau of Labor Statistics, the National Center for Health Statistics, and a variety of other sources, the book offers a series of tables (with brief informational text) on population, families and households, education, the labor force, income and spending, housing, health, and attitudes and behavior. There are a glossary and index, but no maps or any attempt to organize the information geographically, or at any level below the national.

Government statistics are a rich mine of free information that can be put to many productive uses. Whether buying such a shotgun approach as this to U.S. demographics is more useful than consulting the original data is a question for all potential users.—**James R. McDonald**

909. **Population and Development: Directory of Non-Governmental Organisations in OECD Countries. Population et Developpement.** By Development Centre of the Organisation for Economic Co-operation and Development. Washington, D.C., OECD Publications and Information Center, 1994. 360p. index. $73.00pa. ISBN 92-64-04171-0.

The 25 member nations of the Organization for Economic Cooperation and Development (OECD) are frequently referred to as the "rich man's club" of international organizations. Largely grouping the world's wealthiest economies, the OECD seeks to maintain sustainable growth and living standards in member economies, to contribute to responsible expansion of the worldwide economy, and to promote expanded world trade. Among the contemporary problems that impact all of these goals is the critical relationship between population growth and economic development, including the fashionable concept of "sustainable development," which adds an environmental dimension to the equation.

Not surprisingly, most of the funds available to promote development in "less favored" parts of the world are to be found among the OECD membership. Although national governments and international agencies (World Bank, International Monetary Fund) obviously play a major role, there are an impressive number of nongovernmental organizations that often focus on needs that may otherwise be neglected. This useful key to such groups lists 752 organizations from 24 OECD nations (Mexico, the newest member, is not included). Arrangement is alphabetical by country, with contact information, objectives, general information, population action concerns, awareness-enhancing strategies, and comments provided for each group. Cross-referenced indexes to family planning actions, the role of women, health, family issues, and awareness-raising about population issues are provided, along with a select bibliography. This is a useful guide to population-oriented agencies that are often difficult to identify.—**James R. McDonald**

910. **Profiles of America: An Informational, Statistical, and Relocation Encyclopedia of All U.S. Cities, Towns, and Counties. South Region—Volume 4: Kentucky * North Carolina * Tennessee.** Milpitas, Calif., Toucan Valley, 1995. 1v. (various paging). maps. index. $82.00/v.; $1,312.00/set. ISBN 1-884925-34-0 (v.4); 1-884925-03-0 (set).

This is a sample of an ambitious 16-volume set that provides detailed information about all of the counties (or county equivalents), incorporated municipalities, census-designated places, and minor civil divisions—a total of more than 41,000—in the United States. Data are derived largely from the 1990 census, with additional inputs from the U.S. Public Health Service, Bureau of Labor Statistics, National Center for Educational Statistics, Federal Bureau of Investigation, and other agencies as well as from a modest amount of original research.

Data are arranged by county for each state, with communities ranked by population under each county (information for each county typically fills one to two pages). Each entry provides data on geographic location, the local economy (unemployment, industries, number of farms), education levels, housing starts and values, vital statistics (including population breakdowns by race), 1992 presidential election results, and contact addresses and telephone numbers. There is a county base map for each state, as well as a place-name index.

Although data presentations based on the 1990 census age quickly, this is a well-organized and accessible collection that focuses on basics and—unlike several similar recent efforts—allows the consumer to make decisions as to which information is most valuable. The total package is expensive, but compared to (for example) the *American Places Dictionary* (see ARBA 95, entry 500), it is probably a reasonable investment for marketers, merchandisers, and others for whom accurate, small-scale data offer some potential advantage.—**James R. McDonald**

911. Russell, Cheryl. **The Official Guide to the American Marketplace: The Real Facts....** 2d ed. Ithaca, N.Y., New Strategist, 1995. 480p. index. $79.95. ISBN 0-9628092-4-1.

The 2d edition of a comprehensive statistical collection documenting the social condition of the United States, this volume literally paints a portrait of the nation in numbers. In a series of some 150 tables, each prefaced with a modest introduction, the guide provides summaries of trends and projections in the areas of education, health, income, labor force characteristics, living arrangements, population, race and ethnicity, and spending habits. A final section provides telephone contacts (although no addresses) for more information, and a glossary and a general index complete the work. Data sources for each table are credited (most of the information is from census and other federally collected statistics), but there is no overall bibliography.

Based on its title and promotional materials, the book is designed to help marketing strategists better target a specific potential audience of consumers. As such, it falls short in several areas. First, most of the information is presented only at the national level: Relatively few of the tables break down data by state, and there is no effort to display trends by county (although a few tables feature metropolitan areas). Second, a great deal of the information presented would be much more useful in cartographic form—several recent atlases have dramatically mapped the same social trends—yet there are no maps at all. In short, this is a well-researched and well-presented volume that offers data relevant to the American experience, yet seems to fall short of its objectives.—**James R. McDonald**

912. **The Sex and Age Distribution of the World Populations: The 1994 Revision.** By the Department of Economic and Social Information and Policy Analysis, Population Division. New York, United Nations, 1994. 858p. $45.00pa. ISBN 92-1-151274-3. S/N E.95.XIII.2.

This is strictly a data book. A compilation made under the auspices of the United Nations, it contains exactly the information conveyed by its title. For most UN member nations, a few nonmembers such as Switzerland, and a few other areas such as Hong Kong and Puerto Rico, as well as for each continent and the world, this 1994 revision lists population data for every fifth year from 1950 to 2050. For past years, estimates are given, whereas three future cases are presented; these are the high, medium, and low variant cases, as defined in the brief introduction. In every case, the populations are divided by sex and by ages within five-year intervals, as well as totals. This volume is of limited interest and not likely suitable for general readership. However, it is a valuable reference for any application of these kinds of facts.—**Arthur R. Upgren**

913. **The Sourcebook of Zip Code Demographics.** 10th ed. Arlington, Va., CACI Marketing Systems; distr., Detroit, Gale, 1995. 596p. $495.00pa. ISBN 0-918417-56-2.

This is the 10th annual edition of a detailed and comprehensive marketing guide that arranges its comparative data by zip code numbers for each state, thus providing an unusually fine-mesh net for catching useful information. Most competing works provide resolution only to a county or metropolitan area level, thereby allowing only a fairly broad approach to marketing decision making. For each residential zip code (nonresidential codes are included for locational reference), some 70 demographic variables are presented. These are grouped into four categories: population change, population composition, income, and "purchase potential profiles." The basic data, as for similar publications, are derived from the 1990 census. Because the census does not aggregate information by zip code, the compilers have devised a geodemographic system by which census tracts and block numbering areas are superimposed on the zip code map, resulting in reasonably accurate interpolation.

Another feature of the work is its projection of 1990 data to 1995 (which can be fairly easily verified), and to the year 2000. Given the variables at work, this sort of extrapolation carries a certain risk, but it seems here to be done cautiously, and provides a potentially valuable tool for future planning. The data are very densely packed on each page, and the absence of zip code location maps for each state makes combining them into larger geographical units a rather tedious exercise. Nonetheless, this imaginative and functional compilation should be helpful for fine-tuning marketing strategies.—**James R. McDonald**

914. **Statistical Forecasts of the United States.** 2d ed. Sean R. Pollock, ed. Detroit, Gale, 1995. 813p. index. $95.00. ISBN 0-8103-8935-5.

The 1st edition of this work was published in 1993 and reviewed in ARBA 94 (see entry 932). The present edition has 15 topical chapters, such as agriculture; business, banking, and finance; and construction and housing—similar to the 1st edition. Statistical projections cover practically all aspects of U.S. life through the year 2000 and beyond. Material is taken from governmental and private sources with some 800 tables, charts, graphs, and narratives. The volume concludes with an index of forecasts by year and a subject index. The coverage is uneven; for example, acid rain has 2 entries and agriculture has 48. In the 1st edition, crime had only 10 entries while education offered more than 100. This work is handy for the uninitiated.—**Bohdan S. Wynar**

915. Weiss, Michael J. **Latitudes & Attitudes: An Atlas of American Tastes, Trends, Politics, and Passions.** New York, Little, Brown, 1994. 224p. maps. $29.95; $14.95pa. ISBN 0-316-92915-8; 0-316-92908-5pa.

For people of the United States obsessed with the increasingly complex trivial details of the nation's endless sociological variety, this work is the ideal bedtime reading. Filled with catchy one-liners and breezy conversation, the atlas enables the reader to surf through the intricacies of the cultural landscape without ever getting wet feet. There is an underlying suggestion throughout the book that it might somehow be of value to sophisticated marketing campaigns; but the best way to approach the volume is as (often outrageous) fun.

Following an introduction, the first section of the book consists of a series of some 87 brightly colored maps of the United States showing consumer habits and using Arbitron Ratings' "Areas of Dominant Influence" (ADIs), a system of county clustering based on one or a group of geographically related central cities. The data are derived from several opinion sampling firms, notably Claritas, Inc., Simmons Market Research Bureau, R. L. Polk & Co., and Yankelovich Partners, Inc. The maps often deliberately group consumption patterns of widely disparate products (dolls versus Nintendo games; classical versus country music); a half-page discussion follows each map.

The second half gives each ADI (plus Alaska and Hawaii) a quarter-page of brief (and arbitrary) lifestyle and consumption habits ("what's hot/what's not"), along with some basic demographics. This section concludes with a simplistic four-level ratings chart of the ADIs that largely rehashes the material from the maps. Much of the cultural identity of various parts of the nation is highly stereotyped, and the ADI system tends to paint many kinds of people with the same brush. The author's opening sentence suggests that readers should "forget the Rand McNally view of the United States"; but this is not exactly the publication to make that happen.—**James R. McDonald**

STATISTICS

916. **Florida Statistical Abstract, 1994.** 28th ed. By the Bureau of Economic and Business Research, College of Business Administration, University of Florida. Gainesville, Fla., University Press of Florida, 1994. 794p. maps. index. $44.95; $29.95pa. ISBN 0-8130-1311-9; 0-8130-1312-7pa. ISSN 0071-6022.

Largely unchanged in format from its previous editions (see ARBA 93, entry 107, for a review of the 25th ed.), this annual publication continues to provide up-to-date census statistics on the social, political, and economic structure and organization of the state of Florida. It continues as a first-rate source of information and ranks among the best of all state abstracts. Data are organized under five major divisions: human resources, which contains sections on population, housing, vital statistics, and education; physical resources, with sections on geography and environment, agriculture, forestry, and construction; services, with sections on wholesale and retail trade, tourism and recreation, and health; public resources and administration, covering government and elections, courts and law enforcement, and government finance; and economic and social trends, providing data on economic indicators with comparisons by state. Data are presented in more than 400 tables identifying sources and publications from which the tables were constructed. New tables provide timely focus on such topics as domestic violence, immigration, public assistance recipients, Hispanic faculty and students in public universities, military retirees, and so forth. The work opens with statewide maps of counties and metropolitan statistical areas, county seats, and population percentages of those 65 and over; it closes with a glossary, indexes, and explanatory notes/sources for each of the sections.—**Ron Blazek**

917. Mitchell, B. R. **International Historical Statistics: Africa, Asia, & Oceania, 1750-1988.** 2d ed. New York, Stockton Press, 1995. 1089p. $295.00. ISBN 1-56159-063-0.

A librarian's search for historical statistics has been aided immensely by Mitchell's efforts to compile these elusive figures (his newer editions on Europe and the Americas were reviewed in ARBA 93 [see entry 911] and ARBA 94 [see entry 936], respectively). The 1st edition of this work appeared in 1982 (see ARBA 83, entry 724), but did not cover Oceania, so its inclusion here is a welcome addition. The introduction discusses the trouble Mitchell encountered as he gathered these numbers and explains why there are so many gaps in the data. There is also a section on national boundary and jurisdictional changes, as well as a title list of national statistical sources consulted for this book. The source list can be supplemented with Gloria Westfall's *Bibliography of Official Statistical Yearbooks and Bulletins* (see ARBA 88, entry 869).

This volume is not arranged by country but by broad subject category ("Industry," "Education," and so on), and within that by geographical region, with even narrower topical subdivisions (e.g., "Numbers of Livestock"). At the end of each category are explanatory footnotes, which can be of great help for those wishing to continue their research. There is no index. While one might wish that the coverage was a bit more up-to-date, many countries do not compile or report statistics promptly or completely, so it takes a long time for the data to become available. Stockton Press is also preparing CD-ROM versions of their statistical reference sources. This sturdily constructed title is a must purchase for reference collections in all academic, most public, and interested special libraries.—**Daniel K. Blewett**

918. **Services: Statistics on International Transactions 1970-1992. Services: Statistiques sur les Échanges Internationaux.** By Organisation for Economic Co-operation and Development. Washington, D.C., OECD Publications and Information Center, 1995. 461p. $65.00pa. ISBN 92-64-04350-0.

The Organization for Economic Cooperation and Development (OECD), which prepares this reference, is a Paris-based international organization of industrialized, market economy countries. At OECD, representatives from member country governments meet to exchange information and coordinate policy in a wide variety of areas. Country data, for this volume, are listed in two sections. Section A gives comparative information, from 1970 through 1992, about overall trends, travel, transportation, and government and private services. Section B, the larger section, contains more extensive data for each country—one table for each participating country, with the United States listed first. A small amount of the data in section B is duplicated from section A. Definitions or explanations are given for each category in both sections. The data listed in the book are also available on diskette, either $5\frac{1}{4}$-inch or $3\frac{1}{2}$-inch, and can be used with software packages such as Lotus 1-2-3, Microsoft Excel, or Quattro-Pro. This book will be useful for any library with patrons seeking comparative data about industrialized countries.—**Nathan M. Smith**

919. **Statistical Abstract of the ESCWA Region 1983-1992.** 14th ed. By Economic and Social Commission for Western Asia. New York, United Nations, 1994. 586p. $30.00pa. ISBN 92-1-128143-1. ISSN 0252-4333. S/N 94-II-L-8.

This statistical source provides detailed economic and social indicators, as available, on a country-by-country basis for member nations of the Economic and Social Commission for Western Asia (ESCWA). Included are Bahrain, Egypt, Iraq, Jordan, Kuwait, Lebanon, Oman, Palestine, Qatar, Saudi Arabia, Syria, the United Arab Emirates, and Yemen. The introduction and notes accompanying tables indicate that data are drawn from national statistical offices, regional organizations, various United Nations publications, and such recognized sources as the International Monetary Fund.

While some of the information provided on population and finance is readily available in general international reference resources, data on some topics such as tourism and communication would be more difficult to locate. The country-specific arrangement, scope, and level of detail (40 or more tables on each country), and range of years covered by this source will make it useful for general researchers as well as collections supporting Middle East studies.—**Ahmad Gamaluddin**

920. **Statistical Abstract of the United States 1995.** 115th ed. Austin, Tex., Reference Press, 1995. 1045p. maps. index. $24.95. ISBN 1-878753-92-4.

As a U.S. government publication, *Statistical Abstract of the United States* has been compiled by the Bureau of the Census annually since 1878. It has long been recognized as the standard summary of statistics—both governmental and private sources—on the social, political, and economic organization of the United States. It truly is, as the preface to the 115th edition notes, designed to serve as a convenient volume for statistical reference and as a guide to other statistical publications and sources. The guide function is served by the introductory text to each section, the source note appended to tables, and appendix 1, which comprises guides to sources of statistics, state statistical abstracts, and foreign statistical abstracts. As a Government Printing Office (GPO) product, the hardcover version of *Statistical Abstract* is $42.00; this commercial reprint is $24.95.

New to this edition is a section of 92 tables previously published in *U.S. Industrial Outlook* (see ARBA 94, entry 218). Other new tables, which appear throughout the volume, include data from the 1992 Economic and Agriculture Censuses, union membership by state, and home ownership rates. As in the 1994 edition, appendixes 2 through 4 discuss metropolitan area concepts and components and give population figures for these areas, discuss limitations of the data, and provide an index to tables having *Historical Statistics, Colonial Times to 1970* (a related Census Bureau publication). Appendix 5 (a list of 1994 *Statistical Abstract* tables omitted form the 1995 edition), appendix 6 (a guide to new tables), and a detailed index conclude this indispensable collection of statistical data, which is now offered commercially in a far less-expensive version than that published by the GPO.—**Wiley J. Williams**

921. **Statistical Abstract of the World.** Marlita A. Reddy, ed. Detroit, Gale, 1994. 1111p. maps. index. $49.95. ISBN 0-8103-9199-6. ISSN 1077-1360.

Gale has produced another handy volume of statistical information. The alphabetized list of the 185 countries covered in the volume includes all United Nations members, plus Hong Kong, Switzerland, and Taiwan. For each nation, the volume provides approximately 5 to 6 pages of national data organized into 42 panels. When data for a given subject category are not available, the subject panel for that country is shaded in gray. This simple feature enhances the user friendliness of the volume.

The statistical data cover a wide range of subject areas, including geographical facts on matters pertaining to land area, climate, and natural resources; demographic data with birth/death and life expectancy rates for males and females; health personnel and expenditure statistics; ethnicity, religion, and language groupings data; and a variety of educational, science and technology, government, labor, production, and trade data. Much of the information in the volume is taken from UN, World Bank, International Monetary Fund, and U.S. State Department sources. Two jagged, computer-generated maps are also provided for each country.

Statistical Abstract presents an abundance of hard-to-find data in an attractive format. As researchers become more familiar with CD-ROM products, however, volumes such as this one will become less appealing. Despite its attractive format, it is easier to access this type of information via a computer search command than by manually scanning through a bound, 1,000-plus-page volume. [R: BR, Mar/Apr 95, pp. 29-34]

—**Terry D. Bilhartz**

922. **Statistical Handbook of Working America: Statistics on Occupations, Careers, Employment, & the Work Environment.** Charity Anne Dorgan, ed. Detroit, Gale, 1995. 1099p. index. $99.00. ISBN 0-7876-0087-3. ISSN 1083-1398.

This compilation of more than 900 tables of statistics—each with a source note appended—on occupations, careers, employment, and the work environment provides an overview of working life in the United States as of the early to mid-1990s. The most frequently cited sources are U.S. government agencies, especially the Bureau of the Census and the Bureau of Labor Statistics. Nongovernmental sources include academic institutions (e.g., Queen's College Program for Applied Research); associations (e.g., American Management Association, American Medical Association); trade and professional journals (e.g., *ABA Journal, AFL-CIO News, Business Week, Fortune, Industry Week, Information Week, Working Woman*); and newspapers (e.g., *The Christian Science Monitor, The Detroit Free Press, The Los Angeles Times, The New York Times, USA Today, The Wall Street Journal*).

Following a list of abbreviations and acronyms, an introductory chapter of summary indicators (1 table for each of the handbook's 10 other chapters) highlights certain aspects of the U.S. workplace. Chapters 2 through 11 deal in considerable detail with statistics by more than 600 occupations; statistics by industry; employment and unemployment; earnings and costs of employment; employee benefits; skills, training, and education; health and safety; legal and ethical issues (e.g., affirmative action, discrimination, sexual harassment, workplace attire, worker satisfaction); production and technology; and industrial relations. While statistics are most frequently shown at the national level (often with a breakdown, such as by sex or race), many tables provide state or metropolitan area data. In other tables, data are by selected companies or by county, and in at least two tables, the data are for named individuals (e.g., Whoopi Goldberg's average 1993 earnings, Cal Ripkin's 1995 baseball strike salary loss).

The handbook concludes with a glossary of terms used; a list of sources cited; an occupation index; and a keyword index (providing access to all subjects, government agencies, companies, unions, personal names, geographical locations, and so forth. *Statistical Handbook of Working America*, by bringing together a comprehensive variety of statistics with source notes appended, should be of particular interest to economists, human resources and legal professionals, corporate and government executives, researchers, and students—all part of the clientele of large public and academic libraries.—**Wiley J. Williams**

923. **Statistics Sources 1996: A Subject Guide to Data on Industrial, Business....** 19th ed. Jacqueline Wasserman O'Brien and Steven R. Wasserman, eds. Detroit, Gale, 1995. 2v. $385.00/set. ISBN 0-8103-9091-4. ISSN 0585-198X.

This ready-reference source has been reviewed in ARBA several times (see ARBA 93, entry 913, for the most recent one). There is a modest increase in price, and citations have increased from 95,000 to almost 100,000. The information for well-known countries is updated, and some improvements can also be found in statistics from Eastern Europe and the former Soviet Union. Nevertheless, the available information is sketchy, and much of it is simply obsolete. For example, in examining a number of entries for Ukraine, one determines that most of the information is taken from the *CIS Market Atlas*, *Demographic Yearbook* (see ARBA 95, entry 886), *Statistical Yearbook* (see ARBA 95, entry 898), and other similar sources. Not a single Ukrainian statistical source was consulted. Similar situations exist with other former Soviet Republics. The editors consulted international or Russian sources that provided dated information. Nevertheless, there is nothing else similar in scope.—**Bohdan S. Wynar**

924. Thomas, G. Scott. **The Rating Guide to Life in America's Fifty States.** Amherst, N.Y., Prometheus Books, 1994. 575p. $39.95; $19.95pa. ISBN 0-87975-938-0; 0-87975-939-9pa.

Thomas rates the 50 states in 125 statistical categories that are arranged into 25 topical areas. The broad topics, which are the names for the 25 chapters in the text, include such categories as history, environment, female equality, personal finances, and national relations. From these rankings, Thomas awards each state from 0 to 100 points for each statistical category, totals the combined points, and gives each state a report card grade, "A" to "F", for each category. On the last page of chapter 1 (history), for instance, we learn that Massachusetts deserves an "A+" for having the richest past in the nation, while 17 unnoteworthy states, including Iowa, Oregon, Utah, Oklahoma, and Hawaii, failed to pass on Thomas's grading scale. In his 14-page introduction, Thomas attempts to provide a rationale for the statistical categories he selected to study and for the arbitrary rules he used to arrive at the final grade for each state. However, only readers from Vermont, the ultimate winner in Thomas's rating game, will likely be persuaded by the author's pretense to scientific objectivity.

Buried within this volume is a treasure trove of tantalizing information. Unfortunately, as with most long-lost buried treasures, the valuable material in this text is difficult to find and even more difficult to put to practical use. Recommended for public libraries in Vermont.—**Terry D. Bilhartz**

925. **UNCTAD Statistical Pocket Book.** By the United Nations Conference on Trade and Development. New York, United Nations, 1994. 102p. $15.00pa. ISBN 92-1-012035-3. S/N E.94.II.D.32.

This concise handbook offers statistics on development, trade, investment, and growth. Not intended to provide comprehensive coverage, the book in fact lists 12 major publications that can be consulted for more detailed information. Many tables or graphs group countries by category (such as oil exporters) rather than giving a country-by-country breakdown of the data. The authors admit in the foreword that the data on Eastern Europe and Socialist Asia are skimpy.

Typically, any statistical publication that tries to cover the whole world will find that some countries have far more timely and accurate data than others. This handbook is fairly up-to-date considering the limitations of attempting worldwide coverage. Most tables present 1992 or 1993 data, although a fair percentage are not updated past 1991. Table 1.3, "Selected Economic and Social Indicators," says that the data are 1992 or the latest year available. Many researchers would want to go to the original source and find out the exact year of each number.

The tables themselves will be of far more interest to international finance or trade officials than to high school students, covering topics such as multinational debt restructuring and debt-to-Gross National Product ratios. Although there are some data on fertility, life expectancy, poverty, and the like, these are a small part of the coverage. Many tables offer historical data going back to the 1970s, for the purpose of showing what sort of progress a region or country has made. The price and format are attractive, and would make this title useful for quick reference by someone who is willing to accept predigested data.

—**Susan V. McKimm**

URBAN STUDIES

926. **America's Top-Rated Smaller Cities: A Statistical Handbook.** 1994-1995 ed. Rhoda Garoogian and Andrew Garoogian, eds. Boca Raton, Fla., Universal Reference, 1994. 732p. $65.00pa. ISBN 1-881220-13-3.

This book rates and provides statistical information for 60 "top-rated smaller cities," a term used to describe communities with core city populations of between 25,000 and 100,000 population, based on the 1990 census. The selection of these cities was based on rankings in various national magazine surveys and seems to favor the Midwest and the South over the two coasts. The metropolitan populations spread from about 100,000 to almost 1 million.

One of the assumptions on which studies such as this rest is that the population of the core city of a metropolitan region is a viable parameter on which to compare one region with another. In the United States, this is scarcely true. City limits vary so much from one city to another that a central city population cannot be used to predict the size or wealth of its total urban area. The data presented are oriented toward the commercial environment and are likely to change to the point where the rankings may need revision in just a few years. Nonetheless, the information is useful to those interested in comparing potential sites for location or relocation of a business. The volume is not as useful as similar sources for more general comparisons. [R: WLB, Mar 95, p. 75]—**Arthur R. Upgren**

927. Beckner, Chrisanne. **100 Great Cities of World History.** San Francisco, Calif., Bluewood, 1995. 112p. illus. maps. index. $7.95pa. ISBN 0-912517-14-X.

This book represents the latest contribution to the 100 Series from Bluewood (see entries 32, 33, 795, and 1602 for reviews of other volumes in the series). Cities, both ancient and modern, are chosen for inclusion based on what the author claims to be their "undefinable quality of greatness." Entries are written in a light, easy-to-read style, each providing a brief description of the history of the city, its cultural heritage, famous landmarks, geographical layout, and significance within world history. When appropriate, descriptions may also include a discussion of the city's trade and commerce activities and its religious origins. All entries include a photograph or reproduction of the city. In addition, important terms are highlighted in bold typeface within the text of each entry to help identify key concepts and points of interest unique to that city. A subject index is included.

This resource has little, if any, value to researchers but is presented as a teaching tool and travel companion. While this resource probably would not fit within the collection development and evaluation parameters of most research libraries, *100 Great Cities* would be an appropriate addition to a young adult collection in a public or school library.—**Robert V. Labaree**

928. Duensing, Edward E. **Information Sources in Urban and Regional Planning: A Directory and Guide to Reference Materials.** New Brunswick, N.J., Center for Urban Policy Research, 1994. 178p. index. $24.95. ISBN 0-88285-146-2.

Duensing brings to this compilation a rich background in the organization of information, being formerly director of the Center for Urban Policy Research library at Rutgers University. Accessed by indexes under author, organization, and title, all entries stress access points for further information specific to the field of urban and regional planning. Publications cited date from 1980 to the present. The author uses four main divisions of information genres: dictionaries and glossaries; directories (both of which he arranges alphabetically by title); and indexes, abstracts, and organizations (approached through a subject arrangement). For practical and comparative purposes he uses consistent subject headings, where applicable, within the latter two divisions. Entries in all four divisions give full information for successful location of the cited item.

The volume is enhanced by the addition of appendixes noting: earlier guides to the literature; online database vendors in the field; state, business, and industry data centers; and colleges and universities offering graduate programs in urban and regional planning. This comprehensive compilation fills a need for current resources invaluable to planners, researchers, public administrators, students, and analysts.

—**Eleanor Ferrall**

929. **The Encyclopedia of Indianapolis.** David J. Bodenhamer and Robert G. Barrows, with David G. Vanderstel, eds. Bloomington, Ind., Indiana University Press, 1994. 1600p. index. $49.95. ISBN 0-253-31222-1.

Indianapolis, the 12th largest city in the United States, survived the 1980s far better than most cities in the northern industrial belt. By the late twentieth century, the city had diversified into pharmaceuticals, amateur sporting events, and insurance while maintaining holds in agricultural and manufacturing industries. Unlike Chicago, Detroit, Cleveland, and Pittsburgh, Indianapolis gained population during the 1980s. This encyclopedia first places Indianapolis into the larger context of a major U.S. city through its 22 authoritative overview essays on broad topics such as cultural institutions, demography and ethnicity, politics, and urban environment. The main body of the work has 1,600 entries of 2 types: miniessays on broad topics such as agriculture, jazz, and climate, and short entries that describe people, places, institutions, and events. Emphasis is on the twentieth century. All entries are signed. Affiliations are given for some authors, but credentials are given for none. Many entries cite books or periodical articles for further reading. A timeline covering 1816 through the summer of 1994, a statistical abstract, a subject guide, a few maps, and 300 small black-and-white photographs complete the text. Cross-references and *see* references are generously provided throughout the text. However, there are no guide words. A 5,000-entry index provides access to much of the content of the encyclopedia. This work will be of interest to those who would like to see how a northern industrial city has managed to thrive in this era and to those who have lived there.—**Donald W. Maxwell**

930. **Gale City & Metro Rankings Reporter: 3,000 Rankings of U.S. Cities and Metro Areas on a Variety of Topics....** Helen S. Fisher, ed. Detroit, Gale, 1995. 1324p. index. $129.00. ISBN 0-8103-9875-3. ISSN 1077-9132.

Gale City & Metro Rankings Reporter (GCMRR) has broad general interest appeal. It is a compilation of rankings of more than 1,500 urban areas in the United States in 3,017 tables. Designed for "serious reference and analytical work," GCMRR covers a broad scope. The table of contents shows the true order of all tables covered in each chapter. The tables are arranged in seven major parts, with chapters on a variety of topics. Part 1, physical profile, supplies chapters on the environment and natural resources and roads and highways. Part 2, social profile, includes chapters on population, immigration, marital status, cost of living, health and health care, housing and construction, living arrangements, and transportation. Part 3, education and culture, provides chapters on education and language and ancestry. Part 4, jobs and income, includes chapters on employment, occupation, income, and poverty. Part 5, economic profile, has chapters on the number of establishments in the construction, manufacturing, service, wholesale, transportation, and retail sectors and a chapter detailing consumer expenditures, income, the banking sector, and other miscellaneous items. Part 6, government, has chapters on local government finances, the federal government, law and criminal justice, and military forces and veterans. Part 7, leisure time, includes chapters on the media and the arts and leisure. Data are included for good or bad categories, but such information is seemingly limitless. Some users will want to know more. Oddly, the listing of sources, unlike the location and keyword indexes that follow it, does not have a color side-tab to ease access.

Although the work shies away from many potentially controversial topics, academic libraries might consider adopting this volume for general interest users. Others may be frustrated by something else the volume does not provide: detailed descriptions of particular urban areas or data for all urban areas on the variables included. These limits aside, one hopes that more attention will be given to "serious and analytical" tasks rather than merely updating the data in existing tables. Here is a suggestion: Future editions might include an extended introductory discussion of city ratings or illustrate various extant quality-of-life rankings of U.S. cities before one updates data on the number of fish or reptiles in city zoos.

In an era when information may be accessed with great ease, print volumes such as this one should provide more than data arranged in a logical format. Until it does so, this volume falls short of its mission. [R: WLB, Mar 95, p.75]—**David V. Waller**

931. **Health and Environment in America's Top-Rated Cities: A Statistical Profile, 1994-1995.** Rhoda Garoogian and Andrew Garoogian, eds. Boca Raton, Fla., Universal Reference, 1994. 666p. $65.00pa. ISBN 1-881220-12-5.

This is an excellent compendium of information regarding the health and environmental conditions in 71 of the major cities in the United States. The cities were selected because they had previously been designated by various major publications as being the best places for business and living. Considerable effort has obviously been expended to gather information from a variety of sources, both governmental and private. The information is quite recent (1990s), and in each case the source is referenced.

The terms *health* and *environment* are defined rather broadly—health includes not only availability of health care facilities and providers, various measures of health care expenditures, and legislation related to health, but also such data as marriage, divorce, and crime rates. Similarly, the environmental section ranges from local recycling rules, the municipal budget for environmental services, and the quality of the water and air, to local climate conditions and a pollen calendar. This resource will probably be most valuable for those who are considering relocation to one of the cities surveyed, but it may also be useful to those who wish to compare the conditions in these cities.—**Harry E. Pence**

932. **World Urbanization Prospects: The 1994 Revision. Estimates and Projections of Urban and Rural Populations and of Urban Agglomerations.** By the Department for Economic and Social Information and Policy Analysis, Population Division. New York, United Nations, 1995. 178p. $37.50pa. ISBN 92-1-151283-2. S/N E.95.XIII.12.

The twentieth century has been marked by no greater revolution than the urbanization of populations in all sections of the world. The rise of the megacity is a modern phenomenon; for example, the number of urban areas of more than 10 million increased from New York City alone in 1950 to 15 cities today. This modest volume, a publication of the United Nations, gives estimates for the populations of all countries and major cities and other urban areas for every five-year interval from 1950 through 2015.

The data for past years are taken from censuses and estimates made for each country, and for the future years, they are based on extrapolations from available estimates. The tables are arranged in an accessible way, both by numbers and percentages of growth from one quinquennial to the next, with considerable explanatory material. The book is useful to many seeking this kind of information for demographic studies or general curiosity. It is one of the best among a number of similar compilations, and is highly recommended as a reference for readership on all levels.—**Arthur R. Upgren**

18 Women's Studies

ATLASES

933. Fast, Timothy H., and Cathy Carroll Fast. **The Women's Atlas of the United States.** rev. ed. New York, Facts on File, 1995. 246p. maps. index. $75.00. ISBN 0-8160-2970-9.

If people liked the 1986 1st edition of this atlas, they will feel the same way about this 1995 revised edition. The new edition still has the same seven sections—demographics, education, employment, family, health, crime, and politics—but with a redistribution of numbers of maps per topic, as the climate of the times dictates. For example, in the 1986 version, "Education" has two maps, "Educated Woman" and "Educating Woman," while the 1995 edition has four—"Literacy," "High School," "Higher Education," and "Role Models in the Classroom." While the maps in the previous edition were created by noncomputer methods and the ones in this edition by computer, they look much the same; however, the colors in the new edition are brighter than in the old one. Titles of maps are the same in tone in either edition, tending toward phrases that are used in mildly humorous ways (e.g., "The Days of Our Lives" and "The Uphill Battle" [the former in "Health," the latter in "Politics"]).

Both editions have an excellent, brief section on reading maps and both are about the same number of pages. Both have a brief index, although it is not listed in the table of contents for the older version. There are maps, such as that on page 135, where the symbols are not sufficiently different in hue to be easily or correctly deciphered, but generally the maps are easy to read. An appendix is composed of tables that summarize maps; it is followed by notes, a bibliography for the maps, suggestions for further reading, and an index. It makes for fascinating reading (e.g., the legal age for sexual consent in various states, starting at the age of 12!), and leaves the reader with at least one question: What would an atlas of men be like?—**Mary Larsgaard**

BIBLIOGRAPHIES

934. Falk, Nancy Auer. **Women and Religion in India: An Annotated Bibliography of Sources in English 1975-92.** Kalamazoo, Mich., New Issues Press, 1994. 295p. index. $30.00; $15.00pa. ISBN 0-932826-36-9; 0-932826-37-7pa.

Written by one of the most respected scholars in the field, this bibliography of women and religion in India is a welcome addition to any library. Falk is largely responsible for this growing area of academic research in this country and was a profound influence on early interest in this area. Bringing together English-language sources from 1975, the beginnings of real study of this field in the United States, until the present, and expertly annotating them, this book is a must for scholars of India in general and religion and women's studies in particular. The index is especially helpful for research. The preface surveys the state of women and women's scholarship in India at present. The book contains 1,015 entries, of which 650 are produced by long-term residents of India. Topics cover law, ritual, transformative experiences, living women, goddesses, and more. The tone of the work goes beyond a protesting voice to one of celebration. This reference work is crucial for scholars and students who approach any facet of the relationship of women to religion both in India and beyond.—**Linda L. Lam-Easton**

935. Nordquist, Joan, comp. **Ecofeminist Theory: A Bibliography.** Santa Cruz, Calif., Reference and Research Services, 1994. 64p. index. (Social Theory: A Bibliographic Series, no.36). $15.00pa. ISBN 0-937855-71-5.

This ecofeminist bibliography provides access to books, articles in journals, articles in books, and dissertations and theses on the topic of ecofeminism—a theory first named by the French feminist writer Françoise d'Eaubonne, who believed that the "destruction of the planet's resources" is linked to the "capitalist patriarchical institutions" and the "Male System" that dominates women and nature. Helpful indexes and guides include a list of bibliographical sources used, a short introduction to ecofeminist theory, and an author index for major theorists. The bibliography also provides a section on "third world" materials.

The Social Theory series is a helpful compilation of major theorists and ideas that would be especially useful for college libraries, especially those with graduate programs in sociology or women's studies. Reference and Research Services also publishes a bibliographical series on contemporary social issues with resource sections for organizations, groups, and publications.

The compilation of social theorists and issues is especially useful because the information is not found elsewhere. One only wishes that the material were available in hardcover to ensure its place on a reference shelf.—**Barbara Jo O'Hara**

936. Nordquist, Joan, comp. **Women and Aging: A Bibliography.** Santa Cruz, Calif., Reference and Research Services, 1994. 76p. (Contemporary Social Issues: A Bibliographic Series, no.35). $15.00pa. ISBN 0-937855-68-5.

This bibliography in the Contemporary Social Issues series is useful because it brings together current materials from diverse sources and organizes them by subject. The inclusion of small-press titles, multicultural and feminist literature, and works by women makes it especially valuable since these sources are frequently excluded from mainstream bibliographies and databases.

The bibliography includes books, pamphlets, government documents, dissertations, and articles in periodicals and books, and is divided into sections by topic: general information, psychology, health, sexuality, women of color, lesbians, and so forth. Some topics, such as women and aging, literature, art, the mass media, and economic conditions, are especially useful because the information is difficult to locate elsewhere. The list of periodicals, databases, and organizations is helpful also. This inexpensive source is a welcome addition to all reference collections.—**Barbara M. Bibel**

937. Nordquist, Joan, comp. **Women in the United States: Economic Conditions: A Bibliography.** Santa Cruz, Calif., Reference & Research Services, 1995. 72p. (Contemporary Social Issues: A Bibliographic Series, no.38). $15.00pa. ISBN 0-937855-74-X.

This is an up-to-date bibliography of books, directories, pamphlets, government documents, reports, dissertations, and articles published in either books or periodical journals on the general and specific economic conditions of women in the United States. There are 763 entries, and its contents are conveniently and logically arranged by topics and issues. The principal subject areas within this concise and easy-to-use guidebook are organized around the employment and general economic conditions of U.S. women taken as a group, along with a further subdivision of entries by race, age, marital status, and the issues of poverty and housing.

The bibliography is the latest in a series of concise reference works that outline scholarly and general published works on significant economic, political, and social issues. Even though a variety of viewpoints are represented, this bibliography has made an explicit and noteworthy effort to include material published by small and alternative presses as well as activist organizations. Consequently, the most obvious benefit of this bibliography is that it brings together and provides access to a wide variety of scholarly and general works that might otherwise be overlooked. It is a useful reference work that will be of value to public and academic libraries alike.—**Timothy E. Sullivan**

BIOGRAPHY

938. Adams, Jerome R. **Notable Latin American Women: Twenty-Nine Leaders, Rebels, Poets, Battlers, and Spies, 1500-1900.** Jefferson, N.C., McFarland, 1995. 191p. index. $28.50. ISBN 0-7864-0022-6.

Most of American history continues the multiethnic character of the indigenous populations, only adding the competition of various Europeans and their slaves. Democracy, the Protestant work ethic, and monogamy are actually rare. Justice and mercy are the victorious values even when gentility is rare. That is what this book on Southern Hemisphere women teaches.

All Americans can learn from these women. There are comparable North American women's stories to be told. Bartira, of ca.1500-1540 Brazil, daughter of a native chief, befriended a shipwrecked Portuguese. Juana Inés de la Cruz, ca. 1648-1695, a fifth-generation Mexican, wrote devotional poetry and theological arguments. Javiera Carrere, 1781-ca. 1862, a descendant of Basque Spanish migrants to Chile, inspired and supported her brothers in struggles toward independence from Spain.

Such stories should be in the literature and other mediums of children and adults. Adams has fused together much Spanish and some English primary sources and scholarship. He knows what facts are to be known. Sometimes he quotes instead of digesting or repeats himself or is not clear for the newcomer. But no matter: a dream of getting women's stories deservedly into our lives is furthered. Its extensive bibliography alone recommends it to help swab up the hurt pride of women who knew all along that the encouraging and leading, pushing and pulling they have done are of the greatest importance.—**Elizabeth L. Anderson**

939. Bailey, Brooke. **The Remarkable Lives of 100 Women Artists.** Holbrook, Mass., Adams Publishing, 1994. 207p. index. (20th Century Women Series). $12.00. ISBN 1-55850-360-9.

Whereas Frank N. Magill's *Great Lives from History: American Women Series* (see entry 942) presents its information in a highly structured, consistently formatted manner appropriate to ready-reference work, this book instead focuses on the stories of the women's lives. Entries generally are one- to two-page narratives that attempt to recount the essential and influential events, people, and ideas that informed each artist's "unique personal vision." Bailey has thrown a wide net, encompassing architects, archivists of indigenous American music, blues performers, classical composers, collage artists, concert pianists, filmmakers, folk dancers, illustrators, jazz singers, muralists, photographers, sculptors, and even a trapeze performer among her women artists. Although each entry concludes with a very brief list of resources "to find out more," this delightful work has been designed more for inspiration than reference-desk duty.—**G. Kim Dority**

940. Bailey, Brooke. **The Remarkable Lives of 100 Women Healers and Scientists.** Holbrook, Mass., Adams Publishing, 1994. 208p. index. (20th Century Women Series). $12.00. ISBN 1-55850-361-7.

According to the author, "The different paths these women took through often inhospitable circumstances were shaped at least as much by their personalities as by the fields they chose" (preface). Therein lies the focus of Bailey's 100 profiles: It is the lives, lived fully and on their own terms, of these women that engage and inspire.

Bailey has thrown a wide net, encompassing anthropologists, archaeologists, astronomers, biochemists, botanists, cancer researchers, conservationists, engineers, home economists, inventors, mathematicians, naturalists, psychiatrists, zoologists, and even a faith healer among her women healers and scientists. Entries generally are one- to two-page narratives that attempt to recount the essential and influential events, people, and ideas that informed each woman's unique contribution. The author takes a balanced approach to her material, downplaying the hostility these women may have felt toward a society that attempted to deny their abilities and instead focusing on their strengths and achievements. Although not really a traditional reference work, this small (roughly $5\frac{1}{2}$-by-$5\frac{1}{2}$-by-$6\frac{1}{2}$-inch) volume can be recommended for young adult collections and all school libraries for its informative, inspiring narratives.—**G. Kim Dority**

941. Bailey, Brooke. **The Remarkable Lives of 100 Women Writers and Journalists.** Holbrook, Mass., Adams Publishing, 1994. 208p. index. (20th Century Women Series). $12.00. ISBN 1-55850-423-0.

This little book provides wonderfully readable biographies of 100 U.S. women writers who worked primarily during the early to mid-twentieth century. Each of the 2-page, 700- to 750-word entries is presented in an easy, conversational style, and gives basic biographical and critical information. Up to four sources for further information are listed at the end of each biography.

The selection of women included is broadly based. Fiction writers, poets, journalists (and photojournalists, in the person of Margaret Bourke-White), screenwriters, biographers and autobiographers, and essayists are all represented. This wide range results in a broader representation than is found in many other selective collections.

As is common among alphabetically arranged reference books, this one has no table of contents. However, it also lacks any comprehensive index and the "Index by Occupation," although interesting, does not make up for this inadequacy. Poor proofreading is another, more minor, problem. Although it is fun to read, interesting, and thoughtful, this book does not present research-level information or sources. Overall, it is best suited to a high school or public library, where it should serve well as an introductory source.—**Susan Davis Herring**

942. **Great Lives from History: American Women Series.** Frank N. Magill, ed. Pasadena, Calif., Salem Press, 1995. 5v. index. $365.00/set. ISBN 0-89356-892-9.

One of the myriad Magill compendiums, this set profiles 409 women who had a major impact on North American society and culture. White Anglo-Saxon women from the United States overwhelmingly predominate, but readers will also find entries for 45 African Americans, 11 Asian Americans, 8 Hispanic Americans, 8 Native Americans, and 7 Canadians. As would be expected in a Magill series, the women draw from diverse walks of life, including education; business; government, diplomacy, and politics; arts, architecture, literature, music, theater, and entertainment; medicine; business; religion; and social reform. Coverage is both interesting and eclectic; although one never knows whether a particular woman being sought after is likely to appear within this set's pages, the exploration is always enlightening. For example, those who have always wondered just how much Ariel contributed to the Durants' *The Story of Civilization*—and at what cost to her own professional goals—will find just this information sensitively presented in volume 2.

A typical 2,000-word entry begins with birth and death dates, areas of achievement, and a short statement on the individual's primary contribution. Three narrative overviews follow: "early life" (two to three paragraphs), "life's work" (about two pages), and "summary" (two to three paragraphs). A bibliography of 5 to 10 works concludes each profile. Concluding materials include a biographical index, an index by areas of achievement, and a timeline (starting with Anne Hutchinson, b. 1591, and ending with Kristi Yamaguchi, b. 1971). Although serious researchers will need to look elsewhere for scholarly materials, this Magill series provides solid, basic information that will meet the needs of most school and public libraries.—**G. Kim Dority**

943. Morin, Isobel V. **Women Who Reformed Politics.** Minneapolis, Minn., Oliver Press, 1994. 160p. illus. index. $14.95. ISBN 1-881508-16-1.

Women Who Reformed Politics is a concise and affordable guide to the political lives of eight noteworthy, although not necessarily well-known, U.S. women. Profiled women are those who overcame various forms of discrimination, and whose efforts clearly demonstrate that despite some very real prohibitions, women have long been politically active in the United States. Despite the fact that women do not now nor have they historically spoken with a solitary voice, women as a group and individually have often been on the forefront of social reforms. The women outlined in this guide are women who, though themselves not public officeholders, did nevertheless champion efforts to end mob violence, abolish slavery, curb alcohol consumption, regulate and improve working conditions, and provide women with increased access to education and political rights. The women profiled in this compact and accessible guide are: Abby Kelley Foster, Frances Willard, Ida Wells-Barnett, Carrie Chapman Catt, Molly Dewson, Pauli Murray, Fannie Lou Hamer, and Gloria Steinem.

The issues and policies that these women advocated were and remain ones that affect the economic and social lives of all U.S. citizens. However, because not all citizens share equally in political and economic power, those who fight for reform invariably encounter harsh opposition and criticism. In the face of such opposition, reforms often require years of struggle along with the voices and efforts of many people. This insightful and useful guide places these interesting and courageous reformers within the context of U.S. history and the evolution of U.S. society.—**Timothy E. Sullivan**

944. Schraff, Anne. **Women of Peace: Nobel Peace Prize Winners.** Springfield, N.J., Enslow, 1994. 112p. illus. index. $17.95. ISBN 0-89490-493-0.

There have been nine peace awards given to women since the first Nobel Peace prize was awarded in 1901. In this collection of brief biographies, Schraff chronicles the achievements of each of them. This book is an especially useful compilation for young readers. The essays are brief, factual, and dramatic. As a starting point for research projects, the author offers a good bibliography; however, some of the older titles listed may prove difficult to obtain by the general reader. With the exception of Mother Teresa's selfless sacrifice, all the Nobel laureates can be described as fearless political activists. This book provides an inspirational message for the younger reader and scholar.—**Mary Hemmings**

CHRONOLOGY

945. Franck, Irene, and David Brownstone. **Women's World: A Timeline of Women in History.** New York, HarperPerennial/HarperCollins, 1995. 654p. illus. index. $22.50pa. ISBN 0-06-273336-2.

This new chronology of women's history covers prehistory through 1993 in increasing detail. Franck and Brownstone list a plethora of important women's births, deaths, discoveries, foundings, publications, and odd facts that bring history alive. From 1830 on, each year is treated separately (earlier periods are grouped), with entries arranged in four broad categories: "Politics/Law/War"; "Religion/Education/Everyday Life"; "Science/Technology/Medicine"; and "Arts/Literature." The entries range from brief statements of birth or death to slightly longer descriptions of notable events, but are rarely more than two sentences. Occasional photographs, drawings, quotes, and short discussions appear in the wide center margin to add flavor and detail. The book has a good index, but the lack of a bibliography or any suggested references is a major weakness.

Women's World is comparable to Kirstin Olsen's *Chronology of Women's History* (see ARBA 95, entry 911), but Olsen's work provides a lengthy list of selected references. Also, her coverage of prehistory and early historical periods is more thorough, although later historical periods have fewer entries overall. Both chronologies are valuable sources in a field of growing interest. The extremely reasonable price of *Women's World* makes it a good buy for any library, although the paperback format will make it vulnerable to damage from frequent use.—**Susan Davis Herring**

DICTIONARIES AND ENCYCLOPEDIAS

946. Fister, Barbara. **Third World Women's Literatures: A Dictionary and Guide to Materials in English.** Westport, Conn., Greenwood Press, 1995. 390p. index. $75.00. ISBN 0-313-28988-3.

This dictionary and guide discusses women writers and their literary works, in English and English translation, from developing countries. Its goal is to provide students access to writers who have been long neglected in literature classes, anthologies, and literary studies in general. Fister attempts to continue and extend the tradition of *The Bloomsbury Guide to Women's Literature* (see ARBA 93, entry 942), which is a comprehensive, global overview of women's literature, but lacks references to secondary sources. Fister's work focuses more specifically on the literature of Third World women and provides bibliographical sources for further study.

Fister admits that the terminology "Third World" is problematic, but opts to use this term over other terms such as "developing countries" and "postcolonial." By "Third World," she means the Caribbean Islands, Central and Latin America, Africa, the Middle East, South Asia and Asia (but not Japan), Australia, and New Zealand—basically, countries that fall outside the general focus of Western literary studies. Profiles are limited to geographical, rather than ideological, boundaries; therefore, writers who were born in, or spent substantial time in, one of the above named countries are given entries, while others who may have ties to or influence in that particular country are not. For example, so-called colonial writers, such as Marguerite Duras and Isak Dinesen, and "First World"-born writers, such as Paule Marshall, receive entries. *Literatures* in this case is defined as not only traditional fictional forms but also autobiography, life stories, testimonial work, and transcribed oral literature. Children's literature is covered to a certain extent. Both established writers of the past and newly emerging writers are profiled.

Entries are arranged alphabetically and come in three kinds. Author entries provide information on the individual's life, review briefly her writings, and note the author's significance. Entries on individual works of literature are based on Fister's own readings and are therefore (admittedly) subjective. They describe the work in question and comment on its style and significance. A few thematic entries, such as *African Diaspora*, *feminism*, and *Sistren*, are also included. Each entry is followed by a bibliography for further research, which is not intended to be exhaustive. Asterisked works in the bibliography represent those featured as main entries elsewhere in the text.

Five appendixes follow the main dictionary: a list of authors by region or country; a chronological list; resources for further research (including reference books, bibliographies, journals, and publishers); anthologies (broken down by geographical region); and a list of criticism (also divided geographically). A 10-plus-page index concludes the volume. This unique work fills an enormous gap in the schema of literary studies. The appendixes alone make its purchase worthwhile. However, the dictionary proper is also extremely valuable to students and researchers. All libraries should acquire this volume.—**Melissa R. Root**

947. Foster, Gwendolyn Audrey. **Women Film Directors: An International Bio-Critical Dictionary.** Westport, Conn., Greenwood Press, 1995. 443p. index. $79.50. ISBN 0-313-28972-7.

For scholars, students, and film enthusiasts, this work documents the important but often-overlooked contributions of women filmmakers from around the world and throughout film history. Reclaiming the legacy of many early female filmmakers, the book offers a worthy contribution to women's and cinema's history.

An alphabetical list of nearly 200 directors provides vital statistics and a short sketch of each woman's career, followed by a select filmography and a select bibliography. The individuals that are included cover a wide spectrum of the film business—from commercial and mainstream directors, such as Jodie Foster and Kathryn Bigelow, to independents and avant-garde filmmakers, such as Maya Deren and Michelle Citron. In spite of her confessed Western Eurocentric bias, the author has made an effort to represent such U.S. minority directors as Julie Dash, as well as such foreign directors as Mira Nair, Jane Campion, and Lina Wertmüller. The author has composed a list of directors organized by nationality and a chronology of directors by decade. These are included as appendixes to the work. There are also a selected bibliography, a title index, and a general index.

This well-written resource is essential for scholars and students of film, popular culture, women's studies, and international studies. It will also appeal to film buffs.—**Barbara Ittner**

948. Humm, Maggie. **The Dictionary of Feminist Theory.** 2d ed. Columbus, Ohio, Ohio State University Press, 1995. 354p. $59.50; $20.00pa. ISBN 0-8142-0666-2; 0-8142-0667-0pa.

One of the current problems with the women's movement is a matter of globalization and reaching the masses of women who fall outside of the academic sphere. This work does little to eradicate the problem. The written word, as opposed to grass roots activism, is emphasized. The book seems firmly rooted in academe, without taking into consideration the fact that many women worldwide have no access to scholarly writings or the education necessary to grasp complex ideas. Also, many of the writings cited are scholarly rather than creative—women's contributions to art, film, and literature are largely ignored, although creative works often promote a feminist agenda. To the author's credit, she has strived to encompass more global entries, moving away from the purely Anglo-American and French focus employed previously.

The 1st edition was reviewed in ARBA 91 (see entry 925). The price has risen substantially, yet the updates do not merit such an increase. There are 72 new entries, including Gloria Anzaldúa, backlash, Barbara Christian, ecofeminism, empowerment, gynesis, logocentrism, Trinh Minh-ha, postcolonialism, queer theory, reproductive technology, and women of colour [sic]. Deleted entries from the previous edition are adultery, alchemy, astrology, definition, incest, love, moon, mysticism, and strength. Updated terms include abortion, censorship, essentialism, first wave, bell hooks, sexual harassment, spiritual feminism, and Third World. Oddly enough, such terms as war and rape are not updated to reflect surfacing questions on women in combat and acquaintance rape. Other ideas or people are lacking entries altogether: single mothers; Camille Paglia; the glass ceiling; political correctness; Take Back the Night; La Malinche (although she is cited in at least two entries, with no explanation of who she is); and RU 486 (the abortion pill). Some people with works listed in the thorough bibliography at the end are not given entries within the text itself. One serious flaw with the 1st edition has not been corrected: the lack of cross-references. Such entries as those on *écriture féminine*, Hélène Cixous, and *writing the body* contain no cross-references to link the ideas together. Some cross-referencing does exist, but it is both sporadic and arbitrary.

The bibliography is more extensive and up-to-date than in the previous edition. Any student of feminist theory will find this bibliography to be the most helpful feature of the reference; it serves as a comprehensive starting place for researchers and general readers. In fact, readers may be better served by consulting the listed works themselves than by this dictionary. The work under review is just as the title states: It concerns feminist theory, but none of the practical applications or diverse branches of the topic at hand. Libraries already owning the 1st edition need not acquire this text. Libraries in search of a definitive work on feminism should look elsewhere.—**Melissa R. Root**

949. **Masterplots II: Women's Literature Series.** Frank N. Magill, ed. Pasadena, Calif., Salem Press, 1995. 6v. index. $500.00/set. ISBN 0-89356-898-8.

This 6-volume set, 11th in the Masterplots II series, is constructed similarly to others in the series (e.g., *Masterplots II: African-American Literature Series* [see ARBA 95, entry 1171]). Characters, themes, and criticism are treated for individual works of literature by women. Genres covered include novels, short story collections, poetry compilations, plays, and nonfiction works.

Entries are alphabetical by title of the work and provide, where applicable, the author's name, the type of work or plot, a contextual date in which the work is set, the location in which the work is set, the date of publication, a list of principal characters, an analysis of the work, the context, and a list of sources for further study. The 536 essays discuss significant literary feats by women from all around the world, from ancient times to the present. An impressive list of contributing reviewers prefaces the first volume. Each volume furnishes a table of contents for the titles described in that particular volume. Comprehensive indexes—by title, author, type of work, and geographical breakdown—complete volume 6.

This set strives to provide a multicultural and multigenre overview of the contributions women have made to the literary world. Such disparate works as *This Sex Which Is Not One* by Luce Irigaray, the *Poems and Fragments* of Sappho, Buchi Emecheta's *In the Ditch*, and *Like Water for Chocolate* by Laura Esquivel are profiled. Academic libraries with strong literary collections should definitely purchase this resource. Students and scholars alike will find the set helpful in starting research projects (although professors should hope that students are not skipping reading assignments by using these annotations!). Other libraries should consider the set as funds warrant—it is an important contribution to both literary and women's studies.—**Melissa R. Root**

950. **Women's Periodicals in the United States: Consumer Magazines.** Kathleen L. Endres and Therese L. Lueck, eds. Westport, Conn., Greenwood Press, 1995. 509p. index. (Historical Guides to the World's Periodicals and Newspapers). $99.50. ISBN 0-313-28631-0.

Women's consumer magazines, 75 in number, published in the United States from the 1800s to the present are profiled in this narrative and bibliographical guide. Some may quibble with the inclusion of *Barbie* as a "women's periodical," since the audience consists of girls ages 5-12, but it qualifies; criteria for selection and inclusion are spelled out in the brief preface and introduction, which also provide historical background and explanations of "families of magazines" such as the "Seven Sisters" (*Ladies' Home Journal, Redbook, Better Homes and Gardens, Good Housekeeping, McCall's, Family Circle,* and *Woman's Day*).

Titles included range from *American Baby* to *Golf for Women*. *Ms.* also is listed, but those seeking a comprehensive examination of women's movement periodicals will be disappointed. Endres notes, however, that periodicals of the women's liberation movement will be explored in a future Greenwood Press volume. Typical of this series, entries are arranged alphabetically and contain notes (some quite lengthy); information sources such as bibliography, indexing, and location; and a useful publication history. Narratives, written by 46 contributors, range in length from 5 to 10 pages, and are generally well written, lively, and informative. Students, researchers, and librarians seeking an accessible introduction to and a selective timeline of women's magazines will be well served, despite its steep price tag.—**Jo A. Cates**

HANDBOOKS AND YEARBOOKS

951. **The Information Please Women's Sourcebook, 1995.** Lisa DiMona and Constance Herndon, eds. New York, Houghton Mifflin, 1994. 591p. index. $13.95pa. ISBN 0-395-70067-1. ISSN 1077-5994.

Women's Sourcebook comprises a highly eclectic and useful mix of more than 1,000 "resources, organizations, and statistics that describe and influence the lives of American women today" (eds.). The materials are organized into 12 broad categories: education, work, childcare, health, well-being, fertility, sexuality and relationships, divorce and custody, retirement years, politics, violence and safety, and activism. Within these categories, readers can find directory listings for such things as adult education resources, regional women's bureaus, activism resources for women of color, and housing for older women, to name but a few. In addition, there are explanatory treatments and overviews of special topics (women and violence, states and jurisdictions with family leave laws, divorce mediation, and so on); listings of women Nobel laureates and other noteworthy individuals; reprints of speeches by such women as Hillary Rodham Clinton, Elizabeth Dole, and Frances Lear; and recommended reading. Appendixes address government and legislative information and agencies as well as citing newsletters, resource books, and magazines of interest to women. It is impossible to adequately describe the scope and diversity of information this sourcebook provides; suffice it to say that every library—if not every woman—can benefit from owning a copy. [R: RBB, 1 Feb 95, p. 1028; WLB, Mar 95, p. 84]—**G. Kim Dority**

952. **National Guide to Funding for Women and Girls.** 3d ed. James E. Baumgartner and others, eds. New York, Foundation Center, 1995. 414p. index. $95.00pa. ISBN 0-87954-608-5.

This volume is one of several subject directories published by the Foundation Center, the leading information source on foundation and corporate giving. The 3d edition retains the basic arrangement and supplementary information (bibliography, glossary, descriptions of Center services and publications, and listing of Center reference collections and cooperating collections) as previous editions (see ARBA 92, entry 865). It contains 902 entries for grantmaking foundations and 72 entries for direct corporate giving programs (down from 946 and 89, respectively, in the 1993 edition).

The directory proper is arranged alphabetically by state and then by foundation. Each entry is numbered and can consist of up to 34 elements. In addition to the basic name, telephone number, address, contact person, officers, donor(s), and financial data, entries also describe the all-important purposes; fields of interest; limitations; publications; application procedures; and types of support (seed money, program development, equipment, scholarships, and the like) of the foundations. More than half the entries list a total of more than 4,000 recent grants, often with a brief description of purpose.

Six indexes provide multiple access points to the directory: donors/officers/trustees, geographical, types of support, foundations and corporate giving programs by subject (new in this edition), individual grants by subject, and foundations and corporate giving programs. The individual grants index is particularly helpful, as it pinpoints successful grants for specific subject areas as well as for African Americans, Hispanics, Native Americans, and gays and lesbians. Geographical subdivisions in this index would have been helpful, because several subjects provide extremely long strings of entry numbers.

Grants for Women and Girls, one of a series of grant guides published annually by the Foundation Center, focuses on foundation grants of $10,000 or more. Gail Schlachter's biennial title, *Directory of Financial Aids for Women* (see entry 879), includes grants as well as scholarships, fellowships, loans, awards, and internships. The 1993-1995 edition lists almost 500 grants with less detailed information. *Who Benefits? Who Decides? An Agenda for Improving Philanthropy: The Case for Women and Girls*, a report published in 1995 by the National Council for Research on Women in collaboration with other women's organizations, examines the recent state of funding (or nonfunding) for programs benefiting women and girls. The *National Guide* compiles useful, recent information and is highly recommended for grant, reference, or women's studies collections.—**Linda A. Krikos**

953. **Statistical Record of Women Worldwide.** 2d ed. Linda Schmittroth, ed. Detroit, Gale, 1995. 1047p. index. $99.00. ISBN 0-8103-8872-3. ISSN 1082-7811.

This 2d edition is formatted similarly to the 1st edition (see ARBA 92, entry 866). Fourteen chapters cover such topics as attitudes and opinions, education, health and medical care, the military, religion, sports and recreation, and sexuality. The chapters contain various tables filled with statistical data. As with the previous edition, the data come from a wide variety of sources, including periodical literature, government documents, and research centers. According to the preface, approximately 60 percent of the information details women in the United States, and 40 percent, women worldwide. Comparative data (e.g., on men, by race, on girls, with historical context) are also provided where available or pertinent.

Each table starts with an entry number, followed by a headline, an explanatory note, the legend, the data, and source notes. An extensive and detailed table of contents provides access to the data; there is also a comprehensive subject and geographical index, complete with references to page and table numbers, and cross-references. Subjects in the index are based on Library of Congress subject headings. A bibliography of sources consulted is also supplied.

The most interesting feature of this work is the chapter on attitudes and opinions, which provides data on anything from whether women consider abortion to be murder, to gift preferences, to Japanese women's views on reasons to work outside the home. Other interesting tidbits of information are found throughout the work; for example, a table in the "Income, Spending, and Wealth" chapter furnishes statistical figures on Barbie dolls, including the number of dolls sold every second (2) and the sales ratio of Barbies to Kens (8:1).

A disclaimer in the preface proclaims "the collection and interpretation of such a vast amount of data are always subject to error," particularly the international statistics, as "the contributions of women to the family, society, and socioeconomic development are often grossly underestimated" (p. xxxv). However, the interest in women worldwide is spreading, and such references as the work under review expedite research into the role women play in societies as a whole. This important volume should find a place in all public, academic, and research libraries.—**Melissa R. Root**

954. **The World's Women 1995: Trends and Statistics.** [2d ed.]. New York, United Nations, 1995. 188p. (Social Statistics and Indicators, Series K, no.12). $15.95pa. ISBN 92-1-161372-8. S/N E.95.XVII.2.

The World's Women is the 2d edition of a publication that, in 1991, began to compile international statistics on women. This edition is cosponsored by 11 United Nations Partners. The year 1995 also marked the Fourth World Conference on Women, which used the book as its official publication.

New topics covered in this edition are media, violence against women, poverty, the environment, and refugees and displaced persons. The target audience includes people in the media and in policymaking, governments and nongovernmental organizations, and academic research institutions. The compilers hope "to provide the numbers and analysis needed to understand how conditions are changing or not changing for women—and to do it in a way that will reach decision makers, the media and women and men everywhere. It provides concerned men and women with information about how much women contribute to economic life, political life, and family life. Information can support appeals to persuade public and private decision makers to change policies that are unfair to women" (pp. vii and xi).

The World's Women contains chapters on population, households, and families; population growth, distribution, and environment; health; education and training; work; and power and influence. There are a list of statistical sources, technical notes on the tables, and groupings according to countries (developed or undeveloped) and regions. There are also helpful charts and graphs in the margins to illustrate the statistics.

What the statistics say, in summary, is that men and women live in different worlds in regard to education and work, in health, in personal security, and in leisure time. Women work more and earn less; generally they work in different occupations than men, almost always with lower status and pay. However, the statistics show that these areas have improved for women since the First World Conference on Women in Mexico in 1975.

The World's Women is a visually appealing and informative source. It will be invaluable for public, academic, and school libraries, and all policymakers and individuals interested in improving the quality of women's lives in the world.—**Barbara Jo O'Hara**

Part III
HUMANITIES

19 Humanities in General

GENERAL WORKS

Bibliography

955. **BHI PLUS. August 1995.** [CD-ROM]. New Providence, N.J., Bowker-Saur/Reed Reference Electronic Publishing, 1995. Minimum system requirements: IBM PC, XT, XT-286, AT, PS/2 Model 25, 30, or compatible 286. CD-ROM drive with MS-DOS CD-ROM Extensions. 3MB hard disk space. 512K memory. $1,300.00. ISSN 0966-8772.

BHI PLUS is an electronic version of the periodical indexing journal *British Humanities Index* (BHI), a publication with a long tradition dating back to 1915. Bowker-Saur purchased BHI in 1990 and two years later released a CD-ROM version in the *A & I* [abstracting and indexing] *PLUS Series*. This CD-ROM database, which is updated quarterly, now features more than 135,000 indexed humanities-related articles from 350-plus newspapers and journals. The database offers citations, and now abstracts, to journal articles dealing with the arts, economics, history, philosophy, politics, religion, and society from journals published in the United Kingdom, written in English. Retrospective coverage on the electronic version dates from 1985.

BHI PLUS employs the same retrieval software as that used by the rest of Bowker's Plus System product line, perhaps best known through *Books in Print PLUS* (see entry 17) and *Ulrich's PLUS*. Installation is a straightforward process with all the required software on the disc itself. The interface is particularly elegant, and searching, retrieving, and displaying information are relatively simple. The Plus System software provides six pull-down menus on the menu bar: search, browse, format, action, options, and databases. Function keys are used to access help, view citations, print, and save citations. The software allows for 12 fielded search categories, as well as a free-text search capability. Search topics can be combined using Boolean operators. This superior product comes with a looseleaf manual of 100-plus pages with index. *BHI PLUS* is a necessary acquisition for any library or information center with an interest in current British periodical literature.—**Owen H. Ellard**

956. Nordquist, Joan, comp. **Jacques Derrida (II): A Bibliography.** Santa Cruz, Calif., Reference and Research Services, 1995. 80p. index. (Social Theory: A Bibliographic Series, no.37). $15.00pa. ISBN 0-937855-73-1.

This book is the 37th volume in Social Theory: A Bibliographic Series published four times a year since 1986 by Reference and Research Services. Each bibliography in the series is devoted to a prominent twentieth-century social theorist or a theory, such as deconstructionism. This volume on Jacques Derrida, the influential and controversial French literary critic and philosopher, updates an earlier volume in this same series, published in 1986 (see ARBA 87, entry 1336). It also supplements the 1992 book *Jacques Derrida: An Annotated Primary and Secondary Bibliography* (see ARBA 94, entry 1491).

Section 1 of this bibliography lists, alphabetically by title, all the books and essays by Derrida translated into English or those originally written in English. Listed under each book title is a selection of English-language book reviews and essays about that book. Section 2 lists alphabetically by title English-language essays, interviews, and excerpts from books by Derrida. A keyword-in-title index makes works in this section more accessible. Section 3 is an alphabetical list by author of dissertations in English about Derrida. Finally, section 4 lists, for the years 1991 to 1995, critical literature in English about Derrida drawn both from essays in books and journal articles. A variety of electronic and printed bibliographies were scanned in compiling these lists.

As noted by the reviewer of the 1986 bibliography, this source is primarily useful to undergraduates and general readers unable or unwilling to read Derrida in the original French. Readers who do read French or other languages will want to consult the 1992 book-length bibliography listed above as well as other sources listing non-English work on Derrida. Because this volume is also best described as a paperbound pamphlet, rather than a book, libraries acquiring it may want to consider rebinding it.—**David Isaacson**

957. Nordquist, Joan, comp. **Simone Weil: A Bibliography.** Santa Cruz, Calif., Reference and Research Services, 1995. 72p. index. (Social Theory: A Bibliographic Series, no.38). $15.00pa. ISBN 0-937855-75-8.

This book is the 38th volume in Social Theory: A Bibliographic Series published four times a year since 1986 by Reference and Research Services. Each bibliography in this series is devoted to a prominent twentieth-century social theorist or a theory, such as deconstructionism. This volume focuses only on English translations and secondary material about Simone Weil, the French philosopher who despite dying at age 34 in 1943 left a considerable corpus of books and essays that have generated much commentary among philosophers, feminists, social theorists, and general readers. The only other substantial bibliographies of Weil are *Simone Weil: A Bibliography* (London: Grant and Cutler, 1973) and *Simone Weil: A Bibliography: Supplement, No. 1* (London: Grant and Cutler, 1979), both by Janet Little.

Section 1 lists alphabetically by title Weil's books translated into English or originally written in English. Under each title are listed book reviews and essays about that book. Section 2 lists alphabetically by title essays, letters, and excerpts from books by Weil, followed by sources of reprints arranged chronologically. A keyword-in-title index, enhanced with "title enrichment terms" when title words do not significantly identify the subject, makes these works more accessible. Section 3 lists books and dissertations about Weil in English. Finally, section 4 lists critical articles in books and journals written in English between 1940 and 1995. A variety of electronic and printed bibliographies were scanned in compiling these lists.

This source will be especially useful to undergraduates and other readers unable or unwilling to read Weil and Weil criticism in languages other than English. It should be noted, however, that this is an unannotated bibliography—the reader receives no guidance in selecting from among the sources listed. Scholars who wish to be thorough probably need to read Weil in the original French and should take into account the commentary in French and other languages about this seminal thinker. Because this is a paperbound pamphlet, libraries may want to consider rebinding it.—**David Isaacson**

958. **The Year's Work in English Studies. Volume 73: 1992.** Elaine Treharne and others, eds. Oxford, England, Blackwell and Atlantic Highlands, N.J., Humanities Press, 1995. 814p. index. $140.00. ISBN 0-631-18668-9.

The editor's preface to the 73d volume of the *Year's Work in English Studies* (YWES) describes it as "a narrative bibliography that records and evaluates scholarly writing on English language and on literature written in English," and states ambitiously that "the authors of the YWES attempt to cover all significant contributions to English studies"—from Old English to Toni Morrison—published during 1992. It is, however, unfortunate that the YWES is not the work it purports to be and is, alas, in many respects a series whose time has passed. Indeed, it would appear that the writers of the bibliographic essays share this realization, for in too many instances, they reveal a methodological laziness exemplified by the statement, "yet another biography of [Anthony] Trollope appeared, written by Victoria Glendinning, but Hutchinson did not respond to my requests for a review copy" (p. 431). (Why not go to the library?) Cursory checking reveals numerous volumes that the reviewer has not had "available for review" (p. 263), has "not seen" (p. 140), has "not yet seen" (p. 296), has been "unable to locate" (p. 556), and "books we are aware of but have not yet seen" (p. 582). The latter includes publications of the Harvard University Press and the University of Chicago Press, publishers that can hardly be deemed obscure.

If one can overlook these shortcomings, the YWES is still a work of some formidability. Its critical judgments are magisterial, the authors being unafraid to state (for example) that a work is a "poorly documented assemblage of pig lore . . . [that] provides no great insight into its subject, though the whimsically executed illustrations might afford fleeting entertainment to some" (pp. 123-24). Nevertheless, there is something unpleasantly patronizing in the belief that it is possible and necessary for contemporary reviewers to identify the "significant contributions" of a given year, and this attitude, coupled with the three-year delay between the article's initial publication and the volume's appearance, renders the YWES an increasingly questionable purchase.—**Richard Bleiler**

Biography

959. **Who's Who in Writers, Editors, & Poets: United States & Canada 1995-1996.** 5th ed. Curt Johnson, ed. Highland Park, Ill., December Press, 1995. 514p. index. $99.00. ISBN 0-913204-30-7. ISSN 1049-8621.

The 5th edition contains brief biographical sketches of some 9,000 individuals. The press release claims that more than 1,000 libraries have subscribed to this publication since 1986 (apparently the date of the 1st edition). The directory "has received numerous publishing awards and notices as a unique literary record" (also stated in the press release). The volume contains no introduction that normally should discuss criteria used for inclusion. The publisher offers special 25 percent discounts for individuals who reserve a copy for themselves, plus biographee certificates on walnut wall plaques (available for $195) and other "goodies."

Upon examining several pages of listings at random, it becomes apparent that there is a real mix—important and not-so-important people—of writers, teachers, educators, editors, and so forth. For example, note Anna Christie Adams's sketch on page 2:

> Adams, Anna Christie, b. Littlefield, TX, Sept. 26, 1952, d. Verna LaJean (Curtis) A. Contrbr. articles: Lifestyle mag., Enterprize mag., various orgn. newsletters. Wrkg. on articles, fiction. BFA, Tex. Tech. U., 1977. Reporter, KCBD-TV, Lubbock, Tex., 1978-82; freelance wrtr., Lubbock, 1985-. Mem. South Plains Wrtrs. Assn. Home: 4904 9th St Lubbock TX 79416

This reviewer was surprised to find his own biographical sketch on pages 507-508. The information was taken from an older volume of *Who's Who in America* (Marquis Who's Who, annual). As this reviewer never cooperated with this publisher and did not send in this biographical sketch, the work is not recommended.—**Bohdan S. Wynar**

Dictionaries and Encyclopedias

960. **The Columbia Dictionary of Modern Literary and Cultural Criticism.** Joseph Childers and Gary Hentzi, eds. New York, Columbia University Press, 1995. 362p. index. $49.50; $19.50pa. ISBN 0-231-07242-2; 0-231-07243-0pa.

There are a number of dictionaries of literary theory available, but the *Columbia Dictionary of Modern Literary and Cultural Criticism* is the first to focus its attention on cultural criticism as well. Literary and cultural criticism and theory are the fastest growing areas in the humanities. The editors determined that the language of literary and cultural criticism has not been defined for untrained theorists and generalists. Therefore, the main objective of the editors was to provide a lexicon of the most widely used literary and cultural terms for the generalists as well as the specialists.

The terms defined in the dictionary cover the subject areas of literature, cultural analysis, film, history, art, and philosophy and psychology. *Abjection* to *Zeugma* are defined in clear, concise definitions. A pronunciation key is provided for most of the terms. The terms are treated with historical references illustrating the usage of the term in the literature of the humanities. Cross-references are depicted with small capitals. Short bibliographies are provided at the end of the definitions for further study, and a cumulative bibliography of these cited references and an index of names are provided at the end of the dictionary.

The *Columbia Dictionary* accomplishes its mission of providing generalists with succinct definitions and bibliographies in a handy paperback format. The work is up-to-date, denoting current terms such as *Visual Pleasure* and *Gynesis*, and will be useful as a humanities ready-reference in an academic library reference collection.—**Kay M. Stebbins**

Directories

961. **National Guide to Funding in Arts and Culture.** 3d ed. Margaret Mary Feczko, Ruth Kovacs, and Carlotta Mills, eds. New York, Foundation Center, 1994. 1055p. index. $135.00pa. ISBN 0-87954-548-8.

Essentially an expansion and update of the 2d edition (see ARBA 91, entry 931), this edition adds almost 800 new entries for a total of 4,142 U.S. foundations and corporate giving programs. Among these are agencies supporting local, national, and international projects such as capital campaigns, building funds, and grants to individuals. Fund-raisers will find listings for corporate givers such as AT&T and the Ford Foundation, as well as hundreds of lesser-known agencies.

Introductory material describes publications and services of the Foundation Center, and includes a listing of its cooperating collections of information on foundations and grants maintained in various libraries throughout the United States. A bibliography focuses on recent articles and books related to funding for the arts and culture. Typical data for each numbered entry include the foundation name and address, purpose and activities, type of support and limitations, fields of interest and sample grants, application information, and publications. Geographic, personal name, type of support, and subject indexes enhance the directory's usefulness. Users can easily identify agencies funding projects in film, dance, literature and writing, and for museums and historic preservation, among others.

Organizations engaged in fund-raising will find the directory invaluable. Most large academic and public libraries will want to purchase it. Certainly, all libraries owning the 2d edition will welcome this update.—**Bernice Bergup**

Handbooks and Yearbooks

962. **Peterson's Professional Degree Programs in the Visual and Performing Arts 1995.** Princeton, N.J., Peterson's Guides, 1995. 555p. index. $21.95pa. ISBN 1-56079-281-7. ISSN 1073-2020.

Profiling more than 400 schools and providing descriptions of more than 900 programs, *Peterson's Professional Degree Programs in the Visual and Performing Arts* is a comprehensive directory of the accredited universities in the United States and Canada offering undergraduate programs in the arts. The focus is on performance rather than general liberal arts. Programs listed offer degrees in music (BM), music education (BME), fine arts (BFA), or industrial design (BID). The resource is divided into four sections: music, art, theater, and dance, each introduced by an interview with a specialist in the field. Questions in boxed sections are aimed at helping readers evaluate their own skills and whether a particular program would be an appropriate choice. The profiles inform prospective students about application information, costs, financial aid, and student life. The question "Who will teach you?" is often followed by the quote, "Graduate students do not teach undergraduate courses." The "More about the university" section describes facilities, performance opportunities, faculty art connections, and famous alumni in the arts. The "Quick Reference Chart" lists programs by state, includes degrees, tuition, and enrollment, and functions as a handy index. An appendix lists all of the bachelor's programs with contacts, addresses, and telephone numbers. Information in this tool was gathered through a questionnaire completed by college program directors during spring/summer 1994. This well-organized, attractively arranged, practical resource invites browsing. It fills a void for talented young people and will be a welcome addition to the public library, high school library, or guidance department.—**Joyce Kasman Valenza**

20 Communication and Mass Media

GENERAL WORKS

Directories

963. **News Media Yellow Book: Who's Who Among Reporters, Writers, Editors and Producers in the Leading News Media. Fall 1994.** Ryan T. McGaughey and others, eds. New York, Leadership Directories, 1994. 813p. index. $225.00pa./yr. ISSN 1071-8931.

The subtitle accurately states this directory's coverage: Emphasis is on identifying people currently working in the United States for news services, newspapers, and periodicals (including independent journalists and syndicated columnists), and television and radio networks, stations, and programs. An international section also identifies selected non-U.S. media personnel. This, the 11th edition, and now published quarterly, claims to provide "direct access to over 25,000 journalists and opinion-makers at the nation's leading newsmedia organizations" (p. v)—which means that telephone numbers are available for the likes of Rupert Murdoch, Dan Rather, Howard Stern, Russell Baker, and Joyce Brothers. Often, of course, the number is simply for the telephone at the front desk or the same for all personnel; nonetheless, listings name people from presidents, chairs, hosts, and anchors down to the social issues reporter at a remote desk.

The personnel listings make this directory unique among more standard reference works, including *Working Press of the Nation* (R. R. Bowker, annual), *Literary Market Place* (see ARBA 95, entry 672), *Gale Directory of Publications and Broadcast Media* (see ARBA 94, entry 988, and ARBA 91, entry 61), and many others. Although each of these typically offers more data about a publication, program, or organization (e.g., bibliographic details, indexing coverage, broadcast frequencies, sales and advertising information, program synopses, and so forth), none identifies more key personnel more specifically. *News Media Yellow Book*'s personnel listing for *The New York Times* extends to more than 10 columns. NBC News gets more than four columns of names and numbers.

News Media Yellow Book replaces no standard source but complements many. Libraries whose clients frequently need to contact key media personnel may find this directory useful. Those with less urgent needs for direct contacts may be satisfied with more standard reference works or local telephone directories.—**James K. Bracken**

Handbooks and Yearbooks

964. **The ABC-CLIO Companion to the Media in America.** By Daniel Webster Hollis III. Santa Barbara, Calif., ABC-CLIO, 1995. 352p. illus. index. (ABC-CLIO Companions to Key Issues in American History and Life). $55.00. ISBN 0-87436-776-X.

In today's world of news hype and sound bites, one does not often associate the notions "news media" and "historical perspective" together. Yet, in some 200 articles focusing on U.S. media, Hollis has placed in meaningful historical and cultural context an abundance of information and insight on such topics as "Associated Press," "Broadsides," and "Pulitzer Prizes." The work is arranged alphabetically by subject and is interspersed with such illustrations as a facsimile of a page from a 1905 issue of *Collier's*, a photograph from a Nixon-Kennedy debate, and a reproduction depicting colonial printer Isaiah Thomas. This one-volume compendium contains highly readable pieces on diverse topics, including schools of journalism, noted muckrakers, and peripheral topics in the wide fields of electronic communications and popular entertainment. Article headings range from "Continental Convention" to "Iran-Contra Hearings"; from "Keith Rupert Murdoch" to "Edward Roscoe Murrow"; and from "Civil War" to "Persian Gulf War." Even "Videocassette Recorders" and "Virtual Reality" have full-page write-ups.

Entries generally range from 800-1,500 words, and almost invariably are followed by one or more citations to other recent articles or books on the subject. Even the articles for such narrow or relatively obscure subjects as the Memphis Commercial Appeal and Thurlow Reed are accompanied by suggestions for further scholarly reading. In the book's back matter, these citations are cumulated in a 200-entry bibliography, followed by a 70-item chronology of (albeit limited) use to serious researchers. Between article entries, *see* references are generously supplied; this feature enhances the subject accessibility afforded by the volume's 18-page analytical index. *See also* references are also provided, but insufficiently so. Although one is referred to "Yellow Journalism" from "Hearst, William Randolph," there is no cross-reference to "Animation" from "Cartoons." Nor is one directed to "Sedition Act" from "Freedom of the Press."

Furthermore, despite its wide coverage, *Media in America* suffers from several other blindspots. There is no discussion of the CBC or other Canadian media, nor of the pioneering investigative television program *60 Minutes*, nor the Movietone shorts that brought the exploits of Charles Lindbergh and propaganda of the Allies' World War II war machine to millions of moviegoers. Inexplicably, Barbara Walters merits her own entry, but Ben Bradlee and the Pentagon Papers scandal do not. Only passing references are made to John Peter Zenger, Tom Wicker, and Newton Minow. Still, for its eclectic content and meticulous marshaling of information, this work is praiseworthy—and even newsworthy—as an item for most library collections.—**Jeffrey E. Long**

AUTHORSHIP

General Works

965. Noble, William. **The Complete Guide to Writers' Conferences and Workshops.** Forest Dale, Vt., Paul S. Eriksson; distr., Chicago, Independent Publishers Group, 1995. 176p. illus. index. $16.95pa. ISBN 0-8397-1840-3.

Noble has published nine books about the craft of writing. In his introduction to this volume, he quotes John Ciardi as saying "Every writer of any consequence in history was a member of a group." For writers of poetry, fiction, and nonfiction looking for such a group, Noble lists details of more than 200 conferences and workshops that will be held in 1996 in 40 states and several Canadian provinces. Most are designed to provide professional assistance and networking to unpublished and aspiring writers, whose numbers seem to be growing yearly.

The author dates the modern writers' conference from the first Bread Loaf conference, held in Middlebury, Vermont, in 1926. The entries are arranged alphabetically by the name of the state in which they are held. Each entry lists the pertinent facts about the conference, including address, dates, contact addresses, founding date, enrollment limits, and ancillary activities. In addition, each entry also contains information about required manuscripts, individual conferencing, marketing guidance, and attendance of and accessibility to agents and editors. Included are interviews with the heads of some of the most prestigious conferences, such as those at Bread Loaf and Sewanee. The entries are well indexed by month or season, genre, and name.

While this volume contains much of interest to those seeking in-depth information about writers' conferences, it is not exhaustive. The most timely source of information about writers' conferences will likely continue to be periodicals.—**Kay O. Cornelius**

Bibliography

966. Brewer, Jeutonne P. **The Federal Writers' Project: A Bibliography.** Metuchen, N.J., Scarecrow, 1994. 160p. index. $25.00. ISBN 0-8108-2924-X.

In this slim volume, students and scholars will find a wonderful guide to the people, publications, and legacy of the Federal Writers' Project. This bibliography is divided into 3 main sections: Section 1 contains works about the FWP—its publications, policies, and relationship with other federal efforts; section 2 lists works published by the FWP, from regional and state guides to local histories, historical studies, nature essays, as well as a list of FWP authors; section 3 provides a list of commercially issued sound recordings sponsored by the FWP, exclusive of the oral history recordings collected by FWP researchers as part of their background studies. A brief name and title index is provided, as well as a chronology and overview of the Works Progress Administration, which oversaw the FWP and many other arts-related efforts.

More than 6,000 writers, journalists, editors, and researchers participated in the FWP from its inception in 1935 until its termination in 1943. Most famous for its *American Guide Series*, the FWP generated new interest in cultural and social history, biography, nature study, and geography, which continued well after the official end of the organization. It was the first federal effort to recognize and encourage the role of the arts in our national society, and its impact has been both positive and desirable. Recent debates concerning the government's role in the cultural life of its people have put the FWP and related efforts in a new perspective, making this bibliography a timely resource indeed.
—**Elizabeth Patterson**

Handbooks and Yearbooks

967. Guiley, Rosemary Ellen. **Career Opportunities for Writers.** 3d ed. New York, Facts on File, 1995. 230p. index. $27.95. ISBN 0-8160-3203-3.

Career Opportunities for Writers lists jobs for those with a degree in English, journalism, or other communication-related areas. The reference is logically arranged, attractively formatted, and packed with information. The cover note describes it well: "Indispensable and realistic information on over 100 specific writing jobs."

The work contains sections for jobs in several general categories, such as the media, book publishing, and arts and entertainment. Within each category, Guiley lists specific jobs. An index provides ample entry points to a particular job. Appendixes furnish lists of educational institutions that offer degrees in communication fields, of professional associations, and of trade periodicals. Guiley also appends a bibliography of other career books.

The entry for each job title covers about two pages. Each begins with a "Career Profile," indicating job duties; salary range; employment prospects (good, fair, or poor); advancement prospects with the same notation; and education or experience required. Printed beside the career profile is a "Career Ladder," listing jobs that serve as entry points to the described job and jobs to which it can lead. Both the career profile and the career ladder are in tabular form. Following this is a narrative description of the job, with more detailed information of each item in the career profile.

Career Opportunities for Writers collates a great variety of jobs. Some are standard and obvious: editorial assistant or senior editor. Others are more unexpected: greeting card writer or alumni communication specialist. While some—such as screenwriter, playwright, or speechwriter—sound like glamour jobs, the clear delineation of training needed and job duties makes these seem attainable, too.

This book is sure to start the user thinking more creatively about job opportunities. It is a good update to older titles that serve as job hunting guides for those with a humanities background: *Aside from Teaching English, What in the World Can You Do?* by Dorothy K. Bestor (University of Washington Press, 1982) or *Career Choices for Students of English* (rev. ed., Walker, 1990). This particular work is recommended for all libraries—school, public, and academic.—**Terry Ann Mood**

Style Manuals

968. Guidelines for Bias-Free Writing. By Marilyn Schwartz and the Task Force on Bias-Free Language of the Association of American University Presses. Bloomington, Ind., Indiana University Press, 1995. 100p. index. $15.00; $5.95pa. ISBN 0-253-35102-2; 0-253-20941-2pa.

This slim, sane book packs more sense into fewer pages than any writing guide since *The Elements of Style* (3d ed.; see ARBA 80, entry 105). As with that classic, the message is simple: "Say what you mean and mean what you say." The examples and explanations ("Man, like other mammals, breast feeds his young") show that bias in writing results mostly from bad habits and lazy thinking. Again and again, this guide reminds writers: Be precise. Be specific. Be accurate. Stay awake.

The term *Hispanic* has a specific meaning; so do the terms *Latin American*, *Mexican American*, and *Spanish*. Differentiating among these terms is not overnice; it is a matter of fact. On the other hand, the overuse of *hearing-impaired* is euphemistic. If someone is deaf, say so. *Hearing-impaired* means what the oxymoron *partially deaf* does not.

In the format of *The Chicago Manual of Style* (14th ed.; see ARBA 94, entry 1001) (albeit an anorexic one), numbered sections are devoted to specific terms or issues of usage or grammar. Chapters focus on sticky distinctions: gender; race, ethnicity, citizenship, nationality, and religion; disabilities and medical conditions; sexual orientation; and age. For each term or issue, the authors offer a definition, a brief discussion of why it is problematic (or appropriate), and suggestions for avoiding difficulty. A detailed index provides access to individual topics, such as the term *teenager* and the use of *they* as a singular term.

The author points out that the use of offensive words and terms (such as *queer* or *old wive's tale*) is sometimes appropriate, as in quotations, reprints of historical works, or in certain contexts in which hate words have been "defiantly revalued by the very individuals against whom they have been directed." Finally, the author warns against torturing the language and the wholesale purging of traditional English expressions and rhetorical devices.

The book was written for writers and editors, but it has much broader appeal. For word lovers, it is an entertaining guide to the vagaries of evolving language. For people involved in the debate about political correctness—regardless of what side they are on—this book clarifies the point of all the fuss. [R: LJ, 1 Feb 95, p. 70]—**Constance Hardesty**

969. Merriam-Webster's Guide to Punctuation and Style. Springfield, Mass., Merriam-Webster, 1995. 343p. index. $4.99pa. ISBN 0-87779-912-1.

This guide is adapted from *Webster's Standard American Style Manual* (see ARBA 86, entry 889). In addition to discussing punctuation and style, the parent volume also provides much guidance about publishing conventions. The *Guide to Punctuation and Style* is a practical, easy-to-use handbook on the most basic rules of written English. Although not stated in the preface, there seems to be an understanding that American usage, rather than British, is the standard followed. The book's eight chapters are devoted to the following matters: punctuation, capitals, italics, and quotation marks; plurals, possessives, and compounds; abbreviations; numbers; grammar and composition; problems in word usage; and notes and bibliographies. Examples illustrate each rule. Brief discussions offer help when rules have exceptions or offer choices. Because this is a concise guide designed for quick reference about the most commonly asked rules, discussion of exceptions is terse. Finding rules is facilitated not only by a fairly extensive index but also by helpful numbered subtopics at the beginning of each chapter.

Writers who need more scholarly detail about usage should consult other sources. If they want considerable discussion of rules plus extensive historical references from another Merriam-Webster source, they should consult *Webster's Dictionary of English Usage* (see ARBA 90, entry 1005). Readers who do not necessarily believe that Merriam-Webster is the ultimate authority, and who are interested in a less detailed, definitely American, more accessibly written, but less scholarly guide, should look at *The Columbia Guide to Standard American English* (see ARBA 94, entry 1085). College students needing term paper guidance as well as rather detailed advice about punctuation and style may prefer the *Harbrace College Handbook* (12th ed., Harbrace, 1993) to any of these sources.—**David Isaacson**

970. **NTC's Handbook for Writers.** By Martin Steinmann and Michael Keller. Lincolnwood, Ill., National Textbook, 1995. 348p. $19.95. ISBN 0-8442-5810-5.

In this work, Steinmann and Keller have bypassed the usual grammar/usage/composition structure of other writing manuals. Instead, they have integrated such disparate language matters as "cases," "concision," and "cause, reason" distinctions into a single alphabetical arrangement of entries. Through example and explanation, "Standard American Written English" is suggested to the reader as the most appropriate type of writing for North America's adult population to use. Unlike the strident, didactic primers of generations past, *NTC's Handbook for Writers* softens its guidelines with such qualifiers and caveats as "sometimes," "caution," and "some readers object."

Among entries, cross-referencing is quite thorough, although none exists, for example, between "comparisons" and "illogical comparisons." Also, consulters of this reference work may not think to look under such terminology as "elegant variation," "hedges," and "WASP language" for needed advice. Significant omissions are few, but include such items as "height/heighth," "elliptical expressions," and "through/thru." Unexpected entries are the terms "fiction" and "edition, issue." Also, the editing for the most part is sound, although there is an occasional error.

Although there is no index, the book does include a valuable "Topical Guide," in which the headings of major entries are classified under "Argument," "Clarity and Style," "Conventions of Writing," "Grammar," "Language," and "Writing Process." Another positive feature of this book is the highlighting of certain entries that the authors recognize as of superior importance to most writers, or which have customarily received short shrift from other writing manuals. In conclusion, this is a sensible, well-executed handbook that would be appropriate for libraries of all sizes—including that of any serious prose writer.—**Jeffrey E. Long**

NEWSPAPERS AND MAGAZINES
Bibliography

971. Henritze, Barbara K. **Bibliographic Checklist of African American Newspapers.** Baltimore, Md., Genealogical Publishing, 1995. 206p. index. $35.00. ISBN 0-8063-1457-5.

This is a comprehensive checklist of 5,539 newspapers and assorted periodicals. The principal value of the checklist is that it combines entries from numerous sources into one volume. These sources include specific African-American newspaper works such as Clarence S. Brigham's *History and Bibliography of American Newspapers, 1690-1820* (Greenwood Press, 1976), union lists, bibliographies, and finding aids. As the name implies, this checklist is intended for the researcher interested in African-American culture and genealogy. Because this is a checklist and not a union list, there are no specific holdings listed for the various repositories or collections cited.

The work apparently began as a list of the African-American newspapers in Cleveland, Ohio, and evolved into this much more comprehensive effort. There is no biographical information regarding the author nor any mention of her background in the introduction provided by Tony Burroughs. As part of the introductory section, the author provides a brief guide to the major reference sources in this area and a clear explanation of the scope and coverage of each category within the checklist itself. The one-line entries consist of title, city, state, frequency, dates of publication, and source codes; the entries are grouped alphabetically by state and subdivided by city.

The work includes a source code directory (appendix A), a useful and complete bibliography of approximately 190 citations (appendix B), and a thorough title index. Because of its scope, this compilation would be particularly valuable for those libraries owning one or more of the standard reference works in this area; by itself it is of limited use. In summary, the *Bibliographic Checklist of African American Newspapers* is a straightforward, comprehensive resource that fills a very real need. The work is recommended for larger academic and public libraries. [R: LJ, 15 Feb 95, p. 150; RBB, 15 Feb 95, p. 1106]—**Anthony J. Dedrick**

972. Linton, David. **The Twentieth-Century Newspaper Press in Britain: An Annotated Bibliography.** New York, Mansell/Cassell, 1994. 386p. index. $120.00. ISBN 0-7201-2159-0.

By combining the entries relating to the twentieth century that appeared in his and Ray Boston's *The Newspaper Press in Britain: An Annotated Bibliography* (see ARBA 88, entry 927) with a significant number of additional titles, Linton has created a new bibliography devoted to newspapers in the United Kingdom from 1900 to the present. In spite of its narrower chronological scope, this work contains almost 900 more entries than its parent volume, thus reflecting Linton's efforts to cast a considerably wider net in selecting materials for inclusion. Whereas the earlier bibliography emphasized works by news journalists, this version also encompasses accounts by sports reporters, drama and film critics, essayists, media scholars, and other writers. It even identifies fictional and dramatic works that portray the newspaper press. Among the broad range of sources cited are books, periodical and newspaper articles, theses, dissertations, pamphlets, reports of government agencies, and microform sets.

The almost 3,800 sequentially numbered entries are divided into 3 sections, each arranged alphabetically by author. Selected reference works appear first, followed by the main portion of the bibliography, and then by a section for late entries. Citations provide standard bibliographic information, and most are accompanied by brief annotations. Although Linton includes a number of 1994 publications, he has missed some important recent works, such as Ralph McCoy's *Freedom of the Press: An Annotated Bibliography* (see ARBA 95, entry 704).

Following the bibliography is a useful chronology that notes significant events in British newspaper history from 1900 to 1994. Unfortunately, the admirably detailed subject index is flawed by the omission of references to entries for which the subject is also the author. This distinction will be lost on most users, who, almost assuredly, will rely on the index references to *Punch* and therefore miss the six important sources listed under *Punch* in the bibliography. An unusually high percentage of inaccurate entry numbers also hampers efficient access. By identifying publications on topics ranging from newspaper censorship during World War I to media coverage of the bombing of Pan American flight 103, this compilation offers a valuable service to historians and journalism scholars alike. Libraries that have found the earlier bibliography useful will want to supplement it with the expanded coverage offered by this volume.—**Marie Ellis**

Biography

973. Riley, Sam G. **Biographical Dictionary of American Newspaper Columnists.** Westport, Conn., Greenwood Press, 1995. 411p. index. $79.50. ISBN 0-313-29192-6.

Covering the Civil War era to the present, this volume treats 600 U.S. newspaper columnists, ranging from Eugene Field, Joel Chandler Harris, and James Thurber to Erma Bombeck, Hodding Carter, and Anna Quindlen. Riley, a professor of communication studies who has compiled a number of reference works pertaining to print journalism, profiles not only nationally syndicated and self-syndicated columnists but also those who write for only one newspaper. His primary focus is on writers of general interest, political, lifestyle, and humor columns. Although he includes well-known advice, etiquette, and society columnists, he excludes other special interest columnists, such as those writing about finance, gardening, or hobbies.

Varying in length from a few brief paragraphs to more than a page, the alphabetically arranged biographical sketches concentrate on the individuals' careers rather than details of their personal lives. When appropriate, entries conclude with bibliographical references to works by and about the columnist. In addition, a selective bibliography of sources relating to newspaper columns and columnists appears near the end of the volume. An excellent index provides access to the columnists treated, individuals mentioned within entries, and other proper names (such as titles of newspapers, periodicals, and columns; awards; and names of organizations).

Although the four volumes of *American Newspaper Journalists* (see ARBA 87, entry 880; ARBA 85, entries 781-782; and Gale, 1984), which cover 1690 to 1950 and are part of the Dictionary of Literary Biography series, offer much greater depth, they treat only a small percentage of the columnists in Riley's compilation. This work also complements other recent biographical sources on journalists, such as the *Biographical Dictionary of American Journalism* (see ARBA 90, entry 905), which provides more detailed biographical information but includes only 75 of the columnists identified by Riley. Especially valuable for its coverage of outstanding local columnists and those just beginning their ascent to national prominence, this dictionary will be particularly useful in academic libraries that support programs in journalism and mass communication.—**Marie Ellis**

Directories

974. **Bacon's Directories on Disc 1995 Update.** [CD-ROM]. Chicago, Bacon's Information, 1995. Minimum system requirements (Windows version): IBM or compatible 386SX. CD-ROM drive. MS-DOS 3.1. Windows. 6MB RAM. VGA monitor. Minimum system requirements (Macintosh version): Motorola 68020 CPU. CD-ROM drive. System 7. 8MB RAM. $995.00.

This is a solid tool for searching identifying information about the media in the United States. It is based on Bacon's media directories in book form and is a text-only database of newspapers, magazines, television (broadcast and cable) stations, radio, news services, and syndicators. The first menu allows the user to view the database, select a mailing list, add to a list, view a list, and give output options. In the view database menu one can select by media type and state to derive an alphabetical list. The user is able to print mailing labels and lists or export saved lists. Addresses, telephone numbers, editors' names, and other media-specific information is provided, such as frequency of issue, circulation, and advertisement rate.

The CD-ROM was easy to install in Windows; it makes its own Program Manager icon. Although a thorough guide is provided, one can learn to use the program by reading the screen, as it is so intuitive. Screen design is clear, crisp, and uncluttered, with helpful on-screen clues. This disc is recommended for any public relations office or college library with an emphasis on the media or public relations. Because of the limited number of people who request this information in a school or public library, it is not recommended for this market. Its ability to create lists for the user makes it an invaluable tool for those dealing with the media every day.—**Sandra L. Doggett**

975. Brewer, Annie M. **Talk Shows and Hosts on Radio: A Directory Including Show Titles and Formats....** 3d ed. Dearborn, Mich., Whiteford Press, 1995. 293p. index. $34.95. ISBN 0-9632341-4-5.

This 3d edition adds 517 more talk shows and 234 more biographies of talk show hosts. It is identical in scope and format to the 2d edition (covering the United States, Guam, and Puerto Rico). The first section geographically lists programs and includes call letters, the name of the show, the format, addresses, telephone numbers, whether guests appear, and the name of the host. The second section provides the same information for syndicated and network programs. Section 3 provides descriptive, noncritical, and brief biographical sketches of 331 talk show hosts summarizing the host's education and background, approach to issues, and on-air style. Subject and name indexes are included as well as a copy of the questionnaire used to gather and update information. The only current directory of its kind, this work belongs in public libraries, communications collections, and interested academic libraries.—**Glynys R. Thomas**

976. **Editor & Publisher Market Guide 1994.** Colin Phillips, ed. New York, Editor & Publisher, 1994. 1v. (various paging). $100.00pa.

977. **Editor & Publisher Market Guide 1994.** [CD-ROM]. New York, Editor & Publisher, 1994. Minimum system requirements (DOS version): IBM or compatible. CD-ROM drive with MS-DOS CD-ROM Extensions. DOS 3.3. 640K RAM. 3MB hard disk space. VGA monitor. Floppy disk drive. Minimum system requirements (Macintosh version): Macintosh Plus or higher. CD-ROM drive. System 6.0.7. 2.5MB RAM. 2MB hard disk space. Floppy disk drive. $495.00 (single user); $690.00 (2-10 users); $890.00 (11+ users). [Other pricing options for addition of listing capabilities.]

This work's goal is to project demographic statistics and forecast retail sales for daily newspaper markets in the United States and Canada. The 1994 edition is the first to appear in both print and CD-ROM formats.

The print version has four sections. Section 1 begins with a publisher's memo, an index to advertisers, a one-page guide, a general index, and other preliminaries. It then defines and presents U.S. metropolitan statistical areas (MSAs), consolidated metropolitan statistical areas (CMSAs), and New England county metropolitan areas (NECMAs). Next, it ranks all 315 MSAs by population estimates, disposable and per-household income, total retail sales, and retail sales by commodity (e.g., lumber, food, gasoline, drugs). Data for the 250 top counties and the 250 top cities where newspapers are published are similarly arranged. Section 1 concludes with two pages listing national newspaper representatives for daily and selected weekly newspapers published in the United States and Canada.

Sections 2 and 3 present surveys of daily newspaper cities for the respective countries. Arrangement is by state (with a listing of MSAs), then city. Each survey has 14 data fields, including location, transportation, population, households, banks, automobiles, electric and gas meters, industries, climate, water quality, retailing and retail outlets, and newspapers. Maps for each state show where daily newspapers are published and indicate county seats having none. A sample survey is given in the front of the first section; a few pages later, a page of definitions and notes provides an interpretation of encoded data and documents secondary sources.

Section 4 presents statistical data in tabular form: population (1980 and 1990 U.S. census, 1994 publisher's estimate), households, age groups, income, and farm products (1987). A U.S. nationwide summary by state is followed by a breakdown by county and city. The same is done for retail sales data, using the 1982 and 1987 U.S. census and giving the number of stores (1987) and retail sales estimates (1994) by commodity. Canadian data are drawn from censuses in 1986 (population), 1981 (farms), 1985 (crops and livestock), and 1992 and 1993 (retail sales).

The print version is easily accessible, although some of the details are buried, and a list of abbreviations would help. The preliminaries should be presented separately rather than in section 1. The CMSAs and NECMAs have no data given for them. The information in section 4 merits two separate sections. The user should note that data are drawn from various sources, including the publisher's own survey, and avoid confusing individual cities and their respective MSAs.

For the CD-ROM version Editor & Publisher selected CD Answer, a database-oriented software package allowing extensive manipulation of the data. Installation on MS-DOS takes a couple of minutes and uses approximately 1MB of disk space. Four display options for data records are available: General and Newspaper for both Canada and the United States. The user can retrieve data from any field in the record. Options for data access are typing in a search key (truncation and Boolean operators are available) and browsing by displaying a list of all headings, from which one or several can be selected. Data from more than one field can be selected simultaneously, using Boolean and other logical operators to compare fields (use of "NOT" is nonstandard); the number of records matching both searches is indicated in the Connections line, and a list is generated. Searches formulated and information from search results can be stored on disk for future use. This search capability gives a wide range of access to the database. For example, within the field "Tap Water," one can search the word *hard* to retrieve a list of newspaper communities with hard water. Such searching capacity also highlights features, such as that terms like *hard* are not uniformly applied in all pertinent records. Once a list of communities has been selected, various associated information (e.g., auto stores, gas and electricity meters) can be displayed in rotation by pressing the space bar. One can also view the entire data record for a community.

The chief deficiency of the CD-ROM software is the comparative inaccessibility of assistance both electronically and in print. Only a six-page insert accompanies the disk. For full explanation of several abbreviations and the like, the print version, indispensable for a proper understanding of the data record, is required. On-disk help is context-sensitive—that is, provided only for options immediately available to the user. Thus, one cannot request help about Windows without already having selected the list of options within which Windows occurs—and mastering the Windows options takes considerable patience. In DOS, no index of help topics is available. Help messages are in technical language, and whereas "You are in a search window entering search criteria" is concise and to the point, it will baffle many users. The authors of the CD Answer software should develop a tutorial to familiarize users with basic function commands, display characteristics, and the database structure. Use of such features as reading several checked data entries from the browse list into the Search Rectangle can exceed the system limit. Not all software options have been implemented: The LIKE logical operator and the LINKS display command line option are listed in the accompanying sheet but not available on disk. Of high potential is the Language option: Only English is now available.

In both versions the *Market Guide* assists persons seeking demographic data on newspaper communities. Among marketing tools its specialty is that it is organized with newspaper markets as the unit of analysis. It answers a surprising range of ancillary questions such as temperature ranges in Augusta, Georgia, and paydays in the lumber industry in Coos Bay, Oregon. Students of marketing, communication, geography, demographics, and social studies will use it. Businesses seeking markets for testing products and developing franchises will find it invaluable, as will college students considering relocating upon graduation.—**Ian Fairclough**

978. **Hudson's Subscription Newsletter Directory.** 12th ed. Joan W. Artz, ed. Rhinebeck, N.Y., Newsletter Clearinghouse, 1994. 450p. index. $140.00pa. ISBN 0-9617642-4-4. ISSN 1046-8110.

More than 4,000 subscription newsletters "in the United States and abroad" are listed in this work. From accounting, advertising, and aerospace to warehousing, wine, and women, and from *The Corset Newsletter* to *Aggressive Hockey Report* (described as covering "the physical side of hockey"), the gamut of subjects is covered. Arranged by subject, then alphabetically by title, entries contain address, telephone and fax numbers, editor, publisher, cost, size, publication frequency, and, in some cases, a brief description. Online sources are not mentioned; in future editions it would be useful to know which newsletters are available full text online. The table of contents and many indexes are useful, as subject arrangement is occasionally curious. Transportation, distribution, warehousing, railroads, and trucking, for example, are lumped into one section, while aviation and aerospace, a mere two pages, rate their own section. There also are some startling omissions. *GreenMarkets*, for example, the primary newsletter of the fertilizer industry, is excluded although it can be found in both *Ulrich's International Periodicals Directory* (see entry 88) and the *Oxbridge Directory of Newsletters* (Oxbridge Communications, 1994). According to the publisher, "verification forms were sent to the lists of newsletters which we have developed over the past 30 years as publishers of *The Newsletter on Newsletters*." The publication also states that "we assume no responsibility, however, for inaccuracies." Use with care.—**Jo A. Cates**

979. Ross, Marilyn. **National Directory of Newspaper Op-Ed Pages.** Buena Vista, Colo., Communication Creativity, 1994. 158p. index. $19.95pa. ISBN 0-918880-17-3.

Touted on the title page as a "new, profitable tool" for freelance writers, public relations practitioners, speakers, entrepreneurs and the like, this is a specialized collection of United States and Canadian newspaper data. The majority of the directory is a state-by-state listing of more than 200 newspapers. Entries include the name of the op-ed page editor or the editor responsible for the opinion page; an address; a telephone number; a fax number; copyright information; pay scale (which was, incidentally, listed as "seldom," "0," or left blank for more than half the listings); word length; comments; and other information. Part 3 (actually "Art 3" on the contents page of this reviewer's copy) focuses on Canadian newspapers arranged by province.

In the introduction, Ross defines op-ed pages, stating that "it doesn't mean that articles oppose the editorial point of view of the paper, rather it literally denotes where these pieces are found: opposite the editorial page." She also offers brief chapters on "The Hows and Whys of Op-Ed Pages" and "Crafting Compelling Essays," in which she urges the user to "be a flame thrower rather than one who timidly lights a pilot." Most useful (and frequently entertaining) are comments supplied by editorial page editors responding to the author's query letter (e.g., to be included in the *Providence Journal*, the op-ed piece must be "mighty splendid and mighty important"). Doomed to be outdated quickly because of high turnover in newsrooms, this source will appeal primarily to beginning freelancers eager to get their names in print.—**Jo A. Cates**

Handbooks and Yearbooks

980. **Editor & Publisher International Year Book 1994.** Ian E. Anderson, ed. New York, Editor & Publisher, 1994. 1v. (various paging). maps. index. $100.00pa. ISBN 9-993-7798-8-1.

981. **Editor & Publisher Year Book 1994.** [CD-ROM]. New York, Editor & Publisher, 1994. Minimum system requirements: IBM or compatible. CD-ROM drive. DOS. Windows. $895.00 w/Year Book (listing capabilities); $495.00 w/Year Book (without listing capabilities).

This comprehensive directory of world newspapers and related services is organized in eight sections covering U.S. (daily, ethnic) and foreign newspapers, syndicates, equipment, organizations, services (e.g., clip art, brokers), and personnel. These are combined into three searchable databases in the CD-ROM version, with an added option for creating labels from the daily newspaper data. The label program will prove useful for those conducting survey research or seeking employment. The excellent introductory material, which describes industry status (e.g., reduction of dailies), trends, and statistics, is not available on the CD-ROM.

The printed directory employs a primarily geographical or topical arrangement, with brief indexes to content and advertisers. Entries offer a combination of basic (e.g., address), standard (e.g., circulation), and unique data fields (e.g., newsprint consumption) that are completely searchable in the CD-ROM version. While there are several industry directories available, some more current (for example, *Standard Rate & Data* [Standard Rate and Data Service, annual]), few identify a newspaper's hardware and software. The alphabetical personnel directory is a useful feature in the printed edition, but the lack of a title index is a serious flaw.

The current CD-ROM version employs a menu-driven, search-and-display capability that is easily loaded in both DOS and Windows formats. Although there are many help screens for both formats, the brief printed directions are to DOS command keys only and the Windows buttons for specific functions initially are unclear and confusing. The database supports Boolean searches of selected criteria; however, effective use of the more unusual fields (e.g., operator-owned CATV, printing equipment) requires a knowledge of or consultation with the printed version. For the most part, it is easy to toggle between the retrieved formats; however, a major software glitch exists in the section on weekly, foreign, and specialty newspapers. While the DOS version can easily locate specialty newspapers, no countries other than Canada and the United States could be retrieved. In Windows, foreign newspapers were searchable by country as well as other features (e.g., language), with the specialty newspaper choice available but unsearchable.

The printed directory has been and will remain a standard, recommended reference tool. Subsequent editions are likely to remedy existing problems with the CD-ROM version; however, the current cost is substantial for essentially an incomplete, flawed product.—**Sandra E. Belanger**

982. **Newspapers Online: A Guide to Searching Daily Newspapers Whose Articles Are Online in Full Text, 1995.** 3d ed. Susanne Bjørner, comp. and ed. Needham Heights, Mass., BiblioData, 1995. 1v. (various paging). $99.00pa. ISBN 1-879258-12-9.

With the proliferation of newspapers available online (ranging from the *South China Morning Post* to *The Denver Post*), this is an expanded and more essential product for librarians and online searchers than the 2d edition published in 1992 (see ARBA 93, entry 975). Nearly 200 daily newspapers available from at least one major database vendor (e.g., DIALOG, DataTimes) are profiled. An overwhelming amount of introductory material is included, but users are advised to wade through it all, especially sections on searching tips for professional and consumer systems; also, arrangement and pagination are confusing, so consulting the "How to Use This Book" and "The Newspaper Pages—Explanation" pages is helpful.

Newspaper profiles are arranged geographically in sections on Asia and Australia, Europe and the Middle East, Canada, and the United States; titles appear alphabetically within each section. Entries typically offer regional information; a brief "Newsmakers" list of significant names, businesses, events; online vendors and CD-ROM systems; background information on the newspaper; and search tips. Information is provided if there is an electronic edition of the paper (e.g., *Atlanta Journal-Constitution* on Prodigy, *The New York Times* on America Online). There are seven exhaustive indexes. Journalists, news librarians, and other searchers who frequently sift through newspaper databases will be bombarded with dates, vendors, tips, and warnings—and very grateful for the information; the sporadic or initial user of newspaper databases, however, might benefit even more.—**Jo A. Cates**

RADIO, TELEVISION, AUDIO, AND VIDEO

Bibliography

983. **Words on Cassette 1995.** New Providence, N.J., R. R. Bowker/Reed Reference Publishing, 1995. 1985p. $144.95pa. ISBN 0-8352-3591-2.

This telephone directory-sized book is a merging of R. R. Bowker's *On Cassette* (see ARBA 92, entry 908) with Meckler Media's *Words on Tape* (see ARBA 90, entry 921). Its 1,900-plus pages list 59,000 audiobook titles, essentially every title in print for this medium. Yellow side tabs separate sections for authors, titles, readers/performers, producers/distributors, and subjects. Title entries contain cassette running times, bibliographical information, prices, reader names, and a content synopsis.

A weakness is that not all of the data elements appear consistently. Fewer than half the main entries contain all the information possible. Other access points refer the reader to the more complete title main entries. Subject headings are broad ("Health and Fitness," "Music"), but logical cross-references are offered. The listing of producers and distributors is impressively comprehensive, with addresses of subsidiaries, toll-free numbers, and everything else necessary to purchase materials from these vendors.

The inclusion of some content synopses adds to the value of this tool for audiovisual acquisitions librarians. Patrons fully expect their libraries to lend books on tape, and this resource would be the only one needed to support informed purchases in the medium. Be forewarned—the binding may be insufficient to support frequent use of this heavy paperback. Prepare to reinforce it with strapping tape, for this will be a book in steady use by both librarians and their patrons.—**Ed Volz**

Dictionaries and Encyclopedias

984. Bognár, Desi K. **International Dictionary of Broadcasting and Film.** Stoneham, Mass., Focal Press/Butterworth-Heinemann, 1995. 268p. $24.95pa. ISBN 0-240-80212-8.

This is a basic guide to the jargon used by broadcasters around the world, although the lingua franca here is still English. Abbreviations, acronyms, technical devices, scientific terms, slang, and titles of positions in the industry—all the important terms seem to be here, in dictionary arrangement and brevity. For example, under *MBC*, there are listed the Malawi Broadcasting Corporation, the Mauritius Broadcasting Corporation, and the Middle East Broadcasting Centre, with no further identification (such as an address).

All of the terms are briefly described in a few lines, sometimes too briefly. There are also many appendixes, with English-metric conversion tables, lists of frequencies, television standards, film speed, and so forth. What they have to do with a dictionary of communications is debatable. However, the book is useful for quick lookups without any description or explanation.—**Dean Tudor**

985. **Dictionary of Image Technology.** 3d ed. Woburn, Mass., Focal Press/Butterworth-Heinemann, 1994. 160p. illus. $32.95pa. ISBN 0-240-51364-9.

This work is a typical, tested British technical/trade society publication that defines *audio/visual* in the broadest possible sense. Although not covered in ARBA previously, this edition is the 3d in 10 years and benefits thereby. In addition to the obvious technologists in the several A/V subfields, a use is seen for students and practitioners in the performing arts fields wishing to broaden their knowledge of "what is going on around them," thus enhancing their potential employability through career goal modification.

Typical entries are short but fully intelligible (for example, "kansas city" [sic], p. 70, "a standard for recording computer data or program on cassette tape"). Where usage is regionalized, the entry may end with "(UK)" or "(USA)." In all, the entries are a credit to the sponsor, The British Kinematographic Sound and Television Society. The dictionary is recommended for A/V and general technology collections.

—**Eugene B. Jackson**

Directories

986. **Bowker's Complete Video Directory 1995.** New Providence, N.J., R. R. Bowker/Reed Reference Publishing, 1995. 3v. index. $229.95/set. ISBN 0-8352-3586-6.

Bowker's Complete Video Directory 1995 was first published as *Variety's Complete Home Video Directory* in 1988 (see ARBA 90, entries 1335-1336). The 2d edition of the work, while still based on the Variety database, was expanded to include additional citations and published as *Bowker's Complete Video Directory 1990*. This present edition has been further expanded and now claims to be the most extensive listing of currently available video titles.

The work is divided into three volumes with two divisions: "Entertainment" (volume 1), and "Education/Special Interest" (volumes 2 and 3). There are more than 41,000 entertainment titles listed, and the "Education/Special Interest" section contains about 65,000 entries. Volume 1 has several indexes in addition to the alphabetical listing of entertainment videos, including ones by cast/director, genre (actually a subject index), series, Spanish language, laser videodisc, 8-mm titles, closed-captioned titles, awards, international standards, manufacturers, and services and suppliers.

The entries in the main body of the sections each include title; date of first release; genre (e.g., western, comedy); color or black-and-white; length; rating; and cast. In addition, complete ordering information is listed. Generally, an overview of the plot is provided, with brief notes on the production if pertinent. Volumes 2 and 3 have a similar format and contain most of the indexing found in volume 1.

Earlier editions of *Bowker's Complete Video Directory* were criticized for failing to be as complete as they could be, and in some cases errors were detected. Also, volumes 2 and 3 in earlier editions contained fewer titles than the *Educational Film and Video Locator* (see ARBA 91, entry 358). It appears that this 1995 edition has overcome all of these previous criticisms. It lists more titles than other current lists, and provides comprehensive indexing. Also, the Bowker directory appears to include only films that are available on video, or were produced on video originally. Some of the other lists include items available only on film.

While the directory is generally well designed and easy to use, some categories are confusing. For instance, religious films (even when a general release) are considered "special interest" and are included in volumes 2 and 3. In addition, there is no attempt to identify videos for children beyond the subject classifications that may appeal to them (e.g., cheerleading, holidays, and the like). Children's entertainment programs are listed in volume 1, and other children's videos are listed in volumes 2 and 3. The Spanish-language index is extremely useful, but no other language indexing is available, although films in other languages are listed.

The directory is recommended for all libraries wishing to have a complete reference section on film and video, and for smaller collections as a single source. The price of the directory makes it impractical for home collections or smaller branches of public libraries.—**Robert L. Wick**

987. Jacobson, Ronald L., comp. **Television Research: A Directory of Conceptual Categories, Topic Suggestions, and Selected Sources.** Jefferson, N.C., McFarland, 1995. 138p. index. $32.50pa. ISBN 0-7864-0033-1.

This directory serves as an excellent starting point for those about to embark on a television-related research project. While not a study of television in and of itself, the book enumerates research possibilities; it presents a conceptual overview of the field, suggests topics that warrant investigation, and offers a selection of potential sources of information. As such, the directory provides a useful framework for beginning and experienced researchers alike.

Organizationally, the work is divided into 29 broad categories covering such areas as advertising, comedy, minorities, politics, regulation, and technology. For each category, a brief theoretical abstract is presented, followed by a list of relevant research and lecture topics, and a bibliography of print sources. Additional sources are included at the end of the directory, listing general reference works, pertinent indexes and databases, scholarly journals, popular magazines, newspapers, and trade publications. The work is further enhanced by the inclusion of a listing of libraries and museums containing special television-related collections. Research in the field of television continues to gain wide acceptance within popular culture scholarship, and a host of television-related courses are now offered on college campuses. These classes generate a demand for critical studies and create the need for tools to facilitate that research. While not intended as a comprehensive bibliography of the subject, this well-written, well-organized directory is sufficiently informative to serve as an initial guide for those beginning a research project. [R: LJ, 15 Feb 95, p. 150]—**Owen H. Ellard**

988. **Power Media Selects: A Guide to the Nation's Most Influential Media.** 9th ed. Alan Caruba, ed. Washington, D.C., Broadcast Interview Source, 1994. 312p. index. $165.50; $298.77/set looseleaf w/binder. ISBN 0-934333-20-3.

989. **Talk Show Selects: A Guide to the Nation's Most Influential Television and Radio Talk Shows.** 1995 ed. Washington, D.C., Broadcast Interview Source, 1994. 335p. index. $185.00; $298.77/set looseleaf w/binder. ISBN 0-934333-22-X. [also available in disk format].

The subtitle of this looseleaf service says it all: a guide to the nation's most influential media. In an age that values the sound bite over the substantive comment, such books are a necessity. *Power Media Selects* (PMS) consists of identifications of syndicated columnists, newspapers, magazines, newsletters, and radio and television stations. Under each category is a further subdivision where warranted. For example, the section on magazines is further divided by subject: national news, women, men, homeowners, medicine, travel, and the like. A considerable number of items are covered even if there is some overlap. With more than 1,000 sources, and the same material available on computer disk for mailing labels, one would think PMS a good choice.

This, however, is not the case. What alerts one to something amiss are the disclaimers of the tool. On the verso of the title page, PMS reveals the following:

> "***DISCLAIMER NOTICE***Broadcast Interview Source has used its best efforts in collecting and preparing data . . . but does not warrant that the information herein is complete, accurate, and does not assume, and hereby disclaims, any liability to any person for any loss or damage caused by errors, omissions, or inaccuracies. . . ."

Further, this disclaimer is repeated and enlarged on page v, where readers are told that even the "best media directories" can "barely keep up with the flow and the flux [of changes in employment] and *Power Media Selects* doesn't even pretend to."

At best, then, librarians will have a guide that identifies places (ABC, NBC, AP, UP International) or people (George Will, Abe Rosenthal). One hardly needs an expensive guide for such purposes when other standard sources are available. Further, some syndicated writers, such as the ever-controversial Joseph Sobran, are not even included. Annotations to the text are lacking and too brief. Under Tribune Media Services, one finds "An extremely influential syndicate that should be on your 'must send' list." Those who should know will know this already; those who do not should not be sending material to this news service in the first place. Further, the index of names is alphabetized by first name, so George Will is under G and the column "On My Mind" under O. More troubling is that the names are not cross-referenced. If people do not already know that A. M. Rosenthal writes under the column "On My Mind," they will not find an entry for Rosenthal under A or R.

Talk Show Selects (TSS), by the same company, offers contact information to more than 700 national talk shows in the top 150 markets in the United States. Each entry contains the name of the contact person, the market identification (e.g., national), its affiliation, host of the show, telephone and fax numbers, and kilowatt and station number data. TSS indicates if fax numbers were withheld.

Four divisions mark off the major portions of this tool. The state and city division alphabetically lists state and city markets. The national television section lists scores of nationwide broadcast and cable coverage, while the national radio section does the same for radio. The index lists stations in alphabetical order by show name or call letters.

Some of the defects of PMS are not readily apparent in TSS. The three-ring binder for this tool, however, failed to survive shipping and is not shelf-worthy, making the quality of materials selected questionable. While TSS provides more esoteric data not easily found in other sources, it does contain material already to be found in *Gale Directory of Publications and Broadcast Media* (see ARBA 94, entry 988), *Broadcasting & Cable Yearbook* (R. R. Bowker, 1994), and *Editor & Publisher Market Guide* (see entry 976-977). Neither PMS nor TSS appears worth the money it would cost to own them. Unless libraries have no other means for locating this material, or have money to burn, neither of these volumes would be worthy of library shelves.—**Mark Y. Herring**

990. Radio Amateur Callbook, 1995: International Listings. 73d ed. New York, Radio Amateur Callbook/Watson-Guptill, 1995. 1840p. $35.00pa. ISBN 0-8230-8720-4.

Essentially a directory of amateur ham radio operators, this volume covers the world, excluding North America and Hawaii. Call letter entries in bold typeface are followed by a name and address of the operator holding that broadcasting license. Addresses list street number and name, city name, state/district, and country—zip codes are lacking. The radio call letters are arranged alphabetically. A one-page guide linking letter codes to country names precedes the directory listings. Another preface is a census of amateur radio operators worldwide by zip code prefix (for example, there are 1,540 licenses in Denver's 802 prefix). Other prefaces list international postal rates; time zones; standard ("Q") radio signals; and telegraph codes.

Published annually to stay as current as possible, this is clearly a standard source for ham radio operators. Its usefulness is limited somewhat by the tiny typeface size. Libraries purchasing this hefty paperback should have a magnifying lens on hand. Although many ham operators will buy their own copies, libraries should still consider this for purchase.—**Ed Volz**

Handbooks and Yearbooks

991. Broadcast News: July 1994 Through June 1995. [CD-ROM]. Woodbridge, Conn., Research Publications, 1995. Minimum system requirements: IBM or compatible 386. CD-ROM drive with 150K/sec transfer rate and MS-DOS CD-ROM Extensions. Windows. 5MB hard disk space. 4MB memory. 2MB extended memory. 256-color VGA monitor (640 x 480 or higher). Windows-compatible mouse. Printer (optional). $2,295.00. ISSN 1074-5483.

Billing itself as the first CD-ROM reference database for network news, *Broadcast News* provides quick and simple access to more than 60 broadcast and cable news programs, ranging from *All Things Considered* to *Washington Week in Review*. At first glance, this database appears to be a dressed-up version of its Internet-based competitor, *Journal Graphics*, but *Broadcast News* furnishes more than just a CD-ROM-based index to current events and news programming and commentary. It offers program, network, host/anchor, keyword, date, and subject access to these programs, as well as word-for-word transcriptions of the actual broadcasts.

The opening screen offers an index of networks and shows, advanced and guided search modes, and a selective list of current issues. Program transcripts can be viewed on-screen, printed off, or downloaded as text files. Transcript layout is clear and easy to understand. Each disc contains 12 months' worth of programs, updated monthly, with slightly more than a 30-day time lag. Programs are professionally transcribed, but in order to meet deadlines, each transcript warns that the transcripts have not been proofread against the original tape.

Broadcast News can be installed as either a DOS or a Windows application; however, the program must be installed on C:\ drive. It is also compatible with Novell 3.X networks. The program can be configured to allow users to print, export, print and export, or neither according to local needs and policies. A password option is also built into the setup program. The Windows and DOS versions have similar functionality, but the Windows display is definitely showier. Both versions allow for Boolean logic, including NOT, WITHOUT, ADJ, NEAR—**Steven J. Schmidt**

992. MacDonald, Ron. A Broadcast News Manual of Style. 2d ed. New York, Longman, 1994. 224p. index. $13.75pa. ISBN 0-8013-1110-1.

The stated reasons necessitating this 2d edition reflect changes in the ways that news is gathered and reported since its predecessor was published in 1987; specifically, the widespread use of computers and satellites in the news business. Certain axioms still apply, however, and MacDonald's compendium of conventions, rules, and guidelines will assist fledgling and experienced newswriters and newscasters in getting it right the first time. He begins with typical script formats for radio and television presentation, giving sound advice such as "simplify, where possible." Then MacDonald, a professor of journalism after 15 years in radio and television, provides rules for such things as indentation, hyphenation, numbers, analogies, acronyms, abbreviations, and initialisms.

By far the largest portion of the book is given over to a selective usage guide, consisting of 116 pages of MacDonald's recommendations concerning when and how to use which words or other language forms. Examples of these distinctions include the subtle differences between word pairs or trios, such as *ability/capacity*, when to say authorities *believe/feel/think*, when something is *blatant/flagrant*, and how to pronounce *endive* and *en route*. Another useful feature is a brief table describing hospital patient conditions, and what connotations are commonly associated with words like *guarded, stable, serious*, and *critical*.

MacDonald also appends a useful pronouncing guide for place-names in the news, designed to assist a newsreader or reporter in saying such names as Canberra, Windhoek, Lisbon, and Bucharest. However, he does not get them all right, counseling that Kabul, the capital of Afghanistan, is pronounced "kuh-BOOL," rather than "KA-bool." Yet, such ambiguities only serve to underscore the problem with all guides of this type: Rules of spelling, usage, pronunciation, and style are really only conventions or guidelines at best, and sometimes merely (flawed) personal advice. However, as such a criticism is equally true of *all* style manuals, this one rates a purchase recommendation for its willingness to tackle tricky questions of usage that frequently trip up even the most seasoned newsreaders.—**Bruce A. Shuman**

993. Sievers, Maurice L. **Crystal Clear Volume 2: Vintage American Crystal Sets, Crystal Detectors, and Crystals.** Chandler, Ariz., Sonoran Publishing, 1995. 244p. illus. index. $29.95pa. ISBN 1-886606-03-X.

In the 1920s and 1930s, people in the United States with nothing better to do put on funny-looking headphones and started playing around with "cat's whiskers" and tiny galena crystals. Soon they were listening via these crystal radio sets to stations across the nation and the world. Sievers has chronicled this period in U.S. history with a two-volume set that describes the radios of the crystal era. Volume 1 of *Crystal Clear* is a detailed history of the 3 most important crystal set manufacturers: Wireless Specialty Apparatus Company, Radio Corporation of America, and Philmore Manufacturing Company. This volume also has hundreds of photographs and magazine advertisements that will help to identify major sets of the period.

Volume 2 of *Crystal Clear* is a continuation of the identification of crystal radio receivers that Sievers started with volume 1. Some 172 additional crystal sets, 91 additional individual crystal detector units, and 26 additional specific crystals are covered. For each item, the author supplies the manufacturer, the model, the year of production, and the original selling price, if known. Some 350 photographs of crystal sets and 160 advertisement reproductions cover crystal sets manufactured between 1910 and 1970. There is some overlap between the two volumes, with volume 2 providing additional research information found on sets covered in volume 1. Volume 2 has a comprehensive index to the set. Several essays accompany the set descriptions and cover topics such as accessories (e.g., headphones, antennas, tuners); Fahnestock clips (e.g., terminals); crystal set look-alikes; set differences; detector differences; crystal containers; and crystal names. Three tables list individual set/crystal information by manufacturer, set/crystal/detector name, price, year, and "reference." The three tables cover crystal sets, detectors, and crystals.

Sievers's set is well done, with many black-and-white illustrations. The volumes are paperback and the size most "collector" books come in. The typeface is, for the most part, large and highly readable. Most libraries with patrons interested in radio collectibles will want this set. Electrical engineering reference collections will find the set the most comprehensive source of crystal radio information available.
—**Ralph Lee Scott**

994. **The Video Annual 1994.** Jean Thibodeaux Kreamer, ed. Santa Barbara, Calif., ABC-CLIO, 1994. 396p. index. $55.00. ISBN 0-87436-741-7. ISSN 1055-0267.

The expressed purpose of this reference source on videos is to provide information for librarians and video professionals. The book is divided into seven sections. The first section, "Reports from the Field," includes what the editor feels were the year's best literature about video. Section 2, "Annual Reports from Organizations Working with Video," represents the annual reports of several key library and educational organizations involved. Section 3, "Festivals and Awards," contains information about major festivals and awards considered significant to the library community.

The fourth section, entitled "Directory of Associations and Organizations," lists those organizations and individuals involved in the use and advocacy of video as a disseminator of information, instruction, and education. Section 5, "Calendar of Video-Related Events," provides an outline of video-related conventions, meetings, and conferences scheduled during the year. Section 6, "Resource Materials," reviews materials such as professional books, reference works, periodicals, videos, and databases (online and CD-ROM). Finally, section 7, "Distributors and Producers," provides an alphabetical video directory for distribution of videos. The index is not comprehensive, but in some cases, cross-references are given. This is a source of information about the general use of video as a technology, not about specific video titles, and as such, will have limited appeal and use for most libraries.—**Gary E. Joseph**

995. **Video Rating Guide for Libraries on CD-ROM 1990-1994: A 5-Year Compilation of Over 8,900 Video Titles and Reviews.** [CD-ROM]. Santa Barbara, Calif., ABC-CLIO, 1995. Minimum system requirements: IBM PC/XT/AT or compatible. ISO 9660-compatible CD-ROM drive with controller and interface cable. MS-DOS or PC-DOS 3.0. 512K memory, 384K free. 20MB hard disk drive, 700K free. Floppy disk drive. $125.00 (single user); $187.50 (network).

The *Video Rating Guide for Libraries on CD-ROM* contains more than 9,000 reviews for educational, special-interest, informational, and children's videos published between the years 1990 and 1994. This easy-to-use guide provides a one- to five-star rating for each video, as well as a descriptive and evaluative review, awards won, production information, availability, and price information. The software interface makes it easy to create a set of video listings applicable to a specific audience group, on a specific topic, and in a certain price range.

There are a variety of subject access points (title, descriptor, and subject) that aid in creating a more comprehensive search. Context-sensitive help screens allow users to work at their own pace without much assistance. The documentation is on the slim side, and could be better with a more detailed chapter on installation in addition to providing an explanatory illustration of a full record and its fields. However, the combination of useful information and the ease of searching the database would make a welcome addition to any school or academic library that supports programs in teacher education.

—**Elizabeth A. Ginno**

996. **The Video Source Book 1996: A Guide to Programs Currently Available on Video....** 17th ed. Terri Kessler Schell and others, eds. Detroit, Gale, 1995. 2v. index. $275.00/set. ISBN 0-8103-9087-6. ISSN 0748-0881.

The overgrown entry in the VideoHound series of reference books, these two volumes list 145,000 video programs available in the National Television Standard Code (NTSC) technical transmission format. Which is to say, if it can be played on North American A/V equipment (VHS, Beta, videodisc, 8mm, and $\frac{3}{4}$-inch U-matic), it is likely to be included here. This edition includes approximately 19,000 more items than the 1993 edition (see ARBA 94, entry 1020). Types of programs listed are feature films, rock videos, educational/instructional shorts, how-to videos, industrial films, anthologies of sports highlights, television programs reissued on video, cartoons, and so forth. The concise yet comprehensive individual entries list program title, year of release, Motion Picture Association of America rating, evaluative/critical rating, brief synopsis, running time, format options, credits, intended audience level, means of acquisition, distributor, price, and more. The "credits" element for the feature film entries alone is of a quality not usually found in such guidebooks.

Among the information here is cast listings that include nearly any actor with a speaking part, full screenwriter listings, and awards won (U.S. and foreign). A subject index uses 480 terms to categorize entries—feature films as well as nonfiction programs. A directors/cast members index notes even brief appearances by actors (e.g., Harrison Ford's one-liner in *Dead Heat on a Merry-Go-Round*) and lists television and feature film credits together (e.g., Lucille Ball's *I Love Lucy* video compilations are combined with her movies). In the general body of the text, all items are thrown together in one alphabet. This eases use but leads to dissonant juxtapositions, such as these entries from page 205: *Begotten* (an obscure 1991 silent feature), followed by Don Siegal's 1970 Clint Eastwood melodrama *The Beguiled*, followed by *Behave, Bernard!*, a 1986 dog etiquette short. Other indexes list programs by their alternate titles (changed in reissue or importation), by distributor name (with complete contact information), and by special format (e.g., captioned).

Bowker's Complete Video Directory (see entry 986), the ongoing challenger to this source, has a superior feature: quarterly updates platformed on CD-ROM. Other reviews of *The Video Source Book* have noted as a flaw the inclusion of out-of-print items, so these volumes are not a "videos in print" tool such as the R. R. Bowker publication. This reviewer wonders if such out-of-print listings could be valuable as archival information, and interesting simply as film history.

Despite its price, libraries of various types and sizes should consider this work for purchase, certainly if the aforementioned R. R. Bowker guide is not owned. Large libraries will want both sources. Few verification/ready-reference tools are as likely to be browsed for fun by staff and patrons alike.—**Ed Volz**

997. **WRTH Satellite Broadcasting Guide.** 1995 ed. New York, Billboard Books/Watson-Guptill, 1995. 384p. illus. maps. $24.95pa. ISBN 0-8230-5955-3.

An ambitious book that covers information on everything about satellite broadcasting from basic information to installing your own satellite system, it also covers satellite information for countries around the world. Descriptions of satellite technology and its history provide a good background for the reader. As the book progresses through information on transmission techniques, receiving satellite signals, broadcasting systems, and installation, the information becomes more technical. Charts, graphs, and a glossary will help most readers use the book, but it may take some effort to understand the information if they are not familiar with broadcasting terms.

A useful section on how to buy a satellite television system is included in one of the chapters. If readers are ambitious enough, they may want to install the system. In addition to helpful instructions on how to do so, a gentle warning is given that it takes a professional several hours to install a satellite system, but the beginner should plan a weekend or longer to install it. One caution about the book is that sometimes the diagrams and information are for European products. One specific example is on the section for installing a VCR: The diagram shows a European video machine with channels 30-39 as the connecting channels. It should not detract from the usability of the book as long as readers are aware that they may have to use the installation information given with the products bought.

Worldwide information is provided on satellite coverage zones and transmission schedules. The future form of the satellite is the direct broadcasting satellite, and a chapter has been added to the book to cover that new technology. For the reader who wants to find additional information, the book also provides a list of organizations around the world related to telecommunications. Public and academic libraries will find this a usable resource where broadcasting and satellites are of interest.

—**Suzanne Julian**

Indexes

998. **Burrelle's Index of Broadcast Transcripts: A Comprehensive Index to Thousands of News Broadcasts....** 1993 ed. Livingston, N.J., Burrelle's Information Services, 1994. 465p. $69.95; $49.95pa.

The 1993 *Burrelle's Index of Broadcast Transcripts* offers a useful subject index to approximately 120 news and public affairs programs. Shows or news programs that already offer transcription services of their own (such as *Oprah*) are not indexed. Subject headings range from the very general to the specific, such as "Health" and "Gangs" to "New-Nazis" and "Christian Coalition." People are listed under their name and are furnished when they are either interviewed or talked about. The index would have been more helpful if it included an additional index that cross-referenced the program to the subject. This would alleviate the tediousness of wading through seven pages of listings under a popular subject like "Medical Care" when the reader only wants a particular episode of *PrimeTime Live*, for example. The index provides easy ordering instructions for each listed broadcast transcript. A five-year cumulation of *Burrelle's Index* on CD-ROM would be of even greater interest. This resource will be very useful for public libraries and those academic libraries supporting a large journalism program.—**Elizabeth A. Ginno**

21 Decorative Arts

COLLECTING

Antiques

999. Johnston, Phillip M. **Catalogue of American Silver: The Cleveland Museum of Art.** Cleveland, Ohio, The Cleveland Museum of Art and Bloomington, Ind., Indiana University Press, 1994. 180p. illus. index. $65.00. ISBN 0-940717-22-0.

  The Cleveland Museum of Art has a collection of American silver, pieces made before 1820, from makers of New England and masters working in the Boston area. This collection is primarily the achievement of Hollis French, an engineer, who was both a collector of silver and a recognized authority and writer on the subject. Records indicate that well more than half of the 103 entries in the original exhibition of 1916 were lent by French. French continued to make silver purchases, and in 1940, shortly before his death, he gave the silver on loan to the museum in addition to 70 other pieces, making a total donation of 200 examples. Although in size and importance French's collection is the most significant segment of the American silver holdings at the museum, other benefactors made worthy contributions.

  New research methods were used to gain information for this catalog. X-ray fluorescence was chosen for analyzing the collection. The catalog gives detailed, specific data and aids in a more complete understanding of the objects. It is extensively illustrated and documented, giving size and weight of each piece, mark, gift, engravings, collection, exhibition, and literature. A bibliography precedes the catalog, and an index of silversmiths and accession numbers follow it. An indispensable reference for collectors, dealers, and scholars of American silver, the catalog should be in every art and museum library collection.—**Kathleen J. Voigt**

1000. **Warman's Antiques and Collectibles Price Guide: The Essential Field Guide to the Antiques and Collectibles Marketplace.** 29th ed. Harry L. Rinker, ed. Radnor, Pa., Wallace-Homestead Book/Chilton Book, 1995. 835p. illus. index. $14.95pa. ISBN 0-87069-734-X. ISSN 0196-2272.

  Intended as a buyer's guide to middle-range prices of objects made from 1700 to the present, *Warman's* is a classic. For prices, the editor has consulted dealers and collectors, read trade literature, visited shows, and scanned price lists from more than 70 auction houses acknowledged in the preliminaries. Anomalies in prices, such as the Warhol cookie jars, are noted. Entries are alphabetical, ranging from an individual manufacturer (Royal Doulton); an object (radios); and a collection specialty (paper ephemera, children's toy dishes, Coca-Cola items); to major categories (e.g., furniture, pattern glass). As well as prices, each entry provides such details as a brief history, references (with other Warman publications much cited), periodicals, collectors' clubs, museums, reproduction alerts, and additional listings that refer to related entries. Almost every opening has a small illustration, either a photograph with caption and price or a line drawing.

  The index is important to locate entries, to pull together all references to a particular item (inkwells are an entry but can also be found in 18 other entries) and to locate items only listed in broader entries (marbles in the index refers to Bennington). With a few exceptions (barber poles are included under architectural elements but not indexed) the index works well. Folk art, which has been popular for several years, is not a strength in *Warman's*, although the two-page entry notes ongoing debate about definitions.

The references do not cite Nina Fletcher Little, whose collections made headlines at Sotheby's in 1994, and no additional listings are identified despite the linking of some folk art objects through the index. Running heads help the browser, although for large entries such as furniture, they do not show subdivisions (candlestands, stands, and tables). *Warman's* remains a public library basic, and it costs less than most works on antiques and collectibles.—**Patricia Fleming**

Books

1001. **ABC for Book Collectors.** 7th ed. By John Carter; revised by Nicolas Barker. New Castle, Del., Oak Knoll Books, 1995. 224p. $25.00. ISBN 1-884718-05-1.

1002. **Antiquarian Books: A Companion for Booksellers, Librarians and Collectors.** Philippa Bernard, with Leo Bernard and Angus O'Neill, comps. and eds. Philadelphia, University of Pennsylvania Press, 1994. 461p. illus. index. $79.95. ISBN 0-8122-3268-2.

Both of these works are intended for use by buyers and sellers of used and rare books. Although *ABC for Book Collectors* and *Antiquarian Books* each contain approximately 450 alphabetically arranged entries, and each book displays a British perspective toward the subject, they differ in important respects. Significant omissions in either are few; however, examples include Eric Gill and noctuary. For U.S. librarians, the absence of such common terms as "front matter" and "prefatory material" (and the lack of cross-references from these terms) is frustrating. Instead, one must look under "Preliminary Leaves" (in *ABC*) or "Prelims" (in *Antiquarian*).

With revisions by internationally revered bookman Barker, *ABC* (first issued in 1952) is a glossary of such terms as "dentelle," "imprimatur," and "provenance." Its language is a model of spareness and clarity, and the entries range from a few sentences to more than 1,000 words (the average appears to be 50-250 words). Despite the text's British bias, such U.S. cognates as "backbone" (for "backstrip") and "call-number" (for "press-mark") are given. For its U.S. audience, the work's intelligibility is also increased by a four-page table of abbreviations in the front matter. Biographical entries are sparse, with bookbinder Samuel Mearne meriting inclusion, but (surprisingly) not William Caxton. No illustrations appear in *ABC*; no bibliographical citations follow respective entries, nor will one find a list of suggested readings elsewhere in the book.

At three times the cost of *ABC*, the sumptuously produced *Antiquarian* is beyond the budget of all but the largest public or academic libraries. Duplicating much of the information in *ABC*, *Antiquarian*'s price is nonetheless justified, due to its dozens of black-and-white illustrations and its 30 discursive articles, which often run 5 to 10 pages each. Written by a commissioned group of subject experts, these signed essays focus on such topics as "Autographs and Manuscripts," "Natural History Books," and "Restoration and Repair." *Antiquarian* also contains dozens of biographical articles (e.g., John Baskerville, Thomas Dibdin, and Michael Sadleir). Many entries are accompanied by a few bibliographical citations. Several appendixes complete the volume; the most valuable back matter, however, is an author bibliography. It should be noted that of its nearly 300 entries, fewer than 10 percent are U.S. writers.

Those libraries owning *The Bookman's Glossary* (R. R. Bowker/Reed Reference Publishing, 1983) may choose to forgo *ABC* or *Antiquarian*, the latter two each containing but one-fourth the number of entries in the former. Despite its datedness, lack of illustrations, and brevity of entries, *The Bookman's Glossary* provides definitions of many technical terms and profiles of many individuals indigenous to U.S. (as opposed to British) publishing, past and present. Libraries catering to the ardent bibliophile will want to purchase *ABC* or *Antiquarian*; few institutions, however, will have the need—or money—for both.—**Jeffrey E. Long**

1003. **Book Prices: Used and Rare 1995.** Edward N. Zempel and Linda A. Verkler, eds. Peoria, Ill., Spoon River Press, 1995. 798p. $69.00. ISBN 0-930358-12-0.

Book collectors, bookdealers, and special collections librarians are constantly in need of the current market value of collectable books. For the past three decades, they have relied on two reference works: the annual *American Book Prices Current* (see ARBA 77, entry 68; ARBA 75, entry 61; ARBA 73, entry 50; and ARBA 70, v. 1, p. 15), which reports auction prices, and the twice-yearly *Bookman's Price Index* (BPI) (see entry 1004), which reports catalog prices. Because both works are expensive, there is a niche for a less expensive reference work that will supply the same information.

Book Prices: Used and Rare 1995 fills one of these niches. It brings together in alphabetical order the catalogs of 170 well-known American and British antiquarian book dealers at a price well below that of its competitor (the latest volume of BPI retails for $240). There is considerable overlap in the dealer catalogs used by both works, and while BPI has special sections for association copies and fine bindings and includes foreign titles, this is not enough to offset the large difference in price. Frugal book collectors and bookdealers are thus advised to make *Book Prices* their priority purchase for personal use and to consult BPI at the nearest library. Perhaps in the near future, *Book Prices* will be able to list auction prices as well as catalog prices, thus becoming an even more useful reference tool.—**Joseph Cataio**

1004. **Bookman's Price Index: A Guide to the Values of Rare and Other Out-of-Print Books. Volume 50.** Anne F. McGrath, ed. Detroit, Gale, 1995. 911p. $240.00. ISBN 0-8103-9147-3. ISSN 0068-0141.

Since its inception in 1964, *Bookman's Price Index* (BPI) has become the most widely used reference work for checking the current market value of collectible books (see ARBA 94, entry 1025, and ARBA 91, entry 981, for reviews of earlier volumes). Published on a twice-yearly basis, each volume collects together in one alphabetical sequence the catalogs of approximately 160 of the best antiquarian bookdealers in the United States and England. Until recently, the only other one-volume source of market value information on collectible books was the yearly *American Book Prices Current* (Bancroft Parkman), which reports auction prices rather than dealer catalog prices.

Now, however, BPI has a worthy competitor—the newly established, annually published *Book Prices: Used and Rare* (BPUAR) (see entry 1003), which collects together in an alphabetical list approximately the same number of top-flight antiquarian book dealer catalogs at one-third the cost of BPI. BPI still provides more comprehensive coverage of the collectible book market since it appears every six months and since it includes foreign-language titles, which are excluded by BPUAR. However, the significantly lower price of BPUAR combined with its more than adequate comprehensiveness may well make it, rather than BPI, the priority purchase among frugal book collectors, bookdealers, and librarians. In light of this possibility, BPI may want to consider reducing its price or significantly increasing the number of bookdealer catalogs included in each volume.—**Joseph Cataio**

1005. Hand, Richard A. **A Bookman's Guide to Archaeology: A Compilation of over 7,000 Books Pertaining to the Scientific Study of Prehistoric and Historic People....** Metuchen, N.J., Scarecrow, 1994. 1022p. index. $110.00. ISBN 0-8108-2946-0.

This interesting but flawed title is a bibliographical price guide for the collector, dealer, librarian, or other book person. It contains the author, title, size, collation, imprint, type of illustration, dust jacket, binding, and valuation of 7,106 entries having a retail price of more than $10. An additional 2,247 variant or duplicate entries are also valued. Some entries have annotations from 200 United States, South African, and German dealers' catalogs that are the foundation of the work. The bibliographical data and annotations are a strength. Entries are in author order and there are separate title and subject indexes. This is Hand's third book price guide and all have the same flaw: There is no indication of the dealer from whom he obtained the valuation. Other price guides, such as Richard L. Collins's *Mandeville's Used Book Price Guide* (Price Guide Publishers, 1994); Zempel and Verkler's *Book Prices: Used and Rare* (see entry 1003); or *Bookman's Price Index* (see entry 1004), use a code to indicate the dealer. In the relatively small antiquarian and used book market, knowing who priced the book is very important. This omission is unfortunate as no other price guides cover the topic as well (e.g., its Bureau of American Ethnology entries are more complete than any other guide). Useful because of its bibliographical strengths for libraries serving institutions with archaeology departments but of questionable value as a price guide, this is a marginal and expensive purchase.—**Patrick J. Brunet**

1006. **Private Libraries in Renaissance England: A Collection and Catalogue of Tudor and Early Stuart Book-Lists. Volume III: PLRE 67-86.** R. J. Fehrenbach, ed. Binghamton, N.Y., Medieval & Renaissance Texts & Studies, State University of New York, 1994. 282p. index. (Medieval & Renaissance Texts & Studies, v.87). $28.00. ISBN 0-86698-170-5.

Volume 3 of *Private Libraries in Renaissance England* (PLRE) continues the work begun in volumes 1 and 2 of the series (see ARBA 94, entries 598 and 599), with descriptions by 16 scholars of the contents of 20 more libraries (numbers 67 through 86 in the continuous listing). The format established with such care in volume 1 is maintained: a brief biography of the owner of the library, a brief list of the books, followed by a more detailed account of them. This more detailed account provides the name of the author; the title of the work; names of other contributors to the work; place of publication; stationer (publisher, printer, bookseller); date or range of dates; STC status, annotations; languages; cost or appraised value and the date on which the evaluation was made; and the current location of the book. Manuscripts held in these libraries are also described.

A list of reference sources cited is provided, and, at the end, a "PLRE Cumulative Catalogue," covering volumes 1-3, provides "Owners of Book-lists Arranged by Owners' Names," "Owners of Book-lists According to PLRE Number," "Dates of Book-lists," and a series of "Summaries and Concordances" that include "Manuscript Types," "Renaissance Locations of Book-lists," "Professions of Owners," and "Social Status of Owners." Indexes to authors and works, editors and compilers, translators, stationers, places of publication, and dates of publication for this volume are also provided.—**Dean H. Keller**

1007. Siegel, David S., and Susan Siegel. **The Used Book Lover's Guide to the Midwest.** Yorktown Heights, N.Y., Book Hunter Press, 1995. 449p. illus. maps. index. $17.95pa. ISBN 0-9634112-3-3.

Covering Illinois, Indiana, Iowa, Kentucky, Michigan, Minnesota, Missouri, Ohio, West Virginia, and Wisconsin, this is the fourth volume in the Siegels' series of regional guides to used book dealers. As in previous editions (see ARBA 94, entries 1027-1028), the information is comprehensive and arranged to provide easy access to the 1,000-plus dealers included.

The helpful preface defines terms and explains the arrangement. Within state chapters, open and by-appointment dealers are listed by location, with mail-order dealers listed alphabetically in a separate section for each state. Some shops in antique malls are included, although the authors state that they have not researched all the antique malls in the Midwest. Only dealers who responded to questionnaires or whom the authors were able to contact by telephone are included.

Information on dealers includes kinds and number of books, specialties, addresses, telephone numbers, hours, services (e.g., searches, want lists, mail orders, catalogs, appraisals), acceptance of credit cards, owner, year established, and, for open shops, detailed instructions on how to drive to the shop. One warning: Given the nature of the used book business, the authors stress telephoning ahead to verify when and whether the shop is indeed open. The authors have also included comments on their visits to open shops. Because their visits seem to have been brief and their viewpoint subjective, some knowledgeable book persons will disagree with their conclusions. These notes do, however, provide useful data and insights.

Additional helpful features include area maps, cross-indexing by dealer name and geographical location, and a specialty index of 250 subject categories. Recommended for libraries, for book buyers and browsers, and particularly for traveling book lovers.—**Mary Lou Unterburger**

Coins and Paper Money

1008. **A Guide Book of United States Coins, 1996.** 49th ed. By R. S. Yeoman. Kenneth Bressett, ed. Racine, Wis., Western Publishing, 1995. 311p. illus. index. $7.95pa. ISBN 0-307-19902-9.

Known simply as the "red book" for almost 50 years, this guidebook to U.S. coins has been the standard for both collectors and dealers. The first 14 pages provide definitions to terminology and an early history of coinage in the Americas. The remainder of the guide is a listing of colonial and U.S. coins, tokens, medals, and related materials. Photographs, variations, coin grades, mintages, history, and suggested market values are given for each. The prices listed reflect only conservative market values at the time of the publication of the guidebook, and are not meant to serve as a price list for dealers' stock or collectors' sales.

Colonial coinage is described first. U.S. government issues are then presented, by denomination and then chronologically by first year of issue. The book closes with commemorative and private issues. This organization allows for easy lookup. Another aid to finding a specific listing is the large boldface headings for each coin type. Even when the headings fall in the middle of a page, they are easy to locate. The photographs are clear and sharp, even when they are small. Most collectors will have personal copies, but as the standard in the field, the guidebook is recommended for all reference collections.—**Margaret F. Dominy**

Guns

1009. Schwing, Ned, and Herbert Houze. **Standard Catalog of Firearms.** 5th ed. Iola, Wis., Krause, 1995. 912p. illus. $27.95pa. ISBN 0-87341-351-2.

Previously reviewed in ARBA 93 (see entry 1004), the current edition builds on the earlier one with updated pricing estimates and new firearms additions. Approximately 10,000 models of guns and more than 1,000 manufacturers are listed. Whenever possible, a brief historical note of the company and the guns is provided. Illustrations of many of the weapons and a pricing classification guide consisting of six categories make up the individual entries. Updated material on the Violent Crime Control and Law Enforcement Act of 1994 is provided so that users of the catalog may be aware of potential problems before making a purchase. Trade name, manufacturer, and importer address listings appear as appendixes. The current edition of this work still remains the single best resource for individuals looking for basic pricing and historical information on firearms. The price is reasonable, and any public library will benefit from the work's inclusion on the shelf.—**Gregory Curtis**

Toys

1010. Oppenheim, Joanne, and Stephanie Oppenheim. **The Best Toys, Books & Videos for Kids: The 1995 Guide to 1,000+ Kid-Tested, Classic and New Products for Ages 0-10.** New York, HarperCollins, 1994. 375p. illus. index. $12.00pa. ISBN 0-06-273315-X. ISSN 1076-433X.

This inexpensive book is more than just a list of new and classic products for children, and more than its title indicates, since it also covers CD-ROMs/software, audio, and special needs materials. The authors state that theirs is the only independent consumer review of children's media; a list of criteria that they and their testers (families "from all walks of life") use when evaluating products is provided in the introduction. Among other things, the product's developmental "fit," safety, encouragement of active learning, and message are considered. A rating system indicates outstanding products of the year, "Blue Chip Classics," and materials that can be used by children with special needs.

Chapters for each type of product are divided into age ranges, such as infants, toddlers, preschool, and so on. A large amount of useful information is provided in chapter introductions (how different toys fit different developmental needs and abilities, basic principles of reading and reading aloud for various age groups) and in "tip" boxes (on safety, shopping, activities, related books) and checklists (of classics, basic gear, things to avoid, best birthday gifts for every age and budget, and more) scattered throughout the text. The short, descriptive reviews also indicate price, publisher/manufacturer (telephone numbers for some), and recommended age range. Publication dates are not provided. The classic "red trike" from Hedstrom gets a Blue Chip award; *Beethoven Lives Upstairs* in both video and book formats are recommended (but the audiotape is not listed); and "a storybook or board game or magazine subscription" is the best birthday gift in the under $15 category for ages 5 to 10.

The subject index could be improved. For instance, "Encyclopedias" refers to the pages for printed versions only, although CD-ROM encyclopedias are also covered, and access to tip/checklist data is not always provided. There is also a brand-name and title index, in which products are annoyingly listed under manufacturer name. To find Play-Doh, one must look under Playskool; American Girls dolls is under Pleasant Company. The Oppenheims' book is designed primarily as a buying guide for parents, and should be placed in most circulating collections. As it is a serial, expect a yearly update. Its lack of full bibliographic citations and poor indexing should be balanced against the need for ratings of kids' products when considering purchase for reference. Similar coverage is provided by the American Library Association's *The Best of the Best for Children* (Random House, 1993), *Play, Learn, and Grow* (see ARBA 94, entry 1184), and *The Elementary School Library Collection* (19th ed.; see ARBA 95, entries 661-662).

—**Deborah V. Rollins**

CRAFTS

1011. Benmour, Linda. **The Bead Directory.** 3d ed. Oakland, Calif., Ben-Stone Press and The Bead Directory, 1995. 247p. illus. $18.95pa. ISBN 1-883153-18-2.

This nationwide mail-order and traveler's shopping guide to more than 400 bead stores and mail-order bead resources in the United States, Canada, England, and Taiwan provides a rich source of information for the craftsperson's search for foreign, Native American, African, and other beads. Bead stores are listed by state, with entries arranged under each state in alphabetical order (by name of store, along with address, telephone number, and fax number; hours of service; owners and contact persons; specialities; retail and wholesale supplies; custom work and bead bazaars/craft show capabilities; retail and mail-order capabilities; payment type accepted; classes offered; finished pieces available; and gallery space provided). Following the section divided by state is a listing of mail-order businesses, arranged alphabetically.

A brief descriptive annotation about each store is included. Advertisements are scattered throughout the entries. Appendixes list associations and organizations, bead societies, bead bazaars, books and videos, classes, conferences/museum exhibits, magazines/newsletters, museums, and cross-references. Although not a comprehensive directory of stores selling beads, it provides an excellent sampling. It will be of use to any artist or craftsperson with a serious interest in beadwork.—**Maureen Pastine**

1012. Boyd, Margaret A. **The Crafts Supply Source Book: A Comprehensive Shop-by-Mail Guide for Thousands of Craft Materials.** 3d ed. Cincinnati, Ohio, Betterway Books/F & W Publications, 1994. 298p. illus. index. $16.99pa. ISBN 1-55870-355-1.

Because public libraries generally seek to serve the many needs of their clientele (beyond current fiction and best-sellers), making a wide range of other materials available is important. One important category is publications that can help users pursue hobbies, home industries, and other activities, whether to make money or simply have fun. This includes a range of publications that describe how to make crafts. *The Crafts Supply Source Book* is a good supplement to those publications because it provides craftmakers with an array of commercial sources for needed materials.

While its nearly 100-page section on supplies for needlecrafts, sewing, and fiber arts is especially strong, its initial section of more than 150 pages provides fair coverage of suppliers for more than 40 general arts, crafts, and hobbies. These cover everything from basketry and seat weaving to kite making, photography, sign making, and even tattooing and taxidermy. A shorter section on resources provides limited information about appropriate associations, books and booksellers, the general craft business, publications, and supportive materials and aids. A lengthy index furnishes access to the contents by the names of the many associations, firms, individuals, and publications listed in the text. Aimed more at amateur than professional craftspeople, the guide is still a useful and valuable addition for many public library collections.—**Norman D. Stevens**

1013. Florence, Gene. **The Collector's Encyclopedia of Depression Glass.** 11th ed. Paducah, Ky., Collector Books, 1994. 223p. illus. $19.95. ISBN 0-89145-554-X.

Authentic depression glass is colored glassware manufactured between the late 1920s and 1940. When it was mass-produced, it usually sold in small stores or was given away for various promotions. Florence, well known in the antiques field, notes that prices for depression glass have soared over the past 20 years. This frequently updated price guide describes 122 design patterns (Adam to Windsor), plus some reproduction pieces. Entries for each pattern include one or more color photographs of full sets or specialty items. The corresponding price lists are for mint-condition pieces and are arranged according to available colors. Dealers generally pay 30 to 50 percent less than prices quoted here. Asterisks warn collectors about reproductions, price variations, or other particulars. In most cases there is a somewhat chatty paragraph that gives useful details about the manufacturer, the rarity of certain items, color variations, and more. Considering Florence's glossy, hardcover format and his attention to detail, this is a better buy than *The Kovels' Illustrated Price Guide to Depression Glass and American Dinnerware* (2d ed.; see ARBA 85, entry 839), which is also frequently updated.—**Gary D. Barber**

1014. **Index to How to Do It Information: 1994 Supplement.** Norman M. Lathrop, comp. Wooster, Ohio, Norman Lathrop Enterprises, 1995. 202p. $35.00pa. ISBN 0-910868-94-8.

Lathrop's index is a supplement that provides citations for how-to and hobby-related articles published during 1994 only. The entries are alphabetical by subject, and each gives a brief description of the article contents. Previous editions include a 1963-1989 cumulation and a 1990 supplement. There is no coverage for 1991 through 1993, however (these supplements are scheduled to appear later). Also provided are a citation appendix that lists the magazines reviewed in alphabetical order and an errata appendix that acknowledges numerous corrections and additions to previous editions. The index is of limited use without access to the periodicals or an available interlibrary loan service. For a fee, the publisher/compiler will try to locate and copy articles for individuals.—**Jean Engler**

1015. Patterson, Alex. **Hopi Pottery Symbols.** Boulder, Colo., Johnson Books, 1994. 272p. illus. index. $17.95pa. ISBN 1-55566-120-3.

Alexander Stephen, a Scot who lived at Keam's Canyon trading post during the 1880s and 1890s, collected Hopi pottery for Thomas Keam. The purpose was to build a collection for sale. To enhance the collection's value, Stephen prepared a "manuscript catalog." This publication is a compilation of material found in the two existing copies of the manuscript and some material from the Bureau of Ethnology archives. While parts of the manuscript have been published in other works on Hopi ceramics, this is the first time the full manuscript has appeared in print.

Patterson did not fully convince this reviewer that Stephen's interpretations of the ceramic designs were accurate. (Ruth Bunzel's study of Southwestern ceramics did not reveal any consistent symbolism.) It would be interesting to read what a Hopi anthropologist thinks about Stephen's material.

Is this a reference book? In a very specialized sense it is. The last 132 pages of the text consist of an alphabetical listing of major symbol categories such as arrow, bear, and cloud. As one would expect, there are ample black-and-white illustrations, as well as eight color plates. Patterson also included a glossary of Hopi, Navajo, Spanish, Greek, Latin, and Old English terms used by Stephen in the manuscript; a short bibliography; and an index. However, the book's primary use would be in a museum setting where a person was studying Hopi pottery, not in a library reference department. Individuals who collect Hopi ceramics will probably buy a copy, as will museum libraries and libraries specializing in southwestern native peoples. This is an interesting but highly specialized book best suited for the circulating collection.
—**G. Edward Evans**

DESIGN

1016. Ruhling, Nancy, and John Crosby Freeman. **The Illustrated Encyclopedia of Victoriana: A Comprehensive Guide to the Designs, Customs, and Inventions of the Victorian Era.** Philadelphia, Running Press, 1994. 208p. illus. index. $24.95. ISBN 1-56138-405-4.

Compiled from the authors' replies to "what-is-it?" queries at the magazine *Victorian Homes*, this work presents about 500 objects and aspects of Victorian life in the United States. Avowedly eclectic, the entries range from architecture and planning through gardens, domestic furnishings, and clothing, as well as biographical notes and subjects such as camp meeting grounds, phrenology, spring cleaning, and women's colleges. Most topics are outlined in a few sentences, some succinctly and others superficially.

There is at least one, and usually two, colored illustrations for each entry; many are full- or half-page, although smaller silhouette photographs and sketches are also used, often on a disconcerting angle. Lush, generic Victorian-style interiors and settings predominate. Despite the profusion, some deserving entries, particularly those on architecture that identify a specific building, are not illustrated; in other examples a stock photograph, such as the shelf of toys with racing cars, an airplane, and an *Oz* book, is merely distracting.

The three-page bibliography includes contemporary and current sources, although reprints of the Victorian works do not appear. Cross-references have not been provided, and indexing is sometimes capricious: The broad term "Schools" covers the entry on colleges and universities, but not the one on women's colleges, while "Building" refers to capitols but not city halls, and warehouses but not banks.

Although the book is attractive and interesting, it falls short as an encyclopedia in the consistency and documentation of entries and illustrations and in access both to the entries and to broader themes and topics. [R: LJ, 15 Apr 95, p. 66]—**Patricia Fleming**

FASHION

1017. **Contemporary Fashion.** Richard Martin, ed. Detroit, St. James Press, 1995. 575p. illus. index. $135.00. ISBN 1-55862-173-3.

Contemporary Fashion is a much-needed addition to the area of biographical fashion reference. It is international in scope, providing access to more than 400 clothing designers, accessory designers, and design houses. Each entry furnishes a personal and professional biography, including awards, exhibitions, and an address; a bibliography of books and articles by and about the designer; a critical essay by a scholar in the field; and in some cases, a designer statement about work and design philosophy.

The scope of this work is 1945 to the present, and it covers early designers such as Fortuny, Elsa Schiaparelli, Rodier, and Liberty of London, to current designers such as Vivienne Westwood and Issey Miyake. This source is illustrated with handsome black-and-white photographs, exemplifying the work of the designers. The editor, the curator of the Costume Institute of the Metropolitan Museum of Art, has assembled an excellent group of fashion experts as contributors. A nationality and a name index are also included. *Contemporary Fashion* is an essential purchase for any library collection fielding questions in the area of fashion.—**Monica Fusich**

PHOTOGRAPHY

1018. **Contemporary Photographers.** 3d ed. Martin Marix Evans, ed. Detroit, St. James Press, 1995. 1234p. illus. index. $160.00. ISBN 1-55862-190-3.

By all positive standards, the 3d edition of this worldwide survey is a remarkable compilation for its depth of coverage as well as for a truly extraordinary gathering of facts and expert opinions. The contemporaneity of the material is stressed up front in a note from the editor, which informs us that more than 140 new entrants have been prepared for this 1995 edition and that photographers who died before 1975, along with some who have not added significantly to their corpus since the 2d edition (see ARBA 89, entry 891) are not included. This is important information for those who now own the 1987 edition, for they should most certainly hold onto it if they are seriously interested in biography and history of the art of photography.

Each entry covers copious material, with many giving a summary of the philosophy and objectives of their work in the photographer's own words. This is frequently followed up with a cogent article by an authority on the photographer's art and career. The text is immensely rewarding and highly readable as it covers the earlier generation—for example, André Kertész, Gyula Brassaï, Ansel Adams, Gordon Parks, Man Ray—through newer and prominent photographers such as Sandy Skoglund and the Bechers. The many contributions by women to the field are frequently noted, and entries are provided for Eve Arnold, Ruth Orkin, Jill Krementz, and Judith Joy Ross, as well as sometimes controversial practitioners such as Andres Serrano and Larry Clark.

The survey is universal, with a nationality index noting entries for scores of nations. The celebrated works of painter/photographers are also recognized with extensive text on David Hockney, Robert Rauschenberg, Ed Ruscha, and Andy Warhol. The richness of the current state of the art of photography when viewed from a global perspective is astounding as revealed in 1,200-plus pages of text and illustration. Electronic innovations including digital manipulation in the realm of photography will undoubtedly change the future of this art as it is known today. However, this publication serves as a definitive reference source for the next decade and well into the next century.—**William J. Dane**

1019. Roosens, Laurent, and Luc Salu. **History of Photography: A Bibliography of Books. Volume 2.** New York, Mansell/Cassell, 1994. 389p. index. $100.00. ISBN 0-7201-2152-3.

This second volume updates information presented in the earlier one (see ARBA 90, entry 943) by providing access to 5,253 additional citations on the history of photography. Books, exhibition catalogs, dissertations, and university publications are listed, as well as brochures and company literature. This volume includes information on photographers born before 1936, as compared to 1914 in the earlier volume. Both volumes are comprehensive for monographs published before 1914, and selective after 1914. The criteria for post-1914 inclusion are that the work should present an original contribution to the field, provide special coverage, or report on new topics such as television and holography.

The volume is arranged in 2,500 alphabetical subject headings and subheadings. *See also* references refer to both volumes, but no references have been made to subjects covered comprehensively in volume 1. The entries are arranged chronologically within the subject headings. The bibliographic entries include the names of author, editor, contributor, title, place and year of publication, pagination, number of illustrations in black-and-white and color, limited and luxury editions, and (in some cases) a brief comment to clarify content. An index refers to both volumes. This publication is recommended for all libraries with significant history of photography collections.—**Monica Fusich**

UPHOLSTERY

1020. James, David. **The Upholsterer's Pocket Reference Book: Materials * Measurements * Calculations.** Lewes, England, Guild of Master Craftsman; distr., New York, Sterling Publishing, 1995. 167p. illus. index. $9.95pa. ISBN 0-946819-71-8.

This is primarily a how-to-do-it book, and is intended to teach beginners the trade of upholstery. However, it does have considerable reference value, particularly in a public library. From a perusal of some of its 200 line drawings, or by a reading of the detailed instructions for assembling, gluing, sewing, or otherwise producing a finely upholstered piece of furniture, a prospective purchaser can make an informed opinion as to the quality of manufacture of a piece being considered for purchase.

Another reference value is in the introductory pages, which give approximate dates of the various European styles and influences, such as baroque, rococo, Gothic Revival, and so on. Several more pages define and illustrate specific periods, chiefly British, such as Elizabethan, Queen Anne, or art nouveau, with remarks as to what wood was used, what specific fabrics, and what types of chairs or sofas were common (for example, the "Regency Couch" or the "Morris Chair"). This information is useful for patrons who attend furniture auctions or showrooms.

The majority of the book constitutes a careful and sensible manual for the would-be upholsterer, with line drawings of works in progress, and detailed instructions for the use of hand- and machine-operated tools. A four-page, double-columned glossary of upholstering terms (e.g., bouclé, dug-roll, kanaf, orris, squab, tub chair, tester, and Turkey work) is included, and an excellent index concludes the book. It is perhaps best classed as a trade-learning book, and many catalogers would want to put it in that section; but its reference value should not be overlooked.—**Raymund F. Wood**

22 Fine Arts

GENERAL WORKS

Bibliography

1021. Piland, Sherry. **Women Artists: An Historical, Contemporary and Feminist Bibliography.** 2d ed. Metuchen, N.J., Scarecrow, 1994. 454p. illus. $59.50. ISBN 0-8108-2559-7.

First published in the heyday of the women's movement in 1976, this is the 2d edition of a pioneering resource on women artists. There have been few reference works that have attempted a biographical and bibliographical summary of women artists' lives throughout the scope of art history: Breadth of coverage continues to be a strong selling point for the new edition. Containing information on 185 artists from the tenth century A.D. to the mid-twentieth century, as well as a 60-page general bibliography, Piland's work will prove to be a useful starting place for undergraduate research.

The scope of this volume makes it worth purchasing, but it is far from a perfect reference book. Inconsistencies in format, omissions of key sources, incomplete and unexamined citations, and superficial biographical information weaken what could have been an outstanding source. At minimum, a good editor or use of a word processing program should have standardized citations that appear in an amazing array of formats and stages of completeness. For Artemisia Gentileschi (the focus of active scholarly work these days), the short biography is misleading and the bibliography omits several sources published before 1992. Perhaps Gentileschi research offers special problems, but it is hard to be confident about the rigorous accuracy of other artist entries. Thus, *Women Artists* will be useful for initiating further scholarship rather than as a defining authority on its subject.—**Stephanie C. Sigala**

Biography

1022. **A Biographical Dictionary of Artists.** rev. ed. Lawrence Gowing, ed. New York, Facts on File, 1995. 784p. illus. index. $50.00. ISBN 0-8160-3252-1.

This well-designed and handsomely printed volume was edited by Gowing, himself a painter and Slade Professor of Art at London University. The length of each of the 1,340 alphabetical entries usually matches the relative importance of the artists (although Vincent van Gogh is given more space than Leonardo da Vinci, and Holman Hunt more than Henri-Marie-Raymond de Toulouse-Lautrec), and each provides a clear, vivid, and perceptive synthesis of both the life and the work. Francis Bacon's "handling of paint [is] heavily worked in smears to suggest the vulnerability and flexibility of flesh and blood"; Goya's *Disasters of War*, which depicts "the inhumanity to which all classes in Spain had been reduced, contrasts with the self-confident sentimentality of official military art in Napoleonic France." Many, although not all, of the entries include an essential bibliography. There are also an extensive chronology, a glossary, and an index. The essays are more elaborate than those in *The Oxford Companion to Art* (see ARBA 71, entry 1079), and much broader in scope than the more individualistic pieces in *Lives of the Great Twentieth Century Artists* (see ARBA 88, entry 1010).

The only errors noticed are minor: [Diego Rodríguez de Silva] Velázquez is misspelled in the Bacon essay, Wyndham Lewis went blind in 1951 (not 1950), and Kenneth Clark's *Leonardo da Vinci* was published in 1939 (not 1967). The only significant artist missing from the book (and supplementary index) is the Italian surrealist Leonor Fini. The volume emphasizes, quite reasonably, English artists and illustrations from British museums. The essays on Jacques Callot, Vittore Carpaccio, Albrecht Dürer, Hans Holbein, Andrea Mantegna, Henry Moore, and Edvard Munch are especially good; and there are also useful articles on critics and impresarios such as Charles Baudelaire, Émile Zola, and Sergey Pavlovich Diaghilev. The illustrations—many of them full- or half-page color plates—are superb, and the book's low price is astonishing.—**Jeffrey Meyers**

1023. **Biographical Dictionary of Saskatchewan Artists: [Volume 2]: Men Artists.** Marketa Newman, comp. and ed. Saskatoon, Sk., Fifth House; distr., Toronto and Cheektowaga, N.Y., University of Toronto Press, 1994. 281p. index. $55.00. ISBN 1-895618-45-2.

Drawing on her years as the fine arts librarian at the University of Saskatchewan, Newman has completed a second guide to the lives and works of Saskatchewan artists. A companion volume on women artists was published in 1990 (see ARBA 92, entry 969). Her dictionary provides the documentation of regional art that every user, whether student, teacher, collector, curator, dealer, administrator, or researcher, hopes to find, perhaps in a well-thumbed card file or here in a neat handbook. Using an inclusive definition of Saskatchewan (as the place of birth, studies, teaching, or career) and a specific time span (born between 1872 and 1950) predating the creation of the province in 1905, Newman presents 188 painters, printmakers, sculptors, and installation artists. Some work in holography and video, while others are creating murals and icons or preserving folk and Plains Cree traditions.

Entries were launched by a questionnaire, then developed with searches of catalogs, gallery records, books, articles, and interviews. The completed entry was then submitted for checking to the artist or a close relative; entries so verified (an overwhelming majority) are marked with an asterisk. The format is standard: biographical note; education and experience; patents; gallery; a statement (sometimes quoted) of media, style, and subject; chronological lists of exhibitions, collections, commissions, memberships, and awards; and selected bibliographies of publications and interviews by and about the artist. No cutoff date is stated; some entries list 1993 events, others end in 1991 or 1992. The work closes with a general bibliography and two name indexes by artists and folk artists. Competent and streamlined, this dictionary is recommended for fine art reference collections.—**Patricia Fleming**

1024. Ergas, G. Aimée. **Artists: From Michelangelo to Maya Lin.** Detroit, U*X*L/Gale, 1995. 2v. illus. index. $38.00/set. ISBN 0-8103-9862-1.

This 2-volume reference work designed for children 10 and up, or grades 5 and up, is an excellent biographical guide to 62 well-known North American and European artists (sculptors, painters, architects, photographers, illustrators, and designers) who have changed the face of art from the Renaissance to the present. It includes many women and minority artists as well. Artists covered range from Ansel Adams to Mary Cassatt, Paul Cézanne, Marc Chagall, Vincent van Gogh, El Greco, Edward Hopper, Maya Lin, Michelangelo, Georgia O'Keeffe, Pablo Picasso, Faith Ringgold, Diego Rivera, and Titian.

Artists are first arranged alphabetically by name with birth and death dates when applicable, followed by the major section, divided first by fields and media, and then alphabetically by artist. This section provides many black-and-white photographs of the artists and selected works. Fields and media treated range from architecture to collage, etching, furniture design, lithography, needlework, photography, sculpture, and wrap art.

The biographical entries attend to the personal experiences, motivations, and social and artistic climates that impacted the artists. Entries are from 5 to 10 pages in length; they are clear and informative. Boxed sidebars are frequently furnished to denote the importance of movements, events, or processes such as impressionism and composition.

A glossary defines such key terminology as abstract art, fauvism, pointillism, rococo, still life, surrealism, and woodcuts. The prefatory pages in each volume include some key times for events in art and history. The end of each volume has a selective reading list for further information, along with a comprehensive index of biographees and illustrations.—**Maureen Pastine**

1025. McEwan, Peter J. M. **Dictionary of Scottish Art & Architecture.** Wappingers Falls, N.Y., Antique Collectors' Club, 1995. 626p. illus. $99.50. ISBN 1-85149-134-1.

McEwan clearly outlines the ambitious scope of his superb dictionary in its introduction: "The intention has been to provide the most relevant details of all painters, engravers and etchers who met a comprehensive range of criteria, and all architects, carvers, designers, draughtsmen, embroiderers, illustrators, jewelry designers, masons, photographers and stained glass window designers who met slightly more rigorous criteria."

McEwan's definition of *Scottish* for the purposes of this work is broad indeed. He covers artists who are Scottish by birth, ancestry, or marriage. However, he expands his parameters by including artists having an important association with Scottish art, or who exerted some influence on the country's artistic tradition. Additionally, all artists listed in the dictionary have exhibited in a major public institution or executed at least one work of repute.

The resulting volume is a detailed and comprehensive reference work on Scottish art with more than 11,000 entries, the majority of which are biographical. Entries range from a single line to several paragraphs and include birth and death dates where appropriate. Selected bibliographies on the artists are provided with details of their major exhibits and where their work may be seen. In addition, McEwan traces the development of artistic movements along with the schools of art that inspired them and provides brief histories of national academies, art societies, and other organizations. The quality of the work is enhanced by the inclusion of black-and-white reproductions of portraits or self-portraits of 86 artists. This book will be a welcome addition to arts and humanities collections, essential to art dealers and collectors, and useful to anyone interested in the artistic heritage of Scotland.—**Jennifer Comi Ellard**

1026. **North American Women Artists of the Twentieth Century: A Biographical Dictionary.** Jules Heller and Nancy G. Heller, eds. Hamden, Conn., Garland, 1995. 612p. illus. index. (Garland Reference Library of the Humanities, v.1219). $125.00. ISBN 0-8240-6049-0.

This much-needed reference source provides information on more than 1,500 women artists from Canada, Mexico, and the United States. Each entry includes concise biographical and exhibition information and a brief bibliography. To be included in this dictionary, an artist must have been born before 1960, have lived or worked in the United States, Canada, or Mexico, and have shown a serious commitment to the arts as proven by participation in exhibitions and a body of literature about that artist. Well-known artists such as Imogen Cunningham, Frida Kahlo, and Georgia O'Keeffe are covered, as well as lesser-known artists such as Grace Medicine Flower, a Native American potter, and Ulayu Pingwartok, a Canadian Inuit graphic artist. A variety of fields are represented, such as painting, performance art, sculpture, printmaking, ceramics, fibers, metals, and photography. More than 100 black-and-white illustrations, revealing the abundance of North American women's artistic output, are included. This is an excellent and timely reference work, filled with important information on women artists. It is an important and basic addition to any art collection.—**Monica Fusich**

1027. **Who's Who in American Art 1995-96.** 21st ed. New Providence, N.J., R. R. Bowker/Reed Reference Publishing, 1995. 1521p. index. $189.00. ISBN 0-8352-3571-8. ISSN 0000-0191.

Nearly 12,000 representatives from all segments of the visual arts profession in North America are profiled in this annual publication. With some 600 entries new to this edition, the book covers artists, administrators, historians, educators, lecturers, collectors, librarians, publishers, critics, consultants, curators, and dealers. Entries are arranged alphabetically and cite vital statistics, professional titles, education and training, and mailing addresses. Also given is a description of professional activities that may include works in public collections; commissions; exhibitions; publications; positions held with schools, museums, or organizations; memberships in art societies; honors and awards; an interest or research statement; media; and the dealer. All entries are indexed by geographical location and professional classification. In addition, a necrology is provided, which is cumulative from 1953.

Criteria for selection are not thoroughly discussed, but the editor states that new names were obtained through nominations of current entrants, and subsequently went through a selection process based on "works in public collections, commissioned works, and exhibitions of an international, national and wide regional scope in noncommercial galleries and museums." Nonartists were chosen on the basis of position and experience in the field. Thus, while some accomplished artists and art professionals are not included, lesser-known individuals may receive full citations. In spite of its inevitable weaknesses, this is an informative work and should be considered for all large public and academic libraries.—**Barbara Ittner**

Dictionaries and Encyclopedias

1028. Apostolos-Cappadona, Diane. **Dictionary of Christian Art.** New York, Continuum Publishing, 1994. 376p. illus. index. $39.50. ISBN 0-8264-0779-X.

For all the bad one hears about religion, one often forgets all the good it has done. The *Dictionary of Christian Art* reminds one of this and more. In more than 1,000 entries, the author explicates the signs, symbols, figures, and topics that have dominated nearly 2 millennia of Christian art. Contained herein are explanations of why certain fauna are placed here or there, the significance of the color blue, numerology, saints, and shapes. The entries vary from a mere 50 words to several hundred. Cross-references are marked by asterisks that clutter the text in longer articles. More than 160 reproductions are included to take the user from the picture to the word and, presumably, The Word. A selected bibliography, list of illustrations, and fulsome index round out this very useful tool.

This book is a must for every college, university, and school library. It also would make a nice addition to one's private library. [R: LJ, Jan 95, p. 82]—**Mark Y. Herring**

1029. **The Book of Art: A Pictorial Encyclopedia of Painting, Drawing, and Sculpture.** rev. ed. Danbury, Conn., Grolier, 1994. 10v. illus. index. $339.00/set. ISBN 0-7172-7356-3.

This 10-volume set is a scholarly survey of the history of art, the national schools, and individual artists. Although the set emphasizes painting, drawing, printmaking, and sculpture, architecture and the decorative arts are also treated. Eight volumes are devoted to Western art, one volume covers Chinese and Japanese art, and the final volume provides a basis for a critical approach to the appreciation and evaluation of all art, the various schools, genres, and periods.

The editorial committee and international advisory board include curators of museums and professors of art history, and the general editor is Herbert Read, who is well known in the field of art criticism. As the editors and authors of each volume worked primarily independently, there is some unevenness in style. The publishers established six criteria for the set: It should include a substantial amount of quality reproductions; it should provide bibliographical information; it should contain the background and interpretation needed in understanding and appreciating art; it should be organized to bring out the various periods and schools of art and their development; it should exemplify the highest standards of scholarship; and it should be easily readable. These criteria have been followed throughout the set.

Each volume contains a brief introduction followed by an illustrated bibliographical section outlining the life and work of the artists, 630 in all. Following this section is a section of color plates, drawings, and sculptures, including nearly 5,000 reproductions in all. Each plate and illustration is captioned with the artist, title, medium or material, size, and location, when known and appropriate.

A brief list of books for further reading is provided in each volume, and most volumes have a short section on "Influences and Development." Volume 10 has a useful illustrated glossary and a general index to the set. Although the cover of the set says it is a revised edition, and the verso of the title page says an updated edition is published in Italy, what the revisions are is unclear. The set is well-bound, attractive, highly readable, and yet scholarly. Both the layperson and student will find this set useful. Public libraries and art libraries should include this set with their encyclopedic art volumes.—**Kathleen J. Voigt**

1030. Carr-Gomm, Sarah. **The Dictionary of Symbols in Western Art.** New York, Facts on File, 1995. 240p. illus. index. $22.95. ISBN 0-8160-3301-3.

The Dictionary of Symbols in Western Art is an alphabetical listing of individuals (religious, historical, and mythological); fictitious characters and their authors; themes; symbols; emblems; attributes; and personifications of abstract qualities used in art from the Renaissance onward. The goal of this work is to serve as an introduction to the meanings of artworks by providing descriptions of symbols and their use in art.

Each entry describes the symbol or individual and then gives examples of its use in a work of art. Footnotes citing literary sources are included. This dictionary is illustrated with 180 drawings that show key aspects of the works of art being discussed. Interspersed with these entries are feature panels on major themes such as flowers, liberal arts, or religious orders. An index of artists cited in the dictionary is included as well as a supplementary word index covering symbols, minor characters, and episodes that are not included as main entries.

This source is a practical introduction to the use of mythological and religious symbols in Western art. The alphabetical arrangement is easy to use, and the illustrations highlight key points in the entries. It would have benefited from closer editing, however, as there are several missing words in entries. The dictionary is recommended for basic art collections.—**Monica Fusich**

1031. Hall, James. **Illustrated Dictionary of Symbols in Eastern and Western Art.** New York, IconEditions/HarperCollins, 1994. 244p. illus. index. $30.00. ISBN 0-06-433314-0.

The author of this source also wrote the *Dictionary of Subjects & Symbols in Art* (2d ed., Harper-Collins, 1979), which focused on the symbolism of Christian and classical art. The scope of his new book is wider, incorporating the art of ancient Egypt and the Near and Far East. The main section of this dictionary is divided into six thematic parts: abstract signs, animals, artifacts, earth and sky, human body and dress, and plants. Each entry in this section describes the use of the symbol in both Eastern and Western art and is accompanied by a black-and-white illustration chosen to focus on a less familiar aspect of the symbol. Entries also list references from the sacred literature, myths, or legends from which the symbol originated. In addition to the illustrated section of the dictionary, a final section entitled "Collectives" is included. It covers topics made up of numerous symbols such as the four seasons or the cardinal virtues. This source also gives a bibliography, chronological tables organized by geographic area, and a useful index.

This is an excellent reference source. The format allows the reader to approach the information in two ways. The thematic section offers a broad subject approach suitable for browsing, while the index allows access to specific entries. This useful and essential source should be added to the collections of all academic and public libraries.—**Monica Fusich**

1032. McCulloch, Alan, and Susan McCulloch. **The Encyclopedia of Australian Art.** rev. ed. Honolulu, University of Hawaii Press, 1994. 879p. illus. index. $115.00. ISBN 0-8248-1688-9.

The 1st edition of this work, which appeared in 1964, was largely historical in scope, with few entries for living artists. In this edition, coverage has been enlarged. More than one-half of the entries are for living persons. Some 3,000 painters, sculptors, printmakers, and other persons, societies, and organizations involved with the arts are included. Entries are arranged alphabetically in the main body of the work. A typical entry for a person gives birth and death dates and locations, studies, awards, positions held, solo exhibitions, and galleries where their works are located. Occasionally, an entry is accompanied by a black-and-white illustration of one of the artist's works. Most are small, usually one-fifth or one-fourth of a column, although some are larger.

Interspersed within the entries are seven sections of color illustrations, ranging in size from 7 to 15 pages and covering time periods from the aboriginal era to the 1990s. Each is introduced by a short descriptive summary. A five-page introduction gives a short history of Australian art. Directories of galleries, collections, exhibitions, festivals, prizes, schools, foundations, and art periodicals are listed in nine appendixes. Abbreviations used in the entries are identified in an alphabetical list in the forematter. Access to specific works that appear as illustrations is provided by two indexes, one for color, the other for black-and-white. The indexes are arranged by artists' names; there are no title indexes. The scope is intended to be comprehensive, the format is attractive, the illustrations are clear, and the colors are true. This will be an essential reference source in subject collections, and will be useful in general collections as well.

—**Shirley L. Hopkinson**

Directories

1033. **ArtNetwork Yellow Pages.** Constance Smith, ed. Penn Valley, Calif., ArtNetwork, 1995. 136p. index. $12.95pa. ISBN 0-940899-25-6.

This is a directory for all fine artists and art world professionals. It lists more than 3,000 resources from hundreds of sources with complete addresses, organized in a simple-to-use manner. Wide margins are left so notes can be written in this paperback if personally owned.

Every facet of producing artwork from the studio to the marketplace, materials, and services is covered, including the following categories: resources, businesses, lawyers and accountants, grants and residencies, catalogs and magazines, publications, printers, organizations, and critics. A useful, detailed index concludes the volume.

It is suggested that one request the many free catalogs listed to start one's own reference library. The publishers state that this directory is to be updated biannually, adding new information and deleting that which is out-of-date. This is a reasonable reference book to help the artist save time and money. It is a compilation that is a must for all art libraries.—**Kathleen J. Voigt**

1034. **Sixth Bi-Annual National Directory of Arts Internships 1995/96: Over 1,000 Host Organizations....** Diane Robinson, ed. Los Angeles, Calif., National Network for Artist Placement, 1995. 401p. $40.00pa. ISBN 0-945941-07-2. ISSN 1043-092X.

This directory provides brief information about existing internships in the following areas: art/design, arts management, consortia, festivals, multidisciplinary approaches, photography, film/video, music, dance, theater, performing arts/design, and technology. The usual information consists of a brief description of the program, a contact person and an address, and deadlines for applicants. All in all, it is a useful directory with some how-to information.—**Bohdan S. Wynar**

1035. Smith, Constance, comp. **Art Marketing Sourcebook for the Fine Artist.** 2d ed. Penn Valley, Calif., ArtNetwork, 1995. 216p. index. $21.95pa. ISBN 0-940899-26-4.

Looking for places to sell artwork? This sourcebook may provide the help needed. The 2d edition of this work includes more than 3,000 listings of galleries, museums, publications, brokers, and art shows. It also adds three new sections on specialty, photography, and craft markets. The specialty markets section is arranged by market types (e.g., animals, aviation, sports), providing niche market information valuable to many individuals working within a particular genre.

Information contained in the entries is that supplied by the museum, gallery, or publication itself in response to a questionnaire circulated by the compiler. This method allows artists direct insight into their business prospects with any organization listed. For example, some of the data in each entry of the gallery section includes commission rates; whether the gallery is insured; what costs the gallery assumes (e.g., openings, brochures); styles and media they deal in; number of artists represented, and target markets. Information in the other sections is as detailed and thorough. A brief subject index completes the volume. As noted in the review of the 1st edition of this work (see ARBA 94, entry 1045), this edition is recommended for all art reference, marketing, and job placement collections in libraries.—**Gregory Curtis**

Handbooks and Yearbooks

1036. **Art & Design Scholarships: A Complete Guide.** Cleveland, Ohio, Conway Greene Publishing, 1995. 324p. index. $20.95pa. ISBN 1-884669-06-2.

This is a new work for which the information was gathered from the academic departments and admissions offices of each college, university, design and fashion institute, film or photography school, museum school, or craft center covered. More than 2,300 scholarships and awards are listed. There is an introduction by Thomas Steffen of the Cleveland Institute of Art. Much of the directory is arranged under the name of the institution, giving addresses, contact people, majors and concentrations, and specific information about scholarships and awards. There are three columns of large print per page; entries vary in length from one-third of a column to more than eight pages (for the Pratt Institute), depending upon the size of the program.

The guide has a 34-page concentration and scholarship index. This index will be useful simply for identifying programs (e.g., "Art Conservation" with only five entries or "Art History" with two pages of entries) as well as sources of financial assistance. There is also a "State-City Locator" (10 pages) and an index of names of institutions (6 pages).

Prospective students can use this directory to narrow choices, but they also should contact individual schools for catalogs, since such directories seldom are exhaustive. This guide is recommended for schools and public libraries where students seek such specialized information.—**William G. Wilson**

1037. **Art on Screen on CD-ROM.** [CD-ROM]. New York, G. K. Hall/Simon & Schuster, 1995. Minimum system requirements: IBM or compatible. CD-ROM drive with MS-DOS CD-ROM Extensions 2.0. 512K RAM. $495.00. ISBN 0-7838-2153-0.

The *Art on Screen on CD-ROM* database is a project of the Columbia University Libraries' Program for Art on Film. This program was founded in 1984 as a joint venture between the J. Paul Getty Trust and The Metropolitan Museum of Art and was relocated to Columbia University in 1994. From its inception, the program's principal activity has been the Art on Screen Database, which has grown each year and has previously only been available at Columbia University. In addition to the Art on Screen Database, the program has published a newsletter and a series of short films and videos. It also presents various workshops and seminars each year.

The database is international in scope and includes more than 23,000 records covering film-based art from 70 countries. A selection must be film, video, or videodisc to be included. Subjects generally cover painting, sculpture, architecture, archaeology, photography, decorative arts, design, crafts, folk arts, costume, and such general topics as creativity and aesthetics. The coverage of the database is generally from 1970 to the present, but some films of importance produced before that date are listed. According to the compilers, about 2,000 new titles are added each year. The cutoff date for the CD-ROM version of the database was April 1994.

Indexing for the database has been drawn from the *Art and Architecture Thesaurus* (see ARBA 93, entry 635, and ARBA 91, entry 618). Where necessary, subject terms have also been drawn from the *Library of Congress Subject Headings*. The database can be searched by subject, artists' names, art forms and styles, and even by materials and techniques. Each entry contains an annotation of the content, general credits, production date, language, country, and format. In some cases, the distribution source is also added. Many of the entries are provided with lists of criticism, reviews, and awards. All fields are searchable. In addition to the basic information concerning each entry, the database includes more than 8,000 names of distributors and producers of moving image productions.

This index is highly recommended for larger fine arts and film collections in major academic and public libraries where in-depth film research is taking place. It probably has less value to smaller academic and public collections that do not have separate film or fine arts collections.—**Robert L. Wick**

1038. **Artist's & Graphic Designer's Market, 1995: Where & How to Sell Your Illustration, Fine Art & Graphic Design & Cartoons.** Mary Cox and Alice P. Buening, eds. Cincinnati, Ohio, Writer's Digest Books, 1994. 709p. illus. index. $23.99. ISBN 0-89879-675-X. ISSN 1075-0894.

This annual publication is an excellent marketing resource for artists and illustrators trying to sell their work. The title has changed from *Artist's Market* to *Artist's & Graphic Designer's Market* (A&GDM) to reflect the broader scope of this edition. A&GDM opens with basic chapters on marketing, self-promoting, organizing your fine art business, and an industry overview. This is followed by chapters on markets, including advertising and public relations firms; art and design studios; art publishers and distributors; galleries; magazines; and syndicates and clip art firms. Similar to previous editions (see ARBA 91, entry 1017, and ARBA 87, entry 999), each entry includes addresses, fax and telephone numbers, personnel, company descriptions, and specific information regarding the submission of one's work. Some entries also cover tips on how best to approach a particular firm. Five helpful symbols are used: a black square indicating a good first market for the beginning artist, a bullet indicating a special comment, a double dagger noting a new listing in this edition, a maple leaf highlighting Canadian listings, and an asterisk noting listings outside the United States and Canada. Each section contains an interview with a professional in that particular area. This edition provides access to 2,500 markets, including 1,000 new listings. The volume is illustrated with examples of successfully marketed artworks. A&GDM ends with a resource section that includes directories of artist's representatives and organizations, a brief bibliography of related publications, a glossary, a humor index for cartoonists, and a thorough general index.

This is a practical, well-thought-out reference source that is useful for practicing artists. Recommended for all reference collections needing to provide this type of information.—**Monica Fusich**

1039. DuBoff, Leonard. **The Art Business Encyclopedia.** New York, American Council for the Arts and Allworth Press, 1994. 320p. index. $29.95; $18.95pa. ISBN 1-880559-14-5; 0-880559-13-7pa.

Attorney DuBoff has made a successful career by filling a need for simple-to-understand legal and business handbooks for the artist businessperson. The latest "encyclopedia" is really a collection of miscellaneous paragraphs of information on such topics as insurance, copyright, employment practices, safety, and grants. The targeted audience is quite varied—artists themselves, collectors, dealers, and galleries—so the information is basic and generic rather than specific or legal. Many entries are avuncular: Stop payment on outstanding checks; do not allow flammable liquids to accumulate; take a tax deduction for business trips; shop around for the best telephone service; use white space in your advertising. Even the most unworldly artist should know these rudimentary rules of business practice.

While some entries provide useful definitions of, for example, the Berne Copyright Convention, *droit de suite*, and the Robinson-Patman Act, it is hard to wade through the basic material to find the lesser-known data. Once factual information is found, many people will want to know more than the quick-read DuBoff provides. The exception to the generally dispensable character of this book is in the indexes, which give several useful sample forms and many good addresses.

In sum, there are many heavy and authoritative tomes on art law and art business issues in the library. Before starting a fledgling art gallery, one should go to one of them rather than trusting DuBoff and this lightweight effort.—**Stephanie C. Sigala**

1040. Grant, Daniel. **The Artist's Resource Handbook.** New York, American Council for the Arts and Allworth Press, 1994. 176p. index. $12.95pa. ISBN 1-880559-17-X.

This handbook was produced to help guide the 11,000-plus graduates from art schools and university art departments to finding jobs, to financial assistance for producing art, to increasing their own income, and a variety of other needs. Although the organization of the handbook is not always easy to follow or comprehensive, it is a resource that any arts student or recent arts graduate should find valuable. Its chatty chapters not only list where much needed information can be obtained but offer valuable advice to someone relatively new to the profession.

The handbook is divided into 10 chapters and ends with an index and brief bibliographies on sources of public and private grants, sources of financial support for artists, career skills for artists, legal information, health and safety information, a few art magazines and journals, and other information. The chapters begin with some narrative on the topics covered in each chapter and are often subdivided into listings of further information by name of agency, or by state and then agency or organization that can provide further help.

Different categories are provided from sources of technical assistance to information on health risks and precautions associated with making art, affordable living and working space for artists, and financial assistance to individual artists for work, travel, emergencies, and cash awards. Additional reference material is offered on every topic covered. There is information on help for artists with disabilities, as well as names of groups and individuals who can provide advice on a number of issues associated with the field. Artist-in-Residence programs and art colonies are discussed, along with sources for product (materials) donations for the arts, legal services for artists by state, and regional and state arts and humanities agencies. In addition, there are addresses for foundations of artists supporting other artists, groups that offer fellowship addresses of a few religious organizations, and practitioners who specialize in health and safety problems caused by use of hazardous materials. Another important aspect is the topic related to ethical codes, an area drawing much public attention today. Along with some of the other resource books in the field (e.g., Leonard DuBoff's *The Art Business Encyclopedia* [see entry 1039]), the business of art can be made easier and more profitable to the beginner.—**Maureen Pastine**

1041. Haubenstock, Susan H., and David Joselit. **Career Opportunities in Art.** rev. ed. New York, Facts on File, 1994. 191p. index. $14.95pa. ISBN 0-8160-2890-7.

One question that arises for college graduates with degrees in art is, "What will I do now?" This volume will answer that question for many individuals. More than 80 career opportunities in the world of art, from advertising art director to translator, are listed in 8 categories. Not all listings are hands-on, creative positions; many relate to the business or research aspects of the art world. Grants officer and librarian are two listings of this type.

The categories include art and design, museums, art galleries, education, funding for the arts, art journalism, auction galleries, and art-related businesses. Each entry is composed of several sections: career profile with an outline of duties, a salary range, employment prospects, opportunities for advancement, and prerequisites; a career ladder; and a position description. Each entry provides substantial information for the career seeker, providing a basis for decisionmaking.

Any academic library supporting an art program or a related program should place this work on the shelf. As the recognition grows that a degree in art opens up possibilities for alternative career paths, the utility of this volume will grow in importance.—**Gregory Curtis**

1042. Rossol, Monona. **The Artist's Complete Health & Safety Guide.** 2d ed. New York, American Council for the Arts, and Allworth Press; distr., St. Paul, Minn., Consortium, 1994. 343p. index. $19.95pa. ISBN 1-880559-18-8.

This new "revised and updated" edition comes 4 years after the 1st edition. The premier edition provided a much-needed, easily readable source on toxicities of artists' materials used in painting, textile arts, ceramics, stained glass, sculpture, welding, smithing, woodworking, photography, and even leather work. It also provided guidelines on working safely with these materials.

The 2d edition is much the same as the 1st, with some, but not much, new material added. This book has 15 more pages. It also includes the new definition of the word *toxic*, along with guidelines, published by the Consumer Product Safety Commission in 1992, for ascertaining when these products could cause cancer and other harm (including flaws in the guidelines). More information on skin protection is provided, as is a longer list of common solvents and their hazards. A longer list of pigments used in paints and inks is here, and more information on lead glazes and how to work with them. The chapter on classroom safety has been reworked, and a new six-page appendix added, containing a glossary of terms such as *autoignition temperature* and *oxidizer*.

For those libraries that already have a copy, this new edition may not be a necessary buy, as the revisions are not major. However, any new material in this area, no matter how small, may be of value. For those without a copy of the 1st edition, the 2d edition is an essential purchase for all academic, public, school, and art or art museum libraries.—**Diane B. Rhodes**

ARCHITECTURE

Biography

1043. **Contemporary Architects.** 3d ed. Muriel Emanuel, ed. Detroit, St. James Press, 1994. 1125p. illus. index. (Contemporary Arts Series). $149.00. ISBN 1-55862-182-2.

The 3d edition of this excellent and classic reference source covers architects and architectural partnerships of the past 50 years and includes 585 entries, 70 of which are new. These entries are written by an impressive list of contributors. The scope of this international work has been broadened to embrace not only architects, but also engineers, theorists, and landscape architects who have influenced twentieth-century architecture. Each entry contains biographical information; awards received; lists of works and projects; major exhibitions; publications by and about the architect; and an evaluative essay by an architectural historian or academic. A black-and-white photograph of a major work is included with each entry. Cross-references to architects in earlier editions are included, which is helpful. Additionally, there is an index of major buildings arranged geographically by country. This is an essential purchase for all libraries supporting research in architecture and art history.—**Monica Fusich**

Dictionaries and Encyclopedias

1044. Carley, Rachel. **The Visual Dictionary of American Domestic Architecture.** New York, Henry Holt, 1994. 272p. illus. index. $40.00. ISBN 0-8050-2646-0.

This dictionary concerns itself exclusively with buildings that, as stated in the introduction, answer their "own distinctive needs and purposes independent of civic, religious, and commercial architecture." The result is a compact and complete examination of the American house beginning with the indigenous dwelling types of Native American groups and concluding with postmodernism and the 1990s.

Architectural styles are presented chronologically and are grouped by chapters according to the names and periods by which they are generally recognized. Each chapter offers several well-rendered exterior views of structures and presents many elements that are integral to the identification and definition of a particular style or type. The dictionary is handsomely illustrated throughout with more than 500 drawings that include floor plans, interior architectural features, and characteristic details, as well as barns, garages, and other outbuildings. Of particular note are the "anatomy" diagrams sprinkled throughout the volume that illustrate the underpinnings of a given building's structural system.

In an effort to comprehensively examine the ever-changing currents and trends in architecture, the dictionary surveys both high-style and vernacular buildings and their urban, rural, and regional variations. Terms and styles are skillfully defined within the context of social, historical, geographic, ethnic, and climatic influences. Clearly, the intention is not only to show what a particular structure looked like, but also to offer an explanation for its design. This book is highly recommended as a reference work for students and practitioners of architecture or art history, but it should not be overlooked as a useful and practical field guide for anyone who delights in the American house.—**Jennifer Comi Ellard**

1045. Packard, Robert T., and Balthazar Korab. **Encyclopedia of American Architecture.** 2d ed. New York, McGraw-Hill, 1995. 724p. illus. index. $89.50. ISBN 0-07-048010-9.

The 1st edition of this title has been a fundamental component in architecture and design libraries since 1980. As written by William Dudley Hunt Jr., no other reference book has had its combination of descriptive data written for the layperson, American architects' biography, and well-chosen bibliographical citations. The revised edition retains a great deal of Hunt's original organization, content, and writing style, though Hunt's name no longer appears on the title page. Despite much useful information, this is a mixed blessing. Hunt preferred long, discursive, general articles (on, say, the history of architecture) rather than shorter, more useful entries. Also, because Hunt's prose was descriptive rather than analytical, it is too bad that many articles are retained virtually unchanged from the earlier edition.

Some changes and updates do make the new edition worth purchase. First, new biographical articles on contemporary architects like Peter Eisenman, Michael Graves, and Romaldo Giurgola have been added. Second, there are new articles on contemporary issues including adaptive use, accessible design, and computers to bring the text closer to contemporary practice. Third, the ho-hum illustrations in the earlier edition have been replaced and amplified by terrific color illustrations of American buildings, photographed primarily by Korab. However one may feel about the sometimes pedestrian text, the illustrations show the best contemporary American buildings to advantage.—**Stephanie C. Sigala**

Handbooks and Yearbooks

1046. Aicher, Peter J. **Guide to the Aqueducts of Ancient Rome.** Wauconda, Ill., Bolchazy-Carducci, 1995. 183p. illus. maps. index. $40.00; $25.00pa. ISBN 0-86516-271-9; 0-86516-282-4pa.

The 11 legendary aqueducts of ancient Rome, while serving a strictly utilitarian purpose, were imposing features of the Roman landscape because of their majestic proportions and huge scale. Of the more than 450 kilometers of structures that carried immense quantities of water required by a large and expanding population in ancient eras, less than 70 kilometers were carried on arches above ground. Today, these structures are still much in evidence. Aicher describes them in detail, outlining their historical perspective in addition to presenting his research on ancient survey techniques to locate sources of water and the construction, distribution, and administration of these engineering marvels. All people interested in the ancient world will find this book fascinating.

The text is highly readable and is interspersed with new maps that focus on today's ruins as well as schematic drawings and black-and-white photographs. Some of the latter are not sharply focused nor crisply reproduced, but this is a minor flaw in an otherwise unique handbook. The book is divided into three major sections, with the first two devoted to clear, concise descriptions of the history of aqueducts in Rome. Part 3 is presented with on-site visitors particularly in mind.

One of the three appendixes gives readers the Latin and English translations of inscriptions on some of the significant surviving aqueducts. As it should be with a historical survey of this nature, the text and illustrations are carefully placed to be relevant to one another. Concisely organized, the book has real reference value to those concerned with the history of engineering, city planning, and the customs of the ancient world, especially centered on Rome itself and the surrounding Campagna.—**William J. Dane**

1047. **America Preserved: A Checklist of Historic Buildings, Structures, and Sites.** Washington, D.C., Library of Congress, Cataloging Distribution Service, 1995. 1152p. illus. index. $79.00. ISBN 0-16-045255-4.

The *National Register of Historic Places*, published in 1976 by the National Park Service (NPS) (see ARBA 77, entry 387), is the standard reference source for historic places in the United States. The *Register* was updated in 1991 by a joint publication of the American Association for State and Local History, the NPS, and the National Conference of State Historic Preservation Officers. It contains a list of places enrolled under the National Historic Preservation Act of 1966. *America Preserved* is the 2d edition of a checklist of historic buildings, structures, and sites recorded by the Historic American Buildings Survey (HABS) and the Historic American Engineering Record (HAER). The 1st edition of the checklist was published under the title *Historic America* in 1983 by the Library of Congress (see ARBA 85, entry 906). The HABS was a public works project, created in 1933 by Franklin Delano Roosevelt's administration, both to provide employment for Americans and "to systematically record America's built environment through graphic and written records." It was a joint project under the NPS, the American Institute of Architects, and the Library of Congress (LC). The enabling legislation was the Historic Sites, Buildings, and Antiquities Act of 1935. The HAER dates from a later period (1969) and was produced under an agreement between the LC, the American Society of Civil Engineers, and the NPS. The written and photographic records of these two projects are stored in the Prints and Photographs Division of the LC.

America Preserved adds more than 14,000 entries to the 1983 edition of the survey. The 2d edition provides more formal documentation for each site and includes a full shelf list record for the file. This will help locate records faster when ordering copies of specific sites. Listed in the volume are some 30,097 structures, 160,517 photographs, 96,242 drawings, and references to 15,464 pages of written information. Each named site is arranged by city, followed by county and then state (e.g., Jacques Dubreuil Guibourd House, Ste. Genevieve, Ste. Genevieve County, Missouri). There is a city-to-county index at the end of the volume. The editors need to look at how they file the site entries, however. While in the example of the Guibourd House, the entry is filed under "Jacques," other entries can be found under the last name "Janis," "Nicolas," "House" or under joint tenant, such as "Janis-Ziegler House." It is hoped these variations can be corrected in the next edition.

America Preserved, while containing a fuller record for each entry, does not have as many illustrations as the earlier *Historic America*. A number of excellent essays on historic preservation are included in the latter work and it should be retained by all libraries. The latest volume is 1,152 pages long and heavy to carry long distances. *Historic America* was produced in paperback in 1983, while the *America Preserved* is in hardcover. Most libraries will want to own both the *National Register of Historic Places* and the HABS/HAER checklists. If they can only afford one set, the *National Register* has perhaps a more attractive illustrated narrative for the houses listed. The HABS/HAER checklist is, however, the more comprehensive of the two sets.—**Ralph Lee Scott**

1048. **Time-Saver Standards for Housing and Residential Development.** 2d ed. Joseph De Chiara, Julius Panero, and Martin Zelnik, eds. New York, McGraw-Hill, 1995. 1114p. illus. $119.50. ISBN 0-07-016301-4.

It has been 10 years since the 1st edition of this important volume in the Time-Saver Standards series was published. Over the years, building regulations and standards, as well as building materials and housing criteria, have improved. This is no more apparent than in the area of housing and residential development. Housing and residential needs in the 1990s are increasingly important in a world reaching for an affordable and comfortable lifestyle and environment. This comprehensive reference work makes accessible to design professionals the spectrum of new design ideas that can be applied to single dwellings, apartments, housing complexes, and neighborhoods. It is chock-full of drawings, plans, charts, tables, and data for practical application to this type of development. While the book is mainly for the professional developer, large public libraries should find many users once the book becomes known. Anyone contemplating building or purchasing a new dwelling could get much information here to make intelligent selections.—**Robert J. Havlik**

1049. Weeks, Christopher. **AIA Guide to the Architecture of Washington, D.C.** 3d ed. Baltimore, Md., Johns Hopkins University Press, 1994. 307p. illus. maps. index. $39.95; $19.95pa. ISBN 0-8018-4712-5; 0-8018-4713-3pa.

This is the new edition of a specialized guide to the architecture of the District of Columbia plus the Arlington National Cemetery, which is outside the geographic limits of the District. While some of the descriptive entries for the 450 historic buildings and sites are outstanding, and many architectural historians of note assisted in various ways in the preparation of this welcome update, the reader wishes that it were somehow more dynamic, more exciting to read, and that many of the notations were not so sparse and limited to little more than basic facts. However, it should be acknowledged that the author prepared this guide for informed tourists and professional architects and preservationists and, above all, the project is sponsored by the Washington Chapter of the American Institute of Architects. Thus, it is truly a specialized handbook and as such has considerable merit.

Organized into 17 walking tours with handy maps designed for each separate walkabout, the guide starts off with a sweeping history of the famed city's architecture from the beginning up to the 1990s. This fine introduction is followed by the suggested tours; these include more than 100 buildings and sites put up over the past 20 years. Major stylistic and technical changes are characteristic of recent decades. The author points out that more attention has been focused on landscape architecture and project review by endless committees during contemporary times.

Special mention goes to the hundreds of updated photographs by Alan Karchner. They are notable for their clarity, uncluttered foregrounds, and overall visual distinction. The architectural community in the U.S. capital will welcome this newest edition of a standard AIA guide. Others may find Oxford University Press's *Buildings of the District of Columbia* (see ARBA 95, entry 1017) broader in scope and decidedly more enjoyable and informative.—**William J. Dane**

Indexes

1050. **American House Designs: An Index to Popular and Trade Periodicals, 1850-1915.** Margaret Culbertson, comp. Westport, Conn., Greenwood Press, 1994. 326p. illus. (Art Reference Collection, no.19). $75.00. ISBN 0-313-29202-7.

A major factor in the appearance of a town or neighborhood is its care for the design of its domestic architecture. The publication of house designs in popular periodicals during the late nineteenth century and early twentieth century did much to influence designs and housing construction across the country. Architectural historians and designers need access to this elusive literature for many reasons. The *Avery Index to Architectural Periodicals* (see ARBA 95, entry 1014) and the *Burnham Index to Architectural Literature* (Garland, 1990) do a good job of indexing the recent professional literature, but there is a large gap in the ways of approaching the older popular literature.

This index, coupled with access to microfilmed copies of journals in *American Periodicals Seventeen Forty-One to Nineteen Hundred* (University Microfilms, 1979), opens up a new and interesting glimpse to this influential source of design ideas. The compiler has reviewed 34 major periodicals published between 1850 and 1915 and has found and indexed more than 6,500 designs published therein, some of which are illustrated in a design sampler. The periodicals indexed include women's, agricultural, house and garden, and carpentry and builders magazines. More than 2,000 architects and designers are identified. There is an architect index to the designs, a geographical index of the architects, and a geographical index to house designs. Local historians may find use for the latter index to help identify some historic landmarks in their area.—**Robert J. Havlik**

1051. **Taunton's Fine Homebuilding Index, Issues 1-85.** Harriet Hodges, comp. Newton, Conn., Taunton Press, 1994. 203p. $14.95pa. ISBN 1-56158-074-0.

Throughout U.S. history, people have been deeply concerned with homebuilding; even during times of war and financial recessions, the task of building and improving shelter has been of prime importance. Since early 1981, Taunton Press has published a subject-oriented periodical created to appeal to the vast and concentrated audience involved in homebuilding. They have also issued 14 books of reprinted articles focused on the ramifications of house design, the technical aspects of building, and timely improvements. The Taunton editors have responded to the reader's need for a summary listing of the 85 issues of the magazine itself and the 14 books. This index arranges the listings logically under particular subjects such as floors, baths, kitchens, or tools. Librarians and individual subscribers who retained the earlier issues and reprinted books will delight in this compilation.

The index includes columns of entries for highly practical topics (e.g., floors, stairs, walls, roofs, doors, foundations, framing, and insulation). Specific materials such as putty, nails, screens, concrete, and hammers are listed, plus popular features for today's homes (e.g., patios, gazebos, fireplaces, and porches). There are also entries for earthquakes, fires, hurricanes, and insects (with a subset for termites). Amateur and professional builders and designers, as well as libraries and specialized organizations concerned with homebuilding, will appreciate the reference function of this listing which supplies accurate information on the art and trade of homebuilding during the past 13 years.—**William J. Dane**

PAINTING

1052. Cumming, Robert. **Annotated Art.** New York, Dorling Kindersley, 1995. 104p. illus. index. $22.95. ISBN 1-56458-848-3.

Forty-five works from the world's greatest artists offer a deeper understanding, appreciation, and enjoyment of paintings. From Giotto's *The Adoration of the Magi* to Picasso's *Guernica*, *Annotated Art* explains the artist's techniques and intentions and clarifies the meaning of obscure subjects, explaining the symbolism that at times makes even the most familiar painting illusive. This oversized book is like a museum full of the world's spectacular paintings. The generous size and faithful color reproduction allow every painting to be displayed accurately and in detail. Each picture is a double-spread page. Dorling Kindersley, publishers of the Eyewitness books, is consistent in its superior quality.

The guidelines that are developed in the commentary for each of the 45 paintings are subject, technique, symbolism, space and light, historical style, and personal interpretation. Included is an explanation of "What makes a masterpiece" (pp. 8-9). The aspects described are virtuosity, innovation, patronage, artistic vision, and the role of the artist. The journey begins on page 10. Each page provides information about the artist with a picture and an explanation of the painting, including, but not limited to, where it is located, why it was painted, and its significance. Important details of the painting are enlarged and further explained. On pages 26-27, Leonardo da Vinci's *Mona Lisa* is presented. Explanation of the landscape, columns, smile, sleeves, chair arm, hands, and somber colors are explained. Her eye is enlarged with a quote by Leonardo. A familiar painting is brought to life by this book. The Sistine Chapel Ceiling shows its restored beauty. *The Creation of Adam and Eve* is explained in-depth.

The book includes a glossary and an in-depth index. Because many of the paintings have frontal nudity, some schools will not be able to display this book on their shelves. This book will be a welcome addition to a high school or college library or as a reference source for teachers. It is highly recommended.
—**Barbara B. Goldstein**

1053. Gottsegen, Mark D. **The Painter's Handbook.** New York, Watson-Guptill, 1993. 320p. illus. index. $24.95pa. ISBN 0-8230-3003-2.

This book will be useful for anyone who likes to paint, including art students and their instructors. It covers everything from good safety habits in the studio or work space to how to build a crate to transport the finished product. It is divided into three parts. Part 1 is entitled "The Basics" and is essential reading for any beginning art student. In this section, the author defines the terms that make up a painter's working vocabulary and describes the tools, accessories, papers, boards, and other materials painters use. He also explains in detail how to take care of the tools, especially the high-quality brushes he recommends, even for beginning painters. Of special interest for the beginner in this section are the tables that clearly chart the durability of the painting supports and the properties and potential health hazards of practically all of the binders, solvents, thinners, varnishes, balsams, driers, paints, and pigments that are presently available to painters. In part 2, "Paint Making and Painting Techniques," readers learn how to make their own paints and how to apply them. In part 3, "Picture Protection and Restoration," the author gives detailed instructions on how to help retard the gradual decay to which every work of art is vulnerable. *The Painter's Handbook* includes a glossary, a bibliography, a list of suppliers, and a comprehensive index. It is an excellent reference book that can easily be adopted for classroom instruction.—**Sandra Adell**

1054. Henkes, Robert. **Native American Painters of the Twentieth Century: The Works of 61 Artists.** Jefferson, N.C., McFarland, 1995. 219p. illus. index. $38.50. ISBN 0-7864-0092-7.

Although limited in breadth of coverage to only 61 artists, this work includes artists from many different tribes, demonstrating a wide diversity of styles, painting media, and themes. Choices of which artist to include and which to exclude are no doubt more subjective than objective, but even so, the work is well chosen in its representative Native American artists. The 61 young, contemporary artists represented have been selected by the author as significant painters in mainstream American art or talented artists who are primarily known within tribal boundaries.

Prefatory and introductory remarks focus on the difficulty that Native American artists have had in moving beyond the ethnic arena into mainstream American art and on defining the need to incorporate the beliefs, traditions, and symbols of the Native American culture into a style that speaks to a wider public. The primary section is arranged alphabetically by artists' surname. Entries for each one focus on the artist's work (specifically what the artist chose as his or her best work) and techniques used to produce it, and a two- to three-page critique of that artist's work, productivity, cultural and political sensibilities evident in his or her art, and the artist's tribal identification, date of birth, and contribution to American life, art, and influence.

The photographs of works presented include title; name of artist; date of work; medium; size of work; and whether it is in the possession of the artist, a museum, a school, or another location. Photographers of the works are mentioned for a majority of the photographs furnished. The artists represented were asked to submit photographs of their best work also. Most photographs are in black-and-white, although 11 are in color. Because the majority are black-and-white, some are difficult to view as clearly as the original work or a color reproduction would allow. Following the main section is a brief conclusion; a short but excellent bibliography of books, articles, brochures, and exhibition catalogs related to these artists' works; and an index including artists and their works, themes, tribes represented, styles of painting, types of works represented, and subject matter of the art.

Although not a biographical directory, use of this volume in conjunction with the recent publication by Patrick D. Lester, *The Biographical Directory of Native American Painters* (SIR Publications; distr., University of Oklahoma Press, 1995) will add to the value of Henkes's work. Lester's directory contains far more entries than this one. It covers all but six of the artists in Henkes's book (Troy Jumping Eagle, Julie Lankford, Debra McConnell, Marie Moore, Annie Nash, and Billy Newman). The directory has no photographs of art works, which is what marks the value of the book under review. The bibliographies in both Lester's and Henkes's references are of great value, with few duplicative entries.

—**Maureen Pastine**

1055. Horne, Alan. **The Dictionary of 20th Century British Book Illustrators.** Wappingers Falls, N.Y., Antique Collectors' Club, 1994. 456p. illus. $79.50. ISBN 1-85149-108-2.

The predecessor of this book was *The Dictionary of 19th Century British Book Illustrators* by Simon Houfe and published by the Antique Collectors' Club in 1994. Designed with collectors in mind, the book is useful to all those interested in children's literature and British illustrators.

The book begins with several informative essays about the state of British book illustration during the years 1915-1985, followed by the main dictionary of more than 1,000 illustrators in alphabetical order. Each entry in the dictionary attempts to outline the major features of the illustrator's life and career, followed by listings of books illustrated; books written and illustrated; books published on subjects relevant to the artist (such as books on art and artistic techniques); journals to which illustrations have been contributed; major exhibitions of the artist's work; locations for major collections of original art; and a bibliography of sources for further information. Almost every page is illustrated with black-and-white drawings of artists' works, and many pages contain full-color illustrations, particularly from works earlier in the century.

In comparing coverage with standard sources covering British illustrators, this work stands out as more inclusive than any other one source. Information on the most famous of illustrators is heavily abridged because there are numerous sources to consult. The strength of the present volume is its coverage of lesser known individuals. More than 10 years in the creation, Horne's work is scholarly and informative with a touch of critical perspective. For libraries that feature British children's books or answer biographical questions extending to British children's illustrators, this volume is an essential addition to the reference collection. [R: LJ, Jan 95, p. 86]—**David V. Loertscher**

1056. **World Painting Index: Second Supplement, 1980-1989.** By Patricia Pate Havlice. Metuchen, N.J., Scarecrow, 1995. 2v. $149.50/set. ISBN 0-8108-3020-5.

World Painting Index is a major reference work that provides access to reproductions of paintings in 697 art books and catalogs published in the United States and abroad from 1980 to 1989. The titles chosen for indexing were obtained from the annual listings in the *American Book Publishing Record* volumes. The original work, which was selected as one of the outstanding reference books of 1978 (see ARBA 78, entry 816), indexed 1,167 art books and catalogs, while the first supplement (see ARBA 84, entry 828) indexed 617, allowing extraordinary access to reproductions of paintings. This supplement builds on the original volume and first supplement, which covered 1945-1979. The arrangement is similar to the earlier volumes, and consists of a numbered bibliography, a listing by title of works by unknown artists, a listing by painter of works appearing in the indexed volumes, and a listing by title of painting giving names of painters. A letter code indicates what type of reproduction is cited: black-and-white and color, color only, black-and-white detail, or color detail. This is an excellent reference source and an essential addition to any library answering questions in this area.—**Monica Fusich**

23 Language and Linguistics

GENERAL WORKS

Bibliography

1057. Campe, Petra. **Case, Semantic Roles, and Grammatical Relations: A Comprehensive Bibliography.** Philadelphia, John Benjamins Publishing, 1994. 645p. index. $125.00. ISBN 1-55619-675-X.

This work is the first in a series titled Case and Grammatical Relations Across Languages. It contains 6,643 bibliographical entries of periodical and monographic publications arranged in an alphabetical list; the majority of the entries are from the twentieth century. The bibliography is the product of an interuniversity research network on linguistic pragmatics begun in 1990; specifically, of the network team working at the Leuven University project on case and thematic relations, concentrating on case phenomena in both Indo- and non-Indo-European languages.

This area of linguistics is highly complex as there is often ambiguity in the use of the word *case* and disagreement about what constitutes case-markers. Because the number of cases and case inflections varies from language to language (some are even noninflected, using word order or prepositions to mark syntactical relationships), research on case, semantic roles, and grammatical relations in linguistics is especially rich. The comprehensiveness of this bibliography makes it a valuable tool for scholars and researchers. The extensive and well-organized subject index, as well as the language index and guide, makes the work exceptional. This bibliography is recommended for academic and large public libraries.
—Edward Erazo

1058. **CCCC Bibliography of Composition and Rhetoric 1992.** Gail E. Hawisher and others, eds. Carbondale, Ill., Southern Illinois University Press, 1994. 199p. index. $29.95; $19.95pa. ISBN 0-8093-1959-4; 0-8093-1960-8pa.

This bibliography contains information about 1,656 items pertinent to the topic. The entries are given in alphabetical order by the authors' names, with complete citations and short annotations indicating the contents. Besides these features, there are registers of names of the authors of single essays. There is also a highly useful topical index that makes it easy for the user to find information on a given subject. The selection of items for the bibliography is quite broad; indeed, occasionally one would think that some items could be left out. For example, item 731 lists a translation of Friedrich Nietzsche's essay on "Truth and Falsity in an Extra-Moral Sense," which is only superficially related to item 739, an overview of Alfred Korzybski's *Collected Writings*. Korzybski can be taken as relevant to rhetoric because of his well-known position on the deceptive uses of language, but Nietzsche has little in common with the field. In the same way, item 724, David McNeill's "Hand and Mind: What Gestures Reveal About Thought," belongs here only if we take *rhetoric* in the original sense; namely, the art of public speaking. However, citing such items could degenerate into unnecessary carping, because it is better to include the borderline cases in a bibliography than to exclude them. No doubt this bibliography will be a very useful reference tool.
—L. Zgusta

1059. Kess, Joseph F., and Tadao Miyamoto. **Japanese Psycholinguistics: A Classified and Annotated Research Bibliography.** Philadelphia, John Benjamins Publishing, 1994. 357p. index. (Amsterdam Studies in the Theory and History of Linguistic Science, series 5; Library & Information Sources in Linguistics, v.24). $89.00. ISBN 1-55619-254-1.

Psycholinguistics is labeled a cognitive science and is the interdisciplinary activity that searches for answers to how a natural language is learned, produced, stored, and recalled. This volume consists of more than 1,000 entries, contributed by more than 700 scholars. The classified bibliography of Japanese psycholinguistics points to research carried out in Japan, mostly by Japanese scholars, as well as by mixed teams of international and Japanese scholars who targeted the Japanese language as the focal point of empirical approaches in psychology, linguistics, psycholinguistics, and cognitive science. The majority of entries concern published articles. Each entry includes the main points made by the publication or its conclusions, both provided in English. Japanese titles are provided together with their English translations. The bibliography is divided into several sections. Section 1 introduces the relevant Japanese journals and Japanese university publications. The remaining sections cover the history of psycholinguistics; speech perception and speech production; morphology, word recognition, and the mental lexicon; syntax and sentence processing; discourse and text processing; semantics and the organization of meaning; metaphor; language and thought; lateralization and hemispheric specialization in the brain; first language acquisition; second language acquisition; orthography skills and reading aphasis; linguistic disabilities; computational models of language; and social psycholinguistics. Each section is subdivided into thematic subsections. The volume will be helpful to graduate students of linguistics and psychology as applied to oral expression.—**Seiko Mieczkowski**

1060. Nevis, Joel A., and others. **Clitics: A Comprehensive Bibliography 1892-1991.** Philadelphia, John Benjamins Publishing, 1994. 274p. index. (Amsterdam Studies in the Theory and History of Linguistic Science, series 5; Library & Information Sources in Linguistics, v.22). $69.00. ISBN 1-55619-252-5.

One of the projects that gives linguistics a bad name, this bibliography was compiled by a marginal group of impassioned linguists for linguists of like temperament. Attempting to apply scientific methods to a field of linguistic study that is (by their own admission) quite unscientifically confused, they necessarily do little to advance the knowledge of language structure.

The study of clitics is a late child of the search for a universal grammar that occupied the energies of a number of linguists in the 1960s. It is essentially an extension of J. Wackernagel's much earlier study of (en)clitics in Homeric Greek grammar to other languages, where it does not easily apply. The jointly written preface attests to difficulties even in the definition of a clitic and acknowledges problems from cross-classification: "clitics . . . are generally quite hard to define and identify in any way that allows for fruitful cross-linguistic application . . . (W)hat one researcher calls a clitic based on one set of criteria may be considered something else by another set" (p. viii). With such poor definition, it is not surprising that little clarity is forthcoming. Examples of clitics are quoted, unhelpfully, from Tagalog, but none from the more accessible and particle-rich Polynesian languages!

The bibliographical entries are followed by an analytical index of contents. This is essential, although many of the authors of the articles (e.g., an article on "The Spanish Impersonal *se*" by John Knowles) might be surprised to learn that they are writing about clitics.—**John B. Beston**

Dictionaries and Encyclopedias

1061. **The Cambridge Encyclopedia of the English Language.** By David Crystal. New York, Cambridge University Press, 1995. 489p. illus. maps. index. $49.95. ISBN 0-521-40179-8.

Once in a while a reference book is published that is so informative, so generally well done, and so joyful that one wishes it had been available for years instead of just months. *The Cambridge Encyclopedia of the English Language* is such a book. This handsomely illustrated volume—there are color photographs, maps, and imaginative cuts and reproductions on almost every page—tells the story of the English language. This is done, according to linguistics professor Crystal, by considering the structural story (how sounds and grammar have developed), the social story (how the language has come to serve a variety of functions), the literary story (how writers use language), and the chronological story (how language has changed over time). All of this is developed in a series of chapters starting with "History," moving on to "Structure" (English vocabulary and grammar), and concluding with "Use" (spoken and written English, using English, and learning about English).

To make things easier for the user, each chapter is subdivided into specific topics, each treated in a double-page spread. In the chapter on "The Sound System," for example, the user is presented with subsections on consonants, vowels, syllables, connected speech, prosody, and sound symbolism. For the specialist, there are full-page, colored charts showing how English vowels and consonants are articulated, using "Received Pronunciation" as a model. For the general browser, there is a cartoon illustrating "Comic Onomatopoeia" (whizz, whoosh, whump, and whiff) and an insert on "The Sound of Swearing." It appears that the best swear words are constructed from short vowels, plosives, and high-pitched fricatives. For those who do not know what a fricative is, a helpful index of topics will guide them to an explanation.

Since the title of the book is *The Cambridge Encyclopedia of the English Language*, it is not surprising that the emphasis, in both text and illustration, is on England rather than the United States. The editor has allocated 12 pages to a discussion of the differences between American and British English, and twice that many to variations of British, Scottish, and Welsh English. This book can be used as a reference source or a general reading text. In either case, it will please those who love the language. The encyclopedia is highly recommended for academic, public, and school libraries.—**Donald C. Dickinson**

ENGLISH-LANGUAGE DICTIONARIES
Abridged

1062. **The American Heritage Talking Dictionary.** 3d ed. [CD-ROM]. Cambridge, Mass., Softkey, 1994. Minimum system requirements (Windows version): IBM or compatible 386/25MHz. CD-ROM drive. Windows 3.1. 4MB RAM. 2MB hard disk space. 8-bit sound card (MPC-compliant). Minimum system requirements (Macintosh version): Macintosh System 6.02 or higher. CD-ROM drive. 1MB RAM System 6.X; 2MB RAM System 7. 500K hard disk space. $59.95. ISBN 1-56434-380-4.

This is a wonderful idea for an electronic product. It provides a multitude of options that range far beyond the standard print one of looking up the definition for a specific word and finding not only its definition(s) but also pronunciation, part of speech, proper usage, hyphenation, inflection, and etymology. One can also, with the click of a button, check a word in the 500,000-term thesaurus, then hot link to its definition in the dictionary (or use a split-screen option to see both the word's definition and synonyms at the same time). The disc's "wordhunter" feature allows the user to type in one or more words likely to occur in the definition of the sought-after word (it will then suggest possibilities), while the "anagram" feature finds alternative words that can be created from the letters of a current word or any group of letters the user specifies.

Words or phrases can be easily copied from the dictionary to word processing documents. If the entered word is misspelled, the dictionary will suggest possible alternatives. If a word is only known by its abbreviation, for example *mph*, the dictionary will provide the full phrase in response to the abbreviation entered. One can search for alternative spellings with the click of a button, and search for words using wild card characters (a feature sure to be cherished by crossword-puzzle enthusiasts). In terms of scope, the dictionary defines more than 200,000 terms, including 8,000 biographical and 13,000 geographical entries as well as entries for U.S. colleges and universities.

What more could a user wish for? Well, one could wish for the pronouncing feature to work! This disc was installed on four different multimedia computers, none of which were able to get the dictionary fully functioning. Two locked up, one had the program's "exit" feature close down when the pronouncing option was on, and one briefly supported the voice-pronunciation audio before locking up. (It should be noted that the pronunciation sound is that of trained linguists, rather than computer synthesization, and the quality of the audio is excellent.) All four of the machines tested used the same sound card, a standard one recommended for multimedia machines, and it may be that there is some sort of conflict with this particular brand. However, libraries planning to purchase this title—and it is definitely recommended for every collection—will want to check with Softkey first to ensure compatibility with the library's existing system. [R: BR, Jan/Feb 95, p. 64] —**G. Kim Dority**

1063. **Cambridge International Dictionary of English.** Paul Procter and others, eds. New York, Cambridge University Press, 1995. 1773p. illus. $24.95; $19.95pa. ISBN 0-521-48236-4; 0-521-48421-9pa.

Differing from the usual language dictionary, this dictionary is for foreign learners of English, concentrating on the three varieties of Australia, the United States, and Great Britain. For the foreign speaker, this is a guide to usage, pronunciation, spellings, grammatical patterns, and new words and phrases. Definitions are clear and concise, based on a controlled vocabulary of fewer than 2,000 words. Sample sentences illustrate usage with emphasis on collocation (i.e., the use of words that sound natural together).

With only one meaning per entry, words with differing meanings are easily distinguished by a guide word; for example, *adopt*, meaning to "take child," is followed by an entry for the meaning to *start*. A supplementary phrase index leads to entries that explain idiomatic expressions. For example, the expression *around the clock* is keyed to the definition for *clock*, where the phrase is explained and illustrated. Front-end pages add details on word labels and usage, and the introduction has an excellent guide to grammar.

Entries stand out in bold typeface, while sample sentences and phrases are differentiated in italics. The two-column format is clean and attractive. Line numbers between the columns promote quick location of passages identified in the phrase index. A minor flaw mars the phrase index: The print here is especially small and difficult to read.

Interspersed throughout the text are black-and-white line drawings illustrating words with multiple meanings for everyday things. The word *rack*, for example, is illustrated with pictures for a clothes rack, a plate rack, a toast rack, a bath rack, a luggage rack, and a magazine rack. Variants between British and American usage are also indicated. For example, what the British refer to as a *plate rack* is what Americans call a *dish rack*.

Beginning students of English can also consult charts for various languages of what are called "false friends"; words that look similar to words in another language but have very different meanings. The word *absolve* in English appears similar to the Czech word *absolvovat*, but the meaning in Czech is "graduate." Another useful feature is the numerous charts called "language portraits," showing the practical use of language, such as outlining common ways of listing dates.

With its compact presentations, the dictionary makes an excellent textbook, not only for students of English but for native speakers as well. Cambridge University Press identifies it as "the first in a new line of English-language reference books" (foreword). Subsequent works maintaining this high standard will be most welcome. Libraries serving diverse populations may want circulating copies as well as one for the reference collection.—**Bernice Bergup**

1064. **The Chambers Dictionary on CD-ROM. PC Windows Version.** [CD-ROM]. New York, Larousse Kingfisher Chambers, 1994. Minimum system requirements: IBM or compatible 386SX. CD-ROM drive with MS-DOS CD-ROM Extensions 2.2. DOS 3.1. Windows 3.1. 2MB RAM. VGA monitor. $40.00. ISBN 0-550-10260-4.

The Chambers Dictionary on CD-ROM is the electronic version of the British dictionary (Larousse Kingfisher Chambers, 1993) that allows the user to find information within the dictionary rapidly and conveniently, and provides search methods that are not possible with the printed book. The use of wildcards (* and ?) in a search could be a big asset to a crossword puzzle aficionado. Additional indexes such as by idiomatic phrases, foreign phrases, and capitalized words make it even more useful. The keyword index allows the user to find all the phrases in the dictionary containing a particular word. One can do Boolean searches using AND, NOT, and OR through the search dialog. Individual entries may be printed on a printer, although this reviewer was unable to get that function to work.

The CD-ROM was easy to install on the computer, with directions provided on the screen. The program makes its own icon in Program Manager for later ease of use. A complete, easy-to-understand guide is included, along with on-screen help if one prefers that method of learning the features. The guide says that the program may be linked to Microsoft Word for Windows or Microsoft Word 6, which allows the writer to look up words in the dictionary from within the word processing environment. Color cues in the entries denote part of speech (purple), main entry (green), pronunciation (brown), and definitions (blue).

The search engine works quickly and was easy to learn to use. The on-screen icons help the novice learn the features quickly. For a word having several definitions, the various meanings are not numbered. The definitions are short and concise, less complete than *The American Heritage Dictionary of the English Language* (3d ed.; see ARBA 93, entry 1056). The Chambers CD-ROM has more searching features than the *World Book Dictionary* on CD-ROM (World Book, 1993 [print version]). Because the scope is British, there is less coverage of typically American words; for example, *FBI* is listed, but not *NSA*. *Cicerone* is indented under *Cicero*, while it is a separate entry in *The American Heritage Dictionary*.—**Sandra L. Doggett**

1065. **The Concise Oxford Dictionary of Current English.** 9th ed. Della Thompson, ed. New York, Oxford University Press, 1995. 1673p. index. $29.95. ISBN 0-19-861320-2.

The 9th edition of this dictionary is about 14 percent larger than the 8th edition (see ARBA 91, entry 1048), including about 9,000 new words and phrases for a total of 150,000 entries and 230,000 definitions. As the title states, this source provides concise, rather than lengthy, word information, emphasizing current rather than historical meanings. The *Concise Oxford Dictionary* draws on the constantly updated files of its illustrious parent, the 20-volume *Oxford English Dictionary* (see ARBA 90, entry 1006). Discriminating users should realize, however, that if they want a more detailed abridgment of the OED they should consider the two-volume *New Shorter Oxford English Dictionary* (see ARBA 94, entry 1099).

The COD emphasizes British English, although numerous English words from other countries, especially the United States and Canada, are also included. Main entries are in boldface, followed by pronunciation represented with International Phonetic Alphabet symbols, part of speech designation, with separate meanings designated by numbered subentries. Definitions are brief, although major variant forms are noted. The basic editorial view is descriptive rather than prescriptive; however, a few usage notes are provided for disputed words (e.g., "hopefully").

The COD is current enough to cover quite a variety of both technical and popular new terms such as "post-traumatic stress," "chill out," "political correctness," and "ethnic cleansing." Prefatory matter provides clearly written examples of how to read entries (a great deal of information is coded by numerous typographical conventions and abbreviations) and a remarkably accessible four-page history of the English language. Numerous appendixes include lists of countries, states of the United States, chemical elements, and other tables especially useful for home reference. While U.S. readers should use this dictionary with some caution (especially for pronunciation), the COD continues to be a useful, current general dictionary of the English language.—**David Isaacson**

1066. **Merriam-Webster's Collegiate Dictionary Deluxe.** electronic ed. [CD-ROM]. Springfield, Mass., Merriam-Webster Electronic Publishing, 1994. Minimum system requirements (Windows version): IBM or compatible 386SX. CD-ROM drive with MS-DOS CD-ROM Extensions 2.1. DOS 5.0. Windows 3.1. 4MB RAM. Hard disk space. VGA/SVGA monitor. Mouse. Minimum system requirements (Macintosh version): Motorola 68030 processor System 7. CD-ROM drive. 4MB RAM. Hard disk space. 12-inch monitor. Mouse. $49.95.

This CD-ROM provides the full text of the print editions of *Merriam-Webster's Collegiate Dictionary* (10th ed.; see ARBA 94, entry 1076) and *Merriam-Webster's Collegiate Thesaurus* (1993). In some sense, therefore, the strengths and weaknesses of these two print tools define the parameters of this electronic version and make an extensive overview of the contents unnecessary.

As with the print versions, this tool is based on the continuing Merriam-Webster lexical database. It provides 214,000 definitions, 35,000 etymologies, 75,000 dates of first recorded use, 34,000 illustrative quotations, and 700 illustrations, and represents no significant reworking. The black-and-white line-drawing illustrations are infrequent and drab, and most of the illustrative quotations are manufactured rather than taken from actual authors. Those that come from actual sources are attributed to the author but not to a particular work.

On the plus side, the CD-ROM offers word jumbles, cryptograms, trademarks, foreign words, and geographical terms, all of which indicate the marketing of this tool for home and student use. The disc is a great improvement over its CD-ROM predecessor, *Webster's Ninth New Collegiate Dictionary*, which sold for $199.95 and offered little in the way of searchability. If this new tool were nothing but a CD-ROM version of the printed volumes, it would have little to recommend it. However, this electronic version is different from the printed volumes because of its search fields, hypertext, and Boolean capabilities. Each major element of the entries is in a searchable field. A double-click on any word in a definition will lead to a definition of that word. "M-W Link," software that comes with this package, can be invoked from a Windows document, and the dictionary can be used to check spelling or meaning. In other words, this tool releases the power of electronic, nonlinear searching of the database, allowing a variety of results that would not be possible in the print versions.

For the scholar (but perhaps not the average person), this version of the dictionary opens up whole new avenues for inquiry, despite the relative limitations of the database. For the nonscholar, this dictionary makes for enjoyable searching, which will promote learning. Hypertexting from definition to definition is quick and easy. The basic dictionary is relatively easy to install and use, although the more complex searches are not self-evident and require study and experimentation. The basic searching mechanisms, screen appearance, and pop-up menus are similar to *Microsoft Encarta* (see ARBA 95, entry 60) and therefore will be intuitively familiar to a wide range of users.

The CD-ROM comes with a thorough manual and tutorial and a toll-free telephone help-line used with considerable success by this reviewer. Movement between the dictionary and the thesaurus requires just a click, and the size of the typeface and the colors on the screen can be customized. These and other features mark this tool as qualitatively different from its print sources and add value to something that is reasonably priced. One hopes that other dictionary publishers will follow Merriam-Webster's lead.—**Bill Miller**

1067. **Merriam-Webster's Dictionary of Basic English.** Springfield, Mass., Merriam-Webster, 1995. 717p. illus. $7.95pa. ISBN 0-87779-605-X.

As its title suggests, this dictionary's focus is only on the most often used English words. Definitions and other information about each word are presented as concisely as possible. The 32,000 entries include some new words as well as long-established ones. The standard format for each entry covers pronunciation, part of speech label, and definition, often followed by a phrase illustrating how the word is typically used.

The primary audience for this dictionary is adults. While college students may find it somewhat useful, they would probably appreciate the greater detail provided by a somewhat larger dictionary, such as *Merriam-Webster's Collegiate Dictionary* (10th ed.; see ARBA 94, entry 1076). For example, the *Collegiate* defines *gallows* as "a frame usually of two upright posts and a crossbeam from which criminals are hanged—called also *gallows tree*," while *Basic English* defines it as "a structure from which criminals are hanged." Two hundred and fifty words have been selected for extended "word histories." The criteria used to select these words are puzzling. *Slave* is a politically astute choice, but why include *nausea*, a much rarer word? Illustrative phrases are well chosen (e.g., "a slave to alcohol" illustrates "one who is like a slave in not being his or her own master"). Additional helpful information includes paragraphs discriminating among synonyms for some words, clear graphic illustrations, and useful lists of abbreviations, signs and symbols, and proper names at the end of the main dictionary.

One potential liability of this otherwise very useful book, especially for users whose first language is not English, is that when a word has more than one meaning, those meanings are listed in chronological order. Readers who do not read the preface, and who might therefore expect the most recent meaning to be listed first, may be confused by this rather scholarly convention.—**David Isaacson**

1068. **The Oxford Desk Dictionary.** American ed. Laurence Urdang, ed. New York, Oxford University Press, 1995. 691p. illus. $12.95. ISBN 0-19-509153-1.

The American edition of *The Oxford Desk Dictionary* defines approximately 100,000 words, a figure that includes a number of geographical terms and biographical entries. Many colloquial and slang terms are defined, as are terms from the computer and medical fields. Syllabication, part of speech, and pronunciation (including variants) are given; nouns and verbs have their plural(s) and past and participle forms given, and there are approximately 200 primitive illustrations. Finally, the dictionary contains lists of weights and measures, metric equivalents, signs and symbols, U.S. presidents, countries of the world, chemical elements, and zip and area codes.

The flaws in *The Oxford Desk Dictionary* are surprising, disturbing, and manifestly apparent. It contains neither the traditional four-letter obscenities nor the words that are likely to prove offensive to racial and ethnic minorities, a lexicographical irresponsibility that is thoroughly annoying, as ignoring such words will not make them go away. Indeed, when Urdang does take a stance, he is often ambivalent. *Ain't*, for example, is "regarded as highly informal, if not outright incorrect, and should be avoided in a formal context" (p. 12). Older Oxford dictionaries—in particular *The Concise Oxford Dictionary* (see ARBA 84, entry 934)—are less equivocal, stating bluntly that "*ain't* for *is not, are not,* is wrong" (p. 94). Equally serious, *The Oxford Desk Dictionary* provides neither complex etymologies nor the date the word first entered the English language, although such information is now routinely given in desk dictionaries, and its illustrations are too few and too primitive to be particularly helpful.

Finally, the quality of the definitions occasionally leaves something to be desired. *Grout* and *ice cream,* for example, are defined only as nouns, and the definitions (respectively, and in their entirety: "creamlike mortar used between ceramic tiles" [p. 248] and "sweet, creamy frozen food, usually flavored" [p. 277]) are not particularly helpful. Purchasers needing an inexpensive hardcover desk dictionary may find *The Oxford Desk Dictionary* serves their purpose and makes a convenient gift, but at barely twice the price, the 10th edition of the *Merriam-Webster's Collegiate Dictionary* (10th ed.; see ARBA 94, entry 1076) is vastly superior.—**Richard Bleiler**

1069. **The Oxford Encyclopedic English Dictionary.** 2d ed. Judy Pearsall and Bill Trumble, eds. New York, Oxford University Press, 1995. 1765p. illus. maps. $35.00. ISBN 0-19-521158-8.

Similar to its predecessor, this updated and expanded edition combines a comprehensive dictionary of current English with a concise encyclopedia, the entries conveniently interfiled in one alphabetical sequence. The encyclopedic entries add 4,000 biographical entries; 5,000 place-names taken from the *Oxford Dictionary of the World*; and 4,000 other proper names, such as political parties, religious organizations, historical events, treaties, celestial bodies, and fictional and mythological characters. This is essentially an updated *Concise Oxford Dictionary of Current English*, 8th ed. (see entry 1065), enhanced by the addition of 3,000 new words, 1,000 of them from science and technology. The short encyclopedic articles cover most fields of knowledge, including current affairs, science and technology, medicine, history, the arts, philosophy, sports, and so on.

While the dictionary covers current English used throughout the world, as a British publication, spellings, pronunciations, definitions, and usage give precedence to the English of Great Britain. Additional encyclopedic information is covered in more than 100 pages of tabular appendixes, which have information on ecology; presidents of the United States; Indo-European languages; chemical elements; musical notation; astronomy; a chronology of world events from the Paleolithic Age to the present; a chronology of scientific achievements in medicine, telecommunications, computer technology, and space exploration; and 15 full-color maps. Appendix 3, "Countries of the World," now supplies population figures in addition to area, capital city, and currency units. This dictionary is highly recommended for any library needing an authoritative, comprehensive desk dictionary of the English-speaking world, made even more useful by the concise encyclopedic entries.—**Blaine H. Hall**

1070. **The Oxford English Minidictionary.** 4th ed. Helen Liebeck and Elaine Pollard, eds. New York, Oxford University Press, 1995. 634p. $5.95pa. ISBN 0-19-861324-5.

Although it is the smallest member of what its 1-page preface refers to as "the Oxford family of dictionaries" (p. iv), the *Minidictionary* nevertheless defines approximately 50,000 words, including current abbreviations, slang expressions, and technical terms. Syllabications are not given, but clarifications are provided when potential ambiguity exists in pronunciation or in the formation of the plural. The volume concludes with a series of appendixes: a "word-games supplement" lists two-letter words, words containing a *q* not followed by a *u*, and words beginning with an *x*. In addition, there are separate appendixes for Roman numerals, the Greek alphabet, the metric system of weights and measures, conversions between Fahrenheit and centigrade, and rules of English spelling and punctuation.

It is this last appendix that is crucial, for the *Minidictionary* is intended for a British rather than an American audience. Although American alternatives are listed, British spellings are given as preferred, and acronyms such as GNVQ (General National Vocational Qualification), words such as *navvy*, and terms such as *Teddy Boy* are not likely to be in standard American vocabulary. Nor would most Americans consider *police constable* as the first alternative when looking for a definition of *pc*. Finally, the *Minidictionary*'s definitions are occasionally unabashedly prescriptive: *ain't* is "incorrect in standard English," and *fulsome* is "wrongly used" when it is equated with "generous." The standard four-letter obscenities are defined as "vulgar slang."

While this work is an excellent bargain, it is not a volume that belongs in most academic libraries. Its small size invites theft, and its narrow margins prohibit rebinding. Those who love dictionaries, however, will find the *Minidictionary* a portable delight.—**Richard Bleiler**

1071. **Webster's New World Vest Pocket Dictionary.** 2d ed. Katherine Soltis, ed. New York, Macmillan/Simon & Schuster, 1994. 187p. $3.00pa. ISBN 0-671-88993-1.

At half the size of *Webster's New World Pocket Dictionary* (2d ed., Prentice Hall General Reference, 1993), the *Vest* version is less than half as nice. For one thing, the *Pocket* has a flexible vinyl cover that makes it easy to stuff into a jeans pocket or purse. The *Vest* is "perfect-bound" (a term not noted in either dictionary), which means that it has been glued without signatures directly into a flimsy, posterboard cover. But how, one asks, does the *Vest* achieve its economy over the *Pocket*? What could one leave out?

An example is the word *paddle*. The *Pocket* marks the pronunciation, cites a part of speech (noun), provides two definitions, cites another part of speech (verb), and gives another two definitions. The *Vest* stops after the definitions for the noun. The *Pocket* provides a few more extras—the population of certain U.S. cities and a bigger list of abbreviations, for example—but the greatest economy is in the *Vest*'s selective excision of multiple meanings and the omission of entire terms. *Gab*, *gabardine*, *gabble*, and *gable* head the "G" section of the *Pocket*. The *Vest* starts with *gable*. This book is not so much a serious reference work as it is an editorial tour de force.

It is hard to argue in favor of the existence of the *Vest*. People who speak and spell at about the fifth grade level will not find words that challenge them in this tiny reference book, and anybody younger than that probably ought not to have a dictionary so poorly bound or in such a small font. At the price, it is not the first choice for a party favor, either.—**Judith M. Brugger**

Anagrams

1072. Daintith, John. **The Scrambled Word and Anagram Finder.** New York, HarperPerennial/HarperCollins, 1994. 787p. $12.00pa. ISBN 0-06-273277-3.

Originally published as *The Bloomsbury Anagram Finder* (London: Bloomsbury, 1994), this collection of some 200,000 words and phrases is designed for puzzle enthusiasts. The scrambled entries are arranged by the number of letters, from 2 to 28, from "AB" through "AAAEEEEEEFGHHHMOOPPRRSSSTTTT"—the scrambling for "Separate the sheep from the goats." Entries in each section are alphabetical, letter by letter. Selections range from single and compound words to phrases, including some scientific and medical terms, geographical entries, and foreign words; for example, among 10-letter entries, "spring roll" and "gippy tummy" appear as well as "stertorous," "hieroglyph," "Montevideo," "felt-tip pen," "indophenol," and "peridotite." The columnar format, boldface entries, and clear typeface enhance this convenient resource for the home library and the public library reference collection.—**Bernice Bergup**

Etymology

1073. Lyman, Darryl. **Dictionary of Animal Words and Phrases.** Middle Village, N.Y., Jonathan David, 1994. 280p. index. $19.95. ISBN 0-8246-0378-8.

An updated version of Lyman's *The Animal Things We Say* (see ARBA 84, entry 1040), the *Dictionary of Animal Words and Phrases* consists of two parts. Part 1 alphabetically lists animals, parts of animals, or things produced by animals. Each entry begins with an etymology of the word. Origins of words are extensively traced, many harking back to Indo-European or Latin roots. This is followed by various expressions relating to the word. The origin and first known usage of the expression are indicated, as well as the way it is currently used, and other sundry details. For instance, under the phrase "albatross around one's neck," readers learn the mythical status the albatross once held for sea voyagers, and also the story of *The Rime of the Ancient Mariner* by Samuel Taylor Coleridge—the basis of this particular metaphor. Cross-references to other entries are evident throughout. Part 2 concentrates on more obscure animal-related terms. Words derived from animal homes, movements, and sounds are described. For example, the history of the verb *to canter* dates back to the action of horses bearing pilgrims to the shrine of St. Thomas à Becket in Canterbury. Words whose relation to animals is not immediately apparent are detailed also (e.g., personal names that are derived from names for animals).

This dictionary runs neck and neck with such other dictionaries as *Speaking of Animals* (see entry 1074). However, the book under review is generally more readable and more accessible. The format and congenial language provide for easy searching and reading—in fact, a brief perusal of the book will quickly hook readers and lure them to read more. The index proves useful by listing not only animals, but also words and phrases. *Speaking of Animals* is arranged alphabetically by phrase or metaphor, making accessibility more difficult due to variations in expression (e.g., "barking dogs seldom bite" as opposed to "her bark is worse than her bite"). In addition, the format is less user friendly: It lists rather than expounds in sentence form, and therefore is less enjoyable to browse. One benefit *Speaking* has over the *Dictionary* is its inclusion of slang terms. Additionally, some phrases found in the former were not found in the latter, or were not as fully traced. For example, under "Buck," Lyman's work lists "pass the buck" but not Harry S Truman's quote "The buck stops here."

However, the book does not profess to be exhaustive; in any case, it is hands-down a unique study of the way animals have colored human speech and writing since language began. The work is ideal for fledgling writers at the end of their rope searching for colorful turns of phrase. Lyman's dictionary will also prove useful to students, linguists, and anyone else interested in animals or the etymologies of words or metaphors.—**Melissa R. Root**

1074. Palmatier, Robert A. **Speaking of Animals: A Dictionary of Animal Metaphors.** Westport, Conn., Greenwood Press, 1995. 472p. index. $69.50. ISBN 0-313-29490-9.

During the last decade or so, English dictionaries have been becoming simultaneously more specialized and more comprehensive. This dictionary of metaphors drawn from the animal world is the fourth, and the most comprehensive, since the 1980s. Its special feature is that the metaphors are arranged by alphabet rather than by the animal that suggested the metaphor. If that were the only system of classification, it would not be altogether satisfactory—who would expect "tell it to the marines" to be a horse metaphor, or recognize "cynic" as a dog metaphor?—but there is a supplementary index in which metaphors are grouped according to their animal origin. From that index it emerges that the most common source of animal metaphors is the horse, followed by the dog.

The dictionary includes words or terms that appear to be of animal origin but are not. The city of Buffalo, for instance, gets its name from the French *beau fleuve* and not from the animal. The date of the first appearance of a metaphor is provided whenever it can be determined. Surprisingly, perhaps, the 1970s produced a considerable number of new animal metaphors.

Beyond its value to linguists, the dictionary makes for interesting and diverting general reading. It owes much of its attractiveness to the personality of the writer, who conveys his information in a lively, down-to-earth way, with assurance and good humor. He acknowledges with appreciation his debt to the animals in his backyard.—**John B. Beston**

General Usage

1075. Cutts, Martin. **The Plain English Guide.** New York, Oxford University Press, 1995. 162p. illus. $19.95. ISBN 0-19-869259-5.

Directed at an audience of students and memorandum writers, this brief guide discusses all the basics of clear written communication. The author explains the value of short sentences, simple words, and unobtrusive punctuation. He makes a case for active verbs and the use of vertical lists. More general advice is given regarding issues such as avoiding sexist language, planning a written document, and the composition of readable legal text.

This book does address issues not typical for this sort of guide. The author tells how to manage the writing of coworkers through team meetings and regular feedback. He also discusses the physical layout of text and dismisses a variety of writing myths ("don't start sentences with 'and' "). The book has bibliographical notes but no index.

This reviewer would have preferred multiple examples when points were being illustrated; the author seemed content with one per lesson. Aside from that, and the book's modest length, this work is recommended to libraries as an office reference text. Cutts follows his own advice to write clearly and communicate well.—**Ed Volz**

1076. **The Little Oxford Guide to English Usage.** E. S. C. Weiner, Andrew Delahunty, and Janet Whitcut, comps. New York, Oxford University Press, 1994. 249p. index. $11.95. ISBN 0-19-861301-6.

Based on the latest information in Oxford's English-language dictionaries, including the *Oxford English Dictionary* (see ARBA 90, entry 1006), and their extensive language files, this pocket-sized work covers usage guidance related to word formation (spelling), pronunciation, vocabulary (meaning), and grammar, with appendixes on basic punctuation principles and 70 or so clichés and inflated expressions to avoid in good writing. Yet, buyers beware: Despite the "New" on the dust jacket, this work is a miniaturized version of *The Oxford Guide to English Usage* (1993), with some shortened introductory paragraphs, an appendix on English usage in other English-speaking countries eliminated, and fewer examples in some entries, but essentially the same work. However, Oxford University Press fails to note this connection anywhere in the work.

As with all the Oxford English-language dictionaries, this one is authoritative and reliable, but its focus is on British usage. While American usage is noted frequently in the entries, most American users will find it far easier to use an American English usage dictionary, such as *Webster's Dictionary of English Usage* (see ARBA 90, entry 1005), where American usage recommendations do not always appear as the exceptions. Recommended for libraries wanting a shorter authoritative English usage dictionary, most libraries will likely prefer its full-sized, almost-identical twin.—**Blaine H. Hall**

1077. **NTC's Dictionary of American English Pronunciation.** By Bernard Silverstein. Lincolnwood, Ill., National Textbook, 1994. 326p. $12.95pa. ISBN 0-8442-0727-6.

The primary purpose of this dictionary, based on the International Phonetic Alphabet (IPA), is to provide nonnative English speakers with a guide to standard English pronunciation. The first section of the book consists of a pronunciation guide with interpretation for each phonetic symbol in the IPA system. The second section is made up of a 22,000-item vocabulary with the pronunciation given on the basis of the IPA symbols. As an aid to the use of the printed text, Silverstein, a professor of audiology, proposes that users may want to use a model speaker or an audiocassette made for the book. This seems a helpful suggestion, as learning a whole new alphabet by simply reading a text would appear to be a daunting task—especially for non-English speakers trying to learn the Roman alphabet. The IPA approach, as demonstrated in the volume, may be useful for teaching purposes; for example, in the case of an instructor trying to correct speech problems or a nonnative speaker teaching English to other nonnative speakers. The use of the audiocassette will no doubt enhance the use of the printed text. As a stand-alone text this work is of dubious utility.—**Donald C. Dickinson, Dianna Thor, and Jonathan Seeley**

1078. **The Oxford Minireference Dictionary & Thesaurus.** Sara Hawker with Chris Cowley, eds. New York, Oxford University Press, 1995. 742p. $6.95pa. ISBN 0-19-863149-9.

The Oxford Minireference Dictionary & Thesaurus combines a dictionary and a thesaurus in one alphabetical sequence. The dictionary defines approximately 40,000 words, including some slang and colloquial terms, some geographical locations, and some technical terms. Syllabications are not provided, although clarifications are given when potential ambiguity exists in pronunciation or in the formation of the plural. The definitions are descriptive rather than prescriptive, and the standard obscenities are not present. The thesaurus lists approximately 120,000 synonymous terms; antonyms are not provided, and the alphabetical dictionary arrangement prohibits the categorization of terms occasionally used by larger thesauruses.

If *The Oxford Minireference* can be said to have any significant problems, they are those of lack of comprehensiveness. Definitions occasionally lack depth: *aquarium*, for example, is defined solely as "a tank for keeping living fish etc." (p. 28), and the definition for *drone* neglects completely the parasitic aspects of the word. Similarly, thesaurus listings occasionally omit significant synonyms (i.e., the listing for *dream* fails to mention such related terms as "vision" and "fancy"). It must be emphasized, however, that gaps are inevitable in any small reference volume, and *The Oxford Minireference* is a smaller-than-average paperback book. Indeed, for a volume of its size, it is remarkably thorough.

This work is similar to *The Oxford English Minidictionary* (see entry 1070) in size and appearance, as well as in being an excellent bargain that will be useful to students. Nevertheless, as with the *Minidictionary*, the *Minireference* is not a volume that belongs in most academic libraries. Its small size invites theft, and its narrow margins prohibit rebinding. Like its companion, however, the *Minireference* is a portable delight.—**Richard Bleiler**

1079. **Webster's II: New College Dictionary.** New York, Houghton Mifflin, 1995. 1514p. illus. $18.95. ISBN 0-395-70869-9.

Webster's II: New College Dictionary is a slightly updated revision of *Webster's II: New Riverside University Dictionary*, published by Houghton Mifflin in 1984 (see ARBA 86, entry 1045) and slightly revised in 1988. At the price, this hardbound dictionary represents a valuable purchase for the average student or adult. Its derivations and definitions will satisfy 95 percent or more of the average person's daily dictionary needs. However, it lacks currency and its crowded format, sparse margins, lack of color or photography, and flyspeck-sized typeface make it visually unappealing. The editorial staff is all new, but the content, which apparently derives from a common Houghton Mifflin database, is virtually identical to that of the 1984 and 1988 editions, including the line-drawing illustrations, the number of pages, and the number and content of the definitions. The format also remains nearly identical to the previous editions.

The dictionary's preface is only one page long and consists largely of braggadocio. The explanatory notes section does a sufficient job of explaining the way the dictionary works and how to use it, but there is no discussion of criteria for inclusion or exclusion of entries. Occasionally, an entry includes a short illustrative phrase, and in rare cases, the quotation is not made up but is rather literary and attributed. Several hundred entries contain not only an etymology but also a word history

The review of the 1988 edition of this dictionary in *Encyclopedias, Atlases, & Dictionaries* (see entry 48) takes that edition to task for its lack of currency and includes a list of entries expected but not found. Remarkably, 8 of the 15 terms listed still do not appear in this edition. When entries in this dictionary are compared with those in dictionaries of new English words, the inadequacies become apparent. For instance, there is no entry here for *gunboat diplomacy*, *Nudie* (a motion picture or play in which actors perform in the nude), *pierced earring*, or *pig* as a slang term for a law enforcement official, all of which can be found in *The Barnhart Dictionary of New English Since 1963* (see ARBA 74, entry 1234). All obscenities and curse words are lacking here except for *damn*—a sure sign that scholarship gave way to considerations of mass marketing.

This dictionary contains extensive separate sections for biographical and geographical entries. The review of the 1988 edition above noted the omission of a number of prominent individuals, such as Violeta Chamorro, Michael Jackson, and Boris Yeltsin. Yeltsin has made it into this edition, but the other two apparently are not yet prominent enough to merit consideration. Of course, it would be impossible for any dictionary to include every name a user might expect to find in a biographical dictionary or encyclopedia.

The section "Geographic Entries" is similarly unsatisfactory. The review of the 1988 edition cites its failure to list "Germany" (as a unified country) or "Burkina Faso" as the new name for Upper Volta. These lapses have been corrected in this edition, but the entry for Burma does not mention the names "Myanmar" or "Union of Myanmar," although the latter has been the official English name for the country since June 1989, according to *The Statesman's Year-Book* (see entry 102). Unbelievably, there are no entries for Chechnya or Ingushetia, despite the long-standing political turmoil and media prominence of these areas.

In sum, this dictionary is essentially a reprinting of the 1988 edition with some minor updating. It is sturdy and inexpensive, but not suitable for scholarly inquiry.—**Bill Miller**

Grammar

1080. **The Oxford Dictionary of English Grammar.** By Sylvia Chalker and Edmund Weiner. New York, Oxford University Press, 1994. 448p. $25.00. ISBN 0-19-861242-7.

The majority of books on grammar attempt to explain word relationships with the use of structural rules and examples. The purpose of this work is different and more basic, because it provides brief definitions for the terms used by grammarians and other linguists. The authors, both with experience in the production of other language guides, have supplied definitions for nearly 1,000 wide-ranging terms.

In addition to terms employed by grammarians, users of this book will find definitions that clarify meanings in the specialized vocabularies of related disciplines, such as phonetics, linguistics, phonology, semantics, and morphology. In some cases, the authors have supplemented their definitions with quotations from the writings of noted linguists. The term *recursive*, for example, is defined as "a linguistic feature or grammatical rule that can be used repeatedly in sequence." This is followed by further explanation by Robert A. Palmatier as quoted from his *Glossary for English Transformational Grammar* (see ARBA 73, entry 1214) and a statement that the term was originally introduced from mathematics into linguistics by Noam Chomsky in 1955.

The dictionary supplies frequent cross-references in the case of overlapping meanings, so that one can, for example, understand the differences between elision, assimilation, compression, contraction, and haplology. This is a unique reference work that will provide guidance for students and general readers needing assistance in understanding the complex language sometimes used by grammarians and their colleagues.—**Donald C. Dickinson**

1081. Venolia, Jan. **Write Right! A Desktop Digest of Punctuation, Grammar, and Style.** 3d ed. Berkeley, Calif., Ten Speed Press, 1995. 153p. illus. index. $6.95pa. ISBN 0-89815-676-9.

Now in its 3d edition, *Write Right!* is still a useful compendium of commonsense rules and pointers on matters of punctuation, grammar, and style. Its core is unchanged, but some rules have been added or deleted, and the section on frequently misused words has been expanded (of necessity, alas!). Finding help with semicolons is simple: Turn to the chapter on punctuation, where each mark of punctuation is treated alphabetically; under "Semicolon" there are five numbered, clearly expressed rules with examples of usage. The section on grammar is admirably brief and emphasizes quick resolution of problems rather than lengthy explanation of the rules themselves. It includes a helpful glossary of grammatical terms.

The author is particularly good on style. In a handful of pointed, no-nonsense rules, she covers the basic elements of lucid writing. The list of misused words is a handy tool for learning the latest on *hopefully* or *disinterested/uninterested*. Although this is but one of many guides to good writing, *Write Right!* has the virtue of being small, short, sensible, and devoid of pretense and unnecessary detail. It is designed, above all, to be useful.—**Jeffrey R. Luttrell**

Idioms, Colloquialisms, and Special Usage

1082. Hunter, John, and Claudine Dervaes. **The UK to USA Dictionary.** Tampa, Fla., Solitaire Publishing, 1994. 81p. $7.50pa. ISBN 0-933143-18-4.

Dervaes has written several books in the area of travel, including a dictionary of travel. This tiny book is a glossary of British and American English. It simply lists British terms in one column and the American equivalents in another column, and vice versa. Some slang is included on the condition that it is used throughout Great Britain or the United States. No examples of usage or assistance in pronunciation are provided. Terms used in Scotland and Northern Ireland are labeled. The appendixes include a list of birds found in Europe and North America and conversion tables for temperatures and measures.

The pocket-size, paperback format was inexpensive to produce, hence the more-than-reasonable price. The information found in this book is helpful, but unfortunately the format takes away from any significant value it might have.—**Carl Pracht**

1083. **A Dictionary of American Idioms.** 3d ed. By Adam Makkai, M. T. Boatner, and J. E. Gates; revised by Adam Makkai. Hauppauge, N.Y., Barron's Educational Series, 1995. 455p. $12.95pa. ISBN 0-8120-1248-8.

This 3d edition contains more than 8,000 idiomatic words, expressions, regionalisms, and informal English expressions, and it claims to be the largest dictionary of its kind. More than 2,000 entries, many relating to slang, popular culture, and computer technology, have been added since the last edition (see ARBA 89, entry 949). The most likely readers will be those to whom American English is a second language. To that end, a helpful preface that defines *idiom* and explains how to use the entries is written in English, Arabic, Chinese, French, German, Italian, Japanese, Russian, and Spanish.

Each alphabetically arranged entry contains information about the part of speech and definition and gives examples from current usage. Usage labels are helpful, as are *compare to* and *see* cross-indexing. No effort is made to give the source of the idioms, but only their approximate meanings. Because people seldom regard their own way of speaking as idiomatic, the native-English speaker may find this volume to be odd and filled with many phrases that have come to be clichés. "Fit as a fiddle" and "a flash in the pan" are but two examples.

Despite its 8,000 entries, this dictionary is hardly exhaustive. Southern expressions such as "Come back y'all," and "I'm fixing to do that" are unaccountably missing. Neither is there any mention of the differences in meaning between words such as *pickle* and *preserve*, which are often confused. However, non-native-American English speakers seeking to penetrate the mysteries of everyday English will no doubt find this volume indispensable.—**Kay O. Cornelius**

1084. Rees, Nigel. **Dictionary of Catchphrases.** London, Cassell; distr., New York, Sterling Publishing, 1995. 230p. $21.95. ISBN 0-304-34563-6.

How many phrase books and etymologies does a collection need? Probably as many as users call for and the budget can afford, for it seems that two such books rarely have the same, or even similar, entries and explanations. For example, this dictionary is the only one of three—picked at random—published in this decade to cite "I've seen the elephant," meaning that the speaker has been bloodied by experience and has seen all there is to see. Yet two of the three list Harry Truman's advice "If you can't stand the heat, get out of the kitchen," with one explanation more comprehensive (and amusing) than the other.

Alphabetically arranged word-by-word, this reasonably priced volume is a well-planned collection of phrases from the military ("If it moves, salute it, if it don't, paint it!"); from politics ("I'm mad as hell and I'm not taking any more"); from cinema/television/radio ("Frankly, my dear, I don't give a damn!," "All we want is the facts, ma'am," "Faster than a speeding bullet"); from sports ("Back to square one" and "Nice guys finish last"); and from various other categories. What can be either an attraction or a detraction is the fact that many of the entries are heavily British-oriented. As in too many phrase books, a *Dictionary of Catchphrases* lacks an index, definitely a minus. Nevertheless, most academic and public libraries will want to add this useful, attractively formatted volume to their reference collections.—**Charles R. Andrews**

1085. Swanfeldt, Andrew. **Crossword Puzzle Dictionary.** 6th ed. New York, HarperCollins, 1994. 858p. $14.00pa. ISBN 0-06-272053-8.

Crossword puzzle purists must object to dictionaries such as this, as much as traditional poets disdain rhyming dictionaries. Nevertheless, the fact that this is the 6th edition of the book tells one that there must be numerous crossword puzzle workers willing to "cheat" now and then. Although a patient and resourceful user of conventional dictionaries and thesauruses will eventually discover many answers to crossword puzzle clues, a dictionary such as Swanfeldt's is often going to be easier to use.

No definitions of words are provided in this source. That is understandable, because puzzle solvers are more interested in locating a match for the puzzle's sometimes beguilingly worded clue than they are in verifying word meanings. Most entries include more than one word that in some way relates to the word one is looking up. Some of these words are synonyms that could be found in a thesaurus. Many others, however, are much more tangential than synonyms. Thus, among the entries under the word *light* are: *airy, agile, alight, pastel, brighten, frivolous,* and *capricious*. But categories are also sometimes specified, so that if the clue asked for the science of light, the answer is *optics*, or if it asked for words meaning units of light, answers include: *lux, pyr, phot,* and *lumen*. This dictionary also specifies how many letters there are in a word, so if one is looking for a four-letter word or five-letter word meaning without light, one encounters *dark* before *blind*. Most of the book consists of alphabetically arranged word lists. The last few pages provide separate lists of prefixes, suffixes, and combining forms. This is a reference book definitely more useful to patrons who can check it out of the library, although reference librarians may occasionally use it to answer some word questions unrelated to crossword puzzles.—**David Isaacson**

Juvenile

1086. **The American Heritage Children's Dictionary.** By the Editors of the American Heritage Dictionaries. New York, Houghton Mifflin, 1994. 842p. illus. index. $14.95. ISBN 0-395-69191-5.

The American Heritage Children's Dictionary is intended for children between the ages of 6 and 12 and contains approximately 37,000 definitions. For each word, syllable divisions are given, as are its part of speech and its pronunciation (including variants); nouns have their plural(s) given; verbs have past and participle forms given; useful idioms are listed; and frequently, the word is used in a sample sentence. The dictionary also contains approximately 800 attractive color illustrations, as well as numerous boxes and sidebars containing simple etymologies, helpful lists of synonyms, and vocabulary builders describing basic linguistic principles. The supplementary material is immediately noticeable, and although occasional errors in it exist (the "clamp" is more properly a vise, the "turtle" is clearly a tortoise), it is impressive and will prove enticing.

The dictionary, however, is flawed on several grounds. First, although a few minorities are present in the illustrations, the vast majority of the pictures tend to feature only white people. Equally serious, too many words receive inadequate definitions. *Indian*, for example, is defined as "a member of one of the peoples who lived in North, Central, or South America long before explorers and colonists arrived"; there is no cross-referencing to the entry for *Native American*, and a curious user might wonder why Indians are described only in the past tense. Similarly, the entry for *dodo* states that it was "a large, heavy bird that formerly lived on an island in the Indian Ocean and was unable to fly"; the word *extinct* is not used in the definition, although *extinct*'s definition uses the dodo in its sample sentence. *Indian Ocean* is neither explained nor located, for few geographical regions are defined.

Attractive pictures do not a successful dictionary make, but few children's dictionaries are without flaws, real or perceived. School libraries may find this dictionary a useful beginning, and it has the virtue of being very inexpensive.—**Richard Bleiler**

1087. **The Kingfisher Illustrated Children's Dictionary.** John Grisewood, John Bollard, and Joanne Grumet, eds. New York, Larousse Kingfisher Chambers, 1994. 480p. illus. maps. $19.95. ISBN 1-85697-841-9.

This nicely illustrated dictionary containing more than 12,000 dictionary entries and 1,000 encyclopedic entries is aimed at children aged 9 and up. The 1,000 illustrations are full-color drawings, and quite entertaining. The preface furnishes instructions on making the most of the dictionary, and a brief history of the English language. Most entries include the word divided into syllables, pronunciation, part of speech, and definition. Definitions are short and at an appropriate reading level. Occasionally, words are used in complete sentences, and some cross-references are given. Encyclopedic entries are usually boxed and provide slightly more expanded coverage of a topic. Pages are broken down into two columns, with each page usually containing two or three illustrations placed in various locations on the page. The appendixes provide brief information on countries, states, United States presidents, important dates in history, weights and measures, and information on leaders of Canada and the United Kingdom. Students will enjoy this dictionary with its many illustrations; therefore, it is recommended to libraries serving young children. [R: SLJ, Feb 95, pp. 129-30; RBB, 1 Feb 95, p. 1025]—**Carl Pracht**

1088. **The Kingfisher Illustrated Thesaurus.** By George Beal. New York, Larousse Kingfisher Chambers, 1994. 144p. illus. $14.95. ISBN 1-85697-520-7.

The age group for which this thesaurus is intended is not indicated, but it appears to be targeted to primary and intermediate students. With 5,000 main entries, it would seem to outdistance its recent competitors, *Roget's Student Thesaurus* (see ARBA 92, entry 1062) and *The Harcourt Brace Student Thesaurus* (see ARBA 95, entry 1050), but falls far short of these in usefulness and attractiveness.

Main entries and synonyms are neither defined nor used in context, except for a few sample sentences with some synonyms; Roget's defines all main entries and synonyms and gives usage examples, while the Harcourt omits only synonym definitions. Parts of speech are abbreviated and not defined, requiring a student unfamiliar with these to refer to the introduction to learn what *adj.* stands for and to a dictionary for its meaning; both Roget's and the Harcourt spell out parts of speech at each entry and explain them at the front of the book.

Illustrations are crude, cartoonish, two-color line drawings by one artist, as contrasted with Roget's multicolor illustrations from various sources, including sophisticated artwork and excellent photographs. Lacking also are a table of contents, indexes, and the many other user-friendly features found in Roget's and the Harcourt. With prices about the same for all three thesauruses, both Roget's and the Harcourt are much better values than the Kingfisher. [R: SLJ, Feb 95, p. 128]—**Larry Lobel**

Obsolete Words

1089. Grambs, David. **The Endangered English Dictionary: Bodacious Words Your Dictionary Forgot.** New York, W. W. Norton, 1994. 264p. $23.00. ISBN 0-393-03623-5.

This is a strange book, essentially of antiquarian interest. If most of the words here recorded are moribund or endangered, then judgment has already been democratically rendered by the English-speaking public. But "endangered" is not in any case an accurate description of the words listed here. Some are still in common enough use, like *pursy, distrait, dishabille* (or, more commonly, *déshabillé*), and *uxorious*. Some are French words current in France that were simply not absorbed into English, such as *affiche, balbutient, commère, chantage, corvée,* or *tintamarre*. Some words will be recognized from Spanish, such as *impavid, idoneous, jactation, indument*, but these words, lacking English relatives, never found more than a cold welcome. Most of the words recorded here, as Grambs points out, are of Latin origin, a language rarely studied nowadays. In consequence, they seem remote and stiff, already set in *rigor mortis*. Few of them seem to bear out the editor's view of them as delightful or as linguistic gems. Rather, most of them strike one as harsh-sounding and ugly. Thus one page, opened at random, lists *apolaustic, aponic, apopathetic, apopemptic, aporetic*, and *apositic*.

In his preface Grambs claims that without these words our vocabulary would be pedestrian. But with them, one could object, it would be prissy and stilted. Grambs's attempt to revive academically created words has some interest as a contemporary version of the actual creation of "inkhorn terms" during the English Renaissance, but he is trying to revitalize a cause already lost.—**John B. Beston**

Other English-Speaking Countries

1090. **The Cambridge Australian English Style Guide.** By Pam Peters. New York, Cambridge University Press, 1995. 848p. $69.95. ISBN 0-521-43401-7.

Australia, now 200 years old, is able to look at contemporary usage without excessive respect for the past, and to consider British, American, and Australian usage with equal detachment. Therefore, one is not surprised that the author of this most important work should come from down under. Peters trained in historical linguistics and well-suited by temperament to such a work: Whether relaxed or lively, she is always sensible and displays a sense of humor. She steers an assured course between the dogmatism of prescriptive grammar and the sometimes excessive liberalism of descriptive grammar. Also, she is careful not to let her personal preference suggest what is correct: Normally, she gives readers the facts and lets them decide which of the variants appears best.

The work covers a wide range: grammar, idiom, punctuation, and spelling. Inevitably, there are some omissions and some observations not quite up-to-date. Nowhere, for instance, does she comment on the tendency to equate the subordinating *together with* or *along with* with the coordinating *and* (e.g., "This novel, along with the two final novels, show signs of . . . "). And while Peters is current in sanctioning the spelling of *alright*, she seems unaware that the word itself is in the process of obsolescence, becoming replaced by the universal *OK*.

The work seems intended as an international guide to English usage. Indeed, it can be considered the standard reference work of its kind, essential for all libraries. Its appearance is timely, as a new century is about to begin.—**John B. Beston**

Terms and Phrases

1091. **Metaphors Dictionary.** Elyse Sommer and Dorrie Weiss, eds. Detroit, Gale, 1995. 833p. index. $65.00. ISBN 0-8103-9149-X.

The editors have succeeded in producing a comprehensive compendium of metaphors having universal scope and applicability. More than 6,000 metaphors (of which at least 600 are from Shakespeare) compose this thick volume. Basic arrangement is by theme or topic, listed in alphabetical order. At the beginning of each section, appropriate cross-references are supplied to guide the reader to other pertinent metaphors. All metaphors within a thematic section are numbered sequentially, providing metaphor, author or speaker, source, and sometimes date. These numbered entries are keyed to extensive subject and author/speaker indexes that complement the volume.

In addition to pure metaphors, this work also includes examples of mixed metaphors, extended metaphors, similes, personification, allusion, metonymy, and antonomasia—all provided to serve a potential audience of writers, speakers, and others who may need to enhance their own work. Also provided is a brief listing of sources for further consultation and a bibliography of sources used to cull the present metaphors.

Any library serving patrons involved in creative writing, composition, public speaking, or literary criticism should add this volume. Although not exhaustive, it provides enough variety and access to render itself of value.—**Edmund F. SantaVicca**

1092. Sisson, A. F., and Barbara Ann Kipfer. **Sisson's Word and Expression Locater.** 2d ed. Englewood Cliffs, N.J., Prentice Hall/Career & Personal Development, 1994. 404p. index. $27.95; $14.95pa. ISBN 0-13-814088-X; 0-13-814096-0pa.

Sisson has published many works, including *Sisson's Synonyms* (Parker Publishing, 1969) and *The Unabridged Crossword Puzzle Dictionary* (Doubleday, 1963). *Sisson's Word and Expression Locater* is a thesaurus that provides the word from its meaning rather than the meaning of the word. This "dictionary of reverse" is intended for people looking for better power of expression and description. Unlike an ordinary synonyms dictionary, this book provides subheadings of related words under the main-entry word, enabling users to find a word from just an idea. To quote an example from the introduction, to locate a word for the age of a tree, one will find *dendrochronology* from the subheading *Time* under the main entry *TREE*.

Another good feature of the book is an index by category, which divides all main-entry words into 10 broad categories and appears in alphabetical order at the end. This allows users to search for words or expressions in more than one way, as well as to browse through words quickly. The boldface main-entry words are written in uppercase letters; the spacious arrangement of words and bigger fonts also make this book valuable.

This user-friendly thesaurus provides more than 3,700 main-entry words that lead to 100,000-plus words and expressions. Unfortunately, this book lacks scientific and technical terms, including computer-related words, now used in everyday life. Despite this, *Sisson's Word and Expression Locater* is a necessary companion to readers, writers, speakers, and word puzzle/game players for building vocabulary and making their works expressive, clear, and original.—**Sung Ok Kim**

Thesauri

1093. **NTC's Thesaurus of Everyday American English.** By Anne Bertram. Lincolnwood, Ill., National Textbook, 1995. 480p. $12.95pa. ISBN 0-8442-5826-1.

This volume purports to be a "practical resource" for readers who are trying to find and understand the correct words for each particular situation. It aims to supplement dictionaries and other thesauruses (the preface assures us that using the word *thesauri* is also correct) by providing what the casual user needs. Bertram is partially successful. The best feature of the book is the inclusion of brief phrases that show how a particular word might be used. For example, under *obscure* there are the following examples: "Several dark stains obscured the writing on the page." "A veil obscured the visitor's face." Roughly 50 percent of the entries send the browser somewhere else. The first seven entries at the beginning of the letter G look like this: *gab* See the entry for *talk*; *gag* See the entry for *joke*; *gaggle* See the entry for *herd*; *gain* See the entry for *benefit, get*; *gale* See the entry for *wind*; and *gallery* and *gallop* follow in the same vein. No risqué words are included, and current slang words and expressions are not represented. Neither are words such as *gay* (any meaning—the word simply does not exist), *maven, super,* and the like. *Offense* exists only in its criminal implications, while *officer* exists only as a member of the police force. *Fleece* sends you to *fur* and nowhere else. On the other hand, both *imply* and *infer* are properly represented and explained. In showing the proper usage for words that are included, the thesaurus may prove extremely valuable to many people who find it hard to compose a proper sentence.—**Koraljka Lockhart**

1094. **The Oxford Desk Thesaurus.** American ed. Laurence Urdang, ed. New York, Oxford University Press, 1995. 660p. $12.95. ISBN 0-19-509960-5.

This desk thesaurus is a condensation of its parent, *The Oxford Thesaurus* (American ed.; see ARBA 94, entry 1107). Similar to the parent volume, entries are selected for their frequency in the language. They are arranged alphabetically, and where an entry has more than one meaning, synonyms are placed in sense groups. Each sense group within an entry is illustrated by use of a sample sentence, providing the reader with the correct choice of words.

Extensive cross-references provide gateways to further clarity regarding words and their proper use. Labels also assist in identifying special uses of a word (e.g., colloquial, taboo, archaic, technical, slang, and so on). These labels are further clarified regarding use in both American and British English. The editor also has enhanced the volume by including unusual words or phrases. This is a handy, portable, one-volume guide to words and word choices, suitable for any ready-reference collection or home or office library.—**Edmund F. SantaVicca**

1095. **Roget's II: The New Thesaurus.** 3d ed. By the Editors of The American Heritage Dictionaries. New York, Houghton Mifflin, 1995. 1200p. index. $16.95. ISBN 0-395-68722-5.

Roget's has as much authority among thesauruses as Webster's has among dictionaries. Yet, just as Merriam-Webster cannot prevent other publishers from trading on the Webster's name, HarperCollins cannot prevent other publishers from trading on the name Roget's. The closest thesaurus to the original (1852) Roget's is *Roget's International Thesaurus* (see ARBA 93, entry 1075), which groups about 350,000 words and phrases into 15 large classes and 1,073 subcategories. Although this book offers many fine distinctions among synonyms or near-synonyms, general users sometimes are annoyed by the fact that the standard editions of Roget's do not include definitions and sometimes offer too many choices in too many subcategories.

Roget's II has neither of these disadvantages. All of the synonyms appear in one alphabetical list. There is a category index, but it is much shorter than *Roget's International*. *Roget's II* is quite up-to-date, and is based on the 3d edition of the *American Heritage Dictionary of the English Language* (see ARBA 93, entry 1056). Main entries are in boldface, followed by a word (not an abbreviation) denoting part of speech. Definitions are brief—just enough to identify the meaning. There are bountiful *see* references to related words. Different senses of synonyms are separated by numbered subentries. Special senses, such as slang and idioms, are included at the end of entries. A favorite lookup in a thesaurus is the word *drunk*, because, according to Paul Dickson (*Dickson's Word Treasury* [Wiley, 1992, p. 253]) there are at least 2,660 synonyms in English for this word, qualifying it for the *Guinness Book of Records*. *Roget's II* does a fair job with *drunk*, listing 41 synonyms, distinguishing denotative terms such as *inebriated* from such informal words as *cockeyed* and such slang terms as soused.

Another recent competitor to *Roget's II* is *Roget A to Z* (see ARBA 95, entry 1069), which is also arranged alphabetically, but does not include definitions or a category index. *Roget's II* is a handy book for general users who do not want as many choices as *Roget's International*. However, discriminating users will need to remember that no one thesaurus can ever hope to answer the sometimes puzzling usage questions posed when one word is used as a substitute for another.—**David Isaacson**

Visual

1096. The Oxford-Duden Pictorial English Dictionary. 2d ed. New York, Oxford University Press, 1995. 811p. illus. index. $17.95pa. ISBN 0-19-861311-3.

When reference workers are called upon to produce a picture of a machine, a tool, or almost any specialized piece of equipment, they turn to a pictorial dictionary, often identified by the trademark name as a Duden. The *Oxford-Duden Pictorial English Dictionary* includes 384 plates with facing-page vocabulary identifying everything from a discotheque layout (dance floor, barstool, long drink) to the dials on the instrument panel of a single-engine airplane (turn indicator, right tank fuel gauge, accelerometer). For the bookbinding machine, an accompanying plate gives 71 specific parts. Seventy-three items are identified as tools used by the wood joiner. All of the terms are then included in a comprehensive index.

According to the preface, the current edition contains 1,500 new items not present in the 1981 version (see ARBA 82, entry 1188). This may be true, but an examination of both editions shows much duplication. In a 13-page section on papermaking and printing, the editors have added only one new page. The two pages for "The Butcher Shop" and the two pages for "The Bakery" stand line-for-line as they were previously. The illustrations are clear, but the small typeface may pose problems for some users. For American users, it is convenient that the British English vocabulary has been rendered into American English so that one finds, for example, "*dustbin* (Amer. garbage can)." This dictionary would be a useful addition to any library lacking the 1981 edition, and as the price is reasonable, it may even be considered for those institutions holding the earlier edition.—**Donald C. Dickinson**

NON-ENGLISH-LANGUAGE DICTIONARIES

Azerbaijani

1097. Mamedov, Seville. **English-Azerbaijani/Azerbaijani-English Concise Dictionary.** New York, Hippocrene Books, 1995. 144p. $14.95pa. ISBN 0-7818-0244-X.

Azerbaijani is one of the Turkic languages of the former Soviet Union. Indeed, it is so close to Turkish (as spoken in Turkey) that it is mostly only the orthography that makes any difference. This is not surprising, since Azerbaijani spelling was constructed in the Soviet era with the specific purpose of stressing differences in pronunciation from Osman Turkish in order to set the two idioms on diverging paths. The other area of disparity is the far greater number of Russian loanwords in Azerbaijani. The situation of the other Turkic languages of the former Soviet Union is not much different; one cannot help but wonder whether the differentiating trend will be sustained under the new regime.

Be that as it may, this is a small, but good, dictionary. There is no grammar either in the front matter or in the entries (aside from indication of word classes), but there are pronunciation indications in both parts of the dictionary. Like many Hippocrene dictionaries, the present one also uses Azerbaijani symbols to indicate English pronunciation, and English spellings to indicate the Azerbaijani sounds. Naturally, this scheme does not work too well, as is particularly evident for the English entries; the greatest weakness here is the absence of any indication of English stress.

However, the equivalents indicated are numerous and well chosen, and there is some disambiguation of meaning. For instance, *girlfriend* [qiz dostu] is disambiguated by the gloss ([oǧlanin] "of a boy") from all the other possible meanings of this entry word. On the whole, this is a well-printed, elementary dictionary.—**L. Zgusta**

Bosnian

1098. Uzicanin, Nikolina S. **Bosnian-English, English-Bosnian Concise Dictionary.** New York, Hippocrene Books, 1995. 331p. $14.95pa. ISBN 0-7818-0276-8.

The main language of the former Yugoslavia was called Serbo-Croatian, of which there are two varieties—the Eastern (or Serbian) kind and the Western (or Croatian) one. The two varieties are mutually intelligible; granted, there are lexical differences, but these are less extensive than those between British and American English. As the ethnic tension escalated, the Croats started reversing the sequence of the elements of the name, calling the language alternately Croato-Serbian and Serbo-Croatian, but toward the end of their coexistence with the Serbs, they took to calling the language simply Croatian. Bosnia-Herzegovina is a transition zone in which adherence to the Eastern or to the Western variety is determined by geography, religion, and other circumstances. Naturally, there are local dialects spoken there, but in writing, the standard language is used.

This dictionary makes the claim that it gives a Bosnian variety of the standard language, but the claim is not substantiated. The foreword tries to prove the claim by drawing the reader's attention to *kumšiluk* [neighborhood] (a borrowing from Turkish) and *putar* [butter] (a borrowing from German) as specifically Bosnian terms. However, both words are known and used outside of Bosnia as well, just as are other Turkish borrowings. In contrast, such specifically Muslim expressions as [mosque] and [minaret] are not listed at all.

The vocabulary and the entries are minimal; in addition, they tend to be tailored to the local conditions. For example, the verb [to market] is translated *prodavati/kupovati na tržištu*, which means "to sell/buy at the marketplace"; this, however, is hardly the modern meaning of the English verb, not to mention the fact that the user has no way to disambiguate the two verbs. The choice of collocations is not particularly felicitous either. English pronunciation is indicated in the Serbo-Croatian-English part by quite good characters; in fact, ones closer to the International Phonetic Alphabet system than is usual in American English dictionaries.—**L. Zgusta**

Chickasaw

1099. Munro, Pamela, and Catherine Willmond. **Chickasaw: An Analytical Dictionary.** Norman, Okla., University of Oklahoma Press, 1994. 539p. $39.95. ISBN 0-8061-2662-0.

The Chickasaw Indians are one of the original "Five Tribes" who were moved by the U.S. government to the Indian Territory of Oklahoma in the 1830s from their earlier home to the southeast. Their language belongs to the Muskogean family, which also includes Choctaw, a closely related but separate tongue. Chickasaw is now spoken by fewer than 1,000 people, mostly in the area of the original Chickasaw Nation in south-central Oklahoma.

This volume, the first scholarly dictionary ever to be prepared for the language, is the result of a 17-year collaboration between Munro, who is a professor of linguistics at UCLA and a specialist in American Indian languages, and Willmond, a native speaker of the language. The research that went into the work is based on the speech not only of Willmond, but of more than 40 other Chickasaw speakers in Oklahoma who were interviewed by the authors. The book begins with a 52-page introduction that describes pronunciation, orthography, and word structure. Then follows the main body of the book, a Chickasaw-English dictionary with some 12,000 entries, plus subentries and cross-references. The work ends with a 172-page English-Chickasaw index, making this in effect a two-way dictionary. This book meets the highest standards of linguistic acumen, practical usefulness, and lexicographic sophistication; it will be of equally high value both to professional linguists and to the Chickasaw language community. The work is clearly not only the definitive dictionary of Chickasaw, but a model for dictionaries of American Indian languages in general.—**William Bright**

French

1100. The Compact Oxford-Hachette French Dictionary. Marie-Helene Correard and Mary O'Neill, eds. New York, Oxford University Press, 1995. 1007p. index. $13.95pa. ISBN 0-19-864535-X.

In the past couple of years, foreign-language dictionaries have become highly refined. The widespread use of computers has given compilers a database to draw from, one that finds and displays the contexts in which a word is used and the frequency of specific usages. Also, recent dictionaries are being directed toward English speakers, so that there is no longer any need to provide phonetic transcriptions of English words.

With English speakers in mind, the dictionary can concentrate on the particular difficulties of translating English structures into French. Therefore, there are whole pages devoted to such difficulties as the translation of English modal auxiliaries *should, might,* and *have to* and such diversely used auxiliaries as *do* and *get*. In addition, there are pages providing sample letters of invitation in French, the acceptance or declining of invitations, applications for jobs, typical job advertisements and the abbreviations used in them, and a curriculum vitae in French. These are immensely helpful additions that previous dictionaries have not offered.

The vocabulary is reasonably up-to-date, although not as much as one would expect from a database-compiled dictionary. The most common computer terms, which are usually quite different in French, are listed, but by no means all of them. In addition, although a symbol is provided to indicate vulgarities, a check of such terms did not find any listed; even if vulgar, these are an important part of a language. Phrasal verbs, which have proliferated since World War II, are thoroughly and intelligently listed. As the concept of dictionaries is undergoing radical revision, it is a pleasure to have such useful compilations as this available.—**John B. Beston**

1101. The Oxford Paperback French Dictionary and Grammar. By William Rowlinson and others. New York, Oxford University Press, 1995. 506p. $12.95pa. ISBN 0-19-864529-5.

The name "Oxford" implies a towering reputation for excellence, and this work is no exception. Curiously, however, this title is almost identical to a 1992 Oxford University Press publication, *The Oxford Guide to the French Language*, reviewed in ARBA 94 (see entry 1083). The grammar section, in fact, seems to have been copied verbatim from the earlier work. It would be interesting to know the thinking that went into a title change with so little change in content, but because there is no front matter whatsoever (the work just begins with a table of contents and launches into its discussion of French grammar), no explanation is provided. The assumption is that the publishers, while changing the title, for whatever reason hoped to get some extra mileage out of the material, and they have done so. Whatever the motive, Oxford University Press still does a wonderful job of organizing, simplifying, and presenting material.

The French grammar has sections that provide easy-to-understand rules, with examples taken from everyday speech, newspapers, and magazines, and help in resolving the vexing problem of noun gender for those whose native tongue lacks such distinctions. Separate portions treat parts of speech, word order, verb tables, translation problems, and pronunciation traps. Commendably, the pronunciation is described phonetically, rather than with the complicated symbology of lexicographers (for example, *boeuf* is rendered as "berf"), making it easier for anglophones to deal with the tricky sounds of spoken French.

While the dictionary section at first shows little substantive change, the compilers state in their brief introduction that "some entries have been substantially revised, and we have been able to incorporate a large proportion of new material." Perhaps this is true. The cover boasts "over 50,000 words and phrases," whereas its predecessor had only 45,000. While the compilers are not particularly prescriptive, usage notes (e.g., nonstandard usage termed "argot") abound. The juxtaposition of a dictionary and a grammar handbook in one handy paperback results in a somewhat smaller lexicon than one would ordinarily expect to find in a good reference dictionary.

None of the foregoing is intended to be criticism. This handy, authoritative paperback will be of equal value for the traveler and the student. It is highly recommended, but libraries already holding the 1992 work may want to skip this one.—**Bruce A. Shuman**

1102. **Standard French-English, English-French Dictionary.** Faye Carney and others, eds. New York, Larousse Kingfisher Chambers, 1994. 996p. $29.95. ISBN 2-03-420260-0.

Larousse published new editions of both their unabridged and their concise and pocket French-English dictionaries in 1993 (see ARBA 95, entries 1074-1076), and this standard edition fills a niche somewhere between them. It is designed for use by students and teachers at the high school and university level, and for those who use French regularly in their work or leisure activities. With 220,000 entries, it concentrates on current everyday usage and vocabulary. New words and proper nouns, and the language of business and computing (*infographie*, *download*, *idiot-proof*) are well represented.

United States terms and usage are included, as are British, Swiss, Belgian, and Canadian terms. English compounds ([horse sense], [ice show]) are frequently treated as main entries, not buried in long lists of examples, and are therefore easy to find. Explanatory definitions and usage glosses are provided for many difficult-to-translate words and phrases. Vulgar and colloquial terms are easily identified. Conjugation tables are provided for French verbs, with cross-references from the text. There is a table of English irregular verbs as well.

Interspersed throughout the text are "usage modules"—practical tips for handling everyday situations, consisting primarily of sample phrases and their translations. For example, the module on using the telephone includes how to ask for a person, how to explain a wrong number, and typical answering machine messages. There are more than 50 of these usage modules in each half of the dictionary for such topics as introductions, giving advice, thank-yous, good-byes, numbers, correspondence, and many more. By virtue of its clarity, currency, scope, and ease of use, this dictionary is ideally suited for its intended audience.—**Emily L. Werrell**

Fulani

1103. **Hippocrene Practical Fulani-English Dictionary.** By F. W. Taylor. New York, Oxford University Press, 1932; repr., Hippocrene Books, 1995. 242p. $14.95pa. ISBN 0-7818-0404-3.

Fulani is spoken along the west coast of Africa, from Guinea to Cameroons. This 10,000-entry dictionary is a reprint of a 1932 work. The definitions range from 1 to 100 words, with synonyms adding much to the length of some entries. The pronunciation guide is limited; long and short vowels are marked, but nothing more. The use of words in sample sentences is helpful, however. An appendix lists the names for different kinds of cattle (e.g., a *guddiri* is a bull that lacks a tail). A second appendix delineates the months of the year. Cross-references are used freely to direct the reader among words with similar meanings. Libraries needing a Fulani dictionary will likely have to select from a limited number of available titles. This paperback, while by no means comprehensive, is an adequate source.—**Ed Volz**

German

1104. **Collins German-English, English-German Dictionary.** 2d ed. Peter Terrell and others, eds.; revised by Eva Vennebusch and Robin Sawers. New York, HarperCollins, 1994. 613p. $20.00. ISBN 0-06-275515-3.

What a fine dictionary this is! Gone is the staidness that was a hallmark of German dictionaries earlier this century. The introduction is lively and entertaining, and the editors even warn of the limitations of dictionaries used incautiously.

This dictionary is unusually up-to-date on current vocabulary with such words as *sneakers*, *skateboard*, *grunge*, *wimp*, *pantyhose*, and *crack* (the drug). Nearly all computer terms are here, many more than are found in other recent dictionaries that claim to be current. Also, the editors are inventive in translating English words that do not easily render themselves into other European languages, such as *sip*, *scurry*, *cower*, *wry*, *supercilious*, *slink*, and *sleazy*. The vulgarities are translated also, including sexual ones, with a cautionary distinction between (*col*), colloquial, (*col!*), potentially offensive, and (*col!!*), highly offensive. Phrasal verbs, the nightmare of students of present-day English, are entered in accordance with a simple, accurate system that reflects the editors' thorough training in structural linguistics.

It should also be noted that the phonetic transcription of English words records British pronunciation, not American. This work constantly gives the sense of a living language in quick and constant change, not of an honored entity that is gathering dust even as it is being preserved. It is the one German dictionary that deserves to be the standard in any library.—**John B. Beston**

Greek

1105. **The Pocket Oxford Greek Dictionary: Greek-English, English-Greek.** J. T. Pring, comp. New York, Oxford University Press, 1995. 572p. $15.95pa. ISBN 0-19-864197-4.

A revision of the compiler's *Oxford Dictionary of Modern Greek* (see ARBA 84, entry 1049), this new edition features the use of the monotonic accent system, an increase in the proportion of demotic to puristic forms, and the addition of new material to both sections. The definitions are spare but adequate, and there are plentiful examples of idiomatic usage, especially in the English-Greek section. The U.S. user should be advised, however, that these idiomatic usages, along with diction and spelling, are British.

Unfortunately, despite its revisions and updating, this dictionary still falls victim (as did its predecessor) to that nemesis of modern Greek lexicography, the demotic/puristic dichotomy. Although the compiler has purged many puristic forms from this new edition, he has unaccountably allowed many to remain. For example, *ekthesis* has been modernized to *ekthese*, but *ektelesis* remains unchanged. Both *ichthys* and *psari* are defined as fish, but with no indication that the former is a strictly puristic word. Under [fish] in the English-Greek section, readers are referred only to *psari*. Is this the dictionary's roundabout way of informing that *ichthys* is not in current use? Apparently not, since in the similar case of *oinos* and *krasi*, they are both defined as wine, yet under [wine] both words are found. There is no way for a beginner to know which of these two words to use in speech.

The appendixes on personal and place-names are a similar mishmash of demotic and puristic forms. In addition, sometimes words are used as definitions in one section but are not themselves defined in the other section (e.g., under [jailer] one finds *desmophylakas*, but the latter is not defined in the Greek-English section). The Greek-English and English-Greek learner's dictionaries of D. N. Stavropoulos remain unchallenged as the finest in this field.—**Jeffrey R. Luttrell**

Haitian

1106. **Hippocrene Concise Haitian Creole-English, English-Haitian Creole Dictionary.** By Charmant Theodore. New York, Hippocrene Books, 1995. 291p. $11.95pa. ISBN 0-7818-0275-X.

A reasonably priced, pocket-sized word book, this tightly bound dictionary lists a maximum of 26 Haitian-Creole words per page (e.g., *fatra* [fahtrah] *n* trash, mess, refuse; *ill* [ihl] *adj.* malad). The simple h-base pronunciation system makes the book accessible to young readers and persons less familiar with complicated diacritical markings. However, the failure to syllabify or to indicate major and minor stresses leaves some doubt about placement of emphasis. Also, the grave accent appears regularly over words with no explanation as to its use or meaning (e.g., *rebò, sèkèy, lasajès, lekòls*). Entry style is also a puzzle: [forsake] is followed by *v lage, abandone*; [fork] is followed by *n fouchèt, n ranmase*. The repetition of the symbol for *noun* suggests two instruments (table fork or agricultural fork), whereas the paired meanings by [forsake] imply synonyms. Also, there is no explanation of notation for *tròk {twòk}*.

Information about the Haitian-Creole language is limited because of the absence of basic terms (ankle, spine, car, sweater, luggage, taxi, airport, newspaper, painting, library) and because of a lack of a guide to grammar, particularly regular and irregular plurals. Some of the words listed seem bizarre for a beginning list (vogue, espionage, ragamuffin, sluggard, qualm, kindling, xenophobia). The pronunciation of English words is unclear (e.g., *clothe* [klotfv]; *my* [may]. The blurb on the back cover indicates that an introduction appears in the text; however, the last 13 pages contain advertisements for other Hippocrene books rather than the promised syntactical helps.—**Mary Ellen Snodgrass**

Hamito-Semitic

1107. Orel, Vladimir E., and Olga V. Stolbova. **Hamito-Semitic Etymological Dictionary: Materials for a Reconstruction.** New York, E. J. Brill, 1995. 578p. index. (Handbook of Oriental Studies; The Near and Middle East, no.18). $200.00. ISBN 90-04-10051-2.

This is a succinct etymological dictionary that marshals before the user an array of compared forms, which are listed in the basic canonical form, usually the root: One form is allotted one meaning. All literature is quoted in the reference section, and no references appear in the individual entries. Without doubt, the subtitle "Materials for a Reconstruction" is quite accurate. The preface to the main text gives tables of sound correspondences considered plausible among the Hamito-Semitic languages. This information allows scholars who are more at home in the Semitic part of the family (or phylum, as the authors prefer to call it) to refresh their memories concerning the African area, or the other way around. There are few scholars who would have an equal mastery of all the disparate languages of this large phylum, which is also termed the "Afro-Asiatic phylum" of languages.

There are 2,672 reconstructed roots in the book, which constitute a rich harvest. The authors display a laudable constraint in the respect of focusing on Hamito-Semitic languages and to not allow speculations to enter their selection of what they consider more solid facts. Such reasonable constraint permeates the entire book. For instance, any effort at constructing a Hamito-Semitic and Indo-European genetic relation would capitalize on attempts at finding traces of something like Indo-European ablaut in the Hamito-Semitic languages, but the authors coolly resist that temptation.

Occasionally, the authors use a terminology that requires some getting used to by the reader. For instance, roots such as *ab-* [father] or *am* [woman] are referred to as cases of onomatopoeia, whereas the term more generally used in English is "nursery words" or "lallnamen." There can be no doubt that this will be a useful tool for the stated purpose.—**L. Zgusta**

Hebrew

1108. **Harduf's Transliterated English-Hebrew Dictionary. Third Volume: H-K.** Willowdale, Ont., Harduf Books, 1995. 495p. $45.50pa. (U.S.). ISBN 0-920243-27-4.

This third segment of a large English-Hebrew/Hebrew-English dictionary project, similar to the preceding two volumes, presents in an easy-to-use, clear, well-printed form Hebrew equivalents of English words. The entries include the English headword, the part of speech, the Hebrew word, and its transliteration into English. For some of the Hebrew words, biblical and literary sources are given. At the beginning of the volume there is a pronunciation key for vowels, diphthongs, and consonants.

Different typefaces are used for the English word and its Hebrew transliteration, which eases reading. The page layout and typography are pleasing to the eye. The information is presented in two columns, which also helps readability. The book is printed on certificate linen writing paper. The wide inner margins are important for future binding decisions.

The author is a recognized scholar, linguist, and lexicographer. He has published many other books, including a transliterated Yiddish-English dictionary. This dictionary is most appropriate for academic and special libraries, including synagogue libraries, with strong Hebrew language collections. It serves as a useful complement to other Hebrew dictionaries currently available on the market.—**Susan J. Freiband**

Hungarian

1109. **The Oxford-Duden Pictorial Hungarian-English Dictionary.** New York, Oxford University Press, 1994. 1v. (various paging). illus. index. $55.00. ISBN 0-19-864511-2.

This is one in a series of foreign-language, pictorial dictionaries based on the 3d revised edition of the German *Bildwöterbuch*, published as volume 3 of the 10-volume Duden series of dictionaries. This volume contains the same pictures as the other dictionaries in this series, such as *The Oxford-Duden Pictorial Portuguese-English Dictionary* (see ARBA 94, entry 1127).

The dictionary has a detailed table of contents that lists 11 major subject areas such as "atom, universe, earth"; "man and his social environment"; "trades, crafts and industry"; "transport, communications, and information technology"; and "animals and plants." Listed under each are from 7 to 90 specific subjects such as *atom, astronomy, moon landing*, and *atmosphere* under "atom, universe, earth." Each subheading can usually be found on two pages that include a plate with numbered illustrations and a list of words with corresponding numbers, first in Hungarian, then English. British English is used, but if there is a different word in American usage, then it is listed and so indicated in parentheses. There is a thorough Hungarian and English word index that refers the reader to the subject and item number. Unfortunately, the index is letter-by-letter, which results in such confusing listings as "Maya temple" between "may" and "may bug."

Since this dictionary contains the same pictures as those in previously published volumes, it also means that some of the pictures are dated, especially those dealing with technology (computers, typesetting, telecommunications, and audio and video equipment). These areas, however, are updated in the newly published editions of the German and Spanish pictorial dictionaries. Unfortunately, this was not done for the present volume. There are individual pictures that could also use updating; for example, the pictures of libraries and election places. Some of the terms referring to native peoples under "ethnology" should also be updated to reflect current usage and sensitivities. There are some other problematic translations. This could be due to the preponderance of British usage, but not always. There are some strange usages, such as *motor ship* for a large passenger/cargo ship and *Indio* for a Central or South American Indian. Also, the picture of a pumpkin is so identified, but *squash* is given in parentheses as an American usage. Despite some misleading meanings, the number of pictures and words in this dictionary makes it very useful, as one can visualize what is meant. In case of doubt as to a correct word, one can always go to a regular dictionary. (See entries 1096, 1110, and 1140 for other dictionaries in the series.)—**Kathleen Farago**

Italian

1110. **The Oxford-Duden Pictorial Italian and English Dictionary.** New York, Oxford University Press, 1995. 1v. (various paging). $39.95; $19.95pa. ISBN 0-19-864516-3; 0-19-864517-1pa.

Learning a second language is sometimes frustrating in that often one knows what to look for but cannot quite remember what the correct name of the item is in the native language, which makes trying to find it in a second language all the more frustrating. What if one could just point? That is possible with this dictionary.

The work lists approximately 28,000 objects in its numbered illustrations, divided into the following major headings: the atom, the universe, and the earth; man and his social environment; nature as environment, agriculture, and forestry; trades, crafts, and industry; printing industry; transport, communications, and information technology; office, bank, and stock exchange; community; recreation, games, and sport; entertainment, culture, and art; and animals and plants. Each major heading is subdivided into many subheadings, with their illustrations and translations in both Italian and British English—American English is in parentheses.

Coverage ranges from the familiar to the highly specialized. The illustrations are excellent, most in black-and-white. There are two indexes, one in Italian, the other in English. This will be an indispensable supplement to any Italian-English, English-Italian dictionary, and is highly recommended. [R: Choice, May 95, p. 1401]—**Robert L. Turner Jr.**

Japanese

1111. **Kodansha's Furigana Japanese-English Dictionary.** New York, Kodansha America, 1995. 572p. $28.00pa. ISBN 4-7700-1983-1.

Students who have studied the Japanese language for several months find it easier to read hiragana or katakana scripts than roman letters, which were so far the generally accepted form in Japanese-English dictionaries. Japanese is written with a combination of kanji (Chinese characters), hiragana, and katakana scripts, and *furigana* refer to the small hiragana or katakana scripts added above or alongside kanji to show their pronunciation. *Kodansha's Furigana Japanese-English Dictionary* has been published to serve nonnative students who are already familiar with the hiragana and katakana scripts, and *furigana* have been printed above every kanji appearing in the dictionary.

The *Dictionary* includes kanji (such as *oogesa*, *oomisoka*, and *kirei*) likely to be known by educated Japanese but not on the official list of 1,945 kanji for general use; thus, it goes beyond the minimum requirements for Japanese literacy. Each entry of the dictionary is given first in hiragana or katakana, and then—where appropriate—is provided in kanji. Some of the helpful features of the work are: labels of speech-level, such as "colloquial," "formal," and "honorific"; cross-references; antonyms; synonyms; and many entries that are illustrated by short sentences, phrases, and compounds. Appendixes consist of "Conjugation," "Numerals, Counters, and Numbers," and "Place Names."

The entries are not arranged in alphabetical but in Japanese syllabary order, which may cause some confusion for the user. For example, "u" and "o" are the fourth and fifth scripts in the Japanese syllabary order, and the entries that begin with "u" and "o" appear according to that order and not according to the order of the Latin alphabet. Except for this potential problem, the *Dictionary* is very useful, and is recommended for students who want to enjoy reading the actual Japanese writing as commonly used.
—Seiko Mieczkowski

1112. **Kodansha's Pocket Kanji Guide.** New York, Kodansha America, 1994. 542p. index. $15.00pa. ISBN 4-7700-1801-0.

The Japanese people use kanji (Chinese characters), hiragana, and katakana scripts in writing; kanji are used to indicate meanings of nouns and the stem part of verbs and adjectives. Most kanji characters are pronounced several ways in addition to *on* and *kun* readings, and among kanji there are many homonyms. *Kodansha's Pocket Kanji Guide* contains 1,006 kanji that form the core of elementary school education in Japan, and that are used by the Japanese in their newspapers, magazines, and other communications.

The majority of kanji is made up from a part called the *radical*, which indicates the fields of meanings, such as water, fire, hand, and so on, to which kanji belong. Reflecting the editors' awareness of this point, in the *Guide* the *radicals* are shown on the margins of every page with the marks to which the kanji in the page belong, or from which they originated. An English translation is affixed to each *radical* when it is first used. Each kanji is introduced with *on* and *kun* readings and compounds, the number of which varies according to kanji. The number of strokes and the stroke order of each kanji are shown.

The review of the "Japanese Writing System" and "User's Manual" in the introductory part of the *Guide* as well as the "Radical" and "Stroke" indexes at the end of the volume are helpful for the user. The *on* and *kun* index should have been arranged in an English alphabetical order instead of Japanese syllabary order. A more comprehensive alternative is the thorough *NTC's New Japanese-English Character Dictionary* (see ARBA 94, entry 1121), with more than 4,000 kanji and a great number of compounds and example sentences. The present *Kodansha's Pocket Kanji Guide* can be called a concise version of a Japanese-English kanji dictionary, and it will be helpful to the students who want to enhance their knowledge of the Japanese language.—**Seiko Mieczkowski**

1113. Martin, Samuel E. **Martin's Concise Japanese Dictionary: English-Japanese, Japanese-English, Fully Romanized with Complete Kanji & Kana.** Rutland, Vt., Charles E. Tuttle, 1994. 736p. $16.95. ISBN 0-8048-1912-2.

Martin, one of the outstanding teachers of Japanese language and the author of *Essential Japanese* (Tuttle, 1954), *Easy Japanese* (Tuttle, 1957), and *A Reference Grammar of Japanese* (Yale University Press, 1975), has now introduced one of the most up-to-date and comprehensive dictionaries ever published. Some features of his dictionary are as follows: more than 18,000 entries; both English-Japanese and Japanese-English sections; English entries written in romanized Japanese and Japanese-English sections; English entries written in romanized Japanese and in kanji and kana for the English word; precise definitions of entries, including sample phrases and sentences; Japanese verbs cited in both the polite and plain forms, as well as in the *te*- or *de*- form; and accent marks, which are critically useful for correctly pronouncing the words.

The dictionary contains words closely associated with Japanese life, including popular dishes, facial expressions, clothes, and Japanized English verbs. These entries are a reflection of Martin's profound knowledge of Japan and the Japanese language. Martin also discusses—in the introduction—pronunciation, grammar, and kanji and kana in Japanese language. This dictionary renders great assistance to students of Japanese, and is highly recommended for students, businesspeople, and college and university libraries. Individual speakers of Japanese will also find this dictionary highly rewarding.—**Seiko Mieczkowski**

Kurdish

1114. Amindarov, Aziz. **Kurdish-English/English-Kurdish Dictionary.** New York, Hippocrene Books, 1994. 313p. $11.95pa. ISBN 0-7818-0246-6.

This is a dictionary of modern Northern Kurdish, Kurdish spoken and written predominantly in Turkey. Hence it is spelled in a Roman alphabet of Turkish inspiration (e.g., c=[dzh], ç=[tsh]). There are divergences from the Turkish orthography, however; for example, the voiced velar fricative is not symbolized by a ğ as in Turkish, but by an x̌. Alphabetization is the same as in Turkish: The diacritically marked letters follow the simple ones.

The information, apart from the equivalents, is restricted to the indication of the morphological word class and pronunciation. Given the regularity of the Turkish/Kurdish alphabet, the pronunciation of the Kurdish words is largely predictable. English pronunciation is given in a way that avoids strange symbols. The simplification is sometimes excessive; for example, *circumference* is given as [surkumfruns]. The pronunciation given is the American one, as are the spellings.

The greatest drawback of the dictionary consists of the lack of discrimination in meanings. Frequently, there are many translations; this is caused not only by the entry word's polysemy, but also by the fact that Kurdish is not a fully stabilized language. Rich synonymy is typical in such a situation. The entry for *circle* [surkl] gives the following translations: *xelak, çembar, hal, hawir, çarme, daîre, helqe, hol, mafir*. Since many of these words are not listed as entry words in the Kurdish-English section, the dictionary is more useful for the Kurdish user. However, the Kurdish-English section is not much better in this respect. Some difference is indicated by the commas and semicolons, whereas the English-Kurdish section uses commas only.

The vocabulary selected is modern and covers the conversational and reading needs of the user. Despite its flaws and given the lack of dictionaries of Kurdish in general and contemporary Kurdish in particular, this well-printed dictionary is a welcome addition.—**L. Zgusta**

Latin

1115. Blaise, Albert. **A Handbook of Christian Latin: Style, Morphology, and Syntax.** Belgium, Brepols and Washington, D.C., Georgetown University Press, 1994. 157p. index. $45.00. ISBN 0-87840-237-3.

The content of this volume is set forth in a straightforward manner by its title and subtitle. The first quarter of this handbook contains a clear discussion of Christian Latin (as distinguished from the narrower focus of Ecclesiastical Latin) and of its distinctive stylistic features in the areas of symbolic, figurative, and emotional language. The remainder of the book is taken up with grammatical observations, primarily in the area of syntax. Readers will easily be able to note differences between the writers surveyed here and earlier authors whose works are traditionally included within the corpus of classical Latin literature. Moreover, it is possible to detect developments in Christian Latin during the many centuries of its use.

This English edition is a translation, by Grant C. Roti, of a study by Blaise that originally appeared in French. By its very nature and in any language, this is a technical work, and Roti has succeeded to a remarkable degree in making this material accessible and readable for its intended audience. Roti has further enhanced its value by compiling two appendixes (the first detailing principal spelling variants; the second, listing authors and works cited) that appeared earlier in another of Blaise's French texts. Libraries that serve students and specialists in this area will certainly want to acquire this handbook. It is not likely to be superseded or to become out-of-date anytime soon.—**Leonard J. Greenspoon**

1116. Ehrlich, Eugene. **Veni, Vidi, Vici: Conquer Your Enemies, Impress Your Friends with Everyday Latin.** New York, HarperPerennial/HarperCollins, 1995. 297p. illus. index. $13.00pa. ISBN 0-06-273365-6.

As with its highly regarded predecessor *Amo, Amas, Amat, and More* (HarperCollins, 1985), this compendium of Latin expressions intends to both instruct and entertain. Ehrlich starts with pronunciation notes and brief biographies of 33 notable Romans, from Julius Caesar to Virgil, who are quoted in the book. The roughly 1,000 alphabetically arranged entries follow; each includes the phrase, its pronunciation, its translation, and then Ehrlich's explanation of the true meaning of the words in context. For example, *fac et excusa* translates literally into "do it and make excuses later," that timeworn but effective approach to managerial decisionmaking. A browser's delight as well as an inexpensive and informative reference, *Veni, Vidi, Vici* will make a useful addition to all libraries.—**G. Kim Dority**

1117. **The Oxford Latin Minidictionary.** James Morwood, ed. New York, Oxford University Press, 1995. 693p. $6.95pa. ISBN 0-19-864225-3.

The 8th fascicle of the *Oxford Latin Dictionary* was published in 1982, thus completing the long-awaited replacement of the standard dictionary of Lewis and Short (see ARBA 83, entry 1094; ARBA 79, entry 1144; and ARBA 77, entry 1095, for previous reviews). This small and handy dictionary is a modest abbreviation in a portable, minidictionary format. It will be popular with high school and college students.—**Bohdan S. Wynar**

1118. Stelten, Leo F. **Dictionary of Ecclesiastical Latin: With an Appendix of Latin Expressions Defined and Clarified.** Peabody, Mass., Hendrickson, 1995. 330p. $24.95. ISBN 1-56563-131-5.

There are a handful of Latin expressions—for example, "*Spiritus Sanctus*" or "*Dum spiro, spero*" (the latter is on the state seal of South Carolina)—that are widely known and used. Such general knowledge of this ancient language is sufficient for most people in most situations, but clearly more is expected of those who serve the Roman Catholic Church in priestly or legal roles. It is this audience that Stelten addresses, and he does so in a manner that is clear and practical.

A dictionary devoted to ecclesiastical Latin properly emphasizes the vocabulary found in the Vulgate, in Canon Law, in the liturgy, and in significant Church documents such as those relating to Vatican II. Stelten supplies abbreviated grammatical descriptions and a fairly full range of English meanings for each of the Latin words or phrases he lists. In an appendix following the main portion of the work, he provides more extensive definitions or descriptions of terms of particular importance for those working in chancery offices. There is some overlap between material covered here and in the larger dictionary that precedes it.

Stelten's research, which extended beyond the documents themselves to a survey of people who interpret these documents, assures readers of this volume that its contents will be useful in their day-to-day activities of study and service. Libraries and resource centers frequented by individuals engaged in such work would be performing a service of their own by acquiring this dictionary and making it as accessible as possible.—**Leonard J. Greenspoon**

Lushootseed

1119. Bates, Dawn, Thom Hess, and Vi Hilbert. **Lushootseed Dictionary.** Seattle, Wash., University of Washington Press, 1994. 381p. maps. $30.00pa. ISBN 0-295-97323-4.

Lushootseed is the name of an American Indian language spoken in the vicinity of Seattle, Washington; it is also called Puget Salish and Skagit-Nisqually. It is a member of the Salish family of languages, spoken at one time from central British Columbia to western Montana. The present dictionary is the work of Hilbert, a native Lushootseed speaker; Hess, a linguist who published an earlier *Dictionary of Puget Salish* (University of Washington Press, 1976); and Bates, also a linguist, who coordinated and edited the work. The main body of the volume is a Lushootseed-English dictionary of great lexicographical sophistication, organized in terms of roots. Abundant information is given on grammatical classifications, derived stems (with example sentences), dialect variants, and related forms. A diversified typographical system assists the reader's orientation to the wealth of data provided. The volume ends with an English-Lushootseed index and list of personal names.—**William Bright**

Norwegian

1120. **Norwegian Dictionary: Norwegian-English, English-Norwegian.** 2d ed. New York, Routledge, 1994. 553p. $24.95pa. ISBN 0-415-10801-2.

The authorship of this book is not clear, as the only name on the title page is that of Kari Bråtveit as the author of a supplement. However, no supplement can be found in the book; perhaps what is meant is additions included in this 2d edition. Be that as it may, this is an excellent dictionary, prepared with all the attention a good lexicographer pays to every detail and with all the typographical differentiation of various categories of information. The dictionary is prepared primarily for the Norwegian user; hence, all the explanatory glosses in both sections are in Norwegian. However, the anglophone user is also well served. Indeed, it is clear that the two versions are not a mechanical, computer-generated reversal of the entry words and their translations, but were prepared and edited separately. This can be seen clearly when one compares the Norwegian-English version, which gives *karbon-papir* [carbon paper] with the English-Norwegian [carbon] *karbon-papir*. As a translation of *karbon-papir*, [carbon paper] is more explanatory, whereas an entry word [carbon] is the English expression used.

The English pronunciation is given in International Phonetic Alphabet symbols, and British pronunciation is the standard employed, in that only British spellings are indicated. (Norwegian pronunciation being rather predictable on the basis of the orthography, it is treated in the front matter by general rules and examples.) Yet American lexical units are also indicated; for example, [elevator], which gets the translation of both meanings, *heis* (British "lift") and *kornsilo*. This example shows the degree of fineness that the indications of polysemy in the dictionary reach.

Much space is given to set expressions. Under the entry word *stå* there is the term for the "set phrase" itself, *et stående uttrykk*. There are many useful indications; indeed, ones that can be read for pleasure. In short, the work is a very good, modern, detailed dictionary. The next edition could perhaps use a larger font to make the print more easily readable.—**L. Zgusta**

Occult

1121. Hulse, David Allen. **The Key of It All: An Encyclopedic Guide to the Sacred Languages & Magickal Systems of the World. Book Two: The Western Mysteries.** St. Paul, Minn., Llewellyn, 1994. 577p. illus. $24.95pa. ISBN 0-87542-379-5.

This companion volume to *Book One: The Eastern Mysteries* (see ARBA 95, entry 789) is designed for the student of the occult, and as with the first volume, it will frustrate the scholars of the languages it presents. Investigating four complex languages and three symbol systems, the book purports to be the "key to it all," and as such professes the ability to unlock the language of the gods. Greek includes the Gnostic cosmology, Pythagorean metaphors, and the number codes. Coptic contains astrological symbolism and Egyptian hieroglyphs. Runes are presented in Germanic, Icelandic, Scandinavian, and English versions. Latin shows the Renaissance model of the three worlds. Enochian gives the true pattern behind Watchtower symbolism and the Golden Dawn correspondences for this alphabet. Tarot is presented in detail. English includes an attempt at an English Cabalah. Numerology is again a key to interpreting the language and symbol systems. The lists and tables are not explained. As with the first volume, use for its self-stated purpose by an occultist is possible, but use by scholars is quite limited. The general reader should be aware of its limitations.—**Linda L. Lam-Easton**

Russian

1122. English-Russian Comprehensive Dictionary. Oleg P. Benyukh, ed. New York, Hippocrene Books, 1995. 789p. $60.00. ISBN 0-7818-0353-5.

Making foreign-language dictionaries is an expensive undertaking. Soviet Russia, with its low labor costs, had a strong tradition in both dictionary production and translation. Since the advent of glasnost, U.S. publishers have attempted to draw on this to (re)print Russian-made dictionaries. The procedure makes for lower-cost reference works and has the advantage of providing durable paper and bindings—areas in which Russian publications are weak. There are also disadvantages. Such dictionaries are designed for Russians, not English speaker. This is why Russian-made "one-way" English-Russian dictionaries have substantial defects for non-Russian users. In the case at hand, for example, each English entry is accompanied by a phonetic transcription—a feature useless for the English-speaking user. On the other hand, there is insufficient attention to Russian phraseology from the English-speaking point of view.

These general matters aside, this dictionary is a welcome addition to the translator's shelf. Russian vocabulary has been expanding rapidly, and many new terms are to be found here (e.g., fax, floppy disk, and AIDS). On the other hand, much is still missing (e.g., modem, e-mail, hard disk, and gay). Titling the work "comprehensive" is a misnomer, but at 40,000 words, it is one of the fuller one-volume lexicons. The dictionary includes such usual features as appendixes of personal and geographical names, weights and measures, and temperature conversions. A final indication of the work's orientation to the Russian native is the inclusion of a list of Latin tags translated into English, but not Russian. The native English speaker would probably do better with the *Oxford English-Russian Dictionary* (see ARBA 85, entry 974).—**D. Barton Johnson**

1123. HarperCollins Russian Dictionary: Russian-English, English-Russian. college ed. Maree Airlie and others, eds. New York, HarperCollins, 1994. 563p. $20.00pa. ISBN 0-06-276528-0.

This is an excellent medium-sized dictionary for both understanding Russian texts and for producing them. Because both the English and the Russian parts are equally provided with grammatical information (such as irregular forms and syntactic patterns); with semantic discriminations (such as glosses, ranges of application, typical collections); and, last but not least, with the pronunciation (in the International Phonetic Alphabet [IPA]) of the English headwords, this dictionary will be useful to Russian speakers as well.

In comparing the *HarperCollins Russian Dictionary* with dictionaries most similar to it, such as the *Oxford English-Russian Dictionary* (see ARBA 85, entry 974), one finds that in some respects, there is more information in the Oxford work (e.g., more syntactic patterns in the entry of Eng. *a* [indef. art.]), while there is a greater range of modern abbreviations in HarperCollins. The latter dictionary bears the note "college edition," a designation that explains the plethora of abbreviations and other encyclopedic information it contains, such as the Russian versions of English place-names (laudably, along with the names of the inhabitants, as for *Aberdeen/Aberdonian, Manchester/Mancunian*), and vice versa.

The Russian verbal aspects are treated well, with a clear distribution of forms and meanings in the entry and its subentries. Equally useful is the treatment of important formal words in both languages (called "keywords") in boxes. The information provided is not substantively different from what is offered in the Oxford dictionary, but the box simply attracts readers' attention, inviting them not only to seek the concrete bit of information under search but to read the whole entry as well—a useful habit to adopt toward these formal words.

The editors subscribe to the concept of generality of meaning; hence, they treat in one entry homomorphic words belonging to different grammatical classes. Thus, the entry *like* contains in one uninterrupted text the preposition, the adjective, and the verb, the categories being separated by a rhombus; however, the illustrative examples and collocations follow without any orderly distribution.

There are things about the dictionary that leave one wondering, but fortunately they are few. For example, it is difficult to believe that Russian [kak] requires the accusative, nor that the Russian letter [shch] is pronounced "as in Engl. fresh sheets" (p. xxviii). Pronunciations are given, in both the Russian and the English sections, in a broad, phonemic understanding, yet some indications (e.g., on pp. xxvi-xxvii) are in a quite narrow, phonetic transcription. To call "=" the sign of "cultural equivalence" is peculiar wording; what is meant is that the sign indicates equivalence within the same language, as in *NZ = New Zealand*. However, this modern, highly usable dictionary will prove a good tool for any user.—**L. Zgusta**

1124. Katzner, Kenneth. **English-Russian, Russian-English Dictionary.** rev. ed. New York, John Wiley, 1994. 1098p. $60.00; $32.50pa. ISBN 0-471-05677-4; 0-471-01707-8pa.

Bilingual dictionaries are almost by definition intended for language students. Katzner's revised and expanded version of his 1984 work is the only reasonably comprehensive dictionary specifically designed for U.S. students of Russian (see ARBA 85, entry 976, for a review of the previous edition). The Russian section contains about 40,000 words with information on inflection, aspect, stress, and, importantly, word combinations and set phrases. The English-Russian section, with around 26,000 words, has a generous supply of phrases in English and Russian. Both parts are careful to differentiate between multiple meanings of words (e.g., the meanings of *trunk(s)* are specified as *tree, elephant, torso, footlocker, car,* or *swimming*), each with its proper Russian translation. The English section is also strong in representing those two-word expressions (the bane of student translators) that are so much more frequent in English than in Russian (e.g., *grace period*).

Russian vocabulary has changed rapidly in recent years and such changes are reflected in the dictionary, albeit sporadically. For example, one finds the Russian for *floppy disk* but not for *hard disk*. The dictionary covers mostly everyday, basic vocabulary. Neither the literary nor the technical translator will find it adequate. Even the student trying to read much contemporary (or older) fiction will require a dictionary that is more inclusive in all senses. The work at hand contains neither slang, obscenities, nor the common acronyms that figure so heavily in Russian texts. An appendix does, however, contain lists of geographic and family names. This handsomely printed, well-designed dictionary can be strongly recommended for U.S. students of Russian.—**D. Barton Johnson**

1125. Mertvago, Peter. **The Comparative Russian-English Dictionary of Russian Proverbs & Sayings.** New York, Hippocrene Books, 1995. 477p. index. $50.00. ISBN 0-7818-0283-0.

Russia is closer to its oral traditions than the English-speaking world. One reflection of this is the prevalence of proverbs, which are often a problem to translators. Mertvago's well-designed dictionary contains 5,000-odd Russian proverbs for which equivalent or corresponding English proverbs exist. The more common are starred. Each entry is, where possible, followed by an exact equivalent (e.g., *Mir tesen* [It's a small world]). More commonly, there is a literal translation followed by a corresponding English proverb (e.g., *Kak sneg na golovu*, literally [like snow on the head] corresponds to the English [out of the blue]). This example works well, but many of the English proverbs have long passed out of usage. On occasion, similar or antonymic English proverbs are adduced. Also useful is that each Russian entry is cross-referenced to semantically similar Russian proverbs (e.g., a proverb literally meaning [like a blind man discussing colors] is referenced to [don't send a bachelor to arrange a marriage]). Shared biblical and classical sources are indicated.

An introduction briefly discusses the nature of proverbs. One appendix provides a marginally useful list of proverbs containing personal and geographical names. A second, more valuable, appendix applies U.S. folklorist Alan Dundes's classificatory scheme of English proverb structure to Russian material. Although primarily designed for Russian-to-English use, the volume also contains "An English Proverb Index" arranged by keyword, listing all relevant proverbs with cross-references to their Russian counterparts. It also has a bibliography. This volume is the best available resource for its area.

—**D. Barton Johnson**

1126. **The Oxford Russian Minidictionary.** Della Thompson, ed. New York, Oxford University Press, 1995. 696p. $6.95pa. ISBN 0-19-864188-5.

A new work in the Oxford Minidictionary series, this dictionary is not in itself an altogether new work: It is a reduction of the *Pocket Oxford Russian Dictionary* (see entry 1127), which appeared in 1994. The editor of this dictionary had been largely responsible for the English-Russian section of the pocket dictionary. A careful scholar, she has planned her work well, so that within its more limited scope (45,000 words and phrases versus 70,000) and format (now 3-by-4-by-$\frac{1}{2}$-inch), it is superior to the larger and earlier work.

Although Thomspon has taken care to update entries to contemporary Russian usage, she remains essentially conservative: Her English usage is not always contemporary. There is no entry, for instance, for *al(l)right*, and *to cry* is rendered first as [krichat'] and only second as [plakat'], against current usage.

Even contemporary uses such as *access* and *impact* as verbs do not appear as entries. She has not endeavored to deal with any of the common computer terms such as *online, download, modem,* or *hardwired.*

Nevertheless, the dictionary is useful and in a portable format. It is designed for speakers of English (British English, notably), mainly students and tourists. Businesspeople are likely to be less pleased with the book—but they presumably have their own translators.—**John B. Beston**

1127. **The Pocket Oxford Russian Dictionary.** 2d ed. Jessie Coulson, Nigel Rankin, and Della Thompson, comps.; revised by Colin Howlett. New York, Oxford University Press, 1994, 1995. 623p. $32.50; $11.95pa. ISBN 0-19-864500-7; 0-19-864526-0pa.

As a dictionary for English speakers that contains both English-Russian and Russian-English entries, this dictionary has few competitors. The chief competitor, and a much superior one, is Kenneth Katzner's *English-Russian, Russian-English Dictionary* (see entry 1124). Although the *Pocket Oxford Russian Dictionary* advertises itself as revised and updated, the changes are minimal: A few terms such as *fax* are included, but not such terms as *word processor.* What is more of a limitation in the PORD is that it is oriented toward British speakers, whereas Katzner embraces American usage.

In its spare, unaccommodating preface, the PORD defines its users as those who do not have an advanced knowledge of Russian. However, it is really designed for those who have at the least a good intermediate knowledge, and for them a "pocket" dictionary such as this is not adequate. Katzner's dictionary, hardly bigger in size, is much more precise in its information, devoting more space to the various meanings of a word and their corresponding Russian equivalent (e.g., under *shock,* he includes the important sense of *emotional disturbance,* which the PORD omits). Katzner also provides a useful schema of the regular Russian declension patterns, essential for those who do not have an advanced knowledge of Russian—the audience to which the PORD addresses itself. Essentially, the PORD seems to be relying on the established reputation of the Oxford University Press for quality, a reputation that presently is not always deserved.—**John B. Beston**

1128. Shlyakhov, Vladimir, and Eve Adler. **Dictionary of Russian Slang & Colloquial Expressions.** Hauppauge, N.Y., Barron's Educational Series, 1995. 253p. $11.95pa. ISBN 0-8120-9085-3.

If one pairs a classicist with a Slavicist, will a good dictionary of Russian slang be the result? In this case, the answer is yes. Good, current dictionaries of Russian slang, while not being a dime a dozen, are not completely unavailable. The Research Libraries Information Network (RLIN) system lists 28 (including this one) that have been published since 1992. In Russian, a lot of scholarship has gone into the slang coined in Soviet prisons, the slang of thieves, and obscene slang, in contrast to dictionaries of American slang with their focus on city-speak, black vernacular, and cowboys (in addition to the obligatory obscene slang).

Most slang is, of course, short-lived and local, so it is good that slang dictionaries are continuously produced. D. S. Baldaev's wonderful *Slovar' Tiuremno-Lagerno-Blatnogo Zhargona* (Moscow: Kraĭsoskey, 1992) with its 67-page catalog of tattoos, its reprints of articles by the famous Soviet linguist D. S. Likhachev, its 18-page small-print thesaurus, and the 286-page dictionary itself will probably never be surpassed. This is not the case in Shlyakhov and Adler's work. It is less scholarly in intent, less concerned with conveying a sociological context, and more current. It is intended for an audience of students and travelers. It includes street slang, criminal jargon, army and police expressions, teenagers' slang (as well as the obligatory obscenities). Every entry is used in an illustrative sentence, the very American turn of which is pleasingly colloquial and extraordinarily useful. The authors have struck the perfect compromise between heavy, Soviet Socialist scholasticism and cotton-candy, American commercialism. The only thing one would wish for when the next edition comes out is the addition of etymologies.—**Judith M. Brugger**

Semitic

1129. Hoftijzer, J., and K. Jongeling. **Dictionary of the North-West Semitic Inscriptions.** New York, E. J. Brill, 1995. 2v. (Handbook of Oriental Studies; The Near and Middle East, no.21). $343.00/set. ISBN 90-04-09821-6.

The authors of this dictionary present a vastly expanded version of an earlier work, *Dictionnaire des Inscriptions Sémitiques de L'ouest*, published from 1960 to 1965 by C. F. Jean and Hoftijzer. Everyone having to deal with ancient epigraphy knows how scattered the publications of inscriptions frequently are, particularly when considering short inscriptions on ostraca, bottles, and other materials. In this superb collection, the reader gets a digest of such inscriptions in Old Canaanite, Phoenician, Moabite, Ammonite, Hebrew, the language/dialect of the Deir Alla epigraphic texts, Samalian, Old Aramaic and Official Aramaic, Nabatean, Palmyrenean, the Aramaic of the texts from Hatra, the language of the Waw amulet, and Jewish Aramaic. In addition to these, the Phoenician and Punic glosses and insertions in Greek and Latin texts are also listed—certainly a wise decision.

Each entry consists of the lemma in the canonical form of the verbal root or the absolute form of the noun; if the entry word is borrowed, its origin is indicated. Next come the enumeration of all morphological forms attested in the body of inscriptions covered, the indication of the grammatical category, and the indication of the entry word's meaning; if needed, this last rubric discusses individual forms and collocations and their attested meaning(s). Within the entries there are exhaustive references to literature and summaries of scholars' opinions. On the whole, the dictionary is an indispensable reference book for this area of learning.—**L. Zgusta**

Sign Language

1130. **The American Sign Language Dictionary on CD-ROM.** [CD-ROM]. New York, HarperCollins Interactive, 1994. Minimum system requirements: IBM or compatible 386/20MHz. Windows-compatible CD-ROM drive (double-speed recommended). Windows 3.1. 4MB RAM. 13-inch 256-color monitor. Windows-compatible mouse. Sound card (optional). Keyboard. $69.95.

The problem with most American Sign Language (ASL) dictionaries is that they contain one-dimensional illustrations of a highly fluid and three-dimensional language. The *American Sign Language Dictionary on CD-ROM* provides a visual and dynamic tool to help the user form a basic understanding of ASL. Each word has a QuickTime video of a person signing it in addition to an illustration and definition. Each video can be viewed in slow motion, stopped, or zoomed in on so that complicated signs can be read more easily.

There are three different entertaining and useful exercises available to help the user learn the language and its grammar. In addition to word signs, the "Fingerspelling Guide" allows the user to type in a word or letter and view the individual letter signs. A section describing the history and development of ASL, which includes a lengthy bibliography, provides a useful overview. The tutorial moves a bit fast for slow readers, and with only about 2,200 words, the fast learner may become frustrated with its limited vocabulary. Easy to install and use, this dictionary would be useful for public, school, and academic libraries. [R: RBB, 15 Feb 95, p. 1105]—**Elizabeth A. Ginno**

1131. Hoffman, Cheryl M. **Comprehensive Reference Manual for Signers and Interpreters.** 4th ed. Springfield, Ill., Charles C. Thomas, 1994. 305p. $41.95 spiralbound. ISBN 0-398-05919-5.

This alphabetically arranged manual with more than 6,500 entries is designed as a memory aid for experienced signers and interpreters for the deaf. There are no illustrations of the gestural/visual communication system used by the deaf. This title appears to be the standard work of its kind. In the deaf collection at Gallaudet University, which lists 40 titles under "Sign language—Handbooks, manuals, etc.," there is nothing comparable. However, the five copies of each of the four editions owned by Gallaudet show little use. A presumption is that this manual is more useful in the private collection of a professional signer than in a library reference collection. Only 2 of the libraries of the 11 campuses of the University of Maryland own the 3d edition. The local public library system, which serves a large deaf population, owns no copies.

Among the entries are many phrases, idioms, and proper nouns (e.g., "Baltimore," "Lincoln," "Mickey Mouse"). Where the same common English word has several meanings, this manual will give verbal sign descriptions for making as many as three or four different signs. There are many cross-references, including where the sign for an English word is made by combining two or more signs (e.g., "Fugitive = Escape + Agent").

Many phrases from the *Random House American Sign Language Dictionary*, which is illustrated, do not appear in this manual. Newer terms such as "disk" and "byte," as well as names in the news (e.g., "Bosnia"), are not included in this manual. This is a suitable purchase for comprehensive collections on deafness, but the users of most reference collections will find the Random House dictionary or Martin L. A. Sternberg's *American Sign Language Concise Dictionary* (see entry 1132) more helpful.

—**William G. Wilson**

1132. Sternberg, Martin L. A. **American Sign Language Concise Dictionary.** rev. ed. New York, HarperPerennial/HarperCollins, 1994. 737p. illus. $9.00pa. ISBN 0-06-274010-5.

Depending upon your learning style and level of familiarity with American Sign Language, the *American Sign Language Concise Dictionary* offers a good place to begin your acquisition of a substantial sign vocabulary. Each entry contains a short definition along with a verbal description that adds context and additional visual clues, appropriate sign synonyms, and an illustration of the actual sign. For the most part, the illustrations are computer generated and have more shading and depth than the earlier edition. Where there is more than one picture to a sign, the reader may have difficulty putting the actual movements together to create a fluent sign. This is similar to the problem of really being able to pronounce a foreign language using only a dictionary. If new to sign language, one should augment this dictionary with a videotape to help with the kinetic flow of signing. At a hefty 737 pages and containing more than 4,000 words, this pocket dictionary represents a substantial portion of American Sign Language signs and would be very useful for a personal library. Academic and public libraries will want to have the more comprehensive *American Sign Language Dictionary* (see entry 1133) for their shelves.—**Elizabeth A. Ginno**

1133. Sternberg, Martin L. A. **American Sign Language Dictionary.** rev. ed. New York, Harper-Perennial/HarperCollins, 1994. 614p. illus. $18.00pa. ISBN 0-06-273275-7.

As praiseworthy as the 1st edition of Sternberg's *American Sign Language: A Comprehensive Dictionary* (see ARBA 82, entry 1196), this revised edition is instead an "abridged edition." In spite of the inclusion of more than 1,000 new terms and illustrations, the omission of the noteworthy foreword, bibliography, and numerous English-/foreign-language indexes found in the original edition renders this resource more a supplement to the initial edition than an actual revision.

Libraries currently owning the 1981 resource will want to purchase this edition. For those libraries not already owning Sternberg's 1981 resource, purchasing the *American Sign Language Dictionary* is not recommended—consider instead purchasing the 1993 printing of the comprehensive dictionary. Better yet, if technology permits, libraries may want to wait and purchase *The American Sign Language Dictionary on CD-ROM* (see entry 1130) rather than the revised edition.—**Renée J. LaPerrière**

Somali

1134. Korshel, Mohamud, comp. **English-Somali, Somali-English Dictionary.** New Delhi, Star Publications; distr., New York, Hippocrene Books, 1994. 444p. (Languages of the World Series). $29.50. ISBN 0-7818-0269-5.

Both sections, English-Somali and Somali-English, are simple word lists giving translations in the target language. There is no indication of English pronunciation, but the dictionary cannot have been planned for the anglophone user either, because there is no discrimination of meanings. Nor is there any indication of morphological word classes. The only additional information the user gets is the indication of some irregular forms, which are given not under the entry of the basic form (e.g., an irregular plural under the singular, or the past tense under the present), but in separately alphabetized entries. The idiosyncratic selection of these irregular forms is another drawback. For example, there is not only the entry *man* [nin], but also another for *men* [rag, niman]; however, there is only a singular entry for *woman*.

It is perfectly natural for the lexicographer of any pair of languages to be unable to find a good equivalent in the target language and thus resort to an explanation. Such is the case with this dictionary, yet the wording of the explanations is sometimes odd; for instance, *ache* [xanuun sida "headache" (madax-xanuun)], which is in English "pain like 'headache' (head-pain)." There is no doubt that this dictionary, given the scarcity of sources for Somali, offers quite a number of modern expressions and will be useful in this respect. However, for an English speaker, the dictionary by R. David Zorc, *Somali-English Dictionary* (see ARBA 93, entry 1099), will offer much more grammatical and other information.

—L. Zgusta

Sotho

1135. Wilken, Pam, comp. **Understanding Everyday Sesotho: A Vocabulary and Reference Book. Buka ya Tlotlontswe le Katoloso ya Tsebo.** Cape Town, South Africa, Maskew Miller Longman; distr., New York, Hippocrene, 1994. 94p. illus. $16.95pa. ISBN 0-636-01700-1.

Sesotho (also known as Southern Sotho or Suto) is a Bantu language spoken by some 3 million speakers in South Africa and Lesotho. This short dictionary gives Sesotho translations of some 1,000 English words and expressions. They are organized by topics; in each section there is a list of the words themselves, followed by a section called "Usage" (i.e., topically related phrases and short sentences). The topics start with forms of greeting, time and numbers, seasons, months, days, and holidays (including the signs of the Zodiac), then proceed on to the human body, family relations, emergency situations, and so forth. Areas such as government, the judicial system, church and the Bible (with all the names of the books of both Testaments), and even funeral terms are covered. The dictionary ends with a separate listing of the most frequently used verbs and particularly useful phrases. All this material is accompanied by illustrations that are useful in making the reading livelier; they are not, however, indexed to the words themselves and are very general. The illustrations provide no hint through any of their details that the language is spoken in Africa. There are no grammatical indications, but there is an instructional section on how to pronounce the rather predictable and regular Sesotho spellings.—**L. Zgusta**

Spanish

1136. Galván, Roberto A., and Richard V. Teschner, comps. **The Dictionary of Chicano Spanish. El Diccionario del Español Chicano.** 2d ed. Lincolnwood, Ill., National Textbook, 1995. 244p. $12.95pa. ISBN 0-8442-7967-6.

Dictionaries such as this one provide a useful service in supplying translations of words and phrases commonly used in a particular time or place but not included in standard Spanish dictionaries. But no slang dictionary can be really comprehensive as slang varies so much from place to place and over time. This work was previously published in 1975 under the title *The Dictionary of the Spanish of Texas*, and the present edition contains much the same vocabulary as *Vocabulario Español de Texas*, by Gilberto Cerda, Berta Cabaza, and Julieta Farias (Austin, University of Texas Press, 1953, 1974). By contrast, there is much less overlap in vocabulary with Rubén Cobos's *Dictionary of New Mexico and Southern Colorado Spanish* (see ARBA 85, entry 978) or *El Libro de Calo*, by Harry Polkinhorn, Alfredo Velasco, and Malcolm Lambert (see ARBA 88, entry 1108), which covers the Tijuana-San Diego area.

This work contains definitions of approximately 9,000 Spanish words and phrases with an English translation. Many definitions are labeled with terms indicating their social connotations, such as colloquial, vulgar, or euphemistic. Numerous examples show nonstandard uses of common Spanish words, such as *echar habladas* [to insinuate]. Some words or place-names are adapted from English (e.g., *lonchear* [to eat lunch]); some others are Spanish words pronounced in such a way that they are most easily found under a variant spelling (e.g., *degual* instead of *desigual*). An appendix lists 650 commonly used proverbs; a bibliography is also included.

The Dictionary of Chicano Spanish is recommended for any library wishing to supplement its standard Spanish dictionaries with a dictionary of regional terms. It will be useful for learning to understand local speech or for literary or linguistic scholars.—**Marit S. MacArthur**

1137. **NTC's Dictionary of Common Mistakes in Spanish.** By John Pride. Lincolnwood, Ill., National Textbook, 1995. 248p. $14.95. ISBN 0-8442-7255-8.

A traveler to a Spanish-speaking nation, a student, or a translator of the language must be knowledgeable of the pitfalls that result from the countless variations and nuances to be found that differ from a direct and literal translation of Spanish. Errors of speech can be embarrassing, costly to the businessperson, or at the least, misleading. Common language usage mistakes may not only result in sales losses, but may lead to travel delays and countless other problems that might be avoided by studying ahead of time the common mistakes explained and exemplified in this easy to use, lightweight, "carry-on" handbook.

For ease of access, arrangement is alphabetical, and careful consideration has been given to anglicisms, false cognates, words, and phrases needed for everyday situations. The text is suitable for quick reference, browsing, practicing the language, choosing the right word, and identifying parts of speech. This dictionary does not replace a standard dictionary, but is designed to provide a supplemental guide to correct everyday usage for the English-speaking person, especially in meeting the needs of spoken Spanish. A readily understandable, abbreviated coding assists in identifying major usage variations between Spain and the Latin American nations. This convenient and practical reference is highly recommended for students, classrooms, libraries, and travelers.—**Louis G. Zelenka**

Swedish

1138. Prisma, Bokförlaget. **Prisma's Abridged English-Swedish and Swedish-English Dictionary.** Minneapolis, Minn., University of Minnesota Press, 1995. 467p. $24.95. ISBN 0-8166-2734-7.

As both English and Swedish enjoy a rich lexicographical tradition, it is no wonder that this dictionary holds to an excellent standard in regard to both the vocabulary and the information within the entries. It is certain to prove readily usable by, and useful to, an anglophone speaker, in spite of the fact that the dictionary's real target is the Swedish user. This is easily demonstrated with a comparison of an English-to-Swedish entry with a Swedish-to-English one. For example, the English *fine* gets 10 Swedish equivalents with meanings that are not discriminated, whereas the Swedish [fin] has 8 English equivalents, all of them well discriminated by semantic glosses and other means.

All the lexical material is well chosen and modern, with the equivalents selected at appropriate stylistic levels. Particularly valuable is the rich indication of collocations and idioms. The sequence in which the collocations are presented here is the same as that followed in the dictionary; hence, one can see that they are organized alphabetically by the head noun, with the sentential idiomatic expressions having their own sequence. For a small dictionary of this sort, in which the whole entry is composed in a few lines and can be easily surveyed, the disregard of semantic classification is acceptable to anyone, and even preferred by some lexicographers.

Given the expected educational level of both the anglophone and the Swedish user, the front matter is rather short: basically, there is a survey of pronunciation of both languages (laudably in International Phonetic Alphabet), and tables of Swedish paradigms of nouns, adjectives, and verbs. There are no lists of irregular verbs, but their unpredictable forms are listed as separate entries, with reference provided there to the canonical form. The focus on the needs of the Swedish user explains the fact that the abbreviations are in that language only. This setup will not cause too much difficulty for the Anglophone user. However, gloss abbreviations such as [mots.]=[motsvarande] *equivalent (to)* will have to be checked in the list, unless one knows Swedish well. On the whole, this is an excellent, well-organized dictionary.—**L. Zgusta**

Tatar

1139. Shakhmayev, Sergey. **Tatar-English/English-Tatar Dictionary.** New York, Hippocrene Books, 1994. 197p. $11.95pa. ISBN 0-7818-0250-4.

This dictionary marks an exception among those published in the Hippocrene series, in that it is printed on good paper so that one can easily read the Cyrillic characters. This is important, as the Tatar alphabet makes use of several modified characters for a few specifically Tatar phonemes, most of them quite difficult to read. It is for this reason that the pronunciation is indicated in both the Tatar-English and English-Tatar sections. These indications, however, are highly approximative, because the transcription on both sides is kept so simple that it borders on the misleading. For instance, on the English-Tatar side, the pronunciation of the two English *th* sounds is given thus: English thin as [sin] and this as [zis]. On the Tatar side, the pronunciation of several modified characters is indicated as if they were not modified at all.

The entries are so thoroughly simplified that the loss of one letter can occasion difficulties for the user. For example, the Tatar-English entry [iangartu] v. *renewal; restore* surely involves a misprint and should read: [iangartu] n.v. *renewal; restore*. Similarly, an entry in the English-Tatar section, *knee* n. [tez]; [tezlenu] might prompt the reader to wonder about the precise nature of [tezlenu]. Presumably, the text here should correctly entail two entries: *knee* n. [tez]; *kneel* v. [tezlenu]. There are other sources of uncertainty. For example, Tatar-English [khatyn] *wife* is no doubt correct, but is [khatyn-kyz] really *woman; female*? Is it not rather *young woman, young female*? Or should one perhaps read something like [khatyn-keshe]?

The vocabulary is modern, but with lacunae. Tatar-English [futbol] laudably gives both British *football* and American *soccer* as equivalents, but the English-Tatar part has neither *lift* nor *elevator*, although there must be such devices in Kazan. The English-Tatar part has *thanks* n. [rekhmet] but not *goodbye*. Probably the greatest accumulation of error is found on page 197, where the unbelieving eye reads that there is a state whose English name is *Zugoslavia*, which is pronounced [dzhugouslavia], in Tatar [Iugoslavia].—L. Zgusta

Thai

1140. **The Oxford-Duden Pictorial Thai & English Dictionary.** Bangkok, Thailand, River Books, 1994 and New York, Oxford University Press, 1995. 1v. (various paging). illus. maps. index. $55.00. ISBN 974-89007-5-4.

This is the newest dictionary in the series of pictorial dictionaries based on the drawings originally provided by the famous Duden Publishing House in Germany (see ARBA 90, entries 1039 and 1055; ARBA 84, entries 1056 and 1063; and ARBA 82, entry 1188, for reviews of other dictionaries in the series). The drawings, as usual, are good, detailed, clear, and instructive. Only occasionally does one get the feeling that some modernization is in order (e.g., *Grocery Shop* [American Grocery Store] shows an over-the-counter shop of a kind that is now quite rare, even in Germany). Nevertheless, there is considerable genuine modernization (e.g., the French *TGV* is shown instead of the older drawings of locomotives). Occasionally, more detailed drawings have been added, and there is some societal modernization as well, reflecting new hairdos and fashion trends. Few changes have been effected by PC-proclivities; the outstanding cases are *Kitchen*, in which the central female figure performing the chores has been replaced with a microwave, and the new title for *Human Anatomy* (formerly *Man*). The English nomenclature of the dictionary is both British and American. The pictures cannot be quite so encompassing; there is a certain, if subtle, European slant to them.

The most distinguishing feature of this dictionary, however, is its attempt to represent the Thai world as well. Information is interspersed in the drawings, some of it not easily found elsewhere in such completeness and clarity. Most welcome are the designations of the elements of Thai architecture, musical instruments, dancers' garments, and other pieces of information on Thai fauna and flora. All told, the drawings provide some 30,000 pictorial definitions of English and Thai nomenclature. This dictionary, prepared with the cooperation of specialists from a Thai university and other institutions, will render excellent services through both its English and its Thai components.—L. Zgusta

Uzbek

1141. Khakimov, Kamran M. **Uzbek-English, English-Uzbek Concise Dictionary.** New York, Hippocrene Books, 1994. 329p. $11.95pa. ISBN 0-7818-0165-6.

This is one of the minimal dictionaries in the series published by Hippocrene. It contains some 8,000 entries in both parts, Uzbek and English. It is minimal in the sense that pronunciation is given in both parts, and simple parts of speech are indicated as well. Otherwise, there is no discrimination of jointly indicated equivalents, and there are no examples of collocations, let alone syntactic patterns.

The pronunciation is indicated in a simplistic transcription that will not be particularly helpful. To mention an example from the English part alone (where the pronunciation indications of entrywords are transcribed with Cyrillic letters, converted here into their Roman equivalents), the dental fricatives, voiceless and voiced, are transcribed by the Cyrillic letters for *t* and *d*, respectively, both cross-barred; the *r* is represented by the Russian nonpalatalizing *e* or by other symbols. Misprints are frequent. Hence, one finds transcriptions like the following: there [ɖee], thick [ŧik], thickness [ŧiknis], thief [ŧif], thing [ŧing], think [ŧink], thirst [ŧëst], thirteen [ŧë:ti:n], thirtieth [ŧë:ti:t], this [ɖi:z], these [ɖi:z], and thorough [ŧa:re].

Some Uzbek complex lexical units and similar expressions are listed, but there is vacillation about the decision as to which entryword these expressions should be listed under. Hence, under bola *child* we find oghil bola *boy* and qiz bola *girl*, whereas under bosh *head, top; main*, bosh ministr *prime minister* shows up.

Outside of the pronunciation symbols, misprints are not so frequent as in some other dictionaries of this series, but they do occur. The vocabulary is modern, containing even xudo *God*. Included also are a few toponyms from the area, such as Qobil *Kabul*.—**L. Zgusta**

24 Literature

GENERAL WORKS

Bibliography

1142. Miller, R. H. **Handbook of Literary Research.** 2d ed. Metuchen, N.J., Scarecrow, 1995. 103p. index. $25.00. ISBN 0-8108-2977-0.

Miller's guide to literary research is a step-by-step introduction for the beginning student in British and American literature. Following short introductions, chapters concentrate on standard bibliographies and scholarly resources; compilations of criticism; and literary manuscripts, special collections, and guides to dissertations. Entries are annotated with brief critical comments. Where appropriate, sample problems at the end of chapters illustrate practical usage; some conclude with three or four suggested exercises.

Although billed as a 2d edition, this update remains largely unchanged from the previous edition (see ARBA 88, entry 1122). The singular noticeable change notes the availability of electronic versions of standard printed sources. While heavy on traditional sources, the handbook pays almost no attention to contemporary trends in literary studies. For this aspect, Miller refers the student to James Harner's *Literary Research Guide* (2d ed.; see ARBA 94, entry 1139): "For coverage of the new fields of ethnic and boundary studies and feminist and gender studies . . . consult Harner . . . ." (p. 6). Many of the works cited predate contemporary writers and criticism. To take but one typical example, the latest period covered in *The New Cambridge Bibliography of English Literature* (see ARBA 78, entry 1156; ARBA 76, entry 1260; ARBA 73, entry 1301; and ARBA 72, entry 1381) is 1900-1950.

Annotations show little change and continue certain inaccuracies. *British Books in Print* is referred to as "Formerly *Whitaker's Books in Print*" (entry 321), which is, however, the present title. And *Readers' Guide to Periodical Literature* is still listed as "Available on computer data base from 1959 on as the *Magazine Index*" (entry 326). The handbook serves better as a textbook in an introductory bibliography course than as a reference source in a library collection. Libraries owning the 1st edition need not acquire this.
—**Bernice Bergup**

1143. **MLA International Bibliography: 1981-November 1994.** [CD-ROM]. Norwood, Mass., Silver-Platter Information, 1994. Minimum system requirements: IBM or compatible 386SX. ISO 9660 or compatible CD-ROM drive and controller (interface) card (capable of reading 680MB compact discs) with MS-DOS CD-ROM Extensions 2.1. MS-DOS or PC-DOS 3.1. Windows 3.1. 4MB RAM. 8MB hard disk space. Monochrome VGA monitor (color recommended). Windows-compatible mouse. Windows-compatible printer (recommended). High-density floppy disk drive. $1,995.00.

Produced by the Modern Language Association of America (MLA), the CD-ROM version of the *MLA International Bibliography* corresponds to the print index. It provides access to scholarly research in literature, language, linguistics, and folklore by indexing more than 3,000 journals and series, as well as monographs, bibliographies, proceedings, working papers, and other formats. The disc tested covered 1981 to November 1994.

Both the PC SPIRS 3.3 for DOS and WinSPIRS 1.01 for Windows were loaded and tested. Installation was both quick and easy. The print and on-screen documentation is also easy to follow, and it is helpful in understanding the fields used and potential search strategies. The familiar SilverPlatter software commands and features, such as an index, a thesaurus, exploding terms, and lateral searching, are all available.

Additional features that are particularly helpful in literary and linguistic research include role indicators in the descriptor field and searchable descriptor subcodes. Both allow the searcher to be more precise by specifying how terms are connected rather than simply requiring both to be present in the descriptor field. Unfortunately, a recent change in the indexing has made the subcode used to identify the influence of one author on another temporarily inoperable, but both SilverPlatter and the MLA are working to correct the problem. Any library owning the print bibliography or having an interest in literary or linguistic research will want to own this automated version.—**Barbara E. Kemp**

Biography

1144. **Wilson Author Biographies on Disc 1995.** [CD-ROM]. Bronx, N.Y., H. W. Wilson, 1994. Minimum system requirements: CD-ROM drive. $299.00. ISBN 8242-0865-X.

Wilson Author Biographies is the CD-ROM version of five publications in the Wilson Author series, covering some 4,300 writers who lived from 800 B.C. until the early twentieth century. It includes authors from many parts of the world. Contemporary authors are not included. It is similar to other Wilson CD-ROM products, and uses the same software. If one presently has Wilson products on disc, with Wilsondisc 3.0 or higher, this will run. For those who do not have 3.0 or higher, installation is reasonably simple.

Like other Wilson products, this has three levels for searching: name and title; Wilsearch mode, which allows the user to search multiple subject terms; and Wilsonline, which allows sophisticated search methods such as truncation and Boolean operators. By using the author/title mode and typing in either an author's name or the title of a work, the user immediately retrieves the author biography requested, as it appears in the appropriate Wilson publication. In multiple subject search, the user can type in more than one word for retrieval, and also use various qualifiers such as century, nationality, or genre. Truncation also is allowed in this mode. Searching by subject word, however, is done only as a keyword search: If the word searched appears in a certain biographical sketch, that sketch is retrieved. No assigning of subject terms has been done.

Searching on Wilsearch is clearly the most powerful. In that mode, the user retrieves all mentions of the author searched, including many bibliographical citations. The use of the "neighbor" command in Wilsearch is especially helpful, as it allows one to expand a search term and see all nearby terms. Thus, searching (Charles) Dickens with a neighbor command reveals that the system holds records relating to "Dickens - stage adaptations" and "Dickens - sources," among others. Exploring one of those terms usually reveals a list of further sources on the topic.

This is an easy-to-use CD-ROM, especially at the author/title search level, and especially for those already familiar with Wilson products. Unfortunately, the more powerful modes will be seldom used; most will use the author/title search to display what can easily be retrieved in book form. Of course, using the disc allows one to search all five titles simultaneously, obviously an advantage. Whether that advantage is enough to justify its purchase—or whether a library's clientele will make sufficient use of the sophisticated search mode—must be an individual decision. This is a fine source if it will be used.—**Terry Ann Mood**

Dictionaries and Encyclopedias

1145. **Larousse Dictionary of Writers.** Rosemary Goring, ed. New York, Larousse Kingfisher Chambers, 1994. 1070p. $40.00. ISBN 0-7523-0006-7.

A valuable compendium covering international writers "from Cicero to Salinger," this dictionary, composed by 36 contributors, features 6,000 entries and offers essential biographical data plus succinct critical commentary, selected titles, and a severely cropped bibliography in a delightfully fluent, perceptive style. The introduction admits to a "British and American bias" and notes that foreign titles are frequently paired with translations. Goring concludes that reliability has been her hallmark and that she relied on the "most trustworthy sources."

In clear, unfussy typefaces and bicolumnar arrangement, the alphabetical listing of authors covers an impressive array, the first page naming a Danish dramatist, Danish poet, Indian novelist, American dramatist, Iraqi short-story writer, and Turkish dramatist. To Goring's credit, she offers a balanced blend with poets François Villon, Gwilym Dafydd, Catullus, Derek Walcott, and Yevgeny Yevtushenko; playwrights Robert Anderson, Wole Soyinko, and Karel Capek; nonfiction writers N. Scott Momaday and both Plinys; dystopists Ayn Rand and Yevgeny Zamyatin; and fiction writers Bernard Malamud, Colleen McCullough, and Sandra Cisneros. Surprising omissions include Edith Hamilton, Lao Tzu, Dee Brown, Jeanne Wakatsuki Houston, Walter Dean Myers, Gloria Steinem, Jerome Lawrence and Robert E. Lee, Farley Mowat, Yoko Kawashima Watkins, Rudolfo Anaya, Fred Chappell, and T. Coraghessan Boyle. Attention to young adult literature is minimal; Goring mentions Rudyard Kipling, James Barrie, and Scott O'Dell but ignores Gary Paulsen, Beverly Cleary, Robert Cormier, Lois Lowry, Theodore Taylor, and Cynthia Rylant. A serious omission of significant titles fails to capture some writers' most noteworthy accomplishments, such as Randall Jarrell's "The Woman at the Washington Zoo" or Ray Bradbury's "There Will Come Soft Rains." Overall, the selection demonstrates a fair attempt at inclusion of the most significant literary voices. [R: Choice, Feb 95, p. 918; RBB, 15 Feb 95, pp. 1110-11]—**Mary Ellen Snodgrass**

1146. **Merriam-Webster's Encyclopedia of Literature.** Springfield, Mass., Merriam-Webster, 1995. 1236p. illus. $39.95. ISBN 0-87779-042-6.

Like the venerable *Benet's Reader's Encyclopedia* (see ARBA 89, entry 816), *Merriam-Webster's Encyclopedia of Literature* (MWEL) consists of alphabetically arranged, unsigned articles on critically acclaimed world writers (living and deceased), as well as major literary works, terms, characters, illustrators, movements, schools, and awards. Author entries average 150-300 words, with some extended pieces approaching 1,000 words. The work contains an abundance of authors born since World War II; *Benet's* lists few—if any—authors born since 1940, exceptions being John Irving, Stephen King, and Alice Walker. *Benet's* even excludes such writers as Thomas Pynchon, Annie Dillard, Jim Harrison, Ann Beattie, Raymond Carver, Robertson Davies, William Maxwell, Joan Aiken, M. F. K. Fisher, and Pierre Boulle, despite recent, substantial critical recognition of them. Besides providing profiles of all of these, MWEL also covers such popular nineteenth-century writers as F. Marion Crawford and Margaret Oliphant, and such peripheral figures as Natalie Barney and Buffalo Bill.

Linguistic and etymological information abounds in MWEL. Five acceptable pronunciations are given for *Brougham* and three pluralizations for *Arimasp* are shown. Helpful word derivations are given for *hermeneutics*, *epithalamium*, and *palimpsest*, among many other terms. Translations for such words as *Kojiki* and *weltschmerz* are supplied, as are definitions for such esoteric items as *prodromus* and *apocope*. However, a number of terms with rather self-evident definitions also appear; for example, *authorcraft*, *novelization*, and *limited edition*.

Because MWEL mainly confines its entries to persons and things related to novels, short stories, poems, essays, biographies, and literary criticism, the interdisciplinary territory of *Benet's* is not covered. *Benet's* has information on such subjects as Albert Einstein, the *Lusitania*, Søren Kierkegaard, the Rosetta stone, the Sacco-Vanzetti case, and Johannes Gutenberg. However, MWEL does provide a more generous sampling of avant-garde, multicultural, and women writers. (Also, some unexpected entries occasionally do crop up in MWEL, such as those on Moll Cutpurse, Lincoln Kirstein, preciosity, and the Eleusian Mysteries.) Further, unlike *Benet's*, this newcomer has many illustrations of writers, as well as scenes from such literary works as Rudyard Kipling's *Just So Stories* and Charlotte Brontë's *Jane Eyre*.

Inevitably, one must second-guess the presence or omission of certain entries in as ambitious a survey as this. For instance, why include Daniel Berrigan, but not William F. Buckley? Why Beatrix Potter but not Thornton Burgess? Why Alistair Cooke but not Bernard Berenson? In their apparent determination to embrace writers from as many cultures as possible, the editors have, unfortunately, disregarded dozens of accomplished writers on whom North American students (and other researchers) would likely require information.

Certain articles could be merged to save space (e.g., *skeleton dance* and *dance of death*, *literary sketch* and *sketch*, and *Dickens* and *Dickensian*). With such consolidation, accommodation could be made for excluded non-English-language writers such as Bruno Schulz, Milovan Djilas, Cezar Petrescu, André Chamson, and Ai Ching. Important titles absent from the work include the *Book of Common Prayer*, *Madame Solario*, *The Strange Case of Dr. Jekyll and Mr. Hyde*, and *Like Water for Chocolate*. Most conspicuous is the absence of both author and title entries for Michael Shaara's *The Killer Angels*, Robert Schenkkan's *Kentucky Cycle*, and Marsha Norman's *'night Mother*. The *Prix Sainte-Beuve*, the Edgar, and the O. Henry literary awards are also missing.

Some unevenness is evident in certain entries. Under *poet laureate*, for example, are the names of only British poet laureates; their United States counterparts do not appear. The lengthy article on Troy fails to mention that the existence of this fabled city was confirmed by Heinrich Schliemann—nor does the entry on Abraham Lincoln refer to his Gettysburg Address. The articles under the headings *postmodern* and *subliterature* provide no examples of written works. Perhaps a victim of political correctness, the entire subject of Indian captivity tales is not found here. Finally, the editors' idiosyncratic system of internal cross-referencing is annoying at best, confounding at worst. Despite these criticisms, MWEL, with its 10,000 entries, is the finest, most comprehensive one-volume resource on important world authors, past and present. Libraries owning *Benet's* should buy this work as an update and complement to it. Libraries that can afford to purchase only one of these two reference works should opt for MWEL.—**Jeffrey E. Long**

1147. Snodgrass, Mary Ellen. **Encyclopedia of Utopian Literature.** Santa Barbara, Calif., ABC-CLIO, 1995. 644p. illus. index. (ABC-CLIO Literary Companion). $65.00. ISBN 0-87436-757-3.

Most of the entries in this encyclopedia focus on authors, titles, characters, or belief systems. Appendixes cover primary sources, featured titles (listed alphabetically and by date), and a bibliography of secondary sources. Since this is the first reference book on utopian literature meant for the general reader, it is unfortunate that it is not more balanced in its choice of material. The author, who evidently wrote all the entries, provides useful information on the standard warhorses from Plato's *Republic* to George Orwell's *1984*, but her treatment of twentieth-century works is erratic. Ayn Rand receives multiple entries, and Margaret Atwood's dystopian *The Handmaid's Tale* merits no fewer than six separate entries plus a substantial discussion under "Women in Utopia," whereas other important women authors such as Charlotte Perkins Gilman, Joanna Russ, and Ursula K. Le Guin are ignored. Other utopists not discussed include Robert Owen, Thomas Disch, Frederik Pohl, Frank Herbert, Kurt Vonnegut, and Austin Tappan Wright.

Authors' bio-bibliographies seem to be drawn from secondary sources that do not emphasize the utopian aspects of their work. The bibliography lists a few useful contemporary studies, but omits more basic sources, including *British and American Utopian Literature, 1516-1985* (see ARBA 89, entry 984) and *Dystopian Literature* (see ARBA 95, entry 1109).

The basic problem seems to be that Snodgrass has such a broad definition of utopia that almost anything can be included, from The Sermon on the Mount to *Peter Pan*. This leads to a multiplication of peripheral entries to the detriment of more central material. Nevertheless, there is a place for this book in high school and public libraries. Students looking for basic information on classic utopias will find clear and useful summaries of authors, plots, and characters that may even encourage the reading of the originals.—**Lynn F. Williams**

1148. Snodgrass, Mary Ellen. **An Illustrated Dictionary of Little-Known Words from Literary Classics.** Santa Barbara, Calif., ABC-CLIO, 1995. 343p. illus. index. $49.50. ISBN 0-87436-809-X.

Bibliophiles know the frustration of reading a novel and being stopped time and again by little-known or archaic words. The impediment can be the nautical terminology in a Herman Melville novel, a description of Victorian clothing by Charles Dickens, or the casual Spanish spoken by a Rudolfo Anaya character. Snodgrass has compiled a single source to answer readers' grumbled, late-night queries about definitions. Each word is defined and then placed in context via historical background or derivation. Etymology, pronunciation, and alternate spellings are listed. The word is then used in an excerpt of a specific literary work (e.g., "homeboy" from *The Autobiography of Malcolm X*, or "nosegay" from *Great Expectations*). A bibliography of works cited is one of the book's appendixes. The range of terms runs the gamut: medical terminology, insults, games, architectural terms, body parts, dances, clothing, and weights and measures, to name some examples. The words included here are not ones coined by the authors cited; that is not the book's purpose. Effective line drawings illustrate 800 of the terms. Indexes are provided for access by author, title, and subject.

This is a useful resource for reference librarians and general readers of literature. While its most obvious purpose may be to define arcane and antiquated terms, it fulfills a subtler role in enhancing text. Clearly defining these unusual words, and putting them in an appropriate context, adds to the resonance and meaning of the literary experience. Snodgrass has done a favor for librarians and general readers. This is recommended to same.—**Ed Volz**

Handbooks and Yearbooks

1149. **Classical and Medieval Literature Criticism: Excerpts from Criticism of the Works of World Authors....Volume 14.** Jelena O. Krstović and others, eds. Detroit, Gale, 1995. 511p. illus. index. $110.00. ISBN 0-8103-4877-2.

Catoptric images are those images created when a mirror is held up to reflect in another mirror. Likewise, Gale books begin to look alike after the first one, only the content distinguishing one from the other. Even in the case of the content, however, one finds yet more catoptric images: excellence, one right after the other. Volume 14 of this medieval series contains only 4 entries: Roger Bacon, the English philosopher; the prosaic works; the Book of Job and the *Dream of the Rood*; and Terence, a Roman playwright of the second century B.C. Given both the scope and the pace, one can expect this series to end in the Year of Meton, a mythical year that never comes.

But that is certainly all right by scholars, for only Gale could provide such expansive, high-quality coverage of the texts involved. Even G. K. Chesterton is highlighted on the Book of Job—perhaps the most cogent exegete ever to speak about it. Furthermore, Gale cannot be charged with lack of balance. Voltaire will comment in one place, while John Calvin is brought to bear on another. This is true balance, par excellence! What more can be said about simply one of the best publishers of reference tools? While those of us paying for them will always carp about price and endless production, ad infinitum, pound for pound, Gale is a driving wind that blows the others to dust.—**Mark Y. Herring**

1150. **Contemporary Authors: A Bio-Bibliographical Guide to Current Writers in Fiction.... New Revision Series, Volume 43.** Susan M. Trosky, ed. Detroit, Gale, 1994. 491p. $122.00. ISBN 0-8103-9137-6. ISSN 0275-7176.

Volume 43 of Gale's well-established Contemporary Authors New Revision Series continues to update biographical and bibliographical information on authors previously included in one or more earlier volumes. The brief preface states that the New Revision Series "authors are included on the basis of specific criteria that indicate the need for significant revision." Based upon detailed comparisons of revised entries for some two dozen authors and a sampling of bibliographical entries on some dozen more, this reviewer is tempted to question the extent to which the stated guidelines have been consistently applied. Most commonly, the changes consist of an address change or the listing of one to three new primary works or a similar number of biographical/critical sources. Many of the "critical sources" continue to be book reviews rather than scholarly critiques. A core of the "Sidelights" sections checked were simply reprinted from the previous entry with no revision whatsoever, even though close to a decade has passed since their last inclusion, while others have been significantly rewritten.

Not all bibliographies of writings are complete through the volume's 1994 publication date (neither Nelson Mandela's 1990 *One Nation, One Struggle* nor his 1994 *Long Walk to Freedom* [either as a published work or as a work in progress] is included). Bibliographical databases such as OCLC should assure completeness for new writings through the publication date of the new volume. There is no question that this series continues to be a valuable title for academic and public libraries alike. However, given the fiscal limitations faced by most libraries, Gale would be well advised to apply more strictly its criterion of "need for significant revision" before asking subscribers to invest additional funds for multiple "revision" volumes each year.—**Nancy S. Weyant**

1151. **Contemporary Literary Criticism Annual Cumulative Title Index for 1995.** Detroit, Gale, 1995. 400p. free w/purchase of CLC. ISBN 0-8103-4994-9.

1152. **Contemporary Literary Criticism: Excerpts from Criticism of the Works of Today's Novelists, Poets....Volume 84.** James P. Draper and others, eds. Detroit, Gale, 1995. 530p. illus. index. $115.00. ISBN 0-8103-4993-0.

This volume of *Contemporary Literary Criticism* highlights the most recent and useful pieces of critical reviews and discussions on the current works of a diverse group of writers who have received recognition among readers of academic or public audiences. The authors (currently living or having died after 1959) include Native American writers Paula Gunn Allen and John Joseph Mathews, Chicano dramatist Luis Valdez, U.S. poet and critic Hayden Carruth, the French Guianese poet Leon Gontran Damas, U.S. historian Arthur M. Schlesinger Jr., Japanese novelist Banana Yoshimoto, Nigerian poet Christopher Okigbo, Canadian poet and novelist Margaret Atwood, and U.S. writers John Grisham, Laurie Colwin, and Henry Miller. The entry on Miller concentrates on his novel *Tropic of Cancer*.

Each section includes excerpts from scholarly sources, some of which are otherwise difficult to find. Especially valuable are the recent assessments of the works of Okigbo and Yoshimoto, whose literary accomplishments are becoming more appreciated by a worldwide audience. Prefacing each entry is an introductory passage stating the author's significance, along with a brief biographical sketch, and a listing of major works and their critical reception. Other valuable aids include explanatory notes, full bibliographical citations for the critical essays, and a record of other useful sources for further investigation by the reader. The entries for Allen, Atwood, Damas, Okigbo, and Valdez include interesting and enlightening interviews with those authors.

Some of the other features of this reference guide are the excellent cumulative indexes arranged according to authors, their nationalities, titles of their works, and topics dealt with that appear in the entire Gale Literary Criticism series. Also included in the lists are cross-references to the Gale biographical and dictionary volumes.

Accompanying this volume in a separate paperbound edition is the *Annual Cumulative Title Index for 1995* that conveniently lists the more than 60,000 titles of critical pieces covered in Volumes 1-85 of the literary series. This compact, easy-to-consult reference work will serve its useful purpose quite well until it is replaced in December 1995 by the 1996 index covering all volumes from 1-90.—**Angelo Costanzo**

1153. **Contemporary Literary Criticism: Excerpts from Criticism of the Works of Today's Novelists, Poets....Volume 85.** Christopher Giroux and others, eds. Detroit, Gale, 1995. 494p. illus. index. $115.00. ISBN 0-8103-4995-7.

This reference work of general information and excerpts from criticism of contemporary authors (now living or who died after 1959) began with volume 1 in 1973. Volume 85 contains 12 authors: Maria Campbell, Douglas Coupland, Federico Fellini, Frank Herbert, Irving Howe, Masizi Kunene, Bernard Malamud, N. Scott Momaday, Sharon Olds, Wendy Rose, Randy Shilts, and Mario Vargas Llosa. To date, more than 2,000 authors have been included in the series.

Coverage is primarily American and English authors, but many other nationalities are also included throughout each volume, from Albanian to Czech and Russian. Critical coverage usually spans the career of an author, but selected entries may critique only one work (as in the entry on Herbert, which focuses on *Dune*). This volume, as in earlier volumes, includes criticism of novels, dramatic works, films, poetry, record albums, short stories, essays, monographs, books, and similar genres. The excerpts of criticism are taken from such sources as *American Book Review*, *Booklist*, *Canadian Literature*, *The Christian Science Monitor*, *Studies in American Jewish Literature*, *Esquire*, and *New Republic*.

Entries are arranged alphabetically by author (with birth and death dates when applicable, and always with nationality and genres in which each author has written). The brief biographical and critical introduction (e.g., reputation of the critic, importance of the work of criticism, and critical trends) to each author's work precedes the focus on significant excerpts from published popular and scholarly criticism. This critical commentary is excerpted from the beginning of each writer's career to the present. Author interviews accompany each entry if recent and previously unpublished. Following this is a list of major works and critical reception related to each author. Each entry also includes a list of "Further Reading," in addition to pieces reprinted in CLC with brief annotations on the content of the article. There are also references to other useful sources of information such as *Contemporary Authors* and the *Dictionary of Literary Biography*.

Each new volume of CLC includes cumulative topic, author, and nationality indexes. Although the preface states that there is a title index to all titles reviewed in the current CLC volume, that is not true of volume 85; it is true of earlier volumes and of volume 86. However, there is a separate publication entitled *Contemporary Literary Criticism Annual Cumulative Title Index for 1995*, which covers volumes 1-85 (see entry 1151). The lack of the title index in volume 85 is not a major problem as the cumulative index covers it; but because the preface states that each volume includes a title index, some may find this frustrating if unaware of the annual cumulative index.

Writers are often included in more than one volume if their work falls into a critically acclaimed network, if they have received major literary awards, if their work has gained new interest, or if their work has been adapted for the cinema or television. There is some attention to writers who may not yet have received much critical acclaim or who write in genres such as mystery and science fiction. However, this is selective, as some noteworthy authors are not yet included in this or earlier volumes. Some examples are Julia Alvarez, Cathie Pelletier, Duncan Dayton, Laura Esquivel, Terry Kay, and Mary McGarry Morris. Complete bibliographical citations to original sources of information are provided for the approximately 500 individual excerpts in each volume. Portraits are furnished when available.—**Maureen Pastine**

1154. **DiscLit: World Authors.** [CD-ROM]. New York, G. K. Hall/Simon & Schuster, 1994. Minimum system requirements: IBM or compatible. ISO 9660 CD-ROM drive with MS-DOS CD-ROM Extensions 2.0. DOS 3.1. 640K RAM (512.7K free). $995.00.

Complementing the previously issued *DiscLit: American Authors* and *DiscLit: British Authors*, this CD-ROM contains the complete texts of 146 volumes in Twayne's World Authors series. In addition, it provides access to almost 200,000 bibliographical records for materials by and about these writers from the OCLC Online Union Catalog. Ranging from ancient times to the present, the diverse selection of authors includes Homer, Plutarch, Saint Augustine, Victor Hugo, Lev Tolstoy, Karl Marx, Wole Soyinka, and Margaret Atwood.

Because the interface software is loaded directly from the compact disc, this program is fast and simple to install. It offers two searching levels: one for new or casual users that works primarily from a menu system, and the other for more experienced users, which allows for formulating more sophisticated search statements through the use of Boolean operators and qualifiers. Searching in either mode is relatively easy to learn, but the experienced level is more efficient, since limiting can be done more quickly through commands than from pull-down menus. A brief tutorial provides a basic introduction to the *DiscLit* system, and additional assistance is available through a help menu, screen-specific help options, and an extensive manual. However, all of this documentation was prepared for use with any *DiscLit* product, and, consequently, it does not provide a description of the contents of the *World Authors* disc itself.

Users may choose to search either the "Books" or the "Catalog" unit of the disc. Because many of the libraries that will be interested in this product will already have some type of access to the OCLC database, the "Books" component has greater potential value since it offers a means of searching the texts for common themes, literary movements, influences of historical events or other writers, or specific aspects of an author's work. The user can search all books on the disc, a single book, or a selection of books based on certain characteristics, such as the author's time period, nationality, or principal genre. Thus, one can search all books for references to utopias or dystopias, the books on nineteenth- and twentieth-century authors for allusions to Charles Darwin's theory of evolution, the nine books on women authors for the term *feminism*, or the book on Aristophanes for information regarding staging and costume in his plays. However, a serious drawback in all but the last of these searches is the incomplete picture obtained due to the exclusion of writers from Great Britain and the United States. Perhaps the publishers should consider dropping the OCLC records from future versions and issuing a disc devoted to major writers of all nationalities. This would make searching for common themes and influences more meaningful.

Although the software is easy to use, it is somewhat dated and clunky. For example, a user cannot move from the last occurrence of a search term in one book directly to the first match in the next book. Instead, one must go back to the list of books that matched the search and select the next book. Since the price of this disc is considerably lower than the cost of the print volumes, libraries that do not have standing orders for the print series may find this to be an attractive alternative. However, librarians need to be aware that this CD-ROM is designed for single-user access on a stand-alone workstation rather than for use on a local area network.—**Marie Ellis**

1155. Howes, Kelly King. **Characters in 20th-Century Literature, Book II.** Detroit, Gale, 1995. 509p. index. $54.95. ISBN 0-8103-9203-8.

Characters in 20th-Century Literature, Book II is a continuation of *Book I*, which came out in 1990 (see ARBA 91, entry 1103). It covers contemporary novels, short stories, and plays that were not in the earlier volume, and updates entries on previously covered writers who have written new books. Each entry, arranged alphabetically by author, contains a summary of the book's plot, a brief critical commentary, a description of the main characters, and a bibliography of critical works. Regrettably, it does not refer to *Book I*, so the reader does not know whether to look back to it for more information on the same author.

The entries are surprisingly accurate, up-to-date, and well written. Although the focus is supposedly on characters, Howes actually includes a good deal of information on the authors' themes and critical reception. This volume will be useful to high school and college students who want information about books they do not have time to read.—**Lynn F. Williams**

1156. **Literature Criticism from 1400 to 1800: Excerpts from Criticism of the Works of Fifteenth....** Volume 27. James E. Person Jr., Jelena O. Krstović, and Michael Magoulias, eds. Detroit, Gale, 1995. 549p. illus. index. $119.00. ISBN 0-8103-8943-6.

Although the Literature Criticism from 1400 to 1800 series is now clearly a standard reference resource, its scope stretches significantly with this particular volume organized on the theme of "Renaissance Natural Philosophy." With the possible exception of the frequently anthologized metaphysical poet Henry Vaughan, one of the "School of Donne," the remaining figures in the volume—Heinrich Cornelius Agrippa von Nettesheim, Giordano Bruno, William Lilly, and Nostradamus—are in fact more the stuff of footnotes and commentaries in scholarship on the likes of Christopher Marlowe, William Shakespeare, Ben Jonson, John Donne, Francis Bacon, and John Milton than writers actually "considered classics in every secondary school and college or university curriculum" (p. vii)—unless "classics" is now synonymous with obscure.

Agrippa and Bruno in particular underlay the fabric of the English Renaissance, as shown by excerpts from such standard works as Hardin Craig's *The Enchanted Glass: The Elizabethan Mind in Literature* (Oxford University Press, 1936) and Marjorie Hope Nicolson's *The Breaking of the Circle: Studies in the Effect of the "New Science" upon Seventeenth-Century Poetry* (Columbia University Press, 1960) in the topical entry on "Renaissance Natural Philosophy." Nonetheless, it remains difficult to beat this and earlier volumes in the series for convenient biographical sketches with handsome illustrations and useful bibliographical coverage of minor writers. The volume quickly identifies more commentaries on the likes of Agrippa, Bruno, and Lilly than the *New Cambridge Bibliography of English Literature* (see ARBA 78, entry 1156; ARBA 76, entry 1260; ARBA 73, entry 1301; and ARBA 72, entry 1381), for example.

On the other hand, this volume perhaps suffers more than others from the series' restriction to English-language criticisms. In that the bulk of Bruno criticism is in Italian, the selection, at best, represents only a partial "historical survey of critical response" (p. vii). Although noting periodic commentary "since the seventeenth century" (p. 149) on Nostradamus, the first excerpt date is from 1874. More serious, the selections for Agrippa give the misimpressions that Agrippa and Desiderius Erasmus corresponded in English and that Agrippa criticism began in 1853 with an anonymous essay in *Chamber's Edinburgh Journal*. Quite simply, the series' limitation to English-language criticisms reduces the authority and value of its coverage of non-English-language writers.—**James K. Bracken**

1157. **Modern Black Writers: Supplement.** Steven R. Serafin, comp. and ed. New York, Continuum Publishing, 1995. 813p. index. (Library of Literary Criticism). $95.00. ISBN 0-8264-0688-2.

This supplemental volume to the 1978 work by the same name (see ARBA 79, entry 1186) updates and continues the tradition of providing critical profiles of the world's greatest black writers. Designed to complement the 1978 volume, as stated in the introduction, this volume emphasizes creative and fictional writing, rather than nonfiction. Approximately 75 percent more authors are treated in this updated work; 27 of the original authors are treated again, stressing their more recent contributions or recent critical reception. New additions include Toni Cade Bambara, Buchi Emecheta, Werewere Liking, and Ntozake Shange.

The volume consists of excerpts from scholarly criticism on an author's works or motifs present throughout the author's career. The excerpts are written by such well-known critics as Elliott Butler-Evans, Barbara Christian, and Deborah McDowell, as well as authors such as Erica Jong, Milan Kundera, and writers featured in the text itself. For each author covered, there are approximately 10 excerpts of varying length; at least 1 entry contains some sort of biographical information, and the individual entries describe various works by the author.

The table of contents furnishes an alphabetical list of the authors treated, followed by a list by country. Authors are from the United States, Africa, and Caribbean locales. A list of periodicals from which the excerpts were culled appears in the front matter; however, the book sources are listed in back. An irritating aspect of the book is that the sources listed there (described as "Copyright Acknowledgments") are not by work, but instead by publisher or journal. Therefore, tracking down the book or article may prove difficult. However, bibliographical information follows each excerpt. Other useful features of the work are the "Works Mentioned" section, which lists the fictional works alphabetically by author, complete with date published; the index to critics; and the listing of authors as critics.

Coverage is, for the most part, comprehensive and up-to-date; however, there seem to be some inconsistencies. Toni Morrison's *Jazz* (1992) and Ernest Gaines's *A Lesson Before Dying* (1993) are covered; Alice Walker's 1992 *Possessing the Secret of Joy* is not. Notable author omissions include Ann Petry, Alan Paton, and Phyllis Wheatley (nor are they covered in the 1st edition); relative newcomers Bebe Moore Campbell and Tsitsi Dangarembga are also missing. Also, the nonfiction criteria are not always clear-cut. The entries on Audre Lorde cover only her poetry, and not her feminist writings; discussion of Ngugi wa Thiong'o details his fictional novels, but not his prison diary *Detained*; yet Morrison's *Playing in the Dark* receives treatment. Excerpts are well rounded in that they cover a variety of perspectives: Feminist, Marxist, modernist, and deconstructionist viewpoints are as frequent as more traditional critical responses.

Frank N. Magill's duo *Masterpieces of African-American Literature* (see ARBA 93, entry 1164) and *Masterplots II: African-American Literature Series* (see ARBA 95, entry 1171) cover some of the same ground as *Modern Black Writers*. However, the former embraces only African-American writers, the latter some Caribbean authors; neither covers writers from Africa proper. The benefit of the Magill works is that coverage is extended to nonfiction works; such people as Martin Luther King Jr., Frederick Douglass, and Eldridge Cleaver are profiled. Also, the essays included provide more factual information, but are less technical than those in MBW. However, entries are alphabetical by work, rather than author, making access more difficult than in MBW.

People looking for a brief overview of works by major African-American writers will benefit from the Magill volumes. Also, those interested in nonfiction writings will want to consult them. On the other hand, more serious scholars will wish to use MBW. Many scholars will want to explore the primary sources excerpted in MBW, but the volume provides a good starting point for learned research.
—**Melissa R. Root**

1158. **Nineteenth-Century Literature Criticism: Excerpts from Criticism of the Works of Novelists, Poets....Volume 46.** Joann Cerrito and others, eds. Detroit, Gale, 1994. 499p. illus. index. $119.00. ISBN 0-8103-8937-1.

Once again, this latest volume of *Nineteenth-Century Literature Criticism* (NCLC) is international in scope. Covered writers are William Cullen Bryant, Georg Wilhelm Friedrich Hegel, Karel Hynek Macha (a Czech poet), George Augustus Sala (an English journalist), Stendhal (the entry is devoted to *The Red and the Black*), and Ludwig Tieck (a German short story writer). Entries follow the customary format: a brief biographical sketch, a list of principal writings, then excerpts from critical essays arranged chronologically, followed by a list of further readings. The excerpts are substantial and interpretive, tending to be drawn from literary journals and monographs by established scholars. This arrangement facilitates a quick survey of the author's work and reputation and conveniently points the reader toward sources for a more thorough study.

The fact that this series has reached its 46th volume—well beyond its original plan—is a testament to both the fecundity of the nineteenth century and to the popularity of the series with students, researchers, and reference librarians. Issued with this volume is Gale's first separately published cumulative title index. Henceforth, cumulative title indexes will no longer be published in each volume of NCLC; instead, these paperbound indexes will arrive yearly, with each new index superseding its predecessor.
—**Jeffrey R. Luttrell**

1159. **Twentieth-Century Literary Criticism: Excerpts from Criticism of the Works of Novelists, Poets....Volume 56.** Joann Cerrito and others, eds. Detroit, Gale, 1995. 497p. illus. index. $119.00. ISBN 0-8103-2438-5.

Recent volumes of *Twentieth-Century Literary Criticism* have included many figures less-than-universally known. Reputation, admittedly, is a debatable proposition; but how many readers will respond readily to Der Nist, a Ukrainian novelist; Arthur Schendel, a Dutch novelist; Lev Shestov, a Russian philosopher and critic; or Cesar Vallejo, a Peruvian poet? Eight more writers also represented are hardly widely read or studied in literature courses. Still, it should be noted that an entry devoted to Virginia Woolf's novel *Orlando*, and another that evaluates Antoine de Saint-Exupéry's classic fairy tale of philosophical dimensions, *The Little Prince*, have special value.

Since its inception more than 15 years ago, TCLC has covered more than 500 authors, representing some 58 nationalities, and listed 25,000-plus titles. The series has been purchased by nearly 10,000 schools, colleges, and university libraries. TCLC is such a trove of information culled from thousands of books and periodicals not shelved by most collections, that it may be readily assumed that the series—which serves as an excellent introduction to authors who died between 1900 and 1960 and the most significant interpretations of their works—is often consulted. Libraries that already have the first 55 volumes of TCLC will of course wish to obtain this latest edition.—**G. A. Cevasco**

1160. **Twentieth-Century Literary Criticism: Excerpts from Criticism of the Works of Novelists, Poets....Volume 57.** Joann Cerrito and others, eds. Detroit, Gale, 1995. 500p. illus. index. $119.00. ISBN 0-8103-2439-3.

Since its beginning more than 15 years ago, Gale's *Twentieth-Century Literary Criticism* has gradually expanded its coverage, and the series now includes criticism of notables whose achievements involve neither literature nor creative writing. The primary criterion for inclusion in the series has, however, remained constant: The subject must have died between 1900 and 1960. The 57th volume of TCLC thus surveys and critiques the work of 8 people, 6 of whom were noted as writers. Four of these six—Australian novelist Barbara Baynton, English dramatist John Drinkwater, German poet Else Lasker-Schüler, and English novelist Edgar Wallace—have not previously been profiled in TCLC, although the latter three have been analyzed in Gale's *Dictionary of Literary Biography*. The final two writers—Joseph Conrad and Ford Madox Ford—have been profiled several times each by TCLC, but in Volume 57, the criticism focuses on Conrad's "The Secret Sharer" and Ford's *Parade's End*, works that have received relatively cursory attention in previous volumes. The last two subjects—filmmaker Sergey Eisenstein and psychoanalyst Wilhelm Reich—are not remembered for being litterateurs, nor have they been profiled in prior volumes of TCLC. As in all of Gale's Literary Criticism series, the criticism is arranged chronologically, allowing researchers to trace the subject's rise (or decline) in academic reputation. Each entry begins with a bibliography listing principal works and concludes with a brief annotated list of secondary and tertiary sources; the entry for Wallace fails to cite any of the several excellent existing bibliographies. A title index specific to this volume and cumulative indexes to author, nationality, and TCLC topic volumes conclude the book. TCLC and Gale's companion series belong in all academic libraries.—**Richard Bleiler**

Indexes

1161. **Magill Index to Critical Surveys: Cumulative Indexes, 1981-1994.** rev. ed. Pasadena, Calif., Salem Press, 1994. 379p. $12.95pa. ISBN 0-89356-698-5.

Brought up-to-date since the previous edition (covering 1981-1988), this cumulative index to Magill's Critical Surveys series adds coverage of the revised editions of *Critical Survey of Drama* (see ARBA 95, entry 1156), *Critical Survey of Long Fiction* (1991), *Critical Survey of Short Fiction* (see ARBA 94, entry 1215), and *Critical Survey of Poetry* (see ARBA 93, entry 1236). In all, discussions of "books, plays, stories, poems, and authors appearing in the eighty-seven volumes of the series" are indexed. Works are indexed by author and title, with cross-references from foreign-language titles and pseudonyms. The Critical Surveys series has grown to such size and complexity over the years that any library owning a substantial portion of the run would be well advised to acquire this inexpensive and handy index.—**Jeffrey R. Luttrell**

CHILDREN'S AND YOUNG ADULT LITERATURE

General Works

Bibliography

1162. Berman, Matt. **What Else Should I Read? Guiding Kids to Good Books, Volume 1.** Englewood, Colo., Libraries Unlimited, 1995. 211p. index. $24.50pa. ISBN 1-56308-241-1.

Aimed at teachers, this useful book should help both new and experienced teachers who want to develop in their students a love of reading. After a concise introduction to the art of conducting book discussions, the author devotes most of the book to listings of related books for children to read. Thirty novels are used as the basis for book webs that contain listings of other books dealing with themes and issues raised in the central web book. These webs are designed to be photocopied and displayed in classrooms so that children have a guide to further reading. Reproducible bookmarks listing the suggested titles with brief annotations are also provided.

The quality of the suggested central web books is high. Titles include such classics as *Bridge to Terabithia*, *Julie of the Wolves*, and *The Planet of Junior Brown*, and even reach back to the nineteenth century with *Little Women* and *The Secret Garden*. The related books cover some more recent titles, but on the whole, the book sticks to well-known older books likely to be found in any school library. No guidelines are given for the grade or age level of the books suggested, but the reading levels tend to be high. The book will be most useful for senior elementary and high school students, especially those who are already good readers.—**Adele M. Fasick**

1163. Dunkle, Margaret. **Black in Focus: A Guide to Aboriginality in Literature for Young People.** Deakin, Australia, ALIA Press and Port Melbourne, Australia, D. W. Thorpe/Reed Reference Publishing; distr., New Providence, N.J., R. R. Bowker/Reed Reference Publishing, 1994. 181p. illus. index. $25.00pa. ISBN 1-875589-47-3.

Some 300 books published between 1960 and 1994 are considered: Most have plot summaries, comments on illustrations, and judgments on their political correctness (as determined by the author-compiler), becoming clear from the introduction, which replaces "white settlement" with "white invasion" and decries the former government policy of assimilation as motivated by a desire to make the Aborigines "invisible." While the author uses "whitefella," she inveighs against the use of "blackfella"; while she stereotypes white attitudes toward the indigenous people, she insists that others should not: Although anthropologists and photographers have documented aboriginal physical characteristics (thick lips, broad, flat noses, mop hair), these are called "stereotypically racist" descriptions.

Dunkle insists that Aborigines be considered individually (thus eliminating all generalizations); however, she says that they are all "handsome and unmistakably Aboriginal"—whether full-blooded or self-described. Yet she demands that fictionists be realistic. Those who have seen Aborigines in Darwin, Redfern, Narrabri, or Central Australia are not to mention their physical and emotional distress, their drunkenness and dissolution—and their use of pidgin should be discouraged. The "white oppressors" who maintained the slave trade on Queensland canefields should be condemned, as should those who depict "cuddly little primitive black babies." The author is a Rousseauesque romanticist of strident partisanship—and this seriously injures what could have been a more appealing guide to recent literature for young readers.
—**Marian B. McLeod**

1164. Hall, Susan. **Using Picture Storybooks to Teach Literary Devices: Recommended Books for Children and Young Adults. Volume Two.** Phoenix, Ariz., Oryx Press, 1994. 239p. index. $24.95pa. ISBN 0-89774-849-2.

In an attempt to broaden the potential purchasing audience for this annotated bibliography, it has been mistitled. It is not suitable either interest-wise or pedagogically for young adults. Its premise that "picture storybooks can effectively illustrate many of the common literary elements found in mature literature" with regard to young adults is seriously flawed. Unfortunately, young adults are only too cognizant of their rather precarious designation as young adults. They can easily cite a host of obvious and even subtle changes that mark their developmental passage from childhood to young adulthood. One of these, most certainly, is the absence of pictures in their reading material. With the exception of comic books, all young adult literary material is characterized by a dearth of illustration. Adolescents seen reading storybooks by their peers, even for literary thematic purposes, will consider the activity a descent from their eagerly anticipated advancement on the developmental ladder. They will participate with great reluctance and, perhaps, even truculence in such an endeavor.

The second problem relates to pedagogical aspirations. The titles chosen to model literary devices such as imagery, metaphor, parody, symbol, and understatement are appropriate for children because the vocabulary and story are easily comprehensible by this age group. Young adults, on the other hand, require less cliché-ridden vocabulary and more sophisticated plots and themes to challenge and stretch their comprehension and appreciation of literature. Symbolism, for example, is more aptly demonstrated in the passages of Herman Melville's *Moby-Dick* than it is in Roger Duvoisin's picture book *Petunia*—"the story of a silly goose that carries around a book thinking that it will make her look smart." Jonathan Swift's famous, satirical essay, "A Modest Proposal," is a far better young adult vehicle for conveying "understatement" than Ruth Brown's picture book *Our Puppy's Vacation*.

The use of picture storybooks for explaining and demonstrating various literary devices is an excellent idea providing it is used at grade levels where these books are normally being read. Beyond this age, it is pedagogically inappropriate. More challenging materials that advance vocabulary and the critical thinking process should be employed.

Given these parameters for acquisition, this book is still an outstanding resource. It lists more than 300 new titles since publication of the 1990 volume 1 (see ARBA 91, entry 1113) and includes many classic works as well. An introduction concerning the differences among a "picture storybook, picture book and illustrated storybook" is helpful. Thirty-one literary devices are listed, ranging from alliteration and aphorism to simile, theme, and tone. Each title under a specific theme contains a complete bibliographic citation, an annotation of the story, and a passage from the story that aptly illustrates the defined literary device. Other literary devices illustrated by the same title are listed along with curriculum tie-ins to specific subject areas such as social science (e.g., jealousy, siblings). The section concludes with an individual list of titles pertinent to all ages, illustrative of artistic styles and techniques, and useful as curriculum tie-ins. An index follows. This outstanding volume is recommended only for elementary school librarians and teachers and children's librarians in public libraries.—**Kathleen W. Craver**

1165. Holsinger, M. Paul. **The Ways of War: The Era of World War II in Children's and Young Adult Fiction: An Annotated Bibliography.** Metuchen, N.J., Scarecrow, 1995. 487p. index. $57.50. ISBN 0-8108-2925-X.

Holsinger believes that young people suffer from "gross historical ignorance" about World War II, which is, according to him, the most critical event in this century and perhaps any other century. His partial solution to this cultural impoverishment is to expose young people to fiction, acquainting them with events and issues of the period. This annotated bibliography therefore contains more than 750 numbered (and occasionally lettered) entries listing fiction published in the United States that focuses on military and domestic life during the war years (extending from events in China in 1937 to beyond the end of actual fighting). Each entry presents bibliographical information about the original edition and recent paperback reprints. It also suggests the basic reading level and indicates the historical and literary merit of the work by assigning from one to four asterisks. Supplementing the main section is a title index, a geographical and thematic index, and an appendix discussing and listing relevant works never republished in the United States.

This thorough bibliography contains superb annotations that range from about 100 words to a page and a half in length. One could quibble with Holsinger's relative weighting of historical information and literary merit, but he is clear about his reasons and their subjectivity. This is a highly specialized work, but anyone wishing to learn about juvenile fiction treating World War II will appreciate this excellent resource.

—**Raymond E. Jones**

1166. Khorana, Meena. **Africa in Literature for Children and Young Adults: An Annotated Bibliography of English-Language Books.** Westport, Conn., Greenwood Press, 1994. 313p. index. (Bibliographies and Indexes in World Literature, no.46). $59.95. ISBN 0-313-25488-5.

This carefully researched and annotated bibliography fills a big gap in multiculturalism and African literary studies. It focuses on anglophone African literature (dating from 1873 to 1994) for children and young adults and includes 676 entries on works by European, American, and African writers. The entries are divided geographically and generically. For example, works listed under North Africa are subdivided into four genres: traditional literature, fiction, biography, and informational books. Many of the works listed under traditional literature are illustrated and will be of particular interest to readers who enjoy folklore and myths. Similarly, the informational books have been evaluated for their photographs, graphics, maps, and so forth, as well as for the quality and style of the information that is being presented. The informational books cover a wide range of topics, and although most of them are targeted for young readers, researchers will find them useful as quick references. For readers with little or no knowledge of African literature generally, Khorana's introductory essay provides the necessary background in a scholarly yet easily accessible language. Of particular interest are her definitions of *colonial, postcolonial*, and *pan-African* literature. She defines these terms within a historical context that shows how African literature for children has developed almost simultaneously with that for adults and is now firmly established as its own scholarly discipline. She also points out one of the difficulties in dealing with colonial literature in an era that demands greater sensitivity to cultural differences: how to avoid pejorative terms without violating the integrity of texts such as those by Doctor Doolittle and other colonial writers whose enthnocentric biases are unacceptable by today's literary and moral standards. Khorana does not attempt to resolve the problem; instead, she presents it as something that needs to be investigated more fully as these and other texts are reissued and revised. Khorana concludes her introduction by remarking that both African and Western authors who write for children recognize the shifting social, political, and economic paradigms of contemporary African societies, and are responding by experimenting with new forms to represent these ever-changing realities and new ways to disseminate their writing to their large and diverse reading public. The work is highly recommended.—**Sandra Adell**

1167. Lynn, Ruth Nadelman. **Fantasy Literature for Children and Young Adults: An Annotated Bibliography.** 4th ed. New Providence, N.J., R. R. Bowker/Reed Reference Publishing, 1995. 1092p. index. $50.00. ISBN 0-8352-3456-8.

As in the earlier editions, the 4th edition of *Fantasy Literature for Children and Young Adults* is really two bibliographies. The first documents fantastic literature written for children and young adults during the (approximately) last 100 years and contains 3,148 citations listing more than 4,800 works; series are accorded a single entry. A typical citation gives the volume's suggested readership and provides a brief but generally accurate annotation. Bibliographical data include the dates of first and reprint editions, the ISBN(s), and if the book is in print; reviews from professional journals are also cited. Although certain authors and books are not present (e.g., Robert E. Howard, Fritz Leiber) or probably should not have been included (Talbot Mundy's Jimgrim/Ramsden series), the most significant problem of this section stems from the arrangement, for the citations have been grouped by subject. While this arrangement has merit—younger readers often read fantasy by subject—the 13 subjects Lynn has used are neither mutually exclusive nor well considered. Mark Helprin's *Winter's Tale* (another highly dubious inclusion) features a great white flying horse (there is a section for "Animal Fantasy"), is a complex allegory (there is a section for "Allegorical Fantasy and Literary Fairy Tales"), and is partially set in the future (there is a section for "Time Travel Fantasy"), but it is listed as "High Fantasy—Alternate Worlds or Histories," with no cross-referencing. There are, however, excellent author-illustrator and title indexes; a subject index is less than helpful.

The second bibliography is a selective guide listing bio-critical information about the subjects and writers appearing in the first section. The citations in this section are unnumbered, but approximately 10,400 books, dissertations, chapters, and journal articles are cited, making this section about 60 percent larger than it was in the 3d edition. Many of these sources are not accessible via database search, and the data in this section will significantly assist many researchers. Although it is flawed, *Fantasy Literature for Children and Young Adults* is nevertheless a monumental achievement. It belongs in all public libraries; academic libraries supporting studies in education will also want it.—**Richard Bleiler**

1168. **More Kids' Favorite Books: A Compilation of Children's Choices 1992-1994.** New York, Children's Book Council and Newark, Del., International Reading Association, 1995. 126p. illus. index. $8.00pa. ISBN 0-87207-130-8.

Since 1975, the International Reading Association and the Children's Book Council have afforded children ages 4 to 13 the opportunity to recommend their favorite books to the Children's Choices list. More than 2,000 children participate in the project annually and choose the titles for the list. The resulting publication has proved itself a unique and tremendously illuminating selection tool created from the input of children. *More Kids' Favorite Books*, an updated version of the International Reading Association's *Kids' Favorite Books* (see ARBA 94, entry 1174), presents the Children's Choices lists from 1992-1994, and offers an excellent annotated bibliography for the more than 300 titles.

The book's introduction traces the history of the Children's Choices list and outlines the criteria for inclusion, as well as the selection process itself. Titles are organized by 5 suggested reading levels: all ages, beginning independent reading, young readers (ages 5-8), middle grades (ages 8-10), and older readers (ages 10-13). Each of these five sections contains an alphabetical listing of titles with each work given a brief annotation. Additionally, books are indexed by title, author, and illustrator. This work is an effective, practical, and easy-to-use reader's guidance tool. A valuable resource not only for its wealth of up-to-date material aimed at a variety of interest levels, the book is worthy because the included titles are child tested, approved, and sure to make for popular and fun reading. *More Kids' Favorite Books* will be a useful addition to libraries, media centers, and classroom collections.—**Jennifer Comi Ellard**

1169. **Research & Professional Resources in Children's Literature: Piecing a Patchwork Quilt.** Kathy G. Short, ed. Newark, Del., International Reading Association, 1995. 272p. index. $16.00pa. ISBN 0-87207-126-X.

Frustrated in their own attempts at locating a comprehensive synthesis of research on children's literature, due in part to the fact that studies cut across so many disciplines, the authors fill the void with this compilation of research and other professional resources dated 1985-1993. The authors not only conducted a thorough computer search, but also did an extensive hand search of journals across the various disciplines in order to pull in studies done in other disciplines often overlooked by educators. The scope of the project is limited to children's literature through grade 8, or age 14.

The book is divided into three sections. Section 1 lists and annotates the major research studies reported in journals across the disciplines. Section 2 lists the various journals that have contained research on the topic, along with an annotation and typical contents, including the address and telephone number. Section 3 is a selected, annotated bibliography of professional books. Both an author and a subject index are provided.

As a basic synthesis of the research on children's literature, this book is an excellent resource for the researcher, teacher, librarian, or administrator interested in supportive evidence for programs in place, as a tool for curricula development, and a starting point for further research in the field. It is thematically organized and well annotated with complete references. Although limited by the authors' own necessity to narrow the scope of the project, its usefulness as a reference guide to key research studies and other resources is its greatest value. The authors have completed the foundation for research and brought together the many disciplines interested in children's literature, fulfilling their goal of a useful research synthesis.

—**Susan Zernial**

1170. Stephens, Elaine C., Jean E. Brown, and Janet E. Rubin. **Learning About ... The Holocaust: Literature and Other Resources for Young People.** North Haven, Conn., Library Professional Publications/Shoe String Press, 1995. 198p. index. $29.50; $18.50pa. ISBN 0-208-02398-4; 0-208-02408-5pa.

Exposing children to one of the darkest chapters in history with its unimaginable brutality and horror is a particular challenge. This valuable reference work will assist greatly with that process by providing a guide to Holocaust literature and by suggesting teaching strategies and activities to help young people understand these crimes against humanity. It is intended for teachers, librarians, youth leaders, counselors, parents, and others who want to select and use materials about the Holocaust with children from kindergarten through high school.

The bibliography references 170 works that include informational books, photo-essays, picture books, biographies, personal narratives, poems, historical fiction, plays, and realistic fiction. The work is organized into seven chapters. The first chapter presents a historical overview of the Holocaust and a rationale for using Holocaust literature with young people. The next five chapters provide annotated plot summaries of selected literary works and suggestions for using these works in the classroom. These chapters are organized thematically by genre and grade level. Works have been chosen on the basis of their literary quality, historical authenticity, and effectiveness. The final chapter provides information on additional resources, including other media, curriculum materials, organizations, institutions, and journals. This excellent resource book and teaching guide will be a valuable asset to anyone selecting or using materials about the Holocaust with children and young adults.—**Jennifer Comi Ellard**

Biography

1171. **Authors & Artists for Young Adults. Volume 14.** E. A. Des Chenes, ed. Detroit, Gale, 1995. 253p. illus. index. $67.00. ISBN 0-8103-5730-5. ISSN 1040-5682.

This guide to artists of interest to young adults follows the format of previous volumes (see ARBA 95, entry 1144; ARBA 92, entry 1126; and ARBA 90, entries 1091-1092). Each of its 24 entries lists biographical and career information, and provides bibliographies of publications, adaptations, works cited, and suggestions for further reading. The main section, "Sidelights," is actually a biocritical sketch.

Design and content problems weaken this attractive volume. Two typographical lapses are particularly annoying. First, in some entries, a space comes between a hyphen and the word following it. Second, the asterisk indicating that the subject has not examined an entry is confusingly placed with the last item listing further readings. The major weakness, however, is the book's inclusiveness. In addition to writers for young adults, entries cover classic writers studied in high school (Arthur Conan Doyle and Edgar Allan Poe); popular writers read by adolescents (John Grisham and Peter Benchley); photographers (Ansel Adams and Dorothea Lange); movie directors (Tim Burton and Harold Ramis); journalists (Dave Barry and Frank Deford); a film composer (Danny Elfman); a fantasy illustrator (Frank Frazetta); and a nonfiction writer (James S. Haskins).

Although the entries lean to biography rather than criticism, they are well-written and entertaining introductions. Nevertheless, the indiscriminate inclusiveness is disturbing. Too many entries cover artists who do not produce works specifically for young adults or, worse, are of questionable significance. The editorial board needs to reexamine the inclusion of film directors, columnists, and cartoonists, and to readdress the question of what constitutes artists *for* young adults.—**Raymond E. Jones**

1172. **Something About the Author: Facts and Pictures About Authors and Illustrators of Books for Young People. Volume 78.** Kevin S. Hile, ed. Detroit, Gale, 1994. 263p. illus. $85.00. ISBN 0-8103-2288-9.

1173. **Something About the Author: Facts and Pictures About Authors and Illustrators of Books for Young People. Volume 79.** Kevin S. Hile, ed. Detroit, Gale, 1995. 324p. illus. index. $85.00. ISBN 0-8103-2289-7.

1174. **Something About the Author: Facts and Pictures About Authors and Illustrators of Books for Young People. Volume 80.** Kevin S. Hile, ed. Detroit, Gale, 1995. 255p. illus. $85.00. ISBN 0-8103-2290-0.

Something About the Author (SATA) is the standard reference source for authoritative biographical information on authors who write for children. The set began 20 years ago and is still issued in 4 sturdily bound volumes each year. Subset cumulations of the entire set are available as *Major Authors and Illustrators for Children and Young Adults*, published by Gale in 1993 (see ARBA 94, entry 1187), and a CD-ROM version (entitled *Contemporary Authors on CD* [see ARBA 95, entry 1110]).

The format and information for each author have not changed for some time and include personal data; author addresses; a description of career, membership, awards, and honors; a chronological bibliography of writings/illustrations; adaptations of writings in other media; a list of works in progress; and a bibliography for more information. Most sketches contain photographs of the author, book cover art, and sample illustrations from the author's or illustrator's books. An index to the entire set appears in every other volume. Sketches are compiled from information supplied by the authors and illustrators, both through questionnaires and from telephone interviews. Extensive research is conducted on all authors as sketches are compiled.

SATA continues its coverage of early figures from children's literature to contemporary and emerging authors and illustrators primarily from English-speaking countries. Authors and illustrators from the entire spectrum of children's literature are featured. From time to time, the volumes will update previous articles of prolific and well-known authors, and obituary notices are supplied for the most famous persons covered in the set. Prominent authors appearing in volumes 78-80 include Michael Hague, Matt Christopher, Marc Brown, Francine Pascal, Barry Moser, and Joan Lowry Nixon.

Libraries needing complete coverage of children's authors and illustrators must include this set and keep it up-to-date. No other source is as comprehensive and authoritative. For new libraries and libraries whose subscriptions have lapsed but want to pick up coverage, the CD-ROM, the *Major Authors and Illustrators for Children and Young Adults* set, or the one-volume *Twentieth-Century Children's Writers* (3d ed.; see entry 1175) could be purchased, and the subscription to SATA picked up with the 1995 calendar year.—**David V. Loertscher**

1175. **Twentieth-Century Children's Writers.** 4th ed. Laura Standley Berger, ed. Detroit, St. James Press, 1995. 1272p. index. (Twentieth-Century Writers Series). $132.00. ISBN 1-55862-177-6.

Using a panel of experts, the editor of *Twentieth-Century Children's Writers* has again chosen thousands of English-language authors of fiction, nonfiction, poetry, and drama to chronicle. Since the publication of the 3d edition of this work, a companion, *Twentieth-Century Young Adult Writers* (see ARBA 95, entry 1147), has been published, so the contents of this volume have been adjusted more toward the younger set. The writers included are, for the most part, those writing in the twentieth century, although a section on nineteenth-century greats is covered in the appendix. The entry for each author consists of a biography, a complete list of published works, and a signed critical essay. Information is accurate when compared to works such as *Something About the Author* (see entries 1172-1174). Coverage is mainly of British and U.S. writers; however, a number of Australian and Canadian authors are included, as are a smattering of Third World authors.

For a one-volume quick source for information about children's authors, this is the best source. Addresses of the authors or their agents are particularly valuable for those wishing to correspond with these people. There are no references to further information about the authors, so *Something About the Author* or *Biographical Index to Children's and Young Adult Authors and Illustrators* (see ARBA 93, entry 1144) will need to be consulted. Because this source is rather expensive, it begs to be compared to the CD-ROM product *Junior DISCovering Authors* (see ARBA 95, entry 1145), although that product only covers 300 authors. If the library has the right technology, the CD-ROM product would be attractive because of its lengthier biographical sketches, photographs of the authors, and references to further information. However, if the library is still fairly print-oriented, cannot afford *Something about the Author*, and wants extensive coverage, then *Twentieth-Century Children's Writers* is the perfect source. Larger libraries will want all the biographical sources possible to provide the best coverage. Owners of the previous edition will want to add this volume for the additional names and current addresses.—**David V. Loertscher**

Handbooks and Yearbooks

1176. **Canadian Book Review Annual 1994: Children's Literature.** Joyce M. Wilson and Kelly L. Green, eds. Toronto, Canadian Book Review Annual, 1995. 1v. (unpaged). index. $16.95pa. ISBN 0-9697390-5-2.

Children's Literature, developed from *Canadian Book Review Annual*, is an evaluative guide to English-language books by Canadian authors and illustrators. Its 350 original reviews of both fiction and nonfiction titles are arranged in 13 categories, ranging from picture books to works on science, technology, and mathematics. The reviews contain standard bibliographical data, prices, ISBN and cataloging numbers, and suggested ages of readers. The reviews conclude with one of five verbal ratings: "highly recommended," "recommended," "recommended with reservations," "not a first-choice purchase," or "not recommended." Reviews are numbered consecutively, so finding them after consulting the index of subjects, authors, and titles is fast and simple. The volume also lists publishers' addresses.

The reviews, which range in length from 150 to 300 words, follow a pattern, moving from an overview to a critical analysis. The analyses justify the final rating through perceptive comments on the value of the illustrations, the quality of the writing, the suitability for the target audience, or the plausibility of characterization. Because these reviews are written in clear and jargon-free prose, they will be useful to students and members of the general public, as well as to teachers and librarians. This affordable guide brings together reliable information not otherwise available in a single source. If future volumes are available soon after the year they review, Canadian schools and libraries will find them indispensable. This work is highly recommended for Canadians; it is also recommended for others interested in things Canadian.—**Raymond E. Jones**

1177. Kuipers, Barbara J. **American Indian Reference and Resource Books for Children and Young Adults.** 2d ed. Englewood, Colo., Libraries Unlimited, 1995. 230p. index. $27.50pa. ISBN 1-56308-258-6.

When she was a school library media specialist, Kuipers discovered that many books in her library contained stereotypes and misinformation about the American Indian. Because the school population where she worked was predominantly Native American, she suspected that these books contributed to the apathy and lack of self-esteem she found among the students. After she withdrew the poor books and could not locate any bibliographies that would help her replace them with better books, she decided to compile one herself. This volume, produced after studying scholarly publications on the subject, and countless hours of reading and evaluating nonfiction books, is the result of her efforts.

Using the evaluation criteria set forth in the *Encyclopedia of Library and Information Science* (see ARBA 94, entries 601-608), she devised an evaluative checklist that she used on every volume considered for inclusion. Her checklist went beyond the basic elements and was concerned with the treatment of the American Indian in each work. Among the items rated were: whether the culture described was evaluated by American Indian values and attitudes; whether there was an accurate portrayal of American Indians as individuals, not groups; whether there was a realistic description of American Indian life, past or present; and whether there was a recognition of diversity among tribes, cultures, and lifestyles. In evaluating objectivity, the checklist was concerned with unbiased positive values; stereotypes; portrayals of human strengths and weaknesses; and the presentation of both sides of an event, issue, or problem. In addition, the illustrations were required to authentically depict the American Indian way of life.

As to the question of whether an author should be an American Indian to write authentic, accurate material, Kuipers quotes authorities pro and con, but acknowledges that excellent books have been produced by persons who are not Native Americans. Therefore, it is absolutely essential that each work be evaluated according to her checklist to determine the merits, no matter who the author is. Each of the 200-plus titles included in the bibliography has full bibliographical information, a reading level determined by the Fry Readability Formula, and suggested Sears subject headings. Lengthy annotations indicate not only the content but also why the work is important in a collection, and how it may be incorporated into the curriculum.

The bibliography is arranged according to Dewey Decimal Classification, then alphabetically by author with an author/title index. There is a subject index to annotations and a list of publishers with their addresses. Highly recommended, this bibliography and its evaluative checklist should be used by school library media specialists and public librarians to acquire accurate quality books about the American Indian.
—**Sara R. Mack**

Indexes

1178. **Children's Authors and Illustrators: An Index to Biographical Dictionaries.** 5th ed. Joyce Nakamura, ed. Detroit, Gale, 1995. 811p. (Gale Biographical Index Series, no.2). $156.00. ISBN 0-8103-2899-2.

Those people who teach children's literature are forever looking for new sources of biographical information other than *Something About the Author* (see entries 1172-1174), which has been the standard work looked to. Scholastic has issued a two-volume set, *Meet the Authors and Illustrators* by James Preller (1993), and Libraries Unlimited has Jim Roginski's *Behind the Covers* (1985-89) in two volumes, which are in interview format. *Meet the Authors and Illustrators* also has photographs of the artists and writers along with some quotations. Now available is a hefty tome—the 5th edition of *Children's Authors and Illustrators*, which updates the 1987 4th edition by quite a bit. More than 200,000 biographies of some 30,000 authors and illustrators in 650 sources are listed in this reference work. This will be a welcome addition to all the indexes of biographical material for authors and illustrators of children's literature.

A key to the source codes is given on the end pages, followed by a 92-page section of the complete bibliographical listing of the sources. An index of the authors and the illustrators listed follows in alphabetical order. As in any work of this comprehensiveness and size, there are bound to be omissions; neither the Preller nor the Roginski books are listed. Serious researchers and graduates and undergraduates will find this index useful; the more casual reader will still want to look at the Preller and Roginski references as an introduction. This is the type of solid reference work that libraries and research collections eagerly await.—**Anne F. Roberts**

1179. **An Index to Historical Fiction for Children and Young People.** By Janet Fisher. Brookfield, Vt., Scolar Press/Ashgate Publishing, 1994. 192p. illus. index. $44.95. ISBN 1-85928-078-1.

Attempting to encourage the reading of quality historical novels for children by providing easier access to them, the author selected the titles on their merits of meeting strict criteria for historical fiction, which are outlined in the introduction. These included an excellent story, drawing the reader into a world in which the facts unfold along with the characters, and an adherence to the details of the period including place, food, clothing, and dialogue. Bias is noted in entries. The oldest copyright date of a title is the 1937 edition of *Little House on the Prairie*, while the most recent is 1992. The vast majority of entries fall between 1960 and 1990. The titles selected cover history up to the end of World War II. Although all books selected have been published in the United Kingdom, many were originally published elsewhere. This does not limit the subjects either, as countries around the world are included.

The author section is the main portion of the book, containing 461 books arranged alphabetically by author. Each entry is numbered and includes bibliographical information, a summary of approximately 100 words, and the suitable age level of the reader. No prices are given. The author notes those titles out of print, and unfortunately 75 percent are; however, some of those are now appearing in paperback reprints and bibliographical information for those is given. With this large number of out-of-print titles, the volume will not be useful as a buying guide. Awards won by some titles are given; however, these are few and inconsistent. Title and subject indexes follow the main text. The subject index includes specific subjects, places, time periods, and cross-references. Nineteen black-and-white illustrations reprinted from selected titles illustrate the book. [R: Choice, Mar 95, p.1082]—**Elaine Ezell**

Children's Literature

Bibliography

1180. Barstow, Barbara, and Judith Riggle. **Beyond Picture Books: A Guide to First Readers.** 2d ed. New Providence, N.J., R. R. Bowker/Reed Reference Publishing, 1995. 501p. index. $47.00. ISBN 0-8352-3519-X.

This new edition of an annotated bibliography lists well-written children's books containing attractive illustrations and stories or subjects that are of interest to children ages four to seven. The work profiles almost 2,500 first reader titles that the authors have found to be both challenging and entertaining. Reading levels ranging from the easier A (sentences with three to five single-syllable words) to the more challenging C (more text, fewer illustrations, sentences with compound words) are furnished for each title.

Beyond Picture Books is arranged alphabetically by author and provides such information as title, illustrator, publisher, date, ISBN, subjects, reading category, and a brief annotation. Approximately 1,000 new entries have been added to this edition. The inclusion of a list of 200 outstanding first readers makes this work especially useful for collection development.

The annotations provide a brief plot summary in the case of fiction titles and an indication as to the type of illustrations that can be found in the story. Nonfiction titles are dealt with in a similar way, although the emphasis is on content. Almost half of the bibliography is devoted to a series of indexes by subject, title, illustrator, readability, and series. *Beyond Picture Books* is a valuable reference guide and selection tool for librarians, teachers, and parents.—**John B. Romeiser**

1181. Blake, Barbara. **A Guide to Children's Books About Asian Americans.** Brookfield, Vt., Scolar Press/Ashgate Publishing, 1995. 223p. $49.95. ISBN 1-85928-014-5.

The purpose of this book is to provide the reader with specific titles of children's books to be used at home, in the classroom, in story times, and in the library to help children better understand Asians and Asian Americans. In the introductory part of the book, the author presents a concise and interesting demographic picture of Asian Americans according to the 1990 U.S. census. This is followed by part 1, in which Blake focuses on refugees and immigrants from East Asia, Southeast Asia, and South Asia in three separate chapters. For each country of origin, she gives the following helpful information: immigration overview of each important Asian-American group plus notes on its culture.

Part 2 is the main section of the book. It is a briefly annotated bibliography divided into four sections: fiction—preschool through third grade; fiction—fourth through sixth grade; nonfiction—preschool through third grade; and nonfiction—fourth through sixth grade. Interestingly, there are a few Australian and New Zealand entries. There are no entries for media materials. The book entries give basic bibliographical information except price, indicate culture, and include a short descriptive summary. Reviews are noted, but curiously no specific dates or paginations are given.

Four appendixes conclude the book. These are listings by author; title; culture, category, and grade; and a "select list of sources of Asian children's books" (publishers and bookstores). The author is the director of library services at the Rowlett Public Library in Texas. She has written a serviceable and unique bibliography: It is the only one of its kind currently available. The only other remotely comparable title is Rudine S. Bishop's *Kaleidoscope: A Multicultural Booklist for Grades K-8* (see entry 1182). However, the book under review is somewhat overpriced.—**Marshall E. Nunn**

1182. **Kaleidoscope: A Multicultural Booklist for Grades K-8.** Rudine Sims Bishop, ed. Urbana, Ill., National Council of Teachers of English, 1994. 169p. illus. index. (NCTE Bibliography Series). $14.95pa. ISBN 0-8141-2543-3.

Teachers and librarians who wish to offer children in grades K-8 books that reflect diverse cultures and life experiences would be interested in this annotated bibliography. The 400 titles included were published between 1990 and 1992 and the editor compiled them in conjunction with the National Council of Teachers of English, Multicultural Booklist Committee—a group of teachers and librarians. The term multicultural, in this title, is limited to the four nonwhite groups classified by the federal government as minorities: African Americans, Asian Americans, Hispanic Americans/Latinos, and Native Americans. It also covers a limited number of background materials related to the countries of origin of these groups.

Arrangement of entries is by genre (poetry; biographies; histories; folktales, myths, and legends; wonder tales; picture books; fiction; anthologies) or theme (the arts, ceremonies and celebrations, people, immigrants and immigration), rather than by ethnic group. However, titles related to a particular group (e.g., Puerto Ricans or Korean Americans) can be identified through the subject index. The purpose of the arrangement is to point out cultural similarities and differences when studying a particular topic. The annotations are primarily descriptive, providing a brief synopsis of the story or work. A useful list of award-winning books covered in *Kaleidoscope* follows the bibliography, including the name and date of the award received. A directory of publishers and four indexes (author, illustrator, subject, and title) conclude the work.

As Sims points out, the percentage of books published each year about minorities is increasing, but is still quite low. Any tools that help educators at the elementary, secondary, undergraduate, or graduate level are important. They are equally useful to librarians who are participating in selection and development of the collection or providing guidance to readers. The reasonable price of this list also makes it an attractive purchase for school or public libraries, or for academic libraries where children's literature courses are taught.—**Lois J. Buttlar**

1183. Marantz, Sylvia S., and Kenneth A. Marantz. **The Art of Children's Picture Books: A Selective Reference Guide.** 2d ed. Hamden, Conn., Garland, 1995. 293p. index. (Garland Reference Library of the Humanities, v.1636). $38.00. ISBN 0-8153-0937-6.

As implied by the title, this book is designed to be used as a reference source focusing on the history, construction, criticism, artists, and collections of picture books. In addition to the sections mentioned above, the Marantz's include special sections on individual picture book artists, guides to further research, and cross-referenced indexes of artists, editors, compilers, and titles mentioned in the text. Each entry is fully annotated, alphabetized, and in continuous numerical order (for indexing purposes). The annotations vary in length from a few sentences to several paragraphs—the average entry is approximately 50 to 60 words in length. The entries, particularly in the historical section, are highly descriptive of the contents of each title.

Particular emphasis is placed in this work upon children's books as an art form, rather than as literature. As a result, artists and illustrations are highlighted rather than authors or stories. In the introduction, the authors explain this focus by stating that "because the picture book is much more a visual art object than a piece of literature, book selection should focus more on the visual attributes than on the text." Working from this perspective, *The Art of Children's Picture Books* works well as a reference tool, offering much information in a clear, well-ordered text.—**Teresa Holten**

1184. McElmeel, Sharron L. **Great New Nonfiction Reads.** Englewood, Colo., Libraries Unlimited, 1995. 225p. illus. index. $21.00pa. ISBN 1-56308-228-4.

Guided by the premise that "there is no magic list of books that all children must hear before they pass out of childhood" (p. 7), this educator and consultant has assembled more than 600 appealing and accurate nonfiction titles under such topics as inventions, sports, various animals and their behavior, hyphenated-Americans, and personalities such as Sojourner Truth, Johannes Gutenberg, and King Louis XIV.

To stimulate the sense of inquisitiveness that children demonstrate, she features 120 books in-depth, suggesting extensions to further reading, activities, or investigations. For example, "Homelessness" features *Erik Is Homeless* by Keith E. Greenberg (Lerner, 1992), a photo-essay for upper-elementary-aged students about a boy and his mother in transitional housing, which the author connects to three novels for older students and a picture book. However, her nonfiction extension titles (a *Reader's Digest* first-person account and a powerful but difficult-to-read exposé, *Rachel and Her Children* by Jonathan Kozol) are not especially useful for the targeted audience of grades one through six. Better to include a balanced overview such as *Homeless or Helpless?* by Margery G. Nichelason (Lerner, 1993) and *No Place to Be: Voices of Homeless Children* by Judith Berck (Houghton Mifflin, 1992), both accessible to upper-elementary students. In contrast, her excellent entry on "Pollution" suggests using the controversy surrounding *Brother Eagle, Sister Sky: A Message from Chief Seattle* by Susan Jeffers (Dial Books, 1991) to provoke discussion about the credibility of a "message" when the medium has been identified as a hoax. An extensive subject index (as well as an author/title/illustrator index) extends the book's usefulness for curriculum development.

While McElmeel's suggestions are guided by her personal taste and experiences, her instincts are excellent. This paperback provides librarians, teachers, and parents with 620 titles for reading aloud or sharing, criteria for evaluating nonfiction, ideas for thematic curriculum units, and ways to stimulate continued learning through informational reading.—**Debbie Abilock**

FICTION

General Works

1185. Henry, Laurie. **The Fiction Dictionary.** Cincinnati, Ohio, Story Press/F & W Publications, 1995. 324p. index. $18.99. ISBN 1-884910-05-X.

This dictionary will be especially useful to readers needing extended definitions of terms used in the interpretation of fiction. Included are many standard terms, such as *legend*, *plot*, and *omniscient narrator*, as well as numerous contemporary terms, such as *Kmart fiction*, *cyberpunk*, and *flash fiction*. Typical entries begin with a concise definition, followed by a detailed discussion, which also usually includes a substantial excerpt from fiction. Synonyms are included in parentheses and related terms defined in the dictionary are noted with asterisks. An alphabetical list of entries appears at the end of the book (it would be more useful at the front).

Henry, herself a writer and teacher, clearly enjoyed writing the entries: Those sampled were not only clear but fun to read. The extended discussions of terms, cross-references, and literary excerpts establish a rich context for these entries. The selection of terms necessarily reflects the writer's interests, which may not be shared by all of her readers. Despite the authority of the late John Gardner, whose *Art of Fiction* (Alfred A. Knopf, 1984) is frequently quoted here, it is doubtful that many readers will be looking up *crot*, a term Gardner defined as the white space sometimes separating sections of text or asterisks indicating disconnections in the sequence of the story. It would be useful to have a bibliography of the works cited in the definitions. To avoid sexist stereotypes, pronouns are inconsistently used—sometimes the generic "she" replaces "he," and sometimes "they" substitutes, awkwardly, for either pronoun. On the whole, however, this dictionary contains quite a number of terms more old-fashioned dictionaries of literary terms omit, as well as providing more extended definitions. Writers of fiction who are scrupulous about technique may find this book as useful as scholars and students.—**David Isaacson**

1186. Herald, Diana Tixier. **Genreflecting: A Guide to Reading Interests in Genre Fiction.** 4th ed. Englewood, Colo., Libraries Unlimited, 1995. 367p. index. $38.00. ISBN 1-56308-354-X.

Herald continues the solid tradition of predecessor and former coauthor Betty Rosenberg in this latest edition of a work that is key to reader's advisory services in many libraries. The primary audience of this volume is the reader, a fact that is evident in both the structure and style of this guide.

The work is arranged in eight major sections. The first of these explains the nature of the "common reader" and genre fiction. The other sections each treat a specific genre: Westerns, crime, adventure, romance, science fiction, fantasy, and horror. Herald divides each section into two categories: themes and types, and topics. Within each of these, further breakdown is by subgenre or type of secondary material, such as anthologies, bibliographies, history and criticism, awards, and so forth. A wide range of authors, titles, and annotations are presented throughout. In this edition, a new subsection is "D's Picks," wherein the author identifies a few titles that she personally has found to be great reading.

In general, criteria for inclusion of an author are prolific output (a characteristic of genre fiction) and availability in either hardcover or paperback. However, classic authors in a genre who are not prolific are included as appropriate (e.g., mystery writers Dorothy L. Sayers, Dashiell Hammett, and Raymond Chandler). All in all, there is no comparable guide to genre fiction. It is highly recommended for all libraries collecting in this area.—**Edmund F. SantaVicca**

1187. Hicken, Mandy, and Ray Prytherch. **Now Read On: A Guide to Contemporary Popular Fiction.** 2d ed. Brookfield, Vt., Scolar Press/Ashgate, 1994. 442p. index. $46.95. ISBN 1-85928-008-0.

As a guide to authors of contemporary popular fiction (under genres from adventure stories, detective stories, gothic romances, and historical novels to police work, sea stories, thrillers, and women detective stories), this reference work will be particularly useful in public libraries. This edition adds 60 new authors as well as listing new titles by authors included in the 1st edition.

The authors chosen for inclusion are personal favorites of the compilers, but include many best-selling authors in addition to many lesser-known writers. Selection was also partially based on a sample of fiction chosen by public library users. A majority of the authors are British, but there are also a number of American, Australian, and African novelists. The majority of authors are still writing, while a few others are deceased. There will be regular revisions to this work as new titles and authors appear.

Although 20 genres are included, writers of westerns and light romantic novels are purposely excluded, as are more literary-styled novels. Entries are arranged alphabetically by genre and then alphabetically by author within the genre. Entries include brief biographical information and comments regarding content, style, and quality of the novels listed. All titles published by an author are included, along with a few names of authors writing in a similar vein.

There are two indexes, one for every author mentioned (along with pseudonyms) and another for series and recurring characters in an author's work. An appendix lists literature prizes and award winners for specific genres.

Many names will be recognizable: Maeve Binchy and Belva Plain (family stories); Jean M. Auel and Irving Stone (historical novels); Stephen King and Dean Koontz (horror stories); Frank Herbert and Ray Bradbury (science fiction); and John Harris and Leo Kessler (war stories). There are just as many less-known names under each category, opening up new reading possibilities. At any rate, selections may not have been scientifically chosen or be comprehensive in number, but peering into another librarian's bookshelf favorites is always interesting.—**Maureen Pastine**

1188. Weaver, Bruce L. **Novel Openers: First Sentences of 11,000 Fictional Works, Topically Arranged....** Jefferson, N.C., McFarland, 1995. 986p. index. $75.00. ISBN 0-7864-0050-1.

For the shelf of the consummate litterateur, this volume could serve as an opposing bookend to Georgianne Ensign's *Great Endings: Closing Lines of Great Novels* (HarperCollins, 1995). Weaver has culled his opening lines from works of fiction (principally novels) that were originally written in English and that aspire to being recognized by critics as literary in nature. Although the majority of represented titles come from the pens of deceased authors, many others derive from living writers. Minority and genre writers are not shunned, as is evident from excerpts from Ralph Ellison's *Invisible Man* and R. F. Delderfield's *Theirs Was the Kingdom*. As promised in Weaver's introduction, the work also contains many neglected works, such as those by noted writers Sinclair Lewis and John P. Marquand.

More than 300 alphabetically ordered topic headings make up the main body of the book. These headings range from such emotions as "bewilderment" and "excitement" to such concrete nouns as "bells" and "vehicles." Even such abstractions as "chance and luck," "motives," and "waiting" are included. The opening lines themselves appear beneath these rubrics, arranged from older to newer publication dates. Works released during the same year are ordered alphabetically by author. Back matter comprises two indexes: one of subjects, keywords, and key phrases, and one of authors and titles.

Although Weaver has extracted first lines from the finest literary icons, he has occasionally omitted some significant titles: Edgar Allan Poe's *Narrative of Arthur Gordon Pym*, Mark Twain's *A Connecticut Yankee in King Arthur's Court*, and Robert Louis Stevenson's *Catriona*. Also disappointing to note is the absence of such quality novelists as Algernon Blackwood and Thomas Tryon. Despite such flaws, Weaver's reference merits a place on the shelf of all serious literature collections.—**Jeffrey E. Long**

Crime and Mystery

1189. **The Crown Crime Companion: The Top 100 Mystery Novels of All Time.** By Otto Penzler. Mickey Friedman, comp. New York, Crown, 1995. 190p. $12.00pa. ISBN 0-517-88115-2.

This small bibliography is an enjoyable compilation of responses by 200 members of the Mystery Writers of America (MWA) who were asked to choose their 50 favorite mysteries—5 in each of 10 categories. The titles receiving the most votes overall constituted the "Top 100." While one may delight in debating the inclusion of a particular writer on the list, the best of the best are definitely present. Classic and contemporary luminaries such as Arthur Conan Doyle, Edgar Allan Poe, and Wilkie Collins justifiably share the spotlight with Josephine Tey, Agatha Christie, John Le Carré, and Ruth Rendell.

Surprisingly, the annotations are not typical plot summaries. Only a few sentences are devoted to descriptions of the books' contents. The remaining text discusses the contribution the works make to a specific mystery genre, such as spy stories, faction or "true novels," and melodrama. The final paragraph mentions the film version(s), if there is one, the actors and actresses, and an evaluation of the media's treatment of the work on the big screen.

Not content with a simple "Top 100" list, the compiler tabulated and distributed the rest of the responses into 10 categories: classics, suspense, hardboiled/private eye, cozy/traditional, historical, humorous, and legal/courtroom. Each of these categories is introduced by a master of the genre, including Mary Higgins Clark, H. R. F. Keating, Joseph Wambaugh, and Richard Condon. Lest this handy bibliography sound dry, a perusal of MWA members' favorite murder weapon illuminates "a frozen leg of lamb, later served for dinner, in Roald Dahl's short story, 'Lamb to the Slaughter.' " All types of libraries should purchase this inexpensive treat and use it for reading guidance, contests, bulletin boards, book clubs, displays, and the incentive to create one's own personal list of favorite mysteries.—**Kathleen W. Craver**

Historical Fiction

1190. Murph, Roxane C. **The Wars of the Roses in Fiction: An Annotated Bibliography, 1440-1994.** Westport, Conn., Greenwood Press, 1995. 209p. index. (Bibliographies and Indexes in World History, no.41). $69.50. ISBN 0-313-29709-6.

Despite efforts to cover comprehensively English-language fictional prose, verse, and plays written from 1440 to 1994 about "the conflict between the houses of Lancaster and York for the throne of England" (p. vii), this volume substantially amounts to a fairly pricey popular reader's guide to modern historical novels. Of the 364 entries in the largest section for novels and short fiction (the volume includes 566 total entries), about 300 identify novels published after 1900. It cites only about a dozen prose works dating from the seventeenth and eighteenth centuries and about 50 from the nineteenth century. The sections for verse and plays include 137 and 65 entries, respectively.

The total number of entries, however, is inflated by duplicate entries for variant United States-British titles, and, particularly in the section for verse, by separate entries for specific poems and the collections containing them. Sources for fully half of the verses are about two-dozen early and modern collections, including the several editions of *A Mirror for Magistrates*, first published in 1559; Bishop Percy's *Reliques of Ancient English Poetry* (1765); Joseph Ritson's *Ancient Songs and Ballads* (1877); and *Historical Poems of the XIVth and XVth Centuries* (1959), edited by Rossell Hope Robbins. The arrangement of entries for verse by author and, mainly, by title (as most are anonymous), leads to tracking through sequential cross-references to identify the sources of most verses. At the other extreme, at least 1 entry (456) cross-references itself.

While the arrangement by genre is perhaps appropriate for the intended audience of "both students and general readers" (p. viii), a chronological scheme for the verse (at least, and maybe the prose and plays as well), possibly along the lines of Nancy A. Gutierrez's *English Historical Poetry, 1476-1603* (see ARBA 85, entry 1132), may have increased the volume's usefulness for scholars. Indexing is perfunctory at best: "Shore, Jane" references only three entries—and none of the ones titled "Jane Shore," *Jane Shore*, and variants ranging from "Ballad of Jane Shore" to *Witchery of Jane Shore*. This volume may be most useful in libraries with large popular fiction collections where readers are eager to find another novel on the subject; most academic libraries, however, can pass on it.—**James K. Bracken**

Science Fiction, Fantasy, and Horror

1191. **Anatomy of Wonder 4: A Critical Guide to Science Fiction.** Neil Barron, ed. New Providence, N.J., R. R. Bowker/Reed Reference Publishing, 1995. 912p. index. $52.00. ISBN 0-8352-3288-3.

The 1st edition of *Anatomy of Wonder* (see ARBA 77, entry 1173) won deserved acclaim for being the first critical guide to the important primary and secondary literature of science fiction. Successive editions have become increasingly lengthy, testifying not only to the growing number of good writers but also to the increased academic recognition of a hitherto largely marginalized literature. The contents of the 4th edition of *Anatomy of Wonder* have been extensively revised and rewritten, but its basic arrangement is similar to that of earlier editions. The first section of the book thus surveys the significant primary literature: It contains six chapters, each consisting of a superior historical essay followed by a lengthy annotated bibliography. In all, approximately 2,100 novels and short stories are cited, and the result is not only a list of key works but also a developmental history of a literary genre. New to this edition is a survey of science fiction poetry.

The second section also consists of essays and annotated bibliographic lists, but it documents the secondary literature, the important research aids that will assist in locating, studying, and teaching science fiction. Approximately 800 secondary works are identified and described in 11 chapters, and as before, these chapters have been extensively revised and rewritten. Dated studies have been dropped; the section devoted to science fiction illustration has been expanded to include material studying science fiction comics; and Barron has compiled an extensive list of best books, awards, notable series, important English translations of foreign-language works, and the addresses of major science fiction organizations. Useful indexes listing authors, titles, subjects, and key themes used in the fiction conclude the volume.

Although some may disagree with specific items chosen for annotation, few will dispute that the *Anatomy of Wonder* belongs in all academic libraries: It remains unquestionably the finest one-volume guide to the literature of science fiction. Its focus, however, remains entirely print-based, and one hopes that the 5th edition of this superlative work acknowledges the substantial number of Internet and World Wide Web sources devoted to science fiction and its writers.—**Richard Bleiler**

1192. Clute, John. **Science Fiction: The Illustrated Encyclopedia.** New York, Dorling Kindersley, 1995. 312p. illus. index. $39.95. ISBN 00-7894-0185-1.

In his brief introduction, Clute states that "*SF: The Illustrated Encyclopedia* is a guided tour of stories about a million tomorrows" (p. 7). More prosaically, it is an amiable coffee-table book, a volume in which the many illustrations take precedence over the text. There are color pictures of important science fiction books, magazines, comic books, and authors, and there are numerous color stills from significant movies and television shows. As an illustrated volume, it is superior to such earlier books as the 1978 *Encyclopedia of Science Fiction* (edited by Robert Holdstock) and *The Visual Encyclopedia of Science Fiction* of the same year (see ARBA 79, entry 1202).

As an encyclopedia, however, the volume is not without significant flaws. First, its arrangement is broadly thematic, with eight chapters surveying such subjects as future visions, influential magazines, major authors, classic titles, genre films, and international television. Each of these chapters contains text and chronologies, but each treats its subject in isolation. There are too few cross-references, few attempts at integration of data, and the indexing is inadequate: Discussion of Algis Budrys's *Who?* can be found on pages 133, 151, and 276, but the entry for *Budrys* cites pages 133 and 151, and the entry for *Who?* cites pages 151 and 276. Next, there are odd omissions. The pulp magazine *The Shadow* is mentioned in the text (although not in the index), but the more relevant *Doc Savage* is not present. To mention only the major works—the pieces that are today critically accepted—is to paint a portrait of the genre that is at best unbalanced. Finally, there are numerous factual errors. For example, Owen Gregory's name is given as "Gregory Owen," and Hugo Gernsback was not "a German who emigrated to the US" (p. 214); he was from Luxembourg.

Clute's work would have benefited from a greater historical perspective and better editing, but despite its shortcomings, it provides a sense of the development and maturation of a literary genre. It belongs in libraries in which there is significant interest in the history of science fiction.—**Richard Bleiler**

1193. MacNee, Marie J. **Science Fiction, Fantasy, and Horror Writers.** Detroit, U*X*L/Gale, 1994. 2v. illus. index. $38.00/set. ISBN 0-8103-9865-6.

The U*X*L line of books for middle schools are digests of larger Gale monographs. *Science Fiction, Fantasy, and Horror Writers* is no exception, as it presents short, concise, and easy-to-read biographical sketches of this genre of writers. The coverage of a sample biography gives the pattern for the whole. Robin McKinley fills three pages (which have plenty of white space), including a photograph of the author; a "Best Bets" sidebar suggesting her most well-known titles; and a photograph of the cover of *Beauty*, her most famous book. The text is written like a story and covers her early life and her motivation to write. The plots of her most well-known works are mentioned ever-so-briefly, and the article ends with a bibliography of sources for more information (both from Gale sources and from periodicals). Thus, the entries are targeted toward the young person who wants a first introduction to the author, not a more thorough analysis as is done in the Gale sets *Authors & Artists for Young Adults* (see entry 1171) or *Something About the Author* (see entries 1172-1174), or in compilations such as *Major Authors and Illustrators for Children and Young Adults* (see ARBA 94, entry 1187).

Eighty authors are covered in this two-volume set: a taste of the coverage includes Douglas Adams, Piers Anthony, Isaac Asimov, Natalie Babbitt, Clive Barker, Ray Bradbury, Edgar Rice Burroughs, Octavia Butler, Eleanor Cameron, Lewis Carroll, Mary Higgins Clark, and Arthur C. Clarke. Most are popular with the middle and upper elementary school level reader and definitely written for this audience. The challenge today is often to find reference books that are suitable for the young person who is not a particularly strong reader. This set fills the bill and could be used by high school-age youth without fear of "talking down" to this audience.

For libraries who need introductory biographical material wrapped up in an attractive and easy-to-read format, this set is recommended. It does not take the place, however, of the more sophisticated biographical sources for children and young adult authors published by Gale.—**David V. Loertscher**

1194. **The Supernatural Index: A Listing of Fantasy, Supernatural, Occult, Weird, and Horror Anthologies.** By Mike Ashley and William G. Contento. Westport, Conn., Greenwood Press, 1995. 933p. (Bibliographies and Indexes in Science Fiction, Fantasy, and Horror, no.5). $195.00. ISBN 0-313-24030-2.

As aficionados of the genre are sorely aware, the study of weird fiction has until recent decades been hindered by a lack of informed reference tools. Now, to the elite ranks of such pioneers in this shunned field as H. P. Lovecraft, E. F. Bleiler, and S. T. Joshi, readers may consecrate the names of Ashley and Contento for their landmark volume.

More than 2,100 anthologies of English-language supernatural fiction, as well as their contents of nearly 22,000 stories, novellas, and related items, receive serious bibliographical enumeration and scholarly comment. No single-author collections are embraced by Ashley and Contento. The literature is indexed by anthology editor, anthology title, author of anthologized work, and title of anthologized work—the last index including chronologically arranged citations of all known collection appearances of the work, often beginning with the work's initial publication of such now-defunct periodicals as *Smart Set* or *New England Magazine*. Following these indexes, anthologies that are new or of peripheral relevance are listed by author: For example, volumes whose fiction features themes that merely intimate supernatural forces or entities, or volumes whose stories' supernatural elements are blended with those of suspense, science fiction, adventure, or mythology.

Nearly 8,000 authors are represented in *The Supernatural Index*, and the variety of their work in the domain of horror fiction alone is staggering. There are the dimly lit Victorian parlor tales of M. R. James and chilling offerings from mainstream writers such as Charles Dickens. Foreign masters are heard from in the work, as are such weird fiction nouveau writers as Thomas Ligotti and Terri Windling. Also accommodated are anthologies of traditional Gothic works, as are many works of brooding Gothic ambiance that lack supernatural contrivance. Fairy tale collections appear, as well as prominent juvenile anthologies of supernatural fiction (for children at least 11 years old).

Notable ancillary features of the book include the listing together (by title keyword) of citations on the respective volumes of well-known series. Also, authors' years of birth and (if deceased) death are provided, with currency through 1994. Hundreds of anonymously written works are included in *The Supernatural Index* as well.

A check against more than 30 anthologies in hand turned up but one discrepancy. The verso of *Ghost Stories*, edited by A. L. Furman, shows that work to have been issued by Belmont in 1964 rather than 1965, as stated in Ashley and Contento's work. Despite arduous searching, no fiction collection of consequence was found to have been omitted by the authors. The addition of such weird poetry anthologies as *Dark of the Moon*, edited by August Derleth (Books for Libraries Press, 1947), as well as a subject index, would but enhance an already superb work. These suggestions aside, all that remains to be said is that, although this work's format is that of an index, in application *The Supernatural Index* is truly a manual for all fans of supernatural fiction.—**Jeffrey E. Long**

Short Stories

1195. Aycock, Wendell M. **Twentieth-Century Short Story Explication, New Series. Volume II: 1991-1992.** North Haven, Conn., Shoe String Press, 1995. 295p. index. $49.50. ISBN 0-208-02370-4.

After Warren Walker completed the original series of Twentieth-Century Short Story Explication (1961-1991) in 1992, as well as volume 1 of the New Series (1989-1990) (see ARBA 94, entry 1218) in the same year, he chose colleague Aycock to continue the New Series. Like its predecessors, this volume is a bibliography of interpretations that have appeared since 1900 of stories published since 1800. It carries forward the coverage through December 1992 and includes more than 4,940 entries. Of the 662 authors cited, 175 appear here for the first time, 115 of them with Hispanic surnames. Regardless of the language in which the stories were written, these explications are limited to those published in the major languages of western Europe.

Following the arrangement of the earlier volumes, entries here are alphabetical by author, followed by alphabetically arranged short story titles. Each explication cited includes the name of the critic or scholar, the short title of the work in which the explication appears, and the pagination therein. Full bibliographic information appears in an alphabetical author appendix, "A Checklist of Books Used." If the explication appears in a journal or an essay in a critical collection, full publication information is supplied for the initial citation, with the journal title abbreviated. Full titles of journal abbreviations appear in an alphabetically arranged appendix. Subsequent citations carry only an author, a short title, and the pagination. An index of the short story writers concludes the volume. Libraries with earlier editions will likely want to acquire this useful continuation, with its blend of familiar authors and those less well known.

—Charles R. Andrews

1196. **Short Story Criticism: Excerpts from Criticism of the Works of Short Fiction Writers. Volume 17.** Drew Kalasky and others, eds. Detroit, Gale, 1995. 536p. illus. index. $88.00. ISBN 0-8103-9281-X.

Volume 17 of Gale's Short Story Criticism series retains the basic format of the series with a few new features. Each volume in the series contains information on approximately 10 authors, of all nationalities and time periods. Each entry begins with a background essay, a portrait of the author if available, a list of the author's principal works, excerpts from criticism, and a bibliography for further reading. The critical excerpts are arranged chronologically, to allow the reader to track changes in the critical response to the author. Some excerpts are preceded by notes in which the critic's reputation or the scope of the essay is discussed.

The new features are minimal. Comments by the authors themselves on their work are included if available, and a bibliography of general sources on short fiction is appended. While not major changes, these are useful additions. Gale, of course, is well known for its series on literary criticism, such as Contemporary Authors (see entry 1150) and Twentieth-Century Literary Criticism (see entries 1159-1160). A percentage of the articles in *Short Story Criticism* are reprints from other Gale series, but no more than 20 percent of any one volume. This is Gale's only ongoing series covering short fiction.

Titles from other publishers do provide access to short story criticism. *Short Fiction Criticism* (Swallow, 1960) is still useful, although obviously not for contemporary criticism. The other major relevant series, *Twentieth-Century Short Story Explication* (see entry 1195), is perhaps more inclusive in its listings of criticism, but provides bibliographical information only. It is less suitable for high school libraries than *Short Fiction Criticism*, which provides lengthy excerpts. It also, of course, is limited to criticism written in the twentieth century, although the short story authors themselves are from both the nineteenth and twentieth centuries. This series is recommended for high school, academic, and public libraries.

—Terry Ann Mood

NATIONAL LITERATURE

American Literature

General Works

Bibliography

1197. Fabre, Michel, and others, comps. **French Critical Reception of African-American Literature from the Beginnings to 1970: An Annotated Bibliography.** Westport, Conn., Greenwood Press, 1995. 310p. index. (Bibliographies and Indexes in Afro-American and African Studies, no.33). $75.00. ISBN 0-313-25368-4.

This is a helpful reference work for students and scholars interested in learning about how African-American writers have been viewed outside the country of their origin. Fabre and his assistants dug for more than 20 years in Paris libraries and publishers' archives, where they found and gathered hundreds of French critical reviews and essays about African-American authors. Most of the periodical and journal items had appeared between the years 1900 and 1970.

Fabre, who is a distinguished French scholar of African-American literature at the University of Paris, provided the insightful introduction to the bibliography and also wrote most of the informative annotations for the entries. The result is a useful, fascinating revelation of how the French academic and reading public grew to appreciate and understand the major African-American works, such as Richard Wright's *Native Son*, Ralph Ellison's *Invisible Man*, James Baldwin's *Go Tell It on the Mountain*, and Chester Himes's *Lonely Crusade*. All of these writers, except Ellison, were longtime residents of France, and, of course, their preference for the more tolerant French cultural and racial climate helped the expatriates' literary reputations among the French. This reference work is an indispensable guide for readers involved and interested in African-American literary and cultural studies.—**Angelo Costanzo**

Biography

1198. **American Diversity, American Identity: The Lives and Works of 145 Writers Who Define the American Experience.** John K. Roth, ed. New York, Henry Holt, 1995. 709p. index. $45.00. ISBN 0-8050-3430-7.

What does it mean to be a citizen of the United States? What does the term "American" say about a person's identity? This reference work strives to answer these questions, emphasizing that the "American identity" is not a "one-size-fits-all" pattern, and attempts to portray the U.S. identity in all its complexity, diversity, and, the editor hopes, cohesion. The book covers 145 writers that Roth feels epitomize the various aspects of the "American experience."

The text is organized into 13 sections, based on regionalism, ethnicity, gender, and sexual preference; one section discusses writers who concentrate on life during wartime. Each section provides an introduction to the topic at hand and then proceeds to profile individual authors who embody the approach. Each essay supplies a biography of the author, including principal fiction written; achievements; an analysis of how the writer promotes the viewpoint in question; and a bibliography for further reading. The primary text is followed by "A Catagorized [sic] Listing of Writers" and a comprehensive index by titles of works and names of authors. The bibliographies at the ends of the essays are helpful, as is the categorized list of authors.

Interesting as this work is, there are problems. Some authors transcend the boundaries under which they have been placed, while others seem to be questionably distinguished. Writers such as Mark Twain, James Baldwin, Toni Morrison, Alice Walker (why put Walker under "Bearers of the African American Tradition" and Morrison under "Renewing Visions of America," but neither under "Women's Voices"?), Barbara Kingsolver, Audre Lorde, and Adrienne Rich could be placed in different categories than the ones they are assigned. Interestingly, the categorized list at the end of the text provides names of other writers who fit these categories, and places individuals in more than one category as they fit. Another flaw concerns the lack of visions based on religious experience beyond Jewish American voices (which goes beyond mere religious identity)—Do not different religions also contribute to the American identity? Also, no mention is made of Canadian authors, although the broad definition of "American" includes them, and many Canadians also live the "American experience."

The format and goal of the book seem best suited for a high school library, where students could be exposed to new authors and ideas. However, the language used may be a bit advanced for many high school students; it seems more appropriate for undergraduate or graduate institutions. Therefore, the audience to whom this book is directed is questionable; libraries should carefully consider their patrons' needs before purchasing the volume.—**Melissa R. Root**

1199. **Contemporary Poets, Dramatists, Essayists, and Novelists of the South: A Bio-Bibliographical Sourcebook.** Robert Bain and Joseph M. Flora, eds. Westport, Conn., Greenwood Press, 1994. 642p. index. $95.00. ISBN 0-313-28765-1.

Describing and assessing the achievements of 49 modern southern writers of poetry, drama, essays, and novels, this bio-bibliographical sourcebook presents a preliminary report on the excellent work these authors have produced during the last 3 decades. Although none of those whose careers are highlighted here have the reputation of William Faulkner, Eudora Welty, or Tennessee Williams, many of them are already well-known heroes and heroines of southern literary culture: Maya Angelou, Beth Henley,

William Morris, Ishmael Reed, and Tom Wolfe. Only time will tell whether or not the fame of the other authors will last well into the twenty-first century. A companion volume, *Contemporary Fiction Writers of the South: A Bio-Bibliographical Sourcebook* (see ARBA 94, entry 1222), works along with this literary guide as the number of southerners writing well exceeds that which can be treated in-depth in a single book.

Editors Bain and Flora observe that "unlike the writers of the Southern Renascence, most of whom were white males and from the upper middle class, many contemporary poets, dramatists, essayists and novelists come from the middling or rising middle classes." Of course, "formidable work by women and black authors plays a much more important role in the current flowering than it did in the Renascence" (p. xviii). Also clearly evident in the work of this diverse group of southern writers are their responses to such radical changes in the South as the decline of rural living; the rise of urban and suburban environments; the influence of mass media and popular culture (such as sports events, shopping malls, hunting traditions, and auto racing); the preoccupation with gaining wealth; and the social mobility that comes once it is achieved. Faulkner's eternal verities of love, honor, courage, and sacrifice are omnipresent, but so also are themes emphasizing the importance of place, the values of religion and politics, a fascination with the comic grotesque, and the impact of the past on the present.

Each entry includes five parts: a biographical sketch, a discussion of the author's major themes and forms, an assessment of reviews and scholarship, a chronological list of the author's works, and a bibliography of selected criticism. This reference guide will be of help to casual readers as well as lifelong scholars of southern literature and culture. In its coverage of modern trends in poetry, drama, essays, and fiction, it goes beyond its southern focus and will be of interest to modernists of every age, race, class, and gender.—**Colby H. Kullman**

Dictionaries

1200. **The Oxford Companion to Women's Writing in the United States.** Cathy N. Davidson and Linda Wagner-Martin, eds. New York, Oxford University Press, 1995. 1021p. index. $45.00. ISBN 0-19-506608-1.

A useful collection of biographies and essays on literary movements, genres, and ethnic influence, this reference work rivals *The Bloomsbury Guide to Women's Literature* (see ARBA 93, entry 942) and other current overviews of female literary contributions in depth, scope, fairness, and quality of analysis. Opening with an introduction, statement of purpose, and explanation of a remarkably pragmatic layout, the book presents concise, timely coverage of literary figures as well as such writers as Betty Friedan and Rachel Carson, who have contributed to other fields. Appendixes offer parallel timelines of social history and U.S. women's publications as well as an extensive bibliography and exhaustive indexing.

The strength of this desk reference is its forthright language, even tone, and far-ranging bibliographies. Signed essays on temperance, postmodernism, feminist films, conservatism, multiculturalism, the Black arts movement, and gender-based writing avoid ponderous diction and pontification. Weighty, complex topics such as Jewish-American writing and poetry introduce subdivisions by name (e.g., 1650-1850, religious poetry) and cross-reference to additional information (e.g., lesbian writing, Native American writing). Several lapses suggest areas that were passed over or neglected (e.g., female Caldecott and Newbery award-winners, notably Lois Lowry, author of *The Giver*, an unflinching dystopian novel that led to division among teachers, librarians, and readers over the appropriateness of a severely oppressive landscape for children). Overall, this meticulous work deserves a place among the best of literary reference works.—**Mary Ellen Snodgrass**

Handbooks and Yearbooks

1201. **Dictionary of Literary Biography Documentary Series: An Illustrated Chronicle. Volume 12: Southern Women Writers: Flannery O'Connor, Katherine Anne Porter, Eudora Welty.** Mary Ann Wimsatt and Karen L. Rood, eds. Detroit, Gale, 1995. 358p. illus. index. $128.00. ISBN 0-8103-5561-2.

The 300 double-column pages of this portentous volume contain many unpublished photographs, manuscript, typescript, and proof facsimiles as well as printed letters, notebooks, interviews, contemporary reviews and articles, lectures, panel discussions, and obituaries of Flannery O'Connor, Katherine Anne Porter, and Eudora Welty. Although Porter visited O'Connor in Milledgeville (and was crazy about her peacocks) and corresponded with Welty, who reviewed Porter's novel *The Never-Ending Wrong* (1977), the brief, woefully inadequate preface does not show the significant connections between these three writers, whose differences seem more striking than their similarities. The Catholic O'Connor died at the age of 39; the Protestant Welty is still alive at 86. The worldly, stylish, and beautiful Porter, who was born in Texas, was married and divorced three times, and lived in Mexico, France, and Germany, wrote—in *Ship of Fools* (1962)—a moral allegory about the nature of evil and died at the age of 90. She provides a vivid contrast to the dowdy, provincial, maidenly gothic and grotesque writers from Georgia and Mississippi.

Although the printed material—including reviews by Richard Poirier, Guy Davenport, and Alfred Kazin on O'Connor; Louise Bogan, Allen Tate, and Edmund Wilson on Porter; John Crowe Ransom, V. S. Pritchett, and C. Vann Woodward on Welty—is interesting and judiciously selected, it is also readily available, to those willing to do a bit of work, in most university libraries. This book, no bargain at its price, seems patched together. It merely adds to the seemingly endless profusion of this series.—**Jeffrey Meyers**

Drama

1202. **American Playwrights, 1880-1945: A Research and Production Sourcebook.** William W. Demastes, ed. Westport, Conn., Greenwood Press, 1995. 494p. index. $85.00. ISBN 0-313-28638-8.

What kinds of obstacles did Abram Hill encounter when he founded the Harlem-based American Negro Theatre in 1940? Did critics Brooks Atkinson, John Mason Brown, and Joseph Wood Krutch take to Clifford Odets's agitprop, pro-union play *Waiting for Lefty* when it opened in 1935? Where would a scholar look to find information about the influence of German expressionism on Elmer Rice's 1923 classic *The Adding Machine*? Although Paul Green's reputation as a regional dramatist and writer of popular historical pageants has resulted in his neglect by theater scholars, why was he once considered on a par with Eugene O'Neill? What part is played by typical African-American children's games in Zora Neale Hurston and Langston Hughes's *Mule Bone: A Comedy of Negro Life* (first performed in 1991)? The answers to such questions and thousands more may be easily found in *American Playwrights, 1880-1945*, which summarizes the work of 40 outstanding playwrights who were active during the U.S. theater's vital, formative years.

Joining forces with C. W. E. Bigsby (*A Critical Introduction to Twentieth Century American Drama* [Cambridge University Press, 1982-85]) and Brenda Murphy (*American Realism and American Drama* [Cambridge University Press, 1987]), Demastes further strengthens the belief that from 1880 to 1945, U.S. theater underwent a native birth and development that is underscored by this wide variety of impressive playwrights. They established a U.S. theater of its own, "creating an independent rather than a derivative tradition, one particularly suited to the cultural and intellectual needs of this 'new' nation" (p. ix). Although a few of the playwrights highlighted are already celebrated for their distinctive contributions to U.S. theater (Lillian Hellman, George S. Kaufman, Odets, O'Neill, Rice, William Saroyan, and Thornton Wilder), many others await well-deserved reconsideration (Rachel Crothers, Zona Gale, Green, James A. Herne, Georgia Douglas Johnson, Langdon Mitchell, and Sophy Treadwell).

Each entry includes overall assessments of the playwright, critical summaries of major plays' initial receptions, significant revivals, critical assessments of each playwright, and archival and bibliographical data. Novice students, theater enthusiasts, and seasoned scholars will find this an invaluable sourcebook for the study of all aspects of U.S. drama.—**Colby H. Kullman**

Fiction

1203. **American Novelists Since World War II. Fourth Series.** James R. Giles and Wanda H. Giles, eds. Detroit, Gale, 1995. 386p. illus. index. (Dictionary of Literary Biography, v.152). $128.00. ISBN 0-8103-5713-5.

The general aim of this series is to offer biographies of literary careers, providing the information in a convenient format and placing figures within literary movements and historical events. The introduction, by editors James and Wanda Giles, provides a useful historical perspective from which to view the authors included in this volume.

Editorial policy, although by no means flabby, could well have been firmer. At times, writers' biographies are prefaced by an account of their career, and on occasion—generally less successfully—details of their life are interspersed throughout a survey of their work. The evaluations of writers that conclude the entries vary in quality: Occasionally skimpy, they tend to retreat behind other critics' evaluations, but at best are forthright and intelligent (as in the entry for Flannery O'Connor). The entry for Sylvia Plath disappoints in that it is unable to free itself from the hagiography and cult-worship that have surrounded her.

The choice of writers is good. There are, of course, various pressures operating upon the decisions, such as the need to discuss writers from various ethnic minorities and religious groups. In the process, women writers have been somewhat overlooked. The entries are professionally done, and if the writing is at times pedestrian, it can be at others lively and compelling, as in the entries on Robert Stone, Cynthia Ozick, and Chaim Potok. The bibliographies have been well selected; they include published interviews.—**John B. Beston**

1204. **American Novelists Since World War II. Third Series.** James R. Giles and Wanda H. Giles, eds. Detroit, Gale, 1994. 405p. illus. index. (Dictionary of Literary Biography, v.143). $128.00. ISBN 0-8103-5557-4.

This volume contains a tediously "correct" and rather incoherent mixture of subjects—16 whites, 5 blacks, and 2 Native Americans (including 16 men and 7 women)—from William Styron and Eudora Welty to Stephen King and Leslie Marmon Silko. The coeditors boast of a richer diversity of achievement than ever before in American literature, but the pedestrian critics, following the current fashion, fail to discriminate between major and minor authors and works. Nor do they explain, for example, why Toni Morrison's *Song of Solomon*, with its intense "denunciation of white values," sold an extraordinary 570,000 copies.

The useful introduction gives the social and historical background of postwar America, discusses the main streams of the contemporary novel, and mentions the current critical theories. The 23 chapters, written by minor academics, provide biographical facts and offer a basic approach to the authors' works. The chapters are interspersed with photographs of the novelists, manuscripts, and dust wrappers, and contain a good bibliography, listing interviews and the location of the writers' papers. The critics' prose is leaden, their plot summaries banal, their insights limited. But the chapters are thorough, clear, competent, and generally accurate (although Wole Soyinka, not Morrison, was the "first black" to win the Nobel prize).

The editors, quoting Norman Mailer, mention the modern novelists' need to create a greater imaginative reality than exists in the daily barrage of movies and television. Traditional writers such as Robert Stone, Tom McGuane, Richard Ford, and Tim O'Brien transcend this formidable obstacle and prove that the contemporary novel is still a vivid and vital force in our cultural life.—**Jeffrey Meyers**

1205. Kich, Martin. **Western American Novelists: Volume 1: Walter Van Tilburg Clark, Dan Cushman, H. L. Davis, Vardis Fisher, A. B. Guthrie, Jr., William Humphrey, and Dorothy M. Johnson.** Hamden, Conn., Garland, 1995. 876p. $120.00. ISBN 0-8240-7389-4.

Of the making of books there is no end, and librarians know this better than anyone else. Such books as the volume under review serve as constant reminders that any sort of specialization is possible. Here is a tool that focuses on writers who lived "for a considerable period [not really defined] in the Great Plains, Mountain, or Desert Southwest regions and published significant [also not defined] work in the 1930, 1940s and 1950s." Moreover, the materials included cover everything from first reviewed works to materials published in 1990 and 1991.

This is not to mock a work that represents an extraordinary amount of time for one writer's life—half a decade. This annotated bibliography, the first of a projected untold number of future volumes (showcasing nine other writers, two with recognized names—Conrad Richter and Jessamyn West), features the novelists that appear in the title. Each section provides an introductory piece (about three pages long), followed by two sections of primary and secondary works. The annotations in these sections are quite lengthy, some exceeding 10 pages. Book reviews, short stories, articles, criticisms, notes, and queries—it is all here, and perhaps every last word of it.

What is dismaying, of course, is whether such a work is needed at all. Most if not all of these writers have been born under the dubious cloud of political correctness, for better or worse. And just where will it all end?—**Mark Y. Herring**

1206. Simone, Roberta. **The Immigrant Experience in American Fiction: An Annotated Bibliography.** Lanham, Md., Scarecrow, 1995. 203p. index. $39.50. ISBN 0-8108-2962-2.

This new bibliographical source annotates 666 books from 41 immigrant groups and 6 combined groups (Asian, Hispanic, Jewish, Scandinavian, Slavic, and West Indian). English and Scottish immigrants are not covered, as they set many of the standards and cultural norms to which other immigrants had to assimilate. Additionally, the African-American experience is not chronicled, not because there is such a vast repertoire of literature in that area, but because Africans' "immigration" was not voluntary. An introduction by the author lays out these guidelines and discusses the significance of immigrant fiction. The work strives to highlight similarities rather than differences among ethnic groups and cultures; common themes and motifs can be found throughout the body of immigrant fiction, regardless of the source.

The main section of the work consists of the annotated bibliography, alphabetical by ethnic group. Groups from Armenian to Italian to West Indian are featured. The combined groups contain *see also* references to the more specific groups, and vice versa: The Croatian entry references the Slavic entry, while Slavic references Croatian, Czech, Polish, Russian, Serbian, Slovenian, Slovakian, and Ukrainian. Each group may be further subdivided into listings for individual authors, secondary sources, anthologies, and bibliographies. The books highlighted cover publications from the late nineteenth century through the first half of 1994. Books made into movies are so noted (e.g., *Moscow on the Hudson*, *The Joy Luck Club*, *The Mambo Kings [Play Songs of Love]*). A final category of the general immigrant experience completes the bibliography. Indexes at the close of the work (to entry rather than page number) are by author, title, theme and genre, and publication date.

This interesting and important source should find a home in public and university libraries. However, libraries on a strict budget may be put off by the price, which is substantial for so thin a volume.
—Melissa R. Root

Individual Authors

Robert Benchley

1207. Ernst, Gordon E., Jr., comp. **Robert Benchley: An Annotated Bibliography.** Westport, Conn., Greenwood Press, 1995. 290p. index. (Bibliographies and Indexes in Popular Culture, no.6). $59.95. ISBN 0-313-29321-X.

A member of the legendary Algonquin Round Table, Robert Benchley (1889-1945) was a comic essayist, parodist, critic, and actor. This bibliography contains chapters on his books, essays, newspaper writings, dramatic critiques, films, sound recordings, and also literature about him. The entries are numbered, cross-referenced, and indexed. Performing yeoman work, the compiler tracked down Benchley's writings in obscure publications and attempted to verify every citation listed. Any citation not found is noted, as are annotations taken from other sources. Ernst also notes the writings not included in this bibliography. There are some quibbles: The work would have been enhanced with a short biographical introduction; the reader cannot easily locate the titles of the book-length biographies or theses on Benchley; and the list of primary sources should have been included in the text, not in the introduction. Despite these minor shortcomings, this work is useful and the most comprehensive bibliography on this U.S. humorist.—**Donald Altschiller**

Rachel Crothers

1208. Lindroth, Colette, and James Lindroth. **Rachel Crothers: A Research and Production Sourcebook.** Westport, Conn., Greenwood Press, 1995. 141p. index. (Modern Dramatists Research and Productions Sourcebooks, no.8). $59.95. ISBN 0-313-27815-6.

As a playwright, Rachel Crothers was a popular and influential figure on Broadway from 1906 to the late 1930s; her career is well documented here. The authors of the work, professors of English, display an understanding of Crothers's personal life as well as her plays. The former is detailed in a brief biographical chapter; synopses of the latter make up the majority of the book. The individual play synopses give the following: a list of characters; a plot summary; and a thorough, critical overview with excerpts of newspaper and magazine reviews. Crothers's 24 plays and her only film are treated thus. The film—1935's *Splendor*—was her one successful venture in the medium.

A bibliography lists Crothers's plays in single-text format, as magazine publications (one-act plays), and within anthologies. Manuscript holdings and other significant library collections on Crothers are listed. The playwright also wrote newspaper and magazine articles; those are also listed. An annotated bibliography of reviews is also included in this source. Those, combined with the critical excerpts used in the play synopses, give the reader a strong sense of Crothers's critical reception by her peers. A list of play productions and credits, always a useful element in this type of book, is provided. The Crothers novice can learn that *Expressing Willie*, *The Three of Us*, *Susan and God*, and *A Little Journey* were her most-performed plays. A general index and an index to critics who are quoted in the book close out the text.

—Ed Volz

William Eastlake

1209. **The Work of William Eastlake: An Annotated Bibliography & Guide.** By W. C. Bamberger. Boden Clarke and Daryl F. Mallett, eds. San Bernardino, Calif., Borgo Press, 1994. 104p. index. (Bibliographies of Modern Authors, no.21). $25.00; $15.00pa. ISBN 0-89370-398-2; 0-89370-498-9pa.

Assuming that this item, although no. 21 of a series, is the first to be reviewed in ARBA, a few lines of comment are not out of place. These are annotated and bibliographically complete listings of the considered writer's books, articles, ephemera, film scripts, and so on. For the listing of books, reviews are also given, as well as all reprints. Each writer's works are categorized by type: in the present instance, into A, books; B, short fiction; C, short nonfiction; D, poetry; E, other media; and F, unpublished works. This is followed by G, honors and awards; H, interviews with the author; I, secondary sources; and J, miscellanea. Each entry under these categories is numbered, with the index using this alphanumeric system for location.

William Eastlake was born in New York in 1917, entered the army from Los Angeles in 1941, and fought in Europe until 1945. Returning west in 1950, he began to write of his wartime experiences in California and in Europe, finally settling down in western New Mexico and Arizona. His writings deal largely with natives and residents of these two states, such as *The Bronc People* (1958), and an article, "The Medicine Men," in *Harper's Magazine* in 1955.

The value of this extensive bibliography may be shown by the fact that although Richard Etulain's *Bibliographical Guide to the Study of Western American Literature* (see ARBA 83, entry 1166) does list 8 critical references to Eastlake's work, the volume under review lists 90 such references. This in-depth bibliography of an often overlooked Western novelist and story writer will be welcomed by all students of the literature of the West, and should find a place in all academic libraries, west or east.

—Raymund F. Wood

Allen Ginsberg

1210. Morgan, Bill. **The Works of Allen Ginsberg 1941-1994: A Descriptive Bibliography.** Westport, Conn., Greenwood Press, 1995. 456p. index. (Bibliographies and Indexes in American Literature, no.19). $75.00. ISBN 0-313-29389-9.

Allen Ginsberg calls this bibliography an "enormous meticulous catalogue" (p. ix); that it certainly is. Compiled over two decades with the cooperation and assistance of Ginsberg and his staff (and a legion of others), this is now the best guide to Ginsberg's works, superseding the coverage of *A Bibliography of Works by Allen Ginsberg, October, 1943 to July 1, 1967* by George Dowden and Laurence McGilvery (City Lights Books, 1971) and Michelle P. Kraus's *Allen Ginsberg: An Annotated Bibliography, 1969-1977* (Scarecrow, 1980). Separate chapters provide entries for Ginsberg's 66 book and pamphlet first editions; 42 broadsides; 249 first book appearances; 1,228 first periodical appearances; 139 published individual or collected photographic works; 369 miscellaneous publications (such as play and film scripts, flyers, and posters); 131 audio recordings; 60 film appearances; and 26 selected radio and television appearances.

Exacting and complete bibliographic descriptions follow the principles of Fredson Bowers and G. Thomas Tanselle: quasifacsimile title page transcriptions and detailed collations, binding descriptions, and publication histories provide essential data for identifying each of Ginsberg's works and, in the larger sense, for documenting Ginsberg's nearly 50 years of poetical activity. The volume may well contain the more than 10,000 entries that Ginsberg claims, as most of the chronologically arranged main entries include myriad subentries (e.g., entry A3 for the 1st edition of *Howl and Other Poems* [1956] describes 41 printings and 1 reissue; and entry D101 for *Allen Ginsberg: Photographs* [1991] describes each of 91 photographs). The title and first-line index and general index are serviceable, but the latter is not as useful as possible; for example, it lacks headings for the various forms of miscellaneous publications. Morgan's bibliography will stand as a basic and important resource for research collections on Ginsberg and contemporary American poetry.—**James K. Bracken**

Ernest Hemingway

1211. Mandel, Miriam B. **Reading Hemingway: The Facts in the Fictions.** Metuchen, N.J., Scarecrow, 1995. 592p. illus. index. $72.50. ISBN 0-8108-2870-7.

All nine of Hemingway's novels (but none of his short stories) are covered by this encyclopedic and readable guide to nearly every person, animal, or cultural construct mentioned therein. The persons include both real people and fictional characters, while the cultural constructs cover items such as newspapers, poems, movies, and organizations. Entries are arranged first by novel, then alphabetically. Each entry contains explanatory information, notes on sources, and details on the context in which Hemingway uses the item. There are ample cross-references to other relevant material and an excellent index. The guide's most impressive feature is its comprehensiveness. The author has drawn on a vast and diverse array of sources—libraries, university archives, museums, as well as persons and organizations connected with areas such as sports, medicine, the military, nautical life, and diplomacy. Not only are both real and fictional people covered, but so are generic or nameless characters such as policemen, bartenders, boys, customers, flower-sellers, and so forth. Thus, virtually any person, animal, or proper noun found in the novels will have an entry in the guide. This comprehensiveness also serves to fulfill a secondary purpose of the work—to demonstrate that Hemingway was both exceptionally intelligent and prodigiously well-read, something that until quite recently critics either did not realize or were reluctant to concede.
—**Jeffrey R. Luttrell**

Herman Melville

1212. Gale, Robert L. **A Herman Melville Encyclopedia.** Westport, Conn., Greenwood Press, 1995. 536p. index. $79.50. ISBN 0-313-29011-3.

Several encyclopedias on Melville have been published in the past five years, but this includes new material, particularly on Melville's poetry. The volume is clearly organized, beginning with a four-page chronology of major events pertinent to Melville's life from the marriage of his grandparents in 1774 and 1778 to his own death in 1891. Although there is a listing of titles and abbreviations of works cited by the author, there is no listing of works written by Melville. Encyclopedia entries are extensive. In addition to relevant background, plots are summarized in detail. The entry for *Clarel* alone is nine pages long. Cross-references are marked with an asterisk. Proportionately too much space is devoted to artists, writers, and historical figures briefly mentioned by Melville. While the author claims in his preface that material is intended to be informational, not critical, his comments and word choices usually make his opinions clear.

The general bibliography of more than 40 items stresses works published since 1990, although some earlier standard major studies are listed. A 27-page index includes the alphabetically listed entries as well as the cross-references. Despite being designed for beginning students of Melville, *A Herman Melville Encyclopedia* will prove equally useful to scholars and teachers who wish to review plots or check facts.
—**Charlotte Lindgren**

James A. Michener

1213. Roberts, F. X., and C. D. Rhine, comps. **James A. Michener: A Checklist of His Works, with a Selected, Annotated Bibliography.** Westport, Conn., Greenwood Press, 1995. 125p. index. (Bibliographies and Indexes in American Literature, no.20). $49.95. ISBN 0-313-29453-4.

This checklist/bibliography of the works and criticism of Michener is composed of two main parts: a listing of novels and other writings by Michener, and a selected, annotated bibliography of books and articles about him. A third section includes a selected listing of reviews of the novels and other books by the author. Part 1 consists of an alphabetical listing by title of the novels and other works from 1938 to 1993. Also listed in this section are works that include Michener as a contributing author (e.g., the contribution of an introduction, a foreword, or a postscript or afterword). Part 2 describes books and parts of books about Michener. This section lists articles that have appeared in periodicals and newspapers from 1923 to 1993. The items are arranged alphabetically by author if an author exists, otherwise by title. Part 3 consists of a selected list of reviews of each of Michener's major works. The reviews have been chosen at random in what the compilers call "an attempt to give users a feel for the way Michener has been treated by the critics" (p. xiv).

In addition to the sections listed above, a list of adaptations is included, containing writings that have been adapted for film and television. Indexes include an author index, which covers the names of all the authors who appear either as main entries or in one or more parts of the works listed; a subject index that provides terms appearing in bibliographical information or in annotations; and finally, a source index that brings together in one alphabetical order the titles of the books, periodicals, journals, and newspapers from which entries in the checklist/bibliography have been gleaned. In all there are more than 700 items in this checklist. The annotations are generally brief but informative. Roberts and Rhine have provided a valuable source for scholarship concerning Michener. The work is recommended for both public and academic libraries of every size. It is especially recommended for larger academic libraries, as Michener is becoming more accepted as a major U.S. novelist.—**Robert L. Wick**

John Milton

1214. Jones, Edward. **Milton's Sonnets: An Annotated Bibliography, 1900-1992.** Binghamton, N.Y., Medieval & Renaissance Texts & Studies, State University of New York, 1994. 147p. index. (Medieval & Renaissance Texts & Studies, v.122). $20.00. ISBN 0-86698-127-6.

Although not the most comprehensive annotated bibliography possible on John Milton's sonnets, this book offers the widest coverage and most convenient access to all significant notes, articles, monographs, and books available under a single cover. The first of the 2 parts subdivides into 3 sections: 300 general criticisms of Milton's sonnets; about 30 entries on the Italian sonnets; and 47 entries on translated publications (including items from the extensive Milton industry in Japan—many of which do not appear previously in English bibliographies on Milton). The second part treats the English sonnets chronologically. This volume also includes three helpful indexes, by author, sonnet, and subject. The work is strongly recommended for all collections housing Milton, Renaissance, and seventeenth-century British literature collections.—**C. B. (Bob) Darrell**

Eugene O'Neill

1215. **The Proverbial Eugene O'Neill: An Index to Proverbs in the Works of Eugene Gladstone O'Neill.** George B. Bryan and Wolfgang Mieder, comps. Westport, Conn., Greenwood Press, 1995. 359p. (Bibliographies and Indexes in American Literature, no.21). $75.00. ISBN 0-313-29794-0.

Bryan and Mieder provide a foundational tool for advanced study of language in Eugene O'Neill's works—a research area, they contend in their 77-page introductory essay, "Eugene O'Neill and the Proverb," that heretofore has largely drawn "negative comments" (p. 5). The keyword index references some 2,509 "proverbial utterances" found in all of O'Neill's published and unpublished dramatic works and fragments as well as in the major portion of his other writings, comments, conversations, and words otherwise recorded. It must be emphasized that Bryan and Mieder do not index proverb texts in all of the primary works identified in Jenniver McCabe Atkinson's *Eugene O'Neill: A Descriptive Bibliography* (see ARBA 75, entry 1362); on the other hand, they index many more texts (albeit only the proverbs) than the 28 plays included in J. Russell Reaver's 3-volume *An O'Neill Concordance* (see ARBA 70, v.2, entry 77).

Copy texts for the 70 individual and collected texts indexed by Bryan and Mieder include the standard edition of O'Neill's plays, the 3-volume *Eugene O'Neill: Complete Plays* (Library of America; distr., Viking Press, 1988), as well as standard collections of his poetry, fictional and nonfictional prose, letters, and works otherwise recorded. Each of O'Neill's proverbs, proverbial expressions, and proverbial comparisons is in turn verified by reference to the full range of standard English proverb collections and phrase dictionaries.

The introductory essay is more successful for its "fundamental observations" on the types of proverbs in O'Neill's life and works rather than for "exhaustive explication," which Bryan and Mieder directly admit (p. 2). The introduction should, in fact, be read with some caution: Whether O'Neill was in fact "one of the most 'proverbial' dramatists of the modern age" (p. 77), as Bryan and Mieder state, is unsupported here. More seriously, they leave unresolved if O'Neill's use of proverbs in the text of stage directions and personal letters can be accurately viewed as conscious and intentional or simply reflective of a language. Bryan and Mieder seem to straddle the issue, calling O'Neill's dramatic use of proverbs, on the one hand, a "preoccupation" (p. 5), and on the other, noting that "in O'Neill's own persona . . . he talked as he wrote" (p. 85). This reservation aside, the introductory essay presents several interesting approaches for further study; and the keyword index to proverb texts referenced to standard editions makes the volume useful in collections supporting advanced research on O'Neill.—**James K. Bracken**

John Steinbeck

1216. **John Steinbeck: Dissertation Abstracts and Research Opportunities.** Tetsumaro Hayashi and Beverly K. Simpson, comps. and eds. Metuchen, N.J., Scarecrow, 1994. 194p. index. $27.50. ISBN 0-8108-2940-1.

Hayashi and Simpson's claim "to record and make available in one volume all known reprinted American abstracts of Steinbeck-related doctoral dissertations written in English from 1946 to 1993" (p. viii) is accurate enough. Including some 102 entries taken nearly verbatim from *Dissertation Abstracts*, *Dissertation Abstracts International*, and *Dissertation Abstracts CD-ROM* (University Microfilms International), it seems to omit only one dissertation, Kurt Max Hochenauer's "Armadillo Highway" (1991), a fictional parody of *The Grapes of Wrath*; and, of course, it ignores the several master's theses also included in these sources. Author, chronology, subject, title, and degree-granting university indexes are also listed.

The collection's rationale of convenience, however, undermines the volume's significance: What is so special about dissertations on Steinbeck to merit separate treatment? Nothing similar has been considered necessary for the larger dissertation literature on Ernest Hemingway or William Faulkner, for example. Likewise, although the volume's concluding essay, "Research Opportunities" by Christopher S. Busch, amounts to a nearly 50-year history of Steinbeck dissertations and may in fact reveal "trends and new directions in Steinbeck scholarship" (p. xiii), is so limited a survey of greater independent value than that provided annually for published Steinbeck criticism in *American Literary Scholarship* (Duke University Press, annual)? In fact, *ALS* has covered a great many dissertations on Steinbeck when they became books. In 1987, the some 200 entries in Robert B. Harmon's *Steinbeck Bibliographies: An Annotated Guide* (see ARBA 88, entry 1188) clearly showed that despite much bibliographical ado, no comprehensive annotated secondary bibliography for Steinbeck was available. In 1995, as useful as Hayashi and Simpson's new compilation of dissertation abstracts may be, what Steinbeck research still badly needs is a comprehensive annotated bibliography of Steinbeck scholarship—one that cumulates both published criticisms and unpublished dissertation research. Abstracts included by Hayashi and Simpson's volume are all available in the standard dissertation sources: Scholars and students can access them in a variety of ways without buying this volume.—**James K. Bracken**

Mark Twain

1217. Rasmussen, R. Kent. **Mark Twain A to Z: The Essential Reference to His Life and Writings.** New York, Facts on File, 1995. 552p. illus. index. $45.00. ISBN 0-8160-2845-1.

This book features 1,300 entries: synopses of all Twain's books and major short stories; character analyses; actors who have played in screen versions of Twain's works; fictional and actual settings; and a dizzying chronology of historical, biographical, and literary fact. Textual entries are brief and readable; small capital letters mark cross-references to additional data—for example, names of steamboats that Twain piloted or traveled on; Huck Finn's aliases; publications for which Twain wrote; possible locations for a real Jackson's Island; and biographies of Twain's friends, illustrators, and business associates. Drawings and photographs, especially the riveting chiaroscuro of the portrait on page 509, enliven the lucid commentary, which is easily accessible to teenage and adult readers. The volume concludes with a chronological list of Twain's first editions, an extensive bibliography with most valuable works starred, and a detailed index.

A remarkably exhaustive study of Twain, both the man and the author, Rasmussen's work tackles the known and the questionable (e.g., the name and relationship of Mary to Tom and Sid Sawyer and to Aunt Polly, and the number of times "nigger" appears in *Huckleberry Finn*, a perennial question among book banners). The compiler also connects names such as Valet du Chambre with a notebook in which Twain collected unusual names. Except for maps of Twain's world travels, there is little more that a Twain reader could ask of a work so exhaustive in scope and detail. As in Facts on File's *Shakespeare A to Z* (see ARBA 92, entry 1209), the book ranks among the most useful of reference works in recent times.
—**Mary Ellen Snodgrass**

Jack Vance

1218. **The Work of Jack Vance: An Annotated Bibliography & Guide.** By Jerry Hewett and Daryl F. Mallett. Boden Clarke, ed. San Bernardino, Calif., Borgo Press, 1994. 293p. index. (Bibliographies of Modern Authors, no.29). $35.00; $25.00pa. ISBN 0-88733-165-3; 0-8095-1509-1pa.

From his first story published in 1945 to his 1992 short story collection, Jack Vance, now approaching 80, has had an illustrious career as a science fiction, fantasy, and mystery writer. This descriptive, fully annotated bibliography attempts to include all the editions of Vance's work in that 47-year span. The work is divided into 14 sections, the largest being those that cover the books and the short fiction. Other sections list Vance's nonfiction, his work in other media, his maps and drawings, honors and awards, and many secondary sources.

Each of the 86 chronologically arranged book entries begins with the publisher, date of publication, number of pages, edition (cloth or paper), and literary type, followed by contents (where appropriate), collation, binding, and notes. The notes describe features such as cover art, translator, cost at issue, and numbered copies. The same information is included in each reprint. A list of secondary sources and reviews concludes each entry. The short fiction entries list the magazine in which the story first appeared, with appropriate bibliographic information, followed by all editions and collections in which the story has appeared. An introduction by Robert Silverberg and an afterword by Tim Underwood help to acquaint the reader with Vance's personal and professional life. Preceding the comprehensive, well-designed index is a 16-page outline for a Vance novel. This modestly priced, attractively formatted guide is recommended primarily for those academic and research libraries with significant science fiction holdings.
—**Charles R. Andrews**

Kurt Vonnegut

1219. Leeds, Marc. **The Vonnegut Encyclopedia: An Authorized Compendium.** Westport, Conn., Greenwood Press, 1995. 693p. index. $75.00. ISBN 0-313-29230-2.

This is a comprehensive catalog of the characters in Vonnegut's works up to and including *Hocus Pocus* (Ulverscroft, 1991). As Vonnegut is still writing, the compendium is somewhat premature, a fact that Leeds acknowledges. The entries in the encyclopedia are alphabetically arranged. The plots of the novels are summarized, but do not directly help to identify themes and recurring images. That is possible through the index, which lists entries such as humor (various types), schizophrenia, spiral, tunnel, and uncritical love. Regrettably, there is no biography of Vonnegut prefaced to the encyclopedia, and no indication of the circumstances in which he wrote. There is a list of his works in a preface, but without any indication of their genre.

Leeds's style is lively, even slangy—not inappropriate for dealing with an author of Vonnegut's fervid imagination. But again and again Leeds reveals a disturbing unawareness of English syntax. Such errors as inconsistencies, incorrect tense sequences, and false correlatives abound. Errors in English idiom are especially frequent (e.g., *at* whatever terms, analogy *between x with y, for* whom he dedicated a work, despondent *with* her life). If the errors are Leeds's, it was also the responsibility of his editor to have overseen and corrected a conspicuously weak sense of syntax in the author.—**John B. Beston**

Tennesee Williams

1220. Crandell, George W. **Tennessee Williams: A Descriptive Bibliography.** Pittsburgh, Pa., University of Pittsburgh Press; distr., Ithaca, N.Y., CUP Services, 1995. 673p. illus. index. (Pittsburgh Series in Bibliography). $195.00. ISBN 0-8229-3769-7.

Limited to writings by Tennessee Williams, this descriptive bibliography does not discuss works about Williams except in cases where they include something by Williams published for the first time. Here a book collector or modern drama scholar will find answers to questions such as the following: How many first editions of *Cat on a Hot Tin Roof* were published by New Directions in 1955? Where and when was *Small Craft Warnings* first performed? The text of the first British edition of *The Glass Menagerie* (1948) differs from the first U.S. edition (1945) in more than 1,100 substantive instances. What are some of the major variants, and what do they suggest about Williams's changing concept of the play? How might the typography, paper, binding, and slipcase of the 1st edition of Williams's collection of poems called *In the Winter of Cities* be described?

Section A chronologically lists all books, broadsides, and pamphlets by Williams, including all printings of all editions in English through 1991; section B describes and lists all material by Williams published for the first time in a book, pamphlet, or occasional publication written or edited by another author; section C is a chronological list of writings by Williams first appearing in a magazine or newspaper, excluding interviews and articles quoting Williams; and section D lists interviews and articles, including previously unpublished quotations from Williams. Subsequent sections list titles by Williams set to music, blurbs from Williams about the works of others, sound recordings of Williams reading from his works, recorded interviews with Williams offered for sale, and translations of Williams's works.

Because of a comprehensive index, cross-referencing is limited throughout. This newest edition in the Pittsburgh Series in Bibliography is of importance to scholars and book collectors alike. Those interested in Williams, southern culture, and modern U.S. drama will find Crandell's descriptive bibliography a valuable reference tool.—**Colby H. Kullman**

Virginia Woolf

1221. Hussey, Mark. **Virginia Woolf A to Z: A Comprehensive Reference....** New York, Facts on File, 1995. 452p. illus. index. $50.00. ISBN 0-8160-3020-0.

The well-cross-referenced entries in this encyclopedia designed for "students, teachers, and common readers" of Virginia Woolf include literary terms associated with her writing (e.g., stream of consciousness, formalism); relatives and friends; fictional characters; the history of the Hogarth Press; and places, real and fictional. The essays on her individual works are 10 or 12 double-columned pages in length and are divided into an outline of plot, the genesis, the factual background, critical responses, any adaptations, and a bibliography.

The volume is enlivened with black-and-white illustrations of the dust jackets of books, portraits and photographs of people and places, and a two-page reproduction of a holograph letter by Virginia Woolf never before published. Supplementary material includes a chronology of events in Woolf's life from 1882 to 1941, a 32-page alphabetical listing of works cited by both authors and topics, an index, and 2 appendixes. Appendix A alphabetically lists material under 16 different topics ranging from "Allusions in Woolf's Novels" to "Writers and Painters." Appendix B has nine charts of "family" trees showing the complicated relationships of the Bloomsbury Group. Entertainingly written in simple prose, the book is, at the same time, erudite and highly informative, useful alike to serious scholars and to those just looking for basic information about Virginia Woolf.—**Charlotte Lindgren**

Poetry

1222. Sakelliou-Schultz, Liana. **Feminist Criticism of American Women Poets: An Annotated Bibliography, 1975-1993.** Hamden, Conn., Garland, 1994. 332p. index. (Garland Bibliographies of Modern Critics and Critical Schools, v.17; Garland Reference Library of the Humanities, v.1312). $50.00. ISBN 0-8240-7084-4.

Sakelliou-Schultz comes to her bibliographic task with outstanding credentials: Her dissertation, *Comprehensive Annotated Bibliography of Denise Levertov's Works and Secondary Criticism* (Pennsylvania State University, 1988), was later published as *Denise Levertov: An Annotated Bibliography* (see ARBA 90, entry 1150). The present work includes both U.S. and foreign criticism of poetry by U.S. women. Covering a vital period in U.S. feminist activity, this comprehensive guide cites theoretical U.S. feminist texts and their influence on U.S. women poets born after 1900.

Sakelliou-Schultz's introduction to her work deals with "The Most Discussed Issues in Feminist Criticism and Theory (1975-1993)." The most significant of these include the goals of feminist scholarship, a definition of feminist criticism, whether feminist criticism should look to other approaches to develop its methods, the distinctive features of American feminist criticism, and whether women have a different literature because they have a different body and experience. The author discusses the literature on these issues, providing full annotated citations for each in the body of the bibliography.

The bibliography is divided into two main parts. The first three chapters cover U.S. theory; the last three are on the practice of analyzing poetry written by twentieth-century U.S. women authors. In the practical chapters, writings are listed that interpret works of poetry. Books, dissertations, and periodical articles are cited in both sections. The author provides complete bibliographical citations for all entries, as well as annotations for most of the significant items. Annotations are sometimes 100 words in length. An author index and a name and subject index provide access to the poets, critics, and works covered.

This bibliography would have benefited from annotations for all entries cited. However, the author may well have experienced difficulty in obtaining copies of all items for such a comprehensive project. Her important contribution to the field of feminist criticism is highly recommended for all undergraduate and graduate English collections.—**Mark Padnos**

British Literature

General Works

Bibliography

1223. Topp, Chester W. **Victorian Yellowbacks & Paperbacks, 1849-1905. Volume 1: George Routledge.** Denver, Colo., Hermitage Antiquarian Bookshop, 1993. 557p. illus. index. $135.00. ISBN 0-9633920-0-X.

1224. Topp, Chester W. **Victorian Yellowbacks & Paperbacks, 1849-1905. Volume II: Ward & Lock.** Denver, Colo., Hermitage Antiquarian Bookshop, 1995. 456p. illus. index. $135.00. ISBN 0-9633920-1-8.

Yellowbacks were pocket-sized, inexpensive books with glazed yellow covers sold at British railroad stations during the second half of the nineteenth century. They were read on train trips and were usually reprints of popular or classic novels (although some early detective novels were first published as yellowbacks) or were nonfiction books dealing with current events, sports, self-improvement, or natural history. Yellowbacks were extremely popular in England from the late 1840s to about 1900, and, as reflections of the reading tastes of their times, are of decided interest to historians.

The publishing firms of George Routledge and Ward & Lock were the two most prolific publishers of yellowbacks, and it is to the output of these firms that the two bibliographies under review are confined. Each volume is arranged chronologically by year and by month of publication within a given year. Each entry gives the author; the title; the original cost; the date of publication; and, where applicable, the true first edition, the first American edition, and important later editions. The bibliographies each have name and title indexes, a brief introduction discussing publishing history, and a portfolio of color plates showing the covers of some of the more pictorially interesting items. These bibliographies, based on the author's huge personal collection, are part of a multivolume series that, when completed, will provide bibliographical information for almost all yellowbacks and paperbacks published during the Victorian era.

The entries in these volumes surpass in number and bibliographical detail the listings found in Michael Sadleir's *XIX Century Fiction* (University of California Press, 1951) and Robert Wolff's five-volume catalog *Nineteenth Century Fiction* (Garland, 1981-86). When completed, this series will be the definitive bibliography of the yellowback-paperback genre of Victorian England.—**Joseph Cataio**

Biography

1225. **Late Nineteenth- and Early Twentieth-Century British Literary Biographers.** Steven Serafin, ed. Detroit, Gale, 1995. 367p. illus. index. (Dictionary of Literary Biography, v.149). $128.00. ISBN 0-8103-5710-0.

This is the 3d volume on British literary biographers in the Dictionary of Literary Biography series (others are *Eighteenth-Century British Literary Biographers* [volume 142] and *Nineteenth-Century British Literary Biographers* [volume 144; see ARBA 95, entry 1204, and entry 1226, respectively]). Format and treatment are the same as in other DLB volumes: Each subject receives a 6- to 24-page biographical and critical essay preceded by a primary bibliography, and ends, in most cases, with a secondary bibliography accompanied by 1 or 2 illustrations—usually a portrait or a title page reproduction. An appendix includes essays on the writing of literary biography by Sidney Lee, Harold Nicolson, Virginia Woolf, and Lytton Strachey, and a 120-plus item "Checklist of Further Readings." A cumulative subject index to the entire DLB set is included.

Twenty-seven biographers are treated, the majority of them forgotten except by specialists. Most of the exceptions, such as G. K. Chesterton and Herbert Read, are covered by other DLB volumes. Strachey is probably the only biographer whose books are still read and who is not covered elsewhere in the DLB. The essays, written by American and British academics, are generally readable, but pedestrian. A few minor errors were noted (e.g., John Masefield is referred to as "Maysfield" twice on p. 86). Larger public and academic libraries already subscribe to the DLB. Most other libraries will not feel the need to pay for material on such writers as George Paston, Charles Harold Herford, and Edward Tyas Cook.

—**Jonathan F. Husband**

1226. **Nineteenth-Century British Literary Biographers.** Steven Serafin, ed. Detroit, Gale, 1994. 387p. illus. index. (Dictionary of Literary Biography, v.144). $128.00. ISBN 0-8103-5558-2.

Continuing the coverage of biographers begun with *Eighteenth-Century British Literary Biographers* (see ARBA 95, entry 1204), this volume focuses on 26 nineteenth-century writers whose works include biographies of literary figures. Also covered in the appendixes are 2 major biographical sources conceived during the nineteenth century: the *Dictionary of National Biography* and the 39-volume first series of *English Men of Letters*, published by Macmillan. Additional literary biographers associated with the Victorian era are treated in yet another volume, *Late Nineteenth- and Early Twentieth-Century British Literary Biographers* (see entry 1225).

Eighteen of the writers in this volume are also included in one or more of the previous volumes of the Dictionary of Literary Biography (DLB). The majority of these are authors who are better known for their writings in other genres, such as Thomas Carlyle, Elizabeth Gaskell, and Sir Walter Scott. Among the eight individuals for whom this volume marks the first appearance in the DLB series are Lucy Aikin, John Forster, George Gilfillen, and George Trevelyan.

Following the now-familiar format of other volumes in this series, the signed essays, which range in length from 7 to 20 pages, provide both biographical information and critical analysis. Each essay is preceded by a bibliography of primary works and followed by a selected list of secondary sources. Locations of manuscript collections are also noted. The cumulative index covers volumes 1-144 of the DLB, its *Yearbook* through 1993, and its Documentary Series through volume 11.

Because so many of these authors have been the subject of articles in other DLB volumes, libraries that are purchasing this series selectively may not need to add this volume. It will be of interest primarily to academic libraries that support graduate programs in English literature.—**Marie Ellis**

1227. **Twentieth-Century British Literary Biographers.** Steven Serafin, ed. Detroit, Gale, 1995. 413p. illus. index. (Dictionary of Literary Biography, v.155). $128.00. ISBN 0-8103-5716-X.

This is the third Dictionary of Literary Biography (DLB) volume on British literary biographers. Both earlier entries were published in 1994—*Eighteenth-Century British Literary Biographers* (see ARBA 95, entry 1204) and *Nineteenth-Century British Literary Biographers* (see entry 1226). Now, literary biographers of the twentieth century receive the standard DLB treatment, and happily, the group of 40 chosen for this volume is much more noteworthy (and familiar) than the earlier groupings. Scholars, novelists, poets, and popular writers dominate the selection; among them are Peter Ackroyd, Quentin Bell, Humphrey Carpenter, Margaret Drabble, P. N. Furbank, Victoria Glendinning, Ian Hamilton, Ronald Hingley, Elizabeth Longford, Nigel Nicolson, Peter Quennell, A. L. Rowse, Norman Sherry, Julian Symons, John Wain, A. N. Wilson, and Angus Wilson. Several of the writers are also covered in other DLB volumes.

While the study of biography as a literary art may be blossoming, this remains an area that is pretty much ignored by students of literature. Therefore, this volume (and its predecessors) will have a limited audience, and it will be a marginal purchase for most academic libraries despite the high quality of writing and research found on its pages.—**Thomas A. Karel**

Dictionaries and Encyclopedias

1228. **British Short-Fiction Writers, 1945-1980.** Dean Baldwin, ed. Detroit, Gale, 1994. 388p. illus. index. (Dictionary of Literary Biography, v.139). $128.00. ISBN 0-8103-5398-9.

This worthy installment of the Dictionary of Literary Biography demonstrates again the editor's belief that virtue lies in redundancy. Of the 30 postwar fiction writers assayed, 23 have appeared earlier in the series. J. B. Priestly alone now appears in six DLB volumes, while Kingsley Amis is in four. Not surprisingly, many of these writers are better known for their contributions in other genres; for example, Dylan Thomas, John Fowles, Doris Lessing, and Ruth Prawer Jhabvala. However, others are recognized as true masters of the short story (e.g., V. S. Pritchett and William Trevor). Their commonality is that all contributed short fiction that revealed a world transformed by war and the modern condition, leavened by local color, antiheroes, and the storyteller's art.

Covered here are the so-called Angry Young Men, such as Alan Sillitoe, John Wain, Stan Barstow, and Amis; exceptional regional writers such as Iain Crichton Smith of Scotland, George McKay Brown of the Orkney Islands, Trevor of Ireland, and Gwyn Jones and Thomas of Wales; and international figures who portray a modern rootlessness, such as Frank Tuohy and Jhabvala.

Each essay cogently describes the author's life, influence, career, and critical reception. There are brief synopses of many of the stories, chronologically presented. Bibliographies of primary sources include monographs and collections, but not the individual short stories. Criticism and bibliographies appear in a separate listing at the end of each chapter. The contributors write clear and accessible critical essays, useful to students as well as scholars. They place the writers in their cultural milieu, examine the evolution of themes during the course of their careers, and evaluate each writer's contribution to the short story form. Despite duplication within the series and a high list price for individual volumes, the DLB features high-quality essays and great breadth among British and American writers. The series continues to stand out as the leading collection to turn to for literary biography.—**John P. Schmitt**

1229. Carty, T. J. **A Dictionary of Literary Pseudonyms in the English Language.** London, Mansell/Cassell, and Chicago, Fitzroy Dearborn, 1995. 623p. $75.00. ISBN 0-7201-2221-X.

Besides citing famous English-language pseudonymous authors such as George Orwell (Eric Blair), Saki (Hector Hugh Munro) and John Le Carré (David Cornwell), this dictionary lists hundreds of writers who wish or wished to conceal their identities—perhaps to evade either prosecution, labels of prolificness, association with their subject, invasion of their privacy, fame and notoriety, or academic censure. They are included in the first section of the book by pseudonym and in the second part by real name. The latter division also provides the user with birth and death dates, the author's main occupation, and a listing of significant publications.

Although the compiler does not lay claim to total comprehensiveness in this volume, it is quite inclusive. Users will not only discover eighteenth-century pseudonymous writers whose pen names consisted simply of "A Layman," but also most of the pseudonymous writers associated with contemporary romance, crime, science fiction, and fantasy genres. A thorough search performed by consulting pen name lists and other pseudonymous dictionaries revealed the absence of only two people, Judith Barnard and Michael Fain, who have assumed the pseudonym of Judith Michael to write such romances as *Pot of Gold* (1994) and *A Ruling Passion* (1991).

The problem, however, with this accessible, current compendium of English-language literary pseudonyms is its cost and breadth versus its potential for use. Most pseudonym dictionaries in this price range are international in scope. By this criterion, they also include notable pseudonymous writers such as Shalom Aleichem (Sholem Rabinowitz), Émile Zola (Edouard Charles Antoine), and Pablo Neruda (Neftalí Ricardo Reyes Basoalto), all of whom have been translated into English. Their global span makes these dictionaries much more useful for original catalogers, book traders and collectors, reference work, and even whimsical consultation.

Many of these international pseudonym dictionaries, while somewhat dated, are still in print and in the case of Adrian Room's *A Dictionary of Pseudonyms & Their Origins* (see ARBA 90, entry 404) and Harold Sharp's *Handbook of Pseudonyms & Personal Nicknames* (see ARBA 74, entry 117), cost less. Only large public and academic libraries with original cataloging departments or substantial book trade collections should consider purchasing this dictionary.—**Kathleen W. Craver**

1230. **Old and Middle English Literature.** Jeffrey Helterman and Jerome Mitchell, eds. Detroit, Gale, 1994. 550p. illus. index. (Dictionary of Literary Biography, v.146). $128.00. ISBN 0-8103-5707-0.

This volume covers all of the major and most of the minor writers and works of Old and Middle English literature; Mitchell's foreword notes the few exceptions. Generally, most entries provide far less biographical data than those in other Dictionary of Literary Biography (DLB) volumes. Several contributors quite directly admit that little is known about early writers' lives: What few facts are certain about John Barbour and Thomas Malory, for example, amount to one or two paragraphs. Likewise, nothing outside their writings is known of Layamon or John Mandeville, while the four poems of the Gawain-Poet might have been written by "four different poets" (p. 156). Consequently, with only a few exceptions (such as William Dunbar, Geoffrey Chaucer, and Margery Kempe), entries offer much more information on works than lives, typically summarizing plots and surveying critical issues.

Approximately half of the entries cover specific writers, ranging from Saint Bede and Caedmon of the late seventh century, through Dunbar and Robert Henryson, who died in the early sixteenth century. The longest entries are for Chaucer, the Gawain-Poet, John Gower, William Langland, John Lydgate, and Malory. The remaining entries cover specific works and groups of works, such as *Beowulf*, *The Castle of Perseverance*, Old English heroic poems, Breton lays, romances on the matters of England and Rome, and the Chester, Towneley, York, and N-Town play cycles.

Appendixed entries assess the development of the English language from 410 to 1500 and the Celtic and Anglo-Norman influences on Middle English literature. The volume's indexing at the nominal entry level is unfortunate in that it essentially buries discussions of specific writers and works in entries for groups of works; for example, those on the "Wakefield Master" in the entry for the "Towneley Plays" and on *Havelock the Dane* in the entry on "The Matter of England": The volume contains much more than the index reveals.

With useful bibliographies of manuscripts, first published editions, and standard modern editions as well as of secondary materials, and many full-page illustrations of manuscripts, the volume's scope and treatment of Old and Middle English literature is encyclopedic and more similar to that of a general handbook than a biographical dictionary. Offering much less sophisticated critical interpretations than, for example, Malcolm Godden and Michael Lapidge's recent *Cambridge Companion to Old English Literature* (Cambridge University Press, 1991), the volume is favorably reminiscent of David M. Zesmer's study guide, *Guide to English Literature from Beowulf Through Chaucer and Medieval Drama* (Barnes & Noble, 1961): It provides a useful set of introductory readings for the full range of courses in Old and Middle English literature.—**James K. Bracken**

1231. **The Oxford Companion to English Literature.** rev. ed. Margaret Drabble, ed. New York, Oxford University Press, 1995. 1171p. $49.95. ISBN 0-19-866221-1.

With its 5th edition published a decade ago, *The Oxford Companion to English Literature* (see ARBA 86, entry 1162) underwent the most thorough revision since its debut in 1932. With that edition, the torch was passed from Paul Harvey and his steady purpose (but rather diffuse approach to the *Companion*'s contents) to Margaret Drabble's continuation of that steady purpose and narrower approach. Changes from the 5th to the 6th edition is incremental and much more modest than the changes from the 4th to the 5th. By legacy and design, the *Companion* remains, as Harvey intended, "a useful companion to ordinary everyday readers of English literature."

Drabble has augmented the work by including 59 new authors, most of them British writers, such as Peter Ackroyd, Salman Rushdie, and P. D. James. Rushdie, of course, personifies how vexing a problem categorization of writers by nationality can be, especially as modern transportation and communications systems facilitate frequent cross-fertilization among the literatures and cultures of the English-speaking world. Thus, Drabble discusses other writers for whom the "British" label would be a misnomer but whose contemporary significance in the world of letters demands they be included. Among these are American Gore Vidal, South African J. M. Coetzee, New Zealander Janet Frame, Australian Thomas Keneally, and American Paul Theroux. Entries on other living or recently deceased writers have been updated to reflect their activities during the past decade.

Marion Wynne-Davies's *The Bloomsbury Guide to English Literature* (Prentice Hall General Reference, 1990) focuses even more decidedly on British authors and major works. While no longer the eclectic collection of information that it was under Harvey, *The Oxford Companion to British Literature*, by virtue of its more numerous entries on individual characters and writers from other cultures whose names a reader of English literature is apt to encounter, is a more useful reference tool to the general reader whom Harvey wrote for and whom Drabble continues to serve well. They can turn to it for basic information on writers, major works, influential thinkers, national myths, significant periodicals, and other matters of fact that will help them in their understanding of English literature's primary and secondary texts. This fundamental literary reference source retains not just its spirit but also its importance.

—**James Rettig**

Handbooks and Yearbooks

1232. **British Prose Writers of the Early Seventeenth Century.** Clayton D. Lein, ed. Detroit, Gale, 1995. 397p. illus. index. (Dictionary of Literary Biography, v.151). $128.00. ISBN 0-8103-5712-7.

Editor Lein's extensive introduction describes the period's prose as a reflection of "the mind in motion" (p. x): a "restless prose" that sought to convey "more matter" with "fewer words" (p. ix) and balanced wit with penetrating self-examination. This essential vitality of British prose from the early seventeenth century is most evident in the range and variety of the 32 writers included in the volume. Foremost, of course, are the likes of John Milton, John Donne, Francis Bacon, Thomas Browne, Robert Burton, Thomas Hobbes, and Thomas Fuller, whose works both collectively and individually address the full range of the age's interests. Just as certainly, the works of lesser-known writers show considerable and oftentimes a no less paradoxical range. The works of James I cover political theory and practice, spiritual devotion and meditation, and the evils of tobacco. Likewise, Alexander Ross wrote in astronomy, anatomy, natural history, mythology, conservative theology, and yet was responsible for the first English translation of the Koran.

Not unexpectedly, sermon literature predominates in the volume just as it did in seventeenth-century London: Lancelot Andrewes, John Hales, and Richard Sibbes are here. Included also, however, are John Earle and Thomas Overbury for pioneering the character; James Howell, William Cornwallis the Younger, and Abraham Cowley for the essay; and Joseph Hall, who is often identified as the first English satirist. Also covered is Anne Clifford, whose diary unpublished in her lifetime amounts to "a secular version of a spiritual autobiography" (p. 81); as well as the likes of Richard Brathwaite, Henry Peacham, Thomas Coryate, and Samuel Purchas; capable and entertaining writers of prose, it seems, on whatever might appeal to the market.

This volume provides for 32 writers of British prose from the early seventeenth century exactly what has come to be expected from the several Dictionary of Literary Biography series: full, detailed, and authoritative bio-bibliographical entries with exacting bibliographies of primary and secondary works and copious and relevantly captioned illustrations. The volume can readily support undergraduate- and graduate-level courses on early seventeenth-century literature.—**James K. Bracken**

1233. Cooper, Robert M. **The Literary Guide and Companion to Northern England.** Athens, Ohio, Ohio University Press, 1995. 381p. maps. index. $34.95. ISBN 0-8214-1095-4.

Part guidebook, part literary history, this book is wholly fascinating. Cooper covers some 20 counties, arranged geographically, in this guide to northern England. He planned three such guidebooks. *The Literary Guide and Companion to Southern England* (see ARBA 86, entry 451) was published by Ohio University Press in 1986, before Cooper's death; he had done the research and writing for *The Literary Guide and Companion to Middle England* (Ohio University Press, 1992), and for this book, but had not done the supplemental material. His widow, Polly Cooper, has finished the works.

He begins this volume in Shropshire and travels north to the Scottish border. Within each section, he gives a brief history of the location and the people associated with it. He also includes directions for getting to out-of-the-way places, some town and village maps for walking tours, and information on lodging, pubs, and restaurants.

This is a very personal guidebook. The obvious connections are here: D. H. Lawrence in Nottinghamshire; Elizabeth Cleghorn Gaskell in Cheshire; Arnold Bennett and the claypits and potteries of Staffordshire. Yet Cooper includes minor items as well: How many readers know that A. E. Housman mentioned the tiny village of Much Wenlock in his poetry? Cooper also includes references by authors other than ones associated with a particular area, such as Elizabeth Bennet's tour of Derbyshire in Jane Austen's *Pride and Prejudice*. The result is a three-dimensional picture of an area—who lived there, who wrote there, who wrote about it from a distance, and what there is to see.

The indexing is useful, arranged by title, author, and place-name, as well as landmarks and tourist needs. The literary pilgrim will find this book essential and enticing.—**Terry Ann Mood**

Fiction

1234. Harbottle, Philip, and Stephen Holland. **British Science Fiction Paperbacks and Magazines 1949-1956: An Annotated Bibliography and Guide.** San Bernardino, Calif., Borgo Press, 1994. 232p. index. (Borgo Literary Guides, no.7). $30.00; $20.00pa. ISBN 0-89370-821-6; 0-89370-921-2pa.

The heart of this bibliography is a complete listing of paperback science fiction books published in Great Britain between the years 1949 and 1956. This period is remarkable for the explosion of cheaply produced pulp paperbacks occasioned by the lifting of postwar paper restrictions. Many of the titles were written by hack writers working for fly-by-night "publishers" and, not surprisingly, much of the writing is truly awful, something the annotations gleefully point out ("abject rubbish"; "pass the barf bag"; "a ghastly space opera mish-mash"; "as silly as it sounds"). Nevertheless, this body of work is the focus of increasing activity among book collectors, an endeavor in which this painstakingly thorough bibliography (the authors read *every* book and story mentioned therein) will be an invaluable aid. Books are arranged by author, with cross-references to the numerous and often quaint pseudonyms (e.g., Volsted Gridban, Bengo Mistral, Kris Luna) rife during this period. Biographical data are provided where known, along with information on interior and cover artists—an important feature as many of these works are notable only for their illustrations. In addition, there are sections on reprint SF paperbacks, SF magazines, and an index to magazine stories and articles. The authors have produced an admirable guide of the postwar British publishing world.—**Jeffrey R. Luttrell**

1235. **Late-Victorian and Edwardian British Novelists. First Series.** George M. Johnson, ed. Detroit, Gale, 1995. 420p. illus. index. (Dictionary of Literary Biography, v.153). $128.00. ISBN 0-8103-5714-3.

Although for decades the writings of Thomas Hardy, William Makepeace Thackeray, and the Brontës have undergone continual appraisal and reappraisal by successive waves of literary critics, hardly any significant scholarship has focused on the works of such deserving contemporaries of theirs as E. F. Benson, Richard S. Hitchens, or Beatrice Harraden. Strides to redress this oversight have now been made with this collection of biocritical essays and bibliographies. Although volumes 18, 34, and 36 of the Dictionary of Literary Biography (DLB) have previously touched on the works of some of these figures, 20 of the writers discussed in the book have heretofore received no treatment in the series.

Johnson, in his 13-page introduction, displays an informed appreciation of these unheralded authors. Herein he explores the cultural biases (including the everpresent disdain of the literati toward the popular writer) that have obscured such classics as George du Maurier's *Peter Ibbetson* or William Hope Hodgson's *The Nightland* from the view of generations of readers. The 35 articles contained in this volume reflect a refreshingly wide array of critical perspectives held by an international field of scholars who are affiliated with universities in the United States, Canada, Great Britain, the Netherlands, and Portugal. Indeed, only about half of the contributors are tied to U.S. institutions. Also, in this work it is pleasing to encounter such heaven-sent matches of scholar and subject as the study of W. H. Hudson by George Woodcock.

As is customary with the DLB, each article contains a black-and-white illustration of the writer under consideration, usually accompanied by reproductions of manuscript leaves, title pages from first editions, and so forth. Extensive (if not comprehensive) bibliographies of books, play productions, and appearances of shorter works in periodicals and collections precede each biocritical essay; citations for such suggested reading and scholarship sources as letters, interviews, biographies, and papers conclude the study of each writer. A forthcoming companion volume is promised, which would treat neglected writers from this period who are realists as opposed to the mostly neoromantic writers included in the present work. Libraries serving appreciable numbers of college students should consider purchasing this excellent book.

—**Jeffrey E. Long**

1236. Letellier, Robert Ignatius. **A Bibliography of the English Novel from the Restoration to the French Revolution: A Checklist of Sources and Critical Materials, with Particular Reference to the Period 1660 to 1740.** Salzburg, Austria, Institute for English and American Studies, University of Salzburg and Lewiston, N.Y., Edwin Mellen Press, 1994. 428p. index. (Salzburg English & American Studies, v.17). $109.95. ISBN 0-7734-1280-8.

This bibliographical source, based on a work by James Harner (*English Renaissance Prose Fiction, 1500-1660* [see ARBA 93, entry 1203, and ARBA 86, entry 1158]), was funded by the senate of Salzburg University. It explores the rise of the novel in England from the restoration of the Stuart monarchy in 1660 to the French Revolution in 1789; the more specific focus is on the period 1660-1740. The aim of the work is "to provide a comprehensive, complementary and up-to-date context of sources, critical materials and background for the wider period, 1660-1800" (p. xxxi).

The book is divided into two parts, and each part is further subdivided into sections. Part A covers miscellaneous works about the general period, including bibliographies, anthologies, and general studies (historical, cultural); there are also briefer sections that focus on American fiction, women's studies, and different types of fiction (e.g., epistolary novels, Oriental tales, utopian novels, gothic novels). Part B consists of a year-by-year chronological list of principal works of prose fiction for individual authors between the years 1600 and 1740 (that being the date of publication of *Pamela* by Samuel Richardson, "the first universally celebrated major novel in English" [p. xxix]). This is followed by two sections on "literary giants": a section on John Bunyan that contains a list of his works, a bibliography to 1970, and a bibliography of criticism from 1970 to 1990; and a section on Daniel Defoe, which also lists works, bibliographies, and criticism from 1980 to 1990 (as Defoe warrants many studies, and information prior to 1980 is readily available elsewhere).

The majority of the study consists of entries on individual authors for the more specific time period, listing critical sources and articles written about them. The entries are alphabetical by author or anonymous work, with definite or indefinite articles in titles included (i.e., works beginning with "The" are sandwiched between *Terrasson, Jean* and *Theobald, Lewis*). An entry contains a list of works by the author with a brief synopsis, the different editions available (e.g., if the works are included in anthologies or have been reissued), and studies or articles done by critics. Some entries are longer than others, as certain authors have a larger critical scope or are more familiar to more people. The book concludes with an index of scholars as well as an extensive thematic index.

Although the author does not claim to have provided an exhaustive study, the book is thorough, furnishing entries on both the well known and the obscure. A conscious effort has been made to profile women, indicating their important role in the rise of this literary form. Any student of literature would benefit from a perusal of this bibliography; however, the price may be prohibitive toward that end. Therefore, all college and university libraries should consider purchasing it.—**Melissa R. Root**

Individual Authors

Joseph Addison and Richard Steele

1237. Knight, Charles A. **Joseph Addison and Richard Steele: A Reference Guide 1730-1991.** New York, G. K. Hall/Simon & Schuster, 1994. 561p. index. (Reference Guide to Literature). $60.00. ISBN 0-8161-8980-3.

This annotated bibliography covers works written about Addison and Steele that appeared after Steele's death (in 1729) through 1991. Knight begins his study with lists of the works of both Addison and Steele in separate bibliographies, and then continues with the writings about both authors. The guide does not establish separate categories for Addison and Steele, but treats them as if they were a single author. The author points out in the introduction that "although Addison and Steele were distinctly and fully individual, they were, as authors, mutually constituting agents, each to a degree really and figuratively creating the authorial identity of the other." Most entries for the years between 1730 and 1991 have at least one listing. Annotations range from a sentence or two to full-page analyses of important writings. The works listed cover anthologies, textbooks, collections of works in the theatrical repertoire, and literary histories. Writings published in English, French, German, and Russian are listed. Two indexes are provided, one for the authors, and the other for the topics they discussed. The topical index is useful. This bibliography is designed for both scholars of Addison and Steele and others interested in these important eighteenth-century authors. The most comprehensive source available on the subject, the guide is recommended for all larger public and academic libraries, and for scholars interested in Addison and Steele specifically.—**Robert L. Wick**

George Herbert

1238. Ray, Robert H. **A George Herbert Companion.** Hamden, Conn., Garland, 1995. 223p. $35.00. ISBN 0-8240-4849-0.

This literary handbook divides into five sections: research tools, Herbert's life chronology, Herbert's works, the Herbert dictionary (which encompasses most of the book), and a selected bibliography. The dictionary identifies, defines, and explains the most significant and frequently read poems and prose; persons and places in Herbert's life and works; characters, allusions, and ideas in his work and time; words and phrases significant to Herbert; and other important writers and persons contemporary with him.

Although this handbook does not pretend to be exhaustive or aspire to deal with all aspects of Herbert of interest to scholars, it does provide a reliable, extensive, easy-to-read guide for undergraduate students, graduate students, and persons teaching or wishing to read Herbert in the context of a survey or introductory course. Thus, purchase is strongly recommended for libraries serving those audiences, as well as audiences with extensive religious interests (e.g., seminaries, religious bookstores, and so forth).—**C. B. (Bob) Darrell**

William Shakespeare

1239. Lamb, G. F. **Shakespeare Quotations.** New York, Larousse Kingfisher Chambers, 1994. 352p. index. $10.95pa. ISBN 0-7523-5004-8.

This collection of more than 2,000 quotations takes a topical approach to Shakespeare's memorable lines. Arranged under 197 subjects, each selection briefly notes the context, the source, the speaker, and the person addressed. Topics begin alphabetically with "Absence" and "Action" and run through to "The World" and "Youth." Within subjects, quotations are entered alphabetically by the title of the play, with quotations from the poems following.

Additional sections include a dictionary of characters; a section of quotations about Shakespeare and Shakespearean performances; a single-page biography of Shakespeare; a one-page chronological list of the plays; and finally, an index of the plays with their respective subjects. Sources give act and scene but not line numbers. Contexts are brief, often merely a phrase.

A more comprehensive work covering the same subjects plus many more is Burton Stevenson's *The Home Book of Shakespeare Quotations* (Scribner's, 1937; reprinted as *The Macmillan Book of Shakespeare Quotations* [Macmillan, 1987]). Libraries owning Stevenson need not consider Lamb for their reference collection.—**Bernice Bergup**

1240. Quennell, Peter, and Hamish Johnson. **Who's Who in Shakespeare.** New York, Oxford University Press, 1995. 228p. $14.95pa. ISBN 0-19-521081-6.

An old friend returns. This is a reissue of the 1973 edition of *Who's Who in Shakespeare* (see ARBA 74, entry 1396). The text is the same, but this paperback edition is minus the numerous pictures and photographs that studded the original edition: pictures of playhouses, particular productions, actors in signature roles, frontispieces of early editions, and playbills.

The text includes all characters in the Shakespeare canon, even including some animals; it gives a summary of each and a discussion of the character's action and purpose. Often the editors give background on why a certain play was written, or on whom a particular character was based. The book is thorough and reliable.

Although it was the pictures that made this book different from the several other Shakespeare dictionaries (for example, Robin May's *Who's Who in Shakespeare* [see ARBA 74, entry 1376] and *The Hutchinson Shakespeare Dictionary* [Oxford University Press, 1993]), it remains a sturdy and valuable reference. The original hardback version is out of print; this reissue in an inexpensive paperback makes it more widely available, which is to be applauded. Even if a library owns the original edition, this would be useful as an extra or circulating copy.—**Terry Ann Mood**

1241. **The Shakespeare Dictionary.** Sandra Clark, ed. Lincolnwood, Ill., National Textbook, 1994. 291p. $27.95. ISBN 0-8442-5755-9.

Clark's guide to William Shakespeare's plays is divided into five parts: a short Shakespeare biography, theater and play production in Shakespeare's time, Shakespeare's major poetry, a selected bibliography, and an alphabetical listing of entries (the heart of the book).

The first three chapters are essays that offer standard, encyclopedia-style information. The fourth chapter lists approximately 145 bibliographical items. The fifth identifies all Shakespeare's characters, persons, and places mentioned in the plays; principal actors, acting companies, and theaters of the time; other playwrights, writers, and Elizabethan historical figures relevant to Shakespeare; and contemporary writings mentioning Shakespeare. Each play entry discusses possible sources, stage history, characters, and plot summaries. Each character also receives a separate alphabetical entry. Section 5 includes approximately 1,130 entries.

Although not a book for scholars or advanced graduate students in Shakespeare, this compilation should serve advanced literary students in high school, college students, and the general public. [R: SLJ, Feb 95, pp. 128-29]—**C. B. (Bob) Darrell**

1242. **Shakespearean Criticism: Excerpts from the Criticism of William Shakespeare's Plays and Poetry....Volume 26.** Michael Magoulias and others, eds. Detroit, Gale, 1995. 423p. illus. index. $124.00. ISBN 0-8103-8946-0. ISSN 0883-9123.

Perhaps the greatest testimonial to any author's work is that it stands the test of time. William Shakespeare's work is so influential in English literature that a full 400 years after his earlier plays were written, they are still continuously performed, and new things are being written about them all the time. This volume is the 26th in an ongoing series of Shakespearean criticism, designed to provide students, teachers, and other interested readers with valuable insight into Shakespeare's plays and nondramatic poems. The first 10 volumes of the series provided a broad range of facts about, interpretations of, and responses to each of Shakespeare's published and performed works. Beginning with volume 11, the series tackled individual plays in greater detail.

Other volumes in this set deal with tragedies—kings driven mad with grief or tormented by witches—but this one treats the happier themes of rollicking comedic drama, mistaken identity, and Shakespearean social commentary. Specifically delineated are the production records of three comedies: *All's Well That Ends Well* (1602-3), *The Comedy of Errors* (1592-94), and *Twelfth Night* (1601-2). The work begins with a chronological guide to selected productions of those works, providing years, artist(s), and theaters/companies. There is nothing uniform about those chronologies, however; the earliest date supplied for the production of *All's Well* is 1741, while *Comedy*'s listings date back to 1594, and *Twelfth Night*'s to 1602. There follows, for each play, a compendium of as much available information on productions, theaters, persons responsible, and critical reception as the publisher could cram into 100 or so pages of small print. Excerpts from reviews (many in their entirety), with citations and sources, are seamlessly integrated with factual text and commentary.

The book is divided into three major sections, one each for the plays under discussion. The reviews, themselves, date back 50 or so years, and detail the reception of the plays in a number of countries, and under various circumstances. The scholarship is impeccable throughout, and Gale pays commendable attention to proofreading and presentation, as not all publishers bother to do. Strewn throughout the book are full-, half-, and quarter-page black-and-white photographs, captioned to identify both the actors and their dramas.

For the Shakespearean student or scholar seeking criticism of specific plays, conveniently gathered between two covers, this series is ideal. Volume 26 is only another in a fascinating collection of information about the English-speaking world's most enduring playwright. If a library's collection is at all serious about English literature, they should buy this volume—but not just this one; they will want to collect the entire set.—**Bruce A. Shuman**

1243. Williams, Gordon. **Dictionary of Sexual Language and Imagery in Shakespearean and Stuart Literature.** London, Athlone Press; distr., Atlantic Highlands, N.J., Humanities Press, 1994. 3v. $699.00/set. ISBN 0-485-11393-7.

This dictionary, 3 volumes totaling more than 1,600 pages, provides the clearest lexical pathway to date into the fertile field of language and imagery in Shakespearean and Stuart literature. In a brief but provocative eight-page essay, Williams reviews the historical context (e.g., the impact of printing; the shift from almost exclusive agrarian terms of sexual ideas and acts to increasingly urban- and machine-related images and terms; the changing political and religious scene; the impact of the Renaissance) and describes the tools, procedures, and limitations characterizing this enterprise.

Although not intended to be definitive according to Williams, this massive project certainly is comprehensive in its collection of terms likely to carry sexual overtones as evidenced by drama, fiction, poetry, political, religious, and other nonfiction prose printed during the period covered. In most instances,

Williams defines an entry, cites sometimes numerous printed examples, and discusses variations of nuances possible, if not likely. A bibliography of almost 50 pages follows the text. This set is required for all collections of Elizabethan and Stuart literature—undergraduate, graduate, and specialized collections.

—C. B. (Bob) Darrell

Poetry

1244. Bentley, G. E., Jr. **Blake Books Supplement: A Bibliography of Publications and Discoveries About William Blake 1971-1992.** New York, Oxford University Press, 1995. 789p. index. $135.00. ISBN 0-19-812354-X.

Bentley's singular devotion to William Blake remains undiminished in this latest work, a continuation of his magisterial *Blake Books* (Oxford, England: Clarendon Press, 1977). The latter was itself a revised and expanded edition of his earlier *A Blake Bibliography*, edited with M. K. Nurmi (University of Minnesota Press, c.1964).

The *Supplement* follows the same six-part structure as *Blake Books*: editions of Blake's writings (original and reprinted); reproductions of his drawings and paintings; commercial book engravings; catalogs and bibliographies; books owned by Blake; and finally, biography and criticism of the man and his work. Bentley's bibliography is intended in part to update the earlier census of Blake's illuminated books compiled by Sir Geoffrey Keynes and Edwin Wolf (*William Blake's Illuminated Books: A Census* [Grolier Club of New York, 1953]). Aside from newly recorded copies of Blake's work and some earlier items not picked up in *Blake Books*, the secondary materials entered in the *Supplement* comprise more than half of the bibliography.

Of particular note is Bentley's bibliographical essay on "Blake Discoveries, Scholarship, and Criticism 1971-1992," which traces the recent explosion of Blake studies worldwide, particularly in Japanese, but also in French, German, Italian, Hungarian, Polish, Czech, Swedish, Bulgarian, Greek, Finnish, Korean, Catalan, Spanish, and Russian. As Bentley notes, "this bibliography, covering mainly 1975-92, records almost as many works about Blake as did *Blake Books* (1977), which dealt with a period ten times as long (1757-1975)" (p. 10).

Meticulousness in the bibliographer is counted as a virtue rather than a fault. Also, Bentley may in no way be faulted as a critical bibliographer pursuing Blake's primary works, nor disparaged for his energy as a descriptive bibliographer in tracking secondary works. Scholars may disagree with some of his interpretations and conclusions, but they can only applaud his thoroughness as Blake's premier bibliographer. No serious collection on Blake can do without this indispensable addition, despite its exorbitant price.—**Bernice Bergup**

1245. Martinez, Nancy C., Joseph G. R. Martinez, and Erland Anderson. **Guide to British Poetry Explication. Volume 4: Victorian-Contemporary.** New York, G. K. Hall/Simon & Schuster, 1995. 720p. (Reference Publication in Literature). $60.00. ISBN 0-8161-8988-9.

This is the final volume in the Guide to British Poetry Explication series, and it should be purchased by every library owning the previous three volumes: *Old English-Medieval*, *Renaissance*, and *Restoration-Romantic* (see ARBA 94, entries 1265-1266, and ARBA 92, entry 1221). All four volumes are genre derivatives from *Poetry Explication: A Checklist*, edited by Joseph M. Kuntz and Nancy C. Martinez (see ARBA 82, entry 1299). Unlike the *Checklist*, however, this volume contains many more explications for each of the 230 poets cited. Critical explication starts ca. 1925 (a date considered by Kuntz and Martinez to signify the acknowledgment of explication as a necessary evaluative literary tool) and extends through 1993.

Poets cited in this volume range from such standard luminaries as Christina Rossetti, Gerard Manley Hopkins, Philip Larkin, and W. H. Auden, to the more obscure poets such as James Riley and W. E. Henley. Poets are cited alphabetically by last name, followed by an alphabetical listing of their respective poems and attendant explicatory criticism. Books, periodicals, and journals containing criticism are abbreviated, and full publication information is provided in a "Periodicals, Journals and Abbreviations" list or "Main Sources Consulted" index.

Diversity in explications characterizes this compilation. The authors have searched diligently for criticism of various poems, and have been totally inclusive with regard to their citation criteria. They have listed criticism from perspectives that can be considered either historical, biographical, psychological, deconstructionist, religious, Marxist, or linguistic. The acceptance of these differing viewpoints and willingness to cite them provide the user with rich literary criticism about not only lesser-known poets but also prominent ones who may be evaluated differently given the passage of time.

Public and academic librarians purchasing this excellent source will want to consider acquiring the previous volumes if they have not already done so. This volume, however, can stand as a valuable resource on its own merits.—**Kathleen W. Craver**

1246. Reilly, Catherine W. **Late Victorian Poetry 1880-1899: An Annotated Biobibliography.** New York, Mansell/Cassell, 1995. 577p. index. $120.00. ISBN 0-7201-2001-2.

The amount of research required to complete a volume such as this is enormous. Reilly spent an inordinate number of hours in libraries all over Britain and at the University of California—both the Los Angeles and Davis campuses, which have vast collections of Victorian materials—to complete this work. An immense variety of style and theme is found in the volumes that appear in this bibliography. This study identifies nearly 3,000 poets, some only by initials or pseudonyms. Of the authors, it is interesting to note, some 600 were women.

Much of the verse reflected is religious, some contemplative and philosophical. There are narrative poems listed, of which Greek, Roman, Norse, and Arthurian materials provided the initial influence. In addition, there are poems concerned with social conditions. The most popular theme, as might be expected, is love, surpassing the "in memoriam" poems that were a feature of an age when infant mortality was high and life expectancy was short.

This bibliography, which fills a long-existing gap in the history of English literature, is arranged alphabetically by author, with anonymous works listed by title. Brief biographical notes are given for each poet where possible. The titles supplied are those of 1st editions unless otherwise annotated. Publishers and dates of publication are included for all entries, except for those privately printed.

This book is a reference tool of value to scholars and students, librarians, and cultural historians.
—**G. A. Cevasco**

African Literature

1247. Lindfors, Bernth. **Black African Literature in English, 1987-1991.** New Providence, N.J., Hans Zell/Reed Reference Publishing, 1995. 682p. index. $125.00. ISBN 1-873836-16-3.

Lindfors's bibliography is indebted to the 1967 work *Black African Literature in English Since 1952* by Barbara Abrash. In 1979, he published his first work, a bibliography of titles published between 1967 and 1976 (see ARBA 80, entry 1287). Another supplement (1977-1981) appeared in 1986, followed by the 1982-1986 update in 1989 (see ARBA 90, entry 1190); and finally, the present work covering 1987-1991.

Lindfors has maintained the same general criteria for inclusion through each period, emphasized by numbering the entries consecutively. Short review articles are excluded, as are creative works unless accompanied by a critical introduction. Other materials are included if they have "some literary significance" (p. ix). Lindfors has examined most materials and identified those he has not. Some entries deemed spurious have been omitted from the numbering.

The bibliography is arranged into two parts: Part 1 includes genre, topical studies, and reference sources; part 2 covers individual authors. Some entries are annotated by a word or phrase, some to identify black African authors in a work or to point out the relevance of a particular item (for example, entry 14294, "Okara, Soyinka, Tutola, et al."). Complete citations appear only once; cross-references are by entry number. In a few cases, entries from previous supplements are listed among the cross-references.

Over the years, the number of titles perused has increased substantially. This latest numbers approximately 900 serial titles. The scope is truly international, covering a wide range of literature, encompassing theses and dissertations, with sources in French, German, Italian, Spanish, and Portuguese. Titles in languages other than these have been translated into English.

The author index contains authors, editors, and translators. Other indexes are by title and subject. These indexes and a geographic index divided by region, and then by individual African country, provide a range of entry points. A major bibliography, Lindfors's work is preeminent in the field of African literature in English, and should be found in research collections for African studies.—**Bernice Bergup**

Australian Literature

1248. **The Oxford Companion to Australian Literature.** 2d ed. By William H. Wilde, Joy Hooton, and Barry Andrews. New York, Oxford University Press, 1994. 833p. $79.00. ISBN 0-19-553381-X.

This substantially expanded edition is every bit as good as the 1st (see ARBA 88, entry 1233). New entries, including major articles on crime fiction and the immigrant experience, as well as entries for a new generation of writers, bring the total to 3,050 entries. All existing entries have been reviewed and updated with a special emphasis on writers who were in mid-career when the 1st edition was prepared.

This continues to be a splendid companion not just to Australian literature, but to many other aspects of Australian culture and history as well. Many of the entries remain relatively brief, but there are some lengthy essays on major topics that are outstanding expositions of a theme (e.g., the Aborigine in white Australian literature). Arranged alphabetically by author, character, literary work, or topical subject, this volume is so easy to use that the lack of an index is no handicap at all. Libraries with only an incidental interest in Australian literature may be tempted to make do with the 1st edition; however, the strength of this companion as the major reference source in its area, and the quantity and quality of the additions in the 2d edition, suggest that purchase of the new edition is fully warranted.—**Norman D. Stevens**

Canadian Literature

1249. **The George Ryga Papers: George Ryga Fonds, Renée L. Paris Fonds, George Ryga & Associates Fonds. An Inventory of the Archive at the University of Calgary Library.** Juanita Walton and Sandra Mortensen, comps. Marlys Chevrefils and Apollonia Steele, eds. Calgary, Alta., University of Calgary Press, 1995. 463p. index. price not reported. ISBN 1-895176-66-2.

An archival inventory prepared as part of the University of Calgary's inventory series with the support of the Social Sciences and Humanities Research Council of Canada, *The George Ryga Papers* is composed of three separate fonds with acquisitions beginning in 1976 and completed in the early 1990s. Integrated intellectually are four accessions of the George Ryga fonds covering the period from 1944-1988 and documenting Ryga's professional writing career; the Renée L. Paris fonds acquired in 1976, which includes correspondence and legal documentation for the period when she functioned as Ryga's literary agent; and the George Ryga & Associates fonds, the latest acquisition that documents the period from 1976 when the firm became Ryga's literary agent and continued as agent for his literary estate. This latter fond is expected to have future accruals, and there is considerable overlap between the three fonds.

Probably best known in Canada for his play *The Ecstasy of Rita Joe*, Ryga also wrote a number of other dramatic works as well as fiction and poetry until his death in 1987. The inventory is prefaced by a substantial biocritical essay that provides an analytical and biographical introduction to Ryga's career. Interspersed throughout the volume are reproductions of various materials included in the Ryga documentation. Arrangement and description of the inventory follow standard archival methodology, with original order maintained whenever possible. A short appendix lists various materials donated in 1988 from two other sources. Two indexes are included in the compilation. The first is an alphabetical index of Ryga's titles with genre designations to simplify identification of the many works adapted by the author. A substantial general index follows, which allows location by means of a variety of access points. For students, researchers, and reference staff members, this inventory will be an invaluable asset.—**Virginia S. Fischer**

European Literature

1250. Glomski, Jacqueline, and Erika Rummel. **Annotated Catalogue of Early Editions of Erasmus at the Centre for Reformation and Renaissance Studies, Toronto.** Toronto, Centre for Reformation and Renaissance Studies, 1994. 153p. illus. index. $18.00pa; $25.00pa.(U.S.). ISBN 0-9697512-1-4.

Perhaps no one else epitomizes the idealized modern man more than Desiderius Erasmus—scholar, humanist, and sardonic church wit. Not only are his tête-à-têtes with Martin Luther studied, but so also is his early work as a greatly admired New Testament translator and developer of the critical apparatus, which are studied for their measured skills. The book under review is an annotated edition of the works of one of the most influential men of the sixteenth century. Forming the core of the Centre for Reformation and Renaissance Studies are about 3,000 early (pre-1700) editions of the works of Erasmus. This slender book covers collections, original compositions, editions, translations, commentaries, biographies on Erasmus, and works addressed to him. For each entry, the title, place of publication, date, collation, and characteristics (such a whether the book was previously owned) are listed. Marginalia are also included when pertinent, reminding the librarian that doodling found in a text is not necessarily the marks of a sophomoric delinquent. These added features make the tool a must for the scholar wanting a particular edition, or for the social historian searching for clues about the culture of the times.—**Mark Y. Herring**

French Literature

1251. Doss-Quinby, Eglal. **The Lyrics of the Trouvères: A Research Guide (1970-1990).** Hamden, Conn., Garland, 1994. 264p. index. (Garland Medieval Bibliographies, v.17; Garland Reference Library of the Humanities, v.1423). $42.00. ISBN 0-8153-0085-9.

Doss-Quinby covers editions and anthologies of, and studies on, the lyric production of the medieval French *trouvères* (the northern French counterparts of the troubadours) from their inception to the middle of the fourteenth century. The word *lyric* is taken strictly: Nonmusical literary forms are therefore excluded from this guide's purview. Influence and reception studies outside of French literature are not included, and, except for a few reference works, everything listed was published in or after 1970. Almost all the 825 entries are annotated; North American dissertations are cited along with references to their summaries in *Dissertation Abstracts International*; other unpublished dissertations are noted simply with university and date; and a few items not seen are so noted with an asterisk. The quality of the annotations is high, and there is generous internal cross-referencing.

The guide is organized into discrete sections covering general topics (e.g., literary history, metrics, music and literature, poetics) or individual primary authors (approximately the final third of the bibliography). References to primary authors outside of the sections focusing specifically upon them are not indexed and thus only findable by browsing or skimming. Indeed, this is not so much a work of ready-reference as a date-limited subject guide. One would guess that its intended primary audience is teachers of medieval French literature, though advanced students of medieval French or medieval music may also find it useful.—**John B. Dillon**

1252. **The New Oxford Companion to Literature in French.** Peter France, ed. New York, Oxford University Press, 1995. 865p. $49.95. ISBN 0-19-866125-8.

Entirely new and not just an updated version of the 1976 *Concise Oxford Dictionary of French Literature* (see ARBA 78, entry 1188), this work covers 10 centuries of the literary heritage in the French language. Conceived to be more than a dictionary, this Oxford companion provides not only literary and cultural information but the stimulation to learn more about the French-speaking people—more than half of whom now live outside of France. This work views literature from the perspective of its greater cultural context. Accordingly, topics discussed go beyond the poets, novelists, and dramatists of the traditional French canon, and include philosophy, science, art, history, linguistics, and cinema. Even strip cartoons and pamphlets are treated.

The inclusion of this new material as well as the various countries of origin is the chief difference between this Oxford companion and its predecessor. The more than 3,000 entries are written by approximately 130 international experts. In addition to brief entries, there are long articles on general topics, such as Québec, feminism, Occitan literature, and the history of the French language. A timeline of political and cultural history plus authors covering the years 481-1993 adds to the usefulness of this reference. Also, there are several maps of France and the French-speaking world. This excellent new work is highly recommended for all libraries.—**Edward Erazo**

1253. Romeiser, John B. **André Malraux: A Reference Guide 1940-1990.** New York, G. K. Hall/Macmillan, 1994. 370p. index. (Reference Publication in Literature). $45.00. ISBN 0-8161-9071-2.

This well-produced guide to scholarship on the French literary figure and cultural politician André Malraux (1901-1976) is an impressive achievement. Covering slightly fewer than 1,300 contributions in English, French, German, Italian, and Spanish published from 1940 through 1990, it is the work of a knowledgeable specialist in Malraux studies and, while intentionally not exhaustive, very thorough for the period and languages of its purview. For an author already active in the 1920s and honored with the prestigious Prix Goncourt in 1933, the exclusion of pre-1940 matter may seem unduly arbitrary, though one consequence of the limitation is that the first item in the main sequence is one by Haakon Chevalier, a richly symbolic figure in the present context.

After a brief survey of Malraux's life and critical reception and a chronological list of Malraux's more important writings (including English-language translations but not German, Italian, or Spanish ones, though these may be thought important for some of the criticism written in those tongues), most of the bibliography is devoted to year-by-year listings of writings on Malraux, arranged alphabetically by author within each year and intelligently annotated. The book concludes with author and subject indexes to the main sequence. Hierarchical features of the subject index are not always compensated for (as they should be in some cases) by cross-references from the alphabetical sequence, and are not always predictably located in view of the different treatment accorded notionally parallel terms. Such cavils aside, this is an important and extremely useful guide. It belongs in all liberal arts college, university, and major public libraries.
—**John B. Dillon**

German Literature

1254. **German Writers and Works of the Early Middle Ages: 800-1170.** Will Hasty and James Hardin, eds. Detroit, Gale, 1995. 414p. illus. index. (Dictionary of Literary Biography, v.148). $128.00. ISBN 0-8103-5709-7.

Volume 148 of the distinguished Dictionary of Literary Biography (DLB) series deals with significant German writers and anonymous works from 800 to 1170. Where little is known about an author, entries stress the author's work. In addition to providing essential biographical and bibliographical information, authors are assessed in the light of the critical reception of their works. The treatment of the works provides readers with a sense of their atmosphere, language, and significance. Works are discussed individually and in chronological order, rather than thematically.

The Germanists who have written chapters for this work are, generally speaking, leaders in the field. For example, Hasty, one of the volume's editors, is the author of a dissertation on the theme of adventure in the German court epic. He has also written articles on the medieval German love epic and Andreas Gryphius. Robert Levine, who covers the Archpoet and Einhard, is an accomplished medieval literary scholar, whose articles discuss Latin literature in England, Geoffrey Chaucer's *Troilus and Criseyde*, Wolfram von Eschenbach, and *Gawain and the Green Knight*.

Each entry is headed by the full name by which the author is generally known, or the title of the anonymous work. Dates of birth and death appear below the author's name; in the case of an anonymous work, the approximate date of the work's composition appears below the work's title. The author's major works are listed in chronological order with their approximate dates of composition. The titles are listed as they generally appear in standard editions and are italicized. The title of a work is followed by a brief description of the age and location of significant manuscripts. In general, disputes on the merits of various manuscripts of a work are not given much space. The first printing dates, standard or critical editions of the original Middle High German text, modern German editions, and English translations follow. Each essay assesses the author's or anonymous work's place in the literary history of the period. Biographical information on medieval German authors is provided wherever possible. All quotations are in the original, accompanied by parenthetical idiomatic translations. Each entry concludes with a reference section of representative writings on the author or work. At the end of the volume, a list of books for further reading in the field of early German literature is provided.

This DLB volume, edited by Hasty and Hardin, is nothing less than an outstanding collection of well-organized essays on early German authors and anonymous works. It is all the more significant because the editors have so successfully attempted to keep everything in the volume comprehensible to a reader unfamiliar with German language, history, and culture. It is highly recommended for all German and medieval literature collections in university libraries, as well as major public libraries.—**Mark Padnos**

Indic Literature

1255. Zvelebil, Kamil V. **Lexicon of Tamil Literature.** New York, E. J. Brill, 1995. 782p. $228.75. ISBN 90-04-10072-5. ISSN 0169-9377.

The author of this dictionary is one of the best scholars in the field of Tamil and Dravidian linguistics and philology generally, so the reliability and solidness of the information offered here are guaranteed. The entry words in the dictionary are arranged by English alphabetical order. This is a clear-sighted decision, since an arrangement in terms of the sequence of the indigenous script would impede access for many users.

The majority of the entries are of biographical character, with the main stress given to the works of the authors discussed. This is done very adroitly; for instance, the entry concerning the politician and author Kurunaniti is constructed in such a way that one not only learns about his politics and his publications, but also gets a synopsis of one of his typical works, with the result that an impression of the whole oeuvre is conveyed. The entries contain a rich bibliography, and again, the most important opinions are succinctly reported, so it is not necessary to seek information constantly in other books. There are useful entries that contain unexpected information. For instance, the entry on grammarians of the seventeenth and eighteenth centuries informs the reader that these were not just ordinary grammarians. This is the designation of a specific group of grammarians who tried to transfer categories of Sanskrit grammar to Tamil.

There is, however, yet another component of the dictionary. Many entries deal with terms and notions developed by Tamil philologists over the centuries. For example, *yamaka* is a rhetorical term referring to repetition in a stanza with changes of meaning effected by changes in division of words. The front matter of the dictionary provides useful surveys of the history of Tamil literature, an analysis of its typical idiosyncrasies, and similar topics. The usefulness of this dictionary for any reference library is obvious.
—**L. Zgusta**

Irish Literature

1256. Crawford, Gary William. **J. Sheridan Le Fanu: A Bio-Bibliography.** Westport, Conn., Greenwood Press, 1995. 155p. index. (Bio-bibliographies in World Literature, no.3). $59.95. ISBN 0-313-28515-2.

This first full bibliography of Le Fanu is divided into three parts: a brief biography, a primary bibliography, and a secondary bibliography. In the biographical section, Crawford speaks of the anxiety and guilt that seemed to follow the Irish Protestant throughout his life and was strongly evidenced in his fiction of horror and the supernatural; of his devotion to the women in his life, which was also shown in his tales; and of his involvement in the publishing world, especially through his ownership of *The Dublin University Magazine*.

The annotated primary bibliography lists Le Fanu's magazine appearances and his books (both chronologically arranged), anthology appearances (alphabetically arranged by story title), and manuscript sources. The secondary bibliography, annotated and often evaluative, begins with a research overview. It is alphabetical by author and divided into books devoted to Le Fanu, essays in books, general studies containing extended discussions of Le Fanu's works, journal and magazine articles, introductions to editions of Le Fanu's works, book reviews, and dissertations and master's theses. A well-annotated appendix of films and plays based on Le Fanu's works rounds out the volume, followed by a title index to the primary bibliography and an author index to the secondary bibliography.

This bio-bibliography of a minor Victorian writer well known for his ghost stories and mystery novels should easily find a place in most university and larger college libraries, alongside two other studies of the last decade: W. J. McCormack's *Sheridan Le Fanu and Victorian Ireland* (Oxford University Press, 1980) and Ivan Melada's *Sheridan Le Fanu* (Twayne, 1987). On the one hand, this volume is sturdy and particularly well bound; on the other hand, its typeface is pedestrian, and its price may be prohibitive for many budgets.—**Charles R. Andrews**

1257. O'Brien, George. **Brian Friel: A Reference Guide 1962-1992.** New York, G. K. Hall/Simon & Schuster, 1995. 136p. index. $40.00. ISBN 0-8161-7273-0.

Brian Friel: A Reference Guide is a useful addition to this G. K. Hall series. Several full-length studies of Friel have been published recently, which include brief bibliographies. However, Friel has not been the focus of a complete bibliography since Kimball King's *Ten Modern Irish Playwrights* (Garland, 1979).

In this reference guide, O'Brien includes writings about Friel from 1962, when his first book of short stories was published, to 1992, when *Dancing at Lughnasa* won several Tony awards. It thus excludes criticism of Friel's very early plays, produced in regional Irish theaters, as well as criticism of his two latest works, *Wonderful Tennessee* and *Molly Sweeney*. What it does include, however, is extensive: a complete chronology of both biographical and critical information on Friel during his long career, after he first began to command serious attention from critics.

Entries are arranged chronologically by year, with the entries in each year arranged alphabetically by title. Each entry is annotated, usually with a brief one-sentence synopsis capturing the focus and critical judgment of the review. Some of the annotations are longer and contain quotations from the work cited. On the critical side, the bibliography encompasses books, scholarly journal articles, and journal and newspaper reviews, while biographical citations are drawn from news stories, interviews, and profiles.

O'Brien provides both subject and author indexes. The subject index is arranged to facilitate retrieving reviews of particular plays. Supplementary material consists of an introductory critical essay, a list of Friel's works, and a list of the major productions of each of his plays, principally in Ireland, London, and New York.

As Friel is considered one of the premier playwrights of the day, this reference guide will be welcomed by most academic and public libraries with an interest in Irish or English literature or in modern drama.

—**Terry Ann Mood**

Latin American and Caribbean Literature

1258. **Modern Latin-American Fiction Writers. Second Series.** William Luis and Ann González, eds. Detroit, Gale, 1994. 413p. illus. index. (Dictionary of Literary Biography, v.145). $128.00. ISBN 0-8103-5559-0.

The editors' main concern, according to their introduction, is to make this second series collection a complement to the first volume by veering attention from the "boom" and its literary giants. Instead, the collection focuses on the inclusion of well-known figures from underrepresented and marginalized groups or nations. The 39 bio-bibliographical essays—each executed by a different scholar—include a short biography; a list of works; a look at major novels or short story collections; and a selected bibliography on authors born between 1900 and 1951, from 19 nations. Although on a three-to-one ratio in men's favor, women are well represented.

Apart from the well-crafted analytical summaries of each author's major works, an attractive and humanizing touch is the inclusion of photographs of the authors and covers of their books' editions. The look at works of authors such as Lino Novás Calvo, Demetrio Aguilera Malta, and Alfredo Pareja Diezcanseco, who are often overshadowed by high-profile or young writers and overlooked by recent criticism, enriches this collection. Despite a deficient job of proofreading, the volume offers novices a look at an interesting variety of Latin American writers across North, Central, and South America. The essays on lesser-known figures from small nations, and the carefully selected bibliographies, provide a useful tool for proficient scholars in the field.—**Stella T. Clark**

Native American Literature

1259. **Native North American Literature: Biographical and Critical Information on Native Writers and Orators....** Janet Witalec, ed. Detroit, Gale, 1995. 706p. illus. index. $99.00. ISBN 0-8103-9898-2.

The reading public has had two new major guides to Native American literature appear within six months of one another. *Dictionary of Native American Literature* appeared first (see ARBA 95, entry 1175). There are certainly many similarities in the structure and content between this publication and the *Dictionary*, as one would expect due to subject matter. Both encompass oral and written literature, as well as having biographical essays about some of the leading individuals in the field. This volume provides in-depth essays on 78 people, 4 entries under oral autobiography: Black Elk, Black Hawk, Maria Chona, and Lame Deer; and 4 entries under oratory: Chief Joseph, Chief Seattle, Sitting Bull, and Tecumseh. The balance of entries are for writers, most of whom are actively writing. The oral literature section has a 45-page introduction that discusses the character of the oral literature as well as exploring the differences between stories, myths, and song.

Biographical entries are long, a minimum of four pages, meaning excellent depth. The volume is selective, but one finds entries for all of the major contemporary Native American authors (e.g., Vine Deloria, Joy Harjo, N. Scott Momaday, Duane Niatum, and Leslie Marmon Silko). There is also a good selection of authors whose works are readily available, if one goes to a first-rate bookstore or places a special order. Witalec also included a reasonable cross section of deceased authors.

Each entry provides basic biographical information; a biographical essay; a chronological list of major works; a discussion of the criticism of the individual's works excerpted from published reviews, articles, and books (also arranged chronologically); and a "sources for further study" section. There is an explanatory notes section with the criticism material that enables users to place the material in a broader context, such as who the critic was and the purpose of the criticism. Separate genre and title indexes provide additional useful means of access. If a choice must be made, this volume provides more biographies and excerpts of criticism; the *Dictionary* has more essays about Native American literature. Libraries with large reference collections, as well as those serving communities with a strong interest in Native Americans, should have both titles.—**G. Edward Evans**

Oceanian Literature

1260. Goetzfridt, Nicholas J. **Indigenous Literature of Oceania: A Survey of Criticism and Interpretation.** Westport, Conn., Greenwood Press, 1995. 347p. index. (Bibliographies and Indexes in World Literature, no.47). $75.00. ISBN 0-313-29173-X.

As a sourcebook for writings on the indigenous literature of Oceania that has emerged and developed so rapidly during the last 30 years, this work, a product of long and dedicated commitment, is invaluable. As an annotated survey of the writings, however, it is only of limited value: The summaries are prolix and plodding, difficult at times to slough through.

The thorough survey of more than 700 books and articles on Pacific literature does command respect: There is no other single work in existence that offers both bibliographical data and summaries of the contents of critical writings. What one has to deplore is the lack of conciseness in the summaries, their pointless thoroughness. The brief foreword by Fijian playwright Vilsoni Hereniko is of great assistance in that it both provides a lively and succinct account of the emergence and rapid development of Pacific literature, and outlines the ongoing argument over the kind of standards by which the new literature should be judged: whether by European standards or by indigenous standards. Neither Hereniko nor Goetzfridt in his introduction, however, has the clarity of perspective or the assertiveness to say that Eurocentric critics do indeed have some right to assess forms taken from European literature and to point out that indigenous standards still remain distressingly vague in their articulation.

Goetzfridt's introduction is marred by the jargon and abstract writing that make so much of the writing on literature of developing countries a chore to read. Elsewhere, within the main text, his long sentences and syntactic irregularities are the chief causes of the unattractiveness of his style. There are conspicuous failures of agreement between subject and verb, but far more distracting is his recurring inability to incorporate relative clauses into the structure of his sentences. The result is a ragged quality that continually disrupts the reader's train of thought.

The book is an indispensable reference work. One wishes, however, that the scholarly dedication could have been couched in a more lucid style.—**John B. Beston**

Russian Literature

1261. **Early Modern Russian Writers, Late Seventeenth and Eighteenth Centuries.** Marcus C. Levitt, ed. Detroit, Gale, 1995. 465p. illus. index. (Dictionary of Literary Biography, v.150). $128.00. ISBN 0-8103-5711-9.

For most people, modern Russian literature begins with Aleksandr Pushkin in the 1820s. In fact, Russian literature has a substantial tradition starting from the mid- to late-seventeenth century and flourishing in the reign of Catherine the Great (1762-1796). This crucial period saw the transition of Russia from an isolated medieval state to one adopting Western models. Although there are two standard literary histories in English—William E. Brown's *A History of Russian Literature of the Romantic Period* (Ardis, 1986) (volumes on the seventeenth and eighteenth centuries), and Harold B. Segel's history-cum-anthology *Twentieth-Century Russian Drama* (Johns Hopkins University Press, 1993) for the latter period—as well as various more specialized studies, there are virtually no general-purpose English reference works. This gap has now been filled.

Admirably edited by Levitt (University of Southern California), 20-odd North American and Russian scholars provide solid bio-bibliographical articles on 49 writers. Levitt's introduction surveys the historical context, and judiciously presents the issues raised by differing scholarly assessments of the period and its literature. Each of the alphabetically ordered entries opens with a bibliography of the subject's books, followed by an interpretive essay. Lists of biographies, references, and, where available, archival resources are appended to the handsomely illustrated essays. Most of the references are, perforce, in Russian, but English publications are also cited, where possible. The volume concludes with a "Checklist of Further Readings," which constitutes a model bibliography for the field. The attractively printed and durably bound volume is a major addition to the relatively modest repertoire of books devoted to this area of Russian cultural studies.—**D. Barton Johnson**

Slavic Literature

1262. **South Slavic Writers Before World War II.** Vasa D. Mihailovich, ed. Detroit, Gale, 1995. 368p. illus. index. (Dictionary of Literary Biography, v.147). $128.00. ISBN 0-8103-5708-9.

The South Slavs include the Slovenes, Croatians, Serbs, Macedonians, and Bulgarians. All were part of the Ottoman or Austro-Hungarian Empires prior to World War I, when all but the Bulgarians were incorporated into the newly established Yugoslavia. Although the Croatians can trace the origins of their belletristic tradition to the sixteenth century and the Serbs to the eighteenth, the "classic" fiction of the South Slavic peoples really begins in the mid- to late nineteenth century. Of the 43 figures profiled in this volume, 32 died in this century—1 as recently as 1991. Apart from Nobel prize-winner Ivo Andrić, almost none of the writers is familiar to English readers. Editor Mihailovich has made an evenhanded selection: Croatian and Serbian writers are represented by about 13 entries each, while the less-numerous Bulgarians and Slovenes rate about half that number.

The volume observes the standard Dictionary of Literary Biography format. Each handsomely illustrated profile begins with a list of the author's works, including English translations, and concludes with a critical bibliography. Essays open with a brief estimate of the writer's place in his or her national literature, followed by a biographical sketch, a chronological survey of works, and a summation. The entries assume only a general knowledge of historical circumstances. An introductory thumbnail sketch of the national literatures is provided. Aftermatter contains a checklist of histories of the national literatures, a bibliography of English-language collections of each literature, and a chronology of major historical and literary data.—**D. Barton Johnson**

POETRY

1263. **The Columbia Granger's Guide to Poetry Anthologies.** 2d ed. By William Katz, Linda Sternberg Katz, and Esther Crain. New York, Columbia University Press, 1994. 440p. index. $75.00. ISBN 0-231-10104-X.

An updating of the 1994 volume (see ARBA 95, entry 1245), this guide to poetry collections presents teachers, students, librarians, and general readers with a concise overview of anthologies printed between 1970 and 1993. Following the preface, the book groups verse by type: African poetry, ballads and songs, young adult poetry, death poetry, poetry: Study and teaching, and English poetry c. 450-1500. Layout is attractive; overviews are descriptive, as with the entry on William Cole's *A Book of Animal Poems* (1973), which is labeled "an enchanting and delightful anthology of children's poetry." Information includes number and range of contributors to each volume, titles of specific works, and relationship to movements, such as women's verse and religious poetry. The bibliographic data cover title, author, editors, date and place of publication, and page numbers.

For maximum assistance to the poetry reader, the editors append a useful list of highly recommended anthologies. The list, divided into two manageable units for all libraries and for medium to large libraries, guides book buyers toward the best selections to meet the strictures of a limited budget. Indexing covers anthologies in italics; editors, compilers, and translators in roman type; and subject categories in small capital letters. Internal cross-referencing helps readers locate works that could fit numerous categories, such as *In the Midst of Winter: Selections from the Literature of Mourning*, which suits both world poetry and death poetry. Overall, this is an invaluable reference tool.—**Mary Ellen Snodgrass**

1264. Drury, John. **The Poetry Dictionary.** Cincinnati, Ohio, Story Press/F & W Publications, 1995. 324p. index. $18.99. ISBN 1-884910-04-1.

This is as much an anthology of poetry as it is an important reference for literature students. As a poetry anthology, Drury's *Dictionary* includes poems, many of them in their entirety, from a wide range of poetic traditions, covering every literary epoch from Sappho (ca.610-ca.580 B.C.E.) to the present. Brief, historical overviews of those traditions are provided, as are commentaries about the major poets of each tradition. Readers will find definitions of the more familiar elements of poetry such as *alliteration* and *metaphor*, as well as such terms as *tanka* (a Japanese verse form) that do not appear regularly in glossaries or handbooks of poetry and literary terms.

The dictionary is easy to use. The alphabetized terms are all printed in boldface type, while related cross-referenced terms are italicized and marked with an asterisk. All of the terms are listed in the index and are easy to find. Much less helpful are the parenthetical phonetic transcriptions of some of the less familiar words. They detract somewhat from the etymology of the terms themselves, but certainly not from the overall quality of the book. Also, although it is doubtful that the reference will be of as much use to poets as Dana Gioia claims in the foreword, poetry lovers and general readers alike will find that *The Poetry Dictionary* is enjoyable to read. It is highly recommended.—**Sandra Adell**

1265. **Poetry Criticism: Excerpts from Criticism of the Works of the Most Significant and Widely Studied Poets of World Literature. Volume 10.** Drew Kalasky and Jane Kelly Kosek, eds. Detroit, Gale, 1994. 557p. index. $83.00. ISBN 0-8103-5614-7. ISSN 1052-4851.

Collections that already shelve the first nine volumes of *Poetry Criticism* (PC) will of course wish to obtain this latest addition to a useful series. Because PC provides substantial critical excerpts and biographical information on figures studied in undergraduate courses, reference librarians often recommend neophytes in the study of poetry to consult these volumes. They provide not only an excellent overview but also vital information of use in the writing of research papers, saving the student hours of time that would be required to ferret the material out of books and journals. While some of the entries overlap (but never more than 10 or 15 percent) listings found in *Contemporary Literary Criticism* (see entries 1151-1153), *Nineteenth-Century Literary Criticism* (see entry 1158), and *Twentieth-Century Literary Criticism* (see entries 1159-1160), PC obviously offers more focused attention.

Among the 10 poets represented in this volume, 4 are from the United States: Anne Bradstreet, Hayden Carruth, Carolyn Forché, and Thomas Merton. Of the remaining six, one is Romanian (Paul Celan); one Italian (Guido Gozzano); one Japanese (Ishikawa Takuboku); one British (Andrew Marvell); one Russian (Aleksandr Pushkin); and the Roman epigrammatist Martial. Each is sufficiently covered, the length of entry and annotated bibliography reflecting the amount of attention the poet has received from critics writing in English and from foreign critics in translation.—**G. A. Cevasco**

25 Music

GENERAL WORKS

Bibliography

1266. Weaver, Robert Lee. **A Descriptive Bibliographical Catalog of the Music Printed by Hubert Waelrant and Jan de Laet.** Warren, Mich., Harmonie Park Press, 1994. 264p. illus. index. $40.00. ISBN 0-89990-058-5.

Waelrant (ca. 1517-1595) and de Laet (ca. 1524-1566) were specialty music publishers in sixteenth-century Antwerp. Major composers of the period had works published by Waelrant and de Laet, among the most notable a young motet composer, Orlando de Lassus. Weaver, who currently serves as chair of the Music Department at Centre College in Danville, Kentucky, is nationally known for his work in the American Musicological Society.

Weaver uses a special bibliographic technique he devised that is based on the standard techniques developed by Fredson Bowers at the University of Virginia, and those used by the *Repertoire International des Sources Musicales: Recueils Imprimes XVIe-XVIIe Siècles*. Weaver has enhanced the standard Bowers/*Repertoire* form by expanding his entries with additional information on topics such as watermark, collation, size, and binding. A typical entry consists of: the *ideal copy* format in the traditional Bowers style; an expanded format and copy section; an expanded listing of the contents of each volume; a section called "notes" (Weaver calls the "notes" section "general items of interest"); and a final section containing data on the paper, type, binding, and other miscellaneous information on the volume in hand.

Weaver's work is divided into four parts: works printed by Waelrant and de Laet, music printed by de Laet and his widow, Waelrant compositions printed by other presses, and Waelrant compositions in manuscript sources. A watermark guide and indexes by short title, first line (in Latin, French, Italian, and Dutch), and composer are provided by Weaver. Prefatory material includes a guide to Weaver's entry style, a modern siglum, and a type siglum. The descriptive annotations in this work are excellent and a credit to the author and modern bibliographical scholarship.

The Weaver work is well bound and attractive in type and layout. Users will find it a valuable addition to the bibliographic scholarship of sixteenth-century music publishing. Music librarians will want to add this publication to their collections because of the importance of the publishers. General collections will find this volume an excellent example of modern bibliographic scholarship.—**Ralph Lee Scott**

Biography

1267. **International Who's Who in Music and Musicians Directory (In the Classical and Light Classical Fields).** 14th ed. David M. Cummings, ed. Cambridge, England, Melrose Press; distr., Bristol, Pa., Taylor & Francis, 1994. 1296p. $175.00. ISBN 0-948875-71-2.

This "who's who" documents some 8,000 musicians, teachers, librarians, and others connected with music, perhaps prominent but not necessarily so. Information is primarily compiled from questionnaires sent to the biographees. One can learn birthdays, addresses, and hobbies. In between are a range of data, including education; debut dates (for performers); career (including, for opera singers, roles played); lists of compositions and publications; memberships; recordings; honors; and management. Telephone numbers and e-mail addresses are, perhaps mercifully, omitted. Organized by country and state, appendixes list orchestras; opera companies; festivals; music organizations (scholarly societies, professional associations, unions, and the like); major competitions and awards; music libraries; and conservatories (that is, any academic or performance school). The list of Masters of the King's/Queen's Music (dating from their beginnings in 1660) seems quaintly anachronistic (the incumbent has held the position since 1975).

It is instructive to read back through reviews of various editions of this work (see ARBA 94, entry 1346; ARBA 91, entry 1254; and ARBA 86, entry 1233) and see how the work has matured over the years from a provincial British publication into an international resource that serves a wide range of purposes. Previous editions will also prove indefinitely useful to biographers, authors of program notes, and so forth. Future editions would benefit from statements of scope and selection criteria: Is anyone who returns a questionnaire included? Such statements would also either justify or warrant exclusion of the appendixes. In the absence of indexes that might allow access to, for example, the signers who have performed the title role of a given opera, the publisher should consider migrating to an electronic format so as to provide keyword access to the entire database.—**Ian Fairclough**

1268. **The Portable Baker's Biographical Dictionary of Musicians.** By Nicholas Slonimsky. Richard Kostelanetz and Michael Stutzman, eds. New York, Schirmer Books/Simon & Schuster, 1995. 291p. index. $20.00pa. ISBN 0-02-871225-0.

Baker's Biographical Dictionary of Musicians is approaching its 100th birthday. It was first published by G. Schirmer in 1900 and has since gone through several major revisions. The 8th edition was published in 1991 (see ARBA 93, entry 1244) and contained more than 2,000 pages and some 2 million words. *Baker's*, as it is known to music students and professionals, is still the major source for biographical information on musicians and other music professionals. The problem has been that it has only been available in larger libraries due to its size and cost. Kostelanetz and Stutzman have put into one small volume the major entries of the larger *Baker's*. In some cases entries have had to be abridged to keep the volume small, but most of the original flare of Slonimsky's writing has been retained. Also, much of the additional material found in the larger *Baker's* is missing (e.g., the large bibliographies, prefaces, and lists of compositions).

For the most part the selections from the larger work appear to be good ones. Most of the well-known musicians and composers can be found, including some popular music performers such as Janis Joplin and Elvis Presley. While many of the entries are abbreviated from the larger work, they provide valuable information concerning the life of the individual, place of birth, positions held, and an analysis of major works. The narrative form of the original *Baker's* has been maintained, along with many of the witty comments.

The Portable Baker's makes an ideal reference for home and office, and it will delight all music enthusiasts, from the casual concertgoer to the professional musician. While it probably is not a logical purchase for academic and public libraries that already own the larger *Baker's*, smaller branches and special music collections not owning the larger title will find it a useful addition.—**Robert L. Wick**

Dictionaries and Encyclopedias

1269. Baker, Richard. **Richard Baker's Companion to Music: A Personal A-Z Guide to Classical Music.** New York, BBC/Parkwest, 1994. 208p. illus. $28.95. ISBN 0-563-36414-9.

Richard Baker's *Companion to Music* is well titled, having a delightful and individualistic personality reflecting the author's broad, yet eclectic, taste. In compiling the work, Baker had in mind the audience of his BBC radio program, "Melodies for You." Primarily on classical music (a term whose proper usage the author defines), entries are provided also for jazz and musicals. In dictionary format, Baker provides a medley of facts about composers, individual works and musical genres, terminology, concert halls, instruments, and vocal types. Coverage ranges from three lines to double-page spreads, of which those for composers (such as Johann Sebastian Bach, Edward Elgar, and Gilbert and Sullivan) contain sidebars with a chronology and list of favorite works. Other entries cover choral, film, and folk music. The book is liberally illustrated with photographs, several of which are full-page and in color. Text reference to other entries is indicated in bold typeface. In back is a timeline of composers, commencing with Giovanni Pierluigi da Palestrina. As one might expect, English topics and personalities are prominently represented.

Rather than in the reference collection of a research library, this work belongs on browsing shelves and in the circulating collections of public and high school libraries. It also would make an excellent gift for music lovers. [R: RBB, 1 Jan 95, p. 844]—**Ian Fairclough**

1270. **The Oxford Dictionary of Music.** 2d ed. Michael Kennedy and Joyce Bourne, eds. New York, Oxford University Press, 1994. 985p. $35.00. ISBN 0-19-869162-9.

The 1st edition of Kennedy's *Oxford Dictionary of Music* was published in 1985 and quickly became a standard reference work in academic and larger public libraries. It was the most comprehensive and detailed single-volume dictionary of music available. This edition has been extensively revised and expanded and now contains 900-plus new entries out of more than 12,000 total. More than 2,000 composers of all countries and nationalities are included. Also, according to the editors, there are more than 2,200 definitions of musical terms and forms along with 550-plus descriptions of musical instruments. In all, more than 80 percent of the existing entries are completely revised or updated. In addition, the lists of works at the end of the entries have, whenever possible, been brought up to date.

The 2d edition has placed more emphasis on U.S. composers and performers. Finding most prominent jazz composers and performers is now possible, although few popular musicians are present. Also, many more living composers and performers who are in the process of making their names in the concert circuit have been included. Additionally, one can find entries on individuals sometimes thought of as peripheral to the music world, such as opera producers and designers, musicologists, and orchestra managers.

The Oxford Dictionary of Music is written for both general readers and more experienced people in the world of music, and is an indispensable reference source for both the home and libraries of all types and sizes. Published in an easy-to-read format, the book contains some illustrations, although no pictures of individuals are included. Much of the value of the work stems from the stature of Kennedy, who is one of the foremost authorities on music.—**Robert L. Wick**

1271. **Schirmer Pronouncing Pocket Manual of Musical Terms.** 5th ed. Theodore Baker, ed.; revised by Laura Kuhn. New York, Schirmer Books/Simon & Schuster, 1995. 341p. $5.95pa. ISBN 0-02-874567-1.

This small (14-by-10-by-2-centimeter) book is arranged in alphabetical order, with an introduction that presents the rudiments of music (elements of notation, the structure of chords, scales, keys, and tempo) and a pronouncing guide. Noteworthy musicians are listed in a separate section in back. Oriented toward the musical layperson, the tool reflects the multinational nature of Western classical music, listing terms in several European languages, and in some cases referring to a translation. Some terms and people from music outside the Western classical mode are also included.

Rather than a scholarly work, the book is obviously oriented toward musical dilettantes or beginning students. It will serve them handily for checking the meaning of terms that they encounter in printed music and brushing up on the inversions of triads and the like (without prior instruction, some of this material is too technical for the uninitiated). No criteria for the inclusion of a term or musician are specified.

As the title indicates, the book will indeed fit into many pockets. Whether it will fit into a particular library's reference collection is another question. A library serving users such as those mentioned above may want it; others may prefer to invest in more sophisticated tools.—**Ian Fairclough**

1272. Strahle, Graham. **An Early Music Dictionary: Musical Terms from British Sources, 1500-1740.** New York, Cambridge University Press, 1995. 469p. $90.00. ISBN 0-521-41688-4.

More than just a dictionary, this unique and fascinating volume makes interesting reading for the music scholar or performer of early music. Drawing on printed and manuscript sources from general dictionaries to treatises to personal papers, Strahle has compiled a dictionary of musical terms and related matters from British writings appearing during the period 1500-1750. Unlike the early music dictionaries of Jeffrey Pulver (*Biographical Dictionary of Old English Music* [see ARBA 74, entry 1106] and *A Dictionary of Old English Music* [Gordon Press, 1972]) or Jerome and Elizabeth Roche (*A Dictionary of Early Music* [see ARBA 83, entry 932]), Strahle's handsomely presented volume quotes his sources directly, leaving original spellings, punctuation, and capitalization intact. The emphasis here is on objects and terms; specific musicians given independent entries are almost all from the realms of mythology or ancient times. Multiple definitions of a single term are printed in chronological order, making it possible for the reader to determine whether (and how) a term changed meaning over the years.

The dictionary proper is preceded by an extensive and helpful introduction in which Strahle not only presents an overview of the sources he consulted but puts these sources in perspective. Here one learns that some definitions may not in fact represent the way a term was understood at the time they were written, and that sources may have concentrated on obscure or difficult matters to the exclusion of ordinary practices that were in common use. Some treatments of the same topic may be extremely short or quite extended: for example, *accent*, which a 1708 dictionary defines simply as "a warbling of the voice," receives several inches of coverage in a 1728 encyclopedia.

To say that this book has a British orientation is to misrepresent the scope of its coverage. While all of Strahle's sources were written or published in Great Britain, they often deal with ideas and practices from continental Europe or draw on foreign-language terms defined for British readers. This excellent reference book will both delight and enlighten anyone interested in Renaissance and Baroque music.

—**Karin Pendle**

Discography

1273. Charosh, Paul, comp. **Berliner Gramophone Records: American Issues, 1892-1900.** Westport, Conn., Greenwood Press, 1995. 290p. index. (Discographies, no.60). $75.00. ISBN 0-313-29217-5.

A catalog of the phonograph discs published by Emile Berliner must be of paramount interest to students of the art of sound recording, since it was he who created the "gramophone," or record player, in the form in which it survived until it has virtually been superseded by digital playback technology during the past decade. Completion of the project by examination of company catalogs, supplements, and so forth, proved impractical because of the scarcity of such items, and so Charosh's work is based additionally on archival research and investigation of private collections. He claims to have identified about 70 percent of the universe of data—a remarkable task given that the artifacts are a century old.

A seven-page introduction describes pertinent discographical events of the period 1892 to 1900. Next, Charosh describes the discs themselves, with 10 full-page photographs. In back are a list of reproductions on LP and compact disc; resources for further study; and extensive indexes by title, artist, and recording date. The body of the work covers one hundred seventy-four pages and describes "more than three thousand takes of twenty-three hundred different catalogue numbers appearing on seven-inch discs in the United States." The arrangement is in two parts: the "Block" series (in which ranges of numbers were reserved for various combinations of performers); and the "0" series (discs numbered consecutively). Each section is arranged by catalog number. Data include, where available, title and composer, "take" symbol and recording date, recording artist, performance type, language if not English, and source codes (for information taken from published items). Some entries contain summaries, evaluations, and other descriptive notes. The eight-page user's guide lists the various "blocks" and presents sample entries for both the "Block" and "0" series, along with lists of codes for each data element.

The work is primarily oriented toward the scholar of discography. Although it will not be much wanted at a general reference desk, all libraries with specialist music collections should consider acquiring it, principally on account of the historical significance of the data presented.—**Ian Fairclough**

1274. **Goldmine's Celebrity Vocals: Attempts at Musical Fame from 1500 Major Stars and Supporting Players.** By Ron Lofman. Iola, Wis., Krause Publications, 1994. 448p. illus. index. $16.95pa. ISBN 0-87341-292-3.

The purpose of this discography is to help identify, as stated in the preface, "surprising, unexpected and obscure recordings by actors, sports heroes and celebrities." A subject index contains entries for would-be singers better known in other fields. Only dedicated fans will remember such personalities as Ben Lyon, Marie McDonald, and Lizbeth Scott as singers. There are also some surprises for browsers looking at the record covers used as illustrations throughout the work: Anthony Perkins, Jack Palance, Robert Mitchum, and Jack Webb. Individual entries contain birth and death dates and the briefest possible career descriptions. In a long entry, sound recordings are arranged using the following method: solo long-playing albums, songs on the following film soundtracks, anthologies, and singles. Record labels and format (LPs and 45s) are identified. Suggested purchase price is given for every recording listed; condition categories are "very good" and "near mint." Another useful feature of the work is the identification of dubbed voices on film soundtracks. There is a listing of film vocal performances that have not been issued on record, a birthplace index, and a brief, unannotated bibliography.—**Milton H. Crouch**

Handbooks and Yearbooks

1275. Bloom, Ken. **Hollywood Song: The Complete Film and Musical Companion.** New York, Facts on File, 1995. 3v. index. $195.00/set. ISBN 0-8160-2002-7.

The author describes this work as the second volume of the "American Song" series. Actually, the earlier publication is his *American Song: The Complete Musical Theatre Companion* (see ARBA 86, entry 1359). Strictly, the present work is not related to the first one as a member of a bibliographic series. In its first 2 volumes, *Hollywood Song* has 7,039 entries (including *see* references) for U.S.-made films, foreign films released by U.S. companies, unproduced films for which songs or scores were written, films in which instrumental pieces were later given lyrics, and silent films that had songs written for them.

Except for Columbia, studios allowed Bloom access to all their cue sheets, the principal data source. He includes rock musicals and cowboy pictures, but excludes short subjects and most documentaries, concert films (other than those for which songs were expressly written), films produced for video, and films including a song that was not written for the film. Arrangement is alphabetical by film title. Volume 3 has a chronology by year (one entry for 1922, then 1927-1990); an index of personnel follows, with labels stating each person's function and *see also* references linking individuals and their performing groups; in back is a song index. Identical prefatory material in each volume consists of acknowledgments and a one-page introduction. Individual entries list personnel for musical score, composer, lyricist, choreographer, producer, director, screenwriter, cast, and each song title. A section of notes contains such data as earlier titles and songs written for a film but not used, as well as songs used that were not originally composed for the movie.

As a tool, *Hollywood Song* is remarkably easy to use by consulting the index and noting the entry number (the publisher should have noted that index references are to entries, not pages). In contrast to the ease of access, understanding the scope is more difficult. Yet, for a comprehensive survey of such a medium, the difficulties are inherent in the nature of the material. Also, some studios evidently proved more helpful than others in the quality of their record-keeping. For example, the entry "Popeye films" represents not one film but several cartoons for which the cue sheets cannot be matched to each cartoon. For mainstream movies, however, the user will have no problem, and in his notes Bloom does a good job of compensating for inconsistencies. Explanation is wanted for some abbreviations in the text, such as C: and C/L:.

This work will be especially useful for persons seeking to track down a movie in which a song appears, or songs in a movie. It also gives quick and easy answers to many other questions about motion pictures that include songs. Nevertheless, users should be cautioned about the vacillations in scope. Its encyclopedic appearance and Facts on File imprint may lead one to attribute greater comprehensiveness to this work than is warranted.—**Ian Fairclough**

1276. Field, Shelly. **Career Opportunities in the Music Industry.** 3d ed. New York, Facts on File, 1995. 274p. index. $27.95. ISBN 0-8160-3047-2.

Career Opportunities in the Music Industry offers comprehensive career information to music professionals. It examines more than 90 career options and describes in a uniform format the duties, salary ranges, employment and promotion prospects, necessary training and experience, and best geographical locations for employment. Professional associations relevant to each career are also provided. The major change of the 3d edition from the 2d (published in 1992) lies in the adjustment of salary ranges.

This book has much to recommend it. However, entries may not be entirely accurate. For example, the description of a music librarian, while generally sound, lists the American Library Association and the Special Library Association first as professional organizations of use to them. In fact, most music librarians belong to the Music Library Association, which is noted, but not as the primary association.

Another error appears in the listing of schools with music business programs. The president of National Association of Music Business Schools (NAMBI) is a professor at Western Illinois University, whose program is not even listed!

These errors and omissions are relatively minor when compared to the value of the collection of this information in one source. This book is recommended for public and academic libraries, although collections with the 2d edition may not need this newer edition.—**Allie Wise Goudy**

Thesauri

1277. Johnson, Jeffrey. **Thesaurus of Abstract Musical Properties: A Theoretical and Compositional Resource.** Westport, Conn., Greenwood Press, 1995. 332p. index. (Music Reference Collection, no.45). $75.00. ISBN 0-313-29392-9.

This reference source is an accumulation of abstract musical properties arranged by set-class that will assist the serious musician in studying groupings of notes and their interrelationships. This base of information is informative to the serious musician both in the analysis of specific musical works as well as in composition.

This well-organized book is divided into two parts. Part 1 includes set-class reference tables, set-class invariance vectors, invariance vectors between set-classes and literal complements, and set-classes arranged by ascending interval-classes. Part 2, the major portion of the book, will probably prove to be the most useful. It is organized by cardinality and contains specific and referential information about individual set-classes. The cross-referenced information makes locating desired set-classes easy and allows for quick comparisons.

The information is thorough and logically presented. This allows the researcher to move easily from one set-class analysis chart to another. It appears to be more helpful in analysis than in composition. Appendixes prove useful for listings of chromatic set-class listings, set-classes listed in ascending order by cardinality, and a listing of transformational cycles.

While it is well produced, this thesaurus has a very limited audience. Advanced graduate students in theory, composition, and analysis may find it useful. Acousticians, physicists, and mathematicians may also find this sort of quantitative information valuable. Other users would find this information too advanced and the book too costly to add to their collections.—**Vik Brown**

CHILDREN'S

1278. Reid, Rob. **Children's Jukebox: A Subject Guide to Musical Recordings and Programming Ideas for Songsters Ages One to Twelve.** Chicago, American Library Association, 1995. 225p. index. $25.00pa. ISBN 0-8389-0650-8.

Children's Jukebox is a much-needed discography of approximately 2,400 recommended recorded children's songs grouped by specific topics. Of these, 308 recordings listed in this practical guide are currently available, and distributor information provided in the appendixes makes locating these recordings easy.

The largest and most useful portion of this resource is the subject listing. Organized around 47 popular themes and curriculum units from "Anatomy" to "Weather," this listing recommends "kid-tested" songs to incorporate into each unit. The entries provide an annotation of the song, appropriate age levels, and suggested activities for programs and classroom use. Numerous performers, including such favorites as Raffi and Gary Rosen and Bill Schontz, give a wide variety to the songs listed.

Those who find the discography overwhelming will find "The Robbie Award Hall of Fame" useful. This is a core collection of the author's top 20 children's musical recordings, which is especially useful in starting a collection. The section on song formats should not be overlooked. These can be used at any time with children, and include call-and-response songs, cumulative songs, songs in foreign languages, rounds, and songs that feature sound effects.

The practical nature of this book mirrors Reid's 11 years as a children's librarian and 14 years as a children's entertainer. His background as a reviewer of children's audiovisual materials and a recording artist has exposed him to many useful recordings. *Children's Jukebox* is an invaluable resource highly recommended for elementary teachers and librarians, music teachers, storytellers, children's entertainers, and day-care providers.—**Vik Brown**

COMPOSERS

1279. Craggs, Stewart R. **William Mathias: A Bio-bibliography.** Westport, Conn., Greenwood Press, 1995. 246p. index. (Bio-bibliographies in Music, no.58) $65.00. ISBN 0-313-27865-2.

Welsh composer William Mathias (1934-1992) was prolific in his craft. He composed an opera, all types of orchestral music (concerti for various solo instruments, strings, and combinations; four symphonies; and so forth), chamber music, solo instrumental music, and a great number of choral works. His compositional style is basically tonal. Mathias was invited to write a wedding anthem for the marriage of the Prince of Wales and Lady Diana Spencer. *Let the People Praise Thee, O God*, Opus 87, was seen and heard on television by more than 750 million people around the world. The anthem was an immediate success and was enthusiastically adopted by many church choirs throughout the world.

Craggs provides in his neat package of the composer a preface, a rather succinct biography of the composer, a detailed and informative section on the composer's works and performances, a discography, a sparsely annotated bibliography, an alphabetically arranged list of compositions, a chronologically arranged list of compositions, and a name index. The most notable unit in this volume is the list of the composer's works; it contains all the essential data regarding Mathias's compositions, including dates of first performances, artists who participated in the concerts, instrumentation, duration, publishers, and the like. The text will be of special interest to composers and choral conductors, and should be included in music library reference divisions.—**Robert Palmieri**

1280. Green, Jonathan D. **Carl Ruggles: A Bio-bibliography.** Westport, Conn., Greenwood Press, 1995. 148p. index. (Bio-bibliographies in Music, no.59). $55.00. ISBN 0-313-29456-9.

Green presents an informative and well-documented survey of the U.S. composer Carl Ruggles (1876-1971). As a composer, Ruggles is often mentioned with Charles Ives, Edgard Varèse, and Henry Cowell. All were musical innovators and experimenters and in many ways ahead of their time. Ruggles does not have a long list of compositions to his name; his entire published output is approximately 80 minutes in length; however, he is an important composer because he had his own particular idea of atonal music, which is apparent from his musical scores and his writings. Green mentions that in recent years there has been a resurgence of performances of Ruggles's works.

Carl Ruggles: A Bio-bibliography contains a biography of the composer, a list of works and performances (with pertinent data), a discography, an annotated bibliography that is well organized and highly informative, and a list of institutions that house archival materials about Ruggles. The volume also provides a preface, a name index, and a photograph. Green states that Ruggles's works showcase some of the twentieth century's grandest accomplishments in the art of composition. One hopes performing artists will take notice and investigate the music of Ruggles. The bio-bibliography is highly recommended for reference sections in libraries of music conservatories and university and colleges.—**Robert Palmieri**

1281. Nettl, Paul. **The Beethoven Encyclopedia.** New York, Carol Publishing Group, 1994. 325p. $12.95pa. ISBN 0-8065-1539-2.

With the possible exception of a thorough musicologist or Beethoven scholar, anybody who needs to look up facts on this protean composer should keep this volume in the library. The book is arranged alphabetically, in dictionary fashion, and it features facts, insignificant and highly significant, that made up Ludwig van Beethoven's life and life's work. A long time searching did not reveal any item not represented. Fascinating and trivial details abound. Under "Smoking," readers find out that Beethoven was a mild smoker. A complete list of books found in his library at the time of his death is included. There is also a reprint of a detailed contemporary report on his funeral.

Composers whose works are relevant to Beethoven's output are represented in well-written thumbnail sketches; personalities of the time are likewise documented; and, yes, there is even an entry on the film *Immortal Beloved*. The complete text of the *Heiligenstadt Testament* is furnished, and several entries are also peppered with excerpts from Beethoven's letters. In the back of the book is a complete chronology of the composer's life. The author, a professor of musicology at Indiana University, has provided us with one of those books that could go under the heading "If one only wants one book on the subject, this one will do nicely."—**Koraljka Lockhart**

1282. Smith, Carolyn J. **Peter Maxwell Davies: A Bio-bibliography.** Westport, Conn., Greenwood Press, 1995. 343p. index. (Bio-bibliographies in Music, no.57). $75.00. ISBN 0-313-26831-2.

Contemporary British composer/conductor Davies is given a comprehensive treatment in this text, no mean feat given his productivity and interest to scholars. The discography lists 158 recordings; there are 288 entries for works and premiere performances; and the bibliography of writings about Davies is 200-plus pages. A chronology of works is included as well, a valuable addition to those tracing the career of this prominent and popular figure in British music.

Entries for individual compositions list the title, the year, publication information (if published); premiere performance data (if known), and a cross-reference to both related bibliographical citations and recording information. Discography citations give recording label; catalog number; date; available formats (LP, cassette, or CD); album title; contents; and performers' names. The bibliographical section of the book is generously annotated. One black-and-white photograph of Davies precedes the text, and a brief biography gives a capable overview of Davies's personal and professional life. A comprehensive index concludes the book.

The author acknowledges that this is a provisional work, given that the composer is relatively young and famously prolific. This remains the most complete source of information about the work of England's (arguably) preeminent composer. Smith's writing is suitable; her research is excellent. Hers is the book of record regarding Davies through 1994, which is recommended for music libraries of any size.
—**Ed Volz**

1283. Sposato, Jeffrey S. **William Thomas McKinley: A Bio-bibliography.** Westport, Conn., Greenwood Press, 1995. 303p. index. (Bio-bibliographies in Music, no.56). $69.50. ISBN 0-313-28923-9.

McKinley, born in 1938, is a prolific composer as well as a jazz pianist. *The New Grove Dictionary of American Music* (see ARBA 88, entry 1277) devotes approximately two paragraphs to his biography but includes no bibliography. Author Sposato, in his desire to publicize McKinley's music, has documented and organized his musical output. Following a biographical sketch, the main section of the book extensively details his compositions and their performances, including program notes (mostly by McKinley) and bibliographical references, such as reviews, that describe each work. A discography lists recordings of McKinley's works, many released through a publishing cooperative that he started. A bibliography and several appendixes complete the volume. This bio-bibliography, which is chiefly a catalog of McKinley's works, is well crafted and is recommended to libraries with users interested in this composer and have the budget to purchase it.—**Allie Wise Goudy**

1284. Young, W. Murray. **The Sacred Dramas of J. S. Bach: A Reference and Textual Interpretation.** Jefferson, N.C., McFarland, 1994. 213p. index. $45.00. ISBN 0-89950-812-X.

This is the second reference work Young has produced dedicated to the vocal works of J. S. Bach. The present effort follows much the same tone and format as the earlier book titled *The Cantatas of J. S. Bach* (see ARBA 90, entry 1256). The new work includes vocal works not covered in his earlier publication. In particular, Young discusses the *Magnificat in D*, 6 Masses, 4 Passions, 8 Motets, 82 Motet movements from the cantatas, and the chorales found in the Christmas oratorio. The author provides an overview of each work before discussing its component parts. The overviews give historical background and highlight significant musicological information gleaned from Bach research. The data are sound but not particularly recent. No citation later than 1986 appears in this bibliography, and the research of one of the foremost Bach scholars, Christoph Wolff, is conspicuously absent.

Despite this, Young uses his sources to good advantage and makes concise and convincing arguments. Elsewhere he is freer with his commentary. This is especially true when dealing with individual choruses or arias from larger works. Here we find insightful remarks sprinkled amid statements of the obvious; this work appears to be geared toward undergraduate-level readers. Young does not seem interested in presenting new material, but rather in helping those learning about Bach or performing his choral works to gain a greater appreciation of the master's handiwork. In this he succeeds well, making this a useful handbook for church musicians, college teachers and students, and those looking for a brief but accurate introduction to Bach's sacred choral works.—**Gregg S. Geary**

CONDUCTORS

1285. Handy, D. Antoinette. **Black Conductors.** Metuchen, N.J., Scarecrow, 1995. 557p. illus. index. $69.50. ISBN 0-8108-2930-4.

This book profiles more than 100 black conductors or instrumental ensemble leaders from both the classical and jazz worlds. The main, 50-plus profiles are extensive and well documented, and each includes a photograph of the conductor. Those remaining are significantly briefer because, as Handy states, they were secondarily conductors, or because not enough information was available for a more in-depth profile.

Handy acknowledges a heavy reliance on Eileen Southern's *Biographical Dictionary of Afro-American and African Musicians* (see ARBA 83, entry 961), but she has extended Southern's coverage and included additional information provided by the conductors themselves, their families, and their staffs. Another publication, *Blacks in Classical Music* (see ARBA 89, entry 1224), also offers sources of information on some of the symphony orchestra conductors covered here, but Handy's book is more up-to-date and comprehensive for conductors, and her format provides information as well as access to information.

Black Conductors is an interesting and useful book, especially for the less readily available information on classical conductors. It is, however, fairly expensive, and academic and public libraries will have to balance its purchase with their public's needs.—**Allie Wise Goudy**

INSTRUMENTS

Cello

1286. Homuth, Donald. **Cello Music Since 1960: A Bibliography of Solo, Chamber, & Orchestral Works for the Solo Cellist.** Berkeley, Calif., Fallen Leaf Press, 1994. 451p. index. (Fallen Leaf Reference Books in Music, no.26). $69.50. ISBN 0-914913-27-1.

Donald Homuth has played and studied the cello professionally for more than 50 years. He is currently professor emeritus at San Jose State University and performs with the Opera San Jose and the San Jose Chamber Orchestra. He has been principal with a number of American orchestras.

Cello Music Since 1960, as the title says, lists more than 5,200 works for the cello written since 1960. Some 3,100 composers are included in this bibliography. Chamber ensembles, solo works, and accompanied compositions for piano, harpsichord, organ, harp, guitar, percussion, and electronic media are all covered.

The entries in this work consist of composer, title, date, publisher, first performance, and recordings. Basic entries are expanded where needed with special data on the instrumentation, new playing techniques, and difficulty. The main body of the work is divided into 18 categories according to scoring, followed by two indexes: one of composers, and one of cellists involved in premieres or recordings. Helpful lists include a list of music publishers and a list of record, disc, and tape labels, each with addresses.

The book is well-made, the typeface, layout, and binding typical of what one would expect. Music librarians will want to add this volume to their cello sections. General collections will find it useful as a community reference tool for local musicians.—**Ralph Lee Scott**

Harp

1287. Govea, Wenonah Milton. **Nineteenth- and Twentieth-Century Harpists: A Bio-Critical Sourcebook.** Westport, Conn., Greenwood Press, 1995. 330p. index. (Bio-Critical Sourcebooks on Musical Performance). $79.50. ISBN 0-313-27866-0.

Harps have been around for a long time. The contemporary double-action harp that covers the full range of musical notes is a product of a long tradition. While early cultures had harps in a primitive form, the nineteenth century saw the invention of the modern concert harp. Govea's work covers in a biographical format the contributions of many notable harpists of the last two centuries. Biographies include such memorable performers as Elias Alvars, Nicolas Bochsa, Jean-Baptiste Cardon, Oslan Marie-Claire Jamet, and Lilly Laskine. The biographies, numbering almost 70, contain, where possible, critical reviews, discographies, and selected bibliographies. The volume has an extensive index. Govea is professor emeritus of music at California State University, Hayward, and directs the university harp program. She has initiated the American Harp Society Summer Institute program and has assisted in the development of the American Harp Society Foundation. The volume is well crafted, and it is a delight to read the biographies. Music libraries will not want to be without this important work.—**Ralph Lee Scott**

Harpsichord and Clavichord

1288. Elste, Martin, comp. **Modern Harpsichord Music: A Discography.** Westport, Conn., Greenwood Press, 1995. 319p. index. (Discographies, no.58). $79.50. ISBN 0-313-29238-8.

With the revival of harpsichords as performance instruments beginning about 1890, two schools of thought arose among builders of new instruments. One favored the heavy, steel-framed, and resonant hybrid harpsichord devised by nineteenth-century European piano manufacturers, while the other group modeled their instruments on original harpsichords of the Renaissance and Baroque, emulating their light wood frames and more complex tones. The apparent victory of the latter school, according to the author, has created the need for this discography. Because most twentieth-century harpsichord music has been written for the modern, soon-to-be-extinct instrument, this compilation aims at being a complete listing of every recorded performance (including video) on instruments considered authentic for contemporary harpsichord compositions.

Front matter includes the table of contents; a list of abbreviations, a how-to-use section clearly explaining the book's scope and organization; a key to entries—which would have been easier to access on an inside cover; and an introduction stating the premises described above plus a short discussion of some significant composers, performers, and recordings among the entries.

The 825 entries are followed by 6 indexes, 4 of which provide alternative access to entries—by types of composition, by record companies and numbers, by performing artists, and by harpsichord makers. A chronological list of compositions and a list of recordings with three or more modern harpsichord pieces seem superfluous. Musicians would undoubtedly prefer to see this space devoted to information about harpsichord makers and descriptions of instruments, which are scanty. The references section also skimps on harpsichords. Most of the citations are discographies—although a glaring omission is *Harpsichord and Clavichord Music of the Twentieth Century* (see ARBA 94, entry 1335), which lists sources for musical scores and recorded performances, lacking in the present work.

Readability of the entry section is poor. Running heads placed only on right-hand pages in small typeface make locating information difficult. Although there is plenty of blank space around entries, typeface legibility is poor. Despite these flaws, its uniqueness makes this a reasonable choice for reference collections of scholarly music libraries.—**Larry Lobel**

Organ

1289. Arnold, Corliss Richard. **Organ Literature: A Comprehensive Survey.** 3d ed. Metuchen, N.J., Scarecrow, 1995. 2v. maps. index. $97.50/set. ISBN 0-8108-2970-3.

Many years after its 1st edition (see ARBA 74, entry 1063), Arnold's *Organ Literature* has become a basic reference tool for organists throughout the United States. Each subsequent edition has been expanded, and the present 2-volume 3d edition provides nearly 1,400 pages of information. While the focus is purely on the music literature for the organ, the discussion includes relevant references to the instrument's history and technical features.

Volume 1 provides a historical survey of organ music from 1300 to the present, while volume 2 gives biographical information on organ composers. The historical survey includes discussions of style periods and national schools of organ composition. Each chapter has a historical background box that provides a list of historical events, often nonmusical, which help provide a context for the discussions. There are also timelines listing the major organ composers of major periods, which help the reader place composers in proper chronological relationship to one another. Also distributed throughout volume 1 are useful charts and graphs of such data as stop lists of organs by significant organ builders; lists of important treatises on organ performance; and useful maps, such as the one that locates the German cities connected with Johann Sebastian Bach. Substantial bibliographies of cited material and corollary reading close each chapter. A special feature of note is an appendix that contains a chart of all of Bach's organ works and cites their location in 14 different editions.

While volume 2 is identified as the biographical catalog, it may better be called the list of works because more biographical information is often presented in volume 1. Instead, volume 2 contains only brief biographical information, usually confined to birth and death dates, education, and career highlights. The lists of works are significant, nonetheless, for they present ample organ music contained in separate publications, collected works, anthologies, and monuments of music. Each entry also provides publication information to aid those wishing to order. What is lacking, however, is a list of addresses for the major organ publishers, which would have been a welcome addition. Both volumes have their own indexes.

The writing style is a bit dull and uninspired but remains loyal to the facts. Discussions of musical style could be enhanced by the inclusion of musical examples. For instance, the discussion of ornamentation in the French School, 1600-1800, provides no notation to show this technique. One or two examples could quickly illustrate this essential stylistic trait that the author fails to adequately describe. Also, with reference to so many foreign terms and unique names of organ stops, a glossary of organ terms would also be a useful addition. Despite room for improvements, this edition represents a major expansion and update of the previous edition. It is a valuable resource for students of the organ and professional organists alike. Aside from its value as a reference tool, this work could be used as a text for organ literature classes.

—Gregg S. Geary

Other

1290. Holston, Kim R., comp. **The Marching Band Handbook: Competitions, Instruments, Clinics....** 2d ed. Jefferson, N.C., McFarland, 1994. 172p. illus. index. $28.50pa. ISBN 0-89950-922-3.

This excellent handbook hardly requires a review. Compiled by a librarian, and laden with clear photographs of bands, color guards, flag drills, baton twirlers, and other marching band activities, it presents to newly appointed or veteran band leaders all that they might wish to know about the subject. Included are such items as where to buy equipment, instruments, and uniforms; location of national or local competitions; a national directory of parades, with addresses of their organizers; how to arrange travel for large groups of musicians and their baggage; and a chapter on awards, medals, and so on. One chapter deals with musical instruments and their care, while another presents a long list of names of musical pieces that "have been used successfully by indoor color guards, marching bands, and dance-twirl squads." Each chapter has its own topical bibliography, and there is a nine-page general bibliography at the end.

For ease in finding a specific musical item, address of an event, or title of an agency or association, each entry in the book's directories and bibliographies is numbered. The index then lists by item number the titles of all books and articles in the chapter and general bibliographies, as well as all agencies, dealers, clinics, workshops, and other items. The book is highly recommended for high school and college libraries and for all agencies that are affiliated with band music. [R: VOYA, Feb 95, p. 371]—**Raymund F. Wood**

Percussion

1291. **Encyclopedia of Percussion.** John H. Beck, ed. Hamden, Conn., Garland, 1995. 436p. illus. index. (Garland Reference Library of the Humanities, v.947). $75.00. ISBN 0-8240-4788-5.

Thirty contributors make this up-to-date resource a suitable, but fairly pricey, addition to school, music, academic, and public libraries. It is a useful guide for general knowledge as well as for research. Focusing on percussion as defined by the Western tradition, it also includes the world at large with the more common percussion instruments. Entries are to instruments whose sound is percussion (e.g., snare drums, triangles); concussion (e.g., castanets, claves); friction (e.g., cuica, claves); and special sound effects (e.g., aerophones, chordophones).

The text is divided into three major divisions. The first is an extensive alphabetical list of percussion instruments and terms. The second consists of illustrations of percussion instruments, and the final section has articles on all the major instruments, from the basel drum to the xylophone. Three appendixes and a detailed alphabetical index conclude the work. Appendix A supplies definitions of symbols and the range of mallet instruments; appendix B consists of a table of percussion instruments and terms in English, French, German, and Italian; and appendix C provides a selected list of published writings on methods for percussion that date from as early as 1588.—**James M. Murray**

Piano

1292. Edel, Theodore. **Piano Music for One Hand.** Bloomington, Ind., Indiana University Press, 1994. 121p. $19.95. ISBN 0-253-31905-6.

Pianists have long been intrigued by works written for one hand alone. In attempting to perform such compositions, the pianist accepts the challenge of not only being able to physically perform the work, which is a trick in itself, but also of treating the music sensitively, and at the same time attempting to make the piece sound like it is being played by two hands. *Piano Music for One Hand* is an excellent volume that covers this subject in an interesting and thorough style. In Edel's book, the art of performing with one hand is divided into two sections: Part 1 deals with the history of the art, which is well covered and most interesting, and a look at four noteworthy pianists who were historically important in the field. The four pianists are: Alexander Dreyschock, Adolfo Fumagalli, Geza Zichy, and Paul Wittgenstein. Edel discusses their careers as performing pianists and comments on how intrigued the public was with this phenomenon.

Part 2 lists compositions written for one hand: solo works for left hand alone, solo works for right hand alone, works for one hand and orchestra, and chamber music. This second unit lists works under the composer's name, with compositions receiving critical commentary by the author. The volume offers bibliographical material on the subject along with data regarding publishers and date of composition. All in all, it would be difficult to find a book written as well as this one on the art of one-hand piano music. Bravo to Edel on his excellent presentation of the subject! This volume is highly recommended to performing pianists, piano teachers and their students, and composers. *Piano Music for One Hand* is a must for inclusion in libraries of music schools/conservatories and allied performing arts.—**Robert Palmieri**

1293. Gillespie, John, and Anna Gillespie. **Notable Twentieth-Century Pianists: A Bio-Critical Sourcebook.** Westport, Conn., Greenwood Press, 1995. 2v. illus. index. (Bio-Critical Sourcebooks on Musical Performance). $125.00/set. ISBN 0-313-25660-8.

The idea of interviewing musical artists—in this case pianists and pedagogues—has become a popular part of keyboard magazines and journals. People want to know everything about a celebrity; therefore, there is interest in this type of essay. The work discussed here is not based on interviews, but is a compilation of detailed examinations of 100 pianists, with information derived from years of library research and correspondence. Authors John and Anna Gillespie, in their 2-volume set *Notable Twentieth-Century Pianists*, delve into the lives, performances, and recordings of 100 notable twentieth-century pianists. Those chosen to be included were first named on a list compiled by pianists and pedagogues in music conservatories and colleges throughout the United States. The authors then tabulated the results and supplied their own choices as well.

The Gillespies admit that the final list of 100 pianists could not possibly please everyone, but the list does cover the major pianists of this century, from the earliest (by date of birth) pianist listed—Francis Planté (1839-1934)—to the latest pianist—Barry Douglas (b.1960). This sourcebook contains biographical material; style analyses (taken from reviews, recordings, articles, and the like); references and reviews; and a representative discography. The material in the volumes makes for fascinating reading, as it not only discusses the artists' backgrounds but also looks into their performance styles, which can vary greatly from artist to artist.

The volumes include a preface, a general bibliography for the set, illustrations, and a name index (in volume 2). *Notable Twentieth-Century Pianists* will be of interest to pianists and pedagogues and should be included in reference sections of music conservatory libraries and university/college music libraries.
—**Robert Palmieri**

Recorder

1294. Griscom, Richard, and David Lasocki. **The Recorder: A Guide to Writings About the Instrument for Players and Researchers.** Hamden, Conn., Garland, 1994. 504p. index. (Music Research and Information Guides, v.19; Garland Reference Library of the Humanities, v.1026). $70.00. ISBN 0-8240-2945-3.

The recorder had developed as a mainstream instrument by the beginning of the fifteenth century, and played an important role during the baroque period in vocal and pastoral music, sonatas, concertos, and chamber music, performed both by amateurs and professionals. This book provides a guide to writings about the recorder for researchers and performers. More than 1,500 items have been included. Emphasis has been placed on materials concerning the repertory, design, and technique of the instrument. The authors point out in the preface that their emphasis in selecting sources "has been on what is relevant, what is significant, and what is readily available in the United States."

Articles, books, dissertations, and theses devoted to the recorder are covered. In addition, some works that have large sections devoted to the recorder are also included. The book is divided into 33 chapters arranged by subject. The first eight chapters are devoted to general topics including bibliographies of writings, general surveys, studies of etymology, symbolism, and literary references to the recorder. A second section of eight chapters is concerned with the recorder as a physical object and lists recorder makers both present and historical, collections of historical instruments, biographies of recorder makers, and technical studies. The third section is concerned with performance and includes chapters on historical methods, historical performance practices, modern technique and performance, new techniques in twentieth-century music, recorder ensembles, and pedagogy and study. The fourth section includes biographical chapters on performers, writers, and composers both historical and modern. The final section concludes with four miscellaneous chapters on fipple flutes, relevant periodicals, recorder societies, and essays on the future of the recorder.

Appendixes contain a list of theses, dissertations, and similar works not consulted. A complete index is also provided. *The Recorder* provides a much-needed source for research concerning this instrument. It is even more welcome considering the recent revival of interest in the recorder and Renaissance and Baroque music. This book is recommended for all library collections and for individuals who have an interest in playing or researching recorder music.—**Robert L. Wick**

Voice

1295. Ord, Alan J. **Songs for Bass Voice: An Annotated Guide to Works for Bass Voice.** Metuchen, N.J., Scarecrow, 1994. 218p. index. $32.50. ISBN 0-8108-2897-9.

Ord, a member of the music faculty of the University of Alberta, states that he compiled this guide because of his own difficulties in finding true bass solo music. Many songs supposedly for basses are more appropriate for baritones. His list includes more than 2,000 entries, arranged in thematic chapters. Most works are in print, and Ord includes a list of publishers' addresses. The first chapters list anthology contents by difficulty level. Subsequent chapters provide guidance to songs by a variety of approaches, such as song cycles, opera excerpts, church music, Broadway musical selections, and sea chanteys. Songs range from the obscure to the familiar, the latter often being listed several times, sometimes in more than one collection (e.g., "O Isis und Osiris" from Wolfgang Amadeus Mozart's *Die Zauberflöte* has six listings). Each entry includes the collection in which it can be found, language, tessitura, range, tempo, meter, difficulty, and a brief annotation. Indexes list songs by composer, title, and genre. Indexing is careful, thorough, and generally accurate (although five songs by Arnold Schoenberg do not appear in the composer index). Basses from beginners to professionals, and their teachers, will find numerous useful suggestions and discover previously unknown repertoire. The book is appropriate for conservatories and other academic music libraries.—**Richard S. Watts**

1296. Switten, Margaret L. **Music and Poetry in the Middle Ages: A Guide to Research on French and Occitan Song, 1100-1400.** Hamden, Conn., Garland, 1995. 452p. index. (Garland Medieval Bibliographies, v.19; Garland Reference Library of the Humanities, v.1102). $73.00. ISBN 0-8240-4797-4.

In creating this research guide, Switten has done a great service to all persons interested in the medieval French or Occitan lyric. She begins with a lengthy introduction that lays out in a clearly organized fashion the state of research in areas of both poetry and music, for her central tenet is that this repertoire must be studied from an interdisciplinary perspective. After a summary of the repertoire and of responses to it over the centuries, Switten goes on to discuss the perspectives presented by published editions of both poetry and music. Perhaps the most challenging section of the introduction is that devoted to the ways in which modern critical theories have been applied to the study of the medieval lyric. Here she not only deals with ideas as diverse as semiotics and intertextuality, but presents the advantages and disadvantages of each theoretical approach to the study of medieval song. Finally, she discusses issues of performance practice as they apply to medieval music.

The bibliography that follows is arranged into several general categories and emphasizes literature (books, facsimiles, editions, articles) of the last 15 years, although major research published before 1980 is also included. Most listings include annotations that describe the item's contents, and sometimes present evaluations as well. Then comes an excellent discography, with entries that list all performers and all relevant pieces on each recording. Most bear brief annotations as well. The book closes with two indexes that enable the reader to locate specific lyrics, poets, composers, and researchers dealt with in the body of the book.

This excellent book has few flaws, and only one that is particularly troublesome: Quotations from foreign-language sources are almost always left untranslated, thus limiting the book's usefulness to those unacquainted with several ancient and modern tongues. This problem is most annoying in the discography, where the names of instruments are given as they appear in the liner notes, a great many of which are in German or French.

Despite these problems, however, Switten's book is a valuable resource for a wide spectrum of users. Specialists in medieval music or literature will find it a helpful guide to major research in fields not their own. Students will consult it often in their work in medieval poetry or music, as will those performing and recording this music, and even those educated amateurs who are drawn to the repertoire.

—**Karin Pendle**

MUSICAL FORMS
Choral

1297. Green, Jonathan D. **A Conductor's Guide to Choral-Orchestral Works.** Metuchen, N.J., Scarecrow, 1994. 307p. $37.50. ISBN 0-8108-2712-3.

Based on Green's doctoral dissertation, this is a practical performing handbook of 90 works written between 1900 and 1972 by 49 composers. To be included a work must be for full mixed chorus and orchestra (many also include solo voices), have English words (at least in part), be at least 15 minutes in duration, and have performance materials commercially available. Both sacred and secular works are covered.

The entries, arranged alphabetically by composer and subarranged by date of composition, normally include title; date of composition; performance time; source of text; detailed list of performing forces; date, place, and principal performers of the first performance; editions available; location of the composer's autograph score; historical notes; extensive commentary on performance issues; a discography; and a selected bibliography of reviews and criticism. The author assigns each work a performance difficulty rating on a five-point scale from easy (accessible to inexperienced musicians) to difficult (challenging even to first-rate professionals). An introductory chapter surveys major trends in twentieth-century choral composition, and there are brief biographies (with a bibliography) of each composer. An annotated listing of text sources (including translators), a directory of publishers, and a general bibliography are appended. The audience is primarily practicing choral directors and libraries serving them.

—Paul B. Cors

Classical

1298. Heller, Craig. **From Metal to Mozart: The Rock and Roll Guide to Classical Music.** San Francisco, Calif., Chronicle Books, 1994. 223p. index. $9.95pa. ISBN 0-8118-0576-X.

Rock fan Heller began to love classical music when, discouraged by a lack of interesting alternatives in his music of choice, he set out systematically to explore the classical repertoire. In this book he shares his thoughts and experiences with other rock and roll enthusiasts who, like him, wish to expand their musical horizons. The book is divided into two parts. In part 1, Heller lists and defines basic classical music terminology and introduces a number of important composers active from ca.1700 to the present, proposing rock and roll equivalents to make the reader feel comfortable with the material. Part 2, subtitled "Help!" outlines 3 purposeful approaches to learning about classical music. Heller recommends works that are of good-to-great quality and does not shrink from including pieces that are not easy listening, such as Gustav Mahler's 2d symphony or Arnold Schoenberg's *Five Pieces for Orchestra*.

Heller's style is direct, casual, and nonthreatening, his commentary written by a nonmusician for nonmusicians. At times the writing can be rather glib, giving the impression that the author is talking down to his audience. This is most evident in the opening chapters, particularly in the annotated list of composers who seem to have been chosen as much for their possible parallels in the world of rock as for their intrinsic merits. More often, however, the comments are sound and sensible, as in "Classical Music: Your Basic Moves."

One major flaw of the work is Heller's insistence, to the point of phobia, on avoiding any type of vocal music. Not only does he fail to include vocal works among those recommended to his readers, but he does not even define opera, oratorio, cantata, or art-song in his otherwise basic glossary. Even so great a master of vocal music as George Frideric Handel is represented by a single instrumental work. In fact, Heller touts as an advantage of classical music that one need not be concerned about lyrics because there are none. Surely the hypothetical rock fan would not be terribly harmed by listening to a CD of selections from *Messiah* or watching a video of *La Bohème* or *Amahl and the Night Visitors*. On the whole, however, the positive features of this beginner's guide to outweigh the negative ones.—**Karin Pendle**

1299. Klaus, Kenneth S. **Chamber Music for Solo Voice and Instruments 1960-1989: An Annotated Guide.** Berkeley, Calif., Fallen Leaf Press, 1994. 222p. index. (Fallen Leaf Reference Books in Music, no.29). $35.00. ISBN 0-914913-30-1.

Based on Klaus's doctoral dissertation, this volume covers some 700 works of more than 600 contemporary composers for solo voice and two or more instruments. The title could be more precise: The volume covers music composed, as well as published, between 1960 and 1989. Moreover, it is selective, not comprehensive, although no real criteria are given for inclusion or omission. Arrangement is by voice type with data, as appropriate, for title, text, publisher, series, instrumentation, difficulty, vocal range, duration, language, and comments. More than half the entries have annotations; these comments are often no more than a couple of words, but are informative and sometimes intriguing (e.g., "Soprano must whistle accurately and play some percussion instruments"). There are indexes for composers, literary sources, music publishers, and instruments. The typography and layout are handsome compared to many music bibliographies.

There are several other books that cover portions of this topic, but these largely focus on voice with a particular instrument. An exception is Patricia Lust's *American Vocal Chamber Music, 1945-1980: An Annotated Bibliography* (see ARBA 86, entry 1265), which this volume complements but does not replace. Klaus extends Lust's coverage by a decade, but Lust has longer annotations, and includes scores for voice and single as well as multiple instruments. Where they overlap in scope, each has items not in the other.

—**Robert Skinner**

Operatic

1300. Osborne, Charles. **The Bel Canto Operas of Rossini, Donizetti, and Bellini.** Portland, Oreg., Amadeus Press/Timber Press, 1994. 378p. index. $29.95. ISBN 0-931340-71-3.

The term *bel canto* generally refers to a method of singing taught by the Italian masters during the seventeenth and eighteenth centuries that is noted for its beauty and smoothness of presentation. While the term was not generally used until the early nineteenth century, it is now used mainly to describe Italian opera from Verdi through the featured composers of this book: Rossini, Donizetti, and Bellini. The work is divided into three sections, one for each of the composers. Each man's operas are taken one at a time, beginning with a list of the principal characters, the libretto composer (if separate), a short performance history, and a plot outline. More than 115 operas are covered in the book: 40 by Rossini, 66 by Donizetti, and 10 by Bellini. Appendixes include a selective discography (89 items); a selective bibliography (17 items); a list of the works of Rossini, Donizetti, and Bellini in the order of composition; and an index.

Osborne is an international authority on opera and a Verdi specialist. His book is well presented and clearly written. It is highly recommended for opera buffs and for public and academic libraries with music collections of almost any size. It will make an excellent home reference work on bel canto opera.

—**Robert L. Wick**

1301. Smith, Eric Ledell. **Blacks in Opera: An Encyclopedia of People and Companies, 1873-1993.** Jefferson, N.C., McFarland, 1995. 236p. illus. index. $49.95. ISBN 0-89950-813-8.

The difficulties of compiling any specialized encyclopedia are staggering to contemplate. The best of such works are marked by a consistency from entry to entry using the same format and covering the same data, as well as by the accuracy of the information provided. This work is too inconsistent and incomplete in the way the entries are handled to be a successful guide to its subject. Its fullest entries are reserved for the most famous, which is a pity because it is not hard to locate solid information about the careers of singers such as Leontyne Price or Kathleen Battle. The entries for the famous include birth data (frequently incomplete) and sections devoted to education, awards, opera companies and orchestras with which the singer has appeared, debuts, a repertoire, videos, recordings (without label information), reviews, a bibliography, and an obituary. Almost no entries contain all of these sections, and the review section is often left out.

Information provided in each of the sections is often spotty. The entry for Grace Bumbry's repertoire excludes any mention of the soprano roles that dominated the last half of her career and is limited to the mezzo soprano roles of her early years. The recordings section for Marian Anderson gives no indication of her huge output of recordings, which have remained in print in their original 78 format through LP and current CD compilations. Some important singers are all but passed over. Ella Lee, a soprano with a distinguished career, receives note of her birth in Texas, appearances with three opera companies, one review, and one bibliographical entry. More should be mentioned about Altonell Hines than her birth and death dates, where she studied, and the fact that she created an important role in *Four Saints in Three Acts*. She is on the original recording of excerpts, which is not mentioned despite its historical importance as having been conducted by composer Virgil Thomson.

This work will certainly be useful to many users. The range of its coverage, including composers, directors, conductors, and others in the opera world, is impressive. The frustration lies in the lack of information about many of the artists discussed in the work. It certainly gives an impressive overview of just how strong and important the black gift to the world's opera houses has been and continues to be. The book does have a superb index that leads the reader to information within the entries perfectly. The encyclopedia is useful as far as it goes.—**George Louis Mayer**

1302. Zietz, Karyl Lynn. **Opera Companies and Houses of the United States: A Comprehensive, Illustrated Reference.** Jefferson, N.C., McFarland, 1995. 335p. illus. index. $49.95. ISBN 0-89950-955-X.

Information concerning larger opera companies in the United States is generally available in a number of sources, including *New Grove Dictionary of Opera* (see ARBA 94, entry 1356) and David Ewen's *Encyclopedia of the Opera*, and others. But when it comes to the smaller opera companies, reliable data has been much harder to come by. Zietz has relieved this condition to a great extent with this reference source. *Opera Companies and Houses of the United States* provides information on 92 opera companies in 41 states. Some of the smaller opera companies included are not represented in any other sources generally available. And, as Zietz points out in the introduction, there is "difficulty in compiling a reference book on opera [because] so much contradictory and unreliable information has been published . . . [and] the problem is compounded because someone else . . . uses this unreliable material . . ." passing it on from one source to another. To guard against the proliferation of incorrect information, Zietz has verified all data presented and avoided including questionable information on companies.

Each opera company is presented with a brief explanation of its history and support sources. Also, a chronicle of premiere performances and major presentations by the company is listed. A separate section on each company's opera house or performance facility is usually provided, along with a photograph. Finally a section listed the company staff and repertory through 1994 is supplied. Appendixes include a selected bibliography (143 items), opera company and opera house booklets and pamphlets (21 items), a list of opera company and opera house magazines and newsletters (47 items), and a brief bibliography of magazines and journals devoted to opera worldwide (11 items). The book is well indexed. One missing feature of interest is a table showing which companies have performed which operas and when, to provide an interesting look at their popularity historically and geographically.

This work is highly recommended for all libraries. Because it lists opera companies large and small, it will serve as a basic reference source on opera for smaller collections, and at the same time be a valuable addition for resources on the seldom-listed companies for large public or research libraries.

—**Robert L. Wick**

Popular

General Works

1303. **Billboard Music Yearbook 1994.** Joel Whitburn, comp. Menomonee Falls, Wis., Record Research, 1995. 239p. illus. $29.95pa. ISBN 0-89820-110-1.

The productivity of Record Research continues. Here are the chart performances of all the major music activity of 1994, as reported by *Billboard* magazine. There are three major sections: the singles, the albums, and the number one hits. Under the singles, Whitburn has listed all the "Hot 100" action, and all the airplays for the top 100 tunes, with further subdivisions for country singles, R & B singles, adult contemporary singles, and tracks lifted from rock albums. The arrangement is by artist, and there are chronological listings. In addition, there is an alphabetically arranged listing of every song title.

The albums section is arranged by genre (pop, country, R & B) and subarranged by artist name. The "Number One Hits" section is a chronological listing of all the 1994 hits in 17 categories not covered by the other 2 sections of singles and albums. These have fewer fans (e.g., rap, New Age, jazz, classical, gospel, Latin, and others). Whitburn also provides updates, such as charting the 1993 hits that lasted through part of 1994, and even charting the 1994 hits that lasted through May of 1995, when the book was put together—impressive.

Record Research has also assembled a necrology for 1994, but not everybody listed was in the music business. There are death notices for the likes of Cesar Romero and Henry Morgan, neither of whom (as this reviewer understands it) could carry a tune. Other useful items include black-and-white reproductions of album covers and a general look at the recording scene in 1994. The overview provided by the introduction does a good job in describing the charts, for they do look complicated to use. However, there are lots of explanations, so it is merely a question of reading the prefaces.—**Dean Tudor**

1304. Claghorn, Charles E. **Popular Bands and Performers.** Lanham, Md., Scarecrow, 1995. 467p. $75.00. ISBN 0-8108-2976-2.

Compiled from books, magazines, and newspapers, this resource is a dictionary of popular music performers. Its brief entries give the artist's name and other relevant information. Entries contain some, but never all, of the following: birth and death dates, album or singles titles, birthplace, music awards won, marital data, and so on. The types of music covered are rock, jazz, pop, rhythm and blues, and rap. Presumably, one would use this book to verify names of singers and musical groups and read a nugget of career information.

This reviewer spent an hour with the book in hand, trying to find a mistake-free page. That errorless page went undiscovered. For example, on page 110, Thomas Dolby's "The Golden Age of Wireless" is listed as "Golden Age of the Wilderness"; on page 122, John Cale is named "John Cole"; on page 294, the band NRBQ is listed as "NRBO"; on page 320, the rock band Wolfgang Press is filed under "Press, Wolfgang." There are hundreds more of these simple factual miscues. Errors of omission abound—cross-references are not made, band membership line-ups are incomplete, and album titles are given as names of songs and the reverse. This reviewer's favorite enigmatic entry is for the English band Sloan: "Hot Single 'Smeared' on WFIT Playlist in March 1993." Correct information on musicians is available in a host of publications. The reader is advised to look elsewhere.—**Ed Volz**

1305. **Contemporary Musicians: Profiles of the People in Music. Volume 13.** Suzanne M. Bourgoin, ed. Detroit, Gale, 1995. 322p. illus. index. $63.00. ISBN 0-8103-5737-2. ISSN 1044-2197.

Written in the same format as previous volumes in the series, volume 13 profiles 81 personalities who create or influence the music heard today. The information for each person or group includes a photograph, a brief biography, and a history of career highlights with examples of critical response to the artist's work. A selected discography of recordings and sources of additional information in books and periodical articles are also listed for each biographee. A wide range of musical talent is presented, from Lawrence Welk to Easy-E, including band leaders, rock groups, and opera singers.

Most of the major contributors to the popular music scene are found here and easily located through the cumulative index in the back of all volumes. A cumulative subject index classifies the information by type, such as instrument, kind of music, and occupation (conductor, producer, and so forth). The advantage of this series is that a great deal of information can be found easily in one source. It is easy to read and entertaining. The information is not exhaustive, as much information will also be available elsewhere, and serious researchers will have to use other sources. However, this source will satisfy the information needs of most people. Some listees have been on the music scene long enough to have new and revised listings (which began with volume 11). This series will be appreciated in every library where information is sought about the makers of contemporary music.—**Marilyn Strong Noronha**

1306. **The Da Capo Companion to 20th-Century Popular Music.** rev. ed. By Phil Hardy and Dave Laing. New York, Da Capo Press, 1995. 1211p. index. $29.50pa. ISBN 0-306-80640-1.

This revised edition of *The Da Capo Companion to 20th-Century Popular Music* contains profiles of more than 2,000 recording artists who have contributed to popular music in the twentieth century. Individuals listed include singers, band leaders, instrumentalists, vocal groups, and some important figures who are generally behind the scenes in the popular music industry. Individuals from all branches of popular music have been included—pop, jazz, old time, rock and roll, easy listening, and so on—and groups are listed in addition to individual members.

This edition has more than 200 new entries, generally of individuals who became prominent in the 1980s or 1990s. Each entry contains the name of the individual or group, date and place of birth, lists of recordings, and a brief biography. In addition, boldfaced items in each entry indicate that they may be looked up in the *Companion* for additional information. The connections between genres and individuals make this volume unique in music reference works, and the writing is entertaining and exceptionally readable. Appendixes include a glossary of styles and genres, an index of entries and cross-references, and an index of song and album titles.

The premier edition of this work was published as *The Faber Companion to 20th-Century Popular Music* (1990) and immediately became a standard reference work in the field. Hardy and Laing have improved the volume with this edition, which is destined to become even more important as a reference work in the area of popular music. It is recommended for personal libraries and is especially recommended for smaller academic and public libraries where each music reference book must provide as much information as possible.—**Robert L. Wick**

1307. DiMartino, Dave. **Singer-Songwriters: Pop Music's Performer-Composers, from A to Zevon.** New York, Billboard Books/Watson-Guptill, 1994. 306p. illus. index. (Billboard Hitmakers Series). $21.95pa. ISBN 0-8230-7629-6.

While there is no shortage of biographical reference works on popular musicians, this work is a notable addition to the field. The author has managed to identify performers who have attained some measure of stability and endurance in a profession that is accustomed to transitory fame. DiMartino is refreshingly candid about this selection process. To begin, he focused only on singer-songwriters who are pop artists as opposed to those who perform R & B or country. They must also have made solo recordings, be regarded as solo artists, write a majority of the songs they sing, and enjoy some commercial success or have made a significant contribution to the field of songwriting. Even after a candidate survived this winnowing process, the author exercised a measure of personal discretion to pare the list to 208 artists.

Thankfully, this is not another list of top-selling artists with only the scantiest data on each personality. Because of the author's selection process, he is able to devote an average of one-and-a-half double-column pages to each performer. The writing style is informal but not without authority, typical of the author's other venues, which include *Musician*, *Entertainment Weekly*, *Rolling Stone*, and *Village Voice*. The insightful details and evaluative commentary in most entries place this work above other similar reference tools. In addition to biographical information and a discussion of the subject's artistic development, each entry includes a profile of the artist's significant songs and albums. These titles are gleaned from *Billboard* charts and provide label name and year of release. Most entries are accompanied by a generously sized black-and-white photo of the singer. A copious index allows users to locate quickly a favorite song and the singer who wrote it. This work should prove valuable to any public, college, or university library.—**Gregg S. Geary**

1308. Elrod, Bruce C. *Your Hit Parade* **& American Top Ten Hits: A Week-by-Week Guide to the Nation's Favorite Music, 1935-1994.** 4th ed. Ann Arbor, Mich., Popular Culture, Ink., 1994. 655p. illus. index. $80.00. ISBN 1-56075-037-5.

The preface by Elrod in this edition is a nostalgia trip in itself. This reference work has its origins in the radio and television programs of the same name. The first radio broadcast of *Your Hit Parade* was on April 20, 1935. Entries are arranged in chronological order, week by week, with most entries providing the top 10 hits. Some list the top 15 favorites. For each title the entry also includes the top hit recording artist, group, or band/orchestra. Nicely dispersed are black-and-white photographs—some are full page—of selected artists. A variety of trivia quizzes (fortunately with the answers provided on separate pages) is thrown in from time to time.

Because of the diversity of popular music as it has evolved since the 1960s, there are a number of tables showing the top hits year by year in specific categories—adult contemporary, country and western, rhythm-and-blues, easy listening, pop albums, and even the top classical albums. The indexing is wonderfully simple with two indexes offered: by performer and by song title. A six-digit numerical citation refers the user to the weekly chart dates.

With the current trend in radio programming toward considerable retrospective broadcasting of popular music, this volume should be included in the reference collection of most public and academic libraries.—**Louis G. Zelenka**

1309. Goodfellow, William D. **SongCite: An Index to Popular Songs.** Hamden, Conn., Garland, 1995. 433p. $60.00. ISBN 0-8153-2059-0.

This index identifies more than 7,000 popular songs, all recently published, or republished, in 248 music books. All of the selected publications represent piano and vocal arrangements. Although most selections are works of twentieth-century composers, more than 350 of the songs are listed as anonymous compositions.

Indexing is convenient by bibliography of the indexed collections; composers; title and first line; and motion pictures, television productions, or musicals. Librarians and researchers will find this index to be an excellent source for locating the words and music to recent and standard popular songs that have been published since 1988.—**Louis G. Zelenka**

1310. **The Guinness Encyclopedia of Popular Music.** 2d ed. Colin Larkin, ed. Enfield, England, Guinness Publishing and New York, Stockton Press/Grove's Dictionaries of Music, 1995. 6v. index. $495.00/set. ISBN 1-56159-176-9.

This encyclopedia has been revised and expanded from 4 volumes to 6 with more than 40,000 entries. The work is strictly alphabetical and not divided by class or category. According to the editor, more than 70 percent of the entries have been expanded. When appropriate, books about the person or topic have been added at the end of entries in a "Further Reading" list. Videos are now listed, and record labels have begun to be added to the album section. The number of contributors to the set has been pared from about 82 to 30. International in scope, the encyclopedia covers all facets of popular music, including bands, musical groups, vocalists, lyricists, composers, record companies, and definitions of terms. It also includes stage productions and films featuring pop stars and pop music, with information about the plots.

The majority of entries focus on biographical information and musical groups. The biographical information includes birth and death dates if known, along with highlights of careers that discuss successes and disappointments, noting performances and important recordings. Entries vary from several paragraphs to several pages in length for stellar persons or groups such as the Beatles. Bold typeface within the entry acts as a cross-reference to related articles. The major emphasis is still on the United Kingdom and the United States. The most commonly accepted opinion is the one expressed.

There are more listings for music groups and artists after 1960 because more bands and vocalists emerged during this period and became famous. Several new areas covered include Latin music from Cuba and Puerto Rico, reggae from Jamaica, and African pop. Light opera has been omitted unless the composers and singers of this medium have done significant work in pop. Volume 6 has an extensive bibliography by artist and subject, allowing the user to easily locate additional information on a chosen topic. A 239-page subject index follows this with topics having an entry indicated in bold typeface. A quick reference guide at the end of the volume lists all the entries alphabetically. The entries are well researched and well written. This encyclopedia remains the most comprehensive reference work devoted to twentieth-century popular music. It will be a necessary purchase in any music library and in all libraries where there are many questions about popular music.—**Marilyn Strong Noronha**

1311. Haggerty, Gary. **A Guide to Popular Music Reference Books: An Annotated Bibliography.** Westport, Conn., Greenwood Press, 1995. 210p. index. (Music Reference Collection, no.47). $59.95. ISBN 0-313-29661-8.

As another volume in the impressive Greenwood Press Music Reference Collection, Haggerty's book provides a guide for locating information on popular music composers, musicians, and the popular music industry in general. Popular music is defined as "musical styles that have developed measurable commercial success through recordings and live performances. It is music that was (and is) produced for mass dissemination. Classical or art music is of course excluded" (introduction).

The work includes jazz, musical theater, rhythm and blues, rockabilly, Tin Pan Alley, and country music in addition to what is usually referred to as rock music. There are more than 400 annotated entries. These are limited to recent publications, usually works published within the past 20 years, which cover bibliographies, indexes to periodicals, indexes to printed and recorded music, dictionaries and encyclopedias, biographies, dictionaries of terms, directories, general discographies, critical discographies, guidebooks, almanacs and chronologies, and yearbooks. Haggerty points out that the book is modeled after *The Guide to Reference Books* (10th ed.; see ARBA 87, entry 17), but its focus is on popular music styles (preface). Each entry contains author, title, place and publisher, date, Library of Congress catalog and classification numbers, ISBNs, and an annotation.

Well-researched, annotated bibliographies on popular music have been few and far between, only a few titles come to mind. They include Mark Booth's *American Popular Music* (see ARBA 84, entry 913), Roman Waschkin's *Popular Music* (Garland, 1986), and Paul Taylor's *Popular Music Since 1955* (see ARBA 86, entry 1283). However, all of these works have sparse annotations and are not as inclusive as the volume under review. In this guide the annotations are generally brief and informative and often include references to sources of published reviews of the individual works. Appendixes provide a list of individual discographies, individual bibliographies, and an index. The work is recommended for personal libraries and large public and academic libraries where in-depth reference collections on popular music are maintained.—**Robert L. Wick**

1312. Hoffman, Frank, and George Albert. **The Cash Box Charts for the Post-Modern Age: 1978-1988.** Metuchen, N.J., Scarecrow, 1994. 589p. $62.50. ISBN 0-8108-2850-2.

This perplexing book appears to be nothing more than a compilation of the information presented in the weekly publication *Cash Box Charts* between the years 1978 and 1988. From the meager introductory material in this reference, it is not quite clear what kind of publication *Cash Box* is, or what its objectives may be. This is similarly true with this reference. Although nicely bound, with a clear table of contents to guide the reader to the many sections and subsections in this book, one never quite discovers why one should bother with this digest of who-knows-what. If the reader happens to know anything about *Cash Box* (or could find out by any means other than this book), this guide might be a useful reference for music buffs, researchers, librarians, or any others related to the music industry. But without an existing knowledge of the *Cash Box Charts*, this book is close to useless.

There are chart listings for the following charts: compact discs, the jukebox programmer, midline priced albums, music videocassettes, music videos, rap albums/singles, 12-inch singles, video games, and videocassettes. Listings for the jukebox programmer and 12-inch singles take up much of the reference. Record label information, position, and number of weeks on the chart are clearly indicated in each record. Brief introductions to each section offer little explanation as to the calculation techniques of each chart position or why *Cash Box* chose to monitor that market segment in the first place. There is no comprehensive index of the artists mentioned on the charts, despite a good deal of crossover between them, nor is there any cross-referencing of any kind. If the original *Cash Box Charts* is more enlightening about its objectives, methods, and results, researchers will be better served by bypassing this bewildering compilation and directly referencing the original source.—**Daphne Fallieros Potter**

1313. **Joel Whitburn's Pop Hits 1940-1954.** Menomonee Falls, Wis., Record Research, 1994. 398p. illus. $55.00. ISBN 0-89820-106-3.

Whitburn's latest research provides a detailed listing of artists and song titles of the pop hit singles for the 15 years covered by this reference—all compiled from *Billboard's* Pop Singles charts. Fully half of the text is devoted to an alphabetical listing by artist, giving the debut date of a record, peak position on the charts, the number of weeks charted, and the record label and number. As a bonus, some artists rate a snapshot and minimal biographical information. Columnar information also identifies the gold (million-seller) records and the current value of near-mint records of that hit.

A second section lists the peak songs and their final standing for the year in chronological order from 1940 to 1954. This is followed by a third section listing all of the previous hits alphabetically. Thus, there are three separate means of access to the entries of this work, and each entry is cross-referenced. Finally, there are many surprises under Special Sections, where, as Whitburn notes, he has almost "created another book." Under these final sections, there are an assortment of categories, such as Christmas singles, top artists by rank, songs with the longest titles, and finally, for discographers of the period 1890 to 1954, a list of "America's Most Enduring Songs," containing a chronology of recording artists, early duos, and much more trivia. Since there is no clue from the title of this reference that all of this additional material is between the covers, perhaps these really do belong in another book. While this book is not a must-have for a public library's reference collection, nor for an academic or music library, there is no denying that it is well researched, and it contains a wide variety of information. One can say that it does have potential appeal to a widespread variety of users.—**Louis G. Zelenka**

1314. **Joel Whitburn's Top Pop Singles 1955-1993.** Menomonee Falls, Wis., Record Research, 1994. 893p. illus. $74.95; $64.95pa. ISBN 0-89820-104-7; 0-89820-105-5pa.

First published in 1970, *Top Pop Singles 1955-1993* is another in the series produced by Joel Whitburn and published by Record Research. Most of the information in the volume comes from *Billboard*'s major charts research. The work is an artist-by-artist listing of more than 20,000 singles that made *Billboard*'s pop singles charts from 1955 through 1993. Each entry lists the individual record's peak position on the charts, the debut date, the number of weeks charted, the number of weeks at the number one or two position, and the original label and record number. In addition, the book discusses artists' biographies, information concerning the titles of some of the songs, and record price and picture sleeve guides.

Some of the most interesting sections are the listings at the back of the volume including the "Top Artists Section," which lists the top 500 artists in rank and alphabetical order, the "Top Artist Achievements Section," which provides information on artists with the most charted hits, the most top 40 hits, the most weeks at the #1 position, the artists with the longest chart careers, and so on.

Finally, Whitburn has compiled some listings of additional interest (e.g., a section on Christmas songs, the rock & roll hall of fame inductees, and a chronological listing, by peak date, of every title to top *Billboard*'s Pop Singles Chart). As with the other works in this series, the book provides insight into popular culture in general, and is recommended for personal reading, library collections on all levels, and especially for larger public and academic library collections that attempt to provide detailed information sources on the recording industry.—**Robert L. Wick**

1315. Leyser, Brady J., comp. **Rock Stars/Pop Stars: A Comprehensive Bibliography, 1955-1994.** Westport, Conn., Greenwood Press, 1994. 302p. index. (Music Reference Collection, no.43). $59.95. ISBN 0-313-29422-4.

This bibliography lists more than 3,600 books written about individual artists and groups associated with rock and pop music. It also includes books about related personalities, such as record company executives, producers, managers, and disc jockeys. Besides the main body of work that lists all the citations compiled, there are subject, author, and title indexes. The main bibliography lists all the citations. The citation entries are arranged alphabetically by the artist's surname or the group's name. The indexes provide another access to the bibliography.

Besides the main publication information given about a book, there is a physical description or contents line that provides additional information (e.g., whether it includes illustrations, an index, or has been revised). Of special note is the way various types of books about an artist or group are subdivided. For example, there are subject subdivisions for works of bio-bibliography, caricatures and cartoons, chronology, collectibles, concordances, correspondence, criticism and interpretation, discographies, fiction, films, and others. The majority of books listed were published in Canada, England, or the United States between 1955 and 1994. Books published in other countries are included only if the majority of the text is in English and after being physically examined by the authors.

There is a useful supplement that includes citations added since the original manuscript was completed. Those additions are books published in 1994, announced for 1994, or published between 1955 and 1994 and not included in the bibliography. This bibliography is an easy-to-use comprehensive guide to books that concern rock and pop stars, and should be useful as a reference guide to collectors and anyone else interested in the subject. [R: WLB, Feb 95, p. 71]—**Francis Poole**

1316. Reuss, Jerry, comp. **Joel Whitburn's Top Pop Singles CD Guide 1955-1979.** Menomonee Falls, Wis., Record Research, 1995. 270p. $24.95pa. ISBN 0-89820-107-1.

Based on the titles that appeared on the *Billboard* charts from January 1955 through December 1979, this new guide lists more than 10,000 singles on compact disc, by more than 2,100 artists. Reuss, a former major league pitcher, has attempted to locate CDs available from around the world but has excluded bootleg recordings. The majority of the work is devoted to an artist-by-artist listing, which gives the charted single titles now available on CD, the playing time, the disc title, and the label and number of the CD. Only one disc is listed, although a song title may actually be available on more than one. Criteria used to decide which CD to list are provided in a brief introduction.

A second section lists all of the song titles and gives the names of the artists. Similar to the recent *Top 40 Music on Compact Disc, 1955-1981* (see ARBA 95, entry 1290), which is based on *Cash Box* magazine's Top 40 charts, there is bound to be some overlap between the titles. More comprehensive collections and true enthusiasts will want to consider both titles, although the volatility of the music industry means that each will have a somewhat limited span of usefulness as a buying guide.
—**Barbara E. Kemp**

1317. Smith, John L., comp. **The Johnny Cash Record Catalog.** Westport, Conn., Greenwood Press, 1994. 255p. index. (Music Reference Collection, no.44). $49.95. ISBN 0-313-29506-9.

This is a companion volume, of sorts, to Smith's *The Johnny Cash Discography* (see ARBA 95, entry 1301). Here he lists more than 2,200 releases. There are about 1,000 song titles on 228 different record labels (1955-1993): 431 singles, 108 extended-play albums, 1,408 LPs, and 254 compact discs from the United States, Canada, New Zealand, Sweden, Malaysia, South Africa, and 22 other countries. The arrangement is by format, with sections for singles, LPs, and compact discs. There are also a couple of interesting appendixes listing the liner notes written by Cash as well as music videos he has appeared on. Omitted are references to radio transcriptions, but these are not normally available commercially. They are expected to be done in a later volume. The work is useful for the Cash collector or for southern U.S. music/folklore collections.—**Dean Tudor**

1318. **Song Finder: A Title Index to 32,000 Popular Songs in Collections, 1854-1992.** Gary Lynn Ferguson, comp. Westport, Conn., Greenwood Press, 1995. 344p. (Music Reference Collection, no.46). $79.50. ISBN 0-313-29470-4.

Song Finder began as a project by the State Library of Louisiana in 1978. Over time, it evolved from catalog cards and indexed entries to its present form as an electronic database. This book represents that database, as of 1992. It is an index to the contents of 621 songbooks published between 1854 and 1992 as acquired by the library. This title-only index to 32,000 songs contains appropriate cross-references. A third of the individual songs, in addition to about three quarters of the books, have never been indexed before, so the work is a complementary tool to Sears and Havlice, as well as other song indexes.

As mentioned, this is a basic index by title, showing the location of the song in a book annotated in Song Finder. Additional data within each entry draw attention to whether there is music only, words only, or both words and music. Lyrics in foreign languages and in English translation are also noted. Cross-references deal with variant spellings and alternate titles; these are highlighted. Compiler Ferguson also notes the 15 published song indexes, which can be accessed for data about other songs. In fact, indexes to songs seem perfectly adapted to CD-ROM technology (or even floppy disks). One can only hope that Greenwood Press or Louisiana State Library will offer this useful tool in electronic format—or that, perhaps, someone will combine all 16 song indexes into 1 file for computer retrieval.—**Dean Tudor**

1319. Whitburn, Joel. **Joel Whitburn Presents Billboard's Top 10 Charts 1958-1995.** Menomonee Falls, Wis., Record Research, 1995. 726p. index. $49.95pa. ISBN 0-89820-113-6.

I can think of no higher praise than to say that this book turned an ordinary car ride into an adventure in trivia and singing; it is a delight. As the title implies, it is essentially a reprinting of all *Billboard* Top 10 lists in the years 1958-1995. Given the current obsession with top 10s, and the success of such books by David Letterman, this book is a natural.

Relentlessly following simple chronological order, the week-by-week lists stand as a document to at least three eras and types of U.S. popular music: rock, disco, and rap. Elvis Presley appears on the first list, while Boyz II Men are on the last. Highlights between these bookends include the week in April 1964 when the Beatles held the top five slots. An index of song titles works well enough, but this is a book that cries out to be put onto CD-ROM with even more data than are currently provided. There are a number of questions that the book's present structure cannot answer. An artist index would be welcome, and a CD-ROM could easily include a keyword index.

Supplemental lists are found in the back, including most #1 hits and most top 10 hits. A list such as this misses out on subtleties that cannot always be reflected in raw sales broken down by week. The classic "American Pie" is on the list for only seven weeks but got radio airplay for months. More subtle, but more significant, artists who do not always sell millions are lost by such bean counting. It also ignores the effects music videos have had. Nonetheless, if experience is any indication, this book will cause instant fits of nostalgia and singing. This work is appropriate for general and music libraries.—**Bob Craigmile**

Country

1320. McCloud, Barry, and others. **Definitive Country: The Ultimate Encyclopedia of Country Music and Its Performers.** New York, Berkley, 1995. 1132p. illus. $40.00; $20.00pa. ISBN 0-399-51890-8; 0-399-52144-5pa.

Primary author McCloud tries to live up to the ambitious title. He includes Cajun, Zydeco, and gospel artists and country musicians from outside the United States and Canada, mostly from Australia and Great Britain (McCloud is British). Unfortunately, careless editing and proofreading mar McCloud's work. Neither the entry on the Country Music Association (CMA) nor the one on Charlie Rich mentions the infamous incident when Rich burned the CMA ballot naming John Denver "Entertainer of the Year." Pictures with more than one person really need to have everyone identified. Other pictures are mislabeled; a picture captioned "Highway 101 and friends" is actually Paulette Carlson posing with the group Pirates of the Mississippi.

The endnote information, while interesting and welcome, also needs to be more complete. Agent, manager, and label lists need artist rosters. Lists of festivals should supply addresses, not just telephone numbers. "Individual Artist's Awards" lists only a few artists, but does not say why. Conversely, the lists for the Grammy Awards are a little too detailed, containing names at most marginally connected with country music. Still, this is a useful book, if only for the variety of artists it covers. It is cautiously recommended.
—**R. S. Lehmann**

Jazz

1321. Bird, Christiane. **The Jazz and Blues Lover's Guide to the U.S.** updated ed. Reading, Mass., Addison-Wesley Publishing, 1994. 434p. illus. index. $15.00pa. ISBN 0-201-62648-9.

Information about 25 cities and the Mississippi Delta are included in this directory. Entries contain a brief introduction; sources for local information; and annotated lists of clubs, landmarks, record stores, radio stations, and other events and places of interest. Also included are a list of major festivals, a bibliography, and an index.

For the 1st edition (see ARBA 92, entry 1306), Bird spent 4 months visiting the locations he wrote about. This slightly expanded edition is based on repeat visits to nine locations and telephone conversations for the rest. While Bird's directory remains the most comprehensive work of its kind, it is unfortunate that this revision has no additional locations. Also unfortunate, yet unavoidable, is that data become rapidly dated; for example, since publication Tipitina's has closed, George Mayweather has died, and the Jazz Record Mart has moved.

More disappointing is the fact that so few of the errors noted in the 1st edition have been corrected and that new ones appear. For example, Memphis Minnie was not born in Mississippi; Furry Lewis did not follow W. C. Handy to Memphis; Handy did not "arrive on Beale in the early 1920s" (as Bird correctly indicates elsewhere); Tina Turner is not a native of St. Louis; and Muddy Waters never recorded for Sun Records. Other errors are more interpretative; King Biscuit Time, the Delta, and Memphis are discussed but there is no mention of one of their most remarkable and influential musicians, guitarist Joe Willie Wilkins. These are just a sampling of the factual errors and misrepresentations found in this directory.

—**Fred J. Hay**

1322. Campbell, Robert L. **The Earthly Recordings of Sun Ra.** Redwood, N.Y., Cadence Jazz Books; distr., Redwood, N.Y., North Country Distributors, 1994. 252p. index. $25.00pa. ISBN 1-881993-26-4.

Composer/bandleader/keyboardist Sun Ra (Herman "Sonny" Blount, 1914-1993) was one of the most interesting figures in jazz. Ra's innovativeness lay in his unique musical conception enhanced by a mixed-media approach to presentation, which often combined the music with bizarre theatrics reflecting ancient or extraterrestrial themes. The music was extraordinarily inventive, utilizing a variety of electronic instruments in combination with conventional ones, employing nontraditional musical intervals, and featuring free-form improvised solos in unusual orchestral settings. For these reasons, Ra's music was an integral and influential part of the free jazz movement of the 1960s. His amazingly long-lived band (known as the Arkestra) continued to rehearse constantly and to perform sporadically in public until his death.

Although several earlier Ra discographies are available, this one is the most thorough and up-to-date. The author's intent was to present chronologically every known recorded appearance by Ra. Standard discographical information is presented for each recording, along with historical and critical commentary that, taken as a whole, constitutes a history of Ra's musical development. Campbell, a developmental psychology professor, is a longtime enthusiast who has been researching Ra's music for a number of years. His discography of this significant musical figure is an important contribution to scholarship in this area.—**A. David Franklin**

1323. Evans, Philip R., and Larry F. Kiner, with William Trumbauer. **Tram: The Frank Trumbauer Story.** Metuchen, N.J., Institute of Jazz Studies, Rutgers—The State University of New Jersey, and Scarecrow, 1994. 821p. illus. index. (Studies in Jazz, no.18). $79.50. ISBN 0-8108-2851-0.

Even knowledgeable jazz enthusiasts may be unfamiliar with the name Frank "Tram" Trumbauer (1901-1956). His unique contributions to jazz history are most evident in the recordings he made with Bix Beiderbecke and Paul Whiteman. He mostly played C-melody saxophone and was noted for his graceful, light-toned improvisations. Such saxophone colossi as Lester Young and Benny Carter credited Trumbauer as a major influence. His work with Beiderbecke is especially noteworthy. By the late 1930s, however, the swing era had made his style of playing passé.

About one-third of the book is devoted to Trumbauer's biography, accompanied by 16 pages of photographs. A comprehensive discography, chronology of events, and song title index with recording details take up more than 500 pages. The biographical segment incorporates oral histories and the notes Trumbauer wrote in 1953 for a planned autobiography. These notes appear in bold print throughout the text and provide a great deal of insight on the life and career of this highly respected musician.

After World War II, Trumbauer left music and pursued a career in aviation. While most libraries will not care to expend their limited budgets on such an exhaustive study of a minor figure, those with especially strong collections in jazz and U.S. popular music should make room for it on their shelves.

—**Gary D. Barber**

1324. Fujioka, Yasuhiro, with Lewis Porter and Yoh-ichi Hamada. **John Coltrane: A Discography and Musical Biography.** New Brunswick, N.J., Institute of Jazz Studies at Rutgers—The State University of New Jersey and Metuchen, N.J., Scarecrow, 1995. 377p. illus. index. $62.50. ISBN 0-8108-2986-X.

From the mid-1950s on, John Coltrane (1926-1967) exerted perhaps the greatest influence on tenor saxophone sound and improvisational style since the innovations of Lester Young in the 1930s and Charlie Parker in the 1940s, with his only possible rival for that distinction being the still-active Sonny Rollins. During his tenure in Miles Davis's and Thelonious Monk's bands, and later as leader of his own quartet, Coltrane's unique tone and constantly evolving approach to improvisation served as a model for many of his younger contemporaries, as well as for innumerable tenor saxophonists who followed.

Although two earlier Coltrane discographies have appeared (Brian Davis's *John Coltrane: Discography* [2d ed.; Brian Davis, 1976] and David Wild's *The Recordings of John Coltrane: A Discography* [2d ed.; Wildmusic, 1979]), the present effort is by far the most comprehensive and complete to date. It documents the saxophonist's every known recording, including many live recordings that were only recently discovered and appear here for the first time. Every format—vinyl record, audiotape, videotape, film, and compact disc—is included, with the relevant information presented in a clear, easy-to-use display. Also included are a year-by-year chronicle of Coltrane's public performances; 800-plus photographs; and indexes of listed songs, musicians, and record labels. An interesting additional feature is the discographer's occasional commentary, based on his own research or with interviews with participants, on circumstances surrounding certain recordings.

The primary discographer, Fujioka, is an avid collector of Coltrane material who writes for several highly regarded Japanese jazz publications. Porter is a renowned jazz scholar who teaches at the Newark campus of Rutgers University. Their book is the 20th in Rutgers' Institute of Jazz Studies' excellent Studies in Jazz series. As the definitive account of the recorded work of one of the major figures in jazz history, this volume is essential for research libraries, but also will be of value to those who serve general readers interested in jazz.—**A. David Franklin**

1325. Laird, Ross. **Tantalizing Tingles: A Discography of Early Ragtime, Jazz, and Novelty Syncopated Piano Recordings, 1889-1934.** Westport, Conn., Greenwood Press, 1995. 258p. index. (Discographies, no.59). $65.00. ISBN 0-313-29240-X.

This work provides relevant discographical information on all nonclassical piano recordings made throughout the world (including discs and cylinders but excluding piano rolls), from the earliest in 1889 through 1934. Among the performers cited are such figures as Eubie Blake, "Jelly Roll" Morton, James P. Johnson, Thomas "Fats" Waller, Earl Hines, Mary Lou Williams, Art Tatum, Teddy Wilson, "Cow Cow" Davenport, and "Pinetop" Smith from the ragtime, jazz, or boogie-woogie idioms, and Zez Confrey, Roy Bargy, and Rube Bloom from the area of novelty piano. Recordings by such well-known composers as Hoagy Carmichael, Ferde Grofe, and Rudolph Friml, for example, are also listed. In addition to solo recordings, there are duets, trios, quartets, and items that feature a pianist within an orchestra. Because this is the first comprehensive work of its kind, most of the material has never before appeared in print.

The author, a professional librarian, discographer, and archivist who has previously published more than 30 volumes of discographical research, presents the meticulously investigated material in a clear, concise, and easy-to-use format. As number 59 in Greenwood Press's Discographies series, the book helps fill a void in the understanding of the history of nonclassical music styles of the twentieth century and of the role of technological advancements in their development. The work is a valuable resource for researchers in music and U.S. cultural history.—**A. David Franklin**

1326. Lord, Tom. **The Jazz Discography. Volume 9.** Redwood, N.Y., Cadence Jazz Books; distr., Redwood, N.Y., North Country Distributors, 1994. 1v. (various paging). $45.00pa. ISBN 1-881993-08-6.

The latest volume in a series that was previously reviewed in ARBA 93 (see entries 1287-1289) and ARBA 94 (see entries 1373-1374) covers Billy Harper through Claude Hopkins. As previously noted, the purpose of the discography is to provide pertinent information on every known jazz recording, regardless of style, made between 1898 and the publication of the latest volume. This is a departure from previous discographies, which have normally dealt with a single jazz style or a limited time period. Despite the inevitable occasional omissions, this work in progress has garnered high acclaim from jazz scholars. The completed set is expected to contain approximately 20 volumes.—**A. David Franklin**

1327. Meadows, Eddie S. **Jazz Research and Performance Materials: A Select Annotated Bibliography.** 2d ed. Hamden, Conn., Garland, 1995. 806p. index. $90.00. ISBN 0-8153-0373-4.

Unlike the 1st edition, Meadows has excluded the journal literature. Some 2,380 entries are arranged in 16 subject or format chapters, with all but the last 3 (anthologies/collections of sound recordings, a helpful list of current and ceased jazz serials, and a list of jazz libraries) fully annotated. Each numbered citation includes an informed annotation; not included are number of pages, series, or ISBNs.

Meadows's work is a more inclusive canon of jazz than many recent contributions; he includes artists tending more to pop music (e.g., Frank Sinatra) and those who are avant-garde (e.g., Cecil Taylor). Simultaneously, he has been rigorous in his exclusion of any music that might also be classified as blues or rhythm and blues (e.g., jazz, blues, and R & B performer Cousin Joe). Non-American jazz is not covered in-depth, but Meadows does include a chapter on the Harlequin series of recordings of world jazz.

The nearly 300 annotated citations for jazz videos, including distributors, is an asset. Of less interest is the cursory treatment of current research that serves as the introduction. Meadows includes repeated entries for the same book with separate entry numbers and annotations. It would have been a more useful book if repeat citations that were appropriate for more than one chapter had been cross-referenced. Author and subject indexes are furnished. Not exhaustive but thorough, this book with its many expert annotations provides intellectual access that did not previously exist to the monograph and video documentation of jazz.
—**Fred J. Hay**

1328. **The New Grove Dictionary of Jazz.** Barry Kernfeld, ed. New York, St. Martin's Press, 1995. 1358p. illus. $50.00. ISBN 0-312-11357-9.

The New Grove Dictionary of Jazz was originally published as a two-volume work in 1988 (see ARBA 90, entry 1288) and made available to libraries and institutions for $350. The present work is a one-volume reprint of the original, priced at an amazingly affordable $50. The only changes in the new version are the addition of a list of death dates for musicians who have died since the publication of the original, a short list of corrections to article headings, and a correction to the article on Louis Armstrong.

Widely acclaimed on its initial appearance as an indispensable component of any serious collection of music reference books, the work was praised for the comprehensiveness of its 4,500 entries and for the collective expertise of its internationally selected contributors. Although the new version does not take into account the important figures who have come to prominence since 1988, the course of jazz development has not altered significantly, and the book's essential worth remains unchanged.
—**A. David Franklin**

1329. Teubig, Klaus, comp. **Straighten Up and Fly Right: A Chronology and Discography of Nat "King" Cole.** Westport, Conn., Greenwood Press, 1994. 297p. index. (Discographies, no.56). $59.95. ISBN 0-313-29251-5.

Nat "King" Cole was a critically acclaimed, poll-winning jazz pianist and the leader of a highly regarded instrumental trio prior to his emergence in the late 1940s as one of the best and most successful pop singers. After 1950, however, much of Cole's recorded work was only peripherally related to jazz. Discographer Klaus Teubig, a librarian at the German National Music Archive and a longtime collector of Cole recordings, has compiled a listing of all known recordings, transcriptions, and films made by Cole until 1950, as well as some of his later, occasional jazz-oriented recordings. Although the standard discographical data are provided (e.g., personnel, dates, selections, issues), this work goes further, fitting the recordings into a general chronology of Cole's personal life and career. Clippings from newspapers and magazines, with short paragraphs by the compiler, place the record sessions in historical perspective and add special interest.

Also included are a short overview of Cole's personal and professional development; brief biographical sketches of the members of his various trios; song and recording indexes; and a list of other discographies that deal with the musician, including George I. Hall's *Nat "King" Cole—A Discography of Nat Cole Jazz Pianist* (Jazz Discographies Unlimited, 1965).

The book is logically organized, and in spite of an occasional syntactical peculiarity (probably due to the compiler's German background), the text is clearly written.—**A. David Franklin**

Rock

1330. **All Music Guide to Rock: The Best CDs, Albums, & Tapes.** Michael Erlewine, Vladimir Bogdanov, and Chris Woodstra, eds. San Francisco, Miller Freeman; distr., Emeryville, Calif., Publishers Group West, 1995. 973p. index. (AMG All Music Guide Series). $24.95pa. ISBN 0-87930-376-X.

This latest entry in the AMG All Music Guide Series compiles reviews of more than 15,000 rock music recordings. In a format similar to *The Trouser Press Record Guide* (4th ed.; see ARBA 93, entry 1281) and the various Rolling Stone Music Guides, this large paperback encompasses more styles of popular music than any of its critical brethren. While other rock music guidebooks generally ignore rap, soul, and rhythm and blues artists, they are well represented here. Equally impressive is the range of years covered—the music of 1950s rockabilly singers is included along with 1970s disco and the latest grunge and techno albums. Lesser-known acts from throughout the era are covered in-depth. Artist entries begin with a career overview and are followed by briefer reviews of selected individual albums. A coding system that identifies specific albums as "essential recordings," "first purchases," or "landmark recordings" can assist music buyers with modest budgets.

While much of this resource is composed of individual artist reviews, the last 100 pages feature a series of valuable mini-guides. Genres of rock music are defined in 40-plus page-length essays. Influences and precursors to rock are analyzed, and other essays explicate peripheral subjects such as fanzines, reissues, music catalogs, and other reference books. An artist index ends the text.

Designed for use by the general public as well as acquisitions personnel, this resource is recommended to all but the smallest public and academic libraries. Libraries not owning music collections will find this to be a welcome addition to their basic reference collections and a popular circulating item.—**Ed Volz**

1331. Bernadin, Claude, and Tom Stanton. **Rocket Man: The Encyclopedia of Elton John.** Westport, Conn., 1995. 252p. illus. index. $39.95. ISBN 0-313-29700-2.

Elton John, who made his U.S. debut 25 years ago, is a musician who has transcended generations. This well-researched volume, the first reference of its kind devoted to John, provides a comprehensive look at information and trivia related to this classic musician and performer. It chronicles all aspects of the British performer's life and emphasizes the music in its many colors.

The encyclopedia is divided into four sections: "Elton A-Z" highlights explanations, details, and anecdotes that have shaped his career, with entries on celebrity friends, important places, and a wide variety of topics. "Albums" presents a chronological, behind-the-scenes look at 37 of John's U.S. album releases. "Performances" gives a year-by-year look at his concert tours and highlights major performances. Finally, "Songs" compiles a comprehensive alphabetical list of more than 500 songs written or recorded by Elton John throughout his career. Two unique lists—the first noting artists who have recorded his songs and the second detailing songs he has played in concert—are included in the appendixes, which are followed by a bibliography of selected sources and an index.—**Deborah A. Taylor**

1332. Blair, John, comp. **The Illustrated Discography of Surf Music, 1961-1965.** 3d ed. Ann Arbor, Mich., Popular Culture, Ink., 1995. 264p. illus. index. $45.00. ISBN 1-56075-040-5.

Expanded by 100-plus pages, and featuring many additional photographs, illustrations, and publicity stills, the latest edition of what has become a classic discography of California's distinctive surf music continues the high standards set by its predecessor (see ARBA 86, entry 1292). Dick Dale, the artist usually credited with originating surf music, has written a brief preface for this edition. He recalls how he created this unique sound by working with pioneer guitarmaker Leo Fender (whose famous Stratocaster model was played not only by Dale but also by Buddy Holly and Jimi Hendrix) to modify the guitar by repositioning pickups and selecting certain gauges of strings to complement his distinctive staccato picking style.

Photographs depict performers not illustrated in previous editions, including the Jades and the Sunrays. With some of the photographs that are carried over, more information is supplied, such as the caption for The Pyramids, which now identifies each band member by name. Another addition is Blair's designating, with an appropriate surfboard logo, those recordings that he judges to be truly outstanding. The entire discography of truly exceptional artists is so designated, including Dick Dale and the Deltones, Jan and Dean, and of course, the Beach Boys.

While the golden age of surfing music was relatively short-lived, its lasting appeal helps to make Blair's compilation one of the more enjoyable discographies for browsing. It is recommended for record collectors and large music history collections.—**Richard W. Grefrath**

1333. Hoffmann, Frank, and B. Lee Cooper. **Literature of Rock, III: 1984-1990. With Additional Material for the Period 1954-1983.** Metuchen, N.J., Scarecrow, 1995. 1003p. index. $99.50. ISBN 0-8108-2762-X.

The mid- to late 1980s in rock music were marked by the meteoric rise of compact discs, television videoclips, the birth of rap music, and charity projects such as Farm Aid and U.S.A. for Africa. The authors of this work, a librarian and a historian specializing in popular culture, have culled 7,000 prominent items from 700 books and more than 100 periodicals that cover this era in rock music, most of which are reasonably accessible to researchers.

This work divides the genre into 25 major chronological areas such as "Development of Rock and Roll," "Soul Music," "Hybrid Children of Rock," "Disco," "New Wave," and "New Age," and then further divides them into topics such as "Rockabilly," "Blue-Eyed Soul," "Heavy Metal," and "Athens Sound." A final, catch-all chapter covers topics such as awards, drugs, fans, politics, and record album covers. The authors overcome some of the problems of the exclusivity of this subject arrangement by providing a comprehensive index with alphabetical access to topics and names of artists. An appendix suggests a 100-title collection of essential recordings.

This work succeeds in its attempt to provide access to that which represents the best in rock literature from 1984 to 1990. It will be of interest to fans who want to read about an artist or subgenre, but perhaps more importantly, it will be of use to scholars of the present and future who are interested in the history and social impact of this era of rock music.—**Donald W. Maxwell**

1334. Nogowski, John. **Bob Dylan: A Descriptive, Critical Discography and Filmography, 1961-1993.** Jefferson, N.C., McFarland, 1995. 208p. index. $34.50pa. ISBN 0-89950-785-9.

Intended as a comprehensive examination of the creative output of one of the most influential and controversial figures in the history of rock and roll music, this book provides critical analyses of Dylan's recordings, film and television appearances, and books by and about him. The majority of the work is devoted to the recordings, including albums, singles, collaborations with other artists, and bootlegs. A typical entry lists the producer, recording and release dates, top chart position, outtakes, singles released from the album, the album cover and liner notes, a summary evaluation of the record, and analyses and grades for each of the songs. There are three brief appendixes that list the number of weeks on the *Billboard* charts for each album, the chart position reached by each album, and a list of the songs rated "A+" by the author. The grades are admittedly subjective but provide a framework for a critical perspective of Dylan's entire career. An index, which does not reference all names in the body of the work, covers titles and individuals. Dylan fans and libraries with an interest in rock music will want this book for their collections.—**Barbara E. Kemp**

1335. Stanley, David E., with Frank Coffey. **The Elvis Encyclopedia: The Complete and Definitive Reference Book on the King of Rock & Roll.** Santa Monica, Calif., General Publishing Group, 1994. 287p. illus. index. $29.99. ISBN 1-881649-24-5.

Bursting with more than 250 delightful photographs and the excitement of its larger-than-life subject, this glossy, coffee-table compendium will likely become a favorite of fans and researchers alike. Compiler and author Stanley brings a true insider's perspective to the task: He was Elvis's stepbrother, lived with him at Graceland for 17 years, and was the youngest member of the inner circle "Memphis Mafia."

A detailed chronology composes the major section, tracing "The King's" life and career from his humble beginnings to his death in 1977. Embellished with abundant photographs (many in color and some never before published) and numerous sidebars written by Stanley in which he recalls and comments upon the events chronicled, the chronology (and indeed, the entire volume) is suffused with an honesty somewhat surprising from a writer with such close emotional ties. Elvis's generosity and other good qualities are detailed along with his darker, self-destructive side, with an objectivity that neither glamorizes Elvis's excesses nor sermonizes against them. The illustrations are expertly chosen to highlight key events, including a full-page color shot of the triumphant Elvis singing at his fabulously successful 1969 comeback performance in Las Vegas. Yet pictures of the overweight, aging Elvis are furnished as well, documenting his unfortunate decline.

Additional material includes a complete discography with color illustrations of the album covers; Elvis trivia (such as his favorite foods and leading ladies); copies of his birth certificate and autopsy report; and a detailed filmography, which devotes a page to each film and gives cast, credits, synopses, and a list of the songs Elvis sings.

Two previous books are similar in scope, *All Shook Up: Elvis, Day-by-Day, 1954-1977* (see ARBA 86, entry 1294) and Patricia Jobe Pierce's *The Ultimate Elvis: Elvis Presley Day by Day* (Simon & Schuster, 1994). Both feature extensive chronologies, and contain valuable and unique information (such as Pierce's directory of Elvis fan clubs), but with their almanac format and meager collection of black-and-white photographs, they seem rather dry and academic compared to Stanley's colorful extravaganza. [R: WLB, Jan 95, p. 78]—**Richard W. Grefrath**

1336. **The Story of Rock'n'Roll: The Year-by-Year Illustrated Chronicle.** Paul du Noyer, ed. New York, Schirmer Books/Simon & Schuster, 1995. 304p. illus. index. $65.00. ISBN 0-02-860284-6.

The subtitle's claim to be "the year-by-year illustrated chronicle" would seem to qualify this coffee-table-sized book as a reference volume. What it most resembles, however, is an interminable, decades-long gossip column styled after *Rolling Stone* magazine's "Random Notes" column, complete with most of the proper names in boldface and captions with arrows pointing to the pictures they elucidate. Each year from 1954 to 1994 merits roughly four to five pages, with as many photographs. Sidebars on pertinent topics, such as skiffle (1957), Haight-Ashbury (1967), and Live Aid (1985), provide some relief from the chatty text. Feature articles on prominent groups and movements also break up the text. Additionally, each decade is prefaced by a sketchy essay on the fads prevalent at the time and another on the general mood of the decade as reflected in the music.

In an effort to provide historical context, a "headline news" blip runs sideways up the outside margin of each page, so that one will be aware that in July 1988, at the same time Patti Smith was releasing "Dream of Life," 157 workers were dying in a petroleum explosion accident. Libraries seeking to acquire a basic history of rock and roll should not waste their money but should instead look to such works as Robert Palmer's *Rock and Roll: An Unruly History* (Crown, 1995) or to the earlier *Rock of Ages: The Rolling Stone History of Rock and Roll* (Summit Books, 1986) by Ed Ward. The definitive book on rock and roll remains to be written.—**David Dodd**

1337. Whitburn, Joel, comp. **Joel Whitburn's Rock Tracks: Album Rock Tracks 1981-1995, Modern Rock Tracks 1988-1995.** Menomonee Falls, Wis., Record Research, 1995. 285p. illus. index. $34.95pa. ISBN 0-89820-114-4.

The music industry bible for decades, *Billboard* magazine's sales charts are considered the official measurement of success for that business. The oversized weekly also provides charts for broadcasters, tracking the radio airplay of individual songs, not just the sales of singles and albums. The accumulation of two such airplay charts constitutes this latest in a series of similar books by Whitburn.

In 1981, *Billboard* began monitoring the songs played on radio stations featuring an album rock format. The first portion of the book compiles those charts. Seven years later, as a new radio format blossomed in the late 1980s around the popularity of "alternative" music, *Billboard* began tracking songs played on modern rock radio stations. Those accumulated charts make up the second part of the book. The charts are by artist main entry, listing the dates each artist's songs debuted on the chart, peak position attained, number of weeks charted, album label and catalog number, and a brief biographical or career tidbit.

Artists occasionally overlap between the two radio formats, so the book's sections are not always mutually exclusive. While Led Zeppelin and Tom Petty are typical album rock artists, the younger, edgier P. J. Harvey and Sonic Youth are modern rock artists. Pearl Jam's enormous appeal, however, mandates a crossover between the two categories. Simple cross-checking will locate a performer in either or both of the book's sections. Separate lists make note of the most popular artists and songs thus far in the history of these *Billboard* charts. A song title index provides another convenient access point.

While the album rock radio format is nearly 30 years old, *Billboard* did not track airplay information for this format for the first 15 years of its history. Although Whitburn's book is comprehensive in that it reflects the entire history of this specific *Billboard* chart, album rock radio airplay from 1967-1980 (commonly called "progressive rock") remains undocumented. There is no such deficiency with the modern rock charts. This format was not legitimized as a broadcasting category until around the time of the *Billboard* chart's genesis (the latter to some extent causing the former).

This paperback is a valuable name authority tool for libraries with prominent rock music collections in any medium. The biographical and career data for the artists is cogent and not likely to be found in any other single source. *Joel Whitburn's Rock Tracks* is recommended for library collections emphasizing popular music or radio programming and broadcasting.—**Ed Volz**

1338. Wiener, Allen J. **The Beatles: The Ultimate Recording Guide.** 3d ed. Holbrook, Mass., Adams Publishing, 1994. 596p. illus. index. $15.00pa. ISBN 1-55850-414-1.

The enduring appeal of the Beatles has been judged sufficient to warrant an update (through the events of February 1994) of the 1992 edition (see ARBA 94, entry 1380), which itself was an expanded revision of the author's *The Beatles: A Recording History* (see ARBA 87, entry 1271). While books' titles can be endlessly quibbled about, the omission of the keyword "chronology" from these is particularly unfortunate, since they are the best, most comprehensive chronologies of the Beatles' lives and careers, before and after the group disbanded. As in the previous edition, four chronologies are included, a "General Chronology," a "Recording Chronology," "Discographies," and "Bootlegs and Unreleased Recordings," a cumbersome format that results in some duplication of material. Advanced specialists in the field might find the separation convenient, but most would probably prefer collating the four into one. Typically, the reader will be awkwardly flipping back and forth among the four sections. An index is included, but its print is rather small for the large contingent of middle-aged bifocaled Beatles fans, and it provides unhelpful long litanies of undifferentiated page number references after each entry.

Nonetheless, these relatively bare chronologies hold a certain fascination. Scanning the events of 1958, for instance, we easily see what John's activities were when his mother Julia was killed in an automobile accident: it was the early days in Liverpool and he was busy playing with the Quarry Men. There are choice tidbits salted throughout, such as the Fab Four smoking marijuana in a royal bathroom just before being presented the MBE (Member of the Order of the British Empire) by Queen Elizabeth. The march of dates and events in these chronologies eloquently conveys the expansive panorama of the Beatles' significant impact on modern culture, and makes the book an essential reference source for Beatles collections and hardcore fans.—**Richard W. Grefrath**

Soul

1339. Gregory, Hugh. **Soul Music A-Z.** rev. ed. New York, Da Capo Press, 1995. 344p. illus. $17.95pa. ISBN 0-306-80643-6.

The term "soul music" has been more specifically applied to that idiom that absorbed elements from gospel and rhythm-and-blues into the black pop music scene two decades ago. Observers rarely have noted the holistic coexistence of the sacred and secular inherited from African sociology, but the term has suggested proprietorship within the black community. As is true with all other African-American idioms (which have given the country its musical identity), more than mere influences have spread outside of the immediate society. The London-based author acknowledges this among the stylistic and temporal problems his liberal definitions face. This results in the inclusion of David Sanborn and Gladys Knight, but also the artist formerly known as Prince and L. L. Cool J.

Biographical entries, approximately 1,000 in number, cite recordings with sales rankings of tunes (a bow to marketing ventures of the media) and chronological lists of album titles. The shortest sketches are usually more than one inch in length, while some figures claim several columns (James Brown is the longest with six). The 46 full-page press photographs provide graphic interest. Forty-two titles, not all of immediate relevancy, are selected for the brief bibliography. Although this cannot be regarded as a work of major scholarship, it goes beyond the labor-of-love level, assimilating data not readily available in other sources.—**Dominique-René de Lerma**

26 Mythology, Folklore, and Popular Culture

FOLKLORE

1340. Avakian, Anne M. **Armenian Folklore Bibliography.** Berkeley, Calif., University of California Press, 1994. 212p. index. (University of California Catalogs and Bibliographies, v.11). $38.00. ISBN 0-520-09794-7.

This vitally needed bibliography extends beyond its stated scope to be of value to scholars of folklore studies in general, and Russian and European folklore in particular. Before coming to an end with the deportation and genocide of the Armenian peoples during World War I, the Armenian Ethnographic Society's efforts were diligent and are represented in this volume. Because of the lack of skill in the language, most scholars of folklore know little about Armenia despite its antiquity.

The bibliography contains 1,375 citations in several languages besides Armenian. The introduction gives a historical overview as well as an introduction to the materials. Tales, anecdotes, fables, proverbs, oaths, curses, blessings, prayers, songs, and other lore, mostly from village life, make up the body of work. Most were preserved in oral form and collected in the nineteenth century, and biographical notes on the famous Armenian folklorists are interesting.

This bibliography has been carefully and lovingly compiled by an octogenarian retired librarian with the encouragement of the famous folklore theorist Alan Dundes. It is truly an inspired work for presenting an often-ignored body of knowledge. [R: Choice, April 95, p. 1267]—**Linda L. Lam-Easton**

1341. Bartis, Peter T., and Hillary Glatt. **Folklife Sourcebook: A Directory of Folklife Resources in the United States.** 2d ed. Washington, D.C., Library of Congress, American Folklife Center, 1994. 165p. index. (Publications of the American Folklife Center, no.14). $11.00pa. ISBN 0-16-043069-0.

This 2d edition (for a review of the 1st edition, see ARBA 87, entry 1273) incorporates some notable and helpful changes, including updated information about folklife/folklore resources available from federal agencies, archives, higher education programs, societies, different kinds of publications and mail order services, and directories. A notable change appears in the retitling of the section on "State Folk Cultural Programs" as "Public Folk Cultural Programs," and the volume now provides a state-by-state listing of public, educational, and archival folk resources. In addition, Canadian folklife resources now appear in more general form as an appendix, as does a new section on folklife/folklore resources for Mexico, with the suggestion that this latter list be only a beginning for folklife investigations south of the border.

The 2d edition of the *Folklife Sourcebook* is a resource every library—public, academic, or research—that intends to serve the folklore researcher and reader should have, although the authors' caveat regarding the transitoriness of addresses for societies should also be applied to names of contacts for programs in higher education, several of whom are not those listed.—**Susan Tower Hollis**

1342. El-Shamy, Hasan M. **Folk Traditions of the Arab World: A Guide to Motif Classification.** Bloomington, Ind., Indiana University Press, 1995. 2v. $75.00/set. ISBN 0-253-35201-0.

This two-volume guide to motif classification contributes significantly to the scholarly literature of regional folklore. The author employs the detailed classification system developed by Stith Thompson in his *Motif-Index of Folk Literature* (new ed.; see ARBA 95, entry 1317), expanding the categories as necessary to accommodate cultural facets of the Arab folk literature surveyed. The first volume includes a detailed introduction to arrangement and use of the set, a particularly important feature for users unfamiliar with motif indexes. Volume 1 also provides a detailed listing of 12,500 motif classifications grouped within 26 broad categories (e.g., marvels, chance and fate, unnatural cruelty, taboo, and animals).

The motifs identified are followed by appendixes with information on location of tale types in the Arab world and an Islam-based view of supernatural belief-practice systems, as well as an extensive bibliography of resources cited. Volume 2 provides an alphabetical index of the motifs used in the guide. Both folklore studies and Arabic studies reference collections could benefit from this compact but comprehensive scholarly work on folk traditions of the Arab world.—**Ahmad Gamaluddin**

1343. **Larousse Dictionary of World Folklore.** By Alison Jones. New York, Larousse Kingfisher Chambers, 1995. 493p. illus. $27.50. ISBN 0-7523-0012-1.

The objective of this dictionary is to draw together in a single volume the central themes and features of folklore throughout the world; to demonstrate both the similarities and differences that define human cultures; to shed light on some of the ancient beliefs that lie behind many of our traditional customs and celebrations; and to examine the ways in which folklore flourishes in the modern world. The volume is promoted as an invaluable tool for the serious student and an accessible guide to the subject of world folklore for other more general readers. The entries are arranged in strict alphabetical order from *Abandonment* to *Zombi*, and the dictionary offers 468 pages of folkloric motifs, mythic personae, and terms, with a smattering of folklore theory here and there. There are 6 pages of biographical notes on "prominent folklorists," followed by some 21 pages listing ethnographical and folklore museums and a calendar of festivals and folkloric events throughout the world.

This dictionary will indeed prove a useful starting point for the general reader interested in a key to matters folkloric. However, the reader should be aware of a few considerations. When it focuses on the presentation of the well-established body of folkloric "facts," the work is excellent. However, when by accident or design it strays into discussion of folklore theory, the *Dictionary* has a tendency to view folklore in terms of literature or in broad anthropological or even sociological categories rather than the finely focused lens of modern folklore scholarship, which views its subject as the specific, living expression of the beliefs, customs, and meaningful outlook on life of individuals, wherever they may be. The entry on *Motif*, for example, tends to reify folklore when it discusses it in terms of "items" that can be "broken down for analysis." This tendency, and the dust cover suggestion that the volume is "a remarkable guide to the hidden history of humankind," betrays an adherence to outdated folklore theory.

In terms of geographical bias, the dictionary favors the folklore and traditions of people of northern European heritage, with particular emphasis on Celtic and Indo-European folklore and myth. Other countries or regions—Japan, Melanesia, Micronesia, and Polynesia—receive little more than a broad and sometimes historically or sociologically based explanation of the culture and people, and there is scant reference to anything African American. These problems stem, no doubt, from an overly ambitious attempt to present a catalog of "world folklore," a misnomer if there ever was one. Finally, a curious omission from the listing of ethnographical and folklore museums is the internationally renowned, extensive folklore archive of the Department of Irish Folklore, University College, Dublin.

—**Arthur Gribben**

1344. Marley, David F. **Pirates and Privateers of the Americas.** Santa Barbara, Calif., ABC-CLIO, 1994. 458p. illus. maps. index. $54.00. ISBN 0-87436-751-4.

1345. Rogozínski, Jan. **Pirates! Brigands, Buccaneers, and Privateers in Fact, Fiction, and Legend.** New York, Facts on File, 1995. 398p. illus. maps. index. $45.00. ISBN 0-8160-2761-7.

Given the long-term interest of many people in pirates and their exploits, it seems strange that in its first 25 years *American Reference Books Annual* has never reviewed a reference book on pirates. Equally strange is the fact that now, at last, there are two good reference books, both by reputable reference publishers, on brigands, buccaneers, pirates, and privateers. While, as is often the case, there is some overlap in the content, each takes a different approach to the subject. The titles may be similar, but the content is definitely different. Certainly, each is worth judging on its own merits.

Rogozínski's *Pirates!*, which is aimed at a more popular audience, deals with these men, and a few women, from throughout the world as larger-than-life figures portrayed in fact, fiction, and legend. The treatment of important individual pirates who operated in the Americas is far more abbreviated than that in Marley's *Pirates and Privateers*. Henry Morgan, for example, is covered in 5 columns by Rogozínski, as opposed to 19 columns by Marley. Individual pirates are not Rogozínski's primary concern, but he does a good job with both well-known and lesser-known figures. He deals just as adeptly with art, films, novels, plays, short stories, songs, terminology, torture, treasure, types of pirate ships, and many other elements that make the pirate mystique so intriguing. Numerous black-and-white photographs add to the attractiveness of his volume. For public libraries, especially those looking for good reference books that appeal to young adults, Rogozínski's encyclopedia is the better choice.

Marley's treatment of pirates and privateers, which is more scholarly, is limited to approximately 350 alphabetically arranged entries describing the events, people, places, ships, and weapons that helped shape the history of the Americas, especially during the turbulent seventeenth century. The popular aspects of pirate lore, such as films and fiction, are not dealt with, and Marley's emphasis is on the facts and figures derived from standard historical sources. His primary emphasis is on individual biographies for key figures and, for that information as it pertains to pirates operating in the Americas, Marley is unsurpassed. For academic libraries, especially those looking for an excellent addition to their sources of biographical information, Marley's encyclopedia is the better choice. Given the paucity of good standard reference books on pirates, however, many academic and public libraries may well wish to consider adding both volumes to their collections.—**Norman D. Stevens**

MYTHOLOGY

1346. DeLoach, Charles. **Giants: A Reference Guide from History, the Bible, and Recorded Legend.** Metuchen, N.J., Scarecrow, 1995. 313p. illus. index. $39.50. ISBN 0-8108-2971-1.

The author of this dictionary takes the viewpoint that giants, known widely in legend and myth, indeed existed, and he offers photographs and secondary references to real-life giants throughout history. This dictionary has two main features. First, it explains frequent appearances of giants in the Bible with references to archaeological findings. Second, it chronicles examples of individual giants and races of giants since biblical times. The author, a journalist and freelance writer, especially celebrates his findings on Celtic giants, to which he devotes seven full pages. The straw person of DeLoach's book is the historian who would relegate giants to the realm of myth rather than historical reality. So intent is the author on finding accounts of giants in history that he neglects the mythological literature, judging from his bibliography. Naturally, Goliath is there, as are Captain Martin Van Buren Bates and Anna Swan, the world's tallest couple on record. The Cardiff Giant is not there, probably because it proved to be a hoax. Long sections are devoted to "Giants Who Became Gods" and "Israel's Wars with the Giants." Historians and folklorists both are likely to raise eyebrows over statements made in many entries, such as the timeline of 4004 B.C. as Creation. As journalism, the book can be provocative and entertaining, but as a reference it needs to be approached with caution.—**Simon J. Bronner**

1347. **Goddesses, Heroes, and Shamans: The Young People's Guide to World Mythology.** New York, Larousse Kingfisher Chambers, 1994. 159p. illus. maps. index. $19.95. ISBN 1-85697-999-7.

Nicely illustrated, systematically organized, and fairly comprehensive for its target audience, this introductory guide to world mythology should be of interest to parents, librarians, teachers, and young people curious about ancient and contemporary mythology. Various cultures are represented, and entries for more than 500 characters from their cultural myths and legends are included.

Following an "About This Book" page, the guide is introduced by a clear, informative section that discusses "What Is a Myth?" The major portion of the book is divided into six cultural/geographical sections—Northern Lands, Africa, Mediterranean Lands, Eastern Asia, Central and South America, and South Pacific Lands. Most of these sections are further subdivided by country or geographic area (e.g., the Amazon, Egypt, Arctic Lands). Each main section begins with an overview essay and furnishes an area map, a timeline, and illustrations and photographs. The subdivisions each have a specialized essay followed by an alphabetical listing of character entries. Interesting bits of information appear in highlighted boxes, and the many illustrations are well annotated. The volume is concluded by a glossary and a character index.

Attractively presented, clearly written, well organized, and filled with a plethora of information, this guide will be useful to young people and adults alike. It would be a welcome addition not only to all public and school library collections, but to many home libraries as well. For the price, it is an introductory volume that is hard to beat. [R: RBB, 15 Feb 95, pp. 1109-10]—**Kristin Ramsdell**

1348. **Man, Myth and Magic: The Illustrated Encyclopedia of Mythology, Religion and the Unknown.** new ed. Richard Cavendish and Brian Innes, comps. and eds. New York, Marshall Cavendish, 1995. 21v. illus. index. $549.95/set. ISBN 1-85435-731-X.

Much of the content of this encyclopedia is explained in the entry for New Age: "A renewed interest in non-Western beliefs—the chakras of Hinduism, Chinese Tao, the tenets of Zen Buddhism, even the mythology of the North American Indian—combined with a belief in the most esoteric aspects of Western occultism" (p. 1845). The content crosses national borders and covers a wide range of spiritual and spectacular phenomena from ancient tradition to modern science. Unlike more focused dictionaries and encyclopedias for the discipline of folklore, this work focuses on the broad umbrella of spiritual matters. Its main title conveys a mystical quality that is especially manifested in a search for symbol and meaning in primitive rites and tribal wisdom. Its subtitle gives more of a hint of the contents: mythology, religion, and the unknown. Indeed, folklore and its disciplinary relations seem to be avoided, although they appear in the list of major thematic areas found in the first volume.

The bibliography and one of the indexes are organized around some of these thematic areas: magic; alchemy; witches and witchcraft; devils, demons, and angels; birds, plants, and animals in myth and folklore; nature, fertility, and creation myths; rites of passage; mysterious creatures and lands in myth and legend; Western religions; Eastern religions; folklore, primitive beliefs, and customs; psychology and the paranormal; unorthodox Christians; and occultists and theosophists. The reader's guide underscores the sweeping coverage of the reference as an asset to social studies teaching and its multidisciplinary approach to study. In addition to the reader's guide, one will find a comprehensive listing of contents for all the volumes, bibliography, classified subject guide, and list of contributors in the first volume. The last volume contains two indexes—one organized for general subjects and the other for thematic areas.

The contributors are reputable scholars, mostly from British universities, and represent psychology, history, anthropology, sociology, and folklore. The entries encompass short captions (e.g., Mennonites and anti-Semitism), one- to three-page descriptions of beliefs (e.g., Aberdeen witches, purgatory, and Thor), and extended descriptions of subjects as broad as the United States and priests. Longer essays include suggestions of a few titles for further reading. The volumes are illustrated with vivid photographs and drawings, many in color and taking up full pages. The volumes are relatively thin, and with their variety of formats for entries and illustrations, they can appear to be scrapbooks of information. They will be compelling to a popular audience because of the subjects covered and the visual approach to the references.

At least 76 new entries have been added since the previous edition, among them African-American lore, crop circles, urban legends, and near-death experiences. The tone of the entries emphasizes supernatural phenomena in an objective, nonjudgmental manner, although contributors occasionally overstate their case. In the entry for the United States, for example, much is made of belief in sorcery and witchcraft among the Pennsylvania Germans, such as use of traditional hex signs, symbols for warding off the evil eye and hostile supernatural influences, even though most sources view these signs as part of ethnic revivals rather than as supernatural forces. Discussion follows about Pennsylvania-German "powwow doctors," who practiced a form of spiritual healing, but the entry makes them appear to be primarily herbalists. No separate entry about powwowing is found, and the index fails to list powwowing or hex signs.

Although individual encyclopedias and dictionaries can be found for mythology, folklore, and comparative religion, this reference uniquely brings them together and adds consideration of contemporary spiritualist phenomena and movements. Its broad range is both its strength and its weakness. Within the volumes found here, one can make connections between ideas of Western religion and traditional belief, between urban legends and ancient tales, and between the primitive and the modern. However, the volumes also contain an unevenness and cursory treatment that will be frustrating to scholarly users. Their greatest appeal may be to the intelligent public attracted to such subjects, but who find that the subjects often fall between disciplinary, and encyclopedic, cracks. More than most surveys of world traditions, the volumes amply illustrate the phenomena and treat them as part of modern life. They will be appropriate in public libraries and libraries in secondary schools and colleges.—**Simon J. Bronner**

1349. Snodgrass, Mary Ellen. **Voyages in Classical Mythology.** Santa Barbara, Calif., ABC-CLIO, 1994. 478p. illus. maps. index. $49.50. ISBN 0-87436-734-4.

Voyages in Classical Mythology is an unusual work that incorporates much general information about mythological characters, places, and events in recounting voyages, quests, and travels of 44 heroes and deities of Greek and Roman mythology. The journey motif being one of the most pervasive in all mythologies, nearly every leading figure of classical mythology is involved, directly or indirectly, in one or more of these stories. Yet, along with the stories of Odysseus, Dædalus, Helen, and Jason are the lesser-known Canopus, Nauplius, and Teuver, to name a few.

The entries are alphabetically arranged by the names of the travelers. Each provides the character's genealogy and background, a map detailing the location of the travels, a description of the journey, alternate versions of the stories, the symbolism involved, a cross-reference, and a bibliography of ancient sources. Many also contain appropriate quotations from classical literature. Included in the back matter are a glossary, a listing of ancient sources by author, a timeline of ancient works and authors, a bibliography, and general and geographical indexes.

Snodgrass, author of several works on Greek and Roman literature, has provided an interesting and accessible text that deals well with its complex themes. Each story is accompanied by a black-and-white illustration done by a different artist; these vary in quality and usefulness. Students at or above the high school level and nonspecialists of any age with an interest in mythology should find this book both fascinating and informative.—**Kay O. Cornelius**

1350. **Who's Who in Egyptian Mythology.** 2d ed. By Anthony S. Mercatante. R. S. Bianchi, ed. Metuchen, N.J., Scarecrow, 1995. 231p. illus. $32.50. ISBN 0-8108-2967-3.

Bianchi, the editor and reviser of this edition, "decided against a revision . . . and . . . made only those slight changes" needed to reflect more recent scholarship (p. vii). Thus, the comments by the reviewer of the 1st edition (see ARBA 80, entry 1091) still stand. The modifications for this edition occur in the annotated bibliography and involve the elimination of some truly outdated materials (e.g., the works of E. A. Wallis Budge), while adding materials published since 1978. In these revisions, the editor neglected, however, to correct the spelling of Serge Sauneron's name, to add the important 3d volume of Miriam Lichtheim's *Ancient Egyptian Literature* (University of California Press, 1973-1980), and to note that both Alan Gardiner's *Egyptian Grammar* (Oxford University Press) and James Pritchard's *Ancient Near Eastern Texts Relating to the Old Testament* (Princeton University Press) each appeared in 3d editions with significant changes in 1969. Most important, the revised bibliography includes no translation of the *Book of the Dead* (R. O. Faulkner's *Book of the Dead* [1972], being a good example).

Although a library can certainly benefit from having Mercatante's book in either the 1st or 2d edition, George Hart's *Dictionary of Egyptian Gods and Goddesses* (Routledge, 1986), though lacking the annotated bibliography and the full narratives of various tales, provides a better compendium of the mythological world of the ancient Egyptians.—**Susan Tower Hollis**

POPULAR CULTURE

1351. Bati, Anwar, and Simon Chase. **The Cigar Companion: A Connoisseur's Guide.** 2d ed. Philadelphia, Running Press, 1995. 223p. illus. index. $24.95. ISBN 1-56138-657-X.

This 2d edition of *The Cigar Companion* is a well-written and, even for the nonsmoker, intriguing volume by two obvious aficionados of cigars. It is handsomely presented—in colors reminiscent of the cigar itself—with photographs, illustrations, and an index. Chapter 1, "The Story of Cigars," delineates in fascinating detail the history of cigars and the cigar industry, from its possible origins in Central or South America, to the growing and manufacturing process, the introduction of the cigar box, and the cigar band to cigar sizes and even wrapper colors. Chapter 2, "The Cigar Directory," provides a selected list of handmade cigar types and most of the available brands. It also offers notes on flavor and aroma, country of origin, and in some cases, the legend of the originator of a particular cigar. "Buying and Storing Cigars," chapter 3, offers professional advice for the intelligent cigar buyer in terms of examination of the product before leaving the store. The final chapter, "Cigar Merchant Directory," lists the top stores worldwide where quality cigars and paraphernalia may be purchased.

Ostensibly a history of the cigar and the industry associated with it, as well as a handbook for cigar smokers, this guide offers useful insights into the culture of cigar makers and cigar smokers alike. Much of the narrative is devoted to the handmade cigar as a work of art, particularly the world-renowned Havana, but attention is also paid to machine-made cigars and the merits and demerits of one over the other. Finally, a close reading of *The Cigar Companion* indicates a rich industrial and organizational culture and history that lies behind the smoke.—**Arthur Gribben**

1352. Clynes, Tom. **Wild Planet! 1,001 Extraordinary Events for the Inspired Traveler.** Detroit, Gale, 1995. 669p. illus. maps. index. $35.00. ISBN 0-7876-0373-2.

More than just a travel guide, this compilation is a chronicle of celebrations important to people around the world. These celebrations comprise festivals, fairs, unusual sporting competitions, ceremonies, New Year celebrations, and many more special and bizarre events often peculiar to a specific locale. Emphasis tends to be on noncommercial gatherings that encourage community-wide attendance.

Events are grouped first by continent, then by country, then generally in order of annual date of occurrence. The highlighted happening is described, and tips are provided for savvy traveling, including accommodations and transportation advice. Side trips or alternate events are recommended whenever practical. For example, if the "Carnivale at Venice" proves too expensive, there are 19 other *carnivales* in Italy that may be more affordable. For each country, there are resources for further information and addresses of tourism offices. Sidebars give informative facts about related subjects. The index is divided into three parts: by general subject, by chronological grouping (by month and country), and by name of event or place. Unfortunately, these indexes are not as extensive as they should be, and exclude most of the sidebar information boxes, which can cause the user to miss important data.

It is difficult to assess just how comprehensive the work is or what the actual underlying context for inclusion is. The line between what constitutes "commercial" versus "noncommercial" events is seemingly blurred considering some of the events selected in the U.S. section. It also seems highly unrealistic to drop in at an obscure Detroit street fair while visiting a Harley-Davidson motorcycle gathering in Sturgis, South Dakota, as is suggested. Despite this, a wide range of audiences will enjoy the bright writing style and will benefit from either the fascinating cultural insights or the sound travel planning suggestions for those who seek adventure. *Wild Planet!* is suitable for public libraries, and for school and academic sites where there are area studies or international cultures curricula.—**Gary R. Cocozzoli**

1353. Cooper, Gordon. **Festivals of Europe.** London, Percival Marshall, 1961; repr., Detroit, Omnigraphics, 1994. 172p. illus. index. $44.00. ISBN 0-7808-0005-2.

Festivals of Europe describes more than 1,200 festivals and related events in some 25 countries and principalities. Writing as a well-traveled tourist, Cooper informs the reader of the many interesting festivals held throughout Europe each year. The chapters are organized by events of a specific country, with festivals and related activities categorized in this connection. Activities typical of each event, the locale, and the time of year are described, and the volume is supplemented with photographs, a directory of national tourist offices, and an index. The events covered are religious ones, agricultural and horticultural shows, trade fairs, and wine and gastronomic festivities. Cooper's enthusiasm is evident in chapters 1 and 2, where he tries to assist the reader with the choice of festival or with travel hints. His comments seem quaint, however, in an age of sophisticated, frequent, and far-flung travel.

Refreshing as it is to be reminded about things to bring with you on a trip and tipped to sit near the bathroom at an outdoor concert, in places the volume contains simplistic explanations and descriptions of festivals, with some of the information surely lifted from tourist pamphlets prepared to entice tourist dollars (e.g., *Schlercherlaufen* in Austria). For all of Ireland only one custom is offered—the Oyster Festival in Galway—this following earlier mention of other festivals listed under "Cultural Events," leading one to question Cooper's categorizations and distinctions throughout the volume. Though photographs of events are supplied, they are often misplaced and mismatched; an illustration of the Dublin Horse Show appears in the chapter on Italy alongside illustrations of festivals in Bari, Siena, and Venice. While the book will be generally useful to some readers, it must be pointed out that the volume is a reprint of a work originally published in 1961 and shows no evidence of having been updated to reflect current sociopolitical realities.—**Arthur Gribben**

1354. Edwards, Michael. **The Champagne Companion: The Authoritative Connoisseur's Guide.** Philadelphia, Running Press, 1994. 224p. illus. index. $24.95. ISBN 1-56138-440-2.

This guide is actually a directory to some 100 French champagne producers (38 minor ones, being lesser-known brands rarely seen in the United States, are listed in a different directory: This is an inconvenience as both directories need to be consulted). Edwards concentrates on house style approaches, and he handles his brief tasting notes in this manner. Vintage assessments back to 1904 are provided, as well as a description of the basic champagne method process. The harvesting and the history of bubbly wines are here as well, with many French terms and illustrative matter. The author tells how to open a bottle of champagne, but omits the napped cloth feature, which is not only elegant but—on two points—is safer (stronger grip and catches spillage). He also provides tips on how to serve, how to taste, and how to store bottles.

The directory includes names and addresses; annual production in bottles (which he says is estimated, but by whom?); and an overall rating of one, two, or three stars. Food recommendations are sometimes given. Each major house gets about two pages, although some such as Bollinger or Moët & Chandon get four pages. The houses in the lesser directory get about one-quarter of a page each. Most of the pages seem to be full of label reproductions and bottle collars and bottle shapes.

The glossary is short and concise; maybe too concise. "Mousse" does not equal "bubbles": There is more to it than that. The index does not mention most champagne houses. Therefore, this book does the job, but only until the next title on champagne comes along.—**Dean Tudor**

1355. **Fandom Directory. Number 15.** 1995-1996 ed. Mariane S. Hopkins, ed. Springfield, Va., Fandata, 1995. 607p. illus. index. $19.95pa. ISBN 0-933215-15-0. ISSN 8756-8349.

This 608-page edition of *Fandom Directory* is the largest in its history. Intended as a one-stop resource for the fan of almost anything from action/adventure and foreign video/television to Westerns, *Fandom* aims to provide as comprehensive a listing as possible of clubs, publications, stores, and the like. The volume is well organized, with some of the less obvious sections having "How to Use" directions. With sections on computer bulletin boards and electronic communication (such as fax and e-mail), the editors/compilers offer a well-rounded directory that is accessible and easy to use. Indeed, *Fandom* could conceivably be of great potential use as a resource tool for a far greater audience than its more obvious one. Individuals as diverse as market researchers and social scientists, each with their own peculiar need to know, could use this volume to their advantage.

Fandom includes at least four indexes mixed in among its many other categories. In terms of organization, one wonders if it might not have been better to place these in proximity to each other, perhaps later in the volume. Finally, this reviewer was puzzled to read (in July 1995) how the editors of an already published work in hand could indicate in their foreword that they returned to the United States in September 1995. In a volume so rich with detailed information and directions to readers, one can only hope that this is the extent of its errors.—**Arthur Gribben**

1356. Freed, Judith M. **Freed's Guide to Student Contests and Publishing.** 5th ed. Delaware, Ohio, Fountainpen Press, 1994. 121p. illus. index. $13.95pa. ISBN 0-9621647-3-9. ISSN 1074-2522.

Revised for the first time since 1990, this edition contains significant revisions and additions of entries. The result is a useful resource listing almost 200 national academic competitions and contests open for students in grades K-12. Contest and competition listings include the sponsor's name, a description of the event, eligibility requirements, deadlines, evaluation criteria, and contact addresses. Simple icons help to distinguish the categories of contest listings. In addition to the contests that are listed by their general content areas such as art, leadership, and science, this concise work details information on 40 children's and youth magazines that consider submissions from young people. The book also furnishes a brief section on publishing guidelines, as well as an alphabetical index of all listings and a section listing competitions of special interest to high school seniors.

While this book provides an excellent overview of the variety of contests and competitions available for K-12 students to pursue, many of these events require school sponsorship of participating students. For this reason, the book is probably best purchased by a school media center or guidance office. For a more general listing of contests and competitions for children and young adults, try *All the Best Contests for Kids* by Joan and Craig Bergstrom (see ARBA 95, entry 1324). [R: VOYA, Feb 95, p. 371]
—**Carol L. Tilley**

1357. Hoffmann, Frank W. **American Popular Culture: A Guide to the Reference Literature.** Englewood, Colo., Libraries Unlimited, 1995. 286p. index. (Reference Sources in the Humanities Series). $37.50. ISBN 1-56308-142-3.

Another in the stalwart series of guides to specialized topics and literatures, this work brings together a core of titles and formats ranging from general to specific that serve as reference tools in the field of American popular culture. A brief introduction by the author provides a basic explication of the field and major issues concerning libraries and collections of popular culture materials.

The body of the work is composed of 13 chapters, each treating some aspect of reference tools: general references, mass media, performing arts, politics, popular history, popular literature, popular music, religion and psychic phenomena, social phenomena, sports and recreation, special collections, societies and associations, and journals. Within each chapter, works are arranged under subcategories, and then alphabetically by author or title. Each entry is numbered and provides complete bibliographic description and a 50- to 250-word annotation of the reference title. Separate author/title and subject indexes supplement the text and are keyed to numbered entries.

Most academic and public libraries will benefit from adding this title to the collection. As with the other guides in this series, the work will find equal value among the reading public, reference librarians, and collection development and acquisitions professionals. The author covers wide territory in this selective tool. Scholars and students will be most appreciative.—**Edmund F. SantaVicca**

1358. **Holidays and Festivals Index: A Descriptive Guide to Information on More Than 3,000 Holidays....** Helene Henderson and Barry Puckett, eds. Detroit, Omnigraphics, 1995. 782p. $65.00. ISBN 0-7808-0012-5.

This index to more than 3,000 secular and religious holidays, current and ancient, effectively supersedes an earlier work issued by the same publisher (*Holidays, Festivals, and Celebrations of the World Dictionary* [see ARBA 95, entry 1338]). International in scope, this work covers a wide range of current and historical celebrations, excluding commercial and trade events.

Entries are listed alphabetically by event, and include information on the date the event was established and observed, its location, its ethnic or religious affiliation, information on the person or event that is being honored, and an abbreviated reference to the source of the information. In addition to this dictionary listing, four special indexes provide topical access to the entries. They include an ethnic and geographic index; a name index; a religious group and denomination index; and a chronological index that lists events by various calendars such as Chinese, Islamic, and Jewish.

The organization of the work is straightforward, and the special indexes are, for the most part, helpful. The name index does seem somewhat superfluous, virtually duplicating the alphabetical listing in the main body of the work. This publication's greatest competitor, *Chase's Annual Calendar of Events* (see ARBA 91, entry 2), is somewhat more inclusive, especially for U.S. events, and provides considerably more descriptive information concerning each event. As a result, users may find that work more informative for quick reference than this work, while those seeking more detailed information will find the source references included for each citation listed in this *Index* more helpful.—**Elizabeth Patterson**

1359. Rothschild, D. Aviva. **Graphic Novels: A Bibliographic Guide to Book-Length Comics.** Englewood, Colo., Libraries Unlimited, 1995. 245p. illus. index. $30.00. ISBN 1-56308-086-9.

The term "graphic novels" is a bit hard to pin down. In the introduction, Rothschild defines a graphic novel as "a sturdy, lengthy comic book that contains a single story or a set of interrelated stories told by sequential art." She cautions that graphic novels are not aimed at children, and frequently contain highly adult material. She therefore prefers the term both to "comic books," which has juvenile connotations, and to "comix," which often refers to underground or subversive materials. This annotated bibliography of more than 400 English-language graphic novels covers a wide range of stories, with separate chapter headings given to westerns, science fiction, superheroes, action/adventure, fantasy, funny animals, and horror/occult. Such headings overlap somewhat, but they help structure the work's contents.

Rothschild, a lifelong devotee of graphic art and stories, does not merely present plot summaries or characteristics of her entries; she writes personally and colorfully, and is unashamedly subjective in her evaluations. This makes for entertaining reading, especially as she lashes into the ones she does not like (e.g., "This dreadful book is as flat as a shadow from start to finish. How bad is it? I purchased it for 99 cents . . . and I want my dollar back"). She does, however, give praise where she feels it is warranted. Many entries are likely to present unfamiliar authors and characters, but there are some well-known ones here (e.g., Matt Groening [*The Simpsons*]; Robert Crumb [*Fritz the Cat*, which became an X-rated animated feature film]; and art spiegelman [lowercase intentional, *à la* e. e. cummings], whose award-winning *Maus*, a parable of the Holocaust, depicts Jews as mice and Nazis as fanged cats). Controversial here and there? Well . . . yes, but that is in the nature of graphic novels, more often than not. Rothschild provides a glossary of special terms used by graphic novelists and their devotees. Curiously and ironically, the work's only noticeable shortcoming is the lack of pictures, which are unaccountably sparse. More illustrations would have helped the author make her points more strongly . . . if not more graphically.

One great value of a story told visually lies in its use of enticing or inducing reluctant readers or nonreaders to get involved with literature. This book is a very useful buying guide to a genre of literature that libraries have often overlooked or shunned, but should not, if they really want to take part in the struggle against illiteracy.—**Bruce A. Shuman**

1360. Rovin, Jeff. **Aliens, Robots, and Spaceships.** New York, Facts on File, 1995. 372p. illus. index. $35.00. ISBN 0-8160-3107-X.

Nearly 500 science fiction (SF) creations are included in this A-to-Z dictionary. Most are aliens, robots, or spaceships that have appeared in advertisements, comic books, folklore, motion pictures, novels, short stories, television, and trading cards. Others are toys, such as Gobots (humanoid robots) or computer or video game characters (Nintendo or Sega). The selections have been made according to the subject's popularity, an author or filmmaker's notoriety, the character's importance to the genre, and originality. While some may quibble over an entry's importance or originality, Rovin has made an honest effort not to disappoint the fan looking for a favorite alien. Accordingly, he has included some obscure subjects he thought were worthy of wider recognition. Purposely excluded are places and characters covered in *The Encyclopedia of Monsters* (see ARBA 90, entry 1310) or *The Encyclopedia of Super Villains* (see ARBA 88, entry 1151).

The entries include, as appropriate, the subject's first appearance, physical description, and biography, with a brief commentary. Black-and-white line drawings or photographs are on almost every page. Appendixes cover comic book aliens, *Outer Limits* aliens, *Star Trek* aliens, *Star Trek: The Next Generation* and *Star Trek: Deep Space Nine* aliens, and *Star Wars* worlds. The appendix entries are brief. A list of titles for further reading and a detailed index complete the volume. Younger SF fans especially will want to read the book cover to cover; it is recommended for most school and public libraries.

—**Gary D. Barber**

1361. Weaver, Robert S. **International Holidays: 204 Countries from 1994 Through 2015.** Jefferson, N.C., McFarland, 1995. 361p. index. $45.00. ISBN 0-89950-953-3.

A reference book in the truest sense, *International Holidays* covers holidays, religious and political, from 204 countries. The format is clear, concise, and varied, which is evidenced by an excellent table of contents. The main section of the book is devoted to the calendars from 1994 through 2015. These are chronologically arranged by year, month, and day, listing all holidays occurring on a specific date. The remainder of the book is devoted to the four in-depth appendixes.

Appendix A shows holidays with dates that never change, referred to as "fixed multinational holidays," with brief descriptions of each. Appendix B covers holidays with different dates every year, such as Easter, and referred to as "algorithmic holidays." Appendix C contains tables of dates for selected, popular, and commonly known algorithmic holidays with dates from 1900 to 2100 inclusive. In appendix D, each country is listed alphabetically with its fixed and algorithmic holidays. Completing the book is an index that includes reference numbers referring to appropriate appendixes in bold typeface. *International Holidays* is a beneficial addition for multicultural research and a must-have for the frequent international traveler.—**Mary L. Trennery**

27 Performing Arts

GENERAL WORKS

Biography

1362. **Contemporary Theatre, Film, and Television: A Biographical Guide Featuring Performers, Directors, Writers....Volume 13.** Terrie M. Rooney, Brandon Trenz, and Lynn M. Spampinato, eds. Detroit, Gale, 1995. 527p. index. $125.00. ISBN 0-8103-5729-1. ISSN 0749-064X.

The 13th volume of *Contemporary Theatre, Film, and Television* (CTFT) continues the biographical reference series' coverage of the lives and work of performing arts professionals. This volume brings the total number of references in CTFT to about 6,600 and is intended for researchers and general readers. More than 400 entries cover performers, directors, writers, and producers, as well as other specialists in the theater, film, and television industries in the United States and Great Britain. While emphasis is given to individuals who are currently active in these fields, obituaries are included, as are revisions of previous entries.

Entries list biographical and career information, awards, memberships, title-by-title credits, recordings, writings, and sources for further information. Entries vary in length from one column to several pages. A cumulative index provides access to previous volumes in the series, and to Gale's *Who's Who in the Theatre* (see ARBA 82, entry 1099) and *Who Was Who in the Theatre* (see ARBA 80, entry 1022). This ongoing publication gathers information on a wide range of people in the entertainment field and makes it easy to locate.—**Anita Zutis**

1363. **Performing Artists.** Molly Severson, ed. Detroit, U*X*L/Gale, 1995. 3v. illus. index. $57.00/set. ISBN 0-8103-9868-0.

Bubbling with the names, multiracial faces, and performances of living artists in the youth arena, this sensibly priced, three-volume biographical encyclopedia is attractive, informative, and inviting. The layout offers maximum coverage, beginning with a table of contents listing names by volume and by field of endeavor, encompassing comedy, drama, film and television, and music. For young readers, the appeal is instantaneous: Editors establish the validity and dedication of favorites, unfortunately limited to black-and-white photographs, from Snoop Doggy Dogg, Anthony Hopkins, Alvin Ailey, and Gloria Estefan to Janet Jackson, Raul Julia, Arnold Schwarzenegger, Paula Abdul, Ice-T, and the Red Hot Chili Peppers. A concise three-paragraph reader's guide concludes with another upper for young researchers—an address and a telephone number requesting user input on future volumes.

The strongest feature of this set is attractive fonts, wide margins, and clean layout; the work demystifies research by supplying simplified sources, meaningful subheads, consecutive numbering, lively citations by critics and fellow professionals, and sidebars quoting insightful glimpses of the personality and vision of the subjects. For example, under a fluid shot of Axl Rose, Danny Sugerman speaks to the humanistic necessity for celebration of life and art. A cutline under the picture of Maria Tallchief partnering with Jacques d'Amboise connects her with an appropriate honor: a White House performance of *Sylvia*. The index lists titles, performers, and performances followed by volume and page number and boldface to indicate main entries. U*X*L's dedication to racially balanced, stimulating writing provides human models—warts and all—for users to study, learn from, admire, and emulate.—**Mary Ellen Snodgrass**

Handbooks and Yearbooks

1364. **ARCO 100 Best Careers in Entertainment.** By Shelly Field. New York, Macmillan/Simon & Schuster, 1995. 340p. $14.95pa. ISBN 0-02-860017-7.

The entertainment world has a rich mythology replete with romantic tales of discovery, overnight success, fame, and fortune. Often, those aspiring to work in the entertainment industry are blinded by this aura of romance and have little practical understanding of the scope of the job opportunities as well as the talent, training, and skills needed for success. This comprehensive guide to careers in entertainment will remedy this general lack of understanding and serve as a valuable resource for those planning to work in the entertainment industry. The book will also be extremely useful to those professional counselors who dispense career advice.

The work is organized into 10 general sections ranging from opportunities in the business end of the industry to careers in performing and writing, as well as careers in radio, television, film, video, theater, orchestras, opera, and ballet. The 100 individual entries, ranging in length from 3 to 4 pages, follow a clearly established format. Each entry gives a comprehensive job description followed by employment opportunities, earnings, advancement opportunities, education and training, and experience. All the entries conclude with a valuable "tips" section containing advice and information for obtaining that specific job. A directory of trade associations, unions, and other organizations, in addition to listings of television and cable stations and the major entertainment trade publications, are provided in the appendixes.

The book is particularly successful because it never succumbs to the temptation of indulging in the glamour of the subject matter. The approach is practical, the advice is sound, and the expectations are realistic.
—**Owen H. Ellard**

1365. **Music, Dance & Theater Scholarships: A Complete Guide.** Cleveland, Ohio, Conway Greene Publishing, 1995. 493p. index. $20.95pa. ISBN 1-884669-07-7.

This is a new work for which the information was secured from the academic departments and admissions offices of each conservatory, college, university, or professional company covered. More than 5,000 scholarships and awards are listed. In the front are three short pieces written by staff from the Cleveland Institute of Music, the School of Music at the University of Southern California, and the Cunningham Dance Foundation. A majority of the directory is arranged under the name of the institution, giving addresses, contact people, majors and concentrations, and specific information about scholarships and awards. There are four narrow columns per page; entries vary in length from one-third of a column to three pages, depending upon the size of the program.

This guide is well indexed by 3 broad concentrations: music (25 pages), dance (3 pages), and theater (8 pages). These indexes will be useful simply for identifying programs (e.g., accompanying, bagpiping, choreography, and children's theater) as well as sources of financial assistance. There is also a State-City Locator (10 pages) and an index of names of institutions (9 pages).

Prospective students can use this directory to narrow choices, but they also should contact individual schools for catalogs, since directories such as this seldom are exhaustive. A similar directory is *Handel's National Directory for the Performing Arts* (see ARBA 94, entry 1420). But at its price, that work is not as feasible. This guide is recommended for schools and public libraries where students seek such specific information.—**William G. Wilson**

FILM, TELEVISION, AND VIDEO

Bibliography

1366. Paietta, Ann C., and Jean L. Kauppila. **Animals on Screen and Radio: An Annotated Sourcebook.** Metuchen, N.J., Scarecrow, 1994. 385p. index. $42.50. ISBN 0-8108-2939-8.

This compendium notes movies, radio, and television shows in which animals are the focus, and also highlights animal actors in named roles. Live and animated animals are featured, but not insects and prehistoric animals. There are three lists, arranged alphabetically by show title: theatrical and television films (silent to 1993, including non-U.S. films), television series, and radio series. A typical entry lists human cast and crew, running time, year of release, a short nonevaluative summary, and video availability. If appropriate, the name of the animal and its role are given.

A subject index provides theme access and covers a variety of concepts (e.g., deception; deer; the Depression; deserts; detectives), but some entries such as *family life* or *horses* have 250 to 300 entry numbers which are not further subdivided. The other index lists actual and stage animal names such as Tonka (horse), Top Cat (animated cat), and Topo Gigio (puppet mouse). An annotated bibliography of books and popular magazine articles is interesting to browse, but its author arrangement is not practical for reference use.

In works such as these, there can be omissions. "Fred" the dog from *I Love Lucy*, Steven Spielberg's animated *Family Dog* cartoon short and series, cartoon dogs *Ruff and Ready*, *Fer-de-Lance* (snakes-on-the-loose television movie), and the cattle epic *The Rare Breed* with James Stewart were some that failed to appear in a spot-check.

Despite these limitations, this work covers unusual territory and will be welcomed at public and school libraries, and at academic sites with curriculum or interest in popular culture.—**Gary R. Cocozzoli**

Biography

1367. Barson, Michael. **The Illustrated Who's Who of Hollywood Directors. Volume 1: The Sound Era.** New York, Noonday/Farrar, Straus & Giroux, 1995. 530p. illus. index. $27.50pa. ISBN 0-374-52428-9.

Containing more than 150 essays 2-8 pages in length, Barson gives the reader a slightly opinionated and very knowledgeable view of Hollywood film directors whose careers began before 1975. Candid photographs, portraits, movie posters, and promotional shots are used to highlight the insightful essays. This book delves deeper into its subjects than do other film encyclopedias. Each director is given a complete career retrospective, with plot summaries and critical overviews for each of their films. The on-set photographs are gems not likely to have been published elsewhere, whether it is a shot of Mike Nichols sitting with Orson Welles in *Catch-22* or Fritz Lang coaching George Raft in *You and Me*.

The directors are not given equal attention. Logically, career length and degree of prestige affect the extent of coverage warranted. The careers of horror-meister William Castle and funnyman Mel Brooks are surveyed in two pages; John Ford and John Huston are treated in eight-page appraisals. Brief overviews of 44 lesser-known directors follow the main text, and an index to names and film titles ends the book.

Barson has degrees in American culture and popular culture; he has written extensively about Hollywood films. What he has created here is not a book just for director name or film title verification, although it could serve that function. The real values of this resource are its illustrations and plentiful (although individually brief) film summaries. Students would find Barson's book to be an engaging starting point for their research. Fans of a particular director would likely be pleased with this single source.—**Ed Volz**

1368. Doyle, Billy H. **The Ultimate Directory of the Silent Screen Performers: A Necrology of Births and Deaths and Essays on 50 Lost Players.** Metuchen, N.J., Scarecrow, 1995. 346p. illus. $49.50. ISBN 0-8108-2958-4.

Doyle offers an extensive and useful index to the vital statistics of approximately 7,500 performers of the silent screen. The foreword, written by Anthony Slide, provides details of the research methodology employed by Doyle to supply accurate information on the dates of each performer's birth and death as well as where the person died. Along with the short entries of the main section described above, the book contains essays furnishing fuller biographical information on 50 of the performers who intrigued the author the most. Included are such long-forgotten names as Anita Stewart's sister, Lucille Lee Stewart, who worked with Ethel Barrymore and Norma Talmadge; and "rugged outdoorsman" William Stowell, who was killed in a train accident at the peak of his leading-man career in 1919. Each of the essays describes background information on the actors in addition to a filmography and details of their death. This work will be a good first step in research on those silent film actors not commonly included in other film sources (such as *Who Was Who on Screen* by Evelyn M. Truitt [abridged ed., R. R. Bowker, 1984] and John T. Weaver's *20 Years of Silents, 1908-1928* [Scarecrow, 1971]). An invaluable resource to film researchers and enthusiasts, this work is recommended for most libraries.—**Elizabeth A. Ginno**

1369. Vazzana, Eugene Michael. **Silent Film Necrology: Births and Deaths of Over 9000 Performers, Directors, Producers....** Jefferson, N.C., McFarland, 1995. 367p. $55.00. ISBN 0-7864-132-X.

Vazzana is lending his voice to documenting the lives and deaths of silent film figures. More than 9,000 actors, directors, producers, animators, publicists, scenarists, writers, and even Thomas A. Edison, the coinventor of the motion picture camera, appear in this biographical dictionary of silent film, an era that came to an end in the late 1920s. A surprising number of these actors lived until recent years, such as Lillian Gish (1893-1993). Others died under mysterious or obscure circumstances much earlier in their career, which Vazzana attempts to document with historical and contemporary citations. The subjects usually had some connection with the U.S. film industry, although some figures such as Emil Jannings or Charles Pathé were best known in Europe. Some figures are known primarily for their sound pictures or television careers (e.g., Walter Brennan, Ruth Gordon, Charles Farrell), but are included here because of their early years in silent pictures.

Each entry attempts to indicate the individual's birth and death date and place; given name; spouse(s); studio affiliation; and citations to biographies, autobiographies, and obituaries. Vazzana does not list film credits. The author notes instances when biographical information is not available or is in doubt. In addition, Vazzana cites news articles and other notices from sources such as *The New York Times*, *Variety*, and a few dozen film reference books, updating the bibliographical information to recent years. Some details extend beyond what one would expect from a work such as this; for example, by providing the name and address of fan newsletters, citing film tributes and documentaries, including the headlines of obituary notices, and indicating the cause of death.

There is no index or bibliography to *Silent Film Necrology*. Instead, it stands as an index to film industry papers, newspapers of the day, and subsequent film reference works. It also stands on its own as a thorough, well-researched biographical dictionary of the prominent and lesser-known figures from the three decades when pictures moved, but did not speak.—**John P. Schmitt**

Chronology

1370. Berry, David. **Wales and Cinema: The First Hundred Years.** Cardiff, Wales, University of Wales Press; distr., Bloomington, Ind., Indiana University Press, 1994. 567p. illus. index. $49.95. ISBN 0-7083-1256-X.

According to its author, a longtime critic and student of film and its history, this volume is the first book ever published on the cinema of Wales. Covering the history of Wales and film from 1895 to 1994, the work is more of a general history than a reference book. The chapters, 24 in number, are organized into sections covering the silent era, the golden age of the 1930s and 1940s, the postwar cinema of the 1950s and 1960s, and the flowering of Welsh film and television from the 1970s onward. Numerous black-and-white stills and photographs supplement the text.

The appendixes provide useful reference material, including a chronology of Welsh film history, a list of Welsh films, and a filmography of Welsh actors and directors. An index of people, places, and subjects concludes the volume. Libraries interested in Wales, modern British history, or film history will find this specialized study to be a unique and handsome addition.—**Ronald H. Fritze**

1371. **Chronicle of the Cinema.** Robyn Karney and others, eds. New York, Dorling Kindersley, 1995. 920p. illus. index. $59.95. ISBN 0-7894-0123-1.

A century of the cinema is chronicled here, from 1894 to the present, presented in a journalistic style. The volume is intended for the moviegoer, student, and scholar, focusing mostly on the United States, but also including developments in international cinema. Color and black-and-white illustrations, consisting of stills, photographs, and posters, abound throughout the book.

Yearly sections highlight events in the film world, and contain notable births and deaths and, from 1929, Academy Award winners. Each decade is characterized in a unique essay, and there are eight special chapters devoted to unique features in the work of the film industry and its stars. A general index and a film index provide additional access points.

The *Chronicle* is a comprehensive and entertaining history of cinema entertainment, affording many interesting details, as well as overall aspects. It is emphasized that this is a history of an industry and an era, rather than of individual films and performers. Because of the vast scope, some notable movies are omitted (e.g., *Love in the Afternoon*) and any supplementary information on these will have to be sought elsewhere.—**Anita Zutis**

1372. Osborne, Robert. **65 Years of the Oscar: The Official History of the Academy Awards.** rev. ed. New York, Abbeville Press, 1994. 352p. illus. index. $59.95. ISBN 1-55859-715-8.

Intended for the film buff and the scholar, this revised edition of the *Official History of the Academy Awards*, compiled by Osborne under the imprimatur of the Academy of Motion Picture Arts and Sciences, presents the range of movies in competition for an Oscar in each year from 1928 through 1992. Overall, the book is arranged according to decade, with an introductory overview of the accomplishments of and challenges to the Academy and the film industry during each period. The volume opens with "The Beginning...," which is an interesting account of the why and wherefore of the Academy itself. Here, we learn ostensibly the reasons why the Academy had to happen: the swift growth of mass communications after World War I, Hollywood's world leadership in the film industry and a concomitant sense of responsibility, the trend toward unionism, and the move toward the talkies. Each of the 10-year segments of Academy history offers an overview of the challenges and accomplishments of the times, then continues with a listing of the nominees and winners by standard category—best actor, best director, best picture, and so forth—along with the other new and specialized categories introduced in later years. Also described are the staging of the awards ceremony, the highlights and speculation as to potential winners, as well as memorable moments. Dispersed throughout the volume, "Oscar Memories" offer short comments by individuals from Mary Pickford to Norma Shearer, Katharine Hepburn, and more. This interesting feature appears to have been discontinued after 1988.

This handsome coffee-table-sized volume is well executed, easy to read, and well illustrated with interesting stills from both the films and the various Oscar ceremonies through the years. Six hundred rare photos from the Margaret Herrick Library, along with an original movie poster for each year, enhance the volume throughout. [R: Choice, Mar 95, p.1088]—**Arthur Gribben**

Dictionaries and Encyclopedias

1373. **Brewer's Cinema: A Phrase and Fable Dictionary.** Jonathan Law and others, eds. London, Cassell; distr., New York, Sterling Publishing, 1995. 617p. $29.95. ISBN 0-304-34235-1.

The subtitle of this book is misleading: It is not a phrase and fable dictionary. It has about 3,000 entries on actors, producers, directors, screenwriters, major films and genres, and technical terms. The material ranges from fan-magazine gossip by Hedda Hopper to a definition of an anamorphic lens. The style is cliché-ridden and flat, and the content is unilluminating: John Huston's *High Sierra* is "gloomy"; *Key Largo* is a "thriller"; Nicholas Ray's *In a Lonely Place* is a "melodrama"; Emma Thompson in *The Remains of the Day* is Anthony Hopkins's "love interest"—which quite misses the point.

However, the fatal flaw in this book is the appalling abundance of factual errors. The entry on Humphrey Bogart, for example, is a mess. There is a typographical error on the third line: He was 5'9" (not 5'4"); also, he got his scar in a war (not in childhood). Most of his films in the early 1930s were not "routine comedies," *Casablanca* appeared in 1943 (not 1942), and his role as Charlie Allnutt (with two "t"s) in *The African Queen* won an Oscar (not mentioned). The quote attributed to Huston was actually made by the restaurateur Dave Chasen, and the editors fail to see that Bogart's supposedly abusive remarks to his guests were actually meant to be humorous and ironic. All this in one column!

These kinds of factual and typographical errors are found throughout the book, from entries on Audrey Hepburn and Huston to *The Bridge on the River Kwai*. In addition, the description of Beverly Hills—"a town in SW California, close to Los Angeles"—seems written by a Martian. *Brewer's Cinema* is a feeble and pathetic rival to Ephraim Katz's still-valuable *The Film Encyclopedia* (1979) and to David Thomson's superb *A Biographical Dictionary of Film* (3d ed., Alfred A. Knopf, 1994).—**Jeffrey Meyers**

1374. Corey, Melinda, and George Ochoa. **The Dictionary of Film Quotations: 6,000 Provocative Movie Quotes from 1,000 Movies.** New York, Crown, 1995. 434p. index. $24.00pa. ISBN 0-517-88067-9.

As reference works go, a dictionary of film quotations does not seem to be high on the list of usable items. Granted, some movie lines have been significant enough to enter the English lexicon ("Here's looking at you, kid" or "Go ahead, make my day"), but these are rare and so well known that a researcher would not need an entire dictionary to find them. Then, why the need for *The Dictionary of Film Quotations*? Although the compilers do not attempt to answer that question, it appears that the compilation is meant to appease movie buffs' desire to know yet another facet of their favorite art form.

Collected here are 6,000 quips, retorts, declarations, and even social comments sifted from more than 1,000 films, most of them English-language sound features. The compilers claim to have chosen the "most acclaimed, popular, and characteristic films of the day," starting with *The Birth of a Nation* (1915) and finishing with *Forrest Gump* (1994). They limited the number of quotes per film to 15, and in those instances when the maximum number was used, it is possible to follow the plot of the film. To assure accuracy, they watched the films (some repeatedly) and matched spoken dialogue with screenplays.

The Dictionary of Film Quotations is arranged alphabetically by movie title and includes some credit data (studio, year, director, and the like). Quotations are listed in chronological order as they appeared in the film, and both the actor and the character portrayed are given with the quotes. The book, meticulously researched and organized, is sure to revive many memories and provide much entertainment for movie lovers.—**John A. Lent**

1375. Erickson, Hal. **Television Cartoon Shows: An Illustrated Encyclopedia, 1949 Through 1993.** Jefferson, N.C., McFarland, 1995. 659p. illus. index. $75.00. ISBN 0-7864-0029-3.

Encyclopedias, directories, and other reference works have been sprouting at a steady pace in the 1990s, no doubt due to the renewed interest in cartoons on television (e.g., *The Simpsons*), on cable (*Beavis and Butt-Head*, The Cartoon Network), and in the cinema (*Pocahontas*, *The Lion King*). Erickson's work deals with the small screen, being the sole book devoted exclusively to made-for-television animation.

After providing a tightly written, informative introduction about the history and trends of animation, Erickson proceeds to list and describe all made-for-television cartoon shows telecast between January 1, 1949, and December 31, 1993. Each entry includes network or cable affiliation, premiere and final (if any) segment dates, production and voice credits, and a synopsis and critique. The production information is as full as one will find anywhere, providing names of studios or production companies, technical credits, and voice credits.

A perusal of the credits gives some interesting insights into television animation: that much (maybe most) production is done in Asia by first and second generation houses; that, in some cases, a "U.S." animated series will be worked on in three or more countries (e.g., *Care Bear Family* was conceptualized in the United States and parts were done in Taiwan, South Korea, and China); and that stars from the popular music, radio, and live-action movie worlds regularly did the voices (e.g., Ed Asner, Whoopi Goldberg, Dionne Warwick, Jodie Foster, or Bernadette Peters). Erickson pays homage to the regular voice-over brigade (Mel Blanc, June Foray, Frank Welker, Daws Butler) in the book's final chapter.

To call what Erickson writes about the shows "descriptions" is to shortchange him. They are essays blending thorough histories of series with synopses of plots, fascinating vignettes of some producers, and critical commentary. Erickson goes into detail on why series succeeded or failed, embroidering the reasons with humor—sometimes subtle, oftentimes sarcastic—that enlivens the essays. Occasional misspellings (e.g., of Charles Schulz's name) that should have been detected by house editors mar the well-written entries. Overall, comprehensiveness and readability characterize Erickson's book. He shows what few others have: that encyclopedias and other references can be read for their enjoyment, as well as their information.—**John A. Lent**

1376. Hofstede, David. **Hollywood Heroes: Thirty Screen Legends from King Arthur to Zorro.** Lanham, Md., Madison Books/University Press of America, 1994. 282p. illus. index. $22.95. ISBN 1-56833-029-4.

An exuberant but seriously flawed reference work, Hofstede's compendium of screen heroes lists in alphabetical order 30 focal characters ranging on a reality scale from recent history (George S. Patton, Wyatt Earp, Henry V, Davy Crockett) to legend (Robin Hood, King Arthur) to myth (Jason, Hercules, Sinbad the Sailor) to fiction (Batman, Luke Skywalker, Zorro). Each entry contains an overview of the character followed by a history; a discussion of film versions; and a chronological list of screen and television remakes and variations along with dates, producers, variant titles, cast, and a rating from zero to five stars. Beginning with a preface and acknowledgments, the sparsely illustrated text is followed by an equally thin bibliography, a list of four sources of videos, and an index.

For all its good intentions, *Hollywood Heroes* is an amateur's attempt at film critique. Most disturbing of its faults is the poor quality of writing (dangling participles, preponderance of linking verbs, passive voice, weak diction), sophomoric observations, and inadequate editing. A lame justification for paring the list of female entries to one—Joan of Arc—fails to explain the author's preference for Audie Murphy, Bruce Lee, and Billy Jack over Elizabeth I, Cleopatra, and Scarlet O'Hara. The author's ingenuous cheering for his favorite movies leads to questionable conclusions that only *Quo Vadis?*, *Julius Caesar*, and *I, Claudius* qualify as worthy films to compare with *Spartacus*. His unfamiliarity with or dismissal of *The Fall of the Roman Empire*, *Ben Hur*, and *Cleopatra* leaves the impression that this compendium is a scrapbook that should bear the title "My Favorite Movies."—**Mary Ellen Snodgrass**

1377. **Leonard Maltin's Movie Encyclopedia.** Leonard Maltin and others, eds. New York, Dutton, 1994. 976p. $34.95. ISBN 0-525-93635-1.

It may come as a surprise to those who know Maltin only as the likable but slightly overenthusiastic film correspondent on the popular syndicated television program *Entertainment Tonight* that he is also a respected film historian who has written definitive studies on animated films, movie comedians, and cinematography. As such, Maltin is uniquely qualified to edit a film encyclopedia targeted for both the general reader and, to a far lesser degree, the student of cinema. Maltin's encyclopedia features biographical and career profiles (most less than a page) on more than 2,000 actors and filmmakers from the silent era to the present. The biographical entries are perceptive, written in a popular style, and contain vital statistics (birth and death dates, cause of death, and the like), key film credits, and Maltin's informed comments. The volume pays particular attention to Hollywood's new generation of stars (Johnny Depp, Winona Ryder, Uma Thurman), although *Pulp Fiction* director Quentin Tarantino is omitted, even though this 1994 film and his *Reservoir Dogs* (1992) are mentioned in several entries.

Although Maltin's book is entertaining and informative, the best and most comprehensive one-volume source of this kind continues to be Ephraim Katz's *The Film Encyclopedia* (see ARBA 95, entry 1371), first published in 1976 and revised and updated in 1994. Katz's biographical entries are more detailed and the filmographies more complete. In addition to thousands of career profiles, he includes entries on film terms, studios, and styles of filmmaking. Those wishing to complement Maltin's *Movie and Video Guide* (see ARBA 95, entry 1361) should consider purchasing his encyclopedia; for those more interested in reference applications, the Katz work is more useful.—**David K. Frasier**

1378. Miller, Blair. **American Silent Film Comedies: An Illustrated Encyclopedia of Persons, Studios, and Terminology.** Jefferson, N.C., McFarland, 1995. 280p. illus. index. $42.50. ISBN 0-89950-929-0.

The challenge of creating film comedy in silence inspired a unique golden age of clowns and jesters, from the slapstick of Mack Sennett to the pathos of Charlie Chaplin. Although Miller's interest in this field is largely avocational (being a banker by profession), he has compiled a solid if rather limited, A-to-Z, short-entry encyclopedia covering people, places, and events for the approximate period of 1898 to 1930.

While the Essanay Film Company is among those few silent studios that has achieved lasting fame, the entries supplied for the smaller film companies are particularly useful. Many were fly-by-night enterprises about which little is known today, outfits such as the Solax Company and the Flamingo Film Company. However, much of the information about actors and filmmakers is familiar turf, and most of the text is factual rather than analytical, even neglecting to indicate the relative importance of people and events. For instance, the entry on comic pioneer John Bunny simply relates the facts of his career, ignoring the features of his particular variety of comedy and his impact on cinematic history. The comparatively short entry for Harry Langdon gives no indication of his usually being considered one of the four great silent comedians (along with Chaplin, Buster Keaton, and Harold Lloyd), and there is no portrait photograph of him nor a filmography. One may suppose he is less important than the relatively minor actor Lupino Lane, for whom a portrait is included, or the equally lesser-known George Ovey, whose long entry merits a sizable filmography.

Although it covers sound as well as silent comedy, the definitive *Encyclopedia of American Film Comedy* (see ARBA 89, entry 1276) is sufficiently superior to make the present work only necessary for comprehensive cinema collections.—**Richard W. Grefrath**

1379. **The Overlook Film Encyclopedia: Horror.** Phil Hardy, ed. New York, Overlook Press, 1994. 496p. illus. index. $50.00. ISBN 0-87951-518-X.

First published by Harper & Row in 1986 as *The Encyclopedia of Horror Movies* (see ARBA 88, entry 1348), this revised and retitled edition covers the genre from 1896 and updates the original (which only partially covered the films of 1985) through the end of 1992. Hardy, the editor of this work and its recently published companion volumes on Westerns and Science Fiction that currently comprise The Overlook Film Encyclopedia series (see ARBA 95, entries 1375-1376), has corrected many of the errors contained in the 1st edition and has added new entries on some 1970s films such as *Dawn of the Dead*. The current volume now contains complete plot synopses, partial cast and production credits, and variant titles for some 1,300 horror films produced throughout the world.

The entries, which vary in length based upon the film's importance to the genre, were written by five film journalists and are alphabetically arranged under the year in which they were made. This chronological arrangement allows Hardy to trace the evolution of the horror film and to identify its major trends and themes. Lavishly illustrated with more than 450 black-and-white stills and 16 pages of graphic color photographs, this indispensable reference also identifies the "All-Time Horror Rental Champs" and the "Most-Filmed Horror Writers." Absent from this edition is a bibliography and a list of Oscar-winning horror films. Quite simply, this is the best researched and most entertaining reference book written on horror films yet. Long a standard reference source for horror film aficionados, this volume is also an essential purchase for public, college, and academic libraries.—**David K. Frasier**

1380. Palmer, Bill, Karen Palmer, and Ric Meyers. **The Encyclopedia of Martial Arts Movies.** Metuchen, N.J., Scarecrow, 1995. 465p. illus. index. $69.50. ISBN 0-8108-3027-2.

Martial arts movies have been a perennially popular film genre since their first appearance in the United States during the early 1970s. It is the impressive achievement of *The Encyclopedia of Martial Arts Movies* to list 3,281 movies in or related to that genre. Individual movies are listed alphabetically by title, followed by an entry that provides (if available) the name of the production company, lists of cast and crew, the distributor, the date of production, running time, availability on videocassette, a plot synopsis, and the authors' rating of the movie.

Among the types of movies selected for inclusion are the classic Bruce Lee films and their Asian imitators; U.S. productions featuring such actors as Jean-Claude Van Damme and Don "the Dragon" Wilson; mixed-genre films (e.g., martial arts and science fiction, such as *Knights*); and both the classic and low-brow Samurai films of Japan. Extensive cross-referencing allows the reader to navigate through the many alternative titles and locate the main entry for individual movies. Lists of actor aliases, Japanese film series, a brief bibliography, and a detailed index of people acting in and producing martial arts movies all aid the curious reader. A small selection of black-and-white photographs complements the text. The result is a fascinating collection of film listings.

If the authors err, it is in the direction of overinclusiveness. It is doubtful that the classic Japanese films *Rashamon*, *Sansho Daiyo*, and *Loyal 47 Ronin* are even marginal martial arts movies. Kenji Mizoguchi, the director of *Loyal 47 Ronin*, was a pacifist who deliberately excluded all on-screen violence from his film. The authors also need to add *Malibu Express*, *Guns*, and *Enemy Gold* to their listings of Andy Sidaris's movies. Otherwise, this encyclopedia is a unique reference work that achieves the difficult and neglected task of providing an exhaustive filmography for a popular genre.—**Ronald H. Fritze**

1381. Rajadhyaksha, Ashish, and Paul Willemen. **Encyclopaedia of Indian Cinema.** London, British Film Institute and New Delhi, Oxford University Press; distr., Bloomington, Ind., Indiana University Press, 1994. 568p. illus. $49.95. ISBN 0-85170-455-7.

India has the largest film output in the world, but there are few reference books dedicated to it; in the past, one has had to rely on more general works, so this title is a welcome addition to the field. The first, or alphabetical dictionary, part with some 700 entries covers important people in Indian cinema (the majority of the entries in this section), genres, art movements, companies, studios, and organizations. There are filmographies only for directors, actors, and composers. The second section of 1,500-plus entries discusses the films, and is arranged by year, then alphabetically by title, which can be confusing. Data for the film include year of release, length, color or black-and-white, language, director, production company, leading cast and crew members, and a synopsis of the movie. Cross-references are indicated in heavy black typeface.

The index is also confusing: Bold typeface indicates that there is an entry for that subject, but a page number is not provided, only a year for the release of the film. Other films, their directors, release year, and language are also listed in the index but are not described in the book. The 11-page bibliography includes citations for books, articles, catalogs, screenplays, and official reports. The book is completed with lists of abbreviations, dictionary entries, Indian sound feature films for the period 1931-1993, and a 14-page chronology of Indian motion picture history. Sanjit Narwekar's *Directory of Indian Film-Makers and Films* (see ARBA 95, entry 1364) is a comparable reference tool, but it is arranged alphabetically by filmmaker, with biographical information on that person, and a filmography of that person's work. There is no discussion of individual films or photographs. For its price, the item under review is a good buy, with much useful information, but patience is required in mastering its organization. It is recommended for the reference collections of academic and large public libraries, along with special film collections.
—**Daniel K. Blewett**

1382. Rubin, Stephen Jay. **The Complete James Bond Movie Encyclopedia.** rev. ed. Chicago, Contemporary Books, 1995. 482p. illus. $25.00pa. ISBN 0-8092-3268-5.

This revised edition of a 1990 work (see ARBA 92, entry 1354) has been updated with a separate section on the latest (17th) Bond film, *Goldeneye*, starring Pierce Brosnan as the newest 007. Other updates to the encyclopedia include a two-page addendum filled with new details that have come to light since the previous edition, and a general "fine-tuning" of the 1990 text. Another new feature is the scheduled release of the encyclopedia on CD-ROM (with both video and audio components).

Rubin, author of *The James Bond Films* (1977) and three other film histories, has provided "a compendium of thousands of facts, character biographies, definitions, behind-the-scenes information, and bloopers" (introduction). However, he attempts to go beyond mere facts to "delve into the mythology" of Bond and his enormous, long-lived popularity. His assertion that Bond fans are the cinematic equivalents of Shakespearean critics is somewhat questionable; however, there is nothing wrong with indulging in harmless trivia.

At any rate, this encyclopedia is exhaustive in its detail, containing entries on what drinks Bond or his female paramours ordered in certain movies, license plate numbers on various cars, and names of weapons used on the indestructible spy. Entries on the movies themselves furnish the year of release, the running time, plot synopses, cast and crew lists, and films released on the same day (to provide a context of the competition).

The sturdy paperback is formatted in A-to-Z style. Bond fans will delight in the endless trivia and numerous black-and-white photographs and movie stills. Libraries with the original edition need not acquire this idiosyncratic encyclopedia; those not owning it may consider this title for their film or popular culture collections as patron interests warrant. [R: LJ, 15 Sept 95, p. 62]—**Melissa R. Root**

1383. Stephens, Michael L. **Film Noir: A Comprehensive, Illustrated Reference to Movies, Terms and Persons.** Jefferson, N.C., McFarland, 1995. 424p. illus. index. $55.00. ISBN 0-89950-802-2.

Marilyn Monroe, Lucille Ball, Fred MacMurray, Mickey Rooney, and Jim Backus—names you would not normally link with Edward G. Robinson, John Garfield, Humphrey Bogart, or Robert Mitchum—are nonetheless all together in this comprehensive volume on *film noir*, a uniquely U.S. genre that emerged in the 1930s and petered out by 1959.

Stephens is thorough in his search of films, companies, themes, plot devices, characters, and individuals (scriptwriters, actors and actresses, directors, producers, and composers) associated with *film noir*. He includes films and individuals even if they are only marginally related to the genre. Post-*film noir* movies, especially remakes, also make up part of this encyclopedic reference work. Each movie entry lists full filmographic data and an analysis of its place in the genre, while biographical entries focus on the individual's role in *film noir*, with a full filmography of his or her *film noir* work.

The work is sprinkled with about 50 stills from different films and a selected bibliography of about 130 books and articles. A two-page introduction is much too brief to define *film noir* and delineate its development. The book is marred by a few typographical errors, but overall, it is an important source, full of clearly and succinctly written entries that should appeal to both scholars and fans of *film noir*. [R: LJ, Jan 95, p. 92]—**John A. Lent**

Directories

1384. **Film Distribution Guide 1986-1992: Volume One.** Gail McClellan, comp. and ed. Rick Allen, ed. Los Angeles, Calif., Lone Eagle, 1994. 494p. index. $125.00pa. ISBN 0-943728-67-3.

Which distribution company released what film, when (between 1986 and 1992), and how it performed in the theatrical market is documented in this guide, intended for use by the entertainment industry. More than 2,000 films, released in the United States and Canada, and 57 theatrical distribution companies are included.

A title listing provides distributor code, U.S. release date, domestic box office earnings, domestic screens (maximum number), genre code, MPAA rating, and length. In the main section, the "Distributor Listing," films are listed according to distribution company and release year, and have cast, writer, director, and producer information, as well as that given in the previous listing. Following sections contain box office hits (those earning more than $50 million), film titles by genre, top 10 films by genre, and top 20 films by MPAA rating. An index to distributor listing titles lends yet another access point to the guide.

Much information is duplicated here, and its consolidation would result in a more concise and streamlined publication. However, much useful data have been gathered into one volume, and the annual supplements promised will add to the value of this work.—**Anita Zutis**

1385. **Halliwell's Film Guide 1995.** rev. ed. John Walker, ed. New York, HarperCollins, 1994. 1231p. $21.00pa. ISBN 0-06-273318-4. ISSN 1055-7482.

The advent of the VCR and cable television has produced a proliferation of one-volume film guides. *Halliwell's Film Guide* is the patriarch of that genre and still remains the best. The 1995 (10th) edition continues the basic format and typography of earlier editions. It contains some 20,000 entries for individual films, providing dates; running times; brief plot synopses; comparative and critical commentaries; main cast, director, and writer rosters; and excerpts from reviews. Two thousand new films are listed in this edition. New features include alphabetical and chronological lists for four-star movies; notations that a movie's soundtrack is also on CD; and which movies are available in the new Video CD format. While *Halliwell's* is a bit more expensive than the *VideoHound's Golden Movie Retriever* (see ARBA 95, entry 1399) and *Leonard Maltin's Movie and Video Guide* (see ARBA 95, entry 1361), it is worth the extra money to get its more detailed entries and eye-pleasing typography. All 3 guides contain movies not listed in the others, and *VideoHound's* includes 13 useful and imaginative indexes. Therefore, libraries and film lovers may find it desirable to purchase one of the other guides and use it in tandem with *Halliwell's*.—**Ronald H. Fritze**

1386. Turck, Mary C. **A Parent's Guide to the Best Children's Videos and Where to Find Them.** New York, Houghton Mifflin, 1994. 239p. index. $9.95pa. ISBN 0-395-69000-5.

In her book's first chapter, "Taming the One-Eyed Babysitter," Turck states what many people believe: "Television discourages children's physical activity, muffles their imagination and promotes values with which many parents disagree." She then informs parents that they can choose what their children will see as they are "babysat" by the one-eyed monster. Turck helps parents by evaluating more than 200 videos on the basis of how they handle sex, violence, language, gender roles, race, religion, and cultural diversity. In each entry, she provides detailed plot summaries and critical reviews, as well as suggestions and questions for parents.

An initial reaction to the book is that although content (sex, violence, language, and so forth) is important as a concern, perhaps a bigger worry is the notion of using television as a babysitter. The way children (and adults) use leisure time is paramount to what they are watching. However, in reading the first two chapters, it is apparent that Turck recognizes this problem exists. Realizing that children are going to watch television and that the set will be used as a babysitter in the hurly-burly of today's home life, she tells how children can be active while watching television, and how parents can sense a child's reaction to a show. Turck's eagle eye picks up negative nuances of most shows, but she comes down hard on Disney films. In most instances, she gives the reasons why she feels some videos are more acceptable than others, but she does not censor or even prescribe, believing that how children react to a video is a relative, not absolute, situation.

Turck's book is enhanced by a list of tips on how to find more obscure videos; an appendix of distributors, producers, and directors; and a categorization scheme that divides titles by interests. This is a readable, instructive, and informative work, minus the preachiness, that belongs in the homes of all parents who own television sets.—**John A. Lent**

1387. **Variety's Film Reviews. Volume 23: 1993-1994.** New Providence, N.J., R. R. Bowker/Reed Reference Publishing, 1995. 1v. (unpaged). index. $199.00. ISBN 0-8352-3577-7. ISSN 0897-4373.

Rare is the film that escapes the scrutiny of *Variety*, the weekly trade paper for the movie industry. The scope of releases covered in this biannual volume is panoramic: 16 mm. documentaries, animations, foreign films, tributes, retrospectives, sequels, conventional features, and completely unconventional cult films. The pictures may originate in Hollywood or in film festivals from Telluride to Turin. *Variety* reviews each of these 2,900 entries with full credits; gives an assessment of the film's box office potential; and provides a worthy critique of the acting, directing, cinematography, and editing (or as their shorthand has it: thesping, helming, lensing, and cutting). The only forms omitted are made-for-television movies and short subjects.

The trade is most interested in the commercial appeal of these releases and their correct placement on the big screen, in an "art house," on cable, or on video. The reviewer sums up the box office potential in the lead paragraph, then explicates plot, acting, directing, lighting, production design, and overall credibility. R. R. Bowker has reproduced the reviews chronologically in a legible, four-column format. The reviews, averaging 100 to 400 words, are signed and indexed by title and director, improvements over earlier editions (see ARBA 92, entries 1346-1347).

Appropriately, the reviewers are particularly aware of audience, and not simply from the standpoint of box office potential. It is the wise reviewer who warns that the natural world violence of *The Lion King* is not suitable for children who would likely be traumatized by the death of Bambi's mother. Similarly, they discuss the difficulty of a genre film achieving an audience crossover (e.g., *Pulp Fiction* and *The Secret of Roan Inish*). It is also refreshing to see the reviewer challenge the appropriateness of product placement in films targeting children (e.g., *The Flintstones*). While trade sources can be of suspect objectivity, *Variety*'s reviews generally are impartial and frequently insightful.—**John P. Schmitt**

1388. **Variety's Video Directory PLUS.** [CD-ROM]. New Providence, N.J., R. R. Bowker Electronic/Reed Reference Publishing, 1995. Minimum system requirements: IBM or full MS-DOS compatible 286. ISO 9660 or compatible CD-ROM drive with MS-DOS CD-ROM Extensions. MS-DOS or PC-DOS 3.1. (5.0 recommended). Hard disk space. 535K conventional memory. Monochrome or color display monitor. $395.00/yr. ISBN 0-8352-2445-7.

Drawing from the same database used to compile *Bowker's Complete Video Directory* (see entry 986), this electronic version is issued quarterly. The disc reviewed was the spring 1995 release, which provides access to bibliographical records for approximately 109,000 currently available videocassettes and laser discs, and to the addresses and telephone and fax numbers for more than 1,900 publishers and producers. It also contains the full text of 5,092 film reviews that originally appeared in *Variety*. In addition to feature films and documentaries, the directory lists educational, professional, music, exercise, children's, and "how-to" videos.

The disc offers numerous means of access, among them film title; keyword; performer or director; other contributors (e.g., screenwriters, composers); awards; manufacturer or distributor; subject; date; language; and Motion Picture Association of America (MPAA) rating. However, individual records vary considerably in the amount and type of information provided. In addition to the searchable fields mentioned above, some records include such useful elements as length, hue, and brief annotations, while others lack significant data such as production year or director. Review availability is indicated at the beginning of the full display for a title.

Representing both topics and genres, the 581 subject headings tend to be broad rather than specific. For instance, videos about corals are under such headings as "Science—Zoology" or "Oceans," while those on Mark Twain are under "Literature—Biography" or "Literature, American." Fortunately, the ability to search by keyword in a title offers an alternative—albeit not perfect—means of searching for more precise subject terms. This is a distinct advantage over the print version, as is the ability to use Boolean operators and truncation to browse indexes for the various searchable fields.

The disc offers six display formats, including a MARC tagged format, a display similar to a catalog card, and the option to customize the display. Users can also choose between expert and novice search modes. The novice mode provides more prompts but is somewhat cumbersome to use, while expert searching is more straightforward and provides greater flexibility. Records and reviews can be printed out or downloaded to a file, and the software provides the capability of creating an order, which can then either be printed out or submitted electronically. However, the latter option requires the installation of additional software provided by several major video distributors.

While this product's interface may seem outdated and sluggish to those who have grown accustomed to working in a Windows environment, it is functional and relatively easy to use. However, it does include several unfortunate quirks, such as the requirement that titles that include "and" must be searched with an ampersand instead. Help screens are available, but questions can generally be answered more efficiently by consulting the detailed and well-indexed manual that accompanies the CD-ROM.

Although a year's subscription to this directory costs $165 more than its annual print counterpart, the electronic version has the obvious advantage of being more up-to-date. In addition, it offers valuable features not available in the paper edition, such as the film reviews, more sophisticated means of accessing the records, and ordering options. It will be of particular interest to libraries that are developing large video collections, and to those that field frequent inquiries regarding the current availability of particular videos.—**Marie Ellis**

1389. **VideoHound Multimedia.** [CD-ROM]. Detroit, Visible Ink Software/Gale, 1995. Minimum system requirements: IBM or compatible 386/20MHz. ISO 9660-compatible CD-ROM drive with MS-DOS CD-ROM Extensions. DOS 3.1. Windows 3.1. 4MB RAM (8MB recommended). 15MB hard disk space (optional). SVGA monitor and graphics adapter card. Windows-compatible mouse. 8-bit SoundBlaster-compatible sound card and speakers. $79.55. ISBN 0-8103-9042-6.

VideoHound Multimedia is a CD-ROM index of video programs available at the time of its production. There are more than 60,000 video programs represented on the disc, including fitness and exercise, sports, kids, how-to, fine arts, and 22,000-plus feature entertainment films. These programs are listed by title, star or cast member, director, category (genre), and awards on the main menu. In addition, subject searches are possible with a combination of terms (e.g., 1992 + best film, drama + academy award winners). There are more than 1,000 categories that can be searched. Also, the database may be probed by hundreds of themes: World War II films, films on AIDS, films on vampires, and many additional terms that represent commonly found themes in films.

One of the strongest features of the CD-ROM is its extensive biographical information (called "Bio Facts") about Hollywood stars. While these tend to be brief, they do provide basic information on the careers of each star discussed, with a list of films and other interesting data. Finally, there are 2,000-plus still photographs of the movies listed, along with many sound clips that may be played on a computer provided with a sound card. The feature films are rated with a unique system: from four (dog) bones to "Woof." *VideoHound Multimedia* has a convenient printing system. Once a list has been created, it is possible to print it out using a variety of options. It is also possible to print out coupons to save money on the *VideoHound Golden Movie Retriever*, the paperback book from which the information has been taken (see ARBA 95, entry 1399).

It is important to have all the computer capability recommended in order to take advantage of all the *VideoHound Multimedia* options. The program loads relatively easily and provides two options: one for temporary viewing, which runs from the CD-ROM; and a second that allows the database to be partially placed on the hard drive for faster operation. Searching is generally fast and convenient, and the look and feel of the disc are excellent.

The information provided is somewhat less than that available in other publications on movies and videos. Robert Reed's *Encyclopedia of Television, Cable, and Video* (Chapman & Hall, 1992) and *Film Noir* (see entry 1383) provide more detailed biographical information. Also, for home use (at a more reasonable cost), *Leonard Maltin's Movie and Video Guide* (see ARBA 95, entry 1361) is an excellent reference. The only other CD-ROM to offer this kind of versatility in searching is *Cinemania* (Microsoft, 1994), which is more costly and does not provide for the simple searching found on *VideoHound Multimedia*. This disc is recommended for home use; smaller public and academic libraries where it may well be the only source for movie and video information; and larger film collections.—**Robert L. Wick**

Filmography

1390. Billips, Connie, and Arthur Pierce. **Lux Presents Hollywood: A Show-by-Show History of the Lux Radio Theatre and the Lux Video Theatre, 1934-1957.** Jefferson, N.C., McFarland, 1995. 729p. illus. index. $85.00. ISBN 0-89950-938-X.

The *Lux Radio Theatre* ran from 1934 through 1957 and was the longest running radio show ever produced. During the years 1950 through 1957, there was a television companion called the *Lux Video Theatre*. The *Lux Theatres* featured approximately one-hour adaptations of moving pictures. For example, in February 1955 the *Lux Theatre* ran an adaptation of the 1953 Paramount film by Barry Lyndon, based on H. G. Wells's novel *War of the Worlds*. The Billips and Pierce volume, *Lux Presents Hollywood*, is a chronological production-by-production listing of the *Lux* shows. The first part of the work is an excellent history of *Lux Radio Theatre*.

The entries in serial number order give the name of the production, the date, the basis of the screenplay, the network affiliation, the intermission guests, an excellent plot synopsis, and information on the film version of the production. For each production season, the book gives dates, network, time slot, studio (e.g., NBC Studio A, Hollywood, California), host, announcer, musical director, adaptation writer, and sound effects person. Appendixes include a list of *Lux* archives and *Lux* memorabilia sources. Also provided is a bibliography of publications on the *Lux Theatres*. There are two indexes in this volume, one an index to the history portion, the other an index to the programs. Both are structured very well. The work is appropriately illustrated with black-and-white photographs of the *Lux* productions. This work is well written, easy to read, and will enhance public, school, and academic library collections. Collections specializing in the theater arts will find the volume an abundance of screenplay knowledge.—**Ralph Lee Scott**

1391. Kinnard, Roy. **Horror in Silent Films: A Filmography, 1896-1929.** Jefferson, N.C., McFarland, 1995. 278p. illus. index. $39.95. ISBN 0-7864-0036-6.

Horror films as known today owe much to their silent predecessors, especially in visual and thematic presentations. Since the genre officially dates from 1931, this filmography is a catalog of horrific and fantastic elements found in silent movies of this era. Included are films horrific in nature (i.e., having one or more of several standard elements, such as monsters or witches).

Entries are arranged alphabetically by year and are enhanced by black-and-white stills. Each contains the release date, and usually also the running time, the cast and credit information, production notes, and available review quotations. Foreign titles are cross-referenced from the original title to its English translation. Entries, which number more than a thousand, range from a couple of lines to more than a page. Title and name indexes provide further access, and a brief bibliography is included to assist in future research. Many silent films have been either ruined or deformed. This type of documentation is of value in maintaining a history of this form of the performing arts.—**Anita Zutis**

1392. Langman, Larry, and Daniel Finn. **A Guide to American Crime Films of the Forties and Fifties.** Westport, Conn., Greenwood Press, 1995. 372p. illus. index. (Bibliographies and Indexes in the Performing Arts, no.19) $79.50. ISBN 0-313-29265-5.

Film depictions of criminals and criminal activities make up a distinctive segment of U.S. popular culture and reveal a nation captivated by stories of gangsters, cops, gumshoes, and lawyers. However, as the authors of this work point out, what has come to be known as the "crime film" is in fact a composite of many film genres that extends from the gangster movie to the prison drama to *film noir*. In an illuminating introductory essay, the authors trace the development of each of these genres, and in so doing they demonstrate how the various styles were colored by the changing mood of the 1940s and 1950s. The primary objective of this work is to offer a guide to feature-length films with plots chiefly revolving around a crime or criminal intent that were released from 1940 through 1959 and to show, whenever possible, the particular genre to which each belongs.

The body of the work contains more than 1,200 entries and includes both dramas and comedies. Entries are arranged alphabetically, and those with the same title are listed chronologically. Each entry contains a concise plot summary and some brief critical remarks, as well as relevant information on release dates, sources, remakes, and sequels. Also offered are credits that include distributors, directors, screenwriters, and major players. Only feature-length films are discussed; however, a list of serials related to crime and criminals is provided in an appendix. The work includes a bibliography and an excellent index. This entertaining guide will appeal to scholars, students, and film buffs alike.—**Owen H. Ellard**

1393. Langman, Larry, and Daniel Finn. **A Guide to American Crime Films of the Thirties.** Westport, Conn., Greenwood Press, 1995. 347p. illus. index. (Bibliographies and Indexes in the Performing Arts, no.18). $79.50. ISBN 0-313-29532-8.

The authors' present volume continues their excellent 1994 study, *A Guide to American Silent Crime Films* (see ARBA 95, entry 1383), by providing screen credits and plot evaluations for some 1,132 American feature-length crime films released from 1928 through 1939. Langman, a freelance writer who has written several film books, and Finn, a creative writing specialist and former university composition instructor, broadly define the genre as "narratives . . . concerned with the basic questions of 'right' and 'wrong' in human behavior" (p. ix). As such, they identify and include in their compilation of crime films several subgenres, such as cops and robbers films, courtroom dramas, mysteries, detective films, exploitation and cautionary tales, and (perhaps the genre's defining movie type) the gangster film. In a brief introduction, the authors identify these subgenres, cite representative films within them, and discuss the role of women and the importance of settings and locations in crime films.

The book's format is identical to that of its predecessor, with entries alphabetically arranged by title. Each entry identifies the film's production company or studio, director, screenwriter, and principal cast members, and includes a short plot synopsis and historical notes. Appendixes list 33 serials with crime themes and identify 38 series featuring such crime solvers as Boston Blackie, Philo Vance, and Mr. Moto. A bibliography and a detailed index of directors, screenwriters, and principal cast members complete the text. This book is recommended for academic and special libraries supporting strong film studies programs, and those institutions already holding the authors' earlier volume on silent crime films.—**David K. Frasier**

1394. Larson, Randall D. **Films Into Books: An Analytical Bibliography of Film Novelizations, Movie, and TV Tie-Ins.** Metuchen, N.J., Scarecrow, 1995. 608p. index. $69.50. ISBN 0-8108-2928-2.

Frequently, one picks up a new novel with a familiar name or cover and reads, somewhere on the title page, "Based on a screenplay by. . . ." Whereas the original idea had major studios turning successful novels into films such as *Gone With the Wind*, the prevailing trend now is just the opposite. In fact, these "movie tie-ins" have formed a whole new genre of publication: successful screenplays reworked into novels. It is about time, therefore, that somebody did a thorough job of analyzing and referencing the work of those who convert screenplays into fiction, and Larson does it with style. He begins with the extraordinarily candid comment that he—at first, at least—did not consider such "novelizations" of films to be a good thing, pointing out that many novelizations are purely commercial, designed to wring a few extra dollars out of a schlocky or ephemeral film or television property. However, he came to realize that the process of conversion to paper frequently improves the property, and in more than a few cases, adapters actually create masterpieces of fiction from what were less-than-distinguished films. In fact, in supplying narrative descriptions and details, such authors may actually do the reading public a favor by clarifying in print what the viewer could only try to infer from arty directors' attempts to be "deep."

The book's first part is Larson's examination of what occurs when a film or television show is transmuted into a book, listing his personal takes on the joys, sorrows, and problems of such a feat. Part 2, entitled "Viewpoints," is an alphabetical listing by the author's last name, for each of whom a mini-chapter discusses the adapter's comments and observations on the process. Part 3 provides bibliographies, arranged by author and title, and a thorough index.

Most of the fictionalizers are comparatively obscure, but a few are household words (e.g., Isaac Asimov, Arthur C. Clarke, John Jakes). For each named author, there is a list of the films he/she adapted into books, a single, tantalizing excerpt from one of those works, a discussion of what he/she had to say about the challenges faced in effecting such metamorphosis, and his/her satisfaction level with both process and product. Most commonly found here is genre fiction, derived from genre films; frequently selected are novels that grew out of such popular series as *Star Trek*, *Star Wars*, *Planet of the Apes*, and the westerns that starred Clint Eastwood on the big screen, although the range is considerably larger than that.

Larson, who has contributed to—and even edited—several fantasy, science fiction, and horror magazines, writes cleverly and well, and is obviously both well grounded in, and fascinated by, his subject. Remarks he attributes to authors are referenced as having proceeded from personal or telephone interviews, or written responses to letters of inquiry. This book may be of value to the librarian seeking to motivate those who enjoyed a particular film or television show and may wish to read further in the same genre. This book is a winner!—**Bruce A. Shuman**

1395. Lucanio, Patrick. **With Fire and Sword: Italian Spectacles on American Screens 1958-1968.** Metuchen, N.J., Scarecrow, 1994. 529p. illus. index. $67.50. ISBN 0-8108-2816-2.

This comprehensive bibliography and short study of the English-dubbed Italian spectacles produced in the 1960s is a great reference work for researchers and anyone interested in *peplum*. The table of contents is followed by a short preface in which Lucanio presents such data-gathering problems as insufficient screen credits, incomplete production data, multiple titles for the same film, and the anglicizing of performers' names in the credits. In his chapter on neomythology, the author succinctly compares the differences between the neorealist film and the spectacles. In addition, Lucanio characterizes this genre in terms of mythological reality and presents *peplum* as a phenomenon of psychic compensation.

In chapter 2 the author categorizes *peplum* according to exotic opulence, melodrama and fairy tale, and narrative types, and presents his interpretation of the mythical story. He clearly and effectively describes each category in terms of its motifs, iconography, and narrative patterns. Lucanio then presents a comprehensive annotative filmography including title (English and original language), alternate titles, year, cast, credits, production notes, plot, critical responses, historical associations, and personal histories. Appendix 1 contains English-dubbed films produced in countries other than Italy, France, and Spain. Appendix 2 lists English-dubbed European spectacles that are the precursors of *peplum*. Appendix 3 presents major budget spectacles by the U.S. producer Samuel Bronston, and appendix 4 lists films produced in English or post-synchronized in English and released theatrically. Appendix 5 covers foreign films for which reference material was unavailable or inaccessible. Complementing the text are black-and-white stills, advertising artwork, and frame enlargements from featured works. The book also includes reference sources, an index, and a biography of the author.—**Magda Zelinska-Ferl**

1396. Miller, Mark A. **Christopher Lee and Peter Cushing and Horror Cinema: A Filmography of Their 22 Collaborations.** Jefferson, N.C., McFarland, 1994. 437p. illus. index. $45.00. ISBN 0-89950-960-6.

Cushing and Lee, stars of B horror films, have been cast together more than any other horror film stars. This book describes each of their 22 collaborations from bit parts to starring roles. It celebrates their films as well as their friendship. Out of their 22 films, 19 are discussed at length in a chapter devoted to them. Their first two films are discussed together in a chapter, but one is only mentioned in the filmography section since they had unbilled cameo parts. There is one chapter on each actor, giving his history before they started working together in 1948. Each chapter contains a detailed plot synopsis and a critical commentary. Often Miller discusses the book from which the film was made and then compares and contrasts the two. A brief history of each film is given, along with information about how and why it was made and who made it. There is a comprehensive filmography of Lee's and Cushing's works together, giving release date, running time, studio, production information, and full cast and credits. Besides doing original research, Miller interviewed both actors as well as their fellow performers and production personnel. This book will be very useful in comprehensive film collections.—**Robert L. Turner Jr.**

1397. Neibaur, James L., and Ted Okuda. **The Jerry Lewis Films: An Analytical Filmography of the Innovative Comic.** Jefferson, N.C., McFarland, 1995. 285p. illus. index. $37.50. ISBN 0-89950-961-4.

According to the authors, Jerry Lewis (born Joseph Levitch in Newark, New Jersey, in 1926) is one of the most underrated motion picture performers of all time. Certainly, there is little doubt that critical opinion on Lewis's work is deeply divided. While French critics have lionized Lewis, the director, as an auteur and extol his performances as comedic genius, other critics (principally U.S. ones) have chosen to dismiss his work as low and annoying slapstick humor. Neibaur and Okuda, self-professed Lewis fans, examine the totality of the comedian's career: his early pairing with crooner Dean Martin (1949-1956), subsequent solo successes and failures, his self-imposed layoff (1971-1979), and his triumphant return to screen prominence with a brilliant supporting performance in Martin Scorsese's 1983 film *The King of Comedy*.

The authors critically discuss each of Lewis's 47 films, beginning with *My Friend Irma* (1949), the first of his 16 screen pairings with then-night club partner Martin. In addition to cast and credits, the authors supply historical information and incisive analysis on each film. More important, Lewis himself comments on each film in interviews conducted exclusively for this book. Asked if his 1963 masterpiece *The Nutty Professor* was his favorite film, Lewis responds, "That's like asking me which one of my children I love the most—I can't do it."

Appendixes include detailed information chronicling his appearances on television, records, and in other movies. Regardless of the vast critical division over Lewis's work, this book offers a concise and useful overview of one of the world's most versatile and enduring entertainers. It is recommended for large public and academic libraries.—**David K. Frasier**

1398. **VideoHound's That's Amore! Love, Lust, & Longing at the Movies.** Martin Connors, Diane L. Dupuis, and Christine Tomassini, eds. Detroit, Visible Ink Press/Gale, 1995. 126p. illus. $4.95pa. ISBN 0-7876-0086-5.

The material in this inexpensive paperback, which covers "nearly 1,000 classic, neo-classic, steamy, and occasionally platonic movie romances on video" (inside front cover), was culled and repackaged from the massive *VideoHound's Golden Movie Retriever* (see ARBA 95, entry 1399), an annually published directory containing thousands of reviews of currently available videos. Similarly themed movies are grouped under 96 lists bearing cutesy headings such as "Love for Sale" (prostitution), "Amorous Aliens & Sentimental Spirits" (science fiction and the supernatural), and "Love Academy" (romances in scholarly settings).

In addition to supplying basic information on some of the films (year of release, principal cast, director, length, Motion Picture Association of America [MPAA] rating), several also include a brief synopsis. For example, the 1968 film *Rachel, Rachel* is grouped under the heading "Love Academy" and summarized: "Repressed small-town schoolteacher takes love's final exam" (p. 73) Stars (Clark Cable, [Spencer] Tracy and [Katharine] Hepburn) and directors (Billy Wilder, François Truffaut, George Cukor) whose films are commonly associated with love-related themes are spotlighted, and their films listed.

This source is by no means a working reference tool, but rather (as the editors point out) a handy, pocket-sized guide that can be used by a video store patron to select topical entertainment. In fact, in design, format, price, and size it is strikingly reminiscent of the types of guides (diet, astrology, and so on) that can be found in the racks near the checkout counters of supermarkets and discount stores. This guide is not recommended for library purchase except, perhaps, for browsing collections and some public library media centers.—**David K. Frasier**

1399. **Walking Shadows: Shakespeare in the National Film and Television Archive.** Luke McKernan and Olwen Terris, eds. London, British Film Institute; distr., Bloomington, Ind., Indiana University Press, 1994. 269p. illus. index. $45.00; $21.95pa. ISBN 0-85170-414-X; 0-85170-486-7pa.

When films of William Shakespeare's plays began in September 1899, what play was produced and who played the leading role? (*King John*, Herbert Beerbohm Tree.) Televised Shakespeare came of age in the 1970s with two original stage productions that were intelligently restaged with the television screen in mind. What were they? (Trevor Nunn's Royal Shakespeare Company's production of *Antony and Cleopatra* in 1974 and *Macbeth* in 1979.) Thousands of questions and answers such as these are to be found in *Walking Shadows*, a thematic journey through the Shakespeare holdings of the National Film and Television Archive (NFTVA) in Great Britain.

Discussing the more than 400 references to Shakespeare and his plays and characters among the film and television programs preserved by the NFTVA, this invaluable reference guide is not just "an arid list of versions, variations and Shakespearean plot summaries, but a purposely critical, anything-goes anthology of ninety years of parodies, borrowings, quotations, homages, documentaries, operas, ballets, newsfilms, home movies, and comic sketches" (quote from Clyde Jeavons in the introduction). Successfully documenting the phenomenon of Shakespeare on film, this catalog reveals how widely Shakespeare has infiltrated the moving image, as well as how great and varied is the range of his materials.

Easy to use, *Walking Shadows* arranges the plays alphabetically by commonest title (*Henry V* and *Henry VIII*, but *King John* and *King Lear*) and only cites each film's major credits. Each entry begins with a short description of the type of film, which is followed by a combined plot synopsis and critical assessment. Especially useful is a selected bibliographical section at the end of the volume. Whether one's first cinematic adventure into Shakespeare, the scholarly adventure of an enthusiast, or the serious study of a publishing scholar, all will find *Walking Shadows* the perfect guide to the NFTVA's chest of treasures containing filmed versions of Shakespeare's plays.—**Colby H. Kullman**

Handbooks and Yearbooks

1400. Arany, Lynne, Tom Dyja, and Gary Goldsmith. **The Reel List: A Categorical Companion to Over 2,000 Memorable Films.** New York, Dell Publishing, 1995. 316p. index. $12.95pa. ISBN 0-385-31362-4.

In his introduction, legendary film critic Andrew Sarris (whose *Village Voice* reviews in the 1960s helped launch the serious study of cinema) has extravagant praise for this rather lackluster compendium—and it is difficult to know why. Neither the choice of selections nor their short annotations appear particularly "irreverent," as promised by the sub-subtitle, "An Irreverent Guide Arranged by Uncommon Categories." Furthermore, the annotations reflect the conventional wisdom of well-schooled students of cinema history: valuable, but generally unsurprising.

However, the arrangement by categories (hardly any of which seem "uncommon") will prove to be the most enjoyable feature for film buffs. Nearly 200 categories such as "Wars in History," "Diseases," and "Gambling" are listed under broader topics, including "Holidays," "Sports," and "Love & Marriage." This format enables the reader to select films on a certain theme, of a certain type, or (in the "auteur" section, an approach long favored by Sarris, which may account for his favorable introduction) by director, writer, composer, and so on. For instance, if St. Patrick's Day is coming up and one would like to see a good film for the occasion, the suggestions range from the 1930s classic *The Informer*, through *Ryan's Daughter*, to the recent *The Crying Game*. The choices are quite knowledgeable (e.g., for New Year's

Eve, one of the films recommended is *Ocean's Eleven*—while most known for featuring the "Rat Pack" knocking over all the casinos on the Las Vegas Strip, it is a fun New Year's Eve movie because the heist occurs during the celebrations of New Year's Eve).

The format by categories results in duplication. For example, *Paper Moon* is listed under "Cons and Scams," "Kid Stuff" (child stars), and "The Great Depression," although the annotations are different in each case. Still, for those who think along the lines of "I'd like to rent a good detective movie this weekend," or "I'm in the mood for a musical," this will be a handy advisor.—**Richard W. Grefrath**

1401. **BFI Film and Television Handbook 1995.** Nick Thomas, ed. London, British Film Institute; distr., Bloomington, Ind., Indiana University Press, 1994. 328p. illus. index. $28.95pa. ISBN 0-85170-492-1.

The subtitle of this annual indicates its contents: *A Survey of the Year in UK Film, TV and Video with a Directory of Contacts.* The 1995 edition covers these elements of Great Britain's show business industry in 1993. Buyers need to be aware of the lag in publication time.

Combining a statistical look at the year with updated sundry directories, the book offers a name-and-number-packed resource for those curious about the British film industry. Successes are documented through audience numbers and box office totals; productions are noted; multitudinous awards are listed. The majority of the book is composed of directories: production companies, film distributors, booksellers, film festivals worldwide, cable television companies, studios, publicity agents, and many others. The inclusion of photographs from popular feature films and television programs breaks up the statistical nature of the text and makes this a fun book to browse.

Some of the information included is likely to only be found in this source; for example, a complete listing of Great Britain's movie theaters (with addresses and seating capacities); a list of every film released in the United Kingdom in 1993; and every film that started production in the UK in 1993. Primarily of interest to film/television industry insiders, this trade-paperback-sized volume (previously reviewed in ARBA 94, entry 1455) would be appropriate in the directory collections of large public and academic libraries.—**Ed Volz**

1402. **Billboard Video Yearbook 1994.** Joel Whitburn, comp. Menomonee Falls, Wis., Record Research, 1995. 109p. illus. $19.95pa. ISBN 0-89820-111-X.

Best-renting and best-selling videocassettes, compiled from *Billboard*'s weekly charts, are listed in this yearbook, together with other listings of popular consumer choices. All videos debuted on these charts in 1994. Several black-and-white cover illustrations are included.

"Top Video Rentals," arranged alphabetically within feature films, television, and animation categories, supplies year released, date charted, peak position, weeks charted, MPAA rating, total minutes, video company, cast, subject category, plot summary, director, and producer(s). This is followed by compilations of the most popular rentals, by title and by subject category. "Top Video Sales" is identically arranged, with the same information given. However, videos are listed within six additional categories (e.g., classics and sports). There are also lists of the most popular video sales.

An index of stars/performers refers to the appropriate film title(s). Closing sections contain number one videos found on various charts, such as music videos and kid videos, and "Entertainment Obituaries 1994." While a guide to the seemingly endless choices in videos is certainly useful, no qualitative assessment is attempted. Moreover, the index, while providing additional access, would be more helpful if it also provided a page number, signifying which list the video was on.—**Anita Zutis**

1403. Cooper, John. **The Fugitive: A Complete Episode Guide, 1963-1967.** Ann Arbor, Mich., Popular Culture, Ink., 1994. 312p. illus. index. $40.00. ISBN 1-56075-038-3.

As we continue to acknowledge the varied dimensions of television and its contributions to society, specialized reference tools such as this one are likely to abound. Fans, students, and scholars of communication, mass media, and creative writing are likely to find some benefit in this guide to what once was the top-rated television show of its kind.

This episode guide is arranged in five distinct sections, with the first explicating the nature of the pilot episode. Subsequently, episodes are chronologically arranged by season. Details presented for each episode include title and credits, summary and commentary by the author, and the verbatim excerpts (voiceovers) read by the narrator for each episode. Interspersed throughout are a variety of photographs in some way related to the program or its stars. Appendixes include an alphabetical list of episodes and various short yet interesting prose tidbits that Cooper felt compelled to include. These are followed by a complete index.

Although this work can stand on its own as a reference tool, it is enhanced by the enthusiasm of its author, who has felt at liberty to share anecdotal information that many might find tedious but others will find fascinating. The work should certainly be considered for addition to collections in television, mass media, scriptwriting, and cultural history.—**Edmund F. SantaVicca**

1404. Davis, Jeffery. **Children's Television, 1947-1990: Over 200 Series....** Jefferson, N.C., McFarland, 1995. 285p. illus. index. $42.50. ISBN 0-89950-911-8.

Some of television's first screen images (as early as 1931) had young audiences in mind. Once the medium took off in the late 1940s and 1950s, children's television found its place in the forefront of genres with winners such as *Howdy Doody*; *Kukla, Fran, and Ollie*; *Hopalong Cassidy*; *Captain Kangaroo*; and *The Mickey Mouse Club*.

Davis, who viewed these and most of the 200 entries in this book, looks back fondly at the genre. In his entries, he recounts the series' histories, casts of characters, plot summaries, broadcast times and dates, and alternative titles. His writing is fresh, the research thorough, and the organization meticulous. Davis chooses 10 categories in which to place the series: action-adventure, cartoons, circus and magic, comedy, fun and games, informative, kindly hosts and hostesses, puppets and marionettes, westerns, and specials. Each category is preceded by a brief description, followed by titles of shows. Entries are cross-referenced, and the book includes illustrations of some of the shows and characters. Appendixes on awards and citations, landmarks in children's television, children's series appearing in prime time, and live-action shows originating in radio or film add valuable encyclopedic data. Shortcomings are that the introduction is much too brief, and there are some glaring errors (e.g., Fritz Freleng). But, this is a book that will serve well researchers, baby boomers, and others who like to reminisce about these shows.—**John A. Lent**

1405. **Film Directors: A Complete Guide.** 11th international ed. Michael Singer, comp. and ed., and Bethann Wetzel, ed. Los Angeles, Calif., Lone Eagle Publishing, 1995. 738p. index. $65.00pa. ISBN 0-943728-74-6. ISSN 0740-2872.

As the *Guide* enters its second decade of documenting the work of film directors, it has expanded to include more than 41,000 films and 4,500-plus directors. While primarily covering active U.S. filmmakers involved in making full-length features, prominent foreign directors are also listed. The result is a practical reference of selected international film directors and their work.

"From the Director's Chair," including six interviews with diverse filmmakers and illustrated in black-and-white, is followed by lists of directors who are and are not members of the Directors Guild of America. An alphabetical directory of film directors discusses biographical and contact information, as well as the director's films, with the distribution, production company, and year of release. "Notable Directors of the Past" features the careers of selected filmmakers since the end of the nineteenth century, and separate sections list "Academy Awards—Directors" from 1927-1994, and "Foreign-Based Directors" by both name and country. An index by film title provides further access to the directory.

Film directors often do not get the recognition they deserve as integral components of the final product—the movie. Because this is a fairly comprehensive guide, more specific information will have to be obtained by further research. This is a good place to start.—**Anita Zutis**

1406. Harrison, P. S. **Harrison's Reports and Film Reviews.** Hollywood, Calif., Hollywood Film Archive, 1992-1994. 15v. index. $1,985.00/set. ISBN 0-913616-10-9.

Known throughout its 44-year run as "the exhibitors' Bible," the weekly trade paper of Greek emigrant-turned-motion-picture-industry-watchdog Peter S. Harrison (1880-1966) was specifically targeted at independent theater owners. Each four-page issue featured an editorial in which Harrison addressed the economic concerns confronting independent exhibitors, expounded on diverse subjects like censorship (the various production codes) and new technologies (e.g., radio, television, Cinemascope), and reviewed films with an eye to enlightening theater owners as to their "playability." Fiercely independent and iconoclastic, Harrison refused to bow to the wishes of any outside group, as pointedly proclaimed by his publication's masthead: "A Reviewing Service Free from the Influence of Film Advertising."

The complete reprinting in 15 volumes of this long out-of-print source by the Hollywood Film Archive represents a major addition to the literature of film reference. The set not only contains reviews for 17,000 feature films but also, more importantly, chronicles in minute detail various economic and historical developments in the industry. Harrison's reviews, although short on cast and credits, offer some of the most complete plot synopses available. Written as they were for the independent exhibitor, the reviews feature Harrison's own frank critique of the film and its box office prospects. For instance, in a 1924 review of Erich von Stroheim's *Greed*, Harrison decried the movie as "the filthiest, vilest, most putrid picture in the history of the motion picture business" and lobbied film exhibitors to demand that MGM withdraw the film from the theaters "for the benefit of the entire industry." Likewise, superpatriot Harrison attacked the 1941 Frank Capra classic *Mr. Smith Goes to Washington* because he felt it negatively portrayed the United States.

Although volume 15 serves as a complete alphabetical film review index for the set (1919-1962), original indexes are printed on yellow paper at the beginning of each year and include release dates and production information on features, short films, and newsreels. In lieu of a much-needed subject index to Harrison's editorials, the editor has chosen to introduce each volume with a page-long summary of the major issues addressed in the volume.

As this trade paper chronicled more than 40 of the most tumultuous years of an industry that witnessed dramatic technological advancements, agonized over the "Red Scare" of the 1950s, and saw the evolution of film censorship, the lack of a detailed subject index greatly hampers the effective use of this serial reprint. Still, this is an essential purchase for film libraries and those large academic libraries supporting film studies programs.—**David K. Frasier**

1407. Parish, James Robert. **Pirates and Seafaring Swashbucklers on the Hollywood Screen: Plots, Critiques, Casts....** Jefferson, N.C., McFarland, 1995. 228p. index. $39.95. ISBN 0-89950-935-5.

Pirates and Seafaring Swashbucklers on the Hollywood Screen is a specialized reference work that covers its fairly narrow sphere thoroughly. As a genre, pirate movies have not received as much attention as other types of movies, such as science fiction or horror films. For this reason, Parish has hit upon an area that may be ripe for scholarly investigation. In that case, this volume will be highly useful. It lists, alphabetically by title, 137 pirate movies made by Hollywood, including movies made for television. Inclusions begin in the silent era and continue up to the present. Complete credits are given: production staff, cast, length, and so forth. There is a readable plot summary as well as numerous excerpts from criticism contemporary to the film. In the case of early serialized movies, plot information is given for each installment. The author does not skimp where he feels there is interest: The entry for Steven Spielberg's *Hook* takes up eight columns. There is also a chronology of pirate films and an index.

One of the most useful and interesting parts of the book is the introduction, which treats pirate lore both historically and in related arts such as literature. As in the rest of the book, this section is complete and well researched, and would even be useful for researchers investigating pirate lore in genres other than film. The author of this book about film has impressively gone to much trouble to cover background about the subject in general.—**Wendy Waloff**

1408. Phillips, Robert W. **Roy Rogers: A Biography, Radio History, Television Career Chronicle, Discography, Filmography, Comicography, Merchandising and Advertising History, Collectibles Description, Bibliography, and Index.** Jefferson, N.C., McFarland, 1995. 436p. illus. index. $55.00. ISBN 0-89950-937-1.

Seldom has a well-known name in the entertainment world been so thoroughly researched, with details of personal and professional life, and published "works"—chiefly western films, television programs, songs, comic books, endorsements, and memorabilia. The book is well documented; for example, chapter 2, covering the life of Roy and his wife Dale Evans, has 132 endnotes for 34 pages of text.

The first part of the book contains ample biographical data. The remainder of the book lists all professional activities and publications of Roy (and often Dale). It begins with a year-by-year account of all recordings, listing names of musicians, song titles, and identification numbers. Next is a listing of radio performances, including endorsements made by Rogers. The next chapter covers films in which

Roy or Dale appeared or starred from 1935 to 1976, with names of the cast, including his horse Trigger; the titles of songs in the film; and a synopsis of the plot. This is followed by similar coverage of television programs from 1951 to 1993, with somewhat briefer plot summaries.

Chapter 7 deals with comicography, supplying a list of Rogers's 4-color comic books from Dell Publishing from 1944 on. Each entry gives a description of the cover, a synopsis of at least one story inside, and the price that a good copy of the comic book ought to bring. This, like previous chapters, is illustrated with samples. Chapter 8 covers Roy's photographic history, and chapter 9 covers commercial art, arranged by name of artist, and giving name of comic book series or other items for which he regularly drew. The next two chapters cover Rogers-style attire and Trigger memorabilia. The final chapter is "Collectibles and Merchandise History," giving market prices for medals, lunch kits, toys, trading cards, and the like.

There are extensive endnotes for most chapters. An appendix gives dates of name changes and marriages for both Roy and Dale, and names of children, including adoptions; there is even a list of Roy's dogs' names. Business and home addresses are also given. An extensive bibliography and a detailed index complete the work. This is an excellent and well-edited account of the life and influence of two popular western entertainers, suitable for any library with a western-oriented clientele.—**Raymund F. Wood**

1409. **The Political Companion to American Film.** Gary Crowdus, ed. Chicago, Lake View Press, 1994. 524p. illus. index. $60.00. ISBN 0-941702-37-5.

"All films are political," asserts editor Crowdus in the opening sentence of his preface, a critical perspective that explains the far-flung assortment of topics covered in this highly articulate, engrossing collection of essays. While there is the predictable inclusion of "The Communist Party in Hollywood," "Political Assassination Thrillers," and "The Hollywood Blacklist," many of the essays discuss, from a political point of view, subjects that many would not deem especially political, such as "The Drive-In Theater" and "Preston Sturges" (a director more often considered escapist rather than political).

Several of the contributors have been associated in some way with what is arguably the finest politically oriented film journal, the highly regarded *Cineaste*, of which Crowdus is the current editor. There are approximately 100 essays, each concluding with a bibliography of well-chosen key works for further reading. (However, in the omission quibbling department, Kerry Segrave's definitive *Drive-In Theaters: A History from Their Inception in 1933* should have been included.)

The quality of these essays is uniformly superior. While academic and scholarly, there is a pervasive lively, engaging style, which makes for fascinating reading. Even shopworn topics are enriched with fresh insights, such as Foster Hirsch's discussion of the artistic problems experienced by the Marx Brothers in their transition from vaudeville to movies. Mark Finch's "Gays and Lesbians in the Cinema" and Dan Georgakas's "Native Americans in Hollywood Films" are among the commentaries that explore themes of particular contemporary interest. Students of cinema could do no better than to read the essays on "Silent Films" and "Auteur Theory" as concise, knowledgeable introductions to those topics, underscoring the reference value of this absorbing compilation, which, contrary to conventional wisdom about reference books, will likely be read cover to cover.—**Richard W. Grefrath**

1410. Sampson, Henry T. **Blacks in Black and White: A Source Book on Black Films.** 2d ed. Metuchen, N.J., Scarecrow, 1995. 735p. illus. index. $89.50. ISBN 0-8108-2605-4.

The 1st edition of this book received laudatory reviews. This (more than) doubly expanded version deserves additional accolades. Sampson has scoured the literature, especially the African-American press, for information about blacks in films and films by blacks, particularly all-black cast films. He has added substantial new information, including a chapter on whites in blackface; new information on pioneer filmmaker/novelist Oscar Micheaux and on other black and white producers; and additional synopses of films and biographies of black actors. In addition, all five of the appendixes—a filmography of black films, a list of individuals and corporations that produced black-cast films, theaters catering to blacks, black soundies (three-minute musicals), and film credits for featured players—are new or have been enlarged. The historical chapters and synopses quote extensively from the contemporary trade and African-American press.

The work is profusely illustrated with black-and-white photographs, film stills, and reproductions of publicity posters. Unfortunately, there is no list of illustrations. Most illustrations have captions, which are indexed, but the text of advertising copy is not indexed, nor are noncaptioned illustrations. Otherwise, the index is exhaustive for names, titles, and corporations, and selective for subjects. The review of the 1st edition (see ARBA 78, entry 950) noted that Sampson failed to indicate which of these films still exist and are available. That failure has not been rectified. These are admittedly minor criticisms in the face of the major contribution this new edition makes to film scholarship and African-American studies.

—Fred J. Hay

1411. Slide, Anthony. **The Hollywood Novel: A Critical Guide to Over 1200 Works with Film-Related Themes or Characters, 1912 Through 1994.** Jefferson, N.C., McFarland, 1995. 320p. index. $42.50pa. ISBN 0-7864-0044-7.

Not limited simply to fiction about Hollywood, this work identifies more than 1,200 English-language novels with characters, themes, or settings related to the motion picture industry, regardless of their locale. Arranged alphabetically by author, the entries vary greatly in the extent and type of information provided. Some contain brief information about the author, while others do not. Slide, a prolific author of reference works pertaining to film, highlights the titles of film-related novels in boldface and notes the publisher and date. His commentary on each novel ranges from a single sentence to several paragraphs and frequently incorporates quotations from reviews.

A chronology of the novels covered, ranging from the 1912 children's book *Tom Swift and His Wizard Camera* to 18 titles published in 1994, appears near the front of the volume. Other features include preliminary bibliographies of novels pertaining to television and radio and a brief list of general works on Hollywood fiction. In addition to a title index, Slide provides a particularly useful subject index that identifies novels according to genres (e.g., horror, science fiction); themes and motifs (e.g., dance, homosexuality); categories of characters (e.g., child stars, producers); real film personalities whose lives served as the basis of novels (e.g., James Dean, Marilyn Monroe); and locales.

This compilation identifies almost twice as many novels as Nancy Brooker-Bowers's *The Hollywood Novel and Other Novels About Film, 1912-1982* (see ARBA 86, entry 1094), which, however, provides more consistent synopses of the 694 works it covers. The advantages of Slide's guide are its significantly more comprehensive and up-to-date coverage and its useful subject approach. As the annotations reveal only too clearly, many of these novels are forgettable at best and trashy at worst, a situation that limits the value of this guide as a readers' advisory tool. Therefore, it will be of most interest to libraries that are building comprehensive collections of materials pertaining to film.—**Marie Ellis**

1412. Terrace, Vincent. **Television Specials: 3,201 Entertainment Spectaculars, 1939-1993.** Jefferson, N.C., McFarland, 1995. 547p. illus. index. $55.00. ISBN 0-89950-966-5.

This source lists, alphabetically by program title and item number, 3,197 entertainment specials from 1939-1993 that were broadcast on network, cable, or syndicated television. For each show, the cast, including guest star and announcer, is given with production credits (director, producer, writers, and music), formats, dates, running times, and synopses. The book does not cover news specials, documentaries, sports, religious programs, beauty pageants, and parades.

A lengthy index at the end of the volume lists primarily entertainment personalities and the item numbers indicating in which specials they appeared. Some guest stars appear only in the index and not in the main entry. The author indicates that the entries here provide the only source of such information that is currently available to the general public. This book would be of value in large libraries with entertainment collections. The work is also of value for researching the history of television; however, because of the very narrow limits of the subject matter, it is not a necessary item for most libraries.

—**Marilyn Strong Noronha**

Indexes

1413. **An Index to Short and Feature Film Reviews in the *Moving Picture World*: The Early Years, 1907-1915.** Annette M. D'Agostino, comp. Westport, Conn., Greenwood Press, 1995. 407p. (Bibliographies and Indexes in the Performing Arts, no.20). $79.50. ISBN 0-313-29381-3.

First published in New York City on March 9, 1907, the *Moving Picture World* was one of several independent weekly film publications targeted primarily to motion picture exhibitors. Ceasing publication on December 31, 1927, it has since become highly prized by early film historians as a source of detailed information on the technical innovations, musical scores, and production credits and synopses for silent films. Reviews for short and feature films contained in this periodical from its inception in 1907 through December 25, 1915 (volume 26), however, were heretofore inaccessible to scholars as indexing was not begun until 1916. D'Agostino, an adjunct professor of Speech Arts at Hofstra University and the author of the 1994 Greenwood Press book *Harold Lloyd: A Bio-bibliography* (see ARBA 95, entry 1343), has compiled an index to the more than 27,000 films (many no longer extant) reviewed by *Moving Picture World* during these important early years of silent cinema.

Alphabetically arranged by film title, each entry identifies the film's manufacturer or distributor, provides the date the film was reviewed, and cites the page number in the periodical. Reviews for serials such as *The Perils of Pauline* and newsreels such as *Pathe's Weekly* are grouped together chronologically. One criticism, however, is the author's failure to denote whether the title is a short or feature film. Nonetheless, D'Agostino's index provides film scholars unprecedented access to thousands of films reviewed in one of the more respected early film periodicals. *Moving Picture World* is currently available for purchase on microfilm from the Library of Congress. This index is recommended for academic and special libraries that support a film studies curriculum.—**David K. Frasier**

THEATER
Dictionaries and Encyclopedias

1414. **Brewer's Theater: A Phrase and Fable Dictionary.** New York, HarperCollins, 1994. 513p. $35.00. ISBN 0-06-270043-X.

The original dictionary by Ebenezer Cobham Brewer was published in 1870, and the present edition is a direct descendant from that publication. The original title was *Dictionary of Phrase and Fable*, and the work has been kept in print continuously from the date of the original publication. From the beginning, Brewer's dictionary has been a sort of casual mix of information, including literary allusions, etymology, folklore, historical information, and considerable anecdotal material. In the original edition, Brewer stated that he wished to provide "an alms basket of words . . . giving the Derivation, Source, or Origin of . . . Phrases, Allusions, and Words that have a tale to tell" (preface, 1994 ed.). Often criticized by scholars for some of its pronouncements, the dictionary has continued to be popular, and has found its way into thousands of homes, schools, and libraries. Some of the problems in the past may be the emphasis on the humorous and quirky.

The present publication follows Brewer's original system of grouping linguistically related terms under a common head word, and then following it by words related but not necessarily in the same subject area (e.g., the heading "Lady" followed under the same heading with "Lady Bountiful," "Lady Elizabeth's Men," and "Lady's Not for Burning"). Generally, the book covers all aspects of theatrical life such as play histories, plots, biographies, best-known plays, theater buildings, companies, and even theater ghosts, taboos, and superstitions.

The entries are arranged in alphabetical order but follow no set form or inclusion formula. For the most part, they are brief and to the point, but in some cases a topic may provide an entire page of information. Plot summaries are provided for a number of famous plays, and accounts of some of the disastrous opening nights are often detailed. Few, if any, other reference works on the theater attempt to be as inclusive or eclectic as *Brewer's Theater*. The work is entertaining, informative, and humorous, and is highly recommended for the home collection of theater lovers, in addition to small school and medium-sized school and public libraries where few reference sources on the theater are available.—**Robert L. Wick**

1415. **The Cambridge Guide to Theatre.** new ed. By Martin Banham. New York, Cambridge University Press, 1995. 1233p. illus. $49.95. ISBN 0-521-434378.

This resource offers a comprehensive view of the history and present practice of theater in all parts of the world, concentrating on the dynamic interaction of performance traditions from all cultures in today's theater. It also offers both students of the theater and the general theatergoer information, assessment and entertainment, and a base from which each may explore particular interests. This edition contains more than 200 new entries and major reworkings of many other substantial entries. Many of the listings concern theatrical practitioners and national traditions of theater all over the world.

Already well established as the quintessential source for theater data and history, *The Cambridge Guide to Theatre* provides an impressive overview of a varied and multilayered subject. Because of the vastness and complexity of the art, it would be impossible to list all pertinent entries of interest. To create a complete guide to the theater, it would easily require a dozen or more volumes. In this respect, this 1,233-page, 1-volume piece does an exceptional job of including matter the student and theatergoer may wish to know.

If there is a small drawback to this guide, it would be its highbrow approach to defining or essaying certain entries (e.g., *theater theory*, *criticism*, *design*). Those familiar with or working in theater will be able to follow the text, but students and laypeople may become lost in its highly intellectual rhetoric. Also of minor note: Although the book is illustrated, pictures are minimal and in black-and-white—an oversight important only to theater designers and artists. Still, these are minor points to consider. Overall, this guide to theater is an excellent resource for all libraries and theaters.—**Joan Garner**

1416. Hischak, Thomas S. **The American Musical Theatre Song Encyclopedia.** Westport, Conn., Greenwood Press, 1995. 543p. index. $59.95. ISBN 0-313-29407-0.

As the title implies, this is an encyclopedia of theater songs from Broadway shows. It goes from *The Black Crook* (1866) to the end of the 1993-1994 theater season with the Tony Award-winning *Passion*. The guide features more than 1,800 songs from 500-plus musicals, and it provides pertinent information such as the songs' authors, original performers, dates and history of recordings, and an analytical description of each song. Also of value is the index of song titles, shows, authors, and performers; a glossary of theater terms used in the book; a listing of alternate song titles; a bibliography; and a listing of musicals with their respective songs that have been included in this work.

By far, the most useful aspect of this resource is its summary of each song. The author breaks the number down to kind of song (ballad, torch song, I am song, and so on); what the song is about and what purpose it has in the show; how the song came about (if it was a last-minute addition to the musical or if it had been retooled from another, previously discarded song); and what may be unique about the particular number. Hischak's use of colorful adjectives in describing each song makes for fun reading, and the insight and history detailed herein will hold even an expert's interest.

In the back of the book is a listing of the musicals/songs referenced in this guide. Besides giving the date of the musical's opening, it also tells how many performances the production had on Broadway/Off Broadway. This is an especially fascinating quick-reference source. For instance, the lesser-known musical *They're Playing Our Song* had 1,089 performances whereas the now highly popular and well-known *West Side Story* had only 732.

There are, however, a few slight disappointments with this compilation. For one, not all the songs that have been written for musical theater can be put in one book: The author has elected to omit movie musicals that have later made their way to Broadway (such as *Meet Me in St. Louis* and *Gigi*); musical numbers that do not have lyrics (like "Carousel Waltz" and "Slaughter on Tenth Avenue"); and European operettas. Second, the price is a little high. Those libraries with limited budgets will pass on a specialized book of this kind. (This would be their loss.) Finally, on a personal note, the one problem found with the book is that it is so full of interesting tidbits and pieces of information, readers will find themselves meandering through the pages—completely forgetting what they wanted to look up!

The American Musical Theatre Song Encyclopedia is an excellent resource, and libraries, teachers, and theaters alike should invest their precious dollars in it. They will not be disappointed.—**Joan Garner**

1417. White, R. Kerry. **An Annotated Dictionary of Technical, Historical, and Stylistic Terms Relating to Theatre and Drama: A Handbook of Dramaturgy.** Lewiston, N.Y., Edwin Mellen Press, 1995. 254p. $89.95; $69.95pa. ISBN 0-7734-8873-1; 0-7734-8989-4pa.

In the preface to this work, the author draws clear lines of distinction between this annotated dictionary and other theater reference works. While the dictionary contains entries ranging from the conventions of the ancient Greek theater to such postmodern concepts as deconstruction, the work is not intended as a history of the theater and does not follow a chronological sequence. Neither is the work intended as a general encyclopedia with entries on specific people, plays, and theaters. Rather, this dictionary is designed to supplement standard theater encyclopedias and histories by providing more detailed definitions of theatrical terms and thus serve as a resource for people studying the conventions of drama, theater, and performance.

The dictionary contains more than 400 entries that vary significantly in length. Some entries are brief two-line definitions, while others are short essays that address origin, meaning, historical significance, and dramaturgical implications. Thus, while the concept "mixed media" is given a brief definition, an important movement/style such as romanticism is covered in a two-page essay replete with references to particular works, footnotes, and a bibliography. The writing is clear and lively throughout, and complex ideas are rendered understandable without being reduced to simplistic notions. One of the particular strengths of the dictionary is the use of numerous cross-references, which appear in bold typeface and allow for the study of a line of related concepts. Also noteworthy are the illustrative diagrams, which succeed in illuminating a number of complex theories. The dictionary will be particularly useful to students of theater history and dramatic theory.—**Owen H. Ellard**

1418. Yousof, Ghulam-Sarwar. **Dictionary of Traditional South-East Asian Theatre.** New York, Oxford University Press, 1994. 327p. illus. $32.00pa. ISBN 967-65-3032-8.

Labeling this one-of-a-kind book a dictionary is an understatement, as it provides the reader with far more than simple words and phrases. Descriptions of "all South-East Asian theatrical genres, from history to performance, from plays to religious significance, synopses of major literary sources, and important play cycles" (back cover) are provided. Arranged in a two-column letter-by-letter alphabetical order, actual people are presented in boldface capital letters. Headwords for titles of play cycles and literary sources are in upper- and lowercase boldface italics; roman typeface is used for theatrical genres, characters, and terms. The country of origin is indicated in parentheses following the headword. Headwords were compared with entries in *The Cambridge Guide to World Theatre* (see ARBA 90, entry 1362), and *Dictionary of Traditional South-East Asian Theatre* was not found lacking in precise and carefully edited explanations of words, phrases, and concepts important to the development of the theatrical tradition in South-East Asia. The typeface is too small for extended reading, which is unfortunate since the entries are unfailingly interesting, concisely written, and easy to understand. Some entries are encyclopedic in length (e.g., *wayang*—generic name for most theater performances). No pronunciation marks are used.

The relative importance of entries dictates their length, thus *main puteri* (therapeutic dance-theater style found on the east coast of the Malay Peninsula) receives almost four columns, while *jatilan* (dancers using artificial horses fashioned from bamboo or leather) receives only six lines. Sixty-one black-and-white photographs complement the text. Captions (one or two words in native language) do little to explain the subject of the photographs and English translations are sparse. Placement of the photographs does not necessarily correlate with the text; many are outside of their alphabetical sequence (*berjamu*—to feast—is in "S"). Photographic quality is, overall, acceptable. One drawback to the enjoyment of this dictionary is that unless one knows how to spell specific words and what to seek, access is hampered by the lack of an English cross-reference index. No listings were found for modern theatrical luminaries such as Awang Had Salleh and Mustafa Kamil Yassin, directors such as Krishen Jit, or researchers into traditional theater such as Gulam-Sawar Yousof, all of which were located in *Cambridge*. The preface is too brief; an introduction and concise definition of exactly what the compiler included would be helpful.

Preserving a unique and diverse cultural legacy, while providing for the theater's purposes of education, entertainment, commercial viability, and aesthetic vitality, makes this concise dictionary of interest to students, theatergoers, and scholars. It may also act as a stimulus for further research in the performing arts and allied disciplines of world theater, often neglected in contemporary reference works. [R: Choice, April 95, p. 1274]—**Judy Gay Matthews**

Directories

1419. **Directory of Theatre Training Programs: Profiles of College and Conservatory Programs Throughout the United States.** 5th ed. Jill Charles, Debra J. Bromley, and Gene Sirotof, comps. and eds. Dorset, Vt., Theatre Directories, 1995. 217p. index. $24.95pa. ISBN 0-933919-31-X. ISSN 1041-5211.

The 5th edition of this directory has expanded from 380 to 420 entries and claims 85 percent new material after updating its 1993 edition (see ARBA 93, entry 1390). The directory profiles undergraduate and graduate programs for 1995-1997 theater students across the United States, as well as some coverage of Canada and Europe. It includes all schools accredited by the National Association of Schools of Theatre and members of the University Resident Theatre Association.

Alphabetical by state, entries contain a program description that includes training philosophy, admission and scholarship information, enrollment statistics, information about the faculty and the facilities, curriculum, and more. A handy chart at the end of the book displays what degrees are offered by each institution, making it easy for students to locate what they want before delving into the main text. Special articles in this edition discuss making the choice to pursue a career in the performing arts, selecting the right program, and business aspects of the profession. The directory is a valuable resource for prospective theater students.—**Jean Engler**

1420. **Shakespeare Companies and Festivals: An International Guide.** Ron Engle, Felicia Hardison Londre, and Daniel J. Watermeier, eds. Westport, Conn., Greenwood Press, 1995. 568p. illus. index. $95.00. ISBN 0-313-27434-7.

This comprehensive handbook profiles more than 150 U.S. and international Shakespeare festivals and companies, with each profile constituting an essay with a detailed headnote, narrative, and production history. Each headnote includes (with few exceptions) essential information: company or festival name, mailing address, site, administrative office telephone number, box office telephone number, ticket prices, season length, number of productions and performance starting times, principal staff members, physical facilities' description, audition procedures and location, Equity status, annual budget, date of founding, and founder's names. (Note: This survey covers the years 1991-1993; most of the sites were visited by the contributor writing about that site.)

The narrative describes the history of the particular festival or company, including its organization, staffing, and budgeting; its physical facilities and performance site; demographics of its audience and community; and its approach to producing Shakespeare's plays. Most essays also review (briefly) one or more Shakespeare plays attended by the contributor. The production history lists Shakespeare's plays produced usually in chronological order and provides a guide to further information (including a list of selected publications).

Having visited more than a score of these festivals and companies, this reviewer attests to the accuracy, completeness, and objectivity of the festivals in question. Probably, these virtues characterize the book. There exists nothing close to this publication on this subject. The work is strongly recommended for all public and travel libraries and for all libraries collecting Shakespeareana for any purpose.
—**C. B. (Bob) Darrell**

1421. **The Student's Guide to Playwriting Opportunities.** Michael Wright, ed. Dorset, Vt., Theatre Directories, 1995. 136p. index. $14.95 spiralbound. ISBN 0-933919-33-6.

The premier edition of this guide offers a collection of 52 college programs and 72 developmental programs for playwrights, gleaned from a survey of colleges and universities, playwriting labs, writer's colonies, and workshops. Entries for college programs cite available playwriting classes at both undergraduate and graduate levels; reading, production, and critiquing policies; festivals and conferences; outside resources; and a brief, narrative description. The segment of developmental programs lists theater companies, workshops, and the like that may offer internships or other experiental learning situations. The guide is complete with additional resources and several essays with advice for those seeking careers in this field.

The directory is concise in its presentation, serving as a starting point for prospective students. This is a useful addition to the repertoire of Theatre Directories, with plans to update the information every two years.—**Jean Engler**

Handbooks and Yearbooks

1422. **The Cambridge Illustrated History of British Theatre.** By Simon Trussler. New York, Cambridge University Press, 1994. 404p. illus. index. $39.95. ISBN 0-521-41913-1.

Beautifully and generously illustrated with a wide range of color and black-and-white photographs and other graphic materials, this lively, highly readable, and sometimes opinionated account traces the development of British theater from the Roman period to 1990. Trussler, a theater scholar and editor of the *New Theatre Quarterly*, emphasizes the performance aspects of drama as he deftly interweaves the theatrical elements—playwrights, actors, directors, stage managers, audiences, theaters—with the political and social events that surrounded and molded them. Particularly commendable is his treatment of nontraditional theater and the role of women in the theater.

Each of the 22 chapters focuses on a chronological period, generally ranging from 10 to 30 years. Frequent sidebars on topics ranging from Jacobean clowns to the musicals of Andrew Lloyd Webber supplement and enrich the narrative history, as do the lengthy explanatory captions that accompany the illustrative material. Additional features include a chronology of British theater spanning the years from 75 B.C. to 1990; a brief glossary of theatrical terms; a "who's who" section that actually serves as an index to personal names while also providing a brief phrase identifying each individual; and a bibliographic essay. An index to topics, titles, and proper names (other than personal) concludes the volume.

Providing a remarkably detailed yet concise synthesis of the history of theater in Great Britain, Trussler's work will be an excellent addition to the circulating collections of both public and academic libraries. Libraries that have found general theatrical histories, such as Allardyce Nicoll's six-volume *A History of English Drama, 1660-1900* (Cambridge University Press, 1952-1959) and its companion volume, *English Drama 1900-1930* (see ARBA 74, entry 1361), to be useful as reference sources may want to consider purchasing a second copy of this history for the reference collection due to its broad scope and currency.—**Marie Ellis**

28 Philosophy and Religion

PHILOSOPHY

Bibliography

1423. Blackwell, Kenneth, and Harry Ruja. **A Bibliography of Bertrand Russell.** New York, Routledge, 1994. 3v. illus. index. (Collected Papers of Bertrand Russell). $455.00/set. ISBN 0-415-11644-9.

If bibliographies were automobiles, this would be a Rolls Royce. What marks it for such elite status is the uncommon quality and thoroughness of its scholarship. Yet, even the physical attributes of the three-volume set elevate it well above the ordinary: heavy coated paper, gold titles and cover design on blue cloth bindings, gilt-topped edges, a slipcase. Of course, the price is heavy, but the scholarship is admirable. The authors have created in this (exclusively primary) bibliography an authoritative and minutely detailed record of the public output of a figure who easily ranks among this century's five most prominent philosophers, and quite likely its most prolific, to say nothing of outspoken and controversial. It encompasses all sides of Russell's wide-ranging labors and interest: the popular (his work as educator, social critic, moralist, pacifist, and antiwar activist) as well as the technical (logician, philosopher of mathematics, epistemologist, metaphysician).

With painstaking attention to the physical details and publishing history of its subject's remarkable oeuvre, the bibliography serves the bibliophile and book collector or dealer as much as the student or scholar concerned with the substance of Russell's thought, while also placing bibliography at the service of such intellectual endeavors as assessing the popularity and circulation of an individual's ideas and establishing the accuracy and authenticity of texts. Most impressive is volume 1, which in 611 pages catalogs separate publications through 1990—books, pamphlets, and leaflets authored in full or in part by Russell—in every known edition, impression, and translation. Each is meticulously described to distinguish it from others, with descriptions of the extant manuscript remains for each work and listings of all full or partial reprintings (even anthologized extracts) the authors were able to unearth and verify.

Each entry notes locations in one or both of the two foremost Russell library collections, at McMaster University and the University of Toronto. Volume 2 covers serial publications—journal articles, newspaper columns, book reviews, letters to editors, and so forth, again including reprintings—and also contains a number of special sections: reports of speeches, interviews, multiple-signatory publications, original blurbs (endorsements of books published in advertisements or on book jackets), extracts published in booksellers' catalogs, audio recordings, and films. There is even a listing of spurious (falsely or erroneously attributed) publications. Volume 3 provides a comprehensive name, title, and subject index to volumes 1 and 2, and an index to the citations of manuscript files in the Russell Archives at McMaster.—**Hans E. Bynagle**

1424. Manzo, Bettina. **The Animal Rights Movement in the United States, 1975-1990: An Annotated Bibliography.** Metuchen, N.J., Scarecrow, 1994. 296p. index. $39.50. ISBN 0-8108-2732-8.

Balanced information about the fast-growing animal rights movement is hard to find. This annotated bibliography covers the movement from 1975 to 1990 and addresses the movement's goals, organizations, philosophical underpinnings, and political, educational, and legislative activities. Composed of 1,300 citations from magazines, journals, monographs, books, newspapers, government publications, and animal rights literature, it is divided into nine chapters. Headings include circuses, ethics, fur, law, pets, vegetarianism, and a large section on experimentation. The bibliography provides sources predominantly from the United States; however, the movement is global and certain English-language citations from other countries are included. The bibliography is well researched and broadly based. It will be of interest to those concerned with the movement as well as animals in general and ethical social movements. This is an excellent educational source.—**Linda L. Lam-Easton**

1425. Navia, Luis E. **The Philosophy of Cynicism: An Annotated Bibliography.** Westport, Conn., Greenwood Press, 1995. 213p. index. (Bibliographies and Indexes in Philosophy, no.4). $69.50. ISBN 0-313-29249-3.

As Navia (New York Institute of Technology) points out in his preface to the bibliography, Cynicism is not properly characterized as a philosophical *school* of thought. Rather, it constitutes "a philosophical *movement* which manifested itself in various ways at different times, its only pervasive common denominator being a dissatisfaction with the political, social, and moral norms and customs of [its] contemporaries." Thus, it is possible for philosophical Cynicism to whistle through the intellectual climate even today, as this well-written, annotated bibliography amply demonstrates.

Included are 704 substantial annotated entries for more than 600 books, journal articles, and miscellany relating to the Cynical movement. Works pertaining to the ancient Greek and Roman Cynics, as well as to works written throughout the centuries—be they strict philosophical treatises, historical works, or even fictional treatments—up to the present day are annotated. Moreover, the bibliography is international in scope.

The volume is divided into four main sections covering, respectively, "General Studies," "Antisthenes," "Diogenes of Sinope," and "Crates and Other Cynics." There is an index of both authors and names. In all, Navia has compiled a useful and eminently readable annotated bibliography of Cynicism that, while admittedly not a comprehensive work on the topic, should be a welcome addition to graduate-level collections in philosophy and intellectual history.—**Mark Cyzyk**

1426. Verene, Molly Black. **Vico: A Bibliography of Works in English from 1884 to 1994.** Bowling Green, Ohio, Bowling Green State University, Philosophy Documentation Center, 1994. 183p. index. $37.00. ISBN 0-912632-97-6.

This volume, compiled under the auspices of the Institute for Vico Studies at Emory University, provides both a primary and a secondary bibliography of the works of Giambattista Vico (1668-1744), the Italian anti-Cartesian philosopher. Vico studies have come into vogue in recent years due to the interesting parallels between current anti-Cartesian thought and the Vichian philosophy.

The primary bibliography includes English editions of Vico's works, as well as reviews in English of editions of Vico's works in other languages. The secondary bibliography is divided, roughly, into two parts. The first part, "Works on Vico," contains citations to books, essays, dissertations and theses, and entries in reference works. The second part, "Works Citing Vico," is perhaps the more interesting part of the volume; it is also the longer, and was certainly the more difficult to compile. Here one can find citations to books, articles, dissertations, and even works of fiction that cite or merely mention Vico.

The organization of the volume is logical and, conveniently, whenever a book is listed, citations to reviews of that book are also listed. It would be nice to see this well-done bibliography expanded to include works in other languages. Because the subject matter is so specific, it is essential for anyone pursuing Vichian studies. Likewise, it is recommended only for libraries supporting philosophical or historical research at the graduate level.—**Mark Cyzyk**

Biography

1427. Collinson, Diané, and Robert Wilkinson. **Thirty-Five Oriental Philosophers.** New York, Routledge, 1994. 205p. $65.00. ISBN 0-415-02596-6.

As Collinson and Wilkinson admit in their introduction to this slim volume, the term *Oriental* tends to conflate the meaning of several distinct philosophical traditions, suggesting that they all, in some manner, share a common mode of philosophical thought. Apart from a central concern with ethics, however, such is not the case, as this volume, with its brief descriptions of the thought of the main figures of Asian philosophy, will attest.

Divided into five main sections, this work covers representative philosophers from the various Islamic, Indian, Tibetan, Chinese, and Japanese traditions. Each entry provides a three- to five-page elaboration and discussion of a particular philosopher's views. Technical philosophical terms are highlighted within the text, and a glossary is included at the end of the volume to further explain the meaning of these terms. Brief, two- to four-item primary and secondary bibliographies are included at the end of each entry. There is, as well, a general bibliography at the end of the volume.

The main attraction of this work is its concise and readable nature. Its main detractions include a limit to the number of philosophers covered (a few thinkers are conspicuously absent, e.g., Chuang Tzu) and the high price levied by the publishers for this relatively short work. The book is recommended for undergraduate collections in philosophy and religion, but probably not needed for graduate collections.—**Mark Cyzyk**

Dictionaries and Encyclopedias

1428. Caygill, Howard. **A Kant Dictionary.** Cambridge, Mass., Blackwell, 1995. 453p. index. (The Blackwell Philosopher Dictionaries). $59.95; $22.95pa. ISBN 0-631-17534-2; 0-631-17535-0pa.

The Blackwell Philosopher Dictionaries were launched several years ago with a good deal of promise (see review of *A Rousseau Dictionary* [ARBA 93, entry 1396]). Caygill's dictionary on Kant adds substantially to the fulfillment of that promise—but there is one reservation. Ostensibly intended to clarify Immanuel Kant's ideas "for students and general readers alike" (cover blurb), and according to the stated aim of the series, to present "the life and work of an individual philosopher in a scholarly yet accessible manner" (ibid), this work is not in fact as helpful as it may be for the nonspecialist trying to understand this notoriously difficult-to-comprehend philosopher. For instance, a quick reading of the articles on analytical judgments, apperception, or representation will attest that Caygill's presentation of the more technical aspects of Kant's philosophy is often little or no more "accessible" than the original works. That is not to suggest the dictionary has no value: By offering different points of entry to, revealing contexts for, or drawing out relationships among parts of Kant's philosophy, it affords ways of approaching and traversing that complex body of thought that are alternative and complementary to the original writings and the many existing commentaries on it. All this can aid both the specialist and the nonspecialist. For the latter, however, there is too little easing of the struggle with specialized terminology, the dense "network" quality, and the architectonic structure of Kant's philosophizing. These comments do not apply to material on the more popular or at least less technical parts of Kant's thought, such as the articles on enlightenment, federalism, peace, or sex.

Among the work's 250-plus entries, predictably, are such uniquely or characteristically Kantian concepts as a priori/a posteriori, antinomy of pure reason, categorical imperative, heteronomy, synthetic a priori judgment, and thing-in-itself. In addition, there are many terms and concepts in more general currency on which Kant had significant things to say, often redefining or redirecting them in the process: abstraction, causality, discipline, idea, opinion, space, substance, and theodicy, for example. There is also an article on each of Kant's major writings, including the famous three *Critiques*, but also lesser-known works such as the early-written but late-published *Anthropology from a Pragmatic Point of View*. Preceding the alphabetical section are two essays, "Kant and the Language of Philosophy" and "Kant and the 'Age of Criticism,' " the latter providing biographical information and the historical context for Kant's thought generally. Many individual articles, too, have valuable comment on the historical background of his terminology or his treatment of a particular topic (e.g., those on concept and intuition), and in many cases, on the subsequent development of or reaction to his ideas (e.g., the articles on consciousness and infinity). These are among the elements that make Caygill's work worthwhile and welcome despite some caveats.—**Hans E. Bynagle**

1429. **Encyclopedia of Bioethics.** rev. ed. Warren Thomas Reich, ed. New York, Macmillan/Simon & Schuster, 1995. 5v. index. $425.00/set. ISBN 0-02-897355-0.

AIDS, advance directives, animal rights, cryopreservation, the death penalty, ecofeminism, female circumcision, genome mapping, hazardous wastes, hospice care, information disclosure, interpersonal abuse, medical information systems, multinational research, sustainable development, veterinary ethics, xenografts: None of these terms or phrases were even in the index to the 1st edition of this groundbreaking encyclopedia (see ARBA 80, entry 1087). In this revised edition, however, they all show up in the titles of new articles or groups of several related articles. Representing new developments over the last two decades, issues that have gained new prominence or urgency, previously neglected topics, expansions of the field of bioethics or of the encyclopedia's scope, or simply new or newly favored terminology, the above topics signal just some of the more obvious revisions in this thoroughly updated and expanded edition. There are, of course, plenty of other changes. Many topics previously subsumed under broader rubrics have been elevated to independent treatment: conflict of interest, epidemics, and triage, for example. Virtually every one of the hundreds of articles carried forward (if only by title) from the 1st edition has been thoroughly rewritten, in most cases by a different author, to bring information up-to-date and examine the subject from a contemporary perspective. The editor justifiably calls the result "a fresh, new work" (p. xiv). Quantitatively, the encyclopedia has grown from 4 volumes to 5, from 315 articles to 464, and from 285 contributors to 437.

What has not changed are the major virtues that made the original *Encyclopedia of Bioethics* an indispensable resource in its field. Complex topics such as abortion, disability, genetic testing and screening, and population ethics are often covered by multiple articles examining distinct facets (e.g., historical, medical, legal, ethical) or diverse moral and religious perspectives (e.g., Jewish, Roman Catholic, Protestant, Islamic). The roster of editorial advisors still reads like a "who's who" of the field of bioethics, and every article is not only written by an expert on its specific topic, but was reviewed by at least one additional expert. On top of discussions of specific bioethical issues, articles of a more general nature provide essential context and background; for example, those on behaviorism, general ethical theories, and various religious traditions. (These, incidentally, give the encyclopedia considerable usefulness beyond the domain of bioethical concerns.) A valuable appendix containing the texts of major ethical codes, oaths, and directives has doubled from the 1st edition to nearly 200 pages.

Finally, the editors have sought broad representation of divergent views on controversial issues and insisted, they say, "that the contributors give fair representation to a variety of ethical views on a given topic" (p. xxxi). They do not claim complete absence of bias in individual articles, but point to the counterbalancing effect of the breadth of perspectives represented in related entries. Even so, some perspectives (such as those of the so-called Christian Right) may not consider themselves as well represented as they could or should be. It would make an intriguing exercise to see just what biases readers of diverse persuasions may perceive in, for instance, the survey article on Roman Catholicism, written by a prominent Catholic scholar who covers a spectrum of Catholic opinion but is himself well known for his dissent from official Church teachings. No one, in any case, can justly deny the encyclopedia's solid credentials and its immense value in presenting a vast range of bioethical issues, and a still vaster range of hard thinking about them.—**Hans E. Bynagle**

Directories

1430. **The Philosopher's Phone Book, 1995: E-mail Addresses, Department Phone Numbers, University or College Affiliations.** Bowling Green, Ohio, Philosophy Documentation Center/Bowling Green State University, 1995. 320p. $19.95pa. ISBN 0-912632-99-2.

This little volume is no more than its title indicates: a telephone book. It is, however, a telephone book unlike those produced by the baby Bells. There are no extras—no zip codes, no subject thesauruses, and no subject listings. Moreover, it lacks interesting personal or disciplinary information, such as degrees, specialty, or status within the department. If it is not the Brooklyn telephone book of philosophy, neither is it the Martindale-Hubbell of philosophy (*Martindale-Hubbell Law Directory* [see ARBA 91, entry 581]). Maybe a large percentage of the entries are accurate: It is hard to say without invading a lot of privacy. One of the three philosophers with whom this reviewer consorts was correctly listed, and two were missing e-mail addresses. At 320 pages, one ends up with telephone numbers and affiliations for approximately 12,500 philosophers. The next edition could be improved by the addition of an index by institution and another by geographic locale.—**Judith M. Brugger**

Handbooks

1431. **Codes of Professional Responsibility.** 3d ed. Rena A. Gorlin, ed. Washington, D.C., BNA Books, 1994. 816p. index. $75.00. ISBN 0-87179-849-2.

In this edition of *Codes*, Gorlin has updated the 2d edition (see ARBA 91, entry 156) to include the most recent guidelines or codes; she has also added more associations' codes (45, up from 37), developed an expanded list of resources (70 pages, up from 24), and provided more extensive indexing. Indicative of today's societal issues, the section on health has expanded to eight groups with the addition of allied health, chiropractic, and pharmacy. The codes are current as of June 1994, and it is not uncommon to see revisions of the codes dated in the 1990s.

For the most part, the 3d edition has not changed substantively. It lists full texts or significant excerpts of the codes of associations in business, health, and law. Each entry also provides the association's address, telephone number, membership, and its committees or publications concerned with ethics. The resources section covers organizations, government bodies, and educational programs, as well as periodical, bibliographic, and nonprint media resources. Individual indexes to issues, professions, and organizations conclude the volume.

In her introduction, Gorlin cautions that the codes published in this volume are representative of, but may not be the only ones, governing members of a profession. In particular, an individual must be aware of federal, state, and local laws or regulations. Even with this cautionary note, the book is highly recommended as a reference source for public, special, and academic libraries; it is useful as a compilation of ethics codes for people in professions, for consumers, and for students of ethics.—**Joan B. Fiscella**

1432. **A Companion to the Philosophy of Mind.** Samuel Guttenplan, ed. Cambridge, Mass., Blackwell, 1994. 642p. index. (Blackwell Companions to Philosophy). $79.95. ISBN 0-631-17953-4.

This volume, one in the Blackwell Companions to Philosophy series, seeks to serve as a pilot through the notoriously treacherous waters of contemporary Anglo-American philosophy of mind. The book is divided into two main sections. The first is a longish, three-chapter "Essay on Mind" by Guttenplan that admirably introduces and surveys the most salient problems in the philosophy of mind. The second section is the "Companion to the Philosophy of Mind" itself: an encyclopedia of signed articles covering concepts ("agency," "perception," "qualia"), problems ("artificial intelligence," "the unconscious," "weakness of will"), and philosophic positions ("behaviorism," "functionalism," "physicalism") in the philosophy of mind. Topics of considerable controversy (e.g., functionalism) are divided into two segments—each segment authored by a different philosopher—in an attempt to provide the reader with a sense of the scope and the possible theoretical stances surrounding the topic.

Articles in the volume are eminently authoritative; they are authored by some of the most renowned names in Anglo-American philosophy today, such as Noam Chomsky, Donald Davidson, Daniel Dennett, Jerry Fodor, Alvin Goldman, Jaegwon Kim, David Lewis, John Perry, Hilary Putnam, John Searle, and Robert Stalnaker, among others. The most remarkable feature of this volume is that several leading theorists (including many of the aforementioned names) have written articles about their own work. This volume will prove a welcome sight for those navigating the chill and stormy seas of the philosophy of mind and is especially recommended for academic libraries supporting undergraduate and graduate majors in philosophy.—**Mark Cyzyk**

1433. **Great Thinkers of the Eastern World: The Major Thinkers and the Philosophical and Religious Classics of China, India, Japan, Korea, and the World of Islam.** Ian P. McGreal, ed. New York, HarperCollins, 1995. 505p. index. $45.00. ISBN 0-06-270085-5.

Dozens of scholars have contributed to this collection of essays about some of the Eastern world's most influential philosophical and religious thinkers. Concentrating on those individuals whose influence is widely acknowledged (e.g., Confucius, Mao Tse-tung, Rabindranath Tagore), this work contains sections on China, India, Japan, Korea, and the World of Islam. In addition to individuals, the book covers classic writings (e.g., *Upanishads*) whose authorship is unclear or unknown.

Within each geographical section, names are arranged chronologically, purportedly to provide a sense of historical development to the ideas. Readers may question the validity of such a modernist rationale, as they may question the organization by nation, the title (spiritual and philosophical leadership is not necessarily a matter of thought), and the seeming imbalance of sections. Why, for example, is there an essay on Siddhartha Gautama, the Buddha, but none on the Islam prophet Muhammad? Criteria for selection and organization are not clearly defined in the editor's preface.

These concerns aside, the information offered in the essays is valuable. Each listing includes biographical data, a list of major works, a summary statement of major ideas, and suggestions for further reading. A companion to *Great Thinkers of the Western World* (see ARBA 93, entry 950), also edited by McGreal, this book will introduce general readers to the diversity of thought and spiritual traditions in the Eastern world and will stimulate them to explore further.—**Barbara Ittner**

1434. **The Oxford History of Western Philosophy.** Anthony Kenny, ed. New York, Oxford University Press, 1994. 407p. illus. maps. index. $39.95. ISBN 0-19-824278-6.

Where there is need for a reference history of philosophy, *The Oxford History of Western Philosophy* presents an appealing option: an attractive work at, for what one gets, an attractive price. What one gets, more specifically, is a handsome volume printed on heavy, slick paper, illustrated with numerous plates, including 21 in exquisite color. These accompany a text contributed by six eminent British and United States scholars of philosophy under the editorial direction of Kenny, former president of the British Academy and Master of Balliol College, Oxford.

The text covers the history of Western philosophy in five roughly chronological chapters: ancient, medieval, René Descartes to Immanuel Kant, Continental philosophy from Johann Gottlieb Fichte to Jean-Paul Sartre, and John Stuart Mill to Ludwig Wittgenstein. The emphasis in these falls on the central domains of epistemology and metaphysics, with sporadic attention to ethics and other branches of philosophy. The history of political philosophy, from the Greeks to the twentieth century, is handled separately in a sixth chapter by noted Oxford philosopher Anthony Quinton. All of this adds up to a useful, high-quality resource.

Beware, however; this work is not necessarily effective as an introduction for beginners, at least not all its parts. Stephen Clark's chapter on ancient philosophy, for instance, using a manner of presentation that constantly draws connections, comparisons, and contrasts among the various thinkers, schools, and ideas, will be difficult to follow without some prior familiarity with the basic ideas of the philosophers he discusses. And Paul Vincent Spade's treatment of the medieval debate about universals is difficult fare for anyone, let alone the philosophical novice.

Finally, it is important to note the volume's roots in the Anglo-American analytical tradition so strongly associated with Oxford University. True, Roger Scruton makes a brave effort in representing the nineteenth- and twentieth-century Continental tradition, and the very presence of his chapter exemplifies a phenomenon noted in an afterword by editor Kenny: the blurring, bridging, and shifting of established philosophical boundaries during the past decade. Nevertheless, it is clear where this volume's sympathies chiefly lie. [R: Choice, Mar 95, p.1135]—**Hans E. Bynagle**

1435. Sherry, Clifford J. **Animal Rights: A Reference Handbook.** Santa Barbara, Calif., ABC-CLIO, 1994. 240p. index. (Contemporary World Issues). $39.50. ISBN 0-87436-733-6.

As the animal rights movement grows, so does the body of literature connected to it. Accordingly, there is a need for reference works to guide the reader to major works (pro and con) in the field. Sherry is a scientist whose stated goal for this source is to present a balanced overview of the issues. While the book has much useful information, Sherry's bias against animal rights is apparent in the text sections, particularly in the opening overview chapter. For example, he tends to quote the views of extremists in the movement, rather than those of the more moderate groups, such as the Humane Society of the United States. He also includes an inappropriate and graphic discourse on human abortions that appears to be antiabortion.

The book begins with a discussion of the U.S. Constitution, then moves to the philosophical basis for animal rights, including a section on what is acceptable pain. The strengths of the work include: a chronological listing of the steps in the relationship between humans and animals (although it would have been more useful if the author had cited his sources for some of the dates); biographical sketches of the major participants in the movement; a history of animal rights litigation; organizations; and selected print and nonprint sources in such categories as alternative procedures and methods, domestication, entertainment, farm animals, and fur farming/trapping. Sherry's selections, at least in the animal rights section, seem to omit most of the more scholarly works on the subject. Another deficiency is that Sherry does not tell us his criteria for selection, the number of works he has chosen, and the range of publication dates. His annotations, however, are objective, and *Animal Rights* remains a useful, unique work covering the major components of the movement in one source. It will serve beginning researchers and librarians well until a more objective work appears.—**January Adams**

Indexes

1436. **Philosopher's Index: 1940-December, 1994.** [CD-ROM]. Bowling Green, Ohio, Philosophy Documentation Center/Bowling Green State University, 1994. Minimum system requirements: CD-ROM drive. $1,500.00.

Similar to its print counterpart, the *Philosopher's Index* on CD-ROM indexes monographs and more than 300 journals devoted to philosophical topics. Unlike the print version, however, the CD-ROM does not contain citations to book reviews. The inclusion of citations to book reviews would enhance the usefulness of this nevertheless useful index.

Installing the accompanying Digital Library Systems' easy-to-use search software is simple. It can either be installed on a local hard drive by changing to the D:\ drive and typing "install," or, alternatively, it can be run directly from the D:\ drive. The many remarkable features of this DOS-based search software include: menu-driven interface; a straightforward Boolean search function; many options for displaying selected records (including user-defined formats); record marking for future printing or downloading; and the capability of saving search strategies for use at a later date. There are, as well, plenty of useful setup options for systems administrators including password protection, lockout from DOS, page print limits, and forced file saves to the floppy drive.

The database itself—composed of (as of December 1994) more than 155,000 records dating back to 1940—is indexed by word/phrase, subject, title words, author, journal, named person, and publication year. Searches can also be limited by language, publisher, document type, and so on. Although the software used to search the database is to be commended, there are several problems with the database itself. For example, some records appear in all uppercase characters; some do not. It seems that records for items published prior to the fall of 1989 are in uppercase. These records are visually painful to read. Second, the default sort order of retrieved search sets is by accession number. If one desires a retrieved search set to be sorted by another field (e.g., by publication year), one must explicitly request the software to perform a new sort operation. This must be done for each new search set (i.e., there is no way to set the default sort order). Perhaps the most faulty aspect of the database is the so-called subject headings index. The list of terms in the subject headings index in no way resembles a controlled vocabulary. It is unclear how it differs from an inverted index of keywords.

Within the subject headings index, one finds such general (and therefore useless) entries as "thing" and "word." There are entries under "claim," "claim(s)," and "claiming"; "teacher," "teacher(s)," and "teaching"; and "origin" and "origin(s)." One finds an entry for "resemblance" and one for "resenblance." This is clearly not controlled vocabulary. Furthermore, if the terms "oxidation," "chess," "Tay-Sachs," and "bung" are included in the subject headings of a philosophical index, one wonders precisely how such a thesaurus was constructed; these are certainly not philosophical terms.

Despite these problems, however, the *Philosopher's Index* remains the premier index for English-language philosophical literature. Its CD-ROM incarnation provides easier access to several decades of scholarship than does the print version. One hopes that the producers of the database will work toward including citations to philosophical book reviews as well as toward building a strictly philosophical thesaurus of terms to be used in the storage and retrieval of records within the database. The work is recommended for academic institutions supporting both an undergraduate and a graduate curriculum in philosophy. (See ARBA 95, entry 1432, for a review of the print version.)—**Mark Cyzyk**

RELIGION

General Works

Atlases

1437. Halvorson, Peter L., and William M. Newman. **Atlas of Religious Change in America, 1952-1990.** Atlanta, Ga., Glenmary Research Center, 1994. 226p. maps. $49.99pa. ISBN 0-914422-23-5.

This atlas is a most intriguing work, especially due to the amount of information conveyed graphically. Halvorson, a geographer, and Newman, a sociologist, have worked with four data sets covering 1952, 1971, 1980, and 1990 to analyze and portray patterns of denominational change within the United States—at the county level—over the latter half of this century. An introduction clearly outlines the background and procedures. The denominational maps and analyses are grouped by the number of studies available for each denomination. Fifty-seven denominations reporting more than 10,000 adherents at least once during the time frame are included. Thirty-one denominations for which data were available from all four studies are portrayed by five maps each (showing 1990 total adherents, percentage changes over time, and share, or shift in share of populations); the remaining denominations, due to the abbreviated data available, are portrayed by three maps each. This is the third and most comprehensive version of the *Atlas* (1978, 1981). It is an important work for libraries, or anyone, interested in denominational demographics.—**Glenn R. Wittig**

Bibliography

1438. Fenton, John Y. **South Asian Religions in the Americas: An Annotated Bibliography of Immigrant Religious Traditions.** Westport, Conn., Greenwood Press, 1995. 241p. index. (Bibliographies and Indexes in Religious Studies, no.34). $79.50. ISBN 0-313-27835-0.

Focusing on the religions of South Asian immigrants in the Western Hemisphere, this annotated bibliography describes 925 publications from the United States, Canada, and Central and South America. After reviewing the current state of scholarship in the field and identifying areas that warrant further investigation, the author surveys materials about religions of emigrants from India, Pakistan, Bangladesh, Bhutan, Sikkim, Nepal, and Sri Lanka. The religious traditions of Hinduism, Islam, Sikhism, Jainism, Christianity, Buddhism, Zoroastrianism, and several of their charismatic offshoots are addressed. Descriptive bibliographical entries are organized by country for the United States and Canada and by geographical area for Central and South America. Title, author, and a brief subject index complete the work.—**Barbara Ittner**

1439. Haynes, Douglas, and William L. Wuerch. **Micronesian Religion and Lore: A Guide to Sources, 1526-1990.** Westport, Conn., Greenwood Press, 1995. 300p. index. (Bibliographies and Indexes in Religious Studies, no.32). $75.00. ISBN 0-313-28955-7.

Micronesian religion is characterized by its complexity and its pervasiveness in all areas of life. The literature on the subject is scattered throughout a number of disciplines: folklore, art, music, ethnology, anthropology, sociology, religion, and philosophy. Haynes and Wuerch are librarians at the Micronesian Area Research Center at the University of Guam, and Haynes is also an art historian. The goal of the authors of this bibliography was to provide in a single, comprehensive guide access to both published and primary source materials in all languages. Coverage extends from the earliest account, a Spanish manuscript describing a visit to Guam in 1526, to works published or dated in 1990. Printed works, manuscripts, microforms, papers, and audiovisual items, 1,196 in number, are listed. The majority are scholarly or primary source accounts, although some popular magazine and newspaper articles have been included.

Entries in the section devoted to early accounts (to 1872) are arranged in chronological order. In the chapters for specific subject areas, entries are arranged alphabetically. The annotations are descriptive, rather than evaluative or analytical. Some materials in Japanese were unavailable to the authors and are not annotated. An introductory essay by Francis X. Hezel gives general background information on

sources; on the spirit world as seen by the Micronesians; and on cults, shrines, and rituals. Two full-page black-and-white maps show Micronesia's location in the Pacific and the states of Micronesia. Indexes provide geographical, author, title, and subject access. This work will be a valuable tool for researchers and students in all of the related subject areas and for those involved in the preservation of the region's culture.
—**Shirley L. Hopkinson**

1440. Lesser, M. X., comp. **Jonathan Edwards: An Annotated Bibliography, 1979-1993.** Westport, Conn., Greenwood Press, 1994. 189p. index. (Bibliographies and Indexes in Religious Studies, no.30). $65.00. ISBN 0-313-29237-X.

For many Americans, the sum of their knowledge about Jonathan Edwards is the infamous "Sinners in the Hands of an Angry God" sermon that has graced high school literature readers for the last 50 years. With the growth of political correctness, that essay is disappearing from many readers, leaving the next generation of Americans more ignorant of this great Puritan reformer than ever before. While the aforementioned essay does give one the sense of Edwards, it does not give one the man. The current volume is a continuation of the labor of love he began in the 1980s with *Jonathan Edwards: A Reference Guide* (see ARBA 82, entry 1128).

Here Lesser takes up where his last volume left off, adding dissertations, books, parts of books, articles, reviews, and reprints. Cross-referencing is also the same. Subjects covered in the present volume are theology, philosophy, language, and more. While indexing the material chronologically by the year published does give the reader an idea of the amount of material published on Edwards, it leaves those searching for a subject in something of a quandary. The comprehensive index of authors, titles, and subjects is less than satisfactory. This oversight is, however, easily forgiven by the beautifully written and highly informative abstracts. For libraries having the first volume, this addition is essential.
—**Mark Y. Herring**

1441. **Popular Religious Magazines of the United States.** P. Mark Fackler and Charles H. Lippy, eds. Westport, Conn., Greenwood Press, 1995. 595p. index. (Historical Guides to the World's Periodicals and Newspapers). $125.00. ISBN 0-313-28533-0.

In the *Scandal of the Evangelical Mind* (Eerdmans, 1994), Mark Noll complains that evangelical Christians have little by way of printed resources that focus on their particular neck of the religious forest. Certainly he was right, but to judge by the magazines included, although there may be a dearth of intellectual content, there is a spate of journals of every religious genus, not only the evangelical ones.

Fackler and Lippy have provided a tool that will not only be helpful to theological libraries but also to every library that houses religious periodicals, which should cover most any library. Contained herein are popular periodicals of a religious nature, with extensive annotations about the journal, its publisher, and a brief synopsis of the journal's publishing history. Current periodicals and those that have ceased publication are included. Magazines have been selected on the basis of their representative religious slant and their lay popularity. Both in-print and out-of-print serials have been selected. The volume is not necessarily a companion piece to Lippy's earlier *Religious Periodicals of the United States: Academic and Scholarly Journals* (see ARBA 87, entry 135), but the two do make an excellent set.

It should be noted that the annotations are not brief snapshots but a veritable popular religious history. Religious movements can be traced within journals, as can the flavor of religious fervor in the United States. Types of articles are noted, and representative pieces are highlighted. Omissions in such works usually abound for apparent reasons and may be overlooked. Some of the more inexplicable omissions, however, are magazines such as the ever-popular *First Things*, the long-running Jewish monthly *Commentary*, and *Religion and Society Report*. The authors no doubt will argue that these are academic or scholarly works. Yet while that case can be made for one and possibly another of the three, it cannot be made for all; hence, strict selection criteria may need to be made more clear in later editions. All in all, however, this is an excellent tool.—**Mark Y. Herring**

1442. Young, Arthur P., and E. Jens Holley, comps., with Phyllis C. Watts. **Religion and the American Experience, The Twentieth Century: A Bibliography of Doctoral Dissertations.** Westport, Conn., Greenwood Press, 1994. 415p. index. (Bibliographies and Indexes in Religious Studies, no.31). $85.00. ISBN 0-313-27748-6.

Young and Holley earlier published *Religion and the American Experience, 1620-1900* (see ARBA 94, entry 1507). The companion work reviewed here covers the twentieth century to 1993. More than 500 subject terms and 1,000 personal names were used to search *Dissertation Abstracts International* for citations pertaining to historical aspects of religious experience; 4,215 entries were extracted through June 1993. The work is divided into two parts. Denominational and biographical studies are included in part 1; these include groups and movements such as Adventist, Baptist, Charismatic, Fundamentalism, the Keswick Movement, Transcendentalism, and Zen. Any of 72 such categories containing more than 25 entries are further subdivided by broad subject descriptors (e.g., general studies, biography, preaching, and theology). Thematic studies and titles covering more than 1 denomination or movement appear under one of 22 headings in part 2 (e.g., general studies, church and state, cults, death, missions and missionaries, theology, and women). The work is completed by author and subject indexes (38 and 75 pages, respectively). In an age of online bibliographic searching dominated by Boolean logic capabilities, the compilation of unannotated entries from a machine-readable database is a futile exercise. This bibliography, consequently, has only peripheral value.—**Glenn R. Wittig**

Biography

1443. Gervais, Marty. **Seeds in the Wilderness: Profiles of World Religious Leaders.** Kingston, Ont., Quarry Press, 1994. 277p. illus. $19.95pa. ISBN 1-55082-110-5.

Gervais's book on religious leaders fills a felt need for more of this kind of information. The book is better than *Who's Who in Religion* (see ARBA 94, entry 1510) but not as good as *Religious Leaders of America* (see ARBA 92, entry 1402). Gervais's book is different from the latter in that it covers a more intentional flavor of candidates, but far fewer and far more subjective.

Contained herein are leaders such as Rabbi Kahane, Jerry Falwell, Mother Teresa, Charles Templeton, Chuck Colson, Pope John Paul II, Norman Vincent Peale, and more. The net to seine these depths is fathomless: Dr. Benjamin Spock is a religious leader, as is Desmond Tutu and Nancy Manahan and Rosemary Curb (of the Lesbian Nuns) and Andrew M. Greeley (he of the "sex as religious expression" club). The book's strength and weakness are in its chattiness.

These are not scholarly sketches, but they are thoughtful ones. The book may serve collections better as a supplement as one reporter's view of public figures, some of whom are religious, than as a bona fide biographical reference tool.—**Mark Y. Herring**

Dictionaries and Encyclopedias

1444. Leeming, David Adams, with Margaret Adams Leeming. **Encyclopedia of Creation Myths.** Santa Barbara, Calif., ABC-CLIO, 1994. 330p. illus. index. $60.00. ISBN 0-87436-739-5.

This work is the only encyclopedia devoted to creation myths. It consists of a brief introduction discussing the function and types of creation myths, 292 primary entries, 34 *see* references, 30 black-and-white illustrations, a bibliography of 80 myth sources, and an index. Leeming, the principal author, is a professor of English and Comparative Literature at the University of Connecticut, and has written five books on mythology.

The primary entries, arranged alphabetically, vary in length from one sentence to nine pages, and average one page. Diverse time periods (from ancient to modern) and world regions are represented. A majority of the text—166 of the entries—retells the myths of cultures (for example, Babylonian, Navajo, Maori) or major religions, and cites the source upon which the retelling is based. Many entries also give brief background on the type of myth, its origin, or cultural setting. The other 136 primary entries concern: motifs (dreaming, flood); creator figures or principles (earth-diver, Great Mother); types of myths (creation by emergence, creation from nothing); scientific explanations of creation (big bang, evolution); major texts and writers (the Bible, Hesiod); scholars (Mircea Eliade); and technical terms (cosmogony, cosmology). The index includes terms for primary entries, most of the proper names found in them, motifs that are not primary entries, and geographical areas.

The strength of this work lies in the presentation of relationships between myths, through both the cross-references within entries and the index. For example, entries that retell myths refer to other entries for their type of myth, major motifs, and creator figures; and, respectively, these thematic entries refer to representative myths. However, there are weaknesses: The authors do not state why particular myths were chosen. The book jacket only says that the myths are "major." Also, there is geographical imbalance—there are four times as many entries related to North America as to Central and South America combined. There is no explanation of the inconsistency of entry length, ranging from one-fourth of a page to nine pages. In addition, there are entries that significantly consist of quotation or reprinting—inappropriate for an encyclopedia. There are no separate index terms for Asia, Africa, South America, and North America; therefore, myths are not grouped solely by these continents. The index term "Native American creations" merely says "see specific nations" rather than directly listing them. Finally, comparison of a sampling of the retellings with their original sources reveals inconsistency of treatment. In some cases the original is followed closely; in others there is much shortening, or important aspects are omitted.

Because these weaknesses are so substantial, this work cannot be recommended for reference purposes. Researchers may prefer to consult the texts of myths contained in anthologies and anthropological works.
—**John Lewis Campbell**

1445. Lewis, James R. **Encyclopedia of Afterlife Beliefs and Phenomena.** Detroit, Visible Ink Press/Gale, 1994. 420p. illus. index. $37.95; $15.95pa. ISBN 0-8103-4879-9; 0-7876-0288-4pa.

Riding the wave of new reference tools with a focus on New Age, paranormal alternative, and parallel realities, this encyclopedia presents a variety of information—scientific and nonscientific—focused on the afterlife. More than 200 entries are arranged in alphabetical order, explicating a particular topic and providing sources for further reading. Appropriate cross-references are provided.

Among the topics included are funeral rites, angels, voodoo, yoga, American Indian messianic religions, channeling, snake symbols, Orpheus, Zoroastrianism, ghost hunting, out-of-body experiences, and conscious dying. Biographical and association entries are also included. Black-and-white photographs and line drawings, 75 in number, complement the text. Enhancing the work are a brief foreword by Raymond A. Moody (a noted author in the field), an introduction, a full listing of contents, a list of illustrations, a listing of related organizations, and a full index.

For its comprehensiveness and authority, many public and academic libraries should consider this as a serious addition to the collection. However, even within its subject area, it functions as an introduction to the topic, rather than an exhaustive treatment.—**Edmund F. SantaVicca**

Handbooks and Yearbooks

1446. **Eerdmans' Handbook to the World's Religions.** rev. ed. Grand Rapids, Mich., William B. Eerdmans, 1994. 464p. illus. maps. index. $21.99pa. ISBN 0-8028-0853-0.

This revision comes 12 years after the 1st edition appeared, and has been improved greatly by the addition of numerous color illustrations and graphs; the revision of articles (especially those on Judaism, Islam, and Christianity); and the addition of an entirely new section ("Religion in Today's World"). The product is an attractive and engaging guide to religion for the general reader.

The volume has eight parts: religion as a phenomenon; ancient religions (e.g., those of ancient Egypt, Greece, and Rome); primal religions (e.g., those of sub-Saharan Africa, the Americas, and Oceania); Eastern religions (e.g., Hinduism, Buddhism); Judaism and Islam; Christianity; the context of modern religion (e.g., secularism, pluralism, and so on); and a "rapid fact-finder" (an alphabetical list of terms with brief definitions). In these sections, the history, beliefs, and practices of religions are treated, and charts systematically present information on festivals, religious subdivisions, and pantheons. A general index concludes the handbook.

The work is reasonably accurate and, in spite of its Christian authorship, proceeds in a nondogmatic tone, although the Western bias is clear with a chapter labeled "Living Religions of the East." Three other points also deserve mention. First, it may have been better to treat Judaism, Islam, and Christianity in a single section, instead of setting the first two in a part entitled "People of a Book," erroneously suggesting that Christianity (treated in the next part) does not have as much interest in a sacred writing. Second, the section divisions within each part of the handbook are not presented in an adequately hierarchical fashion (for example, the section on the roots of Hinduism is set on the same level as a section treating all of Jainism). Finally, if the paper binding wears out with heavy use, the narrow gutters may not permit rebinding. Nevertheless, the book should be especially useful for public and school libraries, as well as for many church and synagogue libraries.—**M. Patrick Graham**

Periodicals and Serials

1447. Albaugh, Gaylord P. **History and Annotated Bibliography of American Religious Periodicals and Newspapers Established from 1730 Through 1830.** Worcester, Mass., American Antiquarian Society; distr., New Castle, Del., Oak Knoll Books, 1994. 2v. index. $125.00/set. ISBN 0-944026-53-2.

Published by the American Antiquarian Society and distributed by Oak Knoll Books, this annotated bibliography covers U.S. religious periodicals and newspapers published from 1730 through 1830. Volume 1 contains a brief history, "The First Century of American Religious Journalism, 1730-1830," followed by listings of 615 items with fairly long annotations describing the history and content of the periodical. A similar number of annotations is found in volume 2. This project encompasses virtually an entire scholarly lifetime of its compiler. Albaugh is also the compiler of *History and Bibliography of American Newspapers, 1690-1920*, which appeared serially in 18 issues of the *Proceedings of the American Antiquarian Society* from 1913-1927 and was then revised in 1947.—**Bohdan S. Wynar**

Bible Studies

Biography

1448. Duchet-Suchaux, Gaston, and Michel Pastoureau. **The Bible and the Saints.** Paris, Flammarion; distr., New York, Abbeville Press, 1994. 360p. illus. (Flammarion Iconographic Guides). $24.95pa. ISBN 2-08013-575-9.

Christian art has been full of symbolism from its beginning, and those symbols can be bewildering in their number and complexity. Fortunately *The Bible and the Saints*, the first volume in the Flammarion Iconographic Guides series, has appeared to fill the need for a comprehensive introductory guide. Entries are arranged alphabetically and consist of saints, Biblical personages, episodes from the Old and New Testaments, plants, animals, objects, allegorical figures, and ecclesiastical offices. Individual entries begin with alternative forms of the name (e.g., Magi followed by Three Kings and Three Wise Men). Entries are then divided into two main parts. The first part consists of either "Life and Legend" for saints or "Tradition" for Biblical persons or scenes, and provides the historical or legendary background.

The second part is called "Representation and Iconography," which supplies various uses of the hagiographical or Biblical scene through the ages and describes the motif's evolution. A list of cross-references and a brief bibliography conclude the entry. Black-and-white and color photographs of relevant works of art are generously scattered throughout the text. Numerous *see* references also guide the reader. A list of "Attributes and Their Associated Figures" and a bibliography conclude the volume. *The Bible and the Saints* is a well-organized and clearly written work that belongs in any library interested in religion and art history. It is also an attractive browser's delight that many individuals will want to purchase. [R: Choice, Feb 95, p. 914]—**Ronald H. Fritze**

1449. **Who's Who in the Bible.** Pleasantville, N.Y., Reader's Digest/Random House, 1994. 480p. illus. price not reported. ISBN 0-89577-618-9.

This concise, clearly written volume of more than 500 entries of the known and not-so-known personalities mentioned in the Hebrew Bible, the New Testament, and the Apocrypha disproves the cliché that the Bible represents humanity in search of God. Rather, ever since "In the beginning God . . .," the

Holy Scriptures are about God in search of humankind. This biographical dictionary tends to strike a contemporary center as it incorporates aspects of biblical criticism, archaeology, and religious tradition in presenting a plethora of biblical characters, talents and warts alike.

Featuring nearly 400 color illustrations and biblical citations for more than 3,400 people, *Who's Who in the Bible* is a one-stop, educated source in understanding who are the major shakers and brokers of the greatest story ever told. Also, there are appendixes containing brief additional information on biblical events, lore, and passages, and cross-references allow the reader to skip, detour, and revisit items with ease. User friendly and beautifully presented, the work is particularly helpful to the general reader. Nonetheless, gender-exclusive language and a lack of higher criticism render the work an evolution, not revolution, in biblical biographical study.—**Zev Garber**

Dictionaries and Encyclopedias

1450. **Baker Encyclopedia of Bible Places: Towns & Cities * Countries & States * Archaeology & Topography.** John J. Bimson, ed. Grand Rapids, Mich., Baker Book House, 1995. 319p. illus. maps. index. $29.99. ISBN 0-8010-1093-4.

Brightly illustrated with numerous color photographs, maps, and diagrams of ancient structures, this book is for a general audience. More than 70 scholars, most from Great Britain, have contributed to the effort, and the result is an informative and readable guide to the world of the Bible. Bimson, the general editor and an authority on biblical history, archaeology, and culture, calls attention to the difficulty of the task. Aside from such notable exceptions as Jerusalem and Damascus, most biblical cities have not been inhabited continuously since ancient times. This means that the exact location of many biblical towns as well as other sites, such as the place where the Red Sea was crossed, is either unknown or uncertain. There are clues, of course. The Bible frequently suggests a location, as do Egyptian records of military campaigns in the Near East. Other useful information was left by the Jewish historian Josephus and the Christian prelate Eusebius. This kind of evidence is of immense importance to archaeologists.

Arranged alphabetically, the entries in this volume vary in length from a brief paragraph to two or so pages. An index makes the information readily accessible. While this encyclopedia should be added to the reference collections of public, high school, and university libraries, it would also be a worthwhile investment for tourists to the Near and Middle East.—**John W. Storey**

1451. Butcher, Debbie. **Precious Moments Children's Bible Dictionary.** Grand Rapids, Mich., Baker Book House, 1994. 1v. (unpaged). illus. $14.99. ISBN 0-8010-9736-3.

Approximately 225 biblical words are defined in some 40 pages of text that is generously interspersed with cute, illustrative drawings by Samuel Butcher. Words were chosen from the Bible stories most commonly told to children. The book is intended for young children to browse through and for reference with the assistance of older children or adults. Grandparents may enjoy having such a book around the house. It is somewhat conservative in approach; the ambivalent perspective is illustrated by the definitions of heaven, "a *real* place we cannot see," and hell, "a place that cannot be seen." The trinity is defined, although it is not a term found in the Bible, which begs the question of why other important theological terms, such as *Messiah*, *Christ*, and *atonement*, are not included. Likewise, obscure words (e.g., *handmaiden*, *midwife*, *mite*) are not defined, while several words that any child might know (e.g., bear, blind, camel, hate, heal, prison, promise, robber) are included. Man and father are listed, but woman and mother are not.—**Robert T. Anderson**

1452. Ecker, Ronald L. **And Adam Knew Eve: A Dictionary of Sex in the Bible.** Palatka, Fla., Hodge & Braddock, 1995. 192p. illus. index. $35.00. ISBN 0-9636512-4-2.

This slim volume aims to meet the need for information about sex and gender references and themes in the Bible—both the Old and New Testaments and the Apocrypha—and to gather it into one brief, readable work. Its approximately 85 alphabetically arranged entries—from "Aaron and the Golden Calf" to "Yahweh"—range from a paragraph to a page or 2 in length and are accompanies by 16 black-and-white reproductions of paintings featured in the center of the book. The entries include cross-references. The work concludes with a bibliography of items relating to the Bible or sex and gender theory, and indexes of names, subjects, and Scripture passages.

The author has credentials in librarianship and biblical studies and has produced previous works dealing with the creation/evolution debate and *The Canterbury Tales*. Nevertheless, the present work, while of use to scholars, has a popular bent that will probably appeal to public libraries. Although filled with useful information, it is written in part for entertainment. The lighthearted approach to the subject matter is seen throughout the text and is apparent in the headings, as in "CAIN: The First Hell Ever Raised" and "NOAH: Unsunk and Drunk as a Skunk." The work is also gender-correct in its unceasing comparison of ancient customs with present norms. For libraries that cater to such interests, this work will be of interest. Otherwise, good Bible dictionaries and commentaries will do just as well, if not better. [R: LJ, 15 Feb 95, pp. 148-50]—**Donald G. Davis Jr.**

1453. Erickson, Millard J. **Concise Dictionary of Christian Theology.** Grand Rapids, Mich., Baker Book House, 1994. 187p. $8.99pa. ISBN 0-8010-3029-3.

The size of this book is suited to students. Just one-half inch thick, it easily accommodates a backpack or briefcase, and the suggested price will not crowd tight budgets. For the amateur theolog, this small volume will also appeal.

The *Concise Dictionary of Christian Theology* (CDCT) keeps its promise to be concise. Entries are plentiful, are arranged alphabetically, and are rarely more than three sentences in length, providing just enough material to define or identify a particular phrase or person. Historical context, various viewpoints, and chronological developments are all dispensed with. For example, CDCT offers this definition for *Eucharist*: "The Lord's Supper. The term is used especially by sacramentalists." Of course, more involved studies would require reference to more lengthy works.

CDCT tries to avoid bias when possible, although ties are noted if a term arises from some particular denomination. *Consubstantiation*, arising from Lutheran doctrines, is just one example. The book defines theological concepts such as *anthropomorphism*, movements such as the English Reformation, and terms such as *epiphany*, which arise from church history. It also covers biblical terms such as *meekness* and *mercy seat*. Specific religious figures, events, and groups are prolifically salted into the pages, each with dates, significant works, and a summarizing statement. The emphasis on individuals is welcome, with more of the minor theological players identified than found in other theological dictionaries, such as *New Dictionary of Christian Ethics and Pastoral Theology* (InterVarsity Press, 1995) and *The Concise Evangelical Dictionary of Theology* (Baker Book House, 1991), two voluminous alternatives.

CDCT would be an asset during a lecture or class, helping students and laity alike identify confusing terms. It also assists with spellings of names and terms, although not pronunciations. CDCT is a welcome tool.
—**Brad R. Leach**

1454. **Hastings' Dictionary of the Bible.** James Hastings, ed. New York, Scribner's, 1909; repr., Peabody, Mass., Hendrickson, 1994. 992p. $24.95. ISBN 0-943575-22-2.

Biblical scholarship has progressed a considerable distance since the turn of the twentieth century. While there is some good to be gleaned from any reference work, this unrevised reprint of a 1909 classic deserves an honorable place in retirement in the stacks of theological libraries where historical works are of peculiar value. Edited by James Hastings, author of the monumental five-volume *Dictionary of the Bible* (Scribner's, 1898-1904), this outstanding work of 1909 was a ready-reference book of choice for decades and was revised in 1963. The current publisher's claim that this work is "complete, trustworthy and understandable" is surely grounded in the fact that it represents the state of the art of pre-World War I scholarship. Such uncritical acclaim, however, seems to demonstrate either the publisher's nostalgic and ostrich-like reversion to Biblical scholarship of nearly a century ago for religiously correct reasons, or a scam to get the unwary to buy an inexpensively priced Bible dictionary that nets the publisher more profit. Many more current, more readable, and comparable works of high quality, prepared from various religious perspectives, are available for a few more dollars. The price for this work may seem very inexpensive to some institutions. Lay users and general customers in religious bookstores will likely be more gullible.
—**Donald G. Davis Jr.**

1455. **The Hebrew and Aramaic Lexicon of the Old Testament. [Volume] I.** By Ludwig Koehler and Walter Baumgartner; revised by Walter Baumgartner and Johann Jakob Stamm. Kinderhook, N.Y., E. J. Brill, 1994. 365p. $65.00. ISBN 90-04-09696-5.

The present work (hereafter, KB) reflects the real progress that has been made in biblical Hebrew and Aramaic lexicography during the twentieth century and presages the decline of the Hebrew-English lexicon that has been dominant in the English-speaking world since its appearance in 1907 (Francis Brown, S. R. Driver, and Charles A. Briggs, *A Hebrew and English Lexicon of the Old Testament* [Oxford: Clarendon Press]; hereafter, BDB). This version of KB is in fact an English translation of the 3d edition of the German original and is scheduled to appear over a three-year period in five volumes. Its incorporation of scholarly advances in the study of Hebrew (including those made on the basis of the discovery of the Dead Sea Scrolls) and other Semitic languages will ensure its warm reception among its intended audience of students and scholars.

Entries are arranged in strictly alphabetical order (rather than under Hebrew roots, as BDB had done)—making word searches much easier—and supplies for each term the cognates in other Semitic languages, the forms in which the word appears, the various meanings of the term, where it occurs in the Bible, and citations of relevant secondary literature. These have long been the typical elements of a good lexicon for biblical Hebrew and Aramaic. The typeface is clear, the margins comfortable, and the binding both attractive and sturdy.

Packed with a wealth of philological information, KB is another splendid contribution by Brill to biblical studies. The chief competitor to KB is David J. A. Clines's *The Dictionary of Classical Hebrew*, (vol. 1, Sheffield Academic Press, 1993), a larger (eight volumes) and wholly new work (i.e., not a revision of an earlier one) that takes an entirely different approach—one governed by insights from modern linguistics—to their common task. Although ignoring biblical Aramaic, it extends its coverage of Hebrew to inscriptions, Ben Sira, and nonbiblical materials in the Dead Sea Scrolls corpus. Both KB and *The Dictionary of Classical Hebrew* will play important roles in future research and teaching, but as their methods and contributions are so different, most libraries that support the study of the Hebrew Bible will need to purchase both.—**M. Patrick Graham**

1456. McKinsey, C. Dennis. **The Encyclopedia of Biblical Errancy.** Amherst, N.Y., Prometheus Books, 1995. 553p. index. $49.95. ISBN 0-87975-926-7.

From start to finish, McKinsey, the editor of the *Biblical Errancy* newsletter, presents this volume as balanced and objective, when in reality it is one-sided and tendentious. Rather than being a "relevant and comprehensive critique of the Bible" (p. 9), it is an attack on the Bible and those who regard it as scripture. McKinsey's shots are aimed primarily (although not exclusively) at Christians, whom he refers to in derogation as fundamentalists and biblicists. He portrays them as socially unconcerned (or even antisocial), gullible, and intolerant, at the same time displaying an intense intolerance for them.

It is not merely the tone of the book that is objectionable. The content is also of questionable value. It is reasonable to expect that one who attempts to evaluate or critique the Bible would have more than a passing familiarity with it. However, McKinsey repeatedly displays a superficial understanding, and sometimes a total misunderstanding, of the Bible. Rather than reading it with the goal of understanding, it appears that he has combed through it in search of data to discredit it. In fact, in the concluding chapter he urges others to do that very thing. He pulls verses out of context in an attempt to prove that the Bible is a compendium of ignorance and a mass of contradictions. This is evidenced by such assertions as, "So, in essence, human sacrifice is clearly an inseparable part of the biblical message" (p. 273).

McKinsey frequently cites the most conservative proponents of Christianity, such as Hal Lindsey and Harold Lindsell, as though their views are representative of all Christians. In his two chapters on biblical history, he fails time after time to document the "historical facts" with which he contrasts the "historical problems, inconsistencies, improbabilities, and contradictions [which] comprise a significant part of Scripture" (p. 333). Only libraries that aspire to build comprehensive religion collections and have unlimited funds should consider this volume.—**Craig W. Beard**

1457. **Theological Lexicon of the New Testament.** By Ceslas Spicq. James D. Ernest, ed. Peabody, Mass., Hendrickson, 1994. 3v. index. $99.95/set. ISBN 1-56563-035-1.

Unlike comparable New Testament wordbooks, such as *New International Dictionary of New Testament Theology* (NIDNTT) (Zondervan, 1986), *Exegetical Dictionary of the New Testament* (EDNT) (see ARBA 94, entry 1528; ARBA 93, entry 1426; and ARBA 91, entry 1423), and *Theological Dictionary of the New Testament* (TDNT) (see ARBA 86, entry 1387), the *Theological Lexicon of the New Testament* (TLNT) did not begin life as a wordbook. The articles contained here have been gathered from Spicq's previous biblical and theological works, especially his commentaries. The footnotes were updated and expanded when the original volumes were published in French. This translated edition includes references to pertinent entries in standard Greek lexicographical reference works. Although there is some lack of uniformity (due in part, no doubt, to the diverse origins of the material), most of the articles include the etymology of the entry word(s), a summary of the uses in classical and Hellenistic Greek and in the Septuagint, and religious and moral meaning in the New Testament.

This work is not as complete as NIDNTT, EDNT, or TDNT (but then, this was not its intended goal). Not only does TLNT treat fewer words than the other dictionaries, but it also omits several important theological concepts as well: *baptism*, *covenant*, *death*, and *soul* are just a few. Thus, TLNT is by no means a replacement for other New Testament wordbooks; rather, it complements them. Its strong points are Spicq's theological insight and his mastery of contemporary secular and religious literature. This lexicon is recommended for all theological reference collections.—**Craig W. Beard**

Handbooks and Yearbooks

1458. **New Bible Commentary.** 21st century ed. D. A. Carson and others, eds. Downers Grove, Ill., InterVarsity Press, 1994. 1455p. illus. maps. $39.99. ISBN 0-8308-1442-6.

This fully revised edition contains interpretive commentary on all of the books of the Old and New Testaments, plus seven introductory articles dealing with biblical literature and history intended to enhance the reader's understanding of the Bible. Occasional maps, timelines, family trees, and other diagrams provide historical and geographical context for the events.

Introducing each book of the Bible is a discussion of its author and setting, an outline of its contents, and a bibliography for further study. Chapters of each book are broken down by events that are interpreted in a general way rather than by analyses of single words and the like. The intention is to convey an overall picture while addressing details by providing the reader a bibliography of more in-depth sources for independent study. This goal is facilitated by the use of modern vernacular and an easy reading style. The grouping together of passages makes the commentary more unified and narrative in style than verse-by-verse remarks found in many annotated Bibles. The comments are based on the New International Version rather than the Revised Standard Version used in earlier editions, though the volume does not include the biblical text. Assertions are supported with cross-references to other scriptures or Bible reference works. Following each segment, more technical notes define terms and relationships of characters, locate place-names, or describe customs of the era. All of these features make this volume a valuable study aid for both laypersons and clerics.

Each of the 45 contributors prepared the comments for one or more of the books. The authors are well qualified—many are affiliated with Protestant theological institutions in the United Kingdom and United States—and represent a variety of denominations. The format, the wealth of contextual information, and concise and meaty commentary make this an appealing and desirable reference work.
—**Janet J. Kosky**

1459. Porter, J. R. **The Illustrated Guide to the Bible.** New York, Oxford University Press, 1995. 288p. illus. maps. index. $35.00. ISBN 0-19-521159-6.

In an age where just about anything goes, it is refreshing to find a tool such as this one. It reminds us of the important things in life and also serves, inadvertently perhaps, as a lamppost not only to the past but also to the future. The Bible has played an enormous role in the lives of nations, directly or indirectly, affecting every civilized society. This work brings all of that to the fore once more. Arranged as its namesake is, this profusely and beautifully illustrated book takes one literally from creation to the end of the world. In each of the five main sections, one can see how art, literature, and in fact, all culture, has influenced or been influenced by things biblical. From stories in both the Old and New Testaments, readers are treated to a reliquary of scriptural influences in all walks of life.

Throughout each section, beautiful colored photographs, etchings, manuscripts, and the like help readers see what they read. Interspersed among these pages are historical accounts of various Bible stories and historical treatments of the Dead Sea Scrolls, Roman rule, and more. The narrative remains mostly neutral, with occasional lapses into an overly metaphorical interpretation of texts. It is hard to think of a book that makes so valuable and multifaceted an addition as this one does. Its pages are chock-full of art, music, science, history—in short, the fabric of human industry.—**Mark Y. Herring**

Indexes

1460. *Novum Testamentum*, **Volume XXXVIa: An Index to** *Novum Testamentum* **Volumes 1-35.** Watson E. Mills and Joyce H. Mills, comps. New York, E. J. Brill, 1994. 256p. $54.50. ISBN 90-04-10082-2. ISSN 0048-1009.

Novum Testamentum (*NovT*) is in the first rank of scholarly journals devoted to the critical study of the New Testament, and the present book sets out to index the contents of its first 35 volumes (i.e., through 1993). There are indexes to: articles; short notes; authors of articles, notes, book reviews, and books reviewed in the journal; titles of books reviewed; and subjects (including biblical citations). The type is clear, margins adequate, and binding attractive.

There are three obvious problems with the work, one minor and two major. First, the decision to index separately the titles of the 24 short notes in *NovT* is perplexing, since the only result is to complicate searching. More important, though, is the fact that while the subject index is generally accurate and helpful, it typically guides the reader to Scripture references and keywords in the titles of articles but fails to go much beyond this (e.g., Malherbe's article, "Gentle as a Nurse," is listed under "Gentle" and "Nurse" but not under "1 Thessalonians 2:7," the text that the article treats). In addition, since a controlled vocabulary is not used, sometimes articles treating the same subject are listed under different terms (e.g., see listings under "Eucharist" and "Lord's Supper"), and there are no *see* references to link them. Most significant of all for both purchasers and users, though, is the contribution of this book to scholarship: Although it is the first one-volume index to *NovT*, bibliographic access to the contents of the journal is currently available electronically in *Religion Indexes* (ATLA, annual) and *Religion Index One on CD-ROM* (ATLA, annual), and in paper format in *Index to Book Reviews in Religion* (ATLA, 1994). The last factor alone will probably discourage most libraries from purchasing the book.—**M. Patrick Graham**

Christianity

Atlases

1461. **Historical Atlas of Mormonism.** S. Kent Brown, Donald Q. Cannon, and Richard H. Jackson, eds. New York, Simon & Schuster Academic Reference Division, 1994. 169p. maps. index. $37.50. ISBN 0-13-045147-9.

Continuing the model of the clear mapping done for the *Encyclopedia of Mormonism* (see ARBA 93, entries 1420-1421), professors from the religion and geography departments of Brigham Young University have created the first historical atlas of Latter-day Saints Church history. Full-page maps, 75 in number, are presented covering topics from the geographic roots of Joseph Smith and the early places for organization of LDS communities to the location of Mormon temples worldwide as of 1993.

Each map is drawn with clear and uncluttered black lines on white with blue overlays of meaningful data or trends. Every map is accompanied by a full page of descriptive text complete with research sources appended. Numerous scholars prepared data and did research for the various topical maps, and while definitely a Mormon source, the data are both impressive and comprehensive.

While so many Mormon history sources concentrate on the New York, Ohio, Missouri, and Illinois origins of the church, this atlas brings a broader perspective, showing many aspects of Mormon geography, culture, and settlement after 1848 (the arrival of the Mormons in the Salt Lake Valley). Colonization patterns, relations with Native Americans, the spread of polygamy, non-Mormon colonization of Utah, and the growth and spread of the church worldwide are but a few topics covered. Essays are informative and clearly written, providing enough sources for further research. A comprehensive index provides access to the details presented in all the maps.

By combining the maps in the *Historical Atlas* with those in the *Encyclopedia of Mormonism*, the two sources supply the most comprehensive historical/geographical view of Mormonism ever presented. For the library having any significant works on Mormonism, this volume is recommended as a basic source and a first purchase. The clearly drawn maps, illustrated topics, and scholarly, yet interesting, presentation are its best characteristics. The atlas provides a significant source for understanding the growth and development of this religious movement and is highly recommended.—**David V. Loertscher**

Bibliography

1462. Dunn, Maryjane, and Linda Kay Davidson. **The Pilgrimage to Santiago de Compostela: A Comprehensive, Annotated Bibliography.** New York, Garland, 1994. 546p. illus. index. (Garland Medieval Bibliographies, v.18; Garland Reference Library of the Humanities, v.1380). $84.00. ISBN 0-8240-7220-0.

Dunn and Davidson have not only written about things medieval (for example, *Pilgrimage in the Middle Ages: A Research Guide* [Garland, 1992]), they have also made the trek from Roncesvalles to Compostela. The route is more than a journey; it is a true recognition. More than a half-million people a year make this pilgrimage.

Included in the bibliography is everything about Santiago: its art, geography, architecture, literature, history, sociology, and anthropology. The volume is also multilingual, including materials in Portuguese, English, Spanish, German, Italian, Galician, Catalan, French, and Latin. The annotations are informative, scholarly, and well written. Information contained therein is generally more than enough to give users a descriptive overview of the item consulted. A comprehensive index rounds out the volume. This volume is a must for anyone interested in medieval studies and its related areas.—**Mark Y. Herring**

1463. Wyckoff, D. Campbell, and George Brown Jr. **Religious Education, 1960-1993: An Annotated Bibliography.** Westport, Conn., Greenwood Press, 1995. 325p. index. (Bibliographies and Indexes in Religious Studies, no.33). $75.00. ISBN 0-313-28453-9.

The complex and interdisciplinary nature of religious education will make the present annotated bibliography a valuable tool for both the expert and the novice. Compiled by two scholars who have published and taught in this field for many years, it successfully brings together the most important books and articles in the discipline that were published between 1960 and 1993. The authors have not limited themselves to the works of mainline Protestants, but have cast their net broadly to include materials from Catholics, Jews, and Evangelicals, and although most of the works cited are in English, publications in German and French are included as well. A helpful survey of research and publications in the field of religious education precedes the list of bibliographic entries, and indexes of names, subjects, and titles conclude the work. The 1,169 entries have been arranged in alphabetical order by author under seven broad subject categories (e.g., educational theory, administration of religious education), followed by a brief listing of reference works in the field. *See also* references following some entries guide one to additional relevant entries.

The bibliography has been carefully edited and is characterized by complete bibliographic citations and well-written annotations. The latter not only describe the contents of publications but also assess the significance of each and reveal the authors' mastery of their discipline. The primary failing of the work concerns the indexes. The author and title indexes are keyed to entry numbers, but the subject index is keyed to the page numbers of the introductory essay. Consequently, there is no direct subject index for the 1,169 entries. This is a serious problem and detracts from an otherwise excellent work. Although seminary libraries will find the present bibliography helpful, most librarians will look for Greenwood Press to exercise more oversight on future volumes in this series.—**M. Patrick Graham**

Biography

1464. Heffernan, Eileen. **Fifty-Seven Saints.** 2d ed. Boston, St. Paul Books & Media, 1994. 543p. illus. index. $10.95pa. ISBN 0-8198-2656-1.

This title provides colorful narratives on a small selection of saints chosen for their ability to teach children moral lessons. Written from a traditional Roman Catholic perspective, the six- to eight-page entries are composed of stories with imagined dialogue that deal with pivotal moments of the saints. Each story ends with a homily intended to show children how to emulate some behavior of that particular saint. The text is reasonably entertaining and accessible for grade-school-aged children.

Each entry includes the known birth and death dates of the saint and the feast day usually associated with the saint. A nice black-and-white portrait of each saint is also pictured. Otherwise, there is no background on the history of the saint, her or his process of canonization, questions concerning historical evidence, or additional sources to read for further information. Obviously, the purpose is not to offer any sort of critical judgment. Consequently, the reference utility of this title, even in a juvenile literature collection, is quite limited. The extremely small number of saints covered is also a serious drawback for reference use. Those looking for brief dictionaries of Catholic saints that have some reference value may wish to consider *Penguin Dictionary of Saints* (2d ed.; see ARBA 85, entry 1312) or *Oxford Dictionary of Saints* (3d ed.; see ARBA 94, entry 1527). The first has lengthier entries, but the latter provides references to other literature on most saints.—**Christopher W. Nolan**

1465. **Twentieth-Century Dictionary of Christian Biography.** J. D. Douglas, ed. Grand Rapids, Mich., Baker Book House, 1995. 439p. $24.99. ISBN 0-8010-3031-5.

This work contains approximately 800 signed brief biographical sketches of "Christians who lived during, or whose lives extended into, the present century" (p. 12). It includes people, both living and dead, who by profession are (or were) ministers, theologians, and missionaries, as well as lawyers, social reformers, educators, historians, scientists, writers, and so forth. In addition to presenting the basic biographical facts, the writers also evaluate the individual's impact on the world of his or her time. Major writings (if any) are mentioned within each sketch, and when there is a published biography, it is listed at the end of the entry.

Any biographical dictionary that is this brief—even one that is as limited in scope as this one is—cannot discuss everyone who might be designated a twentieth-century Christian. Even among famous or important individuals, choices must be made. No doubt, everyone who looks at this dictionary can find someone who might have been chosen but was not. The editors acknowledge this. However, within the constraints of size, there is fair representation of the theological spectrum. Conservatives and liberals; Catholics and Protestants; and people from the First, Second, and Third Worlds are profiled.

The sketches are well written. Some of them—especially those by general editor Douglas—are even lively. There is one glaring technical omission—no cross-references. Even though mention of one included biographee is frequently made in the entry for another, readers cannot tell immediately if a sketch on the former is included in this dictionary. Also, a factual error was noted: No mention is made of C. Everett Koop's stepping down as surgeon general in 1989.

Biographical information on some of the people chosen for inclusion in this work can be found in other reference volumes, such as *New 20th-Century Encyclopedia of Religious Knowledge* (see ARBA 92, entry 1417); *Dictionary of American Religious Biography* (see ARBA 94, entry 1509); and *Handbook of Evangelical Theologians* (see ARBA 95, entry 1461). In addition, the entries in the latter two—especially *Handbook*—have more information than the work under review. However, the *Twentieth-Century Dictionary of Christian Biography* will serve as a supplemental source.—**Craig W. Beard**

Dictionaries and Encyclopedias

1466. **Concise Dictionary of Christianity in America.** Daniel G. Reid and others, eds. Downers Grove, Ill., InterVarsity Press, 1995. 378p. $16.99pa. ISBN 0-8308-1446-9.

To abridge a work is often difficult. In this case, the present work is one-quarter of the parent work, *Dictionary of Christianity in America* (see ARBA 91, entry 1444). To make this concise dictionary, the editors have completely cut out some of the larger wide-ranging articles and dropped material from the remaining entries. Bibliographies have been left out and the main sentence of most of the paragraphs in the original have been combined to make the entry for this work. Many biographies of religious leaders that appeared in the original are not included here. The primary concern of this work seems to be the history of Christianity in America. The parent work is still in print, and libraries would be better served to purchase that work and leave this one alone.—**Robert L. Turner Jr.**

1467. **Dictionary of Baptists in America.** Bill J. Leonard, ed. Downers Grove, Ill., InterVarsity Press, 1994. 298p. $16.99pa. ISBN 0-8308-1447-7.

The focus of this fine reference work is the United States' largest Protestant community, the Baptists. The dictionary uses a historical approach and contains many biographical sketches of important figures in the Baptist Church. Some entries are taken from the *Dictionary of Christianity in America* (see ARBA 91, entry 1444). This is not an encyclopedic compilation, but rather the first one-volume reference work done on this denomination in America. Additional information may be found by using the helpful bibliographical references at the end of each article. Following the preface is a simple guide to using the dictionary that includes an explanation of the many cross-references found within the entries. The introduction to the dictionary contains an easily readable history of the Baptist community in the United States.

This valuable reference work should be a part of collections in college, university, and public libraries. Useful in answering the general reference question, the dictionary is also a helpful guide for the beginning researcher looking for additional information and details. [R: RBB, 15 Feb 95, p. 1109]

—**Bruce H. Webb**

1468. George, Leonard. **Crimes of Perception: An Encyclopedia of Heresies and Heretics.** New York, Paragon House, 1995. 358p. $29.95. ISBN 1-55778-519-8.

The author of this work describes it as an account of the heresies and heretics that have shaped the development of the conventional worldview in Western culture from the time of Christ to the twentieth century. Judaic, Christian, and occultist traditions are included, but not Islamic, Far Eastern, or primarily political, social, technological, or scientific ideas. The work opens with a 10-page introductory essay entitled "The Value of Heresy" (defining heresy as a crime of perception, hence the title of the book); and closes with 9 listings (9 pages) of entries organized by topic, plus 8 pages of suggestions for further reading. More than 600 entries of varying length from 3 lines to 4 pages, and generously cross-referenced, are presented in the body of the work.

Crimes of Perception suffers in a variety of ways because of its single authorship. George's credentials (Ph.D. in psychology) hardly prepare him as an expert in the field of religion. Some entries offer clear, distinct definitions and explanations, whereas others miss the point entirely. Entries are too frequently uneven in length or emphasis (e.g., *Appollinarianism*, one of the major early church heresies, is addressed in only four lines, whereas *Arianism*, an equally devious heresy, occupies four pages). The *Amish*, a questionable entry, is inadequately dealt with in 24 lines, whereas more than 2 pages are used to cover *Angel Magic*, a curiosity topic at best. The emphasis on *Apostasy* is on the person (apostate) rather than on the belief; *Cadaver Council* was neither a heresy nor a heretic; and *Homoiousians* have always been representatives of the orthodox position. A few entries are out of alphabetical sequence (e.g., *Dolcino* follows *Donatus*) and some cross-references are blind.

This work is possibly 80 percent larger in number of unique entries than the *Encyclopedia of Heresies and Heretics* (see ARBA 94, entry 1530), which includes material only through the sixteenth century and is consequently preferable to it. But neither work is an essential purchase for libraries already possessing the authoritative *Oxford Dictionary of the Christian Church* (2d ed.; see ARBA 75, entry 1220) or the *New International Dictionary of the Christian Church* (see ARBA 79, entry 1056).—**Glenn R. Wittig**

1469. **The HarperCollins Encyclopedia of Catholicism.** Richard P. McBrien and others, eds. New York, HarperCollins, 1995. 1349p. illus. $45.00. ISBN 0-06-065338-8.

Because approximately one in four Americans is Roman Catholic, this comprehensive one-volume encyclopedia has a potentially large audience. Its closest competitor is *The Modern Catholic Encyclopedia* (MCE) (see ARBA 95, entry 1469). Because MCE lacks bibliographies, however, most libraries should have the *HarperCollins Encyclopedia of Catholicism*, which includes brief bibliographies with all feature articles, and many smaller entries as well.

The volume contains 4,200 entries, with 29 extensive essays on broad topics such as God, Christ, the Holy Spirit, and marriage, plus others more directly related to Catholicism such as confirmation, the Eucharist, Mary, the papacy, Vatican II, and women in the Church. Moderately long articles of two to five pages cover Anglicanism, Catholic social teachings, the Counter-Reformation, and miracles in the Bible.

Numerous black-and-white photographs, line drawings, and 16 pages of color plates enhance the overall presentation. Among the various tables are a list of popes with thumbnail sketches, a liturgical calendar, a listing of patron saints, Church statistics, and a timeline (from 1 to 1992) of Catholic and secular persons, events, and developments. Pronunciation of names, places, and terms is provided, as well as cross-references. The entry for "trinity, doctrine of," for example, has seven *see also* references to related entries. The volume is well bound and lies flat for easy reading; it is highly recommended for academic, church, public, and synagogue libraries.—**Gary D. Barber**

1470. **The New Dictionary of Catholic Social Thought.** Judith A. Dwyer, ed. Collegeville, Minn., Liturgical Press, 1994. 1019p. index. $79.50. ISBN 0-8146-5526-2.

This is an excellent (and at times very orthodox) dictionary, despite the fact that of the approximately 150 contributors to this dictionary, only about 15 percent are women. The contributors write from their own clear voice: One is deliberately inclusive, another is a muckraker, another a proselytizer. The writer on *abortion*, for example, makes an undisguised effort to eschew condemnation and polarization, while leaving no doubt that he could ever join the group Catholics for a Free Choice. Indeed, he never even mentions the existence of this group. The writer on *women* goes through all the major encyclicals, picking out illustrations of women's second-class status in Catholic documentation. The writer on *divorce* manipulates some unsophisticated statistics to show that the rate of divorce has climbed steadily since 1960 with no remedy in sight but good, Christian marriage. However, the Census Bureau shows that the "percentage of women whose first marriage will end in divorce [peaks] at 42 percent among those aged 35-39 in 1990" (quoted in *The Official Guide to the Generations* by Susan Mitchell, p. 94 [see entry 908]). Browsers will be intrigued with the selection of topics: love, marginal persons, Jacques Maritain, *Pacem in Terris*, *Sollicitudo Rei Socialis*, and worker priests. Scholars will delight in the bibliographies, librarians in the cross-references. The index is superb.—**Judith M. Brugger**

1471. **Our Sunday Visitor's Catholic Encyclopedia & Catholic Dictionary.** [CD-ROM]. Huntington, Ind., Our Sunday Visitor, 1994. Minimum system requirements: IBM or compatible. CD-ROM drive. Windows 3.0. $49.95. ISBN 0-87973-755-7.

1472. **Our Sunday Visitor's Encyclopedia of Catholic History.** By Matthew Bunson. Huntington, Ind., Our Sunday Visitor, 1995. 1008p. illus. index. $39.95. ISBN 0-87973-743-3.

Our Sunday Visitor's Encyclopedia of Catholic History is a comprehensive history of the Catholic faith and the Catholic Church. This one-volume encyclopedia contains valuable resources, including a complete listing of popes, a survey of the Roman Curia, the major writings of Pope John Paul II, an index of patron saints, a glossary of terms, and a chronology of important dates and events. There are more than 2,600 entries in this volume, which is a current, easy-to-use source. In addition to the above, some key features of this encyclopedia are 200 illustrations and tables, mystics of the Church, and multicultural coverage of all major countries.

Along with the one-volume encyclopedia, a CD-ROM is also available that has combined and hyperlinked the entire text of *Our Sunday Visitor's Catholic Encyclopedia* and *Catholic Dictionary*. One can search any word or phrase and find it instantly. It is easy to combine various searches and print out the findings. Boolean logic can be used to broaden or narrow searches. Each volume can be searched

either separately or simultaneously. This CD-ROM is comprehensive and thorough in scope, and it offers more features than the combined print editions, yet costs less. Either of these resources, whether print or nonprint, will prove to be an exceptional resource for parochial schools, religion classes, or even home use.
—**Barbara B. Goldstein**

1473. Van der Bent, Ans Joachim. **Historical Dictionary of Ecumenical Christianity.** Metuchen, N.J., Scarecrow, 1994. 599p. (Historical Dictionaries of Religions, Philosophies, and Movements, no.3). $69.50. ISBN 0-8108-2853-7.

Besides being an ordained minister in the United Church of Christ, Van der Bent has served as director of the Library and Archives of the World Council of Churches in Geneva, has worked as a librarian at the Harvard Divinity School and Bangor Theological Seminary, and has published 20 books and more than 100 articles on ecumenical topics. He also contributed extensively to the *Dictionary of the Ecumenical Movement* (see ARBA 92, entry 1416).

The primary goal of the ecumenical movement has been to promote the unity of the Christian church. In his introduction, Van der Bent provides a brief overview of the ecumenical movement in the twentieth century, tracing its origin back to the World Missionary Conference in Edinburgh in 1910. The dictionary consists of brief biographies of people active in the movement; short essays on theological concepts such as justice, the Holy Spirit, and the trinity; descriptions of organizations and other religious movements; and essays on broad topics such as "Theology, Late 20th-Century, Trends In," "Social Ethics," and "Women in Church and Society." The essays are generally 5 to 10 pages in length, with numerous short entries of a page or less. The entries on evangelical and pentecostal churches briefly address the critical stances these groups have taken toward the World Council of Churches over the years.

While the lack of a subject index is a definite drawback, the generous use of cross-references ameliorates the problem to some extent. Appendixes include historical and significant ecumenical statements and membership figures for the World Council of Churches from 1948 to 1991. An extensive bibliography of monographs is organized topically. Because the ecumenical movement has had a global impact on race relations, economic development, and peace and justice, most libraries will want to add this dictionary to their shelves.—**Gary D. Barber**

Directories

1474. **Peterson's Choose a Christian College: A Guide to Academically Challenging Colleges Committed to a Christ-Centered Campus Life.** 4th ed. Princeton, N.J., in association with the Christian College Coalition, Peterson's Guides, 1994. 145p. illus. index. $12.95pa. ISBN 1-56079-434-8.

By no means an exhaustive list of all the colleges and universities in the United States that have some religious affiliation, this guide describes 88 regionally accredited 4-year institutions that belong to the Christian College Coalition (CCC). The common goal of these "Christ-centered" schools is to prepare young people "for lives of service to God, the world, and the church" (p. 7) by emphasizing spiritual growth as well as academic learning.

A brief introduction that explains the philosophy of the CCC is interspersed with appealing black-and-white photographs of students participating in college activities. A user's guide is included, along with a geographical listing of the schools, which are located in 29 states of the United States and in Canada. Each one-page college or university profile contains statistical and descriptive information. A special note conveys the school's mission, unique features, and typical campus life. Brief highlights list enrollment figures, costs, entrance difficulty, and denominational affiliation. General information describes student population, faculty, library holdings, financial aid, and athletic programs. Deadlines and contact names are also provided.

Following the profiles is a section outlining 10 special programs available to CCC students, ranging from study-abroad experiences to urban ministries and filmmaking. Four complete indexes allow access by majors, intercollegiate athletics, study-abroad opportunities (arranged by country), and graduate programs. This information-packed guide should be a valuable tool in high school guidance offices for aiding young people seeking a higher education that complements their faith. [R: SLMQ, Winter 95, p. 149]—**Janet J. Kosky**

Handbooks and Yearbooks

1475. **Handbook of Catholic Theology.** [rev. ed.]. Wolfgang Beinert and Francis Schüssler Fiorenza, eds. New York, Crossroad Publishing, 1995. 783p. index. $75.00. ISBN 0-8245-1423-8.

While not pretending to be an imprimatured, rigidly scholastic approach to the numerous themes immanent in Catholic theology, this handbook admirably acquits itself as an evenhanded, well-documented, scholarly compendium. Themes as varied as "Creatureliness," "Entelechy," and "Marriage, Sacrament of" are explored in signed articles ranging from a few paragraphs to several pages, illustrated with tables, punctuated with bibliographies, and extended, where useful, by cross-references. Approximately 400 articles are included, many of which are translations. The translations read well. The authors are for the most part big names in theology, with the Germans seeming to have more grounding in medieval and historical theology (e.g., Wolfgang Beinert, Günter Koch, Josef Finkenzeller). Not all the articles are written by men.

Occasionally, one comes across an abbreviation that is not immediately decipherable except by scholars at a certain level; for example, passages from Irenaeus's *Adversus haereses* and Clement of Alexandria's *Stromata* are cited in the "Entelechy" article (p. 209) as *Adv. haer.* and *Strom.*, respectively, together with something by John Chrysostom abbreviated *Ad pop. Ant. hom*—which appeared neither at the end of the article, nor in the list of abbreviations at the back of the book, nor in this reviewer's library's catalog. On the other hand, the abbreviations at the back of the book do include Vatican documents, documents of the magisterium, reference works, key texts, and journals, and is essentially good.

Late at night when the library is closed, students of Catholic theology who have only the Internet at their fingertips will undoubtedly stumble across the Catholic Resources on the Internet home page (http://www.cs.cmu.edu/Web/People/spok/catholic.html). From this page, they will be able to access quite a number of seminal, full-text works in Catholic theology. After slogging through Pius IX's *Casti connubi*, however, they will gratefully turn to the "Marriage, Sacrament of" article in this handbook and benefit from the learned overview presented there by Koch. They may, in fact, want to read John Paul II's development of a more satisfyingly contemporary view in his *Familiaris consortio*, also full-text on the World Wide Web, or they may instead latch onto one of the excellent secondary sources cited in the bibliography. In any case, they will be glad to have consulted the handbook.—**Judith M. Brugger**

1476. **The Novalis Guide to Canadian Shrines.** By Leonard St. John. Montreal, Novalis, 1994. 213p. illus. maps. index. $14.95pa. ISBN 2-89088-673-5.

Intended for those interested in planning pilgrimages as well as for the "armchair traveler," this pocket-sized paperback from Novalis (Canadian publisher/distributor of religious books, mainly from Bantam-Doubleday-Dell) is the first complete travel guide to Canadian shrines. Arranged geographically by province and then alphabetically by city or village, and traveling east to west, entries include clear travel directions in addition to a brief description, history, and current information on each site. While coverage was not intended to be comprehensive, it is wide-ranging and describes examples of lesser-known though legitimate shrines. When appropriate, contacts for further information are listed.

The guide is prefaced by a 10-page introductory overview of pilgrimages throughout history, and then traces the establishment of shrines in Canada. An appendix lists some interesting facts about Canadian shrines; for example, which Canadian saints have been honored with them. Also included is a substantial bibliography, a short list of pertinent terminology, and an alphabetical index of shrines in each province. For the prospective pilgrim, the handy take-along format will facilitate planning. For general readers, it may provide an introduction to the pilgrimage tradition.—**Virginia S. Fischer**

Islam

1477. **The Oxford Encyclopedia of the Modern Islamic World.** John L. Esposito, ed. New York, Oxford University Press, 1995. 4v. illus. index. $395.00/set. ISBN 0-19-506613-8.

Islam, the second-largest and fastest-growing monotheistic religion in the world, has often been ignored, misunderstood, or feared in the West. This comprehensive work, written by more than 450 international scholars—both Muslim and non-Muslim—helps dispel some common misconceptions about the religion and informs users of Islam's historical, cultural, and political impact throughout the world.

More than 750 articles describe all aspects of Islamic society in the nineteenth and twentieth centuries—from beliefs, institutions, and movements to practices and people. Covering topics that range from abortion and Islamic fundamentalism to Sufism and youth movements, these essays are highly readable and informative. Care has been taken to distinguish those customs (e.g., clitoridectomy) that are attributed to Islamic belief from official doctrine.

Entries are arranged alphabetically, and each is accompanied by a brief bibliography that directs readers to further resources. A thorough index, a synoptic outline of contents, and extensive cross-references increase the work's accessibility. Although more illustrations would enhance the book's appeal, the typography is legible, and the layout is attractive. This outstanding work meets a sore need for accurate and detailed information on the subject. It is an excellent reference for scholars and students of religion, history, and the social sciences, and it is a valuable resource for researchers, journalists, the clergy, and general readers.—**Barbara Ittner**

Judaism

1478. **Encyclopaedia Judaica Decennial Book 1983-1992: Events of 1982-1992.** Geoffrey Wigoder, ed. Jerusalem, Keter Publishing; distr., New York, Macmillan/Simon & Schuster, 1994. 429p. illus. index. $95.00. ISBN 965-07-0396-9.

From Canadian Jewish leader Irving Abella to the 32d Zionist Congress (held at the end of July 1992), this volume attractively packages an amazing amount of information in its 400-plus pages. Most entries are updates of material contained in earlier editions of the *Encyclopaedia Judaica* (EJ) (see ARBA 73, entry 274), but there are many new features reflecting the major changes in Jewish life during the decade that spans the 1980s to the early 1990s.

Among the most valuable features are a 10-year diary of major events and feature articles on American Jewish intermarriage, Eastern European synagogues, and collections from the Ethnographic Museum in St. Petersburg, Russia. The latter two are illustrated by a beautifully reproduced series of black-and-white and color photographs that are both poignant and important. Equally moving in its own way is the seven-page necrology that precedes the full glossary and index at the volume's end.

The entries themselves are uniformly well written and interesting. Discussions of recent developments in Orthodox, Conservative, and Reform Judaism are evenhanded; extended surveys of academic topics such as archaeology and medieval Hebrew poetry are informative; and many Jewish communities worldwide are featured. In connection with the latter, there are some surprises, as with the more than six pages devoted to Los Angeles. Readers will applaud the increased number and scope of biographical sketches, but may nonetheless question the inclusion of so many "personalities," especially popular culture icons whose identification as Jews is marginal at best.

Overall, this volume can be enthusiastically recommended for almost all academic and public libraries. If, by chance, some of them have never purchased the original EJ, the *Decennial Book* should serve as a stimulus to do so long before another decade has passed.—**Leonard J. Greenspoon**

1479. Isaacs, Ronald H., and Kerry M. Olitzky. **Sacred Celebrations: A Jewish Holiday Handbook.** Hoboken, N.J., KTAV Publishing House, 1994. 197p. illus. $19.95; $12.95pa. ISBN 0-88125-484-3; 0-88125-496-7pa.

This book is a concise, basic guide to Jewish religious holidays for cultural Jews. The intended audience is parents who will, in turn, share the information with their children.

Each holiday is explained with words from the Torah, historical background, date when it occurs in the Hebrew calendar, and celebrations for the synagogue and the home. Prayers or blessings are included in three forms: the Hebrew alphabet, the Hebrew phonetic spelling in the English alphabet, and the English translation. Recipes, games, and activities for the family, along with a glossary of terms for particular holidays, are provided. The subtitles and well-organized format make the book easy to use.

Pen-and-ink sketches portray each holiday. No index is provided, although one is not necessary as the holidays are listed in the table of contents. This book is a useful addition to a public library collection.—**Sandra L. Doggett**

1480. Kaganoff, Nathan M. **Judaica Americana: An Annotated Bibliography of Publications from 1960 to 1990.** Brooklyn, N.Y., Carlson Publishing, 1995. 2v. index. $200.00/set. ISBN 0-926019-75-9.

Kaganoff, former librarian at the American Jewish Historical Society (AJHS), for many years published in the Society's journal a biennial bibliography of new U.S. Jewish works. Those 58 bibliographies have been compiled into one work covering 7,400 items, including books, periodicals, articles, pamphlets, and other materials gathered by the AJHS library. U.S. Jewish history is the focus of the majority of the items, but substantial numbers of entries also provide information on the rest of the Americas (North and South) as well. The bibliography is divided into several large topical areas, such as local history, Zionism, and sociology; indexes provide more detailed access.

The entries include complete bibliographical information plus brief annotations, the latter being largely descriptive. Although U.S. Jewish history is the main criterion for inclusion, a significant proportion of the works (almost 45 percent) cite biographical pieces on famous Jews; some may have little to say about Jewish history or culture. Browsing the large categories can be profitable, but the indexes are generally detailed and useful (although more specificity could have been supplied for some entries; e.g., Albert Einstein has more than 50 citation numbers not broken down further by topic).

Kaganoff's work of many years nicely complements *Judaica Americana: A Bibliography of Publications to 1900* (see ARBA 92, entry 380), the best bibliography on this topic for earlier years, and is more exhaustive than the selective *Jewish Heritage in America* (see ARBA 90, entry 378). In spite of its reflection of one archive's collection-building, this work provides an excellent overview of publishing on U.S. Judaism for the 30 years covered.—**Christopher W. Nolan**

1481. **Who's Who in Jewish History: After the Period of the Old Testament.** 2d ed. By Joan Comay; revised by Lavinia Cohn-Sherbok. New York, Oxford University Press, 1995. 407p. index. $15.95pa. ISBN 0-19-521079-4.

This revision of a work first published in 1974 offers brief biographical information on figures of importance in Jewish history from 135 B.C. to the present. Most are deceased. Introductory material includes a glossary of historical terms, a chronology of events and historical figures, and maps of the journeys of Paul of Tarsus and Benjamin of Tudela, as well as of the Russian Pale of Settlement and Israeli-held territory after the 1967 and 1973 wars.

The alphabetical entries range in length from a few sentences to one page. They discuss people from all over the world who have contributed to Jewish life and culture. Non-Jews who have influenced Jewish history also appear. Cross-references to related entries are in small capital letters. Among those covered are scholars (Moses Maimonides, Leo Baeck, Eliezer Ben-Yehudah); authors (Saul Bellow, Marcel Proust, Amos Oz); musicians (Aaron Copland, Otto Klemperer, Isaac Stern); political leaders (Benjamin Disraeli, Golda Meir, Teddy Kollek); and scientists (Richard Feynman, Elie Metchnikoff, Selman Waksman).

Non-Jews include Paul, Jesus, Yasir Arafat, Adolf Hitler, and Tomás de Torquemada. Oddly, there is no entry for Levi Strauss, although British clothing manufacturer Montague Burton has one. Supreme Court Justice Abe Fortas, who died in 1982, is listed as still living. A subject index completes the work. The brevity of the entries and the lack of bibliographies make this work of limited use for large reference collections, but it is an appropriate ready-reference tool for school and synagogue libraries.—**Barbara M. Bibel**

New Age

1482. **New Marketing Opportunities.** 4th ed. Sophia Tarila, ed. Sedona, Ariz., First Editions, 1995. 458p. illus. index. $89.95pa. ISBN 0-944773-10-9.

This do-it-yourself marketing kit is extremely well documented and produced. The New Age/metaphysical market is probably among the fastest growing markets internationally. This guide and how-to book provides valuable information to the curious. The first section on publishers, audio, and video companies provides telephone numbers and addresses as well as company and product descriptions. Of value are the contact names and preferences of each company. This section is useful to consumers who want to research books or tapes and desire a broad range of choice. The next section on products and services will be of use to consumers as well. The resource section contains references, directories, newsletters, files, and clubs, and is followed by associations and networks. The wholesalers and distributors section, in addition to the publishers and reviewers sections, is among the smallest and is not complete. The references included will be of use to the general public as well as specialists and those seeking marketing opportunities. The basic problem is the fluid nature of this information, which will make the data quickly obsolete. As the field grows, its resources will develop concurrently.—**Linda L. Lam-Easton**

Oriental

1483. **The Encyclopedia of Eastern Philosophy and Religion: Buddhism * Hinduism * Taoism * Zen.** Stephen Schuhmacher and Gert Woerner, eds. Boston, Shambhala, 1994. 468p. illus. $22.50pa. ISBN 0-87773-980-3.

This one-volume encyclopedia provides short articles describing concepts, schools, and personalities of the four great "Wisdom teachings of the East": Buddhism, Hinduism, Taoism, and Zen. The title of the volume is misleading, however—the work is more of a dictionary than an encyclopedia, as articles are rarely longer than a few paragraphs. Moreover, the focus on the stated religions to the relative exclusion of the Confucian tradition, Shinto, Ainu religion, and nineteenth- and twentieth-century philosophical developments in China and other areas of the East, make the main title somewhat inappropriate. This volume is not a comprehensive reference work covering the whole of East Asian philosophy and religion, but rather a work with a focus on four specific traditions.

Each entry begins with a clear indication of the tradition to which each definiendum belongs, and definitions are concise and well written; they make for interesting and entertaining reading. Illustrations, appropriately sprinkled throughout, add to the effect and enjoyment this work provides. Transliterations from Sanskrit, Pali, Tibetan, Chinese, and Japanese are included, although the volume would be greatly improved by listing the terms in their original language; this would certainly increase its usefulness as a scholarly reference work. (The fact that they are absent calls into question its scholarly nature.)

In addition to articles and definitions, there are a useful guide to the Pinyin and Wade-Giles systems of transliteration for Chinese characters, helpful bibliographies on each of the major traditions within the subject scope of the volume, and an interesting "Ch'an/Zen Lineage Chart" tracing the East Asian patriarchs of Buddhism from Buddha himself, to the Bodhidharma, and onward through the leaders of the various schools of Zen in Japan. This work is recommended primarily for undergraduate libraries supporting courses in East Asian philosophy, history, and religion.—**Mark Cyzyk**

Part IV
SCIENCE AND TECHNOLOGY

29 Science and Technology in General

BIBLIOGRAPHY

1484. **Scientific & Technical Books & Serials in Print 1995.** 22d ed. New Providence, N.J., R. R. Bowker/Reed Reference Publishing, 1994. 4v. index. $299.95/set. ISBN 0-8352-3530-0. ISSN 0000-054X.

The audience for this work includes professionals and laypeople with an interest in all aspects of the physical and biological sciences and their applications, as well as engineering. Titles are specifically selected for their treatment of technological problems rather than economic, marketing, or management aspects. Business, economics, medicine, and psychology are generally excluded. However, relevant biographies and philosophical and historical works are included.

Volumes 1, 2, and 3 provide access to 157,538 books by subject, title, and author, respectively. These titles were selected from *Books in Print, Books in Print Supplement, Forthcoming Books,* and *Subject Guide to Books in Print* and are limited to books published or exclusively distributed in the United States through April 1995. The subject index follows headings assigned by the Library of Congress and includes *See* and *See also* references. As noted in a previous review (see ARBA 92, entry 1453), these subject headings provide adequate access to the book selections. Entries in the title index include the title, subtitle, number of volumes, edition, author, series information, year of publication, type(s) of binding and price for each, ISBNs, publisher's order number, and publisher's symbol. The author index contains truncated entries providing author, title, and publisher information, with a page reference to the full entry in the title index. The subject index contains full bibliographic entries.

Volume 4 offers subject and title indexes to 29,132 serials published in countries worldwide, including those issued by governments, the United Nations, and the European Communities. Serial titles were selected from the Bowker International Serials Database and provide information included in and received since *Ulrich's International Periodicals Directory* (33d edition). The subject index provides complete entries, including title information; buying and ordering information; abstracting and indexing; author, editor, and publisher information; biographic notes; advertising rates; document type; online or CD-ROM availability; document suppliers (there are nine of them); a brief description of contents and editorial focus; and whether a serial is referenced or not. As noted in the previous review, the subject headings for serial titles are broad and do not allow a user to identify titles in specific subject areas, such as topology or group theory instead of general mathematics. The title index offers only brief information and referral to the complete entry in the subject index. This volume would be easier to use if a colored page clearly denoted separation between the various sections (e.g., between abstracting and indexing codes, publisher codes, the subject index, and the title index), but nevertheless is recommended for academic science and technology collections and large public libraries.—**Janice M. Jaguszewski**

BIOGRAPHY

1485. **American Men & Women of Science 1995-96: A Biographical Directory....** 19th ed. New Providence, N.J., R. R. Bowker/Reed Reference Publishing, 1994. 8v. index. $850.00/set. ISBN 0-8352-3463-0. ISSN 0192-8570.

This set provides personal and professional data on more than 120,000 individuals working in the fields of the biological and physical sciences, engineering, mathematics, statistics, and computer science. Persons covered must have exhibited significant contributions to their disciplines, especially through publications, research activities, and attainment of high professional positions. Currently active scientists are covered; those who have died since the last edition have references to that edition. Retrospective or historical coverage requires libraries to maintain previous editions of this title.

As mentioned in earlier reviews (see ARBA 93, entry 1438), this source certainly ranks among the best titles in its field. Biographies have been verified through contact with the persons discussed and entries show careful proofing. Searches by name are easy, but subject searching is somewhat limited. The index volume lists entrants under one or more of 191 subject specialties (such as inorganic chemistry), subdivided by state of residency. A more detailed keyword index by research interests would facilitate more precise subject searches.

New to this edition is the inclusion of the names of spouses and children, as well as fax and e-mail addresses. Unfortunately, less than 10 percent of the entries include this special address information. Also interesting are the statistical tables and graphs in the index volume that break down the people by discipline and geographical location. The inclusion of gender as a category here would have been quite useful. However, these minor quibbles should not detract from the status of this title as a standard in the field.
—**Christopher W. Nolan**

1486. Bailey, Martha J. **American Women in Science: A Biographical Dictionary.** Santa Barbara, Calif., ABC-CLIO, 1994. 463p. illus. index. $60.00. ISBN 0-87436-740-9.

American Women in Science concentrates specifically on women working in the sciences before 1950. The dictionary is derived from numerous sources, including *American Men & Women of Science* (see ARBA 93, entry 1438; ARBA 90, entry 1420; and ARBA 87, entry 1380), *Women Scientists of America* (Johns Hopkins University Press, 1995), *The Dictionary of American Biography* (see entry 36), *Women Scientists from Antiquity to the Present* (see ARBA 87, entry 1381), and others. Other sources used to compile the dictionary included women listed in other sources who started their employment prior to 1950, women selected for recognition by the National Academy of Sciences, women scientists identified as working for federal or state agencies, and other women who contributed to the development of various sciences in the nineteenth and early twentieth centuries working for companies, museums, arboretums, or associations. In all, more than 400 women scientists are listed in Bailey's work.

Each entry contains the area of scientific specialization, education, an employment record, a brief biography, a list of awards and specific accomplishments, and a bibliography of the sources of information concerning the scientist. When available, a photograph of the scientist is also provided. Appendixes furnish a select bibliography, illustration credits, and an index.

American Women in Science is a welcome addition to the biographical literature in the sciences. The women's entries in *American Men & Women of Science* were all too brief, and often failed to provide vital information. This work contains much more detailed and accurate information on women scientists. It is recommended for libraries on all levels. The dictionary is especially useful for personal collections, and smaller school and public libraries where the larger biographical dictionaries are not collected. [R: BR, Jan/Feb 95, p. 59]—**Robert L. Wick**

1487. **Larousse Dictionary of Scientists.** Hazel Muir, ed. New York, Larousse Kingfisher Chambers, 1994. 595p. index. $35.00. ISBN 0-7523-0002-4.

This compact 1st edition provides access to an impressive amount of biographical information at an affordable price. More than 2,200 descriptions of eminent natural scientists, averaging about 200 words each, are included. Emphasis is given to physics, chemistry, biology, astronomy, and the earth sciences, although mathematics and medicine are well represented also. A selection of ancient natural philosophers and modern technologists completes the work. In its scope and contents, this dictionary is comparable to the *Biographical Encyclopedia of Scientists* (see ARBA 95, entry 1484), but is more compact, less costly, and generally more focused upon the professional accomplishments of the subjects than on personal details.

The dictionary is not completely free of errors; occasional typographical errors and inconsistencies exist (e.g., the famous Biot-Savart law of magnetism is mentioned in Félix Savart's entry but not in Jean-Baptiste Biot's), as well as significant mistakes (such as incorrect first names for Sonya Kovalevskaya and Bernd Matthias). A potentially valuable feature is the subject index, which links important topics to the individuals described in the book. In principle, this would allow readers to easily identify the leading exponents of a scientific subdiscipline. However, the current version of the index is poorly done. For example, having 10 subcategories related to X-rays but just 1 for vision seems unreasonable. Heike Kamerlingh Onnes, the patriarch of low-temperature physics, is not listed under the heading for that field; neither Biot nor Savart appears under magnetism. To make matters worse, the index is difficult to read because the entries and headings are set in nearly indistinguishable fonts. Despite these shortcomings, the volume promises to be a useful reference, and is a welcome addition to the splendid Larousse collection of publications. [R: Choice, Feb 95, pp. 917-18; LJ, Jan 95, p. 89; RBB, 1 Feb 95, p. 1028]—**John U. Trefny**

1488. McKissack, Patricia, and Fredrick McKissack. **African-American Inventors.** Brookfield, Conn., Millbrook Press, 1994. 96p. illus. index. $17.90. ISBN 1-56294-468-1.

1489. McKissack, Patricia, and Frederick McKissack. **African-American Scientists.** Brookfield, Conn., Millbrook Press, 1994. 96p. illus. index. $17.90. ISBN 1-56294-372-3.

These two volumes make excellent gift books, especially for people who are culturally sensitive and who appreciate finding out about less-known biographies of U.S. citizens. Both books are attractive in design, printed on good quality paper, and have indexes and bibliographies. Writing gift books, however, may not be the objective of the authors—who testify to the difficulty of writing these books—but they do not clearly state their objective. Evidently, it is not to write a comprehensive history of African-American scientists and inventors. More apparent is that these books are intended to honor great African-American achievers and to dispel misleading myths about African Americans as incapable in science and creative projects. Unfortunately, these books do not suffice individually or jointly to fulfill either objective.

Only a few of the achievers covered are honored with descriptive essays of their achievements. This unintended slight is augmented by the failure of the authors to explain the selection process for inclusion, and for going beyond a mere mention of the individual to honor as an achiever. On the other hand, noting the achievement of a few individuals over the last two or three centuries of African-American history cannot dispel any negative myth that has been ingrained in that history. Given that they have suffered from discrimination in the form of underendowment, underutilization, and underrewarding, removing such myths would necessitate showing that the frequency of achievement among African Americans is similar to that of people faced with similar constraints. Even more convincing would be an attempt to show that the percentage of African Americans who had an opportunity to achieve in science and technology and were able to do so is comparable to the percentage of others.

The authors could have provided more comprehensive bibliographies of science and creativity than they have. They also could have provided biographical essays of *all* the achievers mentioned in their books. There is an evident bias toward medicine at the expense of other fields of science, though physicists, chemists, entomologists, and other life scientists are sparingly included. These books would be more effective in promoting African-American achievements by listing more achievers and by presenting more detailed essays rather than utilizing space for a history of patents. All this is not to undermine the value of these two attractive and easy-to-read books, but to suggest that they could have been more forceful in promoting the proud heritage of the African American.—**Elias H. Tuma**

1490. **Notable Twentieth-Century Scientists.** Emily J. McMurray, Jane Kelly Kosek, and Roger M. Valade III, eds. Detroit, Gale, 1995. 4v. illus. index. $295.00/set. ISBN 0-8103-9181-3.

Biographical information is always in demand and often difficult to find, particularly when the subject is a living scientist or one who has made relatively recent contributions. For these reasons, *Notable Twentieth-Century Scientists* is a welcome and much-needed addition to any reference collection. This reference work features nearly 1,300 scientists from all over the world and covers the natural, physical, and applied sciences, from biology, mathematics, and chemistry to computer science, ecology, and engineering. Entries include prominent figures, such as Albert Einstein and Marie Curie, as well as lesser-known contemporary scientists working in significant, cutting-edge areas of research. Of particular note is the emphasis on women (17 percent of all profiles), minority (12 percent), and non-Western (6 percent) scientists. Indexes by gender and nationality/ethnicity are especially helpful.

The advisory board for this work, consisting of librarians, academics, and individuals from organizations and associations, developed a comprehensive list of scientists for inclusion according to the following criteria: discoveries, overall contributions, or impact on scientific progress in the twentieth century; receipt of a major science award (e.g., Nobel Prize, National Medal of Science); involvement or influence in education, organizational leadership, or public policy; familiarity to the general public; and notable "first" achievements, including degrees earned and positions held. The biographical sketches are written by over 150 contributors, although it is unclear whether they are scientists or have backgrounds in science. These contributors gathered the biographical information from published sources when available; in many cases, however, a lack of published data required telephone interviews and correspondence with the scientists or with their institutions or families.

Entries are arranged alphabetically by surname and begin with a heading that includes the full name, dates of birth and death, nationality, and area of specialization. The biographical essay then follows, ranging from 400 to 2,500 words. The sketches are of consistently high quality and one well written and well organized. Each entry describes the scientist's personal and professional achievements in a lively and interesting style that is accessible to readers without a background in science. Cross-references to entries on the scientist's colleagues, predecessors, and contemporaries are noted in boldface type. A list of selected writings by the scientist and reference sources for additional information follow the essay. About one-third of the entries provide photographs of the scientists.

Each of the four volumes is prefaced by an alphabetical list of the scientists profiled in all four volumes and by a chronology of important scientific events from 1895 to 1993. In addition to the gender and ethnicity indexes, volume 4 contains a comprehensive subject index to scientific terms used in the text (e.g., *complex analysis*, and *computer-aided design*) and a field-of-specialization index. Not surprisingly, biochemistry, chemistry, engineering, mathematics, medicine, and physics receive the largest number of entries.

Notable Twentieth-Century Scientists complements other biographical sources by offering a number of unique and valuable features. First, it strives to be comprehensive and succeeds by covering scientists who are not well known. Second, its biographical sketches are longer and more complete than many other resources, such as biographical directories or the *Biographical Encyclopedia of Scientists*. Third, the essays are written by contributors, not by the scientists themselves, as in *Modern Scientists and Engineers* (McGraw-Hill, 1980). Therefore, the sketches are more consistent in quality and format and less prone to personal bias. For example, professional setbacks and controversies are discussed forthrightly, as in the essay on Robert Gallo. Finally, *Notable Twentieth-Century Scientists* is the first source of comprehensive scientific biography to recognize and strive to more fully represent the diversity behind scientific achievements. Overall, this reference work is an excellent contribution to scientific biography. Highly recommended! [R: WLB, Feb 95, p. 70]—**Janice M. Jaguszewski**

1491. **Who's Who in European Research and Development 1995.** New Providence, N.J., Bowker-Saur/Reed Reference Publishing, 1995. 800p. index. $400.00pa. ISBN 1-85739-097-0.

This significant work is one of three parts of the new European Research and Development database (ER&D) that exists as two CD-ROMs and two printed titles. The first CD-ROM lists 20,272 organizations and their 120,000-plus staff members who completed the supplied entrant forms asking for 18 categories of information. The second CD-ROM analyzes the above information for the top categories of staff (totaling 10,000 names). This leaves 110,000 remaining names dispersed in CD-ROM 1. However, a hypertext link between the CDs can be exercised so as to obtain an enhanced entry having both organizational and total staff information.

First of the printed works is the two-volume *Directory of European Research and Development* (DER&D), which is reviewed in this edition of ARBA (see entry 1504). Next is the 800-page, softbound *Who's Who in European Research and Development 1995* (WWER&D), with an entry load comparable to *Who's Who in America* (see entry 37) and alphabetical order for the same 10,000 staff members as DER&D and 2 indexes. The preliminary pages are most useful, especially an outstanding statistical study of the database by Jeremy Howells of the Center for Business Research, Cambridge University, and the staff of the European Community. The "Key to Biographical Entries" lists 18 categories of data that can best be summarized as having the elements of an academic promotion memorandum plus communication links. (Listees were expected to respond in English, too.)

In addition to checking organizations and personnel of wide renown and a "Must" category (Nobel prize-winners, Fellows of the Royal Society), the compilers checked organizations in lists of "Small-to-Medium" private businesses. Another concern is the stated prevalence of nonfunded research and development groups in certain Eastern European countries where the staffs no longer reported for work. A point where input personnel evidently erred are the instances of staff of international organizations serving in Geneva invariably listed as being of Swiss nationality. There are about 15 biographical entries per 3-column page; a somewhat larger typeface would have been welcomed for extended-use sessions.

There is a wide range in the names shown per country: Iceland has 2 names, Portugal has 143, and Russia has 443. An even wider range exists in subject specializations, partly because one could list more than a single topic. Overall, the 786 specializations averaged 65 researchers each.

A major consideration in purchase decisions is the 110,000 biographies only on the CD-ROMs. Marketing studies of a less-than-definitive nature could get by with the paper copies, but Fortune 500-type studies would need the CD-ROM regularly.—**Eugene B. Jackson**

1492. **Who's Who in Technology.** 7th ed. Kimberley A. McGrath, ed. Detroit, Gale, 1995. 1701p. index. $195.00. ISBN 0-8103-7467-6. ISSN 0877-5901.

Now in its 7th edition, this large and impressive work contains biographical descriptions of more than 25,000 North American scientists and engineers. Each entry includes personal and employment data as well as affiliations, honors, awards, and special achievements in the individual's areas of expertise. The listed biographees have been selected by virtue of their technical contributions, positions of responsibility, and nominations from professional associates. As no selection process is perfect, it is certainly possible to question numerous entries and omissions in the present work. Nevertheless, the cross-section of "technologists" represented here seems reasonable and undoubtedly improves with each new edition.

Several special sections are provided to aid the reader; for example, lists of entries by geographical location, by employer, and by field of expertise. Another separate section furnishes obituaries of listed individuals who have died since the previous edition. Neither these sections nor the main entries themselves are perfectly up-to-date given the continual changes within the professions. Even so, the attempts to organize the information in multiple ways is a welcome improvement. The work is available in various electronic formats as well as in print. It is a useful complement to other biographical collections for anyone needing to identify the technological leaders of the times.—**John U. Trefny**

DICTIONARIES AND ENCYCLOPEDIAS

1493. Ardley, Neil. **Dictionary of Science.** New York, Dorling Kindersley, 1994. 192p. illus. index. $19.95. ISBN 1-56458-349-X.

In this profusely illustrated and colorfully presented slim "dictionary," the author gives the reader a flavor for a variety of technical terms in the fields of physics, chemistry, mathematics, and technology. The terse definitions and descriptions—especially because of the attractive associated figures—could be of interest to high school students and laypeople who would like to acquire some familiarity with technical terms.

On the one hand, this approach to presenting scientific vocabulary may not be any more effective than *Sesame Street*'s efforts to teach Spanish, in that it is likely to create vague impressions and a feeling for the words rather than any profound understanding or skill in the subject. On the other hand, books of this kind are valuable for a civilization whose everyday vocabulary has been enriched considerably by science and technology. Knowledge and information are expanding at an enormous rate. The average educated person needs books such as this one to refer to for getting at least some understanding of words frequently heard or read in public discourses. From this perspective, the book is worthwhile.

The title of the book is misleading, however, given that not a single term from the life sciences is included in it. Because biology is likely to take center stage in the coming century, it is not appropriate to use the term *science* to the exclusion of biology.—**Varadaraja V. Raman**

1494. **Elsevier's Dictionary of Industrial Technology: In English, German and Portuguese.** H. E. Philippsborn, comp. New York, Elsevier Science, 1994. 943p. index. $300.00. ISBN 0-444-89945-6.

As one would expect from a major publisher dealing with a substantial volume, the book is of technical excellence—attractively bound, adequate margins, appropriate typefaces including italics and boldface, and excellent paper quality. As a reference book, however, one finds several deficiencies. The choice of languages obviously omits several languages of great significance to students of technology (French, Russian, Japanese, and so forth). The narrow choice of technological disciplines further limits its usefulness (e.g., the motor car industry, cleaners, electrical engineering, engineering materials, leather, machinebuilding, nucleonics, nuclear energy, petrochemicals, industrial processes, and textiles). Notable for their omission are such important topics as air and mass transportation, robotics and CAD/CAM, and computers. Indeed, "computer" is not even listed as a primary term despite the pervasiveness of this machine in today's society, although "calculating machines" is listed. The presence of "textiles" as a topic leads to such interesting terms as "chafe marks in cloth" and "collar buttons."

This volume will be useful to technically oriented collections seeking comprehensiveness in interlingual dictionaries. The inclusion of Portuguese is also a plus for those clienteles that might utilize this language. Most libraries, however, will be better advised to purchase more general technical dictionaries such as *Dorian's Dictionary of Science & Technology* (French & European Publications, 1981) or Michel Feutry's *Dictionnaire Technologique* (Martin Publication International, 1976-1981).

—**Edwin D. Posey**

1495. **Encyclopedia of Analytical Science.** Alan Townshend, ed. San Diego, Calif., Academic Press, 1995. 10v. illus. index. $1,950.00/set. ISBN 0-12-226700-1.

The intent of this encyclopedia is to cover all aspects of modern analytical science, which is defined as the "scientific discipline that develops and applies methods, instruments and strategies to obtain information on the composition of matter." The intent was not to produce a procedural manual. Naturally, chemistry constitutes a large part of the focus, but analytical information also comes from biochemistry, physics, electronics, computer science, mathematics, and even economics, and these areas are well represented. A close examination demonstrates both the impact of analytical science on all aspects of modern life from immunoassay to forensic medicine and the wide range of subjects covered.

The encyclopedia consists of more than 750 self-contained articles written by international experts covering three broad categories: specific analytical techniques such as mass spectrometry and chemometrics; specific chemical or material samples, for example asbestos and drugs; and analytes such as aluminum and cholesterol. All of the articles were well edited for readability and clarity. This is well worth the money and should prove useful in many science and technology collections from those with interests in amines to those interested in petroleum. This set intersects beautifully with the Kirk-Othmer et al. *Encyclopedia of Chemical Technology* (4th ed., John Wiley, forthcoming). As with Kirk-Othmer, this is not just for chemists and chemistry students—it is for every scientist and engineer.—**Susan B. Ardis**

1496. **Eureka! Scientific Discoveries and Inventions That Shaped the World.** Linda Schmittroth, Mary Reilly McCall, and Bridget Travers, eds. Detroit, U*X*L/Gale, 1995. 6v. illus. maps. index. $99.95/set. ISBN 0-8103-9802-8.

From the perky salamander on the spine to the appealing layout and rich text, *Eureka!* invites young readers to search for answers and to pause in their research long enough to thumb through subsequent pages in wonder and delight at the set's remarkably diverse coverage. Featuring both familiar and lesser-known inventions and scientific breakthroughs listed alphabetically, the series provides a compendium of varied data alongside photographs, drawings, portraits, sidebars, and charts. The set introduces such topics as types of birth control, purpose and function of an artificial heart, Antoine-Laurent Lavoisier's discovery of oxygen, the atmosphere of distant planets, and mentions male and female scientists of varied racial backgrounds. Simplified notation helps readers access multiple volumes, which are consecutively numbered. Cross-references link ideas that belong together.

The creators of this set have made a worthy addition to science reference works. Two weaknesses inhibit the text: pronunciations of difficult words and names (Röntgen, ionosphere) and small letters on the spine denoting alphabetic range (A-E). Some illustrations are smeared, particularly the sailor anticipating a taste of citrus fruit to cure scurvy. There are always questions about a book's priorities. The dim photograph of windshield wipers seems less important than an entry on the machine gun, a major factor in World War I. A shot of wearers in 3-D glasses seems less informative than a graphic entry on the appliance of dental braces, a procedure common to the target age group.—**Mary Ellen Snodgrass**

1497. **Illustrated Dictionary of Science.** rev. ed. Michael Allaby, ed. New York, Facts on File, 1995. 256p. illus. maps. $29.95. ISBN 0-8160-3253-X.

This newly revised edition of *The Encyclopedic Dictionary of Science* (see ARBA 89, entry 1350) includes thousands of definitions for terms and topics ranging from cell division to the universe. Alphabetically arranged for rapid reference, the work covers theories, events, and breakthroughs, and it provides information on the history of scientific discovery and biographical details on key figures in science. Entries are concise, ranging from a few lines to no more than three or four paragraphs, and are written in clear, nonspecialist language. Of particular note is the addition of 150, 4-color illustrations specifically commissioned for this edition. These illustrations are extensively captioned, each offering a complete, self-contained visual explanation of a specific topic. Cross-references link entries and illustrations. This is a recommended dictionary for any school library and would be appropriate and affordable for small public and home libraries.—**Jennifer Comi Ellard**

1498. Rabkin, Sarah. **My First Science Dictionary.** Los Angeles, Calif., Lowell House, 1994. 61p. illus. $6.95pa. ISBN 1-56565-266-5.

My First Science Dictionary attempts to explain scientific words to primary schoolchildren—grades 1-4. The author has identified words most frequently encountered by young children at home and at school. She balances the focus between the physical and life sciences, purposely avoiding the applied sciences and medicine. Definitions appear in the form of two to five full-sentence explanations. Rabkin includes a number of interesting facts and important concepts in her definitions and fact boxes. A pronunciation key appears in both the front and back.

The work's weakness is primarily its illustrations. Not nearly as attractive as Dorling Kindersley's Eyewitness Visual Dictionaries or *Reader's Digest's How Science Works* (1991), this work will not attract juvenile browsers. The choices made for the illustrations are confusing as well. For the word *cell*, the author shows a generic animal cell, avoiding the distinction between plant and animal cell structure. The entry for *air* pictures a blackboard listing the components of air. The illustration for *climate* features a skier gliding over a palm tree. *My First Science Dictionary* is a reasonably priced, solid—although unattractive—choice for the classroom library or the inquisitive child's home library.—**Joyce Kasman Valenza**

1499. **Routledge French Technical Dictionary. Dictionnaire Technique Anglais.** New York, Routledge, 1994. 2v. $250.00/set. ISBN 0-415-05670-5.

This is a two-volume technical dictionary, volume 1 offering French-to-English translations, volume 2 comprising its English-to-French counterpart. In terms of subjects covered, it is comprehensive, spanning areas of modern technology from acoustics to wave physics. Such traditional areas as mechanical and electrical engineering are included, as well as new areas and emerging fields such as fuelless energy sources, safety engineering, and quality control.

Entries run from *A* (abbreviation for *ampère*) and *A4* (international paper size) to *zymohydrolysis*. A separate section at the end is devoted to acronyms and abbreviations, although these appear in the dictionary proper as well. Conversion tables for standard lengths, areas, volumes, and basic physical terms like mass, force, energy, power, and pressure are provided, along with a list of the periodic table of elements in both French and English (as far as Lawrencium/Lawrencium, #103).

Unique to this dictionary is the relational database system it uses. Files collected separately for terms in French and English are then linked to provide a complex yet thorough set of cross-references, making it possible to trace the various connotations a single word may have in one language to other words used to convey significant distinctions in the second language. Synonyms, antonyms, spelling variants, geographical variants, and abbreviations are all included, along with differences in British and American English, as well as Canadian, Swiss, and Belgian French.

Abbreviations such as CRT are duly explained in both their French and English versions (CRT: *cathode-ray tube*, for example, is TRC: *tube à rayons cathodiques* in French). Care has been taken to cover as many variants of a word as necessary. For example, *field* is given numerous translations into French, including field artillery, field of force, field glasses, field trial, field of view, and field work. Strangely, no translation is given for *field* in mathematics. In fact, despite the claim that mathematical terminology is included, no English equivalents are given for such important concepts as groups or rings, although at a more basic level, *ensemble* (set) is included.

This dictionary has been attractively designed, using easy-to-read text in a double-column format. All grammatical distinctions needed to identify words used as nouns, verbs, adjectives, and so on are clearly marked, and genders for nouns are given for all words in French. An electronic version on CD-ROM is expected in the future.—**Joseph W. Dauben**

1500. **Science Navigator.** [CD-ROM]. New York, McGraw-Hill, 1995. Minimum system requirements (Windows version): IBM or compatible 386. ISO 9660 CD-ROM drive. DOS 3.0. Windows 3.1. 4MB RAM. Hard disk space. Microsoft-compatible mouse (optional). Microsoft-compatible printer (optional). Minimum system requirements (Macintosh version): CD-ROM drive. System 7. llsi. 2MB memory. $149.95 (single user); $295.00 (network).

To be worth using, CD-ROM reference products must do more than the printed resources they supplement. A CD-ROM encyclopedia, for example, cannot be only a book on disc where the pages are simply turned electronically rather than manually. There must be some added value to the awkward method of using a computer to look up a topic. CD-ROM encyclopedias do this by linking entries through hypertext, making pages themselves an ancient concept. *Science Navigator* takes that concept further and links three primary resources for scientists and science students together on one disc: a scientific encyclopedia (8,200 entries), a scientific dictionary (104,300 definitions), and a biographical dictionary of 1,100 scientists. The user can search through all these sources quickly and efficiently.

The amount of information contained in the *Science Navigator* system is impressive. For example, even some of the most obscure extinct animals (e.g., *Coniconchia*, but not, oddly, *mastodonts*) are fully described. The small number of illustrations (750, or about 9 percent of the encyclopedia entries) limits the usefulness of some topics. Plate tectonics theory, for example, is hard to explain without a diagram, as is the use of an abacus. Some included illustrations are hardly worthwhile (*fan*), and others are referred to but not present (*comet*). The list of contributors is long and varied, and most entries are well written. Some authors were an odd choice. Charles Tart, for example, defines *extrasensory perception* and implies it is a scientifically supported concept, and Arthur Jensen was used to describe *intelligence*. There are a few category errors (e.g., the comb-jelly group Platyctenida is listed under "General Anthropology"), but hypertext linking greatly reduces the effects of this sort of problem.

Science Navigator is most effective as a background resource on computer systems running other programs, such as word processing. Be warned, however, that at least the Macintosh version of the program crashes occasionally during searches, sometimes freezing up the entire computer. Save other work frequently when running *Science Navigator*.—**Mark A. Wilson**

1501. Simon, Seymour. **Science Dictionary.** New York, HarperCollins, 1994. 256p. illus. maps. $29.95. ISBN 0-06-025629-X.

The target audience for this science dictionary is elementary and middle school students, and the author serves his audience well. As in Simon's many other science books for children, the key is his simple, clear, and concise use of language. When children attempt to use an adult science dictionary, they invariably have to look up word after word to understand the meaning of the definitions themselves. Although the entries in the dictionary are short (the work is definitely a dictionary, not an encyclopedia), they include enough information, and are written in uncomplicated language, to give the student a good basic understanding of the term defined. Drawings with many entries add to the clarity.

There are approximately 2,000 entries from all fields of science. Areas such as zoology, geology, astronomy, and health, which are emphasized in school curricula, are best represented. Short biographies of many important scientists are also listed. At the back of the book, the author provides several pages of charts and tables, such as a chart of the geological time scale, a periodic table of the elements, and a list of scientific prefixes and suffixes. A minor criticism is that the value of these appendixes would be increased if the dictionary entries referred the reader to them when appropriate.

Because the author has been careful to make this volume accessible to the youngest students, children will soon outgrow it. The recently published *Concise Illustrated Dictionary of Science and Technology* (see ARBA 94, entry 1567) is a good choice for such students. [R: SLJ, Feb 95, p. 132]—**Carol L. Noll**

1502. **Van Nostrand's Scientific Encyclopedia.** 8th ed. Douglas M. Considine, ed. New York, Van Nostrand Reinhold, 1995. 2v. illus. maps. index. $199.95/set. ISBN 0-442-01864-9.

This work covers all fields of science and technology including earth and space sciences, life sciences, energy and environmental sciences, materials and engineering sciences, physics and chemistry, and mathematics and information sciences. Arranged alphabetically, entry length ranges from one or two sentences to several pages. Many of the entries have been revised since the 7th edition (see ARBA 90, entry 1430), although the revisions are often minimal and sometimes merely provide new literature citations.

Entries tend to have a broad focus and one will find that the text describing algae, for example, falls under that heading rather than under specific kinds such as phaeophyta (brown algae). Some plant or animal species, however, are given individual entries. The work is somewhat inconsistent in the amount of space devoted to topics of roughly equal importance. This is partially due to the number of contributors (nearly 300). For the same reason, the quality and technicality of the entries also vary. The work appears to be aimed at the college-level student, and a scientific or subject dictionary may be needed by those without some subject knowledge.

The longer entries often contain "additional reading" references. In general, these are quite up-to-date. In fact, in many cases entries cover only references dated since 1989. While the new references are valuable, in some cases citations to valuable and classic references from the previous edition have been deleted. The many black-and-white photographs and drawings, illustrations, tables, and graphs add to the usefulness and aesthetics of these two volumes. Some of the illustrations are new and some from the previous edition were deleted. Some poor-quality illustrations, unfortunately, have been retained.

Numerous *see* references are included. Entries that have multiple meanings, such as *absorption*, are given separate definitions with the discipline concerned highlighted in parentheses. An index lists entries alphabetically, useful for browsing topics. Some, but not all, of the *see* references are listed here. Not all of the terms in the encyclopedia are indexed; for example, neither *fullerenes* nor *Buckminsterfullerenes* is found in the index, although these molecules are discussed under *carbon*. Despite its faults, this work is a good compromise between a scientific dictionary and a larger, multivolume scientific encyclopedia.
—**T. McKimmie**

1503. **Visual Encyclopedia of Science.** Andrea Moran and Cynthia O'Neill, eds. New York, Larousse Kingfisher Chambers, 1994. 320p. illus. maps. index. (Visual Encyclopedia). $22.95. ISBN 1-85697-998-9.

Condensing a great deal of information on science in one book is not an easy task, but this reference source manages to do it in a visually appealing way. Divided into four major groups covering the planet Earth, the living world, stars and planets, and science and technology, this single volume provides a fascinating look into everything from the abacus to millipedes to zoos. This source gives readers a broad range of information using photographs, charts, beautiful illustrations, tables, maps, and fact boxes.

This is an excellent book for elementary science teachers because it can help them provide students with ideas for science projects. The list of inventions at the end of the book also supplies ideas for research papers on interesting topics. A bibliography would have enhanced the value of this work for those wishing to further their research. The alphabetical index makes it easy to access a multitude of topics in the vast field of science. As this book is reasonably priced, it would be a good reference to have in any home with children, and would be an excellent source for school and public libraries.—**Diane J. Turner**

DIRECTORIES

1504. **Directory of European Research and Development 1995.** New Providence, N.J., Bowker-Saur/Reed Reference Publishing, 1995. 2v. index. $400.00pa./set. ISBN 1-85739-092-X.

This title is a companion to *Who's Who in European Research and Development 1995* (WWER&D) (see entry 1491), with identical forematter in both. Its strength is the unique listing of 20,272 European research organizations of medium to small size. These are frequently overlooked in similar directories. While fully equal in importance to its companion, its prime users will be international marketing staffs who are looking for partners in research and development endeavors. By category of support, the listees are divided into "Business Enterprise," 7,970 firms; "Government," 4,440 units; "Higher Education," 7,550 units; "Consultancies," 316 units; and "Private Non-Profits," 155 units. Sponsors have included familiar firms operating internationally and prestigious universities and units difficult to locate because of peculiar machine sorting. The average page has 55 entries.

Volume 2 consists of an index by country and one by field of research, which has several hundred categories. As usual, German firms lead the listings, followed by the United Kingdom, France, Italy, and Spain. Iceland managed 10 entries. Typically, entries in the main body list a few names of research staff and three to four subject areas of expertise.

In a typical metropolitan area with a strong special library contingent, there may be one set of CD-ROMs, and more libraries with WWER&Ds than *Directory of European Research and Development*'s. Not all would be buying updates annually. This is truly an exceptional publishing enterprise.

—**Eugene B. Jackson**

1505. **Directory of Hyphenated Techniques: TrAC Supplement Number 2.** Z. Deyl, ed. New York, Elsevier Science, 1994. 171p. $78.25pa. ISBN 0-444-82126-0.

"Hyphenated techniques" represents a relatively recent trend in analytical chemistry. It involves the use of various combinations of analytical techniques, such as chromatography and spectrometry, in order to obtain a more powerful set of analytical data. This directory lists approximately 400 researchers worldwide who are using various hyphenated techniques. More than 20 such combinations are represented.

The work is divided into four indexes. The first is alphabetical by researcher name and provides institution, address, telephone number, fax number, and e-mail address, as well as the hyphenated techniques used, research topics, and a few publications. The geographical index is arranged alphabetically by country, then by researcher name, and extends to technique and research topic or application. The company index includes 16 companies categorized by instruments and services provided and the addresses of offices and sales personnel worldwide. The subject index lists the researcher names under each hyphenated technique or research topic. This directory is for libraries serving researchers in chemistry.

—**T. McKimmie**

1506. **State-by-State Biotechnology Directory: Contacts, Centers, and Companies.** 3d ed. Research Triangle Park, N.C., Institute for Biotechnology Information; distr., Phoenix, Ariz., Oryx Press, 1994. 209p. $129.00pa. ISBN 1-886041-00-8.

The Institute for Biotechnology Information (IBI), formerly a part of the North Carolina Biotechnology Center, was created to provide strategic information on commercial biotechnology to interested people. The information in the directory is based on IBI's two databases: the U.S. Companies Database of 1,000-plus small and large companies that work with all aspects of biotechnology; and the Actions Database that tracks the major actions taken by the companies since 1981, including joint efforts, research contracts, patents, and product announcements.

Arranged by state, each entry is divided into four major parts. First, "Contacts" tells the user whom to contact in federal or state government to answer questions dealing with agricultural plants and animals, the environment, education, science and technology, and commercial development. In some instances, Internet addresses are provided. Second, "Regulations" gives information about the responsible entity within the state for regulated issues relevant to biotechnology. Third, "Centers" lists detailed information about state-sponsored centers that try to promote the development of biotechnology. The mission and areas of concentration are included. Last, "Companies" lists some 1,000 corporations that have an interest in biotechnology and genetic engineering. The centers and companies are gathered into single alphabetical listings in the appendixes to assist scanning. The names and addresses of the contacts, companies, and centers are available in electronic format upon request. This is an easy-to-use reference tool, helpful to researchers and those in management and marketing as a first step in resolving any number of questions. Since many of the companies are private and quite small, the directory is very convenient.—**John M. Robson**

1507. **Technology Opportunities: Researching Emerging and Critical Technologies.** 2d ed. By Washington Researchers. Washington, D.C., Washington Researchers, 1995. 488p. index. $275.00pa. ISBN 1-56365-048-7.

An extremely hot topic among business and government leaders, technology transfer is the process of turning government-funded scientific research and development (R&D) into profitable products and services marketed by the commercial sector. *Technology Opportunities* serves as a conduit between the two points—government R&D and those who would like to commercialize it—by identifying and describing those agencies, organizations, universities, and other entities engaged in emerging and critical technologies research. Arranged according to the system or type of organization involved, the directory covers the National Technology Transfer Network; federal departments, federal agencies, and Congress; state, university, and regional sources; and nongovernmental sources. A separate section describes published sources such as directories and books; newsletters, magazines, and journals; databases and CD-ROM titles; and the Internet. Appendixes list publishers and vendors, abbreviations, and federal depository libraries.

A nationally known business research group, Washington Researchers has done a thorough job of providing access to those with research to transfer in the areas of emerging and critical technologies. (As identified by industry and government experts, these include energy, environmental quality, information and communications, living systems, manufacturing, materials, and transportation.) Although expensive, the directory will be well worth the price for those who stand to profit from the resources it cites.—**G. Kim Dority**

HANDBOOKS AND YEARBOOKS

1508. Bridgman, Roger. **Technology.** New York, Dorling Kindersley, 1995. 64p. illus. index. (Eyewitness Science). $15.95. ISBN 1-56458-883-1.

In the early 1990s, Dorling Kindersley initiated a series of guides to science (Eyewitness Science) that are intended for use by junior high and secondary school students. Each title covers a scientific discipline or topic including, among others, light, matter, chemistry, ecology, force and motion, medicine, astronomy, electricity, evolution, and medicine. As noted on the verso of the title page, the series "encourages children to observe and question the world around them," and teachers "will find them especially useful for work in many subjects, and the experiments and demonstrations in the book can serve as an inspiration for classroom activities."

The title under review here is 17th in the series. The physical book is similar to other titles in that it is magazine size, bound in fiberboard, profusely illustrated in color as well as black-and-white, and of a similar length to other volumes in the series. There are 29 2-page articles that describe various aspects of technology, starting with "What Is Technology?" and ending with "Looking to the Future." The book progresses through an uneven spectrum of topics that ranges from definitions of metals, wood, plastics, and composite materials to techniques such as transforming, cutting, using, and shaping metals to a variety of conglomerate categories that vary from "Ingenious Mechanisms" to "Domestic Lives" to "Taste and Smell" to "Personal Communication" to "Discovering Usefulness."

Each two-page section has a limited amount of text and is dominated by illustrations of all sizes and colors. For example, in the section on "Concept and Design," there is an introductory explanation of design with inserts on something called "industrial looks," the jet test, computer-aided design, wind-tunnel testing, and architectural model—no particular pattern or theme is evident. Among the illustrations are a large modern food mixer, a greatly reduced drawing of what is called a nineteenth-century kitchen, an individual at a CAD work station, a car in a wind-tunnel, the Reality Building in Chicago as an example of a clad steel frame structure, and a picture of John Smeaton (identified as possibly the first professional designer).

Although there is a limited index on the final page and cross-references in the text, the narrative has many references that are not indexed (e.g., work hardening, which is mentioned in two sections on metals with slightly differing definitions). The book is readable and replete with information, but adult users cannot help but wonder at what is *not* included as opposed to what *is* included. This volume does not provide a significant number of "experiments for the classroom," although there are lucid drawings of certain processes and how machines operate. Although the books in this series have been regularly cited in the *Junior High School Library Catalog* (H. W. Wilson) with supportive reviews, the work does not serve any useful reference purpose other than providing a far-flung approach to illustrations of technology in our society along with selected examples of how things work. Eyewitness Science as a whole may offer the potential to evolve, as claimed on the back cover, "into an indispensable reference library," but this cannot be determined from an examination of a single title in the series—especially when the criteria for the contents and illustrations are unfathomable.—**Laurel Grotzinger**

1509. Brown, Travis. **Historical First Patents: The First United States Patent for Many Everyday Things.** Metuchen, N.J., Scarecrow, 1994. 216p. illus. index. $39.50. ISBN 0-8108-2898-7.

This book gives an alphabetical list of some 84 items, ranging from the AC induction motor to the zipper, and including such things as the carpet loom, the elevator, and vulcanized rubber, with interesting historical notes on each. It tells about the corresponding inventors and the routes by which the ideas emerged. Aside from brief descriptions of an invention, it also presents many patent drawings.

The book by no means exhausts the subject, but it handles the items it has chosen for discussion in reasonable depth. Based on sound scholarship and much research, it also includes a long bibliography. This is certainly a useful reference work, but more than that, it could be an interesting coffee-table book. It is the kind of book that brings to one's attention the forgotten architects of modern technological civilization. But for a book such as this one, who would recall the names of inventors Pierre Lallement (patent for the bicycle), Ascanio Sobrero (patent for nitroglycerine), Elias Howe Jr. (patent for the sewing machine), and so on?—**Varadaraja V. Raman**

1510. **European Research and Development Database 1995.** [CD-ROM]. New Providence, N.J., Bowker-Saur/Reed Reference Electronic Publishing, 1995. Minimum system requirements: IBM PC or compatible 386/25MHz. MS-DOS CD-ROM Extensions 2.1. MS-DOS or PC-DOS 5.0. Windows 3.1. 4MB RAM. 3MB hard disk space. 640 x 480 x 16-color VGA video adapter and display. Mouse. Printer (optional). $1,595.00/yr. ISSN 1358-6947.

The CD-ROM was mounted on an IBM-compatible 486 machine, and searching was performed by a doctoral student in library/information science who had had an online searching course. Installation was wholly routine and the searcher felt comfortable after five-plus hours. The subjects for searching were "Automotive Engineering" and "Corrosion," as they were in using the printed indexes to the paper products (see entries 1491 and 1504). The results are similar in quantity, in part due to the absence of *see also* and *refer from* references in the printed versions. Stray false drops were due to such factors as typographical errors and non-English-language terms that were missed in the editing processes (and need forgiving in a pioneer work).

The user guide was more helpful than most and freely showed appearance of screens, what button to push, and the result to anticipate. The screen formats and those for the functions such as "Print" and "Save" are typical of those used in Windows applications. While all screens were either "Organizational" or "Biographical" in origin, the linking between the two was not as sophisticated as the term "hypertext" implied.

If one wishes to combine the three terms "Automotive Engineering" (AE), "Automotive Equipment and Materials" (AEM), and "Automotive Safety and Testing" (AST), the "hits" can range from 114 to 24. (Note: One may not combine more than 7 terms for customized searches, generally; however, with care, up to 11 subcategories can be compiled.) Starting from the "Organizations" section of the files, AE has 409 hits, AEM has 149 hits, and AST has 69 hits. Coming from the "Field of Research" section, "Corrosion" has 116 hits and its subfields vary in hits from 150 to 2. One would need to hand sort to differentiate between, for example, "Cancers" and "Carcinogens." It was encouraging that some inquiries that at first seemed impossible turned out to be merely awkward instead. This disc is recommended for sophisticated environments, especially when the next edition appears.—**Eugene B. Jackson**

1511. Freiman, Fran Locher, and Neil Schlager. **Failed Technology: True Stories of Technological Disasters.** Detroit, U*X*L/Gale, 1995. 2v. illus. index. $34.95/set. ISBN 0-8103-9794-3.

Failed Technology collects 44 essays in 2 volumes. This fascinating collection of catastrophes reveals failed technologies in eight fields: ships and submarines; airships, aircraft, and spacecraft; automobiles; dams and bridges; buildings and other structures; nuclear plants; chemical and environmental disasters; and medical disasters. Each volume contains a full table of contents for the set, and a full chronology. The entries are written in a familiar format, giving background and details of the disaster, an assessment of the impact of the catastrophe, and a list of sources for more information. Boldface subtitles highlight additional details of incidents that led up to the catastrophe and occurred in its aftermath. More than 70 photographs are included.

Failed Technology does not include catastrophes that resulted from purely natural phenomena such as hurricanes or earthquakes. Instead, the aim of this work is to remind readers that some of history's most embarrassing and tragic moments have resulted from technical failures, and that society's many technological advancements (and addictions) have been made possible by human error as well as human skill—and human sacrifice.

The table of contents for volume 1 covers ship and air disasters, from the well-known *Titanic* and *Andrea Doria* stories to lesser-known nuclear submarine sinkings; from the *Hindenburg* to the *El Al Boeing 747-200*. The *Apollo 13* and *Challenger* entries are informative for their retrospective assessments of the impact these accidents had on the space program. Volume 2 covers many fascinating, lesser-known incidents, such as major bridge collapses and hotel fires. Nuclear disasters—Three Mile Island, Chernobyl—get good objective coverage, as do such chemical and environmental disasters as Love Canal and the poisonous gas explosion at the Union Carbide plant in Bhopal, India. This reference book is unique in its scope and coverage, and should find avid use in any library.—**JoAnn Balingit**

1512. **The New York Public Library Science Desk Reference.** Patricia Barnes-Svarney, ed. New York, Stonesong Press/Simon & Schuster, 1995. 668p. illus. maps. index. $39.95. ISBN 0-02-860403-2.

Designed as a desk reference for librarians, this volume compiles the most sought-after information in the general sciences. The text divides the sciences into 10 disciplines, supporting the factual data with hundreds of graphs, tables, charts, and other drawings. Chapters conclude with brief biographies relevant to that field, key historic points, glossaries, and bibliographies. The final chapter lists varied resources, from aquariums to wildlife refuges to a list of Nobel prize-winners. The 30-page index, while incomplete, helps guide one through the text.

Each chapter explicates its scientific field in a broad fashion. The "Human Body and Biomedical Science" chapter, for example, opens with a discussion of blood and cells, followed by bodily systems and genetics. Types of health care providers and medical problems are listed next. Then, the text delves into laboratory and dental technology, skims through psychology, and concludes with biomedicine. Familiarity with this tool will enhance its usefulness.

Designed to meet the needs of the reference desk staff of the New York Public Library, this book is a natural addition to library reference collections. It would be useful for quick reference work as well as for high school or college students working on research assignments.—**Ed Volz**

1513. **Peterson's Job Opportunities in Engineering and Technology 1995.** Princeton, N.J., Peterson's Guides, 1994. 436p. illus. index. $18.95pa. ISBN 1-56079-369-4. ISSN 1071-068X.

Job Opportunities provides profiles on 1,800 companies, as well as some government agencies and laboratories. Each profile lists name, address, date founded, number of employees, annual sales, expertise needed, and, most importantly, the name, address, and telephone number of the employment contact person. Included is a prefatory essay with tips on job hunting, finding an emerging company, and limited projections on hiring trends and the engineering and technical specialties with the most potential. Another section consists of 2-page in-depth descriptions of 29 companies. Employers in this section run the gamut from CH2M Hill and TASC to MIT's Lincoln Laboratory and Kodak. Each profile consists of a short discussion of employment opportunities, training requirements, the organization as employer, application information, and some background information on the company. Some descriptions also furnish information on summer jobs, future company directions, and career potential.

All in all, this inexpensive book will be useful in any library where users need information on technical employment. Libraries should also consider the related *Peterson's Guide to Graduate Programs in Engineering and Applied Sciences* (see entry 351). Both answer many questions and provide up-to-date information for many users.—**Susan B. Ardis**

1514. Strauss, Stephen. **The Sizesaurus.** New York, Kodansha America, 1995. 242p. illus. index. $25.00. ISBN 1-56836-110-6.

Formally, this volume is a dictionary/handbook on the science of metrology—the science of weights and measures or of measurement. Informally, this is a fun resource for teachers and counselors who are trying to interest students in the fields of mathematics, science, and technology, not to mention high school journalists seeking to fill science columns in their newspapers.

The following examples give the flavor of this work: "2 gorics = a paragoric" (p. 218), "fingernails grow at 0.05 cm (0.02 in) per week—four times faster than toenails" (p. 201). Body parts are frequently used for size comparisons, and the tendency for sizes of containers to vary from continental to imperial to metric usage is a constant theme. Because the author is a Canadian journalist published by the Japanese firm of Kodansha in North America, he is free to note the superiority of the Canadian adoption of the metric system over the United States' traditional units.

Part 1, "Essays on Assays," includes such things as a "cookingsaurus," which calls Fannie Farmer to task. This section stands up to serial reading as does part 2, "The Sizesaurus," wherein graphics are used skillfully. Needy librarians should note that the author is offering a prize of $250 to the "reader who submits the largest list of possible miscalculations or mistakes in the book by May 1996." Their names will be cited as well.—**Eugene B. Jackson**

1515. **Technological Capacity-Building and Technology Partnership: Field Findings, Country Experiences and Programmes.** By United Nations Conference on Trade and Development. New York, United Nations, 1995. 159p. $22.00pa. ISBN 92-1-112374-7. S/N E.95.II.D.6.

Only government would convene a group of works to talk about fiber optics in countries that have a hard time getting enough fiber in their diets. That notwithstanding, rapid technological advances will eventually have an impact on Tanzania, Ethiopia, Bangladesh, Nepal, Zimbabwe, Chile, India, and the Philippines. The camera-ready text presents articles related to capacity-building in underdeveloped countries and the prospects for the future. Along the way, some country data gleaned from other sources are uncovered. Mildly interesting discussions are revealed in a number of essays with respect to the geographical obstacles facing those who wish to bring these countries into the twenty-first century. Yet by and large, the volume contains mere speculations and hoped-for plans by heads of states maintaining greater or lesser degrees of importance in government funded positions. Because all of the data are available elsewhere, this tool is only for the library that wishes to have to its credit every scrap of writing on technology and its changes.—**Mark Y. Herring**

30 Agricultural Sciences

GENERAL WORKS

Dictionaries and Encyclopedias

1516. **Elsevier's Dictionary of Agriculture and Food Production: Russian-English.** Nazib G. Rakipov and B. Geyer, comps. New York, Elsevier Science, 1994. 900p. $228.50. ISBN 0-444-89929-4.

More than 80,000 Russian terms with brief English definitions fill this dictionary, covering the broad areas of agriculture and food production. The vocabulary includes traditional agricultural terms for plants and crops, animal husbandry, economics, soils, farm management, and veterinary science, as well as modern terms used in genetic engineering, agricultural engineering, agroecology, and cell and tissue culture.

In alphabetical sequence, the dictionary covers agricultural nouns, verbs, adjectives, and adverbs. It goes into some detail for many terms, such as *apricot*, including Russian terms for Manchurian apricot, Briancon apricot, clingstone apricot, freestone apricot, Siberian apricot, black apricot, and Japanese apricot with their Latin names. Each noun gives an indication of its gender (masculine, feminine, or neuter). Abbreviations are also listed next to the word, helping to determine the type of word (e.g., genetics, zoology, agroforestry, dairy science, food industry).

Since this is strictly a Russian dictionary with English definitions, those needing an English-to-Russian dictionary may want to purchase another dictionary by Rakipov with Kozlovsky Vaskhnil, titled *English-Russian Dictionary of Agriculture* (Pergamon, 1985). A less comprehensive dictionary, but one with terms in German, English, French, Spanish, Italian, and Russian, is the *Dictionary of Agriculture* (5th ed., Elsevier, 1986) by Gunther Haensch and Gisela Haberkamp-Anton.

This is the most comprehensive and up-to-date Russian-English dictionary of agriculture available today, and is recommended for all academic libraries, Russian studies libraries, and agriculture libraries.
—**Diane B. Rhodes**

1517. Lipton, Kathryn L. **Dictionary of Agriculture: From Abaca to Zoonosis.** Boulder, Colo., Lynne Rienner, 1995. 345p. $75.00. ISBN 1-55587-523-8.

This dictionary provides definitions to approximately 3,400 agricultural terms. A brief introduction describes the purpose and main features of the work. Definitions vary in length from a sentence to a paragraph, and in each the words that are italicized are defined elsewhere in the dictionary. Where a word has multiple meanings, only those related to agriculture are included. There is no pronunciation key.

An appendix groups the terms under 81 topics. Various appendixes list acronyms, describe U.S. agricultural trade legislation, note the agricultural provisions of the North American Free Trade Agreement (NAFTA), and rank the states in order as top producers of each of nine crops. The remaining appendixes list standard weights and measures, give weights and measures specific to individual commodities, and provide conversion charts (English to metric units and vice versa). References are provided at the end.

A layperson or beginning student can understand the definitions, although they are still useful to professionals. Coverage of agriculture as a discipline is broad, with agricultural economics and legislative aspects of agriculture covered. Collectively, the appendixes represent a valuable resource in a dictionary of this type. It is recommended for all academic libraries with agricultural collections.—**John Laurence Kelland**

Directories

1518. **Key Guide to Electronic Resources: Agriculture.** Wilfred Drew, ed. Medford, N.J., Learned Information, 1995. 123p. index. $39.50pa. ISBN 1-57387-000-5.

This directory covers a broad range of electronic databases, including online databases, CD-ROM databases, magnetic media, online public catalogs, and electronic services. The latter include dial-up, Internet, and Bitnet services. Bulletin boards, listservs, almanac servers (which provide mailing lists), and Gopher servers are covered. An introduction describes the coverage and organization of the book, and discusses future prospects for each of the formats detailed. The book aims to include all major electronic resources in agriculture.

Although the entry formats vary for the many types of resources described here, most entries list producer, vendors, description (generally a brief paragraph), fields in each record in that database, conditions of access, equipment or software requirements, Internet access procedure where appropriate, price, contact person or telephone number, and other information. In addition, many of the databases are briefly evaluated by the author. There is a subject index and an index of database titles.

There is copious information on each electronic resource listed in this guide. It will be useful in agricultural and other academic libraries. The evaluations of these resources are helpful. However, roughly one-third of the resources listed were not evaluated, listed as not seen by the author. The next edition should have these evaluated.—**John Laurence Kelland**

Handbooks and Yearbooks

1519. **The Grain Market: Volume II.** By FAO/ECE Agriculture and Timber Division of the Economic Commission for Europe. New York, United Nations, 1994. 56p. (Agricultural Review for Europe, no.36). $25.00pa. ISBN 92-1-116612-8. ISSN 1011-3363. S/N E.94.II.E.34.

This FAO publication starts with an overall review of grain that is followed by selected issues of the grain sector in the Commonwealth of Independent States, and then a section on state policy related to grain production and the formation of the grain market in Russia. The major portion of the volume is a statistical annex that covers the world, European countries, selected countries of European communities, exporting countries, Baltic countries, countries in the Commonwealth of Independent States, and Russia. The commodities covered include wheat and wheat flour, carryover stocks, grain, barley, maize, rice, oats, sorghum, and coarse grains. Additionally, there are indexes, export prices, consumption, and areas of production. The book is soft covered of average quality, but the printing quality is below average but readable. This information is available from no other source and consequently is a requirement for people interested in grain production around the world.—**Herbert W. Ockerman**

1520. **Prices of Agricultural Products and Selected Inputs in Europe and North America 1992/93.** Prepared by FAO/ECE Agriculture and Timber Division of the Economic Commission for Europe. New York, United Nations, 1994. 202p. (Annual ECE/FAO Price Review, no.43). $36.00pa. ISBN 92-1-116599-7. ISSN 0251-3986. S/N E.94.II.E.21.

A straightforward publication from the annual Price Review series, this title focuses on prices and inputs of various agricultural products. The data were compiled from questionnaires returned by 27 member countries. An entire chapter is dedicated to Hungarian agriculture from 1980 to 1993. The information presented is in an easy-to-read tabular form. Individual prices of various products include average prices and weighted prices received by farmers for various products. Prices are in national currencies and in equivalent U.S. dollars. Tables for the cost of labor, grains, fertilizers, and plant protection products are also given. To use this publication effectively, the reader must pay attention to the introduction, as the publishers emphasize exceptions and other pertinent information to consider.—**Patricia S. Wilson**

1521. UNCTAD Commodity Yearbook 1994: CNUCED Annuaire des Produits de Base. By United Nations Conference on Trade and Development (UNCTAD). New York, United Nations, 1994. 422p. $70.00pa. ISBN 92-1-012033-7. ISSN 1012-0793. S/N E/F.94.II.D.22.

This is the 6th edition of the yearbook. Earlier editions have been reviewed in ARBA 86 (see entry 203) and ARBA 91 (see entry 282). The foreword and introductory notes explain the sources and characteristics of the data. The tables are arranged in three parts. Most tables cover the time period from 1970 to 1992, but this varies. Data for selected countries and regions are listed.

Part 1 provides data on large commodity aggregates such as "all merchandise trade" and "all food items." The tables list trade for each aggregate, in U.S. dollars, for selected countries. Also in part 1 are tables showing share of trade in commodity exports for each country as percentages of total trade. Some tables show the direction (origin to destination) of trade for world regions.

The tables in part 2 deal with selected individual agricultural commodities: food items and agricultural raw materials. Exports and imports are covered (with the value in U.S. dollars and the quantity in metric tons), as well as production and consumption.

Part 3 contains tables covering nine metals, two minerals, and crude petroleum. Coal and natural gas are not covered. These tables also deal with exports and imports, production, and consumption. The brief annex contains several special statistical tables listing commodity prices, processing of raw materials, and other topics. This is an essential reference in academic libraries, especially for programs in business and agricultural economics.—**John Laurence Kelland**

FOOD SCIENCES AND TECHNOLOGY

Bibliography

1522. The Contemporary and Historical Literature of Food Science and Human Nutrition. Jennie Brogdon and Wallace C. Olsen, eds. Ithaca, N.Y., Cornell University Press, 1995. 296p. index. $69.95. ISBN 0-8014-3096-8.

This publication was financed by the Cornell Agricultural Experiment Station, United States Department of Agriculture, and the Rockefeller Foundation. The work is divided into chapters that cover the areas of development and trends, knowledge and changing concerns, determination of core publications, core mimeographs, primary journals and serials, database and nutrient composition, daily intake and food adulteration, and reference updates and primary historical literature from 1850 to 1950. The book is engaging reading for anyone interested in the food science and nutrition area and is well referenced. It has average printing on average paper. The book should be required reading for any students starting in the food science and nutrition area to give them a foundation on how this discipline has evolved. The book would be appropriate for all general-purpose libraries, and particularly food and nutrition specialty libraries.—**Herbert W. Ockerman**

Dictionaries and Encyclopedias

1523. Bloom, Carole. **The International Dictionary of Desserts, Pastries, and Confections: A Comprehensive Guide....** New York, Hearst Books/William Morrow, 1995. 356p. index. $17.95pa. ISBN 0-688-12725-8.

In a search of databases, many books can be found on desserts, pastries, and confections, but no other reference tools such as this dictionary seem to be present. The author states that her impetus for writing this book came from the frustrations of having to search many disparate, and often hard-to-acquire, references to get the information she needed on these foods while she was a student in culinary school and an apprentice chef. Once she had become a chef, and then a teacher, she began organizing her collection of information into this concise, usable reference tool.

Truly international in coverage, this work has entries from the United States, Canada, Eastern and Western Europe, the United Kingdom, South America, Australia, Japan, Russia, Indonesia, and the Middle East, to name a few countries included. A wide variety of subjects are covered: definitions and descriptions of dishes, ingredients, cooking terms, foodstuffs, cooking implements, and cooking procedures. The book is sprinkled with cross-references to other synonymous terms or related subjects and there are recipes and cooking instructions for 86 classic dessert items.

The book is easy to use and has some valuable appendixes at the end. They list equipment and utensils to own, sugar temperatures and stages, temperature equivalents, English and metric weights and measures, a table of volumes for standard cooking pans, conversion tables for metric measures, professional pastry and confectionery schools, and major sources of equipment and ingredients worldwide.

This book should be popular in the public library, with its clear and straightforward language. Written for everyone who cooks, from the novice to the professional, and a bargain, it is a must-own for any culinary or cooking school, as well as any program in dietetics.—**Lillian R. Mesner**

1524. **The Concise Encyclopedia of Foods & Nutrition.** Audrey H. Ensminger and others, eds. Boca Raton, Fla., CRC Press, 1995. 1178p. illus. index. $125.95. ISBN 0-8493-4455-7.

This reference is essentially a reprint of the editors' *Food for Health* (see ARBA 87, entry 1408). Even the pagination is the same. However, many tables have been redesigned for easier understanding or updated with more recent data. There are a few new entries, among them *amaranth, artichoke (jerusalem)*, the food guide pyramid, and a discussion of and example of the new food label. Some of the photographs have been replaced with newer ones, but others appear dated. While most of the 2,700-plus topics covering all aspects of food, health, and nutrition are brief, there are a number of longer, more detailed entries (e.g., *anemia, diabetes, iodine, minerals, vegetables,* and *vitamins*). These sections are preceded by a contents listing. There are cross-references and footnotes where needed, and an adequate index.

This volume could also be considered a condensed version of the same editors' *Foods & Nutrition Encyclopedia* (2d ed.; see ARBA 95, entry 1515), a more comprehensive two-volume source. If libraries have that set, they will not need this one. In spite of its similarity to the other volumes, this is a relatively inexpensive food and nutrition reference. It provides quick, authoritative information, and the entries are readable and understandable to not only food and nutritional personnel but to the layperson as well. It more than adequately fills the gap of information in this area. [R: Choice, Mar 95, p.1161]—**Joy Hastings**

1525. **The Encyclopedia of Beer.** Christine P. Rhodes and others, eds. New York, Henry Holt, 1995. 509p. illus. (A Henry Holt Reference Book). $35.00. ISBN 0-8050-3799-3.

The art of brewing is thousands of years old—it can be traced back to ancient Egypt and Sumer. The editors, who range from writers and beer judges to home brewers, hope that this encyclopedia "will clarify every question you ever had about beer but were afraid to ask" (introduction). The introduction goes on to describe the various beer styles, brewing methods, aging systems, and other interesting tidbits of beer lore.

The encyclopedia itself contains more than 900 entries and is laid out in A-to-Z format, starting with *Abbaye* ("a general name for top-fermented, bottle-conditioned ale of the Trappist order currently available from only six breweries in the world") and ending with *Zythos* ("the Greek name for barley wine from the Egyptian word *zythum*"). Definitions of terms range from a sentence to multipage descriptions. Black-and-white photographs, line drawings, and logos enhance the text. Appendixes on organizations; collectors' clubs; educational organizations; mail-order beer clubs; importers of beer; and magazines, newsletters, and journals conclude the encyclopedia. A four-page bibliography of books and articles is also provided.

More than a mere descriptive guide of different kinds of beer, *The Encyclopedia of Beer* is a useful reference source that details beer styles, brewing terminology, beer festivals, the history of beer, and more. The subject matter is extensive, and the definitions are comprehensive and entertaining to read. Libraries with strong agricultural and popular culture collections should consider purchasing this hardcover volume. Because of its reasonable price, libraries may want to acquire two copies—one for the reference collection, and one to circulate.—**Melissa R. Root**

1526. Ettlinger, Steve, with Melanie Falick. **The Restaurant Lover's Companion: A Handbook for Deciphering the Mysteries of Ethnic Menus.** Reading, Mass., Addison-Wesley Publishing, 1995. 345p. index. $14.95pa. ISBN 0-201-40636-5.

Adventuresome diners seeking to explore the riches of ethnic cuisines will find this a handy guide. Descriptions of a variety of ingredients, dishes, and courses are designed to help users order more intelligently from foreign-language menus, and the inclusion of foreign cooking and dining methods adds an extra dimension to the text. Organized by country or region, chapters cover the Caribbean Islands, China, France, Germany, Greece, India, Italy, Japan, Mexico, the Middle East, Spain, Thailand, Vietnam, and several American regions. Within the chapters there are separate sections for each course. Sidebars draw the reader's attention to common ingredients that may be unfamiliar to many citizens of the United States or to terminology, principles of flavor, foreign influence, service and dining customs, condiments, garnishes, and utensils. Two interesting features of the book are the descriptions of signature dishes and common misconceptions about the cuisine.

The book is not without weaknesses. Although it is a bit too large to be a pocket-sized book, it is not really large enough to serve as a comprehensive reference. The fascinating cuisines of Central and Eastern Europe (e.g., Hungarian, Polish), Scandinavia (e.g., Danish, Swedish), and most of Africa (e.g., Ethiopian) are excluded. Discriminating diners may also find omissions in the material that is presented. For example, in the chapter on Caribbean cuisine, no mention is made of fungi or souse, nor of ingredients such as guava, pigeon peas, and whelks. More important, the index includes ingredients but does not list all dishes covered in the book. Thus, if the reader is curious about a particular dish but uncertain of its origins, there is no way to locate the information without combing the entire book. Aside from these criticisms, this is an entertaining and informative handbook that is certain to make ethnic dining more enjoyable for many readers.—**Barbara Ittner**

1527. **Larousse Encyclopedia of Wine.** Christopher Foulkes, ed. New York, Larousse Kingfisher Chambers, 1994. 608p. illus. maps. index. $40.00. ISBN 2-03-507022-8.

1528. **The Oxford Companion to Wine.** Jancis Robinson, ed. New York, Oxford University Press, 1994. 1088p. illus. maps. $49.95. ISBN 0-19-866159-2.

For many years, the Oxford Companions have been known for their broad, yet detailed, coverage of a topic in one alphabetical arrangement. This companion, edited by a recognized wine writer with the help of more than 80 other authorities, follows a similar standard. The 3,000 entries range from brief descriptions of terms such as *acid* and *aroma* to more extensive essays on *German history* and *pruning*. Wine is presented in a wide context: historical, religious, and literary relationships; growing, cultivating, and harvesting; business aspects such as production, pricing, and transportation; geological, weather, and water considerations; and serving and tasting suggestions. This book also contains numerous illustrations, including 32 color plates and 31 maps of major wine regions. Many articles have brief bibliographies, and some terms have *see* references that compensate for the lack of an index.

Originally published by the reputable French publisher Larousse, the *Larousse Encyclopedia* is edited by a prolific and award-winning British writer of wine books. He is assisted by more than 100 persons, including 20 wine experts, writers, mapmakers, photographers, and illustrators. Michael Broadbent, the well-known wine expert and writer, wrote the lively introductory chapter entitled "The Enjoyment of Wine." The first section of the book deals with the world of wine from these aspects: history; selecting wine; laws; storing, serving, and tasting; the relationship of wine to food; and making wine. The second section describes in detail the lands of the world on which vineyards are open to commerce. Section 3 contains label information, regulations, a quality chart, wine vintages by type, statistics and wine zones, a glossary of wine terms, and a detailed index. The work contains more than 500 attractive illustrations, photographs, and drawings, including 36 new maps prepared for this encyclopedia. The quick-reference section is handy, but lists the wrong page number for sections on choosing a vintage, the glossary of terms, and statistics and regions.

Both titles would be attractive additions to libraries that receive questions on wine. *The Oxford Companion* is recommended as a first consideration for libraries based upon its broad coverage, easily accessible alphabetical arrangement, and the selected bibliographies that lead readers to additional information. Wine connoisseurs will find the *Larousse Encyclopedia* useful in providing current wine information and updating such sources as *Hugh Johnson's Modern Encyclopedia of Wine* (see ARBA 92, entry 1488). [R: LJ, Jan 95, p. 89]—**O. Gene Norman**

1529. Talbot, Ross B. **Historical Dictionary of the International Food Agencies: FAO, WFP, WFC, IFAD.** Metuchen, N.J., Scarecrow, 1994. 169p. (International Organizations Series, no.6). $29.50. ISBN 0-8108-2847-2.

This manuscript starts with abbreviations and acronyms, and then lists chronological information on the international food agencies that is followed by an introduction of Food and Agricultural Organizations (FAO), World Food Programme (WFP), World Food Council (WFC), and International Fund for Agricultural Development (IFAD). The main body of the book is a dictionary that is divided into four sections under the FAO, WFP, IFAD, and WFC. This is followed by a bibliography divided into the same general format. The last section is on charts and tables that again are divided into the various organizations and shows organizational expenditure of funds and funding sources.

This book would be extremely useful for anyone interested in the historical aspects of international food agencies. The author is well qualified and the book has average printing, on average paper and binding. The book should be useful in all professional and advanced libraries.—**Herbert W. Ockerman**

1530. Winter, Ruth. **A Consumer's Dictionary of Food Additives.** 4th ed. New York, Crown, 1994. 425p. $14.00pa. ISBN 0-517-88195-0.

Additives to processed foods can be "good" or "bad," and are sometimes "inadvertent," from processing techniques, pesticides, and so forth. This revision of a classic consumer reference adds new items, summarizes new research and regulations, and thoroughly updates the references. Much of this is explained in the lengthy introduction that also discusses the new food labels required as of May 1994.

Some naturally occurring substances, such as cholesterol, are covered, as are common descriptive food terms, such as low fat. Strong opinions occasionally mar the generally nonjudgmental tone of the presentation, such as the last sentence under estradiol, which states that estradiol implantation in animals should be outlawed. Recommended for all who want to make informed choices leading to a healthier diet, the book aids in understanding the descriptions and effects of chemicals in packaged foods, and the regulations governing their use.—**Harriette M. Cluxton**

1531. Zibart, Eve, Muriel Stevens, and Terrell Vermont. **The Unofficial Guide to Ethnic Cuisine and Dining in America.** New York, Macmillan/Simon & Schuster, 1995. 421p. $13.00pa. ISBN 0-02-860067-3.

The authors (a restaurant columnist, a food critic, and a chef) describe this work as more similar to a traveler's guide to dining than a restaurant guide. Twenty-three geographical regions of the world are listed in seven chapters. Each section provides a historical overview of the country, along with a discussion of how the cuisine has developed.

Within the United States, a seven-page section describes regional cuisine, followed by a selective list of the "best and most authentic ethnic restaurants." Unfortunately, there are no stated criteria for inclusion, and no explanation of how these locales or restaurants were chosen. For example, Salt Lake City, Utah, is included with 12 entries, but not the ethnically mixed cities of either Berkeley or San Jose, California.

More positively, the work does provide sample menus, distinctive dishes, and representative recipes of various cultures and countries. However, it resembles more of a recreational reader than an indispensable reference tool. (No CIP is included.)—**Ilene F. Rockman**

Directories

1532. Johnson, Steve. **On Tap: A Field Guide to North American Brewpubs and Craft Breweries.** 1995 ed. Clemson, S.C., On Tap; distr., Chicago, Login Publishers Consortium, 1994. 266p. index. $12.95pa. ISBN 0-9629368-6-3.

This book is divided into sections that provide an introduction defining brewpubs and craft breweries, information on the beginning of breweries, a discussion of the direction in which the brewery industry is headed, and a description of the three editions of this publication. Johnson covers the United States and Canada, reporting on 371 breweries. He defines beer and discusses its production. Other information and issues covered include beer styles, beer vocabulary, drinking and driving, blood alcohol charts, beer festivals, and brewery count by state and province. Criteria for inclusion and a sample entry of how the coding system works are also given.

The major portion of the manuscript is a state-by-state guide, with detailed information on small individual breweries. This is followed by a brewery index and suggestions for further reading. This book will be of interest to people curious about small-brewery beer.—**Herbert W. Ockerman**

Handbooks and Yearbooks

1533. Ash, Michael, and Irene Ash, comps. **Handbook of Food Additives: An International Guide to More Than 7,000 Products....** Brookfield, Vt., Gower/Ashgate Publishing, 1995. 1025p. $295.00 (with disk). ISBN 0-566-07592-X.

In a search for other reference tools on food additives, most proved to be consumer-type paperbacks, with none approaching this document in terms of extent or comprehensiveness of information. The compilers are co-owners of a chemical products database that has been providing information to the international chemical industry for years. They have published other handbooks in areas such as gardening chemicals and cosmetic chemicals. This work covers trade name products and the chemicals that are used as food additives throughout the world.

The body of the book is divided into four parts. Part 1, "Trade Name Reference," provides information on 5,000 food additive products. The information covers their manufacturers, chemical compositions, Chemical Abstract Service (CAS) numbers, European Inventory of Existing Commercial Chemical Substances (EINECS) numbers, general properties, applications and functions, toxicologies, compliances, and regulatory data.

In part 2, "The Chemical Directory/Cross-Reference," in addition to the CAS and EINECS numbers, there are Flavor and Extract Manufacturer's Association (FEMA) numbers. The entries also contain any synonyms and all of the information given in the entries in part 1. Trade name products from the part 1 that are equivalent to the chemical or contain that compound are cross-referenced.

Additives are listed by their functions (such as colorants or emulsifiers) in part 3, "Functional Cross-References." Each of the 30 categories lists all of the trade name products or chemicals that provide that particular function. Part 4 is the "Manufacturer's Directory." This worldwide list gives all of the information necessary to contact any manufacturer. All four sections are alphabetical, so access to substances or manufacturers is simple. Five appendixes that cross-reference FEMA, CAS, and EINECS numbers to both the trade name products and the chemicals; a table of regulations for the United States, the European Community, and Japan; and a useful glossary conclude this guide.

Accompanying the book is a $3\frac{1}{2}$-inch computer disk that introduces the database format of the handbook. This requires a setup for a CD-ROM, but it does offer another option that may be better for information centers that use this information regularly. It is hoped that this document will be updated regularly, because it seems to be unique. It is good to have a resource that explains what is being ingested and whether it is safe. Written primarily for use in scientific or academic settings, this book is a vital tool for any institution that deals in food science, nutrition, or dietetics.—**Lillian R. Mesner**

1534. **Codex Alimentarius. Volume 5A: Processed and Quick Frozen Fruits and Vegetables.** 2d ed. By the Joint FAO/WHO Food Standards Programme Codex Alimentarius Commission. Rome, Food and Agriculture Organization of the United Nations; distr., Lanham, Md., UNIPUB, 1994. 485p. $60.00pa. ISBN 92-5-103629-2.

1535. **Codex Alimentarius. Volume 13: Methods of Analysis and Sampling.** 2d ed. By the Joint FAO/WHO Food Standards Programme Codex Alimentarius Commission. Rome, Food and Agriculture Organization of the United Nations; distr., Lanham, Md., UNIPUB, 1994. 134p. $17.00pa. ISBN 92-5-103612-8.

The *Codex Alimentarius* is an international publication responsible for executing the joint Food and Agriculture Association of the United Nations (FAO)/World Health Organization (WHO) food standards. The standards exist to protect consumer health and promote international trade in foodstuffs. Food law is a uniform code of international food standards adopted by the Alimentarius Commission. This *Codex* contains provisions regarding the hygiene and nutritional quality of raw and processed food, including norms for microorganisms, food additives, pesticide residues, contaminants, food labeling and presentation, and methods of analysis and sampling.

Published in 14 volumes, the provisions of the *Codex Alimentarius* are advisory—practices, guidelines, and other recommended measures. Volume 5A concerns processed and quick-frozen fruits and vegetables. Volume 13 explains methods of food analysis and sampling. Both volumes are printed with care on high-quality paper. They are, as with all FAO publications, the only sources for this type of information. They are essential purchases for all food libraries, and for any library serving a clientele interested in health and the international food trade.—**Herbert W. Ockerman**

1536. Finch, Christopher, and W. Scott Griffiths. **America's Best Beers.** New York, Little, Brown, 1994. 336p. illus. index. $14.95pa. ISBN 0-316-28204-9.

America's Best Beers by Finch and Griffiths is a valuable resource for persons interested in locating, understanding, and drinking quality beer in the United States. This softbound book is 4.25-by-10 inches in size and very solid. It should hold up well to traveling, which is its intended purpose. In addition, it has a pleasing design and feel. The book consists of the following parts: an introduction (defining what great beer is); a history of beer; the brewing process; styles of beer in the United States; tasting notes; a regional directory; and appendixes—the spectrum of beers, a homebrewer's reference chart (hop varieties), a beer styles table, watering holes, a beer glossary, a bibliography, and an index (to breweries).

The majority of the book is devoted to the regional directory of breweries and brewpubs with address, telephone number, bottle/keg availability, category (restaurant/brewpub/brewery), beer ratings, original gravity of some beers (numbers supplied by brewery), and usually a sentence or two about the establishment. The appendix on watering holes lists the establishments by region, and most of them have their telephone number listed as well.

The only real problem with this book is trying to look up a specific beer. One must know the brewery from which it came or be out of luck. Finding a particular state is frustrating because one must first find its region by thumbing through the book, then the states in that region are listed in alphabetical order. Despite these problems, the work is recommended for public and college libraries.—**Alan N. Livingston**

1537. Klein, Bob. **The Beer Lover's Rating Guide.** New York, Workman Publishing, 1995. 346p. $9.95pa. ISBN 1-56305-682-8.

The Beer Lover's Rating Guide is just that—an alphabetical list of annotations on more than 1,200 beers for the lover of beer. The annotations reflect Klein's personal tastes, yet he provides enough information for readers to make their own decisions regarding beers of preference. The author's goal, aside from sampling 2,000 beers by the year 2000, is to ensure that "You Never Buy A Bad Beer Again—anyplace, anytime, anywhere" (p. 4). The book is a result of Klein's 20-plus years of traveling and beer tasting.

Front matter consists of explanations of different beer styles (ales, bocks, lagers, lambics, malt liquors, pilseners, porters, specialty and combination beers, stouts, and wheats); brewery types; beer glasses, and ideas on pairing beer with food. A description of how beers are rated is also furnished, encouraging readers to rate beers on their own. Next comes the annotations themselves; beers are rated on a scale from 0 to 5, although no beer in this book is rated higher than 4.8 (Rogue Shakespeare Stout, Newport, Oregon). Beers featured are from all over the world, including such exotic locales as the Canary Islands, the Dominican Republic, Greece, Hong Kong, and Tahiti. The annotations discuss such features as appearance, taste, smell, smoothness, fruitiness, fizziness, and what foods go well with the particular beer. A following section reviews nonalcoholic brews (less than $\frac{1}{2}$ of 1 percent alcohol), which are ranked in comparison to each other, not to the beers with alcoholic content.

Several appendixes supply easily accessible data, listing beers alphabetically by state and by country; the best beers by style (these include ratings of 3.5 and above); the best beers for novices; old beer names (e.g., Beer ["the ultimate no-frills name"], Foecking Premium ["pronounce this quietly and discreetly to yourself"], McMenamins Freudian Sip Ale ["Consciously and unconsciously, this beer is ego-enhancing"], and San Andres Earthquake Pale Ale ["The microbrewery serves beer out of the tap for five cents during earthquakes"]); microbreweries and brewpubs (addresses and telephone numbers provided); and rating notes (a chart for the reader's own notes).

Although this work is far more comprehensive and international in scope than *America's Best Beers* (see entry 1536), the reader is still subject to Klein's interpretation. Beers that he has not tasted receive no description, and his judgments on certain beers may not mesh with the reader's own opinion. Even though Klein has traveled extensively, he is bound to have missed some brews. For instance, many brews from Boulder and Fort Collins, Colorado, are profiled, but not many from Denver, despite the recent explosion of brewpubs there. Nonetheless, this guide makes for fascinating reading; it is recommended, however, for personal and not library collections.—**Melissa R. Root**

1538. Sims-Bell, Barbara. **Career Opportunities in the Food and Beverage Industry.** New York, Facts on File, 1994. 240p. index. $14.95pa. ISBN 0-8160-2913-X.

The food industry is one of the largest and fastest growing employment segments in the country. This volume is a selective occupational guide offering a sampling of nearly 70 food careers. Eleven sections profile diverse careers in management, sales, teaching, and writing, including baker, caterer, chef, dietitian, home economist, kitchen designer, plant operations manager, sports nutritionist, and winemaker, to name a few. The format of the guide makes for ease of use and understanding. Arranged alphabetically, each two-to-three-page entry begins with a summary of the career and a "career ladder." Expanding upon this are a more detailed description of the job, employment and advancement prospects, necessary education and training, best geographic locations for work, and tips for entry into the profession. Extensive appendixes listing educational schools offering culinary and food programs, workshops and seminars, professional and trade associations, culinary organizations, and food publications are most useful. All career collections will want this resource.—**Joy Hastings**

1539. Trager, James. **The Food Chronology: A Food Lover's Compendium of Events and Anecdotes, from Prehistory to the Present.** New York, Henry Holt, 1995. 783p. illus. index. (A Henry Holt Reference Book). $40.00. ISBN 0-8050-3389-0.

Packed with information and anecdotal in tone, this book reads like a series of short newspaper clips about important events, people, and products in the history of food. More than 13,000 entries arranged chronologically record milestones from the omnivorous eating habits of *Homo erectus* in 1 million B.C. to the introduction of blue M&Ms in 1995. Within time frames, the author categorizes items into subject areas (e.g., agriculture, human rights, technology) that are designated by small iconic symbols. The text also includes numerous cross-references and a number of black-and-white illustrations.

Although the information presented here is fascinating, and an extensive index helps users locate items within specific subject areas, it is difficult to gain an integrated overview of food history from information in this form. Readers will find a more narrative approach in Maguelonne Toussaint-Samat's *A History of Food* (Blackwell, 1992) and a more topical treatment in Reay Tannahill's *Food in History* (Crown, 1988).—**Barbara Ittner**

1540. Ulene, Art. **The Nutribase Nutrition Facts Desk Reference.** Garden City Park, N.Y., Avery Publishing, 1995. 789p. $17.95pa. ISBN 0-89529-623-3.

As Americans have become more diet- and nutrition-conscious—more aware of food labels and what is in their food—they want to know the food counts of what they eat. This reference will answer those questions. Encyclopedic in format, with nearly 800 pages and 40,000 entries, this volume by a noted television personality and physician, is the most comprehensive single source of food values. Listings in three parts include name brands, generics, specialty, and restaurant items. Part 1 provides general nutrient information such as calories, cholesterol, fat, fiber, and sodium. A most helpful feature is a column giving the percentage of calories from fat. Part 2 provides data on selected vitamins and minerals. Part 3 is an Arbys to Zantigo list of fast-food restaurants and the nutrient content of their food items. The introduction's discussion of nutrition and its explanation of food labels, fat and fiber, and vitamins and minerals are concise and straightforward. A computer version of this information is also available, with ordering details given. Easier to read than Bowes & Church's *Food Values of Portions Commonly Used* (see ARBA 95, entry 1520, and ARBA 86, entry 1451), but not replacing it entirely, this inexpensive but thorough reference should find a place in any size collection.—**Joy Hastings**

FORESTRY

1541. **North American Factbook, 1994-95.** David A. Pease and others, eds. San Francisco, Calif., Miller Freeman, 1994. 448p. index. $257.00pa. ISBN 0-87930-357-3.

Although not obvious from the title, this text is a specialized publication for the wood products industry in Canada and the United States. The statistics and analyses have been gleaned from figures published for the years 1993 and 1994. The book opens with a succinct discussion of the year in review, citing recent political initiatives, legal disputes, market demands, and prices. The organization and operation of the industry are covered in the remaining chapters, with a short analysis preceding every topic. One of the more valuable chapters lists 768 lumber companies in order of level of production in 1993, followed by an alphabetical index.

Users of the text will appreciate the diversity of information presented from engineered lumber and small-log optimizing through corporate profiles, industry organizations, and government agencies. A glossary of terms and an index to company names are included. In addition, the text is enhanced with numerous figures within each chapter. What the book lacks is a list of these figures with the table of contents for quick reference. Despite the price, the work is an invaluable resource for specialized collections.—**Katherine Margaret Thomas**

1542. **Restoration Forestry: An International Guide to Sustainable Forestry Practices.** Michael Pilarski, ed. Durango, Colo., Kivakí Press, 1994. 525p. illus. index. $26.95pa. ISBN 1-882308-51-4.

There is increasing interest in forest restoration, but unfortunately not a concurrent increase in agreement on what restoration forestry actually is. This book does little to advance restoration forestry as a serious science. The Society for Ecological Restoration provides a general definition, stating that ecological restoration involves the alteration of sites in order to establish defined ecosystems. It further states that the goal of this process is to imitate already specified ecosystems. Rather than providing useful information on how to actually achieve this goal, the book is instead an excuse to castigate industrial forestry and plantation silviculture.

Considerable effort went into the book, as it abounds with information on domestic and international environmental organizations, periodicals, and books. The book began as a product of a 1990 restoration forestry conference, but grew as excerpts from books, articles, and other sources were included. However, coverage is not balanced. Many of the contributions are simply essays on individual perceptions concerning preservation, old growth forests, and so forth. Rather than centering on data and research results, anecdotal evidence is usually supplied to support authors' contentions. Societal engineering is even considered as "permaculture." A return to the lifestyle of past centuries favored by some environmentalists is discussed. The intention of the book is made clear where it lists the top 10 books on restoration forestry. Number 5 is *Clearcut: The Tragedy of Industrial Forestry* (Bill Devall, ed., Sierra Club Books and Earth Island Press, 1993). This is a large-format picture book of clear-cuts (areas of forests that have been cleared out), some of which have since been shown to actually be wildfire remnants rather than clear-cuts. The book under review cannot be recommended for use as a technical, balanced reference guide to restoration forestry.—**Michael G. Messina**

HORTICULTURE

Handbooks and Yearbooks

1543. Denckla, Tanya. **The Organic Gardener's Home Reference: A Plant-by-Plant Guide to Growing Fresh, Healthy Food.** Pownal, Vt., Garden Way Publishing/Storey Communications, 1994. 273p. illus. maps. index. $29.95; $19.95pa. ISBN 0-88266-840-4; 0-88266-839-0pa.

The Organic Gardener's Home Reference covers vegetables, herbs, fruits and nuts, and pest and disease control. The book has a good introduction on garden stewardship, followed by chapters on vegetables, fruits and nuts, herbs, macro- and microdestructive agents with organic remedies, and allies and companions. For those who want to know about an edible plant, the book describes growth conditions, harvesting, storage requirements, growing tips, and selected varieties. The appendixes include requirements for an organic garden, seed companies, equipment and pest control companies, state gardening associations, and an updated USDA hardiness zone map, as well as a list of suggested readings. Access is provided by an excellent index. The work compares favorably with *Rodale's All New Encyclopedia of Organic Gardening* (see ARBA 94, entry 1619, and ARBA 93, entry 1489); however, it is not as comprehensive. Denckla's book is more attractive to the eye, making information easier to find. With the increased importance in our society for healthy eating and fitness, this book would be an ideal resource for public library collections and the amateur or professional organic gardener.—**Theresa Maggio**

1544. Hillier, Malcolm. **Container Gardening Through the Year.** New York, Dorling Kindersley, 1995. 160p. illus. index. $24.95. ISBN 1-56458-869-6.

Thematically organized around the four seasons (with a separate concluding section on plant care), *Container Gardening* provides creative ideas and practical advice for year-round gardening in containers such as pots, baskets, and buckets. The work leads off with a discussion of raw materials, choosing the right container, choosing the right plants, the six basic planting shapes, and other similarly useful information. The seasonal chapters, starting with spring, follow. Within these sections, materials are organized by type of plant or planting; for example, a grouping of "camellia, azalea, and hyacinths" or a "woodland windowbox." Growing tips accompany each photo-essay, and site suggestions point out where a given type of planting might be most appropriate. As readers would expect from this publisher, stunning photographs serve as the centerpiece of each single- or double-page spread. The work concludes with a plant list that is organized by type (e.g., trees, shrubs, perennials) and a plant-name index. An enjoyable treatment of a specialized topic, this handbook will be most appropriate for libraries with large gardening collections.—**G. Kim Dority**

1545. Hobbs, Jack, and Terry Hatch. **Best Bulbs for Temperate Climates.** Portland, Oreg., Timber Press, 1994. 196p. illus. index. $32.95. ISBN 0-88192-293-5.

Temperate climate in the context of this book refers to those parts of the world with warm, wet summers and dry, possibly cool, but not intensely cold winters, such as South Africa (especially the Cape Province), western South America, western and southern Australia, California, and the Mediterranean. New Zealand horticulturalists Hobbs and Hatch provide an introduction to growing bulbs in temperate climates, covering cultivation, garden design, containers, propagation, and pests and diseases, followed by an encyclopedia of bulbs suitable for garden use. Most species will be unfamiliar to gardeners in the United States outside of California, although the authors also include such popular bulbs as tulips, daffodils, and crocuses. Encyclopedia entries cover place of origin, suitable garden environment, general description of the genus, culture, notable species and cultivars, and include a full-color photograph. Sometimes the authors' local perspective affects their comments. Generally, however, the text provides ample information to guide readers in selecting bulbs for their own gardens, with the understanding that many must be protected or lifted for indoor storage during the winter. The work is recommended for California libraries and comprehensive gardening collections elsewhere.—**Beth Clewis**

1546. Ogden, Scott. **Garden Bulbs for the South.** Dallas, Tex., Taylor Publishing, 1994. 250p. illus. index. $22.95. ISBN 0-87833-861-6.

Garden Bulbs of the South is an exciting, colorful gardening book with more than 200 color photographs of United States, Mexican, and Central American bulbs. This resource includes such unique chapters as "Petite Afrique," "Rain Lily Day," and "Summer Glories." There is a section that describes where the bulb is native and the genus and family. It contains an appendix describing southern bulb culture, mediterranean beds, and bulbs for hog wallows. A resource appendix covers bulb sources and societies and publications. The index is excellent and detailed. It compares favorably with *Taylor's Guide to Bulbs* (rev. ed., Houghton Mifflin, 1986), but it is more current. It is a must for small and large public libraries, and particularly useful for the warm climates of the South.—**Theresa Maggio**

1547. Pleasant, Barbara. **The Gardener's Guide to Plant Diseases: Earth-Safe Remedies.** Pownal, Vt., Storey Communications, 1995. 188p. illus. index. (A Down-to-Earth Gardening Book). $16.95; $12.95pa. ISBN 0-88266-297-X; 0-88266-274-0pa.

This book is written for the general public, those with small gardens at home. Environmentally sound treatments for more than 50 plant diseases are described. The first chapter provides a general overview of garden plant pathology. The diseases are covered in several chapters, each devoted to a particular category: soilborne, airborne, fungal, insect vectored, bacterial, viral, and nematode caused diseases. For each disease, the type of organism causing it, the geographical range, host plants, the diagnosis, the immediate action, and future (preventative) management are provided. In addition, there is a chapter entitled "Great Masqueraders," dealing with conditions harmful to plants, but not considered by the author to be actual diseases (such as those caused by the organisms listed above). Examples would be insect damage and nutritional disorders. A final chapter contains a chart of 46 plants, listing several diseases for each plant, along with symptoms. This can serve as a cross-reference to the rest of the book, which is organized by disease rather than plant. The index covers scientific names (cross-referenced to common names) and common names, and italicized page numbers indicating illustrations.

This is an excellent and well-written guide for the home gardener growing fruits and vegetables, with much practical information and advice. Although there are not many illustrations, the diseases are well described, and there is a full discussion for each one on how to treat the diseased plants and why each step has to be taken to minimize the overall effect of the pathogen on the garden.—**John Laurence Kelland**

1548. Taylor, Patrick. **The Gardener's Guide to Britain.** new ed. Portland, Oreg., Timber Press, 1994. 320p. illus. maps. index. $19.95pa. ISBN 0-88192-242-0.

This is a most practical guidebook, with maps, directions, opening hours, small color photographs that engender interest, and, best of all, the personal comments of a well-known gardener and author of many practical books on gardening, including *The 500 Best Garden Plants* (Timber Press, 1993). Individual descriptions always point out distinguishing features of a garden—what makes the trip worthwhile. To make sure everyone learns about the best garden to visit, gardens are discussed within a geographic arrangement, indexed by type and features, such as nurseries for specific kinds of plants, those by famous designers, and national collections of plants.

Most library collections will have books on many of the large gardens included here. This guide is designed to travel well and can be torn asunder if people wish to go their separate ways. It is meant to be purchased by individuals and taken along, but it is important for librarians to know about nonetheless.
—**Milton H. Crouch**

1549. Taylor, Patrick. **Gardening with Roses: A Practical and Inspirational Guide.** London, Pavilion Books and Portland, Oreg., Timber Press, 1995. 256p. illus. maps. index. $17.95pa. ISBN 0-88192-286-2.

It is clear that the author has had a love affair with roses for some time. This beautiful book has more than 200 pictures that he has taken of the various varieties of roses in their natural states. Concentrating on old roses and those that have been bred with parallel attributes, Taylor begins the book with a discussion of the history of roses, their classification, cultivation, and planting.

The majority of the text is divided into two chapters that deal with bush roses and climbing roses, respectively. Listed alphabetically by Latin name, each entry has a flowing description that usually contains a "biography" of the specimen, a picture, its virtues and peccadilloes, how to use it effectively in gardens, and other informative tidbits for the gardener. The "Rose Directory" at the heart of the book delineates roses by color; foliage; scent; structure; and whether they work well in shade, small gardens, or informal places. A reading list and a map of hardiness zones for Europe and the United States complete the work.

An obvious labor of love for Taylor, the reader will nearly believe the scents of the roses are rising from the pages as the author's descriptions and interesting discussions are perused. Gardeners of any variety, from amateur to professional to armchair, will find this engaging work to be an enjoyable read as well as a useful reference guide.—**Jo Anne H. Ricca**

1550. **Taylor's Master Guide to Gardening.** Frances Tenenbaum, ed. New York, Houghton Mifflin, 1994. 612p. illus. maps. index. $60.00. ISBN 0-396-64995-1.

As the latest entry in the "one volume does it all" category of gardening books, this large and colorful reference certainly comes close. Taylor is a well-recognized name in gardening guides. This one has more than 30 listed contributors and consultants who are professionals in horticulture, gardening, and landscape design. The volume is similar in size, appearance, and price to *The American Horticultural Society*

Encyclopedia of Gardening (see ARBA 94, entry 1617). There is not nearly the overlap one might expect between these two works, however, and libraries should seriously consider this one even if they have the other. The emphasis of the American Horticultural Society publication is on creating and maintaining all types of gardens; the Taylor's guide, by contrast, features the plants themselves, 1,000 of them in full color in the plant gallery section, and 3,000 (including the 1,000 gallery entries) in the encyclopedia section. Trees, shrubs, vines, ferns, perennials, annuals, and herbs are covered, but few fruits or vegetables. Plants were chosen based on their beauty, practicality, and ready availability, with United States and Canadian gardeners in mind. The encyclopedia entries provide more detailed descriptions than those in the photo gallery, furnish growing information, and mention cultivars, hybrids, and related species, as well as hardiness zones. Plants are arranged by botanical (genus and species) names; common name access is possible by the comprehensive index.

While the gallery and the encyclopedia sections constitute the heart of this guide, there are two smaller sections: one on creating gardens, with many ideas and color photographs, and the other on growing plants, the "how-to" of working with plants and soils for a healthy garden. Highly recommended for all libraries with a gardening clientele, this volume will also be valuable for identifying hundreds of ornamental plant species. [R: RBB, 15 Jan 95, pp. 964-65]—**William H. Wiese**

1551. Thomas, Graham Stuart. **The Graham Stuart Thomas Rose Book.** rev. ed. Portland, Oreg., Sagapress/Timber Press, 1994. 385p. illus. maps. index. $39.95. ISBN 0-88192-280-3.

Interest in growing historic roses has shown a resurgence in the last few years, and gardeners are now eager to find descriptions of these beautiful flowers from the past. This work provides those descriptions as well as those of more modern-day English roses. Lovely color photos and drawings enhance the text. Thomas, a renowned authority on roses, writes with knowledge and affection for the "loveliest of all flowers." This one-volume work compiles, revises, and enlarges three of his popular works on roses that have seen many editions but are now out of print, *The Old Shrub Roses* (C. T. Branford, 1956), *Shrub Roses of Today* (St. Martin's Press, 1962), and *Climbing Roses Old and New* (St. Martin's Press, 1965). It also includes sections on growing roses and works by other authors.

The first part covers the old shrub roses with descriptions of the varieties of Gallica, damask, white, and centifolia roses. The second part describes the species, or wild, roses such as the dog rose, the cinnamon rose, wild yellow roses, rugosa roses, and American wild roses. The author also describes such specimens as the Bourbon rose, hybrid perpetual roses, tea roses, musk roses, and some new English roses being cultivated today. The third part covers climbing roses of all varieties, and the fourth part describes growing and pruning. The final section is a listing of works by other authors on the history of rose species, keys to the cultivated roses, and the botany of climbing roses. Maps of hardiness zones for the United States and Europe, a bibliography of sources, and an index complete the work. A section of 158 beautiful full-color photos and paintings, some by the author, of the roses described in the text are inserted between the first and second sections of the book. Classic rose paintings by Redoute, artist to Josephine Bonaparte, bloom from the pages.

For those libraries and collectors who already own these three books by the author, the works by David Austin, *The Heritage of the Rose* (1988), *Old Roses and English Roses* (1993), and *Shrub Roses and Climbing Roses* (1993) (all published by Antique Collector's Club), would enhance any rose book collection. This work is recommended for public and academic libraries with gardening collections, and for individuals who are discovering, or are experienced in, the beauty and rewards of collecting and growing roses.—**Diane B. Rhodes**

1552. **Western Garden: The Complete Interactive Guide to Your Yard & Garden.** [CD-ROM]. Menlo Park, Calif., Sunset, 1995. Minimum system requirements (Windows version): IBM or compatible 386/25MHz. Double-speed CD-ROM drive. DOS 6.0. Windows 3.1. 4MB RAM (8MB recommended). 640 X 480 256-color display monitor. Mouse. Sound card. Speakers. Video for Windows 1.1d. Minimum system requirements (Macintosh version): Macintosh 68030/25MHz. Double-speed CD-ROM drive. System 7.0. QuickTime 2.0. 4MB RAM (8MB recommended). 640 X 480 256-color display monitor. $49.95. ISBN 0-376-00600-5(Windows); 0-376-00601-3(Macintosh).

The recent popularity of gardening has resulted in a surge in the demand for gardening paraphernalia and information. The Sunset *Western Garden* CD-ROM represents a successful application of the latest technology to this ancient activity. Consisting of three main areas (encyclopedia, plant selector, and garden notebook), the disc includes more than 1,500 photographs and illustrations, videos on various topics, and audio pronunciations for the 6,000 plant entries. The information can be customized to the user's needs and locale. Once the climate zone has been selected (this can be done by typing in the zip code), the user can employ the system's Boolean operators to choose plants or trees by their colors, heights, and other characteristics. The data can then be printed out or stored in the garden notebook. A particularly useful feature is the ability of the system to display the companion plants for other plants in the database. Also included in the package is an attractive 112-page book titled *An Illustrated Guide to Attracting Birds*.

The program is easy to install and generally user friendly. The displays are attractive and informative. Although intended for the western portion of the United States, many of the CD-ROM's features (encyclopedia, garden notebook, quick tips, and so forth) can be used throughout the country. A minor criticism concerns the product's ability to do complex plant specifications. For example, after climate, perennial, height, and the color "white" were selected, the system displayed appropriate perennials of the requested height, but in all colors. This CD-ROM will be welcomed by gardeners everywhere, but will be especially popular and useful to those in the West.—**January Adams**

VETERINARY SCIENCE

1553. **Animal Health Yearbook 1993. Annuaire de la Santé Animale. Anuario de Sanidad Animal.** Rome, Food and Agriculture Organization of the United Nations; distr., Lanham, Md., UNIPUB, 1994. 228p. index. (FAO Animal Production and Health Series, no.33). $55.00pa. ISBN 92-5-003527-6.

An annual publication, this yearbook documents animal diseases throughout the world. Communicable diseases are grouped according to their importance for international trade in livestock or livestock products irrespective of national borders within countries and at the local level. Code lists are provided for animal species, disease occurrence, disease control, and diseases. A separate pamphlet that lists explanatory notes is included. The tables are easy to read if the lists and notes provided are used. Other tables, reports, and lists, such as the Food and Agriculture Organization of the United Nations/World Health Organization Experimental Table and the West Asia Rinderpest Eradication Campaign Coordination, are supplied, as is an index of diseases and causal agents.—**Patricia S. Wilson**

1554. Beaver, Bonnie V. **The Veterinarian's Encyclopedia of Animal Behavior.** Ames, Iowa, Iowa State University Press, 1994. 307p. illus. $29.95. ISBN 0-8138-2114-2.

This is the first encyclopedia specifically on veterinary animal behavior; that is, for domesticated animals such as dogs, cats, horses, cattle, sheep, and goats. It tries to accurately define behavior problems encountered by pet owners, laboratory animal caretakers, and livestock raisers, and often suggests solutions to those problems. The terms are arranged in alphabetical order from abnormal behavior to zoomorphism. Each term is defined in a sentence or up to two pages of text. The author has provided many *see also* references that further explain a term, such as "Finicky Eaters" *see also* "Diet Change, Eating Behavior, Food Preferences." The work ends with three appendixes. One is a blank five-page history form for behavior problems that may be used to fully inform a veterinarian of the problem. Another appendix provides information such as gestation length, estrous cycle length, social behavior type (territorial, linear dominance, and the like), and average number of young for dogs, cats, horses, cattle, swine, sheep, and goats. The last appendix lists drugs commonly used in the treatment of veterinary behavioral problems. A five-page list of references used in the book and for further reading is included at the end.

The author has her doctor of veterinary medicine degree and is a diplomate of the American College of Veterinary Behaviorists—therefore well qualified to provide this reference source. She provides a brief diagnosis and treatment for some behaviors, such as "wind sucking" (a condition in horses of sucking in and swallowing air), for which she provides an entire paragraph on its treatment. For those wanting a more general animal behavior dictionary with more terms, *Animal Behavior Desk Reference* by Edward M.

Barrows (CRC Press, 1995) would be a good choice. For those wanting more information on veterinary animal behavior, *Domestic Animal Behavior for Veterinarians & Animal Scientists* by Katherine A. Houpt (2d ed., Iowa State University Press, 1991) is also suggested. This encyclopedia is recommended for academic, public, and agricultural or veterinary libraries.—**Diane B. Rhodes**

1555. Eby, Vivienne M. **The Horse Dictionary: English-Language Terms Used in Equine Care, Feeding, Training, Treatment, Racing, and Show.** Jefferson, N.C., McFarland, 1995. 256p. illus. $38.50. ISBN 0-89950-912-6.

A small book with more than 6,000 brief definitions of terms related to horses, this work emphasizes on the health of horses. It is illustrated with small line drawings every few pages. A great many definitions are of technical terms concerning body parts, ailments, and training. Some of the more general definitions are too brief to be helpful, and others are in question (e.g., *dressage, cribbing, Irish Hunter*). For most library purposes the broader and more detailed *International Horseman's Dictionary* (see ARBA 76, entry 1566) would probably be more useful. It is well illustrated, includes longer definitions of riding styles, and lists winners of horse competitions. Libraries should carefully consider their need for Eby's more specialized dictionary before paying the price.—**Joann H. Lee**

1556. Vogel, Colin. **The Complete Horse Care Manual.** New York, Dorling Kindersley, 1995. 192p. illus. index. $24.95. ISBN 0-7894-0170-3.

A basic introductory reference to the multiple and varied aspects of horse care and management, this manual begins with a general discussion of the physical characteristics and progresses through handling, shoeing, grooming, stabling, food, tack, disorders, injuries, and much more. Entries are brief, usually just two pages in length. However, the section on diseases, disorders, and first aid is longer and quite informative. As with all Dorling Kindersley books, this one has numerous color photographs that augment the text. The glossary is not extensive, and the inadequate list of horse association addresses and government departments associated with horses appears to have been an afterthought. This section should have been more comprehensive or omitted. A usable but far from complete guide, strictly for the potential or novice horse owner, this book is not a necessary purchase unless no other books on the subject are owned.

—**Joy Hastings**

31 Biological Sciences

GENERAL WORKS

1557. **Elsevier's Dictionary of Biometry: In English, French, Spanish, Dutch, German, Italian and Russian.** D. Rasch, M. L. Tiku, and D. Sumpf, eds. New York, Elsevier Science, 1994. 887p. index. $225.75. ISBN 0-444-81495-7.

Biometry, or "(t)he application of mathematical methods, particularly mathematical statistics, to the life sciences . . ." (p. 59), is the subject of this dictionary. Following the usual format of other Elsevier polyglot dictionaries, entries are in English and consecutively numbered. Foreign-language word indexes at the end of the book refer the user to the numbered English-language entry in which the user will also find the term in each of the six other languages covered. The editors state that the basis for many of the ideas and definitions included here are from the three editions of *Biometrisches Worterbuch* (*Biometrical Dictionary*) (Frankfurt: Harri Deutsch, 1988), and they note that the editor of the 3d edition of *Biometrisches* is the first editor of the dictionary under review here. The 2,430 definitions are succinctly and clearly defined. Boldface terms within definitions lead to other defined terms. As with other Elsevier dictionaries, this one is well bound and the typeface used is highly readable. The high price will probably put it out of reach of many libraries, but it would be a welcome addition to those libraries serving institutions with strong programs in the life sciences, mathematics, and statistics.—**James E. Bird**

1558. Ibelgaufts, Horst. **Dictionary of Cytokines.** New York, VCH, 1995. 778p. $110.00. ISBN 3-527-30042-2.

Cytokines are soluble proteins or peptides, secreted by cells and either inhibiting or stimulating other cells. The first cytokines to be described acted upon cells of the immune system. Now, however, hundreds of such substances have been discovered, involved in a wide variety of biological processes. The study of cytokines is one of the most active, and most confusing, areas of biology today. The study of these factors is yielding understanding of cell growth, behavior, and differentiation in such widely diverse fields as immunology, oncology, neurology, and developmental biology. Because this is such an interdisciplinary (and fast-moving) area of research, the same substance may be discovered, and named, at different times, by different researchers. The result is a confusing hodgepodge of nomenclature.

Although this volume is as technical as one would expect a tome on this subject to be, it is also remarkably well written and interesting. The author includes plenty of background information on cellular and tissue processes (for example, hematopoiesis), as well as the cytokines themselves. The work is in many ways a textbook in dictionary format. There are about 3,200 entries, each cross-referenced from the numerous acronyms and synonyms by which each cytokine is known. Entries define the factor; tell how it is obtained; give its molecular characterization, clinical use, and significance; and cite numerous experimental and review articles. More than 100 color illustrations add to the clarity of the text. Workers in the fields of immunology, cancer research, cellular biology, and related fields will find this an invaluable addition to their libraries.—**Carol L. Noll**

BIOLOGY

1559. Corliss, William R., comp. **Biological Anomalies: Humans III. A Catalog of Biological Anomalies.** Glen Arm, Md., Sourcebook Project, 1994. 206p. illus. maps. index. $19.95. ISBN 0-915554-29-1.

The compiler, editor of the newsletter *Science Frontiers* (1976-), has completed 29 volumes devoted to scientific anomalies. Corliss's purpose is to suggest research areas that need further study. These works offer well-organized lists of anomalies by subject, along with brief discussions and a helpful list of source materials. This latest volume, the third devoted to human anomalies, deals with evolution as inferred from the fossil record and genetics. Although a complex business for many laypeople, the author's organization and discussion promotes understanding. Creationists will find much information that may be of use to them. It is unlikely, however, that information found here is unknown to physical anthropologists, archaeologists, and geneticists.

The work is well organized and contains a subject index, an index to first authors, and an index by source title. Citations to published literature are complete, increasing the work's reference value. Nine pages are devoted to describing other volumes in the series. [R: C&RL, Mar 95, p. 193]—**Milton H. Crouch**

1560. Kress, Stephen W. **The National Audubon Society The Bird Garden.** New York, Dorling Kindersley, 1995. 176p. illus. maps. index. $24.95. ISBN 0-7894-0139-8.

One of the pleasures of garden birding is that it provides an opportunity for people to keep in touch with nature despite the demands of modern living. The varieties of birds visiting a garden can be maximized if one takes advantage of simple landscaping, planting, nest structure, and feeding techniques. These topics are covered in detail throughout this guide, with plenty of accompanying photographs, illustrations, and diagrams.

The majority of the book is taken up with five regional accounts (Northeast, Southeast, Prairies and Plains, Mountains and Deserts, and Pacific Coast) that describe the commonly encountered bird species and the range of bird-attracting plants to be found in that region. A one-page "How to Use This Chapter" precedes this section and includes a color-coded map of the hardiness zones throughout North America. For each region a selection of familiar bird species is depicted, along with a concise description of nest, song, and food preferences. In addition, recommended plants are illustrated and described together with an annotated list of other useful plants. An "ideal" garden is shown for each area, but this is merely a suggestion of what is possible.

The appendixes include a list of plant sources available from mail-order nurseries, a short description of the National Audubon Society, and an index to plant and bird species. This is a well-written and researched guide that both the active and beginning bird gardener will enjoy.—**Katherine Margaret Thomas**

1561. **Molecular Biology and Biotechnology: A Comprehensive Desk Reference.** Robert A. Meyers, ed. New York, VCH, 1995. 1034p. illus. index. $149.95; $59.95pa. ISBN 1-56081-569-8; 1-56081-925-1pa.

A one-volume encyclopedia and contextual dictionary, *Molecular Biology and Biotechnology* provides the novice student or experienced scientist with a useful distillation of the fields of study concerned with the molecular basis of life. A work such as this has been needed because of the interdisciplinary nature of the research. This tool ties together contemporary knowledge and practice. There are 250 signed articles averaging 3-4 pages in length, complete with illustrations, chiefly black-and-white, and short bibliographies.

Each article begins with a listing of defined keywords relevant to the topic. Through the references obtained in the subject index, the user has, in effect, a dictionary of terms placed in a primary context. The subject index also covers tables and figures. *See also* references are inserted after each article, directing users to other pertinent articles. The comprehensiveness of the tool is remarkable for a single volume of modest cost. The editor has done an excellent job in working with 378 authors. The prose is clear and concise.—**John M. Robson**

BOTANY

General Works

Dictionaries and Encyclopedias

1562. Desmond, Ray. **Dictionary of British and Irish Botanists and Horticulturalists: Including Plant Collectors, Flower Painters, and Garden Designers.** rev. ed. London, Natural History Museum and Bristol, Pa., Taylor & Francis, 1994. 825p. index. $250.00. ISBN 0-85066-843-3.

A little different than other directories, this one covers people who worked in the horticultural world as far back as the 1500s. It attempts to be as exhaustive a compilation of British and Irish people involved with plants as possible. This revision of the 1977 edition has more than 3,700 entries. It includes added information for already existing biographical entries and the new categories of flower and botanical artists and garden designers.

The body of the work is arranged in alphabetical entries by name. These range in length from three to four lines to one column, depending on the information available on the individual. To the best of the author's effort, each entry contains the person's name; birth, death, or flourishing dates, where known; education and qualifications; honors and offices held; brief career details; selected publications by the person; locations of any plant collections, herbaria, manuscripts, or portraits; any commemorative plants; and finally, citation information.

Three interesting indexes are included, the first a list of professions (e.g., artists, bryologists, nurserypeople) with appropriate names. The second is a list of particular plants that each person is associated with, and the third is a list of geographical locations where individuals worked with or studied flora. Anyone in the plant world would love to own this dictionary, but it is a really important tool for any institution engaged in the study of botany or horticulture.—**Lillian R. Mesner**

1563. Hyam, R., and R. Pankhurst. **Plants and Their Names: A Concise Dictionary.** New York, Oxford University Press, 1995. 545p. $29.95. ISBN 0-19-866189-4.

This book provides brief information on some 16,000 more commonly occurring scientific and vernacular plant names. The emphasis is on the biodiversity of plants. Biodiversity is usually derived from Latin in an obvious—although not always straightforward—way, reflecting the social backgrounds or hobbies of botanists rather than having anything to do with the plants themselves. There are six types of entries in this dictionary: five cover scientific names, and one is for common names. The five types of scientific name entries are by family names, genus names, species names, common specific epithets, and synonyms. The 6,000 common names that have been included in this work are those that were encountered in the botanical and horticultural literature and should reflect common usage. The whole project was carried out at the Royal Botanic Garden in Edinburgh, Scotland. This dictionary will be of interest to students of botany and horticulture.—**Bohdan S. Wynar**

1564. Isely, Duane. **One Hundred and One Botanists.** Ames, Iowa, Iowa State University Press, 1994. 351p. illus. index. $32.95. ISBN 0-8138-2498-2.

Isely has selected 98 male and 3 female botanists extending chronologically from Aristotle to Winona Hazel Welch (1896-1991). For each scientist, Isely has prepared a three- to five-page essay briefly placing the scientist in history, mentioning any verified personal facts, and his or her major contribution, closing with a three- to five-item bibliography about the subject. Isely stresses the paucity of definitive biographies, eschews autobiographies and obituaries lauding their subjects, and finds published reviews of books by these botanists helpful. Beyond the expected profiles such as Theophrastus, Gregor Mendel, and Adolf Engler, Isley has included both different people such as Nicholas-Théodore de Saussure, the first plant chemist, and unexpected aspects of familiar botanists. For example, Charles Bessey negotiated microscopes for laboratory courses at Iowa State University and stipulated their purchase as a condition for his moving to the University of Nebraska. One disappointment is the omission of Barbara McClintock

(1902-1992), awarded the 1983 Nobel prize for her contribution to maize cytogenetics. Two indexes complete this work, which is enthusiastically recommended for interested amateurs, undergraduates, and botanical historians seeking brief overviews.—**Helen M. Barber**

1565. Wielgorskaya, Tatiana. **Dictionary of Generic Names of Seed Plants.** New York, Columbia University Press, 1995. 570p. $80.00. ISBN 0-231-07892-7.

Wielgorskaya has prepared for both professional and amateur botanists, horticulturalists, foresters, ecologists, and everyone interested in plants a meticulous list of seed plants. The "List of Families" (pp. 1-84) includes the family name, the botanical authority and date of publication, whether the plant is monocotyledon or dicotyledon, the number of genera followed by the number of species, a brief geographical location, and an alphabetical listing of the genera in that family. The "Dictionary of Generic Names of Seed Plants" (pp. 85-570) provides for each genera its name, date, family, number of species, and geographical location.

In contrast to two similar books—*A Dictionary of Flowering Plants and Ferns* by J. C. Willis and revised by H. K. Airy Shaw (International Book Distributor, 1982), which follows the Englerian classification, and D. J. Mabberley's *The Plant-Book: A Portable Dictionary of the Higher Plants* (Cambridge University Press, 1987), following Arthur Cronquist's classification—Wielgorskaya has followed the classification used by her consulting editor, Armen Takhtajan. Careful checking of all available periodicals and monographs published during past decades—modern floras, both editions of *Die Naturlichen Pflanzenfamilien*, *Index Nominus Genericorum*, *Index Kewensis*, *Kew Index*, and the *International Code of Botanical Nomenclature* (1988)—has produced many corrections. Only "living synonyms" found in modern botanical literature and some recently published generic names are included, while generic hybrids are excluded.

Wielgorskaya acknowledges assistance from members of the Missouri Botanical Garden, where Director Peter H. Raven made possible the computerization of this dictionary. Staff members of the Komarov Botanical Institute Library and the Missouri Botanical Garden Library, as well as Cronquist, are also thanked. With almost a fifth of the world's seed plants facing extinction during the next three decades, this dictionary will expedite synthesization of what is known.—**Helen M. Barber**

Handbooks and Yearbooks

1566. Lancaster, Roy. **What Plant Where.** New York, Dorling Kindersley, 1995. 256p. illus. index. $24.95. ISBN 0-7894-0151-7.

As a planting guide, it is doubtful that any other work outshines this publication in presentation. It begins with a "Plant Finder," divided into categories for consideration: size and shape, soil, sunlight, position, seasonal features, color, and other features. The introduction that follows gives general information about plants, shows the features of the book and how to use them, and provides soil and sunlight guides. Five chapters sort out perennials (along with annuals and biennials), climbers, shrubs, conifers, and trees, detailing more than 60 site considerations and landscaping effects. A detailed index completes the work.

Entries within the chapters are arranged alphabetically by Latin name. A picture of the plant is featured, along with a line or two about the special attributes of the plant and a key that details sun/shade requirements, hardiness zones, and sizes (both imperial and metric measurements). If the plant needs an acid soil, this is also noted. Additional pictures are used as needed to detail leaf structure and flowers on trees and shrubs. A particularly satisfying feature is the line drawings in the chapter on trees that show the shape of the mature deciduous tree, along with its appearance in full leaf and during dormancy.

Not enough can be said about the layout of this work, the striking photographs, or the amount of information and detail it contains. Even when types of soil are discussed, there are pictures of soil samples to aid readers in identifying what kind they are dealing with. In typical Dorling Kindersley style, the book is as much a pleasure to behold as it is a depository of knowledge. While not an in-depth resource on all aspects of a particular plant, this work will be a particular delight for the beginning gardener who needs general knowledge, and it is an excellent reference tool for all gardeners in general. Landscapers and plant vendors should find it especially helpful as a visual reference guide for their clients.—**Jo Anne H. Ricca**

Flowering Plants

1567. Fiala, John L. **Flowering Crabapples: The Genus** *Malus*. Portland, Oreg., Timber Press, 1994. 273p. illus. index. $49.95. ISBN 0-88192-292-7.

Incorporating more than 50 years' experience growing and hybridizing crabapples, the late Fiala has prepared a lucid, beautifully illustrated (with 245 color plates) introduction for amateur gardeners, nursery people, and crabapple enthusiasts. Included are a brief history of development from the early species to the newest exclusive polyploids, tree form, culture, diseases and pests, landscaping with companion plants, propagation, and hybridizing.

Taxonomic problems abound throughout this genus. Fiala accepts renaming the toringo crabapple from *Malus sieboldii* to *M. toringo*. Unfortunately, he violated the International Rules of Botanical Nomenclature by proposing the name *M. sieboldii* for a plant previously called *M. xzumi* 'Calocarpa.' The International Ornamental Crabapple Society at The Morton Arboretum declares in the foreword that "The epithet *sieboldii* has already been used for an entirely different crabapple" (p. 11). While discussing accepted botanical species with their related varieties, hybrids, and named clones, Fiala presents his strongest case supporting *M. sieboldii* (Rehder) Fiala 1990 (the year of his death), *M. sieboldii* 'Calocarpa' (Rehder) Fiala, and *M. sieboldii* 'Wooster' (Rehder) Fiala 1954, while *M. sieboldii* (Regel) Rehder and its varieties are clearly labeled "Not an accepted name in this volume" (p. 148). Readers are referred to his earlier taxonomic discussion followed by Fiala's suggestions for combining with or replacing by another *Malus*.

The final chapter concerning named crabapples from unverified sources forms an eloquent plea for further research into crabapple relationships. Appendixes including a list of the best flowering crabapples, nurseries, landscape architects, hybridizers, and a crabapple location key, plus a glossary, bibliography, and indexes, conclude this well-written, meticulous tribute to a confusing genus. The work is recommended for gardening, public, and university libraries.—**Helen M. Barber**

1568. Harris, Marjorie. **Favorite Annuals.** New York, HarperCollins, 1994. 64p. illus. index. $10.00. ISBN 0-00-255404-6.

1569. Harris, Marjorie. **Favorite Flowering Shrubs.** New York, HarperCollins, 1994. 64p. illus. index. $10.00. ISBN 0-00-255394-5.

1570. Harris, Marjorie. **Favorite Perennials.** New York, HarperCollins, 1994. 64p. illus. index. $10.00. ISBN 0-00-255399-6.

1571. Harris, Marjorie. **Favorite Shade Plants.** New York, HarperCollins, 1994. 64p. illus. index. $10.00. ISBN 0-00-255409-7.

Written by an enthusiastic gardener, this four-book series provides a useful introduction to the basic types of garden plants. Each book begins with a short section in which topics such as general plant care, propagation, planting, tips about planting seeds, and maintenance are discussed. For example, the *Favorite Annuals* text has a discussion on container gardening, and *Favorite Shade Plants* outlines the different categories of shade preferred by plants.

Each volume has approximately 20 plant descriptions arranged alphabetically by scientific name. The lively text is further enhanced by a clear, full-color photograph of each species. More specific information such as flowering period, watering regime, height of growth, and soil properties are considered for each plant. All the descriptions contain an invaluable text box entitled "Planting and Maintenance Tips" and an annotated list of similar species and cultivars.

Supplementary materials include a bibliography and index for each volume. A listing of topical magazines and addresses where seed catalogs can be obtained is provided for selected volumes. These books cover the author's favorite plants; therefore, the reader should not expect coverage of all garden plants, although many of the plants described are common and easy to obtain anywhere in North America. The user is urged to refer to the list of "Other Species and Cultivars" to determine what is appropriate for their region. Overall, a highly readable set of books and a recommended reference for gardeners of any ability.
—**Katherine Margaret Thomas**

1572. Jefferson-Brown, Michael, and Harris Howland. **The Gardener's Guide to Growing Lilies.** Portland, Oreg., Timber Press, 1995. 159p. illus. index. $29.95. ISBN 0-88192-315-X.

This guide, billed by the authors as "the most comprehensive and up-to-date general account of the genus available," leaves little room for doubting the claim. Concentrating on the genus *Lilium* and some related plant groups, Jefferson-Brown and Howland seem to have covered all the bases in their discussions of cultivation, ecology and life cycles, integration of the different varieties of lilies into different garden types and spaces, and propagation and hybridization. Lilies specific to North America, New Zealand, and Australia are delineated and described separately.

Almost half of the book is devoted to looking at the various species of lilies individually. Line drawings and photographs, which are used effectively throughout the book, are used here to show attributes of the various plants, aiding in identification. Descriptions contain various data for each entry, concerning place of origin, preferred growing area, flowering habit, propagation issues, size, and other information pertinent to the specific entry. Hybrid lilies are discussed in a separate chapter, with wonderful photographs of the flowers in specific hybrid families collected and photographed faceup. Another chapter goes into great detail describing how gardeners can breed their own lilies.

A species checklist; a list of "false" lilies; an appendix that references where to see, buy, and read about lilies; and a useful index conclude this compendium. Readers will be hard-pressed to find a more comprehensive collection of information on this genus.—**Jo Anne H. Ricca**

1573. Kneller, Marianna. **The Book of Rhododendrons.** Portland, Oreg., Timber Press, 1995. 160p. illus. index. $45.00. ISBN 0-88192-322-2.

The primary purpose of this new book devoted to rhododendrons is to help gardeners select cultivated plants from among the 64 selected for inclusion. The guide is based on a series of 50 full-page color illustrations that help show the 8-month growing cycle of each plant. Illustrations show flowering branch, bud, flower division and profile, new leaf growth, and seedhead. These illustrations are uniformly excellent and will be the sum and substance of the work for most users, as this is not intended as a field guide to rhododendrons. For example, there are no detailed winter, spring, or summer identification keys.

Included are the subgenus *Hymenanthes*, azalea-type rhododendrons found in Exbury Gardens, United Kingdom. For each plant there is information on its discovery in the wild, the aspects that make it particularly appealing or "garden-worthy," and usually some personal observation. These descriptions are contributed by professional growers, botanists, and individuals whose love for a particular plant has resulted in expertise. A most helpful feature of the guide is the section devoted to foliage, which contains some of the most exciting illustrations in the work.

Other features include a complete index; useful biographical information on each of the contributors; an abbreviated glossary; a selective bibliography; and a list of major rhododendron gardens, societies, and associations. Professional users may wish to know that taxonomy is based on a scheme developed at the Royal Botanic Garden, Edinburgh.—**Milton H. Crouch**

1574. Kramer, Jack. **Orchids for the South.** Dallas, Tex., Taylor Publishing, 1994. 163p. illus. maps. index. $28.95. ISBN 0-87833-857-8.

Successful orchid growing is not difficult if you choose plants naturally suited to your growing conditions. Kramer, a prolific author on orchids and other horticultural topics, provides a guide to growing particular orchid species and hybrids that have performed well for him in Florida. Topics covered include how orchids grow, how to buy them, growing them indoors and outdoors, and orchids as cut flowers, as well as individual information on more than 200 species and hybrids. There is a glossary and bibliography, and useful appendixes covering commonly asked questions, lists of U.S. and international orchid suppliers, equipment suppliers and book dealers, and orchid societies and periodicals. Charts covering individual species provide information on plant size, flower color and size, time of bloom, and suggested exposure.

This is a source for horticultural rather than detailed botanical information; its greatest strengths are in its beautiful color photographs, particular plant recommendations for warm climates, and cultural information suitable for novices. More detailed cultural, if less climatically specific, information may be found in a number of sources, including Rick Bond's *All About Growing Orchids* (Ortho Books, 1988) or the venerable handbook *Home Orchid Growing* by Rebecca Tyson Northern (4th rev. ed., Prentice-Hall, 1990). Nonetheless, this is a beautiful book filling a useful purpose; it is recommended for libraries with horticultural collections, especially in warm climates.—**Marit S. MacArthur**

1575. **Manual of Climbers and Wall Plants.** J. K. Burras, ed. London, Macmillan Press and Portland, Oreg., Timber Press, 1994. 282p. illus. index. (The New Royal Horticultural Society Dictionary of Gardening). $39.95. ISBN 0-88192-299-4.

Most of the contents of this volume are derived (but not strictly copied) from *The New Royal Horticultural Society Dictionary of Gardening*, published in 1992. This manual focuses on ornamental climbing plants and is one in a planned series that will be adapted from the 1992 four-volume work. Approximately 300 genera are covered, including annuals and perennials, herbs, shrubs, trees, and ferns. Arrangement is alphabetical by genus name. A popular name index is provided that refers users to the plants' proper genus and species names. A typical entry gives a general description of the genus and instructions for cultivation, followed by a listing and brief description of each species within the genus. Popular cultivars are often mentioned, and safe climatic zones are indicated.

As botanical terms are used extensively in the genus and species descriptions, it is unfortunate that this manual does not supply the seven-page botanical glossary found in the four-volume dictionary. Although the manual does not have the glossy full-color photography that one often finds in new gardening books, there are some fine detailed black-and-white drawings. A recent book that covers climbing plants and does contain some color photographs is *Ornamental Shrubs, Climbers and Bamboos, Excluding Roses and Rhododendrons* (see ARBA 94, entry 1632).

Manual of Climbers and Wall Plants carries the full authority of the Royal Horticultural Society and its careful attention to detail. This new volume will be a worthwhile addition to botanical, horticultural, and serious gardening collections.—**William H. Wiese**

1576. **Manual of Orchids.** Joyce Stewart, ed. Portland, Oreg., Timber Press, 1995. 388p. illus. (The New Royal Horticultural Society Dictionary of Gardening). $49.95. ISBN 0-88192-334-6.

This volume, intended to describe virtually all orchid species, grexes, and cultivars in cultivation, is derived from the four-volume *New Royal Horticultural Society Dictionary of Gardening* (Macmillan, 1992). An introductory section provides general information on plant structure and cultivation techniques as well as peculiarities of orchid cultivar and hybrid nomenclature. Other useful features include an outline of orchid classification based on Robert L. Dressler's *The Orchids: Natural History and Classification* (2d ed., Harvard University Press, 1990); a glossary; abbreviations; a list of names no longer in use; an index of popular names; and an excellent bibliography.

The principal part of the book is an alphabetical listing of genera and species, grexes, and cultivars that provides botanical descriptions and advice on cultivation requirements. The term *grex* refers to a group of plants that are the progeny of a particular artificial hybrid; this work's inclusion of grexes and cultivars is useful as orchid breeding involves so many intergeneric hybrids. More than 100 detailed botanical drawings are furnished; unfortunately, there are no illustrations for many genera and no color illustrations.

Even without benefit of illustrations, botanical descriptions are sufficiently detailed to assist in identification, although those seeking a botanical key would need to consult *The Orchid Book* (see ARBA 94, entry 1652). This is a work not for beginners but for the dedicated orchid grower, with its strength in species, grex, and cultivar descriptions rather than entertainment. Those who are seeking color illustrations showing the exotic beauty of orchid flowers or language easily understood by the uninitiated may prefer works such as *The Illustrated Encyclopedia of Orchids* (see ARBA 94, entry 1658). Nonetheless, because of its detailed information on so many species and hybrids, this is a valuable book, and it is recommended for libraries collecting extensively in botany and horticulture and for individual orchid enthusiasts.—**Marit S. MacArthur**

1577. Rogers, Allan. **Peonies.** Portland, Oreg., Timber Press, 1995. 296p. illus. maps. index. $34.95. ISBN 0-88192-317-6.

One of the most familiar garden perennials, peonies are most often seen in a variety of pink, white, red, or yellow showy flowers. As described in the opening chapter, historically and to the present day, the peony has been an important medicinal plant in herbal therapies worldwide.

The focus of the book is on the cultivation, breeding, and identification of these plants. The chapters on species and recommended cultivars provide short descriptions for each species and selected cultivar, and most are conveniently cross-referenced to 143 high-quality, color photographs. The more than 150 cultivars recommended for description are chosen for their ability to grow in a variety of climatic and cultural conditions. The chapter on propagation is well illustrated with black-and-white line drawings showing details of root systems and grafting methods. Basic topics such as growing season, fertilization, watering, diseases, and pests are covered in a chapter on peony culture.

The appendixes are extensive and include lists and descriptions of peonies in cultivation internationally, nursery sources, landscaping, a conversion table, and a hardiness map. The book concludes with an index to cultivars and a selected bibliography. What the book lacks is a comprehensive subject and species index, which would help the reader to find information more efficiently. Physically, the text is sturdily bound. Both the beginner and commercial grower of peonies will appreciate what this informative text has to offer.—**Katherine Margaret Thomas**

1578. Sheehan, Tom, and Marion Sheehan. **An Illustrated Survey of Orchid Genera.** Portland, Oreg., Timber Press, 1994. 421p. illus. maps. index. $99.95. ISBN 0-88192-288-9.

This beautiful and useful volume results from the Sheehans' articles on orchid genera published in the *American Orchid Society Bulletin* over 25 years. An earlier compilation entitled *Orchid Genera Illustrated* was published in 1979 (see ARBA 80, entry 1382); this edition has been enlarged to cover 158 commonly grown genera, and taxonomic changes have been updated.

Marion Sheehan's superb colored botanical illustrations provide detailed views of all flower parts for at least one type species in each genus: For large genera such as cattleya she provides additional illustrations. The illustrations, besides being beautiful, furnish much more botanical detail than the photographs in such works as Alec Pridgeon's *Illustrated Encyclopedia of Orchids* (see ARBA 94, entry 1658), although Pridgeon's work covers more genera.

Tom Sheehan provides a well-written, informative description of each genus, including identification characteristics, taxonomic history, distribution, and culture, and a list of the more popular species and their flowering seasons. His writing style manages to use minimal technical language while still providing a clear description.

A map showing geographic distribution is provided for each genus. An introductory section includes a description of the basic structure of orchid flowers and an outline of orchid classification; there are also an excellent illustrated glossary, a bibliography, and an index. This work is highly recommended for libraries with horticultural or botanical collections.—**Marit S. MacArthur**

1579. Valder, Peter. **Wisterias: A Comprehensive Guide.** Portland, Oreg., Timber Press, 1995. 160p. illus. index. $32.95. ISBN 0-88192-318-4.

This delightful, informative, and well-illustrated text is the product of one man's dedication to the genus *Wisteria*, a colorful and fragrant vine of the pea family that graces temperate gardens. It is written in a conversational style, yet contains much information on the basic biology and horticulture of these plants. While it is not sufficiently detailed for the professional botanist, serious horticulturalists will find it a pleasure.

The introductory material covers the systematics of the genus and introduces the basic biology of the plant. Thereafter, the author launches into species-by-species coverage of the genus (including cultivational varieties), organized by geographical source areas (North America, China, and Japan). Each of these chapters encompasses a horticultural history of the species together with an excellent description of its morphology and the distinguishing characters of its cultivars, all illustrated by fine color photographs. Two chapters deal with cultivated wisterias of unknown biological provenance and "summer" wisterias, similar plants in the related genus *Millettia*. A chapter on cultivation provides hints on propagation, pests, and pruning, and a final chapter lists situations in which particular cultivars do best.—**Bruce H. Tiffney**

1580. Zomlefer, Wendy B. **Guide to Flowering Plant Families.** Chapel Hill, N.C., University of North Carolina Press, 1994. 430p. illus. index. $49.95; $24.95pa. ISBN 0-8078-2160-8; 0-8078-4470-5pa.

There are more than 200,000 species and 12,000 genera of living flowering plants, but only a little more than 400 families. Thus, most courses in angiosperm identification focus on the family level, generally using native examples. While this work is primarily intended as a textbook for such classes in North America, it is so detailed and well illustrated that it also is a useful, if geographically specialized, reference.

The book commences with an explanation of the coverage and the conventions used, followed by an excellent introduction to the logic of dissecting and illustrating botanical specimens. The majority of the book is given to the description and illustration of 115 families of angiosperms. Each family entry is beautifully organized and detailed, commencing with a full description of the family, followed by a summary of important characteristics and comments on its systematics, distribution, uses, and interesting references. The descriptions are paired with outstanding line drawings illustrating all the salient characters of a representative genus of the family. The book ends with a comparative chart of the characters of the families treated, with an illustrated glossary of botanical terms. All of the material is presented in light of recent, if occasionally controversial, knowledge. The text not only communicates what is known but also what is open to further research in angiosperm systematics. This work deserves a place in every teaching library, and in all botanical research collections.—**Bruce H. Tiffney**

Fungi

1581. Hall, G. S., and D. W. Minter. **International Mycological Directory.** 3d ed. Wallingford, England, published for the International Mycological Association and the International Mycological Institute, CAB International; distr., Tucson, Ariz., University of Arizona Press, 1994. 163p. index. $30.00pa. ISBN 0-85198-947-0.

Consisting of 227 listings, this directory represents a compilation of mycological organizations found throughout the world. Because this work was compiled from questionnaires, a total of 163 of the 227 entries provide descriptive material. The remaining 64 consist only of the name, contact, and address of the organization. All of the 227 entries are listed alphabetically.

For each of the 163 entries, the status, organization type, scope, contact, address, telephone and fax numbers, e-mail addresses, mycological interests, and applied interests are given. In addition, information about the organization, meetings held, culture collections, herbarium information, publications, library information, databases, and courses given are considered. It should be noted that not every descriptive entry will give the same amount of information as stated above.

A geographical index to the organizations can be found near the beginning of the organizational listings. Indexes to the organizations near the end of the work consist of mycological interests, applied interests, living collection holdings, dried reference collection holdings, organizations having databases, organizations holding meetings, producing journals and periodicals, producing newsletters, and producing miscellaneous publications. A nine-page bibliography, the statutes of the International Mycological Association, and the questionnaire for the 4th edition complete the volume. Recommended for college and university libraries, those with strong programs in botany will especially want the directory. Large public libraries may also wish to purchase a copy.—**George H. Bell**

Grasses and Weeds

1582. Boulos, Loutfy, and M. Nabil El-Hadidi. **The Weed Flora of Egypt.** rev. ed. Cairo, Egypt, American University in Cairo Press; distr., New York, Columbia University Press, 1994. 361p. illus. index. $40.00. ISBN 977-424-323-4.

In common parlance, a weed is a plant that is growing where one does not want it, usually in association with cultivated plants. Technically, a weed is an aggressively opportunistic plant that grows to the exclusion of other taxa, often in response to environmental disturbance. While some weeds are useful, many can cause substantial economic loss in commercial settings; in either case, the first step in evaluating the situation is to identify the weed.

This is a new edition of the book, and it contains several revisions, along with seven new species descriptions. The book commences with an introduction to weeds, their importance and their study, and concludes with a bibliography and indexes to scientific names and common names in Arabic and English. In between are descriptions of 169 species of dicot, monocot, and fern weeds. These are arranged alphabetically by family, genus, and species within each group and described on two pages. The text presents a taxonomic citation for the species; the derivation of the scientific name; a brief morphological description; and a briefer discussion of its habitat, ecology, geographic distribution, and—occasionally—its economic significance. Each description is accompanied by a line drawing of a part or all of the plant, occasionally with details of important characters. There are no keys; identification is by picture-matching.
—**Bruce H. Tiffney**

1583. **Manual of Grasses.** Rick Darke, ed. London, Macmillan Press and Portland, Oreg., Timber Press, 1994. 169p. illus. index. (The New Royal Horticultural Society Dictionary of Gardening). $39.95. ISBN 0-88192-300-1.

Grasses have generally not received much horticultural attention, save perhaps the bamboos and lawn grasses. However, there has been a growing appreciation for the use of these plants as structural elements or as sources of color in the garden, as seen in several recent publications (e.g., John Greenlee's *The Encyclopedia of Ornamental Grasses* [Rodale Press, 1992] or Nigel J. Taylor's *Ornamental Grasses, Bamboos, Rushes & Sedges* [distributed in the United States by Sterling Publishing, 1992]). The present volume is drawn from the Royal Horticultural Society's *Dictionary of Gardening* and describes representative species in 143 genera of grasses, sedges, rushes, and other families. Because of the great diversity of these plant groups, the book focuses on those taxa that are horticulturally useful and commonly encountered.

Following an introduction and a section on bamboos, the genera are listed in alphabetical order. A general description is provided of the morphology, distribution, and cultivation of each genus. This is followed by morphological descriptions of representative species, often accompanied by line drawings. The technical definitions are rendered accessible through an excellent, illustrated glossary. Note that there are no keys; the book is not intended as an identification manual. Rather, its value lies in its horticultural focus, aided by useful tables detailing grasses to be chosen for foliage color, for smell, for form, for growth in particular environments, and the like. The work concludes with a bibliography of literature on grasses and associated plants, and an index to common names.—**Bruce H. Tiffney**

Herbaceous Plants

1584. Levine, Carole. **A Guide to Wildflowers in Winter: Herbaceous Plants of Northeastern North America.** New Haven, Conn., Yale University Press, 1995. 329p. illus. index. $40.00; $20.00pa. ISBN 0-300-06207-9; 0-300-06560-4pa.

In the late fall and winter, herbaceous weeds and wildflowers of the northeastern United States and eastern Canada fall into their dormant state, but with this guide they can still be identified and appreciated. Each of the nearly 400 detailed entries describes key impressions (e.g., height, shape, color); fruit; leaves; stem; habitat; range; and whether the plant is perennial, annual, or biennial. Often similar species are listed with notes on distinguishing features. These account for nearly 200 additional species described within annotations.

The clearly written descriptions include both common and Latin names for the plants, making the book useful to a broad audience. All entries are illustrated, and black-and-white photographs in a separate section help users identify winter rosettes of some species. In addition, the book includes numerous charts, an illustrated key, and an illustrated glossary. It is a pity that color illustrations such as those on the cover of the book were not used in the interior, but the line drawings should serve the book's purpose.

Traditional field guides for wildflowers do not depict the winter appearance of the plants. This unique guide will help people who enjoy observing and identifying wildflowers do so during the months when they are dormant. The book will appeal to professional botanists; environmental, conservation, and wildlife management practitioners and consultants; teachers; students; researchers; and, of course, amateur naturalists.—**Barbara Ittner**

Herbs

1585. Bown, Deni. **The Encyclopedia of Herbs & Their Uses.** New York, Dorling Kindersley, 1995. 424p. illus. index. $39.95. ISBN 0-7894-0184-3.

The mission of The Herb Society of America is to promote the knowledge, use, and delight of herbs through education, research, and shared experiences in the members' communities. The Society supports its mission in this book by providing comprehensive information for more than 1,000 herbs grown worldwide, including botanical details, domestic and commercial applications, and gardening designs, all fully illustrated with color photographs and artwork.

The major part of the book is composed of two sections: the herb catalog and the herb dictionary. The catalog is arranged alphabetically by genus name with information on distribution, other relevant species, and name derivations. Color photographs show every species or variety listed. Symbols indicate what part of the herb is used; the category of use (i.e., medicinal, culinary, economic, or aromatic); the level of hardiness; and the climatic zone(s) the plants inhabit. The herb dictionary contains information on the research, historical uses, and associations with legend or folklore. Brief notes on growing and harvesting are also given. Warnings on the medicinal use of any herb or restrictions that may apply on the cultivation of an herb are included in the entries in the dictionary portion of the book.

Feature sections appear throughout the book: herb garden designs, illustrated with both photographs and artwork; culinary, medicinal, and commercial uses of herbs, both past and present; a survey of herbs in their native habitats worldwide; and a comprehensive section on growing and propagating herbs. The glossary includes both botanical and medicinal terms. The extensive index includes *see* references from common names to the genus names; page numbers for illustrations are indicated by italics. Although the recommended reading list is not lengthy, it does contain references to some of the more authoritative works on herbs and pharmacognosy. A directory and one-sentence description of herb gardens to visit in North America completes the book. The author has produced a definitive reference work for the herb gardener. Practical gardening information is combined with historical insight, current research findings, and creative garden designs to produce a beautiful coffee-table book for herbal enthusiasts frequenting public libraries and bookstores.—**Vicki J. Killion**

1586. Bown, Deni. **Growing Herbs.** New York, Dorling Kindersley, 1995. 80p. illus. maps. index. $19.95. ISBN 0-7894-0191-6.

This small guide displays and describes exactly 60 different common herbs, often showing several variations. The herbs chosen are popular ones that can be grown easily in home gardens. Parsley, sage, rosemary, and thyme are here, as well as dill, fennel, lavender, spearmint, catnip, comfrey, and 50 others. Entries are arranged alphabetically by scientific name; the index includes common names. This is a visually appealing volume, brimming with detailed color photographs of plants, leaves, flowers, and seeds.

Inside the front cover is a pull-out chart that provides culture basics such as hardiness, preferred soil types, propagation, and maintenance tips for all 60 herbs. The text is brief; this publication is not intended as a detailed treatment of either herbs or gardening. In addition to a short description for each herb, there are a few sentences on care and suggestions on how and where the plant can fit into the garden. There are some introductory comments on herb gardens and how to create one.

The author is a horticultural writer and photographer. This book will serve as a useful introduction to herbs for novice and would-be gardeners who would like some help getting started.—**William H. Wiese**

Molds

1587. Stephenson, Steven L., and Henry Stempen. **Myxomycetes: A Handbook of Slime Molds.** Portland, Oreg., Timber Press, 1994. 183p. illus. index. $34.95. ISBN 0-88192-277-3.

Alternating between a fungus-like stage and an amoeba-like stage, slime molds represent a fascinating and unique type of life form. This work does an excellent job in representing these unique organisms. A series of chapters considers several aspects that define the biology of the myxomycetes. The first five chapters discuss such areas as life cycles, morphology, distribution, ecology, and the collection, culture, and preparation of slime molds. The sixth chapter comprises the taxonomy of the group.

For each organism listed within chapter 6, the scientific name, person who first named it, morphological description (including size and coloration), substrate upon which the slime mold lives, and general comments regarding the species are considered. A brief description of the orders, along with the biological keys to orders and species, is also included. According to the author, virtually all the species one is most likely to encounter are discussed. The entire work is richly illustrated with black-and-white drawings as well as a series of colored plates. These illustrations depict the organisms in various stages of development. All of the illustrations are well crafted. An eight-page glossary, a nine-page bibliography, and a combined subject and scientific name index complete the book.

Although subtitled *A Handbook of Slime Molds*, this work could easily serve as a supplementary textbook in advanced biology classes, such as a class in mycology. It reads extremely well and is written in a textbook manner. This is an admirable treatise that shows the authors' dedication to this unique type of organism. The work may be of interest to high schools; it is highly recommended for all junior college, university, and public libraries as well.—**George H. Bell**

Trees and Shrubs

1588. Brown, George E. **The Pruning of Trees, Shrubs, and Conifers.** [rev. ed.]. Portland, Oreg., Timber Press, 1995. 354p. illus. index. $29.95. ISBN 0-88192-319-2.

This is essentially a reprint of the 1972 edition, with a new foreword added to the beginning of the text, and an update to the nomenclature added at the end. The original is a classic that provides information on growth habits and pruning advice on hundreds of woody plants, arranged in alphabetical order by genus. It has been, and continues to be, the most comprehensive work on pruning, covering more plants than any other work. It is dated, however, and includes only a few black-and-white pictures and drawings. Newer books, such as *Pruning: A Practical Guide* by Peter McHoy (Abbeville Press, 1993) and *The Complete Book of Pruning* by Duncan Coombs et al. (Sterling, 1994), offer full-color illustrations and detailed black-and-white figures. These illustrate the correct pruning techniques and show the desired form of a plant that can be achieved by good pruning. They also describe new tools and techniques. Although these newer books do not cover as many plants as Brown's book does, they do cover the more common trees, shrubs, and vines, and in more depth.

For those who already own a copy of Brown's 1972 book, this new edition will not offer much except an updated nomenclature. Some of the recent books, mentioned above, may be useful to purchase for their updated information, and especially for their illustrations of correct pruning, and how to achieve the desired form for each plant. For those without a copy, it is a classic reference work written by Brown, now deceased, then assistant curator of the Royal Botanic Gardens, Kew, and should be part of any gardening collection, for all public, academic, or agricultural libraries.—**Diane B. Rhodes**

1589. Henderson, Andrew, Gloria Galaeno, and Rodrigo Bernal. **Field Guide to the Palms of the Americas.** Princeton, N.J., Princeton University Press, 1995. 352p. illus. maps. index. $75.00. ISBN 0-691-08537-4.

Palms are among the most important, and most distinctive, components of many tropical landscapes. They also are of great economic and cultural significance. For instance, palms play a central role in the material, artistic, and mythological cultures of many American Indian tribes. Yet, until now, there has been no comprehensive, easy-to-use field guide to the palms of the Americas. Guides exist for a few small areas, and numerous highly technical monographs on particular genera have been published. The authors of this field guide, however, have performed a great service in gathering in one book an authoritative key to the taxonomy and distribution of the 67 genera and 550 species of native American palms.

A simple key, with visual cues, leads the reader into the main text of the book, in which palms are arranged by genera. Further keys then help the user identify the plant to species. Short (two- to three-paragraph) entries then discuss field characteristics, range, and habitat. Many species are pictured in beautiful color plates, and there is a distribution map for all 550 species.

This field guide is a monumental scientific accomplishment. At the same time, it is so clearly and attractively presented that it will be of great use to nonbotanists, including travelers, growers, or anyone else interested in this fascinating group of plants.—**Carol L. Noll**

1590. Innes, Clive. **Alpines: The Illustrated Dictionary.** Portland, Oreg., Timber Press, 1995. 190p. illus. index. $39.95. ISBN 0-88192-290-0.

Photographs of nearly 1,000 alpine plants are accompanied by commentary on each in this informative dictionary. The introduction gives a brief overview of alpines in a narrative that describes Innes's searches and discoveries of different plants through his travels worldwide. General advice concerning soil types, watering, feeding, and propagation of these plants is provided also, with more specific information for individual plants reserved for the individual species entries. The plant entries are listed alphabetically by their currently accepted name, with commonly known synonyms given as well. Information on habitat, distribution, growing habitat, flowering season, and other areas of interest is provided for each plant. A glossary, an index (of all plant names given, including synonyms and alternatives) and a bibliography complete the work.

The photographs that accompany each entry are wonderfully detailed, and the descriptions, while brief, supply the pertinent information anyone interested in cultivating this family of plants will need. This dictionary is highly recommended.—**Jo Anne H. Ricca**

1591. Kricher, John. **Peterson First Guide to Forests.** New York, Houghton Mifflin, 1994. 128p. illus. index. $4.95pa. ISBN 0-395-71760-4.

Part of the Peterson First Guide series (see ARBA 95, entries 1560 and 1577, and ARBA 94, entries 1674 and 1730, for reviews of other books in the series), this slim, "simplified" guide to the ecology of North American forests contains copious information for the beginning naturalist. The introduction has a brief five-page section on identifying plants and animals. Also included are descriptions of the 10 major forest types in North America. The main part of the book is composed of 2-page descriptions of 48 North American forest types. One page illustrates the most common trees, birds, mammals, reptiles, amphibians, and plants. The other page describes these species. These descriptions, although necessarily brief, are very informative. The illustrations are well drawn but one wishes that the sizes of the species pictured were given. It would also have been useful to key the 48 forest type descriptions found in the main text with these 10 major forest types. Another useful feature would have been inclusion of the two-page map of North America numbering the forest types discussed.

Roger Tory Peterson writes in his editor's note that these First Guides use the "Peterson System," which includes arrows pointing to key field marks, making identification of a particular species easier. This volume does not have these arrows. The book is well produced and written. Those wanting to begin their studies of North American forests and the species that inhabit them will welcome this small, reasonably priced book. The work is recommended for public and school libraries.—**James E. Bird**

1592. Tripp, Kim E., and J. C. Raulston. **The Year in Trees: Superb Woody Plants for Four-Season Gardens.** Portland, Oreg., Timber Press, 1995. 204p. illus. index. $44.95. ISBN 0-88192-320-6.

It has been estimated that only 40 shrubs and trees make up more than 90 percent of the plantings in any given region of the United States. The authors would like to change this, by introducing gardeners and horticulturists to little-known but outstanding plants from all over the world. All the shrubs and trees described have been extensively tested in the North Carolina State University Arboretum. Although some may be hard to find, the authors suggest that they are all hardy, trouble-free, and well worth searching for.

The book consists of extensive "portraits" of 150 plants, arranged by the season in which they are most showy (either for their blooms; fruits; or in the case of many winter plants, their colored bark). For each plant there are colored plates, descriptions, tips on transplanting, and discussions of the best uses in different types of landscapes. Because these plants have all been tested in North Carolina, they are most hardy in USDA zone 7, but should do well anywhere where summers are hot and wet. Many are adaptable to other climates, and the authors could increase the usefulness of this book by providing charts suggesting particular plants for particular locales. Future editions also should include a list of possible sources for the rarer plants.—**Carol L. Noll**

Vascular Plants

1593. Brako, Lois, Amy Y. Rossman, and David F. Farr. **Scientific and Common Names of 7,000 Vascular Plants in the United States.** St. Paul, Minn., APS Press, 1995. 295p. (Contributions from the U.S. National Fungus Collections, no.7). $29.00pa. ISBN 0-89054-171-X.

The authors, from the Missouri Botanical Garden (Brako) and the Systematic Botany and Mycology Laboratory, Beltsville Agricultural Research Center (Rossman and Farr), have produced a very useful reference volume. The book is divided into four sections, each in alphabetical order: scientific names by genus; common names with accompanying scientific name (the largest section of the book); important synonyms of a given scientific name; and genera arranged by plant family. In their introduction, the authors point out that common names of plants vary widely, while scientific names are stable. The volume makes it easy to determine the particular species of plant from its common name(s). As an example, the eastern water-leaf, Indian-salad, John's-cabbage, Shawnee-salad, and Virginia water-leaf all refer to *Hydrophyllum virginianum*.

As with any good publication of this kind, the authors list sources used both for identifying vascular plants for inclusion and for determining their scientific names. Although there are many books that give scientific and common names of plants, this is the first one, to this reviewer's knowledge, that is devoted entirely to this effort. The volume is highly recommended for all college and university libraries with a collection interest in botany. Public libraries will also find it useful to own.—**James E. Bird**

1594. Czerepanov, S. K. **Vascular Plants of Russia and Adjacent States (The Former USSR).** New York, Cambridge University Press, 1995. 516p. index. $100.00. ISBN 0-521-45006-3.

This compilation of the vascular plants of Russia and its surrounding areas is a revision and enlargement of the author's 1981 work, *Vascular Plants of the USSR (Plantae Vasculares URSS)*. More than 21,000 species are listed in the new version, and more than 500 species of cultivated plants. This revision reflects the many changes in nomenclature and taxonomy that have occurred since publication of the original work. There are no plant descriptions as the publication is not intended to serve as an encyclopedia or dictionary.

Regions are identified for each species as one or more of the following: Eastern Europe, Caucasus, Western Siberia, Eastern Siberia, the Far East, and Middle Asia. Listing is alphabetical by family, then by genera within family, and finally by species within genus. Subspecies and varieties are reported where relevant. There are numerous references to alternate plant names, with the commonly accepted name clearly indicated. A combined family and genus index appears at the end of the volume. This comprehensive, definitive work will be of interest primarily to plant scientists and libraries with large botany collections.
—**William H. Wiese**

NATURAL HISTORY

1595. Abbott, R. Tucker, and Percy A. Morris. **A Field Guide to Shells: Atlantic and Gulf Coasts and the West Indies.** 4th ed. New York, Houghton Mifflin, 1995. 350p. illus. index. (The Peterson Field Guide Series, no.3). $26.95; $16.95pa. ISBN 0-395-69780-8; 0-395-69779-4pa.

The 4th edition of a popular field guide to shells of the Atlantic and Gulf coasts and the West Indies, this book is aimed at the average shore collector. The introduction discusses how pollution and habitat destruction have changed the practices of collectors in order to protect species. It continues with tips on how and where to collect, preparation for display, arrangement, and labeling of shells. An explanation of nomenclature rules follows, and commonalities of mollusks are discussed. The species, 780 in number, are described in clear text including information on common and scientific name, geographic range, habitat, detailed description, name changes, and life cycle. Color plates visually depict the shells and clarify the detailed text descriptions. The emphasis of earlier editions has shifted from dead shells to the living animals of the mollusks. Plates representing living animals show the novice how the animals appear in their habitat.

Well organized and logically arranged, the text and plates are conveniently cross-referenced for ease of use. A list of shell clubs, a glossary of conchological terms, a bibliography, a comprehensive index of common and scientific names, and a clearly labeled diagram of shell parts add to this edition's value. An inch and centimeter ruler on the back cover is useful to the collector in the field. The guide is a useful resource for collectors trying to identify shells and is suitable for students grades five and up.—**Sandra L. Doggett**

1596. Braun, Elisabeth. **Portraits in Conservation: Eastern and Southern Africa.** Golden, Colo., North American Press/Fulcrum Publishing, 1995. 268p. illus. maps. index. $28.00. ISBN 1-55591-914-6.

Braun's book, published in cooperation with the International Wilderness Leadership Foundation, looks at two dozen people who are working in Africa to save its wildlife and provide that wildlife with a future. It follows their careers and shows the day-to-day struggles in which they are involved. In doing so, it provides a broad array of the kinds of people involved and their varying philosophies of what needs to be done and how best to accomplish it. Included are Africans and non-Africans, people from academia, and people working for governments, nongovernmental organizations, commercial and noncommercial interests, and independently as well. Some of the best-known names, such as Dian Fossey and Jane Goodall, were excluded on the basis that enough information about them is already known.

Not only are animals considered here, especially the "big five"—lions, leopards, elephants, rhinos, and buffalo—but also the peoples of Africa and their relationship to the environment. Obviously, the people of Africa, their attitudes and needs, form an integral part of any hope we have in preserving African wildlife; village-based conservation efforts, often involving entire communities, are often included in these studies. By reading this book, the reader comes away with a respect for and knowledge of the multitude of approaches each of these conservationists is taking in order to find the right balance between the animals, people, and environment of Southern and Eastern Africa. A general introduction to the problems covered in these portraits as well as useful bibliographical references are also furnished. This work will prove of interest to schools, public libraries, and collections dealing with environmental issues.—**Paul H. Thomas**

1597. **The Grolier Student Encyclopedia of Endangered Species.** Danbury, Conn., Grolier, 1995. 10v. illus. maps. index. $279.00/set. ISBN 0-7172-7385-7.

There are some people who still believe that animals and plants should be classified and efforts made for their survival only if they are "useful" to humans. Gradually, this myopic view of the world and the misunderstanding those holding this view have of the complex interrelationships of species, not to mention still-unknown and potential values for human life, is eroding. In part, this occurs as more young people become aware of the great diversity of life and the labyrinthine interactions among living organisms.

This encyclopedia may be one of the tools to help students learn what animal species are "endangered" and why. The 10 volumes seem clearly written for an upper elementary school level; the typeface is large, the written components brief, and the hundreds of photographs superb. Animals, almost exclusively mammals, are listed alphabetically, but members of the same family are grouped together. There are few entries for birds, reptiles, and amphibians.

Each entry begins with a relief map of the area of the world where the animal lives and on which its general range appears in red. The level of the species' endangerment is shown in one of six categories. For each animal, 5 to 10 major headings are included: description, size, habitat, diet, speed, young, interesting facts, estimated remaining population, reasons for endangerment, and conservation measures. A few facts are briefly given under the headings, and the entire section on each species rarely exceeds a page in length.

Often the facts provided are, it seems, simply unusual features of the species rather than part of an effort toward a coherent introduction to the animal's biology. Some of the "facts" are wrong (e.g., the desert tortoise does not have small teeth). The color photographs usually show individual animals, sometimes in groups and frequently in a natural setting. Pictures exceed the text in space. The first volume provides something of an overview of the endangerment problem, a page on the ICUN Red List, several pages describing different habitats, the impact of humans on these habitats, and efforts made toward conservation. This information is essential to understanding how the elimination of individual species is important in the broader conservation picture.

These volumes may be useful in school libraries. A better, more thorough examination of endangered species with much better animal and plant coverage is *Endangered Wildlife of the World* (see ARBA 94, entry 1676). The latter is also a 10-volume work, but designed for students at the high school level as well as the general public.—**David Bardack**

1598. **Habitats.** Tony Hare, ed. New York, Macmillan/Simon & Schuster, 1994. 143p. illus. maps. index. $25.00. ISBN 0-02-548155-X.

This work focuses on the basic features of 14 major ecosystems or habitats, such as oceans, deserts, and rain forests. After a brief overview of basic biology related to ecosystems, each habitat receives a consistent presentation on its major characteristics, dynamics that lead to changes in the habitats, and photographs and illustrations of major habitat residents. The core of the book, and its most appealing feature, is the set of four-page foldouts, one for each of the habitats. These are finely crafted composite panoramas of the habitats, showing a wide variety of flora and fauna in the same picture, looking as if one could view all these life-forms in the same glance. Each habitat is represented by one particular region; for example, the "Rivers and Lakes" section contains a photographic montage of the Amazon River basin. Substantial captions identify and explain the contents of the panoramas.

The text seems most suitable for secondary school age or higher, although the illustrations will appeal to younger audiences as well. The treatment of habitats is limited by the rather small amount of text, but the chapters give a good overview of general characteristics, and especially the effects of human intervention on natural systems. The montages themselves are beautifully done and fun to browse. The foldout format of these montages makes the volume susceptible to damage; bending or tearing of the foldouts is likely if use is frequent. However, this volume is a reasonable purchase, filling a niche between scholarly sources such as *Grzimek's Animal Life Encyclopedia* (see ARBA 76, entries 1403-1407; ARBA 75, entry 1523; and ARBA 73, entry 1459) or the *Encyclopedia of Environmental Biology* (see entry 1856) and juvenile titles such as *The Animal Atlas* by Barbara Taylor (Knopf, 1992).—**Christopher W. Nolan**

1599. **International Wildlife Trade: A CITES Sourcebook.** Ginette Hemley, ed. Washington, D.C., World Wildlife Fund and Island Press, 1994. 166p. illus. index. $16.95pa. ISBN 1-55963-348-4.

Playing the piano used to be called tickling the ivories. These days, however, the keys are plastic, and the elephants are breathing a big sigh of relief. Elephants, like many other animals, are protected under the 1973 Convention on International Trade in Endangered Species (CITES). The World Wildlife Fund (WWF) has compiled a volume that not only gives the full text of the original treaty but also the appendixes, all participants as of March 1994, and all reservations by parties as of October 1993. There is an explanation on how CITES works, its strengths and weaknesses, and status information about a number of highly threatened and heavily exploited species.

The bibliography is handy for those seeking more information on specific species. The index, however, could use some work. It does not include many of the species listed, so to find a particular species, one needs to know what family it is in. Also, animals listed are by complete common name (e.g., black rhinoceros falls under black, not rhinoceros). Users can work around these flaws, however, and find plenty of useful information within the work.—**Angela Marie Thor**

1600. Leitch, Jay A., and Herbert R. Ludwig Jr., comps. **Wetland Economics, 1989-1993: A Selected, Annotated Bibliography.** Westport, Conn., Greenwood Press, 1995. 133p. index. (Bibliographies and Indexes in Economics and Economic History, no.17). $65.00. ISBN 0-313-29286-8.

The purpose of this bibliography is to bring together references to noteworthy works on the economic aspects of wetlands. The emphasis is on wetland economic assessment and valuation as it relates to policy issues. This volume updates the 1989 publication *Wetland Economics and Assessment* (see ARBA 90, entry 1514). Leitch, one of the compilers of these two books, is a wetlands consultant and professor of agricultural economics at North Dakota State University. Although this second book's title indicates coverage through 1993, references to some early 1994 publications are also included.

Entries are grouped into four categories: methodological; empirical (evaluation of dollar values of wetlands); wetland restoration/creation economics; and wetland definition and delineation. Each of these four sections is preceded by a brief overview of issues and trends. Publications cited include journal articles, books, conference proceedings, reports, and theses. There are 462 entries, with an emphasis on

United States and Canadian literature. The compilers' annotations vary in length from a sentence to a long paragraph. Separate author, geographical, and subject indexes are provided. It is refreshing to see in this type of compilation a clear explanation of the search procedures employed, including names of databases searched and keywords used, as well as other approaches taken to identify the important literature. This bibliography will be of interest to scholars and others involved in wetland policy issues.
—**William H. Wiese**

1601. Molloy, Les. **Wild New Zealand.** Cambridge, Mass., MIT Press, 1994. 208p. illus. maps. index. $39.95. ISBN 0-262-13304-0.

This book is as impressive for its text as for its photographs, and is an admirable addition to a fine series of studies of wildlife in India, Indonesia, and Malaysia. A wilderness in its New Zealand sense, as pointed out in the work, conveys the idea of wild, undeveloped land without traces of human construction.

The extensive introduction provides an overview of the country's ancient origins some 80 million years ago when it became separated from Gondwanaland, its geological structure now, and its extraordinary natural diversity. The diversity one would normally find only in a continent is compressed essentially into two rather small islands. The book is thorough, covering the whole extent of New Zealand from the subtropical Kermadec Islands to the subantarctic Auckland Islands and the Chatham Islands 500 miles east of Christchurch. These offshore islands add little to the total landmass, but add enormously to the geological and biological diversity of the country.

Some 1,000 years of pre-European occupation by the Maori had already wrought considerable damage to the New Zealand landscape, but the last 150 years of European settlement have greatly accelerated the devastation. The book discusses present attempts to conserve the natural landscapes and wildlife of New Zealand, by protecting and enhancing its biological diversity and by controlling weeds and pests.—**John B. Beston**

1602. Yenne, Bill. **100 Natural Wonders of the World.** San Francisco, Calif., Bluewood, 1995. 112p. illus. maps. index. $7.95pa. ISBN 0-912517-15-8.

Designed for the student or casual browser, this little book covers 100 interesting places or objects worldwide. The selection seems well made, including both well-known spectacles such as the Grand Canyon and lesser-known places such as the extremely wet region of Meghalaya in India. Other wonders are the aurora borealis, Mt. Chimborazo in Ecuador, the Bay of Fundy off the eastern coast of Canada, and Pulau Batu Hairan in Malaysia. The information provided for each attraction is enough to whet the appetite, but little detail is supplied, nor is there a bibliography.

The information is generally correct, although there are occasional inaccuracies (the tenrec of Madagascar is described as having spines like a raccoon, for instance). While a world map is shown for each place, they are very small and indicate little more than in what quarter of a continent the attraction is found. Most of the illustrations are from the publisher's collection of images, which unfortunately means that many of them are either old (i.e., noncopyright) or unimpressive. All in all, this book is a nice resource for very general information about natural wonders or a nice gift for an inquisitive youngster, but without a bibliography, it is not a necessary reference purchase. School and public libraries may find it useful, however.—**Diane Schmidt**

ZOOLOGY
General Works

1603. **Amazing Animals of the World.** Danbury, Conn., Grolier, 1995. 24v. illus. maps. index. $279.00/set. ISBN 0-7172-7396-2.

An excellent elementary school animal reference set, each volume in the set runs 48 pages and includes a glossary and a "how to use" explanation. Animals are arranged alphabetically with a set index in volume 24. Each entry is one page long with the page divided into three parts. The beginning section of the entry gives the English and Latin (scientific) name; indicates whether the animal is in danger of extinction; and identifies the animal's scientific classification.

The next section provides a 3-by-4-inch illustration of the animal on the right side of the page. The left side lists class, order, family, length, weight, diet, number of young, and home, and it shows the animal's range on a $1\frac{1}{8}$-by-$1\frac{1}{8}$-inch map. The third section covers half a page. In three paragraphs it discusses basic information about the animal. The format, typeface, and page layout are on target except that the maps are a general outline of part of a continent or country, so that younger readers may need help in deciphering them.

Researchers in grades 2-4 will appreciate this set. Older students will find it too simple for their research needs but may enjoy browsing. Special education and English as a Second Language classes for grades 2-12 may also find the set useful.—**Esther R. Sinofsky**

1604. Bailey, Jill. **Animal Life: Form and Function in the Animal Kingdom.** New York, Oxford University Press, 1994. 160p. illus. index. (The New Encyclopedia of Science). $35.00. ISBN 0-19-521084-0.

The great diversity of the world's animal life includes some 10 million species. This richness can be overwhelming unless one emphasizes the major biological principles that organize life, as done in this volume, one of a continuing series of science encyclopedias from Oxford University Press. There are six major reviews, each encyclopedic in nature—biodiversity, basic physiology, feeding, movement, reproduction, and communication. These synthetic topics show how animals have solved the fundamental needs of life through remarkable adaptations in all forms. For example, depending on the kind of animal, communication can be visual, auditory, based on odor, electrical, or pheromonal.

All topics are well illustrated with color photographs, drawings, and diagrams. For the general reader, technical terms are defined in a lengthy keyword glossary. Other helpful features include a timeline of zoological discoveries, and detailed tables for such essentials as digestive enzymes and mammalian hormones. This book is aimed at a wide audience, from the general science browser to the inquisitive student.
—**Charles Leck**

1605. **Fish & Fisheries Worldwide: 1971-August 1995.** [CD-ROM]. Baltimore, Md., National Information Services Corporation, 1995. Minimum system requirements: IBM or compatible 386. CD-ROM drive. 180KB RAM (512KB without extended memory). Color or monochrome monitor. $795.00/yr. ISSN 1069-9309.

1606. **Species Information Library.** [CD-ROM]. Baltimore, Md., National Information Services Corporation, 1995. Minimum system requirements: IBM or compatible. CD-ROM drive. 512K RAM. Monochrome or color monitor. $495.00. ISBN 0-924291-06-0.

1607. **Wildlife Worldwide: 1935-September 1995.** [CD-ROM]. Baltimore, Md., National Information Services Corporation, 1995. Minimum system requirements: IBM or compatible 386. CD-ROM drive. 180KB RAM (512KB without extended memory). Color or monochrome monitor. $795.00/yr. ISSN 1070-5007.

This is a review of three CD-ROM products from the National Information Services Corporation (NISC). This company produces more than 50 science databases, as well as many in psychology, sociology, and other topics, using the same ROMWright software.

Fish & Fisheries Worldwide is a comprehensive database that includes citations and some abstracts on the world's literature on fish, fisheries, and such similar topics as aquaculture. The database is cumulated annually and updated quarterly. It is a composite of six databases: Fisheries Review (1971-present), Fish Database (1960-present), FISHLIT (1985-present), Aquaculture (1970-1984), Fish Health News (1978-1985), and Castell's Nutrition References (1970-present). Although more than half the database is derived from the Fisheries Review database, the other databases add significantly to the body of information. NISC has gotten around the problem of duplicate records by combining them into a "composite record." However, because of differences in author entries from the separate databases, duplicates are still found in this database. The *Fish & Fisheries* disc is well indexed, including good keyword indexing plus many fields to search. It is possible to search by author, author address, title, keyword, taxonomy, publishing year, source, language, database, and record ID. Geographical identifiers allow searches on individual stream names or larger regions.

Wildlife Worldwide covers the literature on mammals, birds, amphibians, and reptiles, primarily from North America, but with some literature on species found worldwide. It is cumulated annually and updated quarterly. It also is composite database made up of records from six separate databases: Wildlife Review, WIS (HERMAN), BIODOC, Waterfowl and Wetlands Database, Wildlife Database, and a small database of Book Reviews. The disc is made up primarily of records from Wildlife Review. The second largest database is from the Wildlife Information Service (HERMAN database) but are mostly duplicates of those from Wildlife Review. The HERMAN database does, however, index articles back to 1935, which goes back further than other CD-ROM products. The duplicate records have been merged into "composite records" similar to those mentioned above. Indexing is adequate and allows for a wide variety of search approaches. The ROMWright software also allows searching of similar genus and species names, such as *Rattus rattus*, which cannot currently be done in SilverPlatter databases.

The final disc is the *Species Information Library*, which provides full-text information on more than 7,000 North American animals, their taxonomy, habitat, food habits, life history, environment, and management. This database is from the Fish and Wildlife Information Exchange (FWIE) located at Virginia Polytechnic Institute and State University. It is also a composite database made up of 10 database: Endangered Species Information System; Marine & Coastal Species Information System; and databases from 8 state agencies (Colorado, Illinois, Missouri, New Mexico, Oregon, Pennsylvania, Utah, and Virginia).

Although it does not cover all states, the database does include the most common fauna found in the United States and those on the endangered species lists. Most species descriptions cover several screens and end in extensive lists of references for further reading. There may be one or several records for the same species (there are more than five records for the black rat), but this provides a broad perspective from its habitats in the different states or regions. Indexing is generally sufficient; however, there is one major flaw. The search category "Species," where one would expect to be able to search by a species name such as *rattus*, turns out to be a common name index. It appears that those who set up the database may not have known the difference between a species name and a common name. The *Species Information Library* disc is a convenient, full-text way to find information quickly on a large number of North American animals in one source. These are not the definitive sources for literature on a particular animal, however. For example, for mammals *Mammalian Species* is the authoritative source, and these are not included in this disc, but they are often referred to in the references section.

The ROMWright software allows for a variety of searching approaches to each database. It has three modes for searching (novice, advanced, and expert), and it is easy to switch between modes or use only one search mode. This often presents problems, however, when the patron is confused about all the different search modes and prefers one interface. Another problem is that for some databases, each update to the database must be reinstalled. This is supposed to allow for installing enhancements to the software, but having to install each update can be annoying. Newer updates on some databases will, however, allow for "auto-install." One final problem is that the software has a timed "bomb" that garbles the data on the disc if the new update is not installed on time. This is done to prevent anyone from using the old discs, but is a hazard when updates do not arrive in time or are not installed in time.

These problems aside, the NISC offers some of the most affordable CD-ROM databases available today. In addition, *Wildlife Worldwide* and *Fish & Fisheries Worldwide* include records not found in some of the major databases, such as Biological Abstracts, and are especially strong in North American animal literature. They include some obscure "grey literature" and make a good addition to large academic libraries' CD-ROM collections. They also cover more types of literature in one database; including not only journals, but also books, book chapters, reports, government documents, conference proceedings, theses, and unpublished materials. *Species Information Library* is what many students are looking for: full-text information in one database. It is a reasonable one-price database and may be of benefit in a large academic library. These discs are available for a free 30-day trial period, so libraries can judge their worth for their own collections.—**Diane B. Rhodes**

1608. **The Kingfisher First Encyclopedia of Animals.** By David Burnie and Linda Gamlin. New York, Larousse Kingfisher Chambers, 1994. 137p. illus. index. $16.95. ISBN 1-85697-994-6.

Catering to kids, this book provides a colorful introduction to a wide variety of animals found throughout the world. The entries are approximately 60 words, arranged alphabetically, and written in an easy-to-read style and typeface. Cross-references are made within the text to related topics. Any child (and many adults) will be intrigued by the full-color illustrations that accompany most subjects. A full page is devoted to subjects that are broader in scope, such as "Camouflage" and "Deciduous Forests."

The binding is sturdy and lies flat when opened, an important consideration if children are to refer to the book while writing. Also, the book is easy to carry and not too heavy for small hands. An index is found at the end of the encyclopedia, with references to the illustrations in italics. All measurements are given in imperial and metric units.

What the book lacks is an introduction or preface stating its purpose. For example, the age range of the intended audience is an invaluable piece of information for librarians, parents, and teachers of young children, and it is not given. All in all, this lively volume is a good starting point for kids, getting them interested in the natural world. [R: SLJ, Feb 95, p. 128]—**Katherine Margaret Thomas**

1609. **A World Alive: A Wildlife Adventure for Kids.** [CD-ROM]. New York, Voyager, 1994. Minimum system requirements (Windows version): IBM or compatible 486SX-25. MPC2-compatible CD-ROM drive. MS-DOS 5.0. Microsoft Windows 3.1. 4MB RAM. 256-color display (accelerator recommended). MPC2-compatible sound card with speakers or headphones. Minimum system requirements (Macintosh version): any color Macintosh. 16MHz 68030. System 7. Double-speed CD-ROM drive. 3,000K of available RAM. $49.95. ISBN 1-559405988.

This multimedia CD-ROM product provides an entertaining way for children to learn about wild animals and their habitats. It features a 30-minute video, narrated by James Earl Jones, of wild animals in their native habitats. It also includes fact sheets on about 100 animals and a game called "What Is That?" that helps to test the child's knowledge in a fun and amusing way about the animals seen on the CD-ROM. This new dimension in learning, which includes sight and sound along with the written word and picture, is sure to keep a child's attention longer and perhaps make a more lasting memory of the facts learned. Navigating through the different screens of information is usually easy enough, although a child may have some trouble with it at first. The information on each animal is indexed by habitat, classification, and geography.

Material on each animal is basic, including common and scientific names, the diet, the life span, the gestation period, and an indication of its status (e.g., endangered). In addition, there is a paragraph of general information and a film clip of the animal (taken from the 30-minute video). The game "What Is That?" poses a question that can be answered by selecting the correct picture, one out of the four offered. If the wrong picture is selected, a big red "X" is placed on the picture. However, if the correct picture is chosen, it becomes a video that runs for a few seconds. One drawback to this game is the often dim or hard to distinguish images given to choose from.

This is a quality CD-ROM product as an introduction to the animal world. For those who want a more complete work, one that covers more animals and gives more detail, *The San Diego Zoo Presents . . . The Animals!* (Software Toolworks, 1993) may be a good choice. The disc under review is recommended for elementary, junior high, and home libraries.—**Diane B. Rhodes**

Bats

1610. **Walker's Bats of the World.** By Ronald M. Nowak. Baltimore, Md., Johns Hopkins University Press, 1994. 287p. illus. index. $19.95pa. ISBN 0-8018-4986-1.

The indication in this book's Library of Congress Cataloging-in-Publication data that portions have been adapted from the 5th edition of *Walker's Mammals of the World* (see ARBA 93, entry 1572) is somewhat of an understatement. The entire chiroptera (bats) section, pictures included, has been lifted out of that work intact, with no changes. Those libraries owning *Walker's Mammals of the World* may therefore want to pass on this spin-off unless there is sufficient interest in bats among their users to warrant purchase of a copy for reference or a circulating copy. On the other hand, here is an excellent opportunity for libraries or individuals needing this focus to obtain an authoritative, thorough, up-to-date reference on bats at a very reasonable price.

The majority of this volume consists of the genus entries. A brief discussion of each family precedes the descriptions of genera within that family. Emphasis is on physical description, geographic distribution, habitat, and feeding and other behavior of bat genera and species. The many black-and-white photographs are of high quality overall and will be of great help in identifying species. References to the professional literature are provided for those needing more detailed information on particular species.

The material new to this book consists primarily of an introductory review article on bats that includes 15 pages of cited references, many from the 1990s. There is also a table indicating world geographic distribution of bat genera. An index provides both common and scientific name access to the text.

—**William H. Wiese**

Birds

1611. Baerg, Harry J. **Common American Birds.** Happy Camp, Calif., Naturegraph, 1994. 63p. illus. index. $8.95pa. ISBN 0-87961-235-5.

Longtime illustrator and natural history writer Baerg has prepared a beginner's guide to the most familiar birds of North America. In 64 pages of compact illustration and text, this book would be most appreciated by youngsters or other novices interested in recognizing more than 300 common species. The full-color paintings generally represent each species with a male in breeding plumage, portrayed in an appropriate habitat. (Omitted plumage variations are thus substantial: females, juveniles, nonbreeding males, color phases, and so forth.) The text comments briefly on important features of identification, including calls and songs. Additional descriptions have behavioral or ecological notes, especially on nesting and diet. This inexpensive introduction will be helpful to beginning bird-watchers as they start to know and appreciate their "feathered friends."—**Charles Leck**

1612. **CITES Identification Guide—Birds. Guide d'Identification CITES—Oiseaux. Guía de Identificación de CITES—Aves.** Ottawa, Canadian Wildlife Service, 1994. 1v. (various paging). illus. index. free to libraries dealing with CITES-related agencies (looseleaf). ISBN 0-662-61183-7.

The identification of birds in international trade, specifically those that are endangered and protected species, is the focus of this manual. A conservation treaty signed by 120 countries, the Convention on International Trade in Endangered Species (CITES), lists controlled plants and animals and is updated every 2 years. This guide for commercially traded birds gives enforcement officers identification keys that are easily applied because of their pictorial nature and simplification. Thus, use of the manual does not require extensive training and will meet the professional needs of those who inspect and issue custom permits, as well as other conservation officers. Throughout, species are clearly distinguished according to their CITES regulation (protection) status. Product use in economic trade is indicated as feathers, eggs (for breeding or consumption), other food products, and the like. Among the groups of most concern are parrots, waterfowl, and birds of prey.—**Charles Leck**

1613. Curson, Jon, David Quinn, and David Beadle. **Warblers of the Americas: An Identification Guide.** New York, Houghton Mifflin, 1994. 252p. illus. index. $40.00. ISBN 0-395-70998-9.

This, the first comprehensive guide to warblers of all the Western Hemisphere, is part of the well-received Helm series on bird groups, which already includes titles on gulls, swallows, waterfowl, shorebirds, and others. The 36 color plates by Quinn and Beadle are excellent, accurately depicting all morphs (male, female, breeding versus nonbreeding plumage, immatures, recognizable races) for each species. Some of the Latin American birds are depicted here for the first time in a popular publication in a thorough fashion. The painting captions themselves are quite thorough and descriptive, and are accompanied by range maps. The small maps show both the breeding and winter ranges. These suffer from the omission of political boundaries, making it difficult to determine the countries the birds occur in, let alone states or provinces, although the range is also described in the text.

Most of the book consists of detailed species accounts that thoroughly describe the birds' appearance, the biggest sections being devoted to identification and description, but with other sections on geographical variation, voice, habitat and habits, breeding, status and distribution, movements, molting, skulls, measurements, and references. There are also several general and useful sentences at the start of each account, which provide an overview of each bird. Interspersed throughout the text are drawings of the tail patterns for species in which this characteristic is useful in identification, especially for banding or other situations when the bird is in hand. All of the text is thorough, well researched, and authoritative. Introductory sections concern taxonomy, evolution, dimorphism and breeding behavior, hybrids, and conservation. Most of the previous works on American warblers are dated and concern only North American species. This monograph on the attractive warblers—often called the butterflies of the bird world, and a most popular group with birders—is a fine contribution and is highly recommended.—**Henry T. Armistead**

1614. Ehrlich, Paul R., and others. **The Birdwatcher's Handbook: A Guide to the Natural History of the Birds of Britain and Europe.** New York, Oxford University Press, 1994. 660p. illus. index. $22.00. ISBN 0-19-858407-5.

This handbook brings together detailed information on 516 breeding bird species known to nest regularly throughout Britain, Europe, North Africa, the Middle East, and Iceland. Like its North American counterpart entitled *The Birders Handbook: A Field Guide to the Natural History of North American Birds* by Paul R. Ehrlich, David S. Dobkin, and Darryl Wheye (Simon & Schuster, 1988), *The Birdwatcher's Handbook* is intended as a companion text to the traditional field identification guides. The focus is on species conservation and ecology, breeding, behavior, and feeding biology. The text is organized around the species accounts and essays. The accounts are restricted to a half page, and contain a summary line of six columns of symbols that aid the reader in determining nest location, nest type, eggs, chick development, diet, and foraging techniques. The textual portion of the account provides a concise description and includes references to companion field guides, relevant essays within the text, and literature citations.

The 170 essays located on the right-hand pages are written on a variety of topics such as nest sanitation, origin of flight, and polyandry. Where applicable, they face a page with a relevant species account.

The end papers are composed of a number of indexes to subject and species names, including one to bird names in German, French, Dutch, Spanish, and Swedish. Especially useful is the bibliography of more than 700 references to scientific papers. The appendix is a compilation of topical articles that discuss legal protection for birds. Unfortunately, becoming familiar with the quick-reference symbols, abbreviations, and definitions takes some practice. Nonetheless, this handbook is a practical size for field or lab, and is recommended for specialized collections.—**Katherine Margaret Thomas**

1615. Howell, Steve N. G., and Sophie Webb. **A Guide to the Birds of Mexico and Northern Central America.** New York, Oxford University Press, 1995. 851p. illus. maps. index. $39.95pa. ISBN 0-19-854012-4.

Covering all of Mexico, Belize, Guatemala, and El Salvador, most of Honduras, northernmost Nicaragua, and isolated Clipperton Island in the Pacific, this handbook treats approximately 1,070 bird species. Following a general introduction to the region's avifauna, the taxonomically arranged species accounts normally include English, Spanish, and scientific names; detailed descriptions emphasizing but not limited to field marks; voice; habitat and habits; population status and geographical distribution; remarks on similar species; and a regional range map. Appendixes briefly treat extinct species, species of doubtful occurrence in the region, and 50 additional species from eastern Honduras. The 71 color plates mostly depict those species that do not also regularly occur in the United States, unless showing them is helpful in identifying similar Mexican/Central American birds; the plates are sometimes a bit crowded but are satisfactory as identification aids. There are also a few line drawings in the text. The work concludes with a 26-page bibliography and indexes of English and scientific (but not Spanish) names.

Compared to the other two currently available regional guides, Ernest Edwards's *A Field Guide to the Birds of Mexico* (see ARBA 90, entry 1534) and Roger Tory Peterson and Edward Chalif's *A Field Guide to Mexican Birds* (see ARBA 90, entry 1535), this work is somewhat broader in geographical coverage (more of Central America, plus Clipperton), has far lengthier and more detailed species descriptions (the other titles are largely limited to field identification), includes detailed range maps, is more fully documented, and is more rigorously scientific in treatment (although quite accessible to experienced amateurs). It is also much larger and (even in paperback) heavier, which may be a drawback in the field. The guide is the most comprehensive study of the region's avifauna currently available, and is an important contribution to ornithology.—**Paul B. Cors**

1616. Reilly, Pauline. **Penguins of the World.** New York, Oxford University Press, 1994. 164p. illus. maps. $16.95pa. ISBN 0-19-553547-2.

Perennially appealing penguins are well served by this fine book. Inexpensive, well illustrated, and authoritatively written, *Penguins of the World* gives an excellent overview of the world's 17 penguin species, and should inform a wide and varied readership. Most of the text consists of the 17 species accounts, each with sections covering description, distribution, dispersal and opulation, behavior, and breeding, plus numerous well-crafted illustrations—both black-and-white photographs and color paintings. Maps also show each species' distribution.

Two general chapters concern the diversity of penguins and threats, conservation, and the future. Much of the information in this monograph is distilled from the *Handbook of Australian, New Zealand and Antarctic Birds* (see ARBA 92, entry 1563), a superb, massive, and expensive compendium in the classic *Handbuch* tradition. Reilly, an experienced naturalist and past president of the Royal Australasian Ornithologists Union, has done a fine service by making this available in a popular format to a much broader audience.

The book also has a glossary, which should have included *protoptile* and *mesoptile*, words used frequently in the captions accompanying the illustrations. There are several other good penguin books, such as *Penguins* by Roger Tory Peterson (Houghton Mifflin, 1979). It is good to now have a book organized by the various penguin species by a genuine penguin authority. It is highly recommended.
—**Henry T. Armistead**

1617. Rosair, David, and David Cottridge. **Photographic Guide to the Shorebirds of the World.** New York, Facts on File, 1995. 175p. illus. index. $29.95. ISBN 0-8160-3309-9.

The world's 212 species of shorebirds present a remarkable diversity within 14 avian families. These include many cosmopolitan groups such as plovers, sandpipers, coursers, jacanas, avocets, oystercatchers, and stilts. This photographic collection shows the shorebird species with more than 700 spectacular color illustrations, many never before published. The illustrations often show variations in plumage with age, reproductive condition, and geographical race.

The accompanying text is organized by species accounts that address field characteristics, with an emphasis on identification, distribution, and habitat preferences. Shorebirds are among the familiar birds of the world's coastlines, wetlands, and estuaries. People interested in identifying these birds can find no better illustration collection than this guide from one of the foremost bird photographers.—**Charles Leck**

Domestic Animals

1618. **The American Animal Hospital Association Encyclopedia of Cat Health and Care.** By American Animal Hospital Association with Les Sussman. New York, Hearst Books, 1994. 291p. illus. index. $25.00. ISBN 0-688-13454-8.

1619. **The American Animal Hospital Association Encyclopedia of Dog Health and Care.** By American Animal Hospital Association with Sally Bordwell. New York, Hearst Books, 1994. 292p. illus. index. $25.00. ISBN 0-688-13455-6.

These books cover as much territory as a young tom cat on a spring evening. From kittenhood or puppyhood to death, in fewer than 300 pages each, the authors discuss a majority of concerns faced by owners of the 109 million cats and dogs in the United States. The books share an identical format. Each is divided into 22 chapters comprising 3 main sections: a guide to the most popular breeds, a manual on everyday care, and a directory of illnesses and diseases. The chapter on first aid is particularly handy. An excellent index and separately captioned paragraphs make it easy to access information. Also, common procedures and tips—trimming nails, removing a tick, preventing tooth decay—are highlighted in boxes interspersed throughout the text. Simple line drawings are used, with uneven success. The only photographs illustrate various breeds in color.

Despite the claims of comprehensiveness, the relative brevity of these books alone negates such a claim. No topic is covered in depth. This is particularly evident in the sections on illnesses and diseases. The discussion of cystitis in cats, for instance, fails to mention the importance of diet. There are more comprehensive books on breeds, medical care, and so forth available, notably Delbert G. Carlson's revised *Dog Owner's Home Veterinary Handbook* (see ARBA 81, entry 1654), his revised *Cat Owner's Home Veterinary Handbook* (Howell Book House, 1995), as well as the *Atlas of Dog Breeds of the World* (see ARBA 94, entry 1710, and ARBA 91, entry 1580) and the *Atlas of Cats of the World* (see ARBA 91, entry 1576). Nonetheless, these new guides have it all under one roof.

The authors, both journalists rather than veterinarians despite the books' sponsorship by the American Animal Hospital Association, have produced readable and easily understood books aimed at pet owners, especially inexperienced ones. However, it is probably old-timers who can best appreciate the common-sense and sensitive chapter on "Saying Good-Bye." These are books to keep handy for quick reference, a sort of "Dr. Spock" for dog and cat owners.—**Hope Yelich**

1620. Fogle, Bruce. **The Encyclopedia of the Dog.** New York, Dorling Kindersley, 1995. 312p. illus. index. $39.95. ISBN 0-7894-0149-5.

Humankind's best friend, in all the many shapes, sizes, weights, heights, and temperaments, is found in this entertaining and informative book that describes and illustrates more than 400 breeds and varieties of dogs. The highlight of the book is the captivating color photographs of dogs found sleeping, playing, running, and posing on every page of this book. Entertaining chapters on the history and evolution of dogs, their anatomy, behavior, and care come before and after the main part of the book, an encyclopedia of the individual dog breeds. These breeds include the rare Prazsky Krysavik (meaning "beautiful Prague dog"), the unusual Labradoodle (Labrador retriever and poodle mix), and hundreds of old favorites. Because this is a British publication, more European breeds are covered than others. The breeds are grouped under headings for primitive dogs, sight hounds, scent hounds, spitz-type dogs, terriers, gundogs, livestock dogs, companion dogs, and random-bred dogs (mutts).

Each of more than 400 breeds is described in a full or half page. In most instances, three full-color photographs (one of the mature dog, and two of the head or other distinguishing detail) illustrate each breed. One paragraph of description, with another paragraph on the breed's history, is included. The work does not, however, list the registry affiliations of each breed. An inset of brief information called "Key Facts" tells the dog's country and date of origin, first use (for example, small game hunting), use today, life expectancy, other names, and weight and height ranges. An added feature of each description is the use of up to six symbols that show important characteristics of the breed. For example, the symbol of two small children with a line through it indicates the breed is unsuitable as a child's companion. Other symbols indicate if the dog is suitable for urban living or for hot or cold climates, requires a lot of grooming, is easy to obedience train, is a good watchdog, and so forth. A feature better left off is a window showing the coat color variations (blue/tan, sandy), since the colors often did not reproduce well and are not true coat colors.

Written by a doctor of veterinary medicine who is also the author of popular dog- and cat-care books, this work is not only fun and appealing, but has an authoritative base. For those who can afford it, a more thorough work entitled *Atlas of Dog Breeds of the World* (see ARBA 94, entry 1710) is available in a 2-volume set that sells for $130. However, for those who just want a good book to browse through, especially when trying to select a new dog, this is a fun book, and is recommended for all public and school libraries.—**Diane B. Rhodes**

Fishes

1621. Hillard, James M. **Aquariums of North America: A Guidebook to Appreciating North America's Aquatic Treasures.** Metuchen, N.J., Scarecrow, 1995. 190p. index. $27.50. ISBN 0-8108-2923-1.

Compiled by an avid visitor of aquariums, this well-bound and reasonably priced guide highlights particular attractions at 59 aquariums in 26 of the United States and the District of Columbia, and 8 aquariums in 6 Canadian provinces. An emeritus librarian, Hillard applies his appreciation of thorough, consistent data presentation in details about how to get there (including by public transportation), admission and parking fees, availability of food and entertainment, and provisions for disabled visitors. Hillard's introductory section provides a glossary defining such basic terms as *fish* and *invertebrate* as used in the guide, while a list of fish hatcheries in 32 states follows the U.S. entries. Families planning vacations may be content with Tim O'Brien's *Where the Animals Are* (see ARBA 94, entry 1688), although Hillard's guide includes 25 aquariums in the United States and 5 in Canada that do not appear in O'Brien's more generalized work. O'Brien, on the other hand, lists six aquariums, mostly small, not included in Hillard's main or fish hatchery sections. This is a valuable addition for public libraries, zoologically oriented libraries, academic libraries able to purchase materials of general interest, service providers in the tourist industry, and enthusiasts of aquariums and aqua culture.—**Kathryn M. Cleland**

1622. Jensen, Gregory C. **Pacific Coast Crabs and Shrimps.** Monterey, Calif., Sea Challengers, 1995. 87p. illus. index. $19.95pa. ISBN 0-930118-20-0.

There are several popular field guides to West Coast intertidal life that include information on crabs and shrimps, but none that focus specifically on these often bizarre and attractive tidal and subtidal creatures. Such reference works that do exist tend to be for professionals. Biologist Jensen provides an accessible introductory volume enabling the amateur naturalist to identify some 163 crustaceans that tide-poolers and, especially, divers may encounter between Alaska and Mexico.

The introductory material describes and illustrates major groups of crustaceans and their reproduction and growth cycles. This is followed by a set of pictorial keys. Unlike technical keys requiring the user to know a great deal of anatomical terminology, Jensen's are based on clear line drawings of easily observable features. Technical terminology used is defined in a glossary or in illustrations. An initial key leads to three further pictorial keys: the Brachyura (true crabs), Anomura (hermit crabs), and Caridea (shrimp). Each category has its own preliminary discussion followed by first-rate, glossy photographs of each species. The color photographs, most by the author, are the heart of the book. Each picture is accompanied by a paragraph listing identifying features, range, depth, habitat, feeding habits, behavior, and commercial significance. The superb pictures not only serve to identify the creatures, but are an aesthetic delight in themselves. Additionally, the volume contains several charming historical illustrations, a bibliography, an index, and a checklist for those wishing to log their sightings of these exquisite creatures whose color and patterning merit our admiration no less than birds.—**D. Barton Johnson**

1623. Last, P. R., and J. D. Stevens. **Sharks and Rays of Australia.** Australia, CSIRO; distr., Portland, Oreg., ISBS, 1994. 513p. illus. maps. index. $59.95. ISBN 0-643-05143-0.

The aim of the authors is to provide an identification guide to the sharks, rays, and chimaeras of the waters surrounding Australia. The 11-page introduction includes background information on chondrichthian fishes, the fauna and biology related to them, and the impact sharks, rays, and humans have upon one another. A clear explanation on how to use the book, a glossary with excellent line drawings of shark and ray terminology with dimensions, and an illustrated family key precede the main portion of the book, which contains 45 chapters arranged by family, then species.

Each family entry contains alternate common and scientific names, species codes, field characteristics, distinctive features, color, size, distribution remarks, synonyms, and references. Cross-references are provided to enable readers to begin their research by going directly to the family or species, if known, or to the color plates, which are closely arranged by the order of the chapters. These 84 color plates contain 343 illustrations that are referenced to the family and species. An additional 1,400 black-and-white illustrations enhance the book. Three indexes—family numerical, scientific name, and common name— conclude the guide and contribute to its usefulness. The authors specifically narrowed their identification to the Australian area; however, maps indicating the geographic distribution of each species around the world make the book helpful in other geographic areas.

Although directed at the fishing industry, the serious researcher and general interest reader will also find the book useful. The funding of the guide by a grant from the Australian Fisheries Research and Development Corporation allowed the printing of an affordable, quality book in terms of physical features, as well as content and organization.—**Elaine Ezell**

1624. Wooding, Frederick H. **Lake, River, and Sea-Run Fishes of Canada.** Madeira Park, B.C., Harbour Publishing, 1994. 303p. illus. index. $32.95. ISBN 1-55017-113-5.

Canada has fewer fishes than the United States but some provide exceptional challenges to anglers. Wooding's popular text is aimed toward this group. A brief introduction to structure, behavior, and reproduction is followed by more than 35 small color illustrations of Canadian fishes. Half are of salmon, trout, and grayling that compose 40 percent of the text. These illustrations will not be useful to identify a specimen in the field, but should help a reader visualize the species. Throughout the text are black-and-white drawings of fish in active movement.

The text is not arranged in the usual biosystematic order but in a way (perhaps) to present groups important to anglers. Thus, lampreys are placed between cod and sturgeon on one side and herring, carp, and suckers on the other. In each chapter, some data on life history, body weight, and length are given. The writing style is simple. Coverage for each species is eclectic but sufficiently informative for the general reader. Several anecdotes about fishes and fishing sprinkle the text. These include stories about the size of particular species, the origins of a fish name, and so on.

Two short sections are written by specialists: Joseph Nelson provides a foreword placing the Canadian fishes in a somewhat broader perspective, and Robert Campbell looks at the status of endangered fishes in Canada, aided by a table of vulnerable, endangered, and extinct species. This book will help anglers and those interested in natural history to appreciate the life of fishes.—**David Bardack**

Insects

1625. Hill, Dennis S., with Jeremy D. Hill. **Agricultural Entomology.** Portland, Oreg., Timber Press, 1994. 635p. illus. index. $89.95. ISBN 0-88192-223-4.

Agricultural entomology encompasses arthropods constructively or destructively associated with domesticated plants and animals throughout the world. There are tens of thousands of such anthropods, and this text broadly examines them systematically by order and family. This provides a good glimpse of many pests across the globe. However, needed information to develop a management plan is invariably lacking, such as overwintering forms, fecundity, generation time or number per year, pest status in relation to other pests, and the like. The excellent indexes do allow construction of partial pest complexes on many commodities, and a fine glossary is also included. There are many illustrations that complement the text. The introductory chapters provide a strong insightful perspective of agricultural entomology based on the authors' field experience and are interesting reading. This is the broadest treatment of agricultural entomology that this reviewer has seen, but the work lacks the depth Hill provided in a more focused earlier work, *Agricultural Insect Pests of Temperate Regions & Their Control* (Cambridge University Press, 1987). Thus, this is a good survey text for a cosmopolitan view of agricultural entomology. [R: RBB, 1 Jan 95, p. 836]—**Marvin K. Harris**

1626. Sasa, Manabu, and Mihoko Kikuchi. **Chironomidae [Diptera] of Japan.** Tokyo, University of Tokyo Press; distr., New York, Columbia University Press, 1995. 333p. illus. index. $105.00. ISBN 0-86008-516-3.

Chironomidae form fundamental links in biological systems, especially freshwater habitats. Their primary role is in scavenging organic matter from the water and bottom sediments. These activities result in large numbers of chironomid flies in many habitats reprocessing organic matter by themselves becoming prey to small fish, other insects, spiders, and so forth. Some species have been implicated in exacerbating asthma in humans. Their greatest direct value to human affairs appears to be as specific indicators of the condition of the waters in which certain species live.

There are 480 species addressed in this taxonomic work, and ultimately, each is expected to have a rather specialized set of requirements identified so that the presence of a particular species or species complex could be used to reflect the conditions present in the water. The initial step in such forensic application is to provide a reliable means of identifying each species, and this work is primarily devoted to that end. Emphasis is on adult male taxonomy, and it integrates well with earlier and other studies outside Japan. The brief introduction discusses collection and preservation, and advocates use of gum-choral (recipe included) as the preservative in slide mounts. This work will be of principal interest to dipterists and chironomid specialists. It contains many black-and-white illustrations. Syntax and tense in the introduction would have benefited from editing, but the meaning is discernible. This appears to be a sound contribution to a specialized area by knowledgeable authors.—**Marvin K. Harris**

1627. Schuh, Randall T., and James A. Slater. **True Bugs of the World (Hemiptera: Heteroptera). Classification and Natural History.** Ithaca, N.Y., Cornell University Press, 1995. 336p. illus. index. $85.00. ISBN 0-8014-2066-0.

Some crawl into beds. Others skate on the open ocean. True bugs—formally, the order Hemiptera or Heteroptera, depending upon one's tradition in entomology—epitomize evolutionary resourcefulness. Apparently, the ability to feed by modes of sucking opens up many opportunities. The related groups of parasites, predators, and plant-eaters fill out 75 families and boast representatives on all continents except Antarctica.

Reading this utilitarian volume will help readers to better appreciate diversity of form and function in the taxon. Collection tips, literature entry points, and true bug repositories (unfortunately, without addresses) undergird the effort; keys to families and subfamilies, a glossary, and an index embellish it. Intelligible diagrams, drawings, and scanned electron micrographs set a high standard.

Broad-brush statements will leave the general reader unaware. For example, the authors' assertion that the last general treatment of all Heteroptera dates to 1971 is technically correct. Yet the claim diminishes a strong and well-written complement to their book, *Hemiptera* by William R. Dolling (Oxford University Press, 1991). Similarly, the authors succumb to torturous selectivity when citing literature. Despite those things, the general reader meets a robust introduction to the true bugs. The etymology of the family and subfamily names is the only omission sure to leave the general reader wanting.

—**Diane M. Calabrese**

1628. Wiebes, J. T. **The Indo-Australian Agaoninae (Pollinators of Figs).** Amsterdam, Koninklijke Nederlandse Akademie van Wetenschappen; distr., New York, Elsevier Science, 1994. 208p. illus. index. $48.50pa. ISBN 0-444-85779-6.

Fig pollinators and figs present a fascinating arena to examine one of the closest insect-plant interactions known. Many figs are entirely dependent on a fig wasp for pollination (and successful reproduction), and the wasp appears similarly dependent on the host fig as a sole food source. Figs initially brought from the Mediterranean to California for cultivation in the nineteenth century were infertile until years later when the correct species of pollinating wasp was also introduced. The discovery inspired many questions of taxonomic, phylogenetic, biological, and agricultural importance of wasps and host figs. Wiebes embarked on research 30 years ago, expecting phylogenetic specificity to be largely demonstrated between wasps and figs; but he notes that discrepancies still remain despite his major contribution to systematics of wasps.

This text provides keys to genera and species of *Agaoninae*, and referenced species descriptions with their host fig(s) if known, for more than 192 taxons (more than half authored by Wiebes). This classically derived wasp classification is a fundamental step in unraveling one of the mysteries of interactions among groups of organisms. With excellent references and illustrations, it will also contribute to other approaches that use newly emerging research tools to attack these important questions.—**Marvin K. Harris**

Mammals

1629. Carwardine, Mark. **Whales, Dolphins, and Porpoises.** New York, Dorling Kindersley, 1995. 256p. illus. maps. index. $29.95; $17.95 flexibinding. ISBN 1-56458-621-9; 1-56458-620-0 flexibinding.

As the popularity of whale-, dolphin-, and porpoise-watching increases, so does the need for a comprehensive pocket-sized field guide that will appeal to both the casual and seasoned observer. This book dubs itself as the "Visual Guide to All the World's Cetaceans" and it is just that. To begin, the author provides an introduction with short sections ranging from "What Is a Cetacean" to topics on anatomy, behavior, conservation, and where and how to watch these remarkable mammals. A useful identification key that enables one to compare similar species at a glance is included in these prefatory pages.

The majority of the book is composed of attractive and accurate species accounts covering all 79 species recognized by the author and illustrator. In addition, each family is treated with an overview that covers all its key characteristics. Each account is packed with information using text, sidebars, illustrations, and photographs to depict natural history and biological details. Some of the larger accounts include additional information and illustrations, notably for the Rorqual Whales—showing dive sequence and blow shape. Each species is superbly illustrated in color by Martin Camm, with all the main features highlighted. Also illustrated are details of the flukes, jawbone, fins, and teeth. An idea of color variation is indicated where necessary.

The binding is sturdy and could withstand many boat trips. All in all, the small format, together with the informative text and lavish illustrations, makes this an invaluable guide to a fascinating group. It is highly recommended.—**Katherine Margaret Thomas**

1630. Choate, Jerry R., J. Knox Jones Jr., and Clyde Jones. **Handbook of Mammals of the South-Central States.** Baton Rouge, La., Louisiana State University Press, 1994. 304p. illus. maps. index. $30.00. ISBN 0-8071-1819-2.

The purpose of this guidebook is to provide information on the distribution, ecology, and current status of all species of nondomesticated mammals that have lived in the area within historic time. The seven states included are Alabama, Arkansas, Georgia, Kentucky, Louisiana, Mississippi, and Tennessee. The usefulness of the guide extends into regions bordering this section of the Southeast. The authors have prepared carefully arranged keys to each of the orders included. There are distribution maps, a black-and-white photograph of each mammal, a glossary of frequently used descriptive terms found in the keys, an index to scientific and vernacular names, and a good bibliography with complete citations to books and journal articles. Individual entries are well thought-out and formatted, with narrative descriptions on one page with a distribution map and photograph on the facing page. Discussion of natural history is the longest section of each entry.

This is a quality product: good typography, pleasing format, good photographs, tabular information that is clearly presented, nicely bound, and printed on quality paper. The book is highly recommended for all college libraries and for middle and high schools throughout the Southeast.—**Milton H. Crouch**

1631. Flannery, Tim. **Mammals of New Guinea.** rev. ed. Chatswood, Australia, Reed Books Australia and Ithaca, N.Y., Cornell University Press, 1995. 568p. illus. maps. index. $75.00. ISBN 0-8014-3149-2.

The only work of its kind, this is a revised and updated edition of the original, which was published in 1990. The new edition adds more than 100 pages and covers the more than 200 known indigenous mammal species of New Guinea. The species accounts include a distribution map and recorded physical measurements of specimens, taxonomic and local names, and a page or two of descriptive information. The accounts are made more interesting by the author's personal observations from his extensive studies and travels in New Guinea (he is a mammalogist at the Australian Museum in Sydney).

Bandicoots, tree kangaroos, ringtails, cuscuses, bats, rats, mice, and other mammals are described, along with the author's own recent discovery of a black-and-white tree kangaroo not known outside the country. The species accounts are accompanied by excellent color photographs. There is a brief introductory discussion of the country that covers its geology, geography, paleontology, flora and fauna, human inhabitants, and introduced mammal species. Black-and-white skull photographs, a list of references, and an index complete the volume. This updated work will be a useful and attractive addition to academic, zoo, and museum libraries.—**William H. Wiese**

1632. Flannery, Tim. **Mammals of the South-West Pacific & Moluccan Islands.** Chatswood, New South Wales, Reed Books and Ithaca, N.Y., Cornell University Press, 1995. 464p. illus. maps. index. $75.00. ISBN 0-8014-3150-6.

With the publication of this scholarly, yet wonderfully approachable work, we now have complete coverage of land mammals living on the small and large islands of the South-West Pacific, encompassing Australia, New Guinea, and New Zealand. The purpose of this work is to provide coverage for the 230 indigenous mammal species living on islands west of Sulawesi, including islands such as Bismarck Archipelago, Manus, the Tubuaï Islands, Fiji, New Caledonia, Samoa, the Solomon Islands, and Tonga. New Zealand is covered, as are many of the islands within the island group known as Micronesia (Guam and the Mariana Islands, for example). This book is intended as a companion volume to the author's *Mammals of New Guinea* (see entry 1631) and Ronald Strahan's *Complete Book of Australian Mammals* (North Ryde, Australia: Angus and Robertson, 1988). Strahan's work will soon appear in a new edition.

Entries for individual species include an excellent face-on color photograph of the animal, the scientific name, the local name and pronunciation, and its status (endangered, secure, unknown, vulnerable, extinct). A table lists size and weight for males and females; subspecies are also listed. Entries contain a description, the distribution, and interesting information on natural history. Furnishing a distribution map in every entry is essential for users attempting to locate geographical areas quickly, and is another indication of the care the author and publisher have taken to produce a successful reference source. A glossary, an index to scientific and common name(s), photographs of skulls, and a bibliography complete the work.

The author adds to the work's reference value by including essay-length descriptions of the area's geology, vegetation, and paleontology. Flannery's brief essays on zoogeography and human colonization help users appreciate what he has accomplished in gathering the scientific material found here. All three of the mentioned titles should be in all college and university library collections.—**Milton H. Crouch**

Marine Animals

1633. Allen, Gerald R., and D. Ross Robertson. **Fishes of the Tropical Eastern Pacific.** Honolulu, University of Hawaii Press, 1994. 332p. illus. index. $65.00. ISBN 0-8248-1675-7.

A small industry is pouring out a stream of fine books, remarkably well printed, on marine and freshwater fishes. Most have a taxonomic organization, adequate descriptions of groups, and standard characteristics sufficient to identify a specimen, at least to family. Excellent photographs of typical specimens in a coffee-table format book help make this particular volume a conversation-starter, and will aid a visitor to the area in identifying specimens. A good portion of the photographs are of specimens in natural settings. There are also 15 plates of paintings of taxonomically mixed groups of fishes. Especially useful are photographs of juvenile and adult stages where sex and color changes characterize the group. With the standard organization and information all well presented, the most important niche this volume fills is regional coverage: namely, the area of the Eastern Pacific principally south of the Sea of Cortez (Gulf of California) to Ecuador and offshore islands including the Galápagos.—**David Bardack**

Reptiles and Amphibians

1634. Bauer, Aaron M., with Klaus Henle. **Familia Gekkonidae (Reptilia, Sauria). Part 1: Australia and Oceania.** New York, Walter de Gruyter, 1994. 306p. maps. index. (The Animal Kingdom, pt.109). $385.00. ISBN 3-11-014114-0.

Bauer's book is the first of five volumes that will summarize taxonomic and distributional information on the lizard family Gekkonidae. The present volume covers the geckos (subfamilies *Gekkoninae* and *Diplodactylinae*) of Australia, New Zealand, New Guinea, and numerous islands referred to as Oceania (Map 1). The five volumes will update, expand, and supplement the information in Hans Wermuth's 1965 gekkonid book (*The Animal Kingdom*, pt. 80).

The text is organized into a preface, a systematic index, a dichotomous key to genera of Pacific geckos, accounts of gekkonid genera and species, a lengthy list of the literature cited, summary tables, and a register of Pacific gecko names. The accounts make up most of the text and are alphabetically arranged by genus and within a genus by species. Each generic account provides a nomenclatural synonymy and sections on distribution, comments, references, and species referred, as well as a dichotomous key to species. Species accounts include a chresonymy and units on distribution, comments, and references. The maps provided for locality records cover one or more species.

This book is not oversize and has only 315 pages. There are no color plates, photographs, or line drawings. Maps are small and locality records are often difficult to discern because of poor printing quality. While it is a useful, comprehensive, and scholarly source of value to saurian specialists, the volume is overpriced, even by today's standards. Because of the high cost and potential small readership, the existence of a user audience should be determined prior to purchase.—**Edmund D. Keiser Jr.**

1635. Bishop, Sherman C. **Handbook of Salamanders: The Salamanders of the United States, of Canada, and of Lower California.** Ithaca, N.Y., Comstock Publishing/Cornell University Press, 1943; repr., 1994. 555p. illus. maps. index. (Comstock Classic Handbooks). $34.95pa. ISBN 0-8014-8213-5.

This is the long-awaited paperback reprint of Bishop's classic volume on salamanders. Originally published in 1943, this remains the only book devoted to the salamanders of the United States. Its detailed accounts of the 88 urodele species known in 1943 remain invaluable references for anyone interested in the life histories of salamanders. A 1994 foreword by Edmund D. Brodie Jr., provides historical perspectives and an up-to-date table comparing the names of today's taxa with those that were used in the 1943 handbook.

The book itself remains unchanged. An introduction discusses salamanders in general, methods of collecting, and use of the keys and map. Dichotomous identification keys precede, where applicable, accounts of families, genera, species, and subspecies. Family descriptions are followed by taxonomically sequenced species accounts. Species accounts include technical and vernacular names, figure and map reference numbers, and sections on type locality, range, habitat, size, description, color, sexual differences, breeding, eggs, and larvae. Most species accounts are accompanied by black-and-white photographs and range maps. A lengthy bibliography has publication titles arranged by states and subjects. An index completes the book. This handbook should be in every library.—**Edmund D. Keiser Jr.**

1636. Ernst, Carl H., Roger W. Barbour, and Jeffrey E. Lovich. **Turtles of the United States and Canada.** Washington, D.C., Smithsonian Institution Press, 1994. 578p. illus. maps. index. $60.00. ISBN 1-56098-346-9.

Ernst, Lovich, and the late Roger Barbour, accomplished chelonian authorities, combined their talents to produce this outstanding volume on the 56 turtle species of the United States and Canada. This book is more comprehensive and detailed than the 1973 predecessor *Turtles of the United States* by Ernst and Barbour (see ARBA 74, entry 1562). Species described in interim years have been added and text accounts are considerably more detailed and current.

The book is organized into a preface, an introduction, an identification section, seven family accounts, a glossary of scientific names, a bibliography, and an index. The preface comments on purpose, content, and acknowledgments. The introduction discusses turtle evolution, systematics, morphology, karyotypes, distribution, habitats, general biology, and conservation. The identification unit is primarily a dichotomous key to families and turtles of North America.

Each family unit initiates with a discussion on content and definitions, followed by species accounts. Each account includes species names and author citation, vernacular name, plate reference, and detailed sections on such topics as recognition, fossil record, geographic variation, habitat, behavior, reproduction, and predators and defense. The accounts have a distribution map and black-and-white photographs. Many species are also illustrated by color photographs.

This is the most detailed publication on U.S. and Canadian turtles to date. It is well written, easy to comprehend, and minimally technical. Anyone with interests in turtles will find the book indispensable, and it is therefore highly recommended for general purchase by municipal, secondary school, and college libraries.

—**Edmund D. Keiser Jr.**

1637. Mattison, Chris. **The Encyclopedia of Snakes.** New York, Facts on File, 1995. 256p. illus. maps. index. $35.00. ISBN 0-8160-3072-3.

This is a sourcebook with much information on snakes of the world. Mattison, a competent, professional herpetologist, has used a well-written, detail-filled narrative and vivid color photographs to produce an entertaining tome that will delight, educate, and hold the attention of readers.

Ten chapters follow a brief introduction and an acknowledgments section. The first chapter defines *snake* and discusses ophidian evolution and an overview of classification. Anatomy, coloration, locomotion, and senses are detailed in chapter 2; habitats and distributional patterns in chapters 3 and 4; and feeding, defense, and reproduction are the focuses of chapters 5 through 7. Human/snake interrelationships, including myths, snake roundups, research, conservation, and snake bites are considered in chapter 8. The closing chapters provide details on nomenclature and taxonomy and include summarization paragraphs on world families, subfamilies, and genera. A brief bibliography and an index conclude the book.

This volume has more than 200 color photographs, nearly all striking and vividly detailed. Most are by the author, although 10 other photographers have contributed. There are many excellent line drawings, a "family tree," and a few range maps and graphs. Technical terms are used sparingly, and the writing style promotes easy comprehension. This is a superb, inexpensive book that will attract a diverse readership. It is highly recommended for purchase by high school, municipal, college, and university libraries.

—**Edmund D. Keiser Jr.**

1638. Rossi, John V., and Roxanne Rossi. **Snakes of the United States and Canada: Keeping Them Healthy in Captivity. Volume 2: Western Area.** Malabar, Fla., Krieger Publishing, 1995. 325p. illus. maps. index. $69.50. ISBN 0-89464-808-X.

The first volume in this series was published in 1992 (see ARBA 94, entry 1751). Volume 2 covers snakes native to the area west of the Ontario/Manitoba border in Canada and the Mississippi River in the United States. Patterned after the format of volume 1, the text is divided into 4 parts—the most extensive of which are the sections on general snake care and the individual species accounts. The "General Snake Care" section is definitely an excellent starting point for preliminary research. Some topics have been updated or are more thorough, such as the information contained under "Choosing a Snake," "Breeding," and "Sexing."

There is a detailed text for 73 of the 90 species discussed. Only brief descriptions are given for the remaining 17 common subspecies, as these are treated more comprehensively in volume 1. Each of the 73 species accounts includes a sidebar that lists in abbreviated format biological facts such as the size, food, substrate, cage size, and a range map of the geographical distribution. Supplementing the descriptions are 106 high-quality color photographs, which include annotations. The book concludes with an excellent list of recent references, an index to common names, and a subject index. Throughout the text, the authors are quick to promote snake conservation, education, and appropriate handling and captivity methods. One drawback to the book, especially for Canadian readers, is that the larger-scale range maps have state but not provincial boundaries. Regardless, this is an essential reference for the student or practitioner of snakes in this region.—**Katherine Margaret Thomas**

1639. Smith, Hobart M. **Handbook of Lizards: Lizards of the United States and of Canada.** Ithaca, N.Y., Comstock Publishing/Cornell University Press, 1946; repr., 1995. 557p. illus. maps. index. (Comstock Classic Handbooks). $39.95pa. ISBN 0-8014-8236-4.

Nearly a half-century has passed since the initial publication of this comprehensive book on the lizards of the United States and Canada. Now reissued as a Comstock Classic Handbook, the contents are relevant and often essential for present-day biological scientists, naturalists, and teachers who need a sourcebook on lizards. Author Smith continues today as a world-renowned, much-published saurian authority.

Technical nomenclature in any reissued classic is always outdated. The 1995 printing has a foreword by Darrel R. Frost that comments on the history and value of the book and compares, in table form, current taxonomy with that used in the original edition. The handbook narrative is organized as in 1946. There is a preface, a 59-page introduction (part 1), and a 422-page "Accounts of Species" (part 2). The introduction discusses lizard taxonomy, distribution, fossil history, anatomy, habitats, life history, and thermoregulation, then historical comments and definitions of terms.

Part 2 begins with an illustrated identification key to families. Each family is described, then dichotomous keys to genera follow. Genera within each family are characterized. Each genus of a given family is discussed and accounts of the species follow. Keys are provided for genera with two or more species. Each species account furnishes nomenclatural designations; figure and plate references; and comments on range, size, color, recognition, habitat, habits, problems, references, line drawings, and, occasionally, monochrome photographs.

Appended sections include species distribution maps, general literature, state lists of species and literature, literature cited, and an index. The book remains today the best single source on United States and Canadian lizards. It is highly recommended for all college libraries, including those that have the 1946 edition.—**Edmund D. Keiser Jr.**

1640. Wright, Albert Hazen, and Anna Allen Wright. **Handbook of Frogs and Toads of the United States and Canada.** 3d ed. Ithaca, N.Y., Comstock Publishing/Cornell University Press, 1949; repr., 1995. 640p. illus. maps. index. (Comstock Classic Handbooks). $39.95pa. ISBN 0-8014-8232-1.

Bulging eyes and hopping gait collectively describe the order referred to as anurans. Frogs and toads are of enduring interest to biologists and vie for serious attention of behavioral ecologists and amateur naturalists alike. Reprinted after nearly half-a-century, the primary function of the text remains the same—identification of species, habits, and habitats. Technical terminology in any reprint is dated. However, a new foreword by Roy W. McDiarmid brings the reprinted materials into historical perspective, and an up-to-date table compares names of species in current use with those used in previous editions. References to the foreword date to 1993; the preface remains unchanged.

Part 1, "General Account," provides classification and scientific name; physical characteristics, vocalization range, summary of sexual characteristics, and breeding behavior; development and transformation; and journal notes. Part 2, "Keys," lists families with one- or two-sentence physical descriptions (e.g., jaw structure, male and female differences, body structure, and so forth). Part 3, "Accounts of Species" (479 pages), includes technical and vernacular names; range and habitat; size and general appearance; color and structure; breeding; biology, including descriptions of eggs, tadpoles, development of young, and metamorphosis; and field notes. The bibliography and index to the main text are unchanged. Black-and-white photographs and useful line maps detail the range of species; native and introduced frogs and toads are noted on some maps. Illustrations are cross-referenced to the text. For the reference collection, this reasonably priced reprint is recommended.—**Judy Gay Matthews**

32 Engineering

GENERAL WORKS

1641. **Concise Encyclopedia of Measurement & Instrumentation.** L. Finkelstein and K. T. V. Grattan, eds. New York, Pergamon Press/Elsevier Science, 1994. 434p. index. (Advances in Systems, Control and Information Engineering). $280.00. ISBN 0-08-036212-5.

This volume is a condensation and update of the relevant portions of Pergamon's *Systems and Control Encyclopedia* (see ARBA 88, entry 1449). The emphasis is on high-tech measurement, with excellent coverage of electronic, optical, and analytical physical tools and techniques. As is typical of a compact reference to broad bodies of information, the depth of specific sections (such as flow measurement) is necessarily incomplete (entire monographs are devoted to the subject elsewhere). However, the information provided is sufficiently detailed and accurate to guide the researcher in selecting appropriate procedures. The short bibliographies appended to many articles are usually adequate to point out additional resources.

The arrangement of the entries and access to specifics may pose difficulties for inexperienced users. The entire work is divided into broad subject categories, arranged alphabetically, with a list of the articles in the front. A subject index is appended. As an example of the possible problems for researchers, the only terms in the subject index beginning with "acoustics" are "Acoustic Impedance" and "Acoustic Measurements—Sensors." The main section devoted to acoustics is, however, "Noise—Physical Sources," which contains neither reference. The user will be well advised to consult the alphabetical list of subject headings along with the index to optimize searching.

Another minor caveat is the apparent absence of coverage of traditional means of mechanical measurement, such as micrometers and "jo blocks," although modern equivalents, such as laser and optical technology, are included. Brief pointers to packaged commercial measuring devices would also have been welcome, although probably outside the scope of the book. The contributors to this volume have impressive credentials, and it should be added to all libraries supporting engineering and technical clienteles.—**Edwin D. Posey**

1642. **Electronic Giecks' Engineering Formulas.** [CD-ROM]. New York, McGraw-Hill, 1995. Minimum system requirements: IBM or compatible 386/MHz. CD-ROM drive. Windows 3.1. 4MB RAM. 5MB hard disk space. $79.95; $99.95 w/book.

This is the electronic version of a familiar engineering classic now in its 6th edition—*Giecks' Engineering Formulas* (Kurt and Reiner Gieck). As in the printed book (see ARBA 84, entry 1487, and ARBA 81, entry 1669), the electronic version coverage includes the formulas and calculations used in electrical engineering, solid bodies, statics and dynamics, kinematics, strength, and hydraulics. Subject access to the material is possible through an index and hypertext links within the text.

In contrast to the book, however, the CD-ROM provides interactive access through MathSoft's MathCad interface to 500 formulas and 400 graphic images. As a result, users can generate solutions to engineering and scientific equations, such as volume, momentum, velocity, and modulus of elasticity, based on their own data. All of these calculations take place in the scratchpad area and cannot be permanently saved. However, some changes can be saved, and these are displayed in a different color from the original. While users can make permanent notes in any white space, they cannot modify the actual text or delete any original material. The original unaltered text is always available by using the "view original" command.

This CD-ROM installed beautifully; the only choice was whether to install the data on the hard drive or to run it directly from the disc. Both worked well; the choice really depends on how much hard drive space an individual wants taken up with this product. The only disadvantage to running off the CD-ROM is that searching is a bit slower.

Libraries with extensive engineering mathematics collections will find this disc a good value. The installation was quick and easy; any user (who can use the Windows "run" command) should be able to get it working in less than two minutes.—**Susan B. Ardis**

1643. **Key Guide to Electronic Resources: Engineering.** Melissa McBurney, ed. Medford, N.J., Information Today, 1995. 196p. index. $39.50pa. ISBN 1-57387-008-0.

Serving as a basic catalog of electronic resources for various fields of engineering, the introduction to this book explains that it is a "starting point" and not all-inclusive. Contents list and describe online databases, CD-ROM products, locally loaded databases, library Online Public Access Catalogs (OPACs), bulletin board systems, and electronic journals. Evaluations are offered whenever possible. Three indexes cover companies, subjects, and titles. Finally, a brief section on further sources for information is included. This is a specialized and basic reference source. For a more comprehensive and rigorously updated source of electronic information, consider *Gale Directory of Databases* (see ARBA 94, entry 1907).—**Jean Engler**

1644. **Standard Handbook of Engineering Calculations.** 3d ed. Tyler G. Hicks, David S. Hicks, and Joseph Leto, eds. New York, McGraw-Hill, 1995. 1v. (various paging). illus. index. $99.50. ISBN 0-07-028812-7.

This edition of a standard aptly demonstrates three major changes that have occurred in engineering since the 2d edition was published in 1985 (see ARBA 86, entry 1548): the emergence of environmental engineering as a field with broad importance and impact, the pervasive influence and use of personal computers, and the continued emphasis on energy conservation. This handbook has several goals. One is to supply the kind of information engineers in one field often need from another. However, the major purpose is to provide all engineers with specific step-by-step calculation procedures for the more common design and operating problems. While more elegant solutions may exist, the idea is to provide safe and usable results. Each procedure has three parts: a description of the problem, a list of numbered calculation procedures to be used, and a worked example of the problem. The text covers 13 separate disciplines from aeronautical and astronomical engineering to sanitary engineering.

Previous editions have been very popular with both engineering students and working engineers. This is the place to find out how to calculate a myriad of things, from structural load to the stability of a retaining wall to storm-water runoff rate. A copy should be in every engineering collection and large public library.—**Susan B. Ardis**

ASTRONAUTICAL ENGINEERING

1645. Kleczek, Josip, and Helena Kleczková. **Space Sciences Dictionary 2: Motion/Space Flight/Data.** New York, Elsevier Science, 1993. 807p. index. $234.50. ISBN 0-444-98818-1.

1646. Kleczek, Josip, and Helena Kleczková. **Space Sciences Dictionary 3: Space Technology/Space Research.** New York, Elsevier Science, 1994. 742p. index. $228.50. ISBN 0-444-98817-3.

Technical language dictionaries covering more than two languages are a challenge for the author/editor and for the user. Kleczek and Kleczková have struck upon the most economical arrangement of this difficult task. The six languages—English, French, German, Spanish, Portuguese, and Russian—chosen by the authors were partially selected because of the technical problems of handling Chinese and Japanese within a reasonably priced dictionary. Either of those languages is more globally useful than Portuguese (for example) in the area of the space sciences. Each volume in the four-title series can be used independently of the others. In the main part of each volume, terms are listed under one of a number of broad subject headings. In the 4-volume set there are 86 headings. For example, in volume 3, devoted to space technology and research, section 54 is rockets. Within that section are 113 terms with the equivalent in each of the 6 languages. The second part lists words in a single alphabetical listing. The user might find that the term "haftbarkeit" will be the 51st term within the 68th section. The tool is, in effect, 30 bilingual dictionaries. There are no comparable reference works of this magnitude for the subject matter covered. The set is sturdily bound and easy to read.—**John M. Robson**

1647. Neal, Valerie, Cathleen S. Lewis, and Frank H. Winter. **Spaceflight: A Smithsonian Guide.** New York, Macmillan/Simon & Schuster, 1995. 256p. illus. maps. index. $24.95; $18.00pa. ISBN 0-02-860007-X; 0-02-860040-1pa.

The Smithsonian and Macmillan have launched an interesting series of books for the home reference shelf that will also find value for pubic libraries and those of schools and community colleges. *Spaceflight* is the first title of the series, and it fills a void in the history of space exploration by covering in a comprehensive manner the topics of space vehicles, space exploration, and space flights all in one slim volume at a marginal price.

Easy to read in clear, spare prose, *Spaceflight* provides an excellent popular history, summarizing the efforts of humankind in the above areas. In many ways, the book has the appearance of a work that is based on an exhibit or television documentary. There are approximately 350 photographs and drawings, chiefly in color, that are closely integrated with the text. Also included are a 40-page glossary; a 15-page chronology of manned and unmanned programs with launch date, crew, and accomplishments; and an 8-page foldout timeline covering the history of spaceflight from the twelfth century to plans for the year 2000. The authors would have increased the value of the book by including a list of references longer than six related titles.—**John M. Robson**

1648. **The World Satellite Almanac, 1995.** 7th ed. Monica L. Kenny and others, eds. Potomac, Md., Phillips Business Information, 1995. 550p. maps. index. $247.00pa. ISBN 1-881537-28-5.

The World Satellite Almanac is a guide to satellite operations worldwide. It provides up-to-date information on satellite operators, transponder frequency plans, coverage maps, transponder brokers and resellers, and telecommunications policy and regulatory organizations. In addition, it has technical and demographic information on more than 500 countries, territories, and islands, and other reference data. New with this edition is the inclusion of two reference works that were formerly published separately: the *Satellite Systems Handbook* and *The World Satellite Annual* (see ARBA 94, entry 1758).

Entries for each system (operational and nonoperational geostationary, and planned geo- and non-geostationary), network, or service provide technical specification data, geographical maps of transmission ranges, and general contact and focus information. Within sections, the entries are arranged by country and then by operator name. Indexes include satellite systems, satellite operators, and geographical areas. Reference material of note are the "Table of Geostationary Orbital Positions" and "Launch Schedule for 1995-1996." Maps are large and easy to understand, and the typeface is bold and readable.

This convenient tool is easy to use for those knowledgeable about this technical topic, and has no comparable competitors. The publisher is well known to the industry and produces a half-dozen companion titles such as *World-, European-, Asia-Pacific-,* and *Latin American Satellite Directory*. There are a limited number of advertisers inserted in the front and back of the volume, considering the price is high for a paperbound publication.—**John M. Robson**

AUTOMATION ENGINEERING

1649. **World Engineering Industries and Automation 1993-1995: Performance and Prospects.** By Economic Commission for Europe. New York, United Nations, 1995. 445p. $75.00pa. ISBN 92-1-116621-7. ISSN 1020-1300.

The Economic Commission for Europe (ECE) produces a number of publications in cooperation with the Organization for Economic Cooperation and Development (OECD). This title replaces the *Annual Review of Engineering Industries and Automation*, which was last issued in 1993. The title analyzes the period 1990-1993, estimates 1994, and forecasts statistics for 1995. It is divided into two parts. Part 1 provides a structural analysis of the engineering industries as a whole for the period 1985-1995. Data for up to 38 countries are provided, primarily European plus Canada, Japan, Turkey, and the United States. Sometimes, meaningful data were not available for all countries.

Part 2 covers production, trade, consumption, and structural changes in 42 major engineering products grouped into 21 sections. The sections include boilers, internal combustion piston engines, agricultural machinery, machine tools, pumps and compressors, computers and information technology, semiconductors, and motor cars. The data originate with questionnaires sent out to the countries by ECE/OECD.

Each section of part 2 begins with a discussion of the implications of the data and any particular problems that may have occurred. For example, 23 well-composed tables of data are given for "Machine Tools." They provide, by country, such information as production, imports, consumption, exports—all in U.S. dollars. For the major countries—Germany, France, Italy, the United Kingdom, Japan, Switzerland, and the United States—more detailed information is given. The data may be further broken down into leading companies in each of the major countries. This is an excellent tool that has no single multinational equivalent.—**John M. Robson**

CHEMICAL ENGINEERING

1650. **Rules of Thumb for Chemical Engineers: A Manual of Quick, Accurate Solutions to Everyday Process Engineering Problems.** Carl R. Branan, ed. Houston, Tex., Gulf Publishing, 1994. 376p. maps. index. $69.00pa. ISBN 0-88415-162-X.

Engineering handbooks chiefly come in the form of large, comprehensive, and often expensive miniencyclopedias. Branan's useful and convenient handbook for chemical and process engineers (at a bargain price) will be much appreciated by students and practitioners. As the subtitle, *A Manual of Quick, Accurate Solutions to Everyday Process Engineering Problems* states, this reference is meant to supplement, not replace, larger standard works (e.g., *Perry's Chemical Engineer's Handbook*).

It is divided into four main sections: equipment design, process design, plant design, and operations. Each is further divided into subsections and units. For example, under "Equipment Design" is the "Pump" subsection. Under this heading the user will find such units as affinity laws, horsepower, efficiency, minimum flow, general suction system, suction system NPSH with dissolved gas, larger impeller, and construction materials.

There are approximately 200 topical units. For each, there are a minimum of often-excellent text, clearly labeled diagrams that are large enough to see (often not found in other works), nomograms, formulas, and tables of values. Appended to each is a two- to three-item list of sources. Appendix 3, "Do-It-Yourself Shortcut Methods," is a reprint of the editor's 1985 American Society for Engineering Education (ASEE) conference paper on "how classic shortcut design methods can be developed, and [to] encourage new and better ones."

The size mitigates against tucking this title into a pocket, although it is softbound. The editor wisely chose a readable font size versus the convenience of a smaller work.—**John M. Robson**

ELECTRIC ENGINEERING AND ELECTRONICS

1651. **Electric Light & Power U.S. Electric Utility Industry Directory, 1995.** 4th ed. Jonelle Guy and others, eds. Tulsa, Okla., PennWell Publishing, 1994. 955p. index. $165.00pa. ISSN 1058-2479.

With the 4th edition of this directory, PennWell continues its coverage of the electric power industry in detail. The directory consists of eight sections: holding companies; investor-owned electric utilities; municipal or other publicly owned electric utilities; rural electric cooperatives; federal, state, and district systems; commissions and power pools; Canadian electric utilities; and regulatory agencies. The entries are listed alphabetically within states in each section. Directory information includes name, address, and telecommunications numbers; executives; financial data such as assets, long-term debt, and equity; physical data such as peak demand, sales, customers, generation, transmission mileage, interconnections, substations, and generation plants. Indexes by company, and company by type of utility, personnel, and geographic area are available to help the user locate specific information.

Definitions of the types of electric power utilities in each section would be helpful to the user. Holding companies always seem to be a problem in utility directories; there are not many listed here. In the investor-owned section, gross holding company revenues for some of the utilities are given, but these holding companies are not listed in the holding company section. The amount of information provided for each entry varies, since not all of the utilities companies supply all of the requested information. There is some lack of quality control in the listings. For example, in the investor-owned electric utility section, Peco Energy Co. has two listings following each other. One listing is probably supposed to be Peco Energy Power Co., which is not found in the index.

The electric power industry is rapidly restructuring. Information on nonregulated subsidiaries would be of interest in new editions of the directory. PennWell, well known for its petroleum industry directories, also has resources in the electric power industry, since it publishes *Electric Light & Power* and *Power Engineering*. This directory provides comprehensive coverage of the industry and should serve as another valuable directory of the industry.—**Anne C. Roess**

1652. **Electric Light & Power U.S. Non-Utility Power Directory, 1995.** Kharma Amos and others, eds. Tulsa, Okla., PennWell Publishing, 1994. 505p. index. $195.00pa. ISSN 1079-3631.

This new PennWell directory covers the U.S. nonutility power industry by listing more than 1,400 plants, 500 ownership/operating companies, and 3,200 service companies that are active in or serve this industry. The directory consists of four sections: plant listings; owners and operators; service and supply companies (service, supply, engineering, and construction companies, manufacturers, and miscellaneous); and associations and commissions. The listing of plants includes qualifying facilities, cogenerators, small power producers, resource recovery plants, independent power producers, and electric wholesale generators.

Plants are listed alphabetically within states by plant names rather than by owner or operator. However, the owners and operators section allows the user to locate a specific plant by looking at the plants listed under each company name. There are also indexes by company, personnel, and geographic area. Plant information covers key personnel and physical data such as plant type, status, inservice date, fuel, rating, capacity, and owner/operator. Definitions of the various types of plants would be helpful to the user. Not all of the information entered for each plant is defined, so the user may need some knowledge of the industry.

This directory fills the need for information on the nonutility generating companies in the rapidly restructuring electric power industry. PennWell has resources in the electric power industry since it published *Electric Light & Power* and *Power Engineering*. The directory provides comprehensive coverage of the industry and will serve as another valuable directory of the industry.—**Anne C. Roess**

1653. Pasahow, Edward. **Electronics Pocket Reference.** 2d ed. New York, McGraw-Hill, 1994. 496p. illus. maps. index. $24.95pa. ISBN 0-07-048737-5.

This handy title belongs in the shirt pockets of trade school students and trade technicians rather than merely being on the shelves of the libraries serving them. (Perhaps this is the reason the 1985 version under a slightly different title was never reviewed in ARBA.) While one can rarely quibble with this publisher's handbooks, calling the mathematics section "Electronics Mathematics" is a bit much.

Illustrative of the Asiatic bias in semiconductors is that of 17 manufacturers listed on pages 73-74: 8 are from the Far East and 1 is from Canada. Some of the layouts are highly reduced (after all, page size is $3\frac{1}{2}$-by-$5\frac{1}{2}$ inches), but most users will have a magnifying glass on their benches. All the usual topics and tables are present save for trigonometric ones built into calculators. The reference is highly recommended.

—**Eugene B. Jackson**

ENVIRONMENTAL ENGINEERING

1654. **Directory of Hazardous Waste Services, 1994-1995.** 5th ed. Lori Brooks and others, eds. Don Mills, Ont., Southam, 1994. 1v. (various paging). index. $95.00pa. ISBN 0-919217-81-8.

One of the offshoots of the world's increasing concern with environmental pollution, and the mounting volume of legislation and bureaucracy designed to combat it, is the dramatic growth of what one may call the "pollution industry." Realizing that there is a huge potential profit to be made by providing the vast range of goods and services applicable to environmental mitigation, entrepreneurs as well as established companies in many fields have moved to fill the gap, from consulting services to pollution monitoring devices, waste disposal systems, engineering contractors, and legal advice services. Countless companies stand ready to help for a profit: The only problem is how to identify and contact them.

Canada is one of the world's most environmentally aware nations, and this directory, now in its 5th edition, would seem indispensable to any organization concerned with the country's environmental quality. Providers are listed alphabetically in 5 chapters (companies, law firms, associations, libraries, government departments), and then reclassified into 38 categories and arranged by province and city. Addresses, telephone and fax numbers, contact persons, and areas of special expertise are provided. This is a necessary reference for anyone professionally concerned with the Canadian environment.

—James R. McDonald

GENETIC ENGINEERING

1655. Dibner, Mark D. **Biotechnology Guide U.S.A.: Companies, Data, and Analysis.** 3d ed. Research Triangle Park, N.C., Institute for Biotechnology Information; distr., Phoenix, Ariz., Oryx Press, 1995. 692p. index. $249.00pa. ISBN 1-886041-02-4.

The 1st edition (1988) of this relatively unique guide was reviewed in ARBA 89 (see entry 212). Since that date, and that of the 2d edition (1991), the biotechnology industry has undergone massive changes. As the preface to the 3d edition states, "At the end of 1994, the picture has changed dramatically. The fortunes of many companies have changed, many biotechnology-derived therapeutics have shown disappointing results in clinical trials, and investor confidence has been shaken" (p. ix). Regardless, the editors believe the information contained in this expensive and comprehensive volume is essential. Therefore, the Institute of Biotechnology Information (Research Triangle Park, N.C.) has revised the last edition completely using other major sources.

The new volume contains more than twice the companies included in the 1st edition, and is organized in a number of ways to retrieve appropriate information. Sections 2 and 3 identify biotechnology firms and other companies that have significant biotechnical interests. Section 4 provides a geographical breakdown; section 5 displays the companies by interest (e.g., aquaculture, cell culture, cosmetics/health/beauty products, energy, medical devices, reagents, vaccines), while section 6 describes mergers, acquisitions, and partnerships in the field. Finally, section 7 provides a thorough analysis of the industry that includes an array of information ranging from financing, employee numbers, research and development budgets, revenues, and strategic actions to a comparison of United States, Japanese, and Western European technology. Useful appendixes add such information as "dead companies," name changes, references, and commonly used abbreviations; the volume ends with a basic index of companies.

The preceding paragraph cannot completely reflect all of the information found in this work, which is built on the 2 directories of companies (biotechnology and others with major involvements)—these 2 sections fill only 284 pages of the 692-page volume. However, these two directories provide essential company information such as address, telephone number, officers, date founded, classification, technologies used, and products in research and development as well as, in some entries, financial data. Obviously, the remaining pages are used to cross-reference the two major sections as well as supply what the editors refer to as "strategic business information" (p. ix). At the same time, the high cost of this information in addition to its temporal nature in the volatile industry encourages purchase only by specialized collections.

—Laurel Grotzinger

1656. **Human Gene Mapping 1994: A Compendium.** A. Jamie Cuticchia, ed. Baltimore, Md., Johns Hopkins University Press, 1995. 1218p. index. $95.00pa. ISBN 0-8018-5180-7. ISSN 1074-5505.

This snapshot of the current state of the human gene map is for those researchers who want an overview of what has happened recently. As in previous compendiums, this report presents a summary of the marker and selected related literature citations for the mapping reagents covered. Citations and markers for most current data are available electronically through either the World Wide Web or by having an account at one of the Genome Data Base (GDB) nodes. Oddly, the exact Uniform Resource Locators (URL) for the GDB are not given; however, several other related sites such as the Image Consortium <http://www-bio.llnl.gov/bbrp/genome.html.> are provided.

The majority of the text consists of reports of chromosomes 1-22, the X and Y genetic constitution committee, and the committees on human mitochondrial DNA and neoplasia. Indexes are by gene and D-segment. This very specialized publication is of limited use to most libraries.—**Susan B. Ardis**

1657. Kahl, Günter. **The Dictionary of Gene Technology.** New York, VCH, 1995. 550p. illus. $90.00. ISBN 3-527-30005-8.

This dictionary defines more than 4,000 terms concerning the modern multidisciplinary science of gene technology, which is a method of changing gene structure or designing and constructing new genes. The definitions are clear and complete, some in one sentence, others of a paragraph-to-a-page length. Illustrations or chemical formulas and structures that accompany the definitions are found on nearly every page. Tables are also included; for example, three tables are provided for amino acids, rare amino acids, and nonprotein amino acids. Acronyms are also defined (e.g., "BLE: see basal level element"). Cross-references are amply provided to connect related terms. An appendix includes units and conversion factors, and tabular information on restriction endonucleases.

Dictionaries are especially useful for newly emerging fields such as gene technology. They are not only valuable for students, but also for those involved in learning and researching in the area. Because this is a multidisciplinary science, it is helpful to a broad range of professionals—from geneticists, microbiologists, and chemists to bioengineers, and helpful regarding ethical aspects of the subject.

This is a comprehensive, up-to-date, and well-illustrated dictionary on one of the most important new sciences today. The work is highly recommended for academic and large public libraries, and for special or industrial libraries involved in this field of research.—**Diane B. Rhodes**

1658. Rapp, Barbara A., comp. and ed. **Biotechnology Information Sources: North and South America.** Medford, N.J., Learned Information, 1994. 144p. index. $32.50pa. ISBN 0-938734-81-4.

This directory provides eight value-packed chapters focused entirely on biotechnology information resources. Each chapter is devoted to a particular type of information, such as primary research databases, journals and newsletters, and patents. Each chapter begins with a clear, thorough, descriptive introduction to the resource type. Individual resource entries are also thoroughly described. The chapter on Internet resources is international in scope. There is an index, an extensive bibliography, and appended lists of online service producers, CD-ROM and magnetic tape providers, and publishers. Because of its user-friendly nature, all types of libraries will find something valuable here. For academic libraries, it is highly recommended as an indispensable resource for collection development and reference service.

—**Barbara Delzell**

1659. Walker, John M., and Michael Cox. **The Language of Biotechnology: A Dictionary of Terms.** 2d ed. Washington, D.C., American Chemical Society, 1995. 296p. illus. $49.95. ISBN 0-8412-2982-1.

Since the 1st edition of this dictionary was published in 1988, there have been a number of changes in the field of biotechnology, primarily in its size and commercial importance. The current edition consists of nearly 2,000 entries that relate in some way to the practical application of biological systems to manufacturing and service industries and management of the environment. The diversity of biotechnology is amply shown by the subjects covered, which include waste treatment and odor reduction, the production of reagents for the diagnosis and treatment of diseases, genetic engineering, and enzyme reactors. A nice touch is the inclusion of a pronunciation guide for each term, including abbreviations such as FET or IgG. The definitions are clear, and about 10 percent have illustrations or mathematical formulas.

Libraries that purchased William Bains's *Biotechnology from A to Z* (see ARBA 94, entry 1790) will find this volume to be more up-to-date and comprehensive. Published by the American Chemical Society, this book is a good value.—**Susan B. Ardis**

MATERIALS SCIENCE

1660. **Alloy Finder.** [CD-ROM]. Materials Park, Ohio, ASM International, 1994. Minimum system requirements: IBM or compatible 386. Double-speed CD-ROM drive. Windows 3.1. 8MB memory. 12.5MB hard disk space. Windows-compatible mouse. $1,200.00. ISBN 0-87170-547-8.

This highly specialized CD-ROM is a machine hog. It is hard to imagine how it would perform on the stated minimal 386 PC when it was so slow on a Pentium 486 with 12MB memory and a disk drive with more than 20MB of free disk space. This should not surprise any users as the information included with the disc states quite clearly that some "operations are both disk- and processor-intensive"—how true. The installation seemed easy until the disc was installed; then, unfortunately, in order to make good use of the data, the user needs knowledge of Borland's Paradox for Windows (a database program). This is not a program every installer or user would be familiar with, and the README.TXT was not helpful in this regard. Consequently, libraries contemplating this title should also purchase and have handy Paradox's manuals, especially if this database is not used much on-site. Several functions were not activated on the test disc and could not be evaluated, such as unified numbering system searches. There were a number of "errors that will be fixed in the next update."

The actual information on the disc comes from a variety of sources, including manufacturers' datasheets, ASTM, SAE, and some metals handbook standbys: *Woldman's Engineering Alloys* (8th ed.; see entry 1671), *Worldwide Guide to Equivalent Irons and Steels* (3d ed.; see ARBA 94. entry 1796), and *Worldwide Guide to Equivalent Nonferrous Metals and Alloys* (2d ed.; see ARBA 89, entry 1501). Searching is possible by manufacturer, proprietary name, number, and keyword. One of the most useful searching functions is keyword by alloy composition. This last search is extremely time-consuming—the insert suggests "you get a cup of coffee" while waiting for results. The data are then presented in a form that can be manipulated by the user familiar with Paradox.

For most libraries, this title is too specialized and difficult to use. Even the largest engineering libraries would be better served at this time by selecting from *Woldman's Alloy Digest* and *ASM Materials Handbook* (paper or CD-ROM). Frankly, this test database did not install or run as easily as their *ASM Handbook CD-ROM* ($250 with purchase of 10th edition of the *Handbook*). Metallurgical or aerospace libraries, or materials specifiers who can afford to either network this or put it on a stand-alone station, may find it useful.—**Susan B. Ardis**

1661. **ASM Handbook. Volume 5: Surface Engineering.** By the ASM International Handbook Committee. Materials Park, Ohio, ASM International, 1994. 1039p. illus. index. $140.00. ISBN 0-87170-384-X.

This handbook is a continuation of *Metals Handbook*, which has been published since 1948. The name was changed with the 10th edition to reflect broader coverage. One oddity is that only the first 2 volumes of this edition carry the 10th edition statement; this notation was dropped with the later volumes (2, 4, 18), and now volume 5. This, along with the volumes being issued as they are published, creates some user confusion—volume 18 has been published, but not volume 7.

Fortunately, volume 5 has been completely revised and expanded as befits this important topic. Now more than 1,000 pages are devoted to a variety of surface treatments, from specific finishing methods such as shot peening to chemical vapor deposition processes. In keeping with the new title, Volume 5 contains surfacing information on nonmetallic materials such as ceramics and carbon-carbon composites, as well as the traditional and nonferrous metals. A definite improvement, along with the extensive revisions, is the addition of more references. For example, in the previous edition *ion plating* covered fewer than 5 pages and had 10 references. The new revision has 9 pages and 115 references. This is a substantial improvement because handbooks are often used as entry points for additional information. Some of the references could have been more complete; for example, in the section on "Compliant Wipe Solvent Cleaners," the authors cite specific standards by number and subject, and in the references they cite only the *Annual Book of ASTM Standards for 1994*. This is not very helpful; while users need the relevant standard number, they also need the title and date. In other chapters specific standards with titles, numbers, and issuance dates are cited.

Users can also buy an index for the entire set (9th and 10th editions) in either paper or CD-ROM. The CD-ROM indexes other ASM books, as well as this handbook. Purchasers of the entire set definitely need an index. This volume (and complete set) should be added to any collection with an interest in plating, rust prevention, brazing, painting, and a host of other metals (and ceramic) topics.—**Susan B. Ardis**

1662. **ASM Specialty Handbook: Stainless Steels.** J. R. Davis, ed. Materials Park, Ohio, ASM International, 1994. 577p. illus. index. $151.00. ISBN 0-87170-503-6.

Like previous ASM Specialty Handbook volumes, this encyclopedic work has been carefully organized to provide convenient access to much up-to-date information about its subject materials. Subject matter, contained in 27 chapters and grouped in 5 sections, was gathered from approximately 65 review articles that have previously appeared in various ASM Handbooks. In each case, the original review articles, as well as numerous references to primary sources, are cited. Wrought and cast stainless steels are included, as are powder-metallurgy stainless steels, stainless-steel cladding, and weld overlays. Among the topics covered are metallurgical and physical properties of all kinds, fabrication and finishing techniques, corrosion behavior, applications, and recycling technologies. The sections are of uniformly high quality, and all are generously illustrated with photographs, tables, and graphs. Nearly 37, 3-column pages are devoted to an extensive subject index. The work will serve as a useful reference as well as provide an excellent introduction to the field and its subdisciplines.—**John U. Trefny**

1663. **ASTM Standards Source.** [CD-ROM]. Philadelphia, Pa., ASTM, 1994. Minimum system requirements: IBM or compatible 386 (486 recommended). Double speed CD-ROM drive with MS-DOS CD-ROM Extensions 2.1. DOS 3.1. 490K low-level memory. VGA monitor. HP Deskjet or compatible printer (HP Laserjet recommended). $4,800.00/yr.

Anyone who has dealt with the ASTM Standards understands that it is past time for them to be available electronically. The CD-ROM version of the ASTM Standards is a welcome and overdue addition. The facsimile copies of the actual standards are well done, and the print quality from them is excellent. The problem with the package begins with the installation.

The CD-ROM version has a straightforward and intuitive installation. For any library or information center that does more than one thing with its computer hardware, the installation rings every bell and whistle in the arsenal. The days of stand-alone programs should have died long ago. This is a DOS-based program that wants your entire machine! With an imprint date of 1994, there is no excuse why the front-end for the standards is not graphically based and Windows-compatible. The result of the decision to use DOS-based programming is that libraries and information centers must dedicate an entire machine to the program. The good points to the search engine, which are numerous, are lost in the lack of interface that would allow graphical capabilities and multitasking.

The demonstration disc offers a limited database from which to search. As noted above, the search engine is satisfactory for a DOS system (it would have been first-rate five or more years ago). The search engine is quick and clean, but the demonstration disc only contains 100 sample standards, so the efficiency of the system is difficult to judge. Boolean searching is straightforward. The system "hides" the standard from the user unless they actively request it. The user is given an abstract of the actual standard and can then make a determination as to relevance. Requesting the actual standard brings up a facsimile image of the standard. Printing is slow given the nature of the facsimile image but produces high-quality output.

The full package has an index disc and six additional discs. The 6 additional discs contain the facsimile page images of 9,100 current ASTM Standards. For network users, it appears that the full package can be used over a network, but this is unclear from the documentation, and it is unclear what the level of staff interaction will be. The index disc will need to be removed and swapped with one of the six additional discs at some point.

Having ASTM Standards in CD-ROM format is a major step forward. One wishes that the front-end for the standards was also a major step forward. ASTM can and should offer better integration with current operating systems. The price of the full package should also include the cost of a dedicated machine. Despite all the difficulties the antiquated front-end presents, this is a significant advance from the paper copies of the ASTM Standards. This package is recommended for any information center that uses the ASTM Standards heavily and can afford to dedicate computer equipment and staff to the package.—**C. D. Hurt**

1664. **The Encyclopedia of Advanced Materials.** David Bloor and others, eds. Tarrytown, N.Y., Pergamon Press/Elsevier Science, 1994. 4v. illus. index. $1,600.00/set. ISBN 0-08-040606-8.

To invest such money in a four-volume reference set is quite a commitment for most libraries. Science and engineering librarians will want to give serious consideration to the *Encyclopedia of Advanced Materials.* Intended to complement the *Encyclopedia of Materials Science and Engineering* (see ARBA 90, entry 1599, and ARBA 87, entry 1570), the tool is the best succinct yet scholarly reference treatment of the burgeoning area of materials science that underpins much of the technological revolution occurring now. The editors define advanced materials as materials for which primary consideration is given to the systematic synthesis and control of the structure that provide a finely tailored set of properties for difficult applications. The emphasis is on integrating the synthesis, evaluation, properties, and performance of new and developing materials.

There are approximately 475 signed articles, which average 6 pages each. Systeme International d'Unites (International System of Units) are standard. Where the Imperial is used, SI equivalents are given. To make the tool more useful, there is a substantial index, both in-text and end-of-text cross references, and a classified list of the articles divided into 28 broad subjects, providing further topical coherence. The appended bibliographies list an average of 12-16 references. The work is well illustrated with quality black-and-white photographs in addition to the tables and figures of compound structures.—**John M. Robson**

1665. **Engineered Materials Handbook.** desk ed. By ASM International Handbook Committee. Materials Park, Ohio, ASM International, 1995. 1317p. illus. index. $154.00. ISBN 0-87170-283-5.

The American Society for Metals (ASM) has, for the last eight years, created a series entitled *Engineered Materials Handbook* (EMH) to parallel its multivolume *Metals Handbook* (10th ed.; see ARBA 92, entries 1618-1619) that covers nonmetallic materials. The book under review is based on the four titles of that series: *Composites* (2d ed.; see ARBA 93, entry 1606), *Engineering Plastics* (2d ed.; see ARBA 95, entry 1636); *Adhesives and Sealants* (1990), and *Ceramics and Glasses* (1991). In addition, it draws on ASM's volume, *Packaging,* from its *Electronic Materials Handbook.* It is meant to be a single-volume tool that accompanies the *Metals Handbook Desk Reference.* The EMH contains the most useful information on the "properties, selection, processing, and applications of the most widely used nonmetallic engineering materials."

The two classes of materials treated in-depth are polymeric materials and glasses and ceramics. The basic construction materials of wood and stone are not the focus of the editors and have limited treatment. The work is divided into 12 main sections, ranging from an extensive glossary to a general overview, properties of plastics, polymer-matrix composites, advanced ceramics, and glasses. It is further subdivided into approximately 70 subsections. The information is presented primarily in metric units with conversion to English units.

The work has an abundance of tables, illustrations, and figures, all easy to interpret and closely tied to the text. Each of the subsections has an extensive bibliography leading the user to underlying research and more extensive data explication. The 80-page index is excellent, quickly taking the reader to needed information. This is a significant distillation of the information found in the volumes listed above and an essential purchase.—**John M. Robson**

1666. **English-German Dictionary of Materials and Process Engineering. Englisch-Deutsches Worterbuch der Industriellen Werkstofftechnik.** By Claus G. Goetzel and Lilo K. Goetzel. Deutsche Gesellschaft fur Materialkunde e.V., ed. Munich, Hanser Publishers; distr., Cincinnati, Ohio, Hanser/Gardner, 1995. 753p. $97.50. ISBN 1-56990-148-1.

Prepared by two well-known scholars in the field of materials science, this book is a by-product of several decades of teaching and translating technical literature. This title also incorporates many examples in the development of polymer chemistry, advanced ceramics, electronics, and other new materials, as well as more recent ecological considerations for the protection of the environment. The work should be of interest to all scholars active in this field.—**Bohdan S. Wynar**

1667. **Handbook of Corrosion Data.** 2d ed. Bruce D. Craig and David S. Anderson, eds. Materials Park, Ohio, ASM International, 1995. 998p. $188.00. ISBN 0-87170-518-4.

Similar to its predecessor (see ARBA 91, entry 1624), the text is divided into two parts: "Corrosion of Metals and Alloys" and the larger section, "Corrosion Media." As with the earlier edition, the data are organized by chemical compound rather than by alloy or metal system, and the data for each agent/compound are presented in tabular form. Generally, each chemical agent is preceded by two or three introductory paragraphs; however, some important ones, such as hydrofluoric and sulfuric acid, have extensive multipage introductions.

This new edition has been greatly expanded in several obvious ways. First, there are more than 200 additional pages; second, part 2 has many more entries. A quick count of entries from "Acetaldehyde to Gelatin" shows 43 additional corrosion agents. Some of the additions include: ammonium oxalate, chromium sulfate, ferric nitrate, and gallic acid. As befits more information, at least 95 additional reference numbers have been added and *every* tabular entry is given a reference number to the "Cited References" section. While most references consist of only 1 title, some have up to 10 different citations. This is helpful to users needing to verify or expand the data.

There are several niggling points—plastics, rubbers, or other nonmetallics are not covered, and there is no general index. However, the table of contents serves as the entry point because each chemical agent is listed. The authors suggest that this book should be used in conjunction with *Corrosion Data Survey* (6th ed., NACE, 1985). However, there is no comparison between this and other seeming competitors such as *Corrosion Resistance Tables* (rev. ed, Marcel Dekker, 1991), *Corrosion and Corrosion Protection Handbook* (2d ed.; see ARBA 90, entry 1602), or even *Metals Handbook* (10th ed.; see ARBA 92, entries 1618-1619). This handbook is much more in-depth and easier to use, and the data are better referenced. Consequently, this should be found in any collection interested in metals or corrosion.—**Susan B. Ardis**

1668. Lawal, Ibironke O., comp. **Metalworking in Africa South of the Sahara: An Annotated Bibliography.** Westport, Conn., Greenwood Press, 1995. 270p. index. (African Special Bibliographic Series, no.19). $79.50. ISBN 0-313-29324-4.

Lawal, a librarian at the University of Virginia, has compiled the 19th title in Greenwood's African Special Bibliographic Series. A 20-year project, the bibliography responds to the interdisciplinary nature of African studies, covering the fields of archaeology, anthropology, ethnology, mining, history, art, and religion. The topics covered include the origins, spread, mining, smelting, smithing, use, functions, aesthetics, significance, and impact of various metals and their alloys on African culture. Most earlier bibliographies covered specific metals, such as gold, or were not annotated; thus, Lawal makes a significant scholarly contribution by being more comprehensive.

Approximately half of the entries have annotations that are 10 to 20 words long. These are primarily in English and French, although German and Russian items are also included. The book is arranged by nine geographical regions and subdivided under each by country. At the country level, entries are arranged alphabetically by author. Publication dates are primarily from the mid-nineteenth century to as late as 1992, and media are also covered. The index provides a useful access to materials by metal type and ethnic group. Lawal has done a commendable job, one that no electronic search of numerous databases could equal.
—**John M. Robson**

1669. **Materials Properties Handbook: Titanium Alloys.** Rodney Boyer, Gerhard Welsch, and E. W. Collings, eds. Materials Park, Ohio, ASM International, 1994. 1176p. illus. $245.00. ISBN 0-87170-481-1.

The ASM has begun an ambitious expansion of its publications with this first volume of the *Materials Properties Handbook* series. The titles will reflect the content of comprehensive electronic databases devoted to the properties and processing information on alloy-specific engineering materials. Titanium was selected for the first volume because of the relatively small number of major alloys. The scope of the work was then expanded to cover virtually all known titanium alloys up to early 1993. For most alloys, the reader will find sections on mechanical, fatigue, fracture, thermal, corrosion, and forming properties; heat treatment; and forging. For the most widely used, the data provided are more extensive. For example, Ti-Al-4V is given 150 pages. For those with little application to date, the data are much less. The title is meant to be a ready-reference for the scientist and engineer. Where more detailed data are needed, the reader is given references to other works. A final section provides recommended procedures in the areas of forging, forming, casting, powder metallurgy, and welding. The book is well bound, clearly printed, and conveniently arranged.—**John M. Robson**

1670. Todd, Robert H., Dell K. Allen, and Leo Alting. **Manufacturing Processes Reference Guide.** New York, Industrial Press, 1994. 486p. illus. index. $42.95. ISBN 0-8311-3049-0.

This is a reference book that fills a real need; it describes more than 130 manufacturing processes used in industry today. Some of the processes described are sputtering, sandblasting, extrusion molding, and vertical boring. While not exhaustive, this work does describe the most common processes. Each entry is heavily illustrated and includes process characteristics, process schematics, and workpiece geometry. Where relevant, time calculations, cost elements, and safety factors are also provided. Illustrations are clear with parts well marked, and the text is well laid out. The clear language can be understood by anyone at a ninth-grade reading level. Many users will appreciate inclusion of bulleted lists and charts.

Here is a book that should be in any technical library, from an academic engineering library to a community college collection. It would also be at home in any medium-sized public library or in any library that gets questions on joining (brazing and welding); surface coating (spraying, vacuum metallizing); or consolidation (mold casting). Design and manufacturing libraries may want several copies—one for the reference shelf and one for circulation. This is an excellent guide at a reasonable price.—**Susan B. Ardis**

1671. **Woldman's Engineering Alloys.** 8th ed. John P. Frick, ed. Materials Park, Ohio, ASM International, 1994. 1374p. $156.00. ISBN 0-87170-544-3.

This edition of *Engineering Alloys* continues the quality and comprehensiveness that engineers have come to expect from the ASM. The work is divided into three sections: alloy data, manufacturer information, and 33 tables. The alloys are listed alphabetically, either under a common name or a trademark. Numerical titles are listed in the beginning. Under each alloy is a statement of ownership (if applicable), a chemical formula with stated range percentages, common applications, and relevant standards if established. The user is also told if the alloy is obsolete. Cross-references are used. The data given were confirmed by the various manufacturing companies. The 40 pages of tables are a useful collection of specifications and property data applicable to various classes of alloys. This book is a useful tool for specialists as a reference in the laboratory.—**John M. Robson**

MECHANICAL ENGINEERING

1672. Berke, Danielle, Ann Chambers, and Susan D. Kerr. **Power Industry Abbreviator.** Tulsa, Okla., PennWell Publishing, 1995. 314p. $29.95pa. ISBN 0-87814-444-7.

This handy minivolume is intended to provide acronym information to technical and nontechnical employees of the power industry. Convenient in size and sturdily bound, this reference tool guides the user through the maze of acronyms that dominate the literature of power engineering. Primarily it is a two-way dictionary: term-to-acronym and acronym-to-term. In addition, the authors have appended an assortment of other data such as the stock exchange symbols for power companies, various conversion factors, mathematical signs and symbols, and a small spelling guide with both technical and common English words that trouble most users. The authors are professional writers and editors active with the technical and trade journals of the industry.—**John M. Robson**

1673. **Mechanical Engineer's Reference Book.** 12th ed. Edward H. Smith, ed. Warrendale, Pa., Society of Automotive Engineers, 1994. 1v. (various paging). illus. index. $155.00. ISBN 1-56091-450-5.

Fifty contributors, all from Great Britain, have made this 12th edition a very large volume. A great deal of information covers solid state electronics, control, and tribology, all well illustrated. Generally, each of the 19 chapters includes a recent bibliography. All too often, however, contributors have been allowed to indulge in sermons and lofty generality, and this severely limits the usefulness of the book. As an example of the latter, an important section on control engineering begins with "Control Engineering is based on the linear systems analysis associated with the development of feedback theory." Nonetheless, this can be a valuable introduction to topics that an individual is not familiar with. [R: Choice, Jan 95, p. 820]
—**Robert B. McKee**

1674. South, David W., and Richard H. Ewert. **Encyclopedic Dictionary of Gears and Gearing.** New York, McGraw-Hill, 1995. 414p. illus. $54.50. ISBN 0-07-059796-0.

This ready-reference source on gears and gearing was designed as an on-the-job aid for the general engineer or technician. The dictionary includes new terminology and covers everything from the fundamentals of gearing to advanced design concepts.

The entries are listed alphabetically, and many provide *see* and *see also* cross-references to give users old and new terms for the same thing to help them avoid confusion. A variety of illustrations enhance the usefulness of this dictionary. Six appendixes define nomenclature specific to grinding, gaging, hob, gear shaving cutter, milling-cutter, and broaching.

The easy-to-use format and clear print make this a useful work for people on the job as well as for public, special, or academic libraries that assist users with information on the basics of the gear industry. As a resource it would be an excellent companion to *Dudley's Gear Handbook* (see ARBA 92, entry 1624) or to the *Handbook of Practical Gear Design* (see ARBA 85, entry 1515).—**Diane J. Turner**

1675. Weingartner, Clarence, comp. **Machinists' Ready Reference.** 8th ed. Ann Arbor, Mich., Prakken, 1994. 294p. index. $14.50 spiralbound. ISBN 0-911168-90-7.

This book compacts a large amount of useful information in a very small package. Designed for the apprentice machinist, the work consists of the tables, charts, and tabular data most likely to be required. It is well printed—the spiral binding, however, is not likely to endear itself to librarians! The information applies mainly to conventional metalworking tools and techniques (lathes, drill presses, milling machines, and so forth). Numerical control, CAD/CAM, and other more modern approaches are not treated. The book is recommended for purchase by libraries supporting vocational courses in machine operation, and for individuals pursuing this type of training.—**Edwin D. Posey**

PETROLEUM ENGINEERING

1676. Langenkamp, R. D. **Handbook of Oil Industry Terms & Phrases.** 5th ed. Tulsa, Okla., PennWell Books, 1994. 512p. $49.95pa. ISBN 0-87814-421-8.

The oil industry is well known for its own highly specialized and inventive terminology. Many new words and phrases have been added to the vocabulary since the 4th edition was published 10 years ago. Nearly 33 percent of the entries of this edition are new. Like its predecessor, this is an unpretentious book with a lot of humor. What other industry has quite so many interesting terms (e.g., snubbers, bristle pigs, dope choppers, mud cups, scouts, and moose and goose men)? With creativity like this, the need for definitions is strong—no one doing business in this field would want to be a boll weevil (an inexperienced worker).

Not only is new slang being developed, but new scientific and technical terms are also coming into common usage. While the new vocabulary is important, one of the major uses of this book is to document and define historical slang and terminology. For example: What is a doormat in the oil business? The term was used in the early days of U.S. exploration, prior to oil field pooling, to describe a piece of land just big enough to place an oil rig on it. There is a dated bibliography, the same used for the 4th edition. No entry later than 1962 is included. This book provides an interesting insight into the slang as well as the scientific, technical terminology and the humor of the oil business.—**Susan B. Ardis**

PLANT ENGINEERING

1677. **Standard Handbook of Plant Engineering.** 2d ed. Robert C. Rosaler, ed. New York, McGraw-Hill, 1995. 1v. (various paging). illus. index. $104.50. ISBN 0-07-052164-6.

This all-encompassing handbook for plant management starts from the ground up, with considerations for planning the site and the physical facility for an industrial plant, and continues with environmental and practical matters such as power requirements, heating/cooling, and water use. The characteristics of the operation of a plant, including materials handling, hydraulic and pneumatic systems, noise control, and safety and sanitation, are the focus of much of the work. The final sections deal with cleaning, maintenance and repair technology, lubrication requirements, and corrosion control. New to this edition is material on facility maintenance and workplace safety.

Chapters vary since each is provided by a different contributor, but typically include an introduction and glossary, a clearly focused and readable text, numerous illustrations and tables, sources of additional information, and a bibliography. The latter tends to be the weakest offering in some chapters, since many show no updated publication dates since the last edition. But overall the collection of information in this volume is impressive and widely useful beyond its intended target audience. Of particular note are the charts and tables of data. Although many are technical, others are practical, such as troubleshooting electric motors or floor-cleaning problems and time estimates for vacuuming. The index is legible and quite serviceable.

Recommended for any engineering or technical collection, and beneficial for management and architecture users, the book will also provide value for any library serving those from the business or industrial community. It is a strong basic work and will fulfill a variety of reference needs.—**Gary R. Cocozzoli**

TOOLS

1678. **ASM Specialty Handbook: Tool Materials.** J. R. Davis, ed. Materials Park, Ohio, ASM International, 1995. 501p. illus. index. $159.00. ISBN 0-87170-545-1.

The ASM Specialty Handbook series primarily brings together information found in the multivolume *ASM Handbook*, formerly the *Metals Handbook*. The third title in the series, *Tool Materials*, also relies mainly on relevant articles and data in various volumes of the latest edition of the *ASM Handbook*, supplemented by lists of references of widely varying lengths to other books, articles, and standards. This reference title is meant to answer questions or pose the problems in selecting the materials suitable for a particular tool. It brings together in a convenient format information on the applications, advantages and limitations, properties, tool geometries, and typical operating parameters for high-speed tool steels, cobalt alloys, cemented carbides, cermets, ceramics, and ultrahard tool materials and wear-resistant coatings.

The longest section deals with summarizing the selection of ferrous and nonferrous materials for hot-work, cold-work tooling, and plastic molding. Other topics include the wear and failure of tools and dies, heat treatment, and secondary processing of tool and die steels. There are numerous photographs, diagrams, and tables for each entry. The editor has also created a lengthy index that would have been enhanced by a greater use of *see* and *see also* references. This is an excellent single-volume reference useful for industry and academic research.—**John M. Robson**

1679. Lee, Leonard. **The Complete Guide to Sharpening.** Newtown, Conn., Taunton Press, 1995. 245p. illus. index. $34.95. ISBN 1-56158-067-8.

Nothing is more frustrating for an amateur woodworker than ruining a beautiful piece of wood by the use of a blunt or incorrectly sharpened tool. The author of this book, who is a woodworker and tool maker, feels that sharpening involves common sense, a few basic principles, some standard abrasives, and a few "cunning jigs." To prove this he has produced a well-illustrated and informative book on tool sharpening that will be of value to amateurs, professional woodworkers, and tool collectors. Starting with the basics, he defines sharpness, the physics of severing wood fibers, the metallurgy of tools, abrasives, and various types of sharpening tools. He then systematically covers various woodworking tools such as chisels, planes, knives, saws, axes, and drill bits, and describes how to sharpen them to work best with the type and grain of the wood. The examples pictured are for everyday operations. He also shows how to make special devices and jigs out of available scrap materials for ensuring correct edge shapes and sharpness. Illustrated side panels also relate to the usage history of many of the tools. Appendixes dealing with chip classification and international grit standards, a glossary, and an index also give added value to this excellent reference book.—**Robert J. Havlik**

33 Health Sciences

GENERAL WORKS

Dictionaries and Encyclopedias

1680. Ammer, Christine. **The New A to Z of Women's Health: A Concise Encyclopedia.** 3d ed. New York, Facts on File, 1995. 562p. illus. index. $40.00. ISBN 0-8160-3121-5.

A worthy addition to the genre of women's health literature pioneered by *Our Bodies, Ourselves*, this encyclopedic dictionary has been updated to reflect medical developments in the 1990s, including some entirely new entries, such as alternative medicine and human immunodeficiency virus (HIV). It is written largely in ordinary lay language, with medical terms clearly explained. At the time of the 1st edition (1983), women's health concerns involved the understanding and control of their own bodies. Today, health care and access to health information are of national concern, along with the recognition that women are the major consumers of health care. This 3d edition reflects these and other changing viewpoints. Although a great deal of general information on diseases, treatment, and diet is included, the emphasis is still on obstetrics and gynecology—the reproductive and gender-oriented aspects of women's lives, as well as related subjects, such as sexually transmitted diseases.

Major subject categories in appendix A list many related terms to refer to in the dictionary itself. The more detailed alphabetical index gives page numbers. Although the book claims to supply data on "all aspects of a woman's well-being—from birth to old age," there is a remarkable lack of keywords for easy location of information about aging and the health concerns of older women. Some entries contain statistics of age-related incidence, and there is an excellent article on menopause. There should be more listings similar to those on skin changes that describe what often happens as women get older; geriatric conditions need to be given more emphasis if the claim of "birth to old age" is to be substantiated.

This authoritative book belongs in public and school libraries, and especially in patient education collections in hospitals. It may also be useful as a quick reference for nurses and resident physicians.
—**Harriette M. Cluxton**

1681. **Encyclopedia of Home Care for the Elderly.** Ada Romaine-Davis, Jennifer Boondas, and Ayeliffe Lenihan, eds. Westport, Conn., Greenwood Press, 1995. 436p. index. $85.00. ISBN 0-313-28532-2.

This is an idiosyncratic collection of 88 short (2- to 5-page), individually authored vignettes on various topics, some of which bear directly on home care for the elderly. While most of the topics are at least potentially relevant to home health care, the essential connections are often missing. A selection on American Indians describes the unique cultural characteristics of the Native American elderly, but draws no implications for home care. The article on Medicare fails to describe the home health benefits included in that program. Similarly, articles on cardiac care and other diseases prevalent among the elderly contain no mention of home care.

The selections are listed alphabetically, but arbitrary titling conventions make it difficult for the reader to find wanted material. The article that describes how home health care agencies are paid is entitled "Home Health Care: Public Policy Issues." This problem may have been avoided with cross-referencing, but there is none. Instead, the editors have provided an appendix that lists entries by topic, but the topical classification is incomplete. However, all is not lost. The book contains a useful appendix listing descriptions of public and private organizations related to home care. Also, despite the lack of overall focus, most of the entries are well written and interesting. [R: LJ, Jan 95, pp. 84-85]—**Bruce Stuart**

1682. **The Marshall Cavendish Encyclopedia of Health.** rev. ed. North Bellmore, N.Y., Marshall Cavendish, 1995. 14v. illus. index. $299.95/set. ISBN 1-85435-203-2.

This edition of the *Encyclopedia of Health* belongs in every high school and middle school library, and wherever youth services are offered. Directed to adolescents, it presents a great deal of health-related information without talking down or preaching to its readers. When medical topics are discussed, the proper terminology is used and clearly explained. General information about the body and how it works; physical and mental illnesses and how they are treated; fitness, diet, sports, and other wellness concerns; sex and substance abuse, and other problems of young people are all intelligently discussed. Topics are arranged alphabetically; their format and length vary considerably. Related items are extensively cross-referenced. The final volume has an outline of first aid procedures and an excellent index to the whole set. Illustrations are copious and of high quality, mostly in color. Regrettably, there are few references. The *Encyclopedia of Health* is highly recommended for its intended audience; adults will also enjoy browsing. (See ARBA 92, entry 1633, for a review of the previous edition.)—**Harriette M. Cluxton**

1683. Walker, Richard. **The Visual Dictionary of the Skeleton.** New York, Dorling Kindersley, 1995. 64p. illus. index. (Eyewitness Visual Dictionaries). $16.95. ISBN 0-7894-0135-5.

Contrary to the impression possibly conveyed by *Visual Dictionary* in the title, this is not juvenile literature, but a book for all ages. Understanding the brief sectional introductions and the specialized vocabulary requires some degree of maturity. The dictionary is the 1st American edition of 1 volume of a British series of illustrated dictionaries, each on a definite subject, not all involving the health sciences. One entitled *The Visual Dictionary of the Human Body* (see ARBA 93, entry 1492) may be most closely related.

The detailed alphabetical index contains anatomical and popular terms, referring to the page where the word appears next to the appropriate illustration. The topics are not discussed in the alphabetical order common to dictionaries; the book may better be described as an atlas. After definitions of *exoskeleton* and *endoskeleton*, varieties are considered. The human skeleton is described throughout the life span. Two facing pages unfold to show one of an adult in a forty-eight-inch space; no actual scale is indicated here or any place in the book.

The next group of pages depict plant skeletons, shells, arthropods, fish, amphibians, reptiles, birds, and mammals. The section on "early human relatives" shows fossil remains, such as "Lucy," or reconstructions. Several pages illustrate the functions of bones and joints. Final sections feature parts of the skeleton—skulls; backbones; the rib cage; the pelvis; and limbs, hands, and feet, comparing forms of these in various animals and explaining their different functions (e.g., bones of the human foot appear with a penguin's foot and a zebra's forelimb).

The quality of the pictures is excellent, and the labeling is satisfactory. This book is highly recommended as a family reference.—**Harriette M. Cluxton**

Directories

1684. **ALA Fingertip Guide to National Health-Information Resources 1995-1996.** reference desk ed. By Beatrice Kovacs. Chicago, American Library Association, 1995. 97p. $12.00pa. ISBN 0-8389-0645-1.

Members of our health-conscious society, including students, are often interested in finding materials on health topics. A great deal of this material, often free, is available from associations involved with specific health problems or diseases. Designed for quick consultation at a library's reference desk, this address and telephone directory with 800-numbers well accomplishes its purpose of providing access to health-related information. The directory is concise, easy to use, and current, and there are plans for regular updating. A subject index and a hot line listing refer to numbered entries, alphabetically arranged, with a marginal note explaining the field of interest (e.g., "Breast Feeding" precedes "La Leche League"). Only national organizations are listed; many, of course, have local affiliates.

Due to its quality and low cost, social workers, educators, and other health counselors may consider the guide for their personal collections. Most libraries serving the general public should find it very useful. Two recent publications, *Healthcare Resource and Reference Guide* (American Medical Association, 1993) and Alan M. Rees's *Consumer Health Information Source Book* (4th ed.; see ARBA 95, entry 1666), may be considered if more information is needed.—**Harriette M. Cluxton**

1685. **Directory of Biomedical and Health Care Grants 1995.** 9th ed. Phoenix, Ariz., Oryx Press, 1994. 662p. index. $84.50pa. ISBN 0-89774-910-3. ISSN 0883-5330.

This is an indispensable guide for researchers in biomedical and health sciences fields, one that is equally valuable to novice researchers who want a survey of funding opportunities and to seasoned veterans who wish to match their programmatic interests to sponsors' objectives. The 9th edition contains an alphabetical list of 3,107 grant programs offered by governmental agencies, foundations, and other private organizations, including relevant international organizations. Each entry contains the following information: the title of the grant; a brief description of the grants program, including objectives and scope of pertinent projects; restrictions on eligibility; requirements for grant candidates; funding amounts; application dates; contact persons with telephone numbers and addresses; and sponsor information. In addition, there are a comprehensive subject index; a list of grants by sponsoring agency; and a list of grants by program type (e.g., awards, basic research grants, research center grants). With this edition, Oryx Press has expanded its focus to include grants designed to promote health care delivery. For online users, Oryx Press offers its Grants database (including all entries in the biomedical and health care directory) on DIALOG. A CD-ROM version is also available from DIALOG (see entry 848).—**Bruce Stuart**

1686. **The Directory of Health Care Professionals, 1995.** Baltimore, Md., HCIA, 1994. 2v. $299.00pa/set. ISBN 1-880678-67-5. ISSN 1049-9253.

This work provides information about more than 7,000 hospitals in the United States. The information is supplemented by HCIA's hospital database, which contains detailed financial and operating information compiled from each hospital's annual Medicare cost report. The directory is divided into two volumes: Volume 1: *Hospitals and Health Care System Professionals*, and Volume 2: *Index of Professionals*. Section A of volume 1 lists more than 183,000 hospital professionals by hospital. These hospitals are arranged alphabetically by city within each particular state. The information provided covers: names of the hospitals; addresses and zip codes; main telephone and fax numbers; number of beds (most listings); system affiliations (if the hospital is affiliated with a health care system, the system name and location are listed); listings of chief administrative officers and chief medical officers; administrative/financial services; clinical services departments/units; and support service departments with their direct telephone numbers. Support service departments include nutrition services, safety and security, and engineering.

Section B consists of two indexes: an alphabetic hospital index and the health care system headquarters index, listing more than 500 system headquarters and more than 3,000 health care system professionals. Entries list the addresses and zip codes; main telephone and fax numbers; lists of chairpersons, CEOs and other health care system officers, as well as participating member hospitals.

The Directory of Health Care Professionals provides data similar to that in *The Register of North American Hospitals* (American Preeminent Registry Publications, 1995) and the *Hospital Phone Book* (U.S. Directory Service, 1993). This work is recommended for college and university libraries and medical libraries.—**Marilynn Green**

1687. **Directory of Medical & Dental Schools Worldwide.** 6th ed. New Providence, N.J., U.S. Directory Service/Reed Reference Publishing, 1995. 280p. $59.95. ISBN 0-916524-48-5. ISSN 0160-6468.

The specific audience for this frequently updated book is the U.S. student considering a medical or dental education abroad. It will also be useful for people interested in applying to such schools in the United States who want accurate addresses and the names of contact people. Including dental schools for the first time, this work does not rate or evaluate any of the schools. Entries are based on responses from individual schools or, lacking that, information from publicly available sources. Some listings also indicate the language of instruction, the amount of the application fee, the cost per credit for the first year, and prerequisites.

Excellent introductory materials (with plenty of caveats) discuss the selection of a school and make suggestions for application. The pros and cons of attending foreign medical schools (defined as those outside the United States, Canada, and Puerto Rico) are discussed, as are special problems that surround translating that coursework into a license to practice in the United States. Appendixes list the names and addresses of U.S. medical and dental boards and such other resources as professional associations. For careers collections and libraries that serve premed students, this is a suitable purchase.—**Edna M. Boardman**

1688. **Key Guide to Electronic Resources: Health Sciences.** Lee Hancock, ed. Medford, N.J., Learned Information, 1995. 494p. index. $39.50pa. ISBN 1-57387-001-3.

Information resources are expanding rapidly, especially in the health professions. Medical librarians, researchers, and doctors must know how to identify, select, and evaluate resources. This directory has been prepared carefully to make it easier for professionals and students who are searching for health-related information online, for research, for clinical studies, and for patient care.

The initial section is on online databases; *online* here means "computer accessible." Typical information under the title of the database includes the language; the type, such as full-text, bibliographical, and so forth; and a description of what is held within it. "Vendors and Pricing" tells how to access it, geographical and time span coverage, frequency of updating, producer, and costs (for such things as connect hours). The chapter introduction mentions databases that are combinations of databases, such as MEDLINE, and how to access them.

Descriptions of CD-ROM and magnetic media databases are presented in similar fashion. Because sometimes the same information is now available in both forms, cross-references to the vendor listing are provided for comparison shopping. Other systems listed are health-oriented bulletin board systems, listservs, and several approaches to the Internet, including Gopher. Vendor contacts are in an appendix. This tremendous bibliographical project should be of great value to its intended users.—**Harriette M. Cluxton**

1689. **Peterson's Job Opportunities in Health Care 1995.** Princeton, N.J., Peterson's Guides, 1994. 295p. index. $18.95pa. ISBN 1-56079-370-8. ISSN 1071-0671.

This book provides general information on more than 1,500 health care and related fields in the United States. Companies listed were chosen based on recent growth in the number of employees and on sales stability. Therefore, the list of companies is not exhaustive. Companies listed typically hire in the fields described but may not have specific immediate openings. Profiled companies were contacted directly for information on type of employee sought and for specific contact information. An alphabetical list of health-related organizational profiles provides the bulk of the information in this book. Profiles include name, address, description of the company, founding date, annual sales, number of employees, expertise needed, and a contact name and telephone number. A short list of government employers follows the general list. Also included are options for health care jobs, occupations for the future, a page of tips on job search strategies, and information on finding jobs in small companies. Three indexes give access to the listings by industry, state, and hiring needs.

This work does not supply a great deal of guidance or specific information to the job seeker, but the list and its indexes are useful and easy to use. The jobseeker is provided with many good leads to consider. Recommended for general employment collections.—**Joanna M. Burkhardt**

1690. **Profiles of U.S. Hospitals, 1995.** [4th ed.]. Baltimore, Md., 1994. 818p. index. $299.00pa. ISBN 1-880678-66-7. ISSN 1062-1946.

This work includes information on nearly 6,500 hospitals and health care facilities in the United States. This 4th edition differs from earlier editions in that the scope of the profiles has been expanded to cover nine new performance measures, and it enhances five existing ones.

The purpose of this work is to allow users to compare costs, determine market shares, and analyze operating margins for hospitals and physicians. The rankings are divided into three major categories: descriptive, financial, and top five diagnosis related groups (DRGs). The DRG indexes catalog a hospital's highest-volume DRGs, and provide length of stay information. Descriptive elements list beds, discharges, occupancy rate percentages, average length of stay (ALOS), case mix index, Medicare percentages, and Medicaid percentages. Indicators in the far left column are a combination of letters and numerals. Where the indicator does not apply, a dash will appear in its place.

Financial elements include outpatient revenue percentages, operating revenue, days in accounts receivable, and average payment period. Appendix A supplies the names of the 492 DRGs used by the Medicare Prospective Payment System in the federal fiscal year 1993. Rankings such as profitability, leverage, liquidity, and efficiency are compiled on a national, state, and metropolitan statistical area (MSA) level; these are found in appendix B.

The hospitals detailed in *Profiles of U.S. Hospitals* are listed alphabetically by state, then by city. Each hospital's address, telephone number, and Medicare provider number are listed in addition to more than 50 key measures of financial, operational, and clinical performance. The introductory pages describe how to use the profiles, as well as an explanation of the indicators. There is an alphabetical index of hospitals and an index of hospitals by provider numbers.

This work can be compared to *Hospitals: The Sourcebook* (Deloitte & Touche, 1994) and *The DRG Handbook* (3d ed., FICIA, 1993). *Profiles* is recommended for those interested in evaluating the financial performance of hospitals and physicians and the analysis of market-demand trends for pharmaceuticals, medical devices, and related diagnostic services.—**Marilynn Green**

1691. **U.S. Health Policy Groups: Institutional Profiles.** Craig Ramsay, ed. Westport, Conn., Greenwood Press, 1995. 456p. index. $79.50. ISBN 0-313-28618-3.

This book makes an important contribution to medical reference work. However, it should have been even more complete. For 121 organizations that have influenced the health care process at the federal level, it gives directory information including history, structure, funding, policy concerns and tactics, and electoral activity, as well as other sources to consult. The preface explains that "the process of selecting the groups to profile was inevitably subjective," with the final decision for inclusion going to groups that "were most frequently mentioned in general media and academic accounts of federal health policy making activities." One wonders why no alternative medicine groups are mentioned. An appendix does list additional groups that were considered for profiling, but the book would have been more useful if these were also included. The information for the groups that are covered is concise, clear, and comprehensive. Since finding this material elsewhere can be a time-consuming process, larger medical and academic libraries with health science programs should obtain this volume.—**Natalie Kupferberg**

Handbooks and Yearbooks

1692. **Woman's Body.** Miriam Stoppard, ed. New York, Dorling Kindersley, 1994. 224p. illus. index. $29.95. ISBN 1-56458-617-0.

This beautifully illustrated volume provides good, current information about the human female. Anatomy, physiology, mental health, social roles, and sexuality are discussed by a group of experts in the health and social sciences, led by contributing editor Stoppard. Diet, exercise, health care, contraception, pregnancy, infertility, and sexually transmitted diseases are also covered. The excellent color photographs, charts, and graphs make the anatomical and physiological concepts and medical procedures very easy to understand. Insets comparing women with men and animals and historical notes offer interesting sidelights.

Unfortunately, the information presented here is less comprehensive and less objective than that in *The New Our Bodies, Ourselves* (Simon & Schuster, 1992). *Woman's Body* does not, for example, discuss the controversy associated with hormone replacement therapy for menopausal women. It also lacks the extensive bibliographies and referral lists offered in *The New Our Bodies, Ourselves*. Despite these shortcomings, the outstanding graphics, accessible language, and interesting historical material in *Woman's Body* make it an excellent companion volume for *The New Our Bodies, Ourselves* in all reference collections.—**Barbara M. Bibel**

1693. Wright, John W., and Linda Sunshine. **The Best Hospitals in America.** 2d ed. Detroit, Gale, 1995. 609p. index. $34.95. ISBN 0-8103-9874-5.

For those with special medical care needs and the ability and flexibility to choose a hospital, this guide will be invaluable. The book provides much valuable information on what the authors describe as the most eminent institutions of the United States and Canada. The hospitals were chosen for inclusion after consultation primarily with physicians representing various parts of the two countries. Arranged alphabetically by state or province, the directory gives a four- to five-page narrative on each institution that includes specialty areas, patient satisfaction, research programs, and admission policies. A highlighted area in the margin of each entry notes the number of beds; occupancy rates and clinic visits; the numbers of physicians, residents, and nurses; charges; and address and telephone numbers.

The appendixes offer lists of hospitals commended by the Joint Commission on Accreditation of Healthcare Organizations, the *U.S. News and World Report* survey results of the 40 top hospitals in specialty areas, and the cancer centers in the United States designated by the National Cancer Institute. A comprehensive general index allows the reader to research an institution by name, special medical problem, or care need. One drawback is that not every state has an identified hospital in the primary section of the book. Also, fewer and fewer patients have the option to choose their hospital with the advent of managed care. However, for those seeking information on this topic, the book is highly recommended. It is especially appropriate for public libraries.—**Mary Ann Thompson**

MEDICINE

General Works

Atlases

1694. **Atlas of the Human Body.** New York, HarperPerennial/HarperCollins, 1994. 140p. illus. index. $20.00pa. ISBN 0-06-273297-8.

This compendium of detailed drawings, diagrams, and cross-sections of human anatomy offers the student, teacher, patient, or medical worker a clear explanation of the body's interlinking systems and their location, size, shape, and function. For example, the explanation of the stomach and duodenum details this region of the digestive tract in color drawings, in a sketch of the human torso, and in a stylized study of the stomach's relationship to the duodenum. In each chapter, text introduces a single focus (e.g., the female reproductive organs) by explaining their purpose and focusing on individual parts—uterus, fallopian tubes, ovaries, vagina, and external organs. A separate diagram details the mechanism of menstruation in cyclical detail.

The book begins with a five-part table of contents and a poorly labeled index focusing on circulation, respiration, digestion, nerves, endocrine, urinary and reproductive processes, and the skeletal system. Following with a simple explanation and diagrams of the book's scope and method, the text consumes most of the pages, relegating the final four pages to indexing. Missing from this slender volume is a pronouncing glossary and even a cursory attempt to include dark-skinned models or people of a variety of ages and body conditions. Another detriment to the book is its graphic display of a brain wound on page 11, an insensitive departure from the intent and purpose as outlined in the introduction. Despite these flaws, the quality of artwork and simplicity of text combine to form a useful reference work.

—**Mary Ellen Snodgrass**

1695. DeSousa, Luís R., and others. **Common Medical Abbreviations.** Albany, N.Y., Delmar, 1995. 267p. $17.95pa. ISBN 0-8273-6643-4.

The complexity of medical vocabulary has given rise to a plethora of abbreviations. Transcriptionists, consultants, and patients may find these cryptic jottings incomprehensible. This book attempts to list the most commonly used standard abbreviations. It includes the Greek alphabet symbols that are used in some abbreviations, and the variations in punctuation and capitalization that differentiate between, for example, *per os*, post-operative, and Polonium. Only the terms themselves are provided for each abbreviation; no definitions or explanations are provided. This will have to be used in conjunction with a good medical dictionary. Appendixes list common medical symbols, the Greek alphabet, common cardinal numbers, metric weights and measures, and common decimal factors. The book is recommended for all medical collections.—**Susan B. Hagloch**

Bibliography

1696. Morton, Leslie T., and Robert J. Moore. **A Bibliography of Medical and Biomedical Biography.** 2d ed. Brookfield, Vt., Scolar Press/Ashgate Publishing, 1994. 333p. index. $99.95. ISBN 0-85967-981-0.

This is a comprehensive bibliography of men and women who have made significant contributions in medicine, surgery, and related biomedical sciences. The 2d edition encompasses 2,368 individuals, and includes some foreign-language biographical material. While the listing is alphabetical, a chronological index of biographees is arranged by disciplines, providing accessibility to data on people in such diverse areas as protozoology and the hospice movement.

Each entry identifies individuals and gives their dates, then lists from one to six biographical sources. Usually these are books and standard reference works such as the *Dictionary of Scientific Biography* (see ARBA 81, entry 1372), but occasionally a scholarly periodical is cited. Coverage goes back to antiquity, but no cutoff date for inclusion is indicated, although there are many twentieth-century listings. Few non-Western figures are included.

The book also contains a short bibliography of works on the history of medicine, subdivided by subject. Both authors are or have been librarians at the National Institute for Medicine in Britain. Recommended, in spite of the price, for academic and medical libraries with collections in the history of medicine.—**Natalie Kupferberg**

Dictionaries and Encyclopedias

1697. **The American Heritage Stedman's Medical Dictionary.** New York, Houghton Mifflin, 1995. 923p. illus. $24.95. ISBN 0-395-69955-X.

Combining Stedman's medical expertise and American Heritage's clear, precise style has resulted in this new medical dictionary uniquely serving both general readers and health care professionals. With clear, technically accurate, and generally jargon-free language, 45,000 definitions are arranged in strict alphabetical order. One hundred black-and-white drawings and diagrams supplement the definitions for such terms as *balloon angioplasty* and *placenta*. Charts, pictures, and tables in the appendixes show systems of the human body, weights and measures, the periodic table of elements, and types of burns.

Near the front of this title is a must-read guide. These four pages explain how to use all parts of the entries, syllabication, pronunciation, part-of-speech, inflected forms, cross-references, order of senses, undefined forms, and eponymous terms. A subentry index leads users to terms that may be main entries in standard medical dictionaries. In order to help nonspecialists find definitions, specific diseases and syndromes are main entries and nontechnical terms such as "undulant fever *see* brucellosis" are cross-referenced. This reasonably priced, easy-to-read dictionary will be extremely useful in home, office or clinic, and public library settings.—**Susan C. Awe**

1698. **A Dictionary of Epidemiology.** 3d ed. John M. Last and others, eds. New York, Oxford University Press, 1995. 180p. maps. $35.00; $16.95pa. ISBN 0-19-509667-3; 0-19-509668-1pa.

Epidemiology is the study of the relationship between disease and the population: how and why given health conditions exist in given populations, and how they may be controlled. The field is gaining in scope and importance as the population ages, as new strains of viruses and bacteria manifest themselves, and as links between disease, environment, and lifestyle become clearer.

This title is the 3d edition of the work, the 2d having been published in 1988 (see ARBA 89, entry 1520). It includes nearly 300 new entries and a like number of revised definitions. Editor Last worked under the auspices of the International Epidemiological Association, with the assistance of a 90-member international editorial team. The result is a cogent compilation of terms, phrases, and abbreviations used in the field. The dictionary is highly recommended for libraries serving such specialists.

—**Susan B. Hagloch**

1699. Everitt, B. S. **The Cambridge Dictionary of Statistics in the Medical Sciences.** New York, Cambridge University Press, 1995. 274p. illus. $54.95; $19.95pa. ISBN 0-521-47382-9; 0-521-47928-2pa.

Words, phrases, and acronyms are defined in entries that range from 2 to 150 words. The book lists 2,000 terms, from the obvious (*sickness absence*: "absence from work attributed to medical incapacity") to the specialized (most other entries). Cross-referencing is signified through differing typefaces and direct *see* commands. The author, a psychiatrist and statistician, has drawn from several standard medical sources to define terms. The writing is succinct but lengthy enough to ensure comprehension. Graphs are used when needed to clarify text that could otherwise be inscrutable.

Directed at the medical student and practitioner, this compact dictionary (or a comparable one) should be in all medical libraries and in large public and academic collections. The field of medicine revolves around research that is justified and explained with statistical data, which are almost willfully obscure. This resource could be used to quickly and routinely answer reference questions that would otherwise be nightmarish. It is the kind of tool that is used infrequently by reference librarians, but one that is usually reached for with a murmur of discovery and relief.—**Ed Volz**

1700. **Magill's Medical Guide: Health and Illness.** By the Editors of Salem Press. Pasadena, Calif., Salem Press, 1995. 3v. illus. index. $270.00/set. ISBN 0-89356-712-4.

These three medical texts, which are the first half of a two-part series, are written in an encyclopedia format. Each text is designed in a similar fashion, and each has an easy-to-use contents section that makes looking up a topic uncomplicated. All three texts present medical information in an easy-to-read format. Hundreds of medical conditions are discussed throughout the texts, with some topics being discussed in more detail than others. The presentation style is consistent, and each condition has similar subheadings. For example, prior to discussing the details of the condition, the authors briefly define the condition, list the system(s) affected, the types of specialists available, and key terms that are found within the text. The text itself addresses issues such as cause and symptoms, treatment and therapy, perspective and prospects, and a list of additional references that relate to the topic.

Illustrations are present throughout all of the texts and help to clarify certain topics. These black-and-white illustrations are understandable and are not overwhelming. Overall, these three texts contain much medical information. The adult reader should be able to comprehend most of the materials, as the topics are presented in an accessible format. These texts will complement most "home" medical libraries as a useful reference. The reader should, however, consider consulting other texts or a physician prior to making any medical decisions.—**Paul M. Murphy III**

1701. **Merriam-Webster's Medical Dictionary.** Springfield, Mass., Merriam-Webster, 1995. 771p. $6.99pa. ISBN 0-87779-914-8.

This paperback medical dictionary is an abridged version of *Merriam-Webster's Medical Desk Dictionary*. It contains 35,000 of the most frequently used words in both human and veterinary medicine. The vocabulary includes common abbreviations, Latin and English names of plants and animals, and generic and brand names for drugs. Compiled for lay users, terms in the lexicon encompass sports terms such as *abs*, *pecs*, and *delts* for common muscle groups, and brief biographical information on important historical figures such as Louis Pasteur and Rudolf Virchow.

The dictionary is easy to use. Entries are in alphabetical order, letter by letter, with main entries in boldface. Entries list syllabication, pronunciation, variant spelling and pronunciation, hyphenation, and definitions. Functional labels, inflected forms, and capitalization and usage notes are part of the text, but etymology appears only in entries for abbreviations and eponyms. Scientific plant and animal names follow the New Latin vocabulary. These entries are at the genus level, with higher orders listed in the definitions. Cross-references in small capitals direct readers to related material. Common prefixes and suffixes have their own entries so that readers may use them to determine the meaning of words not in the lexicon. An appendix contains graphic scientific and medical symbols that are not in the main body of the dictionary.

The text is arranged in two columns with guide words at the top of each page. The typeface is small but not difficult to read. The margins are adequate. Although this dictionary lacks the breadth, detail, and illustrations of larger medical dictionaries such as *Dorland's* (27th ed.; see ARBA 89, entry 1538), *Stedman's* (see ARBA 91, entry 1664), and *Mosby's* (2d ed.; see ARBA 87, entry 1627), it contains the vocabulary that lay users need. This dictionary is inexpensive and well suited for home use. It will also be useful for students, court reporters, and transcribers who need portable dictionaries.—**Barbara M. Bibel**

1702. **The Oxford Medical Companion.** John Walton, Jeremiah A. Barondess, and Stephen Lock, eds. New York, Oxford University Press, 1994. 1038p. illus. $49.95. ISBN 0-19-2623559.

A reference work whose title begins with the prestigious "The Oxford" bears the burden of expected excellence. Most librarians and researchers anticipate top-quality data and comprehensive coverage in Oxford University Press's trademark succinct, objective style. On the surface, this medical compendium appears to cover the subject. Arranged in alphabetical order are 182 signed main entries along with short definitions or explanations that, according to the editors, summarize and update long entries from the 1st edition, which dates to the 1970s. Opening with a brief preface and impressive list of contributors, which is dominated by mostly male U.K. and U.S. experts, the front matter includes an alphabetical list of main entries and a one-paragraph explanation of notation, but no introductory remarks addressing the serious quandaries of the age, such as abortion, surrogate motherhood, malpractice, new bacterial or viral strains, quality of life for the aged, euthanasia, designer genetics, bionics, organ transplant, toxic pollutants, or AIDS.

Main entries blend historical blips (e.g., Hippocrates's opinion of bladder surgery); sparse line drawings, and sparser charts with detailed coverage of diseases (e.g., AIDS, rheumatology); treatments (e.g., keyhole surgery, anti-infective drugs); and related topics from a broad spectrum of life (e.g., sports and medicine, statistics, the military, women in medicine). Certain of these topics seem ill-chosen for individual attention, especially boxing and art and medicine. Other questionable entries offer a cursory glance at perplexing issues, in particular the cause of homosexuality and the place of alternative medical practice (e.g., midwives, herbalism, prayer and spiritual healing, and other fringe practices, the popularity of which writer Roy Porter attributes to capitalism and greed). Chiropractic receives short shrift with the statement that it is a "complementary discipline" to traditional methods of treatment. The shortest entries, such as arthritis, reveal little more than a dictionary definition. Overall, this work presents a minimal, rigid, and strictly orthodox view of modern medicine.—**Mary Ellen Snodgrass**

Directories

1703. **The Directory of Medical Rehabilitation Facilities, 1995.** Baltimore, Md., HCIA, 1995. 349p. index. $195.00pa. ISBN 1-880678-97-7. ISSN 1063-1712.

This annual directory includes both hospital-sponsored and independent facilities that work with patients having one or more conditions—musculoskeletal, neuromuscular, neurological, cardiovascular, pulmonary, or other—that necessitate retraining in everyday activities. Arranged alphabetically by state and city, each entry covers staffing information, number of beds, accreditation, ownership and revenue profile, and a summary of the types of programs offered. The information has been gathered by HCIA Inc., which was established in 1985 to provide the health care industry with a centralized source of timely and reliable information. It maintains the database of these facilities by contacting them annually to update the directory's information. A useful "Diagnosis Treated Index" organizes the facilities according to the specific conditions treated. This title is essential for all hospital libraries, and would be useful to those public libraries that can afford the price.—**Susan B. Hagloch**

1704. **The Official ABMS Directory of Board Certified Medical Specialists 1996.** 28th ed. New Providence, N.J., Marquis Who's Who/Reed Reference Publishing, 1995. 4v. index. $439.95/set. ISBN 0-8379-0539-7. ISSN 0000-1406.

This four-volume set was formed by the merger of Marquis's *Directory of Medical Specialists* and the American Board of Medical Specialists's *Compendium of Certified Medical Specialists*. Issued annually, it is the most comprehensive listing of physicians available. The most recent edition contains profiles of more than 466,000 retired and practicing specialists on its nearly 9,000 pages. Profiles include medical school and year of degree, place and date of internship, place and date of residencies, fellowship training, academic/hospital appointments, professional associations, type of medical practice, and address information. Physicians are listed geographically within specialities, with a single name index at the end of volume 4. A separate necrology index lists physicians who have died since the publication of the directory's previous edition.

With such a comprehensive list of specialities included—even "Family Physician" is employed as a kind of catch-all category—one would be hard-pressed not to find an particular U.S. physician in this reference set. While brief, the individual profiles provide sufficient data to get some sense of a specialist's background. Evaluative/critical information is not the role of this resource; it is a directory only. The various specialty boards are listed preceding the list of physicians in that area of practice. Board members' names and addresses are listed, and board history, policy statements, and general information are provided.

Libraries desiring a comprehensive resource of this kind will either need to buy this title or live without an adequate resource. It stands alone and will be an automatic purchase for libraries with a demand for medical directory information.—**Ed Volz**

1705. **The Princeton Review Student Access Guide to the Best Medical Schools.** 1996 ed. By Andrea Nagy. New York, Princeton Review/Random House, 1995. 318p. index. $25.00pa. (with disk). ISBN 0-679-76149-7. ISSN 1067-2176.

According to the preface, this guide is designed to provide in-depth profiles of 123 accredited medical schools on such topics as academics, admissions statistics, tuition and financial aid, and student life. Published annually, this directory provides occasionally candid evaluations of the schools by some 5,500 students discussing such aspects as faculty, workload, class size, social life, and the like. Similar guides prepared by Princeton Review exist in such areas as business schools, law schools, and so on. Most students are familiar with other Princeton products (e.g., SAT tests, subject tests). This work is recommended.
—**Bohdan S. Wynar**

1706. **REA's Authoritative Guide to Medical & Dental Schools.** Piscataway, N.J., Research & Education Association, 1995. 480p. illus. $19.95pa. ISBN 0-87891-919-8.

Every medical, osteopathic, dental, chiropractic, and podiatric school in the United States and Canada is profiled in this directory. Each entry describes the school: its admissions procedures, undergraduate prerequisites, costs, student aid and associations, and the like. A summary listing at the start of each section provides at-a-glance summaries of the schools' accreditation; degrees offered; enrollment; percentage of male, female, and minority students; mean grade point average (GPA) and Medical College Admission Test (MCAT) scores; tuition for both in-state and out-of-state students; and the application fee and deadline. An introduction to each section describes the field and the general requirements for success. Thorough and concise, this guide provides an excellent overview of the options available to medical students, and is highly recommended for high school, college, and public libraries.—**Susan B. Hagloch**

Handbooks and Yearbooks

1707. **The American Medical Association Family Medical Guide.** [CD-ROM]. New York, Dorling Kindersley, 1995. Minimum system requirements: IBM or compatible PC 386DX/33MHz. MPC-compatible CD-ROM drive. Windows 3.1. 4MB RAM. SVGA 256-color monitor. Mouse. Sound card. Loudspeakers or headphones. $49.95. ISBN 0-7894-0293-9.

The print edition of *The American Medical Association Family Medical Guide* was revised in 1994 by Random House. This CD-ROM contains the text of the revision with visual enhancements and several search options. The disc does not come with an instruction manual, but there is a toll-free technical support line for assistance. Searching the database is easy. Major categories—including diseases, disorders, and other problems; an atlas of the body; symptoms and self diagnosis; injuries and emergencies; diagnostic imaging techniques; and caring for the sick—are available by clicking on them. A toolbar offers a glossary, a drug glossary, a global search option that includes Boolean operators, and help screens.

Within the disease category, one can search alphabetically or by subject. Once a topic is chosen, information about it appears along with pop-up self-help screens. The symptom category has separate sections for men, women, and children. Each of these has subdivisions for pain, body part, and diagnosis. Clicking on the body part brings up a flowchart to help the user make treatment decisions. The body atlas has both line drawings and color animation with sound. Clicking on the cardiovascular system brought up a diagram, "Aneurysms," yielding a three-dimensional color view of an arterial wall that ballooned as the narrator explained the condition and its treatment. The diagnostic imaging section explains the various endoscopies, X-rays, and scans. Some are illustrated. "Injuries and Emergencies" is a first aid guide with animation and illustrations. The healthy body section focuses on prevention, fitness, and nutrition, while caring for the sick deals with choosing health care, providing care, and dying at home.

The American Medical Association Family Medical Guide is simple to use. It provides current information for lay users in a state-of-the-art format. Libraries with appropriate hardware and CD-ROM reference collections should consider it.—**Barbara M. Bibel**

1708. **The Canadian Guide to Clinical Preventive Health Care.** Ottawa, Canadian Task Force on the Periodic Health Examination; distr., Canada Communication Group, 1994. 1009p. index. $90.95pa. (U.S.). ISBN 0-660-15732-2.

The importance of preventive medicine in health care management was acknowledged in 1976 when the Canadian Task Force on the Periodic Health Examination was established. The early years were spent developing a methodology for evaluating intervention in the treatment of disease and disorder. They were years well spent as many of the evaluative criteria were adopted by the U.S. Preventive Services Task Force.

Recognizing the promotion of health through clinical prevention was an important turning point in the doctor-client relationship. By combining counseling, screening, and immunization, the burden of responsibility for health care shifted to the collaborative nature of the relationship. This spirit of collaboration extended to the United States and Canadian task forces. They worked closely together and in 1990 published the book *Preventing Disease: Beyond the Rhetoric*. The U.S. Task Force is currently in the process of updating its 1989 *Guide to Clinical Preventive Services*.

This guide provides the recommended preventive interventions in prenatal, perinatal, pediatric, and geriatric care; neoplasms; metabolic and nutritional disorders; basic psychosocial illness and lifestyle "diseases"; and infectious diseases, among others. Each of the 81 topics has been thoroughly researched and evaluated by the Task Force. Standard maneuvers are presented together with an evaluation of their effectiveness based on levels of evidence reviewed by the Task Force. More importantly, the Task Force offers a recommendation graded on a positive-to-negative scale of "A" to "E" for each of the interventions it has evaluated.

Unfortunately, a large number of these clinical interventions are conservatively graded as "C," which, according to the editors, suggests both areas for further research as well as the need by the physician to consider a number of other external factors. On the other hand, the more forceful "A" recommendations tend to be applied to preventive measures necessary in early stages of human life. Measuring the benefits of prevention is a difficult exercise. As mentioned in the introduction, there are many past examples of interventions that have not been as beneficial as originally hoped. Nonetheless, this publication provides a good guide to health care personnel based on a solid framework of scientific standards and analysis.
—**Mary Hemmings**

1709. Linden, Tom, and Michelle L. Kienholz. **Dr. Tom Linden's Guide to Online Medicine.** New York, McGraw-Hill, 1995. 337p. illus. index. $17.95pa. ISBN 0-07-038055-4.

This text is designed in a manual style and deals directly with online medical services. The reader will probably find this text to be easily read and user friendly. The author has taken the time to explain to the reader, novice or expert, how to use selected medical online services.

Topics covered in this text range from the various commercial online services that are available to gaining access to the Internet. Also included in this text are key medical terms and phrases that will assist the user while conducting medical research online. The author has also provided sections pertaining to gaining access to the latest medical issues, such as alternative medicine techniques, and how to incorporate the private physician's advice with the advice found online. Sections of this text supply both generalized as well as specific information, depending on the topic being discussed. This can help readers use their online time more efficiently.

Overall, this text will be of benefit to individuals who wish to gain access to the online world of medicine. Adult readers may benefit most from this text.—**Paul M. Murphy III**

1710. **Professional Handbook of Diagnostic Tests.** Michael Shaw and others, eds. Springhouse, Pa., Springhouse Publishing, 1995. 694p. illus. index. $27.95pa. ISBN 0-87434-775-0.

Health care providers encounter daily myriad clinical laboratory tests that they must be able to understand and explain to their patients. This pocket-sized reference tool will prove an invaluable asset in accomplishing both these goals. The text is separated into two major formats. Part 1 covers more than 500 major disorders. For each, this volume briefly lists the clinical or laboratory tests that must be run to diagnose the particular disorder and the relevant test results for positive findings.

Part 2, which comprises the vast majority of the text, divides the large number of clinical and laboratory tests into 16 broad categories (e.g., urine tests, cultures, radiography, nuclear medicine scans). The following pertinent information is provided for each test: general description, purpose, patient preparation, procedure and posttest care, precautions, reference values, and abnormal findings. For appropriate tests, an equipment list is included. Special attention is given to patient education aspects of conducting each test.

The book's language is too complicated for the general public. The unusual format and the emphasis on patient education make this an important reference guide for all medical, nursing, and hospital libraries, as well as for individual practitioners. Because of its unique features, this new volume is a useful complementary text to such standard laboratory test guides as Norbert Tietz's *Clinical Guide to Laboratory Tests* (3d ed., Saunders, scheduled for 1997) and *Mosby's Diagnostic and Laboratory Test Reference* (Mosby Year Book, 1991).—**Jonathon Erlen**

1711. Rees, Alan M., ed. **Consumer Health USA: Essential Information from the Federal Health Network.** Phoenix, Ariz., Oryx Press, 1995. 543p. index. $49.50. ISBN 0-89774-889-1.

For libraries that lack access to government documents or even libraries with document collections, this book offers a good starting point for the layperson to find information on common health problems. The volume brings together information put out by key government agencies like the National Institute of Health and the National Heart, Lung, and Blood Institute, and makes it concise and understandable. Topics range from AIDS to Rocky Mountain spotted fever to nutrition and weight loss. Bibliographical information is given at the end of each document, and occasionally there is a glossary of medical terms with a list of further resources. There are also some reprints from *FDA Consumer* magazine.

Of course, since health information changes so rapidly, there is no way any book of medical information can be completely up-to-date (information on yo-yo dieting has already changed since this book was published). Patrons will still need to check periodicals. Also, this book does not replace more comprehensive ones like *The Mayo Clinic Family Health Book* (William Morrow, 1990). However, it is recommended for public libraries.—**Natalie Kupferberg**

1712. Scialli, Anthony R., Armand Lione, and G. K. Boyle Padgett. **Reproductive Effects of Chemical, Physical, and Biological Agents REPROTOX.** Baltimore, Md., Johns Hopkins University Press, 1995. 891p. index. $150.00. ISBN 0-8018-5183-1.

This volume's 2,880 entries mainly describe drug effects on fertility, pregnancy, and lactation. The entries describe how the drug or physical agent normally affects the body and how it may affect the fetus or nursing baby. Also, the effects of the agent on a preexisting medical condition are explained. Where applicable, information is given on male fertility problems from the agent.

Each entry is clear and concise, listing the drug by its generic name and CAS number if available, and includes references. The data used are gathered internationally, and the entries usually specify what countries have contributed information. The index lists both the generic name and product names that refer to the numeric entry in the text section of the book.

This work is the print version of the REPROTOX online database. It is much quicker and easier to use than accessing a database in a "need to know now" patient situation. This volume is easy to use and appropriate for medical school libraries and hospital or medical office libraries that deal with fertility and obstetrics.
—**Betsy J. Kraus**

1713. Zand, Janet, Rachel Walton, and Bob Rountree. **Smart Medicine for a Healthier Child: A Practical A-to-Z Reference to Natural and Conventional Treatments....** Garden City Park, N.Y., Avery Publishing Group, 1994. 470p. illus. index. $17.95pa. ISBN 0-89529-545-8.

This book purports to be a guide for parents to the treatment of common childhood conditions. It offers some useful information. The short section on advice for selecting a physician for a child offers helpful criteria. It appears to be directed to the parent who would not otherwise select a medical doctor to provide this care. The descriptions of common childhood medical problems are well written and easy to follow. Some statements are not well substantiated; for example, the possible relationship between electromagnetic radiation and cancer is far from proven. The general directions for medical care, which the authors refer to as conventional medical care, are brief, but seem accurate. The book spends substantial time on unproven therapies such as homeopathic medicines, herbs, and nutritional therapies. While many of these may be harmless, they are offered without scientific evidence either for their safety or their effectiveness. They pose the serious danger of delaying or denying effective conventional medical treatments to children whose ailment may worsen or even become fatal during that time. The authors do advise that parents seek the help of a qualified medical practitioner for such disorders as cancer; this is a valuable and life-saving message. For parents who are committed to unproven therapies, this book provides some information about medical diagnosis and treatment of childhood conditions. It does not have a place otherwise, as it emphasizes potentially dangerous unproven methods.

—**Margretta Reed Seashore**

Alternative Medicine

1714. **The Information Sourcebook of Herbal Medicine: A Detailed Bibliography....** David Hoffmann, ed. Freedom, Calif., Crossing Press, 1994. 305p. $40.00. ISBN 0-89594-671-8.

British herbalist Hoffmann has edited a guide to sources of information on Western herbal medicine. The book covers indexes, reference books, computer software, online databases, organizations, and other sources. Unfortunately, most of the resources are either merely listed or so briefly described that it would be difficult for inexperienced researchers to determine what resources may meet their needs. Medline is, however, described in detail. In fact, more than one-third of the book (125 pages) consists of Medline searches on various herbal topics. A lengthy bibliography of herbal titles (not annotated) lists primarily books published in the last 15 years. Information on obtaining out-of-print books consists of a reference to *Bookman's Weekly* and the address of one dealer who specializes in books on herbal topics. A glossary contains one-line definitions that are too brief to be of much help (e.g., "coronary heart disease: a serious condition affecting coronary artery"). Given the current interest in herbal medicine, there is a need for a guide of this type. However, this expensive, inadequate, often inaccurate, and inflated volume does not meet that need. Most potential users would be better served by any of several basic guides to library research.—**Gari-Anne Patzwald**

1715. Kusick, James. **A Treasury of Natural First Aid Remedies from A to Z.** Englewood Cliffs, N.J., Prentice Hall Career & Personal Development, 1995. 313p. index. $24.95; $10.95pa. ISBN 0-13-063173-6; 0-13-063181-7pa.

This handy reference directs the user to therapies for first aid emergencies and other common ailments that employ substances most people either have on hand or can acquire from a health food store or large grocery store. They include various kitchen remedies (e.g., vinegar, celery), herbs, baths, homeopathic remedies, and splints. The body of the book consists of alphabetically arranged articles on health conditions (e.g., allergies, colds and flu, rashes). Each article describes the condition, indicates action to be taken, and then recommends appropriate natural treatments, arranged in order of probable efficacy. Shaded warning boxes note contraindications and identify emergencies for which immediate actions (such as the summoning of emergency medical personnel or a call to a Poison Control Center) are imperative. Unlike many guides of this type, this book does not make exclusive claims for natural remedies but presents them as substitutes for or complements to standard allopathic treatments in the context of complete first aid care. The work is recommended as a supplement to standard first aid manuals, and to libraries where there is interest in herbalism or natural healing.—**Gari-Anne Patzwald**

1716. Marti, James, with Andrea Hine. **The Alternative Health & Medicine Encyclopedia.** Detroit, Gale, 1995. 376p. index. $49.95. ISBN 0-8103-9580-0.

Alternative or holistic approaches to health are becoming increasingly popular. In 1992, U.S. citizens spent more than $14 billion on unconventional medical therapy. While the nebulous term "alternative medicine" includes a wide variety of treatment regimens, such as acupuncture, biofeedback, chiropractic, meditation, visualization therapy, and yoga, most approaches depend on taking advantage of the mind-body connection. This encyclopedia attempts to outline for the health consumer the various fields of alternative medicine, and what each has to offer. The authors cite evidence for the efficacy of many of these treatments, although much of it is anecdotal and from less than rigorous scientific sources.

The first chapter gives general information on the various types of holistic medicine. Most of the specialties described have received at least some degree of acceptance by Western medicine. (Many of the more eccentric New Age treatments such as crystal therapy and aromatherapy are not mentioned.) There is useful advice on how to choose and evaluate an alternative medical therapist. Subsequent chapters discuss various health problems, such as obesity, stress-related disorders, cancer, and heart problems, and alternative approaches to their treatment. Much of the advice given in these chapters is strongly based on common sense. One understands why anecdotal evidence for most of these regimes is so strong—most have as their basis reducing stress, exercising more, and eating a healthier diet. Unlike many promoters of alternative medicine, the authors of this guide do not take an "us or them" approach to conventional physicians. They include warnings to health consumers to be educated and involved no matter where they seek treatment, a wise approach in any case.—**Carol L. Noll**

1717. Scalzo, Richard. **Naturopathic Handbook of Herbal Formulas: A Practical and Concise Herb User's Guide.** 3d ed. Durango, Colo., Kivakí Press, 1994. 1v. (various paging). $5.95pa. ISBN 1-882308-42-5.

This handbook is divided into 4 sections, the first of which describes 51 herbal compounds (ingredients, therapeutic actions, indications, dosage, and contraindications). Ingredients are merely listed with no indication of appropriate amounts or proportions, or of method of preparation. A second section lists a wide variety of symptoms and diseases (e.g., Alzheimer's disease, asthma, coughs, various cancers) and indicates what compounds or individual herbs are recommended for treatment. A third section lists single herbs and suggests for which condition(s) each is appropriate. A brief section describes four compounds recommended for "internal cleansing." The last part of the book, entitled "Naturopathic Desk Reference," is designed as an introduction to a proposed quarterly publication that will present natural alternatives to common allopathic drugs. This is a book for the knowledgeable and experienced herbalist or naturopath; others may be misled to treat themselves inadequately or inappropriately. The work is recommended for specialized collections.—**Gari-Anne Patzwald**

Psychiatry

1718. **A Dictionary of Family Therapy.** rev. ed. By Jacques Miermont; revised by Hugh Jenkins. Cambridge, Mass., Blackwell, 1995. 492p. index. $95.00. ISBN 0-631-17048-0.

This monumental scholarly work explores the origin and history of family therapy and its clinical applications. The dictionary format allows the intermingling of brief definitions with treatises of several pages in length. Articles are initialed by the appropriate contributors.

The original French edition came out in 1987. This English translation by Chris Turner claims to be revised and updated by an international group of scholars (mostly French and English—no Americans), under the direction of Jenkins. Only one of the advisory editors is from the United States. Examination of the extensive bibliography does reveal some citations of U.S. authors, as well as the relative scarcity of entries from any sources carrying dates in the 1990s.

The branch of psychiatry known as family therapy is defined and described in all its ramifications, technical vocabulary, developments, and clinical applications. Theories and concepts from various related disciplines, such as biology and anthropology, are considered. Other psychiatric doctrines and methods are not ignored, but interpretations often seem to have a spin toward family and social relationships. Broad knowledge of psychiatric theory and terminology, and familiarity with mathematical thinking and statistical analysis are necessary for effective use. Schematic representations appear frequently (e.g., the *genogram*). Some entries consist entirely of cross-references, without dictionary definitions.

Despite its European slant, this is an excellent resource for researchers, teachers, and other professionals, especially those practitioners involved with family therapy, a relatively young and not always well-understood way of treating mental and emotional problems as they affect individuals and their nuclear or extended families. (Note: For general reference use in psychiatry, see Robert Jean Campbell, *Psychiatric Dictionary* [6th ed., Oxford University Press, 1989].)—**Harriette M. Cluxton**

Specific Diseases and Conditions

AIDS

1719. Russel, Randall P., comp. **Guide to Books on AIDS.** Commack, N.Y., Nova Science Publishers, 1995. 98p. index. $39.00pa. ISBN 1-56072-179-0.

More a bibliography than a guide, this work includes approximately 700 monograph titles that, in one way or another, deal with the subject of acquired immune deficiency syndrome (AIDS). Entries are arranged alphabetically by author or main entry, with full bibliographical description, cataloging notes, and subject headings. In fact, it would appear that the compiler has done little more than download Library of Congress cataloging data into one complete list.

Although the work has value, its reference potential is limited. There is no introduction, nor a preface. Therefore, it is difficult to deduce the scope or the intent of the work. There are no criteria for inclusion or exclusion, and the book lacks a guide to interpreting the citations. In short, there is no explanation of any of the content. Even skilled librarians or researchers knowledgeable of the literature about AIDS might wonder why certain titles appear, while others do not. Author and subject indexes are included, but considering the number of titles, their usefulness is limited.

Given the immense growth in the literature on this subject, patrons would be better served by an annotated guide to the literature that can clearly distinguish and relate titles on this topic and its subtopics. Considering the price of such a brief and limited work, other options should be considered.

—**Edmund F. SantaVicca**

Birth-Related Conditions

1720. Shepard, Thomas H. **Catalog of Teratogenic Agents.** 8th ed. Baltimore, Md., Johns Hopkins University Press, 1995. 542p. index. $110.00. ISBN 0-8018-5182-3.

Teratogenic agents have been directly linked to causes for certain human congenital defects. The author of this seminal reference tool hopes that by surveying the vast, diverse literature on experimental as well as human teratology, he will be providing a guide that will assist researchers and physicians in understanding and dealing with this complex medical problem. The information found in this volume will prove useful to a wide range of specialists, including teratologists, health care providers working in the fields dealing with congenital defects, and chemists who may be at risk in handling specific teratogenic agents.

This 8th edition of this text presents approximately 1,500 additions to the 7th edition, including coverage of 270 newly listed teratogenic agents. Overall, this reference catalog lists 2,571 potential teratogenic agents. Each listing provides a brief summary of some of the known teratogenic effects of specific drugs, chemicals, viruses, and physical factors, as well as bibliographical citations to one or more key article(s) dealing with this topic. Special attention is given to coverage of Russian- and Japanese-language publications. Very useful subject and name indexes make the material in this book easily accessible. The material in this reference work is far too complicated for the general public. However, this volume will be a basic reference tool for all medical and biological sciences libraries.—**Jonathon Erlen**

Chemically-Related Conditions

1721. Schmitz, Cecilia M., and Richard A. Gray. **Smoking: The Health Consequences of Tobacco Use: An Annotated Bibliography with Analytical Introduction.** Ann Arbor, Mich., Pierian Press, 1995. 298p. index. (Science and Social Responsibility Series, no.2). $30.00pa. ISBN 0-87650-343-1.

Key arguments in the controversies surrounding tobacco's possibly harmful health effects appear regularly in both social science and biomedical publications. Until this bibliographical guide, there has not been a basic reference tool to provide access to the current literature in this debate. This volume focuses on three major areas of the tobacco/health discussion: the addictive nature of tobacco; tobacco's direct role in causing specific medical problems (cancers, heart diseases, complications in pregnancy, lung ailments); and what parts of the U.S. public are tobacco users, based on such variables as sex, income, age, and education.

The editors begin this literature review with an extensive historical essay examining tobacco usage in the United States. Particular attention is centered on the warnings about tobacco's medical dangers, beginning with the 1957 governmental report on this topic. The bibliography provides lengthy annotations covering 106 English-language monographs, journal articles, and reports. The citations cover the 1985-1995 period, with the majority of entries being published after 1990. Annotations vary in length from two to four pages, thus presenting extensive coverage of each cited entry. Coverage does not include certain public health aspects of tobacco usage (i.e., ingestion of tobacco products, or the "sin tax" on tobacco products).

This reference work provides the medical and social science support for the surgeon general's warnings concerning the dangers of tobacco usage. All academic, health science, and large public libraries will find this volume an invaluable resource in dealing with tobacco/health-related questions.—**Jonathon Erlen**

Childbirth

1722. **Mayo Clinic Complete Book of Pregnancy & Baby's First Year.** Robert V. Johnson, ed. New York, William Morrow, 1994. 750p. illus. index. $30.00. ISBN 0-688-11761-9.

The Mayo Clinic's *Complete Book of Pregnancy & Baby's First Year*, despite its rather unwieldy title, is a remarkably complete and thorough guide to one of life's most challenging experiences. The book is divided into two sections: the first deals with conception (including infertility) through birth, and the second begins with the delivery experience and continues through the first year of life. There is an additional short section dealing with the effects of a baby on the family unit.

This book is an excellent combination of clear medical and physiological information, presented in a way that laypeople can absorb, and sound parenting tips. The format helps the comprehensibility: wide margins, lots of subtitles, and charts abound. Charts detail such things as aspirin dosages according to age, and typical pregnancy symptoms and what to do about them.

Every possible aspect of the two topics presented by the book is covered in great detail, with the thoroughness and clarity one would expect from the Mayo Clinic. The section on feeding a baby, for example, covers both breast and bottle feeding, explains the sucking reflex, explains lactation with the help of a diagram, discusses the importance of interaction during feeding and the relationship of feeding to sleep, different positions for breastfeeding, the complexities of scheduling, and so on. All topics in the book are presented in this degree of completeness. There are numerous illustrations and photographs. The ones showing the fetus at various stages of pregnancy are particularly clear and effective. A lengthy glossary and an index conclude the work.—**Wendy Waloff**

Chronic Pain

1723. **Classification of Chronic Pain: Descriptions of Chronic Pain Syndromes and Definitions of Pain Terms.** 2d ed. By Task Force on Taxonomy of the International Association for the Study of Pain. Harold Merskey and Nikolai Bogduk, eds. Seattle, Wash., International Association for the Study of Pain Press, 1994. 222p. index. $20.00pa. ISBN 0-931092-05-1.

Many medical subspecialties have found it necessary to develop a system of classification and coding to supplement ICD-10 (International Classification of Diseases). This edition has been extended, revised, and some of the definitions refined for members of the Association and others who deal with chronic pain syndromes in whatever site or medical context they may appear. The intent is to provide standard descriptions of the chronic pain syndromes and a method of codifying them in order to improve communication among scientists in their papers, speeches, and development of research protocols, data banks, and so on. Contributors are scattered worldwide, and their continued participation is requested—a work like this can never be finished.

Users should carefully study part 1. After a section on generalized syndromes, entries are grouped by site (e.g., head and neck). A typical entry includes definition, site, system, main features, causes when known, relief, pathology, differential diagnosis, the code assigned, and references. Another section defines such pain terms as neurogenic pain. Taxonomy is not usually of much concern to most health science libraries unless they are serving researchers, scientists, and clinicians for whom classification of a specific subject is important. This work is not a textbook on pain, and ordinary or acute phases are not considered except coincidentally, but it is a masterpiece for those interested in chronic pain.—**Harriette M. Cluxton**

Depression

1724. Miletich, John J., comp. **Depression: A Multimedia Sourcebook.** Westport, Conn., Greenwood Press, 1995. 217p. index. (Bibliographies and Indexes in Medical Studies, no.11). $69.50. ISBN 0-313-29374-0.

Climbing rates of depressive disorders have made them one of the premier maladies of the twentieth century. This set of selective, annotated bibliographies compiles multifaceted information, spanning nearly seven decades, and is intended to assist professionals, as well as the general public, in their research efforts. Included are books, review papers, articles, government documents, online databases, CD-ROMs, videocassettes, and television programs.

Five main bibliographies, with more than 800 citations, focus on the identification, causes, incidence, and treatment of depression, and on case examples and Prozac. They are alphabetically arranged within media categories. Fictional accounts and self-help materials are included together with more scholarly writings. The 16 appendixes that follow contain national organizations and their publications, media sources, and information in various indexes and abstracts. Author and subject indexes supply additional access by referring to page numbers in the text.

Literature on depression is proliferating with incidence of the disease itself. A guidebook to selective information sources provides direction to study and research, although other journals will have to be consulted for more cutting-edge information.—**Anita Zutis**

Epidemics

1725. **Encyclopedia of Plague and Pestilence.** George C. Kohn, ed. New York, Facts on File, 1995. 408p. index. $40.00. ISBN 0-8160-2758-7.

In the past few years, two major, highly regarded reference texts have been published surveying the broad scope of medical history: *Companion Encyclopedia of the History of Medicine* (see ARBA 95, entry 1654) and *The Cambridge World History of Human Disease* (see ARBA 95, entry 1662). This new encyclopedia, one in a series produced by Facts on File, fails to meet the quality standards established by the two previously mentioned works. Unlike the compilers of the earlier volumes, the editor and listed contributors for this new guide are not history of medicine scholars, and the lack of familiarity with this specialty field is apparent throughout this very disappointing book.

Any volume that claims (as does the dust jacket of this book) to be "... the only volume available that documents all the major, outstanding and unusual epidemics throughout the world, from the down of human history ..." is bound to fail, and this work is no exception. While the editor says his coverage is limited to "... important facts about particular epidemics ..." (p. vi), he does not explain his criteria for inclusion of epidemics and facts about these disease outbreaks. The book's organizational format is confusing, with epidemics arranged alphabetically by either name or geographic location. Thus, entries on one type of disease outbreak (e.g., plague, cholera) are scattered throughout the volume.

The unannotated bibliography for further reading is adequate for beginners, but ignores many studies one would expect to find in such a list; for example, Allan Brandt's *No Magic Bullet*, the major yellow fever studies by John Ellis and Margaret Humphrey, and Gunter Riesse's key work on plague in San Francisco. Coverage of individual epidemics ranges from one paragraph (Scottish smallpox 1823-31) to several pages (AIDS) in length. Further reading suggestions are appended to each full entry. Information presented about specific disease outbreaks focuses on basic causes and effects of that epidemic, while providing minimal mention of pathological and epidemiological aspects. This book's most useful features are the chronological timetable of epidemics and the geographical appendix locating disease outbreaks by country or continent. Even here, one could challenge the dating of epidemics (i.e., why list the AIDS outbreak as beginning in 1987?).

It is unfortunate that so much effort went into creating this unsatisfactory reference work. Potential users need to be aware of the serious weaknesses in this volume's scholarship and coverage, and should rely on the two reference guides previously mentioned, as well as the many high-quality studies readily available on specific epidemics.—**Jonathon Erlen**

Oncology

1726. Potparic, O., and J. Gibson. **A Dictionary of Human Oncology: A Concise Guide to Tumors.** New York, Parthenon, 1994. 173p. $55.00. ISBN 1-85070-472-4.

Directed to physicians and students, this guide describes many of the malignant and benign tumors affecting the human body. Histological and clinical features and sites are briefly summarized in highly scientific vocabulary. Causes (including some possible genetic and environmental factors), age-related incidence, and geographic frequency are added when known. Possible location of metasteses is indicated when appropriate.

Although there are many cross-references to alternate terms, many listed under "tumors" in a general medical dictionary do not appear as entries. Wilms' tumor is one of these; it is not considered under the "renal" listing either. Perhaps the selection of names for a concise dictionary must omit some; no explanation is given for either inclusion or exclusion, or the choice of one name over another. A few terms common to oncology, such as *sarcoma*, are scattered among the specific entries. Various kinds of neoplasms may be listed under a particular site, such as parotid gland tumors. There are eight pages beginning with the adjective "ovarian," and many under "malignant," but this does not cover the many malignancies noted under other terms. This discrepancy may simply reflect common usage in the specialty, but it is inconsistent with normal dictionary format. Differentiating among the large number of adult and childhood tumors, which are variously described in the considerable but widely diverse literature of oncology, is often very difficult. The authors hope to provide a practical starting point for identification and diagnosis. Oncologists will be the chief beneficiaries of their work.—**Harriette M. Cluxton**

Poisoning

1727. Turkington, Carol. **The Home Health Guide to Poisons and Antidotes.** New York, Facts on File, 1994. 372p. index. $12.95pa. ISBN 0-8160-3316-1.

Following the concept that knowledge is the first step in the prevention of poisoning, this book aims to make its readers aware of the great number and variety of toxic substances, both natural and man-made, in our environment. The guide shows how to recognize potential poisons and the symptoms they cause, and the methods and materials used in treatment. Not a first aid guide, it explains how to contact poison control centers or other medical resources when poisoning is suspected. It describes what information to furnish, and urges compliance with whatever directions may be given. The guide encourages following commonsense rules of prevention, such as avoiding hazardous materials and correctly handling foods.

The text is composed of an alphabetical listing of substances known to be poisonous, or that may be poisonous under certain circumstances, such as overdose or harmful combinations. While snake and insect bites are included, it is made clear that bacterial attacks, misuse of medications, and ingestion of harmful chemicals from house and garden plants, household cleaning products, and decorating products are the most important causes of poisoning, especially in children under five. Inhalation of noxious fumes and absorption of toxins through the skin are also considered.

Most entries discuss identification of a single harmful item; they state what about the item is poisonous (e.g., the plant root or chemicals contained), the symptoms, antidotes, and treatment. There are a few longer summaries, such as one on pesticides, and a notable article on food poisoning. The appendixes list poison control centers, sources of information, poisons by symptoms and toxicity ratings, and a bibliography. This book is a good addition to the home reference shelf or a library's consumer health section.

—Harriette M. Cluxton

Skin Conditions

1728. Mallory, Susan Bayliss, with Susana Leal-Khouri. **An Illustrated Dictionary of Dermatologic Syndromes.** New York, Parthenon Publishing, 1994. 250p. illus. $54.95. ISBN 1-85070-458-9.

This new syndrome dictionary will be useful for a broader audience than just dermatology specialists. Syndromes, 716 in number, are described in detail, and more than 150 color illustrations are used throughout the text as an added aid to recognition. The authors use the term *syndrome* to mean findings that run together, which means that any disorder that has any effect on the skin at all is included. Although the information on the syndromes is brief and covers only manifestations and major findings, key references at the end of each entry give the user access to further information. What sets this syndrome dictionary apart is an appendix that lists conditions, followed by disorders that show them. This could be helpful in making a diagnosis. For example, if a patient has pruritus, then 16 disease possibilities are given. This feature and the illustrations make this a worthy addition to medical libraries.

—Natalie Kupferberg

Sports Medicine

1729. Micheli, Lyle J., with Mark Jenkins. **The Sports Medicine Bible: Prevent, Detect, and Treat Your Sports Injuries....** New York, HarperPerennial/HarperCollins, 1995. 339p. illus. index. $20.00pa. ISBN 0-06-273143-2.

This text discusses sports-related injuries and is presented in an easy-to-read format. The first two chapters discuss fitness in the 1990s. Topics include the prevention of various sports injuries, proper clothing, and tips for exercising in various weather conditions, a nice feature for novice athletes.

Chapter 3 discusses strength and flexibility. It outlines flexibility requirements and discusses flexibility exercises and strength training techniques. Several illustrations accompany this section, and topics such as the "no pain, no gain" theory are also addressed. Chapters 4 and 5 provide the reader with useful information regarding the diagnosis, treatment, and rehabilitation of sports injuries. Basic treatment plans and terminology used to describe these injuries are covered. These chapters also address possible home treatments in addition to providing estimates in regard to recovery time.

A majority of this text is dedicated to addressing specific sports-related injuries, ranging from head to toe. For example, causes of injury, type of injury, associated signs and symptoms, treatment options, and physician involvement are just some of the items addressed. The final two chapters of this text provide information in regard to female athletic and geriatric athletic needs. Overall, this text provides the adult reader with much useful information. Most athletes will find this text to be of practical use, and most helpful when used in conjunction with a physician consultation or with other reference sources.

—Paul M. Murphy III

Surgery

1730. Surgeons' Reference for Minimally Invasive Surgery Products. Montvale, N.J., Medical Economics Data, 1994. 238p. illus. $125.00. ISBN 1-56363-073-7.

The rise in popularity and use of minimally invasive surgical techniques—laparoscopy, endoscopy, and the like—in the last five years has been phenomenal. This rapid development is concisely summarized by the editors in the foreword of this catalog. Obviously, a surgeon's knowledge has had to keep pace with the rapid progress. Adaptations of light and energy sources, photographic techniques, and so forth, have been made as a necessary accompaniment. Following the general format of the *Medical Device Register* produced by the same publisher, the *Surgeons' Reference* begins with trade name and keyword indexes and instructions for use.

The major section is the product directory, divided into 57 categories under which devices are listed alphabetically. Suppliers of these devices are listed under each, also alphabetically, with directory information. Where the manufacturer has furnished it, there is a full description of the product, how and when to use it, precautions, and even illustrations. In all, 274 types of instruments and equipment are included. There are occasional editorial comments. The supplier profiles section repeats the contact information for each supplier, lists all its products for this expanding field, and may give additional data about the company itself. (See Medical Device Register for other products beyond this field.)

Administrators, nurses, and especially purchasing agents will find this new compilation valuable, as well as the surgeons who perform various types of minimally invasive surgery. The *Surgeons' Reference* documents well the devices currently available for its practice, and how to obtain them.—**Harriette M. Cluxton**

NURSING

1731. The Directory of Nursing Homes, 1995. Baltimore, Md., HCIA, 1995. 2212p. index. $249.00pa. ISBN 1-880678-95-0. ISSN 0888-7624.

Although only about 5 percent of older adults permanently reside in nursing homes, it is estimated that about 20 percent of this group will spend some time during their life in a long-term care facility. This fact, coupled with the continued mobility of the American family, provides justification for directories of this type. When the need for nursing home care arises, trying to research even the names of facilities can be a challenge for those at a distance. Thus, this annually updated reference continues to provide much-needed information. Data, gathered by questionnaire, are provided on more than 16,000 nursing homes in the United States.

The homes are listed alphabetically by state, city, and facility name. The usual directory information is given for all facilities. The majority of listings also include administrators' names; numbers of beds in various levels of care; numbers of staff; payer mix (e.g., Medicare, Medicaid, private); admissions requirements; facilities and activities available; type of ownership (proprietary, not-for-profit); and certifications and affiliations. All information is not given for each facility, but the majority of listings are comprehensive.

The directory has few limitations. A more distinct designation of the Joint Commission on the Accreditation of Hospitals (JCAHO) accreditation would be recommended, since families may be searching for those homes that meet the highest national standards. The data have been provided by the facilities themselves, and thus the possibility exists for embellishment. This fact, however, is noted by the editors in the introduction. The limitations are easily outweighed by the benefits. Overall, this directory is an excellent resource for initiating the nursing home care process, and is highly recommended, especially for public libraries.—**Mary Ann Thompson**

1732. Powers, Bethel Ann, and Thomas R. Knapp. **A Dictionary of Nursing Theory and Research.** 2d ed. Thousand Oaks, Calif., Sage, 1995. 205p. $46.00; $22.95pa. ISBN 0-8039-5625-8; 0-8039-5626-6pa.

This is a new edition of a work first published in 1990 (see ARBA 91, entry 1706), adding 66 new definitions and revising many others. The intent of the dictionary is to provide a convenient explanation and discussion of terms commonly encountered in nursing science research. Definitions range in length from a short paragraph to several pages for the most basic terms; the authors describe examples of situations in which terms have been employed, and references to books and articles providing even more extended discussions of their meanings. A substantial bibliography is included.

Because nursing is a discipline dealing with people and patient care, nursing research borrows heavily in methodology from the social sciences and statistics. This volume contains very little medical terminology; there is much more overlap in terms covered between this dictionary and W. Paul Vogt's *Dictionary of Statistics and Methodology: A Nontechnical Guide for the Social Sciences* (see ARBA 94, entry 79) than such general nursing dictionaries as *Mosby's Pocket Dictionary of Medicine, Nursing, & Allied Health* (3d ed.; see ARBA 92, entry 1658). This work is a convenient volume that should be useful for its intended audience, including nursing students, faculty, and practicing nurses. The *Dictionary of Nursing Theory and Research* is recommended for health science and academic libraries.—**Marit S. MacArthur**

PHARMACY AND PHARMACEUTICAL SCIENCES

1733. **Biotechnology in the U.S. Pharmaceutical Industry 1995.** 4th ed. By the Institute for Biotechnology Information. Research Triangle Park, N.C., Institute for Biotechnology Information; distr., Phoenix, Ariz., Oryx Press, 1995. 521p. index. $695.00pa. ISBN 1-886041-01-6.

This work provides current in-depth information on biotechnology-related drug development and research in the pharmaceutical industry. The Institute for Biotechnology Information has for the past eight years targeted strategic business information related to biotechnology. The 4th edition of this special report combines information from the Institute's *U.S. Companies Database*, which includes details on more than 1,000 biotechnology firms and corporations, and the *Actions Database*, which covers the activities and alliances of biotechnology and pharmaceutical companies.

The first section is an overview of the industry with detailed analysis, statistics, projections, and commentary on issues facing the two industries. Tables provide concise summaries of such information as largest pharmaceutical corporations with biotechnology efforts; top-selling biotechnology drugs; research and development budgets as a percent of total sales; and estimated U.S. sales.

Company information and actions in section 2 provide the majority of this work. Pharmaceutical companies that have biotechnology products on the market or in development in the United States were surveyed in 1994; approximately one-third of these companies returned the survey. Data on the remaining companies came from previous surveys, annual reports, and business literature. Arranged alphabetically by the parent company name, each entry contains the address, key officers' names, brief descriptions of the products on the market and in development, the research and development budget, the total revenue, and affiliated company names. Alliances with biotechnology companies and a brief synopsis of the agreements are arranged in reverse chronological order through 1988.

A list of biotechnology-based drugs in development comprises section 3 of the book. Arranged by type of drug, each entry gives a description of indications, approval status (ranging from Investigative New Drug submission to FDA-approved), company name, and trade name, if available. The 4th section is a listing of more than 300 biotechnology firms that have either a primary or secondary focus on therapeutic drug development. Arranged alphabetically by company name, address and telephone numbers are included, as well as a brief listing of products on the market and in development. An index of company names follows the last section.

While the impact of biotechnology is probably the greatest in the pharmaceutical industry, this report is priced beyond the acquisitions budgets of most academic and public libraries. Clients of corporate libraries or business schools want this data, but may prefer electronic access to information updated on a more frequent basis.—**Vicki J. Killion**

1734. **Drug Topics Red Book, 1995.** Montvale, N.J., Medical Economics Data, 1995. 732p. illus. index. $49.95pa. ISBN 1-56363-108-3. ISSN 1072-1142.

This annual publication is the product catalog used by most pharmacists. It provides alphabetical listings of the pharmaceuticals currently available, cross-indexed by the generic name. Each entry lists the drug, what forms and strengths are available, the manufacturer, the average wholesale price, and the direct price. There is no information on indications, contraindications, or side effects, as can be found in other drug references, but it contains an excellent series of informational lists: drug information and poison control centers, state by state; poison antidotes; pills that should not be crushed; products that contain sulfites or that are alcohol- or sugar-free; drugs that cause photosensitivity; drug/food, drug/tobacco, and drug/alcohol interactions; and pregnancy and breast milk ratings. The book includes both prescription and over-the-counter products. There is much excellent information here that cannot be readily found elsewhere. It cannot replace classic references such as *Physicians' Desk Reference* (49th ed.; see ARBA 95, entry 1684), but the extra information it provides is well worth the price.—**Susan B. Hagloch**

1735. **Handbook of Therapeutic Interventions.** Springhouse, Pa., Springhouse, 1994. 660p. illus. index. $26.95pa. ISBN 0-87434-480-8.

This handbook provides an overview of hundreds of medical topics, such as various surgeries, medication administration, and wound care. The text itself is presented in an easy-to-use-and-read fashion. Although this handbook contains an ample amount of medical information, discussion of direct airway control (intubation) does not appear to be included.

The foreword of this handbook clearly explains how the book is designed to be used. This text has been created for use by medical professionals (nurses, physicians) and will probably be of benefit to these individuals as a medical resource. As with most medical texts, individuals may want to consult additional resources or professionals prior to making any final medical decisions.—**Paul M. Murphy III**

1736. **The History of Pharmacy: A Selected Annotated Bibliography.** Gregory J. Higby and Elaine C. Stroud, eds. Hamden, Conn., Garland, 1995. 321p. illus. index. (Bibliographies on the History of Science and Technology, v.25; Garland Reference Library of the Humanities, v.1366). $50.00. ISBN 0-8240-9768-8.

A broad overview of the literature emphasizing essential works, this book leads students, teachers, and historians to bibliographies, natural histories, and biographies in the fields of pharmacy, histories of drugs, pharmaceutical company histories, laws and regulations, pharmaceutical practices, and pharmacy in the arts. Comprehensive English-language secondary sources with good references were given preference in the selection process by the editors. Organized by subject into three main sections, each entry contains the standard bibliographic citation and a brief description. The first section includes a general overview of the field and selective references to bibliographies, encyclopedias, dictionaries, national studies, company histories, and biographies. Part 2 is titled "Special Subjects" and covers the scientific, practical, educational, and societal aspects of pharmacy. Finally, pharmacy as reflected in the arts (architecture, painting, sculpture, music, and literature) composes the third section. If an entry can be placed in more than one section, the complete citation is repeated rather than cross-referenced. Despite being a selective list of the major references in the field and lacking a subject index, this book will be useful for the first-time researcher of a particular area. No one section is so extensive that the reader cannot locate relevant information quickly and easily.—**Vicki J. Killion**

1737. Long, James W., and James J. Rybacki. **The Essential Guide to Prescription Drugs 1995.** New York, HarperCollins, 1994. 1151p. index. $18.00pa. ISBN 0-06-273317-6. ISSN 0894-7058.

Aimed at providing the reader with information needed to supplement the direction and guidance received from a physician, this book offers detailed profiles of more than 300 of the most commonly used drugs. Newly approved drugs and revised therapeutics have been included in this edition (see ARBA 92, entry 1695, and ARBA 88, entry 1690, for reviews of earlier editions).

The book consists of six sections. Section 1 serves to orient the user to the complexities of modern drug therapy and how to make the best use of the information contained in the other five sections. The second section contains the profile and drug therapy of 21 common chronic disorders (these have been revised or expanded to reflect the most recent developments). Section 3 is the major portion of the book, with the descriptive entries for more than 300 prescription drugs used in the United States and Canada. Lists of drugs arranged alphabetically by their chemical or therapeutic class designation are found in the fourth section. The fifth section is a glossary, and the final section emphasizes pertinent aspects of drug behavior. The index lists both brand and generic drug names.

Drug selection was governed by several criteria, including the extent of its use, the urgency of the conditions for which it is prescribed, and the volume and complexity of the information essential to its proper utilization. Each profile contains at least 45 separate categories of information, among them benefits versus risks; principal uses; dosage and administration; drug action; safety; possible effects on sexual function; precautions during pregnancy or breastfeeding; and concerns for geriatric patients.

This book will be an excellent substitute for the consumer wanting the same information found in the drug manufacturer's package insert or in the *Physicians' Desk Reference* (see ARBA 95, entry 1684, and ARBA 94, entry 1880), but in lay terms. Any library with consumer health information should consider adding this book to its collection.—**Vicki J. Killion**

1738. **PDR Generics.** Montvale, N.J., Medical Economics Data, 1995. 2887p. index. $69.95. ISBN 1-56363-118-0.

A comprehensive compendium of nearly all single- and multisource prescription drugs in general use, this single volume not only provides the clinician with a complete overview of the drug, but also presents the alternative sources and the comparative costs. Nearly 24,000 drug products are included for rapid selection of the optimum drug at the most advantageous price. The prescribing information found in *PDR Generics* has been selected, integrated, and reviewed by the board of pharmaceutical editors to reflect all major forms and sources of each generic entity. In contrast, the information found in the PDR is supplied by the manufacturers and is usually taken directly from the package insert. The entries are organized alphabetically by generic name and cross-referenced by leading brand names. Each entry gives complete prescribing information (including description, pharmacology, indications and usage, contraindications, adverse reactions); data on available forms and strengths; suppliers and prices; and reimbursement codes. Use in pregnancy ratings, therapeutic equivalency indicators, and controlled substance status are also given when applicable.

The brand and generic name index lists all generic products profiled in the product information section. The names of all associated brands are printed under the appropriate generic name. The product category index organizes the generic entities under a given therapeutic or pharmacologic category (i.e., beta-blocking drugs will be found in the "cardiovascular agents" section). More than 2,300 specific indications and the drugs used for each are found in the indications index. All FDA-approved uses are listed, along with the generally accepted unlabeled or off-label uses documented in the peer-reviewed literature. A manufacturers directory, a product identification guide using imprints, a visual identification guide, and directories for poison control centers and drug information centers are also found in this resource.

The obvious intent of the book is to provide the prescribing clinician with information on the most cost-effective therapeutic modality. Health science librarians will want this resource for their specialized clientele; other librarians may use it as an alternative to the PDR or other drug information resources.

—**Vicki J. Killion**

1739. **PDR Guide to Drug Interactions, Side Effects, Indications, 1995.** 49th ed. Mukesh Mehta, ed. Montvale, N.J., Medical Economics Data, 1995. 1536p. index. $47.95. ISBN 1-56363-094-X.

In increasing numbers, patients are seeking information about the possible side effects and adverse reactions of their prescription drugs. The entries in this guide cover more than 2,600 drug products. Entries are arranged alphabetically by brand or generic name. The boldface entry is followed by a list of brands by which the user may identify the medication. Entries include dosage form and strength, therapeutic indicators, precautions, side effects, information about the relief of symptoms, brief descriptions of interactions with other drugs, brief descriptions of interactions with food or alcohol, and adverse reactions. The *PDR Guide to Drug Interactions* is comprehensive and completely cross-referenced to the 1995 edition of *The Physicians' Desk Reference* (see ARBA 95, entry 1684). For up-to-date information, color pictures, and product information, consult the *PDR* text.

This work is divided into five separate sections: interactions index (white pages); food interactions (blue pages); side effects index (pink pages); indications index (yellow pages); and a list of certified poison control centers.

The first section lists the brand-name entry followed by a summary of the major pharmaceutical categories with which the drug will interact. Look for some duplication, such as Extra-Strength Tylenol and acetaminophen. The side effects section contains an alphabetical list of the more than 3,500 distinct reactions cited throughout *PDR* and its companion volumes. The guide is recommended as a standard reference tool for academic, public, and medical libraries.—**Marilynn Green**

1740. Pettit, George R., Fiona Hogan Pierson, and Cherry L. Herald. **Anticancer Drugs from Animals, Plants, and Microorganisms.** New York, John Wiley, 1994. 670p. index. $94.95. ISBN 0-471-03657-9.

The focus of this reference work is animal, microorganism, and plant constituents as potential sources for anticancer, antiviral, and other drugs. The tabular survey of these constituents continues literature coverage from January 1986 to January 1989, and the general style of *Biosynthetic Products for Cancer Chemotherapy, Volume 6*, by G. R. Pettit, C. L. Herald, and C. R. Smith (Elsevier Science, 1989).

Entries are listed in order of molecular formula, and also include such data as the structure, molecular weight, melting point, bioactivity (if known), organism, location of the organism, and a referral to one or more citations in the extensive bibliography. Two brief chapters precede these pages: The first covers cancer-causing and related human viruses with emphasis on HIV-1 infections; the second summarizes information on the better-known tumor promoters and carcinogens.

Chemists, biologists, and clinicians concerned with the discovery and development of new anti-cancer drugs will find this reference useful to verify chemical structure or locate what should be the first occurrence in the literature of a particular entity.—**Vicki J. Killion**

1741. **Physicians' Desk Reference for Nonprescription Drugs, 1994.** 15th ed. Montvale, N.J., Medical Economics Data, 1994. 768p. illus. $39.95. ISBN 1-56363-065-6.

As more medications become available without prescription, the need for accessible drug information increases. The *Physicians' Desk Reference for Nonprescription Drugs*, an annual publication from Medical Economics Data, covers these medicines. The book is also available in CD-ROM format along with its companion PDR volumes and the 16th edition of the *Merck Manual*.

Organized like the PDR, this book has four color-coded indexes: manufacturers, product name, product category, and active ingredients. It also has a color product identification section with pictures of both the package and the tablet or capsule for drugs in those forms. The main body of the book contains product information arranged alphabetically by manufacturer and brand name. This includes product name, description, composition, actions and uses, administration and dosage, precautions and warnings, and how supplied. Some homeopathic preparations are covered. There is also a brief section on diagnostic devices and medical aids that offers information on selected home pregnancy and ovulation tests.

Although the *Physicians' Desk Reference for Nonprescription Drugs* covers 700 products, the information about them is supplied by their manufacturers. For more comprehensive and objective coverage, the *Complete Drug Reference* (see ARBA 93, entry 1662), *Zimmerman's Complete Guide to Nonprescription Drugs* (see ARBA 94, entry 1886), and the *Handbook of Over-the-Counter Drugs and Pharmacy Products* by Max R. Leber, Robert W. Jaeger, and Anthony J. Scalzo (Celestial Arts, 1994) are excellent supplements.—**Barbara M. Bibel**

1742. Sharp, John. **European Pharmaceutical Technical and Regulatory Compendium: A Dictionary of Words, Terms, Phrases....** Buffalo Grove, Ill., Interpharm Press, 1994. 275p. $89.00pa. ISBN 0-935184-57-0.

The first 97 pages of this work form a dictionary of concisely defined terms and acronyms used throughout the European Union (EU) that are not readily used in the United States. A set of "allowed terms" is included for answering questions on the EU application format for a drug. The second part of the book is a directory of the members of the EU and their committees. General information is given on each country, including size, population, political structure, economics, and the contact people of governmental agencies who administer health care and pharmaceutics within the country. There is a list

of European trade associations, and the appendixes cover major EU medicinal legislation. Designed to be used in conjunction with *Interpharms' FDA-SPEAK*, this specialized book is recommended for pharmaceutical company libraries and libraries that deal with European pharmaceutical trade.
—**Betsy J. Kraus**

1743. Sultenfuss, Sherry Wilson, and Thomas J. Sultenfuss. **A Woman's Guide to Vitamins and Minerals.** Chicago, Contemporary Books, 1995. 270p. index. $16.95. ISBN 0-8092-3509-9.

This book is a review of the scientific literature on vitamins, minerals, and herbs, compiled to give the healthy adult woman sufficient information to make smart decisions on nutritional choices and available supplements. It is not a self-treatment or diet manual. Although some suggestions for buying supplements and such recognized guidelines as RDAs (recommended dietary allowances) are given, seeking professional advice is advocated. No dosages are given.

The sources of information are mostly medical and nutritional journals. These are listed under the section "Notes and Bibliography" at the end of the book, so that the text is easily readable. Literature searches by a professional medical librarian yielded the research the author compiled into this guidebook. Her husband, a board-certified physician, edited it for medical accuracy. The main portion of the book is about nutritional supplements. The usual format under each is primary function, food sources, recommendations, *Woman's Guide* suggestions, antagonists, toxicity, and warnings to be considered.

Topics of prime concern to women, such as hormone replacement therapy, the female heart, and skin and aging, are treated in a separate section. Herbs and their uses are discussed here; many have been used by women for centuries for various purposes, although there is little proof of their efficacy in modern research papers. This current and comprehensive review of the scientific literature on vitamins and minerals should be a valuable reference in many libraries.—**Harriette M. Cluxton**

1744. **USP DI 1995. Volume I: Drug Information for the Health Care Professional.** 15th ed. Rockville, Md., United States Pharmacopeial Convention, 1995. 3279p. index. $109.00. ISBN 0-913595-83-7. ISSN 0740-4174.

1745. **USP DI 1995. Volume II: Advice for the Patient: Drug Information in Lay Language.** 15th ed. Rockville, Md., United States Pharmacopeial Convention, 1994. 1807p. $54.00. ISBN 0-913595-84-5. ISSN 0740-6916.

1746. **USP DI 1995. Volume III: Approved Drug Products and Legal Requirements.** 15th ed. Rockville, Md., United States Pharmacopeial Convention, 1995. 1v. (various paging). $98.00. ISBN 0-913595-85-3. ISSN 1045-8298.

The *USP DI* is a series of three volumes that includes comprehensive information on all drugs (both prescription and over-the-counter) used in the United States. Most importantly, the information in these volumes represents a consensus of opinion from a panel of 33 experts in the health and pharmaceutical fields. These experts go beyond the material provided by the drug manufacturers, and include all possible research and scientific conclusions about each drug. These works are thus as free as possible from promotional hype and commercial bias.

Volume 1 of this series is a highly technical volume of information for pharmacists, doctors, researchers, and other professionals. Drugs are arranged in alphabetical order by broad chemical categories, accessible by an index including all brand and generic names. Entries discuss indications for use; precautions such as age restrictions and warnings for pregnancy and breast-feeding; dosages; possible side effects; and advice on patient instruction. Interestingly, when the advisory panel considers it warranted, nontraditional or "unlabeled" uses are given. The 14 appendixes at the end of the book are invaluable. Among others, there are lists of drugs to beware of in pregnancy, lists of drugs for particular indications, lists of drugs to beware of in geriatric patients, and even a list of drug precautions for athletes (i.e., banned substances).

Volume 2 is exactly as the title states—drug information for the patient, in language the patient can understand. It is meant to be copied by the drug dispenser and given to the patient (copyright permission is given). All of the information in volume 1 is also in volume 2, but in simpler and more understandable form. (Note: This volume is now available on computer disk, so that pharmacists can print out the entries in leaflet form. Preprinted leaflets, in Spanish or English, are available for the most commonly prescribed drugs.) Unfortunately, not all pharmacists and physicians are conscientious about patient education, so careful health consumers should consider owning a copy of this book.

Volume 3 is, once again, very technical information, particularly therapeutic equivalences, state and federal legal requirements, information on safe storage, and lists of sources and manufacturers. All three volumes include medicine charts—pages with color photographs of about 1,400 widely used capsules and tablets. This set should be in any library used by health professionals. In addition, volume 2 (or at least the paperback edition titles *About Your Medicines*), should be on the shelf of every public library.—**Carol L. Noll**

1747. **USP Dictionary of USAN and International Drug Names.** Carolyn A. Fleeger, ed. Rockville, Md., United States Pharmacopeial Convention, 1994. 919p. $109.00pa. ISBN 0-913595-82-9. ISSN 1076-4275.

This dictionary of drug names has been published by the United States Pharmacopeial Convention since 1963. This edition includes all nonproprietary names, brand names, code designations, and Chemical Abstracts Service (CAS) registry numbers for drugs assigned through June 15, 1994. The work is cumulative from June 15, 1961, when the U.S. Adopted Names (USAN) program began.

A preface explains the rules and procedures for drug nomenclature and the role of the United States Pharmacopeia and National Formulary in promoting and maintaining consistency in the process. The main body of the text is an alphabetical list of code numbers and names for drugs. Code number entries list only the drug name. Name entries include molecular and structural formulas, drug class, and brand names and their companies. There is a separate section for Technetium Tc99m radiopharmaceuticals. Lists of drugs by categories and orphan drugs complete the text. Four appendixes cover the principles of coining U.S. Adopted Names for drugs, CAS and National Service Center (NSC) registry numbers, molecular formulas, and names and addresses of U.S. companies concerned with compounds for which USAN have been selected. This directory is a useful resource for medical, chemical, and business reference collections because it provides basic information about generic and brand names of drugs, as well as the names of the companies that own them.—**Barbara M. Bibel**

34 High Technology

GENERAL WORKS

1748. Borman, Jami Lynne. **Computer Dictionary for Kids and Their Parents.** Hauppauge, N.Y., Barron's Educational Series, 1995. 253p. illus. $14.95pa. ISBN 0-8120-9079-9.

There are practically hundreds of books that deal with all aspects of computer science, including at least two dozen computer dictionaries. For example, in 1993, Houghton Mifflin published the *Dictionary of Computer Words* (see ARBA 95, entry 1691). That publication was a modestly priced compilation with readable text and several illustrations.

This present volume is geared to children ages 8-13. It covers 650 key computer concepts, providing readable definitions with color diagrams and illustrations. This handy dictionary explains terms such as *bitmap*, *byte*, *expansion card*, *integrated circuits*, *interface*, and *nanosecond*. It will even explain the differences between some of the various types of computer components. Also contained in this reference book are a brief history of computers as well as several games and puzzles to challenge the reader's understanding of the definitions presented.

Barron's reputation is well known to students and educators. This dictionary is recommended not only for school libraries but also for home use.—**Patricia B. Lutz**

1749. **CorpTech Directory of Technology Companies 1995.** 10th U.S. ed. Woburn, Mass., Corporate Technology Information Services, 1995. 4v. maps. indexes. $525.00/set. ISBN 1-57114-008-5.

The 10th edition of this standard directory of technology companies is published in 4 volumes: Volume 1 includes indexes and company rankings, and volumes 2-4 present corporate profiles A to Z. The information was provided by the companies listed herein, and a copy of each listing was mailed to them for verification. In other words, the publisher does not guarantee or accept responsibility for accuracy or completeness. It is important to know that permission is given to photocopy pages for internal or personal use of specific clients who are registered with the Copyright Clearance Center (CCC), providing that the stated fee is paid per copy directly to the CCC. The printout is clear, and the text is legible. These volumes should be in the hands of all interested parties and large public libraries as well as educational institutions.—**Bohdan S. Wynar**

1750. Dillon, Patrick M., and David C. Leonard. **Multimedia Technology from A to Z.** Phoenix, Ariz., Oryx Press, 1995. 225p. $19.95pa. ISBN 0-89774-892-1.

Dillon and Leonard have produced an outstanding dictionary of multimedia technology. They have attempted to define some 1,000 terms relating to the multimedia industry. Terms are included if they meet broad industry guidelines or are necessary to the understanding of the background of multimedia technology. The work is truly comprehensive in scope, covering terms from *MPEG* to *Foley Effect* to *cabling*. One is likely to find terms that have anything to do with the film, video, computer, recording, or media industries. In the preface, the authors state that their "most concentrated effort in the video realm is in the area of post-production, where the general move toward all-digital, computer-based tools provides us with a reinforcing motive to include these terms." Also listed are digital video effect terms used in postproduction work and background terms from "authoring systems" used to develop current multimedia software.

The explanations are well written and extensively reference other terms defined in the book. The authors' writing style is a true joy to read and conveys much to the reader about the topic. There are no illustrations to assist the reader in understanding terms; interesting, given that the topic of the work is "multimedia." However, given the amount of material packed in this handy volume, the addition of illustrative material may be prohibitive in terms of cost. The volume is in paperback format with a binding that will not stand much library use. Again, this is another compromise for the authors to make in terms of book production cost allocation. All types of libraries will find this excellent volume a valued addition to their collections. It covers a technology that libraries and librarians will be bound up in for the foreseeable future.—**Ralph Lee Scott**

1751. **The International Multimedia Yearbook 1995-1996.** Jim Ayre, Jane Callaghan, and Signe Hoffos, eds. Chicago, Fitzroy Dearborn, 1995. 955p. illus. index. $150.00. ISBN 1-884964-39-7.

1752. **International Multimedia Yearbook 1995-1996 on CD-ROM.** [CD-ROM]. Chicago, Fitzroy Dearborn, 1995. Minimum system requirements: IBM or compatible. CD-ROM drive. Windows. free w/ book purchase. ISBN 1-884964-43-5.

This invaluable source tracks the entire global village of multimedia (e.g., companies, markets, products, distributors) with signed articles and several directory sections in both the printed and CD-ROM versions. The CD-ROM edition employs a well-constructed, easily searchable Windows interface with clearly designated menus and buttons. Introductory articles define multimedia and its operating technologies, followed by editorials on the market and the newest technologies (e.g., Windows 95, the Internet). The interviews with corporate executives focus on product innovations and industry predictions, while the 15 national profiles analyze trends, government involvement, and innovations in countries such as Spain and Japan. The CD-ROM assists searches of specific categories and of all articles by keyword. Results can be viewed in three languages (English, French, German) and various typeface sizes, an attractive feature for libraries serving visually impaired or English-as-a-second-language students.

From information provided by parent organizations and multimedia companies, products and services are identified in three directory sections. The unique company and product numbers, which have cross-references between profiles and other listings in the printed directory, are available but less relevant for CD-ROM searches. For company entries, standard data (e.g., address, fax number, description) is offered along with such categories as the platforms supported and the type of product. All elements are searchable fields in the CD-ROM edition. Distributors and offices for 71 countries are listed in a separate printed directory, but reside within the company section in the CD-ROM edition. Distributors are easily located by specifying distribution in the type of business field and desired country or product in the appropriate fields.

Products can be searched through the 39-category products directory and the name, producer, and distributor indexes. The inadequate arrangement of the indexes is improved by the availability of product numbers and the Boolean capabilities of the CD-ROM. A sizable glossary, outdated events directory, and bibliography complete the volume. The bibliography uses subject headings and refers primarily to works about techniques and applications. The CD-ROM also contains some pleasant surprises among the data files and other samples of multimedia at its best. The printed edition, a finely crafted reference tool designed for specific clientele, will likely be supplanted by demand for the CD-ROM. An excellent example of what can be produced for the reference market, other publishers would do well to use this pair as a model.—**Sandra E. Belanger**

ARTIFICIAL INTELLIGENCE

1753. **The McGraw-Hill Illustrated Encyclopedia of Robotics & Artificial Intelligence.** Stan Gibilisco, ed. New York, TAB Books/McGraw-Hill, 1994. 420p. illus. index. $40.00; $24.95pa. ISBN 0-07-023613-5; 0-07-023614-3pa.

This concise dictionary is aimed at computer/electronics hobbyists and students. The editor, Gibilisco, is the author or coauthor of more than 25 successful electronics reference books, including the 1985 American Library Association award-winning *Encyclopedia of Electronics* (see ARBA 86, entry 1568). What sets this book apart from others, such as *Robotics Sourcebook* by V. Daniel Hunt (Elsevier Science, 1988), is the inclusion of short biographies of important people in this area (for example, Eric Mittelstadt, the first president of GMF Robotics) and a number of short entries describing generic robots, such as molecular or neurosurgery assistance robots. Also included are numerous slang terms, such as *kludgerobot* and the proprietary names of robots.

However, many terms (for example, *monitor*, *real time*, and *servo system*) can be found in any good technical dictionary. There are some illustrations and a bibliography. The bibliography contains nine entries, eight of which were published between 1979 and 1989 and one—*Applied Artificial Intelligence: A Sourcebook*—that was published in 1992 by TAB Books/McGraw-Hill. Still, this book would be useful in any high school or public library because the definitions are clear and do not contain jargon or mathematical formulas. It provides good value for the price. [R: RBB, 1 Jan 95, pp. 843-44]—**Susan B. Ardis**

COMPUTING
General Works
Dictionaries and Encyclopedias

1754. **Dictionary of Computer Words.** rev. ed. New York, Houghton Mifflin, 1995. 332p. illus. index. $11.95pa. ISBN 0-395-72834-7.

This dictionary contains more than 1,200 words and phrases related to computers, networked communication, and multimedia. Definition lengths average about a quarter of a page, but range from a single sentence to a couple of pages. Entries are liberally cross-referenced, and tables supplement the textual definitions. There are a few gray-scale illustrations and a subject index.

Computer dictionaries become outdated quickly, and this is a revision of a 1993 work (see ARBA 95, entry 1691), mostly adding words relating to the Internet and multimedia. Its terms are taken from computer journals, the database of the American Heritage Dictionary of English, and hardware and software advertisements. The entries are clear, nontechnical, and thorough. They begin with a one-sentence definition followed by a clear, succinct discussion that sets the word in context and refers to other entries. No inaccuracies could be found and there were very few missing words, given its scope. The subject index is of questionable value, except perhaps as a memory jogger.

This is an excellent concise dictionary for both new and experienced computer users. However, the reader might want to consider the strengths and weaknesses of other recent computer dictionaries. The *Microsoft Press Computer Dictionary* (Microsoft Press, 1993) is larger (5,000 entries), with several detailed appendixes and photographic illustrations. *Prentice Hall's Illustrated Dictionary of Computing* (1995; see ARBA 94, entry 1902, for an earlier edition) is also larger and contains photographic illustrations, but it seems to be older than its imprint would suggest. Robin Williams's *Jargon: An Informal Dictionary of Computer Terms* (see ARBA 94, entry 1905) contains long, informal, cutesy articles. It does not always get around to defining terms. The *IBM Dictionary of Computing* (see ARBA 95, entry 1695) is very large (20,000 terms) but draws most of its words from an IBM mainframe environment, thereby limiting its usefulness.—**A. Neil Yerkey**

1755. Downing, Douglas A., Michael A. Covington, and Melody Mauldin Covington. **Dictionary of Computer Terms.** 4th ed. Hauppauge, N.Y., Barron's Educational Series, 1995. 357p. illus. $9.95pa. ISBN 0-8120-9023-3.

This pocked-sized dictionary has more than 1,300 terms on computer applications, commands, functions, programming languages, hardware, and operating systems. The definitions range in length from 1 sentence to 3 pages, the average being about 30-50 words. The dictionary contains a well-balanced mix of terms having to do with issues (e.g., computer ethics), applications (e.g., drag and drop), and technology (e.g., RS-232 pin assignments). Entries are supplemented by line drawings, tables, diagrams, and sample computer programs. The authors' stated goal was to explain, not just define, terms. They have succeeded admirably. The entries are well written, informative, accurate, and well cross-referenced. This reviewer found no errors and few obvious omissions.

Although this dictionary is outstanding in terms of clarity and helpfulness of the entries, other recent computer dictionaries may be worth considering: *Dictionary of Computer Words* (see entry 1754) is similar to this one, but its terms are not quite as thoroughly explained; *Microsoft Press Computer Dictionary* (Microsoft Press, 1993) is larger (5,000 entries), more detailed, and contains photographic illustrations. *Prentice Hall's Illustrated Dictionary of Computing* (see ARBA 94, entry 1902) is also larger and contains photographic illustrations, but the definitions seem dated; *Jargon: An Informal Dictionary of Computer Terms* (see ARBA 94, entry 1905) contains long, informal articles that are sometimes not helpful; and the *IBM Dictionary of Computing* (see ARBA 95, entry 1695) is large (20,000 terms) but draws more of its words from an IBM mainframe environment, limiting its usefulness.—**A. Neil Yerkey**

1756. Dyson, Peter. **The PC User's Essential Accessible Pocket Dictionary.** San Francisco, Sybex, 1994. 577p. illus. $12.99pa. ISBN 0-89588-756-8.

Although almost everything the title says it is, this book does not fit into any pockets! However, its small size does fit nicely into a book bag or briefcase. This book is designed to meet the needs of people who use computers but who are not computer professionals (i.e., computer gurus). It includes definitions for all areas of computers (hardware, software, and computer commands). However, this book is not a listing of "arcane mainframe terminology." It is designed for, and succeeds at, supplying easy-to-understand definitions of computer terms.

The dictionary provides *see* and *see also* references with appropriate definitions, but there is no index. The work has 564 pages of terms, plus an appendix of ASCII and extended ASCII character sets; a table of video adapter standards for IBM-compatible computers; a table of common disk and memory terminology (useful); and a table of decimal, hexadecimal, and binary conversions. The book is well designed, and locating terms is made easy after reading the important section on how the book is organized. One useful feature is a phonetical list of terms that are spelled differently than they are pronounced (i.e., *SCSI* is listed under "SCSI" and has a *see* reference under "scuzzy."

No book dealing with computers can be completely current, and this book is no exception (Frame Technology Corporation, which makes FrameMaker, was recently purchased by Adobe, and Ventura Publisher was purchased by Corel some time ago—both of these products were incorrectly listed in the book). Regardless, this book is recommended for public libraries, school libraries for grades 4-12, college libraries, and anyone needing easy-to-understand definitions of computer terms.—**Alan N. Livingston**

1757. Freedman, Alan. **The Computer Glossary: The Complete Illustrated Dictionary.** 7th ed. New York, AMACOM, 1995. 456p. illus. $36.95; $24.95pa; $39.95pa. (with disk). ISBN 0-8144-0268-2; 0-8144-7872-7pa; 0-8144-0127-9pa. (with disk).

This dictionary of computer terms and concepts belongs in every computer library. Useful items include a topics section that "contains the fundamental terms for each subset of the [computer] industry," greatly helping people find terms about certain topics, and a perspective chart "depicting the interrelationship of systems within the computer industry from a manager's point of view." This book contains 456 pages of definitions, and provides many useful (and entertaining) line drawings. There are also a few interesting photographs, such as the picture of ENIAC, "the first operational electronic digital computer," which, as the illustration graphically portrays, "took up 1,800 square feet" of space—"today, the equivalent technology is used in a watch."

As noted on the first and last pages of the definitions, "most of the terms in this book are defined by their acronyms, not their formal names"; therefore, one must think in acronyms. For example, a reader will not find *end of file* under "end," but rather under "EOF." Included in this book are concepts, such as how to select a personal computer. Also furnished are concise histories of some terms that follow the definition and are interesting and informative. One such example is the programming language Ada on page 5. This book is highly recommended for all libraries that have computer-using patrons.—**Alan N. Livingston**

1758. **International Biographical Dictionary of Computer Pioneers.** J. A. N. Lee, ed. Chicago, Fitzroy Dearborn, 1995. 816p. illus. index. $75.00. ISBN 1-884964-47-8.

This excellent reference book provides information on several hundred people who played an important part in the growth and development of the computer industry. Many of the names have been drawn from the *Annals of the History of Computing*, in particular from the work done for the 10th anniversary issue; other sources were also used. The editor has tried to include not only pioneers—defined as those whose contributions were central to the field of computing—but also managers, educators, and financiers. It is unclear when the cutoff date is; for example, Steve Jobs and Steve Wozniak are included, but Bill Gates is not.

Each entry tries to set the person in the context of computer developments of the time and show the impact or influence of the person on the field of computing. The entries are uneven in their completeness, depending on the role of the person and the amount of information the compilers were able to locate. The fullest entries have a brief biographical statement, followed by education, professional experience, and honors and awards. Many of the entries contain articles written by people who personally knew the subject of the entry; these articles have been selected because they help set the people in context and show their importance to the field of computing. The individual bibliographies contain biographical references and lists of significant publications by the person profiled. Some entries have pictures and a quotation from the biographee.

The appendix lists collections of biographies and memoirs. It also references oral interviews conducted for the Charles Babbage Institute Oral History Collection (June 1992). Furnished in the appendix are lists of professional society awards, including the Association for Computing Machinery, IEEE Computer Society, American Association for Artificial Intelligence, American Federation of Information Processing, Computing Research Association, and the Inamori Foundation. The index is comprehensive, and all the biographical entries are also listed alphabetically in the table of contents. This is a useful reference source. It supplies information about lesser-known figures in the field of computing, but it also contains fascinating insights into many of the better-known figures.—**Linda Main**

1759. Malkin, Gary Scott. **Comprehensive Networking Glossary and Acronym Guide.** Greenwich, Conn., Manning; distr., New York, Prentice Hall Trade/Simon & Schuster, 1995. 200p. illus. $29.00pa. ISBN 0-13-319955-X.

Based on a popular Internet glossary, this dictionary offers brief definitions of 1,500 terms and acronyms, with extensive cross-references and some illustrations. Although the alphabetically arranged compilation is intended for both experts and novices, its reliance on other technical terms within definitions (e.g., TCP/IP, AppleTalk) will prove difficult for some novices. They will, however, appreciate the concise explanations for the many acronyms (e.g., ZIP [Zone Information Protocol]) bandied about but rarely explained in the literature.

The appendixes list terms in three categories (e.g., security, protocols, organizations), but are practically useless in their current form. The lack of page numbers and essential data (e.g., e-mail addresses, telephone numbers) is a problem that would be resolved by a comprehensive subject index. This unique resource, despite its limitations, will prove an essential acquisition for many of today's libraries. [R: Choice, April 95, p. 1278]—**Sandra E. Belanger**

1760. **The McGraw-Hill Illustrated Dictionary of Personal Computers.** 4th ed. By Michael F. Hordeski. New York, McGraw-Hill, 1995. 568p. illus. $32.95; $24.95pa. ISBN 0-07-0304092; 0-07-0304106pa.

Anyone with an agenda or an enthusiastic ego can easily quibble endlessly over the many subjective editorial choices that result in the publication of a technical dictionary: This term was not included, or that one was. What matters most is, does it work and for whom? With a current issue of *BYTE* magazine in hand, this reviewer checked how useful this dictionary would be to the average reader (of computer-oriented literature). Actually, this 4th edition passed the test with flying colors.

Except for the trendiest of acronyms and terminology, the dictionary works. There are trademarked names that are not covered, but who can keep track in this marketplace? There are enough adequate definitions and cross-references. For a complete novice, this could be a frustrating reference tool, for it assumes a certain familiarity with things silicon. Nonetheless, this is a useful dictionary worth buying.

On the other hand, the illustrations and schematics are singularly unattractive and add little to the understanding of a particular word or term. A good technical acronym dictionary, access to an online database, or a connection to the World Wide Web would extend the usefulness of this text. This is a comprehensive, worthwhile addition to any reference shelf.—**George M. Cumming Jr.**

1761. **The Network Press Dictionary of Networking.** By Peter Dyson. Alameda, Calif., Network Press/Sybex, 1995. 404p. $22.99pa. ISBN 0-7821-1818-6.

The Network Press Dictionary of Networking is a revision of *Novell's Dictionary of Networking* (Sybex, 1994), intended to be of use to networking professionals and users of computer networks. The entries are organized alphabetically, with some cross-referencing included. Individual entries are sufficiently complete and accurate to be helpful to the beginner. For the professional attempting to fill a gap, however, they are generally too brief to be useful. For both groups, the lack of any references to other resources that would provide more detailed information is a serious omission.

Although the volume contains some discussion of non-Novell networks (e.g., Banyan Vines, TCP/IP, and AppleTalk), the coverage is sketchy, in contrast to the rich and detailed information on Novell Netware. Much of the book describes general computer concepts—terms pertaining to memory allocation, hard disk use, and stand-alone operating systems—rather than networking concepts. Some omissions are striking. Although the period is frequently called a "dot," there is no listing under *dot* to identify the character or explain its uses. The exclamation point is identified as "bang" (standard jargon in the UNIX world), but the "at" symbol (@) is not similarly identified as "glitch."

Although almost every Netware term this reviewer could think of is listed (oddly, *supervisor* is not listed, although it is used in the definition of *ADMIN*), terms equally fundamental to other networking systems are not included. For example, many of the commands fundamental to UNIX networking in a TCP/IP environment are omitted, with no listings for *routed*, *named*, *resolver*, *traceroute*, or (the UNIX command) *host*, all commands important to system administration. On balance, this reference is useful to anyone working with Novell Netware systems and perhaps to some newcomers to networking, but it fails as a reference for the networking professional who works with non-Netware systems.—**Ray Olszewski**

1762. Southerton, Alan, and Edwin C. Perkins Jr. **The UNIX and X Command Compendium: A Dictionary for High-Level Computing.** New York, John Wiley, 1994. 623p. index. $34.95; $19.95pa. ISBN 0-471-01281-5; 0-471-30982-6pa.

This handy volume will save UNIX users of all types a great deal of time and effort in their day-to-day work. UNIX users who know roughly what command or type of command they are looking for, but who do not remember the syntax or how to use it in conjunction with other commands to accomplish a certain task, are certain to benefit from having this book around, whether they are novices or power-users. What this book is not is a UNIX or X primer—it is a dictionary, intended for use by those who already have a grasp of the specialized language.

Getting to the information one needs is easy in this book. Copious introductory material explains the purpose, scope, and how to use the book. The main part of the reference is arranged in dictionary form, alphabetically by command, which is useful if one already knows what command one is looking for. There is also an index by type of command, which is useful if one does not know the command. Each entry presents a UNIX command as an example, rather than an abstract presentation of a command by itself. The example is either an illustration of the command by itself, or a usage of the command combined with others to effect a more complex action.

Additional explanations of what the command/series of commands is trying to do are also given, as well as an indication of what UNIX version a command is applicable to (all the major versions of the file system are covered); the shell it works under (sh, ksh, csh, or all); and the type of user who would most likely be interested in the particular command (end user, power user, system administrator, or shell-script writer). Entries also include keyword references, files referenced, and *see also* references to other related commands.

Appendixes provide quick references to vi and Emacs editors, shell special characters, and an ASCII table. The only complaint after using the book for some time is the slight lack of confidence inspired by the occasional inaccuracy (e.g., the entry for unencode missed a directional statement). This format makes the book useful in a very practical way—instead of having to read about the concept of the command and piece together its usage, then figure out which UNIX version and shell it will work under, one has the information instantly available and immediately useful.

If one is looking for a book to tell everything anyone ever wanted to know about UNIX or X, this is not the book. But for a regular UNIX/X user who wants a full-time, personal UNIX guru close at hand, then this book is a treasure. But do not be surprised if it is found missing—it may become the most popular reference in the office.—**Daphne Fallieros Potter**

1763. Spencer, Donald D. **Illustrated Computer Dictionary for Young People.** Ormond Beach, Fla., Camelot Publishing, 1995. 117p. illus. $16.95pa. ISBN 0-89218-245-8.

With the most recent juvenile dictionary on computing dated in 1985, this volume would appear to serve a great need, but it leaves much to be desired. The author (who is also the publisher) has written numerous books and dictionaries on computing, but appears to have given little thought to what a dictionary for young people should include. A few samples from the 700 terms included are illustrative. To say that *Boolean algebra* is "a branch of symbolic logic which is similar to algebra but, instead of numerical relationships, deals with logical relationships" (p. 18) is hardly clear, jargon-free language as information on the cover would lead one to expect. Or to say that a *clone* is "a computer that can freely exchange software with another" (p. 24) may be approximately valid but says little about contemporary usage or the variability of IBM clones. Inclusion of software brand names appears indiscriminate (e.g., PageMaker and Windows 95 may be found, but not Lotus or Word or WordPerfect). The DOS definition is just the generic disk operating system without mention of IBM or Microsoft (IBM and Apple receive definitions, but not Microsoft).

The volume's main redeeming feature is the sense of history that it conveys, including entries for nineteenth-century pioneers such as Charles Babbage, George Boole, Herman Hollerith, Joseph-Marie Jacquard, and Ada Lovelace, twentieth-century leaders such as Thomas Watson (but not Steven Jobs), and many of the early computers (ENIAC being only the best-known example). Yet it is also timely, covering many Internet terms just entering the public discourse. The illustrations alluded to in the title appear to be all clip art, "pre-drawn graphic images" according to the definition (p. 24) (otherwise known as line drawings). These range from highly illustrative (drawings of the early machines) to the mundane (a mouse) to the irrelevant (a rickshaw scene drawing identified as "bit mapped graphics"). With no contemporary alternatives, this volume may be of limited use for older "young people."—**K. Mulliner**

1764. Spencer, Donald D. **Personal Computer Dictionary.** Ormond Beach, Fla., Camelot, 1995. 184p. illus. $19.95pa. ISBN 0-89218-223-7.

This dictionary fills a niche in the computer world for experienced computer users as well as computer illiterates. Going from "a:" to "zoom," the 1,400 definitions represent nearly all areas of computer language. For the beginning computer user, all the basic terms one needs to know are included, such as "a: A designation for the first floppy disk drive in IBM-compatible microcomputers." To a neophyte who is feeling inundated by unfamiliar jargon, this book will be invaluable for understanding the personal computer and its uses.

The information presented for the experienced user is equally helpful. Seemingly all of those mysterious acronyms that seem to be omnipresent in computer literature are listed with meanings, such as "PGA the acronym for Pin-Grid Array, a chip that has pins that protrude from all along the bottom of the chip." The diagrams are excellent; for example, illustrations present clearly the difference between ring and star networks. Also represented are the major software programs that have been leaders in their fields: Norton Utilities, PC Tools, and so on. For one interested in the history of computers, browsing the pages brings to light many pioneer models that are no longer around, such as the Altair 880 and the Alto. In short, this is a complete dictionary of the personal computer world, which can help any computer user.—**Nancy P. Reed**

1765. Spencer, Donald D. **Spencer's Illustrated Computer Dictionary.** Ormond Beach, Fla., Camelot Publishing, 1995. 237p. illus. $24.95pa. ISBN 0-89218-220-2.

The stated objective of this book is "to present compactly and precisely the most common terms used by computer users.... It is a book for the person who knows little or nothing about computers but wants to learn." In general, the author sticks to this purpose. The definitions are clear and precise and their simplicity is one of the book's strengths. Another plus is the coverage of many personalities and historical terms, making this work appropriate for students.

There are several weaknesses, however. Coverage of some topics is spotty. For instance, the Internet terms *World Wide Web*, *ARCHIE*, and *Gopher* are defined, but *FTP*, *TELNET*, *TCP/IP*, *slip*, and *listserv* are not. Also, the limited and inconsistent cross-referencing hinders access.

The book is of limited value to the more advanced computer user. It is of most use to novices who want basic terms defined without a great deal of technical explanation. Those wanting a comprehensive computer terminology reference should look elsewhere.—**Stephen Haenel**

1766. **Vocabulary of Computer Security and Viruses. Vocabulaire de la Sécurité et des Virus Informatiques.** Ottawa, Canada Communications Group, 1995. 333p. (Terminology Bulletin, no.226). $38.95pa. (U.S.). ISBN 0-660-59791-8.

Our society has become dependent on computer systems, and computer crime is a serious concern to computer specialists worldwide. This is the premise on which the need for a glossary of computer security terms is based. The introductory pages methodically outline why the work is needed, how it was prepared, what is included, how to use it, and how entries are arranged and formatted. The vocabulary is followed by a French-English glossary and the bibliography from which the words and definitions were culled. Overall, the majority of definitions are accurate, clear, and concise. The physical layout of the book is appealing. The arrangement, format, and typeface are clear and readable; unfortunately, the book's text block is oversewn, which causes pages to be cut and fall out easily.

Occasionally, one may have to refer to other terms in the book in order to define words within a definition. There are a few entries that are defined contextually within a sentence rather than by strict definition. The 1,600 words and phrases are not all unique. Many are variations on a theme, such as the 18 entries of words and phrases regarding encryption, or the 89 transmutations of the entry "virus."

This English-French vocabulary was designed for translators, terminologists, and writers. This may indeed be the only audience for the book because, as the name implies, the scope of this work is related only to computer security and viruses. Those knowledgeable on the issues of computer security may find the only benefit of this work to be its bilingual aspect. Therefore, recommendation of this book is limited to the specialized computer library collection or the computer specialist either in a multinational company or in a country in which both English and French are commonly spoken.—**Deborah S. Hatfield**

Directories

1767. Adler, Bill, Jr., and Kristy Fraser. **The Computer Support Directory: Voice, Fax, and Online Access Numbers.** New York, McGraw-Hill, 1995. 295p. index. $12.95pa. ISBN 0-07-000482-X.

Computers fail just when one needs them most. Maybe a person is organized and maintains a file of all the product support information for each piece of computer hardware and software owned. *The Computer Support Directory* is written for those who are not organized enough to find the necessary information in a crisis. Designed as a small pocket guide, the directory purports to include "nearly every IBM/DOS hardware and software company in the country."

The directory lists companies alphabetically by title. Entries include major product lines, voice and fax support numbers, and online support via services such as Prodigy, CompuServe, America Online, the Internet, and bulletin boards. Some entries provide tips about information to have at one's fingertips when contacting support lines and a delineation of free and fee-based services. This reviewer checked the directory three times before locating the manufacturer of the graphics card in the home computer owned because the typeface used for indicating the top of each entry does not stand out on the page. The index lists manufacturers but not product lines; an individual looking for WordPerfect would have to know that Novell had purchased the WordPerfect Corporation for the directory to be useful.

The directory was tested by looking for entries for the hardware in this reviewer's home computer and software products used at home. This reviewer was able to locate most of the entries for software products using the name of the manufacturer, but unable to locate companies such as Intel, Maxtor, and Western Digital. Gateway and other computer packagers/vendors are not listed. Searching the Internet, this reviewer was able to locate World Wide Web addresses with product support information for most manufacturers of the home computer hardware and software and major computer vendors. However, assuming that one was experiencing technical difficulties, one may not be able to access the Internet. The inexpensive price and reasonable (although incomplete) coverage of *The Computer Support Directory* make it a good purchase for ready-reference and home use. Future editions could be improved with an index by product name and manufacturer.—**Peggy Jobe**

1768. **The CD-ROM Directory.** 14th ed. [CD-ROM]. Washington, D.C., TFPL, 1995. Minimum system requirements (Windows version): IBM or compatible. CD-ROM drive with MS-DOS CD-ROM Extensions 2.21. DOS 3.0. Windows 3.1. 2MB RAM. 2MB hard disk space. Color or monochrome monitor. Minimum system requirements (Macintosh version): Apple Macintosh System 6.0.5. CD-ROM drive. 2MB RAM (4MB if running Multifinder or System 7). 1.5MB hard disk space. Foreign file access and ISO 9660 extensions in the System folder. $99.00; $149.00/yr. ISBN 1-870889-54-1.

The CD-ROM Directory provides information on 10,000 CD-ROM and multimedia titles available worldwide, as well as profiles on 8,000 companies in the field. The directory is a guide to all commercially available CD-ROM titles, according to the publisher, and covers such areas as business, science, professional, entertainment, and education. The user may choose Italian, French, German, Spanish, or English as the interface language. The database also includes information on available hardware and software, upcoming conferences, and journals and books in the area of CD-ROMs and CD-ROM technology.

The information provided on companies is most helpful, and furnishes a full description of the firm's activities, products, hardware/software, and a contact person. There are equally informative data in individual CD-ROM titles, including publisher, full description, type of data, subjects covered, educational level, sources (print and online), geographical coverage, system requirements, update frequency, and price. Altogether, 24 variables are searchable.

The user interface is uncluttered and straightforward, providing numerous search and display options at each level. The search variables differ from one content area to another, depending on whether one is in title, journals, company data, and so forth. Location-specific help is available from anywhere in the database. The retrieved information may be printed or downloaded in a wide variety of formats.

Overall, this is an excellent database: up-to-date, thorough, and easy to use. Although it comes with a user manual, it was unnecessary to refer to it even once. Any library or organization that needs information on CD-ROMs currently available should have this impressive directory.—**Gerald L. Gill**

1769. **The CD-ROM Directory 95 with Multimedia CDs.** 13th ed. George Bischiniotis, ed. London, TFPL Publishing; distr., Detroit, Omnigraphics, 1994. 1197p. index. $139.00pa. ISBN 1-870889-46-0.

The explosive growth in CD-ROM publishing has been accompanied by a similar growth in the number of directories identifying them. One of the oldest is *The CD-ROM Directory*, which in this edition describes alphabetically by title some 9,500 CD-ROMs as well as the nearly 6,000 companies who develop, produce, market, or distribute them. Reflecting the industry's dramatic growth, 3,500 of the titles are new to this edition, as well as 2,200 companies. Entries for the CD-ROMs include title; publisher; type (audio, bibliographical images, and so forth); language; geographical coverage; time span; subject; one- to two-sentence descriptions; computer specifications; frequency of update; price; and availability.

In addition to the CD-ROM and company information, other sections within the directory address special-format works (such as CD-i titles) and electronic books; hardware (for example, portable, internal, external, and CD-recordable drives); software (authoring and development, search and retrieval systems, recording); and conferences, exhibitions, journals, and books. The directory concludes with many indexes (by subject, multimedia CD-ROM titles, Macintosh-compatible titles, retrieval software, company activity, country, and advertisers) and a rudimentary glossary. Relative to other CD-ROM directories on the market, this resource's weaknesses are the brevity and uncritical nature of its annotations, but these are more than offset by the vast amount of ancillary information provided, as well as the directory's international scope.—**G. Kim Dority**

1770. **Directory of Computer and High Technology Grants.** 2d ed. Richard M. Eckstein, ed. Loxahatchee, Fla., Research Grant Guides, 1994. 232p. index. $52.50pa. ISBN 0-945078-07-2. ISSN 1070-3950.

After a brief introduction to the Internet, a discussion of the relative benefits of Macintosh or IBM, and a 3-page introduction to grant writing, the editor lists some 600 foundations that fund computer equipment, medical equipment, and other technical resources. The entries, taken largely from *The Foundation Directory* (see ARBA 94, entries 890-891), are listed alphabetically by state and alphabetically within the state, and include name, address, telephone number of the foundation, type of activities funded, and whether the foundation funds regionally or nationally. A large percentage of the foundations listed fund only in a particular locality. The size of grants made by the foundations is small, with very few allocations of more than $50,000.

The second section of the directory lists approximately 30 federal programs in support of science and technology activities, most of which appear in the *Catalog of Federal Domestic Assistance* (published annually by the U.S. Government Printing Office). Entries cover essentially the same information as in the *CFDA*. Careful review of this easily obtainable reference tool would result in a much more comprehensive list of potential programs. Appendixes include a listing of locations of Foundation Center collections, which provide additional information on foundations and a half-page introduction to the Grantsmanship Center, which offers training in proposal writing.

Is this directory an improvement over the sourcebooks or online databases from which the information was taken? Does it help the reader use the Internet to search out grant information? Does it give the potential grant writer sufficient information to write a grant? The answer to each of these questions is no. Those wishing to identify opportunities and write grant proposals would be better advised to look elsewhere for assistance.—**Ann E. Prentice**

1771. **Guide to Free Computer Materials 1995.** 13th ed. Kathleen Suttles Nehmer, ed. Randolph, Wis., Educators Progress Service, 1995. 412p. index. $38.95pa. ISBN 0-87708-273-1.

The shareware section of this standard source for free materials is probably its most outstanding feature and has been greatly expanded from the introduction of this section, new since the 1990 edition. Containing thousands of titles of both shareware and public domain software, this particular section lists 150-plus pages of programs grouped into 20 general subjects, from business, computer education, engineering, and music to word processing and desktop publishing. Approximately 500 free computer materials, with more than 150 titles new to this edition, are currently found in the guide, which includes films, videotapes, disks, pamphlets, magazines, posters, and books.

A few weaknesses include that some materials are only for loan and must be returned, many items are actually just advertising catalogs, and (some may argue) shareware is not truly "free" if the user pays the requested registration fee. However, a number of books for as much as $20 one noted as free, and a large number of demonstration disks and actual full programs are available (e.g., Quick Check Money Manager), not to mention all of the shareware. Therefore, it is hard to believe that if the user obtained even a fraction of the software listed, that the guide's purchase price would not be recouped many times over.

The work is well edited and includes excellent instructions and advice for maximum success in ordering the materials. Three thorough indexes and a glossary of computer terminology complete this useful work. This should probably be a first purchase for schools that must stretch their technology budgets and for public and academic libraries whose patrons will appreciated the extensive free and inexpensive software listings.—**Carol Truett**

1772. Held, Gilbert. **The Complete Cyberspace Reference and Directory: An Addressing and Utilization Guide to the Internet, Electronic Mail Systems, and Bulletin Board Systems.** New York, Van Nostrand Reinhold, 1994. 765p. $29.95pa. (with disk). ISBN 0-442-01913-0.

The directory is a guide to the Internet, electronic mail systems, and electronic bulletin boards. The work begins with definitions, acronyms, terms, and abbreviations used in electronic communications. Explanations are given for using services like UNIX, Bitnet, TELNET, and GlobalNet Bulletin Board System. Tutorials are provided for using the Internet, CompuServe, e-mail, MCI Mail, and Sprint Mail.

In the chapter discussing Bitnet, e-mail addresses are provided; in other parts, telephone numbers are given, as in the section on the GlobalNet Bulletin Board System. Telephone numbers are also supplied for Internet service providers such as America Online. In total, more than 10,000 electronic addresses are provided, and more than 5,000 telephone numbers.

The guide to cyberspace may overwhelm the beginner and challenge the devotee. Nevertheless, there is information valuable to anyone using electronic communication, whatever his or her proficiency. The reasonable cost makes the work accessible to a wide audience.—**William E. Hug**

1773. **Hoover's Guide to Computer Companies.** Austin, Tex., Reference Press, 1995. 667p. index. $34.95pa. (with disk). ISBN 1-878753-79-7.

The latest in the excellent, reasonably priced series of Hoover's Guides from Reference Press (see ARBA 95, entry 192; ARBA 93, entry 208; and ARBA 92, entries 144-145, for other examples), this work provides print and electronic access to information on more than 1,000 computer companies. There are 3 main sections: "Industry Leaders," composed of 77 2-page profiles; "Selected Industry Players," composed of 173 1-page profiles; and "Key Computer Companies," composed of directory information on the 250 companies profiled and on 885 companies not profiled.

Profiles include an overview, a brief history, a list of corporate officers, directory information, a list of selected products and sales, a list of key competitors, and tables showing financial performance for the last 5 to 10 years. The two-page "Industry Leader" profiles include year-end figures for sales, net income, stock prices, dividends, and the like. "Key Computer Companies" includes page references to company profiles.

Prefatory materials contain three essays by the editorial staff of *Upside*: "The Computer Industry in Perspective," "Who's Who in the Digital Revolution," and "Where to Go for High-Tech Help." There are also a list of abbreviations, a list of companies profiled, and a useful list of lists (showing the 200 top companies by sale, by employment, by 1-year sales growth, by 1-year employment growth, the *Upside* 200, the *Datamation* Global 2000, the *Datamation* North American 100, *Software Magazine*'s top 100 independent software vendors, and *Computer Retail Week*'s top 100 computer retailers). There are two good indexes: a geographical index to the headquarters of profiled companies, and an index to people, brands, and companies mentioned in company profiles.

Two floppy disks containing a Windows version of the guide are enclosed in a pocket on the inside back cover. The disks contain data for the 1,136 companies in FileMakerPro format and FileMakerPro reader. The software is easy to load and use, and data can be searched by name, location, sales, and so forth. It is also simple to sort data by various criteria, to print and download records, and to make mailing labels.

The work is paperbound and includes advertisements for various financial services and other materials from Reference Press. Although limited to one part of the high technology industry, it is a part of great interest to most investors, and the book's price and high utility make this an excellent addition to any business collection.—**Richard H. Swain**

1774. Rosenfeld, Louis, Joseph Janes, and Martha Vander Kolk. **The Internet Compendium: Subject Guides to Health and Science Resources.** New York, Neal-Schuman, 1995. 529p. index. $175.00/set; $75.00/v.pa. ISBN 1-55570-219-8.

The goal of this book is to help people access the mass of information on the Internet. It specifically covers health and sciences, including the areas of chemistry, molecular biology, and aerospace engineering. The guide is quick to point out that this is a starting point, and with the rapid change on the Internet, some of the information here can already be obsolete.

The first seven chapters are a source of good basic information, terms, and details for the novice Internet user. These chapters also describe the different navigation tools on the Internet. The main section of the book is an alphabetical listing of subject-oriented guides/files. This area lists the different ways to reach the file, whether by FTP, HTTP, Gopher, or TELNET; the name or title of the file; who is responsible or developed the file; and a brief description of the contents.

There are two indexes, one that is a list of recommended resources. The second index is an alphabetical listing by keyword or organization with the subject area in boldface, such as **WAIS**. This is an extremely useful book, especially for the Internet novice, and also should be useful to the more experienced user due to its large listing of subjects.—**Betsy J. Kraus**

Online

1775. Hahn, Harley, and Rick Stout. **The Internet Yellow Pages.** 2d ed. Berkeley, Calif., Osborne McGraw-Hill, 1995. 812p. illus. index. $29.95pa. ISBN 0-07-882098-7.

One has to be courageous to compile a directory on the Internet, an amorphous, ever-changing, ethereal entity. Hahn and Stout are clearly up to the task—it is evident that they love their work and revel in the anarchical aspects of the Internet. As with the Internet itself, this book is eclectic, wide-ranging, oozing with personality, often silly, and sometimes downright stupid.

Each of the more than 5,000 listings has a brief, usually humorous, annotation. The book is divided into almost 200 subjects, covering nearly every conceivable human activity. If anyone is not convinced of the breadth and depth of Internet topics, one look here will change his or her mind. The listings cover the range of Internet sources: FTP, Gopher, TELNET, and World Wide Web sites; listservs; newsgroups;

mailing lists; and Internet Relay Chats. Topics include the technical (Protein Data Bank) to the practical (weather and travel topics) to the ridiculous (Fabio's Top Ten Pick-Up Lines). Not covered here are many of the more serious or technical Internet databases (which are covered in the *Gale Guide to Internet Databases* [see entry 1779]) and groups from proprietary Internet services such as America Online or Prodigy. Sprinkled throughout the book are illustrations in the form of advertisements for various sites; pithy and hyperbolic comments ("No one understands the Internet, so relax and enjoy" and "The Net is mankind's [sic] greatest achievement"); and "Excerpts from the Net," snippets from newsgroup conversations.

Access to the directory is provided through a detailed, 25-page table of contents and a combined subject/title index. The lack of cross-references in both can be annoying. There is also a list of Usenet newsgroups divided by hierarchy (alt, soc, bionet, rec, and so forth).

Two caveats: This book is not a how-to; it is a where-to. (The authors are not shy about plugging their other Internet book, *The Internet Complete Reference* from the same publisher, for how-to information.) Also, the squeamish or prudish may take offense at the sections on the bizarre, the listings of alternative newsgroups, and frank discussions of sexual topics.

It is hard to find a subject not covered in this book. Of course, a work of this nature cannot be completely up-to-date (a random check of entries uncovered several sites that had moved or were canceled) or comprehensive. However, it has one quality that most reference books cannot claim: It is a fun read. This book is highly recommended for all libraries.—**Stephen Haenel**

1776. Lent, Max. **Government Online.** New York, HarperPerennial/HarperCollins, 1995. 308p. index. $15.00pa. ISBN 0-06-273301-X.

Intended to offer easy-to-use instructions, this manual describes a selection of federal, nongovernmental (e.g., C-Span), state, and local online resources (e.g., bulletin boards, World Wide Web). Employing an organizational structure based on the *U.S. Government Manual*, agency entries are arranged in a descending order of authority. This confusing structure clearly is at odds with an introduction targeting ordinary citizenry. With five parts, the initial descriptions are well written but repetitious of currently available books. For the agency resources, parts 2 through 4, entries consist of basic data, access instructions, agency descriptions, and author's annotation.

Far too few of the annotations analyze a site's usefulness or indicate the completeness of available data. The coverage of state resources, however, will prove a good point from which to begin investigating local ones. The volume is completed by two appendixes (by online lists and acronyms); an inadequate, unannotated bibliography; and a brief index. Clearly, a more complete topical index would offset the volume's confusing organization and focus any serious browsers.

The author has compiled a monumental amount of information; however, it is woefully out-of-date, fails to consider the many advances beyond Mosaic, and contains several key errors. This work is not recommended.
—**Sandra E. Belanger**

1777. O'Leary, Mick. **The ONLINE 100.** Wilton, Conn., Pemberton Press, 1995. 233p. index. $22.95pa. ISBN 0-910965-14-5.

The ONLINE 100 is a guide to the 100 "most important" online databases. O'Leary does not just list the most popular databases on the market; he relies on his experience and knowledge to select the most significant databases in every major subject area. Full-text databases available through major online vendors are favored. O'Leary's list is inherently subjective, but he does a good job of picking his top 100. Business and sci-tech databases are heavily represented—making up more than half of the total—but unusual databases such as the OCLC Union Catalog and Magill's Survey of Cinema are also included. An advisory board made up of a variety of experts adds credibility and authority to the list.

Each entry includes an introduction, content and search notes, and "key facts," including the producer and vendors. The introductions and content notes are good, explaining where the databases come from and what information they contain. The search notes are also good, giving general tips and noting what the databases are not appropriate for. Some key facts are important but others are useless. The "typical search cost," for example, uses "average" search times and numbers of downloads to generate a meaningless and potentially misleading number. A price per minute/price per download figure from a major vendor would be simpler and more useful.

The ONLINE 100 gives an excellent overview of what is available online. It also helps users select the appropriate database and understand its structure. It would be helpful for the beginning online searcher, and most experts could learn a thing or two from it as well.—**Ken Feser**

TELECOMMUNICATIONS
Directories

1778. Bracken, James K., and Christopher H. Sterling. **Telecommunications Research Resources: An Annotated Guide.** Mahwah, N.J., Lawrence Erlbaum, 1995. 173p. index. $36.00; $17.50pa. ISBN 0-8058-1886-3; ISBN 0-8058-1887-1pa.

This book has a wide variety of information, and that is perhaps its greatest weakness. The only thing the book purports not to cover is electronic mass communication. It is a sourcebook for information about telecommunications and for the major entities that comprise the U.S. telecommunications infrastructure.

Entries in the book are arranged in a generalized subject arrangement with subdivisions under the major heading. Normally, there is further division dependent on the topic and the parent division or subdivision. Items are arranged alphabetically and then numbered with *see* references from one location to the numbered entry elsewhere. The work is indexed, but only for main entries.

There is no subject index, but this is less of a problem than with other works because this volume is arranged by subject. Some users may find this more of a problem than others, and the problem will vary with the size of the subject sections in the work. Some overly obvious materials are included that could have easily been left out, such as *Book Review Index*. Also, the typesetting is too busy. This latter point is more personal than the others, but the choice of typography makes a work more or less readable and can detract from the utility of a work.

This is an adequate choice for small public libraries and some school or community college libraries. Larger collections will have other materials that will cover the field both more broadly and more deeply. The sourcebook is in no way a definitive work, and the authors do not claim comprehensibility. Those who need specific or technical information will need to search elsewhere. For what it purports to accomplish, this slim volume does it reasonably well.—**C. D. Hurt**

1779. **Gale Guide to Internet Databases.** Joanna Zakalik and Sara Burak, eds. Detroit, Gale, 1995. 478p. index. $95.00pa. ISBN 0-7876-0198-5. ISSN 1081-2385.

Getting a handle on the Internet's many resources and presenting it to myriad users is a tough, unenviable task. Zakalik, Burak, and Gale, however, have done an admirable job of it.

Each of the 2,000 listings includes some or all of the following parts: database name and acronym; how to access and retrieve files (FTP, TELNET, Gopher, URL, e-mail, and modem); description of the database; data providers; a listing of main files; alternate, foreign, and former name; type (bibliographical, bulletin board, full-text, image, statistical, and so on); language; geographical and time coverage; updating frequency; fees to use the service (many are free); documentation available; alternate (non-Internet) formats; special instructions/limitations; search routines and searchable elements; and the host and contact information (including e-mail address).

Access is provided through five indexes, by host/provider; by alternate format; white pages of contact persons; by subject, listing 1,200 subject entries; and a master index. Also included are a bibliography of more than 50 current Internet resources, an excellent Internet glossary, and a list of specialized home pages, organized under 24 broad subjects such as agriculture, arts and humanities, cultures, history, Internet guides, and library and information science. The introduction also provides some information on accessing and retrieving files, which is useful to intermediate users or the ambitious novice.

The listings are alphabetical by database name. The descriptions are complete enough for the busy researcher to narrow in on just the right information source. Foreign-language works are listed, although the emphasis is on English-language databases. The scope of coverage is impressive. Technical and scientific databases are listed along with those in the social sciences and humanities. Many popular sites are described as well.

This directory does not include Usenet newsgroups or listservs. The content and tone are decidedly more reserved than Harley Hahn and Rick Stout's *The Internet Yellow Pages* (see entry 1775). Just so that users do not think the publication is too highbrow, however, the publishers make sure one knows about "All the Information About *Seinfeld* That Exists on the Internet" (a.k.a., "Vandelay Industries Archive"). (The *Melrose Place* site is not listed, however.)

The coverage is not as comprehensive as the semiannual *Gale Directory of Databases*, which is geared more toward the professional user, although there is a certain amount of overlap between the two publications. There is something here for serious researchers, students, and those looking for some fun on the Internet. In short, this directory is of the usual high quality of similar Gale publications. It is recommended for all libraries.—**Stephen Haenel**

1780. **International Satellite Directory, 1995: The Complete Guide to the Satellite Communications Industry.** 10th ed. Sonoma, Calif., Design Publishers, 1995. 1v. (various paging). illus. maps. index. $240.00pa. ISBN 0-936361-20-4. ISSN 1041-4541.

The *International Satellite Directory* is the most comprehensive guide to this growing industry. It contains more than 1,200 pages of reference information about an industry that has become essential to daily well-being. Every type of contractor in the industry, from satellite launching firms to organizations that specialize in the finance of dishes for receiving signals are listed. Some 25,000 companies are detailed in this 15-section classed directory. Examples of the type of information listed are: government agencies, international agencies, satellite operators (Intelsat), uplink locations, equipment manufacturers for bidirectional Earth stations, launch vehicles available, TV Receive Only (TVRO) equipment manufacturers, consultants, religious networks, common carriers, video and teleconferencing centers, insurance factors, research centers, Global Positioning System (GPS) manufacturers, and licensing agents. Especially useful is the section on 350 satellites in Earth orbit and their corresponding EIRP (Effective Isotropic Radiated Power [e.g., signal strength and where]) maps for most systems in orbit. Some basic information is even provided about military satellites, much to this reviewer's surprise.

This volume is the bible of the industry; in fact, the authors have included several reply forms for unlisted firms to complete and send in, thereby ensuring the comprehensive nature of the work. The book is a rather large perfect-bound paperback, and will require rebinding for heavy use. Despite its high cost, the *International Satellite Directory* is a gold mine of information on the industry, and few libraries with patrons in the communications field will want to be without it. Most general collections will find the material included of a technical engineering reference nature. If, however, there are firms in the area that transmit data or work with these type systems, few other reference books are as handy or comprehensive. The work will be of some use to the home satellite dish owner; however, monthly satellite programs listing magazines will supply more detailed programming information for this type of patron.—**Ralph Lee Scott**

1781. Rutten, Peter, Albert F. Bayers III, and Kelly Maloni. **Net Guide: Your Map to the Services, Information and Entertainment on the Electronic Highway.** New York, Random House Electronic Publishing, 1994. 356p. illus. index. $19.00pa. ISBN 0-679-75106-8.

This is a subject directory of 4,000-plus online resources on 5 major commercial services (America Online, CompuServe, Delphi, Prodigy, and GEnie); Bulletin Board Systems (BBSs); Usenet; mailing lists/listservs; FTP sites; and Gopher sites. The World Wide Web is mentioned only briefly, since it was not fully operational at the time of publication. Resources, selected for their informational or entertainment value, encompass a broad range of subjects, although some receive disproportionately more space than others.

The core of the directory consists of resource entries, organized first by 12 broad subject areas, then by 2 further levels of more specific subjects, with the entries arranged alphabetically within these small areas. Entries supply the essentials: the name of the resource; a subject description (generally brief) and, in some cases, icons indicating the activities found there (games, chatting, shopping, news); and access instructions.

Preceding this core are explanations of what the commercial services, BBSs, and the Internet are and the types of resources they offer; how to perform basic operations (e.g., e-mail, FTP, WAIS [which could be more thorough]); how to pick a commercial service; and how to use the directory. Three appendixes list the authors' choices of the best of resources in various categories, FidoNet BBSs by area code, and commercial Internet providers. A short glossary defines key terms. There is a fairly thorough index of subjects covered in the entries.

A comparison with three print directories that cover the Internet, but not the commercial services and BBSs (*The Internet Yellow Pages* [see entry 1775], *The Internet Directory* [see ARBA 95, entry 1702], and *Internet World's On Internet* [see ARBA 95, entry 1703]), showed that the first is the most similar to *Net Guide* in its popular tone, careful attention to graphic presentation, and detailed table of contents. Both promote effective browsing through their arrangement by subjects, although *The Internet Yellow Pages* is alphabetical, rather than by broad areas. The second and third directories are arranged by type of resource (e.g., mailing lists, FTP sites), permitting subject access only through their highly detailed indexes. Both have substantially more entries, which often provide helpful details about content and access. *The Internet Directory* numbers its entries, making them easy to locate on the page when referring from the subject index—a practice *Net Guide* should follow.

Net Guide's graphic presentation and subject organization would strongly appeal to Internet novices who need an understandable exploratory tool. It is recommended for public and academic libraries, although it should be supplemented by purchase of the second or third directory.—**John Lewis Campbell**

1782. **Telecommunications Directory 1995-96: An International Guide to Organizations....** 7th ed. John Krol, ed. Detroit, Gale, 1995. 1152p. index. $340.00. ISBN 0-8103-9125-2. ISSN 1055-8454.

The 6th edition of *Telecommunications Directory* was reviewed in ARBA 94 (see entry 1922). As its long subtitle indicates, this is "An International Guide to Organizations, Systems, and Services Concerned with the Interactive Electronic Transmission of Voice, Image, and Data." It is a comprehensive, one-stop source of information for current offerings and activities of organizations in the telecommunications field. The present edition is substantially enlarged, featuring 2,500 entries, with some 300 new entries. It has increased coverage of the Internet and organizations that provide access to it. The directory is highly recommended.—**Bohdan S. Wynar**

Handbooks and Yearbooks

1783. **The Internet: An Introductory Guide for United Nations Organizations.** By the Advisory Committee for the Co-Ordination of Information Systems (ACCIS). New York, United Nations, 1994. 140p. $10.00pa. ISBN 92-1-100678-3. S/N GV.E.94.0.12.

The foreword states that this guide is intended as an introduction to the Internet for novice or prospective users of the Internet from within the United Nations (UN) community. As such, it duplicates much of the information contained in well-known guides such as *The Internet: The Complete Reference* by Harley Hahn and Rick Stout (McGraw-Hill, 1993). The meaty chapter for reference is entitled "United Nations System Information." This section identifies Internet-accessible databases of the UN and its affiliate organizations, and provides brief descriptions of the data available at each site. As an example, the guide states that the *Convention on the Rights of the Child* and other public documents of the United Nations International Children's Emergency Fund (UNICEF) are available through Gopher <gopher://hqfaus01.unicef.org:70>. The guide also identifies databases that are not currently available and provides contact information for potential users, including names and e-mail addresses.

Unfortunately for this slim guide, the Internet provides faster access to new sources of information than do printed works. Since the publication of this guide, numerous UN computer servers and electronic publications have appeared that do not get a mention in this volume because they are very recent additions. An excellent link to UN and related organizations is maintained on the Internet's World Wide Web of networked information at <http://www.undcp.org/unlinks/html>. Another extensive collection of links is maintained by the UN International Computing Centre at <http://www.unicc.org>. Both are updated as new sources appear and addresses change, and are much better sources of information about UN electronic resources.—**Peggy Jobe**

1784. Manger, Jason J. **The Essential Internet Information Guide.** New York, McGraw-Hill, 1995. 515p. index. $27.95pa. ISBN 0-07-707905-1.

Manger is a victim of time. His guide to the Internet is perfectly serviceable and contains much useful information. It is also hopelessly out-of-date. *The Essential Internet Information Guide* is carefully organized and relentlessly detailed. It gives a history of the Internet, a thorough introduction to Usenet (although even here his choice of newsreaders covered seems a bit dated), FTP, ARCHIE, TELNET, using compressed files and images, IRC, and electronic mail. He covers Gopher, WAIS, and the World Wide Web. His coverage of UNIX commands is particularly good, and his appendixes include a glossary, a list of service providers, Internet questions and answers, a resource guide, a list of FTP sites, Internet domains, and a list of Usenet newsgroups.

The World Wide Web coverage is the heart of the problem with the book. In a book of 500-plus pages, the Web is covered in 5; moreover, Manger evidently had access to the Web only through character-based browser software. Even though the Web has exploded since the book was written, and generations of Web browser software are almost measured in nanoseconds these days, the author seems to have been particularly lacking in foresight as to the changes that would be wrought by the Web. The Web is making sweeping changes in the way that people use the Internet, and a useful guide needs to recognize that fact. Even seasoned Internet veterans are, for example, using Web search engines to search FTP sites rather than older methods, and such changes are true of almost all older applications. New Web browser software even includes e-mail and newsreading capabilities.

Internet users should still know how the Internet and its protocols work, and Manger's book is good for teaching the underlying history, commands, and protocols. The Internet, however, will never again be portrayed as it is by this guide. One hopes that Manger will rewrite the book with that thought in mind, as he has written a thorough and well-crafted work. The book is recommended for collections where graphical Web capabilities are not available and where a complete understanding of Internet protocols are needed.—**Mary A. Axford**

1785. Maxwell, Bruce. **Washington Online: How to Access the Federal Government on the Internet 1995.** Washington, D.C., Congressional Quarterly, 1995. 402p. index. $19.95pa. ISBN 1-56802-034-1.

Dissemination of government information by the Government Printing Office and federal agencies is in a period of profound transition. Since the mid-1990s, the U.S. government has looked increasingly to the Internet as a primary vehicle for distribution of electronic information products, which would replace many paper and microfiche products. The *Government Printing Office Electronic Information Access Enhancement Act of 1993* (GPO Access) mandated the creation of a Government Information Locator Service (GILS) to provide subject access to federal electronic information. Until such time as the GILS is fully functional, librarians will need to rely on print resources to locate government information available on the Internet.

Washington Online: How to Access the Federal Government on the Internet is a good start. Author Maxwell divides the book into 17 chapters based on broad topics such as "Demographic Data," "Education," and "Science Technology." Within each chapter, Maxwell identifies relevant Internet information and access methods (Gopher, World Wide Web, TELNET, FTP, e-mail). He provides a fairly detailed description of the files and information available at each site. Maxwell builds on work published electronically at the *Clearinghouse for Subject-Oriented Internet Resource Guides* <http://www.lib.umich.edu/chhome.html>. These guides are an excellent resource, but they lack the librarian's favorite tool: an index. Maxwell's book has a detailed index to help the user quickly locate the Internet address for the relevant information. In the introduction, Maxwell promises to update the book each year. With the rapid transition to electronic dissemination of government information, the publisher should consider updates via the World Wide Web between editions.

Washington Online includes only brief descriptions of the various Internet tools; the experienced Internet user can use this book to go straight to the information. Novice users will need to use this book with a good "how-to" guide at their side. Max Lent's *Government Online* (see entry 1776) covers similar material, but Maxwell's book has a superior arrangement, layout, and indexing. Libraries with a strong interest in government information should purchase Maxwell's earlier effort, *Washington Online: How to Access the Government's Electronic Bulletin Boards* (see entry 1786) and *Government Online* as companions to the current title.—**Peggy Jobe**

1786. Maxwell, Bruce. **Washington Online: How to Access the Government's Electronic Bulletin Boards.** Washington, D.C., Congressional Quarterly, 1995. 340p. index. $19.95pa. ISBN 1-56802-000-7.

The U.S. government is making a variety of information available electronically: from census housing to household appliances to a recording of the president's pet cat. Initially, access was largely through direct dial-up Bulletin Board Systems. More recently, many parts of the government have added

Internet access, sometimes revamping their original electronic Bulletin Board Systems into Gopher or World Wide Web systems; in other cases, keeping the same system but allowing it to be accessed directly via Internet protocols, such as Telnet. There are more than 300 such systems today, nearly 200 of which are described in Maxwell's list. He begins with a helpful introduction describing basic concepts of accessing and using these systems. The bulk of the book is devoted to one- to three-page entries for these systems arranged by broad subject areas, such as criminal justice and jobs and employment. The volume concludes with a small glossary and index.

The virtues of this volume include a nontechnical approach, clear write-ups of the covered sites, and a fair price. Disadvantages are largely generic to any printed volume that attempts to list sites on the Internet. Starting with systems beginning with the letter "A" from a comprehensive online listing of government sites, the first five entries checked were not in Maxwell's volume. Several were too new; others just were not there. However, because of the low price, user-friendly style, detailed annotations, and the promise of annual revisions, *Washington Online* is a recommended purchase for libraries.

—**Robert Skinner**

35 Physical Sciences and Mathematics

PHYSICAL SCIENCES

General Works

1787. Lord, John. **Sizes: The Illustrated Encyclopedia.** New York, HarperCollins, 1995. 374p. illus. index. $15.00pa. ISBN 0-06-273228-5.

This traditionally arranged and easy-to-use encyclopedia is extraordinary not only because it addresses the sizes and gauges of such mundane items as bolts to yarn but also because it describes in historical perspective physical units of measurement from angstroms to yards. It contains appendixes of useful conversion factors and graphical conversions and has ample charts and illustrations among the entries. However, this encyclopedia lacks two important features; a good binding and thorough indexing. Although objects and units are emphasized in the index, there is little organization of measurements by type, by country of origin, or by international organizations that set standards.

Lord's encyclopedia is intended for general readers. It is not, according to the author's preface, a substitute for building codes or various standards of industrial organizations. Because the scope of this work is extremely broad, it could be a useful ready-reference item in most academic and public libraries. It definitely fills a need for current, English-only physical measurement encyclopedias and dictionaries.
—C. Michael Phillips

1788. **World Databases in Physics and Mathematics.** C. J. Armstrong, ed. New Providence, N.J., Bowker-Saur/Reed Reference Publishing, 1995. 1085p. index. (World Databases Series). $165.00. ISBN 1-85739-0-38-5.

This volume is part of a series of directories that focus on specific subject disciplines. Included in this volume are astronomy, mathematics and statistics, nuclear science, and physics. Multidiscipline databases are also included, such as materials science. Coverage is international in scope and covers all formats. Chemistry and agriculture are not included in this volume, but will be found in other volumes of this series.

For each database, content, size, access, and pricing are described in detail, and in some cases, third-party evaluative reviews are included. The directory is divided into nine subject sections. A helpful feature for each database is the thorough listing of all the variations/formats that the database has been or is now available in. This will be useful in any retrospective research.

Three indexes allow relatively easy access to this enormous volume. There is a finely tuned subject index. The databases listed under each subject term are further defined by online host, CD-ROM, or diskette format. The second index is by database name. Here are listed file and alternative database names. The third index is a listing of addresses of all the database providers referenced in the directory. This product has brought some organization to the overwhelming scene of physics and mathematical resources. This book should be found on any reference shelf. It will be a valuable aid to collection development of any size science collection.—**Margaret F. Dominy**

Chemistry

Dictionaries and Encyclopedias

1789. **Ullmann's Encyclopedia of Industrial Chemistry. Volume A25: Starch and Other Polysaccharides to Surfactants.** 5th ed. Barbara Elvers, Stephen Hawkins, and William Russey, eds. New York, VCH, 1994. 817p. $325.00. ISBN 3-527-20125-4.

A representative member of the 36-volume set, this volume covers "Starch and Other Polysaccharides to Surfactants." The set is a highly respected German compendium, similar to the well-known Kirk-Othmer encyclopedia. Although the publishers claim internationality, a cursory examination of the author affiliations in this volume indicates that the preponderance are still German.

The articles are encyclopedic in nature—*Steel*, for instance, occupies some 244 pages, the equivalent of a fair-sized monograph. Articles typically include a history of the item, production details, raw materials (if applicable), materials properties, applications, plus copious bibliographies. The publisher claims to have ventured into newer areas such as biotechnology and environmental protection.

Any reference work treating a high-technology subject needs to be evaluated in the light of current information technology: for example, the numerous online databases providing access to current information. Successive editions of encyclopedias, in particular, may not have every article updated—*Sulfur Dioxide*, for instance, lists nothing in the bibliography later than 1983 (although Homer's *Odyssey*, ca.950 B.C., is cited).

This volume provides a sound basis for the fundamental knowledge of the 20 substances treated, but must be supplemented by other means if an accurate depiction is desired.—**Edwin D. Posey**

1790. Winter, Ruth. **A Consumer's Dictionary of Cosmetic Ingredients.** 4th ed. New York, Crown, 1994. 410p. $14.00pa. ISBN 0-517-88196-9.

A number of factors, ranging from corporate downsizing to changing consumer preferences, have combined to make cosmetic purchases even more confusing than they have been in the past. In order to make intelligent decisions, consumers need clear and up-to-date information about the many different cosmetic ingredients, as well as an explanation of widely used but confusing labels, such as *clear*, *light*, or *natural*.

Winter has provided a useful resource for the consumer who wishes to obtain the maximum value as well as avoid the more obvious risks when purchasing cosmetics. This book follows the format of the previous edition (see ARBA 85, entry 1682). A short introductory section gives a general background, but the major portion of the book discusses the possible harmful effects of the various components found in both women's and men's cosmetics. The compounds are listed alphabetically with extensive cross-references. The book provides a great deal of valuable information, although sometimes the discussion may be confusing for those who lack prior background in chemistry or toxicology.—**Harry E. Pence**

Directories

1791. **Chemical Sciences Graduate School Finder 1994-1995: Participating Master's and Doctoral Programs in the United States and Canada.** Washington, D.C., American Chemical Society, 1994. 660p. index. $49.95pa. ISBN 0-8412-3063-3. ISSN 1058-1227.

This is a source for anyone planning to do graduate work in the chemical sciences. The American Chemical Society has put together a well-organized, easy-to-use publication. Each entry includes information on the department, admissions, degree requirements, tuition, financial assistance, research facilities, and faculty with their research areas. A fields-of-study and a geographical index are provided, as is a fields-of-study table.

There is a deficit of which users should be aware. Not all institutions with graduate chemistry programs are listed. Solicitation of information has been done at departmental levels. Only those who responded and paid a fee to help defray costs are discussed. The American Chemical Society confirmed the above information and stated that the 1995-1996 publication lists institutions that do not pay a fee if they respond and give permission to be listed.—**Patricia S. Wilson**

Handbooks and Yearbooks

1792. East, Michael B., and David J. Ager. **Desk Reference for Organic Chemists.** Malabar, Fla., Krieger Publishing, 1995. 492p. $64.50. ISBN 0-89464-818-7.

The title of this work needs to be accepted literally—it includes a minimum of verbiage and a maximum of data for the working organic chemist/practitioner. In addition, it passes a hurdle for chemical reference tools in that it does not duplicate the *CRC Handbook of Chemistry and Physics* (see ARBA 95, entry 1711), which all chemists have.

Stereochemistry is defined in the *McGraw-Hill Encyclopedia of Science and Technology* (6th ed.; see ARBA 88, entry 1448) as "the study of the three-dimensional arrangement of atoms or groups within molecules and the properties which follow such arrangement," and this speciality is treated at length in the book under review (especially in chapter 3, "Glossary of Organic Stereochemical and Synthetic Terms"). There are some 5,100 entries in chapter 1, "Chemical Acronyms," which are cryptic representations of compounds. An example of confusions is *ABS*, which means "alkyl benzene sulfonates" as well as an "acrylonticle copolymer."

Chapter 2, "Physical Acronyms," has some 1,890 entries from the entire field of physics; for example, both *CAR* and *CARC* mean "carcinogenic," and *TQF-COSY* means "triple quantum filtered spectroscopy." Chapter 4, "Named Reactions," has approximately 480 different reactions associated with such names; for example, there are three different Bamberger ones on page 179. There are about 620 references to "Named Reagents" in chapter 5, including "Bruke's Reagent"—an aqueous solution of potassium iodide, sometimes misidentified in the literature. Chapter 6 has review references "for rapid entry to the literature."

Most references are to literature published in well-known journals since 1970. For example, references to the German *Angewandte Chemie* are to the International [English-language] edition. The 5,610 references are worth the cost of the book to professionals. The work merits purchase by libraries supporting organic chemists at the senior-year academic level or higher and in industrial settings. [R: Choice, March 95, p. 1145]—**Eugene B. Jackson**

1793. Gallant, R. W., and Carl L. Yaws. **Physical Properties of Hydrocarbons and Other Chemicals. Volume 4.** Houston, Tex., Gulf Publishing, 1995. 242p. $75.00. ISBN 0-88415-272-3.

The heart of this book is the 264 charts covering, for each group of hydrocarbons, vapor pressure, heat of vaporization, liquid density, surface tension, heat capacity of the gas, heat capacity of the liquid, viscosity of the gas, viscosity of the liquid, thermal conductivity of the gas, thermal conductivity of the liquid, enthalpy of the formation of the gas, and Gibbs free energy of formation of the gas. Each of the 12 chapters gives the literature references for the hydrocarbons, and the curves are extended per the detailed work of Yaws's associates at Lamar University in Beaumont, Texas (located just five miles from the famous Spindletop oil field that "came in" January 10, 1901). Practitioners do prefer to work with charts rather than tables.

Notable among the references cited are number 5, "Daubrert, T. E. and R. P. Danner. *Data Compilation of Properties of Pure Compounds*, Parts 1-4 and Supplements 1-2. DIPPR Project, AIChE, New York, New York, 1985-1992"; and number 14, "*CRC Handbook of Chemistry and Physics*, 66th-74th ed., CRC Press, Boca Raton, FL, 1985-1991"—a favorite reference book of chemical engineers. The water-solubility tables would be of special interest to the safety and environmental staffs. This book would be needed by petro-industry area libraries and those serving graduate programs in chemical engineering.—**Eugene B. Jackson**

1794. **Handbook of Inorganic Compounds.** Dale L. Perry and Sidney L. Phillips, eds. Boca Raton, Fla., CRC Press, 1995. 464p. index. $125.00. ISBN 0-8493-8671-3.

This volume provides numerical values of the basic chemical properties for 3,326 selected gas, liquid, and solid inorganic compounds. Numerical data include solubility, melting point, density, thermal conductivity, and thermal expansion coefficient. Additional data may include vapor pressure, viscosity, hardness, lattice parameters, and certain thermodynamic values. Descriptive information includes form (e.g., color and particle size, preparation or manufacturing procedure, and commercial or other uses). CAS Registry Numbers are also supplied. With some exceptions, minerals, organometallic compounds, the metal alloys, noncrystalline materials, and nonstoichiometric materials are not listed.

The objective of the book is to cover compounds synthesized over the past five decades, or identify new uses for older compounds. As such, this publication supplements additional numerical data for inorganic compounds found in the 75th edition of the *Handbook of Chemistry and Physics* (see ARBA 76, entry 1344), the *Encyclopedia of Chemical Technology* (4th ed., John Wiley, 1984), the *Merck Index* (11th ed., Merck, 1989), *Comprehensive Inorganic Chemistry* (see ARBA 94, entry 1457), *Gmelin* (see ARBA 81, entry 1396), *Lange's Handbook of Chemistry* (14th ed.; see ARBA 93, entry 1716), and *Hawley's Chemical Dictionary* (12th ed.; see ARBA 94, entry 1933). More recent data can be found in the primary research literature. The volume is intended primarily for commercial practitioners, such as chemists, chemical engineers, and materials scientists. Educators may also find the book a valuable reference tool for classroom or laboratory support. [R: Choice, May 95, p. 1398]—**Andrew G. Torok**

1795. Palma, Robert J., Sr., with Mark Espenscheid. **The Complete Guide to Household Chemicals.** Amherst, N.Y., Prometheus Books, 1995. 325p. $24.95. ISBN 0-87975-794-9.

Realizing consumers know little about the chemicals in common household products, the authors seek to provide the background necessary to choose products used in the home; assess media warnings concerning certain chemicals; and safely use, dispose of, and store these products. Their approach is to walk through the home, focusing on the laundry room, the medicine cabinet, the living room, the bar, the kitchen, the car, the garage, and the backyard, with a chapter devoted to each.

Utilizing a question-and-answer format, the authors answer common household questions ranging from freezer burn and why lobsters are boiled alive to what makes paint stick, how aspirin works, and the difference between concrete and cement. A glossary is included, along with several appendixes covering the chemical elements and their symbols, metric equivalents and conversions, toxicity levels of household chemicals, over-the-counter drug interactions, and contact information for pharmaceutical companies and selected manufacturers. The explanations are clear and easily understood. However, without an index this title is more appropriate for circulating collections.—**Barbara E. Clotfelter**

1796. Stricoff, R. Scott, and Douglas B. Walters. **Handbook of Laboratory Health and Safety.** 2d ed. New York, John Wiley, 1995. 462p. index. $69.95. ISBN 0-471-02628-X.

Hazards of various types being an integral part of scientific laboratory work, the need for a guide such as the *Handbook of Laboratory Health and Safety* is obvious. The 2d edition of the book by Stricoff and Walters presents a sound and well-organized survey of the field. It more than meets its objective of providing easy-to-implement guidelines for safe workplaces and protection of the surrounding community and the environment while complying with regulations. Chemical, biological, and radiological hazards are identified and evaluated; medical precautions are listed; administrative details are described; and emergency responses are suggested. This work is essential for libraries that provide information in occupational and industrial safety.—**Natalie Kupferberg**

Earth and Planetary Sciences

General Works

1797. Levinson, David. **Human Environments: A Cross-Cultural Encyclopedia.** Santa Barbara, Calif., 1995. 284p. illus. maps. index. (Encyclopedias of the Human Experience). $49.50. ISBN 0-87436-784-0.

While there are more scholarly treatments of environmental subject matter, such as the *McGraw-Hill Encyclopedia of Environmental Science & Engineering* (see ARBA 94, entry 1999) and Wiley's publication of Andrew Porteous's *Dictionary of Environmental Science and Technology* (rev. ed.; see ARBA 94, entry 2000), this work is intended more for use by students and laypeople, not professionals.

The encyclopedia focuses on human beings and how they adapt to their environment. The author shows the relationship of people to their surrounding climate, weather, landforms, and various natural resources. The entries go into extensive detail on each chosen topic. For example, the entry on mining includes statistics on the amount of materials removed from the Earth each year for mineral extraction. It also explains how mining increases pollution, the types of minerals that are mined, and how mining is influenced by politics. Another example of the range of topics covered here is the entry on totemism. The work defines the term, traces its origins, and relates its relationship to modern cultures. As well as covering a wide range of topics, the publication also includes illustrations, maps, a subject index, and bibliographical entries to further assist the reader. This encyclopedia is recommended for students and school libraries and as an in-house reference resource.—**Patricia B. Lutz**

Astronomy and Space Sciences

1798. **The Cambridge Guide to the Constellations.** By Michael E. Bakich. New York, Cambridge University Press, 1995. 320p. illus. maps. $49.95; $19.95pa. ISBN 0-521-46520-6; 0-521-44921-9pa.

Stellar arrangements in the night sky have provided people the means to navigate land and water and to regulate time. Distinctive stellar groupings and bright individual stars have lent themselves especially to be named and personified by nearly every culture. Modern astronomers still use these constellations, with few changes over the past millennia, to identify locations in the sky. Eighty-eight constellations that are currently recognized by astronomers were approved by the International Astronomical Union in 1928.

Bakich's intention is to pull together fact and myth related to the constellations. What distinguishes this book from the many other sky guides is the arrangement of the information. The author has divided the book into two parts. The first part consists of numerous lists, and the second part provides detailed information about each constellation, accompanied by an ancient and a modern chart. Particularly appreciated is the author's innovative approach to listing facts. Some of the fact sets will be listed two or more different ways. For example, objects compiled by Charles Messier in 1784 are presented three different ways—in numerical order, by constellation, and by right ascension. This re-sorting of the same information is a real convenience in a sky guide.

The narration is delightful and easy to follow. Discovering the constellations will be a joy using this book. It is recommended for public, school, and academic libraries.—**Margaret F. Dominy**

1799. Clark, Stuart. **Stars and Atoms: From the Big Bang to the Solar System.** New York, Oxford University Press, 1995. 160p. illus. maps. index. (The New Encyclopedia of Science). $35.00. ISBN 0-19-521087-5.

This is a short, easy-to-read book for the lay reader, and assumes little prior knowledge. Many other books serve the same overall purpose, but this one places more emphasis on the physics of modern astronomy than most, especially atomic and particle physics, radiation, and relativity. Thus, the title *Stars and Atoms* is appropriate.

The first major section is in the form of an extended glossary defining keywords that form the cores of the individual short essays making up the balance of the volume. The essays are grouped by topics ranging from the big bang, to the life and death of stars, to the fate of the universe, with appendixes at the end. The heavy emphasis on cosmology and stellar astrophysics indicates that this is not the book for those whose primary interests are the moon and the planets, appearance of the sky, constellations, and the achievements of space probes. Nor is it a handbook or guide for those interested in observing with small telescopes.

This is not a text, but it is suitable for readers with a desire to skip from one subject to another. There may not be sufficient continuity between subjects to satisfy the more thorough reader. The size, gloss, and abundance of illustrations and drawings qualify this attractive volume for the coffee table, and it may spark a number of conversational queries. The work is appropriate for any library.—**Arthur R. Upgren**

1800. Lippincott, Kristen. **Astronomy.** New York, Dorling Kindersley, 1994. 64p. illus. index. (Eyewitness Science). $15.95. ISBN 1-56458-680-4.

The cover accurately reveals the contents of Eyewitness Science's *Astronomy*. It tells the book's purpose, to "explore the planets and stars of the Universe and discover the mysteries of the oldest science." It introduces the colored illustrations that support and enrich the text. At the bottom of the cover, the source of many of the illustrations and astronomical information is recognized—this work is produced in association with the Old Royal Observatory, Greenwich.

Association with such a prestigious source enhances the work's quality and veracity. Throughout *Astronomy*, the history of astronomical exploration is emphasized. Important astronomers and their contributions to the science are noted. Information proceeds chronologically from the development of the science to facts about each planet in our solar system. Speculation as to the future of our solar system and galaxies beyond leaves the reader wondering about future celestial exploration and events.

Excellent cutaways and fact charts on each planet are examples of the information that fills this book. Students from the intermediate level on will find *Astronomy*'s basic information easy to access and useful.

—**Marjorie H. Jones**

1801. Peltier, Leslie C. **The Binocular Stargazer: A Beginner's Guide to Exploring the Sky.** Waukesha, Wis., Kalmbach Publishing, 1995. 159p. illus. maps. index. $19.95pa. ISBN 0-913135-25-9.

This volume updates *Leslie Peltier's Guide to the Stars* (AstroMedia/Cambridge University Press, 1986). The unnamed reviser (Peltier died in 1980) changes little except for updating lists of future astronomical events, such as eclipses. The revised content is current enough to mention the July 1994 impacts of Comet Shoemaker-Levy 9 on Jupiter. Peltier was a passionate, articulate advocate of amateur astronomy. His intended audience is the beginning amateur making an initial attempt to explore this hobby using binoculars instead of a telescope.

This approach contrasts with Philip S. Harrington's *Touring the Universe Through Binoculars* (John Wiley, 1990), which is much more thorough and assumes a more knowledgeable readership. The illustrations include simple seasonal star maps and drawings of the night sky, as well as more detailed locator maps for 12 well-known variable stars and a phase-by-phase guide to the moon. Although the work has some reference value, most libraries will want it to circulate. Harrington's title has more potential as a reference tool; nonetheless, Peltier's achieves its more modest goals admirably. This guide is recommended for public, secondary school, and community college collections.—**Richard S. Watts**

1802. Ronan, Colin A. **The Universe Explained: The Earth-Dweller's Guide to the Mysteries of Space.** New York, Henry Holt, 1994. 192p. illus. maps. index. $35.00. ISBN 0-8050-3488-9.

Ronan's extremely well-written and beautifully designed book will assist any interested person in becoming acquainted with the marvels of the universe that have been unraveled by scientific inquiry. In the pages of *The Universe Explained*, the reader will learn of many of the exciting discoveries of this century. Here the reader can glance at and reflect upon sky maps and constellations, planetary orbits and galaxies, and much more. The book also includes pictures of astronauts, brief biographies of some astronomers and physicists, and data on a host of celestial entities.

No matter where the book is opened, the reader will find a spread filled with diagrams, pictures, photographs, and much sound information on a given topic. The topics include such items as sky maps, the moon, high-energy astronomy, double stars, clusters, and galaxies. A concluding chapter entitled "How the Universe Works," is a masterful summary in readable prose on the conceptual bricks on which current cosmology and astrophysics rest. Thus, the reader will learn from these pages about such subjects as gravitation and light, magnetic fields and the curvature of space, and the missing mass and the big bang theory.

With a fine selection of books for further study, this volume could be an eye-opener for the average educated reader with some inquisitiveness about science. It could also serve as an excellent textbook for a course on astronomy for students who wish to take an extra science elective. Anyone who lays hands on this work will be charmed, entertained, and well informed about the universe. [R: RBB, 1 Feb 95, p. 1029]—**Varadaraja V. Raman**

Geology

1803. Cvancara, Alan M. **A Field Manual for the Amateur Geologist: Tools and Activities for Exploring Our Planet.** rev. ed. New York, John Wiley, 1995. 335p. illus. index. $14.95pa. ISBN 0-471-04430-X.

This revised and reformatted edition of a well-received 1985 book for nature enthusiasts, rock hunters, and itinerant geologists presents widespread topics, including how to read geological maps and cross-sections, use mineral and landform keys, and create geological collections. Access is provided by a detailed table of contents and a subject index.

The entries and structure of this edition remain unchanged from the 1st edition, although some rewriting has occurred. More than 200 photographs, drawings, and tables are reprinted from the previous edition. Captions remain unchanged, but illustrations are, on the whole, helpful and easy to use. Each chapter ends with a selected reading list that has been updated. The writing style has been popularized, with references to "you" as opposed to the more scientific syntax utilized previously. Jargon will not overwhelm the average reader.

The main text is supported by five appendixes; three (C, D, and E) are new. Appendix A, geological museums in the United States and Canada, does not provide such basic information as address, telephone number, or hours, and is not very useful. Appendix B reprints a list of United States and Canadian geological surveys from *Geotimes* (October 1994); appendix C provides, by region, geological highway maps and an address from which to order them. Appendix D gives information on location, relief, landforms, rock deformation, age of bedrock, and selected historical highlights for the various geological provinces of the United States. Appendix E lists nontechnical roadside geology guidebooks. The most recent imprint is 1991; the oldest is 1974. Chapter 21 includes a new subhead, "Ethics of Collecting," a nice touch in a world obsessed with conforming to standards of professional conduct in the field.

There is a real need for a concise field guide designed to introduce, connect, and serve as a reference for geology buffs, and this is it. One could get by with the earlier edition, but for any library from middle-school level up, this provides an inexpensive and useful single-volume reference sure to be a hit with students and professionals.—**Judy Gay Matthews**

1804. **Earth-Science Education Resource Directory.** Maeve A. Boland and Leanne Wiberg Milton, eds. Alexandria, Va., American Geological Institute, 1994. 144p. $19.95 looseleaf. ISBN 0-922152-21-7.

This looseleaf publication provides a list of materials and resources that will aid teachers in communicating geological topics to audiences of almost any level. It is derived from a database assembled by its publisher, the American Geological Institute (AGI), which solicited information about the products and services of a wide range of earth science-related organizations. This information has been placed in three alphabetically arranged indexes.

The first, by organization, lists the name of the organization; its address (including telephone number, fax number, and e-mail address, as available); its products; and associated information. The content index is organized first by subject matter (e.g., subheadings encompass atmosphere, hydrosphere, solid earth); and then by the grade level for which the materials are appropriate. Under each heading, reference is made to the appropriate organization and the particular products, throwing the user back to the first index. The third index is to the medium or format of the teaching aids offered (e.g., films, books, computer disks, and the like); and again identifies various organizations and products under each heading, and directs the user back to the first index for further detail.

The collection ends with a brief and incomplete calendar of events of interest to earth science teachers, unfortunately already a year out of date. This points out one aspect of the compilation. The data are presented as received, and they have not been verified for currency or accuracy. However, an updated version is planned, which may allow for tracking changes.—**Bruce H. Tiffney**

1805. Farndon, John. **Dictionary of the Earth.** New York, Dorling Kindersley, 1994. 192p. illus. maps. index. $19.95. ISBN 0-56458-709-8.

Although not claiming to be a visual dictionary, the *Dictionary of the Earth* gives concise, accurate definitions and descriptions of Earth structure and processes illustrated by explanatory charts, diagrams, and high-resolution color photographs. The dictionary is divided into broad themes including scientific investigation, the Earth in space, the Earth's structure, age of the Earth, rocks and minerals, the changing landscape, soil, seas and oceans, atmosphere, the living world, and human impacts. These themes (10 to 20 pages each) consist of 2-page sections on specific topics, with about 10 keywords defined within each topic. For example, the topic "Minerals" provides definitions and photographs of major mineral types, as well as a nicely illustrated Mohs' scale for hardness, and a table of properties of common minerals.

The clearly written descriptions avoid overly technical wording, but do employ accurate scientific terms and a complex, but not confusing, approach to topics. The high-quality diagrams and illustrations enhance the well-written, well-organized text and are consistent with the Dorling Kindersley emphasis on visually oriented readers. The index has entries for every keyword highlighted in the text, and each topic section furnishes a box listing extensive *see also* references with page numbers. Other features of the volume include brief scientific biographies of relevant earth scientists and a world map showing major physical features. The book lacks any bibliography or list of suggested further reading, which would be useful in this type of work. However, this one disadvantage is outweighed by the features noted above, which ensure that this volume will be useful to a wide range of readers. The *Dictionary of the Earth* is recommended as an introductory and ready-reference source for public, school, and college libraries.—**Jean C. McManus**

1806. Pope, Joyce. **The Children's Atlas of Natural Wonders.** Brookfield, Conn., Millbrook Press, 1995. 94p. illus. maps. index. $19.40; $12.95pa. ISBN 1-56294-564-5; 1-56294-886-5pa.

This engaging overview of earth science presents the planet in a pleasing, relaxed, inviting text that is generously dotted with full-color photographs, drawings of plants and animals, how-it-happened sidebars, maps, models, and boxed statistics. A repeated feature, "Where in the World?" introduces young readers, teachers, parents, and librarians to rugged terrain, volcanoes, mountain chains, parks, lakes, seas, wetlands, and water courses. Cutlines, arrows, and map notations make direct connection with text and themes; cross-references offer alternate methods of connecting ideas and subjects. Subjects range from the Venezuelan rain forest to the Giants' Causeway, the Great Rift Valley, Uluru National Park, Mount Fuji, and Lake Baikal in Siberia to the Barrier Reef and the Dead Sea. The text precedes a three-page glossary and a two-page index, which covers weather, geological formations, and specific locales and natural wonders.

There are few weaknesses in this work, which offers more than its share of information, pedagogy, and eye-appeal for the money. The atlas makes little mention of human road builders, geologists, naturalists, or ecologists. It may also profit from a pronouncing gazetteer for unfamiliar terms (e.g., igneous, Aurora borealis, basalt, Mitre Peak, Kilimanjaro, the Orinoco River). Its major selling point is its tone and focus on geological and biological fact rather than on sentiment or political interests. The gloom and doom of current environmental studies gives place to a positive survey, an upbeat mindset tending toward appreciation and reverence for the Earth.—**Mary Ellen Snodgrass**

1807. Smith, Alan G., David G. Smith, and Brian M. Funnell. **Atlas of Mesozoic and Cenozoic Coastlines.** New York, Cambridge University Press, 1994. 99p. maps. $39.95. ISBN 0-521-45155-8.

Reconstructions of past continental configurations, including coastlines, are important in both basic and applied geological research. This book contains 31 such reconstructions in black-and-white, showing coastlines at intervals (mostly at the level of stratigraphic stages) from the early part of the Triassic (245 million years ago) to the Pliocene (5 million years ago). These reconstructions, produced by British research groups associated with British Petroleum, differ somewhat from those produced by the PALEOMAP Project. The latter group has recently published Christopher R. Scotese and Jan Golonka's *Paleogeographic Atlas* (PALEOMAP, 1993), an unbound series of color maps, as well as *Plate Tracker* by David B. Walsh (PALEOMAP, 1994), a program on diskette that allows one to print out a customized map. Different research groups come up with different-looking maps based upon a number of factors, including the duration of the time slice being considered for any individual map. Because of such variables, it is very difficult to compare maps made by different groups. Thus, serious researchers will want to have the set of maps in this book on hand along with maps generated by other major research groups. Also, this book contains pithy chapters discussing global reconstructions, the plotting of paleogeographic data, and related topics. Finally, there is a lengthy bibliography. This book will be a good addition to collections supporting geological research programs.—**Joseph Hannibal**

Meteorology

1808. **Elsevier's Dictionary of Climatology and Meteorology: In English, French, Spanish, Italian, Portuguese, and German.** J. L. De Lucca, comp. New York, Elsevier Science, 1994. 320p. $185.50. ISBN 0-444-81532-5.

For a relatively simple phrase, such as "The rain in Spain falls mainly on the plain," this reference work from Elsevier Science would hardly be necessary. However, when one needs to differentiate between a simple raindrop and a more serious rainsquall, to check on rain intensity, or to locate a pluviograph (a rainfall recorder)—and to do so in any one of these six languages—then this is the volume, especially if one is actively involved or interested in meteorology or any of its related fields.

The format of this volume is straightforward. Its main body or basic table contains an alphabetical listing, in English, of almost 3,100 weather-related terms. Each English word or phrase is followed by its equivalent in French, Spanish, Italian, Portuguese, and German. All the non-English expressions are separately listed by language and in alphabetical order following this portion of the dictionary. With this arrangement, it is possible to start with or end up in any of these languages. This is especially useful for those translating from English, to English, or among any of these major non-English tongues.

Given the hefty cost of this volume (in United States dollars or in German marks), it is not likely that many individuals will be able to acquire it on their own. Therefore, research libraries with clientele working in the scientific and geographical areas covered by this dictionary should make an effort to purchase it.—**Leonard J. Greenspoon**

1809. **The *USA Today* Weather Almanac 1995.** By Jack Williams. New York, Vintage Books/Random House, 1994. 390p. illus. maps. index. $14.00pa. ISBN 0-679-75547-0.

True to *USA Today* style, this new almanac uses a number of interesting charts and graphs to convey much weather data. The author (*USA Today*'s weather page editor) goes beyond graphics to provide narrative that interprets and gives needed background to the facts presented in the charts. The overall goal is to complement *The USA Today Weather Book* (Vintage Books, 1992) that "explains why weather happens" (foreword) with the where, when, and how much.

The almanac begins with a section misnamed "The 1990s Weather Roller Coaster." While much of the section does revolve around such recent news items as the 1993 East Coast blizzard and the Midwest floods, coverage of the National Weather Services' experimental six-month forecasts, new weather radar and satellites, and 1995 weather experiments shows that this is more a hodgepodge of information, albeit a useful one. The next sections are more focused, providing weather guides for vacations and business travel. The former encompasses overviews and month-by-month statistics for recreation areas and national parks arranged alphabetically by state. The latter includes charts for 19 U.S. and 9 non-U.S. airports with information on the odds for good landing weather. Also covered are weather radio information, charts for length of day at various latitudes, and coverage of time zones worldwide. A fine overview of extreme weather is marred by the inclusion of two phenomena—earthquakes and volcanoes—that are geological in nature, not meteorological.

Following a brief section on record-breaking weather, the largest section is a city-by-city statistical guide to 200 U.S. and 50 foreign cities. The *USA Today* graphic style shines here. Each city profile follows a standard format, making it easy to find information quickly and make comparisons between cities. Such data as average and record high and low temperatures; averages for precipitation, snow, relative humidity, wind speed, and other items; and a "percent time sky is clear" chart are provided. The almanac concludes with an appendix of miscellaneous items and an inadequate index that does not provide thorough access to the contents.

While not perfect or comprehensive, this new reference will answer many of the weather-related questions commonly asked in libraries. Although much of the information can be found in such sources as *Weather Almanac* (see ARBA 93, entry 1722), *Weather Handbook* (see entry 1810), and *Weather of U.S. Cities* (see ARBA 94, entry 1947), most libraries should consider this source, especially given its price. Public libraries should also consider an extra copy for the circulating shelves.—**David E. Salamie**

1810. Watts, Alan. **The Weather Handbook.** Dobbs Ferry, N.Y., Sheridan House, 1994. 187p. illus. maps. index. $19.95. ISBN 0-924486-76-7.

The author states that "This is a book for Joe Public." It is the 10th weather book by Watts. Because there is little new material, a library with a couple of his previous books would not need this one. It covers basic observational meteorology and gives some forecasting techniques intended to augment and update media reports. To accomplish this, the reader is introduced to both surface and upper air weather maps, examples of all types of fronts, the relationship between winds and high- and low-pressure systems, the formation of clouds, precipitation, severe weather, and diurnal and seasonal variations.

Some emphasis is placed on local effects, such as sea breezes and differences due to topography. The terms *ana fronts* and *kata fronts*, at least in most literature, have been replaced with *active fronts* and *inactive fronts*, respectively. In the United States, fog is sometimes reported with a visibility of six miles; in Great Britain, it is not called fog unless the visibility lowers to one kilometer. Part 2, "Information and

Explanations," is a useful glossary of terms; a table of contents and index are also provided. There is information on lightning and some safety tips are given. The effects of driving a car into or with the wind during precipitation is a practical discussion.

Watts admits that computers are becoming kings among weather forecasters, but humans still have work to do, and based on current observations, can improve on computer output. A couple of better-colored satellite images should have been included; in this regard, the author states that radiometers see clouds as being white; they only measure radiation and the assignment of colors is a computer programming convention. Another criticism: One chapter is on "Low Winds." Does this mean height, pressure, or wind speed? Readers who understand the crosswinds rules should continue into more advanced books. This is a readable, introductory weather book for the general public. [R: BR, Mar/Apr 95, p. 970]—**Allen E. Staver**

1811. **World WeatherDisc: Climate Data for the Planet Earth.** 1994 ed. [CD-ROM]. Seattle, Wash., WeatherDisc Associates, 1994. Minimum system requirements (DOS version): IBM or compatible. CD-ROM drive. DOS version 3.1. 512K RAM. color monitor with EGA graphics. Minimum system requirements (Macintosh version): System 7. CD-ROM drive. 2MB RAM. $195.00.

The technological miracle of the CD-ROM is the enormous amount of information that can be packed onto it (330,000 pages of data). This medium is nearly ideal for databases that consist almost entirely of numbers. The *World WeatherDisc* is filled with all the meteorological data most people are ever going to reasonably need. Want to know the weather in Chicago on the day someone was born? Was it dry or rainy in Hitler's collapsing Berlin in April 1945? How cold does it really get in Anchorage in December? With a Macintosh or DOS computer, a CD-ROM drive, and some patience, these types of questions can be answered with this product.

The meteorological data on this disc are divided into two categories—one that is accessible through software and one that consists of sheets of numbers to be laboriously decoded. The software-accessible data include simple monthly climate statistics from 3,293 stations around the world, some dating back to the eighteenth century (for example, Edinburgh statistics start in 1765). A set of data from world airfields (5,717 of them) has more climatological details (including humidity, wind speeds, visibility, and other items of interest to pilots). The most detailed information is available for stations in the United States. The data for each set are presented in a series of windows that are clunky but functional. Graphs are available in a standard format that cannot be modified, and even resizing them is inconvenient. The software used for viewing these data sets has the awkward feel of a mainframe program quickly modified for desktop computers—it works, but it is not pretty.

Considerable data are available on the disc as data files alone. These must be opened with a word processing program and formatted to be read in columns of numbers. The *World WeatherDisc* user manual provides the information for reading the codes. These data files include ship observations, upper air records, sunshine levels, tornado and lightning statistics, and other specialized lists. The files are easily viewed, but they are tedious to interpret. The clever programmer could probably write a simple routine to make the files more useful.—**Mark A. Wilson**

Mineralogy

1812. Robbins, Manuel. **Fluorescence: Gems and Minerals Under Ultraviolet Light.** Phoenix, Ariz., Geoscience Press; distr., Missoula, Mont., Mountain Press, 1994. 374p. illus. index. $40.00. ISBN 0-945005-13-X.

This guide to fluorescence provides an explanation of the phenomenon and also includes a catalog of minerals exhibiting fluorescence. The author states that "discussion is concrete, based on first hand observation of fluorescent specimens" (p. xx). References to samples from specific sites form the basis of the descriptive sections and make the guide useful for collectors and those doing fieldwork.

The volume has several sections, including a discussion of fluorescence, localities where specimens are found, descriptions of mineral families that fluoresce, gemstones, a catalog of fluorescing minerals, and a chapter on simple experiments that can be done to learn more. The index mainly includes entries for specific mineral names and localities. General discussion of fluorescence occurs in several sections. Color plates of fluorescing minerals enhance the text, although black-and-white photographs included here are somewhat indistinct.

The organization of this volume makes it of limited use as a ready-reference tool. However, collectors and those interested in specific fluorescent minerals will find this volume very useful.
—**Jean C. McManus**

Paleontology

1813. Briggs, Derek E. G., Douglas H. Erwin, and Frederick J. Collier. **The Fossils of the Burgess Shale.** Blue Ridge Summit, Pa., Smithsonian Institution Press, 1994. 238p. illus. index. $39.95; $24.95pa. ISBN 1-56098-364-7; 1-56098-659-Xpa.

There are perhaps a half dozen fossil sites around the world that provide an abundance of specimens representing many taxonomic groups as well as copious paleoecologic information. These sites are scattered throughout the geological record. Most have been known for a long time and their fossils studied and restudied each time with new techniques that lead to reinterpretations of the anatomy and evolutionary significance of these fossils. The Burgess Shale fossils are a case in point and one of the geologically earliest such sites.

This text is by three paleontologists primarily responsible for the latest regeneration of interest in Burgess Shale fossils, which were first discovered early in this century. The first quarter of the book provides a history of discovery and study of these fossils, their geological setting, and a discussion of Cambrian (the age of the Burgess Shale) evolution. Most of the text comprises a discussion of each of more than 80 genera. The biota is composed of algae, a multitude of invertebrates, a couple of vertebrates, and several *incertae sedis* organisms. Descriptions are informal and informative; one learns about the anatomy, interpretational problems with these often unusual animals, and their probable relationships. Most important, excellent, enhanced photographs and simple drawings of each organism are provided. There is a good bibliography of Burgess Shale literature and a brief index.

Stephen J. Gould in *Wonderful Life* (W. W. Norton, 1989) provided general readers with an analysis of these fossils from his evolutionary perspective; Briggs et al. offer a somewhat different view and a more intensive examination of the specimens. Any library with Gould should have Briggs, and the latter is essential for libraries with any clientele interested in paleontology.—**David Bardack**

1814. Costa, Vincenzo. **Dinosaur Safari Guide: Tracking North America's Prehistoric Past.** Stillwater, Minn., Voyageur Press, 1994. 259p. maps. index. $14.95pa. ISBN 0-89658-231-0.

Old and young kids alike cannot seem to get enough of dinosaurs. For those who want to track down these beasts, try the *Dinosaur Safari Guide*. Here one will find descriptions of more than 160 exhibits in the United States and Canada that deal with the Mesozoic Era, along with a few pre- and post-dinosaur-era sites. Coverage includes sites specific to dinosaurs, as well as general museums that have dinosaur exhibits.

The entries are arranged by geographic location, making it easy to plan a tour when traveling. There is an alphabetical listing of sites to aid you in finding a particular museum, as well as listings by dinosaur/prehistoric animal names. Each entry contains exhibit fees, hours of operation, addresses and telephone numbers, directions from major highways, and highlights of the exhibit. There are also 60 maps available for assistance, but these do not take the place of an atlas. An introduction to the time of dinosaurs and a pronunciation guide are also included. Although one will not find Barney here, one will find dinosaur exhibits both big and small. [R: SLJ, Feb 95, p. 129]—**Angela Marie Thor**

1815. **The Field Guide to Prehistoric Life.** By David Lambert and the Diagram Group. New York, Facts on File, 1994. 256p. illus. maps. index. $14.95pa. ISBN 0-8160-1389-6.

This book is a quick introduction to the study of fossils, and its profuse illustrations and simple text make it easily accessible. Calling it a "true field guide," however, is misleading. In the typical field guide style, there are simple profiles in the margins showing ancient plants, animals, and other organisms. The diagrams found in this work are, for the most part, of reconstructed living organisms, which no one is likely to stumble across in the field. Thus, this book is not useful as a field guide, as fossils usually do not closely resemble the living organisms of which they are remnants. Rather, it is more useful as a brief summary of the major groups of ancient life classified and interpreted by paleontologists.

The book begins with a simple discussion of what fossils are, how they are distributed, and how living things are categorized. There is a short chapter on fossil plants; one on fossil invertebrates; and then separate chapters on fish, amphibians, reptiles, birds, and mammals. As is typical with most books of this kind, there is almost five times more material on fossil vertebrates than invertebrates, even though in the actual fossil record the invertebrates are far more numerous and diverse. Some invertebrates are especially slighted: The extremely common fossil brachiopods and bryozoans are lumped together with conodonts and phoronid worms on just two pages devoted to *tentaculates*.

Probably the most valuable part of the book begins after the brief descriptions of the major organism groups. A chapter is devoted to the geological time periods and epochs, characterizing the typical life forms in each. Another describes the art and science of fossil hunting in terms older children and young adults will quickly understand. The end of the book has a short list of additional readings that will be helpful for anyone with a developing interest in ancient life.—**Mark A. Wilson**

1816. **Prehistoria: A Multimedia Who's Who of Prehistoric Life.** [CD-ROM]. Danbury, Conn., Grolier Electronic Publishing, 1994. Minimum system requirements: IBM or compatible 386/20MHz. 150 KB/sec CD-ROM drive with MS-DOS CD-ROM Extensions 2.21. DOS 5.0. Windows 3.1. 4MB RAM. 4MB hard disk space. VGA color monitor (SVGA recommended). Minimum system requirements (Windows version): Windows 3.1. Windows-supported mouse. Windows-supported sound card. Windows-supported printer. $69.95. ISBN 0-7172-3971-3. [Also available for Macintosh.]

This CD-ROM has much to recommend it for school use. The visuals that show "flying reptiles to woolly mammoths" are excellently done. One can spend a long time browsing the picture gallery. Each graphic has information about the creature depicted; clicking on each picture leads to further information. The creature show, which depicts more than 500 prehistoric animals with a well thought-out, thorough presentation has detailed information about each, covering basic facts, classification, time, locality, and size. The timeline is helpful for placing animals in their proper place in the evolutionary cycle. Information can be saved to disk or printed out easily.

The search engine works well; entering a topic, such as "birds," brings the user much information. There are also audio/visual essays on various subjects. One fascinating example morphs a dinosaur into a bird, so the viewer can see how the development of the bird's skeleton actually evolved. The example of the inside of a fossil egg is equally good, even though the sound did not work for this reviewer.

Initially, the program installed easily, but then caused problems on the system, which necessitated a call to technical support. Although the requirements claim it will run on a VGA monitor, the program will not run on a computer without a Super VGA monitor. Running on a 486 with 8MB of memory, the videoclips were extremely unsatisfactory, hanging after 1 or 2 movements, then zooming to the end with no intermediate movement. The sound did not work at all on a machine equipped with a Sound Blaster sound system. The program is a good one with excellent information and visuals; unfortunately, there are several technical flaws in the bells-and-whistles portion of the CD-ROM that detract from its presentation.
—**Nancy P. Reed**

1817. **The Visual Dictionary of Prehistoric Life.** New York, Dorling Kindersley, 1995. 64p. illus. index. (Eyewitness Visual Dictionaries). $15.95. ISBN 1-56458-859-9.

For many, visual presentation of information is an important means of understanding the meaning of words and their context. In this visual dictionary, each double-page entry on oversized pages focuses on a particular geologic era, a family of plants, amphibians, dinosaurs, or mammals. A structure of a representative fossil dominates each spread and is surrounded by related fossils or parts of fossils, each of which is labeled. In addition to fossil bones, the muscular structure, skin, feathers, and other scientifically correct identifying characteristics are added. Brief descriptive information places the representative illustration in the context of its family of fossils and current living things.

One can either go directly to the page spread of interests—such as flowering plants or primitive fishes—to look at the illustrations and find a particular term, or one can use the index, which will lead to the appropriate page. Because each page includes numerous illustrations and terms, it may take some time to locate the term sought. This is a pleasing presentation, carefully illustrated and with brief but appropriate text. The dictionary is a good introduction to those just beginning to be interested in knowing about prehistoric life.—**Ann E. Prentice**

Volcanology

1818. Simkin, Tom, and Lee Siebert. **Volcanoes of the World: A Regional Directory, Gazetteer, and Chronology....** 2d ed. Tucson, Ariz., Geoscience Press, 1994. 349p. illus. maps. $25.00. ISBN 0-945005-12-1.

While most volcanoes ring the Pacific Ocean, there are volcanoes in Asia, Africa, the Atlantic Ocean, and Europe. They are all named in this detailed encyclopedia that draws upon several sources: *Catalog of Active Volcanoes* (International Volcanological Association), *Bulletin of Volcanic Eruptions* (Volcanological Society of Japan), and Smithsonian Institution bulletins (lately through Geotimes). Approximately one-third of the book comprises a directory of volcanoes organized by geographic region and specific country. Included are maps showing location (latitude/longitude) of specific volcanoes (including components of multifissured ones), elevation, records of (start/stop) times of eruption, type of volcano, and eruptive characteristics.

Another principal section provides a chronology of eruptions over the last 10,000 years. A gazetteer permits finding specific volcanoes by alphabetical name, and access to synonyms. A short section organized by major volcanically active area lists fatalities and evacuations. Finally, there is a list of references organized by geographic area. The introduction provides an overview of the substance of the volume and is essential to the use of tabular material, as this is the only place where specific abbreviations and codes are explained. While this somewhat slows down the use of the tables, persons seeking information on volcanic activity will gain a fine perspective about volcanoes from these explanatory pages. However, these pages are not intended to be an introduction to volcanology. The general reader must seek a basic geology book instead. These remarks aside, this is a valuable addition to any reference library.—**David Bardack**

Physics

1819. Challoner, Jack. **The Visual Dictionary of Physics.** New York, Dorling Kindersley, 1995. 64p. illus. maps. index. (Eyewitness Visual Dictionaries). $16.95. ISBN 0-7894-0239-4.

This colorful and profusely illustrated introduction to basic concepts in physics is presented in a format that is most likely to appeal to school-aged children. It is divided into 24 sections, each occupying a large (12-by-18-inch), 2-page spread. Each section includes a brief introduction and a number of vivid, high-quality illustrations with appropriate labels and captions. Many of these depict demonstration apparatuses (Van de Graaff generators, cathode ray tubes, and the like) typically found in academic stockrooms. Others schematically represent electromagnetic waves, atomic or subatomic particles, and similar abstractions. There is virtually no discussion of mathematics; the only formulas are listed with minimal explanation in an appendix.

Any survey of physics from classical mechanics through elementary particles in just 48 pages necessarily must be sketchy and oversimplified (voltage is not a "measure of force"; motion does not stop at zero Kelvin). There are also a number of errors, particularly in the illustrations. On page 21, the pressure nodes and antinodes of an air column are mislabeled; on page 32, a voltmeter is shown connected in series rather than in parallel; the electric and magnetic field vectors are incorrectly oriented on page 38; the a and g rays are mislabeled in the cloud chamber sketch on page 50. Despite these shortcomings, the book represents a credible and entertaining effort to attract young persons to the wonders of this important field of science.—**John U. Trefny**

1820. Gribbin, John, and Mary Gribbin. **Time & Space.** New York, Dorling Kindersley, 1994. 64p. illus. index. (Eyewitness Science). $15.95. ISBN 1-56458-619-7.

Diverse and complex concepts are presented in this work. General views of time and space introduce this exploration. Ancient ideas about the Earth and the solar system are presented with the history and measurement of time and space. Next, several laws of science from thermodynamics to relativity are mentioned. More abstract theories such as quantum theory, string theory, and the big bang theory follow. Finally, the ultimate merger of time and space, time travel, is introduced. Instructions for building a time machine conclude the work.

The breadth and depth of the above topics make condensation into the Eyewitness Science series format challenging. *Time & Space* follows the guidelines with only 64 pages. Each subject is arranged on opposing pages that contain a general, informational paragraph surrounded by supporting details in smaller type. Colorful illustrations and quality printing make an attractive product.

Appearance does lure the reader, but the contents test the work, especially for instructional value. *Time & Space* reduces its educational benefit due to its fragmentation and incoherence. Many of the details in small print surrounding a topic are not directly related to the subject. Facts are given without correlation to the central point. Explanations of theories are not as clear as in other sources. If the Eyewitness Science series is purchased as a set for a reduced price, this volume will provide some interesting ideas for contemplation.—**Marjorie H. Jones**

1821. Yaws, Carl L. **Handbook of Thermal Conductivity. Volume 1: Organic Compounds C_1 to C_4.** Houston, Tex., Gulf Publishing, 1995. 356p. (Library of Physico-Chemical Property Data). $85.00. ISBN 0-88415-382-7.

1822. Yaws, Carl L. **Handbook of Thermal Conductivity. Volume 2: Organic Compounds C_5 to C_7.** Houston, Tex., Gulf Publishing, 1995. 402p. (Library of Physico-Chemical Property Data). $85.00. ISBN 0-88415-383-5.

1823. Yaws, Carl L. **Handbook of Thermal Conductivity. Volume 3: Organic Compounds C_8 to C_{28}.** Houston, Tex., Gulf Publishing, 1995. 398p. (Library of Physico-Chemical Property Data). $85.00. ISBN 0-88415-384-3.

This handsomely bound, 3-volume set provides the thermal conductivities of more than 2,000 organic compounds, including hydrocarbons, oxygenates, halogenates, nitrogenates, and others, organized according to the number of carbon atoms each contains. The work presents functional fits of the temperature dependence of the thermal conductivity of each compound, both graphically and in the form of tabulated coefficients. In principle, all of the information is contained in the 34 pages of coefficients (also available on disk), but presumably some researchers will find using the graphical representations more convenient. The fits were made to experimental data in some cases and to the results of detailed modeling in others, but references to the original experiments and calculations are not provided. The reader is warned that the values are rough approximations in certain (unidentified) ranges, but the magnitudes of the expected uncertainties are not given. Separate indexes listing all of the compounds both by formula and by name are provided in each volume for convenience. —**John U. Trefny**

1824. Yaws, Carl L. **Handbook of Transport Property Data: Viscosity, Thermal Conductivity, and Diffusion Coefficients of Liquids and Gases.** Houston, Tex., Gulf Publishing, 1995. 203p. (Library of Physico-Chemical Property Data). $65.00. ISBN 0-88415-392-4.

The *Handbook of Transport Property Data* provides six tables of viscosity, thermal conductivity, and diffusion coefficients in air and water for an extensive range of gaseous and liquid organic compounds. More than 1,300 compounds are listed in carbon number order. These data are relevant to chemical and petroleum engineering processing. Extensive references are included for each chapter of published experimental and theoretical data on the compounds listed in the tables. Additional tables are provided in four appendixes ranging from conversion equations to physical property data. The tables are easy to read and the columns are clearly labeled. The tabular data are also available electronically. This book is appropriate for university or special libraries serving chemistry, chemical, and petroleum engineering departments.—**Margaret F. Dominy**

MATHEMATICS

1825. **Combined Membership List 1995-1996: American Mathematical Society, American Mathematical Association of Two-Year Colleges, Mathematical Association of America, [and] Society for Industrial and Applied Mathematics.** Providence, R.I., American Mathematical Society, 1995. 392p. $59.00pa. ISBN 0-8218-0185-6.

Published by the American Mathematical Society (AMS), the *Combined Membership List* (CML) includes the names and addresses of all persons who are members of the AMS, the American Mathematical Association of Two-Year Colleges, the Mathematical Association of America (MAA), and the Society for Industrial and Applied Mathematics. The directory is distributed in even-numbered years to AMS members and in odd-numbered years to MAA members.

The CML is divided into three sections. The first section is an alphabetical list of individual members. Each entry includes a name; a mailing address; society affiliation(s); and, if supplied, a title or position, a place of employment, a telephone number, and electronic addresses. Membership in the three participating societies is indicated by letters placed at the end of each entry. Where no department is specified with academic addresses, readers should assume it is the Department of Mathematics. State and territory names are abbreviated according to U.S. postal regulations and are followed by zip codes.

The second section is organized geographically into three subdivisions: the United States, Canadian provinces, and other countries. Names of members are arranged according to city and state; two or more members employed at the same institution are listed alphabetically after the employer's name. Zip codes immediately follow the names of employers in the United States. The third section is a list of academic, institutions, and corporate members of the participating societies. Telephone numbers of university switchboards and departments in the mathematical sciences, as well as electronic addresses, if provided, have been included.—**Janet Mongan**

1826. Downing, Douglas. **Dictionary of Mathematics Terms.** 2d ed. Hauppauge, N.Y., Barron's Educational Series, 1995. 393p. illus. $10.95pa. ISBN 0-8120-3097-4.

The purpose of this book is to present in one place reference information that is valuable for students of mathematics and for those in careers that use mathematics. The book covers the level of mathematics generally studied in high school and early college. Some of the general subjects included are arithmetic; algebra; geometry; analytical geometry; trigonometry; calculus, including some topics in multivariable calculus; probability and statistics; and logic. Information on several mathematicians who have made major contributions to the field is also given.

A list of entries by subject category is found at the front of the book that leads to more information on a particular branch of mathematics. A list of symbols helps the reader identify any that are unfamiliar. The appendix has a common logarithm table, a trigonometric function table, standard normal distribution tables, a chi square, t and f distribution tables, and a brief table of integrals. Many entries contain cross-references to background information or further applications of the topic.—**Janet Mongan**

1827. **Encyclopaedia of Mathematics. Volume 10: Subject Index—Author Index.** Michiel Hazewinkel, ed. Norwell, Mass., Kluwer Academic, 1994. 732p. $199.00. ISBN 1-55608-009-3.

Volume 10 of the *Encyclopaedia of Mathematics* is the index of this 10-volume set, which is a translation of the Soviet *Mathematical Encyclopaedia* published in five volumes in 1977-1985. The set is a reference work for all parts of mathematics, a dynamic science, which made updates and additional references to Western literature desirable. Therefore, much of the material has been updated since the articles were completed in 1977. This index volume was generated afresh from volumes 1-9. The only attention paid to the smaller index of the original Soviet *Mathematical Encyclopaedia* was a completeness check.

There are two indexes in the volume: an author index and a much larger subject index. The author index is sorted by complete family name. The subject index is made up of 4 kinds of items: article titles (about 7,000 of them); the phrases and words in italics that occur in each article; words and phrases that have been specially marked by the editor or members of the boards of experts as being of sufficient importance to merit inclusion in the subject index; and, finally, partial inversions of all the phrases of the first 3 kinds. The inversions were computer generated, and subsequently edited. All articles have been provided with one or more American Mathematical Society (AMS) classification numbers, as have all items occurring in the index. The index volume contains the inversion of this list, which, for each number, provides a list of words and phrases that serve as a description of the "content" of that classification number.

—**Janet Mongan**

1828. **Mathematical Sciences Professional Directory 1995.** Providence, R.I., American Mathematical Society, 1995. 213p. index. $50.00. ISBN 0-8218-0190-2. ISSN 0737-4356.

Although published by the American Mathematical Society, this directory covers far more than the workings of the AMS. Instead, it is a guide to a wide variety of people and places in the world of mathematics. Aimed at the working mathematician, especially those active in professional organizations, this short but useful volume should be in every university mathematics library and on many mathematicians' personal shelves.

Divided into eight sections, the book begins with information on the AMS, based in Providence, R.I. Listed are current executive staff, officers in the association, council members, board of trustees, and the numerous committees of the organization. The book lists each person in each group and the date their term expires; this section ends with an index to the AMS committees. A large portion of the work is then given over to directory information for 39 other professional mathematics-related organizations ranging from the American Association for the Advancement of Science to the Casualty Actuarial Society to the Institute of Mathematical Statistics. In each case, the organization's address and telephone number are provided, along with a list of officers and committee members.

The book also includes government agencies having a mathematical slant; a list of reciprocity societies (foreign mathematics organizations); a directory of all the people listed elsewhere in the work (their address, telephone number, and 3-mail address); a list of academic math departments in the United States; a directory of nonacademic (but math-related) organizations such as Bell Labs, Batelle Memorial Institute, and TRW Systems; and finally an index to colleges and universities. While by no means a directory of all math professors or scientists working in mathematics, this directory will come in handy for reference work and for various professional uses by mathematicians.—**Robert A. Seal**

1829. Spencer, Donald D. **Key Dates in Number Theory History: From 10,529 B.C. to the Present.** Ormond Beach, Fla., Camelot Publishing, 1995. 126p. illus. index. $18.95pa. ISBN 0-89218-318-7.

This book is an illustrated chronology of the most important number theory events from 10,529 B.C. to the present. It tells what happened, when it happened, who made it happen, and allows one to comprehend the events that have taken place. In a manner that is both fascinating and accessible, it charts the progress and documents the achievements of the men and women of mathematics, computer science, and number theory. Illustrations and photographs are used throughout the book to highlight specific number theory events and to portray some of the people who made important contributions. The comprehensive index allows the book to be used for general and particular reference.

Number theory is a branch of mathematics concerned with the properties of integers, or whole numbers, such as 0, 1, 2, 3, and so on. These properties have been the object of fascination and investigation for thousands of years. It is the only branch of mathematics where there is any possibility that new and valuable discoveries can be made without an extensive acquaintance with technical mathematics. In recent years, high school students have made new and important discoveries with perfect numbers and prime numbers. College students are regularly making important contributions to the number theory field. Personal computer users around the world are using their machines to produce new number theory results on a regular basis. The book will prove a useful guide through the many centuries of number theory historical development. The book is an indispensable reference work for everyone interested in the history of number theory.—**Janet Mongan**

36 Resource Sciences

GENERAL WORKS

Dictionaries and Encyclopedias

1830. **Encyclopedia of Energy Technology and the Environment.** Attilio Bisio and Sharon Boots, eds. New York, John Wiley, 1995. 4v. illus. maps. index. $900.00/set. ISBN 0-471-54458-2.

Energy Technology and the Environment is the first in a series of John Wiley encyclopedias dealing with the environment. This 4-volume set provides 235 articles on various aspects of energy, including the latest technology, and how these impact the environment. This not only provides more up-to-date information than the 2d edition of the *McGraw Hill Encyclopedia of Energy* (see ARBA 82, entry 1507), but has the added hook of relating energy to the environment. Experts from industry and academia authored the articles, which are written for a broad audience, from high school level up. The information is presented in such a way as not to bore a knowledgeable person and not go over the head of a novice. Tables and illustrations are well incorporated, and cross-references lead the reader to related topics. The style and quality of writing remain consistently good despite the various authors, a credit to the editors. Not having the 4th volume at hand, this reviewer cannot comment on the index and whether it enhances accessibility to the information contained within. However, the alphabetical construction, along with the cross-references, do provide some ease of usage. The set is a good jumping-off point for energy issues.
—Angela Marie Thor

Directories

1831. **SYNERJY: A Directory of Renewable Energy. Volume 21: Summer/Fall 1994.** New York, SYNERJY, 1994. 57p. $20.00/yr.; $50.00/yr. (institutions). ISSN 0163-2183.

The purpose of *SYNERJY* is to stimulate progress in practical, nonpolluting sources of energy by providing information about activity in the field. This volume is the 21st in a series dating back to 1974. It includes information from the spring volume but not information reported in previous years. Its largest part is devoted to bibliographical listings (some of which are annotated) of books, articles, reports, and conferences. Manufacturers are also listed. The topics include solar, wind, biomass, geothermal, water, electrical energy utilization, heat pumps, and unconventional heat engines.

This appears to be a very useful guide to current activities in the energy field. A drawback, of course, is the noncumulative nature of the information. However, the publisher offers a complete index to manufacturers in separate volumes.—**Robert B. McKee**

ENERGY RESOURCES

Acronyms

1832. **D & D Standard Oil Abbreviator.** 4th ed. Compiled by the Association of Desk and Derrick Clubs. Tulsa, Okla., PennWell Publishing, 1994. 341p. $29.95pa. ISBN 0-87814-422-6.

This well-known tool for the oil and gas industry, now in its 4th edition, contains more than 11,500 abbreviations and definitions of the growing and changing energy industries. The bulk of the book contains lists of abbreviations (by either abbreviation or term), as well as logging tools and services—Atlas wireline services, Schlumberger well services, Halliburton log service; pipe-coating terminology and definitions; companies and associations; API standard oil-mapping symbols; mathematical symbols and signs; basic conversion factors; and common oilfield spellings. New to this edition is a listing of federal environmental acronyms, mnemonics-service names and mnemonics-computational products, and log heading nomenclature.

This book contains useful information, making it an indispensable tool for oil and gas industry personnel. It meets the purpose of not only helping the secretary and report writer, but also of familiarizing newcomers to the field.—**Anne C. Roess**

Bibliography

1833. Rudolph, Joseph R., Jr. **Energy.** Pasadena, Calif., Salem Press and Metuchen, N.J., Scarecrow, 1995. 177p. index. (Magill Bibliographies). $29.50. ISBN 0-8108-3011-6.

This is a collection of short reviews of approximately 700 books about energy. They are grouped into a number of subject categories, but the classification is self-defeating because it is not obvious what category will contain a given work. For example, two of the categories are "Energy and the Human Condition" and "Energy and Society." Fortunately, both author and subject indexes are supplied. Too often, a book of passionate advocacy is dismissed as "good." The reader will not realize the insistence by some that all radiation of whatever intensity is harmful, nor people's alarm at the prospect of massive starvation.
—**Robert B. McKee**

Directories

1834. **Latin America Petroleum Directory, 1995.** 14th ed. Alvaro Franco and others, eds. Tulsa, Okla., PennWell Publishing, 1994. 125p. maps. index. $150.00pa. ISSN 0193-8738.

1835. **Worldwide Petrochemical Directory, 1995.** 33d ed. Jonelle Guy and others, eds. Tulsa, Okla., PennWell Publishing, 1994. 245p. index. $150.00pa. ISSN 0084-2583.

Both of these texts are members of the PennWell family of energy, petroleum, and petrochemical industry directories. Each is a true directory, not a list of paid advertisers, and both take a broad view of their field. *Worldwide Petrochemical Directory* (WPD), for example, includes an entry for Fisher Controls, a manufacturer of control valves. Like most PennWell directories, these list a preface of statistics and relevant data surveys reprinted from a number of sources such as *Oil & Gas Journal* and the *International Petroleum Encyclopedia*, an extensive alphabetical listing of companies, and a geographical listing of companies by country, state, or province. Each entry lists the names and titles of two to six relevant high-level personnel, and the company's address and telephone number. Most entries describe information about the company's (and subsidiary's) activities or specialties.

The *Latin America Petroleum Directory* (LAPD) covers all aspects of the petroleum industry, including exploration, pipelines, government agencies, and petrochemical companies. On the other hand, the WPD covers only the petrochemical industry, including basic chemicals or intermediates made from crude, refinery products, and manufacturing facilities—whether the company makes a wide range of petrochemicals or only one type. Both provide easily accessible information about companies outside the United States. Addresses of international and U.S. companies can be found in many places; what is more difficult is finding the name and address of a Sudanese fertilizer company.

Even though subsidiaries change hands, new plants are opened, and old ones are closed, a comparison of the all-capped entries in the WPD between the 1992 and 1995 editions shows a net change of less than 5 percent. There was more change in the boldface entries, but not enough to justify most libraries buying the directories every year. As a result, only the largest, most specialized collections need to purchase this every year.—**Susan B. Ardis**

1836. **Randol Mining Directory 1994/95: U.S. Mines & Mining Companies.** Golden, Colo., Randol International, 1994. 790p. illus. maps. index. $115.00pa. ISBN 1-878307-11-8.

This is a commercial publication with many advertisements, but also a great deal of useful information. The first part of the work consists of articles on various topics, including the economics of production, international mining developments, specific metals, changing technology, the environment, pollution, recycling issues, remote sensing, and online and Internet information sources. These articles are informative despite their industry bias. Several maps, graphs, and charts depict the production of coal, metals, industrial minerals, and aggregates, as well as the location of mines. Tables list metals pricing over the past 5 years and the 100 major gold-producing projects in the United States. The major part of the work consists of several directories. These list mines by commodity and by state, and mining companies and exploration companies alphabetically. The thousands of listings cover sites with as few as one employee as well as those with hundreds of workers. Entries include the names of company owners and officers, contact information, the number of employees, the type of mining, stock and shareholder information, and miscellaneous data on geology, reserves, finances, and planning. Also provided are lists of smelters and refineries, industry and professional associations, federal and state agencies, universities with mining programs, and a calendar of events that covers conferences, workshops, and expositions. The work is indexed by mine name. It is recommended for academic and special libraries.—**T. McKimmie**

1837. **Worldwide Pipelines & Contractors Directory, 1995.** 15th ed. Tulsa, Okla., PennWell Publishing, 1994. 316p. index. $135.00pa. ISSN 0146-3349.

The 15th edition of this well-known reference work continues to provide useful information on pipelines and contractors of the world. Its purpose is to list active companies in natural gas, crude oil, and petroleum products pipeline operations, as well as related engineering and construction service companies.

The companies are listed alphabetically within six categories: pipeline contractors, United States natural gas pipelines, United States crude oil pipelines, United States product pipelines, Canadian pipelines, and foreign pipelines. Each entry contains company addresses; telephone, fax, telex, and cable numbers; company description; and names of personnel. Subsidiaries and branch offices are also listed. Company coverage varies. Pipeline contractors cover half the volume; next are United States companies, followed by foreign companies, and then Canadian companies. Company and geographical indexes are provided. In the front of the directory is a worldwide construction survey called Statistical Survey (unfortunately, *statistical* is misspelled).

PennWell directories continue to be one of the main reference sources for company information in the oil and gas industry. This reviewer hopes that PennWell will continue to collect accurate and timely information on the industry.—**Anne C. Roess**

Handbooks and Yearbooks

1838. **Annual Bulletin of Coal Statistics for Europe and North America 1994.** By Economic Commission for Europe. New York, United Nations, 1994. 154p. $35.00pa. ISBN 92-1-016292-7. ISSN 0066-3808. S/N E/F/R.94.II.E.11.

This work presents data on the production, consumption, and use of coal for energy in Europe and the United States. All parts of the work are given in three languages: English, French, and Russian. An introductory section gives an overview of coal as a source of heat and electricity, noting, for example, that coal produces approximately 40 percent of the electricity in Europe. This is followed by graphs and tables displaying the production and consumption of coal and the production of electricity by type of fuel in 51 countries. The largest section of the book is titled "A Balance Sheet of Solid Forms of Energy." Here, a table is devoted to each of 35 countries. Data include import and export figures by type of coal, production by type of coal and type of mine, and size of the labor force. The appendix defines the types of coal produced and consumed and explains how distribution and supply are calculated. The work will be useful for academic and special libraries.—**T. McKimmie**

1839. **Annual Bulletin of Electric Energy Statistics for Europe and North America, 1994. Volume 38.** By Economic Commission for Europe. New York, United Nations, 1994. 170p. $35.00pa. ISBN 92-1-016293-5. ISSN 0066-3816. S/N E/F/R.94.II.E.12.

Since its inception in 1956, this comprehensive annual bulletin prepared by the United Nations Economic Commission for Europe has provided international electric energy statistics. Written in English, French, and Russian, this source details information on electricity and heat statistics in tabular form. Information is accessible through the table of contents or the tables by country. The intent of this publication is to furnish researchers with comparable data on developments and trends about electric energy in the United States, Canada, and European countries. Explanatory notes are provided, detailing units of measurement, sources, time period, and comparability of data. The clear, easy-to-understand graphs and illustrations on topics such as gross consumption in the world, main importers and exporters of electric energy, and other related subjects greatly enhance the usefulness of this statistical source. Since energy and its consumption are important to people worldwide, this reference tool will be of value to academic, special, and large public libraries.—**Diane J. Turner**

1840. **Annual Bulletin of Gas Statistics for Europe and North America 1994. Volume 38.** By Economic Commission for Europe. New York, United Nations, 1994. 133p. $35.00pa. ISBN 92-1-016294-3. ISSN 0066-3824. S/N E/F/R.94.II.E.13.

This 1994 edition continues the statistical series, published by the United Nations since the late 1950s, on natural gas, liquefied petroleum gas, and manufactured gas in Europe and North America. The series covers the 54 member countries in the European Commission for Europe (ECE).

The data, presented mainly in tabular form by country, cover production; stocks; consumption by transformation, energy, and user sectors; imports and exports; and length of pipeline systems. This edition contains data for the years 1990 through 1992, with some coverage for 1980 and 1985. Annex 2 in the back of the publication contains definitions and general notes to help users understand the statistical topics listed in the tables. There is a descriptive table of contents listing graphs and tables and a country index for locating specific tables. This publication is written in English, French, and Russian.

Selection of the type of statistical data is determined by the UN/ECE's Working Party on Gas, which is also the main internal user of the data. Data are compiled from annual questionnaires or from official national sources. Since 1991, the questionnaire has become a joint endeavor of the UN/ECE, the International Energy Agency, the Statistical Office of the European Union, and the United Nations Statistical Division. The extensive experience of the UN/ECE in compiling this gas statistical series continues to make this publication an authoritative reference source for the serious user.—**Anne C. Roess**

1841. **Energy Balances and Electricity Profiles, 1992. Bilans Énergétiques et Profils du Secteur de L'Électricité.** By Department for Economic and Social Information and Policy Analysis, Statistical Division. New York, United Nations, 1994. 490p. $75.00pa. ISBN 92-1-061158-6. S/N E/F.94.XVII.14.

In this 7th edition, the United Nations' Statistical Division continues to present energy data for selected developing countries by showing—in tabular form—the overall picture of energy production, conversion, and consumption for each fuel used in each country. The energy balance tables include total energy requirements (e.g., production, imports, exports, losses); energy converted (e.g., types of industries, losses); and final consumption (by industry and construction, transport, and households). The electricity tables cover production, trade and consumption, net installed capacity, and thermal power plant input by fuel.

The data provided by each country have been converted to common units by the Statistical Division, which has extensive experience in this area. Each item listed in the tables is defined in detail in the introduction, along with each fuel and the conversion factors used for each country. The UN continues to publish comprehensive and reliable energy data series. This publication is one of them.—**Anne C. Roess**

1842. **Mineral Investment Conditions in Selected Countries of the Asia-Pacific Region.** By Economic and Social Commission for Asia and the Pacific and the United Nations Development Programme. New York, United Nations, 1994. 361p. $85.00. ISBN 92-1-119666-3. S/N E.94.II.F.30.

1843. **Minerals Industry Taxation Policies for Asia and the Pacific.** By Economic and Social Commission for Asia and the Pacific and the United Nations Development Programme. New York, United Nations, 1994. 171p. $50.00. ISBN 92-1-119665-5. S/N E.94.II.F.29.

These are two in a series of eight volumes produced by the United Nations Economic and Social Commission for Asia and the Pacific regarding economic restructuring and international trade in the minerals commodities sector in the Asia-Pacific Region. The volume dealing with investment conditions summarizes specific criteria for mining potential for China, India, Indonesia, Malaysia, Mongolia, Myanmar, the Philippines, Thailand, and Vietnam. The criteria are listed under major headings: geographical, political, marketing, regulatory, fiscal, environmental, operational, profit, and other, such as prior company experience in the country. Among the many criteria evaluated are transportation facilities, stability of regimes, hostile borders, tax laws, mineral abundance, and what the requirements are for environmental protection. It is understood that there is no correct answer, as what is acceptable to one group of investors may not be to another. The investors can draw their own conclusions from the facts presented.

Minerals Industry Taxation Policies addresses issues that relate directly or indirectly to the taxation of mineral sectors of the world. In a lengthy summary, consultants discuss mining law changes currently taking place; countries left behind by technological advances; special attributes of the mineral sector that government planners should be aware of when designing policies, legislation, and fiscal systems; problems and opportunities faced by countries changing from a socialist to a free market economy; and dangers of recent tax approaches that may lead to disputes between the foreign investor and the nation.

The second part of *Taxation* presents a brief country report of taxation policies in Bangladesh, China, India, Indonesia, Myanmar, Papua New Guinea, Korea, Thailand, and Vietnam. These two volumes provide thorough reporting of information for a specialized audience and will be useful for that audience. Their continued value will depend on how often they are updated to reflect possible changing conditions in countries.—**Marilyn Strong Noronha**

1844. **Natural Gas Statistics Sourcebook.** 2d ed. Sandra Meyer and others, eds. Tulsa, Okla., PennWell Publishing, 1995. 564p. $230.00pa. ISSN 1074-6730.

The 2d edition of this sourcebook covers essentially the same natural gas data as in the 1st edition (see ARBA 95, entry 1753). New features are an article in which current natural gas statistics are analyzed, and separate commercial and residential consumers by state tables. However, the total consumers-by-state table that appeared in the 1st edition has been left out.

The sourcebook continues to be a convenient one-volume source of statistical data on the natural gas industry for the total United States as well as individual states and regional areas. The data, updated to 1993, are arranged by chapters following the differing segments of the industry. In some areas, the time series goes back to the 1930s, such as for natural gas production. Most of the time series begin in the 1970s and 1980s. Monthly, quarterly, and annual data are available for many time series.

These essential statistics were selected by the experienced staff of the *Oil & Gas Journal* (PennWell Publishing), well known for its comprehensive Oil & Gas Journal Energy Database. The data are nicely presented for the user in easy-to-use tables. This is another excellent and reliable statistical source for the natural gas industry. It gives the user a broad picture of the industry, a good place to start.

—**Anne C. Roess**

1845. **Oil & Gas Journal Data Book.** 1995 ed. Tulsa, Okla., PennWell Publishing, 1995. 411p. $59.95. ISSN 8756-7164.

This 1995 edition of the *Data Book* is essentially a reproduction of surveys and statistics that were published in PennWell's *Oil & Gas Journal* during 1994. Included are rankings of oil and gas companies (the "OGJ 300" and "OGJ 100") according to financial and energy statistics; forecasts and reviews of energy supply and demand; and surveys of gas processing plants, underground natural gas storage, petroleum refineries, petroleum production by fields, and pipelines. Geographic coverage encompasses the United States and other countries in the world.

The statistics section consists of reprints of the statistical tables that appeared in each issue of the *Journal*, such as the American Petroleum Institute refinery report, crude and product stocks, and imports; Baker Hughes and Smith rig counts; and oil and gas production reports. The OGJ 1994 annual index is also included.

This work serves as a statistical sourcebook for the oil and gas industry. It can be used as a supplement to the *Oil & Gas Journal* or as a stand-alone reference source. The index will not help the user locate specific information in the *Data Book*, but will help the user to locate related articles. PennWell is a well-known publisher of oil and gas information.—**Anne C. Roess**

1846. **Pricing Statistics Sourcebook.** Tulsa, Okla., PennWell Publishing, 1995. 621p. maps. $230.00pa. ISSN 1078-4489.

This comprehensive resource pulls together in one large volume a wide range of energy pricing statistics in the oil and gas industry. Monthly, quarterly, and annual data are given for all key price parameters. Eight pages are devoted to a verbal description of the data; the rest of the volume is in table format. A useful appendix includes a substantial chronology of major events in the industry; a glossary of abbreviations and terms; membership lists in the Organization of Petroleum Exporting Countries (OPEC), Organization for Economic Cooperation and Development (OECD), and International Economic Association (IEA); conversion factors; and a map of Petroleum Administration for Defense districts and U.S. refining districts.

Especially recommended for all academic libraries that support any type of environmental studies programs and petroleum engineering, it is also a good general reference for business and engineering programs, for those who can afford it.—**Barbara Delzell**

1847. **The Real Goods Solar Living Sourcebook: The Complete Guide to Renewable Energy Technologies and Sustainable Living.** 8th ed. John Schaeffer and the Real Goods staff, eds. White River Junction, Vt., Chelsea Green, 1994. 656p. illus. maps. index. (Real Goods Independent Living Books). $23.00pa. ISBN 0-930031-68-7.

The previous edition of *Real Goods Solar Living Sourcebook* sold thousands of copies and the new edition is better than ever, with chapters on gardening, home businesses, and health. The publisher's motto is "Knowledge is our most important product," and this source provides a broad range of renewable energy and resource-efficient products for independent living.

More than a product catalog, *Real Goods* contains comprehensive information about solar energy, written by individuals with firsthand experience using innovative technology to live lightly on this planet. Chapter topics include: independent living, land, shelter, managing energy systems, energy conservation, and the nontoxic home.

Michael Potts's *The Independent Home: Living Well with Power from the Sun, Wind and Water* (Chelsea Green, 1993) is a good companion volume. *A Good House: Building a Life on the Land* (Grove Press, 1993) by Richard Manning encourages a "less is more" architectural style for building solar homes.

Real Goods provides instructions for building solar-power systems with a practical, nuts-and-bolts approach. It has a bibliography and other related sources, including national environmental agencies and research organizations. There are subject and product indexes as well. Plans, charts, photographs, and illustrations enhance the book. This book is a useful, practical, how-to manual for amateurs as well as professionals interested in independent living and renewable energy.—**Marilynn Green**

1848. **Renewable Energy Sources Statistics 1989-91.** Brussels, Office for Official Publications of the European Communities; distr., Lanham, Md., UNIPUB, 1995. 80p. $12.00pa. ISBN 92-826-9056-3.

This statistical publication is aimed at specialists in the field and provides renewable energy sources for the years 1989, 1990, and 1991. The countries covered are Belgium, Denmark, France, Germany, Greece, Ireland, Italy, Luxembourg, the Netherlands, Portugal, Spain, and the United Kingdom, which are members of the European Union. Part 1 contains a summary of the various types of renewable energy sources such as hydropower, wind energy, solar energy, geothermal, or biomass/wastes. It also provides detailed tables of the figures on each source for the three years covered.

Part 2 supplies an explanation of the methodology followed to collect the various statistics and some of the technologies used, such as biofuel production, wind energy converters, or geothermal heat plants. No index is furnished in this compact source, but it is easy to read, the tables are clear and informative, and the contents page is helpful. The publication is recommended for special or academic libraries that support energy research.—**Diane J. Turner**

1849. **Refining Statistics Sourcebook.** Tulsa, Okla., PennWell Publishing, 1994. 584p. 185.00pa. ISSN 1074-6838.

Refining Statistics Sourcebook provides the user convenient access to key statistics of the petroleum refining industry. Petroleum product demand, refining capacity and inputs, production, imports and exports, stocks, transportation and petroleum movement, investment, and prices are included for the United States and the world.

More than 2,500 key data series from the Oil & Gas Journal Energy Database and the U.S. Department of Energy's, Energy Information Administration were selected. The arrangement of data in the tables, which contain annual (at least 10 years' worth) and monthly data, are nicely presented in an easy-to-read format. Some of the data is also presented graphically. Brief source citations are given for each table. The glossary of abbreviations and terms is limited in its coverage. Most of the petroleum products, such as still gas, are not defined.

As a one-volume data source on the refining industry, this sourcebook is a handy one. It is a good place to start, especially if the user does not have access to Energy Information Administration publications. The main advantage of the sourcebook series, besides the data series, is that it gives the user a broad statistical picture of an industry.—**Anne C. Roess**

ENVIRONMENTAL SCIENCE

Acronyms

1850. **Environmental Acronyms.** Julie Hong, ed. Rockville, Md., Government Institutes, 1995. 117p. $29.00pa. ISBN 0-86587-458-1.

Environmental Acronyms is a compilation of acronyms, a majority of which are taken from U.S. environmental laws. The brief introduction states that sources for the acronyms include the Internet, Title 40, and Environmental Protection Agency documents. Approximately 2,200 acronyms are listed in alphabetical order with their corresponding meaning. Also noted in the introduction is that the Government Institutes editorial staff welcomes any acronym additions or suggestions for improving the volume. Users looking through most environmental directories, dictionaries, or encyclopedias will readily be able to add additional acronyms missing from this compilation.

This volume would be more useful to environmental researchers and others if this information was appended to another Government Institutes book, *Directory of Environmental Information Sources* (5th ed.; see entry 1864). In this way, users would, perhaps, be able to find out additional information such as addresses of agencies or organizations concerning a particular acronym. *The Green Encyclopedia* (see ARBA 94, entry 1996) contains a list of more than 1,700 environmental acronyms, as well as 400-plus pages of encyclopedic information, and the cost is $9 less for the paperback edition than *Environmental Acronyms*. This work is recommended only for special libraries concerned with the environment.

—**James E. Bird**

Bibliographies

1851. Nordquist, Joan, comp. **Multinational Corporations and the Environment: A Bibliography.** Santa Cruz, Calif., Reference and Research Services, 1994. 68p. (Contemporary Social Issues: A Bibliographic Series, no.36). $15.00pa. ISBN 0-937855-70-7.

In the last 10 years, there has been much written in the mainstream press on the topic of multinational corporations and the environment. This bibliography, of 826 entries, is a convenient source to the more difficult-to-find material published in the lesser-known, alternative, radical, and activist literature. Some mainstream materials are represented but to a lesser extent. The entries are grouped under a series of headings, which are further organized by document type, such as books, pamphlets, and articles. Although unannotated, the entries include the full citation, arranged alphabetically by author or title. The citations are current to 1995, and the average date is around 1992, when the environmental movement was strong. A sampling of the subject areas covered includes the North American Free Trade Agreement (NAFTA), the General Agreement on Tariffs and Trade (GATT), toxic waste dumping, problems in individual countries, and corporate solutions to environmental problems.

A brief introduction describes the organization and subject matter of the text. The book concludes with a list of addresses to various environmental groups located around the globe. Users will like this small, portable text although it has a simple stapled binding that could easily wear out with repeated use. The work is an extremely useful and unique subject-specific bibliography that will be an important addition to academic and research libraries.—**Katherine Margaret Thomas**

1852. Woodside, Gayle, and Dianna S. Kocurek. **Resources and References: Hazardous Waste and Hazardous Materials Management.** Park Ridge, N.J., Noyes, 1994. 295p. $64.00. ISBN 0-8155-1351-8.

This is one of a limited number of technical bibliographies in the field of hazardous waste and materials management. For good reason, the work includes mostly references from 1986 to 1994, since this field and governmental regulations are rapidly changing. The focus of the text is on the management of hazardous waste and materials management in the United States. This resource is divided into three parts: hazardous waste management, hazardous materials management, and additional resources. Under each of these headings are grouped individual topics such as air quality, industrial and municipal wastewater, chemical hazards, workplace safety, instructional and training videotapes, resource libraries, technical journals, and information about publishers. Each of the headings or topics lists annotated bibliographies of the most recent materials and resources available.

This is a reasonably priced resource tool which, when used with the local ordinances, statutes, rules, and regulations of the region or state in question, can prove helpful in answering important questions concerning hazardous materials. Of particular help are the listings of relevant Environmental Protection Agency offices and telephone numbers. While the book lacks an index, necessary information can be located with relative efficiency. This is due in large part to the simple, but straightforward, easy-to-understand, and clear manner in which the subject has been presented. The work is recommended for public, university, and specialized corporate and government libraries.—**James M. Murray**

Chronology

1853. **Great Events from History II: Ecology and the Environment Series.** Frank N. Magill, ed. Pasadena, Calif., Salem Press, 1995. 5v. index. $375.00/set. ISBN 0-89356-751-5.

This 5th set in the Great Events from History series presents 395 chronologically arranged articles in 5 volumes. The articles are original and cover events from 1902-1944. The topics of ecology and the environment include the natural world as well as the effect of humankind upon the environment. Each article lists the categories of event, time, and location of event; a brief summary of the event's significance in the history of ecology; and the impact of the event. Described, also, are the key persons who were participants. A selected, annotated bibliography is provided at the end of each article, along with cross-references to additional information on the topic that appears elsewhere in the set.

The main key to using this set effectively is the indexes located at the end of volume 5. All volumes have the chronological list of events, but volume 5 also has an alphabetical list of events; a subject and keyword index; a category index listing topics under headings such as air pollution, biology, and medicine; a geographical index listing the events in specific areas of the world; and a principal personages index arranged by last name of persons who participated in or had some influential role in the environment.

The user can now quickly find a wide range of information on the environment, including important legislation, acts, and treaties of the United States and other countries; information about endangered species; and summaries of important happenings such as the Armenian earthquake and the *Exxon Valdez* disaster in Alaska. Once they pinpoint the times, dates, places, and key information, they can go to other sources for in-depth information if desired. The work is an important contribution to ecology and will especially be valued in libraries that emphasize the sciences.—**Marilyn Strong Noronha**

Dictionaries and Encyclopedias

1854. **The Concise Oxford Dictionary of Ecology.** Michael Allaby, ed. New York, Oxford University Press, 1994. 415p. $35.00; $12.95pa. ISBN 0-19-211689-4; 0-19-286160-3pa.

This inexpensive, paperback dictionary provides 5,000 brief entries on up-to-date terms on ecology and the environmental sciences. Many entries are taken from *The Oxford Dictionary of Natural History* (see ARBA 87, entry 1460) and cover a multitude of subjects such as animal behavior, environmental pollution, evolution, climatology, and oceanography. The entries are alphabetically arranged with some including beneficial cross-references. The concise biographical entries on major ecologists, such as Frederic Clements, and other scientists such as German chemist Justus von Liebig enhance the usefulness of this compact ready-reference by leading researchers into other areas related to ecology. This source will be useful in any public or academic library. [R: Choice, Jan 95, p. 744]—**Diane J. Turner**

1855. **The Dictionary of Environmental Law and Science.** William A. Tilleman, ed. Toronto, Emond Montgomery, 1994. 337p. $40.00pa. ISBN 0-920722-59-8.

Semantics can, at times, make or break a case. Words do not always mean the same thing to all people, yet, in legal matters, it is important to have an agreed-upon meaning for all involved. Tilleman, a professor of law and environmental legal counsel, tries to reduce the chaos by providing definitions to more than 5,000 legal and scientific words and terms used by lawmakers. Although Canadian based, this cross-disciplinary dictionary draws also from the United States legal system.

Definitions come from a number of sources, including Canadian federal and provincial statutes and regulations, the Canadian Federal Environmental Assessment and Review Office (FEARO), the United States Code of Federal Regulations, and the United States Environmental Protection Agency's definitions and acronyms. *The Dictionary of Ecology and Environmental Science* (Henry Holt, 1993) was also checked for additional terms. Each definition states the source from which it was obtained. If sources differ in their definitions, each definition is included. The individual must determine which definition is in the proper context for a particular problem, and check current law to ensure that the definition is correct. In the rare instance that a term does not have a reference, the editor has offered what he feels is the most suitable definition, based on his experience and education. Acronyms and abbreviations are cross referenced within the dictionary listings, as well as listed separately in the back. *See also* references direct the user to other appropriate terms. Some case references are listed, but these are not the emphasis of this edition. This book contains useful material for libraries serving the environmental and legal communities.
—**Angela Marie Thor**

1856. **Encyclopedia of Environmental Biology.** William A. Nierenberg, ed. San Diego, Calif., Academic Press, 1995. 3v. illus. maps. index. $395.00/set. ISBN 0-12-226730-3.

This set fills a void in reference collections in the area of environmental biology. The 154 entries average more than 10 pages each and include their own glossaries and bibliographies. Each entry has a table of contents; an introduction; tables; diagrams or photographs; and, where applicable, a historical background that brings the topic into the current arena. The entries are readable and easy to understand without being too simplified, making the set appropriate for public, high school, and academic libraries.

Each volume provides the table of contents for the set, and the entries are arranged alphabetically throughout the set. Volume 3 has the list of contributors with the topic they wrote on and their address. The subject index covers all the subtopics within the main entries and includes cross-references. A separate index of related topics lists the main entries and all other related topics, such as how aquatic weeds and river ecology relate; hence, it is a comprehensive *see also* index. The set is highly recommended.—**Betsy J. Kraus**

1857. **Encyclopedia of Environmental Control Technology. Volume 7: High-Hazard Pollutants.** Paul N. Cheremisinoff, ed. Houston, Tex., Gulf Publishing, 1995. 663p. illus. maps. index. $155.00. ISBN 0-87201-291-3.

This volume contains 27 chapters treating selected topics concerning the effects of toxic agents on human health. Chapters are written by authorities from around the world. Some provide overviews, while others treat specific situations in more detail. The opening chapters deal with risk communication and policy. Later chapters develop such topics as reproductive hazards in the workplace, passive smoke, heavy metals, asbestos, survival of bacteria in animal excreta, insecticides, and sound- and temperature-caused disease. Occupational risk is a common theme.

The treatment of physiological effects and toxicity mechanisms is generally excellent and some of the case studies will serve as good general models. The final chapter discusses sources of information. These include computerized databases, Internet forums, clearinghouses and hotlines, and printed periodicals and books. The quality of writing is somewhat uneven, but overall the treatment is good. References are not always current. Some chapters, for example, contain no references from the 1990s. There are many useful data tables, but graphics are often rudimentary. The work includes an index. It is recommended for academic, special, and large public libraries.—**T. McKimmie**

1858. **Encyclopedia of Environmental Control Technology. Volume 8: Work Area Hazards.** Paul N. Cheremisinoff, ed. Houston, Tex., Gulf Publishing, 1995. 804p. index. $155.00. ISBN 0-87201-304-9.

How hazardous are work areas? Can risks be reduced to levels acceptable to the well-being and comfort of employees and communities? Which hazards can be eliminated? Those questions undergird 30 chapters dealing with topics as wide-ranging as radon in homes to occupational safety in Thailand. Yet the varied settings are good teaching tools. For example, the average amount of radon in a home presents a risk of lung cancer equivalent to inhaling passive smoke. Insecticide poisonings are not uncommon in Thailand. Hospitals generate 13-23 pounds of waste per bed per day—the point on the range depends upon who estimates; 30 percent of the amount is infectious.

Making the work area as safe as possible requires time and energy (e.g., the production of "Materials Safe Data Sheets," the development of accident/security response plans). By using this text to put a specific focus on the human elements tied to hazards, the series editor adds an important dimension to the evolving encyclopedia. As in earlier volumes, this one includes a refined index, chapter-end bibliographies, and—unfortunately, but understandably in terms of print queues—dated references (most no more recent than 1991).—**Diane M. Calabrese**

1859. **Encyclopedia of Environmental Control Technology. Volume 9: Geotechnical Applications, Leak Detection, Treatment Options.** Paul N. Cheremisinoff, ed. Houston, Tex., Gulf Publishing, 1995. 1137p. illus. maps. index. $155.00. ISBN 0-87201-327-8.

Turbid water, no mechanical clarification system—no problem: Reach for some *Vicia* (horse bean) seeds. They are just some of the many seeds—and other plant parts—used as natural coagulants. Seeds of species of *Moringa* not only clarify, they can remove cercariae of *Schistosomiasis mansoni*, the deadly liver fluke, from water. Containment and abatement of waste (mostly human-produced) in water and soil require an approach as broad and diverse as the menaces in those spheres.

This 32-chapter volume takes such an approach. "What works and why" might be the subtitle. Whether the solution is as new as geosynthetic fabrics (membranes) used to separate and filter, or as old as the seeds used as clarifiers, it does not escape attention.

A reader finds, for example, the recommendations that mosquitoes in wetlands be controlled by manipulation of temperature and dissolved oxygen, and selection of plants (e.g., duckweed that covers the surface). One should pick up this volume to learn the potential microorganisms that show in degrading oil. Also, use of the text to assess the effects of heavy metals on the vital foundation of the food chain (algae) is possible. Whatever the topic, readers will relish the intelligible, balanced delivery of this robust reference, perhaps the best in the series to date.—**Diane M. Calabrese**

1860. **The Grolier Illustrated Library of the Environment.** By Brian Knapp. Danbury, Conn., Grolier, 1995. 6v. illus. maps. index. $159.00/set. ISBN 0-7172-7509-4.

Schools and public libraries looking for some straightforward facts on the environment should take a look at *The Grolier Illustrated Library of the Environment*. This six-volume set examines the Earth, energy, environment and conservation, industry, resources, and weather in a basic factual manner. There is no name-calling or fault-blaming, but just the facts.

The information is arranged in a way that should make it palatable even to young schoolchildren. Each book is divided into broad subject chapters, such as "Coasts and Coastlines." These, then, are subdivided into narrower topics (e.g., "The Beach"). There are a few small paragraphs on that topic, as well as a sidebar containing a sound bite of information. The facing page contains illustrations and information on an even narrower division of the topic, as in the above case, "Coastal Landforms."

This format, which carries through the full six volumes, provides the user with information from a broad perspective to a narrower one, a great advantage when working with varying age groups. The illustrations enhance the information and aid in learning more about the topic. Each volume has a glossary of sorts, but these contain a minimal number of terms. There is also a serviceable index in each volume, as well as a master index in the last volume.—**Angela Marie Thor**

1861. Simon, Seymour. **Earth Words: A Dictionary of the Environment.** New York, HarperCollins, 1995. 48p. illus. $15.89. ISBN 0-06-020233-5.

Earth Words is a beautifully illustrated beginner's dictionary that seems at first blush to be aimed at the second or third grade. However, the vocabulary the author uses is a bit more sophisticated, putting the actual readability level more at the third or fourth grade. While the author is careful to use accurate terminology (rather than translating words into more simple terms), this tendency makes the assumption that the reader's lexicon is on par with the author's. For example, the definition of *decomposer* includes the following sentence: "Decomposers cause rot and decay and recycle nutrients back into the environment, where they can be used again by living plants and animals" (p. 15).

The text is arranged alphabetically, with most definitions accompanied by illustrations. While most of the illustrations are helpful in demonstrating such concepts as the greenhouse effect, others (such as depicting a boy fishing off a dock next to a factory as an illustration of PCBs [polychlorinated bipheny]) are not as helpful to the reader in clarifying what a term means. The result is that the illustrations seem to be aimed at a slightly younger audience than the text is. As a result, it may be difficult to interest younger readers in the difficult text, while older readers may balk at making use of a resource that looks like it is meant for younger audiences.—**Teresa Holten**

1862. Vásquez, Milton, and Angelina Cazoria. **English-Spanish Glossary of Environmental Terms and Abbreviations. Español-Inglés Glosario de Términos Ambientales y Abreviaciones.** Houston, Tex., Gulf Publishing, 1995. 138p. $75.00. ISBN 0-88415-254-5.

The publicity material accompanying this bilingual glossary claims that the *English-Spanish Glossary of Environmental Terms and Abbreviations* "helps engineers and consultants on both sides of the borders [sic] communicate successfully and avoid costly mistakes." To achieve this end, the glossary provides English and Spanish definitions for 65 environmental terms as well as spelling out some 1,100 abbreviations. In the English-Spanish section of the glossary, each English term is given a definition in English followed by the term in Spanish with a Spanish definition. In the Spanish-English section the above order is reversed.

This method results in unnecessary duplication and produces a book that appears to provide more information than it actually delivers. The section covering abbreviations is more useful for a translator going from English to Spanish because all of the entries are English (U.S.) abbreviations, acronyms, or initialisms. Thus, users of the glossary will find EPA (Environmental Protection Agency) spelled out in English and Spanish, but they will not find an entry for any equivalent Latin American governmental agency. For the price, this glossary should provide more information.—**Donald A. Barclay**

Directories

1863. **Carroll's Environmental Directory 1995.** Neda A. Zawahri and others, eds. Washington, D.C., Carroll Publishing, 1995. 884p. index. $185.00pa.

Looking for an environmental consultant? Check out *Carroll's Environmental Directory*. This biennial directory lists environmental consultants, business/trade associations, nonprofit organizations, lobbyists, research centers, information centers, and government offices that focus on the environment. There is contact information for more than 18,000 individuals, as well as profiles for more than 2,600 U.S. corporations that have at least one senior officer with environmental responsibilities.

The directory is divided into the above-mentioned categories and is arranged alphabetically within each section. Standard directory information (address, telephone, and fax numbers) is given. Unfortunately, no e-mail addresses are provided. Indexes include lobbyists by name, a general name index, and a SIC index. These make the work easy to use and a good place to turn when tracking down someone in the environmental field.—**Angela Marie Thor**

1864. **Directory of Environmental Information Sources.** 5th ed. Thomas F. P. Sullivan, ed. Compiled by the Editorial Staff of Government Institutes. Rockville, Md., Government Institutes, 1995. 299p. index. $79.00pa. ISBN 0-86587-475-1.

Intended primarily as a tool for businesses that use environmental data in their regular operations, this work is divided into six sections: U.S. government agencies; state agencies; professional, trade, and scientific associations; print resources (chiefly serial publications); online databases (excluding the Internet, which is covered by the publisher's *Environmental Guide to the Internet* [see entry 1868]); and (new to this edition) research centers. The federal section is subarranged by type of agency; the other sections are alphabetically organized.

The entries for government agencies, associations, and research centers include name, mailing address, telephone number, and (except for state agencies) a short description of the body's functions and the types of data available from it. Entries for print sources contain title; name, address, and telephone number of publisher; a descriptive annotation; frequency; and price. Entries for databases have the name of the database; name, address, and telephone number of the producer; a descriptive annotation (which tends to be more detailed than those in the other sections); and a list of data services through which access is available. Given the increasing use of faxes and e-mail today, it would have been useful to include information for these as well as telephone numbers. Geographical coverage is essentially limited to the United States, but a few international sources are included. This directory should be useful to all types of libraries.
—**Paul B. Cors**

1865. **EPA Database Book.** Rockville, Md., Government Institutes, 1994. 1v. (various paging). index. $68.00pa. ISBN 0-86587-409-3.

This book contains the U.S. Environmental Protection Agency's (EPA) Information Systems Inventory of about 500 EPA systems, databases, models, modules, and other computer applications. The systems are arranged alphabetically within the 11 responsible EPA offices and 10 geographical regions. Each entry contains the system name and acronym; responsible office and person; hardware/software; numerical codes for system level ([1] major agency, [2] widely accessed, [3] localized, and [4] user-owned); and an abstract describing the system. Three indexes are provided, by system name, system acronym, and system level (i.e., by code number with system name).

The book's purpose is to serve as a pathfinder to computerized information systems and applications within the EPA for EPA personnel, governmental partners and clients, and the general public. If the user is familiar with the organization of the EPA, this book may be not too difficult to use. However, the general public will find the opposite. Since the Inventory also collected database descriptors and keywords, provision of a subject or keyword index would have been helpful and would have made the book a more useful reference tool. A disk format that is also available may perhaps provide better searching capabilities than the printed version. It does provide clear descriptions of EPA databases along with telephone contact persons for more information if needed by the user.—**Anne C. Roess**

1866. Farquhar, Doug, and Linda Gaer, comps. **Lead Poisoning Prevention: Directory of State Contacts 1994.** Denver, Colo., National Conference of State Legislatures, 1994. 198p. $12.00pa. ISBN 1-55516-428-5.

The information in this volume was gathered through a 19-question survey mailed in March 1994 and is the revised edition of the 1992 directory by the National Council of State Legislatures. The introduction lists the survey questions with all their parts, and lists the answers by state in table form. The volume covers all the states, the District of Columbia, and U.S. territories. The body of the book is alphabetical by state, and then by territories. Each entry gives the contact person, organization, address, telephone and fax numbers, facilities available if applicable, and what the organization is responsible for overseeing. This is a specific, concise, and useful reference tool that is a bargain for the price. The work is highly recommended for public and academic libraries.—**Betsy J. Kraus**

1867. Krupin, Paul J. **Krupin's Toll-Free Environmental Directory.** Kennewick, Wash., Direct Contact Publishing, 1994. 121p. index. $14.95pa. ISBN 1-885035-02-0.

"Small but mighty" describes this handy toll-free telephone directory to more than 4,500 environmental companies, consultants, educational programs, organizations, and agencies. The directory is in easy-to-use alphabetical format, arranged by topic. This format is effective for most areas of coverage. However, several large sections such as "Engineers" and "Laboratories" would be easier to use if subindexed by geographical area. There is an index along with appendixes containing environmental job classifications, titles, and government position classifications. This is a very useful and economical general reference tool for all types of environmental information—highly recommended for all libraries.—**Barbara Delzell**

1868. Schupp, Jonathan F. **Environmental Guide to the Internet.** Rockville, Md., Government Institutes, 1995. 252p. index. $49.00pa. ISBN 0-86587-449-2.

This paperback book is a useful resource for anyone wanting to explore the vast amount of environmental information available on the information superhighway. In the preface, the author explains how the Internet is constantly changing and that some items listed may not be available as explained in his book. Broken down into 5 chapters, this guide points the user to 29 bulletin board systems, 11 Usenet newsgroups, 45 electronic journals and newsletters, and 94 Internet mailing lists. Each entry for the electronic mailing lists provides a brief summary about the list, likely audience, how to subscribe, if it has archives, the list manager, and additional information.

Although this guide cites several of the same items that one can find in Don Rittner's less expensive book *Ecolinking: Everyone's Guide to Online Environmental Information* (Peachpit Press, 1992), it also contains many other unique items that will be useful to those researching environmental issues. Throughout this guide, the author gives simple yet valuable advice about such things as accessing Internet guidebooks online, how to keep abreast of new electronic journals, and general advice on how not to be intimidated by the massive amount of information available. The table of contents and alphabetical index provide simple access to the various mailing lists, bulletin boards, and electronic journals. This source will be valuable to public and academic libraries and any researcher looking for environmental information online.—**Diane J. Turner**

Handbooks and Yearbooks

1869. **The ABC-CLIO Companion to the Environmental Movement.** By Mark Grossman. Santa Barbara, Calif., ABC-CLIO, 1994. 445p. illus. index. $55.00. ISBN 0-87436-732-8.

This work, another in the ABC-CLIO Companions series concentrating on key events in American history, will provide the nonspecialist with easily accessible information on the environmental movement in the United States since 1626. Its focus is on the twentieth century and includes groups and federal legislation related to the environment and conservation. Some brief—though interesting—biographical essays on the prominent players in the environmental movement such as Theodore Roosevelt, Henry David Thoreau, Rachel Carson, and Benton MacKay add a human touch. A chronology of key events and nearly 400 alphabetically arranged entries, several with cross-references, aid readers in finding information. The brief introduction, alphabetical index, and bibliography enhance the value of this easy-to-use volume. Although this work is not as comprehensive as the *Environmental Encyclopedia* (see ARBA 95, entry 1764), it provides unique information not listed in the latter source and is much less expensive. The illustrations and readable prose will hold people's interest. Researchers and other academics should use this companion in conjunction with additional works on the environment. Although this book would not be the best choice for academic libraries, it will be useful in all public libraries.—**Diane J. Turner**

1870. Chase, Jayni. **Blueprint for a Green School.** New York, Scholastic, 1995. 670p. illus. index. $59.95. ISBN 0-590-49830-4.

Radon, pesticides, electromagnetic fields. What do these things have to do with schools? Maybe more than one might think. Children spend a large proportion of their time within the confines of our schools. Due to their physiology, children are also more susceptible to environmental problems. *Blueprint for a Green School* provides a guide for anyone interested in advocating for a safe school environment. Chapter by chapter, one is introduced to a potential problem, given the facts, and then provided with possible solutions. The school is looked at both inside and out, right down to the supplies available in the art room. One learns how to do a general assessment and where to get expert help when needed.

A green school also means taking action to promote a greener lifestyle. To this end, there are chapters on how the cafeteria can promote a more nutritious diet, which also promotes less waste and local, seasonal supplies, as well as projects such as school recycling programs and gardens. Each chapter also has a resource list, and there are student/teacher activities, grants and awards, and contacts to receive other resource materials. The information is well presented and well indexed.—**Angela Marie Thor**

1871. **Earth Work: Resource Guide to Nationwide Green Jobs.** By the Student Conservation Association. Joan Moody and Richard Wizansky, eds. San Francisco, Calif., HarperCollinsWest, 1994. 205p. $25.00; $14.00pa. ISBN 0-06-258543-6; 0-06-258531-2pa.

Earth Work is a comprehensive guide for those seeking positions in the environmental workplace, thereby having a positive impact on the planet. The information provided here includes: the top 10 fastest growing environmental positions, names and addresses of organizations that hire environmental workers, suggestions on forming networks to keep abreast of new job prospects, comparisons of jobs and salaries in the public and private sectors, detailed information on the advantage of graduate education, and summaries of graduate opportunities with a listing of "green" graduate schools that offer environmental programs. Short biographies of individuals who have succeeded in environmental fields, an interesting feature, are interspersed throughout the text. The detailed chapters not only include which jobs are available, but also provide application procedures and contact information for part-time volunteers as well as full-time career seekers.

The authors of this volume also publish *Earthwork* magazine and have compiled the best career advice from that publication. Each month, the magazine carries new job listings and career advice, and the authors suggest consulting it for current listings. The table of contents breaks the guide down into nine chapters, a directory of organizations offering jobs, and a booklist on "green" careers. There is no index. This unique resource has more depth than most career books and provides an excellent overview of all facets of environmental careers. It would be a valuable addition to the career collection of any library.
—**Marilyn Strong Noronha**

1872. **Environmental Statutes.** 1995 ed. Rockville, Md., Government Institutes, 1995. 1216p. index. $67.00; $57.00pa. ISBN 0-86587-451-4; 0-86587-452-2pa.

This is a collection of the major environmental laws in the United States as amended through 1994. Some of the areas covered include clean water and air, radon gas, safe drinking water, and pollution. There is a disclaimer at the beginning of the volume to remind readers that laws are constantly changing, and the most current edition of a law may not be contained herein. However, the book is a good starting point. An index is supplied at the end of the volume for each individual law. The work is a good item for libraries not having any other access to laws dealing with the environment, cleanup, or pollution.—**Betsy J. Kraus**

1873. Glenn, William M. **The Health and Safety Manager's A-Z Guide to Environmental Management.** Don Mills, Ontario, Southam, 1994. 319p. $87.50pa. ISBN 0-919217-67-2.

This work is intended as an overview of environmental issues, but there is no indication in the title that the guide pertains exclusively to Canada. The guide contains much valuable material on new regulations, policies, and technologies in the rapidly changing environmental fields in Canada, information on people in authority, and whom to contact if problems arise. This book includes 56 subdivisions, according to the various sources and types of pollutions and pollutants (e.g., air pollution, asbestos in buildings and building products, company fleets, energy). There are data on: the Environmental Bill of Rights; fines and penalties; funding and assistance programs; New Substances Notification (NSN) regulations; the governmental—federal and provincial—and nongovernmental associations and organizations; and the National Statutes and Contacts, as well as statutes and contacts for each of the Canadian provinces and territories. Additionally, the book gives some recommendations relating to the prevention of environmental pollution. Approximately half the text in this volume is devoted to the description of various environmental problems or liabilities that Canadian companies face today: hazardous waste management, radon contamination, chemical spills and other emergencies, toxic real estate, and leaking underground storage tanks, to name a few. The market for the guide is relevant governmental agencies, companies, enterprises, and individuals involved in environmental matters.—**Ludmila N. Ilyina**

1874. Newton, David E. **The Ozone Dilemma: A Reference Handbook.** Santa Barbara, Calif., ABC-CLIO, 1995. 195p. index. (Contemporary World Issues). $39.50. ISBN 0-87436-719-0.

Part of ABC-CLIO's Contemporary World Issues series, *The Ozone Dilemma* is a well-written and researched account of issues concerning ozone. Newton notes in his preface that the purpose of the book ". . . is to outline the main features of this debate and to provide background information. . . ." He has succeeded well in doing this.

The book is divided into 7 sections: "Ozone Layer Depletion: Myth or Reality"; "Chronology" (of events in ozone research); "Biographical Sketches"; "Data, Opinions, and Documents"; "Directory of Organizations"; "Print Resources"; and "Nonprint Resources." There are also a list of acronyms and abbreviations and a glossary of terms used in ozone discussions, as well as a list of formulas and nomenclature of important chemicals. An index completes the volume.

The writing is clear and concise. Newton cites his sources throughout the book, with many references dated in the 1990s. One area that would have been nice to see would be Internet resources available on ozone, as there are many World Wide Web sites out there. This book should find a place in secondary, undergraduate college, and public libraries. Students using this book will find much information to spark their interest on a variety of topics related to ozone. It is highly recommended.—**James E. Bird**

1875. **Patty's Industrial Hygiene and Toxicology. Volume 3, Part B: Theory and Rationale of Industrial Hygiene Practice: Biological Responses.** 3d ed. Lewis J. Cralley, Lester V. Cralley, and James S. Bus, eds. New York, John Wiley, 1995. 765p. index. $195.00. ISBN 0-471-53065-4.

Patty's Industrial Hygiene and Toxicology has had a long and vibrant history (see ARBA 95, entry 1784, for a review of an earlier volume). This revision carries the name of Frank Patty, author of the original comprehensive guide to industrial toxicology. The latest revision has remained faithful to Patty's original purpose of providing access to information about hazardous substances "lurking in every corner of the modern industrial workplace." A new hazard recognized since the last edition (with an entire chapter) is the ergonomics of office and workplace equipment. Other additions and updated materials include the environmental effects of magnetic fields, radio waves, and ionizing and nonionizing radiation. Other interesting chapters are the ones on "Biological Rhythms, Shift Work, and Occupation Health" and "Biological Agents." Both are areas impacting many working people. The latter recognizes the increased potential for the rapid spread of debilitating or lethal infections such as hemorrhagic fever, malaria, and Lyme disease.

This is an important set for any biology, chemistry, industrial, or engineering library. Large public libraries should seriously consider it, especially if they have public interest in industrial contamination, occupational hazards, and the like. The only criticism of this particular volume is its overly broad subtitle, which does not accurately inform users of what is inside. This is too bad, because if the title were more reflective of the actual contents, this volume could be recommended as a stand-alone reference volume for any library interested in biological agents, ergonomics, and reproductive toxicology.—**Susan B. Ardis**

1876. **Peterson's Job Opportunities in the Environment 1995.** Princeton, N.J., Peterson's Guides, 1994. 265p. index. $18.95pa. ISBN 1-56079-371-6. ISSN 1071-183X.

Job hunters with a concern or education in environmental issues will find this source helpful. The book lists and describes more than 1,500 employers in environmentally related businesses and organizations. The employers listed here are primarily private companies, but some federal and state agencies are also included. The employers cover those in pollution control, waste management, environmental engineering, water treatment facilities, air quality control, environmental consulting, and many others (even scrap bales and shears manufacturers).

As with the other popular Peterson job guides (see entries 280, 1513, and 1689), this one is updated annually and therefore provides current information essential when job hunting. Each company is profiled with a brief description, founding date, annual sales, number of employees, expertise needed, and a contact person and telephone number. Indexes to these companies are provided. One is an index by industry type, such as mining and metals, waste management, environmental services and consulting, water treatment and purification, and so on. Under each category is the company name and page number on which its description is found. A geographic index, arranged by state, is useful when trying to find a job in a particular area of the United States (no foreign countries are listed here). An index of hiring needs, such as air quality control, accounting, biology, chemical engineering, and so on, is especially useful when fitting the job applicant's interest or education to a particular company. Preliminary chapters cover topics such as getting a job, "hot jobs" in the environmental industry, and finding jobs in smaller companies.

The environmental field is developing and expanding rapidly, and offers more positions than in the past. This is the only current source for finding jobs in environmentally related companies, and at a very reasonable price. Those looking for jobs with nonprofit organizations, and a more comprehensive source for state and U.S. government agencies, may find the *Gale Environmental Sourcebook* (see ARBA 93, entry 1768) useful. However, the Peterson guide is recommended for school, public, and academic libraries, and all vocational guidance collections.—**Diane B. Rhodes**

37 Transportation

GENERAL WORKS

1877. **Annual Bulletin of Transport Statistics for Europe, 1995. Volume XLV.** By Economic Commission for Europe. New York, United Nations, 1995. 341p. $60.00pa. ISBN 92-1-016303-6. ISSN 0250-9911. S/N E/F/R.95.II.E.9.

This is the 45th volume of transport statistics for Europe published by the United Nations. The coverage of these statistics now includes the Russian Federation, Ukraine, Belarus, Turkey, Malta, Cyprus, Central and Western Europe, as well as Canada and the United States. A convenient country index provides page references for each country, so that users with particular interests can be easily guided. The transport modes covered (in addition to general statistics) are railways, roads, inland waterways, international rivers, seaports, combined (broken, with transshipment) transport, and pipelines. Statistics cover commodity groups transported, national and international transport, loaded and unloaded, and so on. The headings, footnotes, and classifications are in English, French, and Russian. The series is useful for comparative information, but even though it is comprehensive, this reviewer finds national statistics more informative. As a quick source of reference data, however, this volume has much to recommend it, especially for those who are linguistically handicapped. The data are for 1992 and 1993, with 1980 also shown in most tables. A rather galling feature of this volume is the frequency of unavailable information, obviously not the fault of the United Nations.—**Bogdan Mieczkowski**

1878. **Dorling Kindersley Visual Timeline of Transportation.** By Anthony Wilson. New York, Dorling Kindersley, 1995. 48p. illus. index. $16.95. ISBN 1-56458-880-7.

Children and adults will be transfixed by this simple, stunning, and busy 48-page graphic chronology of transportation from 10,000 B.C.E. to the present. Color drawings and photographs crowd each page, along with lively and readable text. It focuses on all modes of transportation, from bicycles and buses to cruise ships and space vehicles. It even addresses, albeit briefly, current transportation infrastructure problems and other topics such as fuels.

The book is divided into chapters on "Traveling at Nature's Pace" 10,000 B.C.E. to 1779 C.E.; "Full Steam Ahead" 1780-1879; "Powered Flight and the Rise of the Automobile" 1880-1959; and "A World on the Move" 1960-2000. Those seeking specific subjects will find the index, with listings ranging from "Reindeer" to "Rickshaw," indispensable. This is a spectacular ready-reference source for school and public libraries, and a useful and inexpensive reference for transportation buffs of all ages.—**Jo A. Cates**

AIR

1879. **The Aviation and Aerospace Almanac 1995.** Richard Lampl, ed. New York, Tab Books/McGraw-Hill, 1995. 660p. index. $50.00pa. ISBN 0-07-003047-2.

The publishers of *The Aviation and Aerospace Almanac* have, without a doubt, positioned this reference book as an absolutely essential purchase for any library or individual with an aviation/aerospace collection. Occupying a third of the book, the first five sections provide historical and current statistics dealing with civil aviation topics as varied as financial data, operational statistics, inventories, and comparisons with other modes of transportation. This information includes data on international and domestic airlines. It covers major, national, and transcontinental airlines and regionals and general aviation, as well as the airports they all use. The statistics and information in these initial five sections alone make the price of the book a bargain. The publishers have drawn these data from dozens of private sector sources and many U.S. government agencies. Avitas, an aviation consulting firm, and the International Civil Aviation Organization also contributed material. Some of the data appear in the *Air Transport Association Annual Report of the U.S. Scheduled Airline Industry*, but parts of the material are not readily available elsewhere.

Sections 6 through 13 contain directories of U.S. government boards and departments relating to transportation and aviation and aerospace matters, along with appropriate statistics collected by the respective agencies. Section 14 provides statistics on the aerospace industry, and section 15 is a directory of selected aviation and aerospace committees in the 103d Congress.

This almanac contains a detailed table of contents and an equally detailed index. It is a welcome addition to the body of reference literature on aviation/aerospace matters.—**Dene L. Clark**

1880. Davies, R. E. G., and I. E. Quastler. **Commuter Airlines of the United States.** Blue Ridge Summit, Pa., Smithsonian Institution Press, 1995. 480p. illus. maps. index. $56.00. ISBN 1-56098-404-X.

Local service airlines appeared on the aviation scene in the 1950s. Today they carry many more passengers than the major carriers accommodated during their infancy. The story of commuter airlines has never before been told in so much detail, making this book a most welcome addition to aviation history. *Commuter Airlines of the United States* is divided into three parts. Part 1 is a history of U.S. passenger commuter airlines. Individual companies are mentioned frequently, but the emphasis is on presenting a broad overall history. Part 2 consists of profiles on 22 of the most important pioneers in commuter aviation. These personalities are people whose deeds are not generally chronicled elsewhere. Each biographical sketch includes a portrait; most are five to six pages in length.

Part 3 is a list of more than 1,000 commuter airlines that specifies such facts as founder's name, home base, routes, equipment, and unusual features of each airline. The characteristics of these carriers vary so widely by region that the authors have chosen to divide the industry into 13 geographical regions. They present a separate table for each region, and each regional table is preceded by a one- to four-page overview describing broad regional issues that affect the industry.

Airlines of the United States Since 1914 by R. E. G. Davies (Smithsonian Institute, 1983) and *The Airline Industry*, edited by William M. Leary (Facts on File, 1992), complement this new title, but do not present the full history of commuter airlines that the reader will find in the work under review. A mandatory purchase for libraries with strong transportation collections, Davies and Quastler's book should also be found in most large academic and public libraries.—**Dene L. Clark**

1881. **Jane's Airports and Handling Agents, 1995-96: United States and Canada.** Paul Portnoi, ed. Alexandria, Va., Jane's Information Group, 1995. 2v. index. $325.00pa./set. ISBN 0-7106-1277-X.

Published by the world's leading expert on the aerospace industry, *Jane's Airports and Handling Agents* is a comprehensive directory of airport data and operational facilities and of airport handling agents and fixed base operators (FBOs). Jane's Information Group publishes this directory for five different regions of the world. The United States and Canada edition includes a designator applied by the Federal Aviation Administration or Transport Canada. The body of the work lists airports in alphabetical order. The directory provides a useful table of abbreviations and a glossary as well as four reference indexes, by airports, airport identifiers, airports by country, and FBO/handling agents.

For the most part, airports appear under the name of a United States or Canadian city. Occasionally, an airport is listed under the name of an airfield. Atlanta International Airport appears under the entry Hartsfield-Atlanta International; the Macon, Georgia airport appears under the entry Middle Georgia Regional. The listing for Cincinnati appears under the entry Covington/Cincinnati, even though Cincinnati is by far the larger and better-known city. The publisher could avoid confusion by inserting cross-references in the index of airports from Atlanta, Macon, and Cincinnati to the name of the airfield under which the information appears.

The directory is highly suitable for large public and academic libraries that collect geopolitical resource material in-depth. Libraries with strong aerospace collections may also consider purchasing this title. The price will be a deterrent to most other libraries.—**Dene L. Clark**

1882. Lopez, Donald S. **Aviation: A Smithsonian Guide.** New York, Macmillan/Simon & Schuster, 1995. 256p. illus. maps. index. $24.95; $18.00pa. ISBN 0-02-860006-1; 0-02-860041-Xpa.

Written by the senior advisor to the director of the Smithsonian's National Air and Space Museum, this is a clearly written and generously illustrated survey of the history of human flight from its mythological beginnings down to the present day. The arrangement is basically chronological, with numerous sidebars presenting special topics; both civil and military aeronautics are given equal coverage. Technical terminology is kept to a minimum.

The book includes an extensive glossary (containing capsule biographies of many important persons in the field, as well as definitions of terms); a thorough index that will enhance its reference value; a directory of major U.S. air museums; a brief bibliography; and a foldout chronological table.

Intended for the general (including young adult) reader, the work is suitable for both public and high school libraries. Because it can be read through as narrative history as well as consulted for specific facts, it may prove most useful in the circulating collection.—**Paul B. Cors**

GROUND

1883. Aird, Forbes. **Racer's Encyclopedia of Metals, Fibers & Materials.** Osceola, Wis., Motorbooks International, 1994. 128p. illus. index. (Motorbooks International Powerpro Series). $17.95pa. ISBN 0-87938-916-8.

While not truly an encyclopedia, this guide presents a comprehensive overview of substances used in racing car construction. The author is well versed in real-life problems that automotive mechanics and constructors encounter. Clearly written in an informal style that explains basic physical systems in a straightfoward manner, this book is precision-designed for the working mechanic, covering materials and properties, metals, and nonmetallic construction alternatives. A well-chosen range of large, detailed monochrome photographs, drawings, and charts complement the descriptive text. The costs, strengths, and drawbacks of each alternative are outlined (surprisingly, for example, there are cases when simple wooden structures can be highly effective), buttressed by comparative tables of material properties permitting ready comparisons among alternatives. Particular care and attention are paid to potential health hazards of these materials, where applicable. The major enhancement for this book would be inclusion of an address list for suppliers (although working mechanics probably already have their own sources). Crisply printed on good-quality paper in a sturdy binding, this title is a useful information source for any library serving a clientele that builds or maintains racing cars, or is interested in how engineering principles become functioning hardware.—**John Howard Oxley**

1884. Bennett, Jim. **The Complete Motorcycle Book: A Consumer's Guide.** New York, Facts on File, 1995. 228p. illus. index. $31.95; $24.95pa. ISBN 0-8160-2899-0; 0-8160-3181-9pa.

Bennett's book is destined to become a classic. This work is one of the most complete and easy-to-read references about purchasing, maintaining, and riding motorcycles. The first chapter deals with whether or not to ride a motorcycle; it is straightforward and written so that people purchasing a motorcycle for the first time have some idea of what they are getting into.

The book contains chapters about motorcycle types and styles; mechanics and mechanisms; selecting the right motorcycle; purchasing new and used bikes; best bets for used bikes; maintenance; safe riding techniques; common motorcycle purchases (oil, gasoline, tires, and so on); women riders; sharing the road (this is for all motorists); a glossary; and an index. This book is recommended for high school, public, and college libraries.—**Alan N. Livingston**

1885. Berliant, Adam. **The Used Car Reliability and Safety Guide.** Cincinnati, Ohio, Betterway Books/F & W Publications, 1994. 359p. index. $12.99pa. ISBN 1-55870-371-3. ISSN 1075-6248.

Designed to assist the consumer in deciding whether a given make and model of a car is generally safe and reliable, or has a reputation for developing a major problem (or problems), this massive review is based on records of complaints made to the National Highway Traffic Safety Administration (NHTSA). Covered are models made from 1983 through the summer of 1993 that have accumulated at least 50 complaints overall; at least 4 concerning a specific component; and various "hot spots." The absence of a particular year and model does not necessarily mean that the car is trouble-free; it could mean that the requisite number of complaints has not been filed yet, especially for 1992 and 1993 models. The user of the volume should carefully read the introduction before consulting the listings.

The entries are arranged alphabetically by make, model, and year; they include a summary, an "accident rating" from 0 (bad) to 5 (good) stars, a "recall alert," and up to five "hot spots." The "recall alert" section lists all relevant campaigns with the NHSTA number. Also furnished are tables of comparisons of overall performance standings, arranged by car type (e.g., "large cars"), and from worst to best of models. There are also indications of theft likelihood as of 1993 (e.g., the 1984 Oldsmobile Cutlass, rated #1). This is a useful resource for the buyer of a domestic or imported used car. At the low price, it is a near-must for public libraries, where it will serve as a companion to the findings of *Consumer Reports*.
—**Walter C. Allen**

1886. Drury, George H., comp. **Guide to Tourist Railroads and Railroad Museums.** 4th ed. Waukesha, Wis., Kalmbach Publishing, 1995. 320p. illus. index. (Railroad Reference Series, no.13). $18.95pa. ISBN 0-89024-246-1.

Listings for about 350 tourist railroads and railroad museums in the United States and Canada are found in this guide. Although the majority are for operational tourist railroads, it covers a wide variety of other railroad attractions, ranging from zoo railroads to collections of railroad equipment, depot museums, and commercial model railroads.

The guide is arranged alphabetically by state and then by city, with Canadian attractions listed in a separate group. Individual entries describe of the various attractions and are supplemented by a wide variety of the kind of specific information tourists need. Included are information on railroad equipment owned, operating schedules, miles covered, ticket costs and other fees, accessibility, parking, gift shops, nearby attractions, food and lodging, addresses, and telephone numbers. Most entries also furnish a well-reproduced photograph of the attraction.

This book is designed to be carried like a travel guide, but it will be useful to libraries as well. The information found here is difficult to find in any other place. Kalmbach Publishing's Railroad Reference Series includes a number of reliable publications issued in a consistent, portable format. They cover everything from railroad radio frequencies and diesel locomotive rosters to guides to major U.S. railroads (see entries 1889 and 1891 for reviews of other books in the series). Although inexpensive, these guides have a reputation for accuracy and are standard works on the subject.—**Frederick A. Schlipf**

1887. **Jane's World Railways.** 36th ed. James Abbott, ed. Alexandria, Va., Jane's Information Group, 1994. 798p. illus. index. $300.00. ISBN 0-7106-1148-X.

This 1994-95 edition of the annual *Jane's World Railways* provides extensive directory and technical information on thousands of manufacturers of railroad equipment, private freight wagon leasing companies, operators of international rail services, international railway associations and agencies, consultancy services, and railroad systems. Of these, the sections on manufacturers and on railroad systems make up the majority of the book.

The manufacturers section is divided into 17 subsections by type of equipment (ranging from locomotives to bearings) and subdivided alphabetically by company name. Information on individual companies varies with the size of the company, but always includes an address, telephone and fax numbers, officers' names, and product information. For people who need information on (for example) Serbian freight car companies, *Jane's* is the place to look.

The railway systems section contains information on railroads in about 130 countries, ranging from Paraguay (where the principal railroad is operated with 26 ancient steam locomotives) to the state-of-the-art systems of western Europe. For countries with more than one railroad company, separate listings are provided for each company. Information includes addresses and telephone numbers; names of officers; and narrative sections on such topics as political background, organization, finance, investment, passenger operations, freight operations, new lines, improvements to existing lines, traffic, traction and rolling stock, track, signaling and communications, loading gauges, intermodal operations, new stations, and so on. For larger systems, *Jane's* furnishes tables of locomotive and railcar types owned. Accompanying the text are nearly 1,000 photographs and drawings.

For libraries, businesses, and government agencies with an interest in transportation, *Jane's* is clearly essential. The vast amount of information and the reputation of the firm make this the standard work on its subject. As with other Jane's Information Group publications, this work also has an important secondary use. Whether reading about fighting ships or aircraft or railroads or a dozen other topics, both mature fans and enamored young people page happily through the publications, soaking up the endless technical information. For this reason, even the most obsolete editions—with names and addresses long out of date—still retain their usefulness in libraries.

A sister publication—*Jane's Urban Transport Systems*—provides information on public transportation systems and the companies that supply them. The current edition of *Jane's World's Railways* is also available on CD-ROM.—**Frederick A. Schlipf**

1888. Karr, Ronald Dale. **The Rail Lines of Southern New England: A Handbook of Railroad History.** Pepperell, Mass., Branch Line Press, 1995. 383p. illus. maps. index. (New England Rail Heritage Series). $22.95pa. ISBN 0-942147-02-2.

Histories and maps of 83 individual railroads that operate or once operated in Massachusetts, Connecticut, and Rhode Island are the focus of this handbook. It includes every common carrier line in the area, but does not cover freight spurs, cog railroads, industrial spurs, tram lines, or other similar topics. Despite their small geographical area, the three states had an amazingly dense network of competing railroads, leaving few towns unserved. By the turn of the century, most of these had been consolidated into three larger railroads, the *New Haven*, the *Boston and Maine*, and the *New York Central*, which survived relatively intact through the 1960s.

For each of the 83 original railroads, the author provides a wide variety of information: a map of the line, indicating what portions are still in use and what have been abandoned; a mileage chart, listing all stations and the distances between them; a list of the times the line was built, including the completion dates for various segments; a list of the various railroads that operated the line, with the dates for each; brief information on passenger service; dates of abandonments of various segments of the line; and a historical narrative, including photographs. The book has a number of pages of maps that show the locations of these lines. All lines on the general maps are coded by number to the railroad listings, and the maps for individual railroads are coded by number to show connections to other lines, making it easy for readers to place individual lines in the context of railroading in the three states.

This handbook contains a vast amount of detailed information, in addition to clearly written histories, and appears to be accurate. The book's weaknesses are primarily the result of the limits imposed by publication. The general railroad maps of the 3 states are spread out over 19 pages, which makes them sometimes awkward to follow, and photographic reproduction is occasionally somewhat muddy. Overall, the book should be a valuable general reference source for railroad historians and rail fans everywhere. It should also be an important general acquisition for almost any New England library.—**Frederick A. Schlipf**

1889. Marre, Louis A., and Jerry A. Pinkepank. **The Contemporary Diesel Spotter's Guide.** 2d ed. Waukesha, Wis., Kalmbach Publishing, 1995. 351p. illus. index. (Railroad Reference Series, no.14). $19.95pa. ISBN 0-89024-257-7.

An identification manual for locomotive enthusiasts, this work covers all models of diesel and electric locomotives produced in North America from 1972 through 1994. In this period, there are only three major firms in the field: Electro-Motive Division of General Motors, General Electric, and Montreal Locomotive Works (later Bombardier). Each is given a chapter; there is also a short chapter covering other builders, mostly European imports. Subarranged by general type of locomotive, the entries for individual models include a technical description of specifications (partly tabular, partly narrative), production statistics, and good photos of typical examples. A basic familiarity with diesel locomotive design, operating characteristics, and terminology on the reader's part is required.

Complicating the issue of identification is the fact that many locomotives were rebuilt, sometimes more than once, and sometimes with radical changes. There were many firms active in rebuilding, including the railroads themselves, and the documentation for rebuilds is often incomplete. However, about one-third of the book deals with this topic, presenting the same type of data found in the chapters on original builders. Coverage is as complete as possible, but the authors acknowledge that there are some rebuilds (known as "zombies" to rail enthusiasts) for which a provenance cannot be accurately determined.

The work concludes with an essay on locomotive performance ratings, a short glossary, and an index. Though intended primarily for use as a field guide by individual railroad enthusiasts, the work's comprehensive coverage and technical detail will make it a valuable addition to serious transportation collections in all types of libraries; it is unique in the subject area.—**Paul B. Cors**

1890. **Statistics of Road Traffic Accidents in Europe and North America 1995.** By Economic Commission for Europe. New York, United Nations, 1995. 121p. $25.00pa. ISBN 92-1-016295-1. ISSN 0497-9575. S/N E.F.R.94.II.E.14.

This annual report on road traffic accidents in European countries, Canada, Israel, and the United States provides basic data on incidents involving personal injury. Each table is presented in English, French, and Russian. Although the publication is purely statistical, the compiler (the secretariat of the United Nations Economic Commission for Europe) is able to provide an unbelievable amount of detail in a minimum of space by prefacing each table with a description. Each variable under the description has a unique number, and these numbers are repeated in columnar form under the name of each country. Country data appear next to the appropriate numbers.

The statistics include details on the nature of the accidents and surroundings, the number of accidents due to the influence of alcohol, and the number of persons killed or injured by category of road user and age group. The 1995 edition contains nine tables, six relating to accidents and casualties, and the balance covering statistics on road vehicles, mileage, and population estimates broken down by age group.

The European Conference of Ministers of Transport (ECMT) issues an annual statistical report on road accident trends in ECMT member, associate, and observer countries entitled *Statistical Report on Road Accidents*. This ECMT report provides data for fewer countries than does the work under review, but the ECMT publication interprets and compares its data while the UN publication does not. *Statistics of Road Traffic Accidents in Europe and North America* is strongly recommended for all large public and academic libraries.—**Dene L. Clark**

1891. Sturm, Gary L., and Mark J. Landgraf. **The Compendium of American Railroad Radio Frequencies.** 13th ed. Waukesha, Wis., Kalmbach Publishing, 1995. 200p. maps. (Railroad Reference Series, no.15). $16.95pa. ISBN 0-89024-231-3.

This new edition of a standard reference tool for railroad enthusiasts (see ARBA 94, entry 2028, for a review of the 12th edition) has been updated throughout to reflect changes made by the railroads, as well as the disappearance of some companies and the creation of others. The scope and arrangement are the same as before: a short introduction; listings for United States and Canadian railroads (subarranged by common carriers, industrial railroads, transit systems, and museum and tourist operations); a selective international section (no additional countries are included); and a special listing of major North American metropolitan areas. In each section, the individual listings are arranged alphabetically by railroad name. Maps of eight major railroads that use many different radio frequencies are provided.

All individual rail enthusiasts who enjoy even occasionally using a scanner to listen to railroad radio broadcasting will want to keep up-to-date by acquiring this revision. Purchase decisions for libraries will probably be determined by patron demand; while there is no comparable work available, its audience is very specialized.—**Paul B. Cors**

1892. Willson, Quentin, with David Selby. **The Ultimate Classic Car Book.** New York, Dorling Kindersley, 1995. 224p. illus. index. $29.95. ISBN 0-7894-0159-2.

U.S. car enthusiasts have wildly different perceptions of what makes a classic car. Some picture the Alfa Romeo Spider being driven by Dustin Hoffman in the film *The Graduate*; others visualize the Aston Martin in the James Bond film *Goldfinger*; and still others remember the 1959 Cadillac convertible, which starred in many films but was immortalized in the Clint Eastwood picture *Pink Cadillac*. These cars and more are showcased in the authors' catholic collection. Striving for the interesting and the diverting, this work includes a number of U.S. automobiles from the 1950s and the 1960s that clearly epitomized the United States post-World War II optimism as well as its stylistic excesses.

Among the 90 international classic cars selected by the authors are two of the car industry's greatest failures—the DeLorean DMC12 and the Ford Edsel—as well as two automobiles that set sales records—the Ford Mustang and the Citroën 2CV. The book ranges from such immensely popular makes as the Volkswagen Beetle Karmann to pedigreed models such as the Maserati Ghibli and the Lancia Aurelia B24 Spider. The authors' selections are subjective and emotional, but the necessary information necessary has been gathered to support the choices and beguile the reader.

Stunning photographs in brilliant color and interestingly phrased documentation make this a suitable purchase for the coffee table, the classic car enthusiast, or the expert. Public libraries with a classic car clientele will need to acquire this book. The book's historical and technical data make it a useful purchase in academic libraries with strong automotive collections as well.—**Dene L. Clark**

1893. Wilson, Hugo. **The Encyclopedia of the Motorcycle.** New York, Dorling Kindersley, 1995. 320p. illus. maps. index. $39.95. ISBN 0-7894-0150-9.

Long before the Ford automobile became the transportation mode of the masses, there was the motorcycle. For a number of years, motorcycles remained considerably cheaper than automobiles, which were largely playtoys of the upper class. This encyclopedia is a comprehensive coffee-table reference work that covers some 3,000 manufacturer's marques. Major cycles have a two-page color photograph, along with the specifications, history, and, in some, early color advertisements.

The work is divided into two parts; the first, an extensive color photography section, covers the major manufacturers such as BMW, Indian, Harley-Davidson, Honda, Suzuki, and Yamaha. The second part is a "comprehensive catalog of every known motorcycle marques listed alphabetically under country of origin." The author, who has also written the best-selling *The Ultimate Motorcycle Book* (see ARBA 95, entry 1793), has included a glossary of motorcycle terms, a list of manufacturer's addresses, a bibliography, and an extensive index.

The volume is attractive and easy to use. It has high appeal value for young readers as well as experienced enthusiasts. Few libraries with patrons interested in motoring will want to miss this excellent book. It is recommended for ages five and up.—**Ralph Lee Scott**

WATER

1894. **Elsevier's Nautical Dictionary: In English/American, French, Spanish, Dutch, and German.** 3d ed. J. -P. Vandenberghe and M. Johnen, comps. New York, Elsevier Science, 1994. 828p. index. $257.25. ISBN 0-444-89604-X.

The main body of the work is "The Basic Table," an alphabetical listing of English/American nautical terms with their equivalents in French, Spanish, Dutch, and German. This is a listing of terms without any definitions. The English terms are numbered and printed in bold typeface, four columns to a page. The equivalent terms in the other languages then follow in regular type. The languages are identified with italic initials: f for French, e for Spanish, n for Dutch, and d for German. The dictionary lists 13,642 terms. The table is followed by sections containing the terms in French, Spanish, Dutch, and German, which are keyed by number to the English list. There are cross-references.

This new edition incorporates the major technological innovations that have occurred in the field of shipping during the 1980s. To make room for these new words, some words that are covered in general dictionaries were dropped. The book includes terms relating to types of ships, onboard equipment, seamanship, navigational aids, seagoing staff, beacons, yachting and racing, calls and commands, and weather and sea conditions. Naval engineering terms and modern fishery terms have been limited to essentials, since there are specialized glossaries available in those fields. The terms listed deal with seagoing ships. Shipbuilding and port terminology are beyond the scope of this volume. There is a 44-item pertinent bibliography, international in scope and mostly of recent vintage.—**Frank J. Anderson**

1895. **The Nautical Almanac for the Year 1996.** London, HMSO; distr., Lanham, Md., UNIPUB, 1995. 318p. $39.95pa. ISBN 0-11-772814-4. ISSN 0077-619X.

The *Nautical Almanac* has been published continuously in one form or another since the eighteenth century. It is the standard almanac used by astronomers and navigators worldwide. The *Nautical Almanac* was published prior to 1981 separately by the Nautical Almanac Office of the United States Naval Observatory and Her Majesty's Nautical Office at the Royal Greenwich Observatory. Now the two governments have combined the work of the two offices into one publication. The current copy in hand has been printed by Her Majesty's Stationery Office, but contains a note that the U.S. edition is for sale by the Superintendent of Documents, Washington, D.C. This British edition is available in the United States through UNIPUB. Tables cover solar and lunar eclipses for the year; the hour angle and right ascension for Aries, Venus, Mars, Jupiter, Saturn, the sun, and the moon hourly and daily for the year; times of civil and astronomical twilight, sunrise, and moonrise by latitude on a daily basis; and sight reduction tables. There is an appendix that provides corrections used in various navigation calculations.

This work contains the standard tables used for celestial navigation. Anyone wanting to calculate marine, or for that matter, land location will have need for the charts contained in this almanac. Often some of the basic data in the *Nautical Almanac* are entered into even the most modern of navigation computers to update the machine memory as to the precise location. This was the navigation book used on the *Apollo 13* flight to update the onboard computers. Astronomers use the almanac to locate celestial objects, such as the planets and main stars in the heavens. The volume is paperback and contains no illustration, simply tables of data. There is a short method section for sight reduction included in case the reader has forgotten how to do the calculation. Most libraries will find patrons who need this book at one time or another. A favorite reference use for this book is to answer questions from young college couples who want to drive to the beach to look at the moonrise over the ocean, and want to know what time to leave town to get to the beach on time. (Hint: Use the Moonrise table.)—**Ralph Lee Scott**

1896. Pickford, Nigel. **The Atlas of Shipwrecks & Treasure: The History, Location, and Treasures of Ships Lost at Sea.** New York, Dorling Kindersley, 1994. 200p. illus. maps. index. $29.95. ISBN 1-56458-599-9.

Pickford is a professional shipwreck researcher. This large-format volume is arranged in two parts. Part 1 covers shipwrecks, with details of significant wrecks, how each sinking occurred, and the specific areas in which they occurred. Fourteen time periods are covered, from the Bronze Age through World War II. Part 2 is a gazetteer, providing 20 maps of various parts of the world with numbered indicators showing where ships went down. These indicators are keyed to a list of 1,400 shipwrecks wherein the ship is identified along with the date of the sinking and the cargo it was carrying. Ships whose cargo has been salvaged are noted. The book is replete with colored maps, photographs, and depictions of particular ships, many in two-page spreads. All is designed to whet one's appetite for treasure hunting. There are a glossary, a bibliography, and an index.—**Frank J. Anderson**

1897. **Review of Maritime Transport 1993.** By the United Nations Conference on Trade and Development. New York, United Nations, 1994. 139p. $30.00pa. ISBN 92-1-112365-8. ISSN 0566-7682. S/N E.94.II.D.30.

This consecutive annual publication can be used both as a review that conveniently summarizes and explains recent developments, and as a comprehensive reference source with abundant statistics. A summary of main developments is followed by 9 chapters and 4 purely statistical annexes, while the main text also has 13 boxes (topical and interesting; for example, on the decline in maritime losses, and on container terminal automation) and 14 graphs (e.g., on forecasts by type of vessel, and on past trends in surplus capacity by vessel types). The use of the standard United Nations notations and abbreviations is reassuring in its constancy.

The standard main chapters cover the development of international seaborne trade; the development of the world fleet (with the continuing growth of the share of container ships, and a recovery of the share of tankers); productivity of the world fleet; shipbuilding, secondhand market, and demolition; port development; freight markets, multimodal transport, and technological developments, such as landbridges and unit trains; and other developments, such as the General Agreement on Tariffs and Trade (GATT), UN conventions, and cooperation and training. East and South-East Asia, with the region's booming economies, merits a separate final chapter; as one indicator, it has almost 43 percent of world calls of container ships. Graphs are lucid, except where two almost indistinguishable shades of black are used. The *Review* is indispensable to practitioners, and useful as illustrative material in courses on the economics of transportation.—**Bogdan Mieczkowski**

1898. Way, Frederick, Jr., comp. **Way's Packet Directory, 1848-1994: Passenger Steamboats of the Mississippi River System....** rev. ed. Athens, Ohio, Ohio University Press, 1994. 625p. illus. index. $34.95pa. ISBN 0-8214-1106-3.

Way is a familiar name to those interested in steamboats and the history of transportation on U.S. rivers. In addition to his monumental packet boat directory, he wrote seven other books on river history. He published the *Inland River Record* for 30 years, and served as president of the Sons and Daughters of Pioneer Rivermen for more than 50 years. He was no armchair historian, since he spent most of his life on the Ohio, Mississippi, and other rivers as a pilot of large and small steamboats. He died in 1992 at the age of 91.

This updated paperback edition of *Way's Packet Directory* contains almost 6,000 entries and a new foreword by Joseph W. Rutter. The ships are described by rig, class, engine, boiler, shipyard, date when built, history of service, and eventual fate. The book includes a compound name index and an alphabetical index to the numbered entries. Way's wonderful original preface has been retained. Basically an unabridged reprint with a new foreword, there are also 61 new numbered entries in a 4-page addendum (including an entry for the *American Queen*, a 420-passenger tourist boat built in 1994). The price of this paperback edition is the same as that of the original hardcover book.—**Frank J. Anderson**

Author/Title Index
Reference is to entry number.

AALL ref bk, 593
Aaseng, Nathan, 410
Abbott, James, 1887
Abbott, R. Tucker, 1595
Abbreviations dict, 9th ed, 2
ABC for bk collectors, 7th ed, 1001
ABC-CLIO companion to the environmental movement, 1869
ABC-CLIO companion to the media in America, 964
Academic focus Japan: programs & resources in N America, 423
Academic lib of the 90s, 620
Academic libs in the UK & the republic of Ireland 1994, 3d ed, 635
Academic yr abroad 1995/96, 368
Accent on living buyer's gd, 1994-95 ed, 853
ACCESS: the supplementary index to pers, 78
ACCESS travel USA: a dir for people with disabilities, 856
Achenbaum, W. Andrew, 846
Adams, Jerome R., 938
Adams job almanac 1995, 265
Adams Publishing, editors of, 265
Adkins, Lesley, 547
Adkins, Roy A., 547
Adler, Bill, Jr., 1767
Adler, Eve, 1128
Adoption dir, 2d ed, 860
Adventure holidays 1995, 18th ed, 460
Adventure vacations, 473
Advisory Committee for the Co-ordination of Information Systems (ACCIS), 769, 1783
Africa, Asia, & S America since 1800, 555
Africa in lit for children & young adults, 1166
Africa on file, 108
African American breakthroughs, 397
African American genealogical sourcebk, 429
African biographical dict, 109
African hist on file, 529
African-American address bk, 52
African-American inventors, 1488
African-American scientists, 1489
African-American sports greats, 792
Ager, David J., 1792
Aggression & conflict, 835
Aging well, 838
Agricultural entomology, 1625
AIA gd to the architecture of Wash., D.C., 3d ed, 1049
Aicher, Peter J., 1046
Aird, Forbes, 1883
Airlie, Maree, 1123
ALA fingertip gd to natl health-info resources 1995-96, ref desk ed, 1684
Albala, Elie, 249
Albala, Leila, 249

Albaugh, Gaylord P., 1447
Albert, Daniel M., 846
Albert, George, 1312
Alcoholism & aging, 897
Alderton, David, 67, 70
Aliens, robots, & spaceships, 1360
All music gd to rock, 1330
Allaby, Michael, 1497, 1854
Allen, Dell K., 1670
Allen, Gerald R., 1633
Allen, Rick, 1384
Alloy finder [CD-ROM], 1660
Alphabet: a handbk of ABC bks, 2d ed, 328
Alpines, 1590
Altbach, Philip G., 370
Alternative health & medicine ency, 1716
Alternative publishers of bks in N America, 2d ed, 668
Alternative realities, 785
Alternatives to the Peace Corps, 868
Alting, Leo, 1670
Alvino, Paola, 170
Amazing animals of the world, 1603
America: hist & life on disc [CD-ROM], 512
America in the 20th century, 499
America preserved, 1047
America votes 21, 735
American Animal Hospital Assn ency of cat health & care, 1618
American Animal Hospital Assn ency of dog health & care, 1619
American Animal Hospital Association, 1618, 1619
American Assn of Colleges for Teacher Educ dir of members 1995, 316
American bus disc, 1995 ed [CD-ROM], 181
American Camping Association, 811
American Civil War, 504
American community colleges, 10th ed, 362
American decades 1930-39, 513
American decades 1940-49, 514
American decades 1960-69, 515
American decades 1970-79, 516
American diversity, American identity, 1198
American export register 1995, 286
American foreign policy index 1995, v.3, no.2, 743
American Heritage children's dict, 1086
American Heritage Dictionaries, editors of, 1086, 1095
American Heritage Stedman's medical dict, 1697
American Heritage talking dict, 3d ed [CD-ROM], 1062
American Histl Assn's gd to histl lit, 3d ed, 554
American house designs: an index to popular & trade pers, 1850-1915, 1050
American Indian ref & resource bks for children & YAs, 2d ed, 1177
American Indian studies, 421

American Library Association Reference Books Bulletin Editorial Board, 12
American Library Association Social Responsibilities Round Table Alternatives in Print Task Force, 668
American Medical Assn family medical gd [CD-ROM], 1707
American men & women of sci 1995-96, 19th ed, 1485
American military hist, 678
American musical theatre song ency, 1416
American novelists since WW II, 3d series, 1204
American novelists since WW II, 4th series, 1203
American playwrights, 1880-1945, 1202
American popular culture, 1357
American salaries & wages survey, 3d ed, 266
American Sign Lang concise dict, rev ed, 1132
American Sign Lang dict, rev ed, 1133
American Sign Lang dict on CD-ROM [CD-ROM], 1130
American silent film comedies, 1378
American stock exchange, 211
American West: a multicultural ency, 505
American women in sci, 1486
America's best beers, 1536
America's intl trade, 239
America's lowest cost colleges, 9th ed, 359
America's royalty, rev ed, 719
America's top-rated smaller cities, 1994-95 ed, 926
Amindarov, Aziz, 1114
Ammer, Christine, 1680
Amos, Kharma, 1652
Amsterdam, 476
Anatomy of wonder 4, 1191
Ancient world lists & nos, 41
And Adam knew Eve: a dict of sex in the Bible, 1452
Anderson, Byron, 668
Anderson, David S., 1667
Anderson, Erland, 1245
Anderson, Ian E., 980
Anderson, Sean, 597
Andre Malraux, 1253
Andrews, Barry, 1248
Animal health yrbk 1993, 1553
Animal life, 1604
Animal rights, 1435
Animal rights movement in the US, 1975-90, 1424
Animals on screen & radio, 1366
Annenberg, Maurice, 666
Annotated art, 1052
Annotated catalogue of early editions of Erasmus, 1250
Annotated dict of technical, histl, & stylistic terms relating to theatre & drama, 1417
Annual bulletin for transport stats for Europe, 1995, v.45, 1877
Annual bulletin of ...
   coal stats for Europe & N America, 1994, 1838
   electric energy stats for Europe & N America, 1994, v.38, 1839
   gas stats for Europe & N America 1994, v.38, 1840
   stats of world trade in steel 1993, 287
Annual review of info sci & tech, v.29, 1994, 622
Anthony Eden, 1897-1977, 759

Anticancer drugs from animals, plants, & microorganisms, 1740
Antiquarian bks, 1002
APELL annot bibliog, 777
Apostolos-Cappadona, Diane, 1028
Applications in criminal analysis, 604
APT for libs 1995: alternative pr titles for the general reader, 79
Aquariums of N America, 1621
Arab women in ESCWA member states, 156
Arany, Lynne, 1400
ARCO 100 best careers in entertainment, 1364
Arctic & Antarctic regions [CD-ROM], 127
Ardley, Neil, 1493
Arkansas hist, 490
Armenian American almanac, 391
Armenian folklore bibliog, 1340
Armored forces: hist & sourcebk, 702
Armstrong, C. J., 225, 453, 587, 1788
Army Times bk of great land battles, 698
Arnold, Corliss Richard, 1289
Arnold, John, 39
Aronson, Marc, 503
Around the world: an atlas of maps & pictures, 443
Art & design scholarships, 1036
Art bus ency, 1039
Art mktg sourcebk for the fine artist, 2d ed, 1035
Art of children's picture bks, 2d ed, 1183
Art on screen on CD-ROM [CD-ROM], 1037
Arthur Andersen N American bus sourcebk, 288
Artist's & graphic designer's market, 1995, 1038
Artist's complete health & safety gd, 2d ed, 1042
Artists: from Michelangelo to Maya Lin, 1024
Artist's resource hndbk, 1040
ArtNetwork yellow pages, 1033
Artz, Joan W., 978
Ash, Irene, 1533
Ash, Michael, 1533
Ash, Russell, 61
Ashley, Mike, 1194
Asian American almanac, 392
Asian American biog, 393
Asian American ency, 394
Asian American genealogical sourcebk, 430
Asian hist on file, 533
ASM handbk, v.5: surface engineering, 1661
ASM International Handbook Committee, 1661, 1665
ASM specialty handbk: stainless steels, 1662
ASM specialty handbk: tool materials, 1678
ASSIA plus [CD-ROM], 97
Associated Press, 485
Association for Library Service to Children, 661
Association for Population/Family Planning Libs & Info Centers - Intl (AFPLIC-I) union list of serials, 861
Association of Desk and Derrick Clubs, 1832
Asteroid name ency, 790
ASTM standards source [CD-ROM], 1663
Astronomy, 1800
Athletes, 410
Athletic scholarships, 799

Atlas & survey of S Asian hist, 534
Atlas of ...
    Indians of N America, 413
    Mesozoic & Cenozoic coastlines, 1807
    religious change in America, 1952-90, 1437
    Russia & the Independent Republics, 445
    shipwrecks & treasure, 1896
    the Civil War, 486
    the human body, 1694
    the mysterious in N America, 786
    westward expansion, 488
    world dvlpmt, 444
    WW I, 2d ed, 675
Atwell, Robert H., 362
Auerbach, Rena R., 425
August, Eugene R., 866
Australian bks in print 1995, 22
Authors & artists for young adults, v.14, 1171
Avakian, Anne M., 1340
Aviation & aerospace almanac 1995, 1879
Aviation: a Smithsonian gd, 1882
Axelrod, Alan, 705
Ayala, Marta Stiefel, 621
Ayala, Reynaldo, 621
Aycock, Wendell M., 1195
Ayre, Jim, 1751

Backstrom, Gayle, 854
Bacon, Donald C., 720
Bacon's dirs on disc 1995 update [CD-ROM], 974
Bad boys: legends of hockey's toughest, meanest, most-feared players, 826
Baerg, Harry J., 1611
Bahamas hndbk & businessman's annual 1995 [35th ed], 170
Bailey, Brooke, 939, 940, 941
Bailey, Jill, 1604
Bailey, Martha J, 1486
Bailey, William G., 599
Bain, Robert, 1199
Baker, Daniel B., 259, 454
Baker, Derek, 813
Baker ency of Bible places, 1450
Baker, Philip, 111
Baker, Richard, 1269
Baker, Theodore, 1271
Bakich, Michael E., 1798
Baldwin, Dean, 1228
Ballendorf, Dirk Anthony, 168
Ballinger, Erich, 598
Bamberger, W. C., 1209
Banham, Martin, 1415
Bankston, Carl L., III, 138
Barbour, Roger W., 1636
Barbuto, Domenica M., 230
Barker, Nicolas, 1001
Barker, Robert L., 890
Barnes, John A., 422
Barnes-Svarney, Patricia, 1512
Barnhardt, Phillip, 267

Barnhart abbrevs dict, 1
Barnhart, Robert K., 1
Barondess, Jeremiah A., 1702
Barr, Catherine, 623
Barron, Neil, 1191
Barron's best buys in college educ, 3d ed, 331
Barron's gd to law schools, 11th ed, 581
Barrows, Robert G., 929
Barson, Michael, 1367
Barstow, Barbara, 1180
Bartis, Peter T., 1341
Baseball & American culture, 806
Baseball ency update, 1995, 803
Baseball ratings, 2d ed, 804
Basic bus lib: core resources, 3d ed, 173
Bates, Dawn, 1119
Bati, Anwar, 1351
Battleships: US battleships, 1935-92, rev ed, 700
Bauer, Aaron M., 1634
Baumgartner, James E., 896, 952
Baumgartner, Walter, 1455
Bayers, Albert F., III, 1781
Bead dir, 3d ed, 1011
Beadle, David, 1613
Beal, George, 1088
Bear, John, 363
Bear, Mariah, 363
Beatles: the ultimate recording gd, 3d ed, 1338
Beaver, Bonnie V., 1554
Beck, John H., 1291
Beckner, Chrisanne, 927
Beer lover's rating gd, 1537
Beethoven ency, 1281
Beinert, Wolfgang, 1475
Bel Canto operas of Rossini, Donizetti, & Bellini, 1300
Benmour, Linda, 1011
Bennett, James R., 605
Bennett, Jim, 1884
Bensen, Clark H., 733
Bentley, Elizabeth Petty, 428, 588
Bentley, G. E., Jr., 1244
Benyukh, Oleg P., 1122
Berens, Ralph, 500
Berger, James L., 376
Berger, Laura Standley, 1175
Berke, Danielle, 1672
Berliant, Adam, 1885
Berliner gramophone records, 1273
Berlow, Lawrence H., 801
Berman, Matt, 1162
Bernal, Rodrigo, 1589
Bernard, Leo, 1002
Bernard, Philippa, 1002
Bernardin, Claude, 1331
Berry, David, 1370
Bertram, Anne, 1093
Best bulbs for temperate climates, 1545
Best hospitals in America, 2d ed, 1693
Best of teams, the worst of teams, 807
Best toys, bks & videos for kids, 1010
Beyer, Gerry W., 580

Beyond picture bks, 2d ed, 1180
BFI film & TV hndbk 1995, 1401
BHI plus [CD-ROM], 955
Bianchi, R. S., 1350
Bianco, David P., 194
Bible & the saints, 1448
Bibliographic checklist of African American newspapers, 971
Bibliographic gd to ...
   black studies 1994, 398
   bus & economics 1994, 174
   govt pubs--foreign 1994, 57
   govt pubs--US 1994, 58
   N American hist 1994, 489
Bibliographic hist of the bk, 664
Bibliography of ...
   American demographic hist, 906
   Bertrand Russell, 1423
   bus/competitive intelligence & benchmarking lit, 175
   medical & biomedical biog, 2d ed, 1696
   museum studies, 11th ed, 82
   Syrian archaeological sites to 1980, 484
   the English novel from the Restoration to the French Revolution, 1236
   works on Canadian foreign relations 1986-90, 748
Big bk of minority opportunities, 6th ed, 891
Biger, Gideon, 455
Billboard music yrbk 1994, 1303
Billboard video yrbk 1994, 1402
Billips, Connie, 1390
Bimson, John J., 1450
Binocular stargazer, 1801
Biographical dict of ...
   American newspaper columnists, 973
   American sports, 1992-95 suppl, 793
   artists, rev ed, 1022
   Saskatchewan artists: [v.2]: men artists, 1023
   the Union, 495
Biography index [CD-ROM], 24
Biography today, 1993 annual cum, 25
Biological anomalies: humans III, 1559
Bionat, Marvin P., 395
Biondi, Joann, 390
Biotechnology gd USA, 3d ed, 1655
Biotechnology in the US pharmaceutical industry 1995, 4th ed, 1733
Biotechnology info sources, 1658
Bird, Christiane, 1321
Birdwatcher's handbk, 1614
Bischiniotis, George, 1769
Bishop, Rudine Sims, 1182
Bishop, Sherman C., 1635
Bisio, Attilio, 1830
Bjorner, Susanne, 982
Black African lit in English, 1987-91, 1247
Black conductors, 1285
Black in focus, 1163
Black studies on disc [CD-ROM], 399
Blackburn, S., 253
Blacks in black & white, 2d ed, 1410
Blacks in opera, 1301

Blackwell hndbk of educ, 325
Blackwell, Kenneth, 1423
Blair, John, 1332
Blair, Judy, 385
Blaise, Albert, 1115
Blake, Barbara, 1181
Blake bks suppl, 1244
Bleaney, C. H., 135, 163
Blewett, Daniel K., 678
Bloom, Carole, 1523
Bloom, Ken, 1275
Bloor, David, 1664
Blueprint for a green school, 1870
Blumberg, Arnold, 706
Boatner, Mark M., III, 506
Boatner, Maxine Tull, 1083
Bob Dylan, 1334
Boczek, Boleslaw Adam, 610
Bodell, Heather C., 882
Bodenhamer, David J., 929
Bogdanov, Vladimir, 1330
Bogduk, Nikolai, 1723
Bognar, Desi K., 984
Boland, Maeve A., 1804
Bollard, John, 1087
Bond markets, 1995 ed, 292
Bondi, Victor, 513, 514, 516
Book of art, rev ed, 1029
Book of rhododendrons, 1573
Book prices: used & rare 1995, 1003
Bookman's gd to archaeology, 1005
Bookman's price index, v.50, 1004
Books in print 1995-96, 15
Books in print with bk reviews plus [CD-ROM], 17
Books out-of-print plus [CD-ROM], 18
Boondas, Jennifer, 1681
Boots, Sharon, 1830
Bopp, Richard E., 647
Bordwell, Sally, 1619
Borman, Jami Lynne, 1748
Born this day, 30
Bosnian-English, English-Bosnian concise dict, 1098
Bosnich, Victor W., 736
Bosoni, Anthony J., 600
Boulos, Loutfy, 1582
Boulton, Susie, 478
Bourgoin, Suzanne M., 1305
Bourne, Joyce, 1270
Bowker annual lib & bk trade almanac, 1995, 40th ed, 623
Bowker's complete video dir 1995, 986
Bowman, Joel P., 310
Bowman, John S., 35
Bown, Deni, 1585, 1586
Boyd, Margaret A., 1012
Boyer, Rodney, 1669
Boyne, Walter J., 698
Bracken, James K., 1778
Brackney, William H., 867
Brako, Lois, 1593
Branan, Carl R., 1650

Branchaw, Bernadine P., 310
Brassey's ency of military hist & biog, 682
Braun, Elisabeth, 1596
Brawer, Moshe, 445
Bremer, Ronald A., 431
Bressett, Kenneth, 1008
Brewer, Annie M., 975
Brewer, Jeutonne P., 966
Brewer's cinema, 1373
Brewer's theater, 1414
Brian Friel, 1257
Bridgman, Roger, 1508
Briggs, Derek E. G., 1813
British pol facts 1900-94, 7th ed, 758
British prose writers of the early 17th century, 1232
British sci fiction paperbacks & mags 1949-56, 1234
British short-fiction writers, 1945-80, 1228
Broadcast news manual of style, 2d ed, 992
Broadcast news [CD-ROM], 991
Brockman, Norbert C., 109
Brogdon, Jennie, 1522
Bromley, Debra J., 1419
Brook, Stephen, 479
Brooklyn Public Library Business Library Staff, 197
Brooks, Lori, 1654
Brooks, Stephen, 71
Brosman, Catharine Savage, 545
Broude, Gwen J., 862
Brown, George E., 1588
Brown, George, Jr., 1463
Brown, Jean E., 1170
Brown, Lorene Byron, 626
Brown, S. Kent, 1461
Brown, Travis, 1509
Brownstone, David, 945
Browsing in info systems, 644
Bryan, George B., 760, 1215
Buchanan, Anne L., 330
Buchanan, Robert J., 855
Buckley, John F., 268, 269
Buening, Alice P., 1038
Building a new South, 98
Building a popular sci lib collection for high school & adult learners, 660
Bunson, Matthew, 1472
Bunson, Matthew E., 565
Bunting, Jane, 43
Burak, Sara, 1779
Bureau of Economic and Business Research, College of Business Administration, University of Florida, 916
Burger, Robert H., 140
Burke, John Gordon, 78, 90
Burnie, David, 1608
Burras, J. K., 1575
Burrelle's index of broadcast transcripts, 1993 ed, 998
Bursac, Kristine M., 841
Burwell dir of info brokers 1994, 646
Burwell, Helen P., 646
Bus, James S., 1875
Business rankings annual, 1995, 197

Business Week, editors of, 332
Business Week gd to the best bus schools, 4th ed, 332
Bustros, Gabriel M., 161, 165
Butcher, Debbie, 1451
Butcher, Devereux, 470
Butcher, Russell D., 470
Butler, David, 758
Butler, Gareth, 758
Button, John, 766
Bybee, Howard C., 484
Byers, Paula K., 429, 430, 432, 433
Bykerk, Loree, 216
Byrne, John A., 332

Cabell, David W. E., 669, 670
Cabell's dir of publishing opportunities in accounting, economics & finance, 6th ed, 669
Cabell's dir of publishing opportunities in mgmt & mktg, 6th ed, 670
Caldwell, John Michael, 440
Callaghan, Jane, 1751
Calloway, Colin G., 414
Cambridge Australian English style gd, 1090
Cambridge dict of American biog, 35
Cambridge dict of stats in the medical scis, 1699
Cambridge ency, 2d ed, 44
Cambridge ency of the English lang, 1061
Cambridge gd to the constellations, 1798
Cambridge gd to theatre, new ed, 1415
Cambridge illus hist of British theatre, 1422
Cambridge intl dict of English, 1063
Camp, Roderic Ai, 763
Campbell, Alta, 191
Campbell, Robert L., 1322
Campe, Petra, 1057
Canadian address bk, 54
Canadian bk review annual 1994: children's lit, 1176
Canadian gd to clinical preventive health care, 1708
Canadian profile: alcohol, tobacco, & other drugs 1995, 898
Canadian representatives abroad, 749
Canadiana in US repositories: a preliminary gd, 136
Cannon, Donald Q., 1461
Career opportunities for writers, 3d ed, 967
Career opportunities in ...
  art, rev ed, 1041
  the food & beverage industry, 1538
  the music industry, 3d ed, 1276
  travel & tourism, 461
Carl Ruggles, 1280
Carley, Rachel, 1044
Carney, Faye, 1102
Carpenter, Kathryn Hammell, 899
Carr, Fred K., 589
Carr-Gomm, Sarah, 1030
Carroll's county dir, 721
Carroll's environmental dir 1995, 1863
Carroll's fed advisory dir 1995, 722
Carroll's fed assistance dir, 892
Carroll's fed dir, 723

Carroll's fed regional dir, 724
Carroll's military facilities dir, 686
Carroll's municipal dir, 725
Carroll's state dir, 726
Carson, D. A., 1458
Carter, April, 536
Carter, Craig, 828
Carter, John, 1001
Carty, T. J., 1229
Caruba, Alan, 988
Carwardine, Mark, 1629
Case, semantic roles, & grammatical relations, 1057
Cash Box charts for the post-modern age, 1312
Cassell dict of cynical quotations, 89
Cassell's queer companion, 864
Cassidy, Daniel J., 333, 334
Castello, Elena Romero, 424
Catalog of teratogenic agents, 8th ed, 1720
Cataloging nonbook materials with AACR2R & MARC, 631
Catalogue of ...
   American silver, 999
   Canadian catalogues, 249
   the 15th-century printed bks in the Harvard Univ lib, v.3, 42
Catling, Christopher, 476, 478
Cavendish, Richard, 784, 1348
Caygill, Howard, 1428
Cazoria, Angelina, 1862
CCCC bibliog of composition & rhetoric 1992, 1058
CD-ROM bk index, 80
CD-ROM dir, 14th ed [CD-ROM], 1768
CD-ROM dir 95 with multimedia CDs, 13th ed, 1769
CD-ROM finder, 8
CD-ROMs rated, 10
CDs, super glue, & salsa: how everyday products are made, 221
Cello music since 1960, 1286
Centre for Development of Instructional Technology (CENDIT), 243
Cerrito, Joann, 1158, 1159, 1160
Chad, 115
Chalker, Sylvia, 1080
Challoner, Jack, 1819
Chamber music for solo voice & instruments 1960-89, 1299
Chambers, Ann, 1672
Chambers dict on CD-ROM [CD-ROM], 1064
Champagne companion, 1354
Champagne, Duane, 415
Chan, Lois Mai, 627
Chandler, Ralph C., 606
Characters in 20th-century lit, bk 2, 1155
Charles, Jill, 1419
Charosh, Paul, 1273
Chase, Jayni, 1870
Chase, Simon, 1351
Checklist of painters c1200-1994, 2d ed, 652
Chemical industry in 1993, 222
Chemical scis graduate school finder 1994-95, 1791
Cheremisinoff, Paul N., 1857, 1858, 1859

Chesler, Andrew, 437
Chevrefils, Marlys, 658, 1249
Chickasaw: an analytical dict, 1099
Chief executives of Tex., 718
Child abuse & neglect [CD-ROM], 616
Child, Greg, 829
Child sexual abuse custody dispute annot bibliog, 900
Childers, Joseph, 960
Childhood sexual abuse, 618
Children's atlas of natural wonders, 1806
Children's atlas of the 20th century, 553
Children's authors & illustrators, 5th ed, 1178
Children's bks in print 1995, 19
Children's jukebox, 1278
Children's media market place, 4th ed, 649
Children's ref plus [CD-ROM], 21
Children's TV, 1947-90, 1404
Children's visual dict, 43
China: a provincial atlas, 452
China bibliog, 535
Chironomidae [Diptera] of Japan, 1626
Choate, Jerry R., 1630
CHOICE reviews on SilverPlatter [CD-ROM], 84
Christian voluntarism in Britain & N America, 867
Christopher Lee & Peter Cushing & horror cinema, 1396
Chronicle financial aid gd, rev ed, 364
Chronicle 2-yr college databk, rev ed, 335
Chronicle of ...
   America, 500
   the cinema, 1371
   the 20th century, 558
Chronicle vocational school manual, rev ed, 381
Chronology of ...
   Hispanic-American hist, 550
   the ancient world, 559
   the expanding world, 560
   the medieval world, 561
   the modern world, 2d ed, 562
   world hist, compact ed, 564
Cibbarelli, Pamela R., 643
Cigar companion, 2d ed, 1351
CITES identification gd - birds, 1612
Citino, Robert M., 702
City crime rankings, 602
Civil rights decisions of the US Supreme Court, the 19th century, 607
Civil rights decisions of the US Supreme Court, the 20th century, 608
Civil War [CD-ROM], 691
Civil War battlefields, 517
Civil War Society, 504
Civilizations of the ancient Near East, 159
Claghorn, Charles E., 1304
Clark, Neil, 68
Clark, Sandra, 1241
Clark, Stuart, 1799
Clarke, Boden, 1209, 1218
Class FC, a classification for Canadian hist, 2d ed, 628
Classical & medieval lit criticism, v.14, 1149
Classification of chronic pain, 2d ed, 1723
Clements, Frank A., 166

Climbing, 829
Clitics, 1060
Cloud nine: a dreamer's dict, 781
Clute, John, 1192
Clynes, Tom, 1352
Codes of professional responsibility, 3d ed, 1431
Codex alimentarius, v.5a, 2d ed, 1534
Codex alimentarius, v.13, 2d ed, 1535
Coffey, Frank, 1335
Cohn-Sherbok, Lavinia, 1481
Coleman, Charles J., 255
Collector's ency of Depression glass, 11th ed, 1013
College degrees by mail 1996, rev ed, 363
Collier, Frederick J., 1813
Collings, E. W., 1669
Collins ency of Scotland, 148
Collins German-English, English-German dict, 2d ed, 1104
Collins, Raymond L., 689
Collins Scottish clan & family ency, 435
Collinson, Diane, 1427
Columbia chronicles of American life, 1910-92, 501
Columbia dict of modern literary & cultural critcism, 960
Columbia Granger's gd to poetry anthologies, 2d ed, 1263
Comay, Joan, 1481
Combined membership list 1995-96, 1825
Committees in the US congress 1947-92, v.2, 733
Common American birds, 1611
Common medical abbrevs, 1695
Communities dir, 1995 ed, 852
Commuter airlines of the US, 1880
Companion to the philosophy of mind, 1432
Comparative Russian-English dict of Russian proverbs & sayings, 1125
Compendium of ...
   American railroad radio frequencies, 13th ed, 1891
   histl sources, rev ed, 431
   the Confederate armies: Ky., Md., Mo., Confederate units & Indian units, 522
   the Confederate armies: La., 523
   the Confederate armies: Miss., 524
   the Confederate armies: S.C. & Ga., 525
   the Confederate armies: Tex., 526
Complete baby & child care, 904
Complete cyberspace ref & dir, 1772
Complete dict of sexology, new expanded ed, 885
Complete dir of nursing facilities for younger adults with chronic physical disabilities, 1994, 855
Complete gd to ...
   Canadian univs, 3d ed, 320
   household chemicals, 1795
   sharpening, 1679
   writers' conferences & workshops, 965
Complete golfer's almanac 1995, 821
Complete horse care manual, 1556
Complete James Bond movie ency, rev ed, 1382
Complete learning disabilities dir, 1995/96, 374
Complete motorcycle bk, 1884
Comprehensive networking glossary & acronym gd, 1759

Comprehensive ref manual for signers & interpreters, 4th ed, 1131
Computer dict for kids & their parents, 1748
Computer glossary, 7th ed, 1757
Computer support dir, 1767
Concise Columbia ency, 3d ed, 45
Concise dict of Christian theology, 1453
Concise dict of Christianity in America, 1466
Concise ency of foods & nutrition, 1524
Concise ency of measurement & instrumentation, 1641
Concise Oxford dict of ...
   current English, 9th ed, 1065
   ecology, 1854
   sociology, 834
Conductor's gd to choral-orchestral works, 1297
Congressional Quarterly's desk ref on American govt, 737
Congressional Quarterly's Political Staff, 738
Congressional Quarterly's pols in America 1996, 738
Congressional voting gd, 5th ed, 736
Congressional yrbk 1993, 739
Conley, Jill, 892
Connecticut, Maine, Mass., [&] R.I.: atlas of histl county boundaries, 438
Connors, Martin, 1398
Considine, Douglas M., 1502
Consolidated list of products whose consumption and/or sale have been banned...., 5th ed, 217
Constitutional law dict, v.1, 606
Constitutions of the world, 611
Consumer Asia 1995 [2d ed], 242
Consumer Eastern Europe 1996, 251
Consumer health USA, 1711
Consumer Research study on bk purchasing, 1993, 673
Consumer's dict of cosmetic ingredients, 4th ed, 1790
Consumer's dict of food additives, 4th ed, 1530
Consumers ref disc [CD-ROM], 218
Container gardening through the yr, 1544
Contemporary African pols & dvlpmt, 110
Contemporary & histl lit of food sci & human nutrition, 1522
Contemporary architects, 3d ed, 1043
Contemporary authors, new revision series, v.43, 1150
Contemporary black biog, v.8, 400
Contemporary black biog, v.9, 401
Contemporary Canadian pols, 1988-94, 751
Contemporary diesel spotter's gd, 2d ed, 1889
Contemporary fashion, 1017
Contemporary literary criticism annual cum index for 1995, 1151
Contemporary literary criticism, v.84, 1152
Contemporary literary criticism, v.85, 1153
Contemporary musicians, v.13, 1305
Contemporary photographers, 3d ed, 1018
Contemporary poets, dramatists, essayists, & novelists of the South, 1199
Contemporary theatre, film, & TV, v.13, 1362
Contento, William, 1194
Cook, Charles, 824
Cook, Chris, 530, 711
Cook, James F., 496

Cooney, Jerry W., 551
Cooper, B. Lee, 806, 1333
Cooper, Cheryl, 319
Cooper, Gordon, 1353
Cooper, John, 1403
Cooper, Robert M., 1233
Copyright hndbk, 2d ed, 590
Corey, Melinda, 1374
Corliss, William R., 1559
CorpTech dir of tech cos 1996, 10th US ed, 1749
Correard, Marie-Helene, 1100
Cortada, James W., 284
Cosmopolitan world atlas, 446
Costa, Vincenzo, 1814
Cottridge, David, 1617
Coulson, Jessie, 1127
Counseling older persons, 843
Countries of the world & their leaders yrbk 1995: suppl, 710
County courthouse bk, 2d ed, 588
County executive dir, 727
Courtroom hndbk on fed evidence, 1995 ed, 591
Covington, Melody Mauldin, 1755
Covington, Michael A., 1755
Cowboy ency, 510
Cowley, Chris, 1078
Cox, Mary, 1038
Cox, Michael, 1659
Cracking the corporate closet, 259
Crafts supply source bk, 3d ed, 1012
Craggs, Stewart R., 1279
Craig, Barbara L., 653
Craig, Bruce D., 1667
Craighead's intl bus, travel, & relocation gd to 78 countries, 231
Crain, Esther, 1263
Cralley, Lester V., 1875
Cralley, Lewis J., 1875
Crandell, George W., 1220
Crane, Janet, 171
Crawford, Gary William, 1256
Crayton, Tabatha, 52
Cremona, Candida H., 856
Crimes & punishment, 573
Crimes of perception: an ency of heresies & heretics, 1468
Criminal justice in Israel, 596
Crossword puzzle dict, 6th ed, 1085
Crow, Laura, 722
Crowdus, Gary, 1409
Crown crime companion, 1189
Crystal clear v.2, 993
Crystal, David, 44, 1061
Cubberley, Carol W., 379
Culbertson, Margaret, 1050
Cultural atlas of Spain & Portugal, 539
Cumming, Robert, 1052
Cummings, David M., 1267
Cumulated indexes to the public papers of the presidents of the US: George Bush, 1989-93, 744
Cumulated indexes to the public papers of the presidents of the US: Ronald Reagan, 1981-89, 745

Current world leaders almanac, v.38, no.3, June 1995, 104
Curson, Jon, 1613
Curtiss, Jon, 336
Custard, Edward T., 357
Cuticchia, A. Jamie, 1656
Cuts in defense jobs in US counties, metropolitan areas, & states, 1992-2003, 270
Cutts, Martin, 1075
Cvancara, Alan M., 1803
Cy Young award winners, 808
Cyprus, rev ed, 130
Czerepanov, S. K., 1594

D & D standard oil abbreviator, 4th ed, 1832
Da Capo companion to 20th-century popular music, rev ed, 1306
D'Agostino, Annette M., 1413
Dahl, Henry Saint, 574
Dahl's law dict, 574
Daintith, John, 1072
Daly, K. S., 142
Dan Cassidy's worldwide college scholarship dir, 4th ed, 333
Dan Cassidy's worldwide graduate scholarship dir, 4th ed, 334
Dangerous sky: resource gd to the Battle of Britain, 544
Daniel, Clifton, 558
Darke, Rick, 1583
Dastrup, Boyd L., 703
Data sources for bus & market analysis, 4th ed, 296
Davidson, Cathy N., 1200
Davidson, Linda Kay, 1462
Davidson, Roger H., 720
Davies, Eryl, 72
Davies, R. E. G., 1880
Davis, Geoffrey V., 122
Davis, J. R., 1662, 1678
Davis, Jeffery, 1404
Day by day: the 80s, 503
Day-Viaud, Valerie, 115
De Chiara, Joseph, 1048
De Laet, S. J., 568
De Lucca, J. L., 1808
De Sola, Ralph, 2
Deaf persons in the arts & scis, 857
Deaton, Wendy, 900
DeBeer, Shane R., 575
Debrett's peerage & baronetage [1995], 426
Decalo, Samuel, 119, 124
Definitive country, 1320
DeFrancis, Beth, 901
Delahunty, Andrew, 1076
Delgado, Jane L., 409
Delmar ref manual: essentials for the electronic office, 310
DeLoach, Charles, 1346
Demastes, William W., 1202
DenBoer, Gordon, 438, 439
Denckla, Tanya, 1543

Denenberg, Dennis, 321
Department for Economic and Social Information and Policy Analysis, Population Division, 912, 932
Department for Economic and Social Information and Policy Analysis, Statistical Division, 1841
Department for Policy Coordination and Sustainable Development, 217
Department of Military Art and Engineering, United States Military Academy, 677
Depression, 1724
Derbyshire, Ian D., 131
Derks, Scott, 198
Dervaes, Claudine, 1082
Des Chenes, E. A., 1171
Descriptive catalog of the music printed by Hubert Waelrant & Jan de Laet, 1266
Desk ref for organic chemists, 1792
Desmond, Ray, 1562
DeSousa, Luis R., 1695
Detective dict, rev ed, 598
Deutsche Gesellschaft fur Materialkunde e.V., 1666
Devaney, Joan, 235
Development Centre of the Organisation for Economic Co-operation, 909
Dever, John P., 680
Dever, Maria C., 680
Deyl, Z., 1505
Diagram Group, 529, 533, 1815
Dibner, Mark D., 1655
Dickson, Nancy, 83
Dickson, Paul, 83
Dictators & tyrants, 705
Dictionary for bus & finance, 3d ed, 180
Dictionary of ...
   accounting, 210
   agriculture, 1517
   alternative defense, 683
   American biog, suppl 10, 36
   American idioms, 1083
   animal words & phrases, 1073
   Baptists in America, 1467
   British & Irish botanists & horticulturalists, rev ed, 1562
   business & legal terms: Russian-English/English-Russian, 575
   business terms, 2d ed, 178
   catchphrases, 1084
   Chicano Spanish, 2d ed, 1136
   Christian art, 1028
   computer terms, 4th ed, 1755
   computer works, rev ed, 1754
   contemporary quotations, vol.8, 3d ed, 90
   cricket, 2d ed, 814
   cytokines, 1558
   ecclesiastical Latin, 1118
   English surnames, 3d ed, 427
   environmental law & sci, 1855
   epidemiology, 3d ed, 1698
   family therapy, rev ed, 1718
   feminist theory, 2d ed, 948
   film quotations, 1374
   finance & investment terms, 4th ed, 220
   gene tech, 1657
   generic names of seed plants, 1565
   human oncology, 1726
   image tech, 3d ed, 985
   Japanese financial terms, 248
   law, 3d ed, 576
   literary biog documentary series, v.12, 1201
   literary pseudonyms in the English lang, 1229
   marketing & advertising, 304
   mathematics terms, 2d ed, 1826
   modern legal usage, 2d ed, 577
   nursing theory & research, 2d ed, 1732
   Portuguese-African civilization, v.1, 532
   Russian slang & colloquial expressions, 1128
   sci, 1493
   Scottish art & architecture, 1025
   sexual lang & imagery in Shakespearean & Stuart lit, 1243
   symbols in W art, 1030
   the Earth, 1805
   the modern pols of SE Asia, 747
   the NW Semitic inscriptions, 1129
   traditional S-E Asian theatre, 1418
   20th century British bk illustrators, 1055
   20th century culture: French culture 1900-75, 545
   20th century culture: Hispanic culture of S America, 406
Diffor, Elaine N., 375
Diffor, John C., 375
Diggs, Anita Doreen, 96
Dillard, Tom W., 490
Diller, Daniel, 764
Dillon, Patrick M., 1750
DiMartino, Dave, 1307
DiMona, Lisa, 951
Dinosaur safari gd, 1814
Diplomatic, consular, & other representatives in Canada, 750
Directory of ...
   American research & tech 1995, 29th ed, 182
   American youth orgs 1994-95, 5th ed, 902
   biomedical & health care grants 1995, 9th ed, 1685
   bus per special issues, 209
   Canadian lib & info sci consultants, 642
   Canadian schools, 6th ed, 319
   Community legislation in force & other acts of the Community insts, 768
   computer & high tech grants, 2d ed, 1770
   cos required to file annual reports with the SEC, 183
   environmental info sources, 5th ed, 1864
   European research & dvlpmt 1995, 1504
   financial aids for minorities 1995-97, 880
   financial aids for women 1995-97, 879
   graduate student employee bargaining agents & orgs, 336
   hazardous waste servs, 1994-95. 5th ed, 1654
   health care professionals 1995, 1686
   hyphenated techniques, 1505
   import regimes, pt.1, 289
   import regimes, pt.2, 290

Directory of ... *(continued)*
   importers in Latin America, 1994 ed, 291
   intl bus, 233
   intl corporate giving in America & abroad 1995, 869
   lib automation sftwr, systems, & servs, 643
   mail order catalogs, 1995, 9th ed, 219
   medical & dental schools worldwide, 6th ed, 1687
   medical rehabilitation facilities 1995, 1703
   new & emerging fndns, 3d ed, 870
   nursing homes, 1995, 1731
   printers, 1994-95 ed, 671
   professional & occupational regulation in the US & Canada, 730
   retirement facilities 1995, 847
   theatre training programs, 5th ed, 1419
   UN info sources, 5th ed, 769
   US labor orgs, 1994-95 ed, 260
   US military bases worldwide, 687
DiscLit: world authors [CD-ROM], 1154
DISCovering careers & jobs [CD-ROM], 271
Distance educ, 377
Divining the future: prognostication from astrology to zoomancy, 791
Doctor of philosophy degree, 330
Dodd, Peter, 759
Dorgan, Charity A., 905
Dorgan, Charity Anne, 922
Dority, G. Kim, 9
Dorling Kindersley visual ency, 46
Dorling Kindersley visual timeline of transportation, 1878
Doss-Quinby, Eglal, 1251
Douchant, Michael, 809
Dougan, Michael B., 490
Douglas, J. D., 1465
Douglas, Livingston G., 292
Dow Jones & Company, editors of, 212
Dow Jones gd to the world stock market, 1995-96 ed, 212
Dower, John W., 537
Downes, John, 220
Downing, Douglas, 1826
Downing, Douglas A., 1755
Doyle, Billy H., 1368
Doyle, Francis R., 569
Dr. Tom Linden's gd to online medicine, 1709
Drabble, Margaret, 1231
Draper, James P., 1152
Dream ency, 779
Drew, Wilfred, 1518
Drug Topics red bk, 1995, 1734
Drury, George H., 1886
Drury, John, 1264
du Noyer, Paul, 1336
DuBoff, Leonard, 1039
Duchet-Suchaux, Gaston, 1448
Duensing, Edward E., 928
Dulin, Robert O., Jr., 700
Duncan, Philip D., 738
Dunkle, Margaret, 1163
Dunn, D. Elwood, 118
Dunn, Maryjane, 1462

Dupuis, Diane L., 1398
Durham, Michael S., 411
Dwyer, Judith A., 1470
Dyja, Tom, 1400
Dyson, Peter, 1756, 1761

Early modern Russian writers, late 17th & 18th centuries, 1261
Early music dict, 1272
Early US-Hispanic relations 1776-1860, 776
Earth words, 1861
Earth work, 1871
Earthly recordings of Sun Ra, 1322
Earth-Science educ resource dir, 1804
East, Michael B., 1792
Eastern Europe: a bibliographic gd to English lang pubs, 1986-93, 140
Eastern Europe: a resource gd, 141
Eastman, Richard M., 845
Eberhart, George M., 624
Eby, Vivienne M., 1555
Eccleshall, Robert, 704
Ecker, Ronald L., 1452
Eckersley, Richard, 667
Eckstein, Richard M., 1770
Ecofeminist theory, 935
Economic & social survey of Asia & the Pacific 1995, 128
Economic and Social Commission for Asia and the Pacific, 128, 295, 1842, 1843
Economic and Social Commission for Western Asia, 129, 156, 157, 158, 919
Economic Commission for Africa, 113
Economic Commission for Europe, 222, 287, 303, 1649, 1838, 1839, 1840, 1877, 1890
Economic Commission for Latin America and the Caribbean, 151, 153, 154
Economic integration in Europe & N America, 232
Economic panorama of Latin America 1995, 151
Edel, Theodore, 1292
Edelheit, Abraham J., 552
Edelheit, Hershel, 552
Eden, Philip, 76
Eden-Green, Monica, 235
Editor & Publisher intl yr bk 1994, 980
Editor & Publisher market gd 1994, 976
Editor & publisher market gd 1994 [CD-ROM], 977
Editor & Publisher yr bk 1994 [CD-ROM], 981
Editorial Staff of Government Institutes, 1864
Education for the Earth, 2d ed, 337
Educators grade gd to free teaching aids 1995, 41st ed, 322
Educators gd to free films, filmstrips, & slides 1995, 55th ed, 375
Educators gd to free videotapes 1995, 42d ed, 376
Edwards, Michael, 1354
Edwards, Richard L., 893
Eerdmans' hndbk to the world's religions, rev ed, 1446
Ehr, Catherine M., 176, 188, 189
Ehrlich, Eugene, 1116

Ehrlich, Paul R., 1614
Eicher, David J., 517
Elazar, Daniel J., 712
Electric light & power US electric utility industry dir, 1995, 4th ed, 1651
Electric light & power US non-utility power dir, 1995, 1652
Electronic Gieck's engineering formulas [CD-ROM], 1642
Electronics pocket ref, 2d ed, 1653
Elementary teachers gd to free curriculum materials 1995, 52d ed, 323
El-Hadidi, M. Nabil, 1582
Ellet, William, 282
Elliott, Sydney, 761
Elrod, Bruce C., 1308
Elsevier's dict of ...
    agriculture & food production, 1516
    biometry, 1557
    climatology & meteorology, 1808
    industrial tech, 1494
Elsevier's nautical dict, 3d ed, 1894
El-Shamy, Hasan M., 1342
Elste, Martin, 1288
Elvers, Barbara, 1789
Elvis ency, 1335
Emanuel, Muriel, 1043
Emergency Librarian index, vs.1-20: 1973-93, 645
Employment of the elderly, 842
Encyclopaedia Judaica decennial bk 1983-92, 1478
Encyclopaedia of ...
    Celtic wisdom, 788
    Indian cinema, 1381
    mathematics, v.10, 1827
Encyclopedia Americana, 1995 [CD-ROM], 47
Encyclopedia of ...
    advanced materials, 1664
    afterlife beliefs & phenomena, 1445
    aging, 850
    American architecture, 2d ed, 1045
    American family names, 437
    analytical sci, 1495
    Australian art, rev ed, 1032
    beer, 1525
    biblical errancy, 1456
    bioethics, rev ed, 1429
    careers & vocational guidance [CD-ROM], 382
    college basketball, 809
    creation myths, 1444
    E philosophy & religion, 1483
    educ info, 1994/95, 324
    energy tech & the environment, 1830
    environmental biology, 1856
    environmental control tech, v.7, 1857
    environmental control tech, v.8, 1858
    environmental control tech, v.9, 1859
    frontier biog on CD-ROM [CD-ROM], 497
    herbs & their uses, 1585
    home care for the elderly, 1681
    Indianapolis, 929
    intl boundaries, 455
    Irish schools, 1500-1800, 315
    marriage & the family, 863
    martial arts movies, 1380
    memory & memory disorders, 780
    NYC, 107
    percussion, 1291
    plague & pestilence, 1725
    police sci, 2d ed, 599
    popular misconceptions, 62
    snakes, 1637
    social work, 19th ed, 893
    the American Revolution, 3d ed, 506
    the dog, 1620
    the Middle Ages, 565
    the motorcycle, 1893
    the N American Free Trade Agreement, 305
    the sword, 816
    the US congress, 720
    utopian lit, 1147
Encyclopedias, atlases, & dicts, 48
Encyclopedic dict of gears & gearing, 1674
Endangered English dict, 1089
Endres, Kathleen L., 950
Energy, 1833
Energy balances & electricity profiles, 1992, 1841
Engineered materials hndbk, 1665
Engle, Ron, 1420
Englefield, Dermot, 540
English-Azerbaijani/Azerbaijani-English concise dict, 1097
English, Deborah L., 669, 670
English-German dict of materials & process engineering, 1666
English-Russian comprehensive dict, 1122
English-Russian, Russian-English dict, rev ed, 1124
English-Somali, Somali-English Dictionary, 1134
English-Spanish glossary of environmental terms & abbrevs, 1862
Enslen, Richard A., 606
Ensminger, Audrey H., 1524
Environmental acronyms, 1850
Environmental gd to the Internet, 1868
Environmental statutes, 1995 ed, 1872
EPA database bk, 1865
Ergas, G. Aimee, 1024
ERIC identifier authority list (IAL) 1995, 629
Erickson, Hal, 1375
Erickson, Judith B., 902
Erickson, Millard J., 1453
Eritrea, 116
Erlewine, Michael, 1330
Ernest, James D., 1457
Ernst, Carl H., 1636
Ernst, Gordon E., Jr., 1207
Erwin, Douglas H., 1813
Espencheid, Mark, 1795
Esposito, John L., 1477
Esposito, Vincent J., 677
Essay & general lit index 1990-94, 81
Essential gd to prescription drugs 1995, 1737
Essential gd to wilderness camping & backpacking in the US, 824

Essential Internet info gd, 1784
Ethiopia, 117
Ethnic dress, 388
Ethnic relations, 389
ETS test collection catalog, v.2, 2d ed, 314
Ettlinger, Steve, 1526
Eureka! scientific discoveries & inventions, 1496
European employment law, 252
European pharmaceutical technical & regulatory compendium, 1742
European research & dvlpmt database 1995 [CD-ROM], 1510
Evangelista, Nick, 816
Evans, Martin Marix, 1018
Evans, Philip R., 1323
Everitt, B. S., 1699
Evinger, William R., 687
Evriviades, Marios L., 130
Ewert, Richard H., 1674
EXEGY: the source for current world info, 49
Explorers & discoverers, 454
Exploring our natl parks & monuments, 9th ed, 470
Exporting to the USA, 1995-96 ed, 297
External trade bulletin of the ESCWA region, 7th ed, 157
External trade monthly stats, 293
Eyewitness atlas of the world, 447
Eyewitness hist of the world [CD-ROM], 567
Eytan, Zeev, 695

Faber, Charles F., 804
Fabre, Michel, 1197
Fackler, P. Mark, 1441
Facts about Canada, its provinces & territories, 137
Facts about the British prime ministers, 540
Facts on File world pol almanac, 3d ed, 711
Fage, J. D., 531
Failed tech, 1511
Falick, Melanie, 1526
Falk, Nancy Auer, 934
Famighetti, Robert, 7
Familia Gekkonidae (Reptilia, Sauria), pt.1, 1634
Fandom dir, no.15, 1995-1996 ed, 1355
Fantasy lit for children & young adults, 4th ed, 1167
FAO/ECE Agriculture and Timber Division of the Economic Commission for Europe, 1519, 1520
Far East & Australasia 1995, 26th ed, 167
Farndon, John, 1805
Farquhar, Doug, 1866
Farr, David F., 1593
Farrell, Michael, 325
Fast, Cathy Carroll, 933
Fast, Timothy H., 933
Faulkner, Benjamin, 436
Favorite annuals, 1568
Favorite flowering shrubs, 1569
Favorite perennials, 1570
Favorite shade plants, 1571
Feczko, Margaret Mary, 870, 871, 875, 878, 961
Federal database finder, 4th ed, 59

Federal legislative hists, 717
Federal regulatory dir, 7th ed, 731
Federal systems of the world, [2d ed], 712
Federal writers' project, 966
Fegley, Randall, 116
Fehrenbach, R. J., 1006
Feinberg, Sandra, 903
Feminist criticism of American women poets, 1222
Fenton, John Y., 1438
Fenwick, Gillian, 26
Ferguson, Gary Lynn, 1318
Festivals of Europe, 1353
Fetishes, Florentine girdles, & other explorations into the sexual imagination, 886
Fiala, John L., 1567
Fiction dict, 1185
Field artillery, 703
Field gd to ...
    current training videos, 282
    prehistoric life, 1815
    shells, 4th ed, 1595
    the palms of the Americas, 1589
Field manual for the amateur geologist, rev ed, 1803
Field, Shelly, 1276, 1364
Fifty-seven saints, 2d ed, 1464
Fiji, 169
Fildes, Robert, 208
Film directors, 11th intl ed, 1405
Film distribution gd 1986-1992, v.1, 1384
Film noir, 1383
Films into bks, 1394
Financial aid for the disabled & their families 1994-96, 858
Financial aid for vets, military personnel, & their dependents 1994-96, 690
Finch, Christopher, 1536
Find anyone fast, 837
Findlay, Allan M., 120
Findlay, Anne M., 120
Finkelstein, L., 1641
Finn, Daniel, 1392, 1393
Fiorenza, Francis Schussler, 1475
First Americans, 386
Fischler, Stan, 826, 827
Fish & fisheries worldwide [CD-ROM], 1605
Fisher, Helen S., 266, 930
Fisher, Janet, 1179
Fishes of the tropical E Pacific, 1633
Fishman, Stephen, 590
Fister, Barbara, 946
Fitzroy Dearborn dir of venture capital funds, 184
Flackes, W. D., 761
Flanagan, Mike, 502
Flannery, Tim, 1631, 1632
Fleeger, Carolyn A., 1747
Flora, Joseph M., 1199
Florence, Gene, 1013
Florida statl abstract, 1994, 28th ed, 916
Flowering crabapples, 1567
Flows & stocks of fixed capital 1967-92, 213

Fluorescence: gems & minerals under ultraviolet light, 1812
Fly-fisher's gd to saltwater naturals & their imitation, 817
Fodor's great American vacations for travelers with disabilities, 471
Fogle, Bruce, 1620
Folk traditions of the Arab world, 1342
Folklife sourcebk, 2d ed, 1341
Folts, W. Edward, 838
Food aid in figures, v.11, 881
Food chronology, 1539
Foran, Dorothy, 853
Foreign descriptions of Muscovy, 147
Foreign trade stats for Africa, 294
Foreign trade stats of Asia & the Pacific 1988-92, 295
Forms of address, 311
Fossils of the Burgess Shale, 1813
Foster, Gwendolyn Audrey, 947
Foulkes, Christopher, 1527
Foundation Center, 883
Foundation dir suppl, 1995 ed, 871
Foundation grants index 1996, 24th ed, 883
Foundation grants to individuals, 9th ed, 872
Foundation 1000 1995/96, 873
Founders of modern nations, 556
Fowler, David J., 654
Frame, Murray, 548
France, Peter, 1252
Francillon, Rene J., 697
Franck, Irene, 945
Franco, Alvaro, 1834
Francoeur, Robert T., 885
Fraser, Kristy, 1767
Frayser, Suzanne G., 887
Free & inexpensive career materials, 383
Freed, Judith M., 1356
Freedman, Alan, 1757
Freed's gd to student contests & publishing, 5th ed, 1356
Freeman, Carla Conrad, 378
Freeman, John Crosby, 1016
Freeman, Judy, 663
Freeze, Gregory L., 247
Freiman, Fran Locher, 1511
French critical reception of African-American lit from the beginnings to 1970, 1197
Frey, Linda, 762
Frey, Marsha, 762
Frick, John P., 1671
Friedman, Jack P., 178
Friedman, Mickey, 1189
Friedmann, Robert R., 596
From Afar to Zulu: a dict of African cultures, 390
From metal to Mozart, 1298
Frommer's comprehensive travel gd: Caribbean '95, 483
Fugitive: a complete episode gd, 1963-67, 1403
Fujioka, Yasuhiro, 1324
Fuller, Sue, 73
Funnell, Brian M., 1807
Furniture assns in N America, 223

Gaer, Linda, 1866
Galaeno, Gloria, 1589
Gale bus resources [CD-ROM], 199
Gale city & metro rankings reporter, 930
Gale country & world rankings reporter, 905
Gale ency of bus & professional assns, 185
Gale ency of multicultural America, 387
Gale gd to Internet databases, 1779
Gale, Robert L., 1212
Galens, Judy, 387
Gale's career guidance system, expanded ed [CD-ROM], 384
Gale's quotations [CD-ROM], 91
Gall, Susan, 392
Gall, Susan B., 393, 396
Gallant, R. W., 1793
Galvan, Roberto A., 1136
Gamlin, Linda, 1608
Ganly, John, 296
Garden bulbs for the South, 1546
Gardener's gd to ...
    Britain, new ed, 1548
    growing lilies, 1572
    plant diseases, 1547
Gardening with roses, 1549
Garee, Betty, 853
Garner, Bryan A., 577
Garoogian, Andrew, 926, 931
Garoogian, Rhoda, 926, 931
Garraty, John A., 528
Garrett, Jenkins, 657
Garzke, William H., Jr., 700
Gates, J. E., 1083
Gause, Ken, 709
Gay & lesbian address bk, 53
Gay 100, 865
Gazit, Shlomo, 695
Geary, James W., 495
Gender equity in educ, 313
Genealogist's address bk, 3d ed, 428
Genreflecting: a gd to reading interests in genre fiction, 4th ed, 1186
Geography on file, 1995 ed, 457
George Herbert companion, 1238
George, Leonard, 785, 1468
George Ryga papers, 1249
George, Timothy S., 537
Gerardi, Pamela, 554
Gerard-Sharp, Lisa, 481
Gerhan, David R., 906
German writers & works of the early Middle Ages, 1254
Gerring, Anthony L., 55, 339, 340
Gervais, Marty, 1443
Geyer, B., 1516
Giants: a ref gd from hist, the Bible, & recorded legend, 1346
Gibilisco, Stan, 1753
Gibson, J., 1726
Gifford, Courtney D., 260
Giglio, James N., 491

Gilbert, Harriett, 886
Gilbert, Martin, 675
Gilbert, Steve, 607, 608
Giles, James R., 1203, 1204
Giles, Wanda H., 1203, 1204
Gillespie, Anna, 1293
Gillespie, John, 1293
Ginsberg, Leon, 894
Giroux, Christopher, 1153
Glatt, Hillary, 1341
Glenn, William M., 1873
Global bks in print plus [CD-ROM], 13
Global refugee crisis, 895
Global trends: world almanac of dvlpmt & peace, 200
Globe & Mail report on bus: Canada co handbk 1994, 250
Glomski, Jacqueline, 1250
Glossary of insurance terms, 5th ed, 226
Glossary of typesetting terms, 667
Glover, Denise M., 402
Glynn, Jeannette, 186
Goalies: legends from the NHL's toughest job, 827
Goddesses, heroes, & shamans, 1347
Goehlert, Robert U., 715
Goetzel, Claus G., 1666
Goetzel, Lilo K., 1666
Goetzfridt, Nicholas J., 1260
Goins, Charles Robert, 440
Goldberg, Marian, 465
Goldmine's celebrity vocals, 1274
Goldschmidt, Arthur, Jr., 162
Goldsmith, Gary, 1400
Gonyea, James C., 272
Gonzalez, Ann, 1258
Goode, Steven, 591
Goodfellow, William D., 1309
Goodman, Jordan Elliot, 220
Goodridge, George E., Jr., 439
Goodwin, Katherine R., 657
Gorder, Cheryl, 317
Gordon, Alan, 501
Gordon, Lois, 501
Gordon, William A., 472
Goring, Rosemary, 1145
Gorlin, Rena A., 1431
Gorman, G. E., 169
Gosling, William A., 136
Gottlieb, Richard, 219, 228
Gottschalk, Jack A., 233
Gottsegen, Mark D., 1053
Govea, Wenonah Milton, 1287
Government affairs yellow bk, v.1, no.1, 187
Government career gds [CD-ROM], 256
Government dir of addresses & telephone nos 1995, 3d ed, 732
Government online, 1776
Governors of Ga., 1754-1995, rev ed, 496
Gowing, Lawrence, 1022
Gozdecka-Sanford, Adriana, 144
Graduate Group's new internships for 1994-95, 261
Graduate school funding handbk, 365

Graham Stuart Thomas rose bk, rev ed, 1551
Grain market, v.2, 1519
Grambs, David, 1089
Grant, Daniel, 1040
Grant, Peter W., 815
Graphic novels, 1359
Grattan, K. T. V., 1641
Gravlin, Erika, 317
Gray, Richard A., 1721
Great athletes, suppl 21-23, 794
Great Britain, 480
Great events from hist 2: ecology & the environment series, 1853
Great leaders, great tyrants?, 706
Great lives from hist: American women series, 942
Great new nonfiction reads, 1184
Great thinkers of the E world, 1433
Green, Jonathan D., 1280, 1297
Green, Jonathon, 89
Green, Kelly L., 1176
Green, Thomas E., 226
Greenaway, Theresa, 75
Greenfieldt, John, 81
Greenwald, Douglas, 179
Gregory, Hugh, 1339
Gregory, Ross, 518
Gribbin, John, 1820
Gribbin, Mary, 1820
Griffith, Susan, 273
Griffiths, W. Scott, 1536
Griscom, Richard, 1294
Grisewood, John, 1087
Grolier illus lib of the environment, 1860
Grolier lib of N American biogs, 27
Grolier student ency of endangered species, 1597
Grossman, Mark, 1869
Growing herbs, 1586
Grumet, Joanne, 1087
Guide bk of US coins, 1996, 49th ed, 1008
Guide to ...
    accredited camps, 1995/96, 39th ed, 811
    American crime films of the 40s & 50s, 1392
    American crime films of the 30s, 1393
    American studies resources, 1994, 338
    ancient Native American sites, 411
    bks on AIDS, 1719
    British naval papers in N America, 679
    British poetry explication, v.4, 1245
    Central American collections in the US, 152
    children's bks about Asian Americans, 1181
    collections on Paraguay in the US, 551
    fed funding for govts & nonprofits, 1995, Native American ed, 882
    fed funding for volunteer programs & community serv, 3d ed, 874
    flowering plant families, 1580
    free computer materials 1995, 13th ed, 1771
    funding for intl & foreign programs, 2d ed, 875
    greater Wash., DC grantmakers 1994-95, 876
    info at the UN, 770
    natl professional certification programs, 267

original sources for precolonial W Africa published in European langs, rev ed, 531
popular music ref bks, 1311
private fortunes, v.2, 188
private fortunes, v.3, 189
ref bks for small & medium-sized libs, 1984-94, 9
summer camps & summer schools 1995/96, 27th ed, 326
the aqueducts of ancient Rome, 1046
the birds of Mexico & N Central America, 1615
the Community initiatives 1994-99, 753
the Fonds d'Archives & collections in the holdings of the York Univ Archives, 653
the Sol Feinstone collection of the David Lib of the American Revolution, 654
tourist railroads & railroad museums, 4th ed, 1886
wildflowers in winter, 1584
Guidelines for bias-free writing, 968
Guidry, Josee G., 385
Guiley, Rosemary Ellen, 786, 967
Guinness ency of popular music, 2d ed, 1310
Gunter, Kahl, 1657
Gutman, Bill, 818
Guttenplan, Samuel, 1432
Guy, Jonelle, 1651, 1835
Gyeszly, Suzanne D., 141
Gypsies, 405

Habitats, 1598
Haggerty, Gary, 1311
Hahn, Harley, 1775
Haider, Thomas John, 322, 323
Hall, Cally, 69
Hall, G. S., 1581
Hall, James, 1031
Hall, L. Victoria, 872
Hall, Rob, 617
Hall, Susan, 1164
Halliwell's film gd 1995, 1385
Halvorson, Peter L., 1437
Hamada, Yoh-ichi, 1324
Hamel, April Vahle, 365
Hamilton, Neil A., 556
Hamito-Semitic etymological dict, 1107
Hammond road atlas America, 441
Hammond road atlas & vacation gd, 442
Hammond students atlas of the world, 448
Hammud, Zicky, 54
Hancock, Lee, 1688
Hand, Richard A., 1005
Handbook of ...
    Catholic theology [rev ed], 1475
    Christian Latin, 1115
    corrosion data, 1667
    food additives, 1533
    frogs & toads of the US & Canada, 3d ed, 1640
    inorganic compounds, 1794
    intl trade & dvlpmt stats 1993, 234
    lab health & safety, 2d ed, 1796
    literary research, 2d ed, 1142

    lizards, 1639
    mammals of the S-central states, 1630
    oil industry terms & phrases, 5th ed, 1676
    private schools 1995, 76th ed, 327
    salamanders, 1635
    the nations, 14th ed, 713
    therapeutic interventions, 1735
    thermal conductivity, v.1, 1821
    thermal conductivity, v.2, 1822
    thermal conductivity, v.3, 1823
    transport property data, 1824
Handbook to life in ancient Rome, 547
Handy, D. Antoinette, 1285
Hansen, Lucia, 649
Harbottle, Philip, 1234
Hardin, James, 1254
Harduf's transliterated English-Hebrew dict, 3d v., H-K, 1108
Hardy, Phil, 1306, 1379
Hare, Tony, 1598
Hargreaves, David, 235
HarperCollins ency of Catholicism, 1469
HarperCollins Russian dict: Russian-English, English-Russian, college ed, 1123
Harris, Laurie Lanzen, 25
Harris, Marjorie, 1568, 1569, 1570, 1571
Harrison, Maureen, 607, 608
Harrison, P. S., 1406
Harrison's reports & film reviews, 1406
Harrold, Ann, 635, 637
Hartel, Lynda Jones, 888
Haskins, Jim, 390
Hastings' dict of the Bible, 1454
Hastings, James, 1454
Hasty, Will, 1254
Hatch, Terry, 1545
Haubenstock, Susan H., 1041
Hauchler, Ingomar, 200
Havlice, Patricia Pate, 1056
Hawisher, Gail, 1058
Hawker, Sara, 1078
Hawkins, Stephen, 1789
Hawks, John, 371
Hawks, John K., 461
Hayashi, Tetsumaro, 1216
Haycock, Ken, 645
Hayes, Melissa, 336
Haynes, Douglas, 1439
Haynes, Theodora T., 255
Hayslip, Bert, Jr., 839
Hazewinkel, Michiel, 1827
Health & environment in America's top-rated cities, 931
Health & safety manager's A-Z gd to environmental mgmt, 1873
Hebrew & Aramaic lexicon of the O.T., v.1, 1455
Hecht, Cheryl S., 383
Heffernan, Eileen, 1464
Heggoy, Alf Andrew, 114
Heiberger, Mary Morris, 365
Held, Gilbert, 1772
Heller, Craig, 1298

Heller, Jules, 1026
Heller, Nancy G., 1026
Helterman, Jeffrey, 1230
Hemley, Ginette, 1599
Hempelman, Kathleen A., 592
Hemsworth, Brian, 815
Henderson, Andrew, 1589
Henderson, Helene, 1358
Hendrickson, Kenneth E., Jr., 718
Henkes, Robert, 1054
Henle, Klaus, 1634
Henning, Bill, 259
Henritze, Barbara K., 971
Henry, Laurie, 1185
Hentzi, Gary, 960
Herald, Cherry L., 1740
Herald, Diana Tixier, 1186
Herbote, Burkhard, 464, 465, 466
Herman Melville ency, 1212
Herndon, Constance, 951
Herubel, Jean-Pierre V. M., 330
Hess, Thom, 1119
Hewett, Jerry, 1218
Hicken, Mandy, 1187
Hicks, S. David, 1644
Hicks, Tyler G., 1644
Higby, Gregory, 1736
Hiking trails, E US, 825
Hilbert, Vi, 1119
Hile, Kevin S., 1172, 1173, 1174
Hill, Carolyn N., 646
Hill, Dennis S., 1625
Hill, Gerald N., 578
Hill, Jeremy D., 1625
Hill, Kathleen Thompson, 578
Hillard, James M., 1621
Hillier, Malcolm, 1544
Hine, Andrea, 1716
Hinkelman, Edward G., 297, 298
Hipp, James W., 515
Hippocrene concise Haitian Creole-English, English-Haitian Creole dict, 1106
Hippocrene practical Fulani-English dict, 1103
Hischak, Thomas S., 1416
Hispanic American biog, 407
Hispanic American genealogical sourcebk, 432
Hispanic 100, 408
Historical atlas of ...
   La., 440
   Mormonism, 1461
   NYC, 487
Historical dict of ...
   Algeria, 2d ed, 114
   ecumenical Christianity, 1473
   Egypt, 162
   European orgs, 139
   Germany, 546
   Guam & Micronesia, 168
   intl tribunals, 610
   Poland, 144
   Sweden, 150
   terrorism, 597
   the intl food agencies, 1529
   the Republic of Croatia, 549
   Uganda, 125
Historical dir of trade unions, v.4, 264
Historical 1st patents, 1509
Historical stats of black America, 403
History & annot bibliog of American religious pers & newspapers, 1447
History of ...
   humanity, v.1, 568
   pharmacy, 1736
   photography, v.2, 1019
Hobbs, Jack, 1545
Hodges, Harriet, 1051
Hoffman, Cheryl M., 1131
Hoffmann, David, 1714
Hoffmann, Frank, 1312, 1333
Hoffmann, Frank W., 1357
Hoffos, Signe, 1751
Hofstede, David, 1376
Hoftijzer, J., 1129
Hogan, Kathleen M., 8
Holberg, Andrea, 311
Holidays & festivals index, 1358
Holland, Stephen, 1234
Hollander, P. Scott, 787
Holley, E. Jens, 1442
Hollis, Daniel Webster, III, 964
Hollywood heroes, 1376
Hollywood novel, 1411
Hollywood song, 1275
Holsinger, M. Paul, 1165
Holston, Kim R., 1290
Homberger, Eric, 487
Home educ resource gd, 3d ed, 317
Home health gd to poisons & antidotes, 1727
Homuth, Donald, 1286
Hong, Julie, 1850
Hooray for heroes!, 321
Hooton, Joy, 1248
Hoover, Gary, 191
Hoover's co & industry database on CD-ROM [CD-ROM], 190
Hoover's gd to computer cos, 1773
Hoover's hndbk of American bus 1995, 191
Hoover's hndbk of world bus 1995-96, 3d ed, 201
Hoover's masterlist of America's top 2,500 employers, 192
Hopi pottery symbols, 1015
Hopkins, Bruce R., 579
Hopkins, Mariane S., 1355
Hordeski, Michael F., 1760
Horne, Alan, 1055
Horning, S. E., 253
Horror in silent films, 1391
Horse dict, 1555
Horton, Carrell Peterson, 403
Houdek, Frank G., 593
Houston, James E., 318, 629
Houze, Herbert, 1009

How to ...
  find co intelligence in state docs, 15th ed, 202
  find info about divisions, subsidiaries & products, 5th ed, 203
  find info about foreign firms, 6th ed, 204
  find info about private cos, 6th ed, 205
  locate anyone who is or has been in the military, rev ed, 688
Howard, Dale E., 831
Howarth, Sarah, 553
Howell, Steve N. G., 1615
Howes, Kelly King, 1155
Howland, Harris, 1572
Howlett, Colin, 1127
HR words you gotta know!, 258
Hsieh, Chiao-min, 452
Hsieh, Jean Kan, 452
Hubbell, John T., 495
Hubbs, Don, 317
Hudson, Alice, 487
Hudson's subscription newsletter dir, 12th ed, 978
Huellmantel, Michael B., 185
Huettner, Janet S., 884
Hulse, David Allen, 1121
Human environments, 1797
Human gene mapping 1994, 1656
Human rights on CD-ROM, 2d ed [CD-ROM], 609
Humm, Maggie, 948
Humorous quotations, 93
Humphrey, Paul, 499
Hunter, Brian, 102
Hunter, John, 1082
Hussey, Mark, 1221
Hussey, R., 210
Hutchison, Kevin Don, 563
Huttner, Harry J. M., 99
Hyam, R., 1563
Hyland, Pat, 519
Hyman, Robin, 94

Ibelgaufts, Horst, 1558
Illinois hist, 492
Illustrated computer dict for young people, 1763
Illustrated dict of ...
  dermatologic syndromes, 1728
  little-known words from literary classics, 1148
  sci, rev ed, 1497
  symbols in E & W art, 1031
Illustrated discography of surf music, 1961-65, 3d ed, 1332
Illustrated ency of Victoriana, 1016
Illustrated gd to the Bible, 1459
Illustrated survey of orchid genera, 1578
Illustrated who's who of Hollywood directors, v.1, 1367
Immigrant experience in American fiction, 1206
Imperial War Museum film catalog, v.1, 557
Importers manual USA, 1995-96 ed, 298
Index to ...
  docs of the Natl Security Council, 774
  histl fiction for children & young people, 1179
  how to do it info, 1994 suppl, 1014
  law school theses & dissertations, 570
  proceedings of the economic & social council, 771
  short & feature film reviews in the Moving Picture World, 1413
  the Roll of Honor, 434
India, rev ed, 131
Indian social & economic dvlpmt 1993, 243
Indigenous lit of Oceania, 1260
Indo-Australian Agaoninae (pollinators of figs), 1628
Indonesia, 134
Industrial Relations Center, University of Hawaii at Manoa, 257
Information please women's sourcebk, 1995, 951
Information sci abstracts, v.29, no.12, 619
Information sourcebk of herbal medicine, 1714
Information sources in urban & regional planning, 928
Ingram, Caroline, 460
Injury prevention for the elderly, 844
Innes, Brian, 1348
Innes, Clive, 1590
Insider's gd to law firms, 2d ed, 582
Institute for Biotechnology Information, 1733
Interinstitutional dir: European Union, 754
Interlibrary loan policies dir, 5th ed, 641
International advertising & mktg info sources, 299
International African Institute, 111
International biographical dict of computer pioneers, 1758
International Boundaries Research Unit, 455
International bus & trade dirs, 228
International dict of ...
  broadcasting & film, 984
  desserts, pastries, & confections, 1523
  historic places, v.1, 467
  historic places, v.2, 468
  historic places, v.3, 469
International dir of ...
  African studies research, 3d ed, 111
  co hists, v.9, 236
  co hists, v.10, 237
  co hists, v.11, 238
  govt 1995, 2d ed, 707
  Indonesianists, 2d ed, 133
  serials specialists, 655
International financial stats locator, 230
International histl stats: Africa, Asia, & Oceania, 1750-1988, 917
International hndbk on servs for the elderly, 851
International holidays, 1361
International intellectual property protection for computer software, 638
International multimedia yrbk 1995-96, 1751
International multimedia yrbk 1995-96 on CD-ROM [CD-ROM], 1752
International mycological dir, 3d ed, 1581
International research centers dir 1996-97, 8th ed, 55
International Rugby Information Centre, 830
International satellite dir, 1995, 10th ed, 1780
International trade fairs & conferences dir 1995, 19th ed, 300

International who's who in music & musicians dir, 14th ed, 1267
International wildlife trade, 1599
Internet: an introductory gd for UN orgs, 1783
Internet compendium: subject gds to health & sci resources, 1774
Internet compendium: subject gds to humanities resources, 100
Internet compendium: subject gds to social scis, bus, & law resources, 101
Internet yellow pages, 2d ed, 1775
Iraq, 2d ed, 135
Ireland, 481
Ireland: an ency for the bewildered, 142
Irish bed & breakfast bk, 482
Irish-American landmarks, 422
Isaacs, Ronald H., 1479
Isely, Duane, 1564
Israel & the Jewish world, 1948-93, 552
Israel & the W Bank & Gaza Strip, 2d ed, 163
ISS dir of overseas schools, 1994-95 ed, 372
Italy, 143

J. Sheridan Le Fanu, 1256
Jackson, Kenneth T., 36, 107
Jackson, Richard H., 1461
Jacobs, Timothy, 795
Jacobson, Ronald L., 987
Jacques Derrida (II), 956
Jakubiak, Joyce, 274
James A. Michener, 1213
James, David, 1020
James Madison & the American nation 1751-1836, 507
James, Peter D., 653
Jane's airports & handling agents, 1995-96, 1881
Janes, Joseph, 100, 101, 1774
Janes, Robert W., 656
Jane's world railways, 36th ed, 1887
Jankowski, Katherine, 262
Jankowski, Katherine E., 869
Japan dir of professional assns, 3d ed, 244
Japan: exploring your options, 373
Japanese hist & culture from ancient to modern times, 2d ed, 537
Japanese psycholinguistics, 1059
Jazz & blues lover's gd to the US, updated ed, 1321
Jazz discography, v.9, 1326
Jazz research & performance materials, 2d ed, 1327
Jefferson-Brown, Michael, 1572
Jenkins, Hugh, 1718
Jenkins, Mark, 1729
Jensen, Gregory C., 1622
Jerry Lewis films, 1397
Jerusalem Center for Public Affairs, staff of, 712
"Jewish question" in German-speaking countries, 1848-1914, 425
Jews & Europe, 424
JIST's electronic gd for occupational exploration [CD-ROM], 275
Job seeker's gd to socially responsible cos, 262

Jobs for people over 50, 276
Joel Whitburn presents Billboard's top 10 chart 1958-95, 1319
Joel Whitburn's pop hits 1940-54, 1313
Joel Whitburn's rock tracks, 1337
Joel Whitburn's top pop singles 1955-93, 1314
Joel Whitburn's top pop singles CD gd 1955-79, 1316
Joffe, George, 115
John Coltrane, 1324
John F. Kennedy, 491
John Holmes Library, staff of, 748
John Steinbeck, 1216
Johnen, M., 1894
Johnny Cash record catalog, 1317
Johns, Robert L., 404
Johnsen, Ferris, 62
Johnson, Curt, 959
Johnson, George M., 1235
Johnson, Hamish, 1240
Johnson, Jeffrey, 1277
Johnson, Richard S., 688, 837
Johnson, Robert V., 1722
Johnson, Salvatore, 820
Johnson, Steve, 1532
Johnson, Willis L., 891
Johnston, Phillip M., 999
Joint FAO/WHO Food Standards Programme Codex Alimentarius Commission, 1534, 1535
Jonathan Edwards, 1440
Jones, Alison, 1343
Jones, Clyde, 1630
Jones, David R., 146
Jones, Dolores Blythe, 661
Jones, Edward, 1214
Jones, Francine, 873
Jones, H. G., 493
Jones, J. Knox, Jr., 1630
Jongeling, K., 1129
Jordan, Barbara, 903
Joselit, David, 1041
Joseph Addison & Richard Steele, 1237
Judaica Americana, 1480

Kadupski, Charlie, 805
Kaganoff, Nathan M., 1480
Kalasky, Drew, 1196, 1265
Kaleidoscope: a multicultural bklst for grades K-8, 1182
Kanellos, Nicolas, 550
Kant dict, 1428
Kanter, Sanford, 719
Kaplan, Steven M., 782
Kapon, Uriel Macias, 424
Karlsten, Christopher M., 734
Karney, Robyn, 1371
Karp, Rashelle S., 173, 620
Karr, Ronald Dale, 1888
Katz, Bill, 85
Katz, Linda Sternberg, 85, 1263
Katz, William, 1263
Katzner, Kenneth, 1124

Kauppila, Jean L., 1366
Keay, John, 148
Keay, Julia, 148
Keegan, John, 681
Kehde, Ned, 78, 90
Keirstead, Richard S., 613
Keller, Michael, 970
Keller, Morton, 720
Kemper, Daniele Renee, 283
Kemper, Robert E., 283
Kennedy, Michael, 1270
Kennedy, Paul, 200
Kennett, Frances, 388
Kenny, Anthony, 1434
Kenny, Michael, 704
Kenny, Monica L., 1648
Kepos, Paula, 236, 237, 238
Kerchelich, Karen, 2
Kernfeld, Barry, 1328
Kerr, Susan D., 1672
Kerry, Carolle, 325
Kerry, Trevor, 325
Kess, Joseph F., 1059
Key dates in number theory hist, 1829
Key gd to electronic resources: agriculture, 1518
Key gd to electronic resources: engineering, 1643
Key gd to electronic resources: health scis, 1688
Key of it all, bk 2, 1121
Khakimov, Kamran M., 1141
Khorana, Meena, 1166
Kich, Martin, 1205
Kidd, Charles, 426
Kids' world almanac of football, 818
Kiefer, Marie, 671
Kienholz, Michelle L., 1709
Kikuchi, Mihoko, 1626
Kim, David U., 674
Kiner, Larry F., 1323
Kingfisher 1st ency of animals, 1608
Kingfisher illus children's dict, 1087
Kingfisher illus thesaurus, 1088
Kingfisher young world ency, 50
Kinnard, Roy, 1391
Kinnear, Karen L., 603, 618
Kipfer, Barbara Ann, 1092
Kipp, Rita Smith, 133
Kirsch, George B., 798
Kirshon, John W., 500
Kitromilides, Paschalis M., 130
Klaus, Kenneth S., 1299
Kleczek, Josip, 1645, 1646
Kleczkova, Helena, 1645, 1646
Klein, Barry T., 412
Klein, Bob, 1537
Klepper, Nancy, 462
Knapp, Brian, 1860
Knapp, Thomas R., 1732
Knell, Simon J., 82
Kneller, Marianna, 1573
Knight, Charles A., 1237

Kocurek, Dianna S., 1852
Kodansha's furigana Japanese-English dict, 1111
Kodansha's pocket kanji gd, 1112
Koehler, Ludwig, 1455
Koenig, Harold G., 840
Koff, Theodore H., 841
Kohn, George C., 1725
Korab, Balthazar, 1045
Korea [CD-ROM], 692
Korean War, 538
Korshel, Mohamud, 1134
Kosberg, Jordan I., 851
Kosek, Jane Kelly, 1265, 1490
Kostelanetz, Richard, 1268
Kovacs, Beatrice, 1684
Kovacs, Ruth, 875, 877, 878, 961
KR Info OnDisc grants database [CD-ROM], 848
Kramer, Jack, 1574
Krantz, Les, 10
Krausse, Gerald H., 134
Krausse, Sylvia Engelen, 134
Kreamer, Jean Thibodeaux, 994
Kress, Stephen W., 1560
Kricher, John, 1591
Krol, John, 1782
Krstovic, Jelena O., 1149, 1156
Kruger, Anna, 46
Krupin, Paul J., 1867
Krupin's toll-free environmental dir, 1867
Kuhn, Laura, 1271
Kuipers, Barbara J., 1177
Kuman, Arthur, Jr., 276
Kurdish-English/English-Kurdish dict, 1114
Kurth, Martin, 644
Kusick, James, 1715

La Boda, Sharon, 467, 468, 469
Labi, Esther, 77
Labor arbitration, 255
Laing, Dave, 1306
Laird, Ross, 1325
Lake, river, & sea-run fishes of Canada, 1624
Lamb, G. F., 1239
Lambert, David, 1815
Lampl, Richard, 1879
Lancaster, Roy, 1566
Landgraf, Mark J., 1891
Landmark docs in American hist [CD-ROM], 498
Lane, James M., 821
Lang, George, 689
Lang, Harry G., 857
Langenkamp, R. D., 1676
Langman, Larry, 1392, 1393
Langton, Mark, 815
Language of biotech, 2d ed, 1659
Language of Canadian pols, 752
Lanzerotti, Rachel, 336
Lapin, Lee, 775
Larkin, Colin, 1310

Larousse dict of ...
  British hist, 541
  N American hist, 508
  scientists, 1487
  20th century hist, 566
  world folklore, 1343
  writers, 1145
Larousse ency of wine, 1527
Larson, Randall D., 1394
Lasocki, David, 1294
Last, John M., 1698
Last, P. R., 1623
Last words: a dict of deathbed quotations, 95
Late 19th- & early 20th-century British literary biographers, 1225
Late medieval England (1377-1485), 542
Late-Victorian & Edwardian British novelist, 1st series, 1235
Late Victorian poetry 1880-99, 1246
Latham, A. J. H., 555
Lathrop, Norman M., 1014
Latin America on file, 155
Latin America petroleum dir, 1995, 14th ed, 1834
Latin American advertising, mktg, & media sourcebk, 301
Latitudes & attitudes, 915
Lauber, Timothy J., 223
Lauer-Bader, Michele, 903
Laurens, Jeannine, 549
Law, Jonathan, 1373
Lawal, Ibironke O., 1668
Lawmen & desperadoes, 571
Lawrance, Alan, 759
Lawrence, Christine C., 738
Layman, Richard, 515
Lazich, Robert S., 240
LC period subdivisions under names of places, 5th ed, 630
Lead poisoning prevention, 1866
Leal-Khouri, Susana, 1728
Leapman, Michael, 480
Learning about the Holocaust, 1170
Lee, J. A. N., 1758
Lee, Leonard, 1679
Lee, Min, 508, 541, 566
Leeds, Marc, 1219
Leeming, David Adams, 1444
Leeming, Margaret Adams, 1444
Leeuwenburgh, Todd, 708
Leeves, Juliet, 636
Legay, Gilbert, 413
Leifer, Michael, 747
Lein, Clayton D., 1232
Leitch, Jay A., 1600
Lenihan, Ayeliffe, 1681
Lent, Max, 1776
Leo Burnett worldwide advertising & media fact bk, 302
Leonard, Bill J., 1467
Leonard, David C., 1750
Leonard Maltin's movie ency, 1377
Leonard, Thomas M., 152

Lesh, Robert W., 126
Lesko, Matthew, 59, 60
Lesser, M. X., 1440
Letellier, Robert Ignatius, 1236
Leto, Joseph, 1644
Leventhal, F. M., 543
Levine, Carole, 1584
Levinson, David, 389, 835, 863, 1797
Levitt, Marcus C., 1261
Lewis, Amy, 48
Lewis, Cathleen S., 1647
Lewis, James R., 779, 1445
Lewis, Kenneth, 855
Lexicon of Tamil lit, 1255
Leyser, Brady J., 1315
L'Heureux, Conrad, 484
Liberia, 118
Librarian's gd to public records, special ed, 778
Libraries in the UK & Republic of Ireland 1995, 637
Library of Congress subject headings, 3d ed, 627
Library systems in Europe, 636
Liebeck, Helen, 1070
Lignor, Amy, 374
Lin, Alvin C., 874, 882
Linden, Tom, 1709
Lindfors, Bernth, 1247
Lindroth, Colette, 1208
Lindroth, James, 1208
Lindsay, William, 68
Linton, David, 972
Lione, Armand, 1712
Lippincott, Kristen, 1800
Lippy, Charles H., 1441
Lipton, Kathryn L., 1517
LISA plus [CD-ROM], 625
Literary gd & companion to N England, 1233
Literature & gerontology, 845
Literature criticism from 1400-1800, v.27, 1156
Literature of rock, 3, 1333
Little Oxford dict of quotations, 92
Little Oxford gd to English usage, 1076
Littlejohn, Alice C., 211
Lobbying, PACs, & campaign finance, 740
Local hist collections in libs, 659
Loescher, Ann Dull, 895
Loescher, Gil, 895
Lofman, Ron, 1274
Londre, Felicia Hardison, 1420
Long, James W., 1737
Long, John H., 438, 439
Long term care, 841
Longman biographical dir of decision-makers in Russia & the successor states, 145
Lonier, Terri, 263
Lopez, Donald S., 1882
Lord, John, 1787
Lord, Tom, 1326
Lovich, Jeffrey E., 1636
Lowenthal, Mark M., 716
Lucanio, Patrick, 1395
Ludwig, Herbert R., Jr., 1600

Lueck, Therese L., 950
Luis, William, 1258
Lundin, Anne H., 379
Lushootseed dict, 1119
Lux presents Hollywood, 1390
Lyman, Darryl, 1073
Lynn, Ruth Nadelman, 1167
Lyrics of the Trouveres, 1251

Mabunda, L. Mpho, 400, 401
MacDonald, Ron, 992
MacDonald-Haig, Caroline, 388
MacHale, Des, 93
Machinists' ready ref, 8th ed, 1675
Mackenzie, Leslie, 324, 374
MacNee, Marie J., 1193
Maddex, Robert L., 611
Maddox, George L., 850
Magazines for kids & teens, 86
Magazines for libs, 8th ed, 85
Magill, Frank N., 741, 836, 942, 949, 1853
Magill index to critical surveys, rev ed, 1161
Magill's medical gd, 1700
Magoulias, Michael, 1156, 1242
Mahadevan, Vijitha, 110
Mahatma Gandhi, 536
Mahler, Gregory, 751
Major cos of Europe 1994/5, 253
Major cos of the Far East & Australasia 1995/96, 245
Making of modern Africa: a gd to archives, 530
Makkai, Adam, 1083
Malawi, 2d ed, 119
Malinin, Eugene D., 246
Malinowski, Sharon, 416
Malkani, Sheila V., 582
Malkin, Gary Scott, 1759
Mallett, Daryl F., 1209, 1218
Mallory, Susan Bayliss, 1728
Maloni, Kelly, 813, 1781
Maltin, Leonard, 1377
Mamedov, Seville, 1097
Mammals of New Guinea, rev ed, 1631
Mammals of the SW Pacific & Moluccan Islands, 1632
Man, myth & magic, new ed, 1348
Managing the publishing process, 665
Mandel, Miriam B., 1211
Maney, Ardith, 216
Manger, Jason J., 1784
Mangrum II, Charles T., 341
Maniguet, Xavier, 812
Manual of ...
    climbers & wall plants, 1575
    grasses, 1583
    orchids, 1576
Manufacturing processes ref gd, 1670
Manzo, Bettina, 1424
Mapping Specialists, Ltd., 108
Mapping the territory, 658
Marantz, Kenneth A., 1183
Marantz, Sylvia S., 1183

Marching band hndbk, 2d ed, 1290
Margiotta, Franklin D., 682
Mark Twain A to Z, 1217
Market trends for selected chemical products 1985-90 & prospects to 1995, 303
Markoe, Arnold, 36
Markoe, Karen E., 36
Markowitz, Harvey, 417
Marley, David F., 1344
Marre, Louis A., 1889
Marriage, family, & relationships, 862
Marsh, Arthur, 264
Marshall Cavendish ency of health, rev ed, 1682
Marshall, Gordon, 834
Martello, Mary Ann, 60
Marti, James, 1716
Martin, Fenton S., 715
Martin, Richard, 1017
Martin, Samuel E., 1113
Martin, Susan Boyles, 177
Martindale-Hubbell dispute resolution dir, 583
Martindale-Hubbell law dir on CD-ROM [CD-ROM], 584
Martinez, Joseph G. R., 1245
Martinez, Nancy C., 1245
Martinique, 171
Martin's concise Japanese dict, 1113
Marzollo, Jean, 28
Mast, Jennifer Arnold, 196
Masterplots II: women's lit series, 949
Masterworks of man & nature, 2d ed, 458
Materials properties handbk: titanium alloys, 1669
Mathematical scis professional dir 1995, 1828
Matthews, Caitlin, 788
Matthews, John, 788
Mattison, Chris, 1637
Matz, David, 41
Maxwell, Bruce, 1785, 1786
Mayo Clinic complete bk of pregnancy & baby's 1st yr, 1722
McBrien, Richard P., 1469
McBurney, Melissa, 1643
McCall, Mary Reilly, 1496
McCauley, Martin, 145
McClellan, Gail, 1384
McCloud, Barry, 1320
McClure, Paul, 734
McCroskey, Marilyn, 631
McCulloch, Alan, 1032
McCulloch, Susan, 1032
McElmeel, Sharron L., 1184
McEwan, Peter J. M., 1025
McGaughey, Ryan T., 963
McGillivray, Alice V., 735
McGrath, Anne F., 1004
McGrath, Kimberley A., 1492
McGraw-Hill ency of economics, 179
McGraw-Hill ency of quality terms & concepts, 284
McGraw-Hill illus dict of personal computers, 4th ed, 1760

McGraw-Hill illus ency of robotics & artificial intelligence, 1753
McGreal, Ian P., 1433
McKeever, Susan, 64
McKenzie, Diane, 898
McKernan, Luke, 1399
McKinsey, C. Dennis, 1456
McKissack, Frederick, 1488, 1489
McKissack, Patricia, 1488, 1489
McKnew & Parker's buyer's gd to sportfishing boats, 1995 ed, 810
McKnew, Ed, 810
McLaughlin, Ben, 877
McLeod, Denise, 883
McMenemy, John, 752
McMurray, Emily J., 1490
McPherson, James M., 486
McQuiston, Judith L., 651
Meadows, Eddie S., 1327
Meath-Lang, Bonnie, 857
Mechanical engineer's ref bk, 12th ed, 1673
Medal of honor recipients 1863-1994, 689
Mehta, Mukesh, 1739
Mellersh, H. E. L., 559, 564
Meltzer, Ellen, 503
Meltzer, Tom, 358
Mercatante, Anthony S., 1350
Merriam-Webster's biographical dict, 29
Merriam-Webster's collegiate dict deluxe, electronic ed [CD-ROM], 1066
Merriam-Webster's dict of basic English, 1067
Merriam-Webster's ency of lit, 1146
Merriam-Webster's gd to punctuation & style, 969
Merriam-Webster's medical dict, 1701
Merskey, Harold, 1723
Mertvago, Peter, 1125
Metalworking in Africa S of the Sahara, 1668
Metaphors dict, 1091
Mexican pol biogs, 1935-93, 3d ed, 763
Mexican-American War of 1846-48, 657
Mexico co hndbk, 1995/96 ed, 254
Meyer, Carol J., 673
Meyer, Sandra, 1844
Meyers, Ric, 1380
Meyers, Robert A., 1561
Micheli, Lyle J., 1729
Micronesian religion & lore, 1439
Middle & jr high school lib catalog, 7th ed, 650
Middle East, 8th ed, 764
Middle East & N Africa 1995, 160
Middle East & N Africa on file, 459
Middle East military balance 1993-94, 695
Mieder, Wolfgang, 760, 1215
Miermont, Jacques, 1718
Migration stats 1994, 907
Mihailovich, Vasa D., 1262
Miletich, John J., 1724
Military ency of Russia & Eurasia, v.5, 146
Miller, Blair, 1378
Miller, E. Willard, 239
Miller, Jay, 414

Miller, Mark A., 1396
Miller, R. H., 1142
Miller, Ruby M., 239
Mills, Carlotta, 875, 878, 961
Mills, J. J., 169
Mills, Joyce H., 1460
Mills, Watson E., 1460
Milton, Leanne Wiberg, 1804
Milton's sonnets, 1214
Minakir, Pavel A., 247
Mineral investment conditions in selected countries of the Asia-Pacific region, 1842
Minerals industry taxation policies for Asia & the Pacific, 1843
Minter, D. W., 1581
Mitchell, B. R., 917
Mitchell, Jerome, 1230
Mitchell, Mary T., 733
Mitchell, Susan, 908
Miyamoto, Tadao, 1059
MLA intl bibliog [CD-ROM], 1143
Modern America 1914-45, 518
Modern black writers: suppl, 1157
Modern dict for the legal profession, 1994 suppl, 580
Modern harpsichord music, 1288
Modern Latin-American fiction writers, 2d series, 1258
Molecular biology & biotech, 1561
Moll, Verna Penn, 172
Moller, Bjorn, 683
Molloy, Les, 1601
Monash biographical dict of 20th century Australia, 39
Mood, Terry Ann, 377
Moody, Joan, 1871
Moore, Jean M., 658
Moore, Robert J., 1696
Moran, Andrea, 1503
More bks kids will sit still for, 663
More kids' favorite bks, 1168
Morelock, J. D., 698
Morgan, Bill, 1210
Morgan, Kathleen O'Leary, 602
Morgan, Scott, 602
Morin, Isobel V., 943
Morocco, rev ed, 120
Morozov, Vladimir, 40
Morris, Betty J., 651
Morris, Deirdre, 39
Morris, Leslie R., 641
Morris, Percy A., 1595
Morriss, Roger, 679
Morrow, Ed, 30
Mortensen, Sandra, 1249
Morton, Leslie T., 1696
Morwood, James, 1117
Moss, Joyce, 509
Mossman, Jennifer, 3
Mound, Laurence, 71
Mountain bikers almanac, 1996, 815
Mudd, Mollie B., 193
Muir, Hazel, 1487

Multilateral treaties deposited with the secretary-general, 612
Multilevel design, 99
Multimedia tech from A-Z, 1750
Multinational corps & the environment, 1851
Municipal executive dir, 728
Munro, Pamela, 1099
Munro-Hay, Stuart, 117
Murph, Roxane C., 1190
Murphy, C. Edward, 849
Murphy, Jennifer L., 245
Music & poetry in the Middle Ages, 1296
Music, dance & theater scholarships, 1365
My 1st bk of biogs, 28
My 1st sci dict, 1498
Myers, Jane E., 843
Myxomycetes: a hndbk of slime molds, 1587

Nagel, Rob, 407
Nagy, Andrea, 1705
Nakamura, Joyce, 1178
National accounts studies of the ESCWA region, 158
National Audubon Society bird garden, 1560
National dir of ...
    addresses & telephone nos, 1995 ed, 56
    newspaper op-ed pages, 979
    nonprofit orgs 1995, 193
    state bus licensing & regulation, 194
National gd to ...
    funding for the environment & animal welfare, 2d ed, 878
    funding for women & girls, 952
    funding in aging, 4th ed, 849
    funding in arts & culture, 3d ed, 961
    funding in substance abuse, 896
National Planning for Special Collections Committee, 661
National profile of community colleges 1995-96, 366
National seashores, rev ed, 475
Native American genealogical sourcebk, 433
Native American painters of the 20th century, 1054
Native N American chronology, 415
Native N American lit, 1259
Natividad, Irene, 392
Natural gas stats sourcebk, 2d ed, 1844
Naturopathic hndbk of herbal formulas, 3d ed, 1717
Nautical almanac for the year 1996, 1895
Naval Institute gd to world military aviation 1995, 697
Naval Institute histl atlas of the US Navy, 701
Navia, Luis E., 1425
Naylor, Phillip Chiviges, 114
NCAA football, 819
Neal, Valerie, 1647
Nebraska hist, 494
Negotiation lit, 283
Nehmer, Kathleen S., 322
Nehmer, Kathleen Suttles, 1771
Neibaur, James L., 1397
Nelson, Garrison, 733
Net games, 813

Net gd, 1781
Nettl, Paul, 1281
Network Development and MARC Standards Office, 634
Network Pr dict of networking, 1761
Nevis, Joel A., 1060
New A to Z of women's health, 3d ed, 1680
New acronyms, initialisms, & abbrevs, v.2, 3
New Bible commentary, 1458
New dict of Catholic social thought, 1470
New ency of Zionism & Israel, 164
New fortunes 1994, 176
New Grolier ency of WW II, 684
New Grove dict of jazz, 1328
New Hampshire [&] Vt.: atlas of histl county boundaries, 439
New intl atlas, 25th ed, 449
New men's studies, 2d ed, 866
New mktg opportunities, 4th ed, 1482
New Oxford companion to lit in French, 1252
New research centers, 1996, 339
New York Public Lib sci desk ref, 1512
New Zealand bks in print 1995, 23d ed, 23
Newman, Barry M., 285
Newman, Marketa, 1023
Newman, William M., 1437
News media yellow bk, 963
Newspapers online, 1995, 3d ed, 982
Newton, David E., 1874
Ng, Franklin, 394
Nierenberg, William A., 1856
Niles, Ann, 80
Nineteenth- & 20th-century harpists, 1287
Nineteenth-Century British literary biographers, 1226
Nineteenth-century lit criticism, v.46, 1158
Noble, William, 965
Nogowski, John, 1334
Noll, Richard, 780
Nonprofit law dict, 579
Nordin, Jorund B., 639, 640
Nordquist, Joan, 833, 935, 936, 937, 956, 957, 1851
Normandy [CD-ROM], 693
North American factbk, 1994-95, 1541
North American women artists of the 20th century, 1026
North Atlantic Treaty Org, 773
North Carolina hist, 493
Northern Ireland: a pol dir 1968-93, 761
Norton, Mary Beth, 554
Norwegian dict, 2d ed, 1120
Notable Asian Americans, 396
Notable corporate chronologies, 177
Notable Latin American women, 938
Notable Native Americans, 416
Notable 20th-century pianists, 1293
Notable 20th-century scientists, 1490
Novalis gd to Canadian shrines, 1476
Novas, Himilce, 408
Novel openers, 1188
Novum Testamentum, v.36a, 1460
Now read on: a gd to contemporary popular fiction, 2d ed, 1187
Nowak, Ronald M., 1610

NPD Group, Inc., 673
NTC's dict of ...
   American English pronunciation, 1077
   common mistakes in Spanish, 1137
   quotations, 94
NTC's hndbk for writers, 970
NTC's thesaurus of everyday American English, 1093
Nunez, Benjamin, 532
Nutribase nutrition facts desk ref, 1540
Nutt, Timothy G., 490
Nyeko, Balam, 123

O'Brien, George, 1257
O'Brien, Jacqueline Wasserman, 923
Ochoa, George, 1374
Ocko, Stephanie, 473
Office for Subject Cataloging Policy, 630
Official ABMS dir of board certified medical specialists 1996, 1704
Official athletic college gd: baseball, 1995 ed, 805
Official celebrity registry 1994-95, 796
Official gd to the American marketplace, 2d ed, 911
Official gd to the generations, 908
Official jl of the European Communities, v.38, English ed, 755
Official US Open almanac, 820
Ogden, Scott, 1546
O'Hara, Scarlett, 69
Oil & gas journal data bk, 1995 ed, 1845
Okuda, Ted, 1397
Old & Middle English lit, 1230
Old farmer's almanac 1995, 4
Old West: day by day, 502
O'Leary, Mick, 1777
Olitzky, Kerry M., 1479
Olsen, Wallace C., 1522
Olson, Annette, 868
Oman, rev ed, 166
On tap, 1995 ed, 1532
On the trail of the buffalo soldier, 699
One hundred & one botanists, 1564
100 athletes who shaped sports hist, 795
100 great Africans, 112
100 great cities of world hist, 927
100 greatest athletes of all time, 797
100 men who shaped world hist, 33
100 natural wonders of the world, 1602
100 women who shaped world hist, 32
1001 free goodies & cheapies, 60
O'Neill, Angus, 1002
O'Neill, Cynthia, 1503
O'Neill, Mary, 1100
On-line job search companion, 272
ONLINE 100, 1777
Opera cos & houses of the US, 1302
Operation Desert Shield/Desert Storm, 563
Oppenheim, Joanne, 1010
Oppenheim, Stephanie, 1010
Opportunities for vocational study, 385
Orchids for the South, 1574

Ord, Alan J., 1295
Orel, Vladimir E., 1107
Organ lit, 3d ed, 1289
Organic gardener's home ref, 1543
Organization for Economic Cooperation and Development, 918
Organized crime, 594
Orzepowski, Lisa G., 12
Osborne, Charles, 1300
Osborne, Robert, 1372
Osgood, Nancy J., 897
OSHA field inspection ref manual, 277
Our Sunday Visitor's Catholic ency & Catholic dict [CD-ROM], 1471
Our Sunday Visitor's ency of Catholic hist, 1472
Out Magazine, editors of, 53
Ovando, Natascha M. L., 882
Overlook film ency: horror, 1379
Overseas summer jobs 1995, 26th ed, 278
Oxford children's bk of famous people, 31
Oxford companion to ...
   Australian lit, 2d ed, 1248
   English lit, rev ed, 1231
   wine, 1528
   women's writing in the US, 1200
Oxford desk dict, American ed, 1068
Oxford desk thesaurus, American ed, 1094
Oxford dict of English grammar, 1080
Oxford dict of music, 1270
Oxford ency of the modern Islamic world, 1477
Oxford encyclopedic English dict, 2d ed, 1069
Oxford English minidict, 4th ed, 1070
Oxford hist of W philosophy, 1434
Oxford Latin minidict, 1117
Oxford medical companion, 1702
Oxford minireference dict & thesaurus, 1078
Oxford paperback French dict & grammar, 1101
Oxford Russian minidict, 1126
Oxford-Duden pictorial English dict, 2d ed, 1096
Oxford-Duden pictorial Hungarian-English dict, 1109
Oxford-Duden pictorial Italian & English dict, 1110
Oxford-Duden pictorial Thai & English dict, 1140
Oxford-Hachette French dict, 1100
Ozone dilemma, 1874

Pacific coast crabs & shrimps, 1622
Pacific War atlas 1941-45, 676
Packard, Robert T., 1045
Padgett, G. K. Boyle, 1712
Paietta, Ann C., 1366
Painter's hndbk, 1053
Palma, Robert J. Sr., 1795
Palmatier, Robert A., 1074
Palmer, Bill, 1380
Palmer, Karen, 1380
Panero, Julius, 1048
Panic, M., 232
Pankhurst, R., 1563
Pankhurst, Richard, 117
Pare, Michael A., 415

Parenting, 903
Parent's gd to the best children's videos & where to find them, 1386
Parents' resource almanac, 901
Parham, Iris A., 897
Parish, James Robert, 1407
Parker, Derek, 783
Parker, Julia, 783
Parker, Mark, 810
Parker, Sybil P., 456
Parkers' complete bk of dreams, 783
Pasahow, Edward, 1653
Pascoe, Robin, 476
Patents handbk, 589
Patoureau, Michel, 1448
Patt, Carol A., 629
Patterson, Alex, 1015
Patterson, Anna Grace, 11
Patty's industrial hygiene & toxicology, v.3, pt.B, 3d ed, 1875
Paul, Ellen, 860
Paul, Kevin, 320
PC Globe maps'n'facts [CD-ROM], 450
PC user's essential accessible pocket dict, 1756
PDR generics, 1738
PDR gd to drug interactions, side effects, indications, 1995, 49th ed, 1739
Peabody, Virginia S., 285
Pearlman, Mickey, 380
Pearsall, Judy, 1069
Pease, David A., 1541
Pederson, Jay P., 397
Peltier, Leslie C., 1801
Penguins of the world, 1616
Penzler, Otto, 1189
Peonies, 1577
Perez, Cristelia, 550
Performers, 419
Performing artists, 1363
Perkins, Edwin C., Jr., 1762
Perry, Dale L., 1794
Perry, Tim, 481
Person, James E., Jr., 1156
Personal computer dict, 1764
Peter Maxwell Davies, 1282
Peters, Pam, 1090
Peters, Thomas A., 644
Peterson 1st gd to forests, 1591
Peterson, Marilyn B., 604
Peterson's choose a Christian college, 4th ed, 1474
Peterson's colleges with programs for students with learning disabilities, 341
Peterson's contract servs for higher educ, 342
Peterson's gd to ...
    colleges in the Midwest 1995, 11th ed, 343
    colleges in the South 1995, 10th ed, 344
    colleges in the West 1995, 9th ed, 345
    grad & professional programs 1995, 29th ed, 349
    grad programs in bus, educ, health, & law 1995, 29th ed, 350
    grad programs in engineering & applied scis 1995, 29th ed, 351
    grad programs in the biological & agricultural scis 1995, 29th ed, 352
    grad programs in the humanities, arts, & social scis 1995, 29th ed, 353
    grad programs in the physical scis & mathematics 1995, 29th ed, 354
    MBA programs, 355
    middle Atlantic colleges 1995, 11th ed, 346
    New England colleges 1995, 11th ed, 347
    NY colleges 1995, 11th ed, 348
    nursing programs, 356
Peterson's job opportunities in ...
    bus 1995, 280
    engineering & tech 1995, 1513
    health care 1995, 1689
    the environment 1995, 1876
Peterson's professional degree programs in the visual & performing arts 1995, 962
Peterson's summer study abroad, 367
Petterchak, Janice A., 492
Pettit, George R., 1740
PGA tour, 1995, 822
Philanthropic studies index, 1995 cum index, 884
Philippsborn, H. E., 1494
Phillippe, Kent A., 366
Phillips, Charles, 705
Phillips, Colin, 976
Phillips, Faye, 659
Phillips, Robert W., 1408
Phillips, Sidney L., 1794
Philosopher's index [CD-ROM], 1436
Philosopher's phone bk, 1995, 1430
Philosophy of Cynicism, 1425
Photographic gd to the shorebirds of the world, 1617
Physical properties of hydrocarbons & other chemicals, v.4, 1793
Physicians' desk ref for nonprescription drugs, 1994, 15th ed, 1741
Piano music for 1 hand, 1292
Pickford, Nigel, 1896
Pierce, Connie, 1390
Pierce, David, 362
Pierson, Fiona Hogan, 1740
Piland, Sherry, 1021
Pilarski, Michael, 1542
Pilgrimage to Santiago de Compostela, 1462
Pinkepank, Jerry A., 1889
Pirates!, 1345
Pirates & privateers of the Americas, 1344
Pirates & seafaring swashbucklers on the Hollywood screen, 1407
Pirouet, M. Louise, 125
Plain English gd, 1075
Plant explorer's gd to New England, 474
Plants & their names, 1563
Playground industry ref dir 1995, 800
Pleasant, Barbara, 1547
Pocket Oxford Greek dict, 1105
Pocket Oxford Russian dict, 2d ed, 1127

Pockets: ancient Egypt, 63
Pockets: ancient Rome, 64
Pockets: birds, 65
Pockets: bldgs, 66
Pockets: cats, 67
Pockets: dinosaurs, 68
Pockets: Earth facts, 69
Pockets: horses, 70
Pockets: insects, 71
Pockets: inventions, 72
Pockets: rocks & minerals, 73
Pockets: space facts, 74
Pockets: trees, 75
Pockets: weather facts, 76
Pockets: world atlas, 77
Poe, Marshall, 147
Poetry criticism, v.10, 1265
Poetry dict, 1264
Policies for publishers, 1995 ed, 674
Political companion to American film, 1409
Political leaders & peacemakers, 418
Political leaders of contemporary W Europe, 756
Political parties of E Europe, Russia, & the successor states, 2d ed, 757
Political parties of the Middle East & N Africa, 765
Political prisoners & trials, 605
Pollard, Elaine, 1070
Pollock, Sean R., 914
Pope, Joyce, 1806
Popular bands & performers, 1304
Popular religious mags of the US, 1441
Population & dvlpmt: dir of non-govtl orgs in OECD countries, 909
Portable Baker's biog dict of musicians, 1268
Porter, Darwin, 483
Porter, David L., 792, 793
Porter, J. R., 1459
Porter, Lewis, 1324
Portnoi, Paul, 1881
Portraits in conservation: E & S Africa, 1596
Posadskov, Eugene L., 246
Postic, Lionel J., 281
Post-release assistance programs for prisoners, 2d ed, 600
Potparic, O., 1726
Powell, Allan Kent, 511
Power industry abbreviator, 1672
Power media selects, 9th ed, 988
Powers, Bethel Ann, 1732
Precious Moments children's Bible dict, 1451
Prehistoria [CD-ROM], 1816
Preimesberger, Jon, 731
Presidential elections in the US, 742
Presidential libs & museums, 519
Price, Anne, 650
Prices of agricultural products & selected inputs for Europe & N America 1992/93, 1520
Pricing stats sourcebk, 1846
Pride, John, 1137
Prince, Danforth, 483
Princeton Review student access gd: the big bk of colleges, 357

Princeton Review student access gd to ...
    the best 309 colleges, 358
    the best law schools, 585
    the best medical schools, 1705
Pring, J. T., 1105
Prisma, Bokforlaget, 1138
Prisma's abridged English-Swedish & Swedish-English dict, 1138
Private libs in Renaissance England, v.3: PLRE 67-86, 1006
Procter, Paul, 1063
Professional hndbk of diagnostic tests, 1710
Professional secretary's hndbk, 3d ed, 312
Profiles in American hist, 509
Profiles in gerontology, 846
Profiles of ...
    America, S region, v.4: Ky. * N.C. * Tenn., 910
    US hospitals 1995, [4th ed], 1690
    worldwide govt leaders 1995, 708
Programs & centers in comparative & intl educ, rev ed, 370
Provence & the Cote D'Azur, 477
Proverbial Eugene O'Neill, 1215
Proverbial Winston S. Churchill, 760
Pruning of trees, shrubs, & conifers, [rev ed], 1588
Prytherch, Ray, 1187
Psychology of aging, 839
Publication Systems Department, 20
Publishing market ref plus 1994-95, 2d ed [CD-ROM], 672
Puckett, Barry, 1358
Puro, George, 828
Pybus, Victoria, 460

Quantum cos, 195
Quastler, I. E., 1880
Quennell, Peter, 1240
Quick ref to ERISA compliance, 285
Quien es quien: a who's who of Spanish-speaking librarians in the US 1994, 4th ed, 621
Quinn, David, 1613
Quinn-Musgrove, Sandra L., 719
Quitno, Neal, 602

R. R. Bowker Bibliographic Group, 20
Rabkin, Sarah, 1498
Racer's ency of metals, fibers & materials, 1883
Rachel Crothers, 1208
Radicalism hndbk, 766
Radicalism in Minn. 1900-60, 767
Radio amateur callbook, 1995, 73d ed, 990
Radloff, Lisa, 140
Rail lines of S New England, 1888
Rajadhyaksha, Ashish, 1381
Rajewski, Brian, 710
Rake, Alan, 112
Rakipov, Nazib G., 1516
Ramsay, Craig, 1691
Randall, Richard C., 206

Randall's practical gd to ISO 9000, 206
Randol mining dir 1994/95, 1836
Rankin, Nigel, 1127
Rape in America, 617
Rapp, Barbara A., 1658
Rasch, D., 1557
Rasmussen, R. Kent, 1217
Ratcliffe, Susan, 92
Rating gd to life in America's 50 states, 924
Ratjar, Steve, 825
Raulston, J. C., 1592
Ray, Robert H., 1238
Reader's Digest atlas of Canada, 451
Reading Hemingway, 1211
Ready ref: American Indians, 417
Real Goods solar living sourcebk, 8th ed, 1847
Real Goods, staff of, 1847
Real life dict of the law, 578
Reams, Bernard D., Jr., 717
Reamy, Martha, 434
Reamy, William, 434
Reaney, P. H., 427
REA's authoritative gd to law schools, rev ed, 586
REA's authoritative gd to medical & dental schools, 1706
Recommended ref bks for small & medium-sized libs & media centers 1995, 11
Recorder: a gd to writings about the instrument, 1294
Redden, Kenneth R., 580
Reddy, Marlita A., 240, 420, 921
Reed, Gretchen, 299
Reel list, 1400
Rees, Alan M., 1711
Rees, Nigel, 1084
Reference and Adult Services Division of the American Library Association, 648
Reference & info servs, 2d ed, 647
Reference assessment manual, 648
Reference bks bulletin 1993-94, 12
Reference ency: India 2001, 132
Reference ency of the American Indian, 7th ed, 412
Reference gd to US military hist: 1945 to the present, 520
Refining stats sourcebk, 1849
Reich, Warren Thomas, 1429
Reid, Daniel G, 1466
Reid, Rob, 1278
Reilly, Catherine W., 1246
Reilly, Pauline, 1616
Reiser, Katie, 873
Religion & the American experience, the 20th century, 1442
Religious educ, 1960-93, 1463
Remarkable lives of ...
 100 women artists, 939
 100 women healers & scientists, 940
 100 women writers & journalists, 941
Renewable energy sources stats 1989-91, 1848
Renstrom, Peter G., 606
Reports required by Congress, 1995, v.2, no.1, 746

Reproductive effects of chemical, physical, & biological agents REPROTOX, 1712
Research & professional resources in children's lit, 1169
Research centers dir 1996, 20th ed, 340
Research on religion & aging, 840
Resource gd for the disabled, 854
Resources & refs: hazardous waste & hazardous materials mgmt, 1852
Restaurant lover's companion, 1526
Restoration forestry, 1542
Reuss, Jerry, 1316
Revenue stats of OECD member countries 1965-93, 772
Review of maritime transport 1993, 1897
Rhine, C. D., 1213
Rhodes, Christine P., 1525
Rich, Elizabeth H., 871
Richard Baker's companion to music, 1269
Rife, John C., 842
Riggle, Judith, 1180
Riley, Sam G., 973
Ring, Trudy, 467, 468, 469
Ritchie, David, 789
Robb, H. Amanda, 437
Robbins, Manuel, 1812
Robert Benchley, 1207
Roberts' dict of industrial relations, 4th ed, 257
Roberts, F. X., 1213
Roberts, George V., Jr., 817
Roberts, Harold S., 257
Roberts, Patricia L., 328
Robertson, D. Ross, 1633
Robinson, Diane, 1034
Robinson, Jancis, 1528
Rock stars/pop stars, 1315
Rocket man: the ency of Elton John, 1331
Roes, Nicholas A., 359
Rogers, Allan, 1577
Rogers, Helen, 642
Roget's 2: the new thesaurus, 3d ed, 1095
Rogozinski, Jan, 1345
Rolka, Gail Meyer, 32
Romaine-Davis, Ada, 1681
Romeiser, John B., 1253
Ronan, Colin A., 1802
Rood, Karen L., 1201
Rooney, Terrie M., 1362
Roosens, Laurent, 1019
Rosair, David, 1617
Rosaler, Robert C., 1677
Roscoe, Lorraine, 321
Rose, Sharon, 221, 407
Rosenberg, Jerry M., 304, 305
Rosenblum, Joseph, 664
Rosenfeld, Louis, 100, 101, 1774
Rosenthal, Joel T., 542
Ross, Carl, 767
Ross, Marilyn, 979
Ross register of Siberian industry 1995, 246
Ross, Robert E., 246
Rossi, John V., 1638
Rossi, Roxanne, 1638

Rossman, Amy Y., 1593
Rossol, Monona, 1042
Roth, John K., 1198
Rothschild, D. Aviva, 1359
Rountree, Bob, 1713
Routledge French technical dict, 1499
Rovin, Jeff, 1360
Rowlinson, William, 1101
Roy Rogers, 1408
Rubel, David, 521
Rubin, Janet E., 1170
Rubin, Stephen Jay, 1382
Rudolph, Joseph R., Jr., 1833
Ruffin, Albert, 723
Ruffin, C. Bernard, 95
Rugby catalogue of info sources, 830
Ruhling, Nancy, 1016
Ruja, Harry, 1423
Rules of thumb for chemical engineers, 1650
Rummel, Erika, 1250
Rundell, Michael, 814
Russel, Randall P., 1719
Russell, Cheryl, 911
Russell, Paul, 865
Russey, William, 1789
Russian far east: an economic hndbk, 247
Russian Revolution, 1905-21, 548
Rutland, Robert A., 507
Rutten, Peter, 1781
Ryan, Patrick J., 594
Ryan, Tracey A., 721, 722, 724, 725, 726, 727, 728, 729
Ryan, Victoria, 264
Rybacki, James J., 1737

Saari, Peggy, 454
Sacred celebrations: a Jewish holiday hndbk, 1479
Sacred dramas of J. S. Bach, 1284
Sader, Marion, 48
Sakelliou-Schultz, Liana, 1222
Salem Press, editors of, 1700
Salkin, Robert M., 467, 468, 469
Salmon, Richard D., 276
Salu, Luc, 1019
Sampson, Henry T., 1410
Sandler, Stanley, 538
Sanford, George, 144
Sao Tome & Principe, 121
Sapp, Gregg, 660
Saretsky, Cecile L., 651
Sasa, Manabu, 1626
Sasson, Jack M., 159
Sattler, Richard A., 414
Sawers, Robin, 1104
Sawinski, Diane M., 224
Saxe, Stephen O., 666
Scalzo, Richard, 1717
Scammon, Richard M., 735
Schaeffer, John, 1847
Schell, Terri Kessler, 996

Schirmer pronouncing pocket manual of musical terms, 5th ed, 1271
Schlachter, Gail Ann, 690, 858, 879, 880
Schlager, Neil, 221, 1511
Schlessinger, Bernard A., 173
Schmidt, Karl J., 534
Schmittroth, Linda, 953, 1496
Schmitz, Cecilia M., 1721
Schobinger, Juan, 386
Scholars' gd to Wash., D.C., for peace & intl security studies, 656
Scholastic ency of the presidents & their times, 521
School lib media annual 1995, v.13, 651
Schraff, Anne, 944
Schubert, Frank N., 699
Schuh, Randall T., 1627
Schuhmacher, Stephen, 1483
Schultz, Jon S., 638
Schupp, Jonathan F., 1868
Schwartz, Jacob, 790
Schwartz, Marilyn, 968
Schwiebert, Valerie L., 843
Schwing, Ned, 1009
Scialli, Anthony R., 1712
Science dict, 1501
Science fiction, fantasy, & horror writers, 1193
Science fiction: the illus ency, 1192
Science navigator [CD-ROM], 1500
Science, tech, & society in the Third World, 138
Scientific & common names of 7,000 vascular plants in the US, 1593
Scientific & technical bks & serials in print 1995, 22d ed, 1484
Scobbie, Irene, 150
Scrambled word & anagram finder, 1072
Searching the law: the states, 2d ed, 569
Seaton, Janet, 540
Secrest, William B., 571
Seeds in the wilderness: profiles of world religious leaders, 1443
Selby, David, 1892
Senior PGA tour, 1995, 823
Serafin, Steven, 1225, 1226, 1227
Serafin, Steven R., 1157
Servaty, Heather L., 839
Services: stats on intl transactions 1970/92, 918
Severson, Molly, 1363
Sex & age distribution of world populations: 1994 revision, 912
Sex & love quotations, 889
Sexual harassment, 888
Shakespeare cos & festivals, 1420
Shakespeare dict, 1241
Shakespeare quotations, 1239
Shakespearean criticism, v.26, 1242
Shakhmayev, Sergey, 1139
Sharks & rays of Australia, 1623
Sharp, John, 1742
Shaw, Caroline S., 121
Shaw, Eva, 791
Shaw, Michael, 1710

Sheehan, Marion, 1578
Sheehan, Tom, 1578
Sheets, Anna, 387
Shelton, James H., 8
Shepard, Thomas H., 1720
Sherrow, Victoria, 418
Sherry, Clifford J., 1435
Shields, Graham J., 149
Shinoda, Gretchen, 423
Shippey, Karla C., 241
Shirk, Martha, 462
Shlyakhov, Vladimir, 1128
Short, Kathy G., 1169
Short story criticism, v.17, 1196
Short-title catalogue of bks printed in England, Scotland, Ireland, Wales, & British America...., v.1, 2d ed, 14
Shot on this site, 472
Shrader, Charles Reginald, 520
Shrum, Wesley, 138
Siebert, Lee, 1818
Siegel, David S., 1007
Siegel, Susan, 1007
Sievers, Maurice L., 993
Sifakis, Stewart, 522, 523, 524, 525, 526
Silent film necrology, 1369
Silver, A. David, 184, 195
Silverburg, Sanford R., 570
Silverstein, Bernard, 1077
Simkin, Tom, 1818
Simon, Seymour, 1501, 1861
Simone, Roberta, 1206
Simone Weil, 957
Simpson, Beverly K., 1216
Sims-Bell, Barbara, 1538
Singer, Michael, 1405
Singer-songwriters, 1307
Single, Eric, 898
Sirotof, Gene, 1419
Sisson, A. F., 1092
Sisson's word & expression locater, 2d ed, 1092
Sixth bi-annual natl dir of arts internships, 1995/96, 1034
65 yrs of the Oscar, rev ed, 1372
Sizes: the illus ency, 1787
Sizesaurus, 1514
Skole, Robert, 83
Slater, James A., 1627
Slatta, Richard W., 510
Slide, Anthony, 1411
Sloan, Stephen, 597
Slonimsky, Nicholas, 1268
Small bus profiles, v.2, 196
Smart medicine for a healthier child, 1713
Smethurst, John B., 264
Smith, Alan G., 1807
Smith, Carolyn J., 1282
Smith, Constance, 1033, 1035
Smith, David G., 1807
Smith, Edward H., 1673
Smith, Eric Ledell, 1301

Smith, Hobart M., 1639
Smith, Jessie Carney, 397, 403, 404
Smith, John L., 1317
Smith, Linda C., 647
Smither, Roger, 557
Smith-Peters, Lise, 730
Smoking: the health consequences of tobacco use, 1721
Smurthwaite, David, 676
Snakes of the US & Canada, v.2, 1638
Snodgrass, Mary Ellen, 1147, 1148, 1349
Soccer stars, 831
Social panorama of Latin America, 1994 ed, 153
Social work almanac, 2d ed, 894
Social work dict, 3d ed, 890
Solorzano, Lucia, 331
Soltis, Katherine, 1071
Something about the author, v.78, 1172
Something about the author, v.79, 1173
Something about the author, v.80, 1174
Sommer, Elyse, 1091
Song finder, 1318
SongCite: an index to popular songs, 1309
Songs for bass voice, 1295
Sonneborn, Liz, 419
Soul music A-Z, rev ed, 1339
Sourcebook of state public records, 2d ed, 714
Sourcebook of zip code demographics, 10th ed, 913
Sourcebook on parenting & child care, 899
South Africa, rev ed, 122
South Asian religions in the Americas, 1438
South, David W., 1674
South Slavic writers before WW II, 1262
Southerton, Alan, 1762
Space scis dict 2, 1645
Space scis dict 3, 1646
Spaceflight: a Smithsonian gd, 1647
Spain, 2d ed, 149
Spain, Patrick J., 191, 201
Spaminato, Lynn M., 1362
SPDCD 1995: the standard per dir [CD-ROM], 87
Speaking of animals, 1074
Special collections in children's lit, 661
Specialty occupational outlook, 274
Species info lib [CD-ROM], 1606
Speck, Bruce W., 665
Spencer, Donald D., 1763, 1764, 1765, 1829
Spencer's illus computer dict, 1765
Spice trade, 308
Spicq, Ceslas, 1457
Sponza, Lucio, 143
Sport lawyer's gd to legal pers, 1995 suppl, 615
Sport thesaurus, 1994 ed, 802
Sporting News complete hockey bk, 1995-96 ed, 828
Sports ethics, 801
Sports in N America: a documentary hist, v.4, 798
Sports medicine bible, 1729
Sposato, Jeffrey S., 1283
Squire, Romilly, 435
St. John, Leonard, 1476
St. Kitts-Nevis, 172
Stahl, Dean, 2

Stallaerts, Robert, 549
Stamm, Andrea L., 126
Stamm, Johann Jakob, 1455
Standard & Poor's, 214, 215
Standard & Poor's 500 gd, 1995 ed, 214
Standard & Poor's midcap 400 gd, 1995 ed, 215
Standard catalog of firearms, 5th ed, 1009
Standard French-English, English-French dict, 1102
Standard hndbk of engineering calculations, 3d ed, 1644
Standard hndbk of plant engineering, 2d ed, 1677
Standish, Peter, 406
Stanley, David E., 1335
Stanton, Tom, 1331
Stark, Richard W., 802
Stark, Sandra M., 492
Stars & atoms, 1799
Start, Hannah, 279
StartSmart small bus advisor [CD-ROM], 207
State by state gd to human resources law, 1994, 268
State by state gd to human resources law, 1994: midyear suppl & workers' compensation laws, 269
State Capital Law Firm Group, 740
State executive dir, 729
State legislative summary, 1994, 595
State-by-state biotech dir, 3d ed, 1506
Statesman's yr-bk, 132d ed, 102
Statistical abstract of ...
    the ESCWA region 1983-1992, 14th ed, 919
    the US 1995, 115th ed, 920
    the world, 921
Statistical forecasts of the US, 2d ed, 914
Statistical hndbk of working America, 922
Statistical record of ...
    black America, 3d ed, 404
    native N Americans, 2d ed, 420
    women worldwide, 953
Statistical survey of insurance & reinsurance operations in developing countries 1983-90, 227
Statistical yrbk for Latin America & the Caribbean, 1994 ed, 154
Statistics of road traffic accidents in Europe & N America 1995, 1890
Statistics sources 1996, 19th ed, 923
Steedman, Scott, 63
Steele, Apollonia, 658, 1249
Steele, Sandy, 796
Steen, Sara J., 368, 369
Stein, Barbara, 649
Steinmann, Martin, 970
Stelten, Leo F., 1118
Stempen, Henry, 1587
Stephen Lock, 1702
Stephens, Elaine C., 1170
Stephens, John F., 338
Stephens, Michael L., 1383
Stephenson, Steven L., 1587
Sterling, Christopher H., 1778
Sternberg, Martin L. A., 1132, 1133
Stevens, J. D., 1623
Stevens, Muriel, 1531

Stevenson, Barbara, 378
Stewart, Joyce, 1576
Stewart, William, 864
Stitt, Beverly A., 313
Stolbova, Olga V., 1107
Stoll, Donald R., 86
Stoppard, Miriam, 904, 1692
Storey, R. L., 561
Story of rock'n'roll, 1336
Stott, Carole, 74
Stout, Rick, 1775
Stradling, R. A., 539
Strahle, Graham, 1272
Straighten up & fly right: a chronology & discography of Nat "King" Cole, 1329
Strauss, Stephen, 1514
Strichart, Stephen S., 341
Stricoff, R. Scott, 1796
Stroud, Elaine, 1736
Strub, Sean O'Brien, 259
Student Conservation Association, 1871
Students' gd to playwriting opportunities, 1421
Studies in human sexuality, 2d ed, 887
Sturm, Gary L., 1891
Stutzman, Michael, 1268
Subject gd to bks in print 1995-96, 16
Subject gd to children's bks in print 1995, 20
Subject headings for African American materials, 626
Subject headings for children 1994, 632
Sugar, Bert Randolph, 797
Sullivan, Fran, 482
Sullivan, Frank, 482
Sullivan, Helen F., 140
Sullivan, Thomas F. P., 1864
Sultenfuss, Sherry Wilson, 1743
Sultenfuss, Thomas J., 1743
Summer jobs Britain 1995, 26th ed, 279
Summer on campus [2d ed], 360
Sumpf, D., 1557
Sunshine, Linda, 1693
Super family vacations, 3d ed, 462
SUPER LCCS CD [CD-ROM], 633
Supernatural index, 1194
Supreme Court justices, 572
Surgeons' ref for minimally invasive surgery products, 1730
Survey of ...
    economic & social conditions in Africa, 1991-92, 113
    economic & social dvlpmts in the ESCWA region 1993, 129
    social sci: govt & pols series, 741
    social sci: sociology series, 836
Survival, 812
Sussman, Les, 1618
Swanfeldt, Andrew, 1085
Swaziland, rev ed, 123
Switten, Margaret L., 1296
Symonds, Craig L., 701
SYNERJY, 1831
Szajkowski, Bogdan, 757

Tachau, Frank, 765
Talbot, James R., 201
Talbot, Ross B., 1529
Talk show selects, 1995 ed, 989
Talk shows & hosts on radio, 3d ed, 975
Talking drums: an African-American quote collection, 96
Tan, Eng Thye Jason, 370
Tantalizing tingles: a discography of early ragtime, jazz....., 1325
Tarila, Sophia, 1482
Tarot for beginners, 787
Tarrago, Rafael E., 776
Task Force on Bias-Free Language of the Association of American University Presses, 968
Task Force on Taxonomy of the IASP, 1723
Tatar-English/English-Tatar dict, 1139
Tate, Michael L., 494
Taunton's fine homebuilding index, issues 1-85, 1051
Taylor, Ann C. M., 361
Taylor, Barbara, 65
Taylor, F. W., 1103
Taylor, Patrick, 1548, 1549
Taylor's master gd to gardening, 1550
Teacher educ policy in the states, 329
Teaching children's lit, 379
Technological capacity-bldg & tech partnership, 1515
Technology, 1508
Technology opportunities, 2d ed, 1507
Teen legal rights, 592
Telecommunications dir 1995-96, 7th ed, 1782
Telecommunications research resources, 1778
Television cartoon shows, 1375
Television research, 987
Television specials, 1412
Tenenbaum, Frances, 1550
Tennessee Williams, 1220
Terrace, Vincent, 1412
Terrell, Peter, 1104
Terris, Olwen, 1399
Terrorist group profiles [CD-ROM], 601
Terry, John V., 180
Teschner, Richard V., 1136
Test Collection, Educational Testing Service, 314
Teubig, Klaus, 1329
Theodor Adorno (II), 833
Theodore, Charmant, 1106
Theological lexicon of the N.T., 1457
Thesaurus of abstract musical properties, 1277
Thesaurus of ERIC descriptors, 13th ed, 318
Third world women's lits, 946
Thirty-Five Oriental philosophers, 1427
Thomas, G. Scott, 924
Thomas, Graham Stuart, 1551
Thomas, Nick, 1401
Thompson, Della, 1065, 1126, 1127
Thompson, Juliet S., 546
Thompson, Susan L., 546
Thompson, Wayne C., 546
Thomsett, Jean Freestone, 889
Thomsett, Michael C., 889

Thomson, Sandra A., 781
Tiku, M. L., 1557
Tilleman, William A., 1855
Time & space, 1820
Time-Saver standards for housing & residential dvlpmt, 1048
Tobiasen, Linda, 870
Tobiasen, Linda G., 883
Todd, Robert H., 1670
Togo, 124
Tomaselli-Moschovitis, Valerie, 155
Tomassini, Christine, 1398
Tong, Diane, 405
Top 10 of everything, 61
Topp, Chester W., 1223, 1224
Toth, Georgetta, 873
Townshend, Alan, 1495
Tracey, William R., 258
Trade data elements dir: UNTDED 1993, v.1, 306
Trager, James, 1539
Tram: the Frank Trumbauer story, 1323
Travers, Bridget, 1496
Treasury of natural 1st aid remedies from A-Z, 1715
Treaties of the War of the Spanish Succession, 762
Treharne, Elaine, 958
Trejo, Arnulfo D., 621
Trenz, Brandon, 1362
Tripp, Kim E., 1592
Tromble, Katherine R., 656
Trosky, Susan M., 1150
Trowers and Hamlins, 252
True bugs of the world (Hemiptera: Heteroptera), 1627
Trumbauer, William, 1323
Trumble, Bill, 1069
Trussler, Simon, 1422
Turck, Mary C., 1386
Turkington, Carol, 780, 1727
Turtles of the US & Canada, 1636
Tuttle dict of legal terms: English-Japanese, Japanese-English, rev ed, 613
Twentieth-century America, 485
Twentieth-century Britain, 543
Twentieth-century British literary biographers, 1227
Twentieth-century children's writers, 4th ed, 1175
Twentieth-century dict of Christian biog, 1465
Twentieth-century literary criticism, v.56, 1159
Twentieth-century literary criticism, v.57, 1160
Twentieth-century newspaper pr in Britain, 972
20th-Century Radicalism in Minnesota Project, 767
Twentieth-century short story explication, v.2, 1195
Twist, Clint, 74, 76
Twiston-Davies, Suzanne, 170
Type foundaries of America & their catalogs, rev ed, 666

UFO: the definitive gd to unidentified flying objects & related phenomena, 789
UK to USA dict, 1082
Ulane, Art, 1540
Ullmann's ency of industrial chemistry, v.a25, 5th ed, 1789

Ulrich's intl per dir 1996, 88
Ultimate classic car bk, 1892
Ultimate dir of the silent screen performers, 1368
UNCTAD commodity yrbk 1994, 1521
UNCTAD Secretariat, 227
UNCTAD statl pocket bk, 925
Understanding everyday Sesotho, 1135
United Nations Commission on Intl Trade law yrbk, v.24, 1993, 307
United Nations Conference on Trade and Development, 234, 289, 290, 925, 1515, 1521, 1897
United Nations Development Programme, 1842, 1843
U.S. Central Intelligence Agency, 713
United States Congress, 715
U.S. consumer interest groups, 216
United States Department of Labor, Occupational Safety and Health Administration, 277
U.S. health policy groups, 1691
United States in the 1st world war, 685
U.S. industry profiles, 224
US intelligence community, 716
USA business: the portable ency for doing bus with the US, 241
U.S. presidents [CD-ROM], 527
Universal almanac 1995, 5
Universe explained, 1802
University of London Lib catalogue of the Goldsmiths' Lib of Economic Lit, v.5, 662
UNIX & X command compendium, 1762
Unofficial gd to ethnic cuisine & dining in America, 1531
Unterburger, Amy L., 409
Unwin, Tim, 444
Upholsterer's pocket ref bk, 1020
Urdang, Laurence, 1068, 1094
Urofsky, Melvin I., 572
Urwin, Derek W., 139
USA Today weather almanac 1995, 1809
Used bk lover's gd to the Midwest, 1007
Used car reliability & safety gd, 1885
Using picture storybks to teach literary devices. v.2, 1164
USMARC format for bibliographic data, 1994 ed, 634
USP DI 1995, v.1, 1744
USP DI 1995, v.2, 1745
USP DI 1995, v.3, 1746
USP dict of USAN & intl drug names, 1747
Utah hist ency, 511
Uzbek-English, English-Uzbek concise dict, 1141
Uzicanin, Nikolina S., 1098

Vacation study abroad 1995/96, 369
Vacic, Aleksandar M., 232
Valade, Roger M., III, 1490
Valder, Peter, 1579
Value of a dollar, 1860-1989, 198
van den Eeden, Pieter, 99
Van der Bent, Ans Joachim, 1473
Van Nostrand's scientific ency, 8th ed, 1502
Van Tuyl, Ian, 585
Vandenberghe, J. -P., 1894
Vander Kolk, Martha, 100, 101, 1774
Vanderstel, David G., 929
Variety's film reviews, v.23, 1387
Variety's video dir plus [CD-ROM], 1388
Vascular plants of Russia & adjacent states (the former USSR), 1594
Vasquez, Milton, 1862
Vassilian, Hamo B., 391
Vazzana, Eugene Michael, 1369
Veltrop, Kyle, 828
Veni, vidi, vici, 1116
Venice & the Veneto, 478
Vennebusch, Eva, 1104
Venolia, Jan, 1081
Venzon, Anne Cipriano, 685
Verene, Molly Black, 1426
Verkler, Linda A., 1003
Vermont, Terrell, 1531
Veterinarian's ency of animal behavior, 1554
Vick, Julia Miller, 365
Vico: a bibliog of works in English from 1884-1984, 1426
Victorian yellowbacks & paperbacks, 1849-1905, v.1, 1223
Victorian yellowbacks & paperbacks, 1849-1905, v.2, 1224
Video annual 1994, 994
Video rating gd for libs on CD-ROM 1990-94 [CD-ROM], 995
Video source bk 1996, 17th ed, 996
VideoHound multimedia [CD-ROM], 1389
VideoHound's that's amore!, 1398
Vienna, 479
Vietnam [CD-ROM], 694
Vigliotta, Joan M., 285
Vincent, Mary, 539
Violent children, 603
Virginia Woolf A to Z, 1221
Visual dict of ...
    American domestic architecture, 1044
    physics, 1819
    prehistoric life, 1817
    the skeleton, 1683
Visual ency of sci, 1503
Visual resources dir, 378
Vocabulary of computer security & viruses, 1766
Vogel, Colin, 1556
Vogel, Frederick G., 696
Voices of the spirit, 402
Volcanoes of the world, 2d ed, 1818
Volvo gd to halls of fame, 83
Vonnegut ency, 1219
VonVille, Helena M., 888
Voss, D. Stephen, 138
Voyages in classical mythology, 1349
Vyse, Ruth, 662

Wagner-Martin, Linda, 1200
Wales & cinema, 1370
Walker, Bonnie L., 844
Walker, Donald E., 806

Walker, John, 1385
Walker, John M., 1659
Walker, Richard, 1683
Walker's bats of the world, 1610
Walking shadows, 1399
Waller, Philip, 562
Walsh, James E., 42
Walsh, Michael F., 582
Walters, Douglas B., 1796
Walton, John, 1702
Walton, Juanita, 1249
Walton, Rachel, 1713
Warblers of the Americas, 1613
Ward, Amie S., 839
Ward, Robert E, 315
Warman's antiques & collectibles price gd, 29th ed, 1000
Wars of the roses in fiction, 1190
Washington info dir, 734
Washington online: how to access the fed govt on the Internet 1995, 1785
Washington online: how to access the govt's electronic bulletin boards, 1786
Washington Researchers, 175, 1507
Wasserman, Steven R., 923
Watermeier, Daniel J., 1420
Watts, Alan, 1810
Watts, Phyllis C., 1442
Way, Frederick, Jr., 1898
Way, George, 435
Ways of war: the era of WW II in children's & YA fiction, 1165
Way's packet dir, 1848-1994, rev ed, 1898
Weather hndbk, 1810
Weaver, Bruce L., 1188
Weaver, Robert Lee, 1266
Weaver, Robert S., 1361
Webb, Sophie, 1615
Weber, R. David, 690, 858, 880
Webster's new world vest pocket dict, 2d ed, 1071
Webster's 2: new college dict, 1079
Weed flora of Egypt, rev ed, 1582
Weeks, Christopher, 1049
Weiner, Edmund, 1080
Weiner, E. S. C., 1076
Weingartner, Clarence, 1675
Weiss, Dorrie, 1091
Weiss, Michael J., 915
Welch, Jeanie, 308
Wellborn, Olin Guy, III, 591
Weller, Carolyn R., 629
Welsch, Gerhard, 1669
West Point atlas of American wars, v.1, 677
Western American novelists, 1205
Western garden [CD-ROM], 1552
Western political thought, 704
Weston, Ronald, 686
Wetland economics, 1989-93, 1600
Wetterau, Bruce, 737
Wetzel, Bethann, 1405
Wexler, Alan, 488
Whales, dolphins, & porpoises, 1629

What else should I read?, 1162
What plant where, 1566
What to name your African-American baby, 436
What to read, 380
Whiffin, Jean I., 655
Whigham, Thomas, 551
Whitaker's almanack 1996, 128th ed, 6
Whitburn, Joel, 1303, 1314, 1319, 1337, 1402
Whitby, Thomas J., 887
Whitcut, Janet, 1076
White, Gerard F., 689
White, Isobel, 540
White, Phillip M., 421
White, R. Kerry, 1417
Whitelegge, Angela, 662
Whiteley, Sandy, 12
Whitney, Ellen M., 492
Who get grants/who gives grants, 877
Who knows who [1996], 186
Whole lib hndbk 2, 624
Whole spy catalog, 775
Who's who 1995, 34
Who's who among Hispanic Americans 1994-95, 3d ed, 409
Who's who in ...
   America 1996, 37
   American art 1995-96, 21st ed, 1027
   Egyptian mythology, 2d ed, 1350
   European research & dvlpmt 1995, 1491
   Jewish hist, 2d ed, 1481
   Lebanon 1995-96, 13th ed, 165
   Russia & the CIS Republics, 40
   Shakespeare, 1240
   tech, 7th ed, 1492
   the Arab world 1995-96, 12th ed, 161
   the Asian-American community 1994-95, 395
   the Bible, 1449
   the European info world 95/96, 2d ed, 639
   the UK info world 95/96, 5th ed, 640
   writers, editors, & poets, 5th ed, 959
   WW II, 681
Who's who of American women 1995-96, 19th ed, 38
Wice, Nathaniel, 813
Wiebes, J. T., 1628
Wiehs, Jean, 137
Wielgorskaya, Tatiana, 1565
Wiener, Allen J., 1338
Wiggers, Raymond, 474
Wigoder, Geoffrey, 164, 1478
Wild New Zealand, 1601
Wild planet!, 1352
Wilde, T. Jesse, 615
Wilde, William H., 1248
Wildlife worldwide [CD-ROM], 1607
Wiley's English-Spanish, Spanish-English dict of psychology & psychiatry, 782
Wilken, Pam, 1135
Wilkinson, Philip, 66
Wilkinson, Robert, 1427
Wilkirson, Hayward, 98
Willemen, Paul, 1381

Willett, Charles, 79
William Mathias, 1279
William Thomas McKinley, 1283
Williams, Dawn Bastian, 126
Williams, Dominic, 248
Williams, Gordon, 1243
Williams, Jack, 1809
Williams, Martha E., 622
Williams, Neville, 560, 562
Williams, Phil, 773
Williams, Roger, 477
Williamson, David, 426
Willmond, Catherine, 1099
Willson, Quentin, 1892
Wilsford, David, 756
Wilson, A., 253
Wilson, Anthony, 1878
Wilson author biogs on disc 1995 [CD-ROM], 1144
Wilson, Craig A., 674
Wilson, Eunice, 544
Wilson, George, 509
Wilson, Hugo, 1893
Wilson, Joyce M., 1176
Wilson, R. M., 427
Wimsatt, Mary Ann, 1201
Windsor, Steven, 638
Wing, Donald, 14
Winig, Laura, 282
Winkel, Lois, 632
Winter, Frank H., 1647
Winter, Ruth, 1530, 1790
Wisterias, 1579
Witalec, Janet, 1259
With fire & sword: Italian spectacles on American screens 1958-68, 1395
Wizansky, Richard, 1871
Woerner, Gert, 1483
Woldman's engineering alloys, 8th ed, 1671
Wolverton, Ruthe, 475
Wolverton, Walt, 475
Womack, Carol Z., 211
Woman's body, 1692
Woman's gd to coping with disability, 859
Woman's gd to vitamins & minerals, 1743
Women & aging, 936
Women & religion in India, 934
Women & the Dict of Natl Biog, 26
Women & the military, 680
Women artists, 2d ed, 1021
Women film directors, 947
Women in the US: economic conditions, 937
Women of peace: Nobel peace prize winners, 944
Women who reformed pols, 943
Women's atlas of the US, rev ed, 933
Women's pers in the US: consumer mags, 950
Women's world: a timeline of women in hist, 945
Wong, Glenn M., 615
Wood, Helen E., 897
Wooding, Frederick H., 1624
Woods, John A., 284
Woodside, Gayle, 1852

Woodstra, Chris, 1330
Woodworth, David, 278, 279
Words on cassette 1995, 983
Work of Jack Vance, 1218
Work of William Eastlake, 1209
Work your way around the world, 7th ed, 273
Working solo sourcebk, 263
Works of Allen Ginsberg 1941-94, 1210
World alive [CD-ROM], 1609
World almanac & bk of facts 1996, 7
World Bk multimedia ency [CD-ROM], 51
World databases in ...
  geography & geology, 453
  industry, 225
  patents, 587
  physics & mathematics, 1788
World dir of exhibitions & trade fairs 1995, 309
World engineering industries & automation 1993-95, 1649
World geographical ency, English lang ed, 456
World index of economic forecasts, 4th ed, 208
World index of resources & population, 235
World list of univ & other insts of higher ed, 361
World market share reporter 1995-96, 240
World of ghosts & the supernatural, 784
World painting index, 2d suppl, 1056
World satellite almanac, 1995, 7th ed, 1648
World tourism dir '95/96, pt.1, 3d ed, 464
World tourism dir '95/96, pt.2, 3d ed, 465
World tourism dir '95/96, pt.3, 3d ed, 466
World urbanizations prospects: the 1994 revision, 932
World War I songs, 696
World weatherdisc, 1994 ed [CD-ROM], 1811
Worldmark ency of the nations, 8th ed, 105
Worldmark ency of the states, 106
World's major cos dir, 229
World's women 1995, [2d ed], 954
Worldwide govt dir with intl orgs 1995, 709
Worldwide petrochemical dir, 1995, 33d ed, 1835
Worldwide pipelines & contractors dir, 1995, 15th ed, 1837
Wright, Albert Hazen, 1640
Wright, Anna Allen, 1640
Wright, John W., 5, 1693
Wright, Michael, 1421
Wright, Philip C., 385
Wright, Russell O., 742, 807
Write right!, 3d ed, 1081
Writings in Indian hist, 1985-90, 414
Wrongful termination, 281
WRTH satellite broadcasting gd, 1995 ed, 997
WTA Tour, 832
WTA Tour Communications Staff, 832
Wuerch, William L., 168, 1439
Wyckoff, D. Campbell, 1463
Wyckoff, Trip, 209
Wynar, Bohdan S., 11

Yaakov, Juliette, 650
Yahnke, Robert E., 845

Yaws, Carl L., 1793, 1821, 1822, 1823, 1824
Year in trees, 1592
Yearbook of ...
   experts, authorities & spokespersons, 12th ed, 103
   the Intl Law Commission 1992, 614
   tourism stats, 46th ed, 463
Year's work in English studies, v.73, 1992, 958
Yenne, Bill, 33, 1602
Yeoman, R. S., 1008
Young, Arthur P., 1442
Young, Ken, 808
Young reader's companion to American hist, 528
Young, Robyn V., 387
Young, W. Murray, 1284
Your hit parade & American top 10 hits, 4th ed, 1308
Yousof, Ghulam-Sarwar, 1418
Youth exchanges, 371

Zaire, 126
Zakalik, Joanna, 1779
Zancani, Diego, 143
Zand, Janet, 1713
Zawahri, Neda A., 1863
Zelnik, Martin, 1048
Zempel, Edward N., 1003
Zia, Helen, 393, 396
Zibart, Eve, 1531
Zietz, Karyl Lynn, 1302
Zimmerman, Michael F., 861
Zomlefer, Wendy B., 1580
Zurndorfer, Harriet T., 535
Zvelebil, Kamil V., 1255

Subject Index
Reference is to entry number.

ABBREVIATIONS. *See also* **ACRONYMS**
Abbreviations dict, 9th ed, 2
Barnhart abbrevs dict, 1
Common medical abbrevs, 1695
New acronyms, initialisms, & abbrevs, v.2, 3

ABNORMALITIES, HUMAN
Biological anomalies: humans III, 1559
Catalog of teratogenic agents, 8th ed, 1720

ABSTRACTS
Information sci abstracts, v.29, no.12, 619

ACADEMIC LIBRARIES
Academic lib of the 90s, 620
Academic libs in the UK & the republic of Ireland 1994, 3d ed, 635

ACCIDENTS
APELL annot bibliog, 777
Sports medicine bible, 1729

ACCIDENTS—PREVENTION
Injury prevention for the elderly, 844

ACCOUNTING
Cabell's dir of publishing opportunities in accounting, economics & finance, 6th ed, 669
Dictionary of accounting, 210

ACHIEVEMENT TESTS
ETS test collection catalog, v.2, 2d ed, 314

ACQUISITIONS (LIBRARIES)
Policies for publishers, 1995 ed, 674

ACRONYMS. *See also* **ABBREVIATIONS**
Comprehensive networking glossary & acronym gd, 1759
Environmental acronyms, 1850
New acronyms, initialisms, & abbrevs, v.2, 3

ACTORS. *See also* **MOTION PICTURE ACTORS & ACTRESSES**
Leonard Maltin's movie ency, 1377

ADDISON, JOSEPH
Joseph Addison & Richard Steele, 1237

ADJUSTMENT (PSYCHOLOGY)
Woman's gd to coping with disability, 859

ADMINISTRATIVE AGENCIES
Carroll's fed regional dir, 724
Carroll's fed dir, 723
Directory of professional & occupational regulation in the US & Canada, 730
Federal regulatory dir, 7th ed, 731

ADOLESCENCE
Teen legal rights, 592

ADOPTION
Adoption dir, 2d ed, 860

ADORNO, THEODOR
Theodor Adorno (II), 833

ADVENTURE FILMS
Hollywood heroes, 1376

ADVERTISING
Dictionary of marketing & advertising, 304
International advertising & mktg info sources, 299
Latin American advertising, mktg, & media sourcebk, 301
Leo Burnett worldwide advertising & media fact bk, 302

AERONAUTICS
Aviation & aerospace almanac 1995, 1879
Aviation: a Smithsonian gd, 1882
Jane's airports & handling agents, 1995-96, 1881

AEROSPACE INDUSTRIES
Aviation & aerospace almanac 1995, 1879

AFRICA
Africa, Asia, & S America since 1800, 555
Africa in lit for children & young adults, 1166
Africa on file, 108
African biographical dict, 109
African hist on file, 529
Contemporary African pols & dvlpmt, 110
Dictionary of Portuguese-African civilization, v.1, 532
Foreign trade stats for Africa, 294
From Afar to Zulu: a dict of African cultures, 390
Guide to original sources for precolonial W Africa published in European langs, rev ed, 531
International histl stats: Africa, Asia, & Oceania, 1750-1988, 917
Making of modern Africa: a gd to archives, 530
Metalworking in Africa S of the Sahara, 1668
Sao Tome & Principe, 121
Survey of economic & social conditions in Africa, 1991-92, 113
Swaziland, rev ed, 123

AFRICA—BIOGRAPHY
100 great Africans, 112

AFRICA, EAST
Portraits in conservation: E & S Africa, 1596

AFRICA, NORTH
Middle East & N Africa 1995, 160

Middle East & N Africa on file, 459
Political parties of the Middle East & N Africa, 765

AFRICA, SOUTHERN
Portraits in conservation: E & S Africa, 1596

AFRICA—STUDY & TEACHING
International dir of African studies research, 3d ed, 111

AFRICAN LITERATURE (ENGLISH)
Black African lit in English, 1987-91, 1247

AFRO-AMERICAN ATHLETES
African-American sports greats, 792

AFRO-AMERICAN CONDUCTORS
Black conductors, 1285

AFRO-AMERICAN INVENTORS
African-American inventors, 1488

AFRO-AMERICAN MUSICIANS
Blacks in opera, 1301

AFRO-AMERICAN NEWSPAPERS
Bibliographic checklist of African American newspapers, 971

AFRO-AMERICAN SCIENTISTS
African-American scientists, 1489

AFRO-AMERICAN SOLDIERS
On the trail of the buffalo soldier, 699

AFRO-AMERICANS
African-American address bk, 52
African American breakthroughs, 397
African American genealogical sourcebk, 429
Bibliographic gd to black studies 1994, 398
Contemporary black biog, v.8, 400
Historical stats of black America, 403
Kaleidoscope: a multicultural bklst for grades K-8, 1182
Subject headings for African American materials, 626
Talking drums: an African-American quote collection, 96
Voices of the spirit, 402
What to name your African-American baby, 436

AGE DISTRIBUTION (DEMOGRAPHY)
Sex & age distribution of world populations: 1994 revision, 912

AGED. *See also* **AGING; GERONTOLOGY; RETIREMENT COMMUNITIES; RETIREMENT INCOMES**
Alcoholism & aging, 897
Counseling older persons, 843
Encyclopedia of home care for the elderly, 1681

AGED—EMPLOYMENT
Employment of the elderly, 842
Jobs for people over 50, 276

AGED—LONG TERM CARE
Long term care, 841

AGED—RELIGIOUS LIFE
Research on religion & aging, 840

AGED—SERVICES FOR
International hndbk on servs for the elderly, 851

AGGRESSIVENESS (PSYCHOLOGY)
Aggression & conflict, 835

AGING
Aging well, 838
Encyclopedia of aging, 850
Injury prevention for the elderly, 844
Literature & gerontology, 845
National gd to funding in aging, 4th ed, 849
Psychology of aging, 839
Research on religion & aging, 840
Women & aging, 936

AGRICULTURAL INDUSTRIES
Prices of agricultural products & selected inputs for Europe & N America 1992/93, 1520

AGRICULTURAL PESTS
Agricultural entomology, 1625

AGRICULTURE
Dictionary of agriculture, 1517
Elsevier's dict of agriculture & food production, 1516
Key gd to electronic resources: agriculture, 1518

AIDS (DISEASE)
Guide to bks on AIDS, 1719

AIR FORCES
Naval Institute gd to world military aviation 1995, 697

AIR WARFARE
Military ency of Russia & Eurasia, v.5, 146

AIRLINES
Commuter airlines of the US, 1880

AIRPLANES, MILITARY
Naval Institute gd to world military aviation 1995, 697

AIRPORTS
Jane's airports & handling agents, 1995-96, 1881

ALCOHOLISM
Alcoholism & aging, 897

ALGERIA
Historical dict of Algeria, 2d ed, 114

ALL TERRAIN CYCLING
Mountain bikers almanac, 1996, 815

ALLOYS
Alloy finder [CD-ROM], 1660

ALMANACS
Old farmer's almanac 1995, 4
Universal almanac 1995, 5
Whitaker's almanack 1996, 128th ed, 6
World almanac & bk of facts 1996, 7

ALPINE FLORA
Alpines, 1590

ALTERNATIVE MEDICINE
Alternative health & medicine ency, 1716
Information sourcebk of herbal medicine, 1714
Naturopathic hndbk of herbal formulas, 3d ed, 1717

AMATEUR RADIO STATIONS
Radio amateur callbook, 1995, 73d ed, 990

AMERICAN ASSOCIATION OF LAW LIBRARIES
AALL ref bk, 593

AMERICAN DRAMA
American playwrights, 1880-1945, 1202

AMERICAN FICTION
American novelists since WWII, 4th series, 1203
American novelists since WW II, 3d series, 1204
Hollywood novel, 1411
Immigrant experience in American fiction, 1206

AMERICAN LITERATURE. *See also names of individual authors*
American diversity, American identity, 1198
Western American novelists, 1205

AMERICAN LITERATURE—AFRO-AMERICAN AUTHORS
French critical reception of African-American lit from the beginnings to 1970, 1197
Modern black writers: suppl, 1157

AMERICAN LITERATURE—INDIAN AUTHORS
Native N American lit, 1259

AMERICAN LITERATURE—RESEARCH
Handbook of literary research, 2d ed, 1142

AMERICAN LITERATURE—SOUTHERN STATES
Contemporary poets, dramatists, essayists, & novelists of the South, 1199

AMERICAN LITERATURE—WOMEN AUTHORS
Oxford companion to women's writing in the US, 1200

AMERICAN POETRY
Feminist criticism of American women poets, 1222

AMERICAN SIGN LANGUAGE
American Sign Lang concise dict, rev ed, 1132
American Sign Lang dict, rev ed, 1133
American Sign Lang dict on CD-ROM [CD-ROM], 1130

Comprehensive ref manual for signers & interpreters, 4th ed, 1131

AMERICAN STOCK EXCHANGE
American stock exchange, 211

AMERICAN STUDENTS—FOREIGN COUNTRIES
Youth exchanges, 371

AMSTERDAM (NETHERLANDS)
Amsterdam, 476

ANAGRAMS
Scrambled word & anagram finder, 1072

ANATOMY, HUMAN
Visual dict of the skeleton, 1683

ANGIOSPERMS
Guide to flowering plant families, 1580

ANIMAL EXPERIMENTATION
Animal rights, 1435
Animal rights movement in the US, 1975-90, 1424

ANIMAL HEALTH
Animal health yrbk 1993, 1553

ANIMAL RIGHTS
Animal rights, 1435
Animal rights movement in the US, 1975-90, 1424

ANIMALS
Amazing animals of the world, 1603
Kingfisher 1st ency of animals, 1608
National gd to funding for the environment & animal welfare, 2d ed, 878
Speaking of animals, 1074
Species info lib [CD-ROM], 1606
World alive [CD-ROM], 1609

ANIMALS IN THE PERFORMING ARTS
Animals on screen & radio, 1366

ANIMATED FILMS
Television cartoon shows, 1375

ANNUALS (PLANTS)
Favorite annuals, 1568

ANONYMS & PSEUDONYMS
Dictionary of literary pseudonyms in the English lang, 1229

ANTARCTIC REGIONS
Arctic & Antarctic regions [CD-ROM], 127

ANTILLES, LESSER
Martinique, 171

ANTIQUARIAN BOOKSELLERS
Used bk lover's gd to the Midwest, 1007

ANTIQUES
Warman's antiques & collectibles price gd, 29th ed, 1000

ANTIQUITIES
Bibliography of Syrian archaeological sites to 1980, 484

ANTISEMITISM
"Jewish question" in German-speaking countries, 1848-1914, 425

AQUARIUMS, PUBLIC
Aquariums of N America, 1621

AQUEDUCTS
Guide to the aqueducts of ancient Rome, 1046

ARAB COUNTRIES
Who's who in the Arab world 1995-96, 12th ed, 161

ARAMAIC LANGUAGE
Hebrew & Aramaic lexicon of the O.T., v.1, 1455

ARBITRATION, INDUSTRIAL
Labor arbitration, 255

ARBITRATION, INTERNATIONAL
Historical dict of intl tribunals, 610

ARCHAEOLOGY
Bookman's gd to archaeology, 1005

ARCHITECTS
Contemporary architects, 3d ed, 1043

ARCHITECTURE
AIA gd to the architecture of Wash., D.C., 3d ed, 1049
America preserved, 1047
American house designs: an index to popular & trade pers, 1850-1915, 1050
Dictionary of Scottish art & architecture, 1025
Encyclopedia of American architecture, 2d ed, 1045
Masterworks of man & nature, 2d ed, 458

ARCHITECTURE, DOMESTIC
American house designs: an index to popular & trade pers, 1850-1915, 1050
Visual dict of American domestic architecture, 1044

ARCHIVAL RESOURCES
Guide to Central American collections in the US, 152
Guide to collections on Paraguay in the US, 551

ARCHIVES
Landmark docs in American hist [CD-ROM], 498
Making of modern Africa: a gd to archives, 530
Mapping the territory, 658

ARCTIC REGIONS
Arctic & Antarctic regions, [CD-ROM], 127

AREA STUDIES
Current world leaders almanac, v.38, no.3, June 1995, 104

International histl stats: Africa, Asia, & Oceania, 1750-1988, 917
Statesman's yr-bk, 132d ed, 102

ARIZONA
Hopi pottery symbols, 1015

ARKANSAS
Arkansas hist, 490

ARMENIA
Armenian folklore bibliog, 1340

ARMENIAN AMERICANS
Armenian American almanac, 391

ARMORED VEHICLES, MILITARY. *See also* **TANKS (MILITARY)**
Armored forces: hist & sourcebk, 702

ART. *See also* **ARTS**
Art & design scholarships, 1036
Art on screen on CD-ROM [CD-ROM], 1037
Book of art, rev ed, 1029
Dictionary of symbols in western art, 1030
Encyclopedia of Australian art, rev ed, 1032
Illustrated dict of symbols in E & W art, 1031
Peterson's professional degree programs in the visual & performing arts 1995, 962
Sixth bi-annual natl dir of arts internships, 1995/96, 1034
Visual resources dir, 378

ART, AMERICAN
Who's who in American art 1995-96, 21st ed, 1027

ART—MARKETING
Art mktg sourcebk for the fine artist, 2d ed, 1035
Artist's & graphic designer's market, 1995, 1038

ART—VOCATIONAL GUIDANCE
Career opportunities in art, rev ed, 1041

ARTIFICIAL INTELLIGENCE
McGraw-Hill illus ency of robotics & artificial intelligence, 1753

ARTILLERY, FIELD & MOUNTAIN
Field artillery, 703

ARTISTS
Artists: from Michelangelo to Maya Lin, 1024
Artist's resource hndbk, 1040
Authors & artists for young adults, v.14, 1171
Biographical dict of artists, rev ed, 1022
Biographical dict of Saskatchewan artists: [v.2]: men artists, 1023
Dictionary of Scottish art & architecture, 1025
Encyclopedia of Australian art, rev ed, 1032

ARTISTS' MATERIALS
ArtNetwork yellow pages, 1033

ARTS
Art bus ency, 1039
National gd to funding in arts & culture, 3d ed, 961
Remarkable lives of 100 women artists, 939

ASIA. See also ASIA, SOUTHEASTERN
Africa, Asia, & S America since 1800, 555
Asian hist on file, 533
Economic & social survey of Asia & the Pacific 1995, 128
International histl stats: Africa, Asia, & Oceania, 1750-1988, 917
Major cos of the Far East & Australasia 1995/96, 245

ASIA—ECONOMIC CONDITIONS
Consumer Asia 1995 [2d ed], 242

ASIA—RELIGION
Encyclopedia of E philosophy & religion, 1483
Great thinkers of the E world, 1433

ASIA, SOUTHEASTERN
Dictionary of the modern pols of SE Asia, 747
Dictionary of traditional S-E Asian theatre, 1418

ASIAN AMERICANS
Asian American almanac, 392
Asian American biog, 393
Asian American ency, 394
Asian American genealogical sourcebk, 430
Guide to children's bks about Asian Americans, 1181
Kaleidoscope: a multicultural bklst for grades K-8, 1182
Notable Asian Americans, 396
Who's who in the Asian-American community 1994-95, 395

ASSOCIATIONS
American Assn of Colleges for Teacher Educ dir of members 1995, 316

ASSOCIATIONS, INSTITUTIONS, ETC. See also TRADE & PROFESSIONAL ASSOCIATIONS
Gale ency of bus & professional assns, 185

ASTEROIDS
Asteroid name ency, 790

ASTROLOGY
Asteroid name ency, 790
Divining the future: prognostication from astrology to zoomancy, 791

ASTRONOMY
Asteroid name ency, 790
Astronomy, 1800
Binocular stargazer, 1801
Cambridge gd to the constellations, 1798
Stars & atoms, 1799
Universe explained, 1802

ATHLETES
Athletes, 410
Biographical dict of American sports, 1992-95 suppl, 793
Great athletes, suppl 21-23, 794
Official celebrity registry 1994-95, 796
100 athletes who shaped sports hist, 795
100 greatest athletes of all time, 797

ATLANTIC OCEAN
Field gd to shells, 4th ed, 1595

ATLASES
Atlas of Indians of N America, 413
Atlas of westward expansion, 488
Atlas of WW I, 2d ed, 675
Cosmopolitan world atlas, 446
Eyewitness atlas of the world, 447
Geography on file, 1995 ed, 457
Hammond students atlas of the world, 448
Historical atlas of La., 440
Middle East & N Africa on file, 459
New intl atlas, 25th ed, 449
PC Globe maps'n'facts [CD-ROM], 450

ATLASES, CHINESE
China: a provincial atlas, 452

AUDIOCASSETTES
Words on cassette 1995, 983

AUDIO-VISUAL EQUIPMENT
Dictionary of image tech, 3d ed, 985

AUREATE TERMS
Endangered English dict, 1089

AUSTRALIA
Australian bks in print 1995, 22
Encyclopedia of Australian art, rev ed, 1032
Familia Gekkonidae (Reptilia, Sauria), pt.1, 1634
Far East & Australasia 1995, 26th ed, 167
Monash biographical dict of 20th century Australia, 39
Sharks & rays of Australia, 1623

AUSTRALIAN LITERATURE
Black in focus, 1163
Oxford companion to Australian lit, 2d ed, 1248

AUSTRALIANISMS
Cambridge Australian English style gd, 1090

AUTHORITY FILES (CATALOGING)
ERIC identifier authority list (IAL) 1995, 629

AUTHORS
Authors & artists for young adults, v.14, 1171
Children's authors & illustrators, 5th ed, 1178
Contemporary authors, new revision series, v.43, 1150
DiscLit: world authors [CD-ROM], 1154
Larousse dict of writers, 1145

Science fiction, fantasy, & horror writers, 1193
Something about the author, v.78, 1172
Something about the author, v.79, 1173
Something about the author, v.80, 1174
Twentieth-century children's writers, 4th ed, 1175
Wilson author biogs on disc 1995 [CD-ROM], 1144

AUTHORS, AMERICAN
Contemporary poets, dramatists, essayists, & novelists of the South, 1199
Dictionary of literary pseudonyms in the English lang, 1229
Herman Melville ency, 1212
Mark Twain A to Z, 1217
Proverbial Eugene O'Neill, 1215
Western American novelists, 1205
Works of Allen Ginsberg 1941-94, 1210

AUTHORS, ENGLISH
Dictionary of literary pseudonyms in the English lang, 1229
Literary gd & companion to N England, 1233
Now read on: a gd to contemporary popular fiction, 2d ed, 1187

AUTHORS, ENGLISH—EARLY MODERN, 1500-1700
George Herbert companion, 1238

AUTHORS, INDIAN
Native N American lit, 1259

AUTHORS, TAMIL
Lexicon of Tamil lit, 1255

AUTHORSHIP. *See also* PUBLISHERS & PUBLISHING
Career opportunities for writers, 3d ed, 967
Complete gd to writers' conferences & workshops, 965
Dictionary of literary pseudonyms in the English lang, 1229
Freed's gd to student contests & publishing, 5th ed, 1356

AUTOMATION
World engineering industries & automation 1993-95, 1649

AUTOMOBILES
Racer's ency of metals, fibers & materials, 1883
Ultimate classic car bk, 1892
Used car reliability & safety gd, 1885

AWARDS
65 yrs of the Oscar, rev ed, 1372

AZERBAIJANI LANGUAGE—DICTIONARIES—ENGLISH
English-Azerbaijani/Azerbaijani-English concise dict, 1097

BACH, JOHANN SEBASTIAN
Sacred dramas of J. S. Bach, 1284

BACKPACKING
Essential gd to wilderness camping & backpacking in the US, 824

BALTIC STATES
Atlas of Russia & the Independent Republics, 445

BANKS & BANKING
Dictionary of finance & investment terms, 4th ed, 220

BAPTISTS
Dictionary of Baptists in America, 1467

BASEBALL
Baseball & American culture, 806
Baseball ency update, 1995, 803
Best of teams, the worst of teams, 807
Official athletic college gd: baseball, 1995 ed, 805

BASEBALL PLAYERS
Baseball ratings, 2d ed, 804

BASKETBALL
Encyclopedia of college basketball, 809

BATS
Walker's bats of the world, 1610

BATTLEFIELDS
Civil War battlefields, 517

BATTLES
Army Times bk of great land battles, 698

BEADS
Bead dir, 3d ed, 1011

BEATLES
Beatles: the ultimate recording gd, 3d ed, 1338

BED & BREAKFAST ACCOMMODATIONS
Irish bed & breakfast bk, 482

BEER
America's best beers, 1536
Beer lover's rating gd, 1537
Encyclopedia of beer, 1525
On tap, 1995 ed, 1532

BEETHOVEN, LUDWIG VAN
Beethoven ency, 1281

BENCHLEY, ROBERT
Robert Benchley, 1207

BEVERAGE INDUSTRY
Career opportunities in the food & beverage industry, 1538

BIBLE
And Adam knew Eve: a dict of sex in the Bible, 1452
Baker ency of Bible places, 1450
Bible & the saints, 1448

Encyclopedia of biblical errancy, 1456
Illustrated gd to the Bible, 1459
Precious Moments children's Bible dict, 1451
Who's who in the Bible, 1449

BIBLE—COMMENTARIES
New Bible commentary, 1458

BIBLE—DICTIONARIES
Hastings' dict of the Bible, 1454

BIBLE—LANGUAGE, STYLE
Hebrew & Aramaic lexicon of the O.T., v.1, 1455

BIBLE. N.T.
Novum Testamentum, v.36a, 1460
Theological lexicon of the N.T., 1457

BIBLE. O.T.
Hebrew & Aramaic lexicon of the O.T., v.1, 1455

BIBLIOGRAPHY
Books in print 1995-96, 15
Books in print with bk reviews plus [CD-ROM], 17
Books out-of-print plus [CD-ROM], 18
Children's bks in print, 19
China bibliog, 535
Global bks in print plus [CD-ROM], 13
Subject gd to bks in print 1995-96, 16
Subject gd to children's bks in print 1995, 20

BIBLIOGRAPHY—BEST BOOKS
Crown crime companion, 1189
More kids' favorite bks, 1168

BIBLIOGRAPHY—EARLY PRINTED BOOKS
Short-title catalogue of bks printed in England, Scotland, Ireland, Wales, & British America....,
v.1, 2d ed, 14

BIBLIOGRAPHY, INTERNATIONAL
Global bks in print plus [CD-ROM], 13
MLA intl bibliog [CD-ROM], 1143

BIOETHICS
Encyclopedia of bioethics, rev ed, 1429

BIOGRAPHERS
Late 19th- & early 20th-century British literary biographers, 1225
Nineteenth-Century British literary biographers, 1226
Twentieth-century British literary biographers, 1227

BIOGRAPHY
Asian American biog, 393
Athletes, 410
Biographical dict of American newspaper columnists, 973
Biographical dict of artists, rev ed, 1022
Biography index [CD-ROM], 24
Biography today, 1993 annual cum, 25
Deaf persons in the arts & scis, 857

Dictionary of American biog, suppl 10, 36
Grolier lib of N American biogs, 27
International biographical dict of computer pioneers, 1758
Merriam-Webster's biographical dict, 29
Mexican pol biogs, 1935-93, 3d ed, 763
My 1st bk of biogs, 28
100 men who shaped world hist, 33
100 women who shaped world hist, 32
Oxford children's bk of famous people, 31
Performers, 419
Political leaders & peacemakers, 418
Profiles in American hist, 509
Who's who 1995, 34
Who's who in America 1996, 37
Who's who in tech, 7th ed, 1492
Who's who of American women 1995-96, 19th ed, 38
Wilson author biogs on disc 1995 [CD-ROM], 1144
Women & the Dict of Natl Biog, 26

BIOGRAPHY—20TH CENTURY
Monash biographical dict of 20th century Australia, 39

BIOMETRY
Elsevier's dict of biometry, 1557

BIOTECHNOLOGY
Biotechnology gd USA, 3d ed, 1655
Biotechnology in the US pharmaceutical industry 1995, 4th ed, 1733
Biotechnology info sources, 1658
Language of biotech, 2d ed, 1659
Molecular biology & biotech, 1561
State-by-state biotech dir, 3d ed, 1506

BIOTIC COMMUNITIES
Habitats, 1598

BIRD WATCHING
Birdwatcher's handbk, 1614

BIRDS
CITES identification gd—birds, 1612
Common American birds, 1611
National Audubon Society bird garden, 1560
Penguins of the world, 1616
Photographic gd to the shorebirds of the world, 1617
Pockets: birds, 65

BIRDS—AMERICA
Warblers of the Americas, 1613

BIRDS—BRITISH ISLES
Birdwatcher's handbk, 1614

BIRDS—CENTRAL AMERICA
Guide to the birds of Mexico & N Central America, 1615

BIRDS—EUROPE
Birdwatcher's handbk, 1614

BIRDS—MEXICO
Guide to the birds of Mexico & N Central America, 1615

BIRTH CONTROL
Association for Population/Family Planning Libs & Info Centers—Intl (AFPLIC-I) union list of serials, 861

BIRTHDAYS
Born this day, 30

BLACKS
Bibliographic gd to black studies 1994, 398
Black studies on disc [CD-ROM], 399
Contemporary black biog, v.8, 400
Contemporary black biog, v.9, 401

BLACKS IN THE MOTION PICTURE INDUSTRY
Blacks in black & white, 2d ed, 1410

BLACKS—STATISTICS
Statistical record of black America, 3d ed, 404

BLAKE, WILLIAM
Blake bks suppl, 1244

BOATS & BOATING
McKnew & Parker's buyer's gd to sportfishing boats, 1995 ed, 810

BOOK COLLECTING
ABC for bk collectors, 7th ed, 1001
Antiquarian bks, 1002
Book prices: used & rare 1995, 1003
Bookman's price index, v.50, 1004

BOOKS
Bibliographic hist of the bk, 664

BOOKS & READING
Private libs in Renaissance England, v.3: PLRE 67-86, 1006

BOOKS—REVIEWS
Children's ref plus [CD-ROM], 21

BOOKS—STATISTICS
Consumer Research study on bk purchasing, 1993, 673

BOOKSELLERS & BOOKSELLING
Bookman's price index, v.50, 1004
Publishing market ref plus 1994-95, 2d ed [CD-ROM], 672
Used bk lover's gd to the Midwest, 1007

BOSNIAN LANGUAGE—DICTIONARIES—ENGLISH
Bosnian-English, English-Bosnian concise dict, 1098

BOTANISTS
Dictionary of British & Irish botanists & horticulturalists, rev ed, 1562
One hundred & one botanists, 1564

BOTANY
Dictionary of generic names of seed plants, 1565
Plant explorer's gd to New England, 474
Plants & their names, 1563
Scientific & common names of 7,000 vascular plants in the US, 1593
What plant where, 1566

BOUNDARY DISPUTES
Encyclopedia of intl boundaries, 455

BREWERIES
On tap, 1995 ed, 1532

BREWERS
Encyclopedia of beer, 1525

BRITISH HISTORY
Larousse dict of British hist, 541

BRITISH LITERATURE
British prose writers of the early 17th century, 1232
Late 19th- & early 20th-century British literary biographers, 1225
Twentieth-century British literary biographers, 1227

BRITISH NEWSPAPERS
Twentieth-century newspaper pr in Britain, 972

BROADCAST JOURNALISM
Broadcast news manual of style, 2d ed, 992
Burrelle's index of broadcast transcripts, 1993 ed, 998

BROADCASTING
International dict of broadcasting & film, 984

BUILDING SITES
Time-Saver standards for housing & residential dvlpmt, 1048

BUILDINGS
Pockets: bldgs, 66

BULBS
Best bulbs for temperate climates, 1545
Garden bulbs for the South, 1546

BUSH, GEORGE
Cumulated indexes to the public papers of the presidents of the US: George Bush, 1989-93, 744

BUSINESS. See also ACCOUNTING; CORPORATIONS
Bahamas hndbk & businessman's annual 1995 [35th ed], 170
Basic bus lib: core resources, 3d ed, 173
Bibliographic gd to bus & economics 1994, 174
Business rankings annual, 1995, 197
Dictionary for bus & finance, 3d ed, 180
Directory of American research & tech 1995, 29th ed, 182
Gale bus resources [CD-ROM], 199

Peterson's job opportunities in bus 1995, 280
USA business: the portable ency for doing bus with the US, 241
World dir of exhibitions & trade fairs 1995, 309

BUSINESS COMMUNICATION
Delmar ref manual: essentials for the electronic office, 310

BUSINESS—DATABASES
Internet compendium: subject gds to social scis, bus, & law resources, 101

BUSINESS—DICTIONARIES
Dictionary of bus & legal terms: Russian-English/English-Russian, 575
Dictionary of bus terms, 2d ed, 178

BUSINESS EDUCATION
Peterson's gd to MBA programs, 355

BUSINESS ENTERPRISES
American bus disc, 1995 ed [CD-ROM], 181
Hoover's co & industry database on CD-ROM [CD-ROM], 190
Hoover's gd to computer cos, 1773
Hoover's hndbk of American bus 1995, 191
Hoover's hndbk of world bus 1995-96, 3d ed, 201
National dir of addresses & telephone nos, 1995 ed, 56

BUSINESS ETHICS
Codes of professional responsibility, 3d ed, 1431

BUSINESS—HISTORY
Notable corporate chronologies, 177

BUSINESS INFORMATION SERVICES
International bus & trade dirs, 228

BUSINESS INTELLIGENCE
Bibliography of bus/competitive intelligence & benchmarking lit, 175
How to find co intelligence in state docs, 15th ed, 202

BUSINESS LIBRARIES
Basic bus lib: core resources, 3d ed, 173

BUSINESS—PERIODICALS
Directory of bus per special issues, 209

BUSINESS RELOCATION
Craighead's intl bus, travel, & relocation gd to 78 countries, 231

BUSINESS SCHOOLS
Business Week gd to the best bus schools, 4th ed, 332

BUSINESS WRITING
Delmar ref manual: essentials for the electronic office, 310

CALIFORNIA
Lawmen & desperadoes, 571

CAMPAIGN FUNDS
Lobbying, PACs, & campaign finance, 740

CAMPS
Guide to accredited camps, 1995/96, 39th ed, 811
Guide to summer camps & summer schools 1995/96, 27th ed, 326

CANADA
Arthur Andersen N American bus sourcebk, 288
Best hospitals in America, 2d ed, 1693
Canadian profile: alcohol, tobacco, & other drugs 1995, 898
Catalogue of Canadian catalogues, 249
Class FC, a classification for Canadian hist, 2d ed, 628
Dinosaur safari gd, 1814
Directory of Canadian schools, 6th ed, 319
Emergency Librarian index, vs.1-20: 1973-93, 645
Facts about Canada, its provinces & territories, 137
Favorite annuals, 1568
Favorite flowering shrubs, 1569
Favorite perennials, 1570
Favorite shade plants, 1571
Great lives from hist: American women series, 942
Lake, river, & sea-run fishes of Canada, 1624
Novalis gd to Canadian shrines, 1476
Opportunities for vocational study, 385
Turtles of the US & Canada, 1636

CANADA—BUSINESS HANDBOOKS
Globe & Mail report on bus: Canada co handbk 1994, 250

CANADA—DIRECTORIES
Canadian address bk, 54

CANADA—ECONOMIC CONDITIONS
Economic integration in Europe & N America, 232

CANADA—HISTORY
Bibliographic gd to N American hist 1994, 489
Larousse dict of N American hist, 508

CANADA—LIBRARY RESOURCES
Canadiana in US repositories: a preliminary gd, 136

CANADA—MAPS
Hammond road atlas & vacation gd, 442
Reader's Digest atlas of Canada, 451

CANADA—POLITICS & GOVERNMENT
Bibliography of works on Canadian foreign relations 1986-90, 748
Contemporary Canadian pols, 1988-94, 751
Language of Canadian pols, 752

CANADIAN LITERATURE
George Ryga papers, 1249

CANADIAN LITERATURE—INDIAN AUTHORS
Native N American lit, 1259

CANCER
Anticancer drugs from animals, plants, & microorganisms, 1740

CAPITAL INVESTMENTS
Flows & stocks of fixed capital 1967-92, 213

CAREER DEVELOPMENT
DISCovering careers & jobs [CD-ROM], 271
Gale's career guidance system, expanded ed [CD-ROM], 384
On-line job search companion, 272

CARIBBEAN AREA
Bahamas hndbk & businessman's annual 1995 [35th ed], 170
Frommer's comprehensive travel gd: Caribbean '95, 483
Statistical yrbk for Latin America & the Caribbean, 1994 ed, 154

CASH, JOHNNY
Johnny Cash record catalog, 1317

CATALOGING
Cataloging nonbook materials with AACR2R & MARC, 631
Class FC, a classification for Canadian hist, 2d ed, 628
SUPER LCCS CD [CD-ROM], 633
USMARC format for bibliographic data, 1994 ed, 634

CATALOGS, COMMERCIAL
Catalogue of Canadian catalogues, 249

CATALOGS, PUBLISHERS'
Descriptive catalog of the music printed by Hubert Waelrant & Jan de Laet, 1266

CATHOLIC CHURCH
Handbook of Catholic theology [rev ed], 1475
HarperCollins ency of Catholicism, 1469
Our Sunday Visitor's Catholic ency & Catholic dict [CD-ROM], 1471
Our Sunday Visitor's ency of Catholic hist, 1472

CATHOLIC CHURCH—DOCTRINES
New dict of Catholic social thought, 1470

CATS
American Animal Hospital Assn ency of cat health & care, 1618
Pockets: cats, 67

CD-ROM
CD-ROM dir, 14th ed [CD-ROM], 1768
CD-ROM dir 95 with multimedia CDs, 13th ed, 1769
CD-ROM finder, 8

CD-ROM BOOKS
CD-ROM bk index, 80
CD-ROMs rated, 10

CD-ROMs
Alloy finder [CD-ROM], 1660
America: hist & life on disc [CD-ROM], 512
American Heritage talking dict, 3d ed [CD-ROM], 1062
American Medical Assn family medical gd [CD-ROM], 1707
American Sign Lang dict on CD-ROM [CD-ROM], 1130
American bus disc, 1995 ed [CD-ROM], 181
Arctic & Antarctic regions, [CD-ROM], 127
Art on screen on CD-ROM [CD-ROM], 1037
ASSIA plus [CD-ROM], 97
ASTM standards source [CD-ROM], 1663
Bacon's dirs on disc 1995 update [CD-ROM], 974
BHI plus [CD-ROM], 955
Biography index [CD-ROM], 24
Black studies on disc [CD-ROM], 399
Books in print with bk reviews plus [CD-ROM], 17
Books out-of-print plus [CD-ROM], 18
Broadcast news [CD-ROM], 991
CD-ROM dir, 14th ed [CD-ROM], 1768
Chambers dict on CD-ROM [CD-ROM], 1064
Child abuse & neglect [CD-ROM], 616
CHOICE reviews on SilverPlatter [CD-ROM], 84
Civil War [CD-ROM], 691
Consumers ref disc [CD-ROM], 218
DiscLit: world authors [CD-ROM], 1154
DISCovering careers & jobs [CD-ROM], 271
Editor & Publisher market gd 1994 [CD-ROM], 977
Electronic Gieck's engineering formulas [CD-ROM], 1642
Encyclopedia Americana, 1995 [CD-ROM], 47
Encyclopedia of frontier biog on CD-ROM [CD-ROM], 497
European research & dvlpmt database 1995 [CD-ROM], 1510
EXEGY: the source for current world info, 49
Eyewitness hist of the world [CD-ROM], 567
Fish & fisheries worldwide [CD-ROM], 1605
Gale bus resources [CD-ROM], 199
Gale's career guidance system, expanded ed [CD-ROM], 384
Global bks in print plus [CD-ROM], 13
Government career gds [CD-ROM], 256
Hoover's co & industry database on CD-ROM [CD-ROM], 190
Human rights on CD-ROM, 2d ed [CD-ROM], 609
International multimedia yrbk 1995-96 on CD-ROM [CD-ROM], 1752
JIST's electronic gd for occupational exploration [CD-ROM], 275
Korea [CD-ROM], 692
KR Info OnDisc grants database [CD-ROM], 848
Landmark docs in American hist [CD-ROM], 498
LISA plus [CD-ROM], 625
Martindale-Hubbell law dir on CD-ROM [CD-ROM], 584
Merriam-Webster's collegiate dict deluxe, electronic ed [CD-ROM], 1066
MLA intl bibliog [CD-ROM], 1143
Normandy [CD-ROM], 693
PC Globe maps'n'facts [CD-ROM], 450

Philosopher's index [CD-ROM], 1436
Prehistoria [CD-ROM], 1816
Science navigator [CD-ROM], 1500
SPDCD 1995: the standard per dir [CD-ROM], 87
Species info lib [CD-ROM], 1606
StartSmart small bus advisor [CD-ROM], 207
SUPER LCCS CD [CD-ROM], 633
Terrorist group profiles [CD-ROM], 601
U.S. presidents [CD-ROM], 527
Variety's video dir plus [CD-ROM], 1388
Video rating gd for libs on CD-ROM 1990-94 [CD-ROM], 995
Vietnam [CD-ROM], 694
Wildlife worldwide [CD-ROM], 1607
Wilson author biogs on disc 1995 [CD-ROM], 1144
World Bk multimedia ency [CD-ROM], 51
World alive [CD-ROM], 1609
World weatherdisc, 1994 ed [CD-ROM], 1811

CELTIC LITERATURE
Encyclopaedia of Celtic wisdom, 788

CENTRAL AMERICA
Guide to Central American collections in the US, 152

CHAD
Chad, 115

CHAMBER MUSIC
Cello music since 1960, 1286
Chamber music for solo voice & instruments 1960-89, 1299

CHAMPAGNE (WINE)
Champagne companion, 1354

CHARACTERS & CHARACTERISTICS IN LITERATURE
Characters in 20th-century lit, bk 2, 1155
Who's who in Shakespeare, 1240

CHARITABLE USES, TRUSTS, & FOUNDATIONS
Food aid in figures, v.11, 881
Who knows who [1996], 186

CHARITIES—DIRECTORIES
Guide to private fortunes, v.2, 188
Guide to private fortunes, v.3, 189

CHEMICAL ENGINEERING
Rules of thumb for chemical engineers, 1650

CHEMICAL INDUSTRY
Chemical industry in 1993, 222
Market trends for selected chemical products 1985-90 & prospects to 1995, 303

CHEMICAL LABORATORIES
Handbook of lab health & safety, 2d ed, 1796

CHEMICALS
Complete gd to household chemicals, 1795

CHEMISTRY
Chemical scis graduate school finder 1994-95, 1791

CHEMISTRY, ORGANIC
Desk ref for organic chemists, 1792

CHEMISTRY, TECHNICAL
Ullmann's ency of industrial chemistry, v.a25, 5th ed, 1789

CHICANO LANGUAGE
Dictionary of Chicano Spanish, 2d ed, 1136

CHICKASAW LANGUAGE—DICTIONARIES—ENGLISH
Chickasaw: an analytical dict, 1099

CHILD ABUSE
Child abuse & neglect [CD-ROM], 616
Child sexual abuse custody dispute annot bibliog, 900
Childhood sexual abuse, 618

CHILD CARE
Complete baby & child care, 904
Sourcebook on parenting & child care, 899

CHILD REARING
Parenting, 903
Parents' resource almanac, 901

CHILDBIRTH
Mayo Clinic complete bk of pregnancy & baby's 1st yr, 1722

CHILDREN
State legislative summary, 1994, 595

CHILDREN—BOOKS & READING
Fantasy lit for children & young adults, 4th ed, 1167
Great new nonfiction reads, 1184
More kids' favorite bks, 1168
Using picture storybks to teach literary devices. v.2, 1164

CHILDREN—DISEASES
Smart medicine for a healthier child, 1713

CHILDREN OF PRESIDENTS
America's royalty, rev ed, 719

CHILDREN—SERVICES FOR
Parents' resource almanac, 901

CHILDREN'S ATLASES
Around the world: an atlas of maps & pictures, 443
Children's atlas of natural wonders, 1806
Children's atlas of the 20th century, 553
Pockets: world atlas, 77

CHILDREN'S ENCYCLOPEDIAS & DICTIONARIES
American Civil War, 504
Computer dict for kids & their parents, 1748
Dorling Kindersley visual ency, 46
Encyclopedias, atlases, & dicts, 48
Kingfisher illus children's dict, 1087
Kingfisher illus thesaurus, 1088
Kingfisher young world ency, 50
Oxford children's bk of famous people, 31
Profiles in American hist, 509
Visual dict of physics, 1819

CHILDREN'S LIBRARIES
More bks kids will sit still for, 663

CHILDREN'S LITERATURE. *See also* **CHILDREN'S STORIES**
American Indian ref & resource bks for children & YAs, 2d ed, 1177
Best toys, bks & videos for kids, 1010
Beyond picture bks, 2d ed, 1180
Canadian bk review annual 1994: children's lit, 1176
Children's authors & illustrators, 5th ed, 1178
Children's bks in print 1995, 19
Children's ref plus [CD-ROM], 21
Magazines for kids & teens, 86
More bks kids will sit still for, 663
More kids' favorite bks, 1168
Research & professional resources in children's lit, 1169
Something about the author, v.78, 1172
Something about the author, v.79, 1173
Something about the author, v.80, 1174
Special collections in children's lit, 661
Subject gd to children's bks in print 1995, 20
Teaching children's lit, 379
Twentieth-century children's writers, 4th ed, 1175

CHILDREN'S LITERATURE—BIBLIOGRAPHY
Africa in lit for children & young adults, 1166
Index to histl fiction for children & young people, 1179
Ways of war: the era of WW II in children's & YA fiction, 1165

CHILDREN'S LITERATURE—ILLUSTRATIONS
Art of children's picture bks, 2d ed, 1183

CHILDREN'S REFERENCE BOOKS
Children's ref plus [CD-ROM], 21

CHILDREN'S SONGS
Children's jukebox, 1278

CHILDREN'S STORIES
Black in focus, 1163
Using picture storybks to teach literary devices, v.2, 1164

CHINA
China: a provincial atlas, 452
China bibliog, 535

CHORUSES WITH ORCHESTRA
Conductor's gd to choral-orchestral works, 1297

CHRISTIAN ART & SYMBOLISM
Dictionary of Christian art, 1028

CHRISTIAN BIOGRAPHY
Seeds in the wilderness: profiles of world religious leaders, 1443
Twentieth-century dict of Christian biog, 1465

CHRISTIAN EDUCATION
Peterson's choose a Christian college, 4th ed, 1474
Religious educ, 1960-93, 1463

CHRISTIAN LITERATURE
Handbook of Christian Latin, 1115

CHRISTIAN PILGRIMS AND PILGRIMAGES
Pilgrimage to Santiago de Compostela, 1462

CHRISTIAN SHRINES
Novalis gd to Canadian shrines, 1476

CHRISTIANITY
Concise dict of Christian theology, 1453
Concise dict of Christianity in America, 1466
Historical dict of ecumenical Christianity, 1473

CHRONIC PAIN
Classification of chronic pain, 2d ed, 1723

CHRONICALLY ILL
Long term care, 841
Resource gd for the disabled, 854

CHRONOLOGY, HISTORICAL
Chronicle of the 20th century, 558
Chronology of world hist, compact ed, 564
Columbia chronicles of American life, 1910-92, 501

CHURCH & SOCIAL PROBLEMS
New dict of Catholic social thought, 1470

CHURCHILL, WINSTON
Proverbial Winston S. Churchill, 760

CIGARS
Cigar companion, 2d ed, 1351

CITIES & TOWNS
America's top-rated smaller cities, 1994-95 ed, 926
City crime rankings, 602
Editor & Publisher market gd 1994, 976
Editor & Publisher market gd 1994 [CD-ROM], 977
Gale city & metro rankings reporter, 930
Health & environment in America's top-rated cities, 931
100 great cities of world hist, 927

CITY PLANNING
Information sources in urban & regional planning, 928

CIVIL RIGHTS. *See also* **HUMAN RIGHTS**
Civil rights decisions of the US Supreme Court, the 19th century, 607
Civil rights decisions of the US Supreme Court, the 20th century, 608

CLANS
Collins Scottish clan & family ency, 435

CLASSICAL LITERATURE
Annotated catalogue of early editions of Erasmus, 1250
Classical & medieval lit criticism, v.14, 1149

CLASSIFICATION—BOOKS—JUVENILE LITERATURE
Subject headings for children 1994, 632

CLEMENS, SAMUEL. *See* **TWAIN, MARK**

CLERGY
Seeds in the wilderness: profiles of world religious leaders, 1443

CLEVELAND MUSEUM OF ART
Catalogue of American silver, 999

CLIMATOLOGY
Elsevier's dict of climatology & meteorology, 1808

COAL
Annual bulletin of coal stats for Europe & N America, 1994, 1838

COASTS
Atlas of Mesozoic & Cenozoic coastlines, 1807

COINS
Guide bk of US coins, 1996, 49th ed, 1008

COLE, NAT KING
Straighten up & fly right: a chronology & discography of Nat "King" Cole, 1329

COLLECTIBLES
Warman's antiques & collectibles price gd, 29th ed, 1000

COLLEGE CHOICE
American community colleges, 10th ed, 362
Princeton Review student access gd: the big bk of colleges, 357
Summer on campus [2d ed], 360

COLLEGE COSTS
America's lowest cost colleges, 9th ed, 359

COLLEGE LIBRARIANS
Academic lib of the 90s, 620

COLLEGE MAJORS
Education for the Earth, 2d ed, 337

COLLEGE SPORTS
Encyclopedia of college basketball, 809

NCAA football, 819

COLLOQUIAL LANGUAGE
Dictionary of Russian slang & colloquial expressions, 1128

COLTRANE, JOHN
John Coltrane, 1324

COMEDY FILMS
American silent film comedies, 1378
Jerry Lewis films, 1397

COMIC BOOKS, STRIPS, ETC.
Graphic novels, 1359

COMMERCE
Data sources for bus & market analysis, 4th ed, 296
Directory of import regimes, pt.1, 289
Directory of import regimes, pt.2, 290
External trade monthly stats, 293
International bus & trade dirs, 228
United Nations Commission on Intl Trade law yrbk, v.24, 1993, 307

COMMERCIAL CATALOGS
Directory of mail order catalogs, 1995, 9th ed, 219

COMMERCIAL CORRESPONDENCE
Forms of address, 311

COMMERCIAL TREATIES
Encyclopedia of the N American Free Trade Agreement, 305

COMMUNAL LIVING
Communities dir, 1995 ed, 852

COMMUNICATION
Broadcast news [CD-ROM], 991
Leo Burnett worldwide advertising & media fact bk, 302
Power media selects, 9th ed, 988

COMMUNITY COLLEGES
Chronicle 2-yr college databk, rev ed, 335
National profile of community colleges 1995-96, 366

COMMUNITY DEVELOPMENT
Alternatives to the Peace Corps, 868
Guide to fed funding for volunteer programs & community serv, 3d ed, 874

COMPOSERS
Singer-songwriters, 1307

COMPOSERS—GERMANY
Beethoven ency, 1281

COMPOSERS—GREAT BRITAIN
Peter Maxwell Davies, 1282
William Mathias, 1279

COMPOSERS—UNITED STATES
Carl Ruggles, 1280
William Thomas McKinley, 1283

COMPOSITE MATERIALS
ASM handbk, v.5: surface engineering, 1661

COMPOSITION (LANGUAGE ARTS)
CCCC bibliog of composition & rhetoric 1992, 1058

COMPUTER BULLETIN BOARDS
Complete cyberspace ref & dir, 1772
Washington online: how to access the govt's electronic bulletin boards, 1786

COMPUTER GAMES
Net games, 813

COMPUTER INDUSTRY
Hoover's gd to computer cos, 1773

COMPUTER NETWORKS
Complete cyberspace ref & dir, 1772
Net games, 813
Network Pr dict of networking, 1761

COMPUTER SECURITY
Vocabulary of computer security & viruses, 1766

COMPUTER SOFTWARE
Guide to free computer materials 1995, 13th ed, 1771
International intellectual property protection for computer software, 638

COMPUTER VIRUSES
Vocabulary of computer security & viruses, 1766

COMPUTERS. *See also* **MICROCOMPUTERS**
Computer dict for kids & their parents, 1748
Computer glossary, 7th ed, 1757
Computer support dir, 1767
Dictionary of computer terms, 4th ed, 1755
Dictionary of computer works, rev ed, 1754
Directory of computer & high tech grants, 2d ed, 1770
Illustrated computer dict for young people, 1763
International biographical dict of computer pioneers, 1758
McGraw-Hill illus dict of personal computers, 4th ed, 1760
Spencer's illus computer dict, 1765

CONFEDERATE STATES OF AMERICA. ARMY
Compendium of the Confederate armies: Ky., Md., Mo., Confederate units & Indian units, 522
Compendium of the Confederate armies: La., 523
Compendium of the Confederate armies: Miss., 524
Compendium of the Confederate armies: S.C. & Ga., 525
Compendium of the Confederate armies: Tex., 526

CONFLICT MANAGEMENT
Negotiation lit, 283

CONIFERS
Pruning of trees, shrubs, & conifers, [rev ed], 1588

CONNECTICUT
Connecticut, Maine, Mass., [&] R.I.: atlas of histl county boundaries, 438

CONSERVATION OF NATURAL RESOURCES
Portraits in conservation: E & S Africa, 1596

CONSTITUTIONS
Constitutions of the world, 611

CONSUMER EDUCATION
Complete gd to household chemicals, 1795
Consumer health USA, 1711
Consumers ref disc [CD-ROM], 218
U.S. consumer interest groups, 216

CONSUMER PROTECTION
Consolidated list of products whose consumption and/or sale have been banned...., 5th ed, 217
U.S. consumer interest groups, 216

CONSUMERS
Latitudes & attitudes, 915

CONTESTS
Freed's gd to student contests & publishing, 5th ed, 1356

CONTRACTING OUT
Peterson's contract servs for higher educ, 342

COPYRIGHT
Copyright hndbk, 2d ed, 590

COPYRIGHT—COMPUTER PROGRAMS
International intellectual property protection for computer software, 638

CORPORATIONS
American bus disc, 1995 ed [CD-ROM], 181
Business rankings annual, 1995, 197
CorpTech dir of tech cos 1996, 10th US ed, 1749
Directory of cos required to file annual reports with the SEC, 183
Globe & Mail report on bus: Canada co handbk 1994, 250
Hoover's co & industry database on CD-ROM [CD-ROM], 190
Hoover's gd to computer cos, 1773
Hoover's hndbk of American bus 1995, 191
Hoover's hndbk of world bus 1995-96, 3d ed, 201
Hoover's masterlist of America's top 2,500 employers, 192
How to find info about foreign firms, 6th ed, 204
How to find info about private cos, 6th ed, 205
Job seeker's gd to socially responsible cos, 262
Major cos of Europe 1994/5, 253
Multinational corps & the environment, 1851
Notable corporate chronologies, 177
Quantum cos, 195

Standard & Poor's 500 gd, 1995 ed, 214
Standard & Poor's midcap 400 gd, 1995 ed, 215
Who knows who [1996], 186
World's major cos dir, 229

CORPORATIONS—POLITICAL ACTIVITY
Government affairs yellow bk, v.1, no.1, 187

CORRESPONDENCE SCHOOLS & COURSES
College degrees by mail 1996, rev ed, 363

CORROSION & ANTI-CORROSIVES
Handbook of corrosion data, 1667

COSMETICS
Consumer's dict of cosmetic ingredients, 4th ed, 1790

COSMOLOGY
Stars & atoms, 1799
Universe explained, 1802

COSTUME
Ethnic dress, 388

COUNSELING
Dictionary of family therapy, rev ed, 1718

COUNTRY MUSIC
Definitive country, 1320

COUNTY COURTS
County courthouse bk, 2d ed, 588

COUNTY GOVERNMENT
Carroll's county dir, 721
Carroll's municipal dir, 725
County executive dir, 727

COWBOYS
Cowboy ency, 510

CRABS
Pacific coast crabs & shrimps, 1622

CREATION
Encyclopedia of creation myths, 1444

CREOLE DIALECTS—DICTIONARIES—ENGLISH
Hippocrene concise Haitian Creole-English, English-Haitian Creole dict, 1106

CRICKET
Dictionary of cricket, 2d ed, 814

CRIME
City crime rankings, 602
Crimes & punishment, 573
Criminal justice in Israel, 596
Detective dict, rev ed, 598
Guide to American crime films of the 40s & 50s, 1392
Guide to American crime films of the 30s, 1393
Organized crime, 594

CRIMINAL INVESTIGATION
Applications in criminal analysis, 604
Detective dict, rev ed, 598

CRIMINAL JUSTICE, ADMINISTRATION OF
Criminal justice in Israel, 596
Post-release assistance programs for prisoners, 2d ed, 600

CRITICISM
Bibliography of the English novel from the Restoration to the French Revolution, 1236
Classical & medieval lit criticism, v.14, 1149
Columbia dict of modern literary & cultural critcism, 960
Contemporary literary criticism, v.84, 1152
Contemporary literary criticism, v.85, 1153
Jacques Derrida (II), 956
Literature criticism from 1400-1800, v.27, 1156
Nineteenth-century lit criticism, v.46, 1158
Poetry criticism, v.10, 1265
Shakespearean criticism, v.26, 1242
Short story criticism, v.17, 1196
Twentieth-century literary criticism, v.56, 1159
Twentieth-century literary criticism, v.57, 1160

CROATIA
Historical dict of the Republic of Croatia, 549

CROSS-CULTURAL STUDIES
Aggression & conflict, 835
Ethnic relations, 389
Marriage, family, & relationships, 862

CROSSWORD PUZZLES
Crossword puzzle dict, 6th ed, 1085

CROTHERS, RACHEL
Rachel Crothers, 1208

CRYSTAL SETS (RADIO)
Crystal clear v.2, 993

CULTURE
Cultural atlas of Spain & Portugal, 539
Wild planet!, 1352

CURIOSITIES & WONDERS
Encyclopedia of popular misconceptions, 62
Top 10 of everything, 61

CUSHING, PETER
Christopher Lee & Peter Cushing & horror cinema, 1396

CUSTODY OF CHILDREN
Child sexual abuse custody dispute annot bibliog, 900

CY YOUNG AWARD
Cy Young award winners, 808

CYNICS (GREEK PHILOSOPHY)
Philosophy of Cynicism, 1425

CYPRUS
Cyprus, rev ed, 130

CYTOKINES
Dictionary of cytokines, 1558

DANCING
Music, dance & theater scholarships, 1365

DATABASES
Arctic & Antarctic regions, [CD-ROM], 127
Dr. Tom Linden's gd to online medicine, 1709
EPA database bk, 1865
Federal database finder, 4th ed, 59
Key gd to electronic resources: agriculture, 1518
Key gd to electronic resources: engineering, 1643
Key gd to electronic resources: health scis, 1688
KR Info OnDisc grants database [CD-ROM], 848
ONLINE 100, 1777
World databases in industry, 225
World databases in geography & geology, 453
World databases in patents, 587
World databases in physics & mathematics, 1788

DAVIES, PETER MAXWELL
Peter Maxwell Davies, 1282

DEAFNESS
Deaf persons in the arts & scis, 857

DEATH
Encyclopedia of afterlife beliefs & phenomena, 1445
Last words: a dict of deathbed quotations, 95

DECORATIVE ARTS
Illustrated ency of Victoriana, 1016

DEGREES, ACADEMIC
Doctor of philosophy degree, 330

DEMOGRAPHY
Bibliography of American demographic hist, 906
Gale country & world rankings reporter, 905
Latitudes & attitudes, 915
Official gd to the American marketplace, 2d ed, 911
Official gd to the generations, 908
Population & dvlpmt: dir of non-govtl org in OECD countries, 909
Profiles of America, S region, v.4: Ky. * N.C. * Tenn., 910
Sourcebook of zip code demographics, 10th ed, 913
Statistical forecasts of the US, 2d ed, 914

DENTISTRY
Directory of medical & dental schools worldwide, 6th ed, 1687
REA's authoritative gd to medical & dental schools, 1706

DEPRESSION GLASS
Collector's ency of Depression glass, 11th ed, 1013

DEPRESSION, MENTAL
Depression, 1724

DERRIDA, JACQUES
Jacques Derrida (II), 956

DESIGN
Art & design scholarships, 1036
Illustrated ency of Victoriana, 1016

DESSERTS
International dict of desserts, pastries, & confections, 1523

DETECTIVE & MYSTERY FILMS
Guide to American crime films of the 40s & 50s, 1392
Guide to American crime films of the 30s, 1393

DETECTIVE & MYSTERY STORIES
Crown crime companion, 1189
J. Sheridan Le Fanu, 1256

DETECTIVES
Detective dict, rev ed, 598

DEVELOPING COUNTRIES
Science, tech, & society in the 3d World, 138
Technological capacity-bldg & tech partnership, 1515
Third world women's lits, 946

DIAGNOSIS
Professional hndbk of diagnostic tests, 1710

DICTATORS
Dictators & tyrants, 705

DICTIONARIES, POLYGLOT
Elsevier's dict of biometry, 1557
Elsevier's dict of climatology & meteorology, 1808
Elsevier's nautical dict, 3d ed, 1894
Space scis dict 2, 1645
Space scis dict 3, 1646

DIESEL LOCOMOTIVES
Contemporary diesel spotter's gd, 2d ed, 1889

DINOSAURS
Dinosaur safari gd, 1814
Pockets: dinosaurs, 68
Visual dict of prehistoric life, 1817

DIPLOMATIC AND CONSULAR SERVICE, CANADIAN
Diplomatic, consular, & other representatives in Canada, 750

DISASTER RELIEF
Global refugee crisis, 895

DISASTERS
Failed tech, 1511

DISCRIMINATION
Guidelines for bias-free writing, 968

DISPUTE RESOLUTION (LAW)
Martindale-Hubbell dispute resolution dir, 583

DISSERTATIONS, ACADEMIC
Index to law school theses & dissertations, 570
Religion & the American experience, the 20th century, 1442

DISTANCE EDUCATION
Distance educ, 377

DIVINATION
Divining the future: prognostication from astrology to zoomancy, 791
Tarot for beginners, 787

DOGS
American Animal Hospital Assn ency of dog health & care, 1619
Encyclopedia of the dog, 1620

DOLPHINS
Whales, dolphins, & porpoises, 1629

DOMESTIC RELATIONS
State legislative summary, 1994, 595

DRAMA
Shakespeare cos & festivals, 1420

DRAMATISTS
Rachel Crothers, 1208
Tennessee Williams, 1220

DREAMS
Cloud nine: a dreamer's dict, 781
Dream ency, 779
Parkers' complete bk of dreams, 783

DRUGS. See also PHARMACOLOGY
Anticancer drugs from animals, plants, & microorganisms, 1740
Drug Topics red bk, 1995, 1734
Essential gd to prescription drugs 1995, 1737
PDR generics, 1738
PDR gd to drug interactions, side effects, indications, 1995, 49th ed, 1739
Physicians' desk ref for nonprescription drugs, 1994, 15th ed, 1741
USP DI 1995, v.1, 1744
USP DI 1995, v.2, 1745
USP DI 1995, v.3, 1746
USP dict of USAN & intl drug names, 1747

DWELLINGS
Time-Saver standards for housing & residential dvlpmt, 1048

DYLAN, BOB
Bob Dylan, 1334

EARTH SCIENCES. See also GEOGRAPHY; GEOLOGYBDOFF
Earth-Science educ resource dir, 1804
Pockets: Earth facts, 69

EAST ASIA
Chironomidae [Diptera] of Japan, 1626
Far East & Australasia 1995, 26th ed, 167

EASTLAKE, WILLIAM
Work of William Eastlake, 1209

ECOFEMINISM
Ecofeminist theory, 935

ECOLOGY
Concise Oxford dict of ecology, 1854
Earth words, 1861
Encyclopedia of environmental biology, 1856
Environmental acronyms, 1850
Great events from hist 2: ecology & the environment series, 1853
Krupin's toll-free environmental dir, 1867

ECONOMIC ASSISTANCE
Directory of biomedical & health care grants 1995, 9th ed, 1685

ECONOMIC DEVELOPMENT
Atlas of world dvlpmt, 444
Population & dvlpmt: dir of non-govtl org in OECD countries, 909
Revenue stats of OECD member countries 1965-93, 772

ECONOMIC FORECASTING
Global trends: world almanac of dvlpmt & peace, 200
World index of economic forecasts, 4th ed, 208

ECONOMIC HISTORY
Countries of the world & their leaders yrbk 1995: suppl, 710
Global trends: world almanac of dvlpmt & peace, 200

ECONOMIC INDICATORS
Bond markets, 1995 ed, 292

ECONOMICS. See also BUSINESS; COMMERCE; FINANCE; INDUSTRY
Bibliographic gd to bus & economics 1994, 174
Cabell's dir of publishing opportunities in accounting, economics & finance, 6th ed, 669
McGraw-Hill ency of economics, 179
Worldmark ency of the nations, 8th ed, 105

ECUMENICAL MOVEMENT
Historical dict of ecumenical Christianity, 1473

EDEN, ANTHONY, EARL OF AVON
Anthony Eden, 1897-1977, 759

EDUCATION
Educators gd to free films, filmstrips, & slides 1995, 55th ed, 375
Educators gd to free videotapes 1995, 42d ed, 376
Encyclopedia of educ info, 1994/95, 324
ERIC identifier authority list (IAL) 1995, 629
Hooray for heroes!, 321
Princeton Review student access gd to the best medical schools, 1705
Thesaurus of ERIC descriptors, 13th ed, 318

EDUCATION, ELEMENTARY
Blackwell hndbk of educ, 325
Educators grade gd to free teaching aids 1995, 41st ed, 322
Elementary teachers gd to free curriculum materials 1995, 52d ed, 323

EDUCATION, HIGHER
Directory of theatre training programs, 5th ed, 1419
Peterson's gd to colleges in the Midwest 1995, 11th ed, 343
Peterson's gd to colleges in the South 1995, 10th ed, 344
Peterson's gd to colleges in the West 1995, 9th ed, 345
Peterson's gd to middle Atlantic colleges 1995, 11th ed, 346
Peterson's gd to New England colleges 1995, 11th ed, 347
Peterson's gd to NY colleges 1995, 11th ed, 348
Princeton Review student access gd to the best 309 colleges, 358
Students' gd to playwriting opportunities, 1421

EDUCATION, PRIMARY
Hooray for heroes!, 321

EDUCATION, SECONDARY
Blackwell hndbk of educ, 325

EDUCATIONAL EQUALIZATION
Gender equity in educ, 313

EDUCATIONAL TESTING SERVICE
ETS test collection catalog, v.2, 2d ed, 314

EDUCATIONAL TESTS & MEASUREMENTS
ETS test collection catalog, v.2, 2d ed, 314

EDWARDS, JONATHAN
Jonathan Edwards, 1440

EGYPT
Historical dict of Egypt, 162
Pockets: ancient Egypt, 63
Weed flora of Egypt, rev ed, 1582
Who's who in Egyptian mythology, 2d ed, 1350

ELECTIONS
America votes 21, 735

ELECTRIC POWER
Annual bulletin of electric energy stats for Europe & N America, 1994, v.38, 1839
Electric light & power US electric utility industry dir, 1995, 4th ed, 1651
Electric light & power US non-utility power dir, 1995, 1652
Energy balances & electricity profiles, 1992, 1841

ELECTRONIC MAIL SYSTEMS
Complete cyberspace ref & dir, 1772

ELECTRONIC PUBLISHING
Encyclopedias, atlases, & dicts, 48
International multimedia yrbk 1995-96, 1751
International multimedia yrbk 1995-96 on CD-ROM [CD-ROM], 1752

ELECTRONICS
Electronics pocket ref, 2d ed, 1653

ELEMENTARY SCHOOLS
Directory of Canadian schools, 6th ed, 319

EMERGENCY LIBRARIAN
Emergency Librarian index, vs.1-20: 1973-93, 645

EMPLOYEE FRINGE BENEFITS
Quick ref to ERISA compliance, 285

EMPLOYEES—DISMISSAL OF
Wrongful termination, 281

EMPLOYEES—TRAINING OF
Field gd to current training videos, 282
Guide to natl professional certification programs, 267

EMPLOYMENT IN FOREIGN COUNTRIES
Overseas summer jobs 1995, 26th ed, 278
Work your way around the world, 7th ed, 273

ENCYCLOPEDIA AMERICANA
Encyclopedia Americana, 1995 [CD-ROM], 47

ENCYCLOPEDIAS & DICTIONARIES. See also CHILDREN'S ENCYCLOPEDIAS & DICTIONARIES
Cambridge ency, 2d ed, 44
Collins ency of Scotland, 148
Concise Columbia ency, 3d ed, 45
Concise dict of Christianity in America, 1466
Encyclopedia Americana, 1995 [CD-ROM], 47
Encyclopedia of snakes, 1637
Encyclopedias, atlases, & dicts, 48
EXEGY: the source for current world info, 49
Grolier student ency of endangered species, 1597
Kant dict, 1428
Larousse dict of world folklore, 1343
Reference ency: India 2001, 132
Schirmer pronouncing pocket manual of musical terms, 5th ed, 1271
World Bk multimedia ency [CD-ROM], 51

ENDANGERED SPECIES. *See also* **ZOOLOGY**
Grolier student ency of endangered species, 1597
International wildlife trade, 1599

ENDOWMENTS
Directory of intl corporate giving in America & abroad 1995, 869
Directory of new & emerging fndns, 3d ed, 870
Foundation grants index 1996, 24th ed, 883
Foundation 1000 1995/96, 873
Guide to funding for intl & foreign programs, 2d ed, 875
National dir of nonprofit orgs 1995, 193
National gd to funding for the environment & animal welfare, 2d ed, 878
National gd to funding for women & girls, 952
National gd to funding in substance abuse, 896
Philanthropic studies index, 1995 cum index, 884
Who get grants/who gives grants, 877

ENERGY INDUSTRIES
World index of resources & population, 235

ENGINEERING. *See also specific types of engineering*
Electronic Gieck's engineering formulas [CD-ROM], 1642
English-German dict of materials & process engineering, 1666
Key gd to electronic resources: engineering, 1643
Peterson's job opportunities in engineering & tech 1995, 1513
Van Nostrand's scientific ency, 8th ed, 1502
World engineering industries & automation 1993-95, 1649

ENGINEERING INSTRUMENTS
Concise ency of measurement & instrumentation, 1641

ENGINEERING MATHEMATICS
Standard hndbk of engineering calculations, 3d ed, 1644

ENGINEERING—MEASUREMENT
Concise ency of measurement & instrumentation, 1641

ENGINEERS
Notable 20th-century scientists, 1490

ENGLAND—CIVILIZATION—1066-1485
Late medieval England (1377-1485), 542

ENGLISH FICTION
British short-fiction writers, 1945-80, 1228

ENGLISH IMPRINTS
Eastern Europe: a bibliographic gd to English lang pubs, 1986-93, 140

ENGLISH LANGUAGE
Cambridge ency of the English lang, 1061
Year's work in English studies, v.73, 1992, 958

ENGLISH LANGUAGE—ADDRESS, FORMS OF
Forms of address, 311

ENGLISH LANGUAGE—ALPHABET
Alphabet: a handbk of ABC bks, 2d ed, 328

ENGLISH LANGUAGE—ARCHAISMS
Illustrated dict of little-known words from literary classics, 1148

ENGLISH LANGUAGE—DIALECTS
UK to USA dict, 1082

ENGLISH LANGUAGE—DICTIONARIES
American Heritage talking dict, 3d ed [CD-ROM], 1062
Cambridge intl dict of English, 1063
Chambers dict on CD-ROM [CD-ROM], 1064
Concise Oxford dict of current English, 9th ed, 1065
Dictionary of modern legal usage, 2d ed, 577
Merriam-Webster's collegiate dict deluxe, electronic ed [CD-ROM], 1066
Merriam-Webster's dict of basic English, 1067
Modern dict for the legal profession, 1994 suppl, 580
Oxford desk dict, American ed, 1068
Oxford dict of English grammar, 1080
Oxford encyclopedic English dict, 2d ed, 1069
Oxford English minidict, 4th ed, 1070
Oxford minireference dict & thesaurus, 1078
Webster's new world vest pocket dict, 2d ed, 1071
Webster's 2: new college dict, 1079

ENGLISH LANGUAGE—DICTIONARIES— AZERBAIJANI
English-Azerbaijani/Azerbaijani-English concise dict, 1097

ENGLISH LANGUAGE—DICTIONARIES— BOSNIAN
Bosnian-English, English-Bosnian concise dict, 1098

ENGLISH LANGUAGE—DICTIONARIES— CHICKASAW
Chickasaw: an analytical dict, 1099

ENGLISH LANGUAGE—DICTIONARIES— CREOLE DIALECTS
Hippocrene concise Haitian Creole-English, English-Haitian Creole dict, 1106

ENGLISH LANGUAGE—DICTIONARIES— FRENCH
Dahl's law dict, 574
Oxford-Hachette French dict, 1100
Oxford paperback French dict & grammar, 1101
Routledge French technical dict, 1499
Standard French-English, English-French dict, 1102
Vocabulary of computer security & viruses, 1766

ENGLISH LANGUAGE—DICTIONARIES— GERMAN
Collins German-English, English-German dict, 2d ed, 1104
Elsevier's dict of industrial tech, 1494
English-German dict of materials & process engineering, 1666

ENGLISH LANGUAGE—DICTIONARIES—GREEK
Pocket Oxford Greek dict, 1105

ENGLISH LANGUAGE—DICTIONARIES—HAMITO-SEMITIC
Hamito-Semitic etymological dict, 1107

ENGLISH LANGUAGE—DICTIONARIES—HEBREW
Harduf's transliterated English-Hebrew dict, 3d v., H-K, 1108

ENGLISH LANGUAGE—DICTIONARIES—HUNGARIAN
Oxford-Duden pictorial Hungarian-English dict, 1109

ENGLISH LANGUAGE—DICTIONARIES—ITALIAN
Oxford-Duden pictorial Italian & English dict, 1110

ENGLISH LANGUAGE—DICTIONARIES—JAPANESE
Martin's concise Japanese dict, 1113
Tuttle dict of legal terms: English-Japanese, Japanese-English, rev ed, 613

ENGLISH LANGUAGE—DICTIONARIES, JUVENILE
American Heritage children's dict, 1086
Kingfisher illus children's dict, 1087

ENGLISH LANGUAGE—DICTIONARIES—KURDISH
Kurdish-English/English-Kurdish dict, 1114

ENGLISH LANGUAGE—DICTIONARIES—LATIN
Oxford Latin minidict, 1117
Veni, vidi, vici, 1116

ENGLISH LANGUAGE—DICTIONARIES—NORWEGIAN
Norwegian dict, 2d ed, 1120

ENGLISH LANGUAGE—DICTIONARIES—PORTUGUESE
Elsevier's dict of industrial tech, 1494

ENGLISH LANGUAGE—DICTIONARIES—RUSSIAN
Comparative Russian-English dict of Russian proverbs & sayings, 1125
Dictionary of bus & legal terms: Russian-English/English-Russian, 575
English-Russian comprehensive dict, 1122
English-Russian, Russian-English dict, rev ed, 1124
HarperCollins Russian dict: Russian-English, English-Russian, college ed, 1123
Oxford Russian minidict, 1126
Pocket Oxford Russian dict, 2d ed, 1127

ENGLISH LANGUAGE—DICTIONARIES—SOMALI
English-Somali, Somali-English Dictionary, 1134

ENGLISH LANGUAGE—DICTIONARIES—SOTHO LANGUAGE
Understanding everyday Sesotho, 1135

ENGLISH LANGUAGE—DICTIONARIES—SPANISH
Dictionary of Chicano Spanish, 2d ed, 1136
NTC's dict of common mistakes in Spanish, 1137
Wiley's English-Spanish, Spanish-English dict of psychology & psychiatry, 782

ENGLISH LANGUAGE—DICTIONARIES—SWEDISH
Prisma's abridged English-Swedish & Swedish-English dict, 1138

ENGLISH LANGUAGE—DICTIONARIES—TATAR
Tatar-English/English-Tatar dict, 1139

ENGLISH LANGUAGE—DICTIONARIES—THAI
Oxford-Duden pictorial Thai & English dict, 1140

ENGLISH LANGUAGE—DICTIONARIES—UZBEK
Uzbek-English, English-Uzbek concise dict, 1141

ENGLISH LANGUAGE—ETYMOLOGY
Dictionary of animal words & phrases, 1073
Speaking of animals, 1074

ENGLISH LANGUAGE—GLOSSARIES, VOCABULARIES, ETC.
Sisson's word & expression locater, 2d ed, 1092

ENGLISH LANGUAGE—GRAMMAR
NTC's hndbk for writers, 970
Write right!, 3d ed, 1081

ENGLISH LANGUAGE—IDIOMS
Dictionary of American idioms, 1083
Dictionary of catchphrases, 1084

ENGLISH LANGUAGE—OBSOLETE WORDS
Endangered English dict, 1089

ENGLISH LANGUAGE—PRONUNCIATION
NTC's dict of American English pronunciation, 1077

ENGLISH LANGUAGE—PROVINCIALISMS
UK to USA dict, 1082

ENGLISH LANGUAGE—PUNCTUATION
Merriam-Webster's gd to punctuation & style, 969
Write right!, 3d ed, 1081

ENGLISH LANGUAGE—STYLE
Plain English gd, 1075
Write right!, 3d ed, 1081

ENGLISH LANGUAGE—SYNONYMS & ANTONYMS
Kingfisher illus thesaurus, 1088
Roget's 2: the new thesaurus, 3d ed, 1095

ENGLISH LANGUAGE—TERMS & PHRASES
Metaphors dict, 1091
Sisson's word & expression locater, 2d ed, 1092

ENGLISH LANGUAGE—USAGE
Guidelines for bias-free writing, 968
Little Oxford gd to English usage, 1076
NTC's hndbk for writers, 970
Plain English gd, 1075

ENGLISH LITERATURE
Bibliography of the English novel from the Restoration to the French Revolution, 1236
Literary gd & companion to N England, 1233
Old & Middle English lit, 1230
Oxford companion to English lit, rev ed, 1231
Year's work in English studies, v.73, 1992, 958

ENGLISH LITERATURE—19TH CENTURY
Victorian yellowbacks & paperbacks, 1849-1905, v.1, 1223
Victorian yellowbacks & paperbacks, 1849-1905, v.2, 1224

ENGLISH LITERATURE—RESEARCH
Handbook of literary research, 2d ed, 1142

ENGLISH POETRY
Columbia Granger's gd to poetry anthologies, 2d ed, 1263
Late Victorian poetry 1880-99, 1246

ENGLISH POETRY—EXPLICATION
Guide to British poetry explication, v.4, 1245

ENTERTAINERS
Performing artists, 1363
Roy Rogers, 1408

ENTOMOLOGY
Agricultural entomology, 1625

ENTREPRENEURSHIP
Working solo sourcebk, 263

ENVIRONMENTAL EDUCATION
Blueprint for a green school, 1870
Education for the Earth, 2d ed, 337
Grolier illus lib of the environment, 1860

ENVIRONMENTAL HEALTH
Health & environment in America's top-rated cities, 931

ENVIRONMENTAL LAW
Environmental statutes, 1995 ed, 1872

ENVIRONMENTAL LAW—CANADA
Health & safety manager's A-Z gd to environmental mgmt, 1873

ENVIRONMENTAL POLICY
Carroll's environmental dir 1995, 1863
English-Spanish glossary of environmental terms & abbrevs, 1862
Environmental gd to the Internet, 1868
National gd to funding for the environment & animal welfare, 2d ed, 878

ENVIRONMENTAL PROTECTION
EPA database bk, 1865
Earth work, 1871
Encyclopedia of energy tech & the environment, 1830
Multinational corps & the environment, 1851
Ozone dilemma, 1874

ENVIRONMENTAL SCIENCES
Concise Oxford dict of ecology, 1854
Dictionary of environmental law & sci, 1855
Directory of environmental info sources, 5th ed, 1864
Earth work, 1871

ENVIRONMENTALISM
ABC-CLIO companion to the environmental movement, 1869

ENVIRONMENTALISTS
Peterson's job opportunities in the environment 1995, 1876

EPIDEMICS
Encyclopedia of plague & pestilence, 1725

EPIDEMIOLOGY
Dictionary of epidemiology, 3d ed, 1698

ERASMUS
Annotated catalogue of early editions of Erasmus, 1250

ERITREA (ETHIOPIA)
Eritrea, 116

ESPIONAGE
Whole spy catalog, 775

ESSAYS
Essay & general lit index 1990-94, 81

ETHIOPIA
Ethiopia, 117

ETHNIC FOOD INDUSTRY
Restaurant lover's companion, 1526

ETHNIC GROUPS. *See also* **MINORITIES**
Ethnic dress, 388

ETHNIC RELATIONS
Aggression & conflict, 835
Ethnic relations, 389

ETHNOLOGY
From Afar to Zulu: a dict of African cultures, 390
Gale ency of multicultural America, 387

EURASIA
Military ency of Russia & Eurasia, v.5, 146

EUROPE
Annual bulletin of coal stats for Europe & N America, 1994, 1838
Annual bulletin of electric energy stats for Europe & N America, 1994, v.38, 1839
Directory of European research & dvlpmt 1995, 1504
European pharmaceutical technical & regulatory compendium, 1742
European research & dvlpmt database 1995 [CD-ROM], 1510
Festivals of Europe, 1353
Library systems in Europe, 636
Major cos of Europe 1994/5, 253
Migration stats 1994, 907
Political leaders of contemporary W Europe, 756
Prices of agricultural products & selected inputs for Europe & N America 1992/93, 1520
Statistics of road traffic accidents in Europe & N America 1995, 1890
Who's who in European research & dvlpmt 1995, 1491

EUROPE, EASTERN
Consumer Eastern Europe 1996, 251
Eastern Europe: a bibliographic gd to English lang pubs, 1986-93, 140
Eastern Europe: a resource gd, 141

EUROPE—ECONOMIC CONDITIONS
Economic integration in Europe & N America, 232

EUROPE—ETHNIC RELATIONS
Jews & Europe, 424

EUROPE, GERMAN-SPEAKING
"Jewish question" in German-speaking countries, 1848-1914, 425

EUROPEAN COMMUNITIES
Directory of Community legislation in force & other acts of the Community insts, 768
Guide to the Community initiatives 1994-99, 753
Interinstitutional dir: European Union, 754
Official jl of the European Communities, v.38, English ed, 755

EUROPEAN COOPERATION
Historical dict of European orgs, 139

EVIDENCE (LAW)
Courtroom hndbk on fed evidence, 1995 ed, 591

EXCAVATIONS (ARCHAEOLOGY)
Bibliography of Syrian archaeological sites to 1980, 484

EXECUTIVE ADVISORY BODIES
Carroll's fed advisory dir 1995, 722

EXECUTIVE DEPARTMENTS—UNITED STATES
Reports required by Congress, 1995, v.2, no.1, 746

EXHIBITIONS
International trade fairs & conferences dir 1995, 19th ed, 300
World dir of exhibitions & trade fairs 1995, 309

EXPERTISE
Yearbook of experts, authorities & spokespersons, 12th ed, 103

EXPLORERS
Explorers & discoverers, 454

EXPORTS
American export register 1995, 286
Exporting to the USA, 1995-96 ed, 297

FAMILY
Dictionary of family therapy, rev ed, 1718
Encyclopedia of marriage & the family, 863
Marriage, family, & relationships, 862

FAMILY RECREATION
Super family vacations, 3d ed, 462

FANTASTIC FICTION
Fantasy lit for children & young adults, 4th ed, 1167
Science fiction, fantasy, & horror writers, 1193
Supernatural index, 1194

FARM PRODUCE
UNCTAD commodity yrbk 1994, 1521

FASHION
Contemporary fashion, 1017

FASTS & FEASTS
Sacred celebrations: a Jewish holiday hndbk, 1479

FEDERAL AID TO EDUCATION
Big bk of minority opportunities, 6th ed, 891

FEDERAL GOVERNMENT
Congressional Quarterly's desk ref on American govt, 737
Federal systems of the world, [2d ed], 712
Government dir of addresses & telephone nos 1995, 3d ed, 732
Washington online: how to access the fed govt on the Internet 1995, 1785

FEDERAL WRITERS' PROJECT
Federal writers' project, 966

FEMINISM & ART
Women artists, 2d ed, 1021

FEMINISM & LITERATURE
Feminist criticism of American women poets, 1222

FEMINIST THEORY
Dictionary of feminist theory, 2d ed, 948

FESTIVALS
Festivals of Europe, 1353
Holidays & festivals index, 1358
Shakespeare cos & festivals, 1420
Wild planet!, 1352

FICTION. *See also* **DETECTIVE & MYSTERY STORIES; HORROR TALES; SCIENCE FICTION**
Crown crime companion, 1189
Fiction dict, 1185
Genreflecting: a gd to reading interests in genre fiction, 4th ed, 1186
Late-Victorian & Edwardian British novelist, 1st series, 1235
Novel openers, 1188
Now read on: a gd to contemporary popular fiction, 2d ed, 1187

FIGURES OF SPEECH
Sisson's word & expression locater, 2d ed, 1092

FIJI
Fiji, 169

FILM ADAPTATIONS
Films into bks, 1394

FILM NOIR. *See also* **DETECTIVE & MYSTERY FILMS**
Film noir, 1383

FINANCE. *See also* **INVESTMENTS**
Cabell's dir of publishing opportunities in accounting, economics & finance, 6th ed, 669
Dictionary for bus & finance, 3d ed, 180
Dictionary of bus terms, 2d ed, 178
Dictionary of finance & investment terms, 4th ed, 220
Dictionary of Japanese financial terms, 248
International financial stats locator, 230

FIREARMS
Standard catalog of firearms, 5th ed, 1009

FIRST AID IN ILLNESS & INJURY
Treasury of natural 1st aid remedies from A-Z, 1715

FISHES
Fish & fisheries worldwide [CD-ROM], 1605
Fishes of the tropical E Pacific, 1633
Lake, river, & sea-run fishes of Canada, 1624
Species info lib [CD-ROM], 1606

FISHING
McKnew & Parker's buyer's gd to sportfishing boats, 1995 ed, 810

FLIES, ARTIFICIAL
Fly-fisher's gd to saltwater naturals & their imitation, 817

FLORIDA
Florida statl abstract, 1994, 28th ed, 916

FLOWERING SHRUBS
Favorite flowering shrubs, 1569

FLOWERING TREES
Flowering crabapples, 1567

FLUORESCENCE
Fluorescence: gems & minerals under ultraviolet light, 1812

FLY FISHING
Fly-fisher's gd to saltwater naturals & their imitation, 817

FOLKLORE
Armenian folklore bibliog, 1340
Atlas of the mysterious in N America, 786
Folk traditions of the Arab world, 1342
Folklife sourcebk, 2d ed, 1341
Larousse dict of world folklore, 1343
Micronesian religion & lore, 1439

FOOD. *See also* **NUTRITION**
Codex alimentarius, v.5a, 2d ed, 1534
Codex alimentarius, v.13, 2d ed, 1535
Concise ency of foods & nutrition, 1524
Contemporary & histl lit of food sci & human nutrition, 1522
Elsevier's dict of agriculture & food production, 1516
Food aid in figures, v.11, 881
Food chronology, 1539
Nutribase nutrition facts desk ref, 1540
Unofficial gd to ethnic cuisine & dining in America, 1531

FOOD ADDITIVES
Consumer's dict of food additives, 4th ed, 1530
Handbook of food additives, 1533

FOOD CONTAMINATION
Home health gd to poisons & antidotes, 1727

FOOD INDUSTRY & TRADE
Career opportunities in the food & beverage industry, 1538
Elsevier's dict of agriculture & food production, 1516

FOOD—INTERNATIONAL COOPERATION
Historical dict of the intl food agencies, 1529

FOOTBALL
Kids' world almanac of football, 818
NCAA football, 819

FORCE & ENERGY
Natural gas stats sourcebk, 2d ed, 1844

Renewable energy sources stats 1989-91, 1848
SYNERJY, 1831

FOREIGN STUDY
ISS dir of overseas schools, 1994-95 ed, 372
Japan: exploring your options, 373
Peterson's summer study abroad, 367

FOREST PRODUCTS
North American factbk, 1994-95, 1541

FORESTS & FORESTRY
Peterson 1st gd to forests, 1591
Restoration forestry, 1542

FORMER SOVIET REPUBLICS. *See also* **RUSSIA; SOVIET UNION**
Atlas of Russia & the Independent Republics, 445
Longman biographical dir of decision-makers in Russia & the successor states, 145
Political parties of E Europe, Russia, & the successor states, 2d ed, 757
Who's who in Russia & the CIS Republics, 40

FOSSILS
Fossils of the Burgess Shale, 1813

FRANCE—HISTORY
Dictionary of 20th century culture: French culture 1900-75, 545

FREE MATERIAL
Educators grade gd to free teaching aids 1995, 41st ed, 322
Educators gd to free films, filmstrips, & slides 1995, 55th ed, 375
Educators gd to free videotapes 1995, 42d ed, 376
Elementary teachers gd to free curriculum materials 1995, 52d ed, 323
Guide to free computer materials 1995, 13th ed, 1771

FREE TRADE
Arthur Andersen N American bus sourcebk, 288
Encyclopedia of the N American Free Trade Agreement, 305

FRENCH LANGUAGE—DICTIONARIES—ENGLISH
Dahl's law dict, 574
Oxford-Hachette French dict, 1100
Oxford paperback French dict & grammar, 1101
Routledge French technical dict, 1499
Standard French-English, English-French dict, 1102
Vocabulary of computer security & viruses, 1766

FRENCH LITERATURE
Andre Malraux, 1253
New Oxford companion to lit in French, 1252

FRENCH POETRY
Lyrics of the Trouveres, 1251
Music & poetry in the Middle Ages, 1296

FRIEL, BRIAN
Brian Friel, 1257

FROGS
Handbook of frogs & toads of the US & Canada, 3d ed, 1640

FRONTIER & PIONEER LIFE
Atlas of westward expansion, 488
Cowboy ency, 510
Encyclopedia of frontier biog on CD-ROM [CD-ROM], 497

FRUIT
Codex alimentarius, v.5a, 2d ed, 1534
Organic gardener's home ref, 1543

FUGITIVE (TELEVISION PROGRAM)
Fugitive: a complete episode gd, 1963-67, 1403

FULANI LANGUAGE—DICTIONARIES—ENGLISH
Hippocrene practical Fulani-English dict, 1103

FUND RAISING
Guide to funding for intl & foreign programs, 2d ed, 875
National gd to funding for the environment & animal welfare, 2d ed, 878
National gd to funding in aging, 4th ed, 849
National gd to funding in arts & culture, 3d ed, 961
Philanthropic studies index, 1995 cum index, 884

FUNGI
International mycological dir, 3d ed, 1581

FURNITURE
Upholsterer's pocket ref bk, 1020

FURNITURE INDUSTRY & TRADE
Furniture assns in N America, 223

FUTURE LIFE
Encyclopedia of afterlife beliefs & phenomena, 1445

GANDHI, MAHATMA
Mahatma Gandhi, 536

GARDENING
Favorite shade plants, 1571
Gardener's gd to plant diseases, 1547
Gardening with roses, 1549
Growing herbs, 1586
National Audubon Society bird garden, 1560
Taylor's master gd to gardening, 1550
Western garden [CD-ROM], 1552
What plant where, 1566

GARDENS
Gardener's gd to Britain, new ed, 1548

GAS INDUSTRY
Annual bulletin of gas stats for Europe & N America 1994, v.38, 1840

D & D standard oil abbreviator, 4th ed, 1832
Oil & gas journal data bk, 1995 ed, 1845

GAYS. *See also* **LESBIANS; HOMOSEXUALITY**
Cassell's queer companion, 864
Cracking the corporate closet, 259
Gay & lesbian address bk, 53
Gay 100, 865

GEARING
Encyclopedic dict of gears & gearing, 1674

GEMS
Fluorescence: gems & minerals under ultraviolet light, 1812

GENEALOGY
African American genealogical sourcebk, 429
Asian American genealogical sourcebk, 430
Collins Scottish clan & family ency, 435
Compendium of histl sources, rev ed, 431
Genealogist's address bk, 3d ed, 428
Hispanic American genealogical sourcebk, 432
Index to the Roll of Honor, 434
Native American genealogical sourcebk, 433

GENERATIONS
Official gd to the generations, 908

GENETIC ENGINEERING
Dictionary of gene tech, 1657
Human gene mapping 1994, 1656
Language of biotech, 2d ed, 1659

GEOGRAPHY
Geography on file, 1995 ed, 457
Pockets: world atlas, 77
World databases in geography & geology, 453
World geographical ency, English lang ed, 456
Worldmark ency of the nations, 8th ed, 105

GEOLOGICAL MUSEUMS
Dinosaur safari gd, 1814

GEOLOGY
Children's atlas of natural wonders, 1806
Dictionary of the Earth, 1805
Field manual for the amateur geologist, rev ed, 1803
World databases in geography & geology, 453

GEOLOGY, STRATIGRAPHIC
Atlas of Mesozoic & Cenozoic coastlines, 1807

GEORGIA
Governors of Ga., 1754-1995, rev ed, 496

GERMAN LANGUAGE—DICTIONARIES—ENGLISH
Collins German-English, English-German dict, 2d ed, 1104

GERMAN LITERATURE
German writers & works of the early Middle Ages, 1254

GERMANY
Historical dict of Germany, 546

GERONTOLOGY. *See also* **AGED; AGING**
Aging well, 838
Encyclopedia of aging, 850
Literature & gerontology, 845
Profiles in gerontology, 846

GIANTS
Giants: a ref gd from hist, the Bible, & recorded legend, 1346

GINSBERG, ALLEN
Works of Allen Ginsberg 1941-94, 1210

GIRLS
National gd to funding for women & girls, 952

GOLF
Complete golfer's almanac 1995, 821
Official US Open almanac, 820
PGA tour, 1995, 822
Senior PGA tour, 1995, 823

GOVERNMENT PUBLICATIONS
Bibliographic gd to govt pubs--foreign 1994, 57
Bibliographic gd to govt pubs--US 1994, 58
Government online, 1776
1001 free goodies & cheapies, 60
Washington info dir, 734

GOVERNORS
Chief executives of Tex., 718
Governors of Ga., 1754-1995, rev ed, 496

GRADUATE STUDENTS
Directory of graduate student employee bargaining agents & orgs, 336

GRAIN
Grain market, v.2, 1519

GRAMMAR, COMPARATIVE & GENERAL
Case, semantic roles, & grammatical relations, 1057
Clitics, 1060

GRAMOPHONE COMPANY
Berliner gramophone records, 1273

GRANTS-IN-AID
Big bk of minority opportunities, 6th ed, 891
Chronicle financial aid gd, rev ed, 364
Dan Cassidy's worldwide college scholarship dir, 4th ed, 333
Dan Cassidy's worldwide graduate scholarship dir, 4th ed, 334
Directory of biomedical & health care grants 1995, 9th ed, 1685

Directory of computer & high tech grants, 2d ed, 1770
Directory of financial aids for minorities 1995-97, 880
Directory of financial aids for women 1995-97, 879
Directory of intl corporate giving in America & abroad 1995, 869
Financial aid for the disabled & their families 1994-96, 858
Foundation dir suppl, 1995 ed, 871
Foundation grants index 1996, 24th ed, 883
Foundation grants to individuals, 9th ed, 872
Guide to fed funding for govts & nonprofits, 1995, Native American ed, 882
Guide to greater Wash., DC grantmakers 1994-95, 876
KR Info OnDisc grants database [CD-ROM], 848
Who get grants/who gives grants, 877

GRAPHIC ARTS
Artist's & graphic designer's market, 1995, 1038

GRAPHIC NOVELS
Graphic novels, 1359

GRASSES
Manual of grasses, 1583

GREAT BRITAIN
Academic libs in the UK & the republic of Ireland 1994, 3d ed, 635
Blackwell hndbk of educ, 325
British sci fiction paperbacks & mags 1949-56, 1234
Cambridge illus hist of British theatre, 1422
Dangerous sky: resource gd to the Battle of Britain, 544
Early music dict, 1272
Gardener's gd to Britain, new ed, 1548
Great Britain, 480
Larousse dict of British hist, 541
Libraries in the UK & Republic of Ireland 1995, 637
Summer jobs Britain 1995, 26th ed, 279
Who's who in the UK info world 95/96, 5th ed, 640
Women & the Dict of Natl Biog, 26

GREAT BRITAIN—HISTORY
Late medieval England (1377-1485), 542
Twentieth-century Britain, 543
Wars of the roses in fiction, 1190

GREAT BRITAIN—POLITICS & GOVERNMENT
Anthony Eden, 1897-1977, 759
British pol facts 1900-94, 7th ed, 758

GREAT BRITAIN. ROYAL NAVY
Guide to British naval papers in N America, 679

GREEK LANGUAGE, BIBLICAL
Theological lexicon of the N.T., 1457

GREEK LANGUAGE—DICTIONARIES—ENGLISH
Pocket Oxford Greek dict, 1105

GUAM
Historical dict of Guam & Micronesia, 168

GULF COAST (U.S.)
Field gd to shells, 4th ed, 1595

GYPSIES
Gypsies, 405

HABITAT (ECOLOGY)
Habitats, 1598

HANDICAPPED
Accent on living buyer's gd, 1994-95 ed, 853
ACCESS travel USA: a dir for people with disabilities, 856
Financial aid for the disabled & their families 1994-96, 858
Fodor's great American vacations for travelers with disabilities, 471

HANDICRAFT
Crafts supply source bk, 3d ed, 1012
Index to how to do it info, 1994 suppl, 1014

HARPISTS
Nineteenth- & 20th-century harpists, 1287

HARPSICHORD MUSIC
Modern harpsichord music, 1288

HAZARDOUS SUBSTANCES
Consolidated list of products whose consumption and/or sale have been banned...., 5th ed, 217
Encyclopedia of environmental control tech, v.7, 1857
Encyclopedia of environmental control tech, v.8, 1858
Encyclopedia of environmental control tech, v.9, 1859
Home health gd to poisons & antidotes, 1727
Resources & refs: hazardous waste & hazardous materials mgmt, 1852

HAZARDOUS WASTES
Directory of hazardous wastes servs, 1994-95. 5th ed, 1654
Encyclopedia of environmental control tech, v.7, 1857
Resources & refs: hazardous waste & hazardous materials mgmt, 1852

HEADS OF STATE
Dictators & tyrants, 705
Great leaders, great tyrants?, 706
Political leaders of contemporary W Europe, 756
Profiles of worldwide govt leaders 1995, 708

HEALTH
ALA fingertip gd to natl health-info resources 1995-96, ref desk ed, 1684
Health & environment in America's top-rated cities, 931
Internet compendium: subject gds to health & sci resources, 1774
Key gd to electronic resources: health scis, 1688
Marshall Cavendish ency of health, rev ed, 1682
New A to Z of women's health, 3d ed, 1680
Woman's gd to vitamins & minerals, 1743

HEALTH RISK ASSESSMENT
Artist's complete health & safety gd, 2d ed, 1042

HEAT
Handbook of thermal conductivity, v.1, 1821
Handbook of thermal conductivity, v.2, 1822
Handbook of thermal conductivity, v.3, 1823

HEBREW LANGUAGE
Hebrew & Aramaic lexicon of the O.T., v.1, 1455

HEBREW LANGUAGE—DICTIONARIES—ENGLISH
Harduf's transliterated English-Hebrew dict, 3d v., H-K, 1108

HEMINGWAY, ERNEST
Reading Hemingway, 1211

HERALDRY
Debrett's peerage & baronetage [1995], 426

HERB GARDENING
Organic gardener's home ref, 1543

HERBERT, GEORGE
George Herbert companion, 1238

HERBS
Encyclopedia of herbs & their uses, 1585
Growing herbs, 1586
Information sourcebk of herbal medicine, 1714
Naturopathic hndbk of herbal formulas, 3d ed, 1717

HERESIES, CHRISTIAN
Crimes of perception: an ency of heresies & heretics, 1468

HEROES
Hollywood heroes, 1376

HIGH SCHOOL STUDENTS
Summer on campus [2d ed], 360

HIGH SCHOOLS
Directory of Canadian schools, 6th ed, 319

HIGH TECHNOLOGY
Directory of computer & high tech grants, 2d ed, 1770
International multimedia yrbk 1995-96, 1751
International multimedia yrbk 1995-96 on CD-ROM [CD-ROM], 1752

HIKING
Essential gd to wilderness camping & backpacking in the US, 824
Hiking trails, E US, 825

HINDUS
South Asian religions in the Americas, 1438

HISPANIC AMERICAN LIBRARIANS
Quien es quien: a who's who of spanish-speaking librarians in the US 1994, 4th ed, 621

HISPANIC AMERICANS
Chronology of Hispanic-American hist, 550
Dictionary of 20th century culture: Hispanic culture of S America, 406
Hispanic American biog, 407
Hispanic American genealogical sourcebk, 432
Hispanic 100, 408
Kaleidoscope: a multicultural bklst for grades K-8, 1182
Who's who among Hispanic Americans 1994-95, 3d ed, 409

HISTORIC BUILDINGS
America preserved, 1047

HISTORIC SITES
America preserved, 1047
International dict of historic places, v.1, 467
International dict of historic places, v.2, 468
International dict of historic places, v.3, 469
Irish-American landmarks, 422
Masterworks of man & nature, 2d ed, 458
100 great cities of world hist, 927

HISTORICAL FICTION
Index to histl fiction for children & young people, 1179
Wars of the roses in fiction, 1190

HISTORICAL FILMS
With fire & sword: Italian spectacles on American screens 1958-68, 1395

HISTORICAL GEOGRAPHY
Atlas of westward expansion, 488
Atlas of WW I, 2d ed, 675
Children's atlas of the 20th century, 553
Encyclopedia of intl boundaries, 455
Historical atlas of La., 440
Naval Institute histl atlas of the US Navy, 701

HISTORY. See also HISTORY under specific subjects and names of countries, states, etc.
American Histl Assn's gd to histl lit, 3d ed, 554
Chronology of the medieval world, 561
History of humanity, v.1, 568
Worldmark ency of the nations, 8th ed, 105

HISTORY, ANCIENT
Chronology of the ancient world, 559

HISTORY, MODERN
Chronology of the expanding world, 560
Chronology of the modern world, 2d ed, 562
Day by day: the 80s, 503
Founders of modern nations, 556
Twentieth-century America, 485

HOBBIES
Index to how to do it info, 1994 suppl, 1014

HOCKEY
Bad boys: legends of hockey's toughest, meanest, most-feared players, 826
Goalies: legends from the NHL's toughest job, 827
Sporting News complete hockey bk, 1995-96 ed, 828

HOLIDAYS
Holidays & festivals index, 1358
International holidays, 1361
Wild planet!, 1352

HOLLYWOOD
Hollywood novel, 1411

HOLOCAUST, JEWISH (1939-1945)
Learning about the Holocaust, 1170

HOME CARE SERVICES
Encyclopedia of home care for the elderly, 1681

HOME SCHOOLING
Home educ resource gd, 3d ed, 317

HOMESITES—PLANNING
Time-Saver standards for housing & residential dvlpmt, 1048

HOMOSEXUALITY. *See also* GAYS; LESBIANS
Cassell's queer companion, 864
Gay 100, 865

HORROR FILMS
Christopher Lee & Peter Cushing & horror cinema, 1396
Horror in silent films, 1391
Overlook film ency: horror, 1379

HORROR TALES
Science fiction, fantasy, & horror writers, 1193
Supernatural index, 1194

HORSES
Complete horse care manual, 1556
Horse dict, 1555
Pockets: horses, 70

HORTICULTURALISTS
Dictionary of British & Irish botanists & horticulturalists, rev ed, 1562

HOSPITALS
Best hospitals in America, 2d ed, 1693
Profiles of US hospitals 1995, [4th ed], 1690

HOUSE CONSTRUCTION
Taunton's fine homebuilding index, issues 1-85, 1051

HOUSEHOLD SUPPLIES
Complete gd to household chemicals, 1795

HUMAN ANATOMY
Atlas of the human body, 1694

HUMAN CAPITAL
Guide to natl professional certification programs, 267
HR words you gotta know!, 258
State by state gd to human resources law, 1994, 268
State by state gd to human resources law, 1994: mid-year suppl & workers' compensation laws, 269

HUMAN ECOLOGY
Human environments, 1797

HUMAN GEOGRAPHY
Atlas of world dvlpmt, 444

HUMAN RIGHTS
Civil rights decisions of the US Supreme Court, the 19th century, 607
Civil rights decisions of the US Supreme Court, the 20th century, 608
Constitutional law dict, v.1, 606
Human rights on CD-ROM, 2d ed [CD-ROM], 609
Political prisoners & trials, 605

HUMANITIES
BHI plus [CD-ROM], 955
Columbia dict of modern literary & cultural critcism, 960
Internet compendium: subject gds to humanities resources, 100

HUNGARIAN LANGUAGE—DICTIONARIES—ENGLISH
Oxford-Duden pictorial Hungarian-English dict, 1109

HYDROCARBONS
Physical properties of hydrocarbons & other chemicals, v.4, 1793

HYGIENE
Marshall Cavendish ency of health, rev ed, 1682

ILLINOIS
Illinois hist, 492

ILLUSTRATED BOOKS
Dictionary of 20th century British bk illustrators, 1055

ILLUSTRATED BOOKS, CHILDREN'S
Art of children's picture bks, 2d ed, 1183

ILLUSTRATORS
Children's authors & illustrators, 5th ed, 1178

IMMIGRANTS
Immigrant experience in American fiction, 1206

IMMUNOLOGY
Dictionary of cytokines, 1558

IMPERIAL WAR MUSEUM (GREAT BRITAIN)
Imperial War Museum film catalog, v.1, 557

IMPORTS
Directory of import regimes, pt.1, 289

Directory of import regimes, pt.2, 290
Directory of importers in Latin America, 1994 ed, 291
Importers manual USA, 1995-96 ed, 298

INCOME
Value of a dollar, 1860-1989, 198

INCUNABULA
Catalogue of the 15th-century printed bks in the Harvard Univ lib, v.3, 42

INDEPENDENT REGULATORY COMMISSIONS
Directory of professional & occupational regulation in the US & Canada, 730

INDEXES
ASSIA plus [CD-ROM], 97
BHI plus [CD-ROM], 955
Biography index [CD-ROM], 24
CD-ROM bk index, 80
Essay & general lit index 1990-94, 81
Holidays & festivals index, 1358
LISA plus [CD-ROM], 625
Magill index to critical surveys, rev ed, 1161
Philosopher's index [CD-ROM], 1436

INDIA
Encyclopaedia of Indian cinema, 1381
India, rev ed, 131
Mahatma Gandhi, 536
Reference ency: India 2001, 132
Women & religion in India, 934

INDIA—ECONOMIC CONDITIONS
Indian social & economic dvlpmt 1993, 243

INDIANAPOLIS (IND.)
Encyclopedia of Indianapolis, 929

INDIANS
First Americans, 386

INDIANS IN LITERATURE
Native N American lit, 1259

INDIANS OF NORTH AMERICA
American Indian ref & resource bks for children & YAs, 2d ed, 1177
American Indian studies, 421
Athletes, 410
Atlas of Indians of N America, 413
Guide to ancient Native American sites, 411
Kaleidoscope: a multicultural bklst for grades K-8, 1182
Native American genealogical sourcebk, 433
Native American painters of the 20th century, 1054
Native N American chronology, 415
Notable Native Americans, 416
Performers, 419
Political leaders & peacemakers, 418
Ready ref: American Indians, 417
Reference ency of the American Indian, 7th ed, 412
Statistical record of native N Americans, 2d ed, 420

Writings in Indian hist, 1985-90, 414

INDONESIA
Indonesia, 134
International dir of Indonesianists, 2d ed, 133

INDUSTRIAL HYGIENE
Patty's industrial hygiene & toxicology, v.3, pt.B, 3d ed, 1875

INDUSTRIAL RELATIONS
Roberts' dict of industrial relations, 4th ed, 257

INDUSTRIAL SAFETY
Handbook of lab health & safety, 2d ed, 1796
OSHA field inspection ref manual, 277

INDUSTRIAL TOXICOLOGY
Patty's industrial hygiene & toxicology, v.3, pt.B, 3d ed, 1875

INDUSTRY
Elsevier's dict of industrial tech, 1494
Ross register of Siberian industry 1995, 246
U.S. industry profiles, 224
World databases in industry, 225

INFANTS—CARE
Complete baby & child care, 904
Mayo Clinic complete bk of pregnancy & baby's 1st yr, 1722

INFORMATION SCIENCE
Annual review of info sci & tech, v.29, 1994, 622
Directory of Canadian lib & info sci consultants, 642
Information sci abstracts, v.29, no.12, 619
LISA plus [CD-ROM], 625

INFORMATION SERVICES
Burwell dir of info brokers 1994, 646
Library systems in Europe, 636
Reference & info servs, 2d ed, 647
Who's who in the European info world 95/96, 2d ed, 639
Who's who in the UK info world 95/96, 5th ed, 640

INORGANIC COMPOUNDS
Handbook of inorganic compounds, 1794

INSCRIPTIONS, SEMITIC
Dictionary of the NW Semitic inscriptions, 1129

INSECT PESTS
Agricultural entomology, 1625

INSECTS
Chironomidae [Diptera] of Japan, 1626
Indo-Australian Agaoninae (pollinators of figs), 1628
Pockets: insects, 71
True bugs of the world (Hemiptera: Heteroptera), 1627

INSTRUCTIONAL MATERIALS CENTERS
Children's media market place, 4th ed, 649
School lib media annual 1995, v.13, 651

INSURANCE. *See also* **REINSURANCE**
Glossary of insurance terms, 5th ed, 226
Statistical survey of insurance & reinsurance operations in developing countries 1983-90, 227

INTELLECTUAL PROPERTY
International intellectual property protection for computer software, 638

INTELLIGENCE SERVICE
US intelligence community, 716

INTENTION—RELIGIOUS ASPECTS
Communities dir, 1995 ed, 852

INTERLIBRARY LOANS
Interlibrary loan policies dir, 5th ed, 641

INTERNATIONAL AGENCIES
Historical dict of European orgs, 139
Interinstitutional dir: European Union, 754
Worldwide govt dir with intl orgs 1995, 709

INTERNATIONAL BUSINESS ENTERPRISES
Directory of intl bus, 233
Globe & Mail report on bus: Canada co handbk 1994, 250
International advertising & mktg info sources, 299
International dir of co hists, v.9, 236
International dir of co hists, v.10, 237
International dir of co hists, v.11, 238
Major cos of the Far East & Australasia 1995/96, 245
Mexico co hndbk, 1995/96 ed, 254
World's major cos dir, 229

INTERNATIONAL COURTS
Historical dict of intl tribunals, 610

INTERNATIONAL ECONOMIC INTEGRATION
Encyclopedia of the N American Free Trade Agreement, 305

INTERNATIONAL ECONOMIC RELATIONS
Revenue stats of OECD member countries 1965-93, 772
Services: stats on intl transactions 1970/92, 918

INTERNATIONAL EDUCATION
Academic yr abroad 1995/96, 368
Encyclopedia of Irish schools, 1500-1800, 315
ISS dir of overseas schools, 1994-95 ed, 372
Japan: exploring your options, 373
Programs & centers in comparative & intl educ, rev ed, 370
Vacation study abroad 1995/96, 369

INTERNATIONAL FINANCE
International financial stats locator, 230

INTERNATIONAL FUND FOR AGRICULTURAL DEVELOPMENT
Historical dict of the intl food agencies, 1529

INTERNATIONAL LAW
Historical dict of intl tribunals, 610
Reports required by Congress, 1995, v.2, no.1, 746
United Nations Commission on Intl Trade law yrbk, v.24, 1993, 307

INTERNATIONAL LIBRARIANSHIP
Library systems in Europe, 636

INTERNATIONAL RELATIONS
Bibliography of works on Canadian foreign relations 1986-90, 748

INTERNATIONAL RELIEF
Guide to funding for intl & foreign programs, 2d ed, 875

INTERNATIONAL TRADE
American export register 1995, 286
America's intl trade, 239
Directory of import regimes, pt.1, 289
Directory of import regimes, pt.2, 290
Exporting to the USA, 1995-96 ed, 297
External trade monthly stats, 293
Foreign trade stats for Africa, 294
Handbook of intl trade & dvlpmt stats 1993, 234
Importers manual USA, 1995-96 ed, 298
International bus & trade dirs, 228
Trade data elements dir: UNTDED 1993, v.1, 306
United Nations Commission on Intl Trade law yrbk, v.24, 1993, 307

INTERNET (COMPUTER NETWORK)
Essential Internet info gd, 1784
Internet: an introductory gd for UN orgs, 1783
Internet compendium: subject gds to health & sci resources, 1774
Internet compendium: subject gds to humanities resources, 100
Internet compendium: subject gds to social scis, bus, & law resources, 101
Net games, 813
Net gd, 1781
Washington online: how to access the fed govt on the Internet 1995, 1785

INTERNSHIP PROGRAMS
Graduate Group's new internships for 1994-95, 261
Sixth bi-annual natl dir of arts internships, 1995/96, 1034

INVENTIONS
Eureka! scientific discoveries & inventions, 1496
Historical 1st patents, 1509
Pockets: inventions, 72

INVESTMENTS
Dow Jones gd to the world stock market, 1995-96 ed, 212
Standard & Poor's 500 gd, 1995 ed, 214
Standard & Poor's midcap 400 gd, 1995 ed, 215

INVESTMENTS, FOREIGN—UNITED STATES
USA business: the portable ency for doing bus with the US, 241

IRAQ
Iraq, 2d ed, 135

IRAQ—KUWAIT CRISIS, 1990—1991
Operation Desert Shield/Desert Storm, 563

IRELAND
Academic libs in the UK & the republic of Ireland 1994, 3d ed, 635
Brian Friel, 1257
Encyclopedia of Irish schools, 1500-1800, 315
Ireland, 481
Ireland: an ency for the bewildered, 142
Irish bed & breakfast bk, 482
Libraries in the UK & Republic of Ireland 1995, 637

IRISH AMERICANS
Irish-American landmarks, 422

ISLAMIC COUNTRIES
Oxford ency of the modern Islamic world, 1477

ISO 900 SERIES STANDARDS
Randall's practical gd to ISO 9000, 206

ISRAEL
Criminal justice in Israel, 596
Israel & the Jewish world, 1948-93, 552
Israel & the W Bank & Gaza Strip, 2d ed, 163
New ency of Zionism & Israel, 164

ITALIAN LANGUAGE—DICTIONARIES—ENGLISH
Oxford-Duden pictorial Italian & English dict, 1110

ITALY
Italy, 143

JAMES BOND FILMS
Complete James Bond movie ency, rev ed, 1382

JAPAN
Chironomidae [Diptera] of Japan, 1626
Dictionary of Japanese financial terms, 248
Japan dir of professional assns, 3d ed, 244
Japan: exploring your options, 373
Japanese hist & culture from ancient to modern times, 2d ed, 537

JAPANESE AMERICANS
Academic focus Japan: programs & resources in N America, 423

JAPANESE LANGUAGE
Japanese psycholinguistics, 1059

JAPANESE LANGUAGE—DICTIONARIES—ENGLISH
Kodansha's furigana Japanese-English dict, 1111
Kodansha's pocket kanji gd, 1112
Martin's concise Japanese dict, 1113
Tuttle dict of legal terms: English-Japanese, Japanese-English, rev ed, 613

JAZZ MUSIC
Jazz & blues lover's gd to the US, updated ed, 1321
Jazz discography, v.9, 1326
Jazz research & performance materials, 2d ed, 1327
New Grove dict of jazz, 1328
Tantalizing tingles: a discography of early ragtime, jazz...., 1325

JAZZ MUSICIANS
Earthly recordings of Sun Ra, 1322
John Coltrane, 1324
Straighten up & fly right: a chronology & discography of Nat "King" Cole, 1329
Tram: the Frank Trumbauer story, 1323

JEWS. *See also* **JUDAISM**
Encyclopaedia Judaica decennial bk 1983-92, 1478
Jews & Europe, 424

JEWS—PERSECUTIONS
"Jewish question" in German-speaking countries, 1848-1914, 425

JOB HUNTING
Adams job almanac 1995, 265
Cracking the corporate closet, 259
DISCovering careers & jobs [CD-ROM], 271
JIST's electronic gd for occupational exploration [CD-ROM], 275
Job seeker's gd to socially responsible cos, 262
On-line job search companion, 272
Peterson's job opportunities in bus 1995, 280
Peterson's job opportunities in engineering & tech 1995, 1513
Peterson's job opportunities in the environment 1995, 1876
Peterson's job opportunities in health care 1995, 1689

JONGLEURS. *See* **TROUVERES**

JOURNALISM
Broadcast news manual of style, 2d ed, 992

JOURNALISTS
Biographical dict of American newspaper columnists, 973

JUDAISM
Encyclopaedia Judaica decennial bk 1983-92, 1478
Jews & Europe, 424
Judaica Americana, 1480
Sacred celebrations: a Jewish holiday hndbk, 1479
Who's who in Jewish hist, 2d ed, 1481

JUDGES
Supreme Court justices, 572

JUNIOR HIGH SCHOOL LIBRARIES
Middle & jr high school lib catalog, 7th ed, 650

JUVENILE DELINQUENCY
Violent children, 603

KANT, IMMANUEL
Kant dict, 1428

KENNEDY, JOHN F.
John F. Kennedy, 491

KINGS & RULERS
Great leaders, great tyrants?, 706

KOREAN WAR, 1950-1953
Korea [CD-ROM], 692
Korean War, 538

KURDISH LANGUAGE—DICTIONARIES—ENGLISH
Kurdish-English/English-Kurdish dict, 1114

LABOR LAWS & LEGISLATION
European employment law, 252

LAET, JEAN
Descriptive catalog of the music printed by Hubert Waelrant & Jan de Laet, 1266

LANDSCAPE GARDENING
Taylor's master gd to gardening, 1550
What plant where, 1566

LANGUAGE & LANGUAGES
Key of it all, bk 2, 1121

LATIN AMERICA
Latin America on file, 155
Latin America petroleum dir, 1995, 14th ed, 1834
Social panorama of Latin America, 1994 ed, 153
Statistical yrbk for Latin America & the Caribbean, 1994 ed, 154

LATIN AMERICA—COMMERCE
Encyclopedia of the N American Free Trade Agreement, 305

LATIN AMERICA—ECONOMIC CONDITIONS
Directory of importers in Latin America, 1994 ed, 291
Economic panorama of Latin America 1995, 151

LATIN AMERICA—FOREIGN RELATIONS—UNITED STATES
Early US-Hispanic relations 1776-1860, 776

LATIN AMERICA—HISTORY
Chronology of Hispanic-American hist, 550

LATIN AMERICAN LITERATURE
Modern Latin-American fiction writers, 2d series, 1258

LATIN AMERICANS
Notable Latin American women, 938

LATIN LANGUAGE
Handbook of Christian Latin, 1115

LATIN LANGUAGE—CHURCH LATIN
Dictionary of ecclesiastical Latin, 1118

LATIN LANGUAGE—DICTIONARIES—ENGLISH
Dictionary of ecclesiastical Latin, 1118
Oxford Latin minidict, 1117
Veni, vidi, vici, 1116

LAW
Courtroom hndbk on fed evidence, 1995 ed, 591
Dahl's law dict, 574
Dictionary of bus & legal terms: Russian-English/English-Russian, 575
Dictionary of law, 3d ed, 576
Dictionary of modern legal usage, 2d ed, 577
Index to law school theses & dissertations, 570
Martindale-Hubbell law dir on CD-ROM [CD-ROM], 584
Modern dict for the legal profession, 1994 suppl, 580
Nonprofit law dict, 579
Real life dict of the law, 578
Searching the law: the states, 2d ed, 569
Sport lawyer's gd to legal pers, 1995 suppl, 615
Teen legal rights, 592
Tuttle dict of legal terms: English-Japanese, Japanese-English, rev ed, 613

LAW ENFORCEMENT
Applications in criminal analysis, 604

LAW LIBRARIES
AALL ref bk, 593

LAW OFFICES
Insider's gd to law firms, 2d ed, 582

LAW REPORTS, DIGESTS, ETC.
Yearbook of the Intl Law Commission 1992, 614

LAW SCHOOLS
Barron's gd to law schools, 11th ed, 581
Princeton Review student access gd to the best law schools, 585
REA's authoritative gd to law schools, rev ed, 586

LE FANU, JOSEPH SHERIDAN
J. Sheridan Le Fanu, 1256

LEAD
Lead poisoning prevention, 1866

LEARNING DISABILITIES
Complete learning disabilities dir, 1995/96, 374

LEARNING DISABLED—EDUCATION (HIGHER)
Peterson's colleges with programs for students with learning disabilities, 341

LEBANON
Who's who in Lebanon 1995-96, 13th ed, 165

LEE, CHRISTOPHER
Christopher Lee & Peter Cushing & horror cinema, 1396

LEEWARD ISLANDS (WEST INDIES)
St. Kitts-Nevis, 172

LEGENDS
Goddesses, heroes, & shamans, 1347

LEGISLATION
Official jl of the European Communities, v.38, English ed, 755
State legislative summary, 1994, 595

LEGISLATIVE HISTORIES
Federal legislative hists, 717

LEGISLATORS
Committees in the US congress 1947-92, v.2, 733

LESBIANS. *See also* GAYS; HOMOSEXUALITY
Cassell's queer companion, 864
Gay & lesbian address bk, 53
Gay 100, 865

LETTER WRITING
Forms of address, 311

LIBERIA
Liberia, 118

LIBRARIANS
International dir of serials specialists, 655

LIBRARIES. *See also* CHILDREN'S LIBRARIES
Whole lib hndbk 2, 624

LIBRARIES—AUTOMATION
Browsing in info systems, 644
Directory of lib automation sftwr, systems, & servs, 643

LIBRARIES—CANADA
Directory of Canadian lib & info sci consultants, 642
Guide to the Fonds d'Archives & collections in the holdings of the York Univ Archives, 653

LIBRARIES—SPECIAL COLLECTIONS
Building a popular sci lib collection for high school & adult learners, 660
Checklist of painters c1200-1994, 2d ed, 652
Guide to collections on Paraguay in the US, 551
Guide to the Fonds d'Archives & collections in the holdings of the York Univ Archives, 653
Local hist collections in libs, 659
Mexican-American War of 1846-48, 657

Special collections in children's lit, 661

LIBRARY CONSULTANTS
Directory of Canadian lib & info sci consultants, 642

LIBRARY RESOURCES
Canadiana in US repositories: a preliminary gd, 136

LIBRARY SCIENCE
AALL ref bk, 593
Bowker annual lib & bk trade almanac, 1995, 40th ed, 623
Directory of lib automation sftwr, systems, & servs, 643
LISA plus [CD-ROM], 625
SUPER LCCS CD [CD-ROM], 633
Whole lib hndbk 2, 624

LICENSES
National dir of state bus licensing & regulation, 194

LILIES
Gardener's gd to growing lilies, 1572

LITERATURE
Essay & general lit index 1990-94, 81
Illustrated dict of little-known words from literary classics, 1148
Literature & gerontology, 845
Magill index to critical surveys, rev ed, 1161
Merriam-Webster's ency of lit, 1146

LITERATURE—BLACK AUTHORS
Modern black writers: suppl, 1157

LITERATURE, MEDIEVAL
Classical & medieval lit criticism, v.14, 1149
Literature criticism from 1400-1800, v.27, 1156

LITERATURE, MODERN
Contemporary literary criticism annual cum index for 1995, 1151
Contemporary literary criticism, v.84, 1152
Contemporary literary criticism, v.85, 1153
Literature criticism from 1400-1800, v.27, 1156
Nineteenth-century lit criticism, v.46, 1158
Twentieth-century literary criticism, v.56, 1159
Twentieth-century literary criticism, v.57, 1160

LITERATURE—WOMEN AUTHORS
Masterplots II: women's lit series, 949

LITTLE PRESSES
Alternative publishers of bks in N America, 2d ed, 668

LIZARDS
Handbook of lizards, 1639

LOBBYING
Lobbying, PACs, & campaign finance, 740

LOCAL GOVERNMENT
Government dir of addresses & telephone nos 1995, 3d ed, 732

LOCAL HISTORY
Local hist collections in libs, 659

LOCK, GEORGE
Victorian yellowbacks & paperbacks, 1849-1905, v.2, 1224

LOUISIANA
Historical atlas of La., 440

LOVE
Sex & love quotations, 889

LUX RADIO THEATRE (RADIO PROGRAM)
Lux presents Hollywood, 1390

LUX VIDEO THEATRE (TELEVISION PROGRAM)
Lux presents Hollywood, 1390

MACHINERY
Machinists' ready ref, 8th ed, 1675

MADISON, JAMES
James Madison & the American nation 1751-1836, 507

MAGIC
Encyclopaedia of Celtic wisdom, 788
Man, myth & magic, new ed, 1348

MAIL-ORDER BUSINESS
Catalogue of Canadian catalogues, 249
Directory of mail order catalogs, 1995, 9th ed, 219

MAINE
Connecticut, Maine, Mass., [&] R.I.: atlas of histl county boundaries, 438

MALAWI
Malawi, 2d ed, 119

MALRAUX, ANDRE
Andre Malraux, 1253

MAMMALS. *See also names of families, genera, species, etc.*
Handbook of mammals of the S-central states, 1630
Mammals of New Guinea, rev ed, 1631
Mammals of the SW Pacific & Moluccan Islands, 1632

MAN
History of humanity, v.1, 568

MANAGEMENT
Cabell's dir of publishing opportunities in mgmt & mktg, 6th ed, 670
McGraw-Hill ency of quality terms & concepts, 284

MANUFACTURES
CDs, super glue, & salsa: how everyday products are made, 221
How to find info about divisions, subsidiaries & products, 5th ed, 203

MANUFACTURING PROCESSES
Manufacturing processes ref gd, 1670
Metalworking in Africa S of the Sahara, 1668

MANUSCRIPTS. *See also* **LIBRARIES— SPECIAL COLLECTIONS**
Guide to British naval papers in N America, 679
Guide to Central American collections in the US, 152
Guide to collections on Paraguay in the US, 551

MARC FORMATS
USMARC format for bibliographic data, 1994 ed, 634

MARCHING BANDS
Marching band hndbk, 2d ed, 1290

MARKETING
Bond markets, 1995 ed, 292
Cabell's dir of publishing opportunities in mgmt & mktg, 6th ed, 670
Data sources for bus & market analysis, 4th ed, 296
Dictionary of marketing & advertising, 304
Directory of import regimes, pt.1, 289
Directory of import regimes, pt.2, 290
Directory of intl bus, 233
Editor & Publisher market gd 1994, 976
Editor & Publisher market gd 1994 [CD-ROM], 977
External trade monthly stats, 293
Foreign trade stats of Asia & the Pacific 1988-92, 295
International advertising & mktg info sources, 299
Latin American advertising, mktg, & media sourcebk, 301
Trade data elements dir: UNTDED 1993, v.1, 306
World market share reporter 1995-96, 240

MARRIAGE
Encyclopedia of marriage & the family, 863
Marriage, family, & relationships, 862

MARTIAL ARTS
Encyclopedia of martial arts movies, 1380

MARTINIQUE
Martinique, 171

MASS MEDIA
ABC-CLIO companion to the media in America, 964

MASSACHUSETTS
Connecticut, Maine, Mass., [&] R.I.: atlas of histl county boundaries, 438

MATERIALS
Encyclopedia of advanced materials, 1664
English-German dict of materials & process engineering, 1666

MATERIALS SCIENCE
Engineered materials hndbk, 1665
Woldman's engineering alloys, 8th ed, 1671

MATHEMATICS
Combined membership list 1995-96, 1825
Dictionary of mathematics terms, 2d ed, 1826
Encyclopaedia of mathematics, v.10, 1827
Mathematical scis professional dir 1995, 1828
World databases in physics & mathematics, 1788

MATHIAS, WILLIAM
William Mathias, 1279

MECHANICAL ENGINEERING
Mechanical engineer's ref bk, 12th ed, 1673
Power industry abbreviator, 1672

MEDAL OF HONOR
Medal of honor recipients 1863-1994, 689

MEDIA PROGRAMS (EDUCATION)
School lib media annual 1995, v.13, 651

MEDICAL CARE
Complete dir of nursing facilities for younger adults with chronic physical disabilities, 1994, 855
Directory of health care professionals 1995, 1686
U.S. health policy groups, 1691

MEDICAL ETHICS
Encyclopedia of bioethics, rev ed, 1429

MEDICAL PERSONNEL
Bibliography of medical & biomedical biog, 2d ed, 1696
Peterson's job opportunities in health care 1995, 1689

MEDICAL REHABILITATION
Directory of medical rehabilitation facilities 1995, 1703

MEDICAL SCIENTISTS
Bibliography of medical & biomedical biog, 2d ed, 1696

MEDICAL STATISTICS
Cambridge dict of stats in the medical scis, 1699

MEDICINE
American Heritage Stedman's medical dict, 1697
Common medical abbrevs, 1695
Directory of medical & dental schools worldwide, 6th ed, 1687
Dr. Tom Linden's gd to online medicine, 1709
Magill's medical gd, 1700
Merriam-Webster's medical dict, 1701
Oxford medical companion, 1702
Princeton Review student access gd to the best medical schools, 1705
Professional hndbk of diagnostic tests, 1710
REA's authoritative gd to medical & dental schools, 1706
Remarkable lives of 100 women healers & scientists, 940
USP DI 1995, v.1, 1744
USP DI 1995, v.2, 1745
USP DI 1995, v.3, 1746

MEDICINE—SPECIALITIES & SPECIALISTS
Official ABMS dir of board certified medical specialists 1996, 1704

MEDICINE, POPULAR
American Medical Assn family medical gd [CD-ROM], 1707
Consumer health USA, 1711

MEDICINE, PREVENTIVE
Canadian gd to clinical preventive health care, 1708

MEETINGS
International trade fairs & conferences dir 1995, 19th ed, 300

MELVILLE, HERMAN
Herman Melville ency, 1212

MEMORY
Encyclopedia of memory & memory disorders, 780

MEN
100 men who shaped world hist, 33

MEN'S STUDIES
New men's studies, 2d ed, 866

MENTAL HEALTH
Depression, 1724

METAL—CUTTING TOOLS
ASM specialty handbk: tool materials, 1678

METAL TRADE
Annual bulletin of stats of world trade in steel 1993, 287

METAPHOR
Metaphors dict, 1091

METEOROLOGY
Elsevier's dict of climatology & meteorology, 1808

METROPOLITAN AREAS
Gale city & metro rankings reporter, 930

MEXICAN WAR, 1846-1848
Mexican-American War of 1846-48, 657

MEXICO
Mexican pol biogs, 1935-93, 3d ed, 763
Mexico co hndbk, 1995/96 ed, 254

MICHENER, JAMES
James A. Michener, 1213

MICROCOMPUTERS
PC user's essential accessible pocket dict, 1756
Personal computer dict, 1764

MICRONESIA
Historical dict of Guam & Micronesia, 168
Micronesian religion & lore, 1439

MIDDLE AGES
Chronology of the medieval world, 561
Encyclopedia of the Middle Ages, 565

MIDDLE ATLANTIC STATES
Peterson's gd to middle Atlantic colleges 1995, 11th ed, 346

MIDDLE EAST
Arab women in ESCWA member states, 156
Civilizations of the ancient Near East, 159
External trade bulletin of the ESCWA region, 7th ed, 157
Folk traditions of the Arab world, 1342
Middle East, 8th ed, 764
Middle East & N Africa 1995, 160
Middle East & N Africa on file, 459
Middle East military balance 1993-94, 695
National accounts studies of the ESCWA region, 158
Political parties of the Middle East & N Africa, 765
Statistical abstract of the ESCWA region 1983-1992, 14th ed, 919
Who's who in the Arab world 1995-96, 12th ed, 161

MIDDLE EAST—ECONOMIC CONDITIONS
Survey of economic & social dvlpmts in the ESCWA region 1993, 129

MIDDLE SCHOOLS
Directory of Canadian schools, 6th ed, 319

MIDDLE WEST
Peterson's gd to colleges in the Midwest 1995, 11th ed, 343
Used bk lover's gd to the Midwest, 1007

MIGRATION, INTERNAL
Migration stats 1994, 907

MILITARY BASES
Carroll's military facilities dir, 686
Directory of US military bases worldwide, 687

MILITARY HISTORY
Army Times bk of great land battles, 698
Brassey's ency of military hist & biog, 682
Operation Desert Shield/Desert Storm, 563
Pacific War atlas 1941-45, 676
West Point atlas of American wars, v.1, 677

MILITARY POLICY
Dictionary of alternative defense, 683

MILITARY READINESS
Middle East military balance 1993-94, 695

MILTON, JOHN
Milton's sonnets, 1214

MINERAL INDUSTRIES
World index of resources & population, 235

MINERALOGY
Pockets: rocks & minerals, 73

MINERALS
Fluorescence: gems & minerals under ultraviolet light, 1812
Mineral investment conditions in selected countries of the Asia-Pacific region, 1842
Minerals industry taxation policies for Asia & the Pacific, 1843

MINES & MINERAL RESOURCES
Randol mining dir 1994/95, 1836

MINNESOTA
Radicalism in Minn. 1900-60, 767

MINORITIES
Big bk of minority opportunities, 6th ed, 891
Directory of financial aids for minorities 1995-97, 880
Kaleidoscope: a multicultural bklst for grades K-8, 1182

MISSING PERSONS
Find anyone fast, 837

MOLECULAR BIOLOGY
Molecular biology & biotech, 1561

MORMON CHURCH
Historical atlas of Mormonism, 1461

MOROCCO
Morocco, rev ed, 120

MOSCOW
Foreign descriptions of Muscovy, 147

MOTION PICTURE ACTORS & ACTRESSES
Christopher Lee & Peter Cushing & horror cinema, 1396

MOTION PICTURE INDUSTRY
BFI film & TV hndbk 1995, 1401
Harrison's reports & film reviews, 1406

MOTION PICTURE MUSIC
Hollywood song, 1275

MOTION PICTURE PRODUCERS & DIRECTORS
Film directors, 11th intl ed, 1405
Illustrated who's who of Hollywood directors, v.1, 1367
Women film directors, 947

MOTION PICTURES
BFI film & TV hndbk 1995, 1401
Billboard video yrbk 1994, 1402
Blacks in black & white, 2d ed, 1410
Brewer's cinema, 1373
Chronicle of the cinema, 1371
Complete James Bond movie ency, rev ed, 1382
Contemporary theatre, film, & TV, v.13, 1362
Dictionary of film quotations, 1374

Encyclopaedia of Indian cinema, 1381
Encyclopedia of martial arts movies, 1380
Film distribution gd 1986-1992, v.1, 1384
Guide to American crime films of the 40s & 50s, 1392
Guide to American crime films of the 30s, 1393
Halliwell's film gd 1995, 1385
Harrison's reports & film reviews, 1406
Hollywood novel, 1411
International dict of broadcasting & film, 984
Jerry Lewis films, 1397
Leonard Maltin's movie ency, 1377
Pirates & seafaring swashbucklers on the Hollywood screen, 1407
Political companion to American film, 1409
Reel list, 1400
Shot on this site, 472
65 yrs of the Oscar, rev ed, 1372
Ultimate dir of the silent screen performers, 1368
VideoHound's that's amore!, 1398
Wales & cinema, 1370
Walking shadows, 1399
With fire & sword: Italian spectacles on American screens 1958-68, 1395

MOTION PICTURES—REVIEWS
Index to short & feature film reviews in the Moving Picture World, 1413
Variety's film reviews, v.23, 1387
VideoHound multimedia [CD-ROM], 1389

MOTORCYCLES
Complete motorcycle bk, 1884
Encyclopedia of the motorcycle, 1893

MOUNTAIN BIKING. *See* **ALL TERRAIN CYCLING**

MOUNTAINEERING
Climbing, 829

MULTICULTURALISM. *See* **PLURALISM**

MULTIMEDIA SYSTEMS
Multimedia tech from A-Z, 1750

MULTIMEDIA SYSTEMS INDUSTRY
International multimedia yrbk 1995-96, 1751
International multimedia yrbk 1995-96 on CD-ROM [CD-ROM], 1752

MUNICIPAL GOVERNMENT
Carroll's municipal dir, 725
Municipal executive dir, 728

MUSEUMS
Bibliography of museum studies, 11th ed, 82
Guide to tourist railroads & railroad museums, 4th ed, 1886
Volvo gd to halls of fame, 83

MUSIC
Berliner gramophone records, 1273
Descriptive catalog of the music printed by Hubert Waelrant & Jan de Laet, 1266
Early music dict, 1272
From metal to Mozart, 1298
Goldmine's celebrity vocals, 1274
Music & poetry in the Middle Ages, 1296
Music, dance & theater scholarships, 1365
Oxford dict of music, 1270
Portable Baker's biog dict of musicians, 1268
Richard Baker's companion to music, 1269
Schirmer pronouncing pocket manual of musical terms, 5th ed, 1271
Thesaurus of abstract musical properties, 1277

MUSIC TRADE
Career opportunities in the music industry, 3d ed, 1276

MUSICALS
American musical theatre song ency, 1416

MUSICIANS
International who's who in music & musicians dir, 14th ed, 1267
Popular bands & performers, 1304

MUSLIMS
South Asian religions in the Americas, 1438

MYCOLOGY
International mycological dir, 3d ed, 1581

MYSTERY & DETECTIVE STORIES. *See* **DETECTIVE & MYSTERY STORIES**

MYSTICISM
Simone Weil, 957

MYTHOLOGY
Encyclopaedia of Celtic wisdom, 788
Goddesses, heroes, & shamans, 1347
Man, myth & magic, new ed, 1348
Voyages in classical mythology, 1349
Who's who in Egyptian mythology, 2d ed, 1350
With fire & sword: Italian spectacles on American screens 1958-68, 1395

MYXOMYCETES
Myxomycetes: a hndbk of slime molds, 1587

NAMES, GEOGRAPHICAL
Baker ency of Bible places, 1450

NAMES, PERSONAL
Collins Scottish clan & family ency, 435
Dictionary of English surnames, 3d ed, 427
Encyclopedia of American family names, 437
What to name your African-American baby, 436

NATIONAL CHARACTERISTICS
Latitudes & attitudes, 915

NATIONAL PARKS & RESERVES
Exploring our natl parks & monuments, 9th ed, 470

NATIONAL SECURITY—UNITED STATES
Index to docs of the Natl Security Council, 774

NATIVE AMERICANS—DIRECTORIES
Guide to fed funding for govts & nonprofits, 1995, Native American ed, 882

NATURAL GAS
Natural gas stats sourcebk, 2d ed, 1844

NATURAL HISTORY
Masterworks of man & nature, 2d ed, 458
Wild New Zealand, 1601

NATURE
100 natural wonders of the world, 1602

NATUROPATHY
Treasury of natural 1st aid remedies from A-Z, 1715

NAUTICAL ALMANACS
Nautical almanac for the year 1996, 1895

NAVAL HISTORY
Naval Institute histl atlas of the US Navy, 701
Pirates!, 1345
Pirates & privateers of the Americas, 1344

NAVIGATION
Elsevier's nautical dict, 3d ed, 1894

NEBRASKA
Nebraska hist, 494

NEGOTIATION
Negotiation lit, 283

NEW AGE MOVEMENT
New mktg opportunities, 4th ed, 1482

NEW ENGLAND
Peterson's gd to New England colleges 1995, 11th ed, 347
Plant explorer's gd to New England, 474
Rail lines of S New England, 1888

NEW GUINEA
Mammals of New Guinea, rev ed, 1631

NEW HAMPSHIRE
New Hampshire [&] Vt.: atlas of histl county boundaries, 439

NEW YORK (N.Y.)
Encyclopedia of NYC, 107
Historical atlas of NYC, 487

NEW YORK (STATE)
Peterson's gd to NY colleges 1995, 11th ed, 348

NEW ZEALAND
New Zealand bks in print 1995, 23d ed, 23
Wild New Zealand, 1601

NEWSLETTERS
Hudson's subscription newsletter dir, 12th ed, 978

NEWSPAPERS
Biographical dict of American newspaper columnists, 973
Editor & Publisher intl yr bk 1994, 980
Editor & Publisher yr bk 1994 [CD-ROM], 981
National dir of newspaper op-ed pages, 979
News media yellow bk, 963
Newspapers online, 1995, 3d ed, 982
Power media selects, 9th ed, 988

NOBEL PRIZES
Women of peace: Nobel peace prize winners, 944

NONPROFIT ORGANIZATIONS
National dir of nonprofit orgs 1995, 193
Nonprofit law dict, 579
Opportunities for vocational study, 385
Who get grants/who gives grants, 877

NORTH AMERICA
Annual bulletin of coal stats for Europe & N America, 1994, 1838
Annual bulletin of electric energy stats for Europe & N America, 1994, v.38, 1839
Arthur Andersen N American bus sourcebk, 288
Bibliographic gd to N American hist 1994, 489
Grolier lib of N American biogs, 27
Larousse dict of N American hist, 508
Prices of agricultural products & selected inputs for Europe & N America 1992/93, 1520

NORTH AMERICA—MAPS
Hammond road atlas America, 441

NORTH AMERICAN FREE TRADE AGREEMENT
Encyclopedia of the N American Free Trade Agreement, 305

NORTH ATLANTIC TREATY ORGANIZATION
North Atlantic Treaty Org, 773

NORTH CAROLINA
North Carolina hist, 493

NORTHERN IRELAND
Northern Ireland: a pol dir 1968-93, 761

NORWEGIAN LANGUAGE—DICTIONARIES—ENGLISH
Norwegian dict, 2d ed, 1120

NOVELISTS, ENGLISH
Late-Victorian & Edwardian British novelists, 1st series, 1235
Virginia Woolf A to Z, 1221

NOVUM TESTAMENTUM
Novum Testamentum, v.36a, 1460

NUMBER THEORY
Key dates in number theory hist, 1829

NUMISMATICS
Guide bk of US coins, 1996, 49th ed, 1008

NURSING
Dictionary of nursing theory & research, 2d ed, 1732
Handbook of therapeutic interventions, 1735

NURSING HOMES
Complete dir of nursing facilities for younger adults with chronic physical disabilities, 1994, 855
Directory of nursing homes, 1995, 1731

NURSING SCHOOLS
Peterson's gd to nursing programs, 356

NUTRIBASE (COMPUTER FILE)
Nutribase nutrition facts desk ref, 1540

NUTRITION
Concise ency of foods & nutrition, 1524
Contemporary & histl lit of food sci & human nutrition, 1522
Nutribase nutrition facts desk ref, 1540

OCCULTISM
Divining the future: prognostication from astrology to zoomancy, 791
Encyclopedia of afterlife beliefs & phenomena, 1445
Man, myth & magic, new ed, 1348
Tarot for beginners, 787
World of ghosts & the supernatural, 784

OCCUPATIONAL APTITUDE TESTS
ETS test collection catalog, v.2, 2d ed, 314

OCCUPATIONAL HEALTH & SAFETY. See INDUSTRIAL SAFETRY

OCCUPATIONAL TRAINING
Opportunities for vocational study, 385

OCCUPATIONS
DISCovering careers & jobs [CD-ROM], 271
Encyclopedia of careers & vocational guidance [CD-ROM], 382
Government career gds [CD-ROM], 256
JIST's electronic gd for occupational exploration [CD-ROM], 275
Specialty occupational outlook, 274

OCCUPATIONS—UNITED STATES
Cuts in defense jobs in US counties, metropolitan areas, & states, 1992-2003, 270

OCEANIA
Familia Gekkonidae (Reptilia, Sauria), pt.1, 1634

International histl stats: Africa, Asia, & Oceania, 1750-1988, 917
Mammals of the SW Pacific & Moluccan Islands, 1632

OCEANIC LITERATURE
Indigenous lit of Oceania, 1260

OFFICE MANAGEMENT
Professional secretary's hndbk, 3d ed, 312

OIL & GAS JOURNAL
Oil & gas journal data bk, 1995 ed, 1845

OMAN
Oman, rev ed, 166

O'NEIL, EUGENE
Proverbial Eugene O'Neill, 1215

ONLINE BIBLIOGRAPHIC SEARCHING
Government online, 1776
Internet compendium: subject gds to health & sci resources, 1774
Internet compendium: subject gds to humanities resources, 100
Newspapers online, 1995, 3d ed, 982

ONLINE DATABASES
Net gd, 1781
ONLINE 100, 1777

OPERA
Bel Canto operas of Rossini, Donizetti, & Bellini, 1300
Blacks in opera, 1301
Opera cos & houses of the US, 1302

OPERATION DESERT SHIELD, MILITARY 1990-1991
Operation Desert Shield/Desert Storm, 563

ORAL READING
Great new nonfiction reads, 1184

ORCHESTRAL MUSIC
Cello music since 1960, 1286

ORCHIDS
Illustrated survey of orchid genera, 1578
Manual of orchids, 1576
Orchids for the South, 1574

ORGAN MUSIC
Organ lit, 3d ed, 1289

ORGANIC GARDENING
Organic gardener's home ref, 1543

ORGANIZED CRIME
Organized crime, 594

ORNAMENTAL TREES
Year in trees, 1592

OUTDOOR RECREATION
Adventure vacations, 473

OUTER SPACE
Pockets: space facts, 74
Spaceflight: a Smithsonian gd, 1647

OUTLAWS
Lawmen & desperadoes, 571

OZONE LAYER
Ozone dilemma, 1874

PACIFIC AREA
Economic & social survey of Asia & the Pacific 1995, 128
Mammals of the SW Pacific & Moluccan Islands, 1632

PACIFIC COAST (NORTH AMERICA)
Fishes of the tropical E Pacific, 1633
Pacific coast crabs & shrimps, 1622

PACIFISTS
Women of peace: Nobel peace prize winners, 944

PAIN
Classification of chronic pain, 2d ed, 1723

PAINTERS
Checklist of painters c1200-1994, 2d ed, 652

PAINTING
Annotated art, 1052
Native American painters of the 20th century, 1054
Painter's hndbk, 1053
World painting index, 2d suppl, 1056

PALEOGEOGRAPHY
Atlas of Mesozoic & Cenozoic coastlines, 1807

PALEONTOLOGY
Biological anomalies: humans III, 1559
Field gd to prehistoric life, 1815
Fossils of the Burgess Shale, 1813
Prehistoria [CD-ROM], 1816
Visual dict of prehistoric life, 1817

PAPERBACKS
British sci fiction paperbacks & mags 1949-56, 1234
Victorian yellowbacks & paperbacks, 1849-1905, v.1, 1223
Victorian yellowbacks & paperbacks, 1849-1905, v.2, 1224

PARAGUAY
Guide to collections on Paraguay in the US, 551

PARAPSYCHOLOGY
Alternative realities, 785
World of ghosts & the supernatural, 784

PARENTING
Mayo Clinic complete bk of pregnancy & baby's 1st yr, 1722
Parents' resource almanac, 901
Sourcebook on parenting & child care, 899

PATENTS
Historical 1st patents, 1509
Patents handbk, 589
World databases in patents, 587

PEACE
Political leaders & peacemakers, 418
Scholars' gd to Wash., D.C., for peace & intl security studies, 656
Women of peace: Nobel peace prize winners, 944

PEACE OFFICERS
Lawmen & desperadoes, 571

PEDIATRICS
Smart medicine for a healthier child, 1713

PENGUINS
Penguins of the world, 1616

PEONIES
Peonies, 1577

PERCUSSION INSTRUMENTS
Encyclopedia of percussion, 1291

PERENNIALS
Favorite perennials, 1570

PERFORMING ARTS
ARCO 100 best careers in entertainment, 1364
Performers, 419
Peterson's professional degree programs in the visual & performing arts 1995, 962

PERIODICALS
ACCESS: the supplementary index to pers, 78
ASSIA plus [CD-ROM], 97
Association for Population/Family Planning Libs & Info Centers—Intl (AFPLIC-I) union list of serials, 861
Bacon's dirs on disc 1995 update [CD-ROM], 974
BHI plus [CD-ROM], 955
Biography index [CD-ROM], 24
CHOICE reviews on SilverPlatter [CD-ROM], 84
Index to how to do it info, 1994 suppl, 1014
Latin American advertising, mktg, & media sourcebk, 301
Leo Burnett worldwide advertising & media fact bk, 302
Magazines for kids & teens, 86
Magazines for libs, 8th ed, 85
News media yellow bk, 963
Power media selects, 9th ed, 988
SPDCD 1995: the standard per dir [CD-ROM], 87
Ulrich's intl per dir 1996, 88
Wildlife worldwide [CD-ROM], 1607

PERSONAL COMPUTERS. See MICROCOMPUTERS

PETROLEUM
Pricing stats sourcebk, 1846
Refining stats sourcebk, 1849

PETROLEUM CHEMICALS INDUSTRY
Worldwide petrochemical dir, 1995, 33d ed, 1835

PETROLEUM ENGINEERING
Handbook of oil industry terms & phrases, 5th ed, 1676

PETROLEUM INDUSTRY & TRADE
D & D standard oil abbreviator, 4th ed, 1832
Handbook of oil industry terms & phrases, 5th ed, 1676
Latin America petroleum dir, 1995, 14th ed, 1834
Oil & gas journal data bk, 1995 ed, 1845

PHARMACEUTICAL INDUSTRY
Biotechnology in the US pharmaceutical industry 1995, 4th ed, 1733

PHARMACOLOGY
Drug Topics red bk, 1995, 1734
European pharmaceutical technical & regulatory compendium, 1742

PHARMACY
History of pharmacy, 1736

PHILOSOPHERS
Bibliography of Bertrand Russell, 1423
Great thinkers of the E world, 1433
Kant dict, 1428
Philosopher's index [CD-ROM], 1436
Philosopher's phone bk, 1995, 1430
Thirty-Five Oriental philosophers, 1427

PHILOSOPHY
Companion to the philosophy of mind, 1432
Oxford hist of W philosophy, 1434
Philosophy of Cynicism, 1425

PHILOSOPHY, ORIENTAL
Encyclopedia of E philosophy & religion, 1483

PHONOGRAPH
Berliner gramophone records, 1273

PHOTOGRAPHERS
Contemporary photographers, 3d ed, 1018

PHOTOGRAPHS
Masterworks of man & nature, 2d ed, 458

PHOTOGRAPHY
History of photography, v.2, 1019
Visual resources dir, 378

PHYSICAL FITNESS
Marshall Cavendish ency of health, rev ed, 1682

PHYSICAL GEOGRAPHY
Children's atlas of natural wonders, 1806

PHYSICAL MEASUREMENTS
Sizes: the illus ency, 1787
Sizesaurus, 1514

PHYSICALLY HANDICAPPED
Complete dir of nursing facilities for younger adults with chronic physical disabilities, 1994, 855
Resource gd for the disabled, 854
Woman's gd to coping with disability, 859

PHYSICIANS—DIRECTORIES
Official ABMS dir of board certified medical specialists 1996, 1704

PHYSICS
Visual dict of physics, 1819
World databases in physics & mathematics, 1788

PIANISTS
Notable 20th-century pianists, 1293

PIANO MUSIC
Piano music for 1 hand, 1292

PICTURE BOOKS FOR CHILDREN
Art of children's picture bks, 2d ed, 1183
Using picture storybks to teach literary devices. v.2, 1164

PICTURE DICTIONARIES
Children's visual dict, 43
Kingfisher illus children's dict, 1087
Oxford-Duden pictorial English dict, 2d ed, 1096
Oxford-Duden pictorial Hungarian-English dict, 1109
Oxford-Duden pictorial Italian-English dict, 1110
Oxford-Duden pictorial Thai & English dict, 1140
Precious Moments children's Bible dict, 1451
Visual dict of prehistoric life, 1817
Visual dict of the skeleton, 1683

PIDGIN LANGUAGES
Hippocrene concise Haitian Creole-English, English-Haitian Creole dict, 1106

PIPELINES
Worldwide pipelines & contractors dir, 1995, 15th ed, 1837

PIRATES
Pirates!, 1345
Pirates & seafaring swashbucklers on the Hollywood screen, 1407

PITCHERS (BASEBALL)
Cy Young award winners, 808

PLANT DISEASES
Gardener's gd to plant diseases, 1547

PLANT ENGINEERING
Standard hndbk of plant engineering, 2d ed, 1677

PLANTS
Dictionary of generic names of seed plants, 1565

Plants & their names, 1563
Vascular plants of Russia & adjacent states (the former USSR), 1594

PLANTS, FOSSIL
Visual dict of prehistoric life, 1817

PLANTS, ORNAMENTAL
Manual of climbers & wall plants, 1575

PLAY ENVIRONMENTS
Playground industry ref dir 1995, 800

PLURALISM (SOCIAL SCIENCES)
Gale ency of multicultural America, 387

POETRY
Columbia Granger's gd to poetry anthologies, 2d ed, 1263
Poetry criticism, v.10, 1265
Poetry dict, 1264

POETS, ENGLISH
Blake bks suppl, 1244

POISONS
Home health gd to poisons & antidotes, 1727

POLAND
Historical dict of Poland, 144

POLICE
Encyclopedia of police sci, 2d ed, 599

POLITICAL ACTION COMMITTEES
Lobbying, PACs, & campaign finance, 740

POLITICAL LEADERSHIP
Founders of modern nations, 556
Political leaders & peacemakers, 418

POLITICAL PARTIES
Political parties of E Europe, Russia, & the successor states, 2d ed, 757
Political parties of the Middle East & N Africa, 765

POLITICAL SCIENCE
Dictionary of contemporary quotations, vol.8, 3d ed, 90
Survey of social sci: govt & pols series, 741
Western political thought, 704
Worldmark ency of the nations, 8th ed, 105

POLITICAL STATISTICS
Statesman's yr-bk, 132d ed, 102

POLITICIANS—UNITED STATES
Congressional Quarterly's pols in America 1996, 738
Cumulated indexes to the public papers of the presidents of the US: George Bush, 1989-93, 744
Cumulated indexes to the public papers of the presidents of the US: Ronald Reagan, 1981-89, 745

POLLUTION
Earth words, 1861
Encyclopedia of environmental control tech, v.9, 1859

POLLUTION CONTROL INDUSTRY
Earth work, 1871

POPULAR CULTURE
American popular culture, 1357
Fandom dir, no.15, 1995-1996 ed, 1355

POPULAR LITERATURE
Genreflecting: a gd to reading interests in genre fiction, 4th ed, 1186
Now read on: a gd to contemporary popular fiction, 2d ed, 1187
What to read, 380

POPULAR MUSIC
American musical theatre song ency, 1416
Billboard music yrbk 1994, 1303
Cash Box charts for the post-modern age, 1312
Contemporary musicians, v.13, 1305
Da Capo companion to 20th-century popular music, rev ed, 1306
Goldmine's celebrity vocals, 1274
Guide to popular music ref bks, 1311
Guinness ency of popular music, 2d ed, 1310
Joel Whitburn presents Billboard's top 10 chart 1958-95, 1319
Joel Whitburn's pop hits 1940-54, 1313
Joel Whitburn's top pop singles 1955-93, 1314
Joel Whitburn's top pop singles CD gd 1955-79, 1316
Johnny Cash record catalog, 1317
Popular bands & performers, 1304
Rock stars/pop stars, 1315
SongCite: an index to popular songs, 1309
Your hit parade & American top 10 hits, 4th ed, 1308

POPULATION
Association for Population/Family Planning Libs & Info Centers—Intl (AFPLIC-I) union list of serials, 861
Population & dvlpmt: dir of non-govtl org in OECD countries, 909
Sex & age distribution of world populations: 1994 revision, 912

POPULATION FORECASTING
World index of resources & population, 235

PORPOISES
Whales, dolphins, & porpoises, 1629

PORTUGAL
Cultural atlas of Spain & Portugal, 539

POSTAL ADDRESSES. *See* **STREET ADDRESSES**

POTTERY
Hopi pottery symbols, 1015

POWER (MECHANICS)
Power industry abbreviator, 1672

POWER RESOURCES
Encyclopedia of energy tech & the environment, 1830
Energy, 1833

PREGNANCY
Mayo Clinic complete bk of pregnancy & baby's 1st yr, 1722

PRESIDENTIAL LIBRARIES
Presidential libs & museums, 519

PRESIDENTS—UNITED STATES
John F. Kennedy, 491
Presidential elections in the US, 742
Scholastic ency of the presidents & their times, 521
U.S. presidents [CD-ROM], 527

PRESLEY, ELVIS
Elvis ency, 1335

PRICES
Value of a dollar, 1860-1989, 198

PRIME MINISTERS
Facts about the British prime ministers, 540

PRINTERS
Directory of printers, 1994-95 ed, 671

PRINTING INDUSTRY
Directory of printers, 1994-95 ed, 671

PRISONERS
Political prisoners & trials, 605

PRIVATE COMPANIES
How to find info about private cos, 6th ed, 205

PRIVATE INVESTIGATORS
Whole spy catalog, 775

PRIVATE LIBRARIES
Private libs in Renaissance England, v.3: PLRE 67-86, 1006

PRIVATE SCHOOLS
Handbook of private schools 1995, 76th ed, 327
Directory of Canadian schools, 6th ed, 319

PRIVATEERING
Pirates!, 1345
Pirates & privateers of the Americas, 1344

PROFESSIONAL EDUCATION
Guide to natl professional certification programs, 267

PROFESSIONAL ETHICS
Codes of professional responsibility, 3d ed, 1431

PROVENCE-COTE D'AZUR (FRANCE)
Provence & the Cote D'Azur, 477

PROVERBS
Proverbial Eugene O'Neill, 1215

PSYCHIATRY
Wiley's English-Spanish, Spanish-English dict of psychology & psychiatry, 782

PSYCHOLINGUISTICS
Japanese psycholinguistics, 1059

PSYCHOLOGY
Psychology of aging, 839
Wiley's English-Spanish, Spanish-English dict of psychology & psychiatry, 782

PSYCHOTHERAPY
Dictionary of family therapy, rev ed, 1718

PUBLIC HEALTH
APELL annot bibliog, 777

PUBLIC LIBRARIES
Emergency Librarian index, vs.1-20: 1973-93, 645

PUBLIC OFFICERS
Government affairs yellow bk, v.1, no.1, 187

PUBLIC RECORDS
Librarian's gd to public records, special ed, 778
Sourcebook of state public records, 2d ed, 714

PUBLISHERS & PUBLISHING
Alternative publishers of bks in N America, 2d ed, 668
Bibliographic hist of the bk, 664
Cabell's dir of publishing opportunities in accounting, economics & finance, 6th ed, 669
Cabell's dir of publishing opportunities in mgmt & mktg, 6th ed, 670
Managing the publishing process, 665
Policies for publishers, 1995 ed, 674
Publishing market ref plus 1994-95, 2d ed [CD-ROM], 672

PUGET SOUND SALISH LANGUAGES—DICTIONARIES—ENGLISH
Lushootseed dict, 1119

QUALITY CONTROL
McGraw-Hill ency of quality terms & concepts, 284

QUALITY OF LIFE
Gale city & metro rankings reporter, 930
Rating gd to life in America's 50 states, 924

QUESTIONS & ANSWERS
Top 10 of everything, 61

QUOTATIONS
Cassell dict of cynical quotations, 89
Dictionary of contemporary quotations, vol.8, 3d ed, 90

Dictionary of film quotations, 1374
Gale's quotations [CD-ROM], 91
Humorous quotations, 93
Last words: a dict of deathbed quotations, 95
Little Oxford dict of quotations, 92
NTC's dict of quotations, 94
Proverbial Winston S. Churchill, 760
Sex & love quotations, 889
Shakespeare quotations, 1239
Talking drums: an African-American quote collection, 96

RA, SUN. *See* SUN RA

RADICALISM
Radicalism hndbk, 766
Radicalism in Minn. 1900-60, 767

RADIO
Crystal clear v.2, 993
Latin American advertising, mktg, & media sourcebk, 301
Leo Burnett worldwide advertising & media fact bk, 302
Power media selects, 9th ed, 988
Talk shows & hosts on radio, 3d ed, 975

RADIO BROADCASTERS
News media yellow bk, 963

RADIO PROGRAMS
Talk show selects, 1995 ed, 989

RADIO STATIONS
Compendium of American railroad radio frequencies, 13th ed, 1891

RADIO TALKSHOWS
Talk shows & hosts on radio, 3d ed, 975

RAILROADS
Compendium of American railroad radio frequencies, 13th ed, 1891
Guide to tourist railroads & railroad museums, 4th ed, 1886
Jane's world railways, 36th ed, 1887
Rail lines of S New England, 1888

RANKING & SELECTION (STATISTICS)
Gale city & metro rankings reporter, 930
Rating gd to life in America's 50 states, 924

RAPE
Rape in America, 617

RAYS (FISHES)
Sharks & rays of Australia, 1623

READING INTERESTS
Genreflecting: a gd to reading interests in genre fiction, 4th ed, 1186
Now read on: a gd to contemporary popular fiction, 2d ed, 1187
What else should I read?, 1162
What to read, 380

REAGAN, RONALD
Cumulated indexes to the public papers of the presidents of the US: Ronald Reagan, 1981-89, 745

RECORDER (MUSICAL INSTRUMENT)
Recorder: a gd to writings about the instrument, 1294

RECREATION
Playground industry ref dir 1995, 800

REFERENCE BOOKS
American Indian ref & resource bks for children & YAs, 2d ed, 1177
American popular culture, 1357
Basic bus lib: core resources, 3d ed, 173
Guide to ref bks for small & medium-sized libs, 1984-94, 9
Information sources in urban & regional planning, 928
Recommended ref bks for small & medium-sized libs & media centers 1995, 11
Reference bks bulletin 1993-94, 12

REFERENCE SERVICES (LIBRARIES)
Reference & info servs, 2d ed, 647
Reference assessment manual, 648

REFUGEES
Global refugee crisis, 895

REGIONAL PLANNING
Information sources in urban & regional planning, 928

REGIONALISM (INTERNATIONAL ORGANIZATION)
Historical dict of European orgs, 139

REINCARNATION
Encyclopedia of afterlife beliefs & phenomena, 1445

REINSURANCE
Statistical survey of insurance & reinsurance operations in developing countries 1983-90, 227

RELIGION
Atlas of religious change in America, 1952-90, 1437
Man, myth & magic, new ed, 1348
Micronesian religion & lore, 1439

RELIGIONS
Eerdmans' hndbk to the world's religions, rev ed, 1446
Encyclopedia of creation myths, 1444
Encyclopedia of E philosophy & religion, 1483
South Asian religions in the Americas, 1438

RELIGIOUS BIOGRAPHY
Thirty-Five Oriental philosophers, 1427

RELIGIOUS NEWSPAPERS & PERIODICALS
History & annot bibliog of American religious pers & newspapers, 1447
Popular religious mags of the US, 1441

RENAISSANCE
Annotated catalogue of early editions of Erasmus, 1250

RENEWABLE ENERGY SOURCES
Real Goods solar living sourcebk, 8th ed, 1847

REPRESENTATIVE GOVERNMENT & REPRESENTATION
Canadian representatives abroad, 749

REPTILES
Familia Gekkonidae (Reptilia, Sauria), pt.1, 1634

RESEARCH
Academic focus Japan: programs & resources in N America, 423
Directory of American research & tech 1995, 29th ed, 182
Directory of European research & dvlpmt 1995, 1504
Directory of hyphenated techniques, 1505
European research & dvlpmt database 1995 [CD-ROM], 1510
International research centers dir 1996-97, 8th ed, 55
New research centers, 1996, 339
Research centers dir 1996, 20th ed, 340
Technology opportunities, 2d ed, 1507
Who's who in European research & dvlpmt 1995, 1491

RESORTS
Super family vacations, 3d ed, 462

RETIREMENT COMMUNITIES
Directory of retirement facilities 1995, 847

RETIREMENT INCOMES
Quick ref to ERISA compliance, 285

RHETORIC
NTC's hndbk for writers, 970

RHODE ISLAND
Connecticut, Maine, Mass., [&] R.I.: atlas of histl county boundaries, 438

RHODODENDRON
Book of rhododendrons, 1573

ROBOTICS
McGraw-Hill illus ency of robotics & artificial intelligence, 1753

ROCK MUSIC
All music gd to rock, 1330
Billboard music yrbk 1994, 1303
Illustrated discography of surf music, 1961-65, 3d ed, 1332
Joel Whitburn's rock tracks, 1337
Literature of rock, 3, 1333
Singer-songwriters, 1307
Story of rock'n'roll, 1336

ROCK MUSICIANS
Beatles: the ultimate recording gd, 3d ed, 1338
Bob Dylan, 1334
Elvis ency, 1335
Rock stars/pop stars, 1315
Rocket man: the ency of Elton John, 1331

ROCKS
Pockets: rocks & minerals, 73

ROGERS, ROY
Roy Rogers, 1408

ROME
Guide to the aqueducts of ancient Rome, 1046
Handbook to life in ancient Rome, 547
Pockets: ancient Rome, 64

ROSES
Gardening with roses, 1549
Graham Stuart Thomas rose bk, rev ed, 1551

ROUTLEDGE, GEORGE
Victorian yellowbacks & paperbacks, 1849-1905, v.1, 1223

RUGBY FOOTBALL
Rugby catalogue of info sources, 830

RUGGLES, CARL
Carl Ruggles, 1280

RUSSELL, BERTRAND
Bibliography of Bertrand Russell, 1423

RUSSIA. See also FORMER SOVIET REPUBLICS; SOVIET UNION
Longman biographical dir of decision-makers in Russia & the successor states, 145
Military ency of Russia & Eurasia, v.5, 146
Russian revolution, 1905-21, 548
Vascular plants of Russia & adjacent states (the former USSR), 1594

RUSSIAN FAR EAST (RUSSIA)
Russian far east: an economic hndbk, 247

RUSSIAN LANGUAGE—DICTIONARIES—ENGLISH
Comparative Russian-English dict of Russian proverbs & sayings, 1125
Dictionary of bus & legal terms: Russian-English/English-Russian, 575
Dictionary of Russian slang & colloquial expressions, 1128
Elsevier's dict of agriculture & food production, 1516
English-Russian, Russian-English dict, rev ed, 1124
HarperCollins Russian dict: Russian-English, English-Russian, college ed, 1123
Oxford Russian minidict, 1126
Pocket Oxford Russian dict, 2d ed, 1127

RUSSIAN LITERATURE
Early modern Russian writers, late 17th & 18th centuries, 1261

RYGA, GEORGE
George Ryga papers, 1249

SACRED VOCAL MUSIC
Chamber music for solo voice & instruments 1960-89, 1299
Sacred dramas of J. S. Bach, 1284
Songs for bass voice, 1295

SAFETY REGULATIONS
Artist's complete health & safety gd, 2d ed, 1042

SAINTS
Bible & the saints, 1448
Fifty-seven saints, 2d ed, 1464

SALAMANDERS
Handbook of salamanders, 1635

SAO TOME AND PRINCIPE
Sao Tome & Principe, 121

SATELLITE POWER TRANSMISSION
WRTH satellite broadcasting gd, 1995 ed, 997

SATELLITES
International satellite dir, 1995, 10th ed, 1780
World satellite almanac, 1995, 7th ed, 1648

SAXOPHONISTS
Tram: the Frank Trumbauer story, 1323

SCHOLARSHIPS
Art & design scholarships, 1036
Athletic scholarships, 799
Big bk of minority opportunities, 6th ed, 891
Chronicle financial aid gd, rev ed, 364
Dan Cassidy's worldwide college scholarship dir, 4th ed, 333
Dan Cassidy's worldwide graduate scholarship dir, 4th ed, 334
Financial aid for the disabled & their families 1994-96, 858
Foundation grants to individuals, 9th ed, 872
Music, dance & theater scholarships, 1365
Official athletic college gd: baseball, 1995 ed, 805

SCHOOL LIBRARIES
Cataloging nonbook materials with AACR2R & MARC, 631
Children's media market place, 4th ed, 649
Emergency Librarian index, vs.1-20: 1973-93, 645
School lib media annual 1995, v.13, 651

SCIENCE
American men & women of sci 1995-96, 19th ed, 1485
Building a popular sci lib collection for high school & adult learners, 660
Dictionary of sci, 1493
Directory of hyphenated techniques, 1505
Encyclopedia of analytical sci, 1495
Environmental acronyms, 1850
Eureka! scientific discoveries & inventions, 1496
European research & dvlpmt database 1995 [CD-ROM], 1510
Illustrated dict of sci, rev ed, 1497
Internet compendium: subject gds to health & sci resources, 1774
My 1st sci dict, 1498
New York Public Lib sci desk ref, 1512
Remarkable lives of 100 women healers & scientists, 940
Science dict, 1501
Science navigator [CD-ROM], 1500
Scientific & technical bks & serials in print 1995, 22d ed, 1484
Van Nostrand's scientific ency, 8th ed, 1502
Visual ency of sci, 1503

SCIENCE—PERIODICALS
Directory of bus per special issues, 209

SCIENCE & STATE
Science, tech, & society in the 3d World, 138

SCIENCE FICTION
Aliens, robots, & spaceships, 1360
Anatomy of wonder 4, 1191
British sci fiction paperbacks & mags 1949-56, 1234
Science fiction, fantasy, & horror writers, 1193
Science fiction: the illus ency, 1192
Work of Jack Vance, 1218

SCIENTISTS
Directory of hyphenated techniques, 1505
Larousse dict of scientists, 1487
Notable 20th-century scientists, 1490
Who's who in European research & dvlpmt 1995, 1491

SCOTLAND
Collins ency of Scotland, 148
Dictionary of Scottish art & architecture, 1025

SEASHORE
National seashores, rev ed, 475

SECURITIES
Directory of cos required to file annual reports with the SEC, 183

SECURITY, INTERNATIONAL. *See also* **PEACE**
Scholars' gd to Wash., D.C., for peace & intl security studies, 656

SELF-EMPLOYED
Working solo sourcebk, 263

SEMANTICS
Case, semantic roles, & grammatical relations, 1057

SEMITIC LANGUAGES—DICTIONARIES
Dictionary of the NW Semitic inscriptions, 1129
Hamito-Semitic etymological dict, 1107

SERIAL PUBLICATIONS
ACCESS: the supplementary index to pers, 78
Association for Population/Family Planning Libs & Info Centers—Intl (AFPLIC-I) union list of serials, 861

SERVICE INDUSTRIES
Services: stats on intl transactions 1970/92, 918

SEX
And Adam knew Eve: a dict of sex in the Bible, 1452
Complete dict of sexology, new expanded ed, 885
Fetishes, Florentine girdles, & other explorations into the sexual imagination, 886
Sex & love quotations, 889
Studies in human sexuality, 2d ed, 887

SEX CRIMES
Childhood sexual abuse, 618

SEX DISCRIMINATION IN EDUCATION
Gender equity in educ, 313

SEX DISTRIBUTION (DEMOGRAPHY)
Sex & age distribution of world populations: 1994 revision, 912
Women's atlas of the US, rev ed, 933

SEXUAL HARASSMENT
Sexual harassment, 888

SHADE-TOLERANT PLANTS
Favorite shade plants, 1571

SHAKESPEARE, WILLIAM
Dictionary of sexual lang & imagery in Shakespearean & Stuart lit, 1243
Shakespeare cos & festivals, 1420
Shakespeare dict, 1241
Shakespeare quotations, 1239
Shakespearean criticism, v.26, 1242
Walking shadows, 1399
Who's who in Shakespeare, 1240

SHARKS
Sharks & rays of Australia, 1623

SHELLS
Field gd to shells, 4th ed, 1595

SHIP REGISTERS
Way's packet dir. 1848-1994, rev ed, 1898

SHIPPING
Review of maritime transport 1993, 1897

SHIPWRECKS
Atlas of shipwrecks & treasure, 1896

SHORT STORIES
British short-fiction writers, 1945-80, 1228
Short story criticism, v.17, 1196
Twentieth-century short story explication, v.2, 1195

SHRIMPS
Pacific coast crabs & shrimps, 1622

SHRUBS
Pruning of trees, shrubs, & conifers, [rev ed], 1588

SIBERIA
Ross register of Siberian industry 1995, 246

SIGNS & SYMBOLS
Abbreviations dict, 9th ed, 2

SIKHS
South Asian religions in the Americas, 1438

SILENT FILMS
American silent film comedies, 1378
Horror in silent films, 1391
Silent film necrology, 1369
Ultimate dir of the silent screen performers, 1368

SILVERWORK
Catalogue of American silver, 999

SKELETON
Visual dict of the skeleton, 1683

SKIN
Illustrated dict of dermatologic syndromes, 1728

SLANG
Dictionary of Russian slang & colloquial expressions, 1128

SLAVIC LITERATURE
South Slavic writers before WW II, 1262

SLIDES (PHOTOGRAPHY)
Visual resources dir, 378

SMALL BUSINESS
Small bus profiles, v.2, 196
StartSmart small bus advisor [CD-ROM], 207
Working solo sourcebk, 263

SMALL LIBRARIES—COLLECTION DEVELOPMENT
Guide to ref bks for small & medium-sized libs, 1984-94, 9

SNAKES
Encyclopedia of snakes, 1637
Snakes of the US & Canada, v.2, 1638

SOCCER
Soccer stars, 831

SOCIAL ACTION
Building a new South, 98

SOCIAL CONFLICT
Aggression & conflict, 835

SOCIAL HISTORY
Atlas of world dvlpmt, 444
Columbia chronicles of American life, 1910-92, 501
Handbook to life in ancient Rome, 547

SOCIAL JUSTICE
Building a new South, 98

SOCIAL PROBLEMS
Encyclopedia of social work, 19th ed, 893

SOCIAL REFORMERS
Radicalism hndbk, 766
Radicalism in Minn. 1900-60, 767

SOCIAL SCIENCES
ASSIA plus [CD-ROM], 97
Multilevel design, 99
Survey of social sci: govt & pols series, 741
Survey of social sci: sociology series, 836

SOCIAL SERVICE
Carroll's fed assistance dir, 892
Post-release assistance programs for prisoners, 2d ed, 600
Social work almanac, 2d ed, 894
Social work dict, 3d ed, 890

SOCIOLOGY
Concise Oxford dict of sociology, 834
Survey of social sci: sociology series, 836

SOCIOLOGY, CHRISTIAN (CATHOLIC)
New dict of Catholic social thought, 1470

SOLAR ENERGY
Real Goods solar living sourcebk, 8th ed, 1847

SOMALI LANGUAGE—DICTIONARIES— ENGLISH
English-Somali, Somali-English Dictionary, 1134

SONGS
Hollywood song, 1275
Music & poetry in the Middle Ages, 1296
Song finder, 1318

SONGS (LOW VOICE)
Songs for bass voice, 1295

SONGS, OLD FRENCH
Lyrics of the Trouveres, 1251

SONGS WITH INSTRUMENTAL ENSEMBLE
Chamber music for solo voice & instruments 1960-89, 1299

SONNETS
Milton's sonnets, 1214

SOTHO LANGUAGE
Understanding everyday Sesotho, 1135

SOUL MUSIC
Soul music A-Z, rev ed, 1339

SOUND RECORDINGS
All music gd to rock, 1330
Joel Whitburn's top pop singles 1955-93, 1314

SOUTH AFRICA
South Africa, rev ed, 122

SOUTH AMERICA
Africa, Asia, & S America since 1800, 555
Dictionary of 20th century culture: Hispanic culture of S America, 406

SOUTH ASIA
Atlas & survey of S Asian hist, 534
South Asian religions in the Americas, 1438

SOUTHERN STATES
Building a new South, 98
Contemporary poets, dramatists, essayists, & novelists of the South, 1199
Dictionary of literary biog documentary series, v.12, 1201
Garden bulbs for the South, 1546
Handbook of mammals of the S-central states, 1630
Orchids for the South, 1574
Peterson's gd to colleges in the South 1995, 10th ed, 344

SOVIET UNION. See also FORMER SOVIET REPUBLICS; RUSSIA
Russian revolution, 1905-21, 548
Vascular plants of Russia & adjacent states (the former USSR), 1594

SPACE & TIME
Time & space, 1820

SPACE FLIGHT
Spaceflight: a Smithsonian gd, 1647

SPACE SCIENCES
Space scis dict 2, 1645
Space scis dict 3, 1646

SPAIN
Cultural atlas of Spain & Portugal, 539
Pilgrimage to Santiago de Compostela, 1462
Spain, 2d ed, 149

SPANISH LANGUAGE—DICTIONARIES— ENGLISH
Dictionary of Chicano Spanish, 2d ed, 1136
NTC's dict of common mistakes in Spanish, 1137
Wiley's English-Spanish, Spanish-English dict of psychology & psychiatry, 782

SPANISH SUCCESSION, WAR OF
Treaties of the War of the Spanish Succession, 762

SPECIAL DAYS
International holidays, 1361

SPECIAL LIBRARIES
Guide to the Sol Feinstone collection of the David Lib of the American Revolution, 654
University of London Lib catalogue of the Goldsmiths' Lib of Economic Lit, v.5, 662

SPICE TRADE
Spice trade, 308

SPIRITUALISM
Encyclopedia of afterlife beliefs & phenomena, 1445

SPORTS
Athletes, 410
Biographical dict of American sports, 1992-95 suppl, 793
Sport lawyer's gd to legal pers, 1995 suppl, 615
Sport thesaurus, 1994 ed, 802
Sports ethics, 801
Sports in N America: a documentary hist, v.4, 798

SPORTS MEDICINE
Sports medicine bible, 1729

ST. KITTS-NEVIS
St. Kitts-Nevis, 172

STANDARDS, ENGINEERING
ASTM standards source [CD-ROM], 1663

STATE GOVERNMENT—PUBLICATIONS
How to find co intelligence in state docs, 15th ed, 202

STATE GOVERNMENTS
Carroll's state dir, 726
Government dir of addresses & telephone nos 1995, 3d ed, 732
State executive dir, 729
State legislative summary, 1994, 595
Teacher educ policy in the states, 329

STATESMEN
Anthony Eden, 1897-1977, 759
Political leaders of contemporary W Europe, 756

STATISTICS
America's top-rated smaller cities, 1994-95 ed, 926
Baseball ratings, 2d ed, 804
Florida statl abstract, 1994, 28th ed, 916
Gale country & world rankings reporter, 905
International histl stats: Africa, Asia, & Oceania, 1750-1988, 917
Official gd to the American marketplace, 2d ed, 911
Services: stats on intl transactions 1970/92, 918
Statistical abstract of the ESCWA region 1983-1992, 14th ed, 919
Statistical abstract of the US 1995, 115th ed, 920
Statistical abstract of the world, 921
Statistical hndbk of working America, 922
Statistical record of native N Americans, 2d ed, 420

Statistical record of women worldwide, 953
Statistics sources 1996, 19th ed, 923
UNCTAD statl pocket bk, 925
World's women 1995, [2d ed], 954

STEEL, STAINLESS
ASM specialty handbk: stainless steels, 1662

STEELE, RICHARD, SIR
Joseph Addison & Richard Steele, 1237

STEINBECK, JOHN
John Steinbeck, 1216

STOCK-EXCHANGE
American stock exchange, 211
Dow Jones gd to the world stock market, 1995-96 ed, 212

STREET ADDRESSES
National dir of addresses & telephone nos, 1995 ed, 56

STUDENT AID
Athletic scholarships, 799
Big bk of minority opportunities, 6th ed, 891
Chronicle financial aid gd, rev ed, 364
Dan Cassidy's worldwide college scholarship dir, 4th ed, 333
Dan Cassidy's worldwide graduate scholarship dir, 4th ed, 334
Financial aid for vets, military personnel, & their dependents 1994-96, 690
Foundation grants to individuals, 9th ed, 872

STUDENT EXCHANGE PROGRAMS
Youth exchanges, 371

STUDENTS—EMPLOYMENT
Directory of graduate student employee bargaining agents & orgs, 336

STYLE, LITERARY
Using picture storybks to teach literary devices. v.2, 1164

SUBJECT HEADINGS
Sport thesaurus, 1994 ed, 802
Subject headings for African American materials, 626
Subject headings for children 1994, 632

SUBJECT HEADINGS, LIBRARY OF CONGRESS
LC period subdivisions under names of places, 5th ed, 630
Library of Congress subject headings, 3d ed, 627

SUBSIDIARY CORPORATIONS
How to find info about divisions, subsidiaries & products, 5th ed, 203

SUBSTANCE ABUSE
National gd to funding in substance abuse, 896

SUMMER EMPLOYMENT
Overseas summer jobs 1995, 26th ed, 278
Summer jobs Britain 1995, 26th ed, 279
Work your way around the world, 7th ed, 273

SUMMER SCHOOLS
Guide to summer camps & summer schools 1995/96, 27th ed, 326
Peterson's summer study abroad, 367

SUN RA (SONNY BLOUNT)
Earthly recordings of Sun Ra, 1322

SUPERNATURAL
Supernatural index, 1194
World of ghosts & the supernatural, 784

SURGERY
Surgeons' ref for minimally invasive surgery products, 1730

SUSTAINABLE DEVELOPMENT
Real Goods solar living sourcebk, 8th ed, 1847

SWAZILAND
Swaziland, rev ed, 123

SWEDEN
Historical dict of Sweden, 150

SWEDISH LANGUAGE—DICTIONARIES—ENGLISH
Prisma's abridged English-Swedish & Swedish-English dict, 1138

SWORDS
Encyclopedia of the sword, 816

SYMBOLISM IN ART
Dictionary of symbols in Western art, 1030
Hopi pottery symbols, 1015
Illustrated dict of symbols in E & W art, 1031

SYMBOLISM OF NUMBERS
Key of it all, bk 2, 1121

SYRIA
Bibliography of Syrian archaeological sites to 1980, 484

TALK SHOWS
Talk shows & hosts on radio, 3d ed, 975

TAMIL LITERATURE
Lexicon of Tamil lit, 1255

TANKS (MILITARY)
Armored forces: hist & sourcebk, 702

TATAR LANGUAGE—DICTIONARIES—ENGLISH
Tatar-English/English-Tatar dict, 1139

TEACHERS
American Assn of Colleges for Teacher Educ dir of members 1995, 316
Teacher educ policy in the states, 329

TEACHING—AIDS & DEVICES
Educators grade gd to free teaching aids 1995, 41st ed, 322
Educators gd to free films, filmstrips, & slides 1995, 55th ed, 375
Educators gd to free videotapes 1995, 42d ed, 376
Elementary teachers gd to free curriculum materials 1995, 52d ed, 323
Encyclopedia of educ info, 1994/95, 324
Teaching children's lit, 379

TECHNOLOGY
Annual review of info sci & tech, v.29, 1994, 622
CorpTech dir of tech cos 1996, 10th US ed, 1749
Dictionary of sci, 1493
Elsevier's dict of industrial tech, 1494
Failed tech, 1511
Peterson's job opportunities in engineering & tech 1995, 1513
Routledge French technical dict, 1499
Science navigator [CD-ROM], 1500
Scientific & technical bks & serials in print 1995, 22d ed, 1484
Technological capacity-bldg & tech partnership, 1515
Technology, 1508
Technology opportunities, 2d ed, 1507
Who's who in tech, 7th ed, 1492

TECHNOLOGY—PERIODICALS
Directory of bus per special issues, 209

TECHNOLOGY & STATE
Science, tech, & society in the 3d World, 138

TELECOMMUNICATION
Comprehensive networking glossary & acronym gd, 1759
Net gd, 1781
Telecommunications dir 1995-96, 7th ed, 1782
Telecommunications research resources, 1778

TELECOMMUNICATION SYSTEMS
International satellite dir, 1995, 10th ed, 1780

TELEPHONE—DIRECTORIES
Krupin's toll-free environmental dir, 1867

TELEVISION
BFI film & TV hndbk 1995, 1401
Broadcast news [CD-ROM], 991
Contemporary theatre, film, & TV, v.13, 1362
Latin American advertising, mktg, & media sourcebk, 301
Leo Burnett worldwide advertising & media fact bk, 302
News media yellow bk, 963
Power media selects, 9th ed, 988
Television research, 987

TELEVISION PROGRAMS
Children's TV, 1947-90, 1404
Fugitive: a complete episode gd, 1963-67, 1403
Shot on this site, 472
Talk show selects, 1995 ed, 989
VideoHound multimedia [CD-ROM], 1389
Walking shadows, 1399

TELEVISION SPECIALS
Television specials, 1412

TENNIS
WTA Tour, 832

TERATOGENIC AGENTS
Reproductive effects of chemical, physical, & biological agents REPROTOX, 1712

TERRORISM
Historical dict of terrorism, 597

TERRORISTS
Terrorist group profiles [CD-ROM], 601

TEXAS
Chief executives of Tex., 718

TEXTILE INDUSTRY
Historical dir of trade unions, v.4, 264

THAI LANGUAGE—DICTIONARIES—ENGLISH
Oxford-Duden pictorial Thai & English dict, 1140

THEATER
American playwrights, 1880-1945, 1202
Annotated dict of technical, histl, & stylistic terms relating to theatre & drama, 1417
Brewer's theater, 1414
Cambridge gd to theatre, new ed, 1415
Cambridge illus hist of British theatre, 1422
Contemporary theatre, film, & TV, v.13, 1362
Dictionary of traditional S-E Asian theatre, 1418
Directory of theatre training programs, 5th ed, 1419
Music, dance & theater scholarships, 1365
Students' gd to playwriting opportunities, 1421

THEATERS
Opera cos & houses of the US, 1302

THEOLOGIANS
Jonathan Edwards, 1440

THEOLOGY
Handbook of Catholic theology [rev ed], 1475

THERAPEUTICS
Handbook of therapeutic interventions, 1735

THERMODYNAMICS
Handbook of thermal conductivity, v.1, 1821
Handbook of thermal conductivity, v.2, 1822
Handbook of thermal conductivity, v.3, 1823

Handbook of transport property data, 1824

THESAURI
NTC's thesaurus of everyday American English, 1093
Oxford desk thesaurus, American ed, 1094
Oxford minireference dict & thesaurus, 1078
Roget's 2: the new thesaurus, 3d ed, 1095
Thesaurus of ERIC descriptors, 13th ed, 318

TITANIUM ALLOYS
Materials properties handbk: titanium alloys, 1669

TOADS
Handbook of frogs & toads of the US & Canada, 3d ed, 1640

TOBACCO
Smoking: the health consequences of tobacco use, 1721

TOGO
Togo, 124

TOTAL QUALITY MANAGEMENT
Bibliography of bus/competitive intelligence & benchmarking lit, 175
McGraw-Hill ency of quality terms & concepts, 284

TOTALITARIANISM
Dictators & tyrants, 705

TOURIST TRADE
Career opportunities in travel & tourism, 461
Yearbook of tourism stats, 46th ed, 463

TOXICOLOGY
Encyclopedia of environmental control tech, v.7, 1857

TOYS
Best toys, bks & videos for kids, 1010

TRADE & PROFESSIONAL ASSOCIATIONS
Gale ency of bus & professional assns, 185
Historical dir of trade unions, v.4, 264
Japan dir of professional assns, 3d ed, 244

TRADE REGULATION
National dir of state bus licensing & regulation, 194

TRADE-UNIONS
Directory of US labor orgs, 1994-95 ed, 260

TRAFFIC ACCIDENTS
Statistics of road traffic accidents in Europe & N America 1995, 1890

TRAILS
Hiking trails, E US, 825

TRANSPORT THEORY
Handbook of transport property data, 1824

TRANSPORTATION
Dorling Kindersley visual timeline of transportation, 1878

TRANSPORTATION—EUROPE
Annual bulletin for transport stats for Europe, 1995, v.45, 1877

TRAVEL
ACCESS travel USA: a dir for people with disabilities, 856
Fodor's great American vacations for travelers with disabilities, 471
Frommer's comprehensive travel gd: Caribbean '95, 483
Jazz & blues lover's gd to the US, updated ed, 1321
Wild planet!, 1352
World tourism dir '95/96, pt.1, 3d ed, 464
World tourism dir '95/96, pt.2, 3d ed, 465
World tourism dir '95/96, pt.3, 3d ed, 466

TREASURE-TROVE
Atlas of shipwrecks & treasure, 1896

TREATIES
Multilateral treaties deposited with the secretary-general, 612
Treaties of the War of the Spanish Succession, 762

TREES. *See also* **FLOWERING TREES**
Field gd to the palms of the Americas, 1589
Pockets: trees, 75
Pruning of trees, shrubs, & conifers, [rev ed], 1588
Year in trees, 1592

TRIALS
Political prisoners & trials, 605

TROUVERES
Lyrics of the Trouveres, 1251

TRUMBAUER, FRANK
Tram: the Frank Trumbauer story, 1323

TUMORS
Dictionary of human oncology, 1726

TURTLES
Turtles of the US & Canada, 1636

TWAIN, MARK
Mark Twain A to Z, 1217

TWENTIETH CENTURY
Chronicle of the 20th century, 558
Larousse dict of 20th century hist, 566

TYPE & TYPE-FOUNDING
Type foundaries of America & their catalogs, rev ed, 666

TYPE-SETTING
Glossary of typesetting terms, 667

UGANDA
Historical dict of Uganda, 125

UNDERGROUND PRESS
APT for libs 1995: alternative pr titles for the general reader, 79

UNIDENTIFIED FLYING OBJECTS
UFO: the definitive gd to unidentified flying objects & related phenomena, 789

UNITED NATIONS
Guide to info at the UN, 770
Index to proceedings of the economic & social council, 771
Multilateral treaties deposited with the secretary-general, 612
United Nations Commission on Intl Trade law yrbk, v.24, 1993, 307
Worldmark ency of the nations, 8th ed, 105
Yearbook of the Intl Law Commission 1992, 614

UNITED NATIONS—INFORMATION SERVICES
Directory of UN info sources, 5th ed, 769

UNITED STATES
Worldmark ency of the states, 106

UNITED STATES—ARMED FORCES
Directory of US military bases worldwide, 687
How to locate anyone who is or has been in the military, rev ed, 688
Medal of honor recipients 1863-1994, 689

UNITED STATES. ARMY
On the trail of the buffalo soldier, 699

UNITED STATES—BIOGRAPHY
Cambridge dict of American biog, 35

UNITED STATES—CIVILIZATION
America: hist & life on disc [CD-ROM], 512
Columbia chronicles of American life, 1910-92, 501
Guide to American studies resources, 1994, 338
Hispanic 100, 408

UNITED STATES. CONGRESS
Committees in the US congress 1947-92, v.2, 733
Congressional Quarterly's pols in America 1996, 738
Congressional voting gd, 5th ed, 736
Congressional yrbk 1993, 739
Encyclopedia of the US congress, 720
United States Congress, 715

UNITED STATES—CONSTITUTIONAL LAW
Constitutional law dict, v.1, 606

UNITED STATES—DEFENSES
Cuts in defense jobs in US counties, metropolitan areas, & states, 1992-2003, 270

UNITED STATES—ECONOMIC CONDITIONS
Economic integration in Europe & N America, 232
Statistical hndbk of working America, 922

USA business: the portable ency for doing bus with the US, 241
Women in the US: economic conditions, 937

UNITED STATES—FOREIGN RELATIONS
American foreign policy index 1995, v.3, no.2, 743

UNITED STATES—FOREIGN RELATIONS—LATIN AMERICA
Early US-Hispanic relations 1776-1860, 776

UNITED STATES—FOREIGN RELATIONS—SPAIN
Early US-Hispanic relations 1776-1860, 776

UNITED STATES—HISTORICAL GEOGRAPHY
Atlas of westward expansion, 488

UNITED STATES—HISTORY
America: hist & life on disc [CD-ROM], 512
Bibliographic gd to N American hist 1994, 489
Chronicle of America, 500
Encyclopedia of frontier biog on CD-ROM [CD-ROM], 497
Landmark docs in American hist [CD-ROM], 498
Larousse dict of N American hist, 508
Modern America 1914-45, 518
Operation Desert Shield/Desert Storm, 563
Profiles in American hist, 509
Young reader's companion to American hist, 528

UNITED STATES—HISTORY—CHRONOLOGY
American decades 1930-39, 513
American decades 1940-49, 514
American decades 1960-69, 515
American decades 1970-79, 516

UNITED STATES—HISTORY—CIVIL WAR, 1861-1865
American Civil War, 504
Atlas of the Civil War, 486
Biographical dict of the Union, 495
Civil War [CD-ROM], 691
Civil War battlefields, 517
Compendium of the Confederate armies: Ky., Md., Mo., Confederate units & Indian units, 522
Compendium of the Confederate armies: La., 523
Compendium of the Confederate armies: Miss., 524
Compendium of the Confederate armies: S.C. & Ga., 525
Compendium of the Confederate armies: Tex., 526
Index to the Roll of Honor, 434

UNITED STATES—HISTORY, MILITARY
American military hist, 678
Naval Institute histl atlas of the US Navy, 701
Reference gd to US military hist: 1945 to the present, 520

UNITED STATES—HISTORY—REVOLUTION, 1775-1783
Encyclopedia of the American Revolution, 3d ed, 506
Guide to the Sol Feinstone collection of the David Lib of the American Revolution, 654

James Madison & the American nation 1751-1836, 507

UNITED STATES—HISTORY—1783-1865
James Madison & the American nation 1751-1836, 507

UNITED STATES—HISTORY—20TH CENTURY
America in the 20th century, 499
Twentieth-century America, 485

UNITED STATES—HISTORY—WORLD WAR, 1914-1918
United States in the 1st world war, 685

UNITED STATES—MAPS
Hammond road atlas & vacation gd, 442

UNITED STATES—POLITICS & GOVERNMENT
America votes 21, 735
Carroll's fed advisory dir 1995, 722
Carroll's fed dir, 723
Carroll's fed regional dir, 724
Congressional Quarterly's desk ref on American govt, 737
Congressional voting gd, 5th ed, 736

UNITED STATES—POPULATION
Bibliography of American demographic hist, 906
Social work almanac, 2d ed, 894

UNITED STATES—RELIGION
History & annot bibliog of American religious pers & newspapers, 1447
Religion & the American experience, the 20th century, 1442

UNITED STATES—SOCIAL CONDITIONS
Radicalism hndbk, 766
Social work almanac, 2d ed, 894

UNITED STATES—SOCIAL LIFE & CUSTOMS
America in the 20th century, 499
Modern America 1914-45, 518

UNITED STATES—STATISTICS
American salaries & wages survey, 3d ed, 266
Rating gd to life in America's 50 states, 924
Statistical abstract of the US 1995, 115th ed, 920

UNITED STATES—STUDY & TEACHING
Guide to American studies resources, 1994, 338

UNITED STATES SUPREME COURT
Supreme Court justices, 572

UNITS
Sizes: the illus ency, 1787

UNIVERSITIES & COLLEGES
America's lowest cost colleges, 9th ed, 359
Complete gd to Canadian univs, 3d ed, 320
Peterson's colleges with programs for students with learning disabilities, 341
Peterson's contract servs for higher educ, 342

Peterson's gd to colleges in the Midwest 1995, 11th ed, 343
Peterson's gd to colleges in the South 1995, 10th ed, 344
Peterson's gd to colleges in the West 1995, 9th ed, 345
Peterson's gd to middle Atlantic colleges 1995, 11th ed, 346
Peterson's gd to New England colleges 1995, 11th ed, 347
Peterson's gd to NY colleges 1995, 11th ed, 348
Princeton Review student access gd: the big bk of colleges, 357
Princeton Review student access gd to the best 309 colleges, 358
World list of univ & other insts of higher ed, 361

UNIVERSITIES & COLLEGES—FINANCE
Barron's best buys in college educ, 3d ed, 331

UNIVERSITIES & COLLEGES—GRADUATE WORK
Chemical scis graduate school finder 1994-95, 1791
Graduate school funding handbk, 365
Peterson's gd to grad & professional programs 1995, 29th ed, 349
Peterson's gd to grad programs in bus, educ, health, & law 1995, 29th ed, 350
Peterson's gd to grad programs in engineering & applied scis 1995, 29th ed, 351
Peterson's gd to grad programs in the biological & agricultural scis 1995, 29th ed, 352
Peterson's gd to grad programs in the humanities, arts, & social scis 1995, 29th ed, 353
Peterson's gd to grad programs in the physical scis & mathematics 1995, 29th ed, 354
Peterson's professional degree programs in the visual & performing arts 1995, 962

UNIVERSITY OF CALGARY
Mapping the territory, 658

UNIX DEVICE DRIVERS
UNIX & X command compendium, 1762

UPHOLSTERY
Upholsterer's pocket ref bk, 1020

URBANIZATION
World urbanizations prospects: the 1994 revision, 932

USED CARS
Used car reliability & safety gd, 1885

UTAH
Utah hist ency, 511

UTOPIAS
Encyclopedia of utopian lit, 1147

UZBEK LANGUAGE—DICTIONARIES—ENGLISH
Uzbek-English, English-Uzbek concise dict, 1141

VACATIONS
Adventure holidays 1995, 18th ed, 460
Adventure vacations, 473

VANCE, JACK
Work of Jack Vance, 1218

VEGETABLE GARDENING
Organic gardener's home ref, 1543

VEGETABLES
Codex alimentarius, v.5a, 2d ed, 1534

VENDORS & PURCHASERS
Peterson's contract servs for higher educ, 342

VENICE (ITALY)
Venice & the Veneto, 478

VENTURE CAPITAL
Fitzroy Dearborn dir of venture capital funds, 184

VERMONT
New Hampshire [&] Vt.: atlas of histl county boundaries, 439

VETERANS
How to locate anyone who is or has been in the military, rev ed, 688

VETERANS—LOANS
Financial aid for vets, military personnel, & their dependents 1994-96, 690

VETERINARY MEDICINE
Animal health yrbk 1993, 1553
Complete horse care manual, 1556
Veterinarian's ency of animal behavior, 1554

VICO, GIAMBATTISTA
Vico: a bibliog of works in English from 1884-1984, 1426

VICTORIANA
Illustrated ency of Victoriana, 1016

VIDEO CASSETTES
Best toys, bks & videos for kids, 1010
Video rating gd for libs on CD-ROM 1990-94 [CD-ROM], 995

VIDEO RECORDINGS
Billboard video yrbk 1994, 1402
Field gd to current training videos, 282
International dict of broadcasting & film, 984
Variety's video dir plus [CD-ROM], 1388
Video source bk 1996, 17th ed, 996
VideoHound multimedia [CD-ROM], 1389

VIDEO RECORDINGS FOR CHILDREN
Parent's gd to the best children's videos & where to find them, 1386

VIDEO TAPES
Bowker's complete video dir 1995, 986
Educators gd to free videotapes 1995, 42d ed, 376
Video annual 1994, 994

VIENNA (AUSTRIA)
Vienna, 479

VIETNAMESE CONFLICT, 1961-1975
Vietnam [CD-ROM], 694

VIOLONCELLO MUSIC
Cello music since 1960, 1286

VITAMINS
Woman's gd to vitamins & minerals, 1743

VOCABULARY
Sisson's word & expression locater, 2d ed, 1092

VOCATIONAL EDUCATION
Chronicle 2-yr college databk, rev ed, 335
Chronicle vocational school manual, rev ed, 381

VOCATIONAL GUIDANCE
Cracking the corporate closet, 259
Earth work, 1871
Encyclopedia of careers & vocational guidance [CD-ROM], 382
Free & inexpensive career materials, 383
Gale's career guidance system, expanded ed [CD-ROM], 384
JIST's electronic gd for occupational exploration [CD-ROM], 275
On-line job search companion, 272

VOLCANOES
Volcanoes of the world, 2d ed, 1818

VOLUNTARISM
Alternatives to the Peace Corps, 868
Christian voluntarism in Britain & N America, 867
Philanthropic studies index, 1995 cum index, 884

VONNEGUT, KURT
Vonnegut ency, 1219

VOTING
Congressional voting gd, 5th ed, 736

WAELRANT, HUBERT
Descriptive catalog of the music printed by Hubert Waelrant & Jan de Laet, 1266

WAGES
American salaries & wages survey, 3d ed, 266

WALES
Wales & cinema, 1370

WAR SONGS
World War I songs, 696

WARD, EBENEZER
Victorian yellowbacks & paperbacks, 1849-1905, v.2, 1224

WARS OF THE ROSES. *See* **GREAT BRITAIN—HISTORY**

WARSHIPS
Battleships: US battleships, 1935-92, rev ed, 700

WASHINGTON (D.C.)
AIA gd to the architecture of Wash., D.C., 3d ed, 1049
Guide to greater Wash., DC grantmakers 1994-95, 876
Washington info dir, 734

WASPS
Indo-Australian Agaoninae (pollinators of figs), 1628

WEALTH
New fortunes 1994, 176

WEATHER
Pockets: weather facts, 76
USA Today weather almanac 1995, 1809
Weather hndbk, 1810
World weatherdisc, 1994 ed [CD-ROM], 1811

WEEDS
Weed flora of Egypt, rev ed, 1582

WEIL, SIMONE
Simone Weil, 957

WEST (U.S.)
American West: a multicultural ency, 505
Cowboy ency, 510
Old West: day by day, 502
Peterson's gd to colleges in the West 1995, 9th ed, 345
Western American novelists, 1205

WEST INDIES
Field gd to shells, 4th ed, 1595
St. Kitts-Nevis, 172

WESTERN STORIES
Work of William Eastlake, 1209

WETLAND CONSERVATION
Wetland economics, 1989-93, 1600

WHALES
Whales, dolphins, & porpoises, 1629

WILD ANIMAL TRADE
International wildlife trade, 1599

WILD FLOWERS
Guide to wildflowers in winter, 1584

WILDERNESS AREAS
Essential gd to wilderness camping & backpacking in the US, 824

WILDERNESS SURVIVAL
Survival, 812

WILDLIFE. *See* **ZOOLOGY**

WILDLIFE CONSERVATIONISTS
Portraits in conservation: E & S Africa, 1596

WILLIAMS, TENNESSEE
Tennessee Williams, 1220

WINE & WINE MAKING
Champagne companion, 1354
Larousse ency of wine, 1527
Oxford companion to wine, 1528

WISTERIA
Wisterias, 1579

WIT & HUMOR
Humorous quotations, 93
Robert Benchley, 1207

WOMEN
Arab women in ESCWA member states, 156
Dictionary of feminist theory, 2d ed, 948
Directory of financial aids for women 1995-97, 879
Great lives from hist: American women series, 942
Information please women's sourcebk, 1995, 951
National gd to funding for women & girls, 952
New A to Z of women's health, 3d ed, 1680
Notable Latin American women, 938
100 women who shaped world hist, 32
Statistical record of women worldwide, 953
Who's who of American women 1995-96, 19th ed, 38
Woman's gd to vitamins & minerals, 1743
Women & aging, 936
Women & the Dict of Natl Biog, 26
Women in the US: economic conditions, 937
Women of peace: Nobel peace prize winners, 944
Women who reformed pols, 943
Women's atlas of the US, rev ed, 933
Women's world: a timeline of women in hist, 945
World's women 1995, [2d ed], 954

WOMEN & LITERATURE
Feminist criticism of American women poets, 1222
Oxford companion to women's writing in the US, 1200

WOMEN & RELIGION
Women & religion in India, 934

WOMEN & THE MILITARY
Women & the military, 680

WOMEN ARTISTS
North American women artists of the 20th century, 1026
Remarkable lives of 100 women artists, 939
Women artists, 2d ed, 1021

WOMEN AUTHORS
Dictionary of literary biog documentary series, v.12, 1201
Oxford companion to women's writing in the US, 1200
Remarkable lives of 100 women writers & journalists, 941
Third world women's lits, 946
Virginia Woolf A to Z, 1221

WOMEN—EDUCATION
Gender equity in educ, 313

WOMEN—HEALTH AND HYGIENE
Woman's body, 1692

WOMEN IN LITERATURE
Masterplots II: women's lit series, 949

WOMEN IN MOTION PICTURES
Women film directors, 947

WOMEN JOURNALISTS
Remarkable lives of 100 women writers & journalists, 941

WOMEN PHYSICIANS
Remarkable lives of 100 women healers & scientists, 940

WOMEN—PHYSIOLOGY
Woman's body, 1692

WOMEN SCIENTISTS
American women in sci, 1486
Remarkable lives of 100 women healers & scientists, 940

WOMEN—SEXUAL BEHAVIOR
Fetishes, Florentine girdles, & other explorations into the sexual imagination, 886

WOMEN SOCIAL REFORMERS
Women who reformed pols, 943

WOMEN SOLDIERS
Women & the military, 680

WOMEN'S PERIODICALS
Women's pers in the US: consumer mags, 950

WOOD
North American factbk, 1994-95, 1541

WOOD WARBLERS
Warblers of the Americas, 1613

WOODWORKING TOOLS
Complete gd to sharpening, 1679

WOOLF, VIRGINIA
Virginia Woolf A to Z, 1221

WORK ENVIRONMENT
Encyclopedia of environmental control tech, v.8, 1858

WORLD HISTORY
Chronicle of the 20th century, 558
Chronology of world hist, compact ed, 564

Eyewitness hist of the world [CD-ROM], 567
Larousse dict of 20th century hist, 566

WORLD POLITICS
Countries of the world & their leaders yrbk 1995: suppl, 710
Federal systems of the world, [2d ed], 712
Handbook of the nations, 14th ed, 713
International dir of govt 1995, 2d ed, 707
Profiles of worldwide govt leaders 1995, 708
Worldwide govt dir with intl orgs 1995, 709

WORLD POLITICS—1945-
Facts on File world pol almanac, 3d ed, 711

WORLD WAR, 1914-1918
Atlas of WW I, 2d ed, 675
Imperial War Museum film catalog, v.1, 557
United States in the 1st world war, 685
World War I songs, 696

WORLD WAR, 1939-1945
Dangerous sky: resource gd to the Battle of Britain, 544
New Grolier ency of WW II, 684
Normandy [CD-ROM], 693
Pacific War atlas 1941-45, 676
Ways of war: the era of WW II in children's & YA fiction, 1165
Who's who in WW II, 681

X WINDOW SYSTEM (COMPUTER SYSTEM)
UNIX & X command compendium, 1762

YELLOWBACK BOOKS
Victorian yellowbacks & paperbacks, 1849-1905, v.1, 1223
Victorian yellowbacks & paperbacks, 1849-1905, v.2, 1224

YOUNG ADULT FICTION
Index to histl fiction for children & young people, 1179
Ways of war: the era of WW II in children's & YA fiction, 1165

YOUNG ADULT LITERATURE
Africa in lit for children & young adults, 1166
American Indian ref & resource bks for children & YAs, 2d ed, 1177
Authors & artists for young adults, v.14, 1171
Biography today, 1993 annual cum, 25
Fantasy lit for children & young adults, 4th ed, 1167
Learning about the Holocaust, 1170
Magazines for kids & teens, 86
Middle & jr high school lib catalog, 7th ed, 650

YOUTH
Directory of American youth orgs 1994-95, 5th ed, 902
State legislative summary, 1994, 595

ZAIRE
Zaire, 126

ZIONISM
New ency of Zionism & Israel, 164

ZIP CODE
Sourcebook of zip code demographics, 10th ed, 913

ZOOLOGY
Animal life, 1604
Species info lib [CD-ROM], 1606
Wildlife worldwide [CD-ROM], 1607
World alive [CD-ROM], 1609